W9-BFU-638

AGING in AMERICA

AGING in AMERICA

Edited by Robert L. Scardamalia

Lanham • Boulder • New York • London

Published by Bernan Press
An imprint of The Rowman & Littlefield Publishing Group, Inc.
4501 Forbes Boulevard, Suite 200, Lanham, Maryland 20706
www.rowman.com
800-865-3457; info@bernan.com

16 Carlisle Street, London W1D 3BT, United Kingdom

ISBN-13: 978-1-59888-702-0
eISBN-13: 978-1-59888-703-7

∞™ The paper used in this publication meets the minimum requirements of
American National Standard for Information Sciences—Permanence of
Paper for Printed Library Materials, ANSI/NISO Z39.48-1992.
Manufactured in the United States of America.

Contents

Preface

The 2010 census was different from any census in recent memory. All American households answered a simple questionnaire with ten questions. No longer did some people get the "long form" with dozens of detailed questions about employment, education, income, previous residence, housing characteristics, and more. The data gleaned from these important questions have long been used by federal, state, and local governments to evaluate their populations and program needs; by large and small businesses and nonprofit organizations for a variety of planning and location purposes; and by academic researchers to study trends in social and economic conditions.

The "long form" has been replaced by the American Community Survey (ACS). Under development for more than a decade, the ACS is an ongoing survey of the American people that ushered in a new era in social and economic data analysis. The census "long form" provided detailed estimates of social and economic characteristics every ten years. The ACS collects this same information on a rolling basis. It takes 5 years of ACS responses to accumulate a sample almost as large as the census "long form" collected at a single point in time. But data users now have the ability to study these characteristics and trends throughout the decade – annually for some areas.

Because the ACS is a sample survey, large numbers of sample cases are needed before reliable estimates can be made for small populations. Each year's sample is large enough to produce estimates for the nation, all the states, most metropolitan areas, and many counties and cities. The tables in this volume include 3-year estimates for the period 2010 through 2012 for the United States, all states and Congressional Districts, as well as, metropolitan areas, counties, and cities of 65,000 or more population.

The richness of the ACS data can be accessed in varying degrees. Much more subject matter detail is available for large geographic areas partly because reliable estimates for large areas can be produced with smaller samples, and partly because more data must be suppressed for the smaller areas to protect the confidentiality of the respondents.

This book is designed to include a sampling of key information about the older population but also help users understand the survey data and resources to access more detailed data available from the Census Bureau and the ACS. The ten subject area tables in this book include 130 data items for each geographic area. This is a small sampling of the detailed data available.

One of the most notable differences between the census "long form" and the ACS is the time frame of the estimates. We are accustomed to the census data that give us specific information every ten years, a snapshot of the country on April 1. The ACS multiyear estimates are different as the Census Bureau surveys nearly 300,000 households every month. The data in this book are from the ACS 3-year 2010 to 2012 estimates which are produced from 36 months of survey data collection. They are not averages, nor do they represent 2011, the midpoint of the 3-year estimates. They are period estimates with sample cases spread evenly throughout the 3-year survey time period.

To help in the understanding of these estimates, we have included a measure of population change for each geographic area. These are from the 2010 census and the 2010–2012 estimates, showing the actual population growth or decline in each geographic area. Each table shows population characteristics as estimated for the 2010 to 2012 ACS period. It should be remembered that the decennial census and the Census Bureau's Population Estimates Program provide the official population counts that underlie the ACS sample. If an area experienced unusually large population growth or decline, we should understand that these short-term population impacts may not be reflected in the ACS 3-year period estimates. Changes due to a city annexing a large tract of land, many people moving into a new development, or many people leaving the area because of a plant closing may be hidden in the short-term.

With the ACS, there is always a trade-off between data currency and data reliability. More current 1-year estimates come from smaller samples and therefore have larger margins of error. Estimates from the 3-year data are based on three times the sample size and have smaller margins of error – but of course, they do not represent as current a period. While 1-year estimates are available for the geographic areas presented here, the tables in this volume represent a conservative approach to reporting ACS data in that they will display greater year-to-year stability and will have smaller margins of error than the use of annual 1-year estimates.

Finally, it is always critical to remember that all estimates are subject to sampling error. On the Census Bureau's website, every ACS number is accompanied by its margin of error. In the interests of space and simplicity, this book does not include the margins of error, but all users are encouraged to consult the Census Bureau's website and to understand some basics: small differences are very likely to represent no difference at all; do not draw conclusions from small numbers; use these numbers as a starting point to explore the wealth of information from the ACS.

Introduction

The American Community Survey (ACS) has ushered in the most substantial change in the decennial census in more than 60 years. It replaced the decennial census long form in 2010, providing more current data throughout the decade by collecting long-form-type information annually rather than only once every 10 years. The ACS provides annual data for states, metropolitan areas, and large cities and counties, and combines 3 years of survey responses **(in this book, 2010–2012)** to produce data for midsize communities. Very small communities (under 20,000 population) and statistical areas like census tracts and zip code tabulation areas require 5 years of survey responses.

The ACS gathers demographic, social, economic, housing and financial information about the nation's people and communities on a continuous basis. The ACS is an ongoing survey conducted by the U.S. Census Bureau in every county, American Indian and Alaska Native Area, and Hawaiian Home Land in the United States. The ACS is also conducted as the Puerto Rico Community Survey in every municipality in Puerto Rico. As the largest survey in the United States, it is the only source of small-area data on a wide range of important social and economic characteristics for all communities in the country. After years of planning, development, and a demonstration period, the ACS began nationwide full implementation in 2005.

Information about the ACS are available on the Census Bureau's website. The ACS main page is http://www.census.gov/acs/www. Data from the ACS is available from American FactFinder at http://factfinder2.census.gov.

A vast amount of information is collected in the ACS. In this publication, selections of these data have been assembled in various tables by subject and geographic type.

VOLUME ORGANIZATION

The data tables in this book pertain to the older population, generally those 60 years of age and over and include a selection of population and housing characteristics from the ACS in twelve subject areas:

- Population summary
- Age structure
- Race and ethnicity
- Household relationships and living arrangements
- Educational attainment and language spoken
- Employment and labor force status
- Income and poverty status
- Disability status
- Housing summary

The 3-year estimates from the American Community Survey provide data **for all areas of 65,000 population or more.** Each subject area includes data for the United States, the 50 states and the District of Columbia and the following:

- Nearly 800 counties, listed alphabetically within state
- 350+ metropolitan areas, listed alphabetically
- 500+ cities, listed alphabetically within state
- All 435 Congressional districts, listed numerically by state

In addition, each part is preceded by highlights, maps and/or summary tables that show how areas diverge from the national norm, as well as the differences among areas. These research aids are invaluable for helping people understand what the census data tell us about who we are, what we do, and where we live.

In the following sections, information about the ACS and how to use the data is included, much of it excerpted from the wealth of information available on the Census Bureau's website. Especially helpful are the instructions, definitions, and guidelines on using the data in the section on "Guidance for Data Users." Readers are encouraged to explore the Census Bureau's website to expand on the information contained here and to keep up to date with this constantly changing dataset.

Robert Scardamalia is President of RLS Demographics, Inc., a firm providing data and analysis to private organizations, government agencies, and not-for-profits, especially in the areas of aging services and business development. He is an adjunct professor in the Sociology Department of the State University of New York at Albany. Prior to forming RLS Demographics, he was Chief Demographer of New York State and directed the Center for Research and Information Analysis in the New York Department of Economic Development. He also directed the New York State Data Center for more than 20 years. Mr. Scardamalia serves on the Board of the Association of Public Data Users and is a past President. He has chaired the national State Data Center Steering Committee and served on numerous Census Bureau committees. He holds a Master of Arts in Demography from Georgetown University and Bachelor of Arts in Sociology from Penn State University.

Understanding the American Community Survey

Every 10 years since 1790, as required by the U.S. Constitution, Congress has authorized funds to conduct a national census of the U.S. population. From 1960 through 2000, censuses have consisted of:

- a "short form," which included basic questions about age, sex, race, Hispanic origin (since 1980), household relationship, and owner/renter status, and

- a "long form" used for a sample of approximately one of every six households that included not only the basic short-form questions but also detailed questions about socioeconomic and housing characteristics.

Beginning with the 2010 census, the American Community Survey (ACS) replaced the decennial census long form by collecting long-form-type information annually rather than only once every 10 years, providing more current data throughout the decade. The 2010 Census counted the population to support the constitutional mandate—to provide population counts needed to apportion the seats in the U.S. House of Representatives. The ACS data now provide, for the first time, a regular stream of updated information for states and local areas, revolutionizing the way we use data to understand our communities. It produces social, housing, and economic characteristics for demographic groups, even for geographic areas as small as census tracts and block groups.

SOME KEY FACTS ABOUT THE ACS

- The ACS annually provides the same kind of detailed information previously available only every 10 years from the census. The ACS is conducted under the authority of Title 13, United States Code, Sections 141 and 193.

- All answers are confidential. Any Census Bureau employee who violates that confidentiality is subject to a jail term, a fine, or both.

- The Census Bureau may use the information it collects only for statistical purposes.

- Addresses are selected at random from the Master Address File to represent similar households in the area. Approximately 290,000 addresses are selected each month and the survey is conducted by mail,

telephone, and personal visit. Response to this survey is required by Section 221 of Title 13.

- Approximately 2.9 percent of U.S. households are surveyed each year. A sample of group quarters (nursing homes, college dormitories, etc.) is included in the ACS as well.

- While the ACS sample size approximates the traditional long-form census sample, it is a smaller sample resulting in somewhat larger margins of error.

The traditional long-form census decade provided the socio-economic portrait of the nation and communities but that portrait was fixed in time for 10 years. Data from the ACS provides a regular update to that portrait which is used for a variety of purposes that include: monitoring the well-being of America's older population, children and families, tracking trends in disability, analyzing the growth in the number of grandparents responsible for their grandchildren, determining the economic well-being of the elderly and working-poor families, or tracking social, economic, and demographic changes in the general U.S. population.

The ACS provides critical information for communities on a current basis, when they need it most. But the ACS is still a relatively new data collection instrument and a different measure of the characteristics of the population and households. Researchers are still working to understand the differences from the traditional census data so it is good to be cautious in the interpretation of differences between areas and across time. Small differences may not be meaningful. On the other hand, the ACS provides annual estimates and the frequency of updates and currency of the data is a far outweighs waiting 10 years for new results.

NEW OPPORTUNITIES

The main benefits of the ACS are timeliness and access to annual data for states, local areas, and small population subgroups. The ACS will deliver useful, relevant data, similar to data from previous census long forms, but updated every year rather than every 10 years. The ACS provides comparable information across and within states for program evaluation and use in funding formulas.

- ACS information is often used to determine the placement of new schools, senior residential services, hospitals, and highways.

- ACS provides information for tracking the well-being of children, families, and the elderly allowing service providers to better target populations in need.

- The data will improve the distribution of aid through federal, state, and local governments. More than $400 billion in federal program funds are distributed each year based, in whole or in part, on census and ACS data.

- The data are used by community programs, such as those for the elderly, libraries, hospitals, banks, and other organizations.

- The data are used by transportation planners to evaluate peak volumes of traffic in order to reduce congestion, plan for parking, and develop plans for carpooling and flexible work schedules.

- Corporations, small businesses, and individuals use these data to develop business plans, to set strategies for expansion or starting a business, and to determine trends in their service areas to meet current and future needs.

- Small towns and rural communities have much to gain from the ACS. Lacking the staff and resources to conduct their own research, many local communities have relied on decennial census information that became increasingly outdated throughout the decade, or used local administrative records that are not comparable with information collected in neighboring areas.

- The ACS also provides tools for those who want to conduct their own research. The ACS includes a Public Use Microdata Sample (PUMS) file each year that enables researchers to create custom universes and tabulations from individual ACS records that have been stripped of personally identifiable information.

- Because the ACS data collection occurs every month, the Census Bureau uses professional, highly trained, permanent interviewers which have improved the accuracy of ACS data compared with those from the decennial census long-form sample. This strategy has effectively reduced the number of refusals to complete the ACS questionnaire and allows interviewers to obtain more complete information than decennial census interviewers.

NEW CHALLENGES

The main challenges for ACS data users are understanding and using multiyear estimates and the relatively large margins of error associated with ACS data for smaller geographic areas and subgroups of the population.

- ACS data will be produced every year, but the sample size of the ACS is smaller than that of the Census 2000 long form sample. Data users need to pay more attention to the margin of error.

- Data users have access to 5-year estimates of ACS data. The sample size based on 5-year period estimates of ACS data is still smaller than the long-form sample in the decennial census, resulting in larger margins of error in the ACS 5-year estimates.

- Because the ACS will produce 1-year, 3-year, and 5-year estimates, areas of 65,000 population or more will receive three estimates of the same characteristics every year. For example, a large city will receive 1-year, 3-year and 5-year estimates of the number of persons 65 and over in poverty. Data users will have to decide which datasets are appropriate for their needs.

- Data users will need to be aware of the implications of multiyear estimates, particularly in analyzing employment and income data that will span a full year or even a 5-year period.

- Multiyear estimates, especially the 5-year estimates will not reflect short-term changes in the population or economy of an area. The recent recession is a good example because the 5-year ACS estimates span both the fall into recession and the resulting growth coming out.

The ACS includes several questions that are very similar to those collected in other federal surveys—especially the Current Population Survey (CPS), the American Housing Survey, and the Survey of Income and Program Participation. In some cases, there are clear guidelines about which data to use. For example, the CPS is the official source of income and poverty data. It includes detailed questions on these topics and should be used in reporting national trends in these subject areas. The Census Bureau recommends that ACS information on income and poverty be used to supplement CPS data for areas below the state level and for population subgroups (such as age, sex, race, Hispanic origin, type of household) at the state level. For an explanation of various income and poverty data sources, see the Census Bureau's guidelines at http://www.census

.gov/hhes/www/poverty/about/datasources/description.html. For states, generally the Census Bureau recommends using the ACS, though the CPS is still valuable as a source for examining historical state income and poverty trends.

DATA COLLECTION VERSUS DATA REPORTING

Results from the ACS are reported each year which is a major advantage over the traditional long-form data from the decennial census. But unlike the release of data only once every 10 years in the decennial census, the annual release of data from the ACS can be quite confusing. The ACS sample size is such that the reliability of the data is greatly affected by the length of the data collection period and the size of geographic reporting areas. In survey sampling, it is well understood that larger samples yield more reliable estimates with smaller margins of error. In order to produce reliable estimates from the ACS, it is necessary to collect the data over differing periods of time in order to provide estimates for all areas, including small areas like census tracts.

Each set of period estimates is released each year, generally between September and December, and reflect data collection ending in the previous calendar year. Thus, the collection year 2012 1-year estimates for areas of 65,000 or more were released in September of 2013. The 2010–2012 3-year estimates and the 2008–2012 5-year estimates follow as processing is completed.

THE ACS SAMPLE

The ACS is sent each month to a sample of roughly 290,000 addresses in the United States and Puerto Rico, or about 3.3 million a year, resulting in more than 2 million final interviews. The sample represents all housing units and group quarters in the United States and Puerto Rico. (Group quarters include places such as college dormitories, prisons, military barracks, and nursing homes.) The addresses are selected from the Census Bureau's Master Address File (MAF), which is also the basis for the decennial census.

The annual ACS sample is smaller than that of the Census 2000 long-form sample, which included about 18 million

housing units. As a result, the ACS needs to combine population or housing data from multiple years to produce reliable numbers for small counties, neighborhoods, and other local areas. To provide information for communities each year, the ACS will provide 1-, 3-, and 5-year estimates.

The ACS sample is not spread evenly across all areas but includes a larger proportion of addresses in sparsely populated rural communities and American Indian reservations and a lower proportion in densely populated areas. Over a 5-year period, the ACS will sample more than 15 million addresses and complete interviews for about 11 million. This sample is sufficient to produce estimates for small geographic areas, such as neighborhoods and sparsely-populated rural counties though the estimates will have larger margins of error than the census long-form data. In a 5-year period no address will be selected for the ACS more than once, and many addresses will never be selected for the survey. It's important to remember that the sample is address based so while a given address will not be in sample again for at least five years, it is possible that individuals who move or have a second home could be surveyed more than once.

GEOGRAPHY

The ACS data are tabulated for a variety of geographic areas ranging in size from broad geographic regions (Northeast, Midwest, South, and West) to cities, towns, neighborhoods, and census block groups. Before December 2008, the ACS data were only available for geographic areas with at least 65,000 people, including regions, divisions, states, the District of Columbia, Puerto Rico, congressional districts, Public Use Microdata Areas (PUMAs)—census-constructed geographic areas, each with approximately a population of 100,000—and many large counties, metropolitan areas, cities, school districts, and American Indian areas. Starting in December 2008, 3-year estimates became available for all areas with at least 20,000 residents, and in 2010, 5-year estimates for geographic areas down to the block group level became available. One-, three-, and five-year estimates—three sets of numbers—are now available and will be refreshed every year. Less populous areas will receive only 5-year estimates. The vast majority of areas will receive only 5-year estimates.

Data Product	Population Threshold	Year of Data Release							
		2006	**2007**	**2008**	**2009**	**2010**	**2011**	**2012**	**2013**
		Year(s) of Data Collection							
1-year Estimates	65,000+	2005	2006	2007	2008	2009	2010	2011	2012
3-year Estimates	20,000+			2005–2007	2006–2008	2007–2009	2008–2010	2009–2011	2010–2012
5-year Estimates	All Areas					2005–2009	2006–2010	2007–2011	2008–2012

The data tables in this book contain data from the 3-year 2010–2012 estimates. These tables are based on the 2010 tabulation geography for political and statistical areas, the same definitions as the 2010 Census. Changes in area boundaries can occur as a result of annexation, new incorporation or disincorporation of cities, towns, and places. For multiyear estimates, the Census Bureau will reports the data based on the most current geographic boundaries incorporating any changes occurring in the multiyear period.

DATA COMPARABILITY

Since the ACS data are collected continuously, they are not always comparable with data collected from the decennial census. For example, both surveys ask about employment status during the week prior to the survey. However, data from the decennial census are typically collected between March and July with a reference date of April 1st, whereas data from the ACS are collected nearly every day and reflect employment throughout the year. Other factors that may also have an impact on the data include seasonal variation in population and minor differences in question wording and question order.

While the categories of income by source are comparable with the decennial long-form data, the monthly collection of ACS data results in a significant difference in concept. In the decennial census, income refers to the previous calendar year whereas the ACS it refers to the previous 12-month period. Most people have a better understanding of what their calendar year income is, especially since the census is taken around tax time. With the ACS, individuals have to report income for a different period each month. A survey response in October of the year will report income from October of the previous year through September of the current year. This may require respondents to actually compute their 12-month income.

In 2006, the ACS began including samples of the population living in group quarters (e.g., jails, college dormitories, and nursing homes) for the first time. As a result, the ACS data from 2008 through 2010 may not be comparable with data from earlier ACS surveys. This is especially true for estimates of young adults and the elderly, who are more likely than other groups to be living in group quarters facilities.

One of the most important uses of the ACS estimates is to make comparisons between estimates – over time or across areas. Several key types of comparisons are of general interest to users:

- Comparisons of estimates from different geographic areas within the same time period (e.g., comparing the proportion of seniors below the poverty level in two counties).

- Comparisons of estimates for the same geographic area across time periods (e.g., comparing the proportion of people below the poverty level in a metropolitan area for 2011 and 2012).

- Comparisons of ACS estimates with the corresponding estimates from past decennial census samples (e.g., comparing the proportion of people below the poverty level in a county for 2010–2012 and 2000).

A number of conditions must be met when comparing survey estimates.

- When comparing data for different geographic areas, always use the same period estimates. When comparing data for an area which only have 5-year estimates to an area with 1-, 3-, and 5-year estimates, it is important to compare only the 5-year estimates.

- When comparing over time for the same geographic area, again, only compare like-year period estimates. For example, it is not appropriate to compare a 1-year estimate for 2012 to a 3-year estimate for 2009–2011.

- Of primary importance is that the comparison takes into account the sampling error associated with each estimate, thus determining whether the observed differences between estimates are statistically significant. Statistical significance means that there is statistical evidence that a true difference exists within the full population, and that the observed difference is unlikely to have occurred by chance due to sampling. A method for determining statistical significance when making comparisons, as well as considerations associated with the various types of comparisons, can be found in Appendix 4 of the *ACS General Handbook*: http://www.census.gov/acs/www/Downloads/handbooks/ACSGeneralHandbook.pdf

- The statistical properties of survey samples like the ACS are dependent upon independence of samples. In the ACS multiyear period estimates, the estimates are based on the sampled households for each year. That means that when comparing estimates for the period 2009–2011 to 2010–2012, two thirds of the sample cases are the same households—those surveyed in 2010 and 2011. The only different (independent) households are those take in 2009 and 2012. When comparisons over time are made, it is best to compare non-overlapping samples. That is, compare estimates for 2007–2009 to the period 2010–1012 because both periods contain independent household samples. To meet this criteria for the use of 5-year estimates, data users should wait for the 2011–2015 data to make time series comparisons.

Finally, the decennial census and the ACS have different residency rules. In the decennial census, population in tabulated by their "usual place of residence" typically where they spend six months or more of the year. This is subject to some seasonal variation due to persons with dual residences. In the ACS, there is a 2-month residency rule. That is, if the respondent has been in the sampled housing unit for 2 months or expects to be resident there for 2 months they are captured in the survey. This can have an impact on communities with highly seasonal populations and college communities.

SUBJECTS COVERED

The topics covered by the ACS focus on demographic, social, economic, and housing characteristics. These topics are virtually the same as those covered by the 2000 census long-form sample data.

Demographic Characteristics
Age, Sex, Hispanic Origin, Race, and Relationship to Householder (e.g., spouse)

Social Characteristics
Marital Status and Marital History; Fertility; Grandparents as Caregivers; Ancestry Place of Birth; Citizenship and Year of Entry; Language Spoken at Home; Educational Attainment and School Enrollment; Residence One Year Ago; Veteran Status, Period of Military Service, and VA Service-Connected Disability Rating; and Disability

Economic Characteristics
Income, Food Stamps Benefit, Labor Force Status, Industry, Occupation, Class of Worker, Place of Work and Journey to Work, Work Status Last Year, Vehicles Available, and Health Insurance Coverage

Housing Characteristics
Year Structure Built, Units in Structure, Year Moved Into Unit, Rooms, Bedrooms, Kitchen Facilities, Plumbing Facilities, House Heating Fuel, Telephone Service Available, and Farm Residence

Financial Characteristics
Tenure (Owner/Renter), Housing Value, Rent, and Selected Monthly Owner Costs

AVAILABILITY OF ACS ESTIMATES

The ACS began in 1996 and has expanded each subsequent year. From 2000 through 2004, the sample included between 740,000 and 900,000 addresses annually. In 2005, the ACS shifted from a demonstration program to the full sample size and design. It became the largest household survey in the United States, with an annual sample size of about 3 million addresses. Beginning with 2005, the ACS single-year estimates are available for geographic areas with a population of 65,000 or more. Three-year period estimates for areas of 20,000 or more were first released for the 2005–2007 time period while 5-year estimates for all areas were first released in 2010. The ACS will continue to accumulate samples over 3-year and 5-year intervals to produce estimates for smaller geographic areas, including census tracts and block groups.

Annually, the ACS produces updated, single-year estimates of demographic, housing, social, and economic characteristics for all states, as well as for larger counties, cities, metropolitan and urban areas, and congressional districts. Geographic areas must have a minimum population of 65,000 to qualify for estimates based on a single year's sample. Every congressional district meets this threshold and therefore new single year estimates are released each year for every congressional district. Some school districts, townships, and American Indian and Alaska Native areas also meet this population threshold.

For areas with populations of at least 20,000, the Census Bureau produces estimates using data collected over a 3-year period. For rural areas and city neighborhoods (including census tracts and block groups) with fewer than 20,000 people, the Census Bureau produces estimates using data collected over a 5-year period, with plans to update these multiyear estimates every year. ACS data are released annually, about 8 months after the end of each calendar year of data collection.

For some geographic areas—including three-quarters of all counties, most school districts, and most cities, towns, and American Indian reservations—only 3-year or 5-year estimates are available because of their population size. Because some federal grant programs allocate funds directly to these areas, Congress can use the 3- and 5-year estimates to evaluate needs at the relevant geographic level, compare characteristics between areas within and among states, and analyze how various formulas distribute funds. The vast majority of areas will receive only 5-year estimates. In partnership with the states, the Census Bureau created *Public Use Microdata Areas (PUMAs)*, which are special, non-overlapping areas within a state, each with a population of about 100,000. These areas will have annual 1-year estimates.

Definitions of these geographic areas are at: http://www.census.gov/acs/www/UseData/geo.htm.

Using the ACS

DIFFERENCES BETWEEN THE ACS AND THE DECENNIAL CENSUS

While the main function of the decennial census is to provide *counts* of people for the purpose of congressional apportionment and legislative redistricting, the primary purpose of the ACS is to measure the changing social and economic *characteristics* of the U.S. population. As a result, the ACS does not provide official counts of the population though users of the data will report the estimate results as though they were counts. In nondecennial census years, the Census Bureau's Population Estimates Program continues to be the official source for annual population totals, by age, race, Hispanic origin, and sex. The ACS sample estimates are controlled to match the decennial census and the Census Bureau's annual population estimates by selected age, sex, race, and Hispanic origin categories. For more information about population estimates, visit the Census Bureau's website at http://www.census.gov/popest/estimates.html.

There are many similarities between the methods used in the past decennial census sample and the ACS but there are also a number of differences in collection method and concepts. Response to both the ACS and decennial census is required by law, a factor that helps improve overall response. Both the ACS and the decennial census sample data are based on information from a sample of the population. The data from the Census 2000 sample of about one-sixth of the population were collected using a "long-form" questionnaire, whose content was the model for the ACS. The sample for the ACS is somewhat smaller, approximately 1 in 7 households, resulting in larger margins of error.

While some differences exist in the specific Census 2000 question wording and that of the ACS, most questions are identical or nearly identical. Differences in the design and implementation of the two surveys are noted below with references provided to a series of evaluation studies that assess the degree to which these differences are likely to impact the estimates. The ACS produces period estimates and these estimates do not measure characteristics for the same time frame as the decennial census estimates, which are interpreted to be a snapshot as of April 1 of the census year.

Some data items were collected by both the ACS and the Census 2000 long form with slightly different definitions

or reference periods that could affect the comparability of the estimates for these items. One example is annual costs for a mobile home. Census 2000 included installment loan costs in the total annual costs but the ACS does not. In this example, the ACS could be expected to yield smaller estimates than Census 2000.

While some differences were a part of the census and survey design objectives, other differences observed between ACS and census results were not by design, but due to nonsampling error—differences related to how well the surveys were conducted. The ACS and the census experience different levels and types of coverage error, different levels and treatment of housing unit and questionnaire item nonresponse, and different instances of measurement and processing error. Both Census 2000 and the ACS had similar high levels of survey coverage and low levels of unit nonresponse. Higher levels of unit nonresponse were found in the nonresponse follow-up stage of Census 2000 while lower levels of item nonresponse were found in the ACS due to a permanent staff of trained interviewers.

Census Bureau analysts have compared sample estimates from Census 2000 with 1-year ACS estimates based on data collected in 2000 and 3-year ACS estimates based on data collected in 1999–2001 in selected counties. In general, ACS estimates were found to be quite similar to those produced from decennial census data.

Detailed information about the ACS methodology can be found at: http://www.census.gov/acs/www/methodology/methodology_main/.

RESIDENCE RULES

The fundamentally different purposes of the ACS and the census, and their timing, led to important differences in the choice of data collection methods. For example, the residence rules for a census or survey determine the sample unit's occupancy status and household membership at the time of collection. Defining the rules in a dissimilar way can affect those two very important estimates. The 2010 census residence rules, which determined where people should be counted, were based on the principle of "usual residence" on April 1, 2010, in keeping with the focus of the census on the requirements of congressional apportionment and state redistricting. To accomplish this, the decennial census attempts to restrict and determine a principal place of residence on one specific date for everyone enumerated. The ACS residence rules are based on a "current residence" concept since data are collected continuously throughout the entire year with responses provided relative to the continuously changing survey interview dates. This method is consistent with the goal of the ACS to produce estimates that reflect annual averages of the characteristics of all areas.

Residence rules determine which individuals are considered to be residents of a particular housing unit or group quarters. While many people have definite ties to a single housing unit or group quarters, some people may stay in different places for significant periods of time over the course of the year. For example, "snow birds" can maintain two residences in different states and do not live in any one location for the entire year. In the decennial census, it is their residence on April 1, or their interpretation of their "usual place of residence," that is the basis for their location. Differences in treatment of these populations in the census and ACS can lead to differences in estimates of the characteristics of some areas.

For the past several censuses, decennial census residence rules were designed to produce an accurate count of the population as of Census Day, April 1, while the ACS residence rules were designed to collect representative information to produce annual average estimates of the characteristics of all types of areas. When interviewing the population living in housing units, the decennial census uses a "usual residence" rule to enumerate people at the place where they live or stay most of the time as of April 1. The ACS uses a "current residence" rule to interview people who are currently living or staying in the sample housing unit as long as their stay at that address will exceed 2 months. The residence rules governing the census enumerations of people in group quarters depend on the type of group quarter and, where permitted, whether people claim a "usual residence" elsewhere. The ACS applies a straight de facto residence rule to every type of group quarter. Everyone living or staying in a group quarter on the day it is visited by an ACS interviewer is eligible to be sampled and interviewed for the survey.

Further information on residence rules can be found at http://www.census.gov/acs/www/Downloads/survey_methodology/acs_design_methodology_ch06.pdf.

The differences in the ACS and census data, as a consequence of the different residence rules, are most likely minimal for most areas and most characteristics. However, for certain segments of the population the usual and current residence concepts could result in different residence decisions. The older population is one of those segments as many retired and active seniors maintain dual residences. Appreciable differences may occur in areas where large proportions of the total population spend several months of the year in what would not be considered their residence under decennial census rules. In particular, data for areas that include large beach, lake, or mountain vacation areas may differ appreciably between the census and the ACS if populations live there for more than 2 months. In addition, college students are to be counted at the location of the college rather than their parent's home. However, during summer months, college students can meet the 2-month residency rule for the ACS and be counted along with their parents rather than at the college.

REFERENCE PERIODS

Estimates produced by the ACS are not measuring exactly what decennial samples have been measuring. The ACS yearly samples, spread over 12 months, collect information that is anchored to the day on which the sampled unit was interviewed, whether it is the day that a mail questionnaire is completed or the day that an interview is conducted by telephone or personal visit. Individual questions with time references such as "last week" or "the last 12 months" all begin the reference period as of this interview date. Even the information on types and amounts of income refers to the 12 months prior to the day the question is answered. ACS interviews are conducted just about every day of the year, and all of the estimates that the survey releases are considered to be averages for a specific time period. The 1-year estimates reflect the full calendar year; 3-year and 5-year estimates reflect the full 36- or 60-month period.

Most decennial census sample estimates are anchored in this same way to the reference date of April 1. The most obvious difference between the ACS and the census is the overall time frame in which they are conducted. The census enumeration time period is less than half the time period used to collect data for each single-year ACS estimate. But a more important difference is that the distribution of census enumeration dates are highly clustered in March and April (when most census mail returns were received) with additional, smaller clusters seen in May and June (when nonresponse follow-up activities took place).

This means that the data from the decennial census, intended to reflect the characteristics of the population and housing on April 1, tend to describe the characteristics in the March through June time period (with an over-representation of March/April). The ACS data describe the characteristics nearly every day over the full calendar year. For employment and income estimates, the decennial census referred to the prior calendar year for all respondents, while the ACS asks about the 12 months preceding the interview.

Those who are interested in more information about differences in reference periods should refer to the Census Bureau's guidance on comparisons that contrasts for each question the specific reference periods used in Census 2000 with those used in the ACS: http://www.census.gov/acs/www/guidance_for_data_users/table_comparisons/.

Some specific differences in reference periods between the ACS and the decennial census are described below. Users should consider the potential impact these different reference periods could have on distributions when comparing ACS estimates with Census 2000.

Income Data

To estimate annual income, the Census 2000 long-form sample used the calendar year prior to Census Day as the reference period, and the ACS uses the 12 months prior to the interview date as the reference period. Thus, while Census 2000 collected income information for calendar year 1999, the ACS collects income information for the 12 months preceding the interview date. The responses are a mixture of 12 reference periods ranging from, in the case of the 2012 ACS single-year estimates, the full calendar year 2011 through November 2012. The ACS income responses for each of these reference periods are individually inflation-adjusted to represent dollar values for the ACS collection year. Further inflation adjustments are made to the 3- and 5-year estimates to reflect dollar values of the final year of the estimate. It's important to note that the rotating reference period for income can result in misreporting. The calendar year reference period of the decennial census coincides with an individual's annual salary and is also collected around tax time. Respondents will have a good idea of what their annual salary is. In the ACS, the respondent has to calculate their income for the previous 12 months, a figure which can vary considerably throughout the year.

School Enrollment

The school enrollment question on the ACS asks if a person had "at any time in the last 3 months attended a school or college." A consistent 3-month reference period is used for all interviews. In contrast, Census 2000 asked if a person had "at any time since February 1 attended a school or college." Since Census 2000 data were collected from mid-March to late-August, the reference period could have been as short as about 6 weeks or as long as 7 months.

Utility Costs

The reference periods for two utility cost questions—gas and electricity—differ between Census 2000 and the ACS. The census asked for annual costs, while the ACS asks for the utility costs in the previous month.

PERIOD ESTIMATES

The ACS produces period estimates of socioeconomic and housing characteristics. It is designed to provide estimates that describe the average characteristics of an area over a specific time period. In the case of ACS single-year estimates, the period is the calendar year (e.g., the 2012 ACS covers January through December 2012). In the case of ACS multiyear estimates, the period is either 3 or 5 calendar years (e.g., the 2010–2012 ACS 3-year estimates cover January 2010 through December 2012, and the 2008–2012 ACS 5-year estimates cover January 2008 through December 2012). The ACS multiyear estimates are similar in many ways to the ACS single-year estimates, but they encompass a longer time period.

The differences in time periods between single-year and multiyear ACS estimates affect decisions about which set of estimates should be used for a particular analysis. While one may think of these estimates as representing average characteristics over a single calendar year or multiple calendar years, it must be remembered that the 1-year estimates are not calculated as an average of 12 monthly values and the multiyear estimates are not calculated as the average of either 36 or 60 monthly values, nor are the multiyear estimates calculated as the average of 3 or 5 single-year estimates. Rather, the ACS collects survey information continuously nearly every day of the year and then aggregates the results over a specific time period—1 year, 3 years, or 5 years. The data collection is spread evenly across the entire period represented so as not to overrepresent any particular month or year within the period.

Because ACS estimates provide information about the characteristics of the population and housing for areas over an entire time frame, ACS single-year and multiyear estimates contrast with "point-in-time" estimates, such as those from the decennial census long-form samples or monthly employment estimates from the Current Population Survey (CPS), which are designed to measure characteristics as of a certain date or narrow time period. For example, Census 2000 was designed to measure the characteristics of the population and housing in the United States based upon data collected around April 1, 2000, and thus its data reflect a narrower time frame than ACS data. The monthly CPS collects data for an even narrower time frame, the week containing the 12th of each month.

Most areas have consistent population characteristics throughout the calendar year, and their period estimates may not look much different from estimates that would be obtained from a "point-in-time" survey design. However, some areas may experience changes in the estimated characteristics of the population, depending on when in the calendar year the measurement occurred. For these areas, the ACS period estimates (even for a single-year) may noticeably differ from "point-in-time" estimates. The impact will be more noticeable in smaller areas where changes such as a factory closing can have a large impact on population characteristics, and in areas with a large natural event such as Hurricane Katrina's impact on the New Orleans area. This logic can be extended to better interpret 3- and 5-year estimates where the periods involved are much longer. If, over the full period of time (for example, 36 months), there have been major or consistent changes in certain population or housing characteristics for an area, a period estimate for that area could differ markedly from estimates based on a "point-in-time" survey. For example, the 5-year estimates for 2008–2012 will be affected by the volatility in the economy and the housing market during those years and may mask shorter term fluctuations.

The tables in this book include 3-year estimates from 2010 through 2012. Some areas will show a more rapid recovery from the recession than others and experience stronger growth between the 2000 and 2010 censuses.

The important thing to keep in mind is that ACS single-year estimates describe the population and characteristics of an area for the full year, not for any specific day or period within the year, while ACS multiyear estimates describe the population and characteristics of an area for the full 3- or 5-year period, not for any specific day, period, or year within the multiyear time period.

Single-year estimates provide more current information

Single-year estimates provide more current information about areas that have changing population and/or housing characteristics because they are based on the most current data—data from the past calendar year. In contrast, multiyear estimates provide less current information because they are based on both data from the previous year and data that are up to 5 years old. As noted earlier, for many areas with minimal change taking place, using the "less current" sample used to produce the multiyear estimates may not have a substantial influence on the estimates. However, in areas experiencing major changes over a given time period, the multiyear estimates may be quite different from the single-year estimates for any of the individual years. Single-year and multiyear estimates are not expected to be the same because they are based on data from two different time periods. This will be true even if the ACS single year is the midyear of the ACS multiyear period (e.g., 2011 single year, 2009–2012 multiyear).

Multiyear estimates are based on larger sample sizes and are therefore more reliable

The 3-year estimates are based on three times as many sample cases as the 1-year estimates. For some characteristics, this increased sample is needed for the estimates to be reliable enough for use in certain applications. For other characteristics, the increased sample may not be necessary.

Multiyear estimates are the only type of estimates available for geographic areas with populations of less than 65,000. Users may think that they only need to use multiyear estimates when they are working with small areas, but this isn't the case. Estimates for large geographic areas benefit from the increased sample, resulting in more precise estimates of population and housing characteristics, especially for subpopulations within those areas. In addition, users may determine that they want to use single-year estimates, despite their reduced reliability, as building blocks to produce estimates for meaningful higher levels of geography. These aggregations will similarly benefit from the increased sample sizes and gain reliability.

Currency	Reliability
1-year estimates provide information based on the most current year	Sample sizes producing estimates may be small and impact statistical reliability
3-year estimates provide information based on the last year and the 2 years before that	3-year estimates are based on 3 times as many sample cases as 1-year estimates
5-year estimates provide information based on the last year and the 4 years before that	5-year estimates are based on 5 times as many sample cases as 1-year estimates

DECIDING WHICH ACS ESTIMATE TO USE

Three primary uses of ACS estimates are:

- to understand the characteristics of the population of an area for local planning needs,

- to make comparisons across areas, and

- to assess change over time in an area.

Local planning could include making local decisions such as where to place schools or hospitals, determining the need for senior services or transportation, and carrying out other infrastructure analysis. In the past, decennial census sample data provided the most comprehensive information. However, the currency of those data suffered through the intercensal period, and the ability to assess change over time was limited. ACS estimates greatly improve the currency of data for understanding the characteristics of housing and population and enhance the ability to assess change over time. At the same time, small differences between ACS estimates can lead to misinterpretation due to larger margins of error.

Several key factors can help users decide whether to use single-year or multiyear ACS estimates for areas where both are available:

- intended use of the estimates

- required precision, or reliability, of the estimates

- currency of the estimates

All of these factors, along with an understanding of the differences between single-year and multiyear ACS estimates, should be taken into consideration when deciding which set of estimates to use.

For users interested in obtaining estimates for small geographic areas, multiyear ACS estimates are the only option. For the very smallest of these areas (less than 20,000 population), the only option is to use the 5-year ACS estimates. Users have a choice of two sets of multiyear estimates when analyzing data for small geographic areas with populations of at least 20,000. Both 3- and 5-year ACS estimates are available. Only the largest areas with populations of 65,000 and more receive all three data series.

The key trade-off to be made in deciding whether to use single-year or multiyear estimates is between currency and precision. In general, the single-year estimates are preferred, as they will be more relevant to the current conditions. However, the user must take into account the level of uncertainty present in the single-year estimates, which may be large for small subpopulation groups and rare characteristics. While single-year estimates offer more current estimates, they also have higher sampling variability. One measure, the coefficient of variation (CV), can help you determine the fitness for use of a single-year estimate in order to assess if you should opt instead to use the multiyear estimate (or if you should use a 5-year estimate rather than a 3-year estimate). The CV is calculated as the ratio of the standard error of the estimate to the estimate, times 100. A single-year estimate with a small CV is usually preferable to a multiyear estimate as it is more up to date. However, multiyear estimates are an alternative option when a single-year estimate has an unacceptably high CV. Single-year estimates for small subpopulations (e.g., grandparents 65 and over who are responsible for grandchildren) will typically have larger CVs. In general, multiyear estimates are preferable to single-year estimates when looking at estimates for small subpopulations.

For the complete discussion on deciding which estimates to use and on calculating the CV, see Appendix 1 of the *ACS General Handbook*: http://www.census.gov/acs/www/Downloads/handbooks/ACSGeneralHandbook.pdf.

Often users want to compare the characteristics of one area to those of another area. These comparisons can be in the form of rankings or of specific pairs of comparisons. Whenever you want to make a comparison between two different geographic areas, you need to take the type of estimate into account. It is important that comparisons be made within the same estimate type. That is, 1-year estimates should only be compared with other 1-year estimates, 3-year estimates should only be compared with other 3-year estimates, and 5-year estimates should only be compared with other 5-year estimates.

You certainly can compare characteristics for areas with populations of 30,000 to areas with populations of 100,000 but you should use the data set that they have in common. In this example you could use the 3- or the 5-year estimates because they are available for areas of 30,000 and areas of 100,000. You should NOT compare the single-year estimate for the area of 100,000 to the 3-year estimate for the area of 30,000. This book includes only the 3-year estimates for 2010 through 2012 so comparisons across geographic areas will be appropriate.

Users are encouraged to make comparisons between sequential single-year estimates. In American FactFinder

(AFF), comparison profiles are available beginning with the 2007 single-year data. These profiles identify statistically significant differences between each year from 2007 through the most recently released year.

Caution is needed when using multiyear estimates for estimating year-to-year change in a particular characteristic. This is because roughly two-thirds of the respondents in a 3-year estimate overlap with the respondents in the next year's 3-year estimate period (the overlap is roughly four-fifths for 5-year estimates). When comparing 3-year estimates from 2009–2011 with those from 2010–2012, the differences in overlapping multiyear estimates are driven by differences in the non-overlapping years (i.e. 2009 and 2012). A more appropriate comparison of change over time would be comparing the 2007–2009 3-year estimate to the 2010–2012 3-year estimate because they include responses from total independent samples. Comparison of overlapping periods should be made with caution.

Users who are interested in comparing overlapping multiyear period estimates should refer to Appendix 4 of the *ACS General Handbook* for more information: http://www.census.gov/acs/www/Downloads/handbooks/ ACSGeneralHandbook.pdf.

Multiyear estimates are likely to confuse some data users, in part because of their statistical properties, and in part because this is a new product from the Census Bureau. The ACS will provide all states and communities that have at least 65,000 residents with single-year estimates of demographic, housing, social, and economic characteristics—a boon to government agencies that need to budget and plan for public services like transportation, medical care, and schools. For geographic areas with smaller populations, the ACS samples too few households to provide reliable single-year estimates. For these communities, several years of data will be pooled together to create reliable 3- or 5-year estimates.

Single-year, 3- and 5-year estimates from the ACS are all "period" estimates that represent data collected over a period of time as opposed to "point-in-time" estimates, such as the decennial census. While a single-year estimate includes information collected over a 12-month period, a 3-year estimate represents data collected over a 36-month period, and a 5-year estimate includes data collected over a 60-month period. Therefore, ACS estimates based on data collected from 2010–2012 should not be called "2011" or "2012" estimates. Nor should 2008–2012 period estimates be labeled "2010" estimates, even though that is the midpoint of the 5-year period. Multiyear estimates should be labeled to indicate clearly

the full period of time (e.g., "The poverty rate for persons 65 and over in 2010–2012 was X percent"). The primary advantage of using multiyear estimates is the increased statistical reliability of the data for less populated areas and small population subgroups.

Multiyear estimates should, in general, be used when single-year estimates have large CVs or when the precision of the estimates is more important than the currency of the data. Multiyear estimates should also be used when analyzing data for smaller geographies and smaller population subgroups in larger geographies. Multiyear estimates are also of value when examining change over non-overlapping time periods and for smoothing data trends over time.

Single-year estimates should, in general, be used for larger geographies and populations when currency is more important than the precision of the estimates. Single-year estimates should be used to examine year-to-year change for estimates with small CVs. Given the availability of a single-year estimate, calculating the CV provides useful information to determine if the single-year estimate should be used. For areas believed to be experiencing rapid changes in a characteristic, single-year estimates should generally be used rather than multiyear estimates as long as the CV for the single-year estimate is reasonable for the specific usage.

Local area variations may occur due to rapidly occurring changes. Multiyear estimates will tend to be insensitive to such changes when they first occur. Single-year estimates, if associated with sufficiently small CVs, can be very valuable in identifying and studying such phenomena.

Data users also need to use caution in looking at trends involving income or other measures that are adjusted for inflation, such as rental costs, home values, and energy costs. Note that inflation adjustment is based on a national-level consumer price index: it does not adjust for differences in costs of living across different geographic areas.

Appendix 5 of the *ACS General Handbook* provides information on the adjustment of single-year and multiyear ACS estimates for inflation: http://www.census.gov/acs/ www/Downloads/handbooks/ACSGeneralHandbook .pdf.

MARGIN OF ERROR

All data that are based on samples, such as the ACS and the census long-form samples, include a range of uncertainty. Two broad types of error can occur: sampling error and nonsampling error. Nonsampling errors can result from mistakes in how the data are reported or coded, problems in the sampling frame or survey questionnaires, or problems related to nonresponse or interviewer bias. The Census Bureau tries to minimize nonsampling errors by using trained interviewers and by carefully reviewing the survey's sampling methods, data processing techniques, and questionnaire design.

Appendix 6 of the *ACS General Handbook* includes a more detailed description of different types of errors in the ACS and other measures of ACS quality: http://www .census.gov/acs/www/Downloads/handbooks/ACSGeneral Handbook.pdf.

Sampling error occurs when data are based on a sample of a population rather than the full population. Sampling error is easier to measure than nonsampling error and can be used to assess the statistical reliability of survey data. For any given area, the larger the sample and the more months included in the data, the greater the confidence in the estimate. The Census Bureau reported the 90-percent confidence interval on all ACS estimates produced for 2005 and earlier. Beginning with the release of the 2006 ACS data, *margins of error (MOE)* are now provided for every ACS estimate. Ninety percent confidence intervals define a range expected to contain the *true* value of an estimate with a level of confidence of 90 percent. Margins of error are easily converted into these confidence ranges. By adding and subtracting the margin of error from the point estimate, we can calculate the 90-percent confidence interval for an estimate. Therefore, we can be 90 percent confident that the true number falls between the lower-bound interval and the upper-bound interval.

Detailed information about sampling error and instructions for calculating confidence intervals and margins of error are included in Appendix 3 of the *ACS General Handbook*: http://www.census.gov/acs/www/Downloads/ handbooks/ACSGeneralHandbook.pdf.

The margin of error around an estimate is important because it helps one draw conclusions about the data. Small differences between two estimates may not be statistically significant if the confidence intervals of those estimates overlap. However, the Census Bureau cautions data users not to rely on overlapping confidence intervals as a test for statistical significance, because this method will not always produce accurate results. Instead, the Census Bureau recommends following the detailed instructions for conducting statistical significance tests in Appendix 4 of the *ACS General Handbook*.

In some cases, data users will need to construct custom ACS estimates by combining data across multiple geographic areas or population subgroups or it may be necessary to derive a new percentage, proportion, or ratio from published ACS data. In such cases, additional calculations are needed to produce confidence intervals and margins of error for the derived estimates. Appendix 3 of the *ACS General Handbook* provides detailed instructions on how to make these calculations. Note that these error measures do not tell us about the magnitude of nonsampling errors.

Some advanced data users will also want to construct custom ACS estimates from the Census Bureau's Public Use Microdata Samples (PUMS). There are separate instructions for conducting significance tests for PUMS estimates, available on the Census Bureau's American FactFinder (AFF) website at: http://www.census .gov/acs/www/Downloads/data_documentation/pums/ Accuracy/2010AccuracyPUMS.pdf and http://www.census .gov/acs/www/Downloads/data_documentation/pums/ Accuracy/2008_2010AccuracyPUMS.pdf.

Accessing ACS Data Online

All ACS data are available through the Census Bureau's American FactFinder (AFF) website at http://factfinder2.census.gov. From the AFF home page, there are three paths to accessing the data:

- Community Facts – this will provide summary data profiles for a single geographic area. It will be important to check the table titles to verify that the ACS is the source of the data presented.

- Guided Search – this path leads the user through six steps to select the characteristics and geography of interest. Guided Search is available for all Census datasets so it is still important to verify that the ACS is the desired source.

- Advanced Search – this path provides the most flexibility for data selection by the user but also requires a basic level of knowledge about Census datasets and characteristics. Clicking on the "Topics" button will allow the user to view and select "Datasets." For each year of available ACS data there are three datasets shown – the 1-year estimates (based on the 2012 ACS), the 3-year estimates (based on the 2010–2012 ACS), and the 5-year estimates (based on the 2008–2012 ACS). The tables in this book were produced from the 3-year estimates for 2010–2012. It is important for all users to understand that once a data set is selected, the accessed tables will all correspond to this specific data set. All tables are clearly labeled, identifying the data set.

Basic information on using the functions and features of American FactFinder can be found at factfinder2.census.gov/faces/nav/jsf/pages/index.xhtml. The *American FactFinder* main page provides information about available data and guidance on using FactFinder, under the tabs *Using American FactFinder* and *What We Provide*. Additional assistance can be found at FactFinder Help (online help, census data information, glossary, and tutorial): factfinder2.census.gov/help/en/american_factfinder_help.htm#.

The various ACS data products are described below.

- **Data Profiles, Quick Tables and Ranking Tables.** The *data profiles, quick tables* and *ranking tables* are good places to start for novice data users. *Data profiles and quick tables* provide separate fact sheets on the social, economic, demographic, and housing characteristics for different geographic areas, while *ranking tables* provide state-level rankings of key ACS variables.

- **Geographic comparison tables.** Those interested in geographic comparisons for areas other than states may be interested in the *geographic comparison tables*, which allow comparison of ACS data across a variety of geographic areas, including metropolitan areas, cities, counties, and congressional districts.

- **Subject tables.** These are similar to *data profiles* but are specific to a more detailed characteristic or topic (e.g., employment, education, and income). *Subject tables* provide pre-tabulated numbers and percentages for a wide variety of topics, often available separately by age (60 and over and 65 and over), gender, or race/ethnicity.

- **Selected population profiles.** The most detailed race/ethnic data are available through the *selected population profiles*, which provide summary tables separately for more than 400 detailed race, ethnic, tribal, ancestry, and country of birth groups.

- **Comparison profiles.** The *comparison profiles* show data side-by-side from multiple years, indicating where there is a statistically significant difference between the two sets of estimates. Comparison profiles are only available for 1-year estimates.

- **Detailed tables and summary files.** The *detailed tables* are the best source for advanced data users or those who want access to the most comprehensive ACS tables. The tables in this book were developed through this option. For more advanced users, *detailed tables* are also available for download through the ACS Summary File: www.census.gov/acs/www/data_documentation/summary_file.

- **Thematic maps.** The *thematic maps* provide graphic displays of the data available through the various tables. Different shades of color are used to display variations in the data across geographic areas. Data users can also highlight areas with statistically different values from a selected state, county, or metropolitan area of interest. If a mapping option is available, it will display as an option when you view a table.

- **Public Use Microdata Sample files.** Those with expertise in using SAS, SPSS, or STATA may also be interested in the *Public Use Microdata Sample (PUMS) files*, which contain a sample of individual records of people and households that responded to the survey (stripped of all identifying information). The PUMS files permit analysis of specific population groups and custom variables that are not available through the summary tables in American FactFinder. For example, PUMS data users can look at the proportion of persons 60 to 69 with a disability by whether they own or rent their home or employment status and occupation of the 55 to 69 population. This flexibility is not provided by the pre-tabulated summary tables provided in American FactFinder. Data users can also combine multiple years of PUMS data to produce data for relatively small population subgroups (e.g., female physicians over age 55). More information about the PUMS is available at http://www.census.gov/acs/www/data_documentation/public_use_microdata_sample.

For readers who are used to data from the traditional decennial census long-form, it is important to note that there are many conceptual and data collection differences in the ACS. The following is a summary of some of these differences which are described more fully in the chapter "Using the ACS."

- The ACS data are complex and cover a broad range of topics and geographic areas. Because this is a relatively new survey, many people do not fully understand how to interpret and use the ACS data. The key points are summarized below.

- Use caution in comparing ACS data with data from the decennial census or other sources. Every survey uses different methods, which could affect the comparability of the numbers.

- The ACS was designed to provide estimates of the characteristics of the population, not to provide counts of the population in different geographic areas or population subgroups. However, counts of the population are often what is required by grant applications and researchers.

- Be careful in drawing conclusions about small differences between two estimates because they may not be statistically different. Statistical testing should always be considered based on the sensitivity of conclusions to differences in the data results.

- Data users need to be careful not to interpret annual fluctuations in the data as long-term trends. Again, statistical testing is necessary to determine if annual fluctuations are real or merely a result of the sample.

- Use caution in comparing data from 2006 and later surveys with data from the 2000–2005 surveys. Unlike earlier surveys, the 2006 and later ACS surveys include samples of the population living in group quarters (e.g., college dorms and nursing homes), so the data may not be comparable, especially for young adults and the elderly, who are more likely than other age groups to be living in group quarters facilities.

- The questionnaire series to define disability changed in 2008 making it impossible to compare disability status for periods before that date.

- Data users should not interpret or refer to 3-year or 5-year period estimates as estimates of the middle year or last year in the series. For example, a 2008–2010 estimate is not a "2009 average."

- Data users should always be consistent in comparing similar period estimates over time or between geographic areas. Compare 1-year to 1-year, 3-year to 3-year, and 5-year to 5-year estimates. Since geographic areas of different population size have different period estimates available, always make comparisons using the same period estimate. Do not compare a 1-year estimate for a large population size are to a 5-year estimate for a small area or census tract.

- Data users should *not* rely on overlapping confidence intervals as a test for statistical significance because this method will not always provide an accurate result.

More ACS Resources

There is a wealth of information about the ACS on the Web with new information available on a regular basis. Each year, the ACS data release represents a new stage in the process. Consequently, many new documents are required to explain the survey, year-to-year changes, and how to use it. These resources cover many of the topics discussed in this book, but in greater detail.

The best place to start is the Census Bureau's ACS main page: http://www.census.gov/acs/www.

BACKGROUND AND OVERVIEW INFORMATION

The American Community Survey site map provides an overview of the links and materials that are available online, including numerous reference documents. http://www.census.gov/acs/www/utilities/sitemap.php

The site map corresponds to the menu headings on the ACS main page and provides much more detail than the "drop-down" categories displayed.

About the Survey provides background and general information about the importance of the ACS, how sampled households are selected, response options, privacy protections and questionnaire information. http://www.census.gov/acs/www/about_the_survey/american_community_survey/

Guidance for Data Users provides detailed information that helps users understand the geographic coverage of the survey data, how and when to use the multiyear estimates and handbooks for users of various types. http://www.census.gov/acs/www/guidance_for_data_users/guidance_main/

Data & Documentation is critical for users who need to understand the details of the data that's available, research, and detailed documentation for the various data file products. http://www.census.gov/acs/www/data_documentation/data_main/

Methodology provides the most detailed information about the survey sample size, response rates, and data quality. http://www.census.gov/acs/www/methodology/methodology_main/

Library is a link to volumes of research and papers describing aspects of survey methodology, research, and analytical reports categorized by year. http://www.census.gov/acs/www/library/by_year/2013/

PUMS Accuracy of the Data (2011)
Provides a basic understanding of the sample design, estimation methodology, and accuracy of the 2010 ACS data. http://www.census.gov/acs/www/Downloads/data_documentation/pums/Accuracy/2011AccuracyPUMS.pdf

ACS Sample Size
Provides sample size information for each state for each year of the ACS. The initial sample size and the final completed interviews are provided. Sample sizes for all published geographic entities starting with the 2007 ACS are available in the B98 series of detailed tables on American FactFinder. http://www.census.gov/acs/www/methodology/sample_size_data

ACS Quality Measures
Multi-Year Estimate Study Quality Measures Definitions: Includes information about the steps taken by the Census Bureau to improve the accuracy of ACS data. Four indicators of survey quality are described and measures are provided at the national and state level. http://www.census.gov/acs/www/Downloads/methodology/special_data_studies/multiyear_estimates/Quality_Measures_Documentation_MYE.pdf

GUIDANCE ON DATA PRODUCTS AND USING THE DATA

How to Use the Data
Includes links to many documents and materials that explain the ACS data products. http://www.census.gov/acs/www/guidance_for_data_users/guidance_main

Comparing ACS Data to Other Sources
Guidance on comparing the ACS data products to other years of ACS data and to Census 2000 long-form data. http://www.census.gov/acs/www/guidance_for_data_users/comparing_data

When to Use 1-year, 3-year, or 5-year Estimates
The availability of multiple characteristic estimates for a given geographic area for different period estimates can be confusing for users of ACS data. Guidance on comparing across geographies and time periods.
http://www.census.gov/acs/www/guidance_for_data_users/estimates/

Information on Using Different Sources of Data for Income and Poverty
Highlights the sources that should be used for data on income and poverty, focusing on comparing the ACS and the Current Population Survey (CPS).
http://www.census.gov/hhes/www/poverty/about/data-sources/description.html

Public Use Microdata Sample (PUMS)
Provides guidance on accessing ACS microdata.
www.census.gov/acs/www/data_documentation/public_use_microdata_sample

OTHER DATA RESOURCES

- FactFinder Help (online help, census data information, glossary, and tutorial)
  http://factfinder2.census.gov/help/en/american_factfinder_help.htm

- Guide to the Data Products (Web page)
  http://www.census.gov/acs/www/data_documentation/product_descriptions

- *A Compass for Understanding and Using American Community Survey Data: What General Data Users Need to Know* provides a complete overview.
  www.census.gov/acs/www/Downloads/handbooks/ACSGeneralHandbook.pdf

- Other Compass handbooks are available for the business community, media, Congress and many other user groups.
  http://www.census.gov/acs/www/guidance_for_data_users/handbooks/

- *Using the American Community Survey: Benefits and Challenges*, edited by Constance F. Citro and Graham Kalton (The National Academies Press, 2007). An excellent overview of the ACS, complete with several chapters of useful information for data users. The book is available for purchase and is also available to read online at no charge.
  books.nap.edu/catalog.php?record_id=11901

PART A
POPULATION SUMMARY

POPULATION SUMMARY

In 1950 at the early stage of the Baby Boom generation, the nation's population stood at 179,323,000. More than 30 percent of the population was under the age of 15 while less than 10 percent was age 65 or older. The median age in 1950 was 29.5 years. By 2010, less than 20 percent of the population was under the age of 15 and 13 percent was 65 or older with a median age of 37.2 years. Based on the Census Bureau's latest projections, by 2030 when the youngest of the Baby Boom generation passes the age of 65, fully one out of every five residents (20.3 percent) will be over the age of 65 while less than 19 percent are under 15 years of age resulting in a median age of 39.6 years.

While the aging of the Baby Boom generation captures a lot of national attention, it's important to note that change is not uniform. As the geographic level of analysis gets smaller, the variation across our communities grows with some areas following national trends while others outpace or lag behind the nation. Analyzing population change is like telling a story of our communities. It's important to look at population change over time, the varying demographic composition of our communities, and how each compares to other areas. The text and tables in this volume are intended to provide the basic demographic portrait of the nation's older population at the state, county, city, metropolitan area, and congressional district levels and allow planners, researchers, and interested individuals to tell their own stories.

The tables in this book are for the **3-year period, 2010–2012,** from the Census Bureau's American Community Survey for **geographic areas of at least 65,000 population.** The one exception is Table A which presents a population summary and includes the population change from the 2010 Census. *It is important to note that the April 1, 2010 Census figures reported here represent various revisions to the originally published Census counts. These populations are labeled "April 1, 2010 Census Population Estimates Base."* Most of these revisions represent the correction of small geographic misallocations.

POPULATION CHANGE

In the few short years from the 2010 Census, the nation's population has grown by nearly 3 million people, or about one percent and totals 311.7 million people. California remains in the largest state with a population of 37.7 million, followed by Texas, New York, Florida and Illinois as the remaining top five states. More than a third (36.8 percent) of the nation's total population lives in these five largest states and they have about the same proportion (35.7 percent) of the population age 65 years or more. The smallest five states (Wyoming, the District of Columbia, Vermont, North Dakota and Alaska) total 3.2 million in population, slightly over one percent of the nation's total. Their share of the 65 and over population is just less than one percent.

The District of Columbia grew the fastest at 2.8 percent followed by the states of North Dakota and Texas increasing at about 2.0 percent. Numerically, the District of Columbia increased by about 17,000 while Texas added nearly 500,000 and North Dakota's growth was about 13,700. Michigan and Rhode Island were the only two states to have lost population over this period.

One third of the nation's population (103.8 million people) lives in cities. New York City remains the largest city with a population of 8.3 million, followed by Los Angeles with 3.8 million, Chicago with 2.7 million and Houston with 2.1 million residents. The data presented here is limited to 505 cities of 65,000 or more in population. The smallest city in this group is Yuba City in California with a population of 65,005. Of the 10 fastest growing cities, only 2, New Orleans, LA and Irvine City, CA are in the top 100 of population size. Springdale, AR had the fastest rate of growth at 6.3 percent but it is the 437th largest city. Nine cities have populations of over 1 million and 33 are over 500,000. There are 222 cities with populations between 65,000 and 100,000. California has the most cities over 65,000 with 125 while Alaska, Delaware, Hawaii, Maine and North Dakota only have one each.

The 364 Metropolitan Statistical Areas over 65,000 shown here total 261.0 million in population or 83.8 percent of the U.S. total. The New York-Northern New Jersey-Long

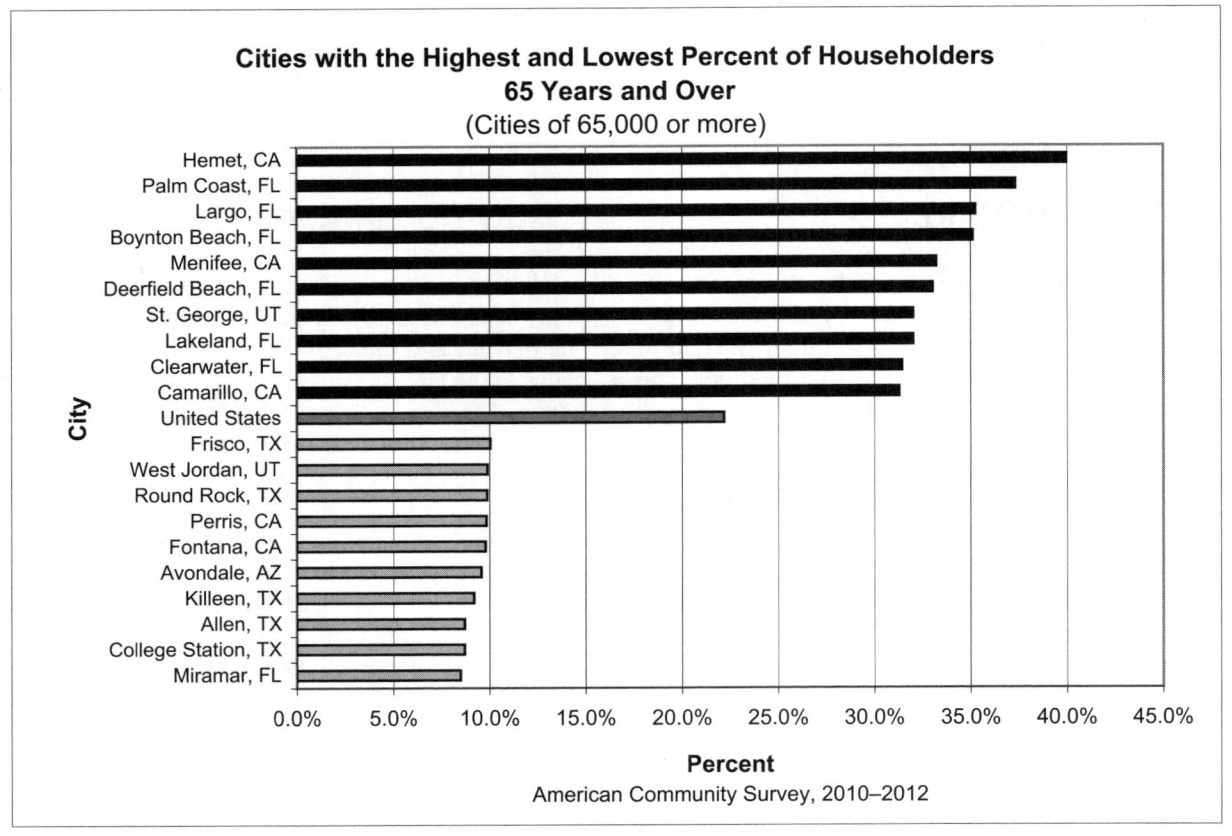

Cities with the Highest and Lowest Percent of Householders 65 Years and Over
(Cities of 65,000 or more)

American Community Survey, 2010–2012

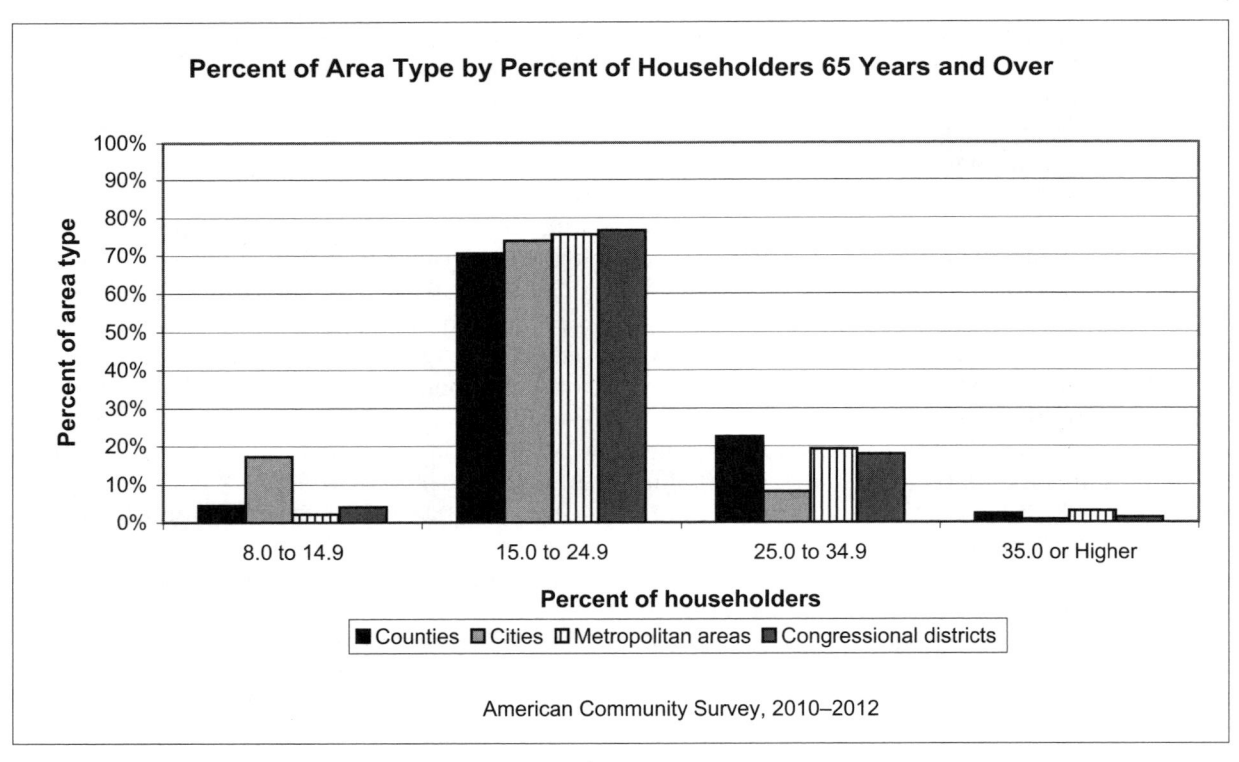

Percent of Area Type by Percent of Householders 65 Years and Over

American Community Survey, 2010–2012

Island metro area is the largest at 19.0 million followed by Los Angeles-Long Beach-Santa Ana at 12.9 million. Fifty-one metropolitan areas have more than 1 million population while twice that number have populations of 500,000 or more. While the New York-Northern New Jersey-Long Island area is the largest, its growth rate ranked only 183rd. The Austin-Round Rock-San Marcos, TX metropolitan area, the 34th largest metro area, was the fastest growing at a rate of 3.6 percent. Pine Bluff, AR, the 344th largest MSA, declined by 1.3 percent.

Nationwide, excluding the District of Columbia, the average population of the 435 congressional districts is 714,921. California has the largest congressional delegation with 53 seats while Alaska, Delaware, Montana, North Dakota, South Dakota, Vermont and Wyoming all have 1 seat each. Wyoming has the smallest population per representative at 563,000 while Montana's single representative represents nearly 1 million residents. Seventy-six congressional districts are estimated to have lost population between the 2010 Census count and the 2010–2012 American Community Survey estimates. Congressional District 3 in Nevada and District 26 in Florida had the fastest growth rates, tied at 4.4 percent. Congressional District 1 in Nevada had the greatest decline in population at 2.1 percent.

Percent of Householders 65 Years and Over Who are Living Alone

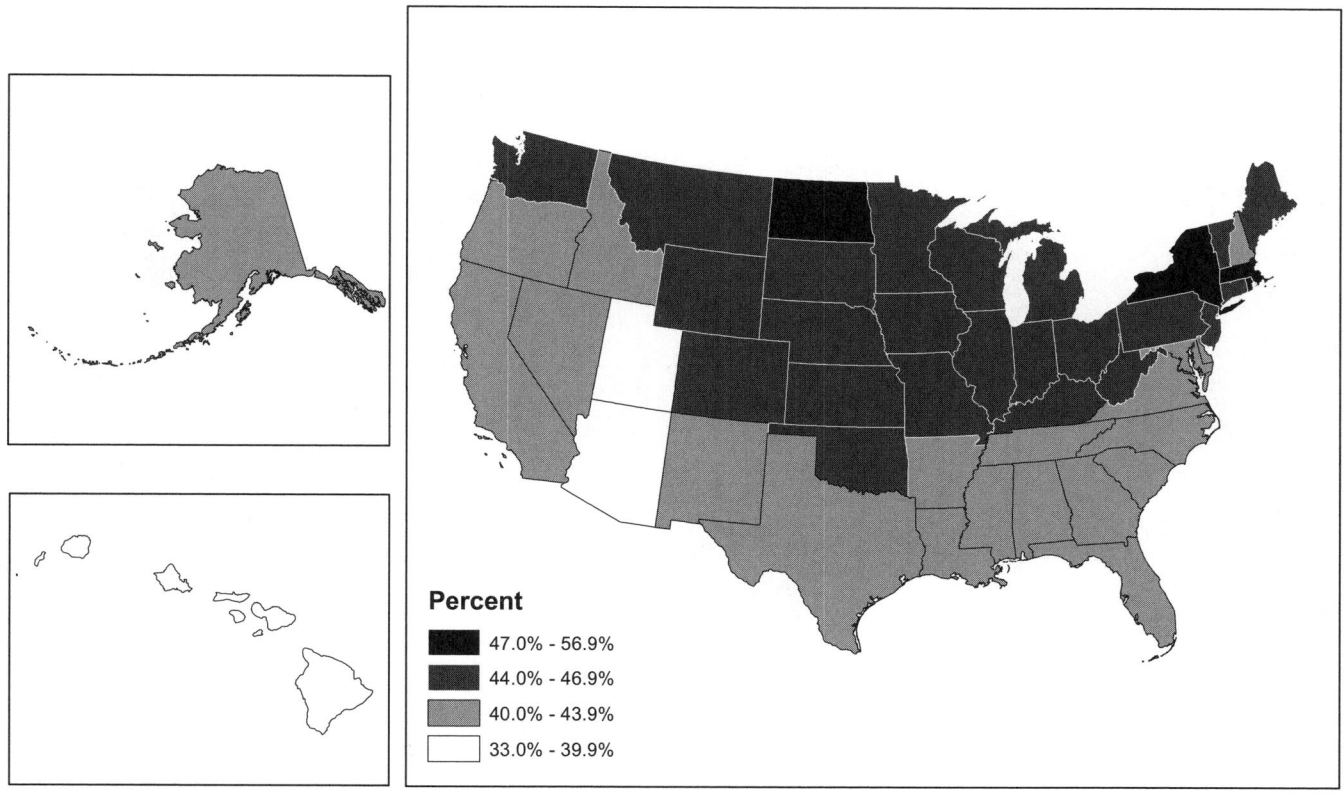

Percent

- 47.0% - 56.9%
- 44.0% - 46.9%
- 40.0% - 43.9%
- 33.0% - 39.9%

Selected State Rankings

State	Total Population 2010–2012	Population Rank	State	Percent Change 2010 to 2010–2012	Percent Change Rank	State	Total Households 2010–2012	Household Rank
Alabama	4,803,488	23	Alabama	0.50	36	Alabama	1,837,823	23
Alaska	723,120	47	Alaska	1.81	5	Alaska	253,718	50
Arizona	6,477,128	16	Arizona	1.33	9	Arizona	2,357,799	17
Arkansas	2,936,822	32	Arkansas	0.72	31	Arkansas	1,129,845	31
California	37,686,586	1	California	1.16	15	California	12,474,950	1
Colorado	5,117,453	22	Colorado	1.75	6	Colorado	1,977,737	22
Connecticut	3,584,561	29	Connecticut	0.29	43	Connecticut	1,355,973	29
Delaware	908,351	45	Delaware	1.16	16	Delaware	334,228	45
District of Columbia	618,777	50	District of Columbia	2.83	1	District of Columbia	261,567	48
Florida	19,081,930	4	Florida	1.49	7	Florida	7,120,273	4
Georgia	9,815,725	9	Georgia	1.32	10	Georgia	3,504,888	10
Hawaii	1,378,239	40	Hawaii	1.32	11	Hawaii	447,566	42
Idaho	1,583,422	39	Idaho	1.01	20	Idaho	580,280	39
Illinois	12,858,490	5	Illinois	0.22	44	Illinois	4,759,131	6
Indiana	6,514,516	15	Indiana	0.47	38	Indiana	2,474,926	15
Iowa	3,062,869	30	Iowa	0.54	35	Iowa	1,224,399	30
Kansas	2,871,709	33	Kansas	0.65	32	Kansas	1,106,960	32
Kentucky	4,364,627	26	Kentucky	0.58	33	Kentucky	1,690,132	26
Louisiana	4,573,595	25	Louisiana	0.89	25	Louisiana	1,706,091	25
Maine	1,328,440	41	Maine	0.01	49	Maine	552,963	40
Maryland	5,837,378	19	Maryland	1.11	18	Maryland	2,141,086	20
Massachusetts	6,605,468	14	Massachusetts	0.88	27	Massachusetts	2,524,028	14
Michigan	9,879,277	8	Michigan	-0.04	50	Michigan	3,805,261	8
Minnesota	5,345,721	21	Minnesota	0.79	30	Minnesota	2,102,761	21
Mississippi	2,977,179	31	Mississippi	0.33	41	Mississippi	1,085,563	33
Missouri	6,009,025	18	Missouri	0.34	40	Missouri	2,354,106	18
Montana	997,852	44	Montana	0.85	28	Montana	404,990	44
Nebraska	1,842,480	38	Nebraska	0.88	26	Nebraska	726,422	38
Nevada	2,727,571	35	Nevada	1.00	21	Nevada	992,757	34
New Hampshire	1,318,455	42	New Hampshire	0.15	45	New Hampshire	518,009	41
New Jersey	8,834,249	11	New Jersey	0.48	37	New Jersey	3,181,881	11
New Mexico	2,076,325	36	New Mexico	0.83	29	New Mexico	765,306	36
New York	19,490,373	3	New York	0.58	34	New York	7,210,095	3
North Carolina	9,654,079	10	North Carolina	1.24	14	North Carolina	3,699,308	9
North Dakota	686,244	48	North Dakota	2.03	2	North Dakota	285,639	47
Ohio	11,541,175	7	Ohio	0.04	48	Ohio	4,542,141	7
Oklahoma	3,786,152	28	Oklahoma	0.93	23	Oklahoma	1,441,163	28
Oregon	3,868,598	27	Oregon	0.98	22	Oregon	1,513,005	27
Pennsylvania	12,739,595	6	Pennsylvania	0.29	42	Pennsylvania	4,949,494	5
Rhode Island	1,051,236	43	Rhode Island	-0.13	51	Rhode Island	409,308	43
South Carolina	4,677,636	24	South Carolina	1.13	17	South Carolina	1,774,128	24
South Dakota	824,391	46	South Dakota	1.25	13	South Dakota	322,005	46
Tennessee	6,404,240	17	Tennessee	0.92	24	Tennessee	2,466,659	16
Texas	25,644,550	2	Texas	1.98	3	Texas	8,852,441	2
Utah	2,814,910	34	Utah	1.85	4	Utah	886,032	35
Vermont	626,172	49	Vermont	0.07	47	Vermont	257,887	49
Virginia	8,105,120	12	Virginia	1.30	12	Virginia	3,007,690	12
Washington	6,821,303	13	Washington	1.44	8	Washington	2,624,689	13
West Virginia	1,854,775	37	West Virginia	0.10	46	West Virginia	741,661	37
Wisconsin	5,708,612	20	Wisconsin	0.38	39	Wisconsin	2,282,454	19
Wyoming	569,380	51	Wyoming	1.02	19	Wyoming	222,558	51

Table A-1: States—Summary Population Characteristics

	April 1, 2010 Census Population Estimates Base	2010–2012 ACS Population	Population Change	2010–2012 ACS				
				Total Households	Population 65 and Over	Population 85 and Over	Householders 65 and Over	Persons 65 and Over Living Alone
United States..........................	308,745,538	311,609,369	2,863,831	115,241,776	41,652,359	5,691,169	25,624,042	11,211,630
Alabama...................................	4,779,735	4,803,488	23,753	1,837,823	677,125	78,797	431,900	185,947
Alaska.....................................	710,231	723,120	12,889	253,718	58,586	4,909	35,129	14,669
Arizona....................................	6,392,013	6,477,128	85,115	2,357,799	927,026	109,961	564,283	223,034
Arkansas.................................	2,915,921	2,936,822	20,901	1,129,845	429,685	52,110	270,357	115,504
California.................................	37,253,956	37,686,586	432,630	12,474,950	4,426,901	631,180	2,544,599	1,061,261
Colorado..................................	5,029,196	5,117,453	88,257	1,977,737	581,315	73,651	364,159	160,601
Connecticut..............................	3,574,097	3,584,561	10,464	1,355,973	518,739	87,038	315,972	146,889
Delaware..................................	897,934	908,351	10,417	334,228	134,601	16,505	81,975	34,426
District of Columbia	601,723	618,777	17,054	261,567	70,302	10,229	49,026	27,518
Florida.....................................	18,801,311	19,081,930	280,619	7,120,273	3,381,499	465,033	2,006,651	838,116
Georgia....................................	9,687,660	9,815,725	128,065	3,504,888	1,083,402	116,840	659,443	275,089
Hawaii......................................	1,360,301	1,378,239	17,938	447,566	203,195	33,761	110,898	36,977
Idaho.......................................	1,567,582	1,583,422	15,840	580,280	203,210	25,619	127,817	51,130
Illinois.....................................	12,830,632	12,858,490	27,858	4,759,131	1,650,052	241,220	1,032,851	472,169
Indiana....................................	6,483,800	6,514,516	30,716	2,474,926	862,979	116,124	543,017	241,696
Iowa..	3,046,350	3,062,869	16,519	1,224,399	460,025	75,126	289,929	133,543
Kansas.....................................	2,853,118	2,871,709	18,591	1,106,960	384,177	60,202	241,937	111,199
Kentucky..................................	4,339,362	4,364,627	25,265	1,690,132	594,220	71,802	379,625	170,292
Louisiana.................................	4,533,372	4,573,595	40,223	1,706,091	575,545	69,178	365,758	158,053
Maine.......................................	1,328,361	1,328,440	79	552,963	218,331	29,104	136,326	62,631
Maryland..................................	5,773,552	5,837,378	63,826	2,141,086	735,175	101,631	447,752	193,997
Massachusetts.........................	6,547,629	6,605,468	57,839	2,524,028	929,928	149,859	576,645	276,642
Michigan..................................	9,883,635	9,879,277	-4,358	3,805,261	1,397,988	197,208	898,838	401,279
Minnesota................................	5,303,925	5,345,721	41,796	2,102,761	705,615	107,530	449,498	207,319
Mississippi...............................	2,967,297	2,977,179	9,882	1,085,563	390,801	45,154	248,897	106,179
Missouri...................................	5,988,927	6,009,025	20,098	2,354,106	859,577	118,662	544,100	241,902
Montana...................................	989,415	997,852	8,437	404,990	151,961	20,461	97,403	44,152
Nebraska..................................	1,826,341	1,842,480	16,139	726,422	250,555	39,161	159,628	74,572
Nevada.....................................	2,700,551	2,727,571	27,020	992,757	342,704	33,000	204,680	83,771
New Hampshire.........................	1,316,472	1,318,455	1,983	518,009	185,440	24,276	113,302	47,992
New Jersey	8,791,894	8,834,249	42,355	3,181,881	1,216,429	184,354	733,601	330,379
New Mexico	2,059,180	2,076,325	17,145	765,306	283,539	33,525	177,448	74,763
New York	19,378,104	19,490,373	112,269	7,210,095	2,683,895	402,881	1,639,609	772,140
North Carolina..........................	9,535,475	9,654,079	118,604	3,699,308	1,288,898	152,016	808,175	348,990
North Dakota............................	672,591	686,244	13,653	285,639	99,040	16,737	62,826	30,835
Ohio...	11,536,502	11,541,175	4,673	4,542,141	1,658,099	236,944	1,060,964	488,877
Oklahoma.................................	3,751,354	3,786,152	34,798	1,441,163	520,281	63,316	331,413	147,735
Oregon.....................................	3,831,074	3,868,598	37,524	1,513,005	557,667	79,856	351,883	153,696
Pennsylvania............................	12,702,379	12,739,595	37,216	4,949,494	1,993,953	316,020	1,248,228	580,494
Rhode Island............................	1,052,567	1,051,236	-1,331	409,308	154,516	26,958	96,289	47,164
South Carolina	4,625,364	4,677,636	52,272	1,774,128	662,509	72,151	416,443	172,388
South Dakota	814,180	824,391	10,211	322,005	119,198	19,915	74,354	34,669
Tennessee	6,346,110	6,404,240	58,130	2,466,659	886,016	102,177	555,184	236,482
Texas.......................................	25,145,561	25,644,550	498,989	8,852,441	2,722,520	321,817	1,628,989	658,137
Utah..	2,763,885	2,814,910	51,025	886,032	260,639	31,441	160,392	59,149
Vermont...................................	625,741	626,172	431	257,887	94,567	12,631	60,018	27,109
Virginia....................................	8,001,030	8,105,120	104,090	3,007,690	1,018,915	127,204	631,149	264,727
Washington..............................	6,724,540	6,821,303	96,763	2,624,689	867,048	120,309	541,768	237,854
West Virginia............................	1,852,996	1,854,775	1,779	741,661	303,310	37,444	196,951	89,892
Wisconsin.................................	5,686,986	5,708,612	21,626	2,282,454	798,387	119,486	510,565	237,472
Wyoming	563,626	569,380	5,754	222,558	72,274	8,656	45,398	20,129

Table A-2: Counties—Summary Population Characteristics

	April 1, 2010 Census Population Estimates Base	2010–2012 ACS Population	Population Change	2010–2012 ACS				
				Total Households	Population 65 and Over	Population 85 and Over	Householders 65 and Over	Persons 65 and Over Living Alone
Alabama								
Baldwin County	182,265	186,965	4,700	73,210	32,060	3,187	19,751	6,600
Calhoun County	118,572	117,845	-727	45,553	17,423	1,905	11,127	4,656
Cullman County	80,406	80,463	57	31,222	13,265	1,651	8,672	3,656
DeKalb County	71,109	71,217	108	25,160	9,998	876	6,209	2,706
Elmore County	79,303	80,107	804	28,370	9,794	1,047	5,647	2,189
Etowah County	104,430	104,381	-49	39,881	16,754	2,400	10,485	4,808
Houston County	101,547	102,538	991	39,172	15,222	1,588	9,594	4,191
Jefferson County	658,466	659,122	656	257,586	87,461	12,702	56,890	25,435
Lauderdale County	92,709	92,638	-71	38,524	15,817	2,004	10,481	4,641
Lee County	140,247	143,866	3,619	55,655	13,450	1,511	8,548	3,414
Limestone County	82,782	85,469	2,687	31,807	10,746	1,206	7,086	3,200
Madison County	334,811	339,640	4,829	132,631	42,421	5,038	26,641	10,894
Marshall County	93,019	94,021	1,002	34,253	14,236	1,558	9,209	4,120
Mobile County	412,990	413,432	442	156,085	54,982	6,289	34,830	14,567
Montgomery County	229,363	230,604	1,241	88,569	28,149	3,495	18,557	8,666
Morgan County	119,490	120,001	511	45,753	17,365	1,904	10,798	4,459
St. Clair County	83,598	84,473	875	31,323	11,339	1,042	7,275	3,011
Shelby County	195,080	198,314	3,234	74,187	22,334	2,264	13,741	5,341
Talladega County	82,291	81,853	-438	31,346	11,956	1,259	7,542	3,295
Tuscaloosa County	194,653	196,794	2,141	67,244	21,613	2,675	12,736	5,545
Walker County	67,023	66,632	-391	25,624	11,137	1,022	7,241	2,765
Alaska								
Fairbanks North Star Borough	97,581	99,275	1,694	36,499	6,666	741	4,117	1,752
Matanuska-Susitna Borough	88,995	91,877	2,882	31,383	7,652	523	4,302	1,690
Arizona								
Apache County	71,518	72,399	881	19,445	8,849	814	5,401	2,001
Cochise County	131,346	132,162	816	49,533	23,510	2,657	15,260	6,415
Coconino County	134,418	134,909	491	44,949	12,670	1,382	7,670	2,496
Maricopa County	3,817,117	3,878,086	60,969	1,404,105	487,207	59,373	293,480	117,820
Mohave County	200,186	202,102	1,916	80,346	48,584	4,700	30,103	11,095
Navajo County	107,449	107,292	-157	34,107	15,077	1,357	9,553	3,524
Pima County	980,263	987,294	7,031	381,827	157,849	21,477	97,843	41,934
Pinal County	375,770	385,577	9,807	122,490	56,499	5,130	33,042	11,373
Yavapai County	211,033	211,339	306	91,813	53,313	7,010	34,015	13,529
Yuma County	195,750	199,061	3,311	70,062	31,751	2,635	18,834	5,641
Arkansas								
Benton County	221,339	227,570	6,231	81,141	27,595	4,028	16,868	5,751
Craighead County	96,443	98,249	1,806	37,834	11,831	1,508	7,167	3,021
Faulkner County	113,237	116,454	3,217	43,040	11,824	1,457	7,091	2,744
Garland County	96,022	96,590	568	38,910	20,125	2,966	12,591	5,134
Jefferson County	77,435	76,023	-1,412	28,592	10,434	1,481	6,807	3,103
Lonoke County	68,354	69,267	913	25,274	7,890	662	4,849	1,995
Pulaski County	382,750	386,435	3,685	154,268	47,384	5,909	29,549	12,623
Saline County	107,120	109,842	2,722	41,717	17,178	1,550	10,363	3,789
Sebastian County	125,744	126,700	956	49,165	16,600	1,985	10,599	4,942
Washington County	203,065	207,763	4,698	79,464	20,480	2,837	13,001	5,917
White County	77,076	77,967	891	29,702	11,245	1,293	7,476	3,398
California								
Alameda County	1,510,271	1,533,311	23,040	543,175	175,805	26,503	101,384	45,117
Butte County	220,000	220,565	565	84,421	34,534	5,476	22,252	9,879
Contra Costa County	1,049,025	1,066,333	17,308	374,552	137,400	19,898	81,300	34,047
El Dorado County	181,058	180,866	-192	67,209	27,846	3,653	16,779	5,848
Fresno County	930,450	940,493	10,043	288,016	96,924	14,407	56,190	23,163
Humboldt County	134,623	135,061	438	52,621	18,302	2,606	11,281	5,165
Imperial County	174,528	175,837	1,309	47,828	18,894	2,533	10,086	4,041
Kern County	839,631	849,101	9,470	254,255	77,955	8,418	45,718	18,950
Kings County	152,982	151,869	-1,113	40,684	12,328	1,452	6,842	2,882
Lake County	64,665	64,331	-334	26,261	11,639	1,699	7,633	3,369
Los Angeles County	9,818,605	9,892,525	73,920	3,211,482	1,106,754	158,945	615,860	256,566
Madera County	150,865	151,827	962	41,702	17,912	1,882	9,464	2,824
Marin County	252,409	254,844	2,435	102,286	44,567	6,098	28,524	13,090
Mendocino County	87,841	87,564	-277	33,791	14,277	1,884	8,852	4,108
Merced County	255,793	259,716	3,923	74,958	25,198	3,093	13,739	5,114
Monterey County	415,057	421,570	6,513	124,727	46,040	7,052	25,539	10,021
Napa County	136,484	137,949	1,465	49,517	21,451	3,557	12,918	5,545
Nevada County	98,764	98,605	-159	41,707	20,068	2,848	12,646	4,928
Orange County	3,010,232	3,054,809	44,577	992,242	365,971	53,885	206,912	80,995
Placer County	348,432	356,331	7,899	132,525	56,811	7,475	34,439	14,060
Riverside County	2,189,641	2,236,158	46,517	679,014	270,278	32,821	155,054	62,984
Sacramento County	1,418,788	1,436,233	17,445	513,594	165,762	24,979	99,171	45,592
San Bernardino County	2,035,210	2,062,483	27,273	601,327	190,389	21,798	103,717	41,544
San Diego County	3,095,313	3,139,726	44,413	1,067,043	365,780	57,661	209,064	87,630
San Francisco County	805,235	815,234	9,999	341,721	112,614	18,043	68,503	34,884
San Joaquin County	685,306	695,251	9,945	214,808	74,322	10,314	41,585	16,422
San Luis Obispo County	269,637	272,034	2,397	100,767	42,727	6,712	25,629	10,423
San Mateo County	718,451	729,489	11,038	257,529	100,065	16,385	56,479	24,534
Santa Barbara County	423,895	427,251	3,356	141,196	56,046	10,019	33,861	14,559
Santa Clara County	1,781,642	1,811,955	30,313	607,217	205,755	28,231	112,271	42,678

Table A-2: Counties—Summary Population Characteristics—*Continued*

	April 1, 2010 Census Population Estimates Base	2010–2012 ACS Population	Population Change	2010–2012 ACS				
				Total Households	Population 65 and Over	Population 85 and Over	Householders 65 and Over	Persons 65 and Over Living Alone
California—Cont.								
Santa Cruz County	262,382	265,057	2,675	92,834	30,785	4,892	19,970	9,121
Shasta County	177,223	177,980	757	68,408	31,209	4,189	19,897	8,677
Solano County	413,344	417,261	3,917	140,669	49,340	5,922	28,831	11,540
Sonoma County	483,878	488,237	4,359	183,773	70,993	11,383	44,296	20,275
Stanislaus County	514,453	518,336	3,883	166,948	56,938	8,517	33,059	13,705
Sutter County	94,737	94,951	214	31,620	12,464	1,366	7,275	3,137
Tulare County	442,179	447,704	5,525	131,426	43,156	5,689	24,691	9,718
Ventura County	823,318	830,828	7,510	266,414	100,859	14,468	59,887	23,335
Yolo County	200,849	202,473	1,624	70,114	20,701	3,215	12,783	5,948
Yuba County	72,155	72,613	458	24,060	7,409	753	4,379	1,589
Colorado								
Adams County	441,603	451,455	9,852	152,332	39,156	4,447	23,266	9,696
Arapahoe County	572,153	585,388	13,235	225,471	61,889	8,355	38,061	16,399
Boulder County	294,567	300,681	6,114	120,203	31,696	4,426	19,981	8,718
Denver County	600,008	619,016	19,008	266,248	64,482	10,683	43,278	23,748
Douglas County	285,465	292,509	7,044	103,574	22,921	1,609	13,496	4,228
El Paso County	622,263	636,034	13,771	237,258	65,360	7,486	40,618	17,299
Jefferson County	534,543	539,836	5,293	218,728	70,648	8,937	44,554	19,006
Larimer County	299,630	305,335	5,705	121,183	37,722	5,129	23,052	9,493
Mesa County	146,723	147,268	545	58,652	22,644	3,281	14,901	7,068
Pueblo County	159,063	160,256	1,193	62,260	25,026	3,150	15,828	7,126
Weld County	252,825	258,708	5,883	90,830	25,925	2,876	15,559	6,382
Connecticut								
Fairfield County	916,829	926,739	9,910	331,766	127,386	20,420	76,458	33,931
Hartford County	894,014	895,987	1,973	348,446	132,472	23,298	81,908	39,355
Litchfield County	189,927	188,731	-1,196	75,801	31,216	4,865	19,301	8,867
Middlesex County	165,676	165,876	200	65,962	26,552	4,337	15,872	6,940
New Haven County	862,477	862,776	299	328,434	126,344	23,684	77,105	37,337
New London County	274,055	274,118	63	106,959	40,149	5,336	24,579	11,555
Tolland County	152,691	152,257	-434	54,537	18,950	2,649	11,494	4,806
Windham County	118,428	118,077	-351	44,068	15,670	2,449	9,255	4,098
Delaware								
Kent County	162,310	165,306	2,996	57,023	23,105	2,511	13,607	5,282
New Castle County	538,479	542,490	4,011	201,107	68,251	9,319	42,316	19,013
Sussex County	197,145	200,555	3,410	76,098	43,245	4,675	26,052	10,131
Florida								
Alachua County	247,336	249,440	2,104	94,455	27,427	3,615	16,705	7,016
Bay County	168,852	170,351	1,499	68,622	25,463	2,599	16,502	6,817
Brevard County	543,372	545,202	1,830	219,293	114,082	14,013	70,245	29,461
Broward County	1,748,066	1,784,340	36,274	664,337	257,655	42,348	154,109	75,583
Charlotte County	159,978	160,602	624	70,035	56,719	8,101	34,637	12,880
Citrus County	141,234	140,174	-1,060	59,783	45,784	5,692	27,506	10,350
Clay County	190,865	192,689	1,824	66,626	23,760	2,549	13,066	4,597
Collier County	321,520	327,537	6,017	121,788	89,552	11,345	52,578	19,384
Columbia County	67,532	67,666	134	23,472	10,695	1,010	6,336	2,522
Duval County	864,263	872,307	8,044	329,194	100,238	13,410	62,242	28,589
Escambia County	297,619	300,150	2,531	110,981	44,259	5,761	28,334	12,371
Flagler County	95,696	97,229	1,533	35,363	25,015	2,962	13,858	4,483
Hernando County	172,778	173,178	400	70,046	45,454	5,567	27,698	10,980
Highlands County	98,786	98,382	-404	39,466	31,966	3,959	19,350	7,317
Hillsborough County	1,229,226	1,260,333	31,107	467,397	151,780	20,045	90,712	39,153
Indian River County	138,028	139,241	1,213	57,183	39,107	6,497	24,390	11,032
Lake County	297,052	300,270	3,218	114,640	74,048	8,557	44,524	16,495
Lee County	618,754	632,499	13,745	238,476	153,513	19,743	87,499	32,859
Leon County	275,487	279,378	3,891	109,003	27,502	3,800	17,555	8,063
Manatee County	322,833	328,231	5,398	131,255	78,467	10,640	48,208	19,355
Martin County	146,318	147,536	1,218	59,741	40,951	6,808	24,833	10,322
Miami-Dade County	2,496,435	2,553,696	57,261	822,746	365,388	49,847	185,793	75,924
Monroe County	73,090	74,007	917	28,341	13,258	1,315	8,057	3,179
Nassau County	73,314	74,096	782	27,937	12,755	1,221	7,596	2,447
Okaloosa County	180,822	184,699	3,877	72,695	25,929	2,704	15,915	6,207
Orange County	1,145,956	1,174,032	28,076	414,460	116,321	14,205	65,171	25,676
Osceola County	268,685	278,254	9,569	90,945	32,023	3,236	17,294	6,428
Palm Beach County	1,320,134	1,339,372	19,238	520,971	291,985	52,039	177,102	79,323
Pasco County	464,697	467,486	2,789	181,324	98,986	13,989	60,399	24,787
Pinellas County	916,542	918,385	1,843	399,785	198,309	32,685	126,874	63,876
Polk County	602,095	609,775	7,680	220,874	111,849	13,506	67,040	26,251
Putnam County	74,366	73,858	-508	28,634	14,415	1,504	8,909	3,321
St. Johns County	190,039	196,491	6,452	75,762	31,942	3,977	19,214	7,593
St. Lucie County	277,789	281,245	3,456	106,641	58,117	7,019	34,902	13,177
Santa Rosa County	151,372	155,782	4,410	57,180	20,326	1,754	12,360	4,195
Sarasota County	379,448	382,652	3,204	169,819	121,625	19,078	75,984	31,529
Seminole County	422,718	426,864	4,146	145,481	53,934	8,092	29,449	11,320
Sumter County	93,420	98,042	4,622	43,178	45,444	3,431	27,991	8,246
Volusia County	494,597	495,284	687	193,177	107,097	14,807	65,197	28,350

Table A-2: Counties—Summary Population Characteristics—*Continued*

	April 1, 2010 Census Population Estimates Base	2010–2012 ACS Population	Population Change	2010–2012 ACS				
				Total Households	Population 65 and Over	Population 85 and Over	Householders 65 and Over	Persons 65 and Over Living Alone
Georgia								
Barrow County	69,367	69,923	556	23,190	6,716	491	3,742	1,248
Bartow County	100,157	100,380	223	34,714	11,214	754	6,660	2,573
Bibb County	155,547	156,088	541	56,393	20,047	2,544	12,547	5,600
Bulloch County	70,217	72,037	1,820	25,786	6,538	638	4,231	1,730
Carroll County	110,527	111,024	497	39,392	12,496	1,039	7,632	3,245
Catoosa County	63,942	64,661	719	23,630	9,266	962	5,795	2,012
Chatham County	265,128	271,443	6,315	102,502	34,187	4,678	21,924	9,969
Cherokee County	214,344	218,189	3,845	76,576	21,237	1,864	12,997	4,805
Clarke County	116,707	118,734	2,027	40,529	10,482	1,229	6,367	2,687
Clayton County	259,423	262,721	3,298	85,801	18,559	1,750	9,931	4,045
Cobb County	688,078	698,168	10,090	260,646	64,367	6,440	39,393	15,433
Columbia County	124,053	128,257	4,204	45,271	13,523	1,070	7,634	2,787
Coweta County	127,317	129,426	2,109	46,706	13,880	1,452	8,188	2,918
DeKalb County	691,893	699,017	7,124	260,968	64,740	7,681	40,015	18,223
Dougherty County	94,565	94,634	69	36,084	11,734	1,533	7,852	3,262
Douglas County	132,403	133,274	871	46,335	12,067	849	6,597	2,621
Fayette County	106,567	107,314	747	37,817	14,593	1,664	8,868	3,427
Floyd County	96,317	96,238	-79	34,961	13,894	1,741	9,051	4,303
Forsyth County	175,511	182,395	6,884	54,017	17,963	1,862	8,366	2,981
Fulton County	920,583	951,157	30,574	365,494	88,653	12,956	56,248	28,643
Glynn County	79,626	80,394	768	31,392	12,564	1,471	8,374	3,261
Gwinnett County	805,321	825,375	20,054	267,526	60,324	5,638	30,096	10,031
Hall County	179,684	182,791	3,107	60,520	21,659	2,307	12,796	4,731
Henry County	203,923	207,215	3,292	69,233	18,174	1,550	9,972	3,728
Houston County	139,911	143,718	3,807	52,077	15,075	1,539	8,976	3,835
Liberty County	63,465	64,540	1,075	22,967	4,061	442	2,671	856
Lowndes County	109,233	112,050	2,817	39,481	10,994	1,249	6,975	2,763
Muscogee County	189,885	194,276	4,391	71,509	22,292	2,991	15,015	7,323
Newton County	99,958	100,833	875	34,208	10,464	1,352	5,917	2,372
Paulding County	142,324	143,802	1,478	47,751	11,194	796	6,247	2,063
Richmond County	200,549	201,592	1,043	71,826	23,487	2,539	14,145	6,356
Rockdale County	85,215	85,619	404	29,104	9,566	847	5,647	2,169
Troup County	67,044	67,816	772	24,738	8,621	1,302	5,337	2,247
Walker County	68,756	68,533	-223	26,323	10,496	1,206	6,583	2,811
Walton County	83,768	84,299	531	29,261	10,511	1,050	5,978	1,980
Whitfield County	102,599	103,068	469	34,409	11,722	1,373	6,887	2,601
Hawaii								
Hawaii County	185,079	187,286	2,207	63,897	28,666	4,449	16,222	6,031
Honolulu County	953,207	966,405	13,198	308,906	143,047	24,044	77,959	25,503
Kauai County	67,091	67,815	724	22,565	10,496	1,869	5,565	1,601
Maui County	154,834	156,670	1,836	52,158	20,965	3,398	11,138	3,831
Idaho								
Ada County	392,365	401,204	8,839	151,822	43,784	6,271	27,658	11,783
Bannock County	82,839	83,439	600	30,098	9,455	984	5,794	2,241
Bonneville County	104,234	105,686	1,452	36,010	11,706	1,858	7,600	3,026
Canyon County	188,923	191,542	2,619	63,130	21,657	2,513	13,265	5,088
Kootenai County	138,494	140,793	2,299	55,713	21,061	2,369	13,114	4,704
Twin Falls County	77,230	78,066	836	28,129	11,062	1,806	6,465	2,456
Illinois								
Adams County	67,103	67,169	66	26,517	11,892	2,170	7,170	3,113
Champaign County	201,081	202,373	1,292	79,246	20,787	2,943	13,396	5,855
Cook County	5,194,675	5,214,942	20,267	1,927,303	633,403	95,088	399,022	190,640
DeKalb County	105,160	104,785	-375	37,386	10,517	1,596	6,674	3,424
DuPage County	916,924	923,503	6,579	334,764	111,162	17,224	66,279	27,793
Kane County	515,269	519,581	4,312	169,535	53,028	6,427	31,517	12,652
Kankakee County	113,449	113,361	-88	41,515	15,361	2,270	9,408	4,398
Kendall County	114,736	116,693	1,957	38,486	8,652	897	5,443	2,109
Lake County	703,462	702,666	-796	240,273	76,078	10,510	45,604	19,025
LaSalle County	113,924	113,423	-501	44,023	18,851	2,882	11,928	5,410
McHenry County	308,760	308,501	-259	108,995	32,664	3,728	19,867	7,792
McLean County	169,572	170,964	1,392	63,314	17,918	2,724	11,076	4,812
Macon County	110,768	110,491	-277	45,580	18,335	2,852	11,817	5,422
Madison County	269,282	268,573	-709	107,047	39,375	5,686	25,080	11,592
Peoria County	186,494	186,755	261	76,007	26,333	4,024	17,184	8,128
Rock Island County	147,546	147,489	-57	60,758	24,334	4,085	16,222	8,393
St. Clair County	270,056	269,786	-270	101,778	34,421	4,507	22,614	11,486
Sangamon County	197,465	198,698	1,233	82,927	27,993	4,443	18,562	9,164
Tazewell County	135,394	135,685	291	54,302	21,454	2,832	13,854	5,982
Vermilion County	81,625	81,225	-400	31,486	13,249	1,936	8,899	4,437
Will County	677,560	680,662	3,102	222,401	66,355	8,244	39,421	15,526
Williamson County	66,362	66,590	228	26,383	11,137	1,298	6,960	3,183
Winnebago County	295,264	293,608	-1,656	112,594	41,803	6,082	25,799	11,471

Table A-2: Counties—Summary Population Characteristics—*Continued*

	April 1, 2010 Census Population Estimates Base	2010–2012 ACS Population	Population Change	2010–2012 ACS				
				Total Households	Population 65 and Over	Population 85 and Over	Householders 65 and Over	Persons 65 and Over Living Alone
Indiana								
Allen County	355,329	358,248	2,919	137,586	43,512	6,120	27,935	12,975
Bartholomew County	76,794	77,946	1,152	29,929	11,140	1,338	6,948	3,311
Clark County	110,232	111,342	1,110	42,689	14,573	1,604	9,165	3,944
Delaware County	117,671	117,599	-72	46,179	17,592	1,931	11,532	5,154
Elkhart County	197,561	198,598	1,037	69,984	24,447	3,734	15,273	6,425
Floyd County	74,578	74,982	404	28,844	10,026	1,436	6,332	2,995
Grant County	70,061	69,661	-400	27,158	11,504	1,684	7,615	3,491
Hamilton County	274,569	283,040	8,471	103,033	25,436	3,343	14,779	5,582
Hancock County	70,002	70,534	532	25,968	9,267	1,030	5,619	2,279
Hendricks County	145,448	148,249	2,801	52,743	16,552	2,027	10,047	4,341
Howard County	82,752	82,799	47	34,446	13,950	1,828	9,030	4,318
Johnson County	139,654	141,550	1,896	52,464	17,932	2,593	11,086	5,211
Kosciusko County	77,356	77,429	73	29,284	10,673	1,417	6,939	3,054
Lake County	496,005	494,961	-1,044	181,174	66,791	9,368	41,018	17,946
LaPorte County	111,467	111,314	-153	42,715	16,122	2,008	10,456	4,743
Madison County	131,636	131,028	-608	49,973	20,715	2,915	13,929	6,710
Marion County	903,393	911,593	8,200	358,923	97,796	13,740	63,430	30,663
Monroe County	137,974	139,880	1,906	53,551	14,539	2,067	9,410	4,504
Morgan County	68,894	69,206	312	25,501	9,510	827	5,550	2,086
Porter County	164,343	165,274	931	61,297	21,201	2,577	12,514	4,780
St. Joseph County	266,929	266,605	-324	101,171	36,042	5,771	22,588	10,117
Tippecanoe County	172,780	175,204	2,424	66,464	16,741	2,584	10,609	4,834
Vanderburgh County	179,703	180,334	631	74,271	26,101	4,492	16,819	8,323
Vigo County	107,848	108,209	361	39,326	14,644	2,292	8,907	4,148
Wayne County	68,917	68,636	-281	28,230	11,421	1,470	7,535	3,636
Iowa								
Black Hawk County	131,090	131,472	382	51,852	18,333	2,903	11,863	5,709
Dallas County	66,135	69,451	3,316	26,221	6,926	1,201	4,323	1,854
Dubuque County	93,653	94,471	818	37,548	14,434	2,116	8,939	4,054
Johnson County	130,882	133,719	2,837	54,073	11,712	1,738	7,794	3,657
Linn County	211,226	213,666	2,440	85,889	28,341	3,965	18,216	8,386
Polk County	430,640	437,941	7,301	171,697	47,984	6,542	30,000	13,831
Pottawattamie County	93,158	93,262	104	36,440	13,462	2,143	8,432	3,663
Scott County	165,224	167,251	2,027	66,945	22,349	3,219	14,428	6,730
Story County	89,542	90,519	977	35,314	9,096	1,547	5,780	2,400
Woodbury County	102,172	102,416	244	38,737	13,359	2,249	8,837	4,724
Kansas								
Butler County	65,880	65,893	13	23,995	8,469	1,493	5,372	2,568
Douglas County	110,826	112,105	1,279	43,566	10,285	1,500	6,461	3,090
Johnson County	544,179	552,886	8,707	215,199	62,589	10,204	39,101	17,147
Leavenworth County	76,227	77,137	910	26,103	8,733	1,293	5,331	2,084
Riley County	71,115	73,398	2,283	25,831	5,281	887	3,449	1,667
Sedgwick County	498,365	501,408	3,043	191,191	58,701	8,419	37,312	17,706
Shawnee County	177,934	178,736	802	72,189	26,288	3,677	16,495	7,258
Wyandotte County	157,505	158,287	782	56,817	17,141	2,688	10,853	4,921
Kentucky								
Boone County	118,811	121,435	2,624	42,680	11,980	1,179	7,509	2,836
Bullitt County	74,319	75,225	906	28,109	8,986	731	5,983	2,296
Campbell County	90,336	90,794	458	35,254	11,732	1,684	7,577	3,275
Christian County	73,950	74,373	423	25,828	7,712	911	4,833	2,170
Daviess County	96,659	97,294	635	37,435	14,464	1,945	9,372	4,357
Fayette County	295,803	301,211	5,408	122,046	32,142	4,219	20,954	10,097
Hardin County	105,549	107,129	1,580	39,246	11,732	1,353	7,210	2,900
Jefferson County	741,096	746,508	5,412	303,988	101,108	14,537	65,238	31,336
Kenton County	159,721	160,710	989	61,671	18,239	2,775	11,711	5,657
McCracken County	65,565	65,616	51	27,159	11,130	1,610	6,928	3,342
Madison County	82,916	84,016	1,100	31,085	9,643	1,027	6,097	2,675
Pike County	65,024	64,635	-389	26,492	9,214	1,064	6,227	2,892
Warren County	113,792	115,586	1,794	44,378	12,841	1,703	8,312	3,890
Louisiana								
Ascension Parish	107,169	110,057	2,888	37,877	10,141	820	6,304	2,337
Bossier Parish	116,979	119,899	2,920	45,632	14,254	1,446	9,301	4,129
Caddo Parish	254,969	256,551	1,582	98,582	35,136	4,688	22,588	10,071
Calcasieu Parish	192,768	193,842	1,074	73,614	25,044	2,772	15,754	6,735
East Baton Rouge Parish	440,178	442,322	2,144	167,220	49,687	6,798	30,978	13,521
Iberia Parish	73,240	73,580	340	26,463	9,215	926	6,097	2,618
Jefferson Parish	432,552	433,283	731	166,467	60,584	8,082	38,072	17,111
Lafayette Parish	221,578	224,469	2,891	86,632	23,524	3,019	14,646	6,106
Lafourche Parish	96,318	96,860	542	35,360	12,426	1,396	7,842	3,295
Livingston Parish	128,069	130,255	2,186	46,185	13,591	1,136	8,216	3,333
Orleans Parish	343,829	359,130	15,301	146,018	40,109	5,790	26,272	13,081
Ouachita Parish	153,720	154,658	938	57,825	19,414	2,615	12,544	5,742
Rapides Parish	131,613	132,132	519	47,148	18,541	2,227	11,646	5,485
St. Landry Parish	83,384	83,540	156	30,940	11,551	1,219	7,576	3,309
St. Tammany Parish	233,740	236,980	3,240	87,583	31,345	3,422	18,763	7,298
Tangipahoa Parish	121,097	122,471	1,374	44,111	14,422	1,379	9,082	3,434
Terrebonne Parish	111,860	111,730	-130	39,436	12,764	1,348	8,315	3,166

Table A-2: Counties—Summary Population Characteristics—*Continued*

	April 1, 2010 Census Population Estimates Base	2010–2012 ACS Population	Population Change	2010–2012 ACS				
				Total Households	Population 65 and Over	Population 85 and Over	Householders 65 and Over	Persons 65 and Over Living Alone
Maine								
Androscoggin County	107,704	107,571	-133	44,502	15,552	2,190	9,997	4,527
Aroostook County	71,870	71,328	-542	30,763	13,965	1,577	8,899	4,353
Cumberland County	281,676	282,689	1,013	117,068	41,790	6,208	25,922	12,903
Kennebec County	122,151	121,959	-192	51,509	19,571	2,680	12,060	5,720
Penobscot County	153,921	153,856	-65	62,186	22,900	2,858	14,088	6,257
York County	197,131	198,155	1,024	80,414	31,686	3,924	20,159	9,122
Maryland								
Allegany County	75,087	74,495	-592	28,829	13,593	1,976	8,459	4,181
Anne Arundel County	537,656	544,889	7,233	199,577	66,751	7,508	40,034	15,969
Baltimore County	805,029	812,043	7,014	313,195	120,243	21,247	74,636	34,896
Calvert County	88,737	89,279	542	30,780	10,165	1,371	5,903	2,222
Carroll County	167,134	167,261	127	59,373	23,043	3,044	13,690	5,577
Cecil County	101,108	101,500	392	35,997	12,395	1,526	7,182	2,777
Charles County	146,551	148,982	2,431	51,274	14,738	1,658	7,861	2,940
Frederick County	233,385	237,037	3,652	85,862	27,310	3,581	16,698	7,219
Harford County	244,826	246,839	2,013	90,302	31,967	4,168	19,247	7,577
Howard County	287,085	293,972	6,887	106,284	31,315	3,419	17,728	6,581
Montgomery County	971,777	990,787	19,010	359,995	124,810	20,747	73,571	31,913
Prince George's County	863,420	873,629	10,209	302,436	86,355	9,127	50,886	20,094
St. Mary's County	105,151	107,482	2,331	37,772	11,417	1,409	6,787	2,391
Washington County	147,430	148,595	1,165	55,790	21,582	2,914	13,680	6,286
Wicomico County	98,733	99,840	1,107	36,019	13,289	1,819	8,249	3,562
Massachusetts								
Barnstable County	215,888	215,681	-207	93,426	55,418	7,009	34,374	14,702
Berkshire County	131,219	130,565	-654	55,573	25,072	4,486	16,435	8,650
Bristol County	548,285	549,972	1,687	209,314	79,940	13,738	48,386	22,459
Essex County	743,159	750,452	7,293	285,412	108,427	18,753	66,454	32,381
Franklin County	71,372	71,495	123	30,159	11,256	1,850	6,942	3,154
Hampden County	463,490	465,177	1,687	177,900	67,146	11,470	41,761	20,481
Hampshire County	158,080	159,575	1,495	58,670	20,996	3,408	13,699	6,722
Middlesex County	1,503,085	1,521,993	18,908	580,358	202,350	31,421	125,401	58,595
Norfolk County	670,850	677,462	6,612	257,153	100,173	16,881	62,632	30,213
Plymouth County	494,919	497,975	3,056	179,835	72,139	10,461	43,633	18,100
Suffolk County	722,023	734,699	12,676	288,162	77,956	12,071	51,273	29,440
Worcester County	798,552	803,429	4,877	298,224	104,748	17,839	63,136	30,662
Michigan								
Allegan County	111,408	111,701	293	41,881	15,160	1,914	9,407	3,696
Bay County	107,771	107,310	-461	43,793	17,937	2,872	11,597	4,955
Berrien County	156,813	156,452	-361	59,373	25,836	3,931	16,237	7,121
Calhoun County	136,146	135,568	-578	52,569	20,385	3,063	13,077	5,765
Clinton County	75,382	75,746	364	28,521	10,328	1,291	6,360	2,421
Eaton County	107,759	107,952	193	42,981	15,669	2,168	9,751	4,094
Genesee County	425,790	421,871	-3,919	165,651	59,719	7,641	39,113	17,371
Grand Traverse County	86,986	88,147	1,161	34,555	13,381	1,861	8,457	3,705
Ingham County	280,895	281,470	575	108,326	30,357	4,222	19,912	9,974
Isabella County	70,311	70,525	214	24,456	6,959	974	4,332	1,967
Jackson County	160,248	160,115	-133	59,781	23,197	3,605	14,626	6,073
Kalamazoo County	250,331	252,546	2,215	99,085	31,522	4,836	20,203	9,374
Kent County	602,622	608,517	5,895	229,328	69,091	11,059	43,911	19,550
Lapeer County	88,316	88,147	-169	32,426	12,339	1,030	7,587	2,722
Lenawee County	99,892	99,324	-568	37,498	15,146	2,023	9,461	3,971
Livingston County	180,967	182,045	1,078	67,112	23,142	2,216	14,436	4,972
Macomb County	840,978	843,852	2,874	331,023	123,166	19,615	79,675	38,001
Marquette County	67,077	67,528	451	27,180	10,139	1,410	6,460	3,019
Midland County	83,629	83,825	196	33,552	12,600	1,665	8,123	3,284
Monroe County	152,021	151,539	-482	57,876	21,131	2,455	13,592	5,803
Muskegon County	172,188	170,724	-1,464	64,394	23,796	3,325	15,242	6,613
Oakland County	1,202,362	1,211,683	9,321	485,367	165,886	24,687	106,767	48,809
Ottawa County	263,801	266,464	2,663	94,154	32,067	4,818	19,807	7,462
Saginaw County	200,169	199,094	-1,075	77,081	31,123	4,628	20,511	9,729
St. Clair County	163,040	161,640	-1,400	64,291	24,312	3,125	15,532	6,728
Shiawassee County	70,648	69,925	-723	27,183	10,426	1,337	6,427	2,445
Van Buren County	76,258	75,887	-371	27,952	10,841	1,130	6,789	2,932
Washtenaw County	344,791	348,311	3,520	134,570	37,073	5,501	24,398	11,302
Wayne County	1,820,584	1,803,251	-17,333	667,145	232,538	35,792	154,962	75,769
Minnesota								
Anoka County	330,844	333,728	2,884	122,793	34,152	3,634	21,874	9,358
Blue Earth County	64,013	64,510	497	24,573	7,666	1,494	4,944	2,506
Carver County	91,042	92,574	1,532	33,166	8,249	931	5,237	2,346
Dakota County	398,552	402,136	3,584	153,554	42,198	5,565	26,628	11,390
Hennepin County	1,152,425	1,169,434	17,009	478,538	135,530	22,715	87,965	43,935
Olmsted County	144,248	145,828	1,580	57,073	18,843	2,831	11,322	4,893
Ramsey County	508,640	514,982	6,342	204,535	62,848	10,130	40,715	20,455
St. Louis County	200,226	200,269	43	84,519	32,330	5,149	20,875	10,671
Scott County	129,928	132,768	2,840	45,770	11,050	1,165	6,480	2,682
Sherburne County	88,499	89,139	640	30,356	7,705	844	4,524	2,026
Stearns County	150,642	151,178	536	56,182	18,731	2,547	11,817	5,164
Washington County	238,136	241,538	3,402	89,096	26,718	3,177	16,953	6,892
Wright County	124,700	126,271	1,571	45,213	12,575	1,652	7,685	3,180

Table A-2: Counties—Summary Population Characteristics—*Continued*

	April 1, 2010 Census Population Estimates Base	2010–2012 ACS Population	Population Change	2010–2012 ACS				
				Total Households	Population 65 and Over	Population 85 and Over	Householders 65 and Over	Persons 65 and Over Living Alone
Mississippi								
DeSoto County	161,252	163,919	2,667	57,912	17,276	1,550	10,554	3,718
Forrest County	74,934	75,944	1,010	27,608	8,871	1,393	5,577	2,564
Harrison County	187,105	190,962	3,857	72,134	23,014	2,629	14,816	6,000
Hinds County	245,285	247,502	2,217	87,736	27,208	3,921	17,118	7,209
Jackson County	139,668	140,062	394	50,558	17,916	1,351	11,224	4,227
Jones County	67,761	68,192	431	24,560	9,880	1,147	6,240	2,343
Lauderdale County	80,261	80,361	100	29,458	11,323	1,542	7,316	3,220
Lee County	82,910	84,080	1,170	31,534	11,165	1,536	7,122	3,194
Madison County	95,203	97,020	1,817	36,617	10,565	1,890	6,612	2,734
Rankin County	141,617	143,637	2,020	52,875	17,092	1,452	10,708	3,840
Missouri								
Boone County	162,642	165,893	3,251	64,944	15,776	2,263	9,695	4,267
Buchanan County	89,201	89,420	219	33,578	12,309	1,978	7,777	3,750
Cape Girardeau County	75,674	76,460	786	29,489	11,033	1,913	6,487	2,738
Cass County	99,478	100,013	535	37,183	14,100	1,786	8,700	3,559
Christian County	77,422	78,786	1,364	29,537	10,098	731	6,348	2,325
Clay County	221,939	225,142	3,203	86,466	26,107	3,401	16,195	6,455
Cole County	75,983	76,299	316	29,288	9,867	1,304	6,589	2,874
Franklin County	101,493	101,543	50	39,448	14,368	1,808	8,825	3,692
Greene County	275,174	277,813	2,639	115,196	39,754	6,273	25,202	11,811
Jackson County	674,158	675,911	1,753	269,581	85,613	12,435	56,156	26,774
Jasper County	117,404	116,957	-447	45,262	15,630	2,282	9,733	4,397
Jefferson County	218,728	219,655	927	81,076	25,707	2,349	15,780	5,722
Platte County	89,322	90,871	1,549	36,355	10,624	1,468	6,619	2,871
St. Charles County	360,485	365,131	4,646	135,386	42,754	5,330	27,199	10,629
St. Francois County	65,364	65,696	332	24,934	9,366	996	6,033	2,848
St. Louis County	998,954	999,595	641	402,680	152,609	25,699	96,508	43,626
Montana								
Cascade County	81,327	81,677	350	32,982	12,936	1,797	8,117	3,667
Flathead County	90,928	91,221	293	36,950	13,704	1,719	8,779	3,809
Gallatin County	89,513	91,193	1,680	36,704	9,014	1,427	5,808	2,234
Missoula County	109,299	110,183	884	45,413	12,935	1,945	8,036	3,318
Yellowstone County	147,972	150,078	2,106	60,814	21,466	3,251	14,161	6,601
Nebraska								
Douglas County	517,110	524,969	7,859	203,592	56,388	8,820	37,242	17,959
Lancaster County	285,407	289,807	4,400	114,964	32,065	4,874	20,392	9,350
Sarpy County	158,840	162,718	3,878	59,930	14,360	1,382	8,953	3,532
Nevada								
Clark County	1,951,269	1,974,036	22,767	703,972	233,408	21,844	137,213	57,180
Washoe County	421,407	425,845	4,438	162,452	54,049	6,169	32,880	13,950
New Hampshire								
Cheshire County	77,117	76,919	-198	30,405	11,680	1,510	7,472	3,384
Grafton County	89,118	89,085	-33	35,102	14,293	1,636	8,927	3,894
Hillsborough County	400,721	401,933	1,212	153,838	49,471	6,877	29,700	12,622
Merrimack County	146,445	146,606	161	57,387	20,842	3,209	12,436	5,304
Rockingham County	295,223	296,427	1,204	116,143	39,341	4,383	24,103	9,498
Strafford County	123,143	123,661	518	46,300	15,212	1,964	9,381	4,339
New Jersey								
Atlantic County	274,549	274,982	433	99,782	40,020	5,176	24,270	11,045
Bergen County	905,116	912,753	7,637	333,711	139,882	22,806	83,020	35,545
Burlington County	448,734	450,454	1,720	164,889	64,071	8,950	39,411	16,776
Camden County	513,657	513,593	-64	187,178	67,424	10,942	41,664	19,671
Cape May County	97,265	96,716	-549	41,459	21,534	2,730	13,676	5,892
Cumberland County	156,898	157,351	453	49,981	20,154	2,843	12,301	5,915
Essex County	783,969	786,363	2,394	276,592	92,329	14,839	55,719	27,563
Gloucester County	288,288	289,167	879	104,568	36,896	4,761	22,640	9,719
Hudson County	634,266	644,288	10,022	243,675	67,536	8,678	40,421	19,440
Hunterdon County	128,349	127,722	-627	47,306	17,173	1,862	10,475	3,952
Mercer County	366,511	367,567	1,056	131,315	47,385	7,261	29,042	13,598
Middlesex County	809,860	816,975	7,115	280,599	102,516	15,846	58,029	24,783
Monmouth County	630,380	630,099	-281	234,366	89,569	13,709	56,213	25,644
Morris County	492,276	495,613	3,337	179,946	70,645	10,793	41,827	18,074
Ocean County	576,567	579,066	2,499	222,796	122,772	19,074	79,232	37,420
Passaic County	501,226	502,431	1,205	162,615	61,904	9,409	34,527	15,741
Salem County	66,083	65,960	-123	24,817	10,175	1,282	6,556	3,072
Somerset County	323,444	325,944	2,500	115,709	41,926	6,901	24,470	10,451
Sussex County	149,265	148,393	-872	54,274	18,525	2,194	11,022	4,133
Union County	536,499	540,650	4,151	184,721	68,570	12,061	40,075	18,144
Warren County	108,692	108,162	-530	41,582	15,423	2,237	9,011	3,801
New Mexico								
Bernalillo County	662,564	669,153	6,589	264,592	84,473	11,004	53,537	24,349
Chaves County	65,645	65,742	97	23,386	9,266	1,297	5,676	2,620
Doña Ana County	209,234	212,571	3,337	73,889	26,999	2,973	16,964	5,980
Lea County	64,727	65,377	650	20,396	7,189	655	4,453	1,720
McKinley County	71,492	72,807	1,315	17,642	7,038	651	4,378	1,850
Otero County	63,797	65,306	1,509	24,463	9,679	971	6,175	2,724
Sandoval County	131,561	134,053	2,492	47,339	17,027	2,102	10,240	4,081
San Juan County	130,044	128,912	-1,132	41,128	14,445	1,702	8,792	3,073
Santa Fe County	144,168	145,378	1,210	61,371	23,581	2,518	15,667	7,558
Valencia County	76,571	76,738	167	27,290	10,321	1,010	6,177	2,414

Table A-2: Counties—Summary Population Characteristics—*Continued*

	April 1, 2010 Census Population Estimates Base	2010–2012 ACS Population	Population Change	2010–2012 ACS				
				Total Households	Population 65 and Over	Population 85 and Over	Householders 65 and Over	Persons 65 and Over Living Alone
New York								
Albany County	304,206	304,694	488	121,548	43,137	7,464	26,694	13,592
Bronx County	1,385,108	1,397,357	12,249	471,665	150,027	20,618	89,776	48,575
Broome County	200,600	199,225	-1,375	80,214	33,185	5,497	20,716	10,191
Cattaraugus County	80,317	79,859	-458	32,114	12,495	1,735	7,955	3,720
Cayuga County	80,027	79,775	-252	30,819	12,491	1,875	8,022	3,674
Chautauqua County	134,905	134,190	-715	54,688	22,528	3,577	14,404	6,872
Chemung County	88,830	88,848	18	35,240	13,656	2,356	8,794	4,569
Clinton County	82,128	81,862	-266	31,901	11,178	1,268	7,230	3,320
Dutchess County	297,488	297,768	280	107,134	41,631	5,536	25,133	10,732
Erie County	919,040	919,268	228	379,140	145,651	22,231	94,461	46,899
Jefferson County	116,229	118,332	2,103	45,679	13,327	2,102	8,655	4,257
Kings County	2,504,700	2,538,529	33,829	908,959	294,324	41,314	180,377	89,713
Livingston County	65,393	65,007	-386	24,065	9,412	1,711	5,743	2,465
Madison County	73,442	72,881	-561	26,523	10,536	1,638	6,509	2,607
Monroe County	744,344	746,442	2,098	296,800	106,484	18,180	68,181	31,987
Nassau County	1,339,532	1,345,448	5,916	441,906	208,405	36,119	118,422	44,949
New York County	1,585,873	1,604,407	18,534	733,765	220,062	31,391	153,315	92,919
Niagara County	216,469	215,837	-632	88,432	34,855	5,421	22,254	10,664
Oneida County	234,878	234,193	-685	90,538	38,570	7,663	23,948	11,940
Onondaga County	467,025	467,263	238	184,224	66,790	11,250	42,609	21,559
Ontario County	107,931	108,374	443	44,113	17,324	2,396	10,730	4,833
Orange County	372,813	374,158	1,345	125,338	42,428	6,170	25,451	11,118
Oswego County	122,112	121,951	-161	44,893	15,690	1,891	9,931	4,127
Putnam County	99,710	99,769	59	34,855	13,030	1,822	7,531	2,840
Queens County	2,230,722	2,254,750	24,028	773,822	293,250	43,495	164,595	72,820
Rensselaer County	159,429	159,719	290	63,991	22,119	3,457	13,772	6,769
Richmond County	468,730	470,402	1,672	162,916	61,773	8,750	35,919	15,200
Rockland County	311,687	315,331	3,644	97,943	43,536	5,918	24,214	8,900
St. Lawrence County	111,944	112,150	206	42,055	15,917	1,869	10,195	4,686
Saratoga County	219,607	221,076	1,469	89,371	31,263	4,168	19,879	8,490
Schenectady County	154,727	154,973	246	58,120	23,143	4,785	14,296	7,118
Steuben County	98,989	99,095	106	41,422	16,051	2,164	10,147	4,786
Suffolk County	1,493,350	1,498,125	4,775	496,396	209,194	28,401	120,129	46,112
Sullivan County	77,545	77,100	-445	29,768	11,951	1,443	7,407	3,256
Tompkins County	101,564	101,989	425	38,530	11,365	1,751	7,172	3,422
Ulster County	182,496	182,256	-240	69,477	28,178	4,304	17,228	8,378
Warren County	65,705	65,653	-52	28,195	11,692	1,565	7,525	3,287
Wayne County	93,772	93,333	-439	36,872	13,836	1,668	8,545	3,432
Westchester County	949,113	956,494	7,381	342,568	142,310	23,448	85,012	39,063
North Carolina								
Alamance County	151,131	152,730	1,599	60,459	22,781	3,757	15,143	7,343
Brunswick County	107,431	110,196	2,765	47,114	25,078	1,552	15,532	4,949
Buncombe County	238,319	241,626	3,307	100,782	39,572	5,914	24,525	11,017
Burke County	90,914	90,713	-201	34,563	14,983	1,702	9,550	4,592
Cabarrus County	178,011	181,358	3,347	64,386	20,765	2,446	12,266	5,182
Caldwell County	83,029	82,380	-649	31,899	13,309	1,490	8,715	4,125
Carteret County	66,469	67,235	766	28,481	13,082	1,465	8,027	3,288
Catawba County	154,356	154,182	-174	58,281	23,003	2,748	13,927	5,935
Chatham County	63,505	65,001	1,496	25,834	12,897	1,653	7,609	3,382
Cleveland County	98,078	97,695	-383	36,958	15,241	1,910	10,113	4,923
Craven County	103,505	104,392	887	39,932	16,486	2,012	10,411	3,878
Cumberland County	319,431	322,532	3,101	120,577	31,376	3,135	20,132	8,832
Davidson County	162,878	163,071	193	64,482	24,684	2,719	15,360	6,169
Durham County	267,587	273,900	6,313	110,642	27,723	4,202	17,478	7,766
Forsyth County	350,670	354,659	3,989	139,085	46,943	6,403	29,928	14,020
Gaston County	206,086	207,039	953	79,259	28,154	3,520	17,191	7,184
Guilford County	488,406	495,297	6,891	196,171	62,583	7,687	40,114	17,795
Harnett County	114,678	119,058	4,380	40,352	12,444	1,221	7,745	3,483
Henderson County	106,740	107,594	854	44,465	24,744	3,326	15,045	5,827
Iredell County	159,437	161,160	1,723	59,408	21,342	2,632	12,673	5,104
Johnston County	168,878	172,463	3,585	60,552	18,658	1,581	11,292	4,657
Lincoln County	78,265	78,848	583	29,724	10,948	699	6,568	2,715
Mecklenburg County	919,628	945,889	26,261	362,469	86,008	11,249	52,955	22,595
Moore County	88,247	89,402	1,155	37,021	20,485	3,131	12,681	5,325
Nash County	95,840	95,838	-2	37,210	13,975	1,738	9,311	4,617
New Hanover County	202,667	206,165	3,498	85,918	29,485	3,442	18,801	8,434
Onslow County	177,772	180,060	2,288	60,656	13,878	1,317	8,668	3,813
Orange County	133,801	135,886	2,085	51,372	13,694	1,387	8,516	3,555
Pitt County	168,148	170,685	2,537	65,837	17,405	2,480	11,087	5,055
Randolph County	141,752	142,122	370	54,744	20,654	1,946	12,944	5,657
Robeson County	134,168	134,961	793	44,706	15,763	1,473	9,833	3,864
Rockingham County	93,640	93,158	-482	37,496	15,663	1,678	9,877	4,617
Rowan County	138,428	138,221	-207	52,290	20,589	2,621	13,295	5,777
Rutherford County	67,809	67,508	-301	27,024	12,047	1,726	7,588	3,375
Surry County	73,673	73,615	-58	30,026	12,520	1,429	8,442	3,882
Union County	201,292	205,292	4,000	67,769	20,603	2,028	11,867	3,874
Wake County	900,993	929,250	28,257	346,096	82,181	9,633	50,571	21,981
Wayne County	122,623	123,656	1,033	48,016	16,464	1,992	10,404	4,888
Wilkes County	69,340	69,250	-90	27,575	12,326	1,496	7,838	3,226
Wilson County	81,234	81,549	315	31,853	11,994	1,631	7,792	3,887

Table A-2: Counties—Summary Population Characteristics—*Continued*

	April 1, 2010 Census Population Estimates Base	2010–2012 ACS Population	Population Change	2010–2012 ACS				
				Total Households	Population 65 and Over	Population 85 and Over	Householders 65 and Over	Persons 65 and Over Living Alone
North Dakota								
Burleigh County	81,308	83,635	2,327	34,391	11,497	1,761	7,417	3,549
Cass County	149,778	153,012	3,234	65,568	15,280	2,040	9,923	5,235
Grand Forks County	66,861	67,006	145	27,483	7,213	986	4,748	2,403
Ohio								
Allen County	106,331	105,701	-630	40,398	15,696	2,573	9,963	4,653
Ashtabula County	101,497	100,967	-530	39,103	16,042	2,694	10,295	4,992
Belmont County	70,400	70,039	-361	28,383	12,501	2,032	7,881	3,815
Butler County	368,130	369,778	1,648	134,423	43,904	5,553	27,637	11,988
Clark County	138,333	137,735	-598	54,969	22,620	3,490	14,890	6,706
Clermont County	197,363	198,437	1,074	74,067	24,388	2,623	15,326	6,515
Columbiana County	107,841	107,190	-651	42,471	18,131	2,294	11,225	4,680
Cuyahoga County	1,280,122	1,271,187	-8,935	531,045	199,199	33,894	131,447	68,499
Delaware County	174,214	178,314	4,100	64,360	17,999	1,686	10,771	3,977
Erie County	77,079	76,700	-379	31,908	13,703	1,779	8,524	3,757
Fairfield County	146,156	147,071	915	54,138	18,641	2,241	11,630	4,345
Franklin County	1,163,414	1,180,276	16,862	467,314	119,415	16,279	76,037	37,004
Geauga County	93,389	93,465	76	34,527	15,046	2,187	8,947	3,167
Greene County	161,573	162,830	1,257	62,924	22,995	2,847	14,111	5,783
Hamilton County	802,374	801,587	-787	323,398	107,723	17,828	70,311	35,360
Hancock County	74,782	75,156	374	29,974	11,172	2,075	6,948	3,134
Jefferson County	69,709	68,965	-744	28,224	12,783	1,786	8,400	3,962
Lake County	230,041	229,836	-205	94,137	38,065	5,283	24,006	10,629
Licking County	166,492	167,159	667	63,875	22,880	2,410	14,450	6,268
Lorain County	301,356	301,611	255	116,604	44,580	6,272	27,906	11,380
Lucas County	441,815	439,826	-1,989	177,384	59,095	8,872	38,251	18,441
Mahoning County	238,823	236,713	-2,110	97,457	42,672	7,684	28,479	13,465
Marion County	66,501	66,411	-90	24,839	9,562	1,419	6,414	2,878
Medina County	172,332	173,217	885	65,591	23,579	3,093	14,720	6,225
Miami County	102,506	102,777	271	40,994	16,212	1,758	10,437	4,313
Montgomery County	535,153	535,057	-96	222,279	82,953	12,325	55,283	27,843
Muskingum County	86,074	86,109	35	33,947	13,274	2,001	8,262	3,865
Portage County	161,419	161,494	75	60,143	21,491	2,376	13,015	4,916
Richland County	124,475	123,331	-1,144	48,336	20,768	2,656	13,532	6,306
Ross County	78,064	77,723	-341	28,074	10,713	1,166	6,824	3,257
Scioto County	79,499	79,079	-420	29,339	12,327	1,380	8,017	3,849
Stark County	375,586	374,871	-715	149,275	61,897	9,674	38,956	17,018
Summit County	541,781	541,230	-551	219,302	80,782	12,364	51,983	24,594
Trumbull County	210,312	208,743	-1,569	86,233	37,110	5,033	23,974	11,364
Tuscarawas County	92,582	92,481	-101	36,140	15,333	2,049	9,621	4,310
Warren County	212,693	215,286	2,593	76,331	24,217	2,747	14,338	5,480
Wayne County	114,520	114,674	154	42,023	17,247	2,617	10,462	4,079
Wood County	125,488	126,871	1,383	48,870	16,009	1,880	10,464	4,660
Oklahoma								
Canadian County	115,541	119,446	3,905	42,386	13,443	1,599	8,051	3,242
Cleveland County	255,757	261,386	5,629	96,150	27,700	3,090	16,651	7,024
Comanche County	124,098	125,850	1,752	44,614	12,964	1,427	8,725	4,008
Creek County	69,967	70,439	472	26,476	10,832	1,256	6,708	2,921
Muskogee County	70,990	70,815	-175	26,604	10,529	1,317	6,568	2,825
Oklahoma County	718,631	730,787	12,156	282,883	87,927	11,975	57,340	27,497
Payne County	77,350	77,921	571	30,218	8,088	1,229	5,209	2,214
Pottawatomie County	69,442	70,209	767	26,043	10,218	1,023	6,421	2,811
Rogers County	86,905	87,729	824	32,902	12,248	1,437	7,325	2,458
Tulsa County	603,409	609,067	5,658	240,665	74,698	10,808	48,412	22,544
Wagoner County	73,085	74,182	1,097	26,749	9,931	783	6,146	2,268
Oregon								
Benton County	85,581	85,989	408	32,925	10,787	1,929	6,771	3,018
Clackamas County	375,992	380,281	4,289	145,555	54,314	7,604	33,314	13,564
Deschutes County	157,733	160,085	2,352	64,982	25,290	3,476	15,950	6,436
Douglas County	107,667	107,420	-247	43,654	23,198	2,906	14,506	5,760
Jackson County	203,206	204,868	1,662	82,524	37,277	5,744	23,740	10,407
Josephine County	82,713	82,825	112	34,151	18,923	2,927	11,849	5,243
Klamath County	66,380	66,186	-194	27,789	11,842	1,165	7,609	2,710
Lane County	351,715	353,315	1,600	145,265	54,955	7,297	34,894	15,537
Linn County	116,672	117,796	1,124	44,926	18,819	2,245	12,108	4,989
Marion County	315,335	317,945	2,610	113,116	42,006	6,420	26,123	11,839
Multnomah County	735,334	748,280	12,946	305,069	81,022	13,346	52,357	26,080
Polk County	75,403	75,987	584	28,501	11,764	1,854	7,109	2,655
Umatilla County	75,889	76,514	625	26,867	9,806	1,291	6,242	2,714
Washington County	529,710	539,525	9,815	201,111	56,477	8,550	35,955	16,609
Yamhill County	99,193	99,803	610	33,574	13,902	2,329	8,356	3,215
Pennsylvania								
Adams County	101,407	101,485	78	37,919	16,630	2,336	9,970	4,155
Allegheny County	1,223,348	1,226,873	3,525	522,238	205,615	36,676	135,087	69,000
Armstrong County	68,942	68,659	-283	28,735	12,928	2,068	8,268	4,097
Beaver County	170,539	170,404	-135	70,787	31,875	4,889	20,859	9,783
Berks County	411,439	412,610	1,171	154,092	60,772	9,371	37,479	16,345
Blair County	127,076	127,131	55	50,990	22,825	3,637	14,484	6,812
Bucks County	625,249	626,494	1,245	230,384	94,503	14,925	56,346	22,641
Butler County	183,862	184,574	712	73,147	28,769	4,188	17,817	7,707
Cambria County	143,679	142,564	-1,115	58,197	27,189	4,525	17,817	8,873
Carbon County	65,249	65,118	-131	25,919	11,798	1,594	7,076	3,029

Table A-2: Counties—Summary Population Characteristics—*Continued*

	April 1, 2010 Census Population Estimates Base	2010–2012 ACS Population	Population Change	2010–2012 ACS				
				Total Households	Population 65 and Over	Population 85 and Over	Householders 65 and Over	Persons 65 and Over Living Alone
Pennsylvania—Cont.								
Centre County	153,985	154,698	713	57,266	17,752	2,566	11,231	5,115
Chester County	498,886	503,325	4,439	184,364	66,785	9,525	39,824	16,322
Clearfield County	81,645	81,422	-223	32,158	14,432	2,259	9,071	4,185
Columbia County	67,296	67,018	-278	26,188	10,849	1,434	7,062	3,495
Crawford County	88,765	88,132	-633	35,042	14,987	1,831	9,560	4,098
Cumberland County	235,408	237,100	1,692	95,126	37,807	6,172	23,269	10,353
Dauphin County	268,100	268,990	890	107,891	37,544	6,060	24,168	11,485
Delaware County	558,979	560,011	1,032	205,185	80,632	14,469	50,131	23,948
Erie County	280,566	280,794	228	109,522	41,308	6,441	25,679	12,037
Fayette County	136,606	136,102	-504	54,372	24,652	3,783	15,556	7,498
Franklin County	149,618	150,691	1,073	57,739	25,484	3,204	15,592	6,536
Indiana County	88,886	88,532	-354	34,652	14,031	2,336	8,758	3,680
Lackawanna County	214,436	214,528	92	85,721	38,470	7,047	23,796	11,507
Lancaster County	519,448	523,676	4,228	193,931	80,119	13,886	47,590	20,147
Lawrence County	91,108	90,411	-697	36,752	17,239	3,004	10,927	5,146
Lebanon County	133,573	134,452	879	51,807	22,939	3,413	14,277	6,204
Lehigh County	349,497	352,948	3,451	133,322	52,617	8,676	31,004	14,131
Luzerne County	320,918	321,013	95	130,097	58,047	9,540	36,834	18,663
Lycoming County	116,108	116,668	560	45,933	19,304	3,409	11,867	5,127
Mercer County	116,638	116,122	-516	46,345	21,759	3,717	14,049	6,505
Monroe County	169,842	169,588	-254	58,173	22,390	2,658	11,953	4,299
Montgomery County	799,874	804,896	5,022	307,618	123,778	20,864	74,581	33,081
Northampton County	297,735	298,618	883	112,120	47,739	7,921	29,061	13,115
Northumberland County	94,517	94,427	-90	39,109	17,551	2,778	11,300	5,227
Philadelphia County	1,526,006	1,538,211	12,205	576,889	186,585	28,788	122,082	67,573
Schuylkill County	148,289	147,618	-671	59,689	26,978	4,328	17,174	7,839
Somerset County	77,742	77,348	-394	29,626	14,685	2,507	9,121	4,184
Washington County	207,820	208,256	436	83,920	37,057	5,452	23,892	11,437
Westmoreland County	365,168	364,357	-811	152,022	69,613	11,376	45,195	20,701
York County	434,972	436,824	1,852	168,566	63,155	8,678	39,794	17,352
Rhode Island								
Kent County	166,158	165,432	-726	68,271	26,590	4,322	17,045	8,609
Newport County	82,888	82,372	-516	34,364	14,503	2,342	9,167	4,206
Providence County	626,667	627,625	958	237,634	85,113	15,615	52,402	26,895
Washington County	126,979	126,394	-585	49,798	19,804	2,950	12,599	5,397
South Carolina								
Aiken County	160,106	161,817	1,711	63,373	25,797	2,290	16,110	6,372
Anderson County	187,122	188,359	1,237	72,891	29,491	3,431	18,798	7,991
Beaufort County	162,233	165,149	2,916	63,600	35,549	3,592	22,118	7,317
Berkeley County	177,843	184,225	6,382	65,396	19,515	1,830	11,717	4,028
Charleston County	350,209	358,009	7,800	142,536	47,190	5,484	30,038	13,233
Darlington County	68,687	68,341	-346	26,568	10,184	1,110	6,784	2,947
Dorchester County	136,555	140,010	3,455	50,323	14,687	1,496	8,916	3,632
Florence County	136,879	137,473	594	51,477	18,568	2,089	11,261	4,324
Greenville County	451,222	459,753	8,531	175,023	60,362	7,557	37,562	16,161
Greenwood County	69,661	69,731	70	26,354	10,839	1,796	7,065	3,353
Horry County	269,291	276,156	6,865	113,314	49,069	4,537	31,520	13,202
Lancaster County	76,652	77,898	1,246	29,268	12,803	984	7,703	2,731
Laurens County	66,540	66,349	-191	24,783	10,202	1,333	6,158	2,619
Lexington County	262,394	266,797	4,403	103,724	33,769	3,872	20,450	8,236
Oconee County	74,275	74,425	150	30,082	14,634	1,165	9,024	3,335
Orangeburg County	92,495	91,835	-660	34,266	14,152	1,411	8,962	3,992
Pickens County	119,226	119,440	214	43,553	16,515	1,906	10,102	4,030
Richland County	384,501	389,648	5,147	142,881	39,434	5,177	24,800	11,267
Spartanburg County	284,307	286,563	2,256	106,734	39,447	3,986	24,662	10,486
Sumter County	107,456	107,642	186	39,766	14,136	1,694	9,106	3,806
York County	226,073	230,600	4,527	86,271	27,017	2,730	17,045	6,562
South Dakota								
Minnehaha County	169,468	172,303	2,835	67,205	19,398	3,019	12,106	5,453
Pennington County	100,948	102,742	1,794	40,606	14,163	2,256	8,758	3,843
Tennessee								
Anderson County	75,118	75,255	137	30,638	13,279	2,717	8,590	3,782
Blount County	123,010	123,676	666	48,349	20,569	2,227	12,826	5,289
Bradley County	98,963	100,080	1,117	37,747	14,689	1,467	9,145	3,993
Davidson County	626,681	637,303	10,622	254,917	67,113	9,196	42,599	20,245
Greene County	68,831	68,901	70	29,192	12,423	1,117	7,888	3,434
Hamilton County	336,463	341,248	4,785	135,018	51,108	7,226	32,214	14,564
Knox County	432,237	437,095	4,858	181,578	58,504	7,110	37,182	18,240
Madison County	98,294	98,364	70	35,185	13,271	1,819	8,034	3,502
Maury County	80,956	81,491	535	31,800	10,993	1,325	6,547	2,857
Montgomery County	172,336	178,227	5,891	64,010	14,271	1,451	8,609	3,344
Putnam County	72,321	72,845	524	28,829	10,849	1,299	6,939	2,649
Robertson County	66,283	66,714	431	24,302	8,107	1,151	5,220	2,123
Rutherford County	262,604	269,144	6,540	95,363	23,173	2,691	14,063	5,290
Sevier County	89,887	91,338	1,451	36,333	14,540	1,258	8,874	3,127
Shelby County	927,644	934,654	7,010	342,124	98,130	12,047	61,462	27,541
Sullivan County	156,823	156,895	72	66,038	30,036	3,763	20,031	8,356
Sumner County	160,645	163,737	3,092	60,301	21,716	2,285	12,748	4,814
Washington County	122,979	124,150	1,171	52,066	19,318	2,503	12,311	5,332
Williamson County	183,182	188,432	5,250	66,153	19,043	2,308	11,552	4,319
Wilson County	113,993	116,756	2,763	42,697	15,060	1,339	9,111	3,100

Table A-2: Counties—Summary Population Characteristics—*Continued*

	April 1, 2010 Census Population Estimates Base	2010–2012 ACS Population	Population Change	2010–2012 ACS				
				Total Households	Population 65 and Over	Population 85 and Over	Householders 65 and Over	Persons 65 and Over Living Alone
Texas								
Angelina County	86,771	87,254	483	31,055	12,215	1,684	7,547	2,912
Bastrop County	74,169	74,713	544	25,097	8,856	1,272	4,902	2,070
Bell County	310,235	317,284	7,049	103,230	28,330	3,140	16,529	6,469
Bexar County	1,714,777	1,754,058	39,281	602,654	183,708	24,257	110,503	45,112
Bowie County	92,565	92,907	342	34,013	13,491	1,836	8,732	4,058
Brazoria County	313,166	319,498	6,332	107,526	31,601	3,916	18,734	6,921
Brazos County	194,851	197,968	3,117	69,824	14,827	1,587	9,419	3,981
Cameron County	406,220	411,930	5,710	118,445	46,553	4,957	25,830	9,071
Collin County	782,341	811,948	29,607	287,166	66,763	6,380	36,949	13,406
Comal County	108,472	111,768	3,296	42,043	17,966	2,214	10,803	3,750
Coryell County	75,402	76,471	1,069	19,793	6,127	434	3,511	1,149
Dallas County	2,368,139	2,411,891	43,752	854,403	216,404	27,091	131,881	56,412
Denton County	662,614	686,622	24,008	242,679	50,590	4,958	28,022	10,766
Ector County	137,130	140,323	3,193	49,495	14,068	1,576	9,061	4,138
Ellis County	149,610	152,258	2,648	50,850	15,922	1,494	9,565	3,373
El Paso County	800,647	816,295	15,648	256,148	84,785	10,499	49,572	18,574
Fort Bend County	585,377	608,747	23,370	189,865	48,089	4,302	24,655	7,835
Galveston County	291,309	296,100	4,791	109,510	34,436	3,987	20,486	8,441
Grayson County	120,877	121,434	557	46,349	19,174	2,535	11,431	4,961
Gregg County	121,730	122,287	557	44,819	16,576	2,547	10,619	5,124
Guadalupe County	131,533	136,021	4,488	46,485	16,215	1,432	10,201	4,146
Harris County	4,092,442	4,178,437	85,995	1,419,274	351,983	39,951	205,093	84,598
Harrison County	65,631	66,832	1,201	23,670	9,151	1,096	5,890	2,740
Hays County	157,103	163,675	6,572	56,282	14,452	1,298	8,277	3,153
Henderson County	78,531	78,843	312	29,673	15,363	1,548	9,403	3,656
Hidalgo County	774,769	793,312	18,543	217,706	75,801	8,386	41,006	13,153
Hunt County	86,129	86,689	560	30,939	12,094	1,703	7,492	3,050
Jefferson County	252,273	252,457	184	92,508	32,227	4,403	21,674	10,531
Johnson County	150,934	152,218	1,284	52,243	18,258	1,550	10,832	3,386
Kaufman County	103,351	105,310	1,959	35,181	11,201	1,155	6,669	2,496
Liberty County	75,643	76,119	476	24,813	8,731	854	5,552	2,036
Lubbock County	278,831	283,082	4,251	105,477	31,501	3,853	20,165	8,782
McLennan County	234,906	237,471	2,565	84,399	30,023	4,469	18,149	8,095
Midland County	136,872	141,207	4,335	50,251	15,298	1,851	9,229	4,180
Montgomery County	455,761	472,014	16,253	163,842	51,133	5,195	30,909	11,317
Nacogdoches County	64,524	65,421	897	23,627	7,752	988	4,957	2,452
Nueces County	340,223	343,697	3,474	122,839	42,309	5,367	25,772	9,844
Orange County	81,837	82,444	607	30,401	11,617	1,287	7,230	2,986
Parker County	116,927	118,462	1,535	42,457	15,347	1,361	9,609	3,442
Potter County	121,073	121,878	805	42,670	13,436	1,993	8,181	3,883
Randall County	120,725	123,283	2,558	48,617	15,476	1,801	10,099	4,214
Rockwall County	78,337	81,054	2,717	27,108	8,153	528	4,518	1,446
San Patricio County	64,806	64,863	57	22,121	8,504	906	5,198	1,865
Smith County	209,714	212,694	2,980	79,299	30,979	4,509	19,347	7,982
Tarrant County	1,809,039	1,847,884	38,845	657,094	170,784	20,334	103,760	44,546
Taylor County	131,506	132,658	1,152	49,159	17,602	2,361	11,015	4,735
Tom Green County	110,224	111,883	1,659	41,907	15,541	1,628	10,089	4,254
Travis County	1,024,272	1,062,335	38,063	409,351	80,410	9,950	49,015	19,832
Victoria County	86,793	87,847	1,054	31,967	11,915	1,310	7,265	3,006
Walker County	67,861	68,254	393	20,601	7,162	677	4,461	1,982
Webb County	250,304	255,135	4,831	67,572	20,230	2,711	10,908	3,597
Wichita County	131,500	131,281	-219	47,266	17,250	2,405	11,069	4,850
Williamson County	422,679	441,748	19,069	154,373	41,340	4,429	23,368	8,731
Utah								
Cache County	112,656	114,454	1,798	35,449	9,042	1,146	5,564	1,986
Davis County	306,479	311,852	5,373	95,457	26,297	3,013	15,780	4,953
Salt Lake County	1,029,655	1,048,261	18,606	344,187	92,822	11,735	57,796	23,566
Utah County	516,564	530,147	13,583	142,724	35,381	4,356	20,809	6,792
Washington County	138,115	141,594	3,479	47,115	25,428	3,421	15,283	4,816
Weber County	231,236	234,303	3,067	79,718	24,310	3,199	15,399	6,067
Vermont								
Chittenden County	156,546	157,675	1,129	62,699	18,518	2,866	11,803	5,459
Virginia								
Albemarle County	98,970	100,757	1,787	37,788	15,021	2,222	9,195	4,051
Arlington County	207,628	215,481	7,853	93,236	18,853	2,506	12,176	6,429
Augusta County	73,750	73,638	-112	28,281	12,395	1,253	7,768	2,693
Bedford County	68,676	69,252	576	27,146	11,913	1,002	7,426	2,768
Chesterfield County	316,236	320,514	4,278	112,630	35,308	4,107	21,476	8,449
Fairfax County	1,081,725	1,103,177	21,452	390,130	113,056	12,982	64,675	23,768
Fauquier County	65,203	66,003	800	22,768	9,036	774	5,124	1,875
Frederick County	78,305	79,483	1,178	28,866	10,369	992	6,175	2,165
Hanover County	99,863	100,255	392	36,329	13,677	1,678	8,435	2,843
Henrico County	306,935	310,972	4,037	123,131	39,428	6,425	25,135	11,980
James City County	67,009	68,048	1,039	26,836	14,492	1,762	8,682	3,125
Loudoun County	312,311	326,222	13,911	106,027	22,693	2,244	11,937	4,412
Montgomery County	94,392	94,800	408	34,718	9,532	1,497	5,998	2,326
Prince William County	402,002	418,759	16,757	132,261	29,852	3,013	15,513	5,187
Roanoke County	92,376	92,748	372	38,024	16,586	2,136	10,426	4,518
Rockingham County	76,314	76,946	632	29,063	12,553	1,564	7,980	3,102
Spotsylvania County	122,397	124,345	1,948	41,892	12,889	1,411	7,813	2,637
Stafford County	128,961	132,152	3,191	41,760	10,202	1,006	5,781	1,879
York County	65,464	65,791	327	23,983	8,195	675	4,985	1,554

Table A-2: Counties—Summary Population Characteristics—*Continued*

	April 1, 2010 Census Population Estimates Base	2010–2012 ACS Population	Population Change	2010–2012 ACS				
				Total Households	Population 65 and Over	Population 85 and Over	Householders 65 and Over	Persons 65 and Over Living Alone
Washington								
Benton County	175,177	179,809	4,632	65,278	21,734	2,623	13,851	5,644
Chelan County	72,453	73,221	768	26,915	11,278	1,842	7,294	3,123
Clallam County	71,404	71,737	333	30,750	17,599	2,484	10,954	4,321
Clark County	425,363	432,801	7,438	158,539	52,173	6,670	32,636	13,070
Cowlitz County	102,410	102,291	-119	39,823	16,595	2,221	10,586	4,651
Franklin County	78,163	82,715	4,552	23,466	5,948	627	3,448	1,551
Grant County	89,120	90,714	1,594	30,367	11,007	1,305	7,157	2,906
Grays Harbor County	72,797	72,289	-508	27,582	12,095	1,222	7,566	3,431
Island County	78,506	78,970	464	32,698	15,084	2,029	9,195	3,519
King County	1,931,249	1,972,284	41,035	796,640	221,540	34,760	139,478	67,295
Kitsap County	251,133	253,763	2,630	98,682	35,096	4,247	21,257	8,685
Lewis County	75,455	75,594	139	29,391	13,363	2,104	8,882	3,852
Pierce County	795,225	803,585	8,360	299,514	91,957	11,896	56,645	24,434
Skagit County	116,901	117,691	790	45,207	19,708	2,652	12,155	4,935
Snohomish County	713,335	723,763	10,428	268,565	77,984	10,667	47,824	20,187
Spokane County	471,221	473,793	2,572	187,863	63,283	8,679	40,702	19,107
Thurston County	252,264	255,927	3,663	101,296	34,479	4,483	21,508	9,488
Whatcom County	201,140	203,482	2,342	79,643	27,966	3,710	17,606	7,528
Yakima County	243,231	245,797	2,566	79,396	29,016	4,420	16,886	7,072
West Virginia								
Berkeley County	104,169	105,863	1,694	40,297	12,474	1,263	7,552	2,934
Cabell County	96,317	96,651	334	39,766	15,474	2,097	10,095	4,493
Harrison County	69,099	69,220	121	27,904	11,634	1,721	7,720	3,589
Kanawha County	193,063	192,432	-631	83,146	32,705	4,259	22,134	10,181
Monongalia County	96,189	98,573	2,384	36,183	9,967	1,324	5,975	2,825
Raleigh County	78,859	79,033	174	31,384	12,926	1,400	8,358	4,010
Wood County	86,956	86,851	-105	35,302	14,901	1,837	9,880	4,848
Wisconsin								
Brown County	248,007	250,712	2,705	98,677	29,647	4,781	18,977	8,865
Dane County	488,073	496,374	8,301	205,451	52,786	7,509	34,303	15,382
Dodge County	88,759	88,596	-163	33,293	13,424	2,162	8,083	3,565
Eau Claire County	98,736	99,769	1,033	39,957	12,758	2,074	8,546	4,355
Fond du Lac County	101,633	101,798	165	41,025	15,621	2,830	9,918	4,453
Jefferson County	83,686	84,046	360	32,115	11,327	1,605	7,181	3,392
Kenosha County	166,426	167,242	816	62,408	19,059	2,949	12,001	5,821
La Crosse County	114,638	115,603	965	46,174	15,680	2,705	10,188	4,804
Manitowoc County	81,442	81,011	-431	34,062	14,066	2,652	8,800	4,223
Marathon County	134,063	134,459	396	52,515	19,728	3,252	11,818	4,956
Milwaukee County	947,735	951,833	4,098	379,601	109,943	17,433	73,522	40,553
Outagamie County	176,695	177,774	1,079	69,255	21,424	3,166	13,975	6,469
Ozaukee County	86,395	86,581	186	34,281	13,648	1,899	8,761	3,584
Portage County	70,019	70,206	187	28,189	9,254	1,451	6,118	2,698
Racine County	195,408	195,086	-322	75,450	26,333	3,575	17,221	8,026
Rock County	160,331	160,240	-91	63,114	22,209	2,999	14,192	6,543
St. Croix County	84,345	84,856	511	32,023	8,892	1,039	5,266	2,019
Sheboygan County	115,507	115,224	-283	46,072	17,184	2,993	10,784	4,750
Walworth County	102,228	102,519	291	39,455	14,110	2,215	8,640	3,723
Washington County	131,887	132,276	389	51,759	18,386	2,953	11,986	5,030
Waukesha County	389,891	391,017	1,126	152,574	57,878	8,728	36,335	16,075
Winnebago County	166,994	167,860	866	67,750	22,787	3,956	14,435	7,320
Wood County	74,749	74,604	-145	31,949	12,944	2,098	8,541	3,935
Wyoming								
Laramie County	91,738	93,030	1,292	37,119	12,078	1,489	7,710	3,736
Natrona County	75,450	76,821	1,371	31,080	9,606	1,300	6,257	2,672

Table A-3: Places—Summary Population Characteristics

	April 1, 2010 Census Population Estimates Base	2010–2012 ACS Population	Population Change	2010–2012 ACS				
				Total Households	Population 65 and Over	Population 85 and Over	Householders 65 and Over	Persons 65 and Over Living Alone
Alabama								
Birmingham city	212,244	211,827	-417	87,407	27,055	4,215	18,290	8,794
Dothan city	65,496	67,269	1,773	25,799	9,820	1,109	6,154	2,670
Hoover city	81,619	82,214	595	31,316	9,964	1,241	6,100	2,319
Huntsville city	180,120	181,734	1,614	75,373	25,490	3,665	16,524	7,247
Mobile city	195,107	194,829	-278	76,621	26,986	3,885	17,863	8,328
Montgomery city	205,771	206,346	575	79,764	24,541	3,096	16,232	7,906
Tuscaloosa city	90,483	92,217	1,734	30,979	9,472	1,507	5,512	2,734
Alaska								
Anchorage Municipality	291,826	296,039	4,213	105,688	22,770	1,777	13,374	5,987
Arizona								
Avondale city	76,238	77,270	1,032	22,330	4,497	293	2,137	530
Chandler city	236,139	240,626	4,487	86,507	20,345	2,299	12,219	4,589
Flagstaff city	65,870	66,400	530	22,385	4,470	584	2,804	1,021
Glendale city	226,724	229,166	2,442	78,437	20,935	2,434	12,528	5,412
Goodyear city	65,275	67,545	2,270	22,141	7,649	590	3,868	820
Mesa city	439,041	445,671	6,478	165,344	68,038	8,643	41,346	17,272
Peoria city	154,067	156,920	2,853	56,220	22,278	3,407	13,410	5,572
Phoenix city	1,445,656	1,467,400	21,744	516,383	129,033	15,505	77,061	32,931
Scottsdale city	217,385	220,293	2,908	99,734	45,320	6,449	28,373	11,555
Surprise city	117,517	119,378	1,861	42,029	23,403	1,587	13,145	3,878
Tempe city	161,719	164,186	2,467	63,328	13,752	1,951	8,421	3,362
Tucson city	520,097	522,770	2,673	200,627	64,634	9,624	41,664	20,581
Yuma city	93,066	95,130	2,064	33,492	12,260	1,235	7,471	2,699
Arkansas								
Fayetteville city	73,580	75,473	1,893	32,050	6,279	983	4,228	2,276
Fort Smith city	86,209	86,981	772	34,062	10,786	1,452	7,098	3,642
Jonesboro city	67,261	68,844	1,583	26,359	7,585	1,176	4,751	2,004
Little Rock city	193,524	195,242	1,718	79,047	22,904	3,427	14,384	6,586
Springdale city	69,792	74,156	4,364	24,286	6,179	978	3,706	1,443
California								
Alameda city	73,812	74,760	948	29,709	9,453	1,309	5,614	2,437
Alhambra city	83,089	83,722	633	29,065	12,420	2,319	6,093	2,233
Anaheim city	336,265	340,306	4,041	98,137	33,105	4,890	17,509	6,474
Antioch city	102,372	104,041	1,669	32,064	9,665	967	5,280	1,928
Bakersfield city	347,462	353,780	6,318	110,198	31,218	3,828	17,566	7,218
Baldwin Park city	75,390	75,914	524	16,846	6,939	903	2,679	726
Bellflower city	76,616	77,006	390	23,088	6,715	755	3,456	1,712
Berkeley city	112,578	114,156	1,578	44,826	14,291	2,062	9,832	5,133
Buena Park city	80,524	81,471	947	22,947	9,293	1,374	4,317	1,263
Burbank city	103,340	103,900	560	40,962	14,713	2,623	9,097	4,656
Camarillo city	65,222	65,671	449	23,854	11,587	2,216	7,463	3,248
Carlsbad city	105,328	107,615	2,287	42,299	16,155	2,843	9,689	3,926
Carson city	91,714	92,358	644	24,849	12,669	1,024	6,307	1,873
Chico city	86,187	86,920	733	33,516	9,386	1,554	5,979	3,230
Chino city	77,983	79,441	1,458	21,625	6,996	627	3,383	1,383
Chino Hills city	74,799	75,762	963	22,897	5,549	416	2,412	775
Chula Vista city	243,916	248,425	4,509	76,159	25,479	3,459	13,541	5,627
Citrus Heights city	83,301	84,192	891	32,472	11,689	1,476	7,453	3,623
Clovis city	95,631	97,434	1,803	33,284	10,801	1,412	6,390	2,688
Compton city	96,455	97,054	599	23,387	7,343	762	4,257	1,524
Concord city	122,067	123,571	1,504	44,492	14,897	2,171	9,029	3,579
Corona city	152,374	155,603	3,229	44,071	11,876	1,396	5,416	1,937
Costa Mesa city	109,960	111,034	1,074	40,576	9,871	1,796	6,028	2,596
Daly City city	101,123	102,417	1,294	30,731	13,905	2,039	6,493	2,420
Davis city	65,622	65,800	178	23,693	5,419	961	3,625	1,972
Downey city	111,772	112,341	569	33,044	11,636	1,915	6,050	2,036
El Cajon city	99,478	100,631	1,153	31,995	10,822	1,964	5,866	2,690
Elk Grove city	153,015	156,190	3,175	47,132	14,455	2,078	6,438	2,025
El Monte city	113,475	114,338	863	28,955	11,767	1,549	4,959	1,372
Escondido city	143,911	145,990	2,079	44,581	14,908	3,112	7,965	3,693
Fairfield city	105,323	106,469	1,146	34,199	11,320	1,181	6,404	2,449
Folsom city	72,203	72,779	576	24,700	6,807	1,145	4,582	2,510
Fontana city	196,069	199,630	3,561	48,176	12,111	1,790	4,711	1,685
Fremont city	214,089	218,160	4,071	70,645	24,028	3,434	11,261	4,093
Fresno city	494,735	501,350	6,615	157,154	46,667	7,248	28,015	12,285
Fullerton city	135,161	136,886	1,725	43,938	16,614	2,740	8,634	2,931
Garden Grove city	170,883	172,868	1,985	46,227	19,428	2,693	9,097	2,929
Glendale city	191,719	193,099	1,380	69,678	30,474	4,479	16,471	7,080
Hawthorne city	84,293	85,016	723	28,451	6,335	834	3,391	1,685
Hayward city	144,186	147,038	2,852	44,815	15,246	2,104	7,670	3,216
Hemet city	78,657	80,140	1,483	30,500	18,184	3,482	12,189	6,855
Hesperia city	90,173	91,307	1,134	26,419	9,075	1,009	5,067	1,905
Huntington Beach city	189,992	193,074	3,082	73,787	28,026	3,872	17,239	6,633
Indio city	76,038	77,953	1,915	23,282	10,563	1,105	5,756	2,183
Inglewood city	109,673	110,528	855	36,350	10,368	1,146	6,548	3,226
Irvine city	212,375	221,358	8,983	79,235	19,093	2,486	10,385	3,748
Jurupa Valley city [1]	95,004	96,465	1,461	24,054	7,366	743	3,998	1,681

[1] Jurupa Valley city was incorporated in 2011. The 2010 population is the U.S. Census Bureau's estimates base figure.

Table A-3: Places—Summary Population Characteristics—*Continued*

	April 1, 2010 Census Population Estimates Base	2010–2012 ACS Population	Population Change	2010–2012 ACS				
				Total Households	Population 65 and Over	Population 85 and Over	Householders 65 and Over	Persons 65 and Over Living Alone
California—Cont.								
Lake Forest city	77,264	78,188	924	27,440	7,983	902	4,442	1,815
Lakewood city	80,048	80,475	427	26,665	9,689	1,347	5,434	2,341
Lancaster city	156,633	158,108	1,475	47,311	13,509	1,670	7,390	3,014
Livermore city	80,968	82,326	1,358	28,999	8,659	1,041	5,198	2,015
Long Beach city	462,257	465,125	2,868	159,984	44,044	6,108	25,039	11,626
Los Angeles city	3,792,625	3,825,653	33,028	1,317,210	409,228	59,670	237,046	107,623
Lynwood city	69,772	70,014	242	14,836	4,566	590	1,648	399
Manteca city	67,171	69,309	2,138	22,128	7,028	929	4,198	1,592
Menifee city	77,519	79,843	2,324	26,686	14,490	1,902	8,860	3,848
Merced city	78,958	79,987	1,029	24,542	7,293	1,106	4,060	1,821
Milpitas city	66,790	67,530	740	19,280	6,720	511	2,848	886
Mission Viejo city	93,305	94,434	1,129	33,255	14,202	2,122	8,517	3,164
Modesto city	201,165	202,400	1,235	68,814	23,450	3,861	14,085	6,258
Moreno Valley city	193,365	197,068	3,703	50,180	13,129	1,386	6,104	1,381
Mountain View city	74,066	75,381	1,315	31,736	8,170	1,221	5,174	2,472
Murrieta city	103,466	105,369	1,903	32,215	10,502	966	6,159	3,049
Napa city	76,945	77,714	769	28,315	10,631	1,806	6,718	3,164
Newport Beach city	85,186	86,259	1,073	38,093	16,120	2,363	10,180	4,066
Norwalk city	105,549	105,961	412	26,703	10,583	1,423	5,292	1,657
Oakland city	390,724	396,030	5,306	154,737	45,885	7,390	29,723	15,086
Oceanside city	167,086	169,530	2,444	57,210	20,928	3,621	12,722	5,847
Ontario city	163,924	165,909	1,985	44,255	12,289	1,393	6,048	2,276
Orange city	136,416	138,220	1,804	43,294	15,186	1,874	8,077	2,782
Oxnard city	197,899	200,015	2,116	50,022	16,693	1,956	8,338	2,764
Palmdale city	152,750	154,383	1,633	40,762	10,733	1,377	5,191	1,882
Palo Alto city	64,403	65,498	1,095	26,426	11,296	2,206	7,239	3,491
Pasadena city	137,122	137,900	778	54,371	19,249	4,120	11,195	5,409
Perris city	68,386	70,174	1,788	15,842	3,126	149	1,558	342
Pleasanton city	70,285	71,366	1,081	24,715	8,045	934	4,777	1,930
Pomona city	149,058	149,961	903	37,883	12,054	1,763	6,121	2,373
Rancho Cordova city	64,805	66,066	1,261	23,679	7,156	925	4,373	1,858
Rancho Cucamonga city	165,269	168,448	3,179	54,680	13,966	1,935	7,504	3,033
Redding city	89,861	90,351	490	34,623	14,970	2,393	9,678	4,586
Redlands city	68,749	69,395	646	24,485	9,027	1,511	5,345	2,467
Redondo Beach city	66,748	67,256	508	28,696	7,620	819	4,936	2,316
Redwood City city	76,815	77,945	1,130	27,731	8,680	1,597	5,268	2,849
Rialto city	99,170	100,663	1,493	24,269	7,428	527	3,995	1,497
Richmond city	103,701	105,304	1,603	36,317	10,244	1,225	6,393	2,854
Riverside city	303,871	309,793	5,922	89,588	28,686	4,001	15,759	6,697
Roseville city	118,788	122,221	3,433	45,049	16,337	1,966	10,180	4,772
Sacramento city	466,488	471,552	5,064	175,723	52,625	8,441	32,016	15,985
Salinas city	150,441	152,650	2,209	40,959	11,562	1,609	5,951	2,653
San Bernardino city	209,947	211,847	1,900	57,865	17,189	1,917	9,607	4,217
San Buenaventura (Ventura) city	106,433	106,994	561	41,174	15,430	2,802	10,104	4,849
San Diego city	1,307,406	1,321,545	14,139	469,700	145,264	21,880	84,219	37,447
San Francisco city	805,235	815,234	9,999	341,721	112,614	18,043	68,503	34,884
San Jose city	952,612	969,324	16,712	305,787	101,942	12,782	52,773	18,653
San Leandro city	84,950	85,958	1,008	30,496	11,556	2,141	6,252	3,048
San Marcos city	83,781	85,213	1,432	27,752	9,526	1,650	5,474	2,543
San Mateo city	97,207	98,499	1,292	37,364	14,337	2,857	8,714	4,505
San Ramon city	72,148	73,160	1,012	25,013	5,414	554	2,920	1,227
Santa Ana city	324,528	328,180	3,652	71,546	21,887	3,035	9,878	3,185
Santa Barbara city	88,409	88,996	587	33,667	12,493	2,791	7,921	4,042
Santa Clara city	116,468	118,010	1,542	41,942	10,904	1,697	6,487	2,871
Santa Clarita city	176,320	177,748	1,428	58,865	17,699	2,495	10,565	4,271
Santa Maria city	99,553	100,529	976	27,417	9,627	1,527	5,330	2,089
Santa Monica city	89,736	90,780	1,044	45,805	13,554	2,290	9,500	5,809
Santa Rosa city	167,821	169,376	1,555	62,249	22,290	4,090	14,615	7,402
Simi Valley city	124,237	125,188	951	41,388	13,589	1,458	8,012	2,811
South Gate city	94,396	94,875	479	23,294	7,413	656	3,404	1,149
Stockton city	291,707	295,354	3,647	90,318	29,433	4,067	16,456	7,019
Sunnyvale city	140,081	143,443	3,362	54,071	15,785	2,265	9,181	3,681
Temecula city	100,146	103,101	2,955	31,409	7,753	761	4,246	1,450
Thousand Oaks city	126,683	127,762	1,079	44,969	19,008	3,009	11,638	4,370
Torrance city	145,438	146,284	846	54,894	23,091	3,762	14,053	5,587
Tracy city	82,922	83,957	1,035	24,014	6,457	462	2,799	1,003
Turlock city	68,549	69,201	652	23,266	8,097	1,378	4,676	2,167
Tustin city	75,540	76,823	1,283	24,902	6,411	541	3,721	1,820
Union City city	69,516	70,700	1,184	20,574	8,138	906	3,817	1,348
Upland city	73,732	74,570	838	26,009	9,783	1,009	5,168	1,526
Vacaville city	92,428	93,276	848	30,946	10,020	1,140	6,089	2,606
Vallejo city	115,940	116,927	987	39,574	14,248	2,194	7,994	3,515
Victorville city	115,921	118,277	2,356	30,780	8,740	756	5,023	1,981
Visalia city	124,442	125,986	1,544	41,823	13,600	1,932	8,055	3,854
Vista city	93,834	95,053	1,219	30,058	9,276	1,884	4,814	2,042
West Covina city	106,098	106,829	731	30,643	13,044	2,496	6,441	2,323
Westminster city	89,701	90,669	968	27,123	13,711	1,585	6,777	2,364
Whittier city	85,331	85,766	435	27,212	10,111	2,000	5,730	2,127
Yorba Linda city	64,234	65,698	1,464	21,943	8,296	1,187	4,885	1,879
Yuba City city	64,925	65,005	80	21,679	8,258	1,025	4,648	2,231

Table A-3: Places—Summary Population Characteristics—*Continued*

	April 1, 2010 Census Population Estimates Base	2010–2012 ACS Population	Population Change	2010–2012 ACS				
				Total Households	Population 65 and Over	Population 85 and Over	Householders 65 and Over	Persons 65 and Over Living Alone
Colorado								
Arvada city	106,433	107,960	1,527	43,522	15,811	1,979	10,077	4,516
Aurora city	325,078	332,532	7,454	121,540	31,056	3,774	19,195	8,731
Boulder city	97,385	100,403	3,018	40,913	9,220	1,627	5,772	2,756
Centennial city	100,377	102,215	1,838	37,985	12,784	1,707	7,538	2,893
Colorado Springs city	416,427	425,725	9,298	167,862	46,940	6,184	29,663	13,342
Denver city	600,008	619,016	19,008	266,248	64,482	10,683	43,278	23,748
Fort Collins city	143,991	146,235	2,244	56,319	12,635	2,112	7,907	3,900
Greeley city	92,889	94,217	1,328	33,494	10,300	1,479	6,143	2,803
Lakewood city	142,980	144,282	1,302	60,712	20,892	3,100	13,204	6,127
Longmont city	86,270	87,474	1,204	33,527	9,902	1,561	6,145	2,764
Loveland city	66,859	68,815	1,956	28,384	9,856	1,590	6,163	3,056
Pueblo city	106,595	107,364	769	42,981	16,758	2,443	10,932	5,604
Thornton city	118,775	121,742	2,967	40,547	8,618	1,164	4,526	1,644
Westminster city	106,114	107,778	1,664	41,399	10,579	1,259	6,626	3,082
Connecticut								
Bridgeport city	144,229	145,555	1,326	49,928	14,345	2,483	8,915	4,931
Danbury city	80,893	82,007	1,114	29,268	9,665	1,548	5,770	3,139
Hartford city	124,775	124,894	119	45,739	11,758	1,679	8,305	4,822
New Britain city	73,206	73,200	-6	27,540	8,955	1,782	5,395	2,813
New Haven city	129,779	130,378	599	49,680	12,721	2,035	8,430	5,058
Norwalk city	85,603	86,632	1,029	37,882	13,131	1,737	8,293	3,738
Stamford city	122,643	123,995	1,352	44,854	15,640	2,359	9,437	4,624
Waterbury city	110,366	110,089	-277	41,419	13,192	2,577	8,254	4,126
Delaware								
Wilmington city	70,852	71,005	153	29,045	8,612	1,553	6,344	3,836
District of Columbia								
Washington city	601,723	618,777	17,054	261,567	70,302	10,229	49,026	27,518
Florida								
Boca Raton city	84,392	86,489	2,097	35,304	18,213	2,570	10,681	4,591
Boynton Beach city	68,217	69,093	876	27,852	15,058	3,607	9,779	4,966
Cape Coral city	154,305	157,933	3,628	55,406	28,419	3,741	14,963	5,204
Clearwater city	107,685	108,403	718	47,178	22,702	3,738	14,824	7,808
Coral Springs city	121,098	123,406	2,308	40,511	11,224	1,198	6,257	2,072
Deerfield Beach city	75,018	76,352	1,334	31,277	16,216	3,112	10,330	5,822
Deltona city	85,182	85,255	73	27,727	11,849	1,861	6,715	2,175
Fort Lauderdale city	165,521	168,405	2,884	72,479	26,951	4,344	17,008	8,580
Gainesville city	124,354	125,273	919	46,374	10,455	1,682	6,416	3,032
Hialeah city	224,669	229,152	4,483	68,760	44,087	6,098	20,913	7,664
Hollywood city	140,768	143,222	2,454	54,825	21,619	3,033	12,296	5,821
Jacksonville city	821,784	829,535	7,751	310,528	93,702	12,180	57,872	26,552
Lakeland city	97,419	98,968	1,549	39,776	20,211	3,282	12,731	6,301
Largo city	77,649	77,769	120	35,622	19,339	3,488	12,557	6,565
Lauderhill city	66,887	68,110	1,223	23,973	8,352	1,310	5,317	2,450
Melbourne city	76,068	76,656	588	32,235	15,941	2,388	10,003	5,243
Miami city	399,457	408,322	8,865	149,591	63,854	9,411	35,694	18,160
Miami Beach city	87,779	89,541	1,762	42,859	13,634	2,435	9,362	5,496
Miami Gardens city	107,167	109,331	2,164	30,757	12,253	1,279	6,720	2,125
Miramar city	122,041	125,351	3,310	37,820	9,310	788	3,210	825
Orlando city	238,304	243,895	5,591	98,916	23,034	2,894	13,677	6,862
Palm Bay city	103,190	103,606	416	36,939	17,017	2,136	9,483	4,080
Palm Coast city	75,176	76,474	1,298	27,054	18,519	2,312	10,098	3,284
Pembroke Pines city	154,750	157,847	3,097	56,871	23,684	3,633	13,710	6,916
Plantation city	84,955	86,708	1,753	33,427	12,514	2,194	6,926	2,749
Pompano Beach city	99,845	101,596	1,751	41,231	18,895	3,823	12,414	6,805
Port St. Lucie city	164,603	166,927	2,324	58,095	27,137	3,543	15,429	5,149
St. Petersburg city	244,769	245,623	854	104,131	39,307	5,585	24,354	12,253
Sunrise city	84,439	86,648	2,209	31,170	13,096	2,669	8,033	4,321
Tallahassee city	181,376	184,079	2,703	72,525	15,094	2,654	9,945	5,182
Tampa city	335,709	343,677	7,968	135,990	37,392	4,937	24,456	12,564
Weston city	65,333	66,603	1,270	20,818	5,107	490	2,607	935
West Palm Beach city	99,920	100,940	1,020	41,680	17,472	3,081	10,164	4,726
Georgia								
Albany city	77,434	77,546	112	29,538	9,071	1,327	6,083	2,726
Athens-Clarke County unified govt (bal)	115,453	117,331	1,878	40,003	10,227	1,193	6,218	2,642
Atlanta city	420,005	432,752	12,747	177,215	42,135	6,528	28,912	16,846
Augusta-Richmond County consolidated govt (bal)	195,844	196,200	356	70,152	22,892	2,515	13,732	6,169
Columbus city	189,885	194,276	4,391	71,509	22,292	2,991	15,015	7,323
Johns Creek city	76,727	79,649	2,922	25,886	6,064	596	3,200	1,232
Macon city	91,346	91,675	329	33,184	10,879	1,599	6,957	3,610
Roswell city	88,347	91,213	2,866	34,440	10,779	1,201	6,430	2,773
Sandy Springs city	93,853	96,890	3,037	40,833	10,701	1,799	6,708	2,908
Savannah city	136,280	139,667	3,387	51,445	16,493	3,137	10,862	5,437
Warner Robins city	66,588	69,489	2,901	26,128	6,794	822	4,253	2,237
Hawaii								
Urban Honolulu CDP	337,256	342,190	4,934	127,145	61,534	12,364	35,645	15,220

Table A-3: Places—Summary Population Characteristics—*Continued*

	April 1, 2010 Census Population Estimates Base	2010–2012 ACS Population	Population Change	2010–2012 ACS				
				Total Households	Population 65 and Over	Population 85 and Over	Householders 65 and Over	Persons 65 and Over Living Alone
Idaho								
Boise City city	205,671	209,292	3,621	86,763	25,172	4,013	16,553	7,670
Meridian city	75,092	77,936	2,844	26,876	7,160	1,007	4,565	1,990
Nampa city	81,565	82,786	1,221	27,068	9,107	1,151	5,623	2,143
Illinois								
Aurora city	197,897	196,491	-1,406	61,135	13,273	1,619	7,685	3,628
Bloomington city	76,610	77,196	586	30,397	7,892	1,595	5,079	2,580
Champaign city	81,055	81,852	797	32,331	6,868	889	4,507	2,008
Chicago city	2,695,598	2,705,981	10,383	1,023,839	283,041	39,266	182,180	90,757
Decatur city	76,122	76,080	-42	31,973	12,738	2,292	8,228	4,021
Elgin city	108,188	110,400	2,212	34,322	9,899	1,562	5,952	2,643
Evanston city	74,486	75,018	532	28,790	8,471	1,518	5,710	2,944
Joliet city	147,440	147,151	-289	46,586	12,914	2,234	7,585	3,725
Naperville city	141,853	143,310	1,457	48,897	13,911	2,035	7,421	2,726
Peoria city	115,025	114,398	-627	47,114	15,110	2,618	10,009	5,114
Rockford city	152,871	152,235	-636	58,379	21,231	3,876	13,412	6,927
Springfield city	116,272	116,824	552	51,264	17,300	3,348	11,949	6,418
Waukegan city	89,078	88,637	-441	28,829	6,856	947	3,931	1,975
Indiana								
Bloomington city	80,407	80,127	-280	29,534	6,568	1,181	4,483	2,555
Carmel city	79,191	82,485	3,294	29,769	8,755	1,293	4,936	1,733
Evansville city	117,429	120,386	2,957	51,410	17,435	3,404	11,492	6,264
Fort Wayne city	253,691	253,795	104	100,418	31,474	4,975	20,604	10,371
Gary city	80,294	79,849	-445	30,229	11,937	1,545	7,903	3,767
Hammond city	80,830	80,218	-612	28,565	8,463	1,322	5,621	2,587
Indianapolis city (bal)	820,442	827,639	7,197	325,624	87,255	12,227	56,836	27,631
Lafayette city	67,140	66,822	-318	28,474	7,667	1,316	5,001	2,474
Muncie city	70,085	69,830	-255	27,611	9,225	1,107	6,280	3,331
South Bend city	101,170	99,803	-1,367	39,167	13,094	2,537	8,609	4,423
Iowa								
Cedar Rapids city	126,326	127,503	1,177	52,438	16,511	2,866	10,513	5,074
Davenport city	99,685	100,643	958	40,894	12,567	2,144	8,009	4,004
Des Moines city	203,433	205,622	2,189	81,018	22,311	3,621	14,491	7,384
Iowa City city	67,873	69,103	1,230	28,050	5,764	1,101	3,932	2,087
Sioux City city	82,695	82,828	133	31,350	10,655	1,834	7,036	3,740
Waterloo city	68,406	68,361	-45	28,283	9,540	1,552	6,487	3,464
Kansas								
Kansas City city	145,786	146,502	716	52,447	15,660	2,464	10,001	4,501
Lawrence city	87,643	88,791	1,148	34,574	6,860	1,095	4,360	2,277
Olathe city	125,872	128,195	2,323	45,072	9,361	1,397	5,755	2,426
Overland Park city	173,372	176,376	3,004	72,431	22,704	4,042	14,305	6,989
Topeka city	127,473	127,895	422	53,366	18,080	2,862	11,733	6,108
Wichita city	382,368	384,025	1,657	149,703	44,713	6,658	28,688	14,177
Kentucky								
Lexington-Fayette urban county	295,803	301,211	5,408	122,046	32,142	4,219	20,954	10,097
Louisville/Jefferson County metro govt (bal)	597,337	601,670	4,333	242,395	76,756	10,904	49,976	24,226
Louisiana								
Baton Rouge city	229,493	229,572	79	87,336	25,953	4,038	16,907	7,725
Kenner city	66,702	66,786	84	24,270	8,989	1,044	5,491	2,418
Lafayette city	120,621	121,744	1,123	49,438	15,071	1,863	9,626	4,184
Lake Charles city	71,993	72,741	748	29,568	10,116	1,303	6,613	3,415
New Orleans city	343,829	359,130	15,301	146,018	40,109	5,790	26,272	13,081
Shreveport city	199,311	201,332	2,021	78,212	25,931	4,108	16,617	7,668
Maine								
Portland city	66,194	66,159	-35	30,846	7,905	1,623	5,304	3,287
Maryland								
Baltimore city	620,961	620,843	-118	240,575	73,112	10,078	50,955	26,900
Frederick city	65,239	65,905	666	26,038	7,338	1,194	4,734	2,571
Massachusetts								
Boston city	617,594	628,365	10,771	248,738	64,953	10,277	42,931	24,822
Brockton city	93,810	94,031	221	33,057	12,044	1,989	7,041	3,601
Cambridge city	105,162	105,733	571	44,598	11,565	1,771	7,952	4,453
Fall River city	88,857	88,885	28	38,292	13,631	2,370	8,833	4,815
Lawrence city	76,377	76,928	551	26,606	6,343	1,211	3,597	2,197
Lowell city	106,519	107,616	1,097	38,913	11,483	1,707	6,538	3,483
Lynn city	90,329	90,885	556	32,900	10,377	1,713	6,702	3,680
New Bedford city	95,072	94,946	-126	38,851	14,345	2,906	9,128	4,869
Newton city	85,146	85,742	596	30,484	13,415	2,629	8,380	3,841
Quincy city	92,271	92,720	449	39,414	13,476	2,277	8,459	4,667
Somerville city	75,754	76,381	627	31,630	6,386	825	4,585	2,324
Springfield city	153,060	153,531	471	55,911	16,969	2,477	11,110	5,552
Worcester city	181,045	182,344	1,299	68,665	22,688	4,556	13,292	7,796
Michigan								
Ann Arbor city	113,934	115,124	1,190	45,974	11,510	1,678	8,021	4,446
Dearborn city	98,153	97,123	-1,030	31,824	10,963	2,226	7,528	4,075
Detroit city	713,777	706,522	-7,255	253,968	83,776	12,635	57,719	28,900
Farmington Hills city	79,740	80,266	526	33,932	13,051	1,935	8,126	3,959
Flint city	102,434	101,423	-1,011	40,853	11,621	1,276	8,223	4,362

Table A-3: Places—Summary Population Characteristics—*Continued*

	April 1, 2010 Census Population Estimates Base	2010–2012 ACS Population	Population Change	2010–2012 ACS				
				Total Households	Population 65 and Over	Population 85 and Over	Householders 65 and Over	Persons 65 and Over Living Alone
Michigan—Cont.								
Grand Rapids city	188,041	189,162	1,121	72,868	20,717	4,314	13,491	6,945
Kalamazoo city	74,262	74,689	427	27,568	7,034	1,813	4,671	2,518
Lansing city	114,297	113,594	-703	47,522	11,568	1,368	7,855	4,429
Livonia city	96,942	96,101	-841	37,094	17,210	2,586	11,070	4,997
Rochester Hills city	70,995	71,650	655	27,546	9,690	1,926	6,177	2,985
Southfield city	71,739	72,131	392	31,386	12,822	2,761	8,403	4,379
Sterling Heights city	129,699	130,037	338	49,577	20,459	3,104	12,444	5,763
Troy city	80,980	81,616	636	30,382	11,601	1,321	7,155	2,992
Warren city	134,056	134,055	-1	52,377	20,880	3,745	13,385	6,604
Westland city	84,094	83,340	-754	33,798	12,300	1,989	7,783	4,171
Wyoming city	72,125	72,741	616	26,908	6,393	725	4,208	2,014
Minnesota								
Bloomington city	82,893	84,347	1,454	35,940	15,767	2,109	10,075	4,703
Brooklyn Park city	75,781	76,868	1,087	26,100	6,201	716	3,527	1,294
Duluth city	86,265	86,221	-44	35,340	12,126	2,298	7,817	4,331
Minneapolis city	382,578	388,054	5,476	165,018	33,141	5,755	22,268	13,183
Plymouth city	70,576	71,771	1,195	28,748	9,006	941	5,630	2,312
Rochester city	106,769	108,024	1,255	43,055	14,063	2,346	8,501	3,775
St. Cloud city	65,842	65,838	-4	25,211	7,113	1,228	4,355	1,986
St. Paul city	285,068	288,347	3,279	111,521	25,859	3,992	16,768	9,117
Mississippi								
Gulfport city	67,793	68,979	1,186	26,288	8,328	1,048	5,444	2,552
Jackson city	173,516	174,706	1,190	61,612	17,946	2,733	11,246	4,833
Missouri								
Columbia city	108,500	111,204	2,704	43,348	9,767	1,597	5,933	2,742
Independence city	116,830	117,028	198	47,939	19,094	3,373	12,340	6,021
Kansas City city	459,787	462,292	2,505	190,467	51,827	7,534	34,840	17,064
Lee's Summit city	91,364	91,979	615	33,846	10,904	1,814	6,916	3,221
O'Fallon city	79,479	80,986	1,507	28,697	7,534	1,035	4,802	1,943
St. Charles city	65,794	66,173	379	26,344	8,779	1,458	5,909	2,956
St. Joseph city	76,803	76,953	150	29,005	10,467	1,840	6,601	3,401
St. Louis city	319,294	318,612	-682	138,981	35,423	4,963	25,167	14,675
Springfield city	159,509	160,748	1,239	70,120	23,361	4,624	15,397	8,313
Montana								
Billings city	104,170	105,648	1,478	43,926	15,711	2,656	10,499	5,142
Missoula city	66,788	67,643	855	28,776	7,567	1,522	4,841	2,270
Nebraska								
Lincoln city	258,381	262,214	3,833	105,019	28,702	4,577	18,487	8,843
Omaha city	408,962	416,374	7,412	164,695	47,588	7,789	31,656	15,676
Nevada								
Henderson city	257,581	261,370	3,789	98,623	39,860	3,196	23,115	8,194
Las Vegas city	583,748	589,541	5,793	210,927	76,125	7,863	45,369	19,687
North Las Vegas city	216,940	219,976	3,036	67,222	16,146	1,206	8,880	3,761
Reno city	225,229	228,658	3,429	89,155	27,363	3,568	17,420	8,463
Sparks city	90,264	91,242	978	34,330	11,064	1,156	6,451	2,635
New Hampshire								
Manchester city	109,565	109,879	314	44,629	13,356	2,382	8,305	4,150
Nashua city	86,494	86,769	275	34,600	11,070	1,679	6,921	3,186
New Jersey								
Camden city	77,344	77,398	54	24,739	6,136	734	4,296	2,050
Clifton city	84,136	84,525	389	28,383	10,870	2,039	6,499	3,042
Elizabeth city	124,969	125,825	856	38,814	11,610	1,772	6,269	3,087
Jersey City city	247,597	251,485	3,888	95,560	23,305	2,378	13,793	6,491
Newark city	277,140	277,627	487	91,552	23,183	2,822	14,658	7,845
Passaic city	69,781	70,066	285	20,530	5,511	919	3,248	1,770
Paterson city	146,199	145,644	-555	43,618	13,595	1,163	7,259	3,444
Trenton city	84,913	84,660	-253	28,218	7,408	975	4,865	2,731
Union City city	66,455	67,193	738	22,440	6,546	972	3,789	1,717
New Mexico								
Albuquerque city	545,852	551,597	5,745	224,766	68,343	9,424	44,318	21,311
Las Cruces city	97,618	99,754	2,136	37,828	12,947	1,714	8,434	3,848
Rio Rancho city	87,521	89,499	1,978	32,137	10,191	1,465	6,090	2,734
Santa Fe city	67,943	68,677	734	31,570	13,122	1,715	9,110	4,897
New York								
Albany city	97,856	97,843	-13	38,841	11,910	2,253	7,417	4,452
Buffalo city	261,310	260,321	-989	111,275	30,087	4,041	20,530	11,340
Mount Vernon city	67,290	67,684	394	26,283	9,071	1,565	5,674	3,026
New Rochelle city	77,062	77,733	671	27,785	11,017	2,116	6,474	3,236
New York city	8,175,133	8,265,445	90,312	3,051,127	1,019,436	145,568	623,982	319,227
Rochester city	210,565	210,548	-17	86,273	19,383	3,264	12,766	7,064
Schenectady city	66,135	66,124	-11	24,486	7,846	1,514	4,988	2,749
Syracuse city	145,170	144,575	-595	54,577	15,206	3,069	9,764	6,023
Yonkers city	195,979	197,514	1,535	73,077	29,033	4,688	17,880	9,029

Table A-3: Places—Summary Population Characteristics—*Continued*

	April 1, 2010 Census Population Estimates Base	2010–2012 ACS Population	Population Change	2010–2012 ACS				
				Total Households	Population 65 and Over	Population 85 and Over	Householders 65 and Over	Persons 65 and Over Living Alone
North Carolina								
Asheville city	83,393	84,661	1,268	36,896	13,344	2,661	8,896	4,869
Charlotte city	731,424	756,725	25,301	292,501	66,451	8,959	41,262	18,101
Concord city	79,066	80,576	1,510	29,364	8,978	923	5,328	2,322
Durham city	228,329	234,160	5,831	95,863	21,670	3,571	13,814	6,398
Fayetteville city	200,564	201,334	770	76,398	20,201	2,112	13,108	5,867
Gastonia city	71,741	72,151	410	26,141	8,484	1,366	4,942	1,971
Greensboro city	269,668	273,641	3,973	111,765	32,361	4,244	20,939	9,887
Greenville city	84,562	86,115	1,553	34,263	6,505	1,372	4,084	2,012
High Point city	104,371	106,164	1,793	40,848	12,556	1,833	8,258	4,019
Jacksonville city	70,145	69,356	-789	20,720	4,449	617	2,617	1,466
Raleigh city	403,903	414,373	10,470	161,309	35,242	4,879	22,166	10,892
Wilmington city	106,476	108,320	1,844	46,561	14,784	2,122	9,696	4,601
Winston-Salem city	229,617	232,090	2,473	90,752	29,362	4,301	19,117	9,860
North Dakota								
Fargo city	105,549	107,752	2,203	47,991	10,971	1,612	7,064	3,928
Ohio								
Akron city	199,110	198,816	-294	82,276	25,344	4,112	17,030	8,983
Canton city	73,014	72,778	-236	29,928	9,790	1,909	6,425	3,168
Cincinnati city	296,950	296,443	-507	127,708	32,832	5,547	22,599	13,209
Cleveland city	396,815	393,288	-3,527	165,887	48,737	7,009	33,934	19,051
Columbus city	787,073	799,357	12,284	324,641	70,515	9,546	46,612	24,369
Dayton city	141,527	141,690	163	56,385	16,744	2,689	11,844	6,463
Parma city	81,601	80,997	-604	32,925	14,696	2,824	9,135	4,147
Toledo city	287,208	285,532	-1,676	117,071	34,360	4,929	23,528	12,013
Youngstown city	66,982	66,005	-977	26,165	10,353	1,921	7,091	3,386
Oklahoma								
Broken Arrow city	98,847	100,497	1,650	36,180	10,776	1,328	6,693	2,710
Edmond city	81,403	83,197	1,794	30,704	9,480	1,028	5,833	2,515
Lawton city	96,867	98,075	1,208	35,159	9,600	1,093	6,506	2,983
Norman city	110,925	113,599	2,674	44,382	12,427	1,495	7,900	3,517
Oklahoma City city	580,001	590,292	10,291	226,306	66,315	8,999	42,365	20,202
Tulsa city	391,901	393,124	1,223	162,791	49,615	7,746	33,014	16,607
Oregon								
Beaverton city	89,806	91,414	1,608	35,730	9,789	1,565	6,308	3,281
Bend city	76,639	77,887	1,248	32,633	11,329	1,938	7,490	3,777
Eugene city	156,191	157,196	1,005	65,952	20,946	3,549	13,664	6,883
Gresham city	105,594	107,505	1,911	39,011	12,008	1,923	7,368	3,342
Hillsboro city	91,611	93,876	2,265	32,267	7,310	955	4,410	2,092
Medford city	74,907	75,704	797	29,771	12,388	2,162	8,144	3,895
Portland city	583,776	594,524	10,748	248,701	63,475	11,012	41,715	21,697
Salem city	154,637	156,155	1,518	57,838	20,075	2,983	12,607	6,043
Pennsylvania								
Allentown city	118,032	118,587	555	42,457	13,948	2,574	8,216	4,215
Bethlehem city	74,982	75,057	75	29,528	11,027	2,310	7,150	4,003
Erie city	101,786	101,419	-367	41,214	13,250	2,516	8,364	4,528
Philadelphia city	1,526,006	1,538,211	12,205	576,889	186,585	28,788	122,082	67,573
Pittsburgh city	305,704	306,006	302	131,719	43,053	8,472	29,182	16,753
Reading city	88,082	88,098	16	30,896	8,356	1,112	5,553	2,911
Scranton city	76,089	75,951	-138	29,585	12,784	2,973	7,982	4,589
Rhode Island								
Cranston city	80,387	80,465	78	30,200	12,207	2,483	7,475	3,646
Pawtucket city	71,148	71,158	10	29,164	9,112	1,321	6,078	3,264
Providence city	178,042	178,299	257	60,526	15,087	2,734	9,006	4,749
Warwick city	82,672	82,222	-450	35,097	14,573	2,293	9,705	5,175
South Carolina								
Charleston city	120,083	123,226	3,143	52,182	15,068	1,963	9,715	4,848
Columbia city	129,272	130,596	1,324	44,324	11,764	2,258	7,637	3,933
North Charleston city	97,471	99,999	2,528	35,889	8,550	978	5,604	2,538
Rock Hill city	66,158	67,348	1,190	26,257	6,790	1,201	4,457	2,307
South Dakota								
Rapid City city	67,956	68,912	956	28,016	10,066	1,909	6,316	3,132
Sioux Falls city	153,890	156,997	3,107	62,651	17,766	2,744	11,068	4,998
Tennessee								
Chattanooga city	167,978	169,718	1,740	69,721	25,216	3,600	16,679	8,261
Clarksville city	132,934	137,588	4,654	49,635	9,977	1,093	6,113	2,456
Jackson city	65,211	67,009	1,798	23,764	8,959	1,311	5,420	2,629
Knoxville city	178,874	180,714	1,840	84,221	25,921	3,684	17,327	9,983
Memphis city	646,889	651,363	4,474	244,775	68,321	8,936	44,272	21,370
Murfreesboro city	108,767	111,813	3,046	41,261	9,804	1,400	5,957	2,497
Nashville-Davidson metropolitan government (bal)	601,222	613,829	12,607	246,103	63,509	8,725	40,491	19,673
Texas								
Abilene city	117,063	120,027	2,964	42,110	14,982	2,231	9,307	4,153
Allen city	84,246	87,343	3,097	28,556	5,380	382	2,485	681
Amarillo city	190,695	193,429	2,734	73,908	23,214	3,250	15,039	6,912
Arlington city	365,438	370,854	5,416	132,177	30,493	3,448	18,636	7,688
Austin city	790,390	818,236	27,846	327,971	58,305	7,986	36,373	16,321
Baytown city	71,802	71,567	-235	23,866	6,803	1,085	4,056	1,705

Table A-3: Places—Summary Population Characteristics—*Continued*

	April 1, 2010 Census Population Estimates Base	2010–2012 ACS Population	Population Change	2010–2012 ACS				
				Total Households	Population 65 and Over	Population 85 and Over	Householders 65 and Over	Persons 65 and Over Living Alone
Texas—Cont.								
Beaumont city	118,296	118,440	144	45,417	14,876	2,187	10,218	5,534
Brownsville city	175,027	178,045	3,018	50,159	17,446	2,095	9,563	3,751
Bryan city	76,201	77,266	1,065	27,502	7,456	864	4,904	2,310
Carrollton city	119,097	122,468	3,371	42,972	10,350	1,141	5,410	1,928
College Station city	93,862	95,960	2,098	33,540	4,785	402	2,918	1,164
Corpus Christi city	305,215	308,497	3,282	110,803	36,661	4,763	22,401	8,884
Dallas city	1,197,816	1,219,879	22,063	456,781	111,981	15,720	69,999	33,168
Denton city	113,379	117,997	4,618	41,474	10,075	1,283	6,081	2,506
Edinburg city	76,960	79,342	2,382	24,104	5,699	588	3,062	1,151
El Paso city	649,152	662,707	13,555	216,792	75,109	9,495	44,679	17,053
Fort Worth city	742,030	761,862	19,832	264,584	63,187	8,379	38,727	18,041
Frisco city	116,989	123,175	6,186	41,055	7,694	622	4,119	1,419
Garland city	226,876	230,317	3,441	72,934	20,891	2,381	12,289	4,281
Grand Prairie city	175,396	178,835	3,439	57,572	12,493	1,037	7,005	2,565
Harlingen city	64,869	65,425	556	20,829	8,769	1,021	5,079	2,127
Houston city	2,099,430	2,130,116	30,686	770,098	196,834	25,014	122,402	54,893
Irving city	216,290	220,677	4,387	82,382	14,627	1,479	8,690	3,365
Killeen city	127,921	131,639	3,718	44,085	6,656	430	4,053	1,712
Laredo city	236,100	240,773	4,673	64,115	19,332	2,599	10,430	3,426
League City city	83,560	86,105	2,545	31,114	7,289	1,038	3,994	1,381
Lewisville city	95,290	97,421	2,131	38,392	7,092	707	4,234	2,250
Longview city	80,455	81,021	566	29,841	11,140	1,918	7,090	3,512
Lubbock city	229,573	233,475	3,902	88,762	25,969	3,159	16,713	7,615
McAllen city	129,877	132,720	2,843	42,241	14,299	1,981	7,802	3,095
McKinney city	131,117	137,971	6,854	44,732	10,073	1,080	5,682	2,042
Mesquite city	139,824	141,533	1,709	48,321	12,312	1,510	7,112	2,772
Midland city	111,147	114,805	3,658	40,862	12,902	1,698	7,578	3,212
Mission city	77,061	79,179	2,118	22,664	8,322	679	4,644	1,727
Missouri City city	67,358	68,004	646	22,382	7,079	488	3,585	1,208
Odessa city	99,940	103,063	3,123	37,223	10,557	1,386	6,972	3,322
Pasadena city	149,043	150,903	1,860	48,255	13,239	1,540	7,980	3,664
Pearland city	91,252	93,887	2,635	32,096	7,289	1,154	4,038	1,365
Pharr city	70,400	72,008	1,608	19,993	7,929	1,175	4,435	1,280
Plano city	259,841	266,857	7,016	99,888	25,850	3,105	14,766	5,635
Richardson city	99,223	101,483	2,260	38,786	12,547	1,673	7,359	2,714
Round Rock city	99,889	104,543	4,654	34,847	6,708	863	3,438	1,229
San Angelo city	93,200	94,684	1,484	35,375	12,983	1,425	8,590	3,804
San Antonio city	1,327,606	1,358,143	30,537	476,131	146,523	19,658	89,493	38,073
Sugar Land city	78,817	81,092	2,275	26,237	8,849	890	4,077	1,149
Temple city	66,130	67,809	1,679	24,155	10,083	1,627	6,009	2,666
Tyler city	96,900	98,296	1,396	38,832	14,596	2,818	9,052	4,468
Waco city	124,805	126,250	1,445	45,326	14,200	2,658	8,666	4,677
Wichita Falls city	104,553	104,348	-205	36,659	12,592	2,046	8,174	3,693
Utah								
Layton city	67,311	68,165	854	21,561	5,210	397	3,023	840
Ogden city	82,825	83,375	550	28,687	7,746	1,259	4,975	2,229
Orem city	88,328	89,712	1,384	26,071	7,523	858	4,539	1,576
Provo city	112,488	114,467	1,979	31,937	6,809	1,411	4,068	1,434
St. George city	72,897	74,225	1,328	25,259	13,140	2,204	8,087	2,722
Salt Lake City city	186,443	187,964	1,521	74,037	17,812	2,899	12,225	7,031
Sandy city	87,540	88,451	911	28,158	8,741	904	5,012	1,536
West Jordan city	103,712	106,387	2,675	30,840	5,172	522	3,049	1,078
West Valley City city	129,480	130,981	1,501	37,418	9,486	719	5,708	1,832
Virginia								
Alexandria city	139,966	143,737	3,771	64,754	13,405	2,086	8,939	4,758
Chesapeake city	222,209	225,844	3,635	78,867	24,382	2,609	14,794	5,666
Hampton city	137,436	136,855	-581	51,699	17,308	2,133	11,080	5,130
Lynchburg city	75,568	76,377	809	28,363	10,473	1,946	6,872	3,673
Newport News city	180,719	180,623	-96	69,003	19,477	2,941	12,796	5,881
Norfolk city	242,803	244,118	1,315	85,626	23,063	3,234	15,010	7,515
Portsmouth city	95,535	95,915	380	36,752	12,762	1,931	8,147	3,528
Richmond city	204,214	206,936	2,722	83,747	23,264	3,875	15,786	9,198
Roanoke city	97,032	96,958	-74	41,819	13,764	2,778	9,667	5,598
Suffolk city	84,592	84,942	350	30,657	10,000	1,309	6,001	2,216
Virginia Beach city	437,994	443,102	5,108	164,066	48,496	5,635	30,003	11,933
Washington								
Auburn city	70,180	71,743	1,563	27,345	8,058	1,036	4,927	2,043
Bellevue city	122,359	124,646	2,287	51,064	17,127	3,089	10,203	4,016
Bellingham city	80,885	81,647	762	33,873	10,535	1,777	7,002	3,691
Everett city	103,019	103,818	799	41,699	10,795	1,754	7,347	4,045
Federal Way city	89,306	90,709	1,403	33,638	9,751	1,575	6,032	2,821
Kennewick city	73,917	75,328	1,411	26,974	8,424	1,301	5,717	2,921
Kent city	118,564	120,964	2,400	41,854	11,529	1,588	6,667	3,280
Renton city	90,995	93,673	2,678	36,182	9,369	1,546	5,793	3,126
Seattle city	608,660	622,273	13,613	284,559	68,854	11,819	46,319	26,546
Spokane city	208,916	209,346	430	88,184	28,661	4,435	19,055	10,176
Spokane Valley city	89,755	90,437	682	36,143	12,971	1,794	8,182	3,897
Tacoma city	198,397	200,090	1,693	77,704	23,185	4,201	14,668	7,834
Vancouver city	161,807	163,964	2,157	65,449	21,672	2,988	14,025	6,875
Yakima city	91,067	92,506	1,439	33,020	12,729	2,450	7,758	3,985

Table A-3: Places—Summary Population Characteristics—*Continued*

	April 1, 2010 Census Population Estimates Base	2010–2012 ACS Population	Population Change	2010–2012 ACS				
				Total Households	Population 65 and Over	Population 85 and Over	Householders 65 and Over	Persons 65 and Over Living Alone
Wisconsin								
Appleton city	72,623	72,689	66	28,620	8,151	1,350	5,622	2,948
Eau Claire city	65,888	66,087	199	26,837	7,424	1,179	5,188	2,997
Green Bay city	104,057	104,494	437	42,755	12,289	2,485	8,094	4,194
Kenosha city	99,226	99,743	517	37,653	10,911	1,914	6,898	3,683
Madison city	233,209	237,136	3,927	101,354	22,627	3,632	14,802	7,049
Milwaukee city	594,832	597,247	2,415	228,852	54,186	7,929	35,948	19,973
Oshkosh city	66,083	66,301	218	25,344	8,277	1,546	5,265	3,144
Racine city	78,860	78,552	-308	30,358	8,651	1,209	5,985	3,077
Waukesha city	70,718	70,752	34	28,645	7,677	1,222	5,269	2,737

Table A-4: Metropolitan Statistical Areas—Summary Population Characteristics

	April 1, 2010 Census Population Estimates Base	2010–2012 ACS Population	Population Change	2010–2012 ACS				
				Total Households	Population 65 and Over	Population 85 and Over	Householders 65 and Over	Persons 65 and Over Living Alone
Abilene, TX	165,252	166,340	1,088	59,894	23,098	2,933	14,532	6,550
Akron, OH	703,200	702,724	-476	279,445	102,273	14,740	64,998	29,510
Albany, GA	157,308	156,878	-430	58,593	19,813	2,338	12,989	5,459
Albany-Schenectady-Troy, NY	870,718	872,935	2,217	345,972	125,011	20,533	78,336	37,876
Albuquerque, NM	887,079	896,196	9,117	344,758	114,446	14,316	71,559	31,353
Alexandria, LA	153,922	154,304	382	54,347	21,281	2,536	13,393	6,298
Allentown-Bethlehem-Easton, PA-NJ	821,173	824,846	3,673	312,943	127,577	20,428	76,152	34,076
Altoona, PA	127,076	127,131	55	50,990	22,825	3,637	14,484	6,812
Amarillo, TX	249,881	253,406	3,525	94,179	30,343	4,035	19,059	8,375
Ames, IA	89,542	90,519	977	35,314	9,096	1,547	5,780	2,400
Anchorage, AK	380,821	387,916	7,095	137,071	30,422	2,300	17,676	7,677
Anderson, IN	131,636	131,028	-608	49,973	20,715	2,915	13,929	6,710
Anderson, SC	187,122	188,359	1,237	72,891	29,491	3,431	18,798	7,991
Ann Arbor, MI	344,791	348,311	3,520	134,570	37,073	5,501	24,398	11,302
Anniston-Oxford, AL	118,572	117,845	-727	45,553	17,423	1,905	11,127	4,656
Appleton, WI	225,666	227,218	1,552	87,466	27,293	4,032	17,635	7,945
Asheville, NC	424,859	428,874	4,015	179,998	80,896	11,076	50,318	21,201
Athens-Clarke County, GA	192,541	194,861	2,320	66,721	20,460	2,385	12,485	5,078
Atlanta-Sandy Springs-Marietta, GA	5,268,860	5,361,152	92,292	1,898,783	503,523	53,291	295,043	121,923
Atlantic City-Hammonton, NJ	274,549	274,982	433	99,782	40,020	5,176	24,270	11,045
Auburn-Opelika, AL	140,247	143,866	3,619	55,655	13,450	1,511	8,548	3,414
Augusta-Richmond County, GA-SC	556,877	563,401	6,524	205,673	72,402	6,648	43,944	17,987
Austin-Round Rock-San Marcos, TX	1,716,289	1,780,890	64,601	656,869	149,824	17,619	88,351	34,845
Bakersfield-Delano, CA	839,631	849,101	9,470	254,255	77,955	8,418	45,718	18,950
Baltimore-Towson, MD	2,710,489	2,734,138	23,649	1,026,413	353,937	50,307	220,901	99,080
Bangor, ME	153,921	153,856	-65	62,186	22,900	2,858	14,088	6,257
Barnstable Town, MA	215,888	215,681	-207	93,426	55,418	7,009	34,374	14,702
Baton Rouge, LA	802,484	809,427	6,943	295,153	90,143	11,004	56,292	23,644
Battle Creek, MI	136,146	135,568	-578	52,569	20,385	3,063	13,077	5,765
Bay City, MI	107,771	107,310	-461	43,793	17,937	2,872	11,597	4,955
Beaumont-Port Arthur, TX	388,745	389,918	1,173	143,517	51,432	6,613	33,882	15,354
Bellingham, WA	201,140	203,482	2,342	79,643	27,966	3,710	17,606	7,528
Bend, OR	157,733	160,085	2,352	64,982	25,290	3,476	15,950	6,436
Billings, MT	158,050	160,174	2,124	65,156	23,429	3,482	15,467	7,216
Binghamton, NY	251,725	250,092	-1,633	100,349	41,571	6,631	25,935	12,235
Birmingham-Hoover, AL	1,128,050	1,132,696	4,646	433,281	150,337	18,963	96,165	41,345
Bismarck, ND	108,779	111,454	2,675	45,762	15,567	2,544	9,938	4,767
Blacksburg-Christiansburg-Radford, VA	162,958	163,302	344	63,179	20,766	2,710	13,742	5,604
Bloomington, IN	192,714	194,445	1,731	75,354	23,319	3,030	15,036	6,709
Bloomington-Normal, IL	169,572	170,964	1,392	63,314	17,918	2,724	11,076	4,812
Boise City-Nampa, ID	616,561	627,845	11,284	228,204	71,521	9,522	44,817	18,350
Boston-Cambridge-Quincy, MA-NH	4,552,402	4,602,669	50,267	1,753,363	615,598	95,934	382,877	182,566
Boulder, CO	294,567	300,681	6,114	120,203	31,696	4,426	19,981	8,718
Bowling Green, KY	125,953	127,739	1,786	49,119	14,943	1,843	9,560	4,337
Bremerton-Silverdale, WA	251,133	253,763	2,630	98,682	35,096	4,247	21,257	8,685
Bridgeport-Stamford-Norwalk, CT	916,829	926,739	9,910	331,766	127,386	20,420	76,458	33,931
Brownsville-Harlingen, TX	406,220	411,930	5,710	118,445	46,553	4,957	25,830	9,071
Brunswick, GA	112,368	113,069	701	43,615	17,681	1,796	11,839	4,753
Buffalo-Niagara Falls, NY	1,135,509	1,135,105	-404	467,572	180,506	27,652	116,715	57,563
Burlington, NC	151,131	152,730	1,599	60,459	22,781	3,757	15,143	7,343
Burlington-South Burlington, VT	211,262	212,711	1,449	84,568	25,657	3,436	16,287	7,294
Canton-Massillon, OH	404,422	403,612	-810	160,501	66,876	10,364	41,933	18,152
Cape Coral-Fort Myers, FL	618,754	632,499	13,745	238,476	153,513	19,743	87,499	32,859
Cape Girardeau-Jackson, MO-IL	96,275	97,241	966	37,306	14,653	2,521	8,706	3,803
Casper, WY	75,450	76,821	1,371	31,080	9,606	1,300	6,257	2,672
Cedar Rapids, IA	257,940	260,340	2,400	104,358	36,006	5,073	23,070	10,728
Champaign-Urbana, IL	231,891	233,025	1,134	91,455	26,270	3,814	16,746	7,422
Charleston, WV	304,282	303,948	-334	125,453	49,372	6,148	32,508	14,170
Charleston-North Charleston-Summerville, SC	664,607	682,244	17,637	258,255	81,392	8,810	50,671	20,893
Charlotte-Gastonia-Rock Hill, NC-SC	1,758,038	1,796,759	38,721	669,746	186,428	22,466	113,854	46,496
Charlottesville, VA	201,559	203,890	2,331	77,535	28,772	3,871	17,931	8,087
Chattanooga, TN-GA	528,143	533,491	5,348	208,240	80,270	10,116	50,496	21,562
Cheyenne, WY	91,738	93,030	1,292	37,119	12,078	1,489	7,710	3,736
Chicago-Joliet-Naperville, IL-IN-WI	9,461,105	9,496,587	35,482	3,419,489	1,111,844	160,222	687,259	310,728
Chico, CA	220,000	220,565	565	84,421	34,534	5,476	22,252	9,879
Cincinnati-Middletown, OH-KY-IN	2,130,151	2,138,136	7,985	814,150	266,872	36,855	169,699	77,537
Clarksville, TN-KY	273,949	280,232	6,283	101,083	26,730	2,701	16,678	6,698
Cleveland, TN	115,788	116,844	1,056	44,368	17,731	1,712	11,151	4,893
Cleveland-Elyria-Mentor, OH	2,077,240	2,069,316	-7,924	841,904	320,469	50,729	207,026	99,900
Coeur d'Alene, ID	138,494	140,793	2,299	55,713	21,061	2,369	13,114	4,704
College Station-Bryan, TX	228,660	231,815	3,155	81,862	21,025	2,321	12,943	5,357
Colorado Springs, CO	645,613	659,419	13,806	246,751	68,685	7,696	42,773	18,125
Columbia, MO	172,786	176,057	3,271	68,745	17,389	2,573	10,703	4,714
Columbia, SC	767,604	777,119	9,515	293,878	92,075	11,127	57,244	24,146
Columbus, GA-AL	294,865	302,508	7,643	109,994	35,039	4,181	23,214	11,087
Columbus, IN	76,794	77,946	1,152	29,929	11,140	1,338	6,948	3,311
Columbus, OH	1,836,536	1,859,697	23,161	714,551	201,981	25,363	127,255	57,824
Corpus Christi, TX	428,185	432,039	3,854	154,476	56,786	6,768	34,267	12,881
Corvallis, OR	85,581	85,989	408	32,925	10,787	1,929	6,771	3,018
Crestview-Fort Walton Beach-Destin, FL	180,822	184,699	3,877	72,695	25,929	2,704	15,915	6,207

Table A-4: Metropolitan Statistical Areas—Summary Population Characteristics—*Continued*

	April 1, 2010 Census Population Estimates Base	2010–2012 ACS Population	Population Change	2010–2012 ACS				
				Total Households	Population 65 and Over	Population 85 and Over	Householders 65 and Over	Persons 65 and Over Living Alone
Cumberland, MD-WV	103,299	102,609	-690	39,882	18,568	2,886	11,888	6,348
Dallas-Fort Worth-Arlington, TX	6,371,774	6,519,849	148,075	2,302,526	594,373	67,366	354,325	143,869
Dalton, GA	142,227	142,540	313	48,332	16,183	1,634	9,721	3,667
Danville, IL	81,625	81,225	-400	31,486	13,249	1,936	8,899	4,437
Danville, VA	106,561	106,132	-429	44,326	19,469	2,450	13,120	5,548
Davenport-Moline-Rock Island, IA-IL	379,690	381,367	1,677	154,594	58,709	8,903	38,299	18,295
Dayton, OH	841,502	842,693	1,191	342,557	128,726	17,788	84,112	39,598
Decatur, AL	153,829	154,078	249	59,078	22,420	2,295	14,058	5,885
Decatur, IL	110,768	110,491	-277	45,580	18,335	2,852	11,817	5,422
Deltona-Daytona Beach-Ormond Beach, FL	494,597	495,284	687	193,177	107,097	14,807	65,197	28,350
Denver-Aurora-Broomfield, CO	2,543,482	2,599,275	55,793	1,009,710	271,402	35,419	170,199	76,324
Des Moines-West Des Moines, IA	569,633	580,572	10,939	226,053	65,905	9,308	41,036	18,610
Detroit-Warren-Livonia, MI	4,296,247	4,290,618	-5,629	1,647,364	581,383	86,465	378,959	177,001
Dothan, AL	145,639	146,721	1,082	57,183	23,272	2,316	14,793	6,274
Dover, DE	162,310	165,306	2,996	57,023	23,105	2,511	13,607	5,282
Dubuque, IA	93,653	94,471	818	37,548	14,434	2,116	8,939	4,054
Duluth, MN-WI	279,771	279,685	-86	117,095	44,189	6,820	28,720	14,455
Durham-Chapel Hill, NC	504,357	514,206	9,849	203,076	60,480	8,124	37,470	16,094
Eau Claire, WI	161,151	162,532	1,381	64,355	21,987	3,495	14,520	7,188
El Centro, CA	174,528	175,837	1,309	47,828	18,894	2,533	10,086	4,041
Elizabethtown, KY	197,561	121,330	-76,231	44,565	13,919	1,625	8,592	3,490
Elkhart-Goshen, IN	88,830	198,598	109,768	69,984	24,447	3,734	15,273	6,425
Elmira, NY	800,647	88,848	-711,799	35,240	13,656	2,356	8,794	4,569
El Paso, TX	119,742	816,295	696,553	256,148	84,785	10,499	49,572	18,574
Erie, PA	280,566	280,794	228	109,522	41,308	6,441	25,679	12,037
Eugene-Springfield, OR	351,715	353,315	1,600	145,265	54,955	7,297	34,894	15,537
Evansville, IN-KY	358,676	359,742	1,066	143,577	52,215	7,683	32,970	14,919
Fairbanks, AK	97,581	99,275	1,694	36,499	6,666	741	4,117	1,752
Fargo, ND-MN	208,777	212,771	3,994	87,920	22,428	3,259	14,513	7,341
Farmington, NM	130,044	128,912	-1,132	41,128	14,445	1,702	8,792	3,073
Fayetteville, NC	366,383	371,706	5,323	136,535	34,763	3,611	22,266	9,804
Fayetteville-Springdale-Rogers, AR-MO	463,207	473,969	10,762	174,789	53,554	7,506	33,426	13,681
Flagstaff, AZ	134,418	134,909	491	44,949	12,670	1,382	7,670	2,496
Flint, MI	425,790	421,871	-3,919	165,651	59,719	7,641	39,113	17,371
Florence, SC	205,566	205,814	248	78,045	28,752	3,199	18,045	7,271
Florence-Muscle Shoals, AL	147,137	147,089	-48	60,826	25,398	3,270	16,800	7,184
Fond du Lac, WI	101,633	101,798	165	41,025	15,621	2,830	9,918	4,453
Fort Collins-Loveland, CO	299,630	305,335	5,705	121,183	37,722	5,129	23,052	9,493
Fort Smith, AR-OK	298,592	298,759	167	112,967	42,570	4,459	26,464	11,385
Fort Wayne, IN	416,257	419,252	2,995	161,610	52,845	7,636	33,792	15,570
Fresno, CA	930,450	940,493	10,043	288,016	96,924	14,407	56,190	23,163
Gadsden, AL	104,430	104,381	-49	39,881	16,754	2,400	10,485	4,808
Gainesville, FL	264,275	266,364	2,089	100,632	30,406	3,928	18,310	7,626
Gainesville, GA	179,684	182,791	3,107	60,520	21,659	2,307	12,796	4,731
Glens Falls, NY	128,921	128,724	-197	52,437	21,670	2,975	13,773	6,131
Goldsboro, NC	122,623	123,656	1,033	48,016	16,464	1,992	10,404	4,888
Grand Forks, ND-MN	98,461	98,516	55	40,165	12,461	1,991	8,067	4,044
Grand Junction, CO	146,723	147,268	545	58,652	22,644	3,281	14,901	7,068
Grand Rapids-Wyoming, MI	774,160	779,682	5,522	292,221	93,323	14,012	58,937	25,547
Great Falls, MT	81,327	81,677	350	32,982	12,936	1,797	8,117	3,667
Greeley, CO	252,825	258,708	5,883	90,830	25,925	2,876	15,559	6,382
Green Bay, WI	306,241	308,878	2,637	122,302	39,452	5,960	25,021	11,428
Greensboro-High Point, NC	723,798	730,577	6,779	288,411	98,900	11,311	62,935	28,069
Greenville, NC	189,510	192,167	2,657	72,876	20,184	2,747	12,947	5,990
Greenville-Mauldin-Easley, SC	636,988	645,542	8,554	243,359	87,079	10,796	53,822	22,810
Gulfport-Biloxi, MS	248,820	253,554	4,734	96,000	32,408	3,227	20,264	7,925
Hagerstown-Martinsburg, MD-WV	269,140	271,937	2,797	103,734	37,326	4,480	23,320	10,493
Hanford-Corcoran, CA	152,982	151,869	-1,113	40,684	12,328	1,452	6,842	2,882
Harrisburg-Carlisle, PA	549,475	551,934	2,459	221,248	81,808	12,914	51,597	23,441
Harrisonburg, VA	125,228	126,824	1,596	44,331	16,371	2,448	10,301	4,208
Hartford-West Hartford-East Hartford, CT	1,212,381	1,214,120	1,739	468,945	177,974	30,284	109,274	51,101
Hattiesburg, MS	142,842	145,103	2,261	53,894	16,933	2,043	10,789	5,031
Hickory-Lenoir-Morganton, NC	365,497	364,335	-1,162	138,692	57,276	6,354	35,767	16,053
Hinesville-Fort Stewart, GA	77,917	79,844	1,927	28,426	5,458	477	3,535	1,223
Holland-Grand Haven, MI	263,801	266,464	2,663	94,154	32,067	4,818	19,807	7,462
Honolulu, HI	953,207	966,405	13,198	308,906	143,047	24,044	77,959	25,503
Hot Springs, AR	96,022	96,590	568	38,910	20,125	2,966	12,591	5,134
Houma-Bayou Cane-Thibodaux, LA	208,178	208,590	412	74,796	25,190	2,744	16,157	6,461
Houston-Sugar Land-Baytown, TX	5,946,839	6,085,873	139,034	2,060,582	543,484	60,514	315,707	124,507
Huntington-Ashland, WV-KY-OH	287,700	287,149	-551	113,187	47,322	5,742	30,945	13,869
Huntsville, AL	417,593	425,109	7,516	164,438	53,167	6,244	33,727	14,094
Idaho Falls, ID	130,374	132,098	1,724	44,153	14,364	2,065	9,202	3,580
Indianapolis-Carmel, IN	1,756,241	1,779,439	23,198	676,095	197,975	26,228	123,762	55,719
Iowa City, IA	152,586	155,534	2,948	63,286	15,517	2,461	10,229	4,807
Ithaca, NY	101,564	101,989	425	38,530	11,365	1,751	7,172	3,422
Jackson, MI	160,248	160,115	-133	59,781	23,197	3,605	14,626	6,073
Jackson, MS	539,057	544,739	5,682	197,138	62,882	8,181	39,518	16,102
Jackson, TN	115,425	115,534	109	41,226	15,792	2,256	9,460	4,133
Jacksonville, FL	1,345,596	1,362,650	17,054	508,115	171,792	21,519	103,893	43,950
Jacksonville, NC	177,772	180,060	2,288	60,656	13,878	1,317	8,668	3,813

Table A-4: Metropolitan Statistical Areas—Summary Population Characteristics—*Continued*

	April 1, 2010 Census Population Estimates Base	2010–2012 ACS Population	Population Change	2010–2012 ACS				
				Total Households	Population 65 and Over	Population 85 and Over	Householders 65 and Over	Persons 65 and Over Living Alone
Janesville, WI	160,331	160,240	-91	63,114	22,209	2,999	14,192	6,543
Jefferson City, MO	149,807	150,133	326	56,756	19,780	2,455	12,941	5,593
Johnson City, TN	198,716	199,784	1,068	83,466	33,365	3,955	21,283	9,448
Johnstown, PA	143,679	142,564	-1,115	58,197	27,189	4,525	17,817	8,873
Jonesboro, AR	121,026	122,682	1,656	46,890	15,824	1,944	9,827	4,381
Joplin, MO	175,518	175,631	113	67,467	25,081	3,393	15,510	6,414
Kalamazoo-Portage, MI	326,589	328,433	1,844	127,037	42,363	5,966	26,992	12,306
Kankakee-Bradley, IL	113,449	113,361	-88	41,515	15,361	2,270	9,408	4,398
Kansas City, MO-KS	2,035,334	2,051,795	16,461	794,615	252,245	36,648	160,004	71,216
Kennewick-Pasco-Richland, WA	253,340	262,524	9,184	88,744	27,682	3,250	17,299	7,195
Killeen-Temple-Fort Hood, TX	405,300	413,662	8,362	130,662	37,782	3,992	22,199	8,464
Kingsport-Bristol-Bristol, TN-VA	309,544	308,895	-649	129,636	57,907	7,019	37,875	15,734
Kingston, NY	182,496	182,256	-240	69,477	28,178	4,304	17,228	8,378
Knoxville, TN	698,030	704,397	6,367	288,027	106,237	13,195	67,028	30,045
Kokomo, IN	98,688	98,600	-88	41,042	16,797	2,199	10,870	5,100
La Crosse, WI-MN	133,665	134,534	869	53,949	19,095	3,199	12,377	5,838
Lafayette, IN	201,789	204,154	2,365	77,987	21,369	3,184	13,741	6,368
Lafayette, LA	273,738	277,061	3,323	105,304	29,895	3,568	18,765	7,873
Lake Charles, LA	199,607	200,378	771	76,053	25,751	2,803	16,269	6,993
Lake Havasu City-Kingman, AZ	200,186	202,102	1,916	80,346	48,584	4,700	30,103	11,095
Lakeland-Winter Haven, FL	602,095	609,775	7,680	220,874	111,849	13,506	67,040	26,251
Lancaster, PA	519,448	523,676	4,228	193,931	80,119	13,886	47,590	20,147
Lansing-East Lansing, MI	464,036	465,168	1,132	179,828	56,354	7,681	36,023	16,489
Laredo, TX	250,304	255,135	4,831	67,572	20,230	2,711	10,908	3,597
Las Cruces, NM	209,234	212,571	3,337	73,889	26,999	2,973	16,964	5,980
Las Vegas-Paradise, NV	1,951,269	1,974,036	22,767	703,972	233,408	21,844	137,213	57,180
Lawrence, KS	110,826	112,105	1,279	43,566	10,285	1,500	6,461	3,090
Lawton, OK	124,098	125,850	1,752	44,614	12,964	1,427	8,725	4,008
Lebanon, PA	133,573	134,452	879	51,807	22,939	3,413	14,277	6,204
Lewiston-Auburn, ME	107,704	107,571	-133	44,502	15,552	2,190	9,997	4,527
Lexington-Fayette, KY	472,099	479,142	7,043	189,976	54,619	6,617	34,928	15,859
Lima, OH	106,331	105,701	-630	40,398	15,696	2,573	9,963	4,653
Lincoln, NE	302,157	306,626	4,469	121,146	34,665	5,190	21,994	10,060
Little Rock-North Little Rock-Conway, AR	699,759	710,321	10,562	274,899	88,696	9,948	54,676	22,308
Logan, UT-ID	125,442	127,244	1,802	39,707	10,763	1,449	6,708	2,469
Longview, TX	214,378	215,688	1,310	76,986	30,550	4,485	18,937	8,754
Longview, WA	102,410	102,291	-119	39,823	16,595	2,221	10,586	4,651
Los Angeles-Long Beach-Santa Ana, CA	12,828,837	12,947,334	118,497	4,203,724	1,472,725	212,830	822,772	337,561
Louisville/Jefferson County, KY-IN	1,283,565	1,293,831	10,266	506,000	169,533	21,639	108,380	48,875
Lubbock, TX	284,890	289,685	4,795	107,820	32,716	4,004	20,867	9,054
Lynchburg, VA	252,638	254,048	1,410	98,070	41,173	5,584	25,581	10,801
Macon, GA	232,293	232,638	345	84,261	31,201	3,513	19,230	8,048
Madera-Chowchilla, CA	150,865	151,827	962	41,702	17,912	1,882	9,464	2,824
Madison, WI	568,593	576,845	8,252	237,824	64,781	9,071	41,825	18,818
Manchester-Nashua, NH	400,721	401,933	1,212	153,838	49,471	6,877	29,700	12,622
Manhattan, KS	127,081	131,648	4,567	46,606	10,509	1,607	6,642	3,194
Mankato-North Mankato, MN	96,740	97,389	649	36,813	11,806	2,216	7,670	3,657
Mansfield, OH	124,475	123,331	-1,144	48,336	20,768	2,656	13,532	6,306
McAllen-Edinburg-Mission, TX	774,769	793,312	18,543	217,706	75,801	8,386	41,006	13,153
Medford, OR	203,206	204,868	1,662	82,524	37,277	5,744	23,740	10,407
Memphis, TN-MS-AR	1,316,100	1,325,160	9,060	481,271	143,766	16,331	89,448	37,756
Merced, CA	255,793	259,716	3,923	74,958	25,198	3,093	13,739	5,114
Miami-Fort Lauderdale-Pompano Beach, FL	5,564,635	5,677,408	112,773	2,008,054	915,028	144,234	517,004	230,830
Michigan City-La Porte, IN	111,467	111,314	-153	42,715	16,122	2,008	10,456	4,743
Midland, TX	136,872	141,207	4,335	50,251	15,298	1,851	9,229	4,180
Milwaukee-Waukesha-West Allis, WI	1,555,908	1,561,707	5,799	618,215	199,855	31,013	130,604	65,242
Minneapolis-St. Paul-Bloomington, MN-WI	3,279,833	3,320,190	40,357	1,283,812	365,949	52,919	233,272	108,252
Missoula, MT	109,299	110,183	884	45,413	12,935	1,945	8,036	3,318
Mobile, AL	412,990	413,432	442	156,085	54,982	6,289	34,830	14,567
Modesto, CA	514,453	518,336	3,883	166,948	56,938	8,517	33,059	13,705
Monroe, LA	176,441	177,278	837	66,201	23,289	2,916	14,969	6,861
Monroe, MI	152,021	151,539	-482	57,876	21,131	2,455	13,592	5,803
Montgomery, AL	374,536	376,964	2,428	141,135	46,361	5,240	29,334	13,178
Morgantown, WV	129,709	132,224	2,515	48,835	15,359	1,933	9,332	4,347
Morristown, TN	136,610	137,261	651	52,773	22,818	2,169	14,596	6,415
Mount Vernon-Anacortes, WA	116,901	117,691	790	45,207	19,708	2,652	12,155	4,935
Muncie, IN	117,671	117,599	-72	46,179	17,592	1,931	11,532	5,154
Muskegon-Norton Shores, MI	172,188	170,724	-1,464	64,394	23,796	3,325	15,242	6,613
Myrtle Beach-North Myrtle Beach-Conway, SC	269,291	276,156	6,865	113,314	49,069	4,537	31,520	13,202
Napa, CA	136,484	137,949	1,465	49,517	21,451	3,557	12,918	5,545
Naples-Marco Island, FL	321,520	327,537	6,017	121,788	89,552	11,345	52,578	19,384
Nashville-Davidson--Murfreesboro--Franklin, TN	1,589,934	1,618,819	28,885	609,320	178,446	21,653	110,342	45,658
New Haven-Milford, CT	862,477	862,776	299	328,434	126,344	23,684	77,105	37,337
New Orleans-Metairie-Kenner, LA	1,167,764	1,190,162	22,398	456,319	148,551	19,252	93,431	41,697
New York-Northern New Jersey-Long Island, NY-NJ-PA	18,897,109	19,048,167	151,058	6,822,864	2,539,430	380,351	1,520,309	704,046
Niles-Benton Harbor, MI	156,813	156,452	-361	59,373	25,836	3,931	16,237	7,121
North Port-Bradenton-Sarasota, FL	702,281	710,883	8,602	301,074	200,092	29,718	124,192	50,884
Norwich-New London, CT	274,055	274,118	63	106,959	40,149	5,336	24,579	11,555
Ocala, FL	331,298	333,001	1,703	132,975	87,503	9,397	53,390	19,525
Ocean City, NJ	97,265	96,716	-549	41,459	21,534	2,730	13,676	5,892

Table A-4: Metropolitan Statistical Areas—Summary Population Characteristics—*Continued*

	April 1, 2010 Census Population Estimates Base	2010–2012 ACS Population	Population Change	2010–2012 ACS				
				Total Households	Population 65 and Over	Population 85 and Over	Householders 65 and Over	Persons 65 and Over Living Alone
Odessa, TX	137,130	140,323	3,193	49,495	14,068	1,576	9,061	4,138
Ogden-Clearfield, UT	547,184	555,816	8,632	178,362	51,625	6,223	31,825	11,143
Oklahoma City, OK	1,252,987	1,276,771	23,784	482,224	152,609	18,977	97,069	43,709
Olympia, WA	252,264	255,927	3,663	101,296	34,479	4,483	21,508	9,488
Omaha-Council Bluffs, NE-IA	865,350	876,971	11,621	336,927	98,887	14,717	63,409	28,932
Orlando-Kissimmee-Sanford, FL	2,134,411	2,179,420	45,009	765,526	276,326	34,090	156,438	59,919
Oshkosh-Neenah, WI	166,994	167,860	866	67,750	22,787	3,956	14,435	7,320
Owensboro, KY	114,755	115,410	655	44,422	17,367	2,264	11,161	4,980
Oxnard-Thousand Oaks-Ventura, CA	823,318	830,828	7,510	266,414	100,859	14,468	59,887	23,335
Palm Bay-Melbourne-Titusville, FL	543,372	545,202	1,830	219,293	114,082	14,013	70,245	29,461
Palm Coast, FL	95,696	97,229	1,533	35,363	25,015	2,962	13,858	4,483
Panama City-Lynn Haven-Panama City Beach, FL	168,852	170,351	1,499	68,622	25,463	2,599	16,502	6,817
Parkersburg-Marietta-Vienna, WV-OH	162,056	161,887	-169	65,023	27,828	3,291	18,054	8,233
Pascagoula, MS	162,246	162,870	624	58,298	20,935	1,646	13,309	5,011
Pensacola-Ferry Pass-Brent, FL	448,991	455,932	6,941	168,161	64,585	7,515	40,694	16,566
Peoria, IL	379,186	379,918	732	152,050	57,552	8,522	36,912	16,357
Philadelphia-Camden-Wilmington, PA-NJ-DE-MD	5,965,343	5,996,101	30,758	2,222,996	811,495	125,351	502,733	234,593
Phoenix-Mesa-Glendale, AZ	4,192,887	4,263,663	70,776	1,526,595	543,706	64,503	326,522	129,193
Pine Bluff, AR	100,258	98,989	-1,269	36,194	13,696	1,836	8,567	3,740
Pittsburgh, PA	2,356,285	2,359,225	2,940	985,221	410,509	68,432	266,674	130,223
Pittsfield, MA	131,219	130,565	-654	55,573	25,072	4,486	16,435	8,650
Pocatello, ID	90,656	91,236	580	32,706	10,500	1,119	6,496	2,452
Portland-South Portland-Biddeford, ME	2,226,009	516,025	-1,709,984	212,336	79,499	11,021	49,863	23,534
Portland-Vancouver-Hillsboro, OR-WA	424,107	2,261,148	1,837,041	866,996	266,798	39,516	168,214	74,634
Port St. Lucie, FL	514,100	428,781	-85,319	166,382	99,068	13,827	59,735	23,499
Poughkeepsie-Newburgh-Middletown, NY	670,301	671,926	1,625	232,472	84,059	11,706	50,584	21,850
Prescott, AZ	211,033	211,339	306	91,813	53,313	7,010	34,015	13,529
Providence-New Bedford-Fall River, RI-MA	1,600,852	1,601,208	356	618,622	234,456	40,696	144,675	69,623
Provo-Orem, UT	526,810	540,458	13,648	145,766	36,447	4,530	21,416	6,995
Pueblo, CO	159,063	160,256	1,193	62,260	25,026	3,150	15,828	7,126
Punta Gorda, FL	159,978	160,602	624	70,035	56,719	8,101	34,637	12,880
Racine, WI	195,408	195,086	-322	75,450	26,333	3,575	17,221	8,026
Raleigh-Cary, NC	1,130,490	1,162,869	32,379	430,065	108,919	12,101	67,021	29,090
Rapid City, SD	126,382	128,421	2,039	50,517	17,359	2,639	10,675	4,698
Reading, PA	411,439	412,610	1,171	154,092	60,772	9,371	37,479	16,345
Redding, CA	177,223	177,980	757	68,408	31,209	4,189	19,897	8,677
Reno-Sparks, NV	425,417	429,841	4,424	164,287	54,704	6,177	33,271	14,123
Richmond, VA	1,258,251	1,270,735	12,484	475,577	160,152	22,140	100,701	43,695
Riverside-San Bernardino-Ontario, CA	4,224,851	4,298,641	73,790	1,280,341	460,667	54,619	258,771	104,528
Roanoke, VA	308,707	309,191	484	127,408	51,554	7,090	33,552	15,336
Rochester, MN	186,011	187,566	1,555	73,332	25,206	3,764	15,468	6,694
Rochester, NY	1,054,323	1,056,072	1,749	417,699	153,409	24,840	97,083	44,397
Rockford, IL	349,431	347,722	-1,709	130,349	48,379	6,539	29,690	12,624
Rocky Mount, NC	152,392	152,041	-351	57,883	22,437	2,791	14,820	7,090
Rome, GA	96,317	96,238	-79	34,961	13,894	1,741	9,051	4,303
Sacramento--Arden-Arcade--Roseville, CA	2,149,127	2,175,903	26,776	783,442	271,120	39,322	163,172	71,448
Saginaw-Saginaw Township North, MI	200,169	199,094	-1,075	77,081	31,123	4,628	20,511	9,729
St. Cloud, MN	210,170	189,905	-20,265	71,572	23,516	3,504	14,791	6,640
St. George, UT	692,942	141,594	-551,348	47,115	25,428	3,421	15,283	4,816
St. Joseph, MO-KS	436,712	127,601	-309,111	46,992	18,214	3,036	11,423	5,503
St. Louis, MO-IL	138,333	2,818,187	2,679,854	1,110,522	385,344	55,390	246,259	112,351
Salem, OR	189,093	393,932	204,839	141,617	53,770	8,274	33,232	14,494
Salinas, CA	138,115	421,570	283,455	124,727	46,040	7,052	25,539	10,021
Salisbury, MD	127,329	126,211	-1,118	44,489	17,045	2,191	10,516	4,597
Salt Lake City, UT	2,812,891	1,144,789	-1,668,102	374,656	100,283	12,192	62,577	25,055
San Angelo, TX	390,738	113,598	-277,140	42,497	15,710	1,642	10,206	4,301
San Antonio-New Braunfels, TX	415,057	2,192,939	1,777,882	758,905	246,536	31,051	148,360	58,462
San Diego-Carlsbad-San Marcos, CA	125,203	3,139,726	3,014,523	1,067,043	365,780	57,661	209,064	87,630
Sandusky, OH	3,095,313	76,700	-3,018,613	31,908	13,703	1,779	8,524	3,757
San Francisco-Oakland-Fremont, CA	1,124,197	4,399,211	3,275,014	1,619,263	570,451	86,927	336,190	151,672
San Jose-Sunnyvale-Santa Clara, CA	111,823	1,868,165	1,756,342	624,110	211,534	29,018	115,635	44,043
San Luis Obispo-Paso Robles, CA	2,142,508	272,034	-1,870,474	100,767	42,727	6,712	25,629	10,423
Santa Barbara-Santa Maria-Goleta, CA	77,079	427,251	350,172	141,196	56,046	10,019	33,861	14,559
Santa Cruz-Watsonville, CA	4,335,391	265,057	-4,070,334	92,834	30,785	4,892	19,970	9,121
Santa Fe, NM	1,836,911	145,378	-1,691,533	61,371	23,581	2,518	15,667	7,558
Santa Rosa-Petaluma, CA	269,637	488,237	218,600	183,773	70,993	11,383	44,296	20,275
Savannah, GA	423,895	355,539	-68,356	131,329	42,188	5,427	26,733	12,030
Scranton--Wilkes-Barre, PA	262,382	563,722	301,340	226,670	101,172	17,073	63,550	31,310
Seattle-Tacoma-Bellevue, WA	144,168	3,499,632	3,355,464	1,364,719	391,481	57,323	243,947	111,916
Sebastian-Vero Beach, FL	483,878	139,241	-344,637	57,183	39,107	6,497	24,390	11,032
Sheboygan, WI	347,616	115,224	-232,392	46,072	17,184	2,993	10,784	4,750
Sherman-Denison, TX	563,630	121,434	-442,196	46,349	19,174	2,535	11,431	4,961
Shreveport-Bossier City, LA	3,439,809	403,273	-3,036,536	154,468	53,345	6,445	34,799	15,294
Sioux City, IA-NE-SD	138,028	143,948	5,920	54,167	18,956	3,009	12,252	6,326
Sioux Falls, SD	115,507	233,298	117,791	90,134	26,322	4,042	16,138	7,099
South Bend-Mishawaka, IN-MI	120,877	318,943	198,066	120,913	44,942	6,767	28,220	12,270
Spartanburg, SC	398,604	286,563	-112,041	106,734	39,447	3,986	24,662	10,486
Spokane, WA	143,577	473,793	330,216	187,863	63,283	8,679	40,702	19,107
Springfield, IL	228,261	211,411	-16,850	88,012	30,049	4,697	19,890	9,792
Springfield, MA	319,222	696,247	377,025	266,729	99,398	16,728	62,402	30,357

Table A-4: Metropolitan Statistical Areas—Summary Population Characteristics—*Continued*

	April 1, 2010 Census Population Estimates Base	2010–2012 ACS Population	Population Change	2010–2012 ACS				
				Total Households	Population 65 and Over	Population 85 and Over	Householders 65 and Over	Persons 65 and Over Living Alone
Springfield, MO	284,307	440,811	156,504	175,502	63,006	8,591	39,922	17,690
Springfield, OH	471,221	137,735	-333,486	54,969	22,620	3,490	14,890	6,706
State College, PA	153,985	154,698	713	57,266	17,752	2,566	11,231	5,115
Steubenville-Weirton, OH-WV	124,454	123,367	-1,087	51,210	23,117	3,201	15,188	7,080
Stockton, CA	685,306	695,251	9,945	214,808	74,322	10,314	41,585	16,422
Sumter, SC	107,456	107,642	186	39,766	14,136	1,694	9,106	3,806
Syracuse, NY	662,579	662,095	-484	255,640	93,016	14,779	59,049	28,293
Tallahassee, FL	367,413	371,927	4,514	141,786	39,930	5,073	25,354	11,176
Tampa-St. Petersburg-Clearwater, FL	2,783,243	2,819,382	36,139	1,118,552	494,529	72,286	305,683	138,796
Terre Haute, IN	172,423	172,476	53	63,535	24,812	3,738	15,187	6,783
Texarkana, TX-Texarkana, AR	136,027	136,546	519	50,759	19,682	2,524	12,536	5,781
Toledo, OH	651,429	650,637	-792	260,021	89,540	12,782	57,899	27,021
Topeka, KS	233,870	234,516	646	94,097	35,398	4,937	22,190	9,761
Trenton-Ewing, NJ	366,511	367,567	1,056	131,315	47,385	7,261	29,042	13,598
Tucson, AZ	980,263	987,294	7,031	381,827	157,849	21,477	97,843	41,934
Tulsa, OK	937,478	945,744	8,266	366,638	124,949	16,103	79,539	35,138
Tuscaloosa, AL	219,458	221,214	1,756	76,828	25,545	3,033	15,326	6,927
Tyler, TX	209,714	212,694	2,980	79,299	30,979	4,509	19,347	7,982
Utica-Rome, NY	299,397	298,723	-674	117,489	49,761	9,381	31,249	15,682
Valdosta, GA	139,584	141,795	2,211	50,708	15,000	1,813	9,597	3,767
Vallejo-Fairfield, CA	413,344	417,261	3,917	140,669	49,340	5,922	28,831	11,540
Victoria, TX	115,384	116,550	1,166	42,995	16,937	1,894	10,442	4,177
Vineland-Millville-Bridgeton, NJ	156,898	157,351	453	49,981	20,154	2,843	12,301	5,915
Virginia Beach-Norfolk-Newport News, VA-NC	1,671,690	1,684,011	12,321	619,344	200,048	24,444	125,196	51,412
Visalia-Porterville, CA	442,179	447,704	5,525	131,426	43,156	5,689	24,691	9,718
Waco, TX	234,906	237,471	2,565	84,399	30,023	4,469	18,149	8,095
Warner Robins, GA	139,911	143,718	3,807	52,077	15,075	1,539	8,976	3,835
Washington-Arlington-Alexandria, DC-VA-MD-WV	5,582,037	5,710,843	128,806	2,063,730	588,571	75,781	350,684	148,886
Waterloo-Cedar Falls, IA	167,819	168,296	477	66,175	24,946	4,039	16,019	7,545
Wausau, WI	134,063	134,459	396	52,515	19,728	3,252	11,818	4,956
Wenatchee-East Wenatchee, WA	110,884	112,118	1,234	41,122	16,803	2,539	10,713	4,258
Wheeling, WV-OH	147,950	147,142	-808	60,933	26,465	3,997	17,078	8,314
Wichita, KS	151,306	625,940	474,634	237,516	76,821	11,698	48,651	23,021
Wichita Falls, TX	623,061	150,783	-472,278	54,797	20,708	2,716	13,139	5,626
Williamsport, PA	116,108	116,668	560	45,933	19,304	3,409	11,867	5,127
Wilmington, NC	362,315	369,711	7,396	152,630	62,904	6,054	39,482	15,342
Winchester, VA-WV	128,472	129,843	1,371	50,363	17,958	2,115	11,457	5,210
Winston-Salem, NC	477,717	481,399	3,682	189,823	68,307	8,563	43,386	19,755
Worcester, MA	798,552	803,429	4,877	298,224	104,748	17,839	63,136	30,662
Yakima, WA	243,231	245,797	2,566	79,396	29,016	4,420	16,886	7,072
York-Hanover, PA	434,972	436,824	1,852	168,566	63,155	8,678	39,794	17,352
Youngstown-Warren-Boardman, OH-PA	565,773	561,578	-4,195	230,035	101,541	16,434	66,502	31,334
Yuba City, CA	166,892	167,564	672	55,680	19,873	2,119	11,654	4,726
Yuma, AZ	195,750	199,061	3,311	70,062	31,751	2,635	18,834	5,641

Table A-5: 113th Congressional Districts—Summary Population Characteristics

	April 1, 2010 Census Population	2010–2012 ACS Population	Population Change	2010–2012 ACS				
				Total Households	Population 65 and Over	Population 85 and Over	Householders 65 and Over	Persons 65 and Over Living Alone
Alabama								
Congressional District 1	682,820	688,249	5,429	261,496	100,507	11,152	63,296	25,095
Congressional District 2	682,820	682,475	-345	260,697	98,176	11,112	62,194	27,605
Congressional District 3	682,819	689,196	6,377	266,942	94,315	10,395	60,439	25,829
Congressional District 4	682,819	680,531	-2,288	260,979	109,146	11,970	70,393	30,129
Congressional District 5	682,819	690,835	8,016	269,779	95,320	10,982	61,062	25,917
Congressional District 6	682,819	683,810	991	259,611	91,264	11,721	57,022	23,827
Congressional District 7	682,820	688,392	5,572	258,319	88,397	11,465	57,494	27,545
Alaska								
Congressional District (at Large)	710,231	723,120	12,889	253,718	58,586	4,909	35,129	14,669
Arizona								
Congressional District 1	710,224	719,827	9,603	236,819	102,031	10,681	61,895	22,191
Congressional District 2	710,224	716,127	5,903	295,532	129,414	18,304	82,408	37,602
Congressional District 3	710,224	718,357	8,133	222,707	66,560	6,933	38,254	13,669
Congressional District 4	710,224	717,210	6,986	278,266	161,536	16,496	98,872	35,420
Congressional District 5	710,224	719,967	9,743	257,942	109,142	11,476	65,598	25,334
Congressional District 6	710,224	723,210	12,986	293,677	106,142	12,710	64,829	25,324
Congressional District 7	710,224	721,604	11,380	219,771	46,883	4,831	27,728	12,362
Congressional District 8	710,225	715,908	5,683	266,360	134,799	17,938	80,030	30,427
Congressional District 9	710,224	724,918	14,694	286,725	70,519	10,592	44,669	20,705
Arkansas								
Congressional District 1	728,765	728,665	-100	280,814	117,546	13,979	74,629	33,358
Congressional District 2	729,192	739,485	10,293	287,673	97,003	11,360	60,603	25,275
Congressional District 3	728,959	740,549	11,590	279,408	93,618	12,134	58,181	23,460
Congressional District 4	729,002	728,123	-879	281,950	121,518	14,637	76,944	33,411
California								
Congressional District 1	702,905	703,517	612	272,812	124,506	17,142	78,841	33,700
Congressional District 2	702,905	705,403	2,498	275,615	113,154	15,495	71,143	31,939
Congressional District 3	702,906	707,542	4,636	239,071	82,747	10,398	50,081	20,855
Congressional District 4	702,906	705,130	2,224	266,828	119,427	14,360	73,173	27,965
Congressional District 5	702,905	712,669	9,764	257,241	99,389	15,649	59,631	27,026
Congressional District 6	702,905	710,032	7,127	259,769	75,852	11,529	46,049	22,511
Congressional District 7	702,904	711,837	8,933	251,698	87,722	13,236	52,070	22,770
Congressional District 8	702,905	705,307	2,402	225,110	80,982	8,481	49,070	20,387
Congressional District 9	702,904	710,682	7,778	220,810	79,074	10,396	44,298	17,766
Congressional District 10	702,905	709,468	6,563	225,284	75,228	10,706	42,739	17,183
Congressional District 11	702,906	716,752	13,846	259,583	99,443	15,865	60,723	25,635
Congressional District 12	702,905	708,026	5,121	309,007	95,959	15,796	60,556	31,937
Congressional District 13	702,906	712,319	9,413	277,262	86,267	13,745	54,816	27,517
Congressional District 14	702,905	716,514	13,609	247,048	99,646	15,777	54,105	23,017
Congressional District 15	702,904	716,070	13,166	234,688	75,584	10,630	40,607	15,698
Congressional District 16	702,904	713,370	10,466	199,680	63,335	8,416	35,459	13,804
Congressional District 17	702,904	717,422	14,518	238,728	76,662	10,148	38,926	14,318
Congressional District 18	702,906	723,643	20,737	269,835	96,943	15,986	57,686	23,764
Congressional District 19	702,904	702,232	-672	214,122	73,386	8,359	38,425	13,666
Congressional District 20	702,906	712,741	9,835	219,660	78,515	12,138	45,790	19,276
Congressional District 21	702,904	705,199	2,295	179,136	53,389	6,444	28,615	10,582
Congressional District 22	702,905	712,793	9,888	228,905	77,990	11,408	45,926	18,768
Congressional District 23	702,904	709,743	6,839	232,662	78,393	9,188	46,736	20,242
Congressional District 24	702,904	709,359	6,455	246,629	99,867	16,788	60,205	25,353
Congressional District 25	702,904	707,791	4,887	216,121	64,992	7,351	35,311	12,753
Congressional District 26	702,905	709,241	6,336	225,123	88,218	13,121	52,466	20,691
Congressional District 27	702,905	707,049	4,144	240,460	105,407	18,467	55,033	21,279
Congressional District 28	702,904	713,520	10,616	294,309	98,991	14,237	58,144	28,376
Congressional District 29	702,905	698,936	-3,969	197,815	61,633	8,068	30,344	12,112
Congressional District 30	702,904	725,109	22,205	266,432	96,711	15,094	54,729	23,127
Congressional District 31	702,905	719,204	16,299	213,301	61,985	8,369	33,895	14,525
Congressional District 32	702,905	706,961	4,056	191,589	79,081	10,899	39,516	14,231
Congressional District 33	702,904	705,606	2,702	297,569	107,873	16,847	67,969	29,437
Congressional District 34	702,904	701,073	-1,831	230,840	70,206	9,832	38,587	17,426
Congressional District 35	702,905	711,969	9,064	179,563	53,148	6,497	24,732	9,144
Congressional District 36	702,905	712,130	9,225	253,338	136,193	18,014	84,960	37,574
Congressional District 37	702,904	716,393	13,489	268,681	80,365	13,479	52,754	27,244
Congressional District 38	702,905	710,784	7,879	203,068	85,926	12,203	46,143	15,460
Congressional District 39	702,905	715,765	12,860	219,754	86,941	11,487	44,798	14,038
Congressional District 40	702,904	701,135	-1,769	174,476	50,219	6,144	24,055	8,448
Congressional District 41	702,904	717,154	14,250	190,721	56,226	6,812	29,365	10,766
Congressional District 42	702,906	722,604	19,698	209,328	71,724	7,284	37,443	13,646
Congressional District 43	702,904	698,157	-4,747	231,001	72,981	9,666	43,125	19,063
Congressional District 44	702,904	708,177	5,273	180,335	59,613	6,189	31,432	11,432
Congressional District 45	702,906	718,596	15,690	254,557	90,423	13,482	52,624	21,328
Congressional District 46	702,906	709,755	6,849	180,486	55,849	8,457	27,832	10,393
Congressional District 47	702,905	714,214	11,309	239,897	81,363	11,492	45,252	19,195
Congressional District 48	702,906	710,815	7,909	263,327	104,415	14,882	62,120	25,179
Congressional District 49	702,906	705,126	2,220	243,959	87,886	14,406	51,672	21,351
Congressional District 50	702,905	717,813	14,908	235,231	87,196	13,934	49,651	19,075
Congressional District 51	702,906	715,432	12,526	195,435	70,177	9,366	37,498	15,004
Congressional District 52	702,904	707,989	5,085	268,778	86,263	13,672	51,293	23,050
Congressional District 53	702,904	720,318	17,414	258,273	81,436	13,349	46,186	20,235

Table A-5: 113th Congressional Districts—Summary Population Characteristics—*Continued*

	April 1, 2010 Census Population	2010–2012 ACS Population	Population Change	2010–2012 ACS				
				Total Households	Population 65 and Over	Population 85 and Over	Householders 65 and Over	Persons 65 and Over Living Alone
Colorado								
Congressional District 1	718,457	736,635	18,178	315,283	78,341	12,655	52,387	27,960
Congressional District 2	718,457	730,276	11,819	291,713	82,009	9,982	50,240	20,363
Congressional District 3	718,457	722,321	3,864	285,958	103,649	12,465	66,323	29,599
Congressional District 4	718,456	727,643	9,187	262,780	80,065	9,789	48,484	19,789
Congressional District 5	718,457	732,004	13,547	274,986	81,970	9,168	51,265	22,105
Congressional District 6	718,456	736,769	18,313	269,284	70,735	8,623	42,773	17,851
Congressional District 7	718,456	731,805	13,349	277,733	84,546	10,969	52,687	22,934
Connecticut								
Congressional District 1	714,820	717,086	2,266	282,280	107,707	19,343	66,372	31,865
Congressional District 2	714,819	713,617	-1,202	269,210	102,946	14,517	62,012	27,304
Congressional District 3	714,819	714,552	-267	275,465	104,522	19,023	64,640	31,394
Congressional District 4	714,819	722,517	7,698	257,711	99,387	16,067	59,564	25,910
Congressional District 5	714,820	716,789	1,969	271,307	104,177	18,088	63,384	30,416
Delaware								
Congressional District (at Large)	897,934	908,351	10,417	334,228	134,601	16,505	81,975	34,426
District of Columbia								
Delegate District (at Large)	601,723	618,777	17,054	261,567	70,302	10,229	49,026	27,518
Florida								
Congressional District 1	696,345	708,435	12,090	267,211	101,989	11,437	63,862	25,869
Congressional District 2	696,345	701,340	4,995	262,081	91,094	10,587	57,302	24,226
Congressional District 3	696,345	700,758	4,413	254,477	106,220	12,529	62,566	24,780
Congressional District 4	696,345	706,238	9,893	266,670	87,437	11,340	53,158	22,788
Congressional District 5	696,345	692,074	-4,271	245,257	74,854	8,645	45,734	20,469
Congressional District 6	696,345	706,412	10,067	276,522	151,827	18,834	91,244	37,198
Congressional District 7	696,345	706,486	10,141	247,253	92,573	14,425	52,401	21,075
Congressional District 8	696,344	699,385	3,041	281,554	154,853	20,529	95,706	40,693
Congressional District 9	696,345	718,149	21,804	242,158	77,152	8,085	42,093	15,265
Congressional District 10	696,345	724,205	27,860	270,101	123,374	14,143	72,215	27,114
Congressional District 11	696,345	699,871	3,526	288,526	213,186	22,913	130,399	47,002
Congressional District 12	696,344	697,696	1,352	274,182	142,428	21,604	86,993	36,625
Congressional District 13	696,345	696,910	565	307,417	155,143	25,177	99,789	50,955
Congressional District 14	696,345	718,783	22,438	279,230	82,835	10,271	50,835	24,019
Congressional District 15	696,345	708,137	11,792	252,019	95,091	12,091	56,084	22,945
Congressional District 16	696,345	704,560	8,215	299,159	199,378	29,680	123,819	50,754
Congressional District 17	696,344	697,323	979	263,066	178,647	24,434	107,005	39,899
Congressional District 18	696,344	700,097	3,753	279,448	159,903	23,084	96,368	39,348
Congressional District 19	696,345	708,108	11,763	275,845	188,998	25,009	109,884	42,272
Congressional District 20	696,345	711,816	15,471	241,489	94,585	16,477	57,393	28,142
Congressional District 21	696,345	710,611	14,266	270,938	156,557	30,258	96,018	43,078
Congressional District 22	696,345	706,089	9,744	303,421	145,605	26,428	90,806	44,789
Congressional District 23	696,345	716,584	20,239	280,920	110,125	16,703	66,819	33,181
Congressional District 24	696,345	695,867	-478	223,313	75,707	8,460	41,211	17,519
Congressional District 25	696,344	704,367	8,023	210,170	103,432	11,936	49,231	16,018
Congressional District 26	696,345	727,073	30,728	217,305	102,763	12,845	47,260	16,187
Congressional District 27	696,345	714,556	18,211	240,541	115,743	17,109	60,456	25,906
Georgia								
Congressional District 1	691,974	702,320	10,346	257,532	84,613	9,572	54,470	23,359
Congressional District 2	691,976	696,235	4,259	251,192	87,496	9,903	57,264	25,497
Congressional District 3	691,974	693,929	1,955	247,961	85,613	9,089	52,125	21,456
Congressional District 4	691,976	709,422	17,446	242,768	62,191	6,855	35,772	14,258
Congressional District 5	691,976	708,096	16,120	272,669	63,743	9,405	42,195	23,105
Congressional District 6	691,975	701,322	9,347	266,110	70,512	8,231	42,234	17,257
Congressional District 7	691,975	705,706	13,731	228,695	54,609	5,301	27,528	9,801
Congressional District 8	691,976	699,402	7,426	252,059	89,986	10,494	55,875	23,767
Congressional District 9	691,975	700,874	8,899	248,408	106,151	10,052	63,534	23,649
Congressional District 10	691,976	698,940	6,964	241,336	82,935	8,330	48,726	18,185
Congressional District 11	691,975	698,290	6,315	258,708	66,643	5,843	41,487	16,666
Congressional District 12	691,975	700,539	8,564	247,864	83,361	8,495	51,734	23,316
Congressional District 13	691,976	706,590	14,614	244,574	60,842	6,288	34,488	14,001
Congressional District 14	691,974	694,060	2,086	245,012	84,707	8,982	52,011	20,772
Hawaii								
Congressional District 1	680,496	687,223	6,727	229,997	110,613	19,581	60,659	21,235
Congressional District 2	679,805	691,016	11,211	217,569	92,582	14,180	50,239	15,742
Idaho								
Congressional District 1	784,132	793,108	8,976	290,123	107,237	12,490	66,692	25,496
Congressional District 2	783,450	790,314	6,864	290,157	95,973	13,129	61,125	25,634
Illinois								
Congressional District 1	712,813	718,265	5,452	261,858	96,833	13,576	63,639	29,033
Congressional District 2	712,813	712,966	153	257,026	93,931	13,786	60,904	27,871
Congressional District 3	712,813	707,476	-5,337	240,265	89,539	14,928	53,766	24,634
Congressional District 4	712,813	711,230	-1,583	217,501	54,981	6,557	32,366	14,530
Congressional District 5	712,813	718,501	5,688	298,220	84,617	14,485	52,736	26,330
Congressional District 6	712,813	719,794	6,981	259,445	89,670	12,538	53,412	21,949
Congressional District 7	712,812	716,884	4,072	282,059	74,370	8,504	49,877	25,420
Congressional District 8	712,812	715,533	2,721	249,855	72,496	10,752	44,160	19,550
Congressional District 9	712,813	720,781	7,968	287,380	111,895	19,467	69,300	33,922
Congressional District 10	712,813	710,409	-2,404	245,779	86,278	13,014	51,370	22,179

Table A-5: 113th Congressional Districts—Summary Population Characteristics—*Continued*

	April 1, 2010 Census Population	2010–2012 ACS Population	Population Change	2010–2012 ACS				
				Total Households	Population 65 and Over	Population 85 and Over	Householders 65 and Over	Persons 65 and Over Living Alone
Illinois—Cont.								
Congressional District 11	712,813	714,699	1,886	241,146	70,597	9,352	42,364	18,528
Congressional District 12	712,813	711,907	-906	275,191	103,683	14,314	67,007	32,418
Congressional District 13	712,813	714,939	2,126	284,995	97,989	15,007	62,715	29,065
Congressional District 14	712,813	722,048	9,235	246,358	72,531	7,754	43,461	16,599
Congressional District 15	712,813	709,304	-3,509	276,978	117,440	17,472	75,149	35,654
Congressional District 16	712,813	711,132	-1,681	268,044	106,334	14,952	65,819	28,996
Congressional District 17	712,813	709,394	-3,419	285,761	114,419	17,414	74,168	34,598
Congressional District 18	712,813	713,228	415	281,270	112,449	17,348	70,638	30,893
Indiana								
Congressional District 1	720,422	720,082	-340	265,074	96,735	12,987	59,248	25,457
Congressional District 2	720,423	721,518	1,095	268,645	99,749	14,467	62,647	26,974
Congressional District 3	720,423	722,426	2,003	274,100	94,945	13,374	60,316	26,870
Congressional District 4	720,422	726,521	6,099	273,345	95,509	12,365	59,975	26,205
Congressional District 5	720,423	727,904	7,481	281,975	89,604	13,443	56,560	25,229
Congressional District 6	720,422	720,862	440	276,467	107,554	13,060	68,201	31,100
Congressional District 7	720,423	728,887	8,464	280,694	75,109	9,648	48,994	23,466
Congressional District 8	720,422	721,040	618	278,038	107,489	15,132	66,676	29,262
Congressional District 9	720,422	725,276	4,854	276,588	96,285	11,648	60,400	27,133
Iowa								
Congressional District 1	761,548	764,571	3,023	304,787	118,999	18,405	74,800	33,998
Congressional District 2	761,624	765,560	3,936	306,936	112,960	18,033	71,833	33,226
Congressional District 3	761,612	771,866	10,254	302,976	98,424	14,786	61,362	27,818
Congressional District 4	761,571	760,872	-699	309,700	129,642	23,902	81,934	38,501
Kansas								
Congressional District 1	713,278	718,540	5,262	277,615	105,616	17,455	66,555	31,852
Congressional District 2	713,272	714,742	1,470	279,092	103,262	15,351	65,186	29,123
Congressional District 3	713,287	723,187	9,900	276,352	81,186	13,083	50,782	22,391
Congressional District 4	713,281	715,240	1,959	273,901	94,113	14,313	59,414	27,833
Kentucky								
Congressional District 1	723,178	724,310	1,132	280,150	114,216	13,500	73,165	33,450
Congressional District 2	723,137	730,024	6,887	276,370	98,109	11,845	62,186	26,619
Congressional District 3	723,171	726,055	2,884	296,996	98,854	14,465	63,933	31,029
Congressional District 4	723,450	731,275	7,825	270,253	89,547	10,917	56,281	23,728
Congressional District 5	723,228	720,359	-2,869	277,298	105,071	10,659	67,095	29,877
Congressional District 6	723,203	732,604	9,401	289,065	88,423	10,416	56,965	25,589
Louisiana								
Congressional District 1	755,445	762,461	7,016	289,472	102,412	13,295	64,336	27,887
Congressional District 2	755,538	768,511	12,973	286,763	85,924	11,031	55,094	24,691
Congressional District 3	755,596	759,525	3,929	284,929	92,733	10,603	58,991	25,168
Congressional District 4	755,605	760,870	5,265	285,674	103,953	11,891	67,450	29,637
Congressional District 5	755,581	758,550	2,969	274,554	104,506	12,938	66,226	28,727
Congressional District 6	755,607	763,678	8,071	284,699	86,017	9,420	53,661	21,943
Maine								
Congressional District 1	664,180	667,366	3,186	276,908	107,561	15,149	67,165	31,338
Congressional District 2	664,181	661,074	-3,107	276,055	110,770	13,955	69,161	31,293
Maryland								
Congressional District 1	722,650	722,293	-357	264,662	113,441	13,533	67,990	25,901
Congressional District 2	723,447	728,536	5,089	275,193	84,857	13,043	52,049	23,403
Congressional District 3	720,094	729,649	9,555	282,010	95,451	15,625	60,493	29,717
Congressional District 4	720,065	730,307	10,242	260,230	76,158	8,559	45,816	18,746
Congressional District 5	720,472	729,639	9,167	249,247	78,778	8,793	44,843	15,908
Congressional District 6	728,448	733,427	4,979	266,143	90,332	12,219	53,783	24,307
Congressional District 7	716,862	723,624	6,762	270,054	94,368	12,974	61,093	29,010
Congressional District 8	721,514	739,903	18,389	273,547	101,790	16,885	61,685	27,005
Massachusetts								
Congressional District 1	727,515	728,828	1,313	286,686	111,910	18,995	70,654	35,103
Congressional District 2	727,514	735,213	7,699	272,295	96,124	16,590	58,359	28,670
Congressional District 3	727,514	734,142	6,628	271,648	90,463	13,989	54,213	25,622
Congressional District 4	727,514	730,756	3,242	266,899	99,335	16,410	59,690	26,178
Congressional District 5	727,515	735,647	8,132	287,629	104,791	17,321	65,582	31,275
Congressional District 6	727,515	736,098	8,583	279,199	111,694	17,866	68,756	32,138
Congressional District 7	727,514	734,126	6,612	280,295	73,035	10,518	48,752	27,556
Congressional District 8	727,514	740,640	13,126	289,935	107,611	18,840	66,721	33,248
Congressional District 9	727,514	730,018	2,504	289,442	134,965	19,330	83,918	36,852
Michigan								
Congressional District 1	705,974	705,808	-166	292,473	135,818	17,061	86,476	36,774
Congressional District 2	705,975	707,806	1,831	263,120	92,958	12,877	58,368	24,418
Congressional District 3	705,974	710,012	4,038	265,469	89,195	13,751	56,348	24,046
Congressional District 4	705,974	703,641	-2,333	269,804	112,216	13,470	70,829	29,244
Congressional District 5	705,975	701,978	-3,997	278,692	107,406	14,713	70,085	31,407
Congressional District 6	705,974	707,698	1,724	269,613	100,920	14,053	63,960	27,734
Congressional District 7	705,974	703,255	-2,719	265,971	101,761	14,073	63,933	26,430
Congressional District 8	705,975	708,452	2,477	266,550	82,972	9,830	52,661	22,193
Congressional District 9	705,975	709,274	3,299	294,154	109,625	18,728	72,707	36,642
Congressional District 10	705,974	703,688	-2,286	268,128	102,115	13,274	63,850	26,831
Congressional District 11	705,974	709,950	3,976	275,428	95,496	13,582	60,804	26,895
Congressional District 12	705,974	705,254	-720	269,593	83,608	12,375	55,781	27,494
Congressional District 13	705,974	698,800	-7,174	260,172	87,355	13,708	59,820	30,655
Congressional District 14	705,974	703,661	-2,313	266,094	96,543	15,713	63,216	30,516

Table A-5: 113th Congressional Districts—Summary Population Characteristics—*Continued*

	April 1, 2010 Census Population	2010–2012 ACS Population	Population Change	2010–2012 ACS				
				Total Households	Population 65 and Over	Population 85 and Over	Householders 65 and Over	Persons 65 and Over Living Alone
Minnesota								
Congressional District 1	662,991	665,310	2,319	261,145	101,113	17,592	64,269	29,565
Congressional District 2	662,991	669,519	6,528	249,329	71,429	9,686	44,625	18,942
Congressional District 3	662,990	672,025	9,035	262,002	81,795	10,728	52,318	23,164
Congressional District 4	662,990	672,201	9,211	262,885	80,444	12,082	52,030	25,256
Congressional District 5	662,991	673,222	10,231	284,460	74,161	14,337	49,190	27,194
Congressional District 6	662,990	669,599	6,609	240,273	66,245	8,231	40,864	17,030
Congressional District 7	662,991	662,441	-550	269,701	116,871	19,815	73,648	33,518
Congressional District 8	662,991	661,404	-1,587	272,966	113,557	15,059	72,554	32,650
Mississippi								
Congressional District 1	741,837	745,626	3,789	272,699	100,583	11,482	63,562	26,646
Congressional District 2	741,862	738,747	-3,115	256,657	90,999	12,333	58,279	26,048
Congressional District 3	741,822	743,109	1,287	279,895	101,570	11,716	65,405	27,956
Congressional District 4	741,776	749,697	7,921	276,312	97,649	9,623	61,651	25,529
Missouri								
Congressional District 1	748,616	745,647	-2,969	313,191	89,830	14,157	61,438	32,445
Congressional District 2	748,616	750,747	2,131	294,616	118,892	19,338	73,521	31,467
Congressional District 3	748,615	756,645	8,030	286,498	99,071	10,941	62,537	24,809
Congressional District 4	748,616	751,805	3,189	285,805	108,676	13,894	67,398	28,465
Congressional District 5	748,616	751,988	3,372	303,785	100,542	14,711	66,508	32,580
Congressional District 6	748,616	750,841	2,225	284,380	106,475	15,515	65,556	28,556
Congressional District 7	748,616	752,854	4,238	296,174	114,802	15,126	71,462	30,277
Congressional District 8	748,616	748,498	-118	289,657	121,289	14,980	75,680	33,303
Montana								
Congressional District (at Large)	989,415	997,852	8,437	404,990	151,961	20,461	97,403	44,152
Nebraska								
Congressional District 1	608,780	615,021	6,241	241,759	80,879	12,535	50,998	23,145
Congressional District 2	608,781	618,941	10,160	238,003	63,721	9,610	41,658	19,570
Congressional District 3	608,780	608,518	-262	246,660	105,955	17,016	66,972	31,857
Nevada								
Congressional District 1	675,138	660,846	-14,292	236,834	81,313	8,168	49,790	24,584
Congressional District 2	675,138	681,152	6,014	258,559	92,739	9,999	57,060	22,892
Congressional District 3	675,138	705,052	29,914	263,425	87,495	8,066	49,698	18,068
Congressional District 4	675,137	680,521	5,384	233,939	81,157	6,767	48,132	18,227
New Hampshire								
Congressional District 1	658,233	658,723	490	260,498	91,778	12,241	55,685	23,213
Congressional District 2	658,237	659,732	1,495	257,511	93,662	12,035	57,617	24,779
New Jersey								
Congressional District 1	732,658	732,198	-460	269,265	97,197	14,905	60,165	28,121
Congressional District 2	732,658	734,501	1,843	268,289	113,956	14,669	70,540	31,125
Congressional District 3	732,658	735,488	2,830	278,313	125,859	18,925	78,363	34,966
Congressional District 4	732,657	734,131	1,474	270,204	123,238	19,632	78,391	36,852
Congressional District 5	732,658	734,079	1,421	261,620	108,929	17,576	62,712	24,905
Congressional District 6	732,657	737,333	4,676	252,577	87,231	12,308	49,969	21,719
Congressional District 7	732,658	736,302	3,644	263,322	98,051	15,510	58,088	24,896
Congressional District 8	732,658	749,007	16,349	268,817	70,575	9,573	41,136	19,999
Congressional District 9	732,658	740,535	7,877	260,735	96,868	15,070	58,242	27,242
Congressional District 10	732,658	727,269	-5,389	262,379	82,333	10,884	51,555	26,416
Congressional District 11	732,658	736,482	3,824	266,675	115,572	19,838	66,166	28,609
Congressional District 12	732,658	736,924	4,266	259,685	96,620	15,464	58,274	25,529
New Mexico								
Congressional District 1	686,393	693,850	7,457	273,346	89,553	11,488	56,382	25,207
Congressional District 2	686,393	696,955	10,562	244,812	101,911	11,506	63,242	25,425
Congressional District 3	686,393	685,520	-873	247,148	92,075	10,531	57,824	24,131
New York								
Congressional District 1	717,707	721,323	3,616	246,159	105,187	13,772	61,352	23,758
Congressional District 2	717,708	721,246	3,538	229,411	95,262	14,253	53,807	20,336
Congressional District 3	717,707	719,371	1,664	251,076	126,715	21,897	72,842	27,413
Congressional District 4	717,708	720,769	3,061	234,801	105,114	18,477	60,479	24,467
Congressional District 5	717,708	748,243	30,535	222,353	89,569	11,771	46,869	17,398
Congressional District 6	717,707	716,781	-926	266,481	109,100	17,342	61,218	28,433
Congressional District 7	717,708	738,965	21,257	244,627	67,061	9,154	40,174	19,295
Congressional District 8	717,708	718,055	347	264,910	90,816	11,653	57,410	29,141
Congressional District 9	717,708	731,894	14,186	270,034	85,664	11,479	52,588	25,563
Congressional District 10	717,707	720,858	3,151	305,765	95,392	14,939	63,915	37,102
Congressional District 11	717,708	720,598	2,890	258,343	104,186	15,646	61,466	28,489
Congressional District 12	717,707	704,688	-13,019	360,384	97,919	12,687	69,281	43,418
Congressional District 13	717,707	742,082	24,375	267,951	82,276	12,939	51,805	29,144
Congressional District 14	717,708	707,577	-10,131	242,520	83,707	11,886	47,181	22,270
Congressional District 15	717,707	728,371	10,663	235,057	61,125	6,274	39,856	22,224
Congressional District 16	717,707	727,727	10,020	265,660	108,448	17,980	65,395	32,735
Congressional District 17	717,708	724,651	6,943	241,101	104,140	15,770	59,751	24,979
Congressional District 18	717,707	720,607	2,900	248,332	91,399	12,898	54,771	22,810
Congressional District 19	717,708	713,514	-4,194	273,623	115,575	15,662	71,306	32,026
Congressional District 20	717,708	721,349	3,641	286,339	103,746	18,159	64,691	32,181

Table A-5: 113th Congressional Districts—Summary Population Characteristics—*Continued*

	April 1, 2010 Census Population	2010–2012 ACS Population	Population Change	2010–2012 ACS				
				Total Households	Population 65 and Over	Population 85 and Over	Householders 65 and Over	Persons 65 and Over Living Alone
New York—Cont.								
Congressional District 21	717,707	718,315	608	282,848	105,185	14,086	66,841	30,132
Congressional District 22	717,708	716,508	-1,200	277,749	114,501	19,126	71,222	34,176
Congressional District 23	717,707	715,848	-1,859	284,145	110,106	16,438	69,521	32,442
Congressional District 24	717,707	715,855	-1,852	279,863	102,817	16,229	65,266	31,242
Congressional District 25	717,707	719,847	2,140	286,461	103,104	17,768	65,975	31,026
Congressional District 26	717,707	716,685	-1,022	303,810	111,987	17,711	74,605	39,213
Congressional District 27	717,707	718,646	939	280,292	113,794	16,885	70,022	30,727
North Carolina								
Congressional District 1	733,499	732,969	-530	281,422	103,676	13,520	66,554	32,357
Congressional District 2	733,499	750,926	17,427	275,084	90,819	10,558	55,632	24,172
Congressional District 3	733,499	745,337	11,838	281,116	98,780	11,191	62,436	25,689
Congressional District 4	733,498	746,310	12,812	289,889	71,250	8,396	45,224	21,486
Congressional District 5	733,499	734,276	777	292,018	112,466	13,691	70,921	30,285
Congressional District 6	733,499	748,094	14,595	295,359	114,690	14,568	72,716	31,438
Congressional District 7	733,499	742,142	8,644	287,340	112,736	10,490	71,476	29,584
Congressional District 8	733,499	741,484	7,985	269,136	98,166	10,823	62,266	25,776
Congressional District 9	733,498	751,710	18,212	283,690	80,611	9,893	48,157	19,678
Congressional District 10	733,499	737,637	4,138	287,270	112,143	14,385	69,278	30,141
Congressional District 11	733,499	732,884	-615	297,541	143,435	16,735	89,001	37,423
Congressional District 12	733,499	747,107	13,608	279,936	64,378	7,832	41,118	19,032
Congressional District 13	733,498	743,203	9,705	279,507	85,748	9,934	53,396	21,929
North Dakota								
Congressional District (at Large)	672,591	686,244	13,653	285,639	99,040	16,737	62,826	30,835
Ohio								
Congressional District 1	721,032	724,310	3,278	274,979	88,952	12,491	56,278	26,015
Congressional District 2	721,031	719,580	-1,451	286,973	102,327	14,717	65,963	31,741
Congressional District 3	721,031	727,948	6,917	284,799	66,582	8,461	43,825	22,530
Congressional District 4	721,032	718,276	-2,756	275,169	106,000	15,025	67,395	29,223
Congressional District 5	721,031	722,141	1,110	285,037	108,969	15,598	69,228	30,604
Congressional District 6	721,032	718,925	-2,107	281,406	123,125	16,616	77,660	34,356
Congressional District 7	721,031	723,018	1,987	275,645	111,120	15,316	68,916	29,052
Congressional District 8	721,032	722,967	1,935	274,002	100,698	13,413	64,548	27,846
Congressional District 9	721,032	716,499	-4,533	295,907	97,460	15,149	64,955	32,592
Congressional District 10	721,032	722,146	1,114	294,969	109,825	15,561	71,934	34,949
Congressional District 11	721,032	712,904	-8,128	299,180	103,702	17,730	69,855	37,557
Congressional District 12	721,031	728,420	7,389	279,646	91,781	11,607	57,210	24,614
Congressional District 13	721,031	720,340	-691	296,097	115,537	18,243	75,629	36,215
Congressional District 14	721,032	718,013	-3,019	281,880	117,668	17,270	73,757	32,414
Congressional District 15	721,031	726,003	4,972	273,311	92,347	11,763	57,635	25,409
Congressional District 16	721,031	719,685	-1,346	283,141	122,006	17,984	76,176	33,760
Oklahoma								
Congressional District 1	750,270	759,361	9,091	297,488	96,729	13,263	62,489	28,471
Congressional District 2	750,270	749,793	-477	285,541	123,553	13,031	77,562	33,206
Congressional District 3	750,270	754,206	3,936	283,089	109,325	13,745	68,953	29,888
Congressional District 4	750,270	760,024	9,754	281,280	96,840	10,963	61,389	27,228
Congressional District 5	750,271	762,768	12,497	293,765	93,834	12,314	61,020	28,942
Oregon								
Congressional District 1	766,216	778,506	12,290	295,030	91,190	13,823	57,497	26,054
Congressional District 2	766,215	769,888	3,673	306,029	133,691	18,806	84,449	35,688
Congressional District 3	766,215	776,688	10,473	307,536	86,085	13,185	54,792	25,139
Congressional District 4	766,214	769,480	3,266	310,730	133,488	17,292	84,442	35,889
Congressional District 5	766,214	774,036	7,822	293,680	113,213	16,750	70,703	30,926
Pennsylvania								
Congressional District 1	705,688	694,882	-10,806	257,956	77,108	10,990	49,999	26,686
Congressional District 2	705,688	720,129	14,441	279,130	92,431	12,825	63,296	35,330
Congressional District 3	705,688	703,488	-2,200	281,381	117,141	18,254	73,915	33,975
Congressional District 4	705,687	709,009	3,322	277,071	105,387	15,491	66,376	29,447
Congressional District 5	705,688	705,821	133	275,805	114,028	16,604	72,084	33,143
Congressional District 6	705,688	714,715	9,027	270,872	102,208	15,249	62,853	27,112
Congressional District 7	705,688	709,405	3,717	258,296	111,067	19,679	66,840	29,359
Congressional District 8	705,688	708,380	2,692	260,477	106,568	16,449	63,106	24,918
Congressional District 9	705,688	705,062	-626	278,421	124,178	18,910	78,422	35,966
Congressional District 10	705,687	709,436	3,749	270,793	120,737	16,598	72,892	29,648
Congressional District 11	705,688	700,354	-5,334	278,991	115,375	17,421	72,457	33,618
Congressional District 12	705,688	705,390	-298	287,084	130,893	21,688	83,948	39,308
Congressional District 13	705,687	716,493	10,806	266,427	104,076	19,620	62,168	30,416
Congressional District 14	705,688	705,793	105	313,023	115,723	21,098	78,595	43,469
Congressional District 15	705,687	713,374	7,687	269,452	109,042	17,780	65,964	29,335
Congressional District 16	705,688	705,511	-177	261,157	101,501	17,345	61,178	27,071
Congressional District 17	705,687	704,634	-1,053	274,563	120,694	19,954	73,422	34,972
Congressional District 18	705,688	707,719	2,031	288,595	125,796	20,065	80,713	36,721
Rhode Island								
Congressional District 1	526,283	526,900	617	206,750	78,453	14,295	48,757	24,670
Congressional District 2	526,284	524,336	-1,948	202,558	76,063	12,663	47,532	22,494

Table A-5: 113th Congressional Districts—Summary Population Characteristics—*Continued*

	April 1, 2010 Census Population	2010–2012 ACS Population	Population Change	2010–2012 ACS				
				Total Households	Population 65 and Over	Population 85 and Over	Householders 65 and Over	Persons 65 and Over Living Alone
South Carolina								
Congressional District 1	660,766	680,440	19,674	263,375	98,295	10,409	60,335	22,880
Congressional District 2	660,766	669,171	8,405	255,964	86,215	9,692	53,496	21,806
Congressional District 3	660,767	665,379	4,612	250,390	103,371	12,030	64,787	27,271
Congressional District 4	660,766	665,915	5,149	253,434	90,379	10,490	56,127	23,764
Congressional District 5	660,766	668,079	7,313	251,829	91,728	9,355	58,130	23,025
Congressional District 6	660,766	661,355	589	238,978	84,860	9,700	54,028	24,015
Congressional District 7	660,767	667,297	6,530	260,158	107,661	10,475	69,540	29,627
South Dakota								
Congressional District (at Large), South Dakota	814,180	824,391	10,211	322,005	119,198	19,915	74,354	34,669
Tennessee								
Congressional District 1	705,123	708,015	2,892	291,506	122,602	13,072	78,559	32,962
Congressional District 2	705,123	711,143	6,020	289,157	107,335	11,713	67,244	30,019
Congressional District 3	705,122	710,362	5,240	279,700	114,531	14,558	71,872	30,858
Congressional District 4	705,123	714,751	9,628	266,485	92,771	10,037	57,673	22,990
Congressional District 5	705,123	715,416	10,293	283,831	77,457	10,451	48,840	22,619
Congressional District 6	705,123	713,695	8,572	271,465	109,705	11,560	67,865	26,365
Congressional District 7	705,123	713,895	8,772	262,860	91,180	10,444	56,764	24,145
Congressional District 8	705,122	703,555	-1,567	257,277	101,575	11,841	61,894	24,913
Congressional District 9	705,123	713,408	8,285	264,378	68,860	8,501	44,473	21,611
Texas								
Congressional District 1	698,488	703,224	4,736	256,209	102,140	13,987	63,924	27,960
Congressional District 2	698,488	723,080	24,592	256,807	63,387	6,548	35,897	13,332
Congressional District 3	698,488	724,712	26,224	258,886	60,135	5,431	33,448	12,129
Congressional District 4	698,488	704,633	6,145	256,954	105,905	12,619	64,787	26,577
Congressional District 5	698,488	711,441	12,953	244,727	86,856	10,546	53,103	22,614
Congressional District 6	698,498	714,545	16,047	251,375	67,250	7,649	40,426	16,166
Congressional District 7	698,488	714,849	16,361	273,576	65,396	9,279	40,123	18,840
Congressional District 8	698,488	723,640	25,152	243,572	83,388	8,866	49,965	18,775
Congressional District 9	698,488	704,014	5,526	235,117	56,277	5,710	31,161	13,195
Congressional District 10	698,487	708,312	9,825	254,746	74,339	9,931	43,255	17,937
Congressional District 11	698,488	706,946	8,458	258,857	105,354	12,153	65,403	28,627
Congressional District 12	698,488	719,711	21,223	267,250	78,330	10,066	48,788	20,819
Congressional District 13	698,488	699,483	995	256,674	96,369	12,089	60,794	26,310
Congressional District 14	698,472	703,773	5,301	253,575	84,102	10,236	52,832	23,009
Congressional District 15	698,488	714,244	15,756	206,932	70,806	7,726	40,468	14,524
Congressional District 16	698,488	711,491	13,003	229,297	77,803	9,581	45,848	17,253
Congressional District 17	698,487	708,910	10,423	257,812	76,778	9,977	46,729	20,228
Congressional District 18	698,488	713,599	15,111	240,694	59,824	6,419	36,168	15,308
Congressional District 19	698,487	704,522	6,035	250,292	90,031	11,482	56,285	24,534
Congressional District 20	698,488	710,016	11,528	238,891	71,347	9,277	43,172	16,846
Congressional District 21	698,488	716,736	18,248	294,788	97,884	13,841	60,200	24,730
Congressional District 22	698,504	727,399	28,895	235,625	60,816	6,644	32,218	10,899
Congressional District 23	698,488	711,152	12,664	220,346	77,355	8,494	45,265	15,963
Congressional District 24	698,488	718,266	19,778	286,423	63,840	7,720	38,054	16,255
Congressional District 25	698,478	718,277	19,799	250,742	84,759	8,601	50,768	18,356
Congressional District 26	698,488	724,499	26,011	246,220	54,122	4,823	30,049	11,234
Congressional District 27	698,487	704,288	5,801	252,052	96,292	11,707	58,692	23,658
Congressional District 28	698,488	717,279	18,791	208,263	70,871	8,074	38,665	12,863
Congressional District 29	698,488	711,135	12,647	204,081	49,961	5,270	28,978	11,480
Congressional District 30	698,487	701,889	3,402	238,321	61,775	6,835	38,028	16,486
Congressional District 31	698,487	721,902	23,415	247,652	69,024	7,569	39,647	15,161
Congressional District 32	698,488	712,074	13,586	269,970	74,688	10,696	44,912	18,186
Congressional District 33	698,488	704,441	5,953	211,469	53,174	5,308	32,269	13,906
Congressional District 34	698,487	705,853	7,366	206,712	85,222	9,861	48,254	16,801
Congressional District 35	698,488	719,739	21,251	238,662	60,611	7,641	37,093	16,739
Congressional District 36	698,488	704,476	5,988	248,872	86,309	9,161	53,321	20,437
Utah								
Congressional District 1	690,971	700,776	9,805	224,978	62,491	6,812	39,016	14,028
Congressional District 2	690,971	697,881	6,910	233,938	79,681	10,522	49,485	18,948
Congressional District 3	690,972	703,988	13,016	206,980	61,532	6,832	36,967	12,246
Congressional District 4	690,971	712,265	21,294	220,136	56,935	7,275	34,924	13,927
Vermont								
Congressional District (at Large)	625,741	626,172	431	257,887	94,567	12,631	60,018	27,109
Virginia								
Congressional District 1	727,366	739,813	12,447	259,594	93,300	10,301	56,291	20,516
Congressional District 2	708,087	723,222	15,135	271,490	85,639	10,498	54,078	22,902
Congressional District 3	746,645	740,966	-5,679	279,072	81,173	11,251	53,307	26,183
Congressional District 4	727,366	733,469	6,103	256,363	88,230	10,109	53,177	20,487
Congressional District 5	727,365	726,253	-1,112	282,162	122,713	14,846	77,295	32,790
Congressional District 6	727,366	732,960	5,594	286,165	115,830	16,068	74,617	33,433
Congressional District 7	727,366	736,332	8,966	274,611	96,737	13,478	59,890	24,293
Congressional District 8	727,366	745,750	18,384	297,774	71,280	10,058	44,714	21,186
Congressional District 9	727,366	724,797	-2,569	290,646	123,793	15,735	80,517	35,542
Congressional District 10	727,365	747,077	19,712	247,126	68,407	6,750	38,090	13,159
Congressional District 11	727,366	754,481	27,115	262,687	71,813	8,110	39,173	14,236

Table A-5: 113th Congressional Districts—Summary Population Characteristics—*Continued*

	April 1, 2010 Census Population	2010–2012 ACS Population	Population Change	2010–2012 ACS				
				Total Households	Population 65 and Over	Population 85 and Over	Householders 65 and Over	Persons 65 and Over Living Alone
Washington								
Congressional District 1	672,444	681,235	8,791	253,640	74,820	9,380	45,144	18,069
Congressional District 2	672,454	682,158	9,704	267,843	89,548	12,954	56,310	24,510
Congressional District 3	672,448	680,576	8,128	256,385	95,521	12,295	60,556	25,007
Congressional District 4	672,456	686,253	13,797	230,498	80,656	10,928	49,062	20,460
Congressional District 5	672,455	676,453	3,998	267,660	96,015	13,385	61,573	28,065
Congressional District 6	672,448	678,817	6,369	270,947	110,213	14,251	68,148	28,677
Congressional District 7	672,457	684,671	12,214	311,279	84,802	14,108	56,152	29,809
Congressional District 8	672,463	677,270	4,807	245,780	71,324	9,014	43,636	17,185
Congressional District 9	672,460	689,251	16,791	262,881	81,270	13,577	49,636	23,631
Congressional District 10	672,455	684,619	12,164	257,776	82,879	10,417	51,551	22,441
West Virginia								
Congressional District 1	615,991	617,339	1,348	245,019	100,993	13,399	66,039	31,627
Congressional District 2	620,862	622,819	1,957	250,725	98,893	11,750	63,481	28,325
Congressional District 3	616,141	614,617	-1,524	245,917	103,424	12,295	67,431	29,940
Wisconsin								
Congressional District 1	710,874	711,976	1,102	272,474	93,940	12,784	59,452	26,686
Congressional District 2	710,874	721,065	10,191	295,118	86,057	12,616	55,307	24,987
Congressional District 3	710,873	711,306	433	282,936	105,860	15,396	67,859	31,519
Congressional District 4	710,873	714,049	3,176	279,002	72,913	10,881	48,766	26,869
Congressional District 5	710,873	713,022	2,149	286,952	106,286	17,907	68,769	33,566
Congressional District 6	710,873	709,754	-1,119	285,007	110,401	18,061	69,461	31,792
Congressional District 7	710,873	712,359	1,486	295,367	121,384	16,775	76,850	33,338
Congressional District 8	710,873	715,081	4,208	285,598	101,546	15,066	64,101	28,715
Wyoming								
Congressional District (at Large)	563,626	569,380	5,754	222,558	72,274	8,656	45,398	20,129

PART B

AGE STRUCTURE

AGE STRUCTURE

Based on the 2010–2012 American Community Survey, 13.4 percent of the national population is age 65 years old or over while 1.8 percent was age 85 and over. This is only a slight change from the 2010 Census results where the 65 and over population was 13.0 percent and the 85 and over percent was unchanged. Though a small change in the 65 and over population, it indicates the coming growth in this segment as the oldest of the Baby Boom generation (age 68 in 2014) has passed this threshold and the numbers will continue to grow quickly.

There are 41.7 million people in the United States over the age of 65 and 5.7 million of them are over the age of 85. The proportion of the population that is over 65 is higher than the national average in thirty-one states while 26 states have a higher proportion of the 85 and over population. As one might expect, Florida leads the nation with the largest proportion of population over 65 but states with older populations aren't all retirement destinations. Among the states with the highest percentage of population 65 and over, most are a result of the existing age structure rather than retirement being a retirement destination as is the case in West Virginia and Pennsylvania. Those states with the lowest proportion of population 65 and over typically reflect high in-migration states attracting a younger population as with Maryland, Virginia, and Nevada.

65 Years and Over – Top 10		65 Years and Over – Bottom 10	
Florida	17.3%	Maryland	12.3%
West Virginia	16.0%	Virginia	12.2%
Maine	15.9%	Nevada	12.0%
Pennsylvania	15.4%	District of Columbia	11.4%
Iowa	14.9%	California	11.4%
Montana	14.8%	Colorado	10.9%
Vermont	14.6%	Georgia	10.7%
North Dakota	14.5%	Texas	10.3%
Rhode Island	14.4%	Utah	9.0%
Arkansas	14.4%	Alaska	7.7%

Only six of the states in the 65 and over top 10 are also among the 85 and over top 10. Connecticut, South Dakota, Hawaii and Massachusetts join the list. Similarly, only five of the bottom 10 states in the 65 and over bottom 10 are also in the 85 and over bottom 10.

85 Years and Over – Top 10		85 Years and Over – Bottom 10	
Rhode Island	2.5%	South Carolina	1.5%
North Dakota	2.5%	Wyoming	1.5%
Iowa	2.5%	Mississippi	1.5%
Pennsylvania	2.4%	Louisiana	1.4%
Connecticut	2.4%	Colorado	1.4%
South Dakota	2.4%	Texas	1.2%
Florida	2.3%	Georgia	1.2%
Hawaii	2.2%	Utah	1.1%
Massachusetts	2.2%	Nevada	1.1%
Maine	2.2%	Alaska	0.7%

Los Angeles County, California and Cook County, Illinois have the largest number of people age 65 and over but rank 627th and 537th, respectively, of the 814 counties in terms of the percent of their total population. Liberty County, Georgia has the smallest number of persons 65 and over at 4,061 but that's also the lowest percentage. The ten counties with the largest 65 and over population account for 10.9 percent of the nation's 41.6 million population or a total of 4.6 million people. The smallest ten counties have only 62,260 people over age 65 and represent only 0.15 percent of the total. More than 400 counties have a larger proportion of their population over the age of 65 and the national average of 13.4 percent.

While cities make up a third of the total population, they contain only 27.9 percent of the 65 and over population, indicating that a relatively larger proportion of the population live outside of the densest urban centers. More than 2.7 million (6.6 percent) people age 65 and over live in the top 10 cities. About the same proportion of the 85 and over population lives in the top 10 cities. Only 53,800 people 65 and over live in the bottom 10 cities and, like counties, account for only 0.13 percent of the total. New York City, Los Angeles and Chicago have the largest

Rank	Top 15 Areas - Percent 85 and Over								
	Counties		Cities		Metropolitan Areas		Congressional Districts	
1	Charlotte County , FL	5.0%	Boynton Beach city, FL	5.2%	Punta Gorda, FL	5.0%	Congressional District 21, FL	4.3%
2	Sarasota County , FL	5.0%	Largo city, FL	4.5%	Sebastian-Vero Beach, FL	4.7%	Congressional District 16, FL	4.2%
3	Indian River County , FL	4.7%	Hemet city, CA	4.3%	North Port-Bradenton-Sarasota, FL	4.2%	Congressional District 22, FL	3.7%
4	Martin County , FL	4.6%	Deerfield Beach city, FL	4.1%	Naples-Marco Island, FL	3.5%	Congressional District 13, FL	3.6%
5	Citrus County , FL	4.1%	Scranton city, PA	3.9%	Pittsfield, MA	3.4%	Congressional District 19, FL	3.5%
6	Highlands County , FL	4.0%	Southfield city, MI	3.8%	Prescott, AZ	3.3%	Congressional District 17, FL	3.5%
7	Palm Beach County , FL	3.9%	Pompano Beach city, FL	3.8%	Barnstable Town, MA	3.2%	Congressional District 18, FL	3.3%
8	Anderson County, TN	3.6%	Urban Honolulu CDP, HI	3.6%	Port St. Lucie, FL	3.2%	Congressional District 11, FL	3.3%
9	Pinellas County , FL	3.6%	Parma city, OH	3.5%	Johnstown, PA	3.2%	Congressional District 4, IA	3.1%
10	Josephine County, OR	3.5%	Clearwater city, FL	3.4%	Utica-Rome, NY	3.1%	Congressional District 12, FL	3.1%
11	Moore County, NC	3.5%	Camarillo city, CA	3.4%	Cape Coral-Fort Myers, FL	3.1%	Congressional District 12, PA	3.1%
12	Sumter County , FL	3.5%	Palo Alto city, CA	3.4%	Hot Springs, AR	3.1%	Congressional District 3, NY	3.0%
13	Collier County , FL	3.5%	Lakeland city, FL	3.3%	Palm Coast, FL	3.0%	Congressional District 7, MN	3.0%
14	Clallam County, WA	3.5%	Asheville city, NC	3.1%	Scranton--Wilkes-Barre, PA	3.0%	Congressional District 14, PA	3.0%
15	Berkshire County, MA	3.4%	Santa Barbara city, CA	3.1%	Deltona-Daytona Beach-Ormond Beach, FL	3.0%	Congressional District 8, FL	2.9%
16	Lawrence County, PA	3.3%	Melbourne city, FL	3.1%	Youngstown-Warren-Boardman, OH-PA	2.9%	Congressional District 1, HI	2.8%
17	Yavapai County, AZ	3.3%	Cranston city, RI	3.1%	Williamsport, PA	2.9%	Congressional District 18, PA	2.8%
18	Ocean County, NJ	3.3%	Sunrise city, FL	3.1%	Pittsburgh, PA	2.9%	Congressional District 17, PA	2.8%
19	Lackawanna County, PA	3.3%	Bethlehem city, PA	3.1%	Altoona, PA	2.9%	Congressional District 3, NE	2.8%
20	Manitowoc County, WI	3.3%	Newton city, MA	3.1%	Ocean City, NJ	2.8%	Congressional District 7, PA	2.8%

populations over age 65 but all rank low in terms of their percent of total population. New York ranks 176th while Los Angeles and Chicago rank 307th and 321st, respectively. Perris City, California has the smallest population 65 and over at 3,126. Of the 505 cities reported here, 119 are above the national percentage of 65 and over.

Four out of every five people age 65 and over lives in a metropolitan area. The total is 33.2 million people or 80.0 percent of this 41.7 million population. A slightly higher proportion, 81.2 percent of the nation's 85 and over population lives in metropolitan areas at 4.6 million. As with the city populations, the New York, Los Angeles and Chicago metropolitan areas have the largest 65 and over populations. Just these three areas account for 12.3 percent of the national total or 5.1 million people. The Hinesville-Ft. Steward, Georgia metropolitan area has the lowest number of people 65 and over at 5,458 which is 6.8 percent of the metropolitan area total population.

Congressional District 11 in Florida has the largest number of persons 65 and over at 213,186. That district also has

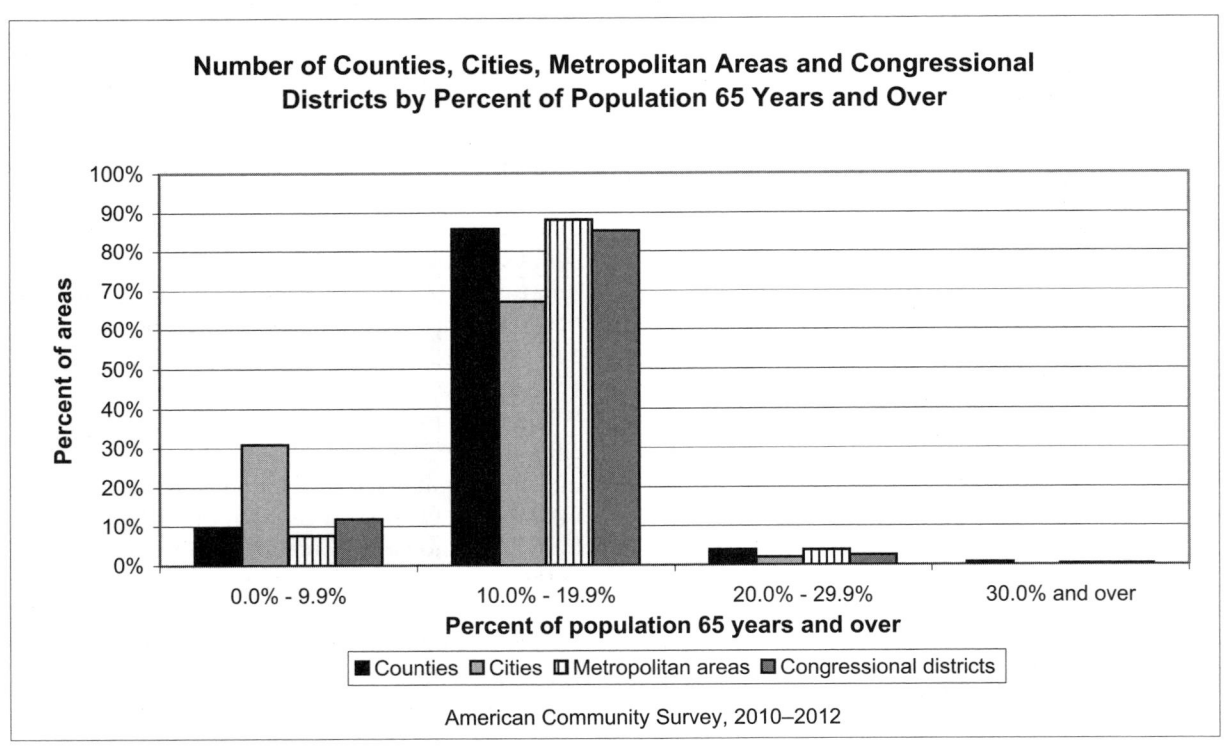

American Community Survey, 2010–2012

the largest proportion of its total population over the age of 65 at 30.5 percent. However, the district includes the City of Tampa and surrounding area which ranks 55th in total size of the 65 and over population and only 289th in its proportion of the total. More than 1.7 million persons 65 and over reside in the 10 congressional districts with the largest older population while just over half a million (526,335) reside in the 10 districts with the smallest population. Congressional district 7 in Arizona has the fewest residents age 65 and over at 46,900 and also the lowest percentage of the total population at 6.5 percent. This district includes the City of Phoenix and surrounding area.

Percent of the Population 65 Years and Over

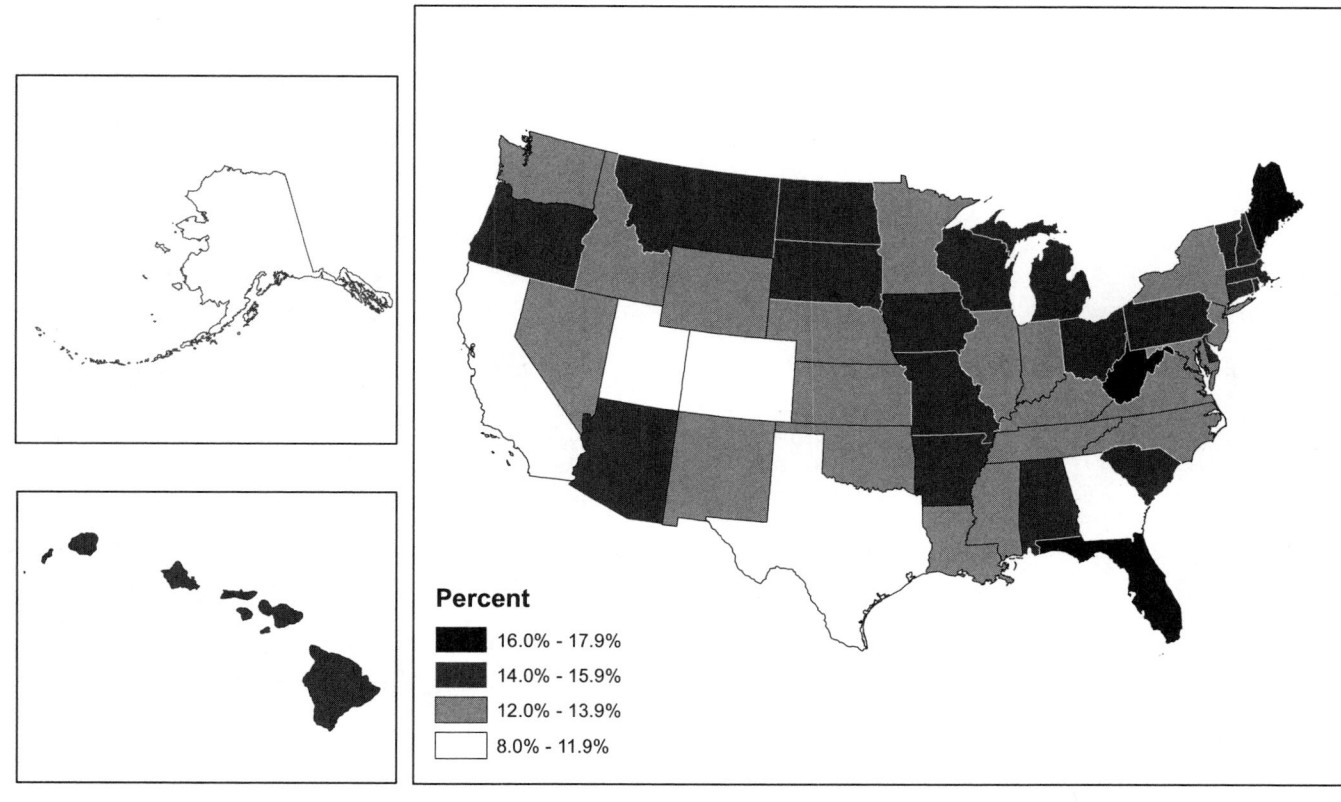

Percent

- 16.0% - 17.9%
- 14.0% - 15.9%
- 12.0% - 13.9%
- 8.0% - 11.9%

Table B-1: States—Older Population by Age

	Total Population	60 to 61 Years	62 to 64 Years	65 to 66 Years	67 to 69 Years	70 to 74 Years	75 to 79 Years	80 to 84 Years	85 Years and Over	65 Years and Over
United States............	311,609,369	7,385,820	10,250,313	5,657,807	7,425,790	9,689,050	7,390,053	5,798,490	5,691,169	41,652,359
Alabama...............	4,803,488	121,522	168,285	94,776	126,933	163,019	124,840	88,760	78,797	677,125
Alaska..................	723,120	17,319	21,417	10,747	11,384	15,489	9,350	6,707	4,909	58,586
Arizona.................	6,477,128	151,462	214,075	126,991	171,268	229,654	165,707	123,445	109,961	927,026
Arkansas...............	2,936,822	72,119	100,326	58,625	77,308	105,860	78,680	57,102	52,110	429,685
California..............	37,686,586	817,545	1,108,472	618,579	771,973	1,014,266	775,282	615,621	631,180	4,426,901
Colorado...............	5,117,453	120,851	162,897	87,324	110,832	134,931	99,949	74,628	73,651	581,315
Connecticut...........	3,584,561	86,270	125,908	68,703	90,152	108,822	88,998	75,026	87,038	518,739
Delaware...............	908,351	22,634	32,278	19,284	25,080	32,054	23,992	17,686	16,505	134,601
District of Columbia	618,777	13,526	18,298	9,704	12,641	15,898	12,570	9,260	10,229	70,302
Florida.................	19,081,930	477,288	693,410	422,615	582,742	799,989	619,502	491,618	465,033	3,381,499
Georgia................	9,815,725	212,316	308,768	166,579	212,381	265,474	188,793	133,335	116,840	1,083,402
Hawaii.................	1,378,239	38,690	48,811	27,780	34,661	43,718	34,481	28,794	33,761	203,195
Idaho..................	1,583,422	37,318	51,604	28,288	38,746	48,999	35,873	25,685	25,619	203,210
Illinois................	12,858,490	295,707	402,548	216,134	292,552	375,693	290,770	233,683	241,220	1,650,052
Indiana................	6,514,516	156,840	209,246	114,663	151,934	203,530	153,570	123,158	116,124	862,979
Iowa...................	3,062,869	78,601	103,777	55,922	72,435	103,018	83,959	69,565	75,126	460,025
Kansas................	2,871,709	65,538	91,782	49,150	64,496	84,278	68,446	57,605	60,202	384,177
Kentucky..............	4,364,627	106,411	153,702	84,121	110,143	144,133	106,896	77,125	71,802	594,220
Louisiana.............	4,573,595	105,026	150,157	82,264	103,009	140,306	103,806	76,982	69,178	575,545
Maine..................	1,328,440	38,940	55,871	29,670	38,162	50,912	39,263	31,220	29,104	218,331
Maryland..............	5,837,378	143,365	192,594	105,889	133,923	167,552	127,999	98,181	101,631	735,175
Massachusetts..........	6,605,468	161,985	224,984	120,204	158,344	202,917	161,228	137,376	149,859	929,928
Michigan..............	9,879,277	252,696	345,055	185,774	250,535	319,161	245,838	199,472	197,208	1,397,988
Minnesota.............	5,345,721	127,823	170,307	92,364	120,122	159,507	126,832	99,260	107,530	705,615
Mississippi............	2,977,179	69,402	99,244	53,511	72,451	96,539	70,779	52,367	45,154	390,801
Missouri...............	6,009,025	144,944	204,825	112,355	152,239	202,458	153,668	120,195	118,662	859,577
Montana...............	997,852	28,745	37,915	21,199	27,999	35,412	26,362	20,528	20,461	151,961
Nebraska..............	1,842,480	45,765	57,283	30,302	40,799	55,494	47,165	37,634	39,161	250,555
Nevada................	2,727,571	64,955	92,620	53,723	68,444	87,793	58,980	40,764	33,000	342,704
New Hampshire..........	1,318,455	35,387	50,620	26,146	33,754	43,002	32,258	26,004	24,276	185,440
New Jersey	8,834,249	211,503	285,542	164,018	206,619	268,832	212,822	179,784	184,354	1,216,429
New Mexico	2,076,325	54,034	72,514	39,271	54,980	67,950	50,152	37,661	33,525	283,539
New York..............	19,490,373	462,140	643,408	353,948	455,734	606,196	470,407	394,729	402,881	2,683,895
North Carolina.........	9,654,079	227,264	330,323	182,602	242,932	312,090	230,696	168,562	152,016	1,288,898
North Dakota..........	686,244	17,128	22,082	11,738	14,867	21,898	17,463	16,337	16,737	99,040
Ohio...................	11,541,175	292,236	408,031	211,738	287,325	383,172	297,330	241,590	236,944	1,658,099
Oklahoma..............	3,786,152	86,990	122,898	69,905	93,000	128,175	94,509	71,376	63,316	520,281
Oregon................	3,868,598	104,895	145,959	79,043	100,517	130,443	93,443	74,365	79,856	557,667
Pennsylvania...........	12,739,595	324,069	453,204	246,998	331,120	436,239	354,617	308,959	316,020	1,993,953
Rhode Island...........	1,051,236	27,360	34,824	19,570	24,582	33,110	26,595	23,701	26,958	154,516
South Carolina	4,677,636	118,449	171,005	96,938	130,467	164,613	116,773	81,567	72,151	662,509
South Dakota	824,391	20,088	27,183	14,573	18,494	26,711	21,196	18,309	19,915	119,198
Tennessee.............	6,404,240	162,114	224,719	124,791	168,656	216,588	160,209	113,595	102,177	886,016
Texas.................	25,644,550	524,245	726,817	396,947	513,004	645,173	487,735	357,844	321,817	2,722,520
Utah..................	2,814,910	47,596	66,193	35,310	47,914	62,722	47,397	35,855	31,441	260,639
Vermont...............	626,172	17,630	25,094	13,437	17,781	21,207	16,374	13,137	12,631	94,567
Virginia...............	8,105,120	196,734	270,493	142,515	193,580	246,465	178,574	130,577	127,204	1,018,915
Washington............	6,821,303	170,773	237,941	127,657	163,738	197,231	144,879	113,234	120,309	867,048
West Virginia...........	1,854,775	56,879	73,355	42,303	53,753	72,142	56,404	41,264	37,444	303,310
Wisconsin..............	5,708,612	138,312	192,660	100,630	136,161	180,549	143,753	117,808	119,486	798,387
Wyoming	569,380	14,391	18,989	10,489	13,124	17,666	12,889	9,450	8,656	72,274

Table B-2: Counties—Older Population by Age

	Total Population	60 to 61 Years	62 to 64 Years	65 to 66 Years	67 to 69 Years	70 to 74 Years	75 to 79 Years	80 to 84 Years	85 Years and Over	65 Years and Over
Alabama										
Baldwin County	186,965	5,079	7,929	4,592	6,913	7,477	5,485	4,406	3,187	32,060
Calhoun County	117,845	3,067	4,001	1,987	3,127	4,581	3,618	2,205	1,905	17,423
Cullman County	80,463	2,219	3,252	1,929	2,939	2,829	2,330	1,587	1,651	13,265
DeKalb County	71,217	1,727	2,851	1,355	1,675	2,787	1,639	1,666	876	9,998
Elmore County	80,107	1,476	2,713	1,607	2,145	2,268	1,732	995	1,047	9,794
Etowah County	104,381	3,100	3,928	1,915	3,138	4,302	2,814	2,185	2,400	16,754
Houston County	102,538	2,554	3,233	2,085	2,709	3,791	3,029	2,020	1,588	15,222
Jefferson County	659,122	16,398	21,535	11,361	14,742	19,525	15,773	13,358	12,702	87,461
Lauderdale County	92,638	3,053	3,300	2,150	2,779	3,785	3,291	1,808	2,004	15,817
Lee County	143,866	3,049	3,920	1,978	2,754	3,403	2,511	1,293	1,511	13,450
Limestone County	85,469	1,845	3,337	1,969	2,045	2,546	2,160	820	1,206	10,746
Madison County	339,640	8,152	10,756	5,212	8,463	10,345	8,167	5,196	5,038	42,421
Marshall County	94,021	2,438	2,958	1,937	2,700	3,548	2,834	1,659	1,558	14,236
Mobile County	413,432	10,158	14,315	8,155	10,823	12,512	10,458	6,745	6,289	54,982
Montgomery County	230,604	6,210	6,568	4,605	4,899	5,697	5,407	4,046	3,495	28,149
Morgan County	120,001	3,149	4,447	2,741	2,954	4,270	3,279	2,217	1,904	17,365
St. Clair County	84,473	2,271	3,064	1,935	2,467	2,595	1,881	1,419	1,042	11,339
Shelby County	198,314	4,248	6,456	3,048	4,821	5,563	3,875	2,763	2,264	22,334
Talladega County	81,853	2,253	3,026	1,706	2,032	3,268	2,266	1,425	1,259	11,956
Tuscaloosa County	196,794	4,260	5,470	3,126	3,512	5,191	3,966	3,143	2,675	21,613
Walker County	66,632	1,829	3,531	1,583	2,034	2,940	2,171	1,387	1,022	11,137
Alaska										
Fairbanks North Star Borough	99,275	2,542	2,349	1,131	1,421	1,803	996	574	741	6,666
Matanuska-Susitna Borough	91,877	2,211	2,678	1,426	1,499	2,143	1,226	835	523	7,652
Arizona										
Apache County	72,399	1,791	2,132	1,216	1,783	2,541	1,494	1,001	814	8,849
Cochise County	132,162	4,022	5,136	3,349	4,477	6,130	4,037	2,860	2,657	23,510
Coconino County	134,909	2,777	3,776	2,227	2,884	2,878	2,033	1,266	1,382	12,670
Maricopa County	3,878,086	81,725	114,726	66,083	90,424	115,644	88,400	67,283	59,373	487,207
Mohave County	202,102	6,269	10,623	6,417	8,859	13,995	8,220	6,393	4,700	48,584
Navajo County	107,292	2,959	3,151	2,385	2,663	4,318	2,799	1,555	1,357	15,077
Pima County	987,294	26,269	35,502	22,507	26,911	36,757	27,626	22,571	21,477	157,849
Pinal County	385,577	9,288	14,992	8,470	12,073	15,624	9,555	5,647	5,130	56,499
Yavapai County	211,339	8,198	11,577	6,584	10,262	13,917	9,047	6,493	7,010	53,313
Yuma County	199,061	3,698	5,856	3,735	4,752	9,228	7,211	4,190	2,635	31,751
Arkansas										
Benton County	227,570	4,975	6,946	3,733	4,920	6,498	4,818	3,598	4,028	27,595
Craighead County	98,249	2,446	3,069	1,375	2,319	2,897	2,204	1,528	1,508	11,831
Faulkner County	116,454	1,938	3,164	1,729	2,464	2,557	1,892	1,725	1,457	11,824
Garland County	96,590	2,518	4,516	2,248	3,507	5,099	4,053	2,252	2,966	20,125
Jefferson County	76,023	2,075	2,796	1,446	2,049	2,345	1,626	1,487	1,481	10,434
Lonoke County	69,267	1,688	1,765	1,126	1,423	2,199	1,377	1,103	662	7,890
Pulaski County	386,435	9,192	12,314	6,809	8,053	11,160	8,508	6,945	5,909	47,384
Saline County	109,842	2,822	3,552	2,459	3,320	4,684	3,400	1,765	1,550	17,178
Sebastian County	126,700	2,978	4,074	2,156	3,211	3,819	3,064	2,365	1,985	16,600
Washington County	207,763	3,573	5,411	2,921	3,204	5,372	3,930	2,216	2,837	20,480
White County	77,967	1,564	2,334	1,910	2,233	2,255	2,206	1,348	1,293	11,245
California										
Alameda County	1,533,311	36,704	47,365	26,195	29,885	40,394	29,144	23,684	26,503	175,805
Butte County	220,565	5,768	9,264	5,056	5,277	7,473	5,694	5,558	5,476	34,534
Contra Costa County	1,066,333	26,045	36,904	19,982	24,174	31,837	23,287	18,222	19,898	137,400
El Dorado County	180,866	6,181	7,866	4,464	5,605	6,355	4,374	3,395	3,653	27,846
Fresno County	940,493	17,803	25,033	13,950	16,567	21,685	16,630	13,685	14,407	96,924
Humboldt County	135,061	3,996	4,833	2,760	3,240	4,222	2,845	2,629	2,606	18,302
Imperial County	175,837	2,672	4,137	2,636	3,094	4,336	3,551	2,744	2,533	18,894
Kern County	849,101	15,590	21,220	11,138	15,055	19,172	14,402	9,770	8,418	77,955
Kings County	151,869	2,346	3,257	2,034	2,358	2,598	2,120	1,766	1,452	12,328
Lake County	64,331	1,799	3,788	1,973	2,044	2,692	1,793	1,438	1,699	11,639
Los Angeles County	9,892,525	204,882	269,556	151,711	191,454	253,021	196,469	155,154	158,945	1,106,754
Madera County	151,827	2,921	4,750	2,908	3,220	4,263	3,474	2,165	1,882	17,912
Marin County	254,844	8,165	11,657	5,877	8,886	10,243	7,376	6,087	6,098	44,567
Mendocino County	87,564	2,791	4,197	2,371	2,886	2,946	2,135	2,055	1,884	14,277
Merced County	259,716	4,628	6,130	3,653	4,650	5,883	4,300	3,619	3,093	25,198
Monterey County	421,570	8,642	12,872	6,298	7,496	10,435	8,355	6,404	7,052	46,040
Napa County	137,949	3,661	4,907	3,491	2,854	4,869	3,511	3,169	3,557	21,451
Nevada County	98,605	3,644	5,567	2,896	3,265	5,227	3,001	2,831	2,848	20,068
Orange County	3,054,809	63,988	89,553	51,067	62,404	85,071	62,524	51,020	53,885	365,971
Placer County	356,331	8,739	13,608	7,287	10,472	13,334	10,589	7,654	7,475	56,811
Riverside County	2,236,158	42,501	60,763	35,550	48,472	64,238	51,216	37,981	32,821	270,278
Sacramento County	1,436,233	31,566	42,463	22,828	27,693	37,980	28,863	23,419	24,979	165,762
San Bernardino County	2,062,483	41,467	51,383	28,342	37,063	44,665	32,877	25,644	21,798	190,389
San Diego County	3,139,726	66,640	89,620	49,644	60,975	81,304	63,554	52,642	57,661	365,780
San Francisco County	815,234	20,796	28,758	13,849	17,150	25,317	21,432	16,823	18,043	112,614
San Joaquin County	695,251	13,077	18,342	10,578	12,658	17,480	12,907	10,385	10,314	74,322
San Luis Obispo County	272,034	7,290	10,670	5,746	7,097	9,668	7,533	5,971	6,712	42,727
San Mateo County	729,489	17,929	24,773	13,584	17,663	21,598	17,293	13,542	16,385	100,065
Santa Barbara County	427,251	8,387	12,444	7,656	8,674	11,713	10,392	7,592	10,019	56,046
Santa Clara County	1,811,955	37,768	49,775	28,132	36,173	47,792	35,469	29,958	28,231	205,755

Table B-2: Counties—Older Population by Age—*Continued*

	Total Population	60 to 61 Years	62 to 64 Years	65 to 66 Years	67 to 69 Years	70 to 74 Years	75 to 79 Years	80 to 84 Years	85 Years and Over	65 Years and Over
California—Cont.										
Santa Cruz County	265,057	8,255	8,557	4,985	5,840	6,483	4,561	4,024	4,892	30,785
Shasta County	177,980	4,971	7,629	4,413	5,819	7,291	5,033	4,464	4,189	31,209
Solano County	417,261	10,801	14,531	7,362	8,951	11,561	9,456	6,088	5,922	49,340
Sonoma County	488,237	14,635	19,789	10,403	12,274	15,927	11,210	9,796	11,383	70,993
Stanislaus County	518,336	10,313	14,086	7,977	10,133	13,091	9,373	7,847	8,517	56,938
Sutter County	94,951	2,209	3,049	1,317	2,262	3,379	2,494	1,646	1,366	12,464
Tulare County	447,704	8,172	10,655	6,585	7,731	9,636	7,390	6,125	5,689	43,156
Ventura County	830,828	19,256	25,269	15,045	18,484	21,117	18,158	13,587	14,468	100,859
Yolo County	202,473	3,877	5,512	2,683	4,338	4,222	3,567	2,676	3,215	20,701
Yuba County	72,613	1,773	2,236	1,365	1,150	1,647	1,184	1,310	753	7,409
Colorado										
Adams County	451,455	7,582	10,662	5,679	8,212	9,061	7,254	4,503	4,447	39,156
Arapahoe County	585,388	13,959	17,850	9,906	11,619	13,737	10,466	7,806	8,355	61,889
Boulder County	300,681	7,226	8,417	5,732	5,875	6,652	5,453	3,558	4,426	31,696
Denver County	619,016	13,338	16,813	9,035	11,176	14,020	10,374	9,194	10,683	64,482
Douglas County	292,509	5,177	8,311	4,001	4,904	6,032	4,217	2,158	1,609	22,921
El Paso County	636,034	13,013	20,138	9,955	12,566	15,226	12,084	8,043	7,486	65,360
Jefferson County	539,836	17,178	18,671	10,602	13,061	16,275	12,013	9,760	8,937	70,648
Larimer County	305,335	7,598	10,291	5,479	6,787	9,034	6,192	5,101	5,129	37,722
Mesa County	147,268	3,341	5,412	2,819	3,987	5,338	3,843	3,376	3,281	22,644
Pueblo County	160,256	4,099	6,115	2,934	4,379	5,783	4,694	4,086	3,150	25,026
Weld County	258,708	5,166	7,370	3,620	4,876	6,810	4,188	3,555	2,876	25,925
Connecticut										
Fairfield County	926,739	21,005	30,342	16,922	22,131	26,270	21,778	19,865	20,420	127,386
Hartford County	895,987	21,071	30,912	17,565	22,220	26,696	22,845	19,848	23,298	132,472
Litchfield County	188,731	5,890	7,008	4,474	5,444	6,823	5,613	3,997	4,865	31,216
Middlesex County	165,876	4,297	7,576	3,363	5,253	5,639	4,471	3,489	4,337	26,552
New Haven County	862,776	20,553	30,248	16,522	21,002	26,234	21,927	16,975	23,684	126,344
New London County	274,118	7,034	10,277	5,508	7,579	8,767	6,417	6,542	5,336	40,149
Tolland County	152,257	3,545	5,304	2,219	3,804	4,708	3,250	2,320	2,649	18,950
Windham County	118,077	2,875	4,241	2,130	2,719	3,685	2,697	1,990	2,449	15,670
Delaware										
Kent County	165,306	3,443	5,951	3,484	4,274	5,585	4,373	2,878	2,511	23,105
New Castle County	542,490	12,242	16,774	9,720	12,401	15,091	12,357	9,363	9,319	68,251
Sussex County	200,555	6,949	9,553	6,080	8,405	11,378	7,262	5,445	4,675	43,245
Florida										
Alachua County	249,440	5,798	7,385	3,578	4,922	6,602	4,785	3,925	3,615	27,427
Bay County	170,351	4,383	5,538	3,425	4,182	6,794	4,923	3,540	2,599	25,463
Brevard County	545,202	14,979	21,473	13,896	19,025	26,860	21,841	18,447	14,013	114,082
Broward County	1,784,340	40,795	59,050	32,790	43,829	55,475	41,790	41,423	42,348	257,655
Charlotte County	160,602	5,089	9,856	6,431	9,104	14,721	11,094	7,268	8,101	56,719
Citrus County	140,174	5,290	7,924	4,380	8,778	11,667	9,045	6,222	5,692	45,784
Clay County	192,689	4,691	6,977	3,525	5,572	5,436	3,759	2,919	2,549	23,760
Collier County	327,537	9,661	14,412	10,105	15,984	22,326	16,939	12,853	11,345	89,552
Columbia County	67,666	2,088	2,423	1,581	2,238	2,466	1,998	1,402	1,010	10,695
Duval County	872,307	19,636	28,393	14,784	19,346	22,109	17,416	13,173	13,410	100,238
Escambia County	300,150	6,902	11,247	6,054	7,888	10,631	8,303	5,622	5,761	44,259
Flagler County	97,229	3,598	4,583	3,110	4,661	6,965	4,393	2,924	2,962	25,015
Hernando County	173,178	4,664	8,268	5,163	7,644	11,107	9,000	6,973	5,567	45,454
Highlands County	98,382	2,762	4,043	3,236	5,552	7,620	6,962	4,637	3,959	31,966
Hillsborough County	1,260,333	27,523	38,585	21,100	27,717	34,358	28,614	19,946	20,045	151,780
Indian River County	139,241	4,284	5,488	3,580	6,335	9,170	7,743	5,782	6,497	39,107
Lake County	300,270	9,277	12,065	9,186	12,763	18,552	14,882	10,108	8,557	74,048
Lee County	632,499	18,174	28,385	18,874	28,527	38,791	27,225	20,353	19,743	153,513
Leon County	279,378	6,172	7,956	4,442	5,443	5,813	4,026	3,978	3,800	27,502
Manatee County	328,231	9,398	13,627	9,555	12,875	18,790	15,061	11,546	10,640	78,467
Marion County	333,001	10,234	16,043	9,946	15,239	23,254	16,909	12,758	9,397	87,503
Martin County	147,536	4,063	6,808	4,392	6,335	9,442	7,846	6,128	6,808	40,951
Miami-Dade County	2,553,696	56,241	77,582	42,757	59,620	91,011	67,487	54,666	49,847	365,388
Monroe County	74,007	3,223	3,587	1,659	2,752	3,799	2,363	1,370	1,315	13,258
Nassau County	74,096	1,537	3,717	2,141	2,240	3,563	1,834	1,756	1,221	12,755
Okaloosa County	184,699	4,261	5,895	3,671	4,406	6,435	5,430	3,283	2,704	25,929
Orange County	1,174,032	22,643	31,156	18,274	20,205	27,029	20,484	16,124	14,205	116,321
Osceola County	278,254	6,692	8,239	4,979	7,034	7,112	5,396	4,266	3,236	32,023
Palm Beach County	1,339,372	32,466	47,317	31,634	43,287	60,438	55,145	49,442	52,039	291,985
Pasco County	467,486	12,264	20,684	11,422	17,042	24,403	18,415	13,715	13,989	98,986
Pinellas County	918,385	27,832	39,902	24,785	31,268	42,555	36,196	30,820	32,685	198,309
Polk County	609,775	15,652	22,431	14,920	20,068	27,837	20,841	14,677	13,506	111,849
Putnam County	73,858	2,181	3,087	1,712	2,749	3,739	2,647	2,064	1,504	14,415
St. Johns County	196,491	5,691	7,581	4,964	6,152	7,215	4,933	4,701	3,977	31,942
St. Lucie County	281,245	7,227	9,940	6,908	10,851	13,248	10,933	9,158	7,019	58,117
Santa Rosa County	155,782	3,823	5,155	3,349	3,847	5,426	3,425	2,525	1,754	20,326
Sarasota County	382,652	11,122	18,982	14,034	18,838	27,713	22,592	19,370	19,078	121,625
Seminole County	426,864	10,740	14,095	7,985	9,728	12,206	9,161	6,762	8,092	53,934
Sumter County	98,042	3,357	8,449	6,282	10,083	13,149	8,309	4,190	3,431	45,444
Volusia County	495,284	14,042	20,277	12,507	17,643	25,775	19,714	16,651	14,807	107,097

Table B-2: Counties—Older Population by Age—*Continued*

	Total Population	60 to 61 Years	62 to 64 Years	65 to 66 Years	67 to 69 Years	70 to 74 Years	75 to 79 Years	80 to 84 Years	85 Years and Over	65 Years and Over
Georgia										
Barrow County	69,923	1,685	1,824	1,198	1,465	1,389	1,309	864	491	6,716
Bartow County	100,380	2,132	2,829	2,019	2,707	2,176	1,923	1,635	754	11,214
Bibb County	156,088	3,447	5,059	3,113	3,315	4,389	3,560	3,126	2,544	20,047
Bulloch County	72,037	1,225	1,507	804	1,096	1,942	1,239	819	638	6,538
Carroll County	111,024	1,817	3,387	1,884	2,359	3,441	2,546	1,227	1,039	12,496
Catoosa County	64,661	1,419	2,752	1,465	1,899	2,118	1,579	1,243	962	9,266
Chatham County	271,443	5,644	9,385	4,748	6,346	7,871	6,132	4,412	4,678	34,187
Cherokee County	218,189	4,536	6,876	3,331	5,471	5,026	3,247	2,298	1,864	21,237
Clarke County	118,734	1,925	2,645	1,528	1,973	2,378	2,154	1,220	1,229	10,482
Clayton County	262,721	5,390	6,628	3,436	3,872	4,521	3,093	1,887	1,750	18,559
Cobb County	698,168	14,582	21,550	11,197	12,896	15,039	11,020	7,775	6,440	64,367
Columbia County	128,257	3,072	4,198	1,999	2,843	3,402	2,322	1,887	1,070	13,523
Coweta County	129,426	3,201	4,702	2,409	2,758	3,536	2,261	1,464	1,452	13,880
DeKalb County	699,017	14,985	20,062	10,426	12,243	14,937	10,391	9,062	7,681	64,740
Dougherty County	94,634	2,103	3,051	1,344	2,256	2,826	2,213	1,562	1,533	11,734
Douglas County	133,274	2,827	4,136	2,050	2,492	3,332	1,960	1,384	849	12,067
Fayette County	107,314	2,392	4,359	2,471	2,908	3,464	2,340	1,746	1,664	14,593
Floyd County	96,238	2,546	3,216	1,383	2,417	3,772	2,986	1,595	1,741	13,894
Forsyth County	182,395	3,859	4,658	2,623	3,713	4,878	3,153	1,734	1,862	17,963
Fulton County	951,157	18,874	27,840	13,393	16,971	20,753	13,970	10,610	12,956	88,653
Glynn County	80,394	2,272	3,827	2,007	2,221	3,070	2,236	1,559	1,471	12,564
Gwinnett County	825,375	15,476	20,729	10,292	11,774	15,561	11,046	6,013	5,638	60,324
Hall County	182,791	3,241	6,171	3,272	4,129	5,334	3,767	2,850	2,307	21,659
Henry County	207,215	3,531	4,977	3,318	3,512	4,726	3,221	1,847	1,550	18,174
Houston County	143,718	2,639	3,976	1,992	2,918	3,836	2,804	1,986	1,539	15,075
Liberty County	64,540	784	1,283	745	1,114	900	600	260	442	4,061
Lowndes County	112,050	2,352	2,898	1,598	2,136	2,731	1,987	1,293	1,249	10,994
Muscogee County	194,276	4,271	5,437	2,827	3,635	5,265	3,781	3,793	2,991	22,292
Newton County	100,833	1,745	2,644	1,233	2,757	2,486	1,516	1,120	1,352	10,464
Paulding County	143,802	2,476	3,399	2,151	1,977	3,195	1,957	1,118	796	11,194
Richmond County	201,592	4,475	5,756	3,234	4,345	5,724	4,389	3,256	2,539	23,487
Rockdale County	85,619	1,970	2,900	1,504	2,246	2,128	1,631	1,210	847	9,566
Troup County	67,816	1,530	2,162	1,380	1,707	1,748	1,479	1,005	1,302	8,621
Walker County	68,533	1,707	2,408	1,750	2,191	2,157	1,988	1,204	1,206	10,496
Walton County	84,299	2,039	2,510	1,373	2,549	2,424	1,854	1,261	1,050	10,511
Whitfield County	103,068	1,778	2,871	1,689	2,172	2,710	2,433	1,345	1,373	11,722
Hawaii										
Hawaii County	187,286	6,661	8,005	4,442	4,704	7,114	3,985	3,972	4,449	28,666
Honolulu County	966,405	25,130	31,819	19,397	23,915	28,821	25,876	20,994	24,044	143,047
Kauai County	67,815	2,007	3,000	1,277	1,878	2,556	1,499	1,417	1,869	10,496
Maui County	156,670	4,892	5,982	2,657	4,164	5,219	3,116	2,411	3,398	20,965
Idaho										
Ada County	401,204	9,306	12,781	6,818	8,040	9,946	7,317	5,392	6,271	43,784
Bannock County	83,439	1,635	2,366	1,094	1,693	2,455	1,731	1,498	984	9,455
Bonneville County	105,686	2,204	3,404	1,646	2,011	2,672	2,115	1,404	1,858	11,706
Canyon County	191,542	3,449	5,360	3,126	4,215	5,233	3,547	3,023	2,513	21,657
Kootenai County	140,793	4,020	5,572	3,054	3,999	5,151	3,801	2,687	2,369	21,061
Twin Falls County	78,066	1,885	2,564	1,038	2,279	2,581	1,966	1,392	1,806	11,062
Illinois										
Adams County	67,169	1,749	2,329	1,518	1,879	2,371	2,259	1,695	2,170	11,892
Champaign County	202,373	4,431	4,990	2,664	3,511	4,800	3,595	3,274	2,943	20,787
Cook County	5,214,942	113,523	154,619	81,931	111,109	143,142	111,187	90,946	95,088	633,403
DeKalb County	104,785	1,876	2,816	1,388	1,959	2,266	1,881	1,427	1,596	10,517
DuPage County	923,503	24,223	29,430	17,282	20,223	23,975	18,236	14,222	17,224	111,162
Kane County	519,581	10,930	15,698	8,201	9,796	12,395	9,809	6,400	6,427	53,028
Kankakee County	113,361	2,372	4,065	1,828	2,961	3,299	2,731	2,272	2,270	15,361
Kendall County	116,693	2,242	2,876	1,324	2,025	1,907	1,314	1,185	897	8,652
Lake County	702,666	15,831	21,870	10,779	14,476	17,403	12,411	10,499	10,510	76,078
LaSalle County	113,423	2,729	3,868	1,951	3,089	4,305	3,604	3,020	2,882	18,851
McHenry County	308,501	6,592	9,760	5,117	6,885	7,762	5,285	3,887	3,728	32,664
McLean County	170,964	3,735	4,755	2,416	3,274	3,889	2,948	2,667	2,724	17,918
Macon County	110,491	3,328	4,092	2,455	3,356	3,579	3,220	2,873	2,852	18,335
Madison County	268,573	6,658	7,765	4,520	6,776	9,411	6,847	6,135	5,686	39,375
Peoria County	186,755	4,819	5,762	3,147	4,679	6,007	5,199	3,277	4,024	26,333
Rock Island County	147,489	4,030	5,672	2,798	4,405	5,501	4,339	3,206	4,085	24,334
St. Clair County	269,786	5,905	8,274	4,539	5,613	7,832	6,749	5,181	4,507	34,421
Sangamon County	198,698	5,353	7,565	3,293	5,044	6,459	4,837	3,917	4,443	27,993
Tazewell County	135,685	3,635	4,562	2,519	3,550	4,933	3,992	3,628	2,832	21,454
Vermilion County	81,225	2,252	2,786	1,865	2,111	3,038	2,408	1,891	1,936	13,249
Will County	680,662	13,379	19,436	9,917	13,319	15,684	11,030	8,161	8,244	66,355
Williamson County	66,590	1,899	2,582	1,645	1,678	2,886	2,011	1,619	1,298	11,137
Winnebago County	293,608	6,794	10,369	5,341	7,972	9,184	7,126	6,098	6,082	41,803

Table B-2: Counties—Older Population by Age—*Continued*

	Total Population	60 to 61 Years	62 to 64 Years	65 to 66 Years	67 to 69 Years	70 to 74 Years	75 to 79 Years	80 to 84 Years	85 Years and Over	65 Years and Over
Indiana										
Allen County	358,248	8,277	11,270	5,640	7,436	10,035	7,644	6,637	6,120	43,512
Bartholomew County	77,946	2,054	2,776	1,658	2,463	2,131	1,791	1,759	1,338	11,140
Clark County	111,342	3,098	3,745	2,011	2,848	3,564	2,377	2,169	1,604	14,573
Delaware County	117,599	2,656	3,838	2,310	2,754	4,414	3,714	2,469	1,931	17,592
Elkhart County	198,598	4,772	5,787	3,433	4,255	5,281	4,031	3,713	3,734	24,447
Floyd County	74,982	1,778	2,417	1,421	1,629	2,567	1,628	1,345	1,436	10,026
Grant County	69,661	1,734	2,604	1,311	2,137	2,762	1,956	1,654	1,684	11,504
Hamilton County	283,040	6,777	7,537	3,966	4,671	6,215	3,817	3,424	3,343	25,436
Hancock County	70,534	2,054	2,330	1,495	1,607	2,346	1,669	1,120	1,030	9,267
Hendricks County	148,249	3,391	3,924	2,124	3,455	3,911	3,174	1,861	2,027	16,552
Howard County	82,799	1,905	3,416	1,986	2,776	2,924	2,521	1,915	1,828	13,950
Johnson County	141,550	3,328	4,655	2,370	3,349	4,349	2,497	2,774	2,593	17,932
Kosciusko County	77,429	1,540	2,694	1,462	1,848	2,738	1,986	1,222	1,417	10,673
Lake County	494,961	12,241	16,358	8,572	11,371	15,528	12,559	9,393	9,368	66,791
LaPorte County	111,314	3,269	3,754	2,148	3,145	3,516	2,953	2,352	2,008	16,122
Madison County	131,028	3,356	4,592	2,577	3,401	5,145	3,816	2,861	2,915	20,715
Marion County	911,593	19,140	23,791	12,960	16,493	22,743	17,818	14,042	13,740	97,796
Monroe County	139,880	2,931	3,648	2,219	2,524	3,021	2,553	2,155	2,067	14,539
Morgan County	69,206	2,106	2,496	1,364	2,094	2,290	1,808	1,127	827	9,510
Porter County	165,274	4,157	6,031	3,253	3,928	4,845	3,743	2,855	2,577	21,201
St. Joseph County	266,605	6,857	7,988	4,574	5,411	7,854	6,057	6,375	5,771	36,042
Tippecanoe County	175,204	3,006	4,650	2,297	2,436	4,349	2,419	2,656	2,584	16,741
Vanderburgh County	180,334	4,254	5,792	2,991	4,234	5,822	4,872	3,690	4,492	26,101
Vigo County	108,209	2,350	3,503	1,774	2,290	3,653	2,339	2,296	2,292	14,644
Wayne County	68,636	1,575	2,304	1,219	2,090	2,787	1,873	1,982	1,470	11,421
Iowa										
Black Hawk County	131,472	3,245	4,522	2,551	2,770	3,893	3,265	2,951	2,903	18,333
Dallas County	69,451	1,645	1,999	978	1,159	1,691	913	984	1,201	6,926
Dubuque County	94,471	2,483	3,211	1,372	2,444	3,386	2,659	2,457	2,116	14,434
Johnson County	133,719	2,992	3,916	1,937	2,090	2,448	1,778	1,721	1,738	11,712
Linn County	213,666	4,664	6,615	3,816	4,624	6,432	5,501	4,003	3,965	28,341
Polk County	437,941	9,793	13,787	6,642	8,349	11,055	8,679	6,717	6,542	47,984
Pottawattamie County	93,262	2,821	2,995	1,805	2,184	3,080	2,320	1,930	2,143	13,462
Scott County	167,251	4,354	6,380	3,117	3,801	5,155	3,992	3,065	3,219	22,349
Story County	90,519	1,589	2,487	1,112	1,371	2,155	1,514	1,397	1,547	9,096
Woodbury County	102,416	2,408	2,790	1,883	1,956	3,073	2,260	1,938	2,249	13,359
Kansas										
Butler County	65,893	1,362	2,175	1,308	1,342	1,652	1,594	1,080	1,493	8,469
Douglas County	112,105	1,943	2,997	1,348	2,039	2,203	1,879	1,316	1,500	10,285
Johnson County	552,886	12,395	17,600	8,954	10,628	14,031	10,202	8,570	10,204	62,589
Leavenworth County	77,137	1,807	2,557	1,341	1,731	1,944	1,025	1,399	1,293	8,733
Riley County	73,398	1,036	1,168	677	877	1,148	992	700	887	5,281
Sedgwick County	501,408	10,825	14,576	8,021	10,535	12,593	10,599	8,534	8,419	58,701
Shawnee County	178,736	5,088	6,177	3,540	4,417	5,759	4,721	4,174	3,677	26,288
Wyandotte County	158,287	3,201	4,760	2,050	2,579	4,671	2,713	2,440	2,688	17,141
Kentucky										
Boone County	121,435	2,634	4,037	1,690	2,727	2,977	1,927	1,480	1,179	11,980
Bullitt County	75,225	1,411	2,682	1,483	2,144	2,147	1,675	806	731	8,986
Campbell County	90,794	1,972	3,078	1,752	1,931	2,679	2,131	1,555	1,684	11,732
Christian County	74,373	1,141	1,941	1,059	1,179	2,001	1,797	765	911	7,712
Daviess County	97,294	2,214	3,428	2,139	2,622	2,864	2,561	2,333	1,945	14,464
Fayette County	301,211	6,256	9,912	4,626	5,525	7,619	5,777	4,376	4,219	32,142
Hardin County	107,129	2,746	2,885	1,746	2,315	2,630	2,071	1,617	1,353	11,732
Jefferson County	746,508	18,713	25,790	13,995	16,711	22,191	18,071	15,603	14,537	101,108
Kenton County	160,710	3,454	5,308	2,259	3,358	4,507	2,955	2,385	2,775	18,239
McCracken County	65,616	1,516	2,287	1,383	2,114	2,440	1,853	1,730	1,610	11,130
Madison County	84,016	1,988	2,296	1,433	1,938	2,215	1,629	1,401	1,027	9,643
Pike County	64,635	1,783	3,000	1,511	1,804	2,212	1,559	1,064	1,064	9,214
Warren County	115,586	2,097	2,869	1,893	2,165	3,254	2,096	1,730	1,703	12,841
Louisiana										
Ascension Parish	110,057	2,181	3,278	1,740	2,358	2,350	2,021	852	820	10,141
Bossier Parish	119,899	2,431	3,237	2,070	2,558	3,621	2,800	1,759	1,446	14,254
Caddo Parish	256,551	6,034	8,375	4,199	5,945	8,434	6,957	4,913	4,688	35,136
Calcasieu Parish	193,842	4,548	7,045	3,552	4,444	6,183	4,581	3,512	2,772	25,044
East Baton Rouge Parish	442,322	9,617	14,180	6,472	9,587	11,702	8,376	6,752	6,798	49,687
Iberia Parish	73,580	1,360	2,131	1,567	1,381	2,257	1,863	1,221	926	9,215
Jefferson Parish	433,283	10,668	15,669	8,853	9,840	14,490	10,467	8,852	8,082	60,584
Lafayette Parish	224,469	4,657	5,740	3,538	4,003	5,421	4,539	3,004	3,019	23,524
Lafourche Parish	96,860	2,206	2,802	1,704	2,564	2,866	2,164	1,732	1,396	12,426
Livingston Parish	130,255	2,983	3,594	2,381	2,577	3,499	2,442	1,556	1,136	13,591
Orleans Parish	359,130	9,024	12,021	6,634	7,194	8,743	6,471	5,277	5,790	40,109
Ouachita Parish	154,658	3,340	4,535	3,129	3,112	4,311	3,650	2,597	2,615	19,414
Rapides Parish	132,132	2,964	4,024	2,774	3,204	4,410	3,503	2,423	2,227	18,541
St. Landry Parish	83,540	2,139	2,878	1,455	2,057	2,952	2,258	1,610	1,219	11,551
St. Tammany Parish	236,980	5,983	8,742	4,878	5,919	7,669	4,909	4,548	3,422	31,345
Tangipahoa Parish	122,471	2,644	4,557	2,353	2,432	3,701	2,632	1,925	1,379	14,422
Terrebonne Parish	111,730	2,387	3,124	2,124	2,235	3,188	2,300	1,569	1,348	12,764

Table B-2: Counties—Older Population by Age—*Continued*

	Total Population	60 to 61 Years	62 to 64 Years	65 to 66 Years	67 to 69 Years	70 to 74 Years	75 to 79 Years	80 to 84 Years	85 Years and Over	65 Years and Over
Maine										
Androscoggin County	107,571	2,781	4,303	2,418	2,262	3,566	2,872	2,244	2,190	15,552
Aroostook County	71,328	1,984	3,210	1,572	2,456	3,486	2,717	2,157	1,577	13,965
Cumberland County	282,689	7,660	10,115	5,428	6,966	9,656	7,641	5,891	6,208	41,790
Kennebec County	121,959	3,391	5,145	2,580	3,676	4,121	3,501	3,013	2,680	19,571
Penobscot County	153,856	4,204	6,238	2,657	3,779	5,769	4,151	3,686	2,858	22,900
York County	198,155	6,117	8,107	4,379	5,581	7,442	5,751	4,609	3,924	31,686
Maryland										
Allegany County	74,495	2,121	2,832	1,524	2,349	3,168	2,597	1,979	1,976	13,593
Anne Arundel County	544,889	12,818	19,515	10,168	13,308	15,921	11,069	8,777	7,508	66,751
Baltimore County	812,043	21,046	29,007	14,209	20,302	24,790	21,332	18,363	21,247	120,243
Calvert County	89,279	2,142	3,062	2,076	1,767	2,122	1,652	1,177	1,371	10,165
Carroll County	167,261	4,888	6,137	3,509	4,072	5,274	4,172	2,972	3,044	23,043
Cecil County	101,500	2,276	4,004	1,916	2,213	3,207	2,037	1,496	1,526	12,395
Charles County	148,982	3,488	4,260	2,402	2,972	3,666	2,220	1,820	1,658	14,738
Frederick County	237,037	6,043	7,205	3,955	5,712	5,614	4,483	3,965	3,581	27,310
Harford County	246,839	5,824	8,543	4,686	6,306	7,363	5,459	3,985	4,168	31,967
Howard County	293,972	6,161	9,035	5,181	5,890	8,028	5,245	3,552	3,419	31,315
Montgomery County	990,787	26,130	31,478	16,595	21,960	27,697	21,514	16,297	20,747	124,810
Prince George's County	873,629	20,026	26,059	14,587	17,737	20,992	14,853	9,059	9,127	86,355
St. Mary's County	107,482	2,230	2,845	1,660	2,415	2,637	1,882	1,414	1,409	11,417
Washington County	148,595	3,521	5,413	2,528	3,507	5,115	3,859	3,659	2,914	21,582
Wicomico County	99,840	2,487	2,781	1,881	2,450	2,897	2,157	2,085	1,819	13,289
Massachusetts										
Barnstable County	215,681	7,240	10,961	6,337	9,059	12,831	10,933	9,249	7,009	55,418
Berkshire County	130,565	3,896	5,711	2,878	3,657	5,860	4,319	3,872	4,486	25,072
Bristol County	549,972	13,927	18,943	10,736	14,416	16,338	13,890	10,822	13,738	79,940
Essex County	750,452	19,392	27,150	14,262	17,889	23,389	18,567	15,567	18,753	108,427
Franklin County	71,495	2,560	3,529	1,825	1,829	2,429	1,715	1,608	1,850	11,256
Hampden County	465,177	11,823	15,874	7,335	11,738	14,467	12,249	9,887	11,470	67,146
Hampshire County	159,575	3,911	5,934	2,857	3,578	4,622	3,664	2,867	3,408	20,996
Middlesex County	1,521,993	35,379	50,292	25,253	34,247	44,949	35,774	30,706	31,421	202,350
Norfolk County	677,462	16,569	22,538	13,214	16,911	20,231	16,597	16,339	16,881	100,173
Plymouth County	497,975	13,446	19,091	10,440	13,771	16,152	11,663	9,652	10,461	72,139
Suffolk County	734,699	13,999	19,053	10,174	12,999	18,199	12,913	11,600	12,071	77,956
Worcester County	803,429	18,973	24,785	14,401	17,415	22,385	18,165	14,543	17,839	104,748
Michigan										
Allegan County	111,701	2,864	3,876	2,014	2,901	3,721	2,621	1,989	1,914	15,160
Bay County	107,310	2,897	4,586	2,335	3,077	4,133	2,976	2,544	2,872	17,937
Berrien County	156,452	4,195	5,678	2,876	4,850	5,902	4,411	3,866	3,931	25,836
Calhoun County	135,568	3,941	4,863	2,594	3,456	4,654	3,622	2,996	3,063	20,385
Clinton County	75,746	1,863	2,565	1,499	1,929	2,488	1,777	1,344	1,291	10,328
Eaton County	107,952	3,152	3,551	2,436	2,839	3,605	2,647	1,974	2,168	15,669
Genesee County	421,871	10,235	15,186	7,814	10,434	13,916	12,314	7,600	7,641	59,719
Grand Traverse County	88,147	2,584	3,296	1,669	2,170	3,232	2,558	1,891	1,861	13,381
Ingham County	281,470	6,556	8,473	4,231	5,891	6,375	5,526	4,112	4,222	30,357
Isabella County	70,525	975	1,890	796	1,266	1,701	1,271	951	974	6,959
Jackson County	160,115	4,323	5,957	3,202	3,972	5,026	4,166	3,226	3,605	23,197
Kalamazoo County	252,546	5,390	8,754	3,692	5,278	7,571	5,889	4,256	4,836	31,522
Kent County	608,517	13,107	17,870	9,312	12,331	14,161	11,452	10,776	11,059	69,091
Lapeer County	88,147	2,587	2,850	1,917	2,134	3,437	2,421	1,400	1,030	12,339
Lenawee County	99,324	2,534	3,923	2,020	3,019	3,257	2,773	2,054	2,023	15,146
Livingston County	182,045	4,479	6,282	3,564	4,745	5,788	3,634	3,195	2,216	23,142
Macomb County	843,852	21,005	29,783	15,231	21,019	27,469	20,952	18,880	19,615	123,166
Marquette County	67,528	1,985	2,394	1,345	1,867	2,176	1,724	1,617	1,410	10,139
Midland County	83,825	2,031	2,877	1,460	2,464	2,653	2,623	1,735	1,665	12,600
Monroe County	151,539	4,107	5,717	3,031	3,637	5,042	3,572	3,394	2,455	21,131
Muskegon County	170,724	4,426	5,302	3,028	4,098	5,608	4,231	3,506	3,325	23,796
Oakland County	1,211,683	31,648	43,095	23,650	30,756	35,388	26,845	24,560	24,687	165,886
Ottawa County	266,464	5,824	7,502	4,130	5,684	7,530	5,684	4,221	4,818	32,067
Saginaw County	199,094	5,391	6,602	3,928	5,876	6,709	5,785	4,197	4,628	31,123
St. Clair County	161,640	4,668	6,414	3,496	4,383	5,544	4,307	3,457	3,125	24,312
Shiawassee County	69,925	2,010	2,559	1,705	1,745	2,370	1,833	1,436	1,337	10,426
Van Buren County	75,887	1,996	2,995	1,636	1,970	2,551	1,954	1,600	1,130	10,841
Washtenaw County	348,311	7,956	10,487	5,222	7,406	8,551	5,572	4,821	5,501	37,073
Wayne County	1,803,251	43,521	58,441	31,173	38,825	50,950	41,365	34,433	35,792	232,538
Minnesota										
Anoka County	333,728	7,773	9,552	5,205	7,094	8,380	6,182	3,657	3,634	34,152
Blue Earth County	64,510	1,455	1,713	852	1,161	1,696	1,203	1,260	1,494	7,666
Carver County	92,574	1,544	2,383	1,192	1,622	1,778	1,510	1,216	931	8,249
Dakota County	402,136	9,691	12,263	6,696	7,635	9,744	6,991	5,567	5,565	42,198
Hennepin County	1,169,434	27,912	35,405	18,449	23,468	28,547	23,239	19,112	22,715	135,530
Olmsted County	145,828	3,159	4,521	2,919	2,752	4,296	3,539	2,506	2,831	18,843
Ramsey County	514,982	11,852	16,407	7,980	9,946	14,011	11,586	9,195	10,130	62,848
St. Louis County	200,269	5,541	7,950	4,587	5,015	6,900	5,964	4,715	5,149	32,330
Scott County	132,768	2,403	3,130	1,638	2,181	2,791	1,636	1,639	1,165	11,050
Sherburne County	89,139	1,554	2,216	1,131	1,356	2,034	1,389	951	844	7,705
Stearns County	151,178	3,313	4,589	2,389	2,744	4,436	3,598	3,017	2,547	18,731
Washington County	241,538	5,949	7,799	4,649	4,886	6,002	4,857	3,147	3,177	26,718
Wright County	126,271	2,302	3,229	1,693	2,515	3,148	2,008	1,559	1,652	12,575

Table B-2: Counties—Older Population by Age—*Continued*

	Total Population	60 to 61 Years	62 to 64 Years	65 to 66 Years	67 to 69 Years	70 to 74 Years	75 to 79 Years	80 to 84 Years	85 Years and Over	65 Years and Over
Mississippi										
DeSoto County	163,919	3,547	4,720	2,526	3,639	4,359	3,179	2,023	1,550	17,276
Forrest County	75,944	1,489	2,510	1,152	1,751	2,033	1,358	1,184	1,393	8,871
Harrison County	190,962	3,986	5,864	3,001	3,969	6,058	4,286	3,071	2,629	23,014
Hinds County	247,502	5,092	7,491	3,785	4,753	6,419	4,807	3,523	3,921	27,208
Jackson County	140,062	2,993	4,839	2,448	3,399	4,929	3,856	1,933	1,351	17,916
Jones County	68,192	1,717	2,410	1,536	1,811	2,043	2,111	1,232	1,147	9,880
Lauderdale County	80,361	1,981	2,521	1,585	1,944	2,458	2,012	1,782	1,542	11,323
Lee County	84,080	1,822	2,851	1,374	1,851	3,195	1,602	1,607	1,536	11,165
Madison County	97,020	1,786	3,283	1,377	2,146	2,429	1,589	1,134	1,890	10,565
Rankin County	143,637	3,088	4,591	3,013	3,135	4,205	3,009	2,278	1,452	17,092
Missouri										
Boone County	165,893	2,989	3,990	2,037	3,073	3,409	2,643	2,351	2,263	15,776
Buchanan County	89,420	2,243	2,780	1,567	2,111	2,646	2,052	1,955	1,978	12,309
Cape Girardeau County	76,460	1,720	2,233	1,368	1,794	2,455	1,624	1,879	1,913	11,033
Cass County	100,013	2,229	2,882	1,899	2,552	3,462	2,431	1,970	1,786	14,100
Christian County	78,786	1,792	2,862	1,649	2,029	2,401	2,099	1,189	731	10,098
Clay County	225,142	4,933	6,945	3,564	5,064	6,005	4,539	3,534	3,401	26,107
Cole County	76,299	1,918	2,778	1,535	1,773	2,091	1,779	1,385	1,304	9,867
Franklin County	101,543	2,225	3,367	2,134	2,438	3,377	2,687	1,924	1,808	14,368
Greene County	277,813	6,567	9,386	4,843	7,308	8,537	7,178	5,615	6,273	39,754
Jackson County	675,911	15,369	22,200	11,479	14,518	19,337	15,434	12,410	12,435	85,613
Jasper County	116,957	2,592	3,225	1,772	2,823	3,865	2,835	2,053	2,282	15,630
Jefferson County	219,655	5,319	7,356	3,942	5,323	6,612	4,186	3,295	2,349	25,707
Platte County	90,871	2,003	3,148	1,539	1,959	2,796	1,519	1,343	1,468	10,624
St. Charles County	365,131	8,166	11,708	6,094	8,281	10,044	7,537	5,468	5,330	42,754
St. Francois County	65,696	1,282	2,209	1,127	1,609	2,443	1,755	1,436	996	9,366
St. Louis County	999,595	25,703	35,636	18,996	24,942	33,296	25,649	24,027	25,699	152,609
Montana										
Cascade County	81,677	2,037	3,095	1,438	2,255	3,142	2,549	1,755	1,797	12,936
Flathead County	91,221	2,912	3,254	2,491	2,244	3,056	2,821	1,373	1,719	13,704
Gallatin County	91,193	1,917	2,503	1,266	1,680	2,171	1,257	1,213	1,427	9,014
Missoula County	110,183	2,420	4,023	2,090	2,492	2,774	1,779	1,855	1,945	12,935
Yellowstone County	150,078	3,830	5,175	2,891	3,541	4,822	3,842	3,119	3,251	21,466
Nebraska										
Douglas County	524,969	12,553	14,559	7,203	10,231	12,430	9,267	8,437	8,820	56,388
Lancaster County	289,807	6,920	8,590	4,543	5,068	7,271	6,195	4,114	4,874	32,065
Sarpy County	162,718	3,193	4,143	2,188	2,606	3,793	2,731	1,660	1,382	14,360
Nevada										
Clark County	1,974,036	44,262	61,743	37,738	46,418	59,451	40,461	27,496	21,844	233,408
Washoe County	425,845	11,330	15,851	8,425	10,798	13,495	8,840	6,322	6,169	54,049
New Hampshire										
Cheshire County	76,919	2,168	3,530	1,591	2,047	2,736	2,166	1,630	1,510	11,680
Grafton County	89,085	2,401	3,514	2,025	2,514	3,282	2,646	2,190	1,636	14,293
Hillsborough County	401,933	9,532	14,234	6,855	8,198	12,142	8,656	6,743	6,877	49,471
Merrimack County	146,606	4,173	5,225	2,670	4,049	4,524	3,584	2,806	3,209	20,842
Rockingham County	296,427	8,055	11,427	6,557	7,476	8,676	6,850	5,399	4,383	39,341
Strafford County	123,661	2,572	3,528	1,779	2,845	3,609	2,725	2,290	1,964	15,212
New Jersey										
Atlantic County	274,982	7,575	9,712	5,688	7,191	9,243	6,569	6,153	5,176	40,020
Bergen County	912,753	23,396	29,081	18,193	23,836	28,518	24,605	21,924	22,806	139,882
Burlington County	450,454	11,080	15,794	7,877	11,027	14,962	12,098	9,157	8,950	64,071
Camden County	513,593	11,393	17,228	9,748	10,716	15,022	11,473	9,523	10,942	67,424
Cape May County	96,716	3,540	4,333	2,485	3,779	5,188	3,916	3,436	2,730	21,534
Cumberland County	157,351	3,254	4,848	2,392	3,537	5,072	3,577	2,733	2,843	20,154
Essex County	786,363	16,638	22,514	13,103	15,183	21,154	15,515	12,535	14,839	92,329
Gloucester County	289,167	7,710	9,288	5,057	6,357	8,872	6,342	5,507	4,761	36,896
Hudson County	644,288	13,209	16,501	9,754	11,572	15,907	11,844	9,781	8,678	67,536
Hunterdon County	127,722	3,296	4,695	2,410	3,530	3,957	2,773	2,641	1,862	17,173
Mercer County	367,567	8,595	11,358	6,876	7,499	10,172	8,278	7,299	7,261	47,385
Middlesex County	816,975	18,489	24,492	13,956	17,263	22,291	18,029	15,131	15,846	102,516
Monmouth County	630,099	15,350	22,807	12,135	14,983	19,881	16,079	12,782	13,709	89,569
Morris County	495,613	12,172	16,971	9,409	12,568	15,524	12,182	10,169	10,793	70,645
Ocean County	579,066	15,360	22,777	13,957	20,120	26,321	23,445	19,855	19,074	122,772
Passaic County	502,431	11,303	14,418	9,364	10,428	13,552	10,259	8,892	9,409	61,904
Salem County	65,960	1,732	2,468	1,427	1,691	2,233	1,934	1,608	1,282	10,175
Somerset County	325,944	7,088	10,936	6,077	7,391	8,820	6,951	5,786	6,901	41,926
Sussex County	148,393	4,005	5,699	2,852	3,820	4,348	2,635	2,676	2,194	18,525
Union County	540,650	13,289	15,551	9,353	11,189	14,505	11,742	9,720	12,061	68,570
Warren County	108,162	3,029	4,071	1,905	2,939	3,290	2,576	2,476	2,237	15,423
New Mexico										
Bernalillo County	669,153	16,899	22,551	10,985	15,444	20,170	14,897	11,973	11,004	84,473
Chaves County	65,742	1,569	1,762	1,258	1,469	2,067	1,735	1,440	1,297	9,266
Doña Ana County	212,571	4,496	5,850	3,525	5,095	6,566	5,158	3,682	2,973	26,999
Lea County	65,377	1,076	1,868	1,023	1,235	1,690	1,523	1,063	655	7,189
McKinley County	72,807	1,653	1,708	863	1,443	1,899	1,340	842	651	7,038
Otero County	65,306	1,785	2,868	1,342	1,745	2,457	1,950	1,214	971	9,679
Sandoval County	134,053	3,519	4,920	2,761	3,507	4,125	2,347	2,185	2,102	17,027
San Juan County	128,912	2,903	3,631	2,244	2,788	3,066	2,642	2,003	1,702	14,445
Santa Fe County	145,378	5,224	6,923	3,949	5,386	5,319	3,884	2,525	2,518	23,581
Valencia County	76,738	1,787	3,129	1,276	2,115	2,774	1,542	1,604	1,010	10,321

Table B-2: Counties—Older Population by Age—*Continued*

	Total Population	60 to 61 Years	62 to 64 Years	65 to 66 Years	67 to 69 Years	70 to 74 Years	75 to 79 Years	80 to 84 Years	85 Years and Over	65 Years and Over
New York										
Albany County	304,694	7,483	10,818	5,517	7,082	8,862	7,119	7,093	7,464	43,137
Bronx County	1,397,357	26,404	35,664	20,562	26,590	35,877	26,299	20,081	20,618	150,027
Broome County	199,225	4,781	7,386	3,557	5,279	7,331	6,366	5,155	5,497	33,185
Cattaraugus County	79,859	2,071	3,251	1,559	2,087	2,993	2,445	1,676	1,735	12,495
Cayuga County	79,775	1,998	3,474	1,530	1,980	2,977	2,337	1,792	1,875	12,491
Chautauqua County	134,190	3,914	5,277	2,298	3,654	5,424	4,007	3,568	3,577	22,528
Chemung County	88,848	2,331	3,475	1,308	2,526	3,002	2,322	2,142	2,356	13,656
Clinton County	81,862	2,052	2,689	1,158	2,127	2,783	2,244	1,598	1,268	11,178
Dutchess County	297,768	8,005	9,414	6,011	7,153	9,099	7,627	6,205	5,536	41,631
Erie County	919,268	21,898	32,100	17,592	22,488	31,850	26,472	25,018	22,231	145,651
Jefferson County	118,332	2,653	3,447	1,975	2,471	2,762	2,119	1,898	2,102	13,327
Kings County	2,538,529	57,074	73,477	41,184	47,507	69,372	51,300	43,647	41,314	294,324
Livingston County	65,007	1,519	2,468	1,273	1,567	2,158	1,615	1,088	1,711	9,412
Madison County	72,881	1,870	2,532	1,325	1,912	2,607	1,746	1,308	1,638	10,536
Monroe County	746,442	17,907	24,287	13,547	18,455	22,743	18,150	15,409	18,180	106,484
Nassau County	1,345,448	35,824	48,282	25,172	32,754	44,177	37,719	32,464	36,119	208,405
New York County	1,604,407	36,450	50,911	29,888	39,267	50,245	39,241	30,030	31,391	220,062
Niagara County	215,837	5,288	8,185	4,694	5,693	7,379	5,952	5,716	5,421	34,855
Oneida County	234,193	5,944	9,740	4,329	6,133	8,576	6,278	5,591	7,663	38,570
Onondaga County	467,263	11,459	15,007	8,949	10,475	13,929	11,839	10,348	11,250	66,790
Ontario County	108,374	3,572	4,763	2,918	3,003	3,516	3,186	2,305	2,396	17,324
Orange County	374,158	9,010	11,931	6,160	7,665	9,965	6,699	5,769	6,170	42,428
Oswego County	121,951	3,276	3,808	1,985	3,171	3,752	2,824	2,067	1,891	15,690
Putnam County	99,769	2,284	3,372	1,750	2,837	3,150	2,012	1,459	1,822	13,030
Queens County	2,254,750	49,383	72,240	39,874	47,888	68,127	51,548	42,318	43,495	293,250
Rensselaer County	159,719	4,331	6,136	2,771	3,972	4,791	3,675	3,453	3,457	22,119
Richmond County	470,402	12,314	16,682	8,637	11,153	14,823	10,628	7,782	8,750	61,773
Rockland County	315,331	8,058	9,484	5,769	7,439	10,064	8,232	6,114	5,918	43,536
St. Lawrence County	112,150	2,506	4,321	2,078	2,769	3,832	2,817	2,552	1,869	15,917
Saratoga County	221,076	5,877	8,055	4,766	5,689	7,346	5,078	4,216	4,168	31,263
Schenectady County	154,973	3,662	5,053	2,515	3,673	4,960	3,070	4,140	4,785	23,143
Steuben County	99,095	2,884	3,993	2,178	3,015	3,385	2,827	2,482	2,164	16,051
Suffolk County	1,498,125	33,580	49,637	27,616	38,931	47,123	37,068	30,055	28,401	209,194
Sullivan County	77,100	1,926	3,106	1,739	2,457	3,053	1,855	1,404	1,443	11,951
Tompkins County	101,989	2,469	3,229	1,547	1,888	2,596	1,924	1,659	1,751	11,365
Ulster County	182,256	5,592	7,604	4,352	5,160	5,616	4,577	4,169	4,304	28,178
Warren County	65,653	1,748	3,238	1,640	2,095	2,555	1,810	2,027	1,565	11,692
Wayne County	93,333	2,141	3,846	1,974	2,845	2,936	2,651	1,762	1,668	13,836
Westchester County	956,494	23,067	31,259	18,259	22,781	30,317	24,882	22,623	23,448	142,310
North Carolina										
Alamance County	152,730	3,332	4,944	3,219	4,152	4,608	3,865	3,180	3,757	22,781
Brunswick County	110,196	4,402	6,709	3,875	6,114	6,770	4,034	2,733	1,552	25,078
Buncombe County	241,626	7,369	8,863	5,075	6,864	9,204	7,143	5,372	5,914	39,572
Burke County	90,713	2,526	3,464	1,872	2,559	4,126	3,063	1,661	1,702	14,983
Cabarrus County	181,358	3,428	5,303	3,168	3,233	5,367	3,776	2,775	2,446	20,765
Caldwell County	82,380	2,192	3,904	1,782	2,304	3,929	2,503	1,301	1,490	13,309
Carteret County	67,235	2,190	3,460	1,817	2,579	3,261	2,242	1,718	1,465	13,082
Catawba County	154,182	3,719	5,756	3,493	4,403	5,178	4,220	2,961	2,748	23,003
Chatham County	65,001	2,544	3,284	2,013	2,414	2,674	2,335	1,808	1,653	12,897
Cleveland County	97,695	2,348	3,718	2,042	2,596	4,210	2,271	2,212	1,910	15,241
Craven County	104,392	2,488	3,832	2,102	2,847	4,205	2,909	2,411	2,012	16,486
Cumberland County	322,532	6,389	7,979	4,706	5,604	8,210	5,748	3,973	3,135	31,376
Davidson County	163,071	4,095	5,905	3,593	4,312	6,726	4,202	3,132	2,719	24,684
Durham County	273,900	5,653	7,892	4,035	4,861	6,500	4,725	3,400	4,202	27,723
Forsyth County	354,659	8,299	11,883	6,408	8,664	10,321	8,503	6,644	6,403	46,943
Gaston County	207,039	4,547	7,879	3,981	5,568	6,351	4,962	3,772	3,520	28,154
Guilford County	495,297	10,774	16,707	7,535	12,041	14,478	12,102	8,740	7,687	62,583
Harnett County	119,058	2,325	3,178	1,738	2,234	3,360	2,283	1,608	1,221	12,444
Henderson County	107,594	3,120	5,006	3,097	3,681	6,171	4,642	3,827	3,326	24,744
Iredell County	161,160	3,859	5,756	3,047	4,160	5,270	3,798	2,435	2,632	21,342
Johnston County	172,463	3,488	5,937	3,321	3,814	4,465	3,029	2,448	1,581	18,658
Lincoln County	78,848	2,085	2,854	1,506	2,322	3,007	2,123	1,291	699	10,948
Mecklenburg County	945,889	18,027	25,601	12,824	15,744	20,564	14,602	11,025	11,249	86,008
Moore County	89,402	2,490	4,066	2,218	3,335	4,811	4,107	2,883	3,131	20,485
Nash County	95,838	2,524	4,055	2,087	2,415	3,500	2,452	1,783	1,738	13,975
New Hanover County	206,165	5,187	6,866	4,024	5,399	7,319	5,400	3,901	3,442	29,485
Onslow County	180,060	2,594	3,611	2,328	2,593	3,310	2,633	1,697	1,317	13,878
Orange County	135,886	3,008	3,686	2,265	2,564	3,415	2,375	1,688	1,387	13,694
Pitt County	170,685	3,790	4,377	2,669	3,392	3,861	2,767	2,236	2,480	17,405
Randolph County	142,122	3,441	5,855	3,252	3,684	5,143	3,915	2,714	1,946	20,654
Robeson County	134,961	2,837	4,588	2,629	2,966	3,954	3,197	1,544	1,473	15,763
Rockingham County	93,158	2,463	3,624	1,898	3,356	3,470	3,107	2,154	1,678	15,663
Rowan County	138,221	3,280	5,070	2,908	3,749	4,689	3,368	3,254	2,621	20,589
Rutherford County	67,508	2,341	2,583	1,637	2,143	3,045	1,898	1,598	1,726	12,047
Surry County	73,615	1,691	3,338	1,779	1,883	3,347	2,418	1,664	1,429	12,520
Union County	205,292	4,159	6,306	2,796	4,864	5,274	3,560	2,081	2,028	20,603
Wake County	929,250	18,108	24,551	13,126	16,335	19,160	13,603	10,324	9,633	82,181
Wayne County	123,656	3,102	4,055	2,093	3,201	4,113	3,088	1,977	1,992	16,464
Wilkes County	69,250	1,836	2,683	1,972	2,112	2,950	2,182	1,614	1,496	12,326
Wilson County	81,549	1,958	3,055	1,814	2,169	2,789	2,022	1,569	1,631	11,994

Table B-2: Counties—Older Population by Age—*Continued*

	Total Population	60 to 61 Years	62 to 64 Years	65 to 66 Years	67 to 69 Years	70 to 74 Years	75 to 79 Years	80 to 84 Years	85 Years and Over	65 Years and Over
North Dakota										
Burleigh County	83,635	2,083	2,897	1,389	1,749	2,661	2,135	1,802	1,761	11,497
Cass County	153,012	3,323	4,167	2,226	2,343	3,159	3,148	2,364	2,040	15,280
Grand Forks County	67,006	1,317	1,708	1,071	1,142	1,629	1,172	1,213	986	7,213
Ohio										
Allen County	105,701	2,638	3,398	2,055	2,310	3,677	2,556	2,525	2,573	15,696
Ashtabula County	100,967	2,774	3,609	2,063	2,961	3,545	2,618	2,161	2,694	16,042
Belmont County	70,039	1,949	3,009	1,370	2,286	2,686	2,168	1,959	2,032	12,501
Butler County	369,778	10,060	11,452	6,302	7,538	10,309	8,475	5,727	5,553	43,904
Clark County	137,735	3,923	5,571	2,348	3,916	5,936	3,991	2,939	3,490	22,620
Clermont County	198,437	4,708	6,271	4,050	4,371	5,938	4,079	3,327	2,623	24,388
Columbiana County	107,190	3,411	4,132	2,097	3,288	4,247	3,200	3,005	2,294	18,131
Cuyahoga County	1,271,187	32,945	45,787	23,787	30,451	43,395	35,937	31,735	33,894	199,199
Delaware County	178,314	4,030	5,898	2,708	3,733	4,472	2,970	2,430	1,686	17,999
Erie County	76,700	2,420	3,327	1,575	2,640	3,158	2,712	1,839	1,779	13,703
Fairfield County	147,071	3,471	5,083	3,042	3,435	4,217	3,427	2,279	2,241	18,641
Franklin County	1,180,276	23,413	34,149	16,825	20,704	28,365	21,079	16,163	16,279	119,415
Geauga County	93,465	2,879	3,759	1,949	3,184	3,336	2,365	2,025	2,187	15,046
Greene County	162,830	4,275	6,041	2,825	3,909	5,661	4,324	3,429	2,847	22,995
Hamilton County	801,587	20,439	25,562	12,673	18,108	23,959	19,021	16,134	17,828	107,723
Hancock County	75,156	1,654	2,565	1,449	1,770	2,694	1,685	1,499	2,075	11,172
Jefferson County	68,965	2,097	2,700	1,451	2,205	3,041	2,211	2,089	1,786	12,783
Lake County	229,836	5,827	8,833	5,113	6,513	8,771	6,845	5,540	5,283	38,065
Licking County	167,159	4,019	5,756	3,417	4,640	5,275	4,122	3,016	2,410	22,880
Lorain County	301,611	8,550	11,537	5,748	8,223	10,155	8,047	6,135	6,272	44,580
Lucas County	439,826	10,782	14,038	7,782	9,552	13,451	10,422	9,016	8,872	59,095
Mahoning County	236,713	7,347	9,593	5,264	6,274	8,846	7,419	7,185	7,684	42,672
Marion County	66,411	1,846	2,670	1,254	1,550	2,246	1,943	1,150	1,419	9,562
Medina County	173,217	4,574	6,143	3,158	4,624	5,671	3,893	3,140	1,758	23,579
Miami County	102,777	2,535	3,888	2,109	2,911	4,076	3,140	2,218	1,758	16,212
Montgomery County	535,057	13,940	20,270	9,164	14,208	19,569	15,463	12,224	12,335	82,953
Muskingum County	86,109	2,073	3,390	1,433	2,362	3,278	2,053	2,147	2,001	13,274
Portage County	161,494	3,881	5,617	2,816	4,458	5,036	4,391	2,414	2,376	21,491
Richland County	123,331	3,495	4,857	2,288	3,347	5,256	4,220	3,001	2,656	20,768
Ross County	77,723	1,562	2,482	1,756	1,954	2,580	1,924	1,333	1,166	10,713
Scioto County	79,079	2,019	3,043	1,475	2,362	2,845	2,197	2,068	1,380	12,327
Stark County	374,871	10,021	13,669	7,793	10,739	13,382	10,877	9,432	9,674	61,897
Summit County	541,230	13,037	20,860	9,837	13,251	18,118	14,568	12,644	12,364	80,782
Trumbull County	208,743	6,109	9,540	4,624	6,185	8,419	6,611	6,238	5,033	37,110
Tuscarawas County	92,481	2,628	3,319	1,649	2,674	3,627	2,782	2,552	2,049	15,333
Warren County	215,286	4,881	7,382	3,268	4,928	5,751	4,586	2,937	2,747	24,217
Wayne County	114,674	3,232	4,082	1,926	3,594	3,933	3,236	1,941	2,617	17,247
Wood County	126,871	3,409	3,699	2,348	2,677	3,434	2,641	3,029	1,880	16,009
Oklahoma										
Canadian County	119,446	2,924	3,479	1,842	2,719	3,446	2,346	1,491	1,599	13,443
Cleveland County	261,386	5,548	7,804	3,661	5,202	7,429	4,549	3,769	3,090	27,700
Comanche County	125,850	1,933	3,357	1,830	2,260	3,044	2,881	1,522	1,427	12,964
Creek County	70,439	2,144	2,172	1,275	2,222	2,818	2,075	1,186	1,256	10,832
Muskogee County	70,815	1,710	2,776	1,600	2,028	2,145	2,149	1,290	1,317	10,529
Oklahoma County	730,787	15,330	22,662	11,803	14,143	21,290	15,585	13,131	11,975	87,927
Payne County	77,921	1,226	2,231	976	1,432	2,030	1,197	1,224	1,229	8,088
Pottawatomie County	70,209	1,670	2,241	1,664	1,884	2,462	1,878	1,307	1,023	10,218
Rogers County	87,729	1,925	3,111	1,903	2,748	2,624	1,982	1,554	1,437	12,248
Tulsa County	609,067	13,568	18,334	10,603	12,515	16,914	13,037	10,821	10,808	74,698
Wagoner County	74,182	2,393	2,608	1,775	2,073	2,584	1,719	997	783	9,931
Oregon										
Benton County	85,989	1,996	3,251	1,755	1,661	2,332	1,636	1,474	1,929	10,787
Clackamas County	380,281	11,552	16,107	8,640	10,331	12,081	8,781	6,877	7,604	54,314
Deschutes County	160,085	4,684	6,658	3,713	4,628	6,764	3,627	3,082	3,476	25,290
Douglas County	107,420	3,867	5,614	3,328	3,898	5,489	3,949	3,628	2,906	23,198
Jackson County	204,868	6,095	8,905	4,797	6,457	8,571	6,699	5,009	5,744	37,277
Josephine County	82,825	2,646	4,149	2,473	3,137	4,739	2,768	2,879	2,927	18,923
Klamath County	66,186	2,087	2,900	1,493	2,238	3,032	2,552	1,362	1,165	11,842
Lane County	353,315	10,423	14,033	7,199	9,460	13,436	9,098	8,465	7,297	54,955
Linn County	117,796	3,424	5,001	2,149	3,480	4,865	3,502	2,578	2,245	18,819
Marion County	317,945	6,951	10,168	5,807	7,052	9,793	7,348	5,586	6,420	42,006
Multnomah County	748,280	17,850	24,301	11,996	14,717	17,599	12,573	10,791	13,346	81,022
Polk County	75,987	2,038	3,035	1,549	2,383	2,429	2,000	1,549	1,854	11,764
Umatilla County	76,514	1,871	2,819	1,633	1,593	2,319	1,827	1,143	1,291	9,806
Washington County	539,525	12,099	15,804	8,733	10,280	12,476	9,092	7,346	8,550	56,477
Yamhill County	99,803	1,983	3,010	1,793	2,545	2,985	2,219	2,031	2,329	13,902
Pennsylvania										
Adams County	101,485	2,621	4,011	2,186	2,707	4,040	3,069	2,292	2,336	16,630
Allegheny County	1,226,873	33,048	44,880	24,388	30,986	42,598	35,968	34,999	36,676	205,615
Armstrong County	68,659	2,091	2,705	1,369	2,124	3,040	2,299	2,028	2,068	12,928
Beaver County	170,404	4,640	6,711	3,082	5,295	7,125	5,943	5,541	4,889	31,875
Berks County	412,610	9,643	13,715	7,575	10,493	12,713	10,834	9,786	9,371	60,772
Blair County	127,131	3,756	4,927	2,544	4,211	4,647	3,736	4,050	3,637	22,825
Bucks County	626,494	16,126	24,082	12,681	17,412	19,481	16,128	13,876	14,925	94,503
Butler County	184,574	4,822	6,473	3,833	4,666	6,360	5,044	4,678	4,188	28,769
Cambria County	142,564	4,038	5,804	3,005	4,328	5,773	4,802	4,756	4,525	27,240
Carbon County	65,118	1,474	3,050	1,707	1,867	2,693	2,005	1,932	1,594	11,798

Table B-2: Counties—Older Population by Age—*Continued*

	Total Population	60 to 61 Years	62 to 64 Years	65 to 66 Years	67 to 69 Years	70 to 74 Years	75 to 79 Years	80 to 84 Years	85 Years and Over	65 Years and Over
Pennsylvania—Cont.										
Centre County	154,698	2,942	4,103	2,064	3,045	4,254	3,240	2,583	2,566	17,752
Chester County	503,325	11,932	16,846	9,239	11,441	15,573	11,387	9,620	9,525	66,785
Clearfield County	81,422	2,422	3,027	1,899	2,637	2,974	2,618	2,045	2,259	14,432
Columbia County	67,018	1,633	2,477	1,433	1,721	2,451	2,098	1,712	1,434	10,849
Crawford County	88,132	2,538	3,366	2,217	2,828	3,129	3,047	1,935	1,831	14,987
Cumberland County	237,100	6,664	8,225	4,413	6,204	8,749	6,710	5,559	6,172	37,807
Dauphin County	268,990	6,824	10,192	5,117	6,050	8,302	6,267	5,748	6,060	37,544
Delaware County	560,011	14,218	17,155	9,357	12,622	16,533	13,953	13,698	14,469	80,632
Erie County	280,794	7,676	9,359	4,437	7,434	9,159	7,579	6,258	6,441	41,308
Fayette County	136,102	4,163	5,259	3,067	3,630	5,816	4,341	4,015	3,783	24,652
Franklin County	150,691	3,426	5,631	3,370	4,398	5,799	5,208	3,505	3,204	25,484
Indiana County	88,532	2,077	3,091	1,521	2,638	3,142	2,581	1,813	2,336	14,031
Lackawanna County	214,528	5,720	7,715	4,973	5,814	7,966	6,114	6,556	7,047	38,470
Lancaster County	523,676	12,458	16,305	9,548	14,081	16,542	14,203	11,859	13,886	80,119
Lawrence County	90,411	2,604	3,539	2,007	2,611	3,617	3,254	2,746	3,004	17,239
Lebanon County	134,452	3,198	5,165	2,462	3,973	5,162	3,944	3,985	3,413	22,939
Lehigh County	352,948	8,497	11,318	5,856	8,469	11,721	9,535	8,360	8,676	52,617
Luzerne County	321,013	8,853	12,282	6,696	9,173	12,575	10,175	9,888	9,540	58,047
Lycoming County	116,668	2,929	4,372	2,415	3,187	4,055	3,361	2,877	3,409	19,304
Mercer County	116,122	3,119	4,470	2,413	3,250	4,902	4,006	3,471	3,717	21,759
Monroe County	169,588	4,855	5,863	3,238	4,252	5,593	3,403	3,246	2,658	22,390
Montgomery County	804,896	20,042	28,012	15,630	20,056	25,557	22,085	19,586	20,864	123,778
Northampton County	298,618	7,026	10,440	5,987	7,942	9,699	7,989	8,201	7,921	47,739
Northumberland County	94,427	2,880	4,321	2,037	2,526	4,315	3,411	2,484	2,778	17,551
Philadelphia County	1,538,211	33,357	44,617	24,756	30,396	41,793	34,129	26,723	28,788	186,585
Schuylkill County	147,618	3,868	6,352	3,412	4,220	5,657	5,078	4,283	4,328	26,978
Somerset County	77,348	2,248	2,934	1,578	2,353	3,470	2,533	2,244	2,507	14,685
Washington County	208,256	6,496	8,436	4,561	5,497	8,629	7,510	5,408	5,452	37,057
Westmoreland County	364,357	10,781	15,364	8,070	11,993	14,705	12,613	10,856	11,376	69,613
York County	436,824	11,126	16,348	8,492	11,819	13,979	10,944	9,243	8,678	63,155
Rhode Island										
Kent County	165,432	4,646	6,325	3,451	4,041	5,741	5,293	3,742	4,322	26,590
Newport County	82,372	2,538	2,793	2,091	2,609	3,048	2,279	2,134	2,342	14,503
Providence County	627,625	15,066	18,695	10,134	12,775	18,382	14,333	13,874	15,615	85,113
Washington County	126,394	3,615	5,479	2,793	3,777	4,340	3,141	2,803	2,950	19,804
South Carolina										
Aiken County	161,817	4,117	6,205	3,811	4,989	6,143	4,937	3,627	2,290	25,797
Anderson County	188,359	4,361	7,211	3,810	5,201	7,808	5,401	3,840	3,431	29,491
Beaufort County	165,149	5,293	7,866	5,304	6,641	9,760	5,922	4,330	3,592	35,549
Berkeley County	184,225	4,189	5,346	3,232	4,278	5,194	2,900	2,081	1,830	19,515
Charleston County	358,009	9,409	12,189	6,608	9,134	11,377	8,243	6,344	5,484	47,190
Darlington County	68,341	1,867	2,778	1,585	1,950	2,472	2,043	1,024	1,110	10,184
Dorchester County	140,010	2,699	4,599	2,259	3,220	3,778	2,545	1,389	1,496	14,687
Florence County	137,473	3,204	5,236	2,629	3,878	4,456	3,321	2,195	2,089	18,568
Greenville County	459,753	10,254	14,117	8,719	11,898	14,093	10,879	7,216	7,557	60,362
Greenwood County	69,731	2,178	2,350	1,246	1,976	2,649	1,664	1,508	1,796	10,839
Horry County	276,156	8,564	13,399	7,388	10,662	12,409	8,444	5,629	4,537	49,069
Lancaster County	77,898	2,223	3,267	2,153	2,651	3,054	2,487	1,474	984	12,803
Laurens County	66,349	1,619	2,744	1,302	2,235	2,261	1,597	1,474	1,333	10,202
Lexington County	266,797	6,820	9,328	5,056	7,180	7,853	5,371	4,437	3,872	33,769
Oconee County	74,425	2,121	3,209	2,123	2,950	3,789	2,844	1,763	1,165	14,634
Orangeburg County	91,835	2,185	3,644	2,035	2,454	3,757	2,492	2,003	1,411	14,152
Pickens County	119,440	2,767	3,747	2,334	2,922	4,159	2,834	2,360	1,906	16,515
Richland County	389,648	7,682	11,828	5,573	7,767	9,438	6,934	4,545	5,177	39,434
Spartanburg County	286,563	7,753	10,039	5,384	7,124	10,522	7,223	5,208	3,986	39,447
Sumter County	107,642	2,552	3,731	2,018	2,366	3,640	2,762	1,656	1,694	14,136
York County	230,600	4,712	7,688	4,089	5,540	6,684	5,196	2,778	2,730	27,017
South Dakota										
Minnehaha County	172,303	3,664	5,394	2,615	2,898	4,422	3,245	3,199	3,019	19,398
Pennington County	102,742	2,571	3,515	1,616	2,150	3,681	2,406	2,054	2,256	14,163
Tennessee										
Anderson County	75,255	2,245	2,840	1,694	2,291	2,878	2,074	1,625	2,717	13,279
Blount County	123,676	3,266	4,832	2,772	3,424	5,769	3,869	2,508	2,227	20,569
Bradley County	100,080	2,424	3,371	1,904	2,880	3,902	2,721	1,815	1,467	14,689
Davidson County	637,303	13,506	18,069	9,159	11,226	16,159	12,397	8,976	9,196	67,113
Greene County	68,901	1,871	3,235	1,712	2,641	3,085	2,160	1,708	1,117	12,423
Hamilton County	341,248	9,915	11,787	6,937	9,689	11,135	8,811	7,310	7,226	51,108
Knox County	437,095	11,207	14,629	7,389	11,644	13,118	11,133	8,110	7,110	58,504
Madison County	98,364	1,949	3,445	1,830	2,403	3,142	2,293	1,784	1,819	13,271
Maury County	81,491	2,224	3,147	1,723	1,911	2,653	2,017	1,364	1,325	10,993
Montgomery County	178,227	2,579	4,327	2,082	2,855	3,463	2,685	1,735	1,451	14,271
Putnam County	72,845	1,642	2,572	1,713	2,135	2,297	2,122	1,283	1,299	10,849
Robertson County	66,714	1,389	2,326	1,213	1,488	2,149	1,277	829	1,151	8,107
Rutherford County	269,144	4,897	7,634	3,491	4,479	5,986	4,041	2,485	2,691	23,173
Sevier County	91,338	2,589	3,721	2,018	3,217	3,674	2,578	1,795	1,258	14,540
Shelby County	934,654	22,008	27,563	14,809	17,787	22,388	16,945	14,154	12,047	98,130
Sullivan County	156,895	4,231	7,026	3,457	5,354	7,883	5,506	4,073	3,763	30,036
Sumner County	163,737	4,303	5,545	3,558	3,768	5,903	3,676	2,526	2,285	21,716
Washington County	124,150	3,009	5,050	2,494	3,463	5,048	3,232	2,578	2,503	19,318
Williamson County	188,432	5,352	5,903	2,874	3,950	4,461	3,797	1,653	2,308	19,043
Wilson County	116,756	2,875	4,429	2,548	3,335	3,587	2,678	1,573	1,339	15,060

Table B-2: Counties—Older Population by Age—*Continued*

	Total Population	60 to 61 Years	62 to 64 Years	65 to 66 Years	67 to 69 Years	70 to 74 Years	75 to 79 Years	80 to 84 Years	85 Years and Over	65 Years and Over
Texas										
Angelina County	87,254	2,175	2,920	1,870	2,192	2,498	2,377	1,594	1,684	12,215
Bastrop County	74,713	1,710	2,810	1,275	1,431	2,242	1,703	933	1,272	8,856
Bell County	317,284	5,000	8,012	4,041	5,247	6,768	4,856	4,278	3,140	28,330
Bexar County	1,754,058	35,443	48,846	25,636	33,869	42,237	32,810	24,899	24,257	183,708
Bowie County	92,907	2,288	3,303	2,037	2,192	3,191	2,471	1,764	1,836	13,491
Brazoria County	319,498	5,820	9,160	4,880	6,671	7,439	5,008	3,687	3,916	31,601
Brazos County	197,968	3,210	4,254	2,177	2,481	3,638	2,773	2,171	1,587	14,827
Cameron County	411,930	7,150	9,888	6,161	7,705	11,597	9,772	6,361	4,957	46,553
Collin County	811,948	14,149	21,782	12,139	14,827	15,891	9,933	7,593	6,380	66,763
Comal County	111,768	3,532	4,723	2,605	3,627	4,418	2,895	2,207	2,214	17,966
Coryell County	76,471	1,263	1,386	943	1,234	1,506	1,213	797	434	6,127
Dallas County	2,411,891	46,235	62,033	31,736	41,526	49,599	37,472	28,980	27,091	216,404
Denton County	686,622	12,303	16,080	9,113	11,823	11,332	8,000	5,364	4,958	50,590
Ector County	140,323	2,924	2,984	1,844	2,846	3,079	2,564	2,159	1,576	14,068
Ellis County	152,258	3,202	4,757	2,673	3,254	4,000	2,848	1,653	1,494	15,922
El Paso County	816,295	15,031	20,413	11,326	14,054	20,253	16,631	12,022	10,499	84,785
Fort Bend County	608,747	12,794	16,870	8,463	10,062	11,982	7,070	6,210	4,302	48,089
Galveston County	296,100	7,411	9,825	4,902	6,978	8,122	6,326	4,121	3,987	34,436
Grayson County	121,434	2,877	4,779	2,165	3,636	4,721	3,424	2,693	2,535	19,174
Gregg County	122,287	3,341	3,529	2,185	2,371	3,875	2,983	2,615	2,547	16,576
Guadalupe County	136,021	2,822	4,592	2,643	3,528	3,201	2,975	2,436	1,432	16,215
Harris County	4,178,437	78,951	107,361	55,828	68,175	84,676	59,201	44,152	39,951	351,983
Harrison County	66,832	1,754	2,341	1,448	1,700	2,090	2,053	764	1,096	9,151
Hays County	163,675	3,116	4,786	2,995	3,075	2,811	2,592	1,681	1,298	14,452
Henderson County	78,843	2,495	3,342	1,930	3,614	3,326	2,681	2,264	1,548	15,363
Hidalgo County	793,312	12,690	17,052	9,788	13,389	18,791	14,179	11,268	8,386	75,801
Hunt County	86,689	2,599	3,181	1,654	2,266	3,150	1,890	1,431	1,703	12,094
Jefferson County	252,457	4,919	8,826	4,090	5,263	6,995	6,702	4,774	4,403	32,227
Johnson County	152,218	3,030	4,436	2,604	4,029	4,613	3,604	1,858	1,550	18,258
Kaufman County	105,310	2,591	3,239	1,346	2,529	3,059	1,796	1,316	1,155	11,201
Liberty County	76,119	1,964	2,172	1,203	1,786	2,278	1,800	810	854	8,731
Lubbock County	283,082	5,104	7,243	4,518	5,370	7,085	6,354	4,321	3,853	31,501
McLennan County	237,471	4,400	7,026	3,877	5,377	6,341	5,572	4,387	4,469	30,023
Midland County	141,207	3,247	3,758	1,867	2,385	3,569	3,084	2,542	1,851	15,298
Montgomery County	472,014	11,040	15,067	9,101	9,590	13,071	8,491	5,685	5,195	51,133
Nacogdoches County	65,421	1,243	1,853	1,020	1,382	1,786	1,330	1,246	988	7,752
Nueces County	343,697	8,139	11,239	5,623	7,755	9,712	8,027	5,825	5,367	42,309
Orange County	82,444	2,077	2,645	1,492	2,143	2,762	2,431	1,502	1,287	11,617
Parker County	118,462	3,092	4,174	2,247	2,965	4,133	2,993	1,648	1,361	15,347
Potter County	121,878	2,439	3,870	1,725	2,165	3,201	2,435	1,917	1,993	13,436
Randall County	123,283	2,872	3,995	1,832	2,858	4,026	3,004	1,955	1,801	15,476
Rockwall County	81,054	2,094	2,467	1,373	1,405	2,266	1,396	1,185	528	8,153
San Patricio County	64,863	1,347	2,358	1,394	1,726	1,732	1,536	1,210	906	8,504
Smith County	212,694	4,901	6,644	4,021	4,711	7,916	5,735	4,087	4,509	30,979
Tarrant County	1,847,884	37,805	51,139	26,804	32,557	39,135	29,722	22,232	20,334	170,784
Taylor County	132,658	2,847	3,543	2,155	3,108	3,935	3,546	2,497	2,361	17,602
Tom Green County	111,883	2,305	3,427	2,341	2,561	3,253	3,297	2,461	1,628	15,541
Travis County	1,062,335	19,636	26,732	12,942	16,639	17,144	13,491	10,244	9,950	80,410
Victoria County	87,847	1,404	3,394	1,499	2,205	2,789	2,436	1,676	1,310	11,915
Walker County	68,254	1,250	1,627	1,224	1,456	1,718	1,352	735	677	7,162
Webb County	255,135	4,059	5,089	2,732	3,722	4,958	3,545	2,562	2,711	20,230
Wichita County	131,281	2,805	3,871	2,288	2,747	3,847	3,674	2,289	2,405	17,250
Williamson County	441,748	8,674	11,491	6,087	8,811	10,419	7,130	4,464	4,429	41,340
Utah										
Cache County	114,454	1,638	1,860	1,275	1,564	2,115	1,658	1,284	1,146	9,042
Davis County	311,852	5,505	6,591	3,663	4,815	6,196	4,941	3,669	3,013	26,297
Salt Lake County	1,048,261	18,387	26,983	12,802	17,709	21,634	16,083	12,859	11,735	92,822
Utah County	530,147	6,457	7,974	4,894	6,452	8,385	6,345	4,949	4,356	35,381
Washington County	141,594	2,354	4,602	2,934	4,253	6,453	5,081	3,286	3,421	25,428
Weber County	234,303	4,146	5,925	3,426	3,978	5,575	4,714	3,418	3,199	24,310
Vermont										
Chittenden County	157,675	3,819	5,044	2,864	3,123	4,105	2,897	2,663	2,866	18,518
Virginia										
Albemarle County	100,757	2,360	3,361	2,032	2,102	3,729	2,671	2,265	2,222	15,021
Arlington County	215,481	4,243	5,516	3,141	3,289	4,469	3,112	2,336	2,506	18,853
Augusta County	73,638	2,269	2,977	1,592	2,513	3,201	2,170	1,666	1,253	12,395
Bedford County	69,252	2,216	2,869	1,703	2,354	3,339	1,973	1,542	1,002	11,913
Chesterfield County	320,514	7,651	10,687	5,846	6,661	8,799	5,770	4,125	4,107	35,308
Fairfax County	1,103,177	27,817	36,971	18,249	22,334	27,326	18,513	13,652	12,982	113,056
Fauquier County	66,003	1,832	2,464	1,387	1,895	2,212	1,474	1,294	774	9,036
Frederick County	79,483	2,260	3,035	1,553	2,089	2,474	2,170	1,091	992	10,369
Hanover County	100,255	2,279	3,811	1,805	2,858	3,172	2,585	1,579	1,678	13,677
Henrico County	310,972	7,292	10,941	4,989	6,337	9,039	6,764	5,874	6,425	39,428
James City County	68,048	1,990	2,979	1,614	3,295	3,100	2,579	2,142	1,762	14,492
Loudoun County	326,222	5,447	6,516	3,887	5,088	4,694	3,583	3,197	2,244	22,693
Montgomery County	94,800	1,871	2,363	1,025	1,883	2,359	1,677	1,091	1,497	9,532
Prince William County	418,759	8,296	10,646	4,980	7,123	7,647	4,615	2,474	3,013	29,852
Roanoke County	92,748	2,952	3,516	1,681	3,176	3,973	3,147	2,473	2,136	16,586
Rockingham County	76,946	1,966	2,920	1,513	1,792	3,386	2,107	2,191	1,564	12,553
Spotsylvania County	124,345	3,251	3,747	2,146	2,683	2,897	1,882	1,870	1,411	12,889
Stafford County	132,152	2,304	2,809	2,076	2,100	2,486	1,568	966	1,006	10,202
York County	65,791	1,678	2,159	965	1,999	1,914	1,605	1,037	675	8,195

Table B-2: Counties—Older Population by Age—*Continued*

	Total Population	60 to 61 Years	62 to 64 Years	65 to 66 Years	67 to 69 Years	70 to 74 Years	75 to 79 Years	80 to 84 Years	85 Years and Over	65 Years and Over
Washington										
Benton County	179,809	4,566	5,917	3,102	4,447	5,073	3,761	2,728	2,623	21,734
Chelan County	73,221	2,020	2,700	1,127	2,080	2,725	2,370	1,134	1,842	11,278
Clallam County	71,737	2,386	3,766	1,826	3,490	4,243	2,882	2,674	2,484	17,599
Clark County	432,801	10,931	15,721	8,262	10,563	11,823	8,529	6,326	6,670	52,173
Cowlitz County	102,291	2,643	4,626	2,225	3,131	4,091	2,791	2,136	2,221	16,595
Franklin County	82,715	1,647	2,266	807	997	1,562	735	1,220	627	5,948
Grant County	90,714	1,909	2,226	1,867	2,047	2,458	1,737	1,593	1,305	11,007
Grays Harbor County	72,289	2,102	3,169	2,062	2,162	2,867	2,251	1,531	1,222	12,095
Island County	78,970	2,535	3,697	2,393	2,817	3,827	2,268	1,750	2,029	15,084
King County	1,972,284	45,798	61,039	33,080	39,593	48,730	36,008	29,369	34,760	221,540
Kitsap County	253,763	7,535	10,250	5,307	6,798	8,794	6,042	3,908	4,247	35,096
Lewis County	75,594	2,728	2,720	1,515	2,644	3,340	1,951	1,809	2,104	13,363
Pierce County	803,585	19,355	25,372	14,188	17,655	20,285	15,741	12,192	11,896	91,957
Skagit County	117,691	3,125	5,164	2,502	4,086	4,397	3,682	2,389	2,652	19,708
Snohomish County	723,763	17,433	24,065	11,339	15,253	17,852	12,410	10,463	10,667	77,984
Spokane County	473,793	11,727	17,550	9,477	11,368	13,436	11,472	8,851	8,679	63,283
Thurston County	255,927	6,858	10,481	4,946	6,230	8,393	6,150	4,277	4,483	34,479
Whatcom County	203,482	5,664	7,684	4,010	5,712	6,012	4,183	4,339	3,710	27,966
Yakima County	245,797	4,963	6,706	4,143	5,623	5,993	4,980	3,857	4,420	29,016
West Virginia										
Berkeley County	105,863	2,889	3,773	2,000	2,434	3,265	2,032	1,480	1,263	12,474
Cabell County	96,651	3,004	3,207	2,181	2,264	3,585	2,911	2,436	2,097	15,474
Harrison County	69,220	1,537	2,842	1,255	1,975	2,954	1,974	1,755	1,721	11,634
Kanawha County	192,432	5,994	7,011	4,050	5,698	7,630	6,773	4,295	4,259	32,705
Monongalia County	98,573	2,277	2,522	1,280	1,876	2,254	1,910	1,323	1,324	9,967
Raleigh County	79,033	2,195	3,666	1,788	1,919	3,118	2,531	2,170	1,400	12,926
Wood County	86,851	2,482	3,357	2,128	2,813	3,446	2,852	1,825	1,837	14,901
Wisconsin										
Brown County	250,712	5,862	6,988	3,578	4,796	7,180	5,517	3,795	4,781	29,647
Dane County	496,374	11,229	15,675	7,412	9,941	11,289	8,782	7,853	7,509	52,786
Dodge County	88,596	2,137	2,842	1,565	1,869	3,263	2,246	2,319	2,162	13,424
Eau Claire County	99,769	2,498	3,335	1,423	2,200	2,890	2,095	2,076	2,074	12,758
Fond du Lac County	101,798	3,000	3,604	2,040	2,614	3,175	2,619	2,343	2,830	15,621
Jefferson County	84,046	2,049	2,576	1,454	1,960	2,934	1,856	1,518	1,605	11,327
Kenosha County	167,242	3,355	4,472	2,260	3,130	4,596	3,002	3,122	2,949	19,059
La Crosse County	115,603	2,454	4,031	2,138	2,288	3,465	2,853	2,231	2,705	15,680
Manitowoc County	81,011	1,889	3,346	1,603	2,164	3,347	2,389	1,911	2,652	14,066
Marathon County	134,459	3,830	4,618	2,552	3,409	4,263	3,314	2,938	3,252	19,728
Milwaukee County	951,833	19,584	26,106	13,726	16,989	22,732	20,612	18,451	17,433	109,943
Outagamie County	177,774	4,114	5,288	2,713	3,977	4,579	4,125	2,864	3,166	21,424
Ozaukee County	86,581	2,733	2,769	1,732	2,686	2,832	2,433	2,066	1,899	13,648
Portage County	70,206	1,865	2,592	1,030	1,585	2,299	1,540	1,349	1,451	9,254
Racine County	195,086	4,592	6,769	3,434	4,809	5,772	4,929	3,814	3,575	26,333
Rock County	160,240	3,307	5,551	2,514	3,905	5,320	4,160	3,311	2,999	22,209
St. Croix County	84,856	2,148	2,270	1,351	1,621	2,050	1,421	1,410	1,039	8,892
Sheboygan County	115,224	2,441	4,225	1,886	2,890	3,968	3,308	2,139	2,993	17,184
Walworth County	102,519	2,555	3,438	2,119	2,526	3,016	2,433	1,801	2,215	14,110
Washington County	132,276	3,694	4,590	2,315	2,988	4,597	2,979	2,554	2,953	18,386
Waukesha County	391,017	10,156	15,420	7,356	9,911	12,950	10,128	8,805	8,728	57,878
Winnebago County	167,860	3,858	5,557	2,701	3,995	4,776	4,200	3,159	3,956	22,787
Wood County	74,604	1,972	2,723	1,542	1,892	3,051	2,465	1,896	2,098	12,944
Wyoming										
Laramie County	93,030	2,227	2,777	1,485	2,359	2,981	2,178	1,586	1,489	12,078
Natrona County	76,821	2,255	2,330	1,631	1,438	1,984	1,898	1,355	1,300	9,606

Table B-3: Places—Older Population by Age

	Total Population	60 to 61 Years	62 to 64 Years	65 to 66 Years	67 to 69 Years	70 to 74 Years	75 to 79 Years	80 to 84 Years	85 Years and Over	65 Years and Over
Alabama										
Birmingham city	211,827	5,109	6,439	3,432	4,273	5,930	5,290	3,915	4,215	27,055
Dothan city	67,269	1,821	1,972	1,312	1,703	2,283	2,064	1,349	1,109	9,820
Hoover city	82,214	2,413	2,735	1,222	2,089	2,237	1,623	1,552	1,241	9,964
Huntsville city	181,734	4,308	5,690	2,793	4,614	6,396	4,968	3,054	3,665	25,490
Mobile city	194,829	4,561	6,282	3,649	4,902	5,856	5,101	3,593	3,885	26,986
Montgomery city	206,346	5,412	5,375	4,023	4,118	5,250	4,799	3,255	3,096	24,541
Tuscaloosa city	92,217	1,673	1,950	1,010	1,385	2,133	2,082	1,355	1,507	9,472
Alaska										
Anchorage Municipality	296,039	6,331	8,613	4,050	4,453	5,766	3,733	2,991	1,777	22,770
Arizona										
Avondale city	77,270	1,238	1,578	1,039	962	1,293	589	321	293	4,497
Chandler city	240,626	4,732	6,605	3,279	4,202	4,757	3,236	2,572	2,299	20,345
Flagstaff city	66,400	1,002	1,295	702	1,062	877	828	417	584	4,470
Glendale city	229,166	4,767	6,374	3,293	3,964	5,110	3,391	2,743	2,434	20,935
Goodyear city	67,545	1,365	1,470	1,074	1,840	2,342	1,209	594	590	7,649
Mesa city	445,671	9,965	15,076	7,879	11,838	15,906	12,876	10,896	8,643	68,038
Peoria city	156,920	3,089	5,040	2,624	3,742	4,860	4,238	3,407	3,407	22,278
Phoenix city	1,467,400	29,205	37,288	20,600	24,314	29,883	22,091	16,640	15,505	129,033
Scottsdale city	220,293	6,436	8,807	5,084	8,345	12,118	7,441	5,883	6,449	45,320
Surprise city	119,378	2,154	3,464	3,495	4,636	6,732	4,353	2,600	1,587	23,403
Tempe city	164,186	3,040	4,386	1,921	2,916	3,340	2,067	1,557	1,951	13,752
Tucson city	522,770	11,576	14,562	9,404	10,137	14,726	10,927	9,816	9,624	64,634
Yuma city	95,130	1,383	2,076	1,634	1,903	3,081	2,623	1,784	1,235	12,260
Arkansas										
Fayetteville city	75,473	1,191	1,786	675	660	1,700	1,372	889	983	6,279
Fort Smith city	86,981	1,798	2,736	1,414	2,044	2,030	2,016	1,830	1,452	10,786
Jonesboro city	68,844	1,541	1,992	806	1,376	1,519	1,548	1,160	1,176	7,585
Little Rock city	195,242	4,483	5,892	3,157	3,712	5,374	3,974	3,260	3,427	22,904
Springdale city	74,156	722	1,646	753	984	1,458	1,250	756	978	6,179
California										
Alameda city	74,760	2,394	2,641	1,320	1,973	1,915	1,523	1,413	1,309	9,453
Alhambra city	83,722	2,294	2,292	1,578	1,926	2,734	1,958	1,905	2,319	12,420
Anaheim city	340,306	6,464	8,675	4,351	5,664	7,735	5,624	4,841	4,890	33,105
Antioch city	104,041	2,484	3,487	1,569	1,906	2,790	1,564	869	967	9,665
Bakersfield city	353,780	5,985	8,115	4,219	6,221	7,169	5,532	4,249	3,828	31,218
Baldwin Park city	75,914	1,574	1,799	1,228	1,056	1,772	1,172	808	903	6,939
Bellflower city	77,006	1,087	2,093	949	1,289	1,317	1,152	1,253	755	6,715
Berkeley city	114,156	2,844	3,576	2,107	2,853	3,647	2,037	1,585	2,062	14,291
Buena Park city	81,471	1,922	1,878	1,520	1,363	2,150	1,323	1,563	1,374	9,293
Burbank city	103,900	2,288	3,040	1,802	2,075	3,222	2,940	2,051	2,623	14,713
Camarillo city	65,671	1,367	2,237	1,605	1,652	2,054	2,057	2,003	2,216	11,587
Carlsbad city	107,615	2,550	3,417	1,615	2,737	3,500	3,256	2,204	2,843	16,155
Carson city	92,358	2,400	3,147	1,628	2,157	3,820	2,523	1,517	1,024	12,669
Chico city	86,920	1,664	2,489	1,237	1,014	1,997	1,602	1,982	1,554	9,386
Chino city	79,441	1,784	1,849	1,184	1,603	1,804	1,108	670	627	6,996
Chino Hills city	75,762	1,874	2,119	1,064	1,270	1,312	751	736	416	5,549
Chula Vista city	248,425	4,284	6,391	3,945	4,447	5,630	4,656	3,342	3,459	25,479
Citrus Heights city	84,192	1,989	2,489	1,566	1,965	2,700	2,198	1,784	1,476	11,689
Clovis city	97,434	1,872	2,940	2,145	1,849	2,103	1,728	1,564	1,412	10,801
Compton city	97,054	1,491	1,906	997	1,573	1,863	1,239	909	762	7,343
Concord city	123,571	2,449	3,888	2,199	2,392	3,209	2,726	2,200	2,171	14,897
Corona city	155,603	2,396	3,636	1,685	2,342	3,077	2,219	1,157	1,396	11,876
Costa Mesa city	111,034	2,100	2,769	1,624	1,732	2,033	1,331	1,355	1,796	9,871
Daly City city	102,417	2,243	4,152	1,767	2,480	3,623	2,526	1,470	2,039	13,905
Davis city	65,800	1,052	1,531	623	1,246	1,116	738	735	961	5,419
Downey city	112,341	1,979	2,958	1,757	1,641	2,834	1,926	1,563	1,915	11,636
El Cajon city	100,631	1,679	2,381	1,743	1,672	2,229	1,737	1,477	1,964	10,822
Elk Grove city	156,190	3,107	3,786	2,048	2,451	3,701	2,145	2,032	2,078	14,455
El Monte city	114,338	2,225	3,163	1,739	2,072	2,743	2,106	1,558	1,549	11,767
Escondido city	145,990	2,375	3,769	1,738	2,042	3,101	2,697	2,218	3,112	14,908
Fairfield city	106,469	1,785	2,563	1,422	2,324	2,235	2,424	1,734	1,181	11,320
Folsom city	72,779	1,697	1,544	902	1,231	1,597	1,189	743	1,145	6,807
Fontana city	199,630	2,901	3,633	2,191	2,014	3,098	1,654	1,364	1,790	12,111
Fremont city	218,160	4,222	5,867	3,132	4,279	5,259	4,590	3,334	3,434	24,028
Fresno city	501,350	9,192	11,865	6,090	8,417	10,575	7,672	6,665	7,248	46,667
Fullerton city	136,886	2,395	3,805	2,427	2,424	3,337	3,296	2,390	2,740	16,614
Garden Grove city	172,868	3,664	4,573	2,170	3,547	4,679	3,461	2,878	2,693	19,428
Glendale city	193,099	4,798	6,489	3,128	5,489	6,288	6,156	4,934	4,479	30,474
Hawthorne city	85,016	1,544	1,661	914	1,369	1,634	1,194	390	834	6,335
Hayward city	147,038	3,134	3,936	2,277	2,018	3,680	2,519	2,648	2,104	15,246
Hemet city	80,140	1,888	2,631	1,924	2,698	3,740	3,152	3,188	3,482	18,184
Hesperia city	91,307	1,967	2,368	1,108	1,640	2,382	1,630	1,306	1,009	9,075
Huntington Beach city	193,074	4,822	7,080	4,332	4,969	6,403	4,991	3,459	3,872	28,026
Indio city	77,953	1,614	2,154	1,363	1,857	3,335	1,363	1,540	1,105	10,563
Inglewood city	110,528	2,153	2,800	1,734	2,218	2,334	1,935	1,001	1,146	10,368
Irvine city	221,358	3,886	6,282	2,936	3,437	5,276	2,914	2,044	2,486	19,093
Jurupa Valley city [1]	96,465	1,686	2,319	1,152	1,709	1,654	1,250	858	743	7,366

[1] Jurupa Valley city was incorporated in 2011. The 2010 population is the U.S. Census Bureau's estimates base figure.

Table B-3: Places—Older Population by Age—*Continued*

	Total Population	60 to 61 Years	62 to 64 Years	65 to 66 Years	67 to 69 Years	70 to 74 Years	75 to 79 Years	80 to 84 Years	85 Years and Over	65 Years and Over
California—Cont.										
Lake Forest city	78,188	1,624	2,220	1,207	1,573	1,962	1,546	793	902	7,983
Lakewood city	80,475	2,098	2,398	884	1,374	2,524	1,881	1,679	1,347	9,689
Lancaster city	158,108	3,065	4,046	1,812	2,453	3,255	2,674	1,645	1,670	13,509
Livermore city	82,326	2,202	2,436	1,443	1,566	1,923	1,820	866	1,041	8,659
Long Beach city	465,125	9,626	13,080	6,089	8,342	9,992	7,422	6,091	6,108	44,044
Los Angeles city	3,825,653	76,499	99,153	57,041	69,088	93,513	72,042	57,874	59,670	409,228
Lynwood city	70,014	913	1,179	635	991	734	923	693	590	4,566
Manteca city	69,309	1,299	2,316	1,096	931	1,980	1,340	752	929	7,028
Menifee city	79,843	1,752	2,201	1,142	3,241	3,159	3,376	1,670	1,902	14,490
Merced city	79,987	1,485	1,992	1,168	1,516	1,607	1,213	683	1,106	7,293
Milpitas city	67,530	1,689	1,789	1,042	1,375	1,431	1,332	1,029	511	6,720
Mission Viejo city	94,434	2,945	3,862	1,722	2,529	3,283	2,655	1,891	2,122	14,202
Modesto city	202,400	4,376	5,933	3,054	3,964	4,814	3,929	3,828	3,861	23,450
Moreno Valley city	197,068	3,346	4,132	2,085	2,275	3,126	2,756	1,501	1,386	13,129
Mountain View city	75,381	1,365	2,042	1,160	1,520	1,854	1,223	1,192	1,221	8,170
Murrieta city	105,369	2,151	2,463	1,362	1,754	2,283	2,124	2,013	966	10,502
Napa city	77,714	1,925	2,737	1,621	1,319	2,254	2,083	1,548	1,806	10,631
Newport Beach city	86,259	2,748	3,534	2,023	2,367	4,320	2,544	2,503	2,363	16,120
Norwalk city	105,961	1,675	2,878	1,578	1,891	2,354	1,806	1,531	1,423	10,583
Oakland city	396,030	8,933	13,027	6,907	7,198	11,240	7,380	5,770	7,390	45,885
Oceanside city	169,530	3,639	4,641	2,534	3,473	4,327	3,525	3,448	3,621	20,928
Ontario city	165,909	2,302	4,364	1,752	2,313	2,450	2,469	1,912	1,393	12,289
Orange city	138,220	2,922	3,782	2,242	2,782	3,692	2,509	2,087	1,874	15,186
Oxnard city	200,015	3,567	4,402	2,321	3,343	3,642	3,199	2,232	1,956	16,693
Palmdale city	154,383	2,293	2,644	1,365	2,096	2,558	2,172	1,165	1,377	10,733
Palo Alto city	65,498	1,463	1,664	1,282	1,909	2,472	1,697	1,730	2,206	11,296
Pasadena city	137,900	2,826	3,965	2,334	3,214	3,439	3,196	2,946	4,120	19,249
Perris city	70,174	372	904	463	507	1,127	382	498	149	3,126
Pleasanton city	71,366	1,671	2,148	1,351	1,340	1,851	1,431	1,138	934	8,045
Pomona city	149,961	2,996	3,161	2,069	1,775	3,043	1,949	1,455	1,763	12,054
Rancho Cordova city	66,066	1,084	2,424	959	1,134	1,756	1,484	898	925	7,156
Rancho Cucamonga city	168,448	4,077	3,783	1,931	2,767	2,858	2,449	2,026	1,935	13,966
Redding city	90,351	2,064	3,508	1,793	2,319	3,493	2,413	2,559	2,393	14,970
Redlands city	69,395	1,841	1,818	942	1,637	2,123	1,592	1,222	1,511	9,027
Redondo Beach city	67,256	1,040	2,022	992	1,526	1,761	1,476	1,046	819	7,620
Redwood City city	77,945	1,597	1,680	1,344	1,681	1,702	1,303	1,053	1,597	8,680
Rialto city	100,663	1,462	2,068	1,435	1,527	1,559	1,157	1,223	527	7,428
Richmond city	105,304	2,358	3,767	1,968	1,986	2,134	1,735	1,196	1,225	10,244
Riverside city	309,793	5,019	6,873	3,790	5,648	6,433	4,652	4,162	4,001	28,686
Roseville city	122,221	2,337	3,403	1,942	2,717	3,498	3,566	2,648	1,966	16,337
Sacramento city	471,552	10,233	12,942	7,159	8,923	11,139	9,014	7,769	8,441	52,625
Salinas city	152,650	2,400	3,280	1,588	1,817	3,127	2,029	1,392	1,609	11,562
San Bernardino city	211,847	3,413	4,395	2,490	3,105	4,334	3,247	2,096	1,917	17,189
San Buenaventura (Ventura) city	106,994	2,565	3,816	2,368	2,414	3,060	2,654	2,132	2,802	15,430
San Diego city	1,321,545	27,364	35,375	19,822	24,194	32,775	24,824	21,769	21,880	145,264
San Francisco city	815,234	20,796	28,758	13,849	17,150	25,317	21,432	16,823	18,043	112,614
San Jose city	969,324	20,258	25,905	14,581	18,792	23,534	18,034	14,219	12,782	101,942
San Leandro city	85,958	2,320	3,363	1,540	2,150	2,219	1,756	1,750	2,141	11,556
San Marcos city	85,213	1,070	2,062	1,391	1,711	1,394	1,685	1,695	1,650	9,526
San Mateo city	98,499	2,471	2,930	1,497	2,127	3,151	2,356	2,349	2,857	14,337
San Ramon city	73,160	959	1,726	751	1,121	1,480	679	829	554	5,414
Santa Ana city	328,180	4,407	5,571	3,261	3,485	5,664	3,500	2,942	3,035	21,887
Santa Barbara city	88,996	1,670	2,822	1,829	2,234	1,957	2,135	1,547	2,791	12,493
Santa Clara city	118,010	1,722	2,944	1,124	1,478	2,648	2,120	1,837	1,697	10,904
Santa Clarita city	177,748	3,703	5,057	2,989	3,579	3,915	2,478	2,243	2,495	17,699
Santa Maria city	100,529	1,230	2,172	1,150	1,517	2,250	1,784	1,399	1,527	9,627
Santa Monica city	90,780	2,312	3,025	1,857	2,284	2,889	2,324	1,910	2,290	13,554
Santa Rosa city	169,376	4,681	5,225	2,707	3,547	4,707	3,559	3,680	4,090	22,290
Simi Valley city	125,188	3,185	3,743	2,054	2,903	3,124	2,356	1,694	1,458	13,589
South Gate city	94,875	1,745	1,810	1,208	1,381	1,959	1,163	1,046	656	7,413
Stockton city	295,354	5,231	7,666	4,212	5,251	6,837	4,698	4,368	4,067	29,433
Sunnyvale city	143,443	2,535	3,435	2,072	2,338	3,706	2,746	2,658	2,265	15,785
Temecula city	103,101	2,152	2,445	1,032	1,433	1,930	1,642	955	761	7,753
Thousand Oaks city	127,762	3,992	4,643	2,625	3,588	4,018	3,474	2,294	3,009	19,008
Torrance city	146,284	3,150	4,201	3,048	3,063	5,676	3,931	3,611	3,762	23,091
Tracy city	83,957	1,378	1,560	924	1,651	1,582	986	852	462	6,457
Turlock city	69,201	1,164	1,762	997	1,340	1,867	1,460	1,055	1,378	8,097
Tustin city	76,823	1,203	1,768	851	1,378	1,641	1,071	929	541	6,411
Union City city	70,700	1,712	2,045	1,326	1,490	1,919	1,427	1,070	906	8,138
Upland city	74,570	1,946	2,196	1,609	1,736	2,254	1,926	1,249	1,009	9,783
Vacaville city	93,276	2,289	2,728	1,442	1,859	2,906	1,794	879	1,140	10,020
Vallejo city	116,927	3,416	4,747	1,959	2,412	3,294	2,558	1,831	2,194	14,248
Victorville city	118,277	2,003	2,237	905	2,253	1,958	1,532	1,336	756	8,740
Visalia city	125,986	2,465	3,596	2,021	2,280	2,982	2,418	1,967	1,932	13,600
Vista city	95,053	1,841	2,102	1,042	1,745	1,752	1,625	1,228	1,884	9,276
West Covina city	106,829	2,514	3,194	1,563	2,268	2,667	2,040	2,010	2,496	13,044
Westminster city	90,669	2,113	2,893	1,460	2,216	3,711	2,665	2,074	1,585	13,711
Whittier city	85,766	1,703	1,876	1,306	1,364	1,799	1,768	1,874	2,000	10,111
Yorba Linda city	65,698	1,588	2,271	1,393	1,926	1,645	1,346	799	1,187	8,296
Yuba City city	65,005	1,591	1,850	874	1,429	2,237	1,563	1,130	1,025	8,258

Table B-3: Places—Older Population by Age—*Continued*

	Total Population	60 to 61 Years	62 to 64 Years	65 to 66 Years	67 to 69 Years	70 to 74 Years	75 to 79 Years	80 to 84 Years	85 Years and Over	65 Years and Over
Colorado										
Arvada city	107,960	3,604	3,527	2,254	2,956	3,541	3,015	2,066	1,979	15,811
Aurora city	332,532	7,061	9,238	5,208	6,073	6,922	5,254	3,825	3,774	31,056
Boulder city	100,403	1,899	2,184	1,408	1,495	1,982	1,485	1,223	1,627	9,220
Centennial city	102,215	3,253	3,764	1,971	2,820	2,363	2,409	1,514	1,707	12,784
Colorado Springs city	425,725	8,958	13,953	6,750	8,515	10,899	8,851	5,741	6,184	46,940
Denver city	619,016	13,338	16,813	9,035	11,176	14,020	10,374	9,194	10,683	64,482
Fort Collins city	146,235	2,960	3,615	1,669	2,207	3,053	1,824	1,770	2,112	12,635
Greeley city	94,217	2,012	2,382	1,030	1,848	2,531	1,758	1,654	1,479	10,300
Lakewood city	144,282	4,241	4,401	2,459	3,567	4,754	3,648	3,364	3,100	20,892
Longmont city	87,474	1,795	2,312	1,538	1,637	2,145	1,655	1,366	1,561	9,902
Loveland city	68,815	1,380	2,302	1,093	1,512	2,252	1,921	1,488	1,590	9,856
Pueblo city	107,364	2,755	3,627	1,811	2,920	3,344	3,394	2,846	2,443	16,758
Thornton city	121,742	2,035	2,465	1,401	1,672	2,099	1,348	934	1,164	8,618
Westminster city	107,778	2,022	3,184	1,420	2,032	2,458	1,745	1,665	1,259	10,579
Connecticut										
Bridgeport city	145,555	2,615	3,730	1,853	2,829	2,838	2,154	2,188	2,483	14,345
Danbury city	82,007	1,434	2,509	1,471	1,623	2,076	1,347	1,600	1,548	9,665
Hartford city	124,894	2,054	3,102	1,840	1,853	2,926	2,173	1,287	1,679	11,758
New Britain city	73,200	1,578	1,780	1,191	1,467	1,577	1,447	1,491	1,782	8,955
New Haven city	130,378	2,167	3,116	1,863	2,069	2,487	2,555	1,712	2,035	12,721
Norwalk city	86,632	2,651	3,662	1,767	2,335	2,858	2,389	2,045	1,737	13,131
Stamford city	123,995	2,097	3,227	1,980	2,572	3,069	3,169	2,491	2,359	15,640
Waterbury city	110,089	2,229	3,456	1,592	2,195	2,957	2,372	1,499	2,577	13,192
Delaware										
Wilmington city	71,005	1,273	2,062	1,116	1,590	2,006	1,455	892	1,553	8,612
District of Columbia										
Washington city	618,777	13,526	18,298	9,704	12,641	15,898	12,570	9,260	10,229	70,302
Florida										
Boca Raton city	86,489	2,640	3,656	2,519	2,887	3,776	3,233	3,228	2,570	18,213
Boynton Beach city	69,093	788	2,218	1,171	1,887	2,882	2,722	2,789	3,607	15,058
Cape Coral city	157,933	4,324	6,162	3,555	6,367	6,562	4,593	3,601	3,741	28,419
Clearwater city	108,403	3,489	4,603	2,811	3,812	4,222	4,030	4,089	3,738	22,702
Coral Springs city	123,406	2,441	4,184	2,521	1,919	2,671	1,370	1,545	1,198	11,224
Deerfield Beach city	76,352	1,858	2,128	1,157	2,803	2,982	3,307	2,855	3,112	16,216
Deltona city	85,255	1,812	2,917	1,546	2,010	2,736	1,920	1,776	1,861	11,849
Fort Lauderdale city	168,405	4,981	6,336	4,126	5,160	5,649	4,638	3,034	4,344	26,951
Gainesville city	125,273	2,593	2,774	1,230	1,492	2,221	2,105	1,725	1,682	10,455
Hialeah city	229,152	5,414	6,410	4,585	5,706	11,765	9,021	6,912	6,098	44,087
Hollywood city	143,222	3,609	4,792	2,927	2,932	4,980	3,945	3,802	3,033	21,619
Jacksonville city	829,535	18,535	26,580	13,936	18,266	20,888	15,906	12,526	12,180	93,702
Lakeland city	98,968	2,532	3,585	2,379	2,974	4,774	4,315	2,487	3,282	20,211
Largo city	77,769	2,077	2,908	2,362	2,667	4,259	3,664	2,899	3,488	19,339
Lauderhill city	68,110	1,450	2,341	1,410	1,371	1,924	1,182	1,155	1,310	8,352
Melbourne city	76,656	1,719	2,302	1,984	2,325	3,187	3,042	3,015	2,388	15,941
Miami city	408,322	8,874	11,862	6,705	9,318	15,013	12,737	10,670	9,411	63,854
Miami Beach city	89,541	2,259	2,401	1,355	2,166	3,083	2,626	1,969	2,435	13,634
Miami Gardens city	109,331	2,682	3,404	1,601	2,203	3,551	2,139	1,480	1,279	12,253
Miramar city	125,351	2,097	2,713	1,085	1,481	2,334	1,715	1,907	788	9,310
Orlando city	243,895	4,068	5,263	3,303	4,165	5,048	4,487	3,137	2,894	23,034
Palm Bay city	103,606	2,961	3,644	1,956	2,869	4,151	3,141	2,764	2,136	17,017
Palm Coast city	76,474	2,686	3,599	2,299	3,329	5,249	3,334	1,996	2,312	18,519
Pembroke Pines city	157,847	2,953	5,513	2,907	3,749	4,844	3,842	4,709	3,633	23,684
Plantation city	86,708	2,191	3,271	1,559	2,319	2,793	2,350	1,299	2,194	12,514
Pompano Beach city	101,596	2,291	3,389	1,600	3,040	3,534	3,338	3,560	3,823	18,895
Port St. Lucie city	166,927	3,639	5,291	3,524	5,377	6,012	5,012	3,669	3,543	27,137
St. Petersburg city	245,623	7,098	9,071	5,659	6,384	8,945	7,054	5,680	5,585	39,307
Sunrise city	86,648	1,921	2,883	1,282	1,967	2,970	2,256	1,952	2,669	13,096
Tallahassee city	184,079	3,183	3,523	2,282	2,558	2,955	2,378	2,267	2,654	15,094
Tampa city	343,677	6,602	9,833	5,188	6,404	8,211	7,288	5,364	4,937	37,392
Weston city	66,603	1,083	1,956	1,243	1,034	921	577	842	490	5,107
West Palm Beach city	100,940	2,823	3,690	2,083	3,014	3,843	3,187	2,264	3,081	17,472
Georgia										
Albany city	77,546	1,500	2,171	869	1,722	2,132	1,725	1,296	1,327	9,071
Athens-Clarke County unified govt (bal)	117,331	1,877	2,586	1,488	1,924	2,352	2,110	1,160	1,193	10,227
Atlanta city	432,752	8,419	11,924	5,991	7,446	10,234	6,371	5,565	6,528	42,135
Augusta-Richmond County consolidated govt (bal)	196,200	4,384	5,692	3,172	4,146	5,589	4,287	3,183	2,515	22,892
Columbus city	194,276	4,271	5,437	2,827	3,635	5,265	3,781	3,793	2,991	22,292
Johns Creek city	79,649	1,582	2,703	1,010	838	1,880	1,274	466	596	6,064
Macon city	91,675	1,821	2,681	1,372	2,059	2,109	2,038	1,702	1,599	10,879
Roswell city	91,213	1,940	2,747	2,140	2,609	2,067	1,756	1,006	1,201	10,779
Sandy Springs city	96,890	1,999	3,091	1,795	2,069	2,140	1,315	1,583	1,799	10,701
Savannah city	139,667	2,877	4,323	2,150	3,020	3,354	2,572	2,260	3,137	16,493
Warner Robins city	69,489	1,279	1,634	940	1,242	1,473	1,442	875	822	6,794
Hawaii										
Urban Honolulu CDP	342,190	10,206	11,658	7,620	9,295	11,079	11,258	9,918	12,364	61,534
Idaho										
Boise City city	209,292	5,190	7,176	3,388	4,593	5,995	4,318	2,865	4,013	25,172
Meridian city	77,936	1,478	2,115	1,548	1,288	994	1,272	1,051	1,007	7,160
Nampa city	82,786	1,198	2,072	1,209	1,734	2,245	1,528	1,240	1,151	9,107

Table B-3: Places—Older Population by Age—*Continued*

	Total Population	60 to 61 Years	62 to 64 Years	65 to 66 Years	67 to 69 Years	70 to 74 Years	75 to 79 Years	80 to 84 Years	85 Years and Over	65 Years and Over
Illinois										
Aurora city	196,491	2,712	4,083	2,430	2,528	3,205	2,261	1,230	1,619	13,273
Bloomington city	77,196	1,666	2,449	1,085	1,187	1,491	1,244	1,290	1,595	7,892
Champaign city	81,852	1,664	1,846	941	1,225	1,532	1,122	1,159	889	6,868
Chicago city	2,705,981	51,369	73,050	36,715	50,711	67,038	50,737	38,574	39,266	283,041
Decatur city	76,080	2,148	2,790	1,577	1,833	2,531	2,244	2,261	2,292	12,738
Elgin city	110,400	2,190	2,926	1,508	2,081	1,880	1,460	1,408	1,562	9,899
Evanston city	75,018	1,609	2,442	1,092	1,516	1,897	1,137	1,311	1,518	8,471
Joliet city	147,151	2,670	2,887	1,773	2,097	2,610	2,136	2,064	2,234	12,914
Naperville city	143,310	3,216	4,733	2,178	2,674	2,944	2,064	2,016	2,035	13,911
Peoria city	114,398	2,461	3,101	1,752	2,531	3,211	3,077	1,921	2,618	15,110
Rockford city	152,235	2,926	4,822	2,562	3,672	4,319	3,358	3,444	3,876	21,231
Springfield city	116,824	3,173	4,532	1,975	2,493	3,966	3,178	2,340	3,348	17,300
Waukegan city	88,637	1,840	2,046	874	1,265	1,380	1,428	962	947	6,856
Indiana										
Bloomington city	80,127	1,049	1,446	870	1,175	1,103	1,058	1,181	1,181	6,568
Carmel city	82,485	2,130	2,767	1,176	1,757	2,532	929	1,068	1,293	8,755
Evansville city	120,386	2,495	3,419	1,671	2,857	3,794	2,958	2,751	3,404	17,435
Fort Wayne city	253,795	5,622	7,893	4,095	5,052	6,659	5,753	4,940	4,975	31,474
Gary city	79,849	1,987	2,699	1,784	1,822	2,852	2,655	1,279	1,545	11,937
Hammond city	80,218	1,828	2,098	939	1,512	1,799	1,512	1,379	1,322	8,463
Indianapolis city (bal)	827,639	17,278	21,739	11,234	14,537	20,956	15,908	12,393	12,227	87,255
Lafayette city	66,822	1,108	1,887	823	1,005	2,112	1,008	1,403	1,316	7,667
Muncie city	69,830	1,411	1,891	1,106	1,412	2,251	2,063	1,286	1,107	9,225
South Bend city	99,803	2,346	3,049	1,683	1,892	2,658	2,187	2,137	2,537	13,094
Iowa										
Cedar Rapids city	127,503	2,610	4,039	2,148	2,423	3,239	3,086	2,749	2,866	16,511
Davenport city	100,643	2,210	3,540	1,612	1,944	2,905	2,290	1,672	2,144	12,567
Des Moines city	205,622	4,552	5,589	3,066	3,589	5,062	3,914	3,059	3,621	22,311
Iowa City city	69,101	1,276	1,541	810	935	1,182	823	913	1,101	5,764
Sioux City city	82,828	1,933	1,924	1,562	1,598	2,401	1,662	1,598	1,834	10,655
Waterloo city	68,361	1,869	2,533	1,324	1,308	1,996	1,678	1,682	1,552	9,540
Kansas										
Kansas City city	146,502	2,869	4,368	1,948	2,327	4,373	2,363	2,185	2,464	15,660
Lawrence city	88,791	1,353	1,827	939	1,176	1,307	1,401	942	1,095	6,860
Olathe city	128,195	2,282	3,651	1,502	1,699	2,193	1,371	1,199	1,397	9,361
Overland Park city	176,376	4,304	5,534	3,084	3,629	5,057	3,761	3,131	4,042	22,704
Topeka city	127,895	3,126	4,064	2,173	2,778	3,781	3,419	3,067	2,862	18,080
Wichita city	384,025	8,540	11,375	6,350	8,006	9,466	7,683	6,550	6,658	44,713
Kentucky										
Lexington-Fayette urban county	301,211	6,256	9,912	4,626	5,525	7,619	5,777	4,376	4,219	32,142
Louisville/Jefferson County metro govt (bal)	601,670	15,433	20,461	10,945	12,391	16,988	13,860	11,668	10,904	76,756
Louisiana										
Baton Rouge city	229,572	4,064	6,628	3,643	4,559	5,819	4,238	3,656	4,038	25,953
Kenner city	66,786	1,770	2,385	1,265	1,891	2,311	1,309	1,169	1,044	8,989
Lafayette city	121,744	2,734	3,240	2,312	2,582	3,429	2,796	2,089	1,863	15,071
Lake Charles city	72,741	1,890	2,690	1,155	1,630	2,542	1,833	1,653	1,303	10,116
New Orleans city	359,130	9,024	12,021	6,634	7,194	8,743	6,471	5,277	5,790	40,109
Shreveport city	201,332	4,714	5,704	3,196	4,277	5,842	4,875	3,633	4,108	25,931
Maine										
Portland city	66,159	1,525	2,120	865	953	1,745	1,281	1,438	1,623	7,905
Maryland										
Baltimore city	620,843	15,189	18,555	11,647	11,245	16,322	13,526	10,294	10,078	73,112
Frederick city	65,905	1,745	2,138	891	1,383	1,627	1,052	1,191	1,194	7,338
Massachusetts										
Boston city	628,365	11,942	15,886	8,365	10,655	15,148	11,061	9,447	10,277	64,953
Brockton city	94,031	1,735	2,654	1,335	1,890	3,044	1,978	1,808	1,989	12,044
Cambridge city	105,733	2,028	3,088	1,575	2,211	2,651	1,848	1,509	1,771	11,565
Fall River city	88,885	2,164	2,603	1,450	2,609	2,694	2,381	2,127	2,370	13,631
Lawrence city	76,928	1,452	1,727	773	1,008	1,586	1,164	601	1,211	6,343
Lowell city	107,616	2,181	2,876	1,505	1,937	2,496	2,199	1,639	1,707	11,483
Lynn city	90,885	1,469	2,077	1,069	1,912	2,485	1,857	1,341	1,713	10,377
New Bedford city	94,946	1,944	3,314	1,871	2,153	2,775	2,517	2,123	2,906	14,345
Newton city	85,742	2,175	2,634	1,466	2,118	2,982	2,126	2,094	2,629	13,415
Quincy city	92,720	2,145	2,890	2,065	2,313	2,616	2,058	2,147	2,277	13,476
Somerville city	76,381	1,335	1,530	795	938	1,437	1,173	1,218	825	6,386
Springfield city	153,531	2,938	4,389	1,889	3,127	4,295	2,802	2,379	2,477	16,969
Worcester city	182,344	3,242	4,961	3,134	3,895	4,155	4,022	2,926	4,556	22,688
Michigan										
Ann Arbor city	115,124	2,110	2,808	1,705	1,885	2,522	1,938	1,782	1,678	11,510
Dearborn city	97,123	1,815	3,288	1,096	1,983	2,155	1,691	1,812	2,226	10,963
Detroit city	706,522	17,759	20,985	11,147	14,199	19,095	15,116	11,584	12,635	83,776
Farmington Hills city	80,266	2,261	3,450	1,645	2,037	2,646	2,402	2,386	1,935	13,051
Flint city	101,423	2,377	3,354	1,648	2,242	2,414	2,589	1,452	1,276	11,621

Table B-3: Places—Older Population by Age—*Continued*

	Total Population	60 to 61 Years	62 to 64 Years	65 to 66 Years	67 to 69 Years	70 to 74 Years	75 to 79 Years	80 to 84 Years	85 Years and Over	65 Years and Over
Michigan—Cont.										
Grand Rapids city	189,162	3,148	4,645	2,426	3,208	3,462	3,507	3,800	4,314	20,717
Kalamazoo city	74,689	1,147	1,774	781	1,003	1,362	999	1,076	1,813	7,034
Lansing city	113,594	2,502	3,648	1,862	2,314	2,323	2,172	1,529	1,368	11,568
Livonia city	96,101	2,430	3,788	1,858	2,753	3,406	3,249	3,358	2,586	17,210
Rochester Hills city	71,650	1,644	2,673	1,430	1,804	1,731	1,468	1,331	1,926	9,690
Southfield city	72,131	2,433	3,193	1,871	2,176	2,397	1,871	1,746	2,761	12,822
Sterling Heights city	130,037	3,033	4,800	3,027	3,355	4,624	3,757	2,592	3,104	20,459
Troy city	81,616	2,319	3,451	1,528	2,472	2,603	1,966	1,711	1,321	11,601
Warren city	134,055	3,275	3,915	2,141	2,910	4,354	4,143	3,587	3,745	20,880
Westland city	83,340	1,939	2,775	1,638	1,992	2,659	2,290	1,732	1,989	12,300
Wyoming city	72,741	1,992	1,968	797	1,119	1,433	1,074	1,245	725	6,393
Minnesota										
Bloomington city	84,347	2,220	3,263	1,981	2,777	3,597	2,659	2,644	2,109	15,767
Brooklyn Park city	76,868	1,481	1,975	1,011	1,329	1,576	881	688	716	6,201
Duluth city	86,221	2,046	2,626	1,634	1,786	2,209	2,280	1,919	2,298	12,126
Minneapolis city	388,054	8,365	9,330	5,116	5,585	7,132	5,185	4,368	5,755	33,141
Plymouth city	71,771	1,617	2,348	1,144	1,855	2,197	1,707	1,162	941	9,006
Rochester city	108,024	2,217	3,240	2,135	1,912	3,061	2,615	1,994	2,346	14,063
St. Cloud city	65,838	1,194	1,628	800	1,020	1,548	1,365	1,152	1,228	7,113
St. Paul city	288,347	5,381	7,714	3,450	4,285	5,764	4,637	3,731	3,992	25,859
Mississippi										
Gulfport city	68,979	1,396	1,837	1,094	1,358	1,989	1,498	1,341	1,048	8,328
Jackson city	174,706	3,592	4,634	2,332	3,191	4,207	2,975	2,508	2,733	17,946
Missouri										
Columbia city	111,204	1,502	1,979	1,239	1,781	1,959	1,595	1,596	1,597	9,767
Independence city	117,028	2,795	3,586	2,291	2,943	4,632	3,160	2,695	3,373	19,094
Kansas City city	462,292	9,884	14,646	6,481	9,475	11,686	9,068	7,583	7,534	51,827
Lee's Summit city	91,979	2,322	2,636	1,498	1,729	2,308	1,707	1,848	1,814	10,904
O'Fallon city	80,986	1,390	2,270	1,095	1,469	1,531	1,109	1,295	1,035	7,534
St. Charles city	66,173	1,273	1,771	901	1,574	1,886	1,609	1,351	1,458	8,779
St. Joseph city	76,953	1,792	2,429	1,223	1,724	2,112	1,786	1,782	1,840	10,467
St. Louis city	318,612	7,816	9,221	4,561	5,793	7,880	6,974	5,252	4,963	35,423
Springfield city	160,748	3,316	4,483	2,679	3,681	4,616	4,184	3,577	4,624	23,361
Montana										
Billings city	105,648	2,726	3,860	1,942	2,530	3,392	2,803	2,388	2,656	15,711
Missoula city	67,643	1,192	1,659	981	1,276	1,521	952	1,315	1,522	7,567
Nebraska										
Lincoln city	262,214	5,954	7,347	3,908	4,460	6,429	5,604	3,724	4,577	28,702
Omaha city	416,374	10,054	11,542	5,484	8,476	10,236	8,240	7,363	7,789	47,588
Nevada										
Henderson city	261,370	7,341	10,243	5,892	8,474	10,553	6,685	5,060	3,196	39,860
Las Vegas city	589,541	13,115	18,181	11,307	14,250	18,790	14,088	9,827	7,863	76,125
North Las Vegas city	219,976	3,565	4,653	3,527	3,102	4,028	2,822	1,461	1,206	16,146
Reno city	228,658	5,302	7,793	4,324	5,080	6,063	4,701	3,627	3,568	27,363
Sparks city	91,242	2,072	3,307	1,720	2,356	2,893	1,696	1,243	1,156	11,064
New Hampshire										
Manchester city	109,879	2,147	3,886	1,918	2,111	3,342	1,964	1,639	2,382	13,356
Nashua city	86,769	1,717	2,829	1,421	1,812	2,547	2,188	1,423	1,679	11,070
New Jersey										
Camden city	77,398	1,438	1,653	1,394	975	1,568	932	533	734	6,136
Clifton city	84,525	2,067	2,460	1,957	1,277	2,364	1,566	1,667	2,039	10,870
Elizabeth city	125,825	2,316	2,624	1,685	2,435	2,490	1,778	1,450	1,772	11,610
Jersey City city	251,485	4,906	6,625	3,368	4,971	5,584	4,152	2,852	2,378	23,305
Newark city	277,627	4,591	6,160	3,423	3,921	5,902	3,998	3,117	2,822	23,183
Passaic city	70,066	1,261	1,088	790	1,255	1,128	850	569	919	5,511
Paterson city	145,644	2,400	3,218	2,290	2,610	3,516	2,377	1,639	1,163	13,595
Trenton city	84,660	1,562	1,916	1,210	1,147	1,652	1,233	1,191	975	7,408
Union City city	67,193	1,377	1,769	1,081	924	1,463	1,128	978	972	6,546
New Mexico										
Albuquerque city	551,597	13,235	17,856	8,819	11,939	16,308	11,952	9,901	9,424	68,343
Las Cruces city	99,754	2,172	2,983	1,545	2,272	3,141	2,546	1,729	1,714	12,947
Rio Rancho city	89,499	1,905	2,622	1,554	1,875	2,742	1,296	1,259	1,465	10,191
Santa Fe city	68,677	2,311	3,442	1,853	2,906	2,784	2,321	1,543	1,715	13,122
New York										
Albany city	97,843	2,110	2,620	1,500	2,034	2,298	1,770	2,055	2,253	11,910
Buffalo city	260,321	5,150	7,544	3,400	4,898	6,904	5,908	4,936	4,041	30,087
Mount Vernon city	67,684	1,461	2,093	1,279	1,377	2,243	1,445	1,162	1,565	9,071
New Rochelle city	77,733	1,560	2,599	1,261	1,675	2,293	1,905	1,767	2,116	11,017
New York city	8,265,445	181,625	248,974	140,145	172,405	238,444	179,016	143,858	145,568	1,019,436
Rochester city	210,548	4,169	5,489	2,594	3,636	4,298	3,379	2,212	3,264	19,383
Schenectady city	66,124	1,004	1,696	855	1,320	1,642	1,136	1,379	1,514	7,846
Syracuse city	144,575	2,841	3,730	2,037	2,254	2,981	2,409	2,456	3,069	15,206
Yonkers city	197,514	5,383	6,813	3,802	4,481	6,591	5,055	4,416	4,688	29,033

Table B-3: Places—Older Population by Age—*Continued*

	Total Population	60 to 61 Years	62 to 64 Years	65 to 66 Years	67 to 69 Years	70 to 74 Years	75 to 79 Years	80 to 84 Years	85 Years and Over	65 Years and Over
North Carolina										
Asheville city	84,661	2,355	2,710	1,571	1,976	2,972	2,246	1,918	2,661	13,344
Charlotte city	756,725	13,922	19,834	9,558	11,967	15,623	11,324	9,020	8,959	66,451
Concord city	80,576	1,172	2,155	1,231	1,821	2,321	1,550	1,132	923	8,978
Durham city	234,160	4,479	6,589	3,372	3,735	4,765	3,600	2,627	3,571	21,670
Fayetteville city	201,334	3,811	4,592	2,766	3,545	5,071	3,846	2,861	2,112	20,201
Gastonia city	72,151	1,504	2,519	1,312	1,735	1,483	1,424	1,164	1,366	8,484
Greensboro city	273,641	5,692	8,624	3,245	5,982	7,184	6,992	4,714	4,244	32,361
Greenville city	86,115	1,481	1,561	953	1,239	1,361	844	736	1,372	6,505
High Point city	106,164	1,837	2,993	1,697	1,999	3,068	2,123	1,836	1,833	12,556
Jacksonville city	69,356	583	738	649	591	1,114	768	710	617	4,449
Raleigh city	414,373	7,602	9,339	5,178	5,928	8,311	6,103	4,843	4,879	35,242
Wilmington city	108,320	2,487	3,576	1,792	2,641	3,548	2,709	1,972	2,122	14,784
Winston-Salem city	232,090	4,826	6,721	3,766	5,214	6,347	5,315	4,419	4,301	29,362
North Dakota										
Fargo city	107,752	2,445	2,803	1,274	1,632	2,199	2,354	1,900	1,612	10,971
Ohio										
Akron city	198,816	3,987	6,935	3,394	3,860	5,837	4,170	3,971	4,112	25,344
Canton city	72,778	1,722	2,081	1,042	1,699	1,808	1,648	1,684	1,909	9,790
Cincinnati city	296,443	6,897	8,094	4,282	5,409	7,364	5,758	4,472	5,547	32,832
Cleveland city	393,288	9,172	12,267	6,286	7,424	11,332	9,353	7,333	7,009	48,737
Columbus city	799,357	14,077	20,936	10,113	12,406	16,754	12,674	9,022	9,546	70,515
Dayton city	141,690	2,761	4,575	1,627	2,906	4,421	2,773	2,328	2,689	16,744
Parma city	80,997	2,039	3,115	1,675	2,144	3,108	2,860	2,085	2,824	44,696
Toledo city	285,532	6,284	7,835	4,376	5,528	7,561	6,366	5,600	4,929	34,360
Youngstown city	66,005	1,653	2,438	1,180	1,326	1,925	1,866	2,135	1,921	10,353
Oklahoma										
Broken Arrow city	100,497	2,311	3,111	1,748	2,091	2,515	1,968	1,126	1,328	10,776
Edmond city	83,197	1,642	2,557	1,364	1,734	2,355	1,906	1,093	1,028	9,480
Lawton city	98,075	1,227	2,601	1,364	1,612	2,201	2,118	1,212	1,093	9,600
Norman city	113,599	2,154	3,581	1,739	2,282	2,959	2,234	1,718	1,495	12,427
Oklahoma City city	590,292	12,597	18,261	8,615	11,239	16,323	10,991	10,148	8,999	66,315
Tulsa city	393,124	9,202	11,606	6,638	8,149	10,836	8,592	7,654	7,746	49,615
Oregon										
Beaverton city	91,414	2,315	2,417	1,738	1,703	2,037	1,486	1,260	1,565	9,789
Bend city	77,887	1,992	2,815	1,631	1,723	2,819	1,778	1,440	1,938	11,329
Eugene city	157,196	4,158	5,137	2,710	3,272	4,855	3,089	3,471	3,549	20,946
Gresham city	107,505	2,206	3,041	1,612	2,352	2,621	1,854	1,646	1,923	12,008
Hillsboro city	93,876	1,584	2,140	1,154	1,580	1,923	958	740	955	7,310
Medford city	75,704	1,578	2,604	1,046	1,980	2,733	2,367	2,100	2,162	12,388
Portland city	594,524	14,139	19,245	9,429	11,217	13,603	9,813	8,401	11,012	63,475
Salem city	156,155	3,498	4,928	2,872	3,642	4,576	3,660	2,342	2,983	20,075
Pennsylvania										
Allentown city	118,587	2,634	2,836	1,905	1,794	2,609	2,735	2,331	2,574	13,948
Bethlehem city	75,057	1,389	2,441	1,330	1,504	1,993	1,851	2,039	2,310	11,027
Erie city	101,419	2,220	2,451	1,538	1,954	2,782	2,357	2,103	2,516	13,250
Philadelphia city	1,538,211	33,357	44,617	24,756	30,396	41,793	34,129	26,723	28,788	186,585
Pittsburgh city	306,006	6,338	9,809	5,217	7,075	8,486	6,436	7,367	8,472	43,053
Reading city	88,098	1,436	2,248	927	1,646	1,780	1,500	1,391	1,112	8,356
Scranton city	75,951	1,809	2,210	1,513	1,560	2,226	2,198	2,314	2,973	12,784
Rhode Island										
Cranston city	80,465	2,261	2,710	1,193	1,794	2,714	2,094	1,929	2,483	12,207
Pawtucket city	71,158	1,507	1,960	1,024	1,388	2,219	1,846	1,314	1,321	9,112
Providence city	178,299	3,200	4,122	2,036	2,647	2,964	2,616	2,090	2,734	15,087
Warwick city	82,222	2,390	3,246	1,777	2,220	3,076	3,090	2,117	2,293	14,573
South Carolina										
Charleston city	123,226	3,015	3,827	1,857	2,419	4,179	2,963	1,687	1,963	15,068
Columbia city	130,596	1,748	3,096	1,482	1,775	2,654	2,211	1,384	2,258	11,764
North Charleston city	99,999	2,041	2,664	1,423	1,798	1,996	1,288	1,067	978	8,550
Rock Hill city	67,348	1,214	2,100	738	1,105	1,471	1,309	966	1,201	6,790
South Dakota										
Rapid City city	68,912	1,722	2,561	1,221	1,224	2,522	1,663	1,527	1,909	10,066
Sioux Falls city	156,997	3,125	5,085	2,455	2,792	3,725	3,017	3,033	2,744	17,766
Tennessee										
Chattanooga city	169,718	4,830	5,689	3,082	4,753	5,370	4,520	3,891	3,600	25,216
Clarksville city	137,588	1,868	2,976	1,452	2,042	2,374	1,838	1,178	1,093	9,977
Jackson city	67,009	1,153	1,889	1,175	1,515	2,097	1,546	1,315	1,311	8,959
Knoxville city	180,714	3,849	5,819	3,015	5,505	5,127	5,001	3,589	3,684	25,921
Memphis city	651,363	14,799	18,527	10,167	11,389	15,436	12,102	10,291	8,936	68,321
Murfreesboro city	111,813	1,944	3,187	1,110	2,130	2,398	1,872	894	1,400	9,804
Nashville-Davidson metropolitan government (bal)	613,829	12,929	17,050	8,840	10,649	15,258	11,544	8,493	8,725	63,509
Texas										
Abilene city	120,027	2,381	3,023	1,788	2,527	3,352	2,948	2,136	2,231	14,982
Allen city	87,343	1,370	1,780	1,099	1,096	1,225	856	722	382	5,380
Amarillo city	193,429	4,069	5,671	2,631	3,810	5,643	4,528	3,352	3,250	23,214
Arlington city	370,854	7,688	9,358	4,583	6,844	6,716	5,067	3,835	3,448	30,493
Austin city	818,236	14,545	19,057	8,800	11,338	12,508	9,858	7,815	7,986	58,305
Baytown city	71,567	1,400	2,663	807	1,200	1,132	1,303	1,276	1,085	6,803

Table B-3: Places—Older Population by Age—*Continued*

	Total Population	60 to 61 Years	62 to 64 Years	65 to 66 Years	67 to 69 Years	70 to 74 Years	75 to 79 Years	80 to 84 Years	85 Years and Over	65 Years and Over
Texas—Cont.										
Beaumont city	118,440	2,287	4,849	2,239	2,408	3,185	3,062	1,795	2,187	14,876
Brownsville city	178,045	2,538	4,073	2,670	3,181	4,015	3,210	2,275	2,095	17,446
Bryan city	77,266	1,279	1,911	977	1,468	1,620	1,509	1,018	864	7,456
Carrollton city	122,468	1,928	3,164	1,795	2,223	2,618	1,384	1,189	1,141	10,350
College Station city	95,960	1,133	1,386	863	608	1,393	649	870	402	4,785
Corpus Christi city	308,497	7,145	9,964	4,917	6,443	8,426	6,734	5,378	4,763	36,661
Dallas city	1,219,879	22,794	30,589	15,764	21,090	24,825	18,445	16,137	15,720	111,981
Denton city	117,997	1,897	2,814	1,652	2,455	2,194	1,337	1,154	1,283	10,075
Edinburg city	79,342	1,149	1,539	973	834	1,474	1,080	750	588	5,699
El Paso city	662,707	12,859	16,758	9,684	12,158	18,246	14,793	10,733	9,495	75,109
Fort Worth city	761,862	13,409	17,926	9,726	10,587	14,852	11,161	8,482	8,379	63,187
Frisco city	123,175	1,844	2,132	1,610	1,673	1,949	1,273	567	622	7,694
Garland city	230,317	4,718	5,624	3,156	4,030	5,148	3,702	2,474	2,381	20,891
Grand Prairie city	178,835	3,485	4,058	2,110	2,586	3,296	2,151	1,313	1,037	12,493
Harlingen city	65,425	1,116	1,683	1,000	1,169	2,404	1,935	1,240	1,021	8,769
Houston city	2,130,114	39,401	52,740	29,766	35,204	46,430	34,240	26,180	25,014	196,834
Irving city	220,677	3,278	4,568	1,934	2,569	3,711	3,002	1,932	1,479	14,627
Killeen city	131,639	1,613	2,013	771	1,540	1,835	1,127	953	430	6,656
Laredo city	240,773	3,950	4,861	2,625	3,581	4,771	3,427	2,329	2,599	19,332
League City city	86,105	1,611	2,264	942	1,685	1,888	1,062	674	1,038	7,289
Lewisville city	97,421	1,814	1,817	1,206	1,781	1,396	942	1,060	707	7,092
Longview city	81,021	1,956	2,225	1,153	1,328	2,445	2,287	2,009	1,918	11,140
Lubbock city	233,475	4,070	5,860	3,547	4,082	6,151	5,499	3,531	3,159	25,969
McAllen city	132,720	2,604	3,699	1,852	2,833	3,511	2,356	1,766	1,981	14,299
McKinney city	137,971	2,007	3,115	1,473	2,044	2,380	1,643	1,453	1,080	10,073
Mesquite city	141,533	2,193	3,624	1,922	2,375	2,507	1,940	2,058	1,510	12,312
Midland city	114,805	2,764	3,009	1,417	1,972	2,872	2,681	2,262	1,698	12,902
Mission city	79,179	1,494	1,780	1,385	1,274	1,831	2,121	1,032	679	8,322
Missouri City city	68,004	2,118	2,356	1,322	1,564	1,673	941	1,091	488	7,079
Odessa city	103,063	2,203	2,464	1,285	1,808	2,301	1,938	1,839	1,386	10,557
Pasadena city	150,903	3,292	3,557	1,733	2,493	2,840	2,641	1,992	1,540	13,239
Pearland city	93,887	1,574	2,225	1,346	1,179	1,512	923	1,175	1,154	7,289
Pharr city	72,008	1,210	1,432	955	1,019	1,507	1,969	1,304	1,175	7,929
Plano city	266,857	5,681	8,560	4,214	5,831	6,055	3,832	2,813	3,105	25,850
Richardson city	101,483	2,424	2,889	1,800	2,464	2,752	2,105	1,753	1,673	12,547
Round Rock city	104,543	1,696	2,078	1,450	1,440	1,640	719	596	863	6,708
San Angelo city	94,684	1,836	2,722	1,943	2,097	2,660	2,813	2,045	1,425	12,983
San Antonio city	1,358,143	26,796	36,898	20,537	26,889	32,960	26,239	20,240	19,658	146,523
Sugar Land city	81,092	1,868	3,924	1,350	1,668	2,361	1,492	1,088	890	8,849
Temple city	67,809	1,325	2,476	1,396	1,636	2,090	1,633	1,701	1,627	10,083
Tyler city	98,296	1,978	3,055	1,468	2,070	3,305	2,644	2,291	2,818	14,596
Waco city	126,250	2,119	2,922	1,630	2,168	2,642	2,792	2,310	2,658	14,200
Wichita Falls city	104,348	2,190	3,081	1,802	1,976	2,601	2,481	1,686	2,046	12,592
Utah										
Layton city	68,165	1,607	1,361	588	869	1,589	890	877	397	5,210
Ogden city	83,375	1,311	1,694	1,142	1,138	1,585	1,517	1,105	1,259	7,746
Orem city	89,712	1,534	1,924	1,052	1,417	1,839	1,279	1,078	858	7,523
Provo city	114,467	1,559	1,230	715	1,206	1,381	1,049	1,047	1,411	6,809
St. George city	74,225	1,205	2,782	1,359	1,880	3,044	2,823	1,830	2,204	13,140
Salt Lake City city	187,964	3,101	5,208	2,273	3,068	4,004	3,153	2,415	2,899	17,812
Sandy city	88,451	2,120	2,806	1,483	1,929	2,280	1,382	763	904	8,741
West Jordan city	106,387	1,918	2,391	1,144	692	1,199	868	747	522	5,172
West Valley City city	130,981	2,046	2,802	1,691	2,212	2,036	1,701	1,127	719	9,486
Virginia										
Alexandria city	143,737	2,895	3,858	2,198	2,713	2,847	2,080	1,481	2,086	13,405
Chesapeake city	225,844	4,801	6,939	3,878	4,334	6,106	4,537	2,918	2,609	24,382
Hampton city	136,855	3,364	3,595	2,439	3,611	3,707	3,093	2,325	2,133	17,308
Lynchburg city	76,377	1,679	2,171	996	1,387	2,614	2,086	1,444	1,946	10,473
Newport News city	180,623	3,749	4,848	2,606	3,237	4,813	3,980	1,900	2,941	19,477
Norfolk city	244,118	4,680	5,624	3,112	3,958	4,880	4,209	3,670	3,234	23,063
Portsmouth city	95,915	2,268	3,238	1,761	1,806	3,031	2,377	1,856	1,931	12,762
Richmond city	206,936	4,427	5,614	3,445	3,923	4,695	4,346	2,980	3,875	23,264
Roanoke city	96,958	2,693	3,528	1,500	2,321	3,008	2,162	1,995	2,778	13,764
Suffolk city	84,942	2,119	2,615	1,211	2,124	2,493	1,643	1,220	1,309	10,000
Virginia Beach city	443,102	9,140	13,143	6,784	8,918	11,538	8,736	6,885	5,635	48,496
Washington										
Auburn city	71,743	1,802	2,207	976	1,408	1,802	1,515	1,321	1,036	8,058
Bellevue city	124,646	2,856	3,787	1,767	2,764	3,592	3,501	2,414	3,089	17,127
Bellingham city	81,647	1,771	2,956	1,316	2,590	1,728	1,334	1,790	1,777	10,535
Everett city	103,818	2,459	3,421	1,713	1,764	2,231	1,726	1,607	1,754	10,795
Federal Way city	90,709	2,069	2,319	1,579	1,289	2,585	1,572	1,151	1,575	9,751
Kennewick city	75,328	1,935	2,002	1,232	1,510	1,742	1,314	1,325	1,301	8,424
Kent city	120,964	2,775	3,084	2,117	2,264	2,282	1,830	1,448	1,588	11,529
Renton city	93,673	1,894	2,344	1,264	1,812	2,018	1,456	1,273	1,546	9,369
Seattle city	622,273	14,453	20,454	11,053	12,180	14,113	10,965	8,724	11,819	68,854
Spokane city	209,346	4,732	6,916	4,114	4,441	5,565	5,685	4,421	4,435	28,661
Spokane Valley city	90,437	2,612	3,443	1,709	2,400	3,149	1,833	2,086	1,794	12,971
Tacoma city	200,090	4,743	5,777	2,859	4,033	4,984	3,821	3,287	4,201	23,185
Vancouver city	163,964	3,725	6,073	2,853	4,181	4,771	3,931	2,948	2,988	21,672
Yakima city	92,506	2,043	2,295	1,906	2,049	2,433	1,965	1,926	2,450	12,729

Table B-3: Places—Older Population by Age—*Continued*

	Total Population	60 to 61 Years	62 to 64 Years	65 to 66 Years	67 to 69 Years	70 to 74 Years	75 to 79 Years	80 to 84 Years	85 Years and Over	65 Years and Over
Wisconsin										
Appleton city	72,689	1,926	2,536	1,028	1,496	1,533	1,700	1,044	1,350	8,151
Eau Claire city	66,087	1,470	1,739	651	1,254	1,727	1,254	1,359	1,179	7,424
Green Bay city	104,494	2,434	2,584	1,343	1,750	2,666	2,375	1,670	2,485	12,289
Kenosha city	99,743	1,919	2,325	1,238	1,641	2,658	1,800	1,660	1,914	10,911
Madison city	237,136	5,044	6,082	2,914	3,844	4,810	3,864	3,563	3,632	22,627
Milwaukee city	597,247	10,976	14,118	7,235	8,563	11,306	10,447	8,706	7,929	54,186
Oshkosh city	66,301	1,232	1,732	1,012	1,266	1,720	1,465	1,268	1,546	8,277
Racine city	78,552	1,417	2,402	1,142	1,649	1,897	1,409	1,345	1,209	8,651
Waukesha city	70,752	1,822	2,517	1,131	1,272	1,589	1,351	1,112	1,222	7,677

Table B-4: Metropolitan Statistical Areas—Older Population by Age

	Total Population	60 to 61 Years	62 to 64 Years	65 to 66 Years	67 to 69 Years	70 to 74 Years	75 to 79 Years	80 to 84 Years	85 Years and Over	65 Years and Over
Abilene, TX	166,340	3,621	4,936	3,270	3,855	5,140	4,460	3,440	2,933	23,098
Akron, OH	702,724	16,918	26,477	12,653	17,709	23,154	18,959	15,058	14,740	102,273
Albany, GA	156,878	3,858	4,960	2,500	4,012	4,822	3,619	2,522	2,338	19,813
Albany-Schenectady-Troy, NY	872,935	22,533	31,581	16,372	21,352	27,260	19,920	19,574	20,533	125,011
Albuquerque, NM	896,196	22,929	31,192	15,490	21,675	27,876	19,090	15,999	14,316	114,446
Alexandria, LA	154,304	3,369	4,661	3,073	3,916	5,062	4,066	2,628	2,536	21,281
Allentown-Bethlehem-Easton, PA-NJ	824,846	20,026	28,879	15,455	21,217	27,403	22,105	20,969	20,428	127,577
Altoona, PA	127,131	3,756	4,927	2,544	4,211	4,647	3,736	4,050	3,637	22,825
Amarillo, TX	253,406	5,612	8,153	3,753	5,190	7,599	5,669	4,097	4,035	30,343
Ames, IA	90,519	1,589	2,487	1,112	1,371	2,155	1,514	1,397	1,547	9,096
Anchorage, AK	387,916	8,542	11,291	5,476	5,952	7,909	4,959	3,826	2,300	30,422
Anderson, IN	131,028	3,356	4,592	2,577	3,401	5,145	3,816	2,861	2,915	20,715
Anderson, SC	188,359	4,361	7,211	3,810	5,201	7,808	5,401	3,840	3,431	29,491
Ann Arbor, MI	348,311	7,956	10,487	5,222	7,406	8,551	5,572	4,821	5,501	37,073
Anniston-Oxford, AL	117,845	3,067	4,001	1,987	3,127	4,581	3,618	2,205	1,905	17,423
Appleton, WI	227,218	5,195	6,793	3,361	4,800	6,215	5,494	3,391	4,032	27,293
Asheville, NC	428,874	12,794	17,757	10,387	13,476	19,668	15,142	11,147	11,076	80,896
Athens-Clarke County, GA	194,861	3,720	5,769	3,138	4,205	4,798	3,659	2,275	2,385	20,460
Atlanta-Sandy Springs-Marietta, GA	5,361,152	109,891	156,586	82,332	102,491	121,948	85,049	58,412	53,291	503,523
Atlantic City-Hammonton, NJ	274,982	7,575	9,712	5,688	7,191	9,243	6,569	6,153	5,176	40,020
Auburn-Opelika, AL	143,866	3,049	3,920	1,978	2,754	3,403	2,511	1,293	1,511	13,450
Augusta-Richmond County, GA-SC	563,401	13,946	18,729	10,662	13,863	17,956	13,434	9,839	6,648	72,402
Austin-Round Rock-San Marcos, TX	1,780,890	34,128	46,952	24,170	30,576	33,777	25,628	18,054	17,619	149,824
Bakersfield-Delano, CA	849,101	15,590	21,220	11,138	15,055	19,172	14,402	9,770	8,418	77,955
Baltimore-Towson, MD	2,734,138	67,012	92,728	50,340	62,787	79,594	62,103	48,806	50,307	353,937
Bangor, ME	153,856	4,204	6,238	2,657	3,779	5,769	4,151	3,686	2,858	22,900
Barnstable Town, MA	215,681	7,240	10,961	6,337	9,059	12,831	10,933	9,249	7,009	55,418
Baton Rouge, LA	809,427	18,371	25,726	12,919	17,579	21,837	15,462	11,342	11,004	90,143
Battle Creek, MI	135,568	3,941	4,863	2,594	3,456	4,654	3,622	2,996	3,063	20,385
Bay City, MI	107,310	2,897	4,586	2,335	3,077	4,133	2,976	2,544	2,872	17,937
Beaumont-Port Arthur, TX	389,918	8,429	13,517	6,685	8,673	11,681	10,538	7,242	6,613	51,432
Bellingham, WA	203,482	5,664	7,684	4,010	5,712	6,012	4,183	4,339	3,710	27,966
Bend, OR	160,085	4,684	6,658	3,713	4,628	6,764	3,627	3,082	3,476	25,290
Billings, MT	160,174	4,279	5,635	3,270	3,977	5,206	4,121	3,373	3,482	23,429
Binghamton, NY	250,092	6,363	9,385	4,773	6,947	9,020	7,633	6,567	6,631	41,571
Birmingham-Hoover, AL	1,132,696	28,253	39,257	20,537	27,410	35,428	26,709	21,290	18,963	150,337
Bismarck, ND	111,454	2,857	4,027	1,699	2,511	3,631	2,681	2,501	2,544	15,567
Blacksburg-Christiansburg-Radford, VA	163,302	3,619	4,912	2,411	4,094	5,413	3,785	2,353	2,710	20,766
Bloomington, IN	194,445	4,831	5,757	3,351	4,251	5,213	4,160	3,314	3,030	23,319
Bloomington-Normal, IL	170,964	3,735	4,755	2,416	3,274	3,889	2,948	2,667	2,724	17,918
Boise City-Nampa, ID	627,845	13,957	19,427	10,757	13,693	16,551	12,014	8,984	9,522	71,521
Boston-Cambridge-Quincy, MA-NH	4,602,669	109,412	153,079	81,679	106,138	135,205	105,089	91,553	95,934	615,598
Boulder, CO	300,681	7,226	8,417	5,732	5,875	6,652	5,453	3,558	4,426	31,696
Bowling Green, KY	127,739	2,404	3,400	2,233	2,590	3,762	2,474	2,041	1,843	14,943
Bremerton-Silverdale, WA	253,763	7,535	10,250	5,307	6,798	8,794	6,042	3,908	4,247	35,096
Bridgeport-Stamford-Norwalk, CT	926,739	21,005	30,342	16,922	22,131	26,270	21,778	19,865	20,420	127,386
Brownsville-Harlingen, TX	411,930	7,150	9,888	6,161	7,705	11,597	9,772	6,361	4,957	46,553
Brunswick, GA	113,069	2,943	5,762	2,712	3,732	4,329	2,997	2,115	1,796	17,681
Buffalo-Niagara Falls, NY	1,135,105	27,186	40,285	22,286	28,181	39,229	32,424	30,734	27,652	180,506
Burlington, NC	152,730	3,332	4,944	3,219	4,152	4,608	3,865	3,180	3,757	22,781
Burlington-South Burlington, VT	212,711	5,161	7,121	3,954	4,521	5,702	4,206	3,838	3,436	25,657
Canton-Massillon, OH	403,612	10,849	14,877	8,479	11,872	14,471	11,689	10,001	10,364	66,876
Cape Coral-Fort Myers, FL	632,499	18,174	28,385	18,874	28,527	38,791	27,225	20,353	19,743	153,513
Cape Girardeau-Jackson, MO-IL	97,241	2,238	3,326	1,961	2,502	3,267	2,045	2,357	2,521	14,653
Casper, WY	76,821	2,255	2,330	1,631	1,438	1,984	1,898	1,355	1,300	9,606
Cedar Rapids, IA	260,340	5,994	8,487	4,635	5,916	8,155	6,978	5,249	5,073	36,006
Champaign-Urbana, IL	233,025	5,292	6,218	3,298	4,299	6,165	4,496	4,198	3,814	26,270
Charleston, WV	303,948	9,490	11,037	6,732	8,217	12,287	9,880	6,108	6,148	49,372
Charleston-North Charleston-Summerville, SC	682,244	16,297	22,134	12,099	16,632	20,349	13,688	9,814	8,810	81,392
Charlotte-Gastonia-Rock Hill, NC-SC	1,796,759	35,551	53,834	27,586	35,514	45,152	32,715	22,995	22,466	186,428
Charlottesville, VA	203,890	5,039	7,215	3,883	4,893	7,216	4,991	3,918	3,871	28,772
Chattanooga, TN-GA	533,491	14,872	19,352	11,556	15,960	17,656	14,142	10,840	10,116	80,270
Cheyenne, WY	93,030	2,227	2,777	1,485	2,359	2,981	2,178	1,586	1,489	12,078
Chicago-Joliet-Naperville, IL-IN-WI	9,496,587	210,624	286,294	151,966	200,676	252,579	192,664	153,737	160,222	1,111,844
Chico, CA	220,565	5,768	9,264	5,056	5,277	7,473	5,694	5,558	5,476	34,534
Cincinnati-Middletown, OH-KY-IN	2,138,136	52,626	69,430	35,406	47,902	62,418	47,756	36,535	36,855	266,872
Clarksville, TN-KY	280,232	4,328	7,336	3,967	5,085	6,502	5,372	3,103	2,701	26,730
Cleveland, TN	116,844	2,857	4,131	2,366	3,557	4,680	3,304	2,112	1,712	17,731
Cleveland-Elyria-Mentor, OH	2,069,316	54,775	76,059	39,755	52,995	71,328	57,087	48,575	50,729	320,469
Coeur d'Alene, ID	140,793	4,020	5,572	3,054	3,999	5,151	3,801	2,687	2,369	21,061
College Station-Bryan, TX	231,815	4,031	5,490	3,030	3,652	4,977	3,929	3,116	2,321	21,025
Colorado Springs, CO	659,419	14,011	21,626	10,800	13,510	15,828	12,500	8,351	7,696	68,685
Columbia, MO	176,057	3,293	4,315	2,298	3,334	3,759	2,883	2,542	2,573	17,389
Columbia, SC	777,119	18,607	25,713	13,237	18,741	21,912	15,787	11,271	11,127	92,075
Columbus, GA-AL	302,508	6,510	9,003	4,760	5,992	8,465	6,217	5,424	4,181	35,039
Columbus, IN	77,946	2,054	2,776	1,658	2,463	2,131	1,791	1,759	1,338	11,140
Columbus, OH	1,859,697	39,194	57,053	29,345	36,858	47,981	35,681	26,753	25,363	201,981
Corpus Christi, TX	432,039	10,125	14,746	7,584	10,569	13,320	10,640	7,905	6,768	56,786
Corvallis, OR	85,989	1,996	3,251	1,755	1,661	2,332	1,636	1,474	1,929	10,787
Crestview-Fort Walton Beach-Destin, FL	184,699	4,261	5,895	3,671	4,406	6,435	5,430	3,283	2,704	25,929

Table B-4: Metropolitan Statistical Areas—Older Population by Age—*Continued*

	Total Population	60 to 61 Years	62 to 64 Years	65 to 66 Years	67 to 69 Years	70 to 74 Years	75 to 79 Years	80 to 84 Years	85 Years and Over	65 Years and Over
Cumberland, MD-WV	102,609	3,173	4,124	2,283	3,269	4,424	3,127	2,579	2,886	18,568
Dallas-Fort Worth-Arlington, TX	6,519,849	129,064	175,288	92,821	119,276	139,436	101,391	74,083	67,366	594,373
Dalton, GA	142,540	2,622	4,244	2,186	3,134	4,070	3,414	1,745	1,634	16,183
Danville, IL	81,225	2,252	2,786	1,865	2,111	3,038	2,408	1,891	1,936	13,249
Danville, VA	106,132	3,290	4,267	2,231	3,936	4,464	3,378	3,010	2,450	19,469
Davenport-Moline-Rock Island, IA-IL	381,367	10,297	14,300	7,344	10,421	13,377	10,566	8,098	8,903	58,709
Dayton, OH	842,693	22,124	32,046	14,853	22,180	31,155	24,007	18,743	17,788	128,726
Decatur, AL	154,078	4,050	5,645	3,402	4,082	5,650	4,009	2,982	2,295	22,420
Decatur, IL	110,491	3,328	4,092	2,455	3,356	3,579	3,220	2,873	2,852	18,335
Deltona-Daytona Beach-Ormond Beach, FL	495,284	14,042	20,277	12,507	17,643	25,775	19,714	16,651	14,807	107,097
Denver-Aurora-Broomfield, CO	2,599,275	60,223	76,140	41,464	51,945	61,894	46,007	34,673	35,419	271,402
Des Moines-West Des Moines, IA	580,572	13,579	18,053	9,096	11,247	15,378	11,722	9,154	9,308	65,905
Detroit-Warren-Livonia, MI	4,290,618	107,908	146,865	79,031	101,862	128,576	99,524	85,925	86,465	581,383
Dothan, AL	146,721	3,792	5,118	3,294	4,075	5,792	4,709	3,086	2,316	23,272
Dover, DE	165,306	3,443	5,951	3,484	4,274	5,585	4,373	2,878	2,511	23,105
Dubuque, IA	94,471	2,483	3,211	1,372	2,444	3,386	2,659	2,457	2,116	14,434
Duluth, MN-WI	279,685	7,900	10,831	6,116	7,055	9,636	8,228	6,334	6,820	44,189
Durham-Chapel Hill, NC	514,206	12,427	16,085	9,287	10,990	13,973	10,469	7,637	8,124	60,480
Eau Claire, WI	162,532	3,970	5,471	2,509	3,949	4,974	3,641	3,419	3,495	21,987
El Centro, CA	175,837	2,672	4,137	2,636	3,094	4,336	3,551	2,744	2,533	18,894
Elizabethtown, KY	121,330	3,138	3,275	2,036	2,705	3,130	2,531	1,892	1,625	13,919
Elkhart-Goshen, IN	198,598	4,772	5,787	3,433	4,255	5,281	4,031	3,713	3,734	24,447
Elmira, NY	88,848	2,331	3,475	1,308	2,526	3,002	2,322	2,142	2,356	13,656
El Paso, TX	816,295	15,031	20,413	11,326	14,054	20,253	16,631	12,022	10,499	84,785
Erie, PA	280,794	7,676	9,359	4,437	7,434	9,159	7,579	6,258	6,441	41,308
Eugene-Springfield, OR	353,315	10,423	14,033	7,199	9,460	13,436	9,098	8,465	7,297	54,955
Evansville, IN-KY	359,742	9,096	12,609	7,073	8,883	11,783	9,661	7,132	7,683	52,215
Fairbanks, AK	99,275	2,542	2,349	1,131	1,421	1,803	996	574	741	6,666
Fargo, ND-MN	212,771	4,478	5,878	2,901	3,402	4,899	4,573	3,394	3,259	22,428
Farmington, NM	128,912	2,903	3,631	2,244	2,788	3,066	2,642	2,003	1,702	14,445
Fayetteville, NC	371,706	7,397	9,125	5,178	6,160	9,246	6,216	4,352	3,611	34,763
Fayetteville-Springdale-Rogers, AR-MO	473,969	9,487	13,568	7,272	9,492	13,231	9,611	6,442	7,506	53,554
Flagstaff, AZ	134,909	2,777	3,776	2,227	2,884	2,878	2,033	1,266	1,382	12,670
Flint, MI	421,871	10,235	15,186	7,814	10,434	13,916	12,314	7,600	7,641	59,719
Florence, SC	205,814	5,071	8,014	4,214	5,828	6,928	5,364	3,219	3,199	28,752
Florence-Muscle Shoals, AL	147,089	4,623	5,459	3,630	4,243	6,175	5,183	2,897	3,270	25,398
Fond du Lac, WI	101,798	3,000	3,604	2,040	2,614	3,175	2,619	2,343	2,830	15,621
Fort Collins-Loveland, CO	305,335	7,598	10,291	5,479	6,787	9,034	6,192	5,101	5,129	37,722
Fort Smith, AR-OK	298,759	7,281	10,091	5,009	8,351	11,321	7,322	6,108	4,459	42,570
Fort Wayne, IN	419,252	10,017	13,346	6,548	9,058	12,365	9,339	7,899	7,636	52,845
Fresno, CA	940,493	17,803	25,033	13,950	16,567	21,685	16,630	13,685	14,407	96,924
Gadsden, AL	104,381	3,100	3,928	1,915	3,138	4,302	2,814	2,185	2,400	16,754
Gainesville, FL	266,364	6,112	8,151	3,941	5,603	7,257	5,425	4,252	3,928	30,406
Gainesville, GA	182,791	3,241	6,171	3,272	4,129	5,334	3,767	2,850	2,307	21,659
Glens Falls, NY	128,724	3,416	5,566	3,065	3,872	4,791	3,771	3,196	2,975	21,670
Goldsboro, NC	123,656	3,102	4,055	2,093	3,201	4,113	3,088	1,977	1,992	16,464
Grand Forks, ND-MN	98,516	2,160	2,685	1,675	1,871	2,862	2,070	1,992	1,991	12,461
Grand Junction, CO	147,268	3,341	5,412	2,819	3,987	5,338	3,843	3,376	3,281	22,644
Grand Rapids-Wyoming, MI	779,682	17,906	23,958	12,642	16,758	20,402	15,458	14,051	14,012	93,323
Great Falls, MT	81,677	2,037	3,095	1,438	2,255	3,142	2,549	1,755	1,797	12,936
Greeley, CO	258,708	5,166	7,370	3,620	4,876	6,810	4,188	3,555	2,876	25,925
Green Bay, WI	308,878	7,662	9,007	4,728	6,602	9,629	7,344	5,189	5,960	39,452
Greensboro-High Point, NC	730,577	16,678	26,186	12,685	19,081	23,091	19,124	13,608	11,311	98,900
Greenville, NC	192,167	4,168	5,029	2,891	4,028	4,479	3,144	2,895	2,747	20,184
Greenville-Mauldin-Easley, SC	645,542	14,640	20,608	12,355	17,055	20,513	15,310	11,050	10,796	87,079
Gulfport-Biloxi, MS	253,554	5,386	8,121	4,482	5,747	8,510	6,239	4,203	3,227	32,408
Hagerstown-Martinsburg, MD-WV	271,937	7,175	9,978	4,962	6,567	9,239	6,391	5,687	4,480	37,326
Hanford-Corcoran, CA	151,869	2,346	3,257	2,034	2,358	2,598	2,120	1,766	1,452	12,328
Harrisburg-Carlisle, PA	551,934	14,749	20,304	10,490	13,465	18,639	14,333	11,967	12,914	81,808
Harrisonburg, VA	126,824	2,508	3,736	1,956	2,223	4,200	2,719	2,825	2,448	16,371
Hartford-West Hartford-East Hartford, CT	1,214,120	28,913	43,792	23,147	31,277	37,043	30,566	25,657	30,284	177,974
Hattiesburg, MS	145,103	2,889	4,211	2,204	3,584	3,929	2,736	2,437	2,043	16,933
Hickory-Lenoir-Morganton, NC	364,335	9,645	14,477	8,054	10,573	14,692	11,011	6,592	6,354	57,276
Hinesville-Fort Stewart, GA	79,844	964	1,911	1,071	1,377	1,182	954	397	477	5,458
Holland-Grand Haven, MI	266,464	5,824	7,502	4,130	5,684	7,530	5,684	4,221	4,818	32,067
Honolulu, HI	966,405	25,130	31,819	19,397	23,915	28,821	25,876	20,994	24,044	143,047
Hot Springs, AR	96,590	2,518	4,516	2,248	3,507	5,099	4,053	2,252	2,966	20,125
Houma-Bayou Cane-Thibodaux, LA	208,590	4,593	5,926	3,828	4,799	6,054	4,464	3,301	2,744	25,190
Houston-Sugar Land-Baytown, TX	6,085,873	121,352	165,164	87,465	106,302	131,767	90,759	66,677	60,514	543,484
Huntington-Ashland, WV-KY-OH	287,149	8,802	11,371	6,572	8,514	10,860	9,191	6,443	5,742	47,322
Huntsville, AL	425,109	9,997	14,093	7,181	10,508	12,891	10,327	6,016	6,244	53,167
Idaho Falls, ID	132,098	2,694	3,949	2,077	2,449	3,434	2,610	1,729	2,065	14,364
Indianapolis-Carmel, IN	1,779,439	40,036	49,615	27,248	35,564	47,219	34,565	27,151	26,228	197,975
Iowa City, IA	155,534	3,631	4,548	2,360	2,714	3,228	2,365	2,389	2,461	15,517
Ithaca, NY	101,989	2,469	3,229	1,547	1,888	2,596	1,924	1,659	1,751	11,365
Jackson, MI	160,115	4,323	5,957	3,202	3,972	5,026	4,166	3,226	3,605	23,197
Jackson, MS	544,739	11,530	17,325	9,156	11,656	14,995	10,790	8,104	8,181	62,882
Jackson, TN	115,534	2,211	3,919	2,135	2,976	3,607	2,596	2,222	2,256	15,792
Jacksonville, FL	1,362,650	32,175	47,577	25,910	34,010	39,049	28,348	22,956	21,519	171,792
Jacksonville, NC	180,060	2,594	3,611	2,328	2,593	3,310	2,633	1,697	1,317	13,878

Table B-4: Metropolitan Statistical Areas—Older Population by Age—*Continued*

	Total Population	60 to 61 Years	62 to 64 Years	65 to 66 Years	67 to 69 Years	70 to 74 Years	75 to 79 Years	80 to 84 Years	85 Years and Over	65 Years and Over
Janesville, WI	160,240	3,307	5,551	2,514	3,905	5,320	4,160	3,311	2,999	22,209
Jefferson City, MO	150,133	3,792	5,394	2,802	3,649	4,531	3,482	2,861	2,455	19,780
Johnson City, TN	199,784	5,362	8,403	4,183	6,009	8,984	5,814	4,420	3,955	33,365
Johnstown, PA	142,564	4,038	5,804	3,005	4,328	5,773	4,802	4,756	4,525	27,189
Jonesboro, AR	122,682	3,000	3,887	2,216	3,089	3,678	2,700	2,197	1,944	15,824
Joplin, MO	175,631	3,917	5,232	3,043	4,800	6,020	4,635	3,190	3,393	25,081
Kalamazoo-Portage, MI	328,433	7,386	11,749	5,328	7,248	10,122	7,843	5,856	5,966	42,363
Kankakee-Bradley, IL	113,361	2,372	4,065	1,828	2,961	3,299	2,731	2,272	2,270	15,361
Kansas City, MO-KS	2,051,795	46,467	66,361	34,202	43,903	59,114	42,870	35,508	36,648	252,245
Kennewick-Pasco-Richland, WA	262,524	6,213	8,183	3,909	5,444	6,635	4,496	3,948	3,250	27,682
Killeen-Temple-Fort Hood, TX	413,662	6,896	10,091	5,552	7,044	9,117	6,568	5,509	3,992	37,782
Kingsport-Bristol-Bristol, TN-VA	308,895	8,899	13,429	6,864	10,712	15,357	10,082	7,873	7,019	57,907
Kingston, NY	182,256	5,592	7,604	4,352	5,160	5,616	4,577	4,169	4,304	28,178
Knoxville, TN	704,397	18,920	25,496	14,038	20,235	25,345	19,546	13,878	13,195	106,237
Kokomo, IN	98,600	2,379	3,991	2,396	3,268	3,614	3,122	2,198	2,199	16,797
La Crosse, WI-MN	134,534	2,979	4,761	2,559	2,721	4,245	3,677	2,694	3,199	19,095
Lafayette, IN	204,154	3,887	5,455	2,984	3,489	5,256	3,167	3,289	3,184	21,369
Lafayette, LA	277,061	5,589	7,998	4,505	5,288	6,991	5,708	3,835	3,568	29,895
Lake Charles, LA	200,378	4,593	7,331	3,648	4,655	6,369	4,689	3,587	2,803	25,751
Lake Havasu City-Kingman, AZ	202,102	6,269	10,623	6,417	8,859	13,995	8,220	6,393	4,700	48,584
Lakeland-Winter Haven, FL	609,775	15,652	22,431	14,920	20,068	27,837	20,841	14,677	13,506	111,849
Lancaster, PA	523,676	12,458	16,305	9,548	14,081	16,542	14,203	11,859	13,886	80,119
Lansing-East Lansing, MI	465,168	11,571	14,589	8,166	10,659	12,468	9,950	7,430	7,681	56,354
Laredo, TX	255,135	4,059	5,089	2,732	3,722	4,958	3,545	2,562	2,711	20,230
Las Cruces, NM	212,571	4,496	5,850	3,525	5,095	6,566	5,158	3,682	2,973	26,999
Las Vegas-Paradise, NV	1,974,036	44,262	61,743	37,738	46,418	59,451	40,461	27,496	21,844	233,408
Lawrence, KS	112,105	1,943	2,997	1,348	2,039	2,203	1,879	1,316	1,500	10,285
Lawton, OK	125,850	1,933	3,357	1,830	2,260	3,044	2,881	1,522	1,427	12,964
Lebanon, PA	134,452	3,198	5,165	2,462	3,973	5,162	3,944	3,985	3,413	22,939
Lewiston-Auburn, ME	107,571	2,781	4,303	2,418	2,262	3,566	2,872	2,244	2,190	15,552
Lexington-Fayette, KY	479,142	10,679	16,131	7,983	9,497	13,209	9,792	7,521	6,617	54,619
Lima, OH	105,701	2,638	3,398	2,055	2,310	3,677	2,556	2,525	2,573	15,696
Lincoln, NE	306,626	7,403	9,085	4,835	5,365	7,989	6,803	4,483	5,190	34,665
Little Rock-North Little Rock-Conway, AR	710,321	16,239	22,166	12,795	15,993	21,813	16,152	11,995	9,948	88,696
Logan, UT-ID	127,244	1,771	2,139	1,433	2,034	2,497	1,892	1,458	1,449	10,763
Longview, TX	215,688	5,613	7,070	4,220	4,901	7,229	5,374	4,341	4,485	30,550
Longview, WA	102,291	2,643	4,626	2,225	3,131	4,091	2,791	2,136	2,221	16,595
Los Angeles-Long Beach-Santa Ana, CA	12,947,334	268,870	359,109	202,778	253,858	338,092	258,993	206,174	212,830	1,472,725
Louisville/Jefferson County, KY-IN	1,293,831	31,861	45,215	24,275	30,533	39,191	29,892	24,003	21,639	169,533
Lubbock, TX	289,685	5,322	7,424	4,749	5,534	7,370	6,562	4,497	4,004	32,716
Lynchburg, VA	254,048	6,887	9,779	5,528	6,890	10,629	7,783	4,759	5,584	41,173
Macon, GA	232,638	5,451	8,148	4,745	5,495	7,110	5,909	4,429	3,513	31,201
Madera-Chowchilla, CA	151,827	2,921	4,750	2,908	3,220	4,263	3,474	2,165	1,882	17,912
Madison, WI	576,845	13,292	18,775	8,951	12,211	13,887	11,224	9,437	9,071	64,781
Manchester-Nashua, NH	401,933	9,532	14,234	6,855	8,198	12,142	8,656	6,743	6,877	49,471
Manhattan, KS	131,648	2,028	2,888	1,489	1,755	2,224	1,848	1,586	1,607	10,509
Mankato-North Mankato, MN	97,389	2,200	2,428	1,203	1,917	2,762	1,779	1,929	2,216	11,806
Mansfield, OH	123,331	3,495	4,857	2,288	3,347	5,256	4,220	3,001	2,656	20,768
McAllen-Edinburg-Mission, TX	793,312	12,690	17,052	9,788	13,389	18,791	14,179	11,268	8,386	75,801
Medford, OR	204,868	6,095	8,905	4,797	6,457	8,571	6,699	5,009	5,744	37,277
Memphis, TN-MS-AR	1,325,160	31,048	40,884	21,549	27,274	33,801	25,391	19,420	16,331	143,766
Merced, CA	259,716	4,628	6,130	3,653	4,650	5,883	4,300	3,619	3,093	25,198
Miami-Fort Lauderdale-Pompano Beach, FL	5,677,408	129,502	183,949	107,181	146,736	206,924	164,422	145,531	144,234	915,028
Michigan City-La Porte, IN	111,314	3,269	3,754	2,148	3,145	3,516	2,953	2,352	2,008	16,122
Midland, TX	141,207	3,247	3,758	1,867	2,385	3,569	3,084	2,542	1,851	15,298
Milwaukee-Waukesha-West Allis, WI	1,561,707	36,167	48,885	25,129	32,574	43,111	36,152	31,876	31,013	199,855
Minneapolis-St. Paul-Bloomington, MN-WI	3,320,190	76,169	98,049	51,930	65,320	82,731	63,688	49,361	52,919	365,949
Missoula, MT	110,183	2,420	4,023	2,090	2,492	2,774	1,779	1,855	1,945	12,935
Mobile, AL	413,432	10,158	14,315	8,155	10,823	12,512	10,458	6,745	6,289	54,982
Modesto, CA	518,336	10,313	14,086	7,977	10,133	13,091	9,373	7,847	8,517	56,938
Monroe, LA	177,278	3,930	5,459	3,590	3,913	5,298	4,325	3,247	2,916	23,289
Monroe, MI	151,539	4,107	5,717	3,031	3,637	5,042	3,572	3,394	2,455	21,131
Montgomery, AL	376,964	9,080	11,211	7,392	8,784	10,341	8,652	5,952	5,240	46,361
Morgantown, WV	132,224	3,520	3,766	2,063	2,737	3,731	2,907	1,988	1,933	15,359
Morristown, TN	137,261	3,728	5,228	3,108	4,747	5,965	3,945	2,884	2,169	22,818
Mount Vernon-Anacortes, WA	117,691	3,125	5,164	2,502	4,086	4,397	3,682	2,389	2,652	19,708
Muncie, IN	117,599	2,656	3,838	2,310	2,754	4,414	3,714	2,469	1,931	17,592
Muskegon-Norton Shores, MI	170,724	4,426	5,302	3,028	4,098	5,608	4,231	3,506	3,325	23,796
Myrtle Beach-North Myrtle Beach-Conway, SC	276,156	8,564	13,399	7,388	10,662	12,409	8,444	5,629	4,537	49,069
Napa, CA	137,949	3,661	4,907	3,491	2,854	4,869	3,511	3,169	3,557	21,451
Naples-Marco Island, FL	327,537	9,661	14,412	10,105	15,984	22,326	16,939	12,853	11,345	89,552
Nashville-Davidson--Murfreesboro--Franklin, TN	1,618,819	36,771	50,043	26,583	33,197	43,990	32,365	20,658	21,653	178,446
New Haven-Milford, CT	862,776	20,553	30,248	16,522	21,002	26,234	21,927	16,975	23,684	126,344
New Orleans-Metairie-Kenner, LA	1,190,162	29,069	41,301	22,696	26,352	34,741	24,999	20,511	19,252	148,551
New York-Northern New Jersey-Long Island, NY-NJ-PA	19,048,167	439,332	599,926	340,808	431,245	570,669	446,631	369,726	380,351	2,539,430
Niles-Benton Harbor, MI	156,452	4,195	5,678	2,876	4,850	5,902	4,411	3,866	3,931	25,836
North Port-Bradenton-Sarasota, FL	710,883	20,520	32,609	23,589	31,713	46,503	37,653	30,916	29,718	200,092
Norwich-New London, CT	274,118	7,034	10,277	5,508	7,579	8,767	6,417	6,542	5,336	40,149
Ocala, FL	333,001	10,234	16,043	9,946	15,239	23,254	16,909	12,758	9,397	87,503
Ocean City, NJ	96,716	3,540	4,333	2,485	3,779	5,188	3,916	3,436	2,730	21,534

Table B-4: Metropolitan Statistical Areas—Older Population by Age—*Continued*

	Total Population	60 to 61 Years	62 to 64 Years	65 to 66 Years	67 to 69 Years	70 to 74 Years	75 to 79 Years	80 to 84 Years	85 Years and Over	65 Years and Over
Odessa, TX	140,323	2,924	2,984	1,844	2,846	3,079	2,564	2,159	1,576	14,068
Ogden-Clearfield, UT	555,816	9,791	12,869	7,274	9,065	12,100	9,812	7,151	6,223	51,625
Oklahoma City, OK	1,276,771	27,865	39,791	20,658	26,497	38,518	26,389	21,570	18,977	152,609
Olympia, WA	255,927	6,858	10,481	4,946	6,230	8,393	6,150	4,277	4,483	34,479
Omaha-Council Bluffs, NE-IA	876,971	21,766	25,393	13,076	17,507	22,725	17,119	13,743	14,717	98,887
Orlando-Kissimmee-Sanford, FL	2,179,420	49,352	65,555	40,424	49,730	64,899	49,923	37,260	34,090	276,326
Oshkosh-Neenah, WI	167,860	3,858	5,557	2,701	3,995	4,776	4,200	3,159	3,956	22,787
Owensboro, KY	115,410	2,698	4,161	2,460	3,299	3,590	3,175	2,579	2,264	17,367
Oxnard-Thousand Oaks-Ventura, CA	830,828	19,256	25,269	15,045	18,484	21,117	18,158	13,587	14,468	100,859
Palm Bay-Melbourne-Titusville, FL	545,202	14,979	21,473	13,896	19,025	26,860	21,841	18,447	14,013	114,082
Palm Coast, FL	97,229	3,598	4,583	3,110	4,661	6,965	4,393	2,924	2,962	25,015
Panama City-Lynn Haven-Panama City Beach, FL	170,351	4,383	5,538	3,425	4,182	6,794	4,923	3,540	2,599	25,463
Parkersburg-Marietta-Vienna, WV-OH	161,887	4,674	5,922	3,833	5,297	6,444	5,478	3,485	3,291	27,828
Pascagoula, MS	162,870	3,581	5,608	2,924	4,073	5,731	4,343	2,218	1,646	20,935
Pensacola-Ferry Pass-Brent, FL	455,932	10,725	16,402	9,403	11,735	16,057	11,728	8,147	7,515	64,585
Peoria, IL	379,918	9,945	12,123	6,825	9,852	13,145	11,054	8,154	8,522	57,552
Philadelphia-Camden-Wilmington, PA-NJ-DE-MD	5,996,101	142,108	196,268	107,408	136,332	178,324	143,923	120,157	125,351	811,495
Phoenix-Mesa-Glendale, AZ	4,263,663	91,013	129,718	74,553	102,497	131,268	97,955	72,930	64,503	543,706
Pine Bluff, AR	98,989	2,633	3,576	1,796	2,670	3,138	2,356	1,900	1,836	13,696
Pittsburgh, PA	2,359,225	66,041	89,828	48,370	64,191	88,273	73,718	67,525	68,432	410,509
Pittsfield, MA	130,565	3,896	5,711	2,878	3,657	5,860	4,319	3,872	4,486	25,072
Pocatello, ID	91,236	1,852	2,621	1,205	1,958	2,670	1,958	1,590	1,119	10,500
Portland-South Portland-Biddeford, ME	516,025	14,830	19,738	10,758	13,691	18,498	14,324	11,207	11,021	79,499
Portland-Vancouver-Hillsboro, OR-WA	2,261,148	56,218	77,500	40,983	50,294	58,958	42,611	34,436	39,516	266,798
Port St. Lucie, FL	428,781	11,290	16,748	11,300	17,186	22,690	18,779	15,286	13,827	99,068
Poughkeepsie-Newburgh-Middletown, NY	671,926	17,015	21,345	12,171	14,818	19,064	14,326	11,974	11,706	84,059
Prescott, AZ	211,339	8,198	11,577	6,584	10,262	13,917	9,047	6,493	7,010	53,313
Providence-New Bedford-Fall River, RI-MA	1,601,208	41,287	53,767	30,306	38,998	49,448	40,485	34,523	40,696	234,456
Provo-Orem, UT	540,458	6,693	8,206	4,995	6,709	8,623	6,464	5,126	4,530	36,447
Pueblo, CO	160,256	4,099	6,115	2,934	4,379	5,783	4,694	4,086	3,150	25,026
Punta Gorda, FL	160,602	5,089	9,856	6,431	9,104	14,721	11,094	7,268	8,101	56,719
Racine, WI	195,086	4,592	6,769	3,434	4,809	5,772	4,929	3,814	3,575	26,333
Raleigh-Cary, NC	1,162,869	22,964	32,439	17,942	21,405	25,730	18,143	13,598	12,101	108,919
Rapid City, SD	128,421	3,470	4,065	2,024	2,844	4,356	3,084	2,412	2,639	17,359
Reading, PA	412,610	9,643	13,715	7,575	10,493	12,713	10,833	9,786	9,371	60,772
Redding, CA	177,980	4,971	7,629	4,413	5,819	7,291	5,033	4,464	4,189	31,209
Reno-Sparks, NV	429,841	11,482	16,359	8,528	10,879	13,740	8,990	6,390	6,177	54,704
Richmond, VA	1,270,735	31,190	44,476	23,172	28,802	38,727	27,305	20,006	22,140	160,152
Riverside-San Bernardino-Ontario, CA	4,298,641	83,968	112,146	63,892	85,535	108,903	84,093	63,625	54,619	460,667
Roanoke, VA	309,191	9,057	12,727	5,872	9,691	12,414	9,409	7,078	7,090	51,554
Rochester, MN	187,566	4,083	5,837	3,618	3,726	6,070	4,758	3,270	3,764	25,206
Rochester, NY	1,056,072	26,123	36,994	20,501	26,989	32,906	26,598	21,575	24,840	153,409
Rockford, IL	347,722	7,931	11,938	6,220	9,429	10,799	8,292	7,100	6,539	48,379
Rocky Mount, NC	152,041	3,791	6,234	3,530	3,921	5,382	4,069	2,744	2,791	22,437
Rome, GA	96,238	2,546	3,216	1,383	2,417	3,772	2,986	1,595	1,741	13,894
Sacramento--Arden-Arcade--Roseville, CA	2,175,903	50,363	69,449	37,262	48,108	61,891	47,393	37,144	39,322	271,120
Saginaw-Saginaw Township North, MI	199,094	5,391	6,602	3,928	5,876	6,709	5,785	4,197	4,628	31,123
St. Cloud, MN	189,905	3,905	5,836	2,988	3,557	5,363	4,459	3,645	3,504	23,516
St. George, UT	141,594	2,354	4,602	2,934	4,253	6,453	5,081	3,286	3,421	25,428
St. Joseph, MO-KS	127,601	3,111	4,099	2,277	3,253	3,995	3,036	2,617	3,036	18,214
St. Louis, MO-IL	2,818,187	68,559	91,890	50,196	66,167	88,340	68,021	57,230	55,390	385,344
Salem, OR	393,932	8,989	13,203	7,356	9,435	12,222	9,348	7,135	8,274	53,770
Salinas, CA	421,570	8,642	12,872	6,298	7,496	10,435	8,355	6,404	7,052	46,040
Salisbury, MD	126,211	3,125	3,727	2,356	3,289	3,768	2,986	2,455	2,191	17,045
Salt Lake City, UT	1,144,789	20,438	30,117	14,268	19,230	23,513	17,161	13,919	12,192	100,283
San Angelo, TX	113,598	2,336	3,502	2,384	2,586	3,275	3,337	2,486	1,642	15,710
San Antonio-New Braunfels, TX	2,192,939	46,807	66,321	35,041	46,446	57,026	43,485	33,487	31,051	246,536
San Diego-Carlsbad-San Marcos, CA	3,139,726	66,640	89,620	49,644	60,975	81,304	63,554	52,642	57,661	365,780
Sandusky, OH	76,700	2,420	3,327	1,575	2,640	3,158	2,712	1,839	1,779	13,703
San Francisco-Oakland-Fremont, CA	4,399,211	109,639	149,457	79,487	97,758	129,389	98,532	78,358	86,927	570,451
San Jose-Sunnyvale-Santa Clara, CA	1,868,165	39,142	51,204	28,709	36,934	49,717	36,593	30,563	29,018	211,534
San Luis Obispo-Paso Robles, CA	272,034	7,290	10,670	5,746	7,097	9,668	7,533	5,971	6,712	42,727
Santa Barbara-Santa Maria-Goleta, CA	427,251	8,387	12,444	7,656	8,674	11,713	10,392	7,592	10,019	56,046
Santa Cruz-Watsonville, CA	265,057	8,255	8,557	4,985	5,840	6,483	4,561	4,024	4,892	30,785
Santa Fe, NM	145,378	5,224	6,923	3,949	5,386	5,319	3,884	2,525	2,518	23,581
Santa Rosa-Petaluma, CA	488,237	14,635	19,789	10,403	12,274	15,927	11,210	9,796	11,383	70,993
Savannah, GA	355,539	7,672	12,085	6,270	7,918	9,921	7,380	5,272	5,427	42,188
Scranton--Wilkes-Barre, PA	563,722	15,394	21,315	12,450	15,871	21,612	17,081	17,085	17,073	101,172
Seattle-Tacoma-Bellevue, WA	3,499,632	82,586	110,476	58,607	72,501	86,867	64,159	52,024	57,323	391,481
Sebastian-Vero Beach, FL	139,241	4,284	5,488	3,580	6,335	9,170	7,743	5,782	6,497	39,107
Sheboygan, WI	115,224	2,441	4,225	1,886	2,890	3,968	3,308	2,139	2,993	17,184
Sherman-Denison, TX	121,434	2,877	4,779	2,165	3,636	4,721	3,424	2,693	2,535	19,174
Shreveport-Bossier City, LA	403,273	9,164	12,702	7,098	9,166	12,878	10,740	7,018	6,445	53,345
Sioux City, IA-NE-SD	143,948	3,470	4,177	2,715	2,930	4,229	3,240	2,833	3,009	18,956
Sioux Falls, SD	233,298	4,770	7,202	3,521	4,360	5,636	4,377	4,386	4,042	26,322
South Bend-Mishawaka, IN-MI	318,943	8,261	10,163	5,937	7,025	10,132	7,350	7,731	6,767	44,942
Spartanburg, SC	286,563	7,753	10,039	5,384	7,124	10,522	7,223	5,208	3,986	39,447
Spokane, WA	473,793	11,727	17,550	9,477	11,368	13,436	11,472	8,851	8,679	63,283
Springfield, IL	211,411	5,812	8,059	3,687	5,375	6,909	5,195	4,186	4,697	30,049
Springfield, MA	696,247	18,294	25,337	12,017	17,145	21,518	17,628	14,362	16,728	99,398

Table B-4: Metropolitan Statistical Areas—Older Population by Age—*Continued*

	Total Population	60 to 61 Years	62 to 64 Years	65 to 66 Years	67 to 69 Years	70 to 74 Years	75 to 79 Years	80 to 84 Years	85 Years and Over	65 Years and Over
Springfield, MO	440,811	10,217	15,440	8,187	12,188	13,707	11,241	9,092	8,591	63,006
Springfield, OH	137,735	3,923	5,571	2,348	3,916	5,936	3,991	2,939	3,490	22,620
State College, PA	154,698	2,942	4,103	2,064	3,045	4,254	3,240	2,583	2,566	17,752
Steubenville-Weirton, OH-WV	123,367	3,985	5,083	2,615	3,939	5,285	4,205	3,872	3,201	23,117
Stockton, CA	695,251	13,077	18,342	10,578	12,658	17,480	12,907	10,385	10,314	74,322
Sumter, SC	107,642	2,552	3,731	2,018	2,366	3,640	2,762	1,656	1,694	14,136
Syracuse, NY	662,095	16,605	21,347	12,259	15,558	20,288	16,409	13,723	14,779	93,016
Tallahassee, FL	371,927	8,340	11,838	5,960	8,099	9,086	6,267	5,445	5,073	39,930
Tampa-St. Petersburg-Clearwater, FL	2,819,382	72,283	107,439	62,470	83,671	112,423	92,225	71,454	72,286	494,529
Terre Haute, IN	172,476	3,877	6,212	3,288	4,014	5,967	4,144	3,661	3,738	24,812
Texarkana, TX-Texarkana, AR	136,546	3,145	4,569	2,756	3,462	4,840	3,438	2,662	2,524	19,682
Toledo, OH	650,637	16,775	21,302	12,149	14,890	20,174	15,502	14,043	12,782	89,540
Topeka, KS	234,516	6,780	8,151	4,730	5,965	8,106	6,439	5,221	4,937	35,398
Trenton-Ewing, NJ	367,567	8,595	11,358	6,876	7,499	10,172	8,278	7,299	7,261	47,385
Tucson, AZ	987,294	26,269	35,502	22,507	26,911	36,757	27,626	22,571	21,477	157,849
Tulsa, OK	945,744	22,709	30,384	17,795	22,740	29,557	22,061	16,693	16,103	124,949
Tuscaloosa, AL	221,214	5,200	6,191	3,575	4,135	6,289	4,728	3,785	3,033	25,545
Tyler, TX	212,694	4,901	6,644	4,021	4,711	7,916	5,735	4,087	4,509	30,979
Utica-Rome, NY	298,723	7,801	12,141	5,709	7,978	11,100	8,444	7,149	9,381	49,761
Valdosta, GA	141,795	2,954	4,036	2,172	2,829	3,769	2,545	1,872	1,813	15,000
Vallejo-Fairfield, CA	417,261	10,801	14,531	7,362	8,951	11,561	9,456	6,088	5,922	49,340
Victoria, TX	116,550	2,176	4,628	2,111	3,025	4,137	3,378	2,392	1,894	16,937
Vineland-Millville-Bridgeton, NJ	157,351	3,254	4,848	2,392	3,537	5,072	3,577	2,733	2,843	20,154
Virginia Beach-Norfolk-Newport News, VA-NC	1,684,011	37,239	51,561	27,517	37,781	47,116	36,623	26,567	24,444	200,048
Visalia-Porterville, CA	447,704	8,172	10,655	6,585	7,731	9,636	7,390	6,125	5,689	43,156
Waco, TX	237,471	4,400	7,026	3,877	5,377	6,341	5,572	4,387	4,469	30,023
Warner Robins, GA	143,718	2,639	3,976	1,992	2,918	3,836	2,804	1,986	1,539	15,075
Washington-Arlington-Alexandria, DC-VA-MD-WV	5,710,843	132,481	170,148	90,978	114,584	136,844	98,282	72,102	75,781	588,571
Waterloo-Cedar Falls, IA	168,296	4,113	5,984	3,321	3,815	5,437	4,321	4,013	4,039	24,946
Wausau, WI	134,459	3,830	4,618	2,552	3,409	4,263	3,314	2,938	3,252	19,728
Wenatchee-East Wenatchee, WA	112,118	2,934	4,258	1,748	3,298	3,928	3,498	1,792	2,539	16,803
Wheeling, WV-OH	147,142	4,685	6,207	3,248	4,525	5,621	4,533	4,541	3,997	26,465
Wichita, KS	625,940	13,370	18,789	10,367	13,470	16,091	14,202	10,993	11,698	76,821
Wichita Falls, TX	150,783	3,214	4,630	2,879	3,350	4,663	4,339	2,761	2,716	20,708
Williamsport, PA	116,668	2,929	4,372	2,415	3,187	4,055	3,361	2,877	3,409	19,304
Wilmington, NC	369,711	11,007	15,800	8,991	13,049	16,432	10,584	7,794	6,054	62,904
Winchester, VA-WV	129,843	3,710	4,759	2,543	3,533	4,167	3,528	2,072	2,115	17,958
Winston-Salem, NC	481,399	11,783	16,908	9,412	12,891	15,420	12,538	9,483	8,563	68,307
Worcester, MA	803,429	18,973	24,785	14,401	17,415	22,385	18,165	14,543	17,839	104,748
Yakima, WA	245,797	4,963	6,706	4,143	5,623	5,993	4,980	3,857	4,420	29,016
York-Hanover, PA	436,824	11,126	16,348	8,492	11,819	13,979	10,944	9,243	8,678	63,155
Youngstown-Warren-Boardman, OH-PA	561,578	16,575	23,603	12,301	15,709	22,167	18,036	16,894	16,434	101,541
Yuba City, CA	167,564	3,982	5,285	2,682	3,412	5,026	3,678	2,956	2,119	19,873
Yuma, AZ	199,061	3,698	5,856	3,735	4,752	9,228	7,211	4,190	2,635	31,751

Table B-5: 113th Congressional Districts—Older Population by Age

	Total Population	60 to 61 Years	62 to 64 Years	65 to 66 Years	67 to 69 Years	70 to 74 Years	75 to 79 Years	80 to 84 Years	85 Years and Over	65 Years and Over
Alabama										
Congressional District 1	688,249	17,353	25,540	14,564	20,367	23,232	17,918	13,274	11,152	100,507
Congressional District 2	682,475	16,735	22,625	14,459	18,678	22,248	18,443	13,236	11,112	98,176
Congressional District 3	689,196	17,952	23,691	13,747	17,876	23,161	17,590	11,546	10,395	94,315
Congressional District 4	680,531	18,072	27,506	15,038	20,408	27,614	19,550	14,566	11,970	109,146
Congressional District 5	690,835	17,492	24,114	13,111	18,070	23,490	18,683	10,984	10,982	95,320
Congressional District 6	683,810	16,440	22,840	12,117	16,989	21,753	16,021	12,663	11,721	91,264
Congressional District 7	688,392	17,478	21,969	11,740	14,545	21,521	16,635	12,491	11,465	88,397
Alaska										
Congressional District (at Large)	723,120	17,319	21,417	10,747	11,384	15,489	9,350	6,707	4,909	58,586
Arizona										
Congressional District 1	719,827	18,704	24,873	15,357	19,970	26,613	17,900	11,510	10,681	102,031
Congressional District 2	716,127	20,873	27,024	17,811	22,131	29,915	22,207	19,046	18,304	129,414
Congressional District 3	718,357	13,984	18,114	11,079	12,228	16,804	12,219	7,297	6,933	66,560
Congressional District 4	717,210	21,781	35,666	21,116	30,347	45,059	28,388	20,130	16,496	161,536
Congressional District 5	719,967	15,113	23,364	13,131	19,880	26,924	21,417	16,314	11,476	109,142
Congressional District 6	723,210	19,647	26,367	15,901	20,303	26,145	18,159	12,924	12,710	106,142
Congressional District 7	721,604	10,969	13,733	7,307	8,997	11,517	8,067	6,164	4,831	46,883
Congressional District 8	715,908	15,315	25,115	15,366	23,587	31,148	26,486	20,274	17,938	134,799
Congressional District 9	724,918	15,076	19,819	9,923	13,825	15,529	10,864	9,786	10,592	70,519
Arkansas										
Congressional District 1	728,665	19,598	25,896	15,658	20,674	29,819	21,437	15,979	13,979	117,546
Congressional District 2	739,485	16,994	23,336	14,221	17,743	22,893	17,703	13,083	11,360	97,003
Congressional District 3	740,549	16,160	23,751	12,628	17,095	22,598	16,872	12,291	12,134	93,618
Congressional District 4	728,123	19,367	27,343	16,118	21,796	30,550	22,668	15,749	14,637	121,518
California										
Congressional District 1	703,517	20,444	31,607	17,754	21,415	29,813	20,460	17,922	17,142	124,506
Congressional District 2	705,403	22,618	31,301	17,029	22,298	25,412	17,657	15,263	15,495	113,154
Congressional District 3	707,542	16,594	22,438	11,417	15,437	19,367	14,908	11,220	10,398	82,747
Congressional District 4	705,130	20,336	29,657	17,097	22,856	28,093	21,964	15,057	14,360	119,427
Congressional District 5	712,669	20,035	27,446	14,691	15,866	22,934	16,791	13,458	15,649	99,389
Congressional District 6	710,032	13,853	19,036	10,501	12,873	16,648	13,273	11,028	11,529	75,852
Congressional District 7	711,837	16,635	22,852	11,904	14,599	20,626	15,254	12,103	13,236	87,722
Congressional District 8	705,307	17,015	21,108	11,329	16,331	19,181	14,510	11,150	8,481	80,982
Congressional District 9	710,682	13,929	19,888	11,507	13,628	18,826	13,565	11,152	10,396	79,074
Congressional District 10	709,468	13,970	18,842	10,714	13,401	17,812	12,692	9,903	10,706	75,228
Congressional District 11	716,752	18,308	25,926	14,219	16,731	22,034	17,044	13,550	15,865	99,443
Congressional District 12	708,026	17,943	24,372	11,642	14,730	21,466	18,257	14,068	15,796	95,959
Congressional District 13	712,319	17,519	23,979	13,000	14,951	20,330	13,364	10,877	13,745	86,267
Congressional District 14	716,514	18,002	25,371	13,376	16,766	21,911	17,709	14,107	15,777	99,646
Congressional District 15	716,070	16,719	21,047	11,517	13,092	17,076	12,207	11,062	10,630	75,584
Congressional District 16	713,370	12,108	16,237	9,012	11,407	14,922	10,929	8,649	8,416	63,335
Congressional District 17	717,422	13,962	18,794	10,416	12,892	17,289	14,741	11,176	10,148	76,662
Congressional District 18	723,643	18,059	22,063	12,401	16,742	21,965	15,870	13,979	15,986	96,943
Congressional District 19	702,232	13,959	18,805	11,087	14,027	17,520	12,338	10,055	8,359	73,386
Congressional District 20	712,741	16,330	21,110	11,020	13,068	17,971	13,652	10,666	12,138	78,515
Congressional District 21	705,199	10,583	15,646	7,824	10,462	12,248	9,300	7,111	6,444	53,389
Congressional District 22	712,793	13,888	19,740	11,781	13,369	16,540	13,536	11,356	11,408	77,990
Congressional District 23	709,743	15,282	19,337	11,364	14,417	19,487	13,760	10,177	9,188	78,393
Congressional District 24	709,359	15,894	23,419	13,695	15,983	21,634	18,088	13,679	16,788	99,867
Congressional District 25	707,791	14,582	17,790	9,897	13,410	15,133	11,296	7,905	7,351	64,992
Congressional District 26	709,241	15,851	21,720	12,842	15,844	18,245	16,104	12,062	13,121	88,218
Congressional District 27	707,049	18,649	23,435	13,160	16,436	23,539	18,684	15,121	18,467	105,407
Congressional District 28	713,520	16,706	21,621	12,111	16,219	22,820	18,111	15,493	14,237	98,991
Congressional District 29	698,936	13,005	15,059	9,575	10,161	14,756	11,043	8,030	8,068	61,633
Congressional District 30	725,109	16,925	23,054	12,863	16,140	21,556	16,942	14,116	15,094	96,711
Congressional District 31	719,204	14,090	15,753	8,967	11,309	13,943	10,841	8,556	8,369	61,985
Congressional District 32	706,961	14,866	20,897	10,860	14,466	18,288	14,044	10,524	10,899	79,081
Congressional District 33	705,606	16,352	23,299	14,965	18,125	23,235	19,026	15,675	16,847	107,873
Congressional District 34	701,073	14,417	18,244	9,571	11,765	16,200	13,103	9,735	9,832	70,206
Congressional District 35	711,969	11,220	15,715	8,858	9,809	12,756	8,614	6,614	6,497	53,148
Congressional District 36	712,130	15,465	24,719	16,845	21,928	32,386	26,701	20,319	18,014	136,193
Congressional District 37	716,393	14,067	18,898	10,023	13,896	18,286	13,692	10,989	13,479	80,365
Congressional District 38	710,784	13,831	19,728	11,299	14,277	19,526	15,481	13,140	12,203	85,926
Congressional District 39	715,765	16,966	22,868	13,638	16,192	19,089	15,111	11,424	11,487	86,941
Congressional District 40	701,135	10,782	13,930	7,820	8,919	11,331	9,424	6,581	6,144	50,219
Congressional District 41	717,154	11,539	15,554	8,099	10,792	13,318	9,628	7,577	6,812	56,226
Congressional District 42	722,604	13,668	18,529	9,752	14,607	17,103	13,537	9,441	7,284	71,724
Congressional District 43	698,157	14,344	17,475	10,650	12,674	16,875	13,261	9,855	9,666	72,981
Congressional District 44	708,177	12,267	16,106	9,280	11,159	14,925	10,480	7,580	6,189	59,613
Congressional District 45	718,596	15,432	24,041	11,907	15,894	21,063	15,681	12,396	13,482	90,423
Congressional District 46	709,755	11,469	13,851	7,616	8,910	13,495	9,226	8,145	8,457	55,849
Congressional District 47	714,214	14,887	20,138	9,998	14,659	18,431	14,578	12,205	11,492	81,363
Congressional District 48	710,815	17,276	24,523	15,151	18,217	25,087	17,054	14,024	14,882	104,415
Congressional District 49	705,126	15,486	20,817	11,252	14,892	19,521	14,900	12,915	14,406	87,886
Congressional District 50	717,813	16,718	22,574	12,440	15,029	18,331	15,442	12,020	13,934	87,196
Congressional District 51	715,432	11,369	16,248	9,356	11,369	16,413	13,292	10,381	9,366	70,177
Congressional District 52	707,989	16,789	20,651	11,404	14,891	19,474	14,832	11,990	13,672	86,263
Congressional District 53	720,318	14,542	21,214	12,083	12,643	18,036	13,285	12,040	13,349	81,436

Table B-5: 113th Congressional Districts—Older Population by Age—*Continued*

	Total Population	60 to 61 Years	62 to 64 Years	65 to 66 Years	67 to 69 Years	70 to 74 Years	75 to 79 Years	80 to 84 Years	85 Years and Over	65 Years and Over
Colorado										
Congressional District 1	736,635	16,396	21,337	10,860	13,871	17,628	12,345	10,982	12,655	78,341
Congressional District 2	730,276	20,213	23,842	14,081	16,358	18,777	13,221	9,590	9,982	82,009
Congressional District 3	722,321	19,099	28,666	14,669	19,898	24,858	18,321	13,438	12,465	103,649
Congressional District 4	727,643	15,634	22,105	11,572	14,541	20,103	13,504	10,556	9,789	80,065
Congressional District 5	732,004	15,969	25,342	12,616	16,468	18,840	14,723	10,155	9,168	81,970
Congressional District 6	736,769	16,283	21,027	11,747	13,844	15,835	12,428	8,258	8,623	70,735
Congressional District 7	731,805	17,257	20,578	11,779	15,852	18,890	15,407	11,649	10,969	84,546
Connecticut										
Congressional District 1	717,086	17,477	25,404	14,349	17,476	21,519	18,915	16,105	19,343	107,707
Congressional District 2	713,617	17,512	27,314	13,372	20,071	23,219	16,978	14,789	14,517	102,946
Congressional District 3	714,552	16,916	25,613	14,223	17,093	21,682	18,007	14,494	19,023	104,522
Congressional District 4	722,517	16,850	23,930	12,948	17,463	20,451	17,433	15,025	16,067	99,387
Congressional District 5	716,789	17,515	23,647	13,811	18,049	21,951	17,665	14,613	18,088	104,177
Delaware										
Congressional District (at Large)	908,351	22,634	32,278	19,284	25,080	32,054	23,992	17,686	16,505	134,601
District of Columbia										
Delegate District (at Large)	618,777	13,526	18,298	9,704	12,641	15,898	12,570	9,260	10,229	70,302
Florida										
Congressional District 1	708,435	17,024	24,783	14,774	18,843	25,167	18,982	12,786	11,437	101,989
Congressional District 2	701,340	16,655	22,611	13,204	16,856	22,360	15,638	12,449	10,587	91,094
Congressional District 3	700,758	18,306	25,624	14,211	20,426	26,150	18,743	14,161	12,529	106,220
Congressional District 4	706,238	15,611	26,525	13,477	17,277	19,604	14,327	11,412	11,340	87,437
Congressional District 5	692,074	14,897	19,448	11,231	13,266	17,873	13,638	10,201	8,645	74,854
Congressional District 6	706,412	21,876	29,693	19,212	27,062	37,869	26,616	22,234	18,834	151,827
Congressional District 7	706,486	17,042	22,354	12,333	15,713	21,507	15,923	12,672	14,425	92,573
Congressional District 8	699,385	19,562	27,603	17,785	25,836	36,422	29,791	24,490	20,529	154,853
Congressional District 9	718,149	14,902	20,927	13,007	15,938	17,726	13,142	9,254	8,085	77,152
Congressional District 10	724,205	18,132	24,232	16,595	21,518	29,701	23,794	17,623	14,143	123,374
Congressional District 11	699,871	21,878	37,518	24,312	39,346	55,500	42,022	29,093	22,913	213,186
Congressional District 12	697,696	19,253	30,602	17,112	24,649	33,633	26,070	19,360	21,604	142,428
Congressional District 13	696,910	20,966	30,352	19,451	24,419	33,230	28,160	24,706	25,177	155,143
Congressional District 14	718,783	15,543	20,597	11,794	15,364	18,499	15,917	10,990	10,271	82,835
Congressional District 15	708,137	17,157	23,704	13,296	16,675	23,100	17,882	12,047	12,091	95,091
Congressional District 16	704,560	20,368	32,336	23,481	31,467	46,282	37,571	30,897	29,680	199,378
Congressional District 17	697,323	17,814	29,712	20,036	30,236	45,369	34,362	24,210	24,434	178,647
Congressional District 18	700,097	18,125	27,784	18,643	27,216	35,673	30,270	25,017	23,084	159,903
Congressional District 19	708,108	20,823	32,990	23,008	34,344	46,702	34,284	25,651	25,009	188,998
Congressional District 20	711,816	15,373	20,492	12,163	15,666	20,878	15,679	13,722	16,477	94,585
Congressional District 21	710,611	15,571	24,443	15,809	22,579	31,861	29,095	26,955	30,258	156,557
Congressional District 22	706,089	19,881	27,455	16,373	23,196	29,768	25,894	23,946	26,428	145,605
Congressional District 23	716,584	16,236	23,348	13,681	17,489	24,686	18,156	19,410	16,703	110,125
Congressional District 24	695,867	14,390	21,012	10,480	13,938	18,664	14,264	9,901	8,460	75,707
Congressional District 25	704,367	15,374	22,141	12,128	17,459	26,945	19,186	15,778	11,936	103,432
Congressional District 26	727,073	16,977	23,148	12,766	17,846	26,344	18,637	14,325	12,845	102,763
Congressional District 27	714,556	17,552	21,976	12,253	18,118	28,476	21,459	18,328	17,109	115,743
Georgia										
Congressional District 1	702,320	14,907	25,032	12,492	16,282	20,494	15,057	10,716	9,572	84,613
Congressional District 2	696,235	15,464	22,279	12,353	16,324	21,361	15,847	11,708	9,903	87,496
Congressional District 3	693,929	15,325	23,983	13,221	17,085	20,753	15,125	10,340	9,089	85,613
Congressional District 4	709,422	15,414	20,653	9,558	13,046	14,835	9,990	7,907	6,855	62,191
Congressional District 5	708,096	14,003	19,684	10,132	11,574	15,037	9,725	7,870	9,405	63,743
Congressional District 6	701,322	15,259	22,789	12,061	13,450	16,743	11,667	8,360	8,231	70,512
Congressional District 7	705,706	12,644	17,655	9,215	10,521	14,491	9,597	5,484	5,301	54,609
Congressional District 8	699,402	15,634	23,329	12,449	17,024	21,870	16,173	11,976	10,494	89,986
Congressional District 9	700,874	17,599	26,365	16,100	20,740	27,289	18,707	13,263	10,052	106,151
Congressional District 10	698,940	15,912	22,978	12,815	17,515	19,973	14,570	9,732	8,330	82,935
Congressional District 11	698,290	13,539	20,196	10,604	16,049	14,510	10,906	8,731	5,843	66,643
Congressional District 12	700,539	17,239	21,460	12,200	15,711	21,495	14,516	10,942	8,495	83,361
Congressional District 13	706,590	14,417	19,892	10,164	11,420	15,583	10,913	6,474	6,288	60,842
Congressional District 14	694,060	14,960	22,473	13,213	15,640	21,040	16,000	9,832	8,982	84,707
Hawaii										
Congressional District 1	687,223	19,064	23,386	14,663	17,919	22,046	19,652	16,752	19,581	110,613
Congressional District 2	691,016	19,626	25,425	13,117	16,742	21,672	14,829	12,042	14,180	92,582
Idaho										
Congressional District 1	793,108	19,834	27,609	16,098	20,576	25,992	18,506	13,575	12,490	107,237
Congressional District 2	790,314	17,484	23,995	12,190	18,170	23,007	17,367	12,110	13,129	95,973
Illinois										
Congressional District 1	718,265	16,820	22,430	12,081	16,633	21,961	17,896	14,686	13,576	96,833
Congressional District 2	712,966	16,100	22,471	12,256	17,094	22,297	16,743	11,755	13,786	93,931
Congressional District 3	707,476	15,019	21,549	10,997	15,700	19,351	14,680	13,883	14,928	89,539
Congressional District 4	711,230	11,351	15,905	8,800	9,720	13,133	9,833	6,938	6,557	54,981
Congressional District 5	718,501	15,102	19,908	11,236	13,398	18,685	14,988	11,825	14,485	84,617
Congressional District 6	719,794	18,602	23,894	12,948	16,043	20,825	15,212	12,104	12,538	89,670
Congressional District 7	716,884	14,685	20,314	10,064	14,611	18,085	13,362	9,744	8,504	74,370
Congressional District 8	715,533	16,774	21,964	10,357	14,340	15,166	12,278	9,603	10,752	72,496
Congressional District 9	720,781	18,300	24,871	13,003	18,986	24,131	19,053	17,255	19,467	111,895
Congressional District 10	710,409	17,034	21,886	10,808	15,958	19,763	14,015	12,720	13,014	86,278

Table B-5: 113th Congressional Districts—Older Population by Age—*Continued*

	Total Population	60 to 61 Years	62 to 64 Years	65 to 66 Years	67 to 69 Years	70 to 74 Years	75 to 79 Years	80 to 84 Years	85 Years and Over	65 Years and Over
Illinois—Cont.										
Congressional District 11	714,699	14,387	20,391	11,287	13,435	15,765	12,074	8,684	9,352	70,597
Congressional District 12	711,907	16,797	23,136	12,919	16,802	24,660	18,894	16,094	14,314	103,683
Congressional District 13	714,939	18,211	21,971	12,025	16,685	22,509	16,808	14,955	15,007	97,989
Congressional District 14	722,048	14,987	22,069	12,283	15,030	16,703	12,246	8,515	7,754	72,531
Congressional District 15	709,304	17,753	24,606	14,272	19,762	27,082	21,639	17,213	17,472	117,440
Congressional District 16	711,132	17,061	25,239	13,236	18,641	24,768	18,929	15,808	14,952	106,334
Congressional District 17	709,394	18,173	24,681	13,863	20,141	25,760	21,165	16,076	17,414	114,419
Congressional District 18	713,228	18,551	25,263	13,699	19,573	25,049	20,955	15,825	17,348	112,449
Indiana										
Congressional District 1	720,082	17,993	24,305	12,953	17,022	22,516	17,770	13,487	12,987	96,735
Congressional District 2	721,518	18,048	23,202	13,288	16,511	22,281	17,323	15,879	14,467	99,749
Congressional District 3	722,426	16,943	24,055	11,833	16,925	22,393	16,674	13,746	13,374	94,945
Congressional District 4	726,521	16,590	22,506	12,920	16,899	22,963	17,186	13,176	12,365	95,509
Congressional District 5	727,904	17,506	22,357	11,767	15,625	20,736	15,462	12,571	13,443	89,604
Congressional District 6	720,862	18,191	24,911	14,798	19,280	25,471	19,689	15,256	13,060	107,554
Congressional District 7	728,887	14,946	18,144	10,529	12,552	18,437	13,473	10,470	9,648	75,109
Congressional District 8	721,040	18,923	25,604	13,688	18,380	25,694	19,467	15,128	15,132	107,489
Congressional District 9	725,276	17,700	24,162	12,887	18,740	23,039	16,526	13,445	11,648	96,285
Iowa										
Congressional District 1	764,571	19,348	26,050	13,876	19,058	26,853	22,271	18,536	18,405	118,999
Congressional District 2	765,560	20,665	27,448	14,707	18,738	24,894	19,669	16,919	18,033	112,960
Congressional District 3	771,866	19,205	24,935	13,008	16,053	22,890	17,907	13,780	14,786	98,424
Congressional District 4	760,872	19,383	25,344	14,331	18,586	28,381	24,112	20,330	23,902	129,642
Kansas										
Congressional District 1	718,540	16,276	22,849	12,739	16,272	22,000	19,799	17,351	17,455	105,616
Congressional District 2	714,742	17,622	23,977	13,058	18,296	23,194	17,992	15,371	15,351	103,262
Congressional District 3	723,187	15,866	22,818	11,132	13,548	19,073	13,135	11,215	13,083	81,186
Congressional District 4	715,240	15,774	22,138	12,221	16,380	20,011	17,520	13,668	14,313	94,113
Kentucky										
Congressional District 1	724,310	18,528	26,554	15,540	21,159	28,026	21,949	14,042	13,500	114,216
Congressional District 2	730,024	16,625	23,839	14,081	18,989	22,973	17,289	12,932	11,845	98,109
Congressional District 3	726,055	18,194	24,748	13,552	16,162	21,656	17,657	15,362	14,465	98,854
Congressional District 4	731,275	16,998	27,396	12,961	17,449	21,941	15,215	11,064	10,917	89,547
Congressional District 5	720,359	19,235	26,904	15,543	20,286	27,353	19,096	12,134	10,659	105,071
Congressional District 6	732,604	16,831	24,261	12,444	16,098	22,184	15,690	11,591	10,416	88,423
Louisiana										
Congressional District 1	762,461	18,682	26,566	14,301	18,186	23,413	17,758	15,459	13,295	102,412
Congressional District 2	768,511	17,911	25,003	13,774	15,421	20,972	14,137	10,589	11,031	85,924
Congressional District 3	759,525	15,807	24,201	13,167	15,631	23,561	17,215	12,556	10,603	92,733
Congressional District 4	760,870	17,170	25,485	13,232	18,834	26,044	20,302	13,650	11,891	103,953
Congressional District 5	758,550	18,512	24,791	15,067	18,286	24,960	19,100	14,155	12,938	104,506
Congressional District 6	763,678	16,944	24,111	12,723	16,651	21,356	15,294	10,573	9,420	86,017
Maine										
Congressional District 1	667,366	19,410	27,248	14,565	18,556	24,575	19,269	15,447	15,149	107,561
Congressional District 2	661,074	19,530	28,623	15,105	19,606	26,337	19,994	15,773	13,955	110,770
Maryland										
Congressional District 1	722,293	18,327	28,063	16,296	21,639	26,901	19,683	15,389	13,533	113,441
Congressional District 2	728,536	17,430	22,742	11,427	14,369	18,606	15,376	12,036	13,043	84,857
Congressional District 3	729,649	17,301	25,888	13,033	15,007	19,956	17,541	14,289	15,625	95,451
Congressional District 4	730,307	16,384	22,492	13,124	15,314	18,523	13,085	7,553	8,559	76,158
Congressional District 5	729,639	18,103	23,121	12,764	16,221	18,647	12,417	9,936	8,793	78,778
Congressional District 6	733,427	17,569	22,899	11,988	16,974	22,462	15,011	11,678	12,219	90,332
Congressional District 7	723,624	17,370	22,590	13,891	16,443	21,564	16,643	12,853	12,974	94,368
Congressional District 8	739,903	20,881	24,799	13,366	17,956	20,893	18,243	14,447	16,885	101,790
Massachusetts										
Congressional District 1	728,828	19,439	27,123	13,203	18,639	24,279	20,184	16,610	18,995	111,910
Congressional District 2	735,213	17,459	23,539	13,578	15,806	20,626	16,333	13,191	16,590	96,124
Congressional District 3	734,142	16,652	24,472	11,654	15,257	21,456	15,815	12,292	13,989	90,463
Congressional District 4	730,756	17,623	25,066	13,500	17,146	21,057	17,285	13,937	16,410	99,335
Congressional District 5	735,647	18,094	25,935	13,236	17,255	21,748	17,831	17,400	17,321	104,791
Congressional District 6	736,098	19,744	26,693	14,657	19,157	24,764	19,600	15,650	17,866	111,694
Congressional District 7	734,126	13,799	17,780	9,194	12,832	16,702	12,716	11,073	10,518	73,035
Congressional District 8	740,640	17,666	24,151	13,764	17,795	22,046	18,168	16,998	18,840	107,611
Congressional District 9	730,018	21,509	30,225	17,418	24,457	30,239	23,296	20,225	19,330	134,965
Michigan										
Congressional District 1	705,808	22,405	30,135	16,584	24,266	33,392	25,469	19,046	17,061	135,818
Congressional District 2	707,806	17,410	21,692	11,992	16,191	21,895	16,486	13,517	12,877	92,958
Congressional District 3	710,012	16,711	22,659	11,850	16,121	19,547	14,840	13,086	13,751	89,195
Congressional District 4	703,641	18,890	26,041	14,600	21,540	26,620	20,756	15,230	13,470	112,216
Congressional District 5	701,978	17,658	26,049	14,381	18,806	24,838	20,557	14,111	14,713	107,406
Congressional District 6	707,698	17,101	25,643	12,758	18,181	24,088	17,683	14,157	14,053	100,920
Congressional District 7	703,255	19,291	26,396	14,293	19,207	22,990	17,136	14,062	14,073	101,761
Congressional District 8	708,452	17,696	23,006	12,736	16,975	19,015	13,772	10,644	9,830	82,972
Congressional District 9	709,274	16,913	24,858	13,381	17,771	23,128	17,943	18,674	18,728	109,625
Congressional District 10	703,688	19,919	26,180	13,813	19,156	24,593	18,004	13,275	13,274	102,115
Congressional District 11	709,950	17,530	24,083	12,998	17,650	20,871	16,169	14,226	13,582	95,496
Congressional District 12	705,254	15,841	22,341	11,219	15,161	18,287	14,366	12,200	12,375	83,608
Congressional District 13	698,800	17,258	21,622	11,659	13,925	19,256	15,922	12,885	13,708	87,355
Congressional District 14	703,661	18,073	24,350	13,510	15,585	20,641	16,735	14,359	15,713	96,543

Table B-5: 113th Congressional Districts—Older Population by Age—*Continued*

	Total Population	60 to 61 Years	62 to 64 Years	65 to 66 Years	67 to 69 Years	70 to 74 Years	75 to 79 Years	80 to 84 Years	85 Years and Over	65 Years and Over
Minnesota										
Congressional District 1	665,310	15,922	21,011	11,601	15,950	22,398	18,575	14,997	17,592	101,113
Congressional District 2	669,519	15,217	19,606	10,579	12,776	16,675	12,262	9,451	9,686	71,429
Congressional District 3	672,025	16,995	22,370	11,551	15,568	17,941	14,533	11,474	10,728	81,795
Congressional District 4	672,201	15,747	21,278	11,121	13,130	18,120	14,589	11,402	12,082	80,444
Congressional District 5	673,222	14,797	17,858	9,733	11,675	15,170	12,535	10,711	14,337	74,161
Congressional District 6	669,599	13,757	19,248	9,503	12,880	16,325	11,606	7,700	8,231	66,245
Congressional District 7	662,441	16,631	23,675	13,664	18,263	25,608	21,366	18,155	19,815	116,871
Congressional District 8	661,404	18,757	25,261	14,612	19,880	27,270	21,366	15,370	15,059	113,557
Mississippi										
Congressional District 1	745,626	17,516	26,081	13,570	19,279	24,716	17,968	13,568	11,482	100,583
Congressional District 2	738,747	16,931	23,067	12,106	16,477	22,151	15,904	12,028	12,333	90,999
Congressional District 3	743,109	18,052	25,678	14,742	17,501	24,733	18,326	14,552	11,716	101,570
Congressional District 4	749,697	16,903	24,418	13,093	19,194	24,939	18,581	12,219	9,623	97,649
Missouri										
Congressional District 1	745,647	18,238	22,860	11,969	14,699	19,758	15,948	13,299	14,157	89,830
Congressional District 2	750,747	19,270	27,387	14,644	19,908	26,257	20,126	18,619	19,338	118,892
Congressional District 3	756,645	18,417	25,705	14,150	19,330	24,355	17,689	12,606	10,941	99,071
Congressional District 4	751,805	16,922	24,002	14,139	19,225	26,583	20,273	14,562	13,894	108,676
Congressional District 5	751,988	17,441	24,790	13,096	16,847	22,835	17,989	15,064	14,711	100,542
Congressional District 6	750,841	17,650	25,576	14,133	18,774	25,013	18,883	14,157	15,515	106,475
Congressional District 7	752,854	18,644	26,628	14,355	22,148	27,692	20,590	14,891	15,126	114,802
Congressional District 8	748,498	18,362	27,877	15,869	21,308	29,965	22,170	16,997	14,980	121,289
Montana										
Congressional District (at Large)	997,852	28,745	37,915	21,199	27,999	35,412	26,362	20,528	20,461	151,961
Nebraska										
Congressional District 1	615,021	15,055	18,518	10,205	12,600	18,540	16,050	10,949	12,535	80,879
Congressional District 2	618,941	14,527	16,834	8,221	11,641	14,291	10,566	9,392	9,610	63,721
Congressional District 3	608,518	16,183	21,931	11,876	16,558	22,663	20,549	17,293	17,016	105,955
Nevada										
Congressional District 1	660,846	14,882	19,769	12,978	15,245	20,693	14,373	9,856	8,168	81,313
Congressional District 2	681,152	18,888	27,088	14,174	18,627	23,426	15,366	11,147	9,999	92,739
Congressional District 3	705,052	17,195	24,181	14,111	18,608	22,670	13,834	10,206	8,066	87,495
Congressional District 4	680,521	13,990	21,582	12,460	15,964	21,004	15,407	9,555	6,767	81,157
New Hampshire										
Congressional District 1	658,723	17,082	25,172	13,204	16,542	21,457	15,816	12,518	12,241	91,778
Congressional District 2	659,732	18,305	25,448	12,942	17,212	21,545	16,442	13,486	12,035	93,662
New Jersey										
Congressional District 1	732,198	16,720	24,615	13,886	15,499	22,106	16,471	14,330	14,905	97,197
Congressional District 2	734,501	20,653	26,705	15,038	20,549	26,896	20,073	16,731	14,669	113,956
Congressional District 3	735,488	19,517	27,806	14,774	21,529	27,375	23,889	19,367	18,925	125,859
Congressional District 4	734,131	16,908	26,010	15,199	19,267	26,858	23,189	19,093	19,632	123,238
Congressional District 5	734,079	19,427	24,901	14,884	19,216	23,204	18,182	15,867	17,576	108,929
Congressional District 6	737,333	17,280	22,478	12,259	14,783	19,936	15,176	12,769	12,308	87,231
Congressional District 7	736,302	17,669	24,857	13,830	17,292	20,604	16,421	14,394	15,510	98,051
Congressional District 8	749,007	13,123	17,501	10,380	11,492	16,150	12,736	10,244	9,573	70,575
Congressional District 9	740,535	16,992	20,459	13,489	16,741	20,328	16,325	14,915	15,070	96,868
Congressional District 10	727,269	16,647	20,656	12,442	15,398	19,513	13,132	10,964	10,884	82,333
Congressional District 11	736,482	19,636	27,132	14,662	18,920	24,826	20,092	17,234	19,838	115,572
Congressional District 12	736,924	16,931	22,422	13,175	15,933	21,036	17,136	13,876	15,464	96,620
New Mexico										
Congressional District 1	693,850	18,172	24,021	12,073	16,728	21,289	15,591	12,384	11,488	89,553
Congressional District 2	696,955	16,305	24,005	12,990	19,302	24,687	19,271	14,155	11,506	101,911
Congressional District 3	685,520	19,557	24,488	14,208	18,950	21,974	15,290	11,122	10,531	92,075
New York										
Congressional District 1	721,323	16,350	26,359	14,227	20,786	23,387	18,490	14,525	13,772	105,187
Congressional District 2	721,246	15,650	21,414	12,275	15,511	20,839	17,617	14,767	14,253	95,262
Congressional District 3	719,371	19,461	27,437	14,722	20,472	26,485	22,444	20,695	21,897	126,715
Congressional District 4	720,769	19,152	24,588	13,094	17,000	22,369	18,542	15,632	18,477	105,114
Congressional District 5	748,243	16,897	23,988	12,971	15,434	21,601	15,740	12,052	11,771	89,569
Congressional District 6	716,781	17,648	25,468	14,224	17,254	25,755	19,028	15,497	17,342	109,100
Congressional District 7	738,965	13,852	17,871	9,020	11,081	15,255	12,767	9,784	9,154	67,061
Congressional District 8	718,055	16,794	20,907	12,684	14,392	22,849	15,962	13,276	11,653	90,816
Congressional District 9	731,894	17,961	23,313	13,115	14,470	20,258	14,218	12,124	11,479	85,664
Congressional District 10	720,858	17,330	25,435	13,431	16,532	20,357	16,196	13,937	14,939	95,392
Congressional District 11	720,598	18,538	24,775	13,704	17,490	24,980	17,911	14,455	15,646	104,186
Congressional District 12	704,688	14,466	21,477	13,615	18,024	21,930	17,955	13,708	12,687	97,919
Congressional District 13	742,082	15,202	18,572	10,647	14,446	19,773	14,179	10,292	12,939	82,276
Congressional District 14	707,577	14,108	20,723	11,136	13,694	19,137	15,213	12,641	11,886	83,707
Congressional District 15	728,371	12,077	16,276	9,788	10,886	16,153	10,655	7,369	6,274	61,125
Congressional District 16	727,727	17,308	24,237	13,241	17,629	24,508	18,348	16,742	17,980	108,448
Congressional District 17	724,651	17,866	22,133	13,667	17,134	22,231	19,676	15,662	15,770	104,140
Congressional District 18	720,607	16,849	23,408	12,773	16,451	20,812	15,351	13,114	12,898	91,399
Congressional District 19	713,514	21,322	28,963	16,673	21,138	26,619	19,452	16,031	15,662	115,575
Congressional District 20	721,349	17,427	25,585	13,358	16,827	21,685	16,334	17,383	18,159	103,746

Table B-5: 113th Congressional Districts—Older Population by Age—*Continued*

	Total Population	60 to 61 Years	62 to 64 Years	65 to 66 Years	67 to 69 Years	70 to 74 Years	75 to 79 Years	80 to 84 Years	85 Years and Over	65 Years and Over
New York—Cont.										
Congressional District 21	718,315	17,954	25,925	13,608	19,643	24,364	18,397	15,087	14,086	105,185
Congressional District 22	716,508	18,063	27,253	13,394	18,922	26,502	19,995	16,562	19,126	114,501
Congressional District 23	715,848	19,611	27,539	13,705	19,331	24,701	19,668	16,263	16,438	110,106
Congressional District 24	715,855	17,719	24,765	13,488	17,241	21,955	18,589	15,315	16,229	102,817
Congressional District 25	719,847	16,968	23,278	13,072	17,564	21,997	17,588	15,115	17,768	103,104
Congressional District 26	716,685	15,803	24,224	12,781	16,896	24,021	20,402	20,176	17,711	111,987
Congressional District 27	718,646	19,764	27,495	15,535	19,486	25,673	19,690	16,525	16,885	113,794
North Carolina										
Congressional District 1	732,969	16,778	24,706	14,510	18,118	23,911	18,936	14,681	13,520	103,676
Congressional District 2	750,926	16,219	23,516	12,894	16,946	22,083	16,574	11,764	10,558	90,819
Congressional District 3	745,337	17,625	25,867	14,094	19,035	24,491	17,058	12,911	11,191	98,780
Congressional District 4	746,310	15,148	18,381	11,035	12,514	17,021	12,914	9,370	8,396	71,250
Congressional District 5	734,276	18,847	26,932	15,328	20,422	27,124	20,461	15,440	13,691	112,466
Congressional District 6	748,094	19,080	27,720	15,398	22,337	25,683	21,194	15,510	14,568	114,690
Congressional District 7	742,142	20,023	28,409	16,786	23,889	28,223	19,462	13,886	10,490	112,736
Congressional District 8	741,484	16,727	26,024	14,567	17,955	24,806	18,118	11,897	10,823	98,166
Congressional District 9	751,710	16,137	24,116	12,338	15,652	19,204	13,405	10,119	9,893	80,611
Congressional District 10	737,637	19,598	28,137	15,230	21,391	26,799	19,279	15,059	14,385	112,143
Congressional District 11	732,884	21,033	32,649	18,054	25,511	37,038	27,302	18,795	16,735	143,435
Congressional District 12	747,107	13,079	18,511	8,767	11,877	15,637	11,848	8,417	7,832	64,378
Congressional District 13	743,203	16,970	25,355	13,601	17,285	20,070	14,145	10,713	9,934	85,748
North Dakota										
Congressional District (at Large)	686,244	17,128	22,082	11,738	14,867	21,898	17,463	16,337	16,737	99,040
Ohio										
Congressional District 1	724,310	16,788	22,281	11,359	16,176	20,669	15,945	12,312	12,491	88,952
Congressional District 2	719,580	18,239	25,855	13,268	17,425	23,441	18,227	15,249	14,717	102,327
Congressional District 3	727,948	12,673	19,066	9,265	11,593	16,024	12,563	8,676	8,461	66,582
Congressional District 4	718,276	18,560	25,781	13,741	17,728	24,770	19,324	15,412	15,025	106,000
Congressional District 5	722,141	19,024	24,585	13,914	18,214	25,140	18,980	17,123	15,598	108,969
Congressional District 6	718,925	21,336	28,719	15,689	23,159	28,436	21,864	17,361	16,616	123,125
Congressional District 7	723,018	19,028	26,928	13,843	20,102	26,050	19,790	16,019	15,316	111,120
Congressional District 8	722,967	19,498	25,036	12,696	17,387	24,881	18,559	13,762	13,413	100,698
Congressional District 9	716,499	17,641	23,783	11,756	16,023	22,276	17,517	14,739	15,149	97,460
Congressional District 10	722,146	18,808	27,125	12,399	18,816	26,272	20,486	16,291	15,561	109,825
Congressional District 11	712,904	17,765	25,623	13,149	15,706	22,379	18,866	15,872	17,730	103,702
Congressional District 12	728,420	18,466	26,186	13,214	16,860	21,698	15,736	12,666	11,607	91,781
Congressional District 13	720,340	18,571	28,430	14,460	17,817	25,774	20,257	18,986	18,243	115,537
Congressional District 14	718,013	19,516	27,659	14,982	21,134	26,051	20,872	17,359	17,270	117,668
Congressional District 15	726,003	15,845	23,763	13,646	16,879	21,853	15,866	12,340	11,763	92,347
Congressional District 16	719,685	20,478	27,211	14,357	22,306	27,458	22,478	17,423	17,984	122,006
Oklahoma										
Congressional District 1	759,361	18,122	23,275	14,022	16,677	22,319	16,957	13,491	13,263	96,729
Congressional District 2	749,793	18,264	27,507	16,515	23,299	31,650	23,577	15,481	13,031	123,553
Congressional District 3	754,206	18,378	24,158	13,896	20,044	26,612	19,876	15,152	13,745	109,325
Congressional District 4	760,024	16,101	24,273	12,648	17,494	24,881	17,377	13,477	10,963	96,840
Congressional District 5	762,768	16,125	23,685	12,824	15,486	22,713	16,722	13,775	12,314	93,834
Oregon										
Congressional District 1	778,506	18,313	24,600	13,818	17,199	20,374	14,548	11,428	13,823	91,190
Congressional District 2	769,888	22,296	32,079	17,923	23,534	33,034	23,230	17,164	18,806	133,691
Congressional District 3	776,688	18,675	26,509	13,093	15,872	18,760	13,819	11,356	13,185	86,085
Congressional District 4	769,480	24,096	33,635	17,430	24,039	32,445	22,703	19,579	17,292	133,488
Congressional District 5	774,036	21,515	29,136	16,779	19,873	25,830	19,143	14,838	16,750	113,213
Pennsylvania										
Congressional District 1	694,882	14,577	19,393	9,939	13,327	18,101	13,789	10,962	10,990	77,108
Congressional District 2	720,129	16,476	21,380	12,458	15,949	20,544	16,631	14,024	12,825	92,431
Congressional District 3	703,488	19,052	25,115	14,116	19,070	26,172	21,722	17,807	18,254	117,141
Congressional District 4	709,009	18,027	26,480	13,619	18,366	23,597	18,644	15,670	15,491	105,387
Congressional District 5	705,821	17,959	25,674	13,610	19,918	26,083	20,563	17,250	16,604	114,028
Congressional District 6	714,715	16,004	25,199	13,574	17,019	22,824	17,724	15,818	15,249	102,208
Congressional District 7	709,405	19,155	23,714	13,052	17,652	22,552	19,858	18,274	19,679	111,067
Congressional District 8	708,380	18,098	27,177	14,232	19,502	22,197	18,227	15,961	16,449	106,568
Congressional District 9	705,062	18,928	27,200	14,759	21,169	27,940	22,310	19,090	18,910	124,178
Congressional District 10	709,436	18,737	28,866	15,682	21,310	28,826	21,371	16,950	16,598	120,737
Congressional District 11	700,354	19,559	27,511	15,399	18,797	26,231	20,528	16,999	17,421	115,375
Congressional District 12	705,390	20,255	26,809	14,697	20,956	27,416	24,152	21,984	21,688	130,893
Congressional District 13	716,493	17,509	23,352	13,187	15,608	21,032	18,892	15,737	19,620	104,076
Congressional District 14	705,793	18,205	25,901	13,365	17,144	24,590	19,318	20,208	21,098	115,723
Congressional District 15	713,374	17,295	24,387	13,039	18,349	24,526	18,464	16,884	17,780	109,042
Congressional District 16	705,511	15,883	20,827	12,280	17,373	21,019	18,175	15,309	17,345	101,501
Congressional District 17	704,634	17,535	25,610	14,765	19,125	25,395	20,642	20,813	19,954	120,694
Congressional District 18	707,719	20,815	28,609	15,225	20,486	27,194	23,607	19,219	20,065	125,796
Rhode Island										
Congressional District 1	526,900	13,564	15,431	9,834	11,948	16,837	13,291	12,248	14,295	78,453
Congressional District 2	524,336	13,796	19,393	9,736	12,634	16,273	13,304	11,453	12,663	76,063

Table B-5: 113th Congressional Districts—Older Population by Age—*Continued*

	Total Population	60 to 61 Years	62 to 64 Years	65 to 66 Years	67 to 69 Years	70 to 74 Years	75 to 79 Years	80 to 84 Years	85 Years and Over	65 Years and Over
South Carolina										
Congressional District 1	680,440	17,748	25,156	14,041	19,679	25,573	16,601	11,992	10,409	98,295
Congressional District 2	669,171	16,121	23,141	13,311	17,757	19,829	14,435	11,191	9,692	86,215
Congressional District 3	665,379	17,192	24,853	14,288	19,512	26,217	18,275	13,049	12,030	103,371
Congressional District 4	665,915	16,118	21,688	12,819	17,306	21,868	16,407	11,489	10,490	90,379
Congressional District 5	668,079	17,120	24,168	13,410	17,778	22,974	17,231	10,980	9,355	91,728
Congressional District 6	661,355	15,360	22,790	12,931	16,067	21,075	15,010	10,077	9,700	84,860
Congressional District 7	667,297	18,790	29,209	16,138	22,368	27,077	18,814	12,789	10,475	107,661
South Dakota										
Congressional District (at Large)	824,391	20,088	27,183	14,573	18,494	26,711	21,196	18,309	19,915	119,198
Tennessee										
Congressional District 1	708,015	19,342	30,101	15,687	23,798	31,886	21,670	16,489	13,072	122,602
Congressional District 2	711,143	19,129	26,097	14,467	20,966	26,213	20,146	13,830	11,713	107,335
Congressional District 3	710,362	20,611	26,742	16,166	21,776	27,007	20,528	14,496	14,558	114,531
Congressional District 4	714,751	17,529	23,832	13,422	18,182	23,253	16,720	11,157	10,037	92,771
Congressional District 5	715,416	15,125	21,038	10,858	13,296	18,633	14,342	9,877	10,451	77,457
Congressional District 6	713,695	18,587	26,754	16,749	20,567	28,082	19,483	13,264	11,560	109,705
Congressional District 7	713,895	18,222	23,646	12,926	18,778	21,204	17,306	10,522	10,444	91,180
Congressional District 8	703,555	17,482	26,668	13,956	19,260	25,022	17,788	13,708	11,841	101,575
Congressional District 9	713,408	16,087	19,841	10,560	12,033	15,288	12,226	10,252	8,501	68,860
Texas										
Congressional District 1	703,224	17,719	23,359	13,860	17,139	24,481	18,972	13,701	13,987	102,140
Congressional District 2	723,080	15,026	22,041	11,655	12,065	15,165	10,774	7,180	6,548	63,387
Congressional District 3	724,712	12,715	19,346	10,841	13,321	14,347	9,249	6,946	5,431	60,135
Congressional District 4	704,633	17,545	26,255	15,621	19,478	25,861	18,890	13,436	12,619	105,905
Congressional District 5	711,441	16,372	21,807	11,093	17,751	20,479	14,737	12,250	10,546	86,856
Congressional District 6	714,545	15,338	21,002	10,823	14,361	14,826	11,375	8,216	7,649	67,250
Congressional District 7	714,849	13,353	19,522	10,044	12,714	14,979	10,016	8,364	9,279	65,396
Congressional District 8	723,640	15,894	23,015	14,033	16,200	20,317	14,531	9,441	8,866	83,388
Congressional District 9	704,014	14,634	17,463	9,357	10,605	13,904	9,007	7,694	5,710	56,277
Congressional District 10	708,312	14,803	20,579	10,968	13,959	17,581	12,579	9,321	9,931	74,339
Congressional District 11	706,946	16,900	22,483	14,589	18,516	24,723	19,973	15,400	12,153	105,354
Congressional District 12	719,711	16,191	20,891	11,578	13,687	18,150	14,270	10,579	10,066	78,330
Congressional District 13	699,483	16,394	22,708	12,207	16,584	23,024	19,589	12,876	12,089	96,369
Congressional District 14	703,773	15,522	23,832	11,932	16,170	19,268	15,723	10,773	10,236	84,102
Congressional District 15	714,244	11,988	16,520	9,804	13,085	16,741	12,968	10,482	7,726	70,806
Congressional District 16	711,491	13,082	17,546	10,438	12,712	18,637	15,326	11,109	9,581	77,803
Congressional District 17	708,910	13,208	19,007	10,801	14,602	17,308	13,666	10,424	9,977	76,778
Congressional District 18	713,599	12,709	18,026	8,677	11,589	14,948	10,302	7,889	6,419	59,824
Congressional District 19	704,522	14,040	19,553	11,511	15,461	20,932	17,908	12,737	11,482	90,031
Congressional District 20	710,016	13,687	18,775	10,389	12,763	16,241	13,455	9,222	9,277	71,347
Congressional District 21	716,736	16,922	26,000	13,322	19,375	21,862	16,429	13,055	13,841	97,884
Congressional District 22	727,399	13,841	19,025	9,568	12,140	15,208	9,599	7,657	6,644	60,816
Congressional District 23	711,152	14,873	20,579	11,166	13,997	19,751	13,871	10,076	8,494	77,355
Congressional District 24	718,266	14,496	19,466	10,399	11,855	15,459	11,038	7,369	7,720	63,840
Congressional District 25	718,277	16,084	20,930	13,297	16,644	19,925	15,631	10,661	8,601	84,759
Congressional District 26	724,499	12,628	17,506	9,285	13,242	12,316	8,454	6,002	4,823	54,122
Congressional District 27	704,288	16,096	24,821	12,540	16,757	23,279	18,412	13,597	11,707	96,292
Congressional District 28	717,279	13,423	18,005	8,959	13,118	18,082	13,286	9,352	8,074	70,871
Congressional District 29	711,135	11,769	13,641	7,930	9,601	11,747	9,213	6,200	5,270	49,961
Congressional District 30	701,889	15,136	18,470	9,272	12,870	14,208	10,889	7,701	6,835	61,775
Congressional District 31	721,902	13,136	19,311	9,981	13,911	17,067	11,893	8,603	7,569	69,024
Congressional District 32	712,074	14,579	20,068	10,793	14,424	16,659	11,888	10,228	10,696	74,688
Congressional District 33	704,441	10,607	15,424	8,305	9,347	13,402	10,104	6,708	5,308	53,174
Congressional District 34	705,853	14,005	19,027	11,029	14,690	20,440	16,721	12,481	9,861	85,222
Congressional District 35	719,739	12,772	17,341	8,800	11,353	13,321	10,796	8,700	7,641	60,611
Congressional District 36	704,476	16,758	23,473	12,080	16,918	20,535	16,201	11,414	9,161	86,309
Utah										
Congressional District 1	700,776	12,155	16,247	9,005	10,827	15,358	11,872	8,617	6,812	62,491
Congressional District 2	697,881	12,447	18,018	10,180	14,533	18,823	14,758	10,865	10,522	79,681
Congressional District 3	703,988	11,955	16,138	9,087	11,726	14,874	10,767	8,246	6,832	61,532
Congressional District 4	712,265	11,039	15,790	7,038	10,828	13,667	10,000	8,127	7,275	56,935
Vermont										
Congressional District (at Large)	626,172	17,630	25,094	13,437	17,781	21,207	16,374	13,137	12,631	94,567
Virginia										
Congressional District 1	739,813	17,100	23,993	13,011	19,689	23,207	16,690	10,402	10,301	93,300
Congressional District 2	723,222	16,182	21,467	11,695	15,784	20,099	16,112	11,451	10,498	85,639
Congressional District 3	740,966	16,786	20,686	11,290	14,187	18,745	14,872	10,828	11,251	81,173
Congressional District 4	733,469	17,342	25,185	13,872	16,110	22,096	15,209	10,834	10,109	88,230
Congressional District 5	726,253	20,607	30,278	15,718	23,871	30,432	21,002	16,844	14,846	122,713
Congressional District 6	732,960	19,081	26,844	13,721	20,176	28,522	21,124	16,219	16,068	115,830
Congressional District 7	736,332	18,352	26,610	13,458	18,015	22,445	16,348	12,993	13,478	96,737
Congressional District 8	745,750	15,998	21,234	10,851	13,559	16,071	11,939	8,802	10,058	71,280
Congressional District 9	724,797	20,486	28,617	15,482	23,034	31,455	22,265	15,822	15,735	123,793
Congressional District 10	747,077	17,243	21,590	11,332	14,248	16,394	11,728	7,955	6,750	68,407
Congressional District 11	754,481	17,557	23,989	12,085	14,907	16,999	11,285	8,427	8,110	71,813

Table B-5: 113th Congressional Districts—Older Population by Age—*Continued*

	Total Population	60 to 61 Years	62 to 64 Years	65 to 66 Years	67 to 69 Years	70 to 74 Years	75 to 79 Years	80 to 84 Years	85 Years and Over	65 Years and Over
Washington										
Congressional District 1.............	681,235	16,921	22,929	11,547	15,678	17,231	11,480	9,504	9,380	74,820
Congressional District 2.............	682,158	17,430	25,592	12,960	17,448	19,305	14,303	12,578	12,954	89,548
Congressional District 3.............	680,576	18,800	26,247	14,089	19,587	22,259	15,290	12,001	12,295	95,521
Congressional District 4.............	686,253	15,290	20,258	11,564	15,687	18,197	13,234	11,046	10,928	80,656
Congressional District 5.............	676,453	17,032	25,953	14,228	17,186	21,192	17,139	12,885	13,385	96,015
Congressional District 6.............	678,817	20,543	28,840	16,510	20,791	26,377	18,541	13,743	14,251	110,213
Congressional District 7.............	684,671	16,540	24,299	13,104	15,577	18,352	12,963	10,698	14,108	84,802
Congressional District 8.............	677,270	16,871	20,599	10,675	13,099	17,941	12,271	8,324	9,014	71,324
Congressional District 9.............	689,251	15,422	19,965	10,971	13,687	17,582	14,304	11,149	13,577	81,270
Congressional District 10.............	684,619	15,924	23,259	12,009	14,998	18,795	15,354	11,306	10,417	82,879
West Virginia										
Congressional District 1.............	617,339	18,084	23,313	13,466	18,102	23,315	17,882	14,829	13,399	100,993
Congressional District 2.............	622,819	18,896	23,722	14,109	17,880	24,432	18,834	11,888	11,750	98,893
Congressional District 3.............	614,617	19,899	26,320	14,728	17,771	24,395	19,688	14,547	12,295	103,424
Wisconsin										
Congressional District 1.............	711,976	16,229	24,721	12,580	16,946	21,779	16,023	13,828	12,784	93,940
Congressional District 2.............	721,065	16,690	23,928	11,652	15,825	18,410	14,836	12,718	12,616	86,057
Congressional District 3.............	711,306	17,410	25,259	13,224	17,648	24,574	19,127	15,891	15,396	105,860
Congressional District 4.............	714,049	13,947	17,677	9,608	11,441	15,323	13,752	11,908	10,881	72,913
Congressional District 5.............	713,022	18,214	25,056	12,264	16,590	23,634	19,091	16,800	17,907	106,286
Congressional District 6.............	709,754	17,863	25,296	13,434	18,786	24,421	19,871	15,828	18,061	110,401
Congressional District 7.............	712,359	19,960	27,673	15,626	21,578	28,196	21,965	17,244	16,775	121,384
Congressional District 8.............	715,081	17,999	23,050	12,242	17,347	24,212	19,088	13,591	15,066	101,546
Wyoming										
Congressional District (at Large)	569,380	14,391	18,989	10,489	13,124	17,666	12,889	9,450	8,656	72,274

PART C
RACE AND ETHNICITY

RACE AND ETHNICITY

While it is clear that the nation's population continues to grow more diverse, these tables show how diversity is not uniform across the country and how large differences occur at smaller geographic levels. Racial and ethnic identification in the Census is obtained in a number of different ways including direct questions on race and Hispanic Origin. Other questions obtain data on ancestry, language spoken at home, and place of birth. The Census and American Community Survey also allow for respondents to identify with more than one racial group. The term "Alone" means the respondent identifies with that single racial group. Those who identify with two or more racial groups are identified here as "Multi-race." Hispanic Origin is obtained in a separate question. The tables in this section present only selected major response categories – White, Non-Hispanic; Black Alone; Asian Alone; Multi-race; and Hispanic. A relatively small number of individuals identify themselves as "some other race" and are not included here. The American Indian and Alaskan Native population is also a relatively small population but very important in specific areas. Summary data for this population is included in a separate table.

Unlike many other tables in this volume, the ACS sample population counts by race and Hispanic Origin are often too small to be reported. As a result, the Census files do not report results for these categories and they are indicated here by "na." It is important to also note that the age structure of many minority populations are younger than the White population due to historic immigration and fertility patterns. "Part C – Race and Ethnicity" presents data only for the population age 65 and over and therefore may exhibit different distributions of the racial and Hispanic origin population than that for the general population. For example, in the White Non-Hispanic population, 16.8 percent are age 65 and over but among the Hispanic population, only 5.7 percent are 65 and over. Those who identify as Multi-race are even lower at 4.7 percent which may result from a larger number of mixed race children.

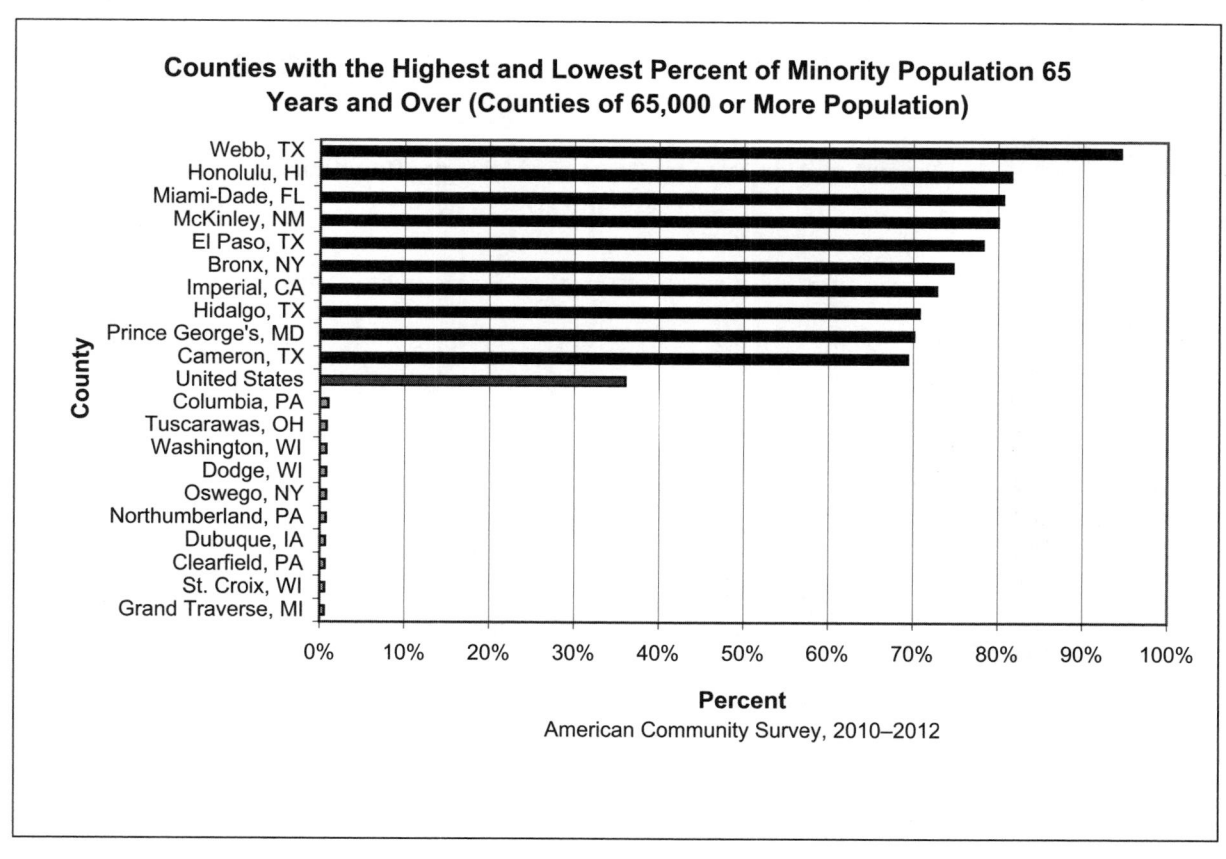

Counties with the Highest and Lowest Percent of Minority Population 65 Years and Over (Counties of 65,000 or More Population)

American Community Survey, 2010–2012

In the nation as a whole, 79.5 percent of the population age 65 and over is White, Non-Hispanic which means that one out of every five people (20.5 percent) over age 65 identifies with some minority group. Across states, the proportion of White, Non-Hispanic ranges from a low of 24.7 percent in Hawaii to a high of 97.9 percent in Maine. Thirty-four states have a higher proportion of White, Non-Hispanic population than the national average. Among the 65 year and over population, Hawaii and the District of Columbia are both "majority minority" which means their proportion of minority populations is actually greater than 50 percent. In Hawaii, 75.3 percent of the population identifies with a minority group (mostly Asian Alone and Multi-race) while in the District of Columbia, 68.9 percent of the 65 and over population is minority and mostly Black Alone.

Four states (Idaho, Montana, North Dakota and South Dakota) have only one-tenth of a percent of their 65 and over population that is Black Alone while in five states, more than one of every five people is Black Alone. Not surprising, Hawaii has the largest Asian Alone population at 58.3 percent with California a distant second at 13.6 percent. Every other state is less than 7 percent Asian Alone and 24 states are less than 1 percent. Hawaii is also the state with the highest Multi-race population at 9.5 percent but Oklahoma has the second highest proportion at 3.7 percent. At 31.4 percent, New Mexico has the highest proportion of Hispanic population age 65 and over followed by Texas (20.9 percent) and California

(18.0 percent). Fifteen states are less than 1 percent Hispanic but nine states have more than the U.S. average of 7.1 percent.

Black Alone

For the age 65 and over population, the District of Columbia, Georgia, Louisiana, Maryland and Mississippi all have proportions over 20 percent. Among counties, 80 are greater than 20 percent Black Alone with Prince George's County, Maryland having the highest proportion at 60.8 percent. There are 299 counties with at least some Black Alone population over age 65 but less than 5.0 percent. Gary, Indiana is the city with the highest proportion of Black Alone population at 84.3 percent followed closely by Detroit, Michigan at 81.5 percent. In 19 cities the Black Alone population is a majority of the total 65 and over population. The Sumter, South Carolina metropolitan area has the highest proportion of Black Alone population at 40.6 percent. More than one out of every five people age 65 and over are Black Alone in 33 metropolitan areas. Congressional District 5 in Georgia has the largest proportion of Black Alone at 63.1 percent followed by district 2 in Pennsylvania at 62.0 percent. Thirteen districts are a majority Black Alone.

Asian Alone

Nationally, 3.6 percent of the 65 and over population is Asian Alone. Eighty-five counties exceed that average with Honolulu, Hawaii having the highest proportion at 68.6 percent. Other counties with at least 25 percent

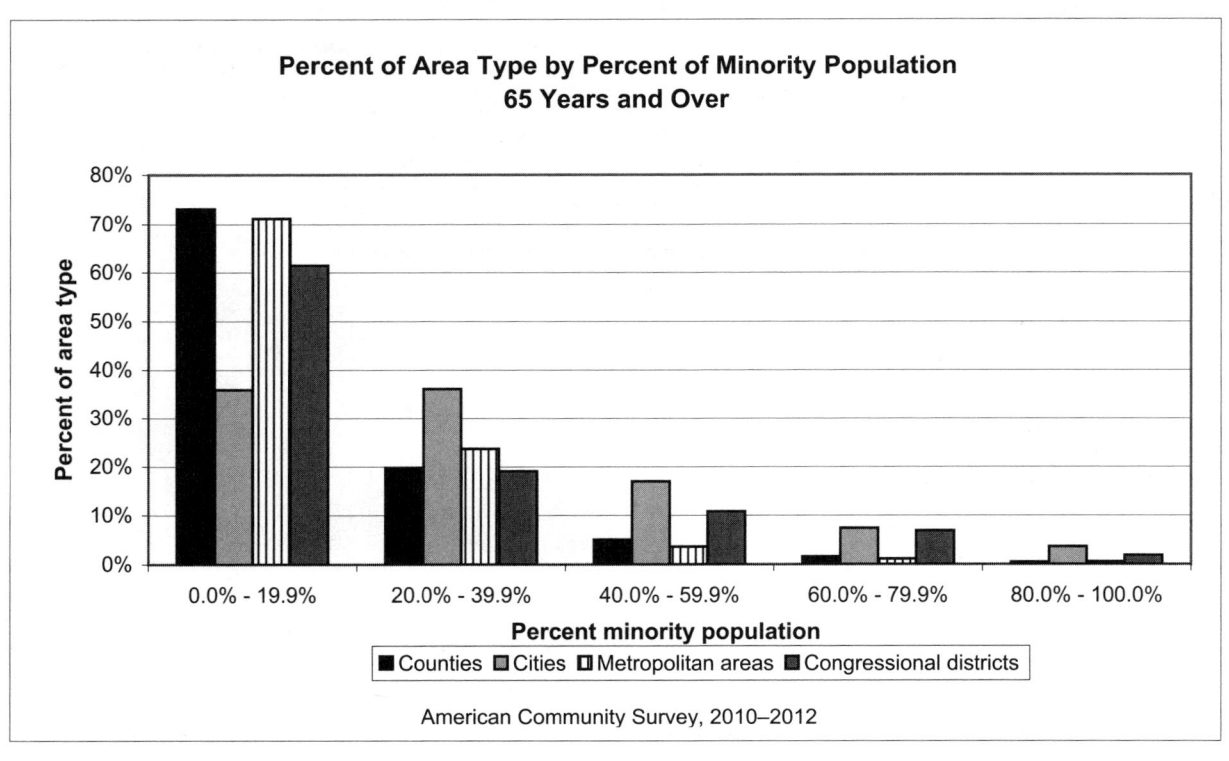

American Community Survey, 2010–2012

Asian Alone include the California counties of Alameda (25.5 percent), San Francisco (42.5 percent), and Santa Clara (28.0 percent) and the Hawaiian counties of Hawaii (36.7 percent), Kauai (51.4 percent) and Maui (41.2 percent). The Honolulu Census Designated Place has the highest proportion of 65 and over that is Asian Alone at 71.8 percent. In addition to Honolulu, four California cities have more than 50 percent Asian Alone population and 90 cities are well above the national average at over 10 percent. Only three metropolitan areas have greater than 20 percent Asian Alone population – San Francisco-Oakland-Fremont, California (23.5 percent), San Jose-Sunnyvale-Santa Clara, California (27.3 percent) and Honolulu, Hawaii (65.6 percent). Congressional District 1 in Hawaii has the highest proportion at 70.7 followed by Hawaii's 2nd Congressional District at 43.5 percent. Thirteen other districts have more than 20 percent Asian Alone: 11 of which are in California with the remaining two in New York.

Multi-race

Hawaii and Maui counties have the largest proportion of Multi-race 65 and over population at 12.4 percent and 11.4 percent, respectively. Creek, Muskogee, and Wagoner counties in Oklahoma have proportions of Multi-race population over 65 greater than 5 percent each. Nationally, about 1 percent of the 65 and over population identifies as Multi-race and 185 counties exceed that level.

Hispanic

The Hispanic population has grown to almost 52 million people in the United States or 16.6 percent of the total population. Among those 65 years and over, 7.1 percent are Hispanic. California has the largest Hispanic population over 65 at nearly 800,000 followed by Texas at almost 570,000 but New Mexico has the largest proportion of Hispanic population over the age of 65 at 31.4 percent. North Dakota has the smallest absolute number and proportion of Hispanic population. Webb County, Texas has the largest proportion of its Hispanic population in the 65 and over age group at 94.4 percent followed by El Paso County, Texas at 74.5 percent. The 65 and over population is more than 25 percent Hispanic in 26 counties, most of which are in California, New Mexico and Texas. Hialeah City, Florida has the largest proportion of Hispanic 65 and over at 95.5 percent. In 15 cities the 65 and over population is a majority Hispanic and 72 cities are more than 25 percent Hispanic 65 and over. At the metropolitan area level, Laredo, Texas is the largest proportion with 94.4 percent Hispanic 65 and over. McAllen-Edinburg-Mission, Texas is the next largest with 69.5 percent. Five metropolitan areas are over 50 percent. Florida's 27th Congressional District has the largest proportion at 75.9 percent and five of Florida's districts are over 30 percent. California has 11 districts more than 20 percent of the 65 and over population is Hispanic.

Percent Native American for Areas with 5 Percent or More Native American Popoulation

Area	Percent of Total Population	Percent of Population 65 Years or Over	Area	Percent of Total Population	Percent of Population 65 Years or Over
Counties					
Anchorage Municipality, Alaska	6.7%	7.5%	Sandoval County, New Mexico	12.5%	8.0%
Fairbanks North Star Borough, Alaska	7.1%	5.8%	San Juan County, New Mexico	37.2%	8.0%
Matanuska-Susitna Borough, Alaska	5.7%	6.1%	Robeson County, North Carolina	37.3%	9.9%
Apache County, Arizona	72.7%	10.0%	Comanche County, Oklahoma	5.3%	7.4%
Coconino County, Arizona	27.2%	7.4%	Creek County, Oklahoma	7.1%	4.9%
Navajo County, Arizona	42.9%	9.0%	Muskogee County, Oklahoma	13.8%	7.7%
Pinal County, Arizona	5.4%	5.0%	Pottawatomie County, Oklahoma	12.0%	7.6%
Humboldt County, California	5.6%	6.2%	Rogers County, Oklahoma	12.8%	7.8%
Terrebonne Parish, Louisiana	5.4%	3.2%	Wagoner County, Oklahoma	8.4%	5.0%
McKinley County, New Mexico	73.9%	8.3%	Pennington County, South Dakota	8.6%	4.9%
Otero County, New Mexico	7.1%	5.0%	Clallam County, Washington	5.4%	8.3%
Places					
Anchorage municipality, Alaska	6.7%	7.5%	Rapid City city, South Dakota	11.0%	5.6%
Flagstaff city, Arizona	11.4%	1.5%			
Metropolitan Statistical Areas					
Albuquerque, NM	5.6%	7.4%	Flagstaff, AZ	27.2%	7.4%
Anchorage, AK	6.5%	7.2%	Lawton, OK	5.3%	7.4%
Fairbanks, AK	7.1%	5.8%	Rapid City, SD	7.3%	5.0%
Farmington, NM	37.2%	8.0%	Tulsa, OK	6.9%	7.4%
113th Congressional Districts					
Congressional District (at Large) (113th Congress), Alaska	14.2%	7.5%	Congressional District (at Large) (113th Congress), North Dakota	5.3%	5.2%
Congressional District 1 (113th Congress), Arizona	23.4%	8.5%	Congressional District 1 (113th Congress), Oklahoma	5.7%	7.1%
Congressional District (at Large) (113th Congress), Montana	6.4%	6.4%	Congressional District 2 (113th Congress), Oklahoma	14.5%	9.2%
Congressional District 2 (113th Congress), New Mexico	5.8%	9.1%	Congressional District 3 (113th Congress), Oklahoma	5.5%	7.7%
Congressional District 3 (113th Congress), New Mexico	17.7%	8.2%	Congressional District 4 (113th Congress), Oklahoma	5.2%	7.4%
Congressional District 8 (113th Congress), North Carolina	7.2%	9.6%	Congressional District (at Large) (113th Congress), South Dakota	8.9%	5.4%

Native American

The American Indian and Alaska Native population is a small proportion of the nation's total and is not included in the data tables because most of the areas would have no data reported. However, the American Indian and Alaska Native population is also concentrated in specific areas and represents an important segment of those communities. Many of these areas are in states with federal or state reservations but not all. Included in the following table are areas where at least five percent of the total population is Native American. This includes 22 counties, 3 cities, 8 metropolitan areas and 12 congressional districts. Within these areas, Apache County, Arizona has the largest proportion of American Indian and Alaska Native population that is 65 and over while Terrebonne Parish, Oklahoma has the lowest. Anchorage, Alaska, the Farmington, New Mexico metropolitan area and North Carolina's 8th Congressional District all have the largest proportions.

Percent of the Population 65 Years and Over Who are Minority (Not - White, Non-Hispanic)

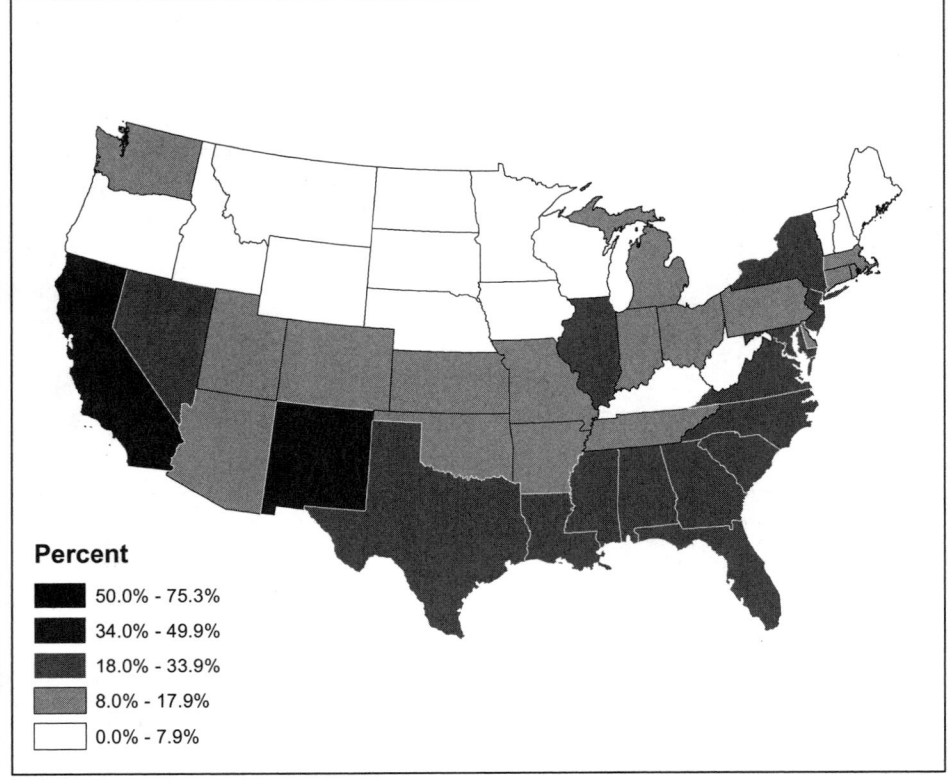

Percent

- 50.0% - 75.3%
- 34.0% - 49.9%
- 18.0% - 33.9%
- 8.0% - 17.9%
- 0.0% - 7.9%

Table C-1: States—Older Population by Race and Hispanic Origin

	Total Population		White, Non-Hispanic		Black, Alone		Asian, Alone		Multi-race, Alone		Hispanic	
	65 Years and Over	85 Years and Over	65 Years and Over	85 Years and Over	65 Years and Over	85 Years and Over	65 Years and Over	85 Years and Over	65 Years and Over	85 Years and Over	65 Years and Over	85 Years and Over
United States..............	41,652,359	5,691,169	33,121,578	4,783,498	3,575,731	404,680	1,504,716	156,970	407,340	38,705	2,965,049	304,258
Alabama......................	677,125	78,797	541,063	62,610	121,147	14,987	3,708	143	4,366	542	5,565	450
Alaska.........................	58,586	4,909	43,585	3,664	1,279	95	3,353	342	1,238	50	1,300	105
Arizona.......................	927,026	109,961	763,506	95,359	18,432	1,688	16,137	1,030	7,503	549	103,887	9,785
Arkansas....................	429,685	52,110	379,430	46,296	38,844	5,187	1,923	3	4,222	248	4,102	251
California...................	4,426,901	631,180	2,716,449	437,750	231,315	27,478	603,921	71,664	80,725	7,710	797,447	87,868
Colorado....................	581,315	73,651	489,760	64,671	15,336	1,692	11,827	1,163	6,340	691	58,257	5,582
Connecticut................	518,739	87,038	451,297	81,083	31,957	3,338	8,771	357	3,387	244	23,875	2,050
Delaware....................	134,601	16,505	110,758	14,208	17,398	1,827	2,592	153	884	100	2,707	308
District of Columbia	70,302	10,229	21,878	3,347	43,449	6,305	1,386	253	884	120	3,032	253
Florida.......................	3,381,499	465,033	2,592,346	379,592	267,109	26,651	46,849	2,945	26,568	2,495	460,013	54,242
Georgia......................	1,083,402	116,840	806,596	90,145	225,985	23,119	21,520	1,183	6,946	620	22,579	1,876
Hawaii........................	203,195	33,761	50,221	6,609	943	130	118,464	23,742	19,202	2,058	6,591	714
Idaho.........................	203,210	25,619	192,292	24,478	224	50	1,586	199	1,956	320	5,729	517
Illinois.......................	1,650,052	241,220	1,308,484	207,761	186,279	21,088	56,420	4,487	10,852	982	88,918	6,838
Indiana.......................	862,979	116,124	787,515	108,308	50,251	5,646	5,678	263	5,166	457	13,566	1,421
Iowa..........................	460,025	75,126	446,262	73,885	4,483	412	2,863	243	1,283	68	4,544	521
Kansas.......................	384,177	60,202	350,370	56,750	13,746	1,634	4,341	200	3,953	528	10,528	1,049
Kentucky....................	594,220	71,802	554,376	67,924	28,947	3,204	2,780	224	3,536	220	4,050	207
Louisiana...................	575,545	69,178	420,886	52,409	130,694	14,766	5,022	342	4,153	324	13,173	1,237
Maine.........................	218,331	29,104	213,851	28,836	470	5	1,086	8	1,286	127	1,086	132
Maryland....................	735,175	101,631	518,878	79,937	160,538	16,190	31,573	2,835	6,323	692	18,213	1,851
Massachusetts.............	929,928	149,859	828,794	139,210	36,605	4,165	26,108	2,666	8,151	740	29,897	2,937
Michigan.....................	1,397,988	197,208	1,208,657	174,389	137,262	18,146	17,341	1,370	10,726	1,006	20,751	2,127
Minnesota...................	705,615	107,530	670,415	103,905	11,218	906	11,423	1,315	3,622	463	6,073	676
Mississippi..................	390,801	45,154	288,842	33,031	95,427	11,467	1,773	110	1,945	240	2,392	341
Missouri.....................	859,577	118,662	771,146	108,906	63,856	7,217	7,062	504	6,441	772	9,383	1,170
Montana.....................	151,961	20,461	144,644	19,823	155	0	615	120	1,103	27	1,496	258
Nebraska....................	250,555	39,161	237,074	38,038	5,587	519	1,746	136	1,045	116	4,673	328
Nevada.......................	342,704	33,000	259,862	27,024	20,231	1,701	23,682	1,724	4,883	285	31,171	2,102
New Hampshire............	185,440	24,276	180,682	23,968	641	40	1,409	81	1,080	101	1,512	32
New Jersey	1,216,429	184,354	927,402	156,707	119,550	12,616	62,694	4,846	11,174	885	100,661	10,018
New Mexico	283,539	33,525	171,471	21,679	3,796	421	2,591	283	4,246	330	89,138	9,649
New York....................	2,683,895	402,881	1,943,893	324,714	326,988	38,715	138,523	13,007	30,798	3,239	264,533	25,733
North Carolina.............	1,288,898	152,016	1,038,394	125,619	203,037	23,241	13,223	844	7,289	410	18,315	1,344
North Dakota...............	99,040	16,737	95,731	16,650	123	0	443	0	445	8	397	15
Ohio..........................	1,658,099	236,944	1,475,534	216,060	141,415	17,230	14,630	1,074	9,470	800	16,391	1,590
Oklahoma...................	520,281	63,316	441,448	56,003	22,834	2,442	5,085	322	19,507	1,736	10,600	791
Oregon......................	557,667	79,856	514,395	75,750	5,183	572	13,004	1,405	6,737	632	14,542	1,372
Pennsylvania...............	1,993,953	316,020	1,790,447	293,123	136,183	16,730	26,603	1,808	9,510	1,311	32,165	3,142
Rhode Island...............	154,516	26,958	140,914	25,547	3,851	459	1,920	150	1,420	155	5,773	410
South Carolina	662,509	72,151	515,083	56,879	131,576	14,257	4,674	117	3,215	365	6,989	401
South Dakota	119,198	19,915	113,210	19,411	163	38	358	0	716	43	795	118
Tennessee	886,016	102,177	775,008	90,585	88,495	9,948	6,814	168	6,503	639	8,307	777
Texas.........................	2,722,520	321,817	1,822,506	233,879	233,537	26,071	73,541	4,700	28,256	2,503	568,529	55,448
Utah..........................	260,639	31,441	239,805	29,472	1,081	63	4,309	575	1,778	180	12,019	1,053
Vermont.....................	94,567	12,631	92,627	12,441	199	12	618	40	390	68	538	10
Virginia......................	1,018,915	127,204	798,945	104,309	153,337	17,773	36,134	2,475	9,178	843	21,094	1,884
Washington.................	867,048	120,309	761,480	110,632	15,958	1,505	48,968	4,956	10,797	1,067	23,336	2,046
West Virginia..............	303,310	37,444	291,875	36,116	6,340	892	1,025	45	2,393	285	1,409	102
Wisconsin...................	798,387	119,486	754,068	115,810	21,744	1,958	6,184	272	3,112	281	10,298	892
Wyoming	72,274	8,656	67,423	8,196	533	84	416	78	637	30	2,710	235

Table C-2: Counties—Older Population by Race and Hispanic Origin

	Total Population		White, Non-Hispanic		Black, Alone		Asian, Alone		Multi-race, Alone		Hispanic	
	65 Years and Over	85 Years and Over	65 Years and Over	85 Years and Over	65 Years and Over	85 Years and Over	65 Years and Over	85 Years and Over	65 Years and Over	85 Years and Over	65 Years and Over	85 Years and Over
Alabama												
Baldwin County	32,060	3,187	29,796	3,004	1,660	183	na	na	177	0	218	0
Calhoun County	17,423	1,905	14,794	1,554	2,161	251	na	na	152	100	246	0
Cullman County	13,265	1,651	12,798	1,583	na	na	na	na	na	na	154	25
DeKalb County	9,998	876	9,733	847	na	na	na	na	na	na	46	0
Elmore County	9,794	1,047	8,694	960	1,068	87	na	na	na	na	na	na
Etowah County	16,754	2,400	14,868	2,032	1,560	359	na	na	na	na	74	0
Houston County	15,222	1,588	12,428	1,270	2,442	285	40	0	99	15	146	14
Jefferson County	87,461	12,702	59,339	9,308	26,686	3,294	438	0	462	74	551	38
Lauderdale County	15,817	2,004	14,621	1,943	970	61	na	na	na	na	na	na
Lee County	13,450	1,511	10,548	1,296	2,522	209	114	0	na	na	170	6
Limestone County	10,746	1,206	9,643	1,071	929	117	na	na	na	na	83	18
Madison County	42,421	5,038	34,859	4,427	6,022	549	663	37	207	7	476	18
Marshall County	14,236	1,558	13,701	1,530	228	7	na	na	na	na	120	0
Mobile County	54,982	6,289	39,041	4,428	14,131	1,673	508	25	483	93	726	95
Montgomery County	28,149	3,495	17,149	2,195	10,231	1,194	341	0	148	20	331	86
Morgan County	17,365	1,904	15,856	1,638	1,113	184	na	na	112	38	234	29
St. Clair County	11,339	1,042	10,759	1,022	509	17	na	na	na	na	na	na
Shelby County	22,334	2,264	20,397	1,983	1,171	260	296	0	na	na	305	21
Talladega County	11,956	1,259	9,349	1,042	2,449	209	na	na	na	na	na	na
Tuscaloosa County	21,613	2,675	16,574	1,958	4,556	605	96	20	na	na	243	76
Walker County	11,137	1,022	10,573	1,005	359	7	na	na	na	na	na	na
Alaska												
Fairbanks North Star Borough	6,666	741	5,733	622	216	0	na	na	0	0	80	0
Matanuska-Susitna Borough	7,652	523	6,913	477	na	na	na	na	97	0	65	11
Arizona												
Apache County	8,849	814	2,828	200	na	na	na	na	na	na	549	9
Cochise County	23,510	2,657	17,988	2,144	459	25	na	na	340	18	4,259	482
Coconino County	12,670	1,382	8,612	979	na	na	na	na	119	0	952	56
Maricopa County	487,207	59,373	410,720	53,067	13,165	1,240	10,944	665	3,426	257	47,028	4,018
Mohave County	48,584	4,700	44,459	4,403	na	na	na	na	832	85	2,698	174
Navajo County	15,077	1,357	9,663	947	na	na	na	na	72	0	879	16
Pima County	157,849	21,477	125,224	18,139	3,045	268	2,603	168	1,455	70	24,511	2,787
Pinal County	56,499	5,130	47,969	4,423	843	61	515	150	466	46	5,981	509
Yavapai County	53,313	7,010	49,851	6,536	na	na	na	na	314	11	2,307	376
Yuma County	31,751	2,635	23,283	1,865	151	4	357	0	210	52	7,547	664
Arkansas												
Benton County	27,595	4,028	26,668	3,847	na	na	88	0	219	29	403	126
Craighead County	11,831	1,508	11,507	1,505	132	0	na	na	na	na	na	na
Faulkner County	11,824	1,457	11,064	1,358	541	84	na	na	na	na	95	0
Garland County	20,125	2,966	19,041	2,824	527	142	na	na	na	na	269	0
Jefferson County	10,434	1,481	6,407	1,049	3,854	432	na	na	na	na	na	na
Lonoke County	7,890	662	7,255	604	469	58	na	na	na	na	na	na
Pulaski County	47,384	5,909	36,543	4,774	9,224	1,083	510	0	412	15	548	0
Saline County	17,178	1,550	16,249	1,508	368	0	na	na	na	na	152	0
Sebastian County	16,600	1,985	15,291	1,913	603	50	304	0	220	4	167	18
Washington County	20,480	2,837	19,373	2,798	172	0	221	0	253	0	409	22
White County	11,245	1,293	10,705	1,208	298	81	na	na	na	na	118	0
California												
Alameda County	175,805	26,503	86,373	14,916	21,849	3,617	44,830	5,174	3,845	598	18,640	2,407
Butte County	34,534	5,476	31,225	5,004	na	na	549	85	830	51	1,766	279
Contra Costa County	137,400	19,898	93,237	15,408	9,886	1,317	17,499	1,687	2,574	39	13,798	1,470
El Dorado County	27,846	3,653	25,300	3,373	na	na	690	46	359	41	1,314	193
Fresno County	96,924	14,407	57,441	9,746	3,674	391	8,284	1,216	2,006	371	25,954	2,825
Humboldt County	18,302	2,606	16,604	2,501	na	na	196	0	458	7	543	17
Imperial County	18,894	2,533	5,142	503	261	22	386	121	489	47	12,735	1,880
Kern County	77,955	8,418	51,707	6,076	3,337	405	3,743	411	850	19	17,702	1,481
Kings County	12,328	1,452	7,411	981	468	0	570	107	270	0	3,712	364
Lake County	11,639	1,699	10,354	1,569	na	na	na	na	na	na	615	0
Los Angeles County	1,106,754	158,945	500,802	87,702	101,178	12,200	191,258	25,542	22,003	2,178	296,121	32,082
Madera County	17,912	1,882	12,525	1,461	414	48	438	37	201	33	4,028	336
Marin County	44,567	6,098	39,838	5,638	622	59	1,784	179	622	28	1,805	199
Mendocino County	14,277	1,884	12,607	1,715	na	na	244	19	370	57	725	72
Merced County	25,198	3,093	14,720	1,977	1,013	79	1,652	208	452	0	7,245	825
Monterey County	46,040	7,052	29,640	5,108	1,331	169	4,250	638	566	27	10,296	1,155
Napa County	21,451	3,557	17,649	3,113	277	48	1,117	105	280	0	2,047	295
Nevada County	20,068	2,848	19,029	2,731	na	na	na	na	na	na	449	85
Orange County	365,971	53,885	242,119	41,305	3,834	385	64,927	6,124	4,521	519	50,288	5,518
Placer County	56,811	7,475	49,819	6,766	390	20	2,469	254	661	21	3,225	414
Riverside County	270,278	32,821	188,668	25,417	12,474	985	13,993	1,328	4,395	439	51,330	4,755
Sacramento County	165,762	24,979	111,342	18,288	11,963	1,404	22,525	2,644	3,844	439	15,665	2,078
San Bernardino County	190,389	21,798	107,221	13,901	13,901	1,100	14,115	1,025	3,581	145	51,979	5,672
San Diego County	365,780	57,661	251,652	44,625	12,332	1,527	38,700	3,882	5,400	603	57,994	7,232
San Francisco County	112,614	18,043	45,142	8,073	7,494	1,028	47,823	7,180	2,008	204	10,425	1,726
San Joaquin County	74,322	10,314	44,246	7,214	4,095	477	10,061	1,054	2,449	223	14,006	1,416
San Luis Obispo County	42,727	6,712	37,755	6,123	343	3	1,082	278	355	28	3,078	275
San Mateo County	100,065	16,385	60,983	12,160	3,122	454	21,836	2,462	1,900	170	11,963	1,185
Santa Barbara County	56,046	10,019	42,229	8,263	891	76	2,157	392	844	100	9,754	1,098
Santa Clara County	205,755	28,231	113,654	17,972	3,816	409	57,604	6,514	3,829	429	27,392	2,858

Table C-2: Counties—Older Population by Race and Hispanic Origin—*Continued*

	Total Population		White, Non-Hispanic		Black, Alone		Asian, Alone		Multi-race, Alone		Hispanic	
	65 Years and Over	85 Years and Over	65 Years and Over	85 Years and Over	65 Years and Over	85 Years and Over	65 Years and Over	85 Years and Over	65 Years and Over	85 Years and Over	65 Years and Over	85 Years and Over
California—Cont.												
Santa Cruz County	30,785	4,892	25,006	4,174	283	0	1,263	184	436	16	3,954	534
Shasta County	31,209	4,189	28,753	3,930	na	na	455	59	690	52	940	145
Solano County	49,340	5,922	28,360	3,898	5,869	565	8,836	935	1,018	58	5,213	498
Sonoma County	70,993	11,383	62,054	10,339	621	97	2,168	142	1,003	106	5,042	626
Stanislaus County	56,938	8,517	40,715	6,578	1,089	167	2,621	179	1,445	169	10,890	1,378
Sutter County	12,464	1,366	8,692	1,067	na	na	1,851	104	295	8	1,385	139
Tulare County	43,156	5,689	27,077	4,101	526	57	1,524	253	1,171	65	13,141	1,212
Ventura County	100,859	14,468	71,743	11,318	1,459	89	7,290	697	1,621	150	19,203	2,210
Yolo County	20,701	3,215	14,889	2,582	315	24	1,482	241	562	76	3,477	328
Yuba County	7,409	753	5,931	603	na	na	426	83	135	0	786	32
Colorado												
Adams County	39,156	4,447	28,734	3,507	776	27	1,297	254	589	60	7,863	640
Arapahoe County	61,889	8,355	51,488	7,437	3,220	231	2,616	241	776	30	3,673	400
Boulder County	31,696	4,426	28,892	4,151	na	na	644	27	271	28	1,670	170
Denver County	64,482	10,683	43,286	8,391	7,118	956	2,017	171	778	161	11,425	1,060
Douglas County	22,921	1,609	21,284	1,523	na	na	548	51	149	0	771	35
El Paso County	65,360	7,486	55,678	6,908	2,628	174	1,830	135	903	81	4,485	228
Jefferson County	70,648	8,937	63,908	8,201	272	82	1,446	152	406	47	4,620	455
Larimer County	37,722	5,129	35,533	4,968	75	0	400	18	177	46	1,535	133
Mesa County	22,644	3,281	20,977	3,108	na	na	na	na	278	39	1,192	131
Pueblo County	25,026	3,150	17,510	2,364	430	86	na	na	383	0	6,819	627
Weld County	25,925	2,876	21,750	2,512	87	0	277	54	309	40	3,597	270
Connecticut												
Fairfield County	127,386	20,420	106,124	18,600	9,856	936	3,089	154	621	53	8,188	713
Hartford County	132,472	23,298	111,504	21,227	10,420	1,255	2,393	143	1,028	76	7,473	624
Litchfield County	31,216	4,865	30,366	4,820	na	na	213	0	66	0	392	31
Middlesex County	26,552	4,337	25,105	4,219	718	89	321	9	98	0	267	0
New Haven County	126,344	23,684	108,316	22,243	9,309	898	1,733	16	881	28	5,966	488
New London County	40,149	5,336	36,767	5,053	1,204	146	757	14	378	61	919	38
Tolland County	18,950	2,649	18,198	2,600	110	0	237	21	165	0	238	28
Windham County	15,670	2,449	14,917	2,321	191	0	na	na	150	26	432	128
Delaware												
Kent County	23,105	2,511	18,049	1,978	3,875	432	539	44	100	26	497	85
New Castle County	68,251	9,319	53,364	7,986	10,821	1,023	1,843	109	534	74	1,667	176
Sussex County	43,245	4,675	39,345	4,244	2,702	372	210	0	250	0	543	47
Florida												
Alachua County	27,427	3,615	21,892	3,051	3,991	466	389	0	170	7	1,059	91
Bay County	25,463	2,599	22,750	2,334	1,587	210	280	0	348	17	415	38
Brevard County	114,082	14,013	99,896	12,922	7,165	731	1,464	79	978	86	4,939	215
Broward County	257,655	42,348	170,989	34,637	38,214	3,432	5,268	224	3,015	313	41,793	4,121
Charlotte County	56,719	8,101	52,535	7,574	1,966	332	na	na	na	na	1,403	109
Citrus County	45,784	5,692	43,345	5,464	634	38	na	na	na	na	1,163	156
Clay County	23,760	2,549	21,014	2,313	1,106	89	569	0	249	15	860	132
Collier County	89,552	11,345	81,802	10,666	1,808	128	489	59	440	83	5,023	409
Columbia County	10,695	1,010	9,209	909	1,058	91	na	na	na	na	293	10
Duval County	100,238	13,410	72,068	10,495	19,930	2,199	3,423	172	968	157	4,010	403
Escambia County	44,259	5,761	35,071	4,815	6,715	741	963	0	611	97	807	72
Flagler County	25,015	2,962	20,395	2,334	2,545	502	na	na	na	na	1,403	103
Hernando County	45,454	5,567	41,130	4,990	1,306	292	na	na	na	na	2,572	265
Highlands County	31,966	3,959	28,903	3,641	1,189	113	na	na	na	na	1,659	145
Hillsborough County	151,780	20,045	105,704	15,183	15,473	1,509	3,791	301	1,890	174	25,954	2,841
Indian River County	39,107	6,497	36,113	6,065	1,359	57	na	na	na	na	1,191	172
Lake County	74,048	8,557	66,336	7,966	3,132	296	823	6	344	17	3,020	272
Lee County	153,513	19,743	139,378	18,381	4,404	415	1,387	29	789	104	7,358	868
Leon County	27,502	3,800	20,818	3,188	5,286	453	462	11	115	35	798	113
Manatee County	78,467	10,640	72,486	10,140	2,337	205	708	64	411	57	2,393	174
Marion County	87,503	9,397	77,153	8,487	5,046	567	722	0	635	19	4,001	304
Martin County	40,951	6,808	38,958	6,685	782	20	na	na	232	36	902	67
Miami-Dade County	365,388	49,847	70,868	12,578	46,928	4,542	4,148	346	3,701	168	246,294	32,640
Monroe County	13,258	1,315	11,037	1,021	409	34	na	na	na	na	1,714	260
Nassau County	12,755	1,221	11,741	1,079	701	142	na	na	na	na	na	na
Okaloosa County	25,929	2,704	23,432	2,470	1,192	91	596	39	138	11	583	93
Orange County	116,321	14,205	69,350	10,060	17,808	1,330	5,004	236	1,768	158	23,844	2,540
Osceola County	32,023	3,236	17,574	2,109	2,778	342	749	101	607	37	10,761	687
Palm Beach County	291,985	52,039	247,887	47,221	18,737	2,308	3,122	193	1,137	103	21,262	2,298
Pasco County	98,986	13,989	90,940	13,251	1,786	183	858	76	816	27	4,686	452
Pinellas County	198,309	32,685	178,612	30,395	8,984	947	2,924	250	1,206	163	6,498	849
Polk County	111,849	13,506	94,882	11,805	8,255	752	1,392	50	678	113	6,782	764
Putnam County	14,415	1,504	12,451	1,299	1,345	79	na	na	na	na	376	126
St. Johns County	31,942	3,977	29,486	3,807	1,231	64	234	38	114	0	864	37
St. Lucie County	58,117	7,019	47,782	6,316	5,631	313	569	17	380	17	3,774	368
Santa Rosa County	20,326	1,754	18,890	1,692	321	0	na	na	348	36	314	26
Sarasota County	121,625	19,078	115,753	18,312	2,202	268	792	47	411	45	2,574	406
Seminole County	53,934	8,092	41,726	6,885	4,132	344	1,390	210	513	38	6,197	615
Sumter County	45,444	3,431	43,602	3,290	709	50	na	na	na	na	857	58
Volusia County	107,097	14,807	94,468	13,214	5,402	723	881	134	546	74	5,901	662

Table C-2: Counties—Older Population by Race and Hispanic Origin—*Continued*

	Total Population		White, Non-Hispanic		Black, Alone		Asian, Alone		Multi-race, Alone		Hispanic	
	65 Years and Over	85 Years and Over	65 Years and Over	85 Years and Over	65 Years and Over	85 Years and Over	65 Years and Over	85 Years and Over	65 Years and Over	85 Years and Over	65 Years and Over	85 Years and Over
Georgia												
Barrow County	6,716	491	5,935	379	539	93	18	0	na	na	224	19
Bartow County	11,214	754	10,080	714	797	40	na	na	na	na	244	0
Bibb County	20,047	2,544	12,369	1,928	7,192	616	na	na	na	na	141	0
Bulloch County	6,538	638	5,185	505	1,283	130	na	na	na	na	17	0
Carroll County	12,496	1,039	10,884	944	1,351	55	na	na	na	na	183	40
Catoosa County	9,266	962	8,857	962	na	na	na	na	na	na	na	na
Chatham County	34,187	4,678	23,143	3,180	9,894	1,375	512	51	183	30	457	42
Cherokee County	21,237	1,864	19,957	1,737	450	0	202	9	101	40	437	78
Clarke County	10,482	1,229	7,454	940	2,406	221	218	0	na	na	348	68
Clayton County	18,559	1,750	8,633	1,187	7,842	532	1,268	0	308	31	747	0
Cobb County	64,367	6,440	52,201	5,308	7,427	737	2,076	164	486	102	2,197	150
Columbia County	13,523	1,070	11,289	1,035	1,306	19	579	0	98	16	252	0
Coweta County	13,880	1,452	11,603	1,119	2,014	288	na	na	na	na	231	45
DeKalb County	64,740	7,681	33,021	5,107	26,926	2,230	2,372	135	665	30	1,703	179
Dougherty County	11,734	1,533	6,307	865	5,056	650	na	na	na	na	na	na
Douglas County	12,067	849	9,221	645	2,429	204	na	na	na	na	324	0
Fayette County	14,593	1,664	12,018	1,449	1,828	141	263	27	na	na	391	47
Floyd County	13,894	1,741	12,337	1,608	1,265	60	na	na	na	na	138	73
Forsyth County	17,963	1,862	15,961	1,688	357	140	649	0	na	na	896	34
Fulton County	88,653	12,956	47,057	8,190	36,526	4,473	2,445	105	843	50	1,942	147
Glynn County	12,564	1,471	10,306	1,284	1,949	182	na	na	na	na	116	5
Gwinnett County	60,324	5,638	42,140	4,310	7,525	424	6,596	620	449	105	3,823	259
Hall County	21,659	2,307	19,328	2,068	1,038	90	247	0	112	0	900	149
Henry County	18,174	1,550	13,268	1,231	3,949	319	377	0	280	0	409	0
Houston County	15,075	1,539	12,131	1,157	2,440	382	na	na	91	0	234	0
Liberty County	4,061	442	2,342	189	1,510	253	na	na	0	0	147	0
Lowndes County	10,994	1,249	7,892	966	2,769	277	na	na	149	0	196	6
Muscogee County	22,292	2,991	13,678	2,084	7,645	838	429	30	216	0	343	39
Newton County	10,464	1,352	7,593	1,234	2,674	118	na	na	na	na	138	0
Paulding County	11,194	796	9,788	740	1,122	56	na	na	na	na	264	0
Richmond County	23,487	2,539	13,059	1,777	9,198	716	464	17	270	29	567	24
Rockdale County	9,566	847	6,727	669	2,529	178	na	na	na	na	123	0
Troup County	8,621	1,302	6,520	983	1,931	319	na	na	na	na	109	0
Walker County	10,496	1,206	10,049	1,162	290	44	na	na	na	na	na	na
Walton County	10,511	1,050	9,200	860	1,090	170	na	na	na	na	na	na
Whitfield County	11,722	1,373	10,716	1,204	356	85	na	na	146	0	442	57
Hawaii												
Hawaii County	28,666	4,449	12,093	1,721	na	na	10,515	2,084	3,545	333	1,298	128
Honolulu County	143,047	24,044	26,364	3,481	809	130	93,897	18,351	12,747	1,406	3,892	330
Kauai County	10,496	1,869	3,666	501	na	na	5,396	1,229	520	67	469	70
Maui County	20,965	3,398	8,098	906	na	na	8,648	2,078	2,388	252	931	185
Idaho												
Ada County	43,784	6,271	41,492	5,938	54	19	619	74	462	154	968	86
Bannock County	9,455	984	8,924	942	na	na	na	na	73	15	163	15
Bonneville County	11,706	1,858	11,286	1,828	na	na	na	na	36	0	302	26
Canyon County	21,657	2,513	19,607	2,321	na	na	na	na	246	38	1,456	110
Kootenai County	21,061	2,369	20,435	2,349	na	na	na	na	166	0	234	20
Twin Falls County	11,062	1,806	10,401	1,652	na	na	na	na	na	na	366	91
Illinois												
Adams County	11,892	2,170	11,530	2,113	246	28	na	na	na	na	na	na
Champaign County	20,787	2,943	18,357	2,687	1,455	193	503	31	198	32	254	0
Cook County	633,403	95,088	385,341	69,772	147,434	17,055	34,280	3,213	5,214	366	62,118	4,723
DeKalb County	10,517	1,596	10,102	1,596	67	0	na	na	na	na	215	0
DuPage County	111,162	17,224	94,706	16,019	1,925	183	9,278	530	502	38	4,490	395
Kane County	53,028	6,427	44,297	5,704	1,821	168	1,578	97	284	82	5,119	344
Kankakee County	15,361	2,270	13,558	2,128	1,495	129	na	na	na	na	179	0
Kendall County	8,652	897	8,056	740	247	157	84	0	na	na	261	0
Lake County	76,078	10,510	64,343	9,631	3,358	219	3,603	240	672	127	4,218	363
LaSalle County	18,851	2,882	18,231	2,854	129	26	na	na	na	na	400	2
McHenry County	32,664	3,728	30,654	3,623	205	0	685	0	288	29	932	76
McLean County	17,918	2,724	16,843	2,645	420	57	210	11	130	0	299	11
Macon County	18,335	2,852	16,532	2,732	1,592	110	na	na	59	0	103	9
Madison County	39,375	5,686	36,715	5,358	1,580	262	287	0	274	48	510	21
Peoria County	26,333	4,024	23,383	3,738	2,279	196	308	26	41	5	295	59
Rock Island County	24,334	4,085	21,820	3,796	1,107	131	162	0	242	14	1,048	144
St. Clair County	34,421	4,507	25,972	3,574	7,397	860	na	na	208	37	419	19
Sangamon County	27,993	4,443	25,958	4,238	1,533	124	185	16	135	26	172	65
Tazewell County	21,454	2,832	21,149	2,813	na	na	na	na	108	19	74	0
Vermilion County	13,249	1,936	12,316	1,895	739	26	na	na	na	na	23	2
Will County	66,355	8,244	55,045	7,442	4,701	329	2,449	201	527	0	3,727	272
Williamson County	11,137	1,298	10,747	1,264	191	24	na	na	na	na	54	0
Winnebago County	41,803	6,082	37,258	5,830	2,609	148	593	17	206	33	1,097	54

Table C-2: Counties—Older Population by Race and Hispanic Origin—*Continued*

	Total Population		White, Non-Hispanic		Black, Alone		Asian, Alone		Multi-race, Alone		Hispanic	
	65 Years and Over	85 Years and Over	65 Years and Over	85 Years and Over	65 Years and Over	85 Years and Over	65 Years and Over	85 Years and Over	65 Years and Over	85 Years and Over	65 Years and Over	85 Years and Over
Indiana												
Allen County	43,512	6,120	38,661	5,778	3,166	214	529	46	249	0	762	82
Bartholomew County	11,140	1,338	10,757	1,324	na	na	75	0	na	na	30	0
Clark County	14,573	1,604	13,738	1,531	581	73	na	na	92	0	45	0
Delaware County	17,592	1,931	16,585	1,852	653	60	na	na	180	14	132	0
Elkhart County	24,447	3,734	23,164	3,601	701	133	na	na	122	0	480	0
Floyd County	10,026	1,436	9,480	1,436	425	0	na	na	na	na	na	na
Grant County	11,504	1,684	10,673	1,602	589	60	na	na	na	na	116	22
Hamilton County	25,436	3,343	23,996	3,281	543	46	712	16	8	0	177	0
Hancock County	9,267	1,030	9,126	1,025	na	na	na	na	na	na	na	na
Hendricks County	16,552	2,027	15,818	1,968	184	0	na	na	na	na	104	21
Howard County	13,950	1,828	12,991	1,775	599	0	na	na	na	na	160	12
Johnson County	17,932	2,593	17,440	2,521	na	na	na	na	193	15	196	55
Kosciusko County	10,673	1,417	10,500	1,400	na	na	na	na	na	na	134	17
Lake County	66,791	9,368	46,423	6,931	13,950	1,663	528	37	473	23	5,473	714
LaPorte County	16,122	2,008	14,919	1,897	845	77	na	na	45	0	218	34
Madison County	20,715	2,915	19,371	2,857	827	30	na	na	206	2	220	26
Marion County	97,796	13,740	73,854	11,088	20,167	2,350	1,245	48	833	91	1,623	163
Monroe County	14,539	2,067	13,965	2,013	143	0	166	12	58	0	189	42
Morgan County	9,510	827	9,151	806	na	na	na	na	na	na	na	na
Porter County	21,201	2,577	20,061	2,419	175	51	245	0	na	na	688	107
St. Joseph County	36,042	5,771	32,261	5,454	2,638	286	303	0	209	6	529	25
Tippecanoe County	16,741	2,584	16,139	2,574	147	0	191	0	100	0	216	0
Vanderburgh County	26,101	4,492	24,329	4,160	1,430	306	na	na	104	24	141	2
Vigo County	14,644	2,292	13,885	2,275	504	12	na	na	129	0	55	5
Wayne County	11,421	1,470	10,872	1,458	307	12	na	na	213	0	na	na
Iowa												
Black Hawk County	18,333	2,903	17,180	2,739	947	139	84	12	21	0	78	13
Dallas County	6,926	1,201	6,812	1,201	na	na	na	na	na	na	72	0
Dubuque County	14,434	2,116	14,341	2,099	na	na	na	na	28	0	21	0
Johnson County	11,712	1,738	11,334	1,695	96	43	199	0	25	0	45	0
Linn County	28,341	3,965	27,529	3,783	248	31	215	91	32	0	222	60
Polk County	47,984	6,542	44,298	6,330	1,571	114	1,005	63	213	0	830	49
Pottawattamie County	13,462	2,143	13,118	2,107	na	na	na	na	na	na	248	28
Scott County	22,349	3,219	20,849	3,146	780	3	275	28	58	0	422	42
Story County	9,096	1,547	8,886	1,533	23	0	151	13	na	na	na	na
Woodbury County	13,359	2,249	12,521	2,177	99	31	317	0	na	na	264	41
Kansas												
Butler County	8,469	1,493	8,237	1,419	na	na	na	na	na	na	56	0
Douglas County	10,285	1,500	9,567	1,401	238	22	184	45	74	0	53	5
Johnson County	62,589	10,204	58,207	9,754	1,128	118	1,355	60	505	102	1,290	174
Leavenworth County	8,733	1,293	7,987	1,187	346	71	na	na	99	0	194	27
Riley County	5,281	887	4,998	878	157	9	55	0	39	0	32	0
Sedgwick County	58,701	8,419	50,317	7,881	3,713	234	1,517	0	765	129	2,230	171
Shawnee County	26,288	3,677	23,196	3,305	1,415	165	185	0	349	11	1,057	196
Wyandotte County	17,141	2,688	10,787	1,868	4,476	633	264	47	260	44	1,373	125
Kentucky												
Boone County	11,980	1,179	11,631	1,179	30	0	na	na	na	na	90	0
Bullitt County	8,986	731	8,733	685	na	na	na	na	na	na	na	na
Campbell County	11,732	1,684	11,497	1,674	107	10	na	na	na	na	83	0
Christian County	7,712	911	6,410	830	1,153	81	na	na	na	na	74	0
Daviess County	14,464	1,945	13,896	1,903	366	42	na	na	na	na	na	na
Fayette County	32,142	4,219	27,686	3,846	3,423	323	506	22	169	0	358	21
Hardin County	11,732	1,353	10,616	1,243	759	110	306	0	13	0	38	0
Jefferson County	101,108	14,537	84,746	12,794	13,250	1,439	1,211	156	653	61	1,166	87
Kenton County	18,239	2,775	17,708	2,740	324	25	na	na	12	0	195	10
McCracken County	11,130	1,610	10,319	1,471	682	139	na	na	na	na	na	na
Madison County	9,643	1,027	9,256	961	256	57	na	na	na	na	na	na
Pike County	9,214	1,064	9,030	1,046	na	na	na	na	na	na	na	na
Warren County	12,841	1,703	11,718	1,657	688	28	na	na	179	0	50	na
Louisiana												
Ascension Parish	10,141	820	7,960	657	1,819	163	na	na	na	na	319	0
Bossier Parish	14,254	1,446	11,971	1,317	1,864	126	na	na	na	na	169	0
Caddo Parish	35,136	4,688	22,711	3,169	11,458	1,427	288	23	252	0	345	69
Calcasieu Parish	25,044	2,772	19,556	2,295	4,489	388	177	0	263	21	303	14
East Baton Rouge Parish	49,687	6,798	32,568	4,788	15,133	1,847	805	87	397	0	875	76
Iberia Parish	9,215	926	6,743	802	2,054	124	na	na	na	na	na	na
Jefferson Parish	60,584	8,082	45,778	6,727	8,340	730	1,540	65	341	48	4,625	535
Lafayette Parish	23,524	3,019	18,803	2,584	3,942	381	167	0	141	0	461	54
Lafourche Parish	12,426	1,396	10,991	1,225	1,028	118	na	na	na	na	136	0
Livingston Parish	13,591	1,136	12,715	1,096	570	23	na	na	na	na	na	na
Orleans Parish	40,109	5,790	14,833	2,730	22,648	2,826	830	91	424	31	1,438	110
Ouachita Parish	19,414	2,615	14,866	2,120	4,107	442	na	na	na	na	na	na
Rapides Parish	18,541	2,227	13,945	1,760	3,883	407	na	na	na	na	287	60
St. Landry Parish	11,551	1,219	7,767	899	3,551	305	na	na	na	na	na	na
St. Tammany Parish	31,345	3,422	27,702	3,118	2,227	182	196	28	254	59	796	35
Tangipahoa Parish	14,422	1,379	11,293	1,075	2,677	256	na	na	na	na	272	48
Terrebonne Parish	12,764	1,348	10,535	1,149	1,697	161	na	na	na	na	289	0

Table C-2: Counties—Older Population by Race and Hispanic Origin—*Continued*

	Total Population		White, Non-Hispanic		Black, Alone		Asian, Alone		Multi-race, Alone		Hispanic	
	65 Years and Over	85 Years and Over	65 Years and Over	85 Years and Over	65 Years and Over	85 Years and Over	65 Years and Over	85 Years and Over	65 Years and Over	85 Years and Over	65 Years and Over	85 Years and Over
Maine												
Androscoggin County	15,552	2,190	15,214	2,173	32	5	na	na	197	12	na	na
Aroostook County	13,965	1,577	13,649	1,577	na	na	na	na	81	0	na	na
Cumberland County	41,790	6,208	40,557	6,188	182	0	476	0	197	0	335	20
Kennebec County	19,571	2,680	19,191	2,625	na	na	na	na	na	na	na	na
Penobscot County	22,900	2,858	22,428	2,823	na	na	na	na	103	0	na	na
York County	31,686	3,924	31,059	3,907	na	na	186	8	na	na	171	0
Maryland												
Allegany County	13,593	1,976	13,113	1,957	300	17	na	na	na	na	na	na
Anne Arundel County	66,751	7,508	56,645	6,515	6,824	707	1,795	138	412	85	1,018	38
Baltimore County	120,243	21,247	97,010	19,068	17,723	1,706	3,431	215	638	82	1,409	152
Calvert County	10,165	1,371	8,573	1,221	1,363	133	na	na	80	0	72	16
Carroll County	23,043	3,044	21,821	2,900	727	111	189	0	108	7	198	26
Cecil County	12,395	1,526	11,682	1,461	534	62	na	na	na	na	60	0
Charles County	14,738	1,658	10,056	1,117	3,902	517	377	10	94	0	201	35
Frederick County	27,310	3,581	24,643	3,476	1,406	41	548	31	259	0	457	33
Harford County	31,967	4,168	28,617	3,711	2,254	316	559	22	46	0	416	36
Howard County	31,315	3,419	22,683	2,649	4,327	474	3,465	201	265	22	614	73
Montgomery County	124,810	20,747	84,867	16,452	14,016	1,566	15,574	1,652	2,190	217	8,603	892
Prince George's County	86,355	9,127	25,840	4,029	52,472	4,185	3,786	439	1,161	134	3,379	319
St. Mary's County	11,417	1,409	9,470	1,261	1,493	148	243	0	25	0	173	0
Washington County	21,582	2,914	20,602	2,782	513	12	164	8	70	14	223	96
Wicomico County	13,289	1,819	10,606	1,539	2,297	280	na	na	51	0	198	0
Massachusetts												
Barnstable County	55,418	7,009	53,571	6,789	487	52	226	49	266	14	357	74
Berkshire County	25,072	4,486	24,146	4,291	334	124	na	na	156	0	270	51
Bristol County	79,940	13,738	75,138	13,285	1,196	116	613	18	784	114	1,392	90
Essex County	108,427	18,753	98,801	17,815	1,803	160	1,707	181	634	82	6,132	618
Franklin County	11,256	1,850	11,002	1,850	na	na	na	na	na	na	83	0
Hampden County	67,146	11,470	57,565	10,663	3,631	235	790	76	477	21	4,693	438
Hampshire County	20,996	3,408	19,971	3,361	325	13	292	0	146	0	239	30
Middlesex County	202,350	31,421	182,183	29,379	4,993	589	9,118	904	1,760	96	4,400	449
Norfolk County	100,173	16,881	90,645	15,875	2,909	345	4,713	440	670	51	1,168	175
Plymouth County	72,139	10,461	66,390	9,877	3,037	251	582	32	661	156	821	44
Suffolk County	77,956	12,071	47,726	8,359	16,211	2,047	6,021	831	1,888	175	7,109	715
Worcester County	104,748	17,839	97,694	17,305	1,406	168	1,817	135	568	31	3,203	253
Michigan												
Allegan County	15,160	1,914	14,598	1,897	na	na	na	na	22	0	246	10
Bay County	17,937	2,872	17,343	2,818	na	na	na	na	137	0	313	11
Berrien County	25,836	3,931	22,831	3,513	2,291	330	196	0	187	51	300	37
Calhoun County	20,385	3,063	18,054	2,733	1,771	308	107	0	71	6	305	16
Clinton County	10,328	1,291	9,993	1,283	na	na	na	na	na	na	168	0
Eaton County	15,669	2,168	14,728	2,103	521	10	67	0	86	12	220	43
Genesee County	59,719	7,641	48,776	6,620	9,044	945	379	14	611	9	795	41
Grand Traverse County	13,381	1,861	13,309	1,851	na	na	na	na	na	na	na	na
Ingham County	30,357	4,222	26,052	3,959	2,203	101	776	44	299	41	1,012	77
Isabella County	6,959	974	6,688	909	na	na	na	na	19	3	19	9
Jackson County	23,197	3,605	21,879	3,458	902	147	na	na	131	0	156	0
Kalamazoo County	31,522	4,836	28,801	4,398	1,876	170	389	165	137	36	283	67
Kent County	69,091	11,059	62,052	10,358	3,836	380	915	27	693	26	1,768	268
Lapeer County	12,339	1,030	12,032	1,014	na	na	na	na	64	16	120	0
Lenawee County	15,146	2,023	14,283	1,960	na	na	na	na	39	0	493	23
Livingston County	23,142	2,216	22,652	2,206	na	na	na	na	99	0	207	10
Macomb County	123,166	19,615	114,973	18,702	3,762	494	2,262	198	751	82	1,111	139
Marquette County	10,139	1,410	9,869	1,382	na	na	na	na	36	0	na	na
Midland County	12,600	1,665	12,273	1,627	na	na	66	0	na	na	87	0
Monroe County	21,131	2,455	20,450	2,404	197	4	na	na	100	29	300	18
Muskegon County	23,796	3,325	21,153	3,095	2,072	174	na	na	157	18	356	38
Oakland County	165,886	24,687	139,502	22,109	17,241	1,883	5,019	381	1,610	39	2,175	251
Ottawa County	32,067	4,818	30,773	4,671	87	25	215	0	205	23	829	116
Saginaw County	31,123	4,628	25,671	4,017	3,905	425	143	4	225	26	1,277	170
St. Clair County	24,312	3,125	23,470	3,041	368	48	na	na	119	13	209	23
Shiawassee County	10,426	1,337	10,150	1,280	na	na	na	na	na	na	102	29
Van Buren County	10,841	1,130	9,911	1,030	551	50	na	na	49	17	236	33
Washtenaw County	37,073	5,501	31,163	4,912	3,239	442	1,646	70	464	32	635	48
Wayne County	232,538	35,792	140,139	22,789	80,813	11,803	3,741	383	2,305	274	5,027	488
Minnesota												
Anoka County	34,152	3,634	32,693	3,469	217	9	667	87	203	28	325	41
Blue Earth County	7,666	1,494	7,576	1,494	na	na	na	na	na	na	48	0
Carver County	8,249	931	7,980	931	na	na	179	0	na	na	10	0
Dakota County	42,198	5,565	39,908	5,409	578	0	907	48	250	70	528	38
Hennepin County	135,530	22,715	122,207	21,299	6,770	528	3,727	422	970	175	1,594	285
Olmsted County	18,843	2,831	17,849	2,665	198	74	535	60	128	26	163	6
Ramsey County	62,848	10,130	55,616	9,325	2,470	106	2,999	469	477	16	1,231	178
St. Louis County	32,330	5,149	31,515	5,125	61	0	206	12	149	12	136	0
Scott County	11,050	1,165	10,175	1,067	209	80	391	18	128	0	68	0
Sherburne County	7,705	844	7,580	844	na	na	na	na	na	na	na	na
Stearns County	18,731	2,547	18,337	2,432	64	15	na	na	na	na	117	13
Washington County	26,718	3,177	25,615	3,002	127	17	499	83	162	41	268	34
Wright County	12,575	1,652	12,398	1,646	na	na	na	na	na	na	84	6

Table C-2: Counties—Older Population by Race and Hispanic Origin—*Continued*

	Total Population		White, Non-Hispanic		Black, Alone		Asian, Alone		Multi-race, Alone		Hispanic	
	65 Years and Over	85 Years and Over	65 Years and Over	85 Years and Over	65 Years and Over	85 Years and Over	65 Years and Over	85 Years and Over	65 Years and Over	85 Years and Over	65 Years and Over	85 Years and Over
Mississippi												
DeSoto County	17,276	1,550	15,104	1,410	1,798	99	106	0	56	41	190	0
Forrest County	8,871	1,393	6,880	1,064	1,864	300	na	na	na	na	55	16
Harrison County	23,014	2,629	18,636	2,071	3,304	499	529	28	220	15	372	63
Hinds County	27,208	3,921	13,811	2,090	12,902	1,754	na	na	na	na	222	65
Jackson County	17,916	1,351	15,074	1,191	2,325	74	114	0	na	na	175	67
Jones County	9,880	1,147	8,050	928	1,803	219	na	na	na	na	0	0
Lauderdale County	11,323	1,542	8,177	1,126	3,004	358	na	na	na	na	na	na
Lee County	11,165	1,536	9,350	1,476	1,657	60	na	na	na	na	na	na
Madison County	10,565	1,890	7,538	1,405	2,814	431	na	na	na	na	na	na
Rankin County	17,092	1,452	14,803	1,290	1,951	162	na	na	na	na	163	0
Missouri												
Boone County	15,776	2,263	14,287	2,160	802	78	365	2	214	23	91	0
Buchanan County	12,309	1,978	11,850	1,831	236	95	na	na	72	4	126	34
Cape Girardeau County	11,033	1,913	10,710	1,908	237	0	na	na	na	na	10	0
Cass County	14,100	1,786	13,488	1,786	na	na	na	na	na	na	170	0
Christian County	10,098	731	9,838	731	na	na	na	na	na	na	na	na
Clay County	26,107	3,401	24,370	3,077	468	99	245	36	165	32	849	153
Cole County	9,867	1,304	9,183	1,277	427	16	na	na	na	na	na	na
Franklin County	14,368	1,808	14,052	1,808	na	na	na	na	na	na	na	na
Greene County	39,754	6,273	38,343	5,937	437	94	201	49	289	114	384	69
Jackson County	85,613	12,435	65,601	10,196	15,586	1,724	963	19	820	126	2,526	323
Jasper County	15,630	2,282	14,811	2,167	na	na	na	na	130	13	182	45
Jefferson County	25,707	2,349	25,075	2,304	na	na	na	na	183	0	124	0
Platte County	10,624	1,468	9,885	1,468	184	0	216	0	na	na	209	0
St. Charles County	42,754	5,330	40,845	5,208	934	110	536	0	151	0	279	8
St. Francois County	9,366	996	9,272	996	na	na	na	na	na	na	na	na
St. Louis County	152,609	25,699	125,454	22,775	22,319	2,309	2,811	262	924	97	1,310	317
Montana												
Cascade County	12,936	1,797	12,325	1,695	na	na	na	na	107	0	107	55
Flathead County	13,704	1,719	13,342	1,699	na	na	na	na	na	na	na	na
Gallatin County	9,014	1,427	8,822	1,415	na	na	na	na	na	na	96	12
Missoula County	12,935	1,945	12,674	1,922	na	na	na	na	80	0	66	23
Yellowstone County	21,466	3,251	20,585	3,187	na	na	na	na	41	0	384	39
Nebraska												
Douglas County	56,388	8,820	49,269	8,251	4,720	439	651	33	193	16	1,561	86
Lancaster County	32,065	4,874	30,494	4,726	246	17	622	77	147	24	518	20
Sarpy County	14,360	1,382	13,427	1,329	426	9	128	0	62	0	347	44
Nevada												
Clark County	233,408	21,844	164,439	16,878	19,020	1,618	20,610	1,519	3,764	179	24,622	1,657
Washoe County	54,049	6,169	45,988	5,570	762	74	2,311	174	832	92	3,761	235
New Hampshire												
Cheshire County	11,680	1,510	11,560	1,450	na	na	na	na	na	na	na	na
Grafton County	14,293	1,636	14,085	1,587	na	na	48	10	69	20	46	0
Hillsborough County	49,471	6,877	47,321	6,786	360	34	760	0	297	35	782	22
Merrimack County	20,842	3,209	20,400	3,188	na	na	na	na	143	21	136	0
Rockingham County	39,341	4,383	38,440	4,314	180	0	188	50	254	19	241	0
Strafford County	15,212	1,964	14,762	1,958	na	na	189	0	na	na	154	0
New Jersey												
Atlantic County	40,020	5,176	30,796	4,253	4,935	515	1,888	173	331	28	2,162	219
Bergen County	139,882	22,806	110,044	20,145	6,131	689	12,371	1,001	1,165	48	10,545	920
Burlington County	64,071	8,950	52,120	8,090	8,189	623	2,020	52	281	35	1,509	150
Camden County	67,424	10,942	51,156	9,090	9,322	1,365	2,718	230	839	56	3,592	201
Cape May County	21,534	2,730	20,344	2,502	681	208	na	na	na	na	287	7
Cumberland County	20,154	2,843	15,279	2,244	2,280	271	na	na	217	10	2,161	216
Essex County	92,329	14,839	46,769	10,316	31,704	3,327	3,394	259	1,441	95	9,938	895
Gloucester County	36,896	4,761	32,467	4,275	3,056	354	711	27	146	12	473	93
Hudson County	67,536	8,678	28,123	4,909	7,235	578	6,112	470	1,476	59	25,763	2,835
Hunterdon County	17,173	1,862	16,158	1,753	222	19	390	23	na	na	375	67
Mercer County	47,385	7,261	34,929	6,172	7,316	704	2,586	256	389	25	2,176	136
Middlesex County	102,516	15,846	74,499	13,500	6,463	431	12,636	1,056	1,042	88	8,218	811
Monmouth County	89,569	13,709	77,356	12,408	5,512	636	3,147	262	662	64	2,983	339
Morris County	70,645	10,793	61,659	10,046	1,614	131	4,217	385	443	76	2,933	248
Ocean County	122,772	19,074	115,909	18,408	1,867	156	1,263	54	656	44	3,102	399
Passaic County	61,904	9,409	41,352	7,540	6,315	641	2,357	156	1,247	121	12,003	1,013
Salem County	10,175	1,282	8,711	1,180	1,221	91	na	na	na	na	186	0
Somerset County	41,926	6,901	33,646	6,274	2,510	340	3,856	188	184	37	1,740	128
Sussex County	18,525	2,194	17,726	2,069	189	54	na	na	na	na	525	97
Union County	68,570	12,061	43,672	9,347	12,586	1,483	2,379	114	409	72	9,730	1,244
Warren County	15,423	2,237	14,687	2,186	202	0	184	12	66	15	260	0
New Mexico												
Bernalillo County	84,473	11,004	52,202	7,332	1,722	128	1,579	226	988	89	26,994	3,114
Chaves County	9,266	1,297	6,471	999	na	na	na	na	na	na	2,568	265
Doña Ana County	26,999	2,973	14,236	1,638	na	na	276	18	435	0	11,910	1,255
Lea County	7,189	655	4,946	566	na	na	na	na	na	na	1,728	89
McKinley County	7,038	651	1,407	129	na	na	na	na	na	na	991	28
Otero County	9,679	971	7,200	788	na	na	na	na	na	na	2,013	136
Sandoval County	17,027	2,102	11,528	1,473	131	48	na	na	385	60	3,677	390
San Juan County	14,445	1,702	8,994	1,338	na	na	na	na	221	0	1,596	51
Santa Fe County	23,581	2,518	15,044	1,622	na	na	na	na	410	28	7,767	799
Valencia County	10,321	1,010	5,476	442	na	na	na	na	274	76	4,317	462

Table C-2: Counties—Older Population by Race and Hispanic Origin—*Continued*

	Total Population		White, Non-Hispanic		Black, Alone		Asian, Alone		Multi-race, Alone		Hispanic	
	65 Years and Over	85 Years and Over	65 Years and Over	85 Years and Over	65 Years and Over	85 Years and Over	65 Years and Over	85 Years and Over	65 Years and Over	85 Years and Over	65 Years and Over	85 Years and Over
New York												
Albany County	43,137	7,464	38,570	6,940	2,944	325	871	43	187	0	513	156
Bronx County	150,027	20,618	37,978	8,541	48,755	6,101	4,786	214	3,515	581	61,556	6,103
Broome County	33,185	5,497	31,803	5,419	402	24	338	19	171	9	443	39
Cattaraugus County	12,495	1,735	12,189	1,683	na	na	na	na	48	0	26	0
Cayuga County	12,491	1,875	12,196	1,875	135	0	na	na	na	na	na	na
Chautauqua County	22,528	3,577	21,913	3,530	314	0	na	na	21	0	201	22
Chemung County	13,656	2,356	13,331	2,311	270	33	na	na	14	12	na	na
Clinton County	11,178	1,268	10,969	1,236	na	na	na	na	na	na	54	0
Dutchess County	41,631	5,536	36,329	5,216	2,515	162	950	0	355	42	1,517	100
Erie County	145,651	22,231	128,329	20,569	12,440	1,305	1,441	34	896	122	2,183	190
Jefferson County	13,327	2,102	12,993	2,081	39	6	na	na	78	0	74	6
Kings County	294,324	41,314	133,042	25,297	97,621	10,614	23,803	1,907	3,426	357	42,222	3,682
Livingston County	9,412	1,711	8,990	1,634	na	na	na	na	na	na	39	0
Madison County	10,536	1,638	10,311	1,605	na	na	na	na	na	na	na	na
Monroe County	106,484	18,180	92,664	16,920	8,949	773	1,771	168	407	44	2,791	308
Nassau County	208,405	36,119	168,399	32,178	16,633	1,708	10,004	980	1,896	236	11,703	1,004
New York County	220,062	31,391	115,254	16,334	35,303	6,167	21,010	3,275	5,728	502	50,699	6,038
Niagara County	34,855	5,421	32,853	5,261	1,240	122	94	0	155	7	213	7
Oneida County	38,570	7,663	36,518	7,446	880	169	467	42	276	4	465	11
Onondaga County	66,790	11,250	60,810	10,677	3,460	361	883	31	520	70	791	134
Ontario County	17,324	2,396	16,683	2,299	225	52	na	na	106	0	221	45
Orange County	42,428	6,170	35,385	5,572	2,879	360	716	36	362	0	3,298	237
Oswego County	15,690	1,891	15,574	1,891	na	na	na	na	38	0	67	0
Putnam County	13,030	1,822	12,061	1,655	na	na	na	na	na	na	736	104
Queens County	293,250	43,495	135,259	27,694	52,135	6,234	52,110	4,879	5,970	612	48,428	4,086
Rensselaer County	22,119	3,457	20,969	3,409	636	10	118	11	105	27	246	0
Richmond County	61,773	8,750	49,596	7,687	3,353	261	4,081	288	524	21	4,358	516
Rockland County	43,536	5,918	34,152	5,051	4,122	553	2,392	108	521	47	2,666	213
St. Lawrence County	15,917	1,869	15,484	1,820	na	na	na	na	72	5	45	11
Saratoga County	31,263	4,168	30,411	4,075	260	27	219	0	134	49	197	26
Schenectady County	23,143	4,785	21,306	4,648	903	54	344	18	218	31	339	34
Steuben County	16,051	2,164	15,680	2,133	117	0	82	0	na	na	122	27
Suffolk County	209,194	28,401	180,938	25,942	9,965	775	4,498	345	1,584	137	12,481	1,233
Sullivan County	11,951	1,443	10,310	1,353	632	70	na	na	229	0	799	14
Tompkins County	11,365	1,751	10,683	1,691	226	23	305	37	43	0	87	0
Ulster County	28,178	4,304	25,859	3,957	819	131	274	48	267	45	943	122
Warren County	11,692	1,565	11,341	1,515	na	na	na	na	na	na	na	na
Wayne County	13,836	1,668	13,240	1,668	252	0	na	na	na	na	200	0
Westchester County	142,310	23,448	108,006	20,002	16,511	1,856	5,411	389	1,398	161	11,951	1,149
North Carolina												
Alamance County	22,781	3,757	18,797	3,321	3,287	381	na	na	324	3	477	56
Brunswick County	25,078	1,552	23,059	1,458	1,640	75	na	na	na	na	122	0
Buncombe County	39,572	5,914	37,062	5,491	1,758	349	na	na	197	0	335	47
Burke County	14,983	1,702	14,081	1,612	694	69	160	21	na	na	27	0
Cabarrus County	20,765	2,446	18,003	2,084	2,117	254	120	0	na	na	468	85
Caldwell County	13,309	1,490	12,472	1,411	639	79	na	na	na	na	na	na
Carteret County	13,082	1,465	12,456	1,327	421	136	na	na	na	na	na	na
Catawba County	23,003	2,748	20,788	2,414	1,292	142	435	84	20	20	430	88
Chatham County	12,897	1,653	11,163	1,467	1,622	186	na	na	na	na	19	0
Cleveland County	15,241	1,910	12,725	1,712	2,235	198	na	na	na	na	148	0
Craven County	16,486	2,012	13,227	1,778	2,608	189	na	na	145	4	317	45
Cumberland County	31,376	3,135	18,765	1,994	10,186	890	866	66	378	15	1,026	59
Davidson County	24,684	2,719	22,432	2,580	1,638	139	na	na	na	na	232	0
Durham County	27,723	4,202	17,266	3,283	8,747	892	800	0	349	11	532	16
Forsyth County	46,943	6,403	36,975	5,482	8,648	841	369	37	136	13	792	30
Gaston County	28,154	3,520	24,888	2,918	2,817	581	196	0	48	0	121	21
Guilford County	62,583	7,687	47,127	6,251	12,934	1,319	1,151	77	309	8	860	52
Harnett County	12,444	1,221	9,894	863	2,089	288	na	na	107	0	212	0
Henderson County	24,744	3,326	23,628	3,142	537	137	na	na	na	na	403	42
Iredell County	21,342	2,632	18,778	2,318	2,093	241	100	36	na	na	339	26
Johnston County	18,658	1,581	15,540	1,226	2,445	247	na	na	na	na	463	41
Lincoln County	10,948	699	10,149	628	482	44	na	na	na	na	83	0
Mecklenburg County	86,008	11,249	60,954	9,211	19,110	1,870	2,318	37	664	0	2,941	138
Moore County	20,485	3,131	18,375	2,858	1,750	227	na	na	na	na	199	46
Nash County	13,975	1,738	9,738	1,393	3,813	345	na	na	na	na	79	0
New Hanover County	29,485	3,442	25,448	2,942	3,416	435	na	na	na	na	234	24
Onslow County	13,878	1,317	10,992	988	2,012	222	361	0	76	0	364	86
Orange County	13,694	1,387	11,087	1,261	1,792	126	354	0	27	0	319	0
Pitt County	17,405	2,480	11,998	1,858	4,896	597	159	0	na	na	241	0
Randolph County	20,654	1,946	19,323	1,879	984	39	na	na	na	na	208	0
Robeson County	15,763	1,473	6,841	762	3,437	392	106	0	101	0	331	34
Rockingham County	15,663	1,678	12,998	1,426	2,362	232	na	na	na	na	121	19
Rowan County	20,589	2,621	17,823	2,319	2,354	279	na	na	80	0	123	23
Rutherford County	12,047	1,726	10,984	1,609	992	79	na	na	na	na	38	38
Surry County	12,520	1,429	11,949	1,398	446	24	na	na	na	na	72	7
Union County	20,603	2,028	17,872	1,818	2,014	62	186	0	7	0	484	148
Wake County	82,181	9,633	63,986	7,983	12,944	1,317	2,800	273	439	27	2,045	33
Wayne County	16,464	1,992	11,383	1,348	4,656	644	na	na	240	0	25	0
Wilkes County	12,326	1,496	11,737	1,394	379	102	na	na	na	na	97	0
Wilson County	11,994	1,631	8,125	894	3,605	724	na	na	na	na	126	0

Table C-2: Counties—Older Population by Race and Hispanic Origin—*Continued*

	Total Population		White, Non-Hispanic		Black, Alone		Asian, Alone		Multi-race, Alone		Hispanic	
	65 Years and Over	85 Years and Over	65 Years and Over	85 Years and Over	65 Years and Over	85 Years and Over	65 Years and Over	85 Years and Over	65 Years and Over	85 Years and Over	65 Years and Over	85 Years and Over
North Dakota												
Burleigh County	11,497	1,761	11,230	1,761	na	na	na	na	na	na	na	na
Cass County	15,280	2,040	14,868	2,040	20	0	234	0	58	0	47	0
Grand Forks County	7,213	986	6,895	979	na	na	na	na	na	na	14	0
Ohio												
Allen County	15,696	2,573	14,368	2,459	1,098	32	na	na	na	na	115	15
Ashtabula County	16,042	2,694	15,430	2,640	334	25	na	na	59	0	156	8
Belmont County	12,501	2,032	12,164	1,989	na	na	na	na	na	na	na	na
Butler County	43,904	5,553	40,926	5,256	1,845	179	596	60	232	0	216	10
Clark County	22,620	3,490	20,780	3,169	1,616	285	na	na	102	0	47	8
Clermont County	24,388	2,623	23,710	2,586	na	na	na	na	na	na	180	37
Columbiana County	18,131	2,294	17,669	2,243	na	na	na	na	na	na	na	na
Cuyahoga County	199,199	33,894	146,114	27,456	45,248	5,755	3,306	226	1,206	134	3,515	336
Delaware County	17,999	1,686	16,779	1,582	537	24	473	46	na	na	140	9
Erie County	13,703	1,779	12,601	1,715	783	39	na	na	na	na	164	25
Fairfield County	18,641	2,241	18,278	2,129	128	47	na	na	129	19	30	0
Franklin County	119,415	16,279	95,537	13,863	18,882	2,118	2,654	160	1,107	74	1,326	76
Geauga County	15,046	2,187	14,784	2,146	na	na	na	na	na	na	na	na
Greene County	22,995	2,847	21,046	2,627	998	49	559	116	184	38	191	0
Hamilton County	107,723	17,828	85,016	14,690	19,984	2,840	1,368	166	540	25	759	63
Hancock County	11,172	2,075	10,736	2,048	na	na	na	na	na	na	215	0
Jefferson County	12,783	1,786	12,000	1,702	583	44	na	na	na	na	na	na
Lake County	38,065	5,283	36,497	5,179	930	71	230	13	133	0	268	20
Licking County	22,880	2,410	22,162	2,324	449	54	na	na	82	0	61	22
Lorain County	44,580	6,272	39,965	5,866	2,315	239	305	0	352	50	1,725	117
Lucas County	59,095	8,872	48,991	7,943	7,772	704	598	43	497	24	1,319	158
Mahoning County	42,672	7,684	37,038	6,993	4,653	570	na	na	173	11	776	110
Marion County	9,562	1,419	9,370	1,400	na	na	na	na	na	na	na	na
Medina County	23,579	3,093	23,200	3,060	na	na	na	na	na	na	136	22
Miami County	16,212	1,758	15,825	1,738	261	0	na	na	na	na	na	na
Montgomery County	82,953	12,325	67,736	10,355	13,256	1,839	880	26	513	42	596	63
Muskingum County	13,274	2,001	12,803	1,924	183	22	na	na	190	28	na	na
Portage County	21,491	2,376	20,643	2,329	509	47	na	na	172	0	29	0
Richland County	20,768	2,656	19,200	2,535	1,052	99	na	na	111	10	na	na
Ross County	10,713	1,166	10,182	1,153	244	12	na	na	185	0	na	na
Scioto County	12,327	1,380	12,041	1,366	na	na	na	na	na	na	na	na
Stark County	61,897	9,674	57,868	9,188	2,937	316	245	0	337	68	427	38
Summit County	80,782	12,364	70,871	11,205	8,155	974	842	48	400	50	441	126
Trumbull County	37,110	5,033	34,633	4,734	2,102	267	na	na	131	13	125	32
Tuscarawas County	15,333	2,049	15,211	2,039	na	na	na	na	na	na	na	na
Warren County	24,217	2,747	23,398	2,713	314	27	223	0	109	7	157	7
Wayne County	17,247	2,617	16,714	2,575	na	na	na	na	na	na	na	na
Wood County	16,009	1,880	15,451	1,880	na	na	na	na	64	0	256	0
Oklahoma												
Canadian County	13,443	1,599	12,205	1,480	256	4	311	13	170	28	199	55
Cleveland County	27,700	3,090	24,790	2,861	306	0	625	119	647	34	622	40
Comanche County	12,964	1,427	10,033	1,273	1,286	40	na	na	313	2	496	69
Creek County	10,832	1,256	9,609	1,148	232	20	na	na	700	57	18	0
Muskogee County	10,529	1,317	8,031	1,105	982	94	na	na	669	38	77	0
Oklahoma County	87,927	11,975	70,317	10,253	8,897	1,063	1,920	74	2,286	276	3,211	274
Payne County	8,088	1,229	7,654	1,184	na	na	na	na	146	7	59	0
Pottawatomie County	10,218	1,023	9,054	968	117	7	na	na	236	13	117	0
Rogers County	12,248	1,437	10,585	1,247	na	na	na	na	582	31	157	0
Tulsa County	74,698	10,808	63,152	9,721	4,624	401	958	62	2,147	276	1,654	142
Wagoner County	9,931	783	8,494	726	259	35	na	na	548	0	200	0
Oregon												
Benton County	10,787	1,929	10,155	1,828	na	na	257	93	152	0	152	0
Clackamas County	54,314	7,604	51,199	7,398	205	23	1,232	78	468	22	937	40
Deschutes County	25,290	3,476	24,336	3,402	na	na	na	na	326	66	444	1
Douglas County	23,198	2,906	22,039	2,855	na	na	na	na	407	36	364	15
Jackson County	37,277	5,744	35,389	5,482	na	na	na	na	396	101	933	101
Josephine County	18,923	2,927	18,004	2,803	na	na	na	na	na	na	496	65
Klamath County	11,842	1,165	10,793	1,138	na	na	na	na	208	0	503	0
Lane County	54,955	7,297	52,107	7,083	126	0	640	13	734	78	1,034	154
Linn County	18,819	2,245	17,769	2,047	na	na	na	na	215	21	469	177
Marion County	42,006	6,420	38,530	6,070	na	na	598	110	630	86	1,920	105
Multnomah County	81,022	13,346	68,854	12,177	3,594	474	5,153	591	774	29	2,019	70
Polk County	11,764	1,854	10,897	1,725	na	na	na	na	121	24	519	103
Umatilla County	9,806	1,291	8,952	1,234	na	na	na	na	184	50	493	4
Washington County	56,477	8,550	50,163	7,845	380	0	3,212	296	617	53	1,962	314
Yamhill County	13,902	2,329	13,060	2,292	na	na	na	na	175	0	368	35
Pennsylvania												
Adams County	16,630	2,336	16,172	2,299	na	na	na	na	na	na	127	6
Allegheny County	205,615	36,676	183,129	33,838	18,002	2,353	2,178	248	1,040	110	1,218	124
Armstrong County	12,928	2,068	12,746	2,033	na	na	na	na	na	na	na	na
Beaver County	31,875	4,889	30,289	4,680	1,302	170	na	na	119	20	175	19
Berks County	60,772	9,371	56,222	9,119	1,561	109	352	50	298	3	2,616	90
Blair County	22,825	3,637	22,536	3,609	136	28	na	na	na	na	na	na
Bucks County	94,503	14,925	88,826	14,245	1,883	201	2,143	104	401	99	1,242	254
Butler County	28,769	4,188	28,153	4,171	189	17	193	0	46	0	144	0
Cambria County	27,189	4,525	26,385	4,460	497	38	na	na	46	8	200	19
Carbon County	11,798	1,594	11,566	1,594	na	na	na	na	na	na	na	na

Table C-2: Counties—Older Population by Race and Hispanic Origin—*Continued*

	Total Population		White, Non-Hispanic		Black, Alone		Asian, Alone		Multi-race, Alone		Hispanic	
	65 Years and Over	85 Years and Over	65 Years and Over	85 Years and Over	65 Years and Over	85 Years and Over	65 Years and Over	85 Years and Over	65 Years and Over	85 Years and Over	65 Years and Over	85 Years and Over
Pennsylvania—Cont.												
Centre County	17,752	2,566	17,413	2,505	33	0	137	0	26	0	97	24
Chester County	66,785	9,525	61,101	8,862	3,180	475	1,174	105	287	24	1,026	59
Clearfield County	14,432	2,259	14,344	2,248	na	na	na	na	na	na	na	na
Columbia County	10,849	1,434	10,742	1,434	na	na	na	na	na	na	na	na
Crawford County	14,987	1,831	14,629	1,821	na	na	na	na	40	0	4	0
Cumberland County	37,807	6,172	36,362	6,014	458	47	473	35	232	31	253	45
Dauphin County	37,544	6,060	31,828	5,469	4,445	457	591	18	229	0	645	173
Delaware County	80,632	14,469	68,631	13,053	8,728	1,111	2,174	144	409	63	780	93
Erie County	41,308	6,441	39,346	6,244	1,190	122	137	0	181	0	357	75
Fayette County	24,652	3,783	23,752	3,740	825	43	na	na	na	na	na	na
Franklin County	25,484	3,204	24,625	3,122	355	31	na	na	na	na	323	3
Indiana County	14,031	2,336	13,828	2,300	80	31	na	na	na	na	na	na
Lackawanna County	38,470	7,047	37,349	7,002	198	0	369	8	162	0	388	37
Lancaster County	80,119	13,886	75,957	13,251	1,102	155	809	153	319	137	1,986	190
Lawrence County	17,239	3,004	16,626	2,979	403	25	na	na	na	na	350	15
Lebanon County	22,939	3,413	22,272	3,398	141	0	na	na	3	0	350	15
Lehigh County	52,617	8,676	47,798	8,179	924	63	790	50	214	58	2,805	271
Luzerne County	58,047	9,540	56,538	9,444	405	26	242	0	200	8	735	46
Lycoming County	19,304	3,409	18,903	3,324	166	43	na	na	32	0	na	na
Mercer County	21,759	3,717	20,854	3,628	699	75	na	na	28	9	na	na
Monroe County	22,390	2,658	19,158	2,300	1,552	143	na	na	341	57	992	158
Montgomery County	123,778	20,864	109,907	19,471	7,478	932	4,230	173	729	49	1,336	239
Northampton County	47,739	7,921	44,289	7,685	1,022	70	597	57	227	3	1,716	87
Northumberland County	17,551	2,778	17,425	2,770	na	na	na	na	na	na	15	8
Philadelphia County	186,585	28,788	94,380	17,880	74,099	9,404	7,625	536	1,845	370	9,543	716
Schuylkill County	26,978	4,328	26,642	4,315	na	na	na	na	78	0	95	9
Somerset County	14,685	2,507	14,499	2,506	na	na	na	na	na	na	na	na
Washington County	37,057	5,452	35,668	5,258	787	127	135	8	248	58	252	1
Westmoreland County	69,613	11,376	68,211	11,223	807	77	172	11	167	54	236	11
York County	63,155	8,678	60,120	8,478	1,524	114	459	0	170	29	838	57
Rhode Island												
Kent County	26,590	4,322	25,826	4,280	na	na	153	0	64	0	261	26
Newport County	14,503	2,342	13,718	2,131	289	105	na	na	124	13	131	47
Providence County	85,113	15,615	73,903	14,626	3,314	322	1,362	73	1,083	142	5,195	308
Washington County	19,804	2,950	19,135	2,823	70	16	165	64	na	na	110	0
South Carolina												
Aiken County	25,797	2,290	20,933	1,848	4,232	378	na	na	na	na	328	24
Anderson County	29,491	3,431	25,742	3,083	3,216	273	na	na	na	na	229	0
Beaufort County	35,549	3,592	31,245	3,101	3,346	440	na	na	45	0	571	51
Berkeley County	19,515	1,830	14,161	1,122	4,308	659	509	28	249	0	162	0
Charleston County	47,190	5,484	33,910	4,036	12,164	1,352	447	0	163	50	473	23
Darlington County	10,184	1,110	6,920	605	3,035	462	na	na	na	na	na	na
Dorchester County	14,687	1,496	11,197	1,239	2,758	193	na	na	148	0	241	44
Florence County	18,568	2,089	12,509	1,468	5,840	593	na	na	na	na	44	28
Greenville County	60,362	7,557	50,971	6,882	7,148	639	617	0	412	17	1,196	19
Greenwood County	10,839	1,796	8,477	1,466	2,132	305	na	na	na	na	11	0
Horry County	49,069	4,537	44,682	4,168	3,453	280	295	0	144	76	503	13
Lancaster County	12,803	984	10,740	847	1,727	137	na	na	na	na	180	0
Laurens County	10,202	1,333	8,113	1,145	2,012	188	na	na	na	na	64	0
Lexington County	33,769	3,872	30,547	3,633	2,455	189	184	33	64	0	407	17
Oconee County	14,634	1,165	13,713	1,103	690	62	na	na	na	na	134	0
Orangeburg County	14,152	1,411	6,949	623	6,937	788	na	na	na	na	86	0
Pickens County	16,515	1,906	15,429	1,804	793	52	na	na	na	na	126	21
Richland County	39,434	5,177	24,282	3,503	13,603	1,574	666	43	205	16	662	41
Spartanburg County	39,447	3,986	33,122	3,352	5,539	634	331	0	136	0	344	0
Sumter County	14,136	1,694	8,173	955	5,733	719	na	na	na	na	na	na
York County	27,017	2,730	22,821	2,282	3,482	415	na	na	57	0	424	28
South Dakota												
Minnehaha County	19,398	3,019	18,928	2,941	93	38	186	0	0	0	61	6
Pennington County	14,163	2,256	13,369	2,226	na	na	na	na	171	0	157	0
Tennessee												
Anderson County	13,279	2,717	12,733	2,620	273	86	na	na	na	na	na	na
Blount County	20,569	2,227	19,907	2,172	429	55	na	na	na	na	na	na
Bradley County	14,689	1,467	13,849	1,450	401	17	na	na	na	na	300	0
Davidson County	67,113	9,196	51,297	7,685	12,915	1,283	1,247	73	510	113	1,129	33
Greene County	12,423	1,117	12,068	1,098	na	na	na	na	na	na	na	na
Hamilton County	51,108	7,226	42,657	6,181	6,900	997	510	31	187	17	674	17
Knox County	58,504	7,110	53,386	6,648	3,422	396	809	0	307	13	530	53
Madison County	13,271	1,819	10,210	1,400	2,884	419	na	na	na	na	144	0
Maury County	10,993	1,325	9,544	1,102	1,101	136	na	na	na	na	35	0
Montgomery County	14,271	1,451	11,686	1,155	1,885	244	349	0	98	0	270	52
Putnam County	10,849	1,299	10,530	1,240	na	na	na	na	na	na	99	18
Robertson County	8,107	1,151	7,417	1,029	568	56	na	na	na	na	119	66
Rutherford County	23,173	2,691	20,542	2,429	1,689	198	403	11	238	29	363	114
Sevier County	14,540	1,258	14,254	1,220	na	na	na	na	na	na	na	na
Shelby County	98,130	12,047	56,624	8,019	38,073	3,839	1,588	35	718	46	1,186	108
Sullivan County	30,036	3,763	29,087	3,620	na	na	na	na	na	na	na	na
Sumner County	21,716	2,285	20,279	2,181	942	86	na	na	na	na	351	0
Washington County	19,318	2,503	18,609	2,402	328	42	na	na	na	na	189	59
Williamson County	19,043	2,308	17,743	2,209	722	19	180	0	na	na	269	34
Wilson County	15,060	1,339	13,917	1,235	725	28	na	na	na	na	170	30

Table C-2: Counties—Older Population by Race and Hispanic Origin—*Continued*

	Total Population		White, Non-Hispanic		Black, Alone		Asian, Alone		Multi-race, Alone		Hispanic	
	65 Years and Over	85 Years and Over	65 Years and Over	85 Years and Over	65 Years and Over	85 Years and Over	65 Years and Over	85 Years and Over	65 Years and Over	85 Years and Over	65 Years and Over	85 Years and Over
Texas												
Angelina County	12,215	1,684	10,098	1,411	1,197	135	na	na	na	na	650	75
Bastrop County	8,856	1,272	7,027	821	678	416	na	na	na	na	1,070	65
Bell County	28,330	3,140	21,065	2,515	3,012	188	907	40	390	11	2,882	386
Bexar County	183,708	24,257	85,562	13,991	11,430	1,349	3,526	172	2,623	392	81,798	8,634
Bowie County	13,491	1,836	10,929	1,428	2,043	287	na	na	na	na	233	87
Brazoria County	31,601	3,916	23,234	2,928	2,507	440	1,324	138	218	83	4,205	327
Brazos County	14,827	1,587	11,496	1,349	1,418	72	336	0	67	0	1,518	166
Cameron County	46,553	4,957	14,276	1,949	na	na	245	21	254	71	31,829	2,977
Collin County	66,763	6,380	54,331	5,513	2,595	281	5,352	351	625	20	3,802	220
Comal County	17,966	2,214	15,322	1,925	na	na	na	na	319	0	2,203	270
Coryell County	6,127	434	4,906	277	464	32	na	na	50	0	439	91
Dallas County	216,404	27,091	134,864	19,934	39,827	3,691	8,551	685	2,944	266	30,487	2,541
Denton County	50,590	4,958	42,132	4,272	1,858	363	2,559	35	757	24	3,475	264
Ector County	14,068	1,576	9,281	1,181	564	57	na	na	182	17	4,012	324
Ellis County	15,922	1,494	13,168	1,299	1,155	119	na	na	255	0	1,394	43
El Paso County	84,785	10,499	18,438	2,700	1,751	222	927	60	1,519	115	63,184	7,480
Fort Bend County	48,089	4,302	25,060	2,753	7,139	550	8,204	438	746	15	7,067	566
Galveston County	34,436	3,987	24,798	2,971	4,469	423	722	28	316	0	4,003	565
Grayson County	19,174	2,535	17,723	2,311	633	190	na	na	286	0	373	34
Gregg County	16,576	2,547	13,621	2,051	2,228	401	na	na	na	na	438	46
Guadalupe County	16,215	1,432	11,794	1,154	766	72	na	na	123	27	3,405	179
Harris County	351,983	39,951	196,985	27,234	60,526	5,676	22,896	1,459	3,684	266	68,460	5,185
Harrison County	9,151	1,096	6,921	854	1,946	233	na	na	na	na	250	9
Hays County	14,452	1,298	11,160	985	322	0	na	na	222	110	2,757	313
Henderson County	15,363	1,548	14,210	1,413	592	107	na	na	na	na	400	0
Hidalgo County	75,801	8,386	22,201	2,505	224	42	498	8	565	94	52,718	5,873
Hunt County	12,094	1,703	11,099	1,674	541	29	na	na	na	na	314	0
Jefferson County	32,227	4,403	20,995	3,290	8,527	808	583	38	286	22	1,924	255
Johnson County	18,258	1,550	16,403	1,440	397	32	na	na	182	0	1,142	91
Kaufman County	11,201	1,155	9,526	1,081	969	56	na	na	124	0	502	3
Liberty County	8,731	854	7,481	687	843	138	na	na	na	na	288	14
Lubbock County	31,501	3,853	24,253	3,223	1,684	199	304	0	300	17	5,111	464
McLennan County	30,023	4,469	23,498	3,698	3,384	432	188	31	224	64	2,674	273
Midland County	15,298	1,851	11,543	1,659	926	57	na	na	na	na	2,529	135
Montgomery County	51,133	5,195	45,214	4,840	1,293	163	713	74	479	44	3,285	60
Nacogdoches County	7,752	988	6,426	849	971	123	na	na	na	na	261	16
Nueces County	42,309	5,367	19,957	2,943	1,533	223	570	12	520	34	20,018	2,169
Orange County	11,617	1,287	10,438	1,209	795	66	na	na	na	na	285	12
Parker County	15,347	1,361	14,443	1,241	na	na	na	na	na	na	476	44
Potter County	13,436	1,993	10,251	1,860	769	45	351	0	290	29	1,844	59
Randall County	15,476	1,801	14,522	1,718	29	3	na	na	196	0	716	46
Rockwall County	8,153	528	7,330	417	281	75	na	na	na	na	301	0
San Patricio County	8,504	906	5,074	513	na	na	na	na	na	na	3,317	393
Smith County	30,979	4,509	25,302	3,794	3,910	515	na	na	308	0	1,123	173
Tarrant County	170,784	20,334	129,177	16,872	16,531	1,689	6,101	378	1,528	141	17,318	1,275
Taylor County	17,602	2,361	15,013	2,183	579	13	270	16	66	0	1,621	149
Tom Green County	15,541	1,628	11,963	1,123	419	36	na	na	na	na	2,958	427
Travis County	80,410	9,950	56,866	7,727	6,424	824	3,115	265	727	0	13,208	1,120
Victoria County	11,915	1,310	8,186	962	570	119	na	na	112	14	3,148	268
Walker County	7,162	677	5,842	579	969	66	na	na	na	na	260	32
Webb County	20,230	2,711	1,116	110	na	na	na	na	na	na	19,088	2,601
Wichita County	17,250	2,405	14,730	2,216	1,111	99	192	0	125	0	1,099	90
Williamson County	41,340	4,429	34,863	3,755	1,258	170	1,118	86	193	0	3,767	406
Utah												
Cache County	9,042	1,146	8,666	1,146	na	na	52	0	26	0	281	0
Davis County	26,297	3,013	24,518	2,878	190	0	427	10	147	41	1,002	59
Salt Lake County	92,822	11,735	82,773	10,705	338	33	2,671	319	780	77	5,820	542
Utah County	35,381	4,356	33,063	4,188	103	0	456	69	176	27	1,494	83
Washington County	25,428	3,421	24,298	3,298	na	na	na	na	na	na	813	77
Weber County	24,310	3,199	21,932	2,857	365	11	382	75	117	12	1,432	235
Vermont												
Chittenden County	18,518	2,866	17,919	2,791	115	3	371	40	23	3	82	0
Virginia												
Albemarle County	15,021	2,222	13,459	1,975	1,074	162	294	25	76	0	118	60
Arlington County	18,853	2,506	13,838	1,998	1,752	101	1,531	182	199	55	1,544	190
Augusta County	12,395	1,253	12,113	1,242	na	na	na	na	na	na	77	0
Bedford County	11,913	1,002	11,079	1,002	607	0	na	na	na	na	na	na
Chesterfield County	35,308	4,107	29,176	3,601	4,258	316	998	147	291	21	605	0
Fairfax County	113,056	12,982	81,149	10,704	6,207	471	16,859	1,073	1,999	153	7,088	598
Fauquier County	9,036	774	7,649	704	839	70	na	na	na	na	193	0
Frederick County	10,369	992	10,067	992	133	0	na	na	na	na	57	0
Hanover County	13,677	1,678	12,143	1,386	1,369	249	na	na	na	na	na	na
Henrico County	39,428	6,425	29,406	5,636	7,894	573	1,141	86	189	14	647	116
James City County	14,492	1,762	12,968	1,689	1,146	73	na	na	na	na	152	0
Loudoun County	22,693	2,244	16,941	1,953	1,449	125	2,627	69	434	84	1,223	13
Montgomery County	9,532	1,497	9,117	1,378	180	100	89	0	na	na	na	na
Prince William County	29,852	3,013	21,235	2,414	3,806	158	2,449	252	405	18	2,114	171
Roanoke County	16,586	2,136	15,694	2,042	546	77	na	na	na	na	na	na
Rockingham County	12,553	1,564	12,280	1,493	na	na	na	na	na	na	121	43
Spotsylvania County	12,889	1,411	10,803	1,346	1,574	45	133	0	126	0	172	20
Stafford County	10,202	1,006	8,518	873	1,070	88	250	45	37	0	239	0
York County	8,195	675	6,897	664	1,026	11	170	0	na	na	73	0

Table C-2: Counties—Older Population by Race and Hispanic Origin—*Continued*

	Total Population		White, Non-Hispanic		Black, Alone		Asian, Alone		Multi-race, Alone		Hispanic	
	65 Years and Over	85 Years and Over	65 Years and Over	85 Years and Over	65 Years and Over	85 Years and Over	65 Years and Over	85 Years and Over	65 Years and Over	85 Years and Over	65 Years and Over	85 Years and Over
Washington												
Benton County	21,734	2,623	19,698	2,591	na	na	na	na	197	0	956	18
Chelan County	11,278	1,842	10,935	1,834	na	na	na	na	na	na	154	6
Clallam County	17,599	2,484	16,793	2,437	na	na	na	na	222	0	173	47
Clark County	52,173	6,670	48,048	6,401	734	37	na	na	414	46	948	58
Cowlitz County	16,595	2,221	15,733	2,154	na	na	na	na	389	54	248	4
Franklin County	5,948	627	4,665	597	na	na	na	na	na	na	1,053	30
Grant County	11,007	1,305	9,332	1,212	na	na	na	na	225	39	1,101	32
Grays Harbor County	12,095	1,222	11,420	1,177	na	na	na	na	166	11	100	7
Island County	15,084	2,029	14,359	1,972	30	0	na	na	139	0	99	0
King County	221,540	34,760	176,093	29,498	9,014	1,011	na	na	2,778	356	5,283	738
Kitsap County	35,096	4,247	31,699	3,985	227	0	na	na	425	21	647	46
Lewis County	13,363	2,104	12,899	2,007	na	na	na	na	176	23	217	58
Pierce County	91,957	11,896	77,925	10,817	3,766	259	na	na	1,275	84	2,039	162
Skagit County	19,708	2,652	18,550	2,581	na	na	na	na	247	18	574	0
Snohomish County	77,984	10,667	68,572	9,873	687	155	na	na	716	42	1,656	189
Spokane County	63,283	8,679	59,931	8,499	364	0	na	na	851	51	836	48
Thurston County	34,479	4,483	31,316	4,275	362	17	na	na	415	85	661	86
Whatcom County	27,966	3,710	26,080	3,620	na	na	na	na	300	28	491	28
Yakima County	29,016	4,420	23,317	3,934	na	na	na	na	612	125	4,190	245
West Virginia												
Berkeley County	12,474	1,263	11,690	1,232	497	26	na	na	34	5	114	0
Cabell County	15,474	2,097	14,836	2,024	447	57	na	na	na	na	na	na
Harrison County	11,634	1,721	11,245	1,636	na	na	na	na	na	na	na	na
Kanawha County	32,705	4,259	30,503	4,101	935	94	na	na	766	42	219	18
Monongalia County	9,967	1,324	9,698	1,284	169	30	na	na	na	na	na	na
Raleigh County	12,926	1,400	11,904	1,281	719	105	na	na	na	na	na	na
Wood County	14,901	1,837	14,616	1,798	na	na	na	na	na	na	na	na
Wisconsin												
Brown County	29,647	4,781	28,622	4,665	30	0	na	na	195	33	367	51
Dane County	52,786	7,509	50,161	7,381	816	71	na	na	149	0	661	30
Dodge County	13,424	2,162	13,324	2,160	na	na	na	na	na	na	71	0
Eau Claire County	12,758	2,074	12,605	2,074	na	na	na	na	na	na	na	na
Fond du Lac County	15,621	2,830	15,345	2,778	na	na	na	na	na	na	122	27
Jefferson County	11,327	1,605	11,187	1,593	na	na	na	na	na	na	64	0
Kenosha County	19,059	2,949	17,861	2,927	503	5	na	na	24	0	549	17
La Crosse County	15,680	2,705	15,369	2,686	na	na	na	na	na	na	51	na
Manitowoc County	14,066	2,652	13,834	2,648	na	na	na	na	na	na	48	4
Marathon County	19,728	3,252	19,228	3,215	na	na	na	na	97	9	105	22
Milwaukee County	109,943	17,433	85,613	15,286	17,225	1,596	na	na	591	83	4,494	319
Outagamie County	21,424	3,166	20,728	3,114	na	na	na	na	96	20	211	28
Ozaukee County	13,648	1,899	13,272	1,893	na	na	na	na	na	na	84	6
Portage County	9,254	1,451	9,073	1,442	na	na	na	na	na	na	60	9
Racine County	26,333	3,575	23,544	3,366	1,606	191	na	na	76	0	901	18
Rock County	22,209	2,999	21,235	2,919	615	80	na	na	102	0	115	0
St. Croix County	8,892	1,039	8,843	1,039	na	na	na	na	na	na	na	na
Sheboygan County	17,184	2,993	16,763	2,935	na	na	na	na	na	na	202	44
Walworth County	14,110	2,215	13,780	2,197	na	na	na	na	na	na	183	7
Washington County	18,386	2,953	18,245	2,933	na	na	na	na	na	na	86	0
Waukesha County	57,878	8,728	56,057	8,537	335	0	na	na	204	28	519	112
Winnebago County	22,787	3,956	22,448	3,896	na	na	na	na	50	0	123	60
Wood County	12,944	2,098	12,703	2,089	na	na	na	na	na	na	54	0
Wyoming												
Laramie County	12,078	1,489	10,518	1,387	na	na	na	na	132	0	1,005	77
Natrona County	9,606	1,300	9,048	1,250	na	na	na	na	77	4	352	50

Table C-3: Places—Older Population by Race and Hispanic Origin

	Total Population		White, Non-Hispanic		Black, Alone		Asian, Alone		Multi-race, Alone		Hispanic	
	65 Years and Over	85 Years and Over	65 Years and Over	85 Years and Over	65 Years and Over	85 Years and Over	65 Years and Over	85 Years and Over	65 Years and Over	85 Years and Over	65 Years and Over	85 Years and Over
Alabama												
Birmingham city	27,055	4,215	8,236	1,744	18,260	2,449	na	na	na	na	228	38
Dothan city	9,820	1,109	7,678	871	1,925	211	na	na	53	9	90	14
Hoover city	9,964	1,241	9,284	1,222	369	19	244	0	na	na	23	0
Huntsville city	25,490	3,665	20,592	3,243	4,172	381	288	16	76	7	316	18
Mobile city	26,986	3,885	16,767	2,563	9,411	1,246	159	25	na	na	324	38
Montgomery city	24,541	3,096	15,027	1,987	8,780	1,003	323	0	131	20	307	86
Tuscaloosa city	9,472	1,507	6,120	1,030	3,064	441	na	na	na	na	na	na
Alaska												
Anchorage Municipality	22,770	1,770	16,582	1,227	868	95	2,208	297	635	0	915	76
Arizona												
Avondale city	4,497	293	2,373	204	229	5	na	na	na	na	1,761	84
Chandler city	20,345	2,299	15,981	2,005	747	88	1,183	103	312	1	2,085	102
Flagstaff city	4,470	584	3,581	493	na	na	na	na	74	0	557	54
Glendale city	20,935	2,434	16,144	2,053	736	117	857	68	263	8	2,798	175
Goodyear city	7,649	590	6,242	373	na	na	na	na	na	na	905	217
Mesa city	68,038	8,643	61,416	8,125	920	115	947	53	251	34	4,308	347
Peoria city	22,278	3,407	19,671	3,136	386	26	739	68	104	22	1,405	165
Phoenix city	129,033	15,505	94,852	12,549	7,629	741	3,614	231	1,221	53	21,191	1,854
Scottsdale city	45,320	6,449	42,968	6,260	275	32	649	41	100	0	1,096	116
Surprise city	23,403	1,587	21,495	1,479	517	37	na	na	na	na	1,118	71
Tempe city	13,752	1,951	10,977	1,696	344	19	723	34	162	0	1,551	159
Tucson city	64,634	9,624	43,798	7,483	1,999	210	1,274	50	798	70	16,671	1,821
Yuma city	12,260	1,235	8,748	874	91	4	na	na	120	20	2,998	318
Arkansas												
Fayetteville city	6,279	983	6,107	966	83	0	na	na	na	na	0	0
Fort Smith city	10,786	1,452	9,765	1,386	592	50	164	0	136	4	129	12
Jonesboro city	7,585	1,176	7,308	1,176	126	0	na	na	na	na	na	na
Little Rock city	22,904	3,427	16,343	2,617	5,504	769	451	0	na	na	359	0
Springdale city	6,179	978	5,919	956	na	na	na	na	na	na	156	22
California												
Alameda city	9,453	1,309	5,611	870	339	157	2,870	176	47	0	488	106
Alhambra city	12,420	2,319	2,464	590	na	na	6,639	1,111	116	0	3,220	608
Anaheim city	33,105	4,890	18,173	3,723	647	44	6,428	462	614	43	7,381	588
Antioch city	9,665	967	5,413	691	1,013	54	1,254	0	252	0	1,805	222
Bakersfield city	31,218	3,828	19,295	2,646	2,381	399	2,283	249	392	10	6,822	536
Baldwin Park city	6,939	903	837	273	na	na	1,829	308	13	13	4,040	266
Bellflower city	6,715	755	3,247	411	490	53	1,000	137	73	36	1,939	140
Berkeley city	14,291	2,062	9,690	1,250	1,975	415	1,662	337	246	0	817	74
Buena Park city	9,293	1,374	4,073	879	na	na	2,854	252	112	22	1,930	156
Burbank city	14,713	2,623	10,741	2,266	na	na	1,637	69	345	25	1,977	271
Camarillo city	11,587	2,216	9,140	1,871	na	na	805	122	198	0	1,322	199
Carlsbad city	16,155	2,843	13,513	2,468	na	na	1,305	82	127	15	1,287	293
Carson city	12,669	1,024	1,936	266	3,098	130	3,788	240	909	52	3,066	372
Chico city	9,386	1,554	8,310	1,407	na	na	218	25	231	24	510	93
Chino city	6,996	627	2,731	386	383	19	1,411	0	98	0	2,311	222
Chino Hills city	5,549	416	2,479	246	243	0	1,819	137	122	16	943	17
Chula Vista city	25,479	3,459	9,818	1,624	935	59	4,018	455	429	66	10,395	1,276
Citrus Heights city	11,689	1,476	9,875	1,280	na	na	na	na	200	0	882	93
Clovis city	10,801	1,412	7,778	1,174	na	na	897	72	157	9	1,463	116
Compton city	7,343	762	na	na	4,740	530	na	na	156	26	2,308	195
Concord city	14,897	2,171	10,943	1,732	453	23	1,734	273	304	7	1,421	138
Corona city	11,876	1,396	5,573	814	913	63	1,936	172	151	15	3,017	313
Costa Mesa city	9,871	1,796	7,896	1,541	na	na	653	55	138	28	1,031	127
Daly City city	13,905	2,039	3,595	972	747	70	7,515	830	279	18	1,843	167
Davis city	5,419	961	4,264	751	na	na	607	158	176	15	251	30
Downey city	11,636	1,915	5,001	1,017	265	46	1,254	87	133	0	5,128	765
El Cajon city	10,822	1,964	9,124	1,810	248	27	352	0	195	36	900	91
Elk Grove city	14,455	2,078	7,059	923	1,186	235	3,864	355	510	218	1,860	322
El Monte city	11,767	1,549	2,029	345	na	na	4,444	473	55	14	5,220	717
Escondido city	14,908	3,112	10,624	2,438	na	na	1,005	146	200	14	2,926	459
Fairfield city	11,320	1,181	6,010	814	1,570	98	2,339	197	307	8	1,035	64
Folsom city	6,807	1,145	5,602	1,029	na	na	689	71	103	0	264	20
Fontana city	12,111	1,790	3,349	602	1,337	181	1,354	218	263	0	5,840	789
Fremont city	24,028	3,434	10,897	2,113	465	39	9,815	825	685	153	2,292	431
Fresno city	46,667	7,248	26,545	4,907	2,860	312	4,910	582	1,112	297	11,686	1,278
Fullerton city	16,614	2,740	9,731	1,916	na	na	4,000	394	202	47	2,525	383
Garden Grove city	19,428	2,693	8,472	1,357	na	na	7,856	907	133	0	2,783	382
Glendale city	30,474	4,479	22,851	3,627	na	na	4,166	374	646	34	2,771	410
Hawthorne city	6,335	834	1,762	263	1,674	190	628	149	38	0	2,218	232
Hayward city	15,246	2,104	6,530	1,203	1,103	72	3,818	476	424	29	3,143	339
Hemet city	18,184	3,482	14,361	3,120	630	96	na	na	365	8	2,392	266
Hesperia city	9,075	1,009	5,971	705	357	80	na	na	110	0	2,376	183
Huntington Beach city	28,026	3,872	21,621	3,071	na	na	3,501	456	313	68	2,368	299
Indio city	10,563	1,105	6,853	657	410	36	na	na	na	na	3,074	345
Inglewood city	10,368	1,146	na	na	6,568	659	na	na	333	43	2,587	226
Irvine city	19,093	2,486	11,937	1,850	231	0	5,360	544	186	0	1,351	92
Jurupa Valley city[1]	7,366	743	3,854	459	416	29	300	59	149	0	2,679	196

[1] Jurupa Valley city was incorporated in 2011. The 2010 population is the U.S. Census Bureau's estimates base figure.

Table C-3: Places—Older Population by Race and Hispanic Origin—*Continued*

	Total Population		White, Non-Hispanic		Black, Alone		Asian, Alone		Multi-race, Alone		Hispanic	
	65 Years and Over	85 Years and Over	65 Years and Over	85 Years and Over	65 Years and Over	85 Years and Over	65 Years and Over	85 Years and Over	65 Years and Over	85 Years and Over	65 Years and Over	85 Years and Over
California—Cont.												
Lake Forest city	7,983	902	5,446	807	na	na	979	56	69	0	1,262	39
Lakewood city	9,689	1,347	5,827	1,054	452	32	1,848	112	146	14	1,420	135
Lancaster city	13,509	1,670	7,977	1,336	1,881	150	803	58	261	0	2,585	121
Livermore city	8,659	1,041	6,886	899	na	na	956	46	71	0	638	76
Long Beach city	44,044	6,108	24,000	4,382	4,220	343	7,283	803	1,006	111	7,573	574
Los Angeles city	409,228	59,670	187,977	32,930	48,048	6,736	64,348	8,789	8,860	727	101,958	10,747
Lynwood city	4,566	590	na	na	879	88	na	na	na	na	3,244	369
Manteca city	7,028	929	5,062	626	199	14	454	48	227	0	1,102	241
Menifee city	14,490	1,902	11,040	1,674	749	71	391	0	na	na	2,202	157
Merced city	7,293	1,106	4,363	683	391	32	451	34	192	0	1,893	344
Milpitas city	6,720	511	1,504	45	na	na	4,253	425	146	0	755	49
Mission Viejo city	14,202	2,122	12,087	1,880	na	na	704	70	249	0	1,003	92
Modesto city	23,450	3,861	17,241	3,003	641	95	1,477	115	566	62	3,461	570
Moreno Valley city	13,129	1,386	4,916	775	2,026	92	1,282	99	284	14	4,680	411
Mountain View city	8,170	1,221	4,833	804	na	na	2,059	219	121	0	806	130
Murrieta city	10,502	966	7,640	672	276	0	889	42	92	0	1,616	252
Napa city	10,631	1,806	9,170	1,567	na	na	na	na	na	na	930	200
Newport Beach city	16,120	2,363	14,867	2,294	na	na	559	25	36	0	597	44
Norwalk city	10,583	1,423	2,965	722	433	0	1,983	228	230	3	5,064	470
Oakland city	45,885	7,390	14,615	2,777	14,735	2,477	11,311	1,603	927	103	4,323	463
Oceanside city	20,928	3,621	15,065	3,134	599	126	1,649	81	302	32	3,086	248
Ontario city	12,289	1,393	4,418	867	1,143	1	722	80	343	23	5,799	445
Orange city	15,186	1,874	10,480	1,465	na	na	2,333	176	189	1	1,898	208
Oxnard city	16,693	1,956	6,243	857	579	31	2,643	217	398	13	7,115	838
Palmdale city	10,733	1,377	5,276	793	1,133	47	593	15	248	53	3,386	481
Palo Alto city	11,296	2,206	8,932	1,925	na	na	1,761	180	na	na	297	37
Pasadena city	19,249	4,120	10,563	2,599	2,253	373	2,610	602	281	69	3,580	499
Perris city	3,126	149	906	49	450	20	na	na	na	na	1,518	75
Pleasanton city	8,045	934	6,353	774	na	na	884	101	51	0	552	51
Pomona city	12,054	1,763	3,571	724	1,746	159	1,614	359	316	107	4,966	508
Rancho Cordova city	7,156	925	4,768	601	622	72	909	74	102	35	649	143
Rancho Cucamonga city	13,966	1,935	7,275	798	776	114	1,756	197	460	37	3,981	809
Redding city	14,970	2,393	13,844	2,269	na	na	266	28	221	16	468	59
Redlands city	9,027	1,511	6,690	1,222	na	na	349	21	71	0	1,624	187
Redondo Beach city	7,620	819	5,530	586	na	na	562	135	256	0	1,070	98
Redwood City city	8,680	1,597	6,071	1,328	na	na	795	138	187	49	1,546	79
Rialto city	7,428	527	2,872	298	1,639	0	na	na	60	0	2,612	229
Richmond city	10,244	1,225	3,366	568	3,545	521	1,938	83	216	17	1,126	77
Riverside city	28,686	4,001	16,750	2,641	2,341	337	1,904	300	618	18	7,263	705
Roseville city	16,337	1,966	13,541	1,725	na	na	938	69	142	5	1,405	159
Sacramento city	52,625	8,441	27,699	5,247	6,336	703	10,588	1,516	1,167	129	6,542	852
Salinas city	11,562	1,609	5,128	999	na	na	1,525	316	144	1	4,581	290
San Bernardino city	17,189	1,917	7,099	798	2,309	256	1,339	104	457	25	6,322	773
San Buenaventura (Ventura) city	15,430	2,802	12,397	2,471	na	na	435	49	151	30	2,299	252
San Diego city	145,264	21,880	88,984	15,658	8,045	957	23,083	2,382	2,112	160	23,332	2,781
San Francisco city	112,614	18,043	45,142	8,073	7,494	1,028	47,823	7,180	2,008	204	10,425	1,726
San Jose city	101,942	12,782	46,070	6,480	2,379	226	34,012	4,056	2,611	372	17,429	1,653
San Leandro city	11,556	2,141	5,768	1,387	867	131	3,351	313	395	91	1,210	236
San Marcos city	9,526	1,650	7,743	1,389	na	na	598	86	99	0	870	147
San Mateo city	14,337	2,857	9,332	2,202	na	na	2,961	402	308	77	1,399	164
San Ramon city	5,414	554	3,384	515	na	na	1,491	39	na	na	350	0
Santa Ana city	21,887	3,035	5,995	1,305	448	65	4,622	383	495	44	10,498	1,300
Santa Barbara city	12,493	2,791	9,596	2,290	na	na	na	na	112	19	2,277	340
Santa Clara city	10,904	1,697	6,892	1,398	98	13	2,376	165	191	0	1,378	121
Santa Clarita city	17,699	2,495	12,824	1,967	429	54	1,325	121	391	71	2,780	282
Santa Maria city	9,627	1,527	5,531	1,012	na	na	800	115	157	41	2,894	298
Santa Monica city	13,554	2,290	10,797	1,911	441	36	762	94	325	2	1,202	247
Santa Rosa city	22,290	4,090	19,613	3,792	217	19	594	75	194	15	1,607	189
Simi Valley city	13,589	1,458	10,817	1,173	na	na	1,077	128	366	46	1,250	83
South Gate city	7,413	656	905	176	na	na	na	na	na	na	6,358	480
Stockton city	29,433	4,067	12,674	2,057	2,984	398	7,116	755	847	131	6,016	788
Sunnyvale city	15,785	2,265	9,622	1,569	na	na	4,380	422	248	0	1,436	254
Temecula city	7,753	761	4,954	492	na	na	569	42	239	28	2,049	199
Thousand Oaks city	19,008	3,009	15,804	2,815	na	na	1,427	79	198	0	1,537	115
Torrance city	23,091	3,762	14,320	2,674	232	48	5,899	739	240	21	2,208	217
Tracy city	6,457	462	3,001	364	435	10	773	40	352	0	1,824	48
Turlock city	8,097	1,378	6,471	1,125	na	na	313	28	191	45	1,045	177
Tustin city	6,411	541	4,073	453	na	na	969	14	131	11	1,054	43
Union City city	8,138	906	1,973	230	374	20	4,120	402	245	2	1,325	252
Upland city	9,783	1,009	6,291	690	291	0	1,264	22	219	0	1,819	297
Vacaville city	10,020	1,140	6,863	925	954	65	511	55	241	26	1,545	95
Vallejo city	14,248	2,194	5,693	1,144	2,313	332	4,524	572	242	0	1,492	128
Victorville city	8,740	756	4,243	474	1,221	25	593	57	83	0	2,644	187
Visalia city	13,600	1,932	9,653	1,463	190	0	683	44	257	9	2,909	416
Vista city	9,276	1,884	6,690	1,496	na	na	678	59	281	57	1,593	297
West Covina city	13,044	2,496	4,532	1,221	591	124	4,017	556	184	12	3,903	583
Westminster city	13,711	1,585	6,261	869	na	na	5,998	556	28	0	1,389	151
Whittier city	10,111	2,000	5,955	1,321	na	na	473	134	177	0	3,468	542
Yorba Linda city	8,296	1,187	6,183	945	na	na	1,267	117	62	23	665	102
Yuba City city	8,258	1,025	5,501	779	na	na	1,540	68	251	0	808	130

Table C-3: Places—Older Population by Race and Hispanic Origin—*Continued*

	Total Population		White, Non-Hispanic		Black, Alone		Asian, Alone		Multi-race, Alone		Hispanic	
	65 Years and Over	85 Years and Over	65 Years and Over	85 Years and Over	65 Years and Over	85 Years and Over	65 Years and Over	85 Years and Over	65 Years and Over	85 Years and Over	65 Years and Over	85 Years and Over
Colorado												
Arvada city	15,811	1,979	14,428	1,847	na	na	na	na	na	na	1,035	50
Aurora city	31,056	3,774	23,294	3,229	2,850	190	1,637	180	569	22	2,692	153
Boulder city	9,220	1,627	8,575	1,560	na	na	252	0	37	6	284	61
Centennial city	12,784	1,707	11,558	1,583	na	na	429	46	147	0	398	42
Colorado Springs city	46,940	6,184	39,879	5,696	1,765	151	1,327	121	571	56	3,536	200
Denver city	64,482	10,683	43,286	8,391	7,118	956	2,017	171	778	161	11,425	1,060
Fort Collins city	12,635	2,112	11,578	2,038	na	na	259	18	78	10	685	46
Greeley city	10,300	1,479	8,609	1,409	na	na	na	na	151	0	1,414	41
Lakewood city	20,892	3,100	18,513	2,681	93	32	604	66	118	40	1,453	281
Longmont city	9,902	1,561	8,911	1,409	na	na	112	0	na	na	734	100
Loveland city	9,856	1,590	9,484	1,567	na	na	na	na	na	na	301	23
Pueblo city	16,758	2,443	10,464	1,714	344	84	na	na	340	0	5,738	572
Thornton city	8,618	1,164	6,235	954	na	na	482	152	99	21	1,642	58
Westminster city	10,579	1,259	8,807	1,069	na	na	627	20	206	0	1,065	170
Connecticut												
Bridgeport city	14,345	2,483	6,883	1,882	4,352	344	249	0	82	0	3,002	315
Danbury city	9,665	1,548	7,746	1,426	565	24	325	41	121	0	985	57
Hartford city	11,758	1,679	3,570	938	4,322	484	211	0	352	16	3,665	263
New Britain city	8,955	1,782	7,002	1,639	583	63	72	13	96	26	1,228	67
New Haven city	12,721	2,035	6,564	1,457	4,010	461	240	0	205	14	1,772	108
Norwalk city	13,131	1,737	10,362	1,589	1,301	65	467	0	na	na	941	58
Stamford city	15,640	2,359	11,220	1,993	1,995	152	826	56	na	na	1,613	148
Waterbury city	13,192	2,577	9,570	2,316	2,080	156	na	na	79	0	1,385	72
Delaware												
Wilmington city	8,612	1,553	3,949	1,005	4,105	506	na	na	45	19	413	23
District of Columbia												
Washington city	70,302	10,229	21,878	3,347	43,449	6,305	1,386	253	884	120	3,032	253
Florida												
Boca Raton city	18,213	2,570	16,348	2,288	409	213	na	na	na	na	1,107	48
Boynton Beach city	15,058	3,607	12,472	3,204	1,461	236	na	na	na	na	951	149
Cape Coral city	28,419	3,741	24,855	3,383	609	68	na	na	na	na	2,484	261
Clearwater city	22,702	3,738	19,924	3,405	1,459	47	na	na	na	na	958	265
Coral Springs city	11,224	1,198	7,676	890	962	164	367	0	na	na	1,980	144
Deerfield Beach city	16,216	3,112	13,544	2,857	1,742	112	na	na	na	na	720	126
Deltona city	11,849	1,861	7,293	1,204	1,302	291	na	na	na	na	3,038	215
Fort Lauderdale city	26,951	4,344	19,549	3,577	4,984	368	na	na	194	0	2,040	358
Gainesville city	10,455	1,682	8,092	1,373	1,868	278	188	0	0	0	292	31
Hialeah city	44,087	6,098	1,625	528	455	56	na	na	na	na	42,104	5,547
Hollywood city	21,619	3,033	14,659	2,513	1,803	83	391	0	375	11	4,924	444
Jacksonville city	93,702	12,180	65,954	9,370	19,709	2,141	3,379	172	934	123	3,910	390
Lakeland city	20,211	3,282	17,147	2,941	1,768	258	246	0	na	na	1,023	32
Largo city	19,339	3,488	18,180	3,363	193	46	246	0	na	na	521	45
Lauderhill city	8,352	1,310	3,071	963	4,504	304	na	na	na	na	286	43
Melbourne city	15,941	2,388	13,913	2,271	918	18	na	na	na	na	675	26
Miami city	63,854	9,411	5,875	1,217	9,056	757	488	15	624	58	49,658	7,445
Miami Beach city	13,634	2,435	4,888	880	379	14	na	na	na	na	8,374	1,508
Miami Gardens city	12,253	1,279	na	na	8,197	827	na	na	na	na	3,198	315
Miramar city	9,310	788	1,469	224	3,555	192	465	0	223	0	3,622	408
Orlando city	23,034	2,894	11,763	2,025	4,910	383	758	59	289	12	5,767	452
Palm Bay city	17,017	2,136	12,389	1,678	2,372	288	na	na	na	na	2,106	170
Palm Coast city	18,519	2,312	14,384	1,716	2,361	470	na	na	na	na	1,102	103
Pembroke Pines city	23,684	3,633	12,032	2,647	2,128	185	832	0	161	0	8,569	836
Plantation city	12,514	2,194	8,961	1,710	1,792	366	135	0	na	na	1,718	233
Pompano Beach city	18,895	3,823	14,985	3,420	2,441	217	na	na	na	na	1,120	118
Port St. Lucie city	27,137	3,543	20,872	3,010	2,699	193	na	na	265	0	2,972	352
St. Petersburg city	39,307	5,585	30,336	4,589	5,836	550	965	150	207	22	1,948	274
Sunrise city	13,096	2,669	7,559	2,071	2,408	162	431	78	na	na	2,589	371
Tallahassee city	15,094	2,654	10,878	2,201	3,478	332	268	11	84	35	355	75
Tampa city	37,392	4,937	19,975	3,114	7,759	602	1,078	37	461	34	8,652	1,166
Weston city	5,107	490	2,974	435	na	na	na	na	na	na	1,853	16
West Palm Beach city	17,472	3,081	12,098	2,027	3,520	617	na	na	na	na	1,689	454
Georgia												
Albany city	9,071	1,327	4,551	742	4,224	567	na	na	na	na	na	na
Athens-Clarke County unified govt (bal)	10,227	1,193	7,199	904	2,406	221	218	0	na	na	348	68
Atlanta city	42,135	6,528	14,288	2,998	26,490	3,476	552	0	263	0	525	54
Augusta-Richmond County consolidated govt (bal)	22,892	2,515	12,594	1,777	9,079	692	464	17	270	29	563	24
Columbus city	22,292	2,991	13,678	2,084	7,645	838	429	30	216	0	343	39
Johns Creek city	6,064	596	4,222	462	493	29	1,066	105	na	na	na	na
Macon city	10,879	1,599	5,457	1,146	5,308	453	na	na	na	na	na	na
Roswell city	10,779	1,201	9,473	1,082	922	119	248	0	na	na	80	0
Sandy Springs city	10,701	1,799	9,474	1,682	542	32	331	0	na	na	259	55
Savannah city	16,493	3,137	8,392	1,996	7,671	1,087	210	27	0	0	186	27
Warner Robins city	6,794	822	5,098	678	1,327	144	na	na	na	na	178	0
Hawaii												
Urban Honolulu CDP	61,534	12,364	10,049	1,394	251	27	44,175	10,155	4,261	575	912	133

Table C-3: Places—Older Population by Race and Hispanic Origin—*Continued*

	Total Population		White, Non-Hispanic		Black, Alone		Asian, Alone		Multi-race, Alone		Hispanic	
	65 Years and Over	85 Years and Over	65 Years and Over	85 Years and Over	65 Years and Over	85 Years and Over	65 Years and Over	85 Years and Over	65 Years and Over	85 Years and Over	65 Years and Over	85 Years and Over
Idaho												
Boise City city	25,172	4,013	23,858	3,875	35	0	538	53	187	85	519	0
Meridian city	7,160	1,007	6,890	942	na	na	na	na	na	na	138	44
Nampa city	9,107	1,151	8,256	1,115	na	na	na	na	na	na	665	33
Illinois												
Aurora city	13,273	1,619	8,330	1,162	1,318	108	715	76	230	60	2,795	237
Bloomington city	7,892	1,595	7,212	1,538	378	57	156	0	na	na	102	0
Champaign city	6,868	889	5,654	796	782	93	290	0	na	na	109	0
Chicago city	283,041	39,266	115,774	21,399	107,284	12,501	16,142	2,065	3,322	252	41,488	3,114
Decatur city	12,738	2,292	11,080	2,176	1,516	110	na	na	na	na	na	na
Elgin city	9,899	1,562	8,043	1,420	466	60	280	0	59	47	1,081	53
Evanston city	8,471	1,518	6,390	1,217	1,620	264	203	37	na	na	238	0
Joliet city	12,914	2,234	9,898	1,991	1,394	148	na	na	146	0	1,271	95
Naperville city	13,911	2,035	11,324	1,859	266	7	2,035	169	24	0	220	0
Peoria city	15,110	2,618	12,441	2,379	2,135	196	242	13	35	5	230	25
Rockford city	21,231	3,876	17,582	3,694	2,263	91	411	17	136	20	799	54
Springfield city	17,300	3,348	15,465	3,161	1,454	110	139	16	106	26	133	61
Waukegan city	6,856	947	3,709	688	1,293	119	318	5	122	0	1,477	135
Indiana												
Bloomington city	6,568	1,181	6,178	1,127	na	na	166	12	na	na	na	na
Carmel city	8,755	1,293	8,211	1,250	na	na	388	0	na	na	na	na
Evansville city	17,435	3,404	15,866	3,117	1,325	285	na	na	62	0	141	2
Fort Wayne city	31,474	4,975	27,047	4,677	3,104	198	421	46	199	0	645	54
Gary city	11,937	1,545	1,363	283	10,058	1,186	na	na	na	na	449	68
Hammond city	8,463	1,322	5,827	1,134	1,220	90	na	na	108	8	1,275	90
Indianapolis city (bal)	87,255	12,227	64,640	9,685	19,348	2,258	1,086	48	769	73	1,369	163
Lafayette city	7,667	1,316	7,421	1,316	43	0	na	na	na	na	110	0
Muncie city	9,225	1,107	8,466	1,028	557	60	na	na	104	14	na	na
South Bend city	13,094	2,537	10,466	2,248	2,074	275	na	na	36	6	391	8
Iowa												
Cedar Rapids city	16,511	2,866	16,042	2,758	159	3	124	63	na	na	160	42
Davenport city	12,567	2,144	11,307	2,071	714	3	212	28	23	0	346	42
Des Moines city	22,311	3,621	19,593	3,460	1,403	98	614	63	105	0	537	14
Iowa City city	5,764	1,101	5,484	1,058	70	43	129	0	na	na	45	0
Sioux City city	10,655	1,834	9,846	1,762	99	31	312	0	na	na	253	41
Waterloo city	9,540	1,552	8,549	1,426	913	113	na	na	na	na	78	13
Kansas												
Kansas City city	15,660	2,464	9,548	1,673	4,380	619	264	47	258	42	1,269	112
Lawrence city	6,860	1,095	6,240	1,023	216	0	184	45	59	0	32	0
Olathe city	9,361	1,397	8,381	1,353	311	44	307	0	117	0	208	0
Overland Park city	22,704	4,042	20,812	3,737	352	51	681	60	214	102	595	96
Topeka city	18,080	2,862	15,233	2,535	1,373	154	185	0	320	11	883	162
Wichita city	44,713	6,658	36,994	6,147	3,529	234	1,464	0	660	116	1,987	157
Kentucky												
Lexington-Fayette urban county	32,142	4,219	27,686	3,846	3,423	323	506	22	169	0	358	21
Louisville/Jefferson County metro govt (bal)	76,756	10,904	62,834	9,507	11,626	1,212	768	64	514	56	913	65
Louisiana												
Baton Rouge city	25,953	4,038	14,476	2,642	10,320	1,347	397	10	266	0	539	39
Kenner city	8,989	1,044	5,839	772	1,468	136	na	na	na	na	1,399	98
Lafayette city	15,071	1,863	11,705	1,581	2,918	280	na	na	na	na	263	2
Lake Charles city	10,116	1,303	6,265	925	3,346	323	na	na	na	na	na	na
New Orleans city	40,109	5,790	14,833	2,730	22,648	2,826	830	91	424	31	1,438	110
Shreveport city	25,931	4,108	15,090	2,722	10,095	1,335	237	0	172	0	266	51
Maine												
Portland city	7,905	1,623	7,521	1,623	141	0	124	0	na	na	51	0
Maryland												
Baltimore city	73,112	10,078	26,097	4,728	44,549	5,018	917	104	597	85	844	119
Frederick city	7,338	1,194	6,139	1,138	678	25	268	31	na	na	243	0
Massachusetts												
Boston city	64,953	10,277	36,316	6,611	16,022	2,033	5,785	811	1,480	175	6,054	703
Brockton city	12,044	1,989	8,352	1,576	2,505	215	227	10	292	74	457	40
Cambridge city	11,565	1,771	8,717	1,442	1,479	173	726	133	333	10	334	23
Fall River city	13,631	2,370	13,155	2,331	na	na	na	na	111	39	195	0
Lawrence city	6,343	1,211	3,096	834	264	8	223	48	128	28	2,924	312
Lowell city	11,483	1,707	9,099	1,526	398	0	1,131	128	120	21	732	32
Lynn city	10,377	1,713	8,168	1,560	740	61	257	49	151	43	1,212	60
New Bedford city	14,345	2,906	12,303	2,589	500	86	na	na	324	66	610	58
Newton city	13,415	2,629	12,370	2,563	na	na	601	11	34	0	163	40
Quincy city	13,476	2,277	11,015	2,189	225	6	2,003	41	na	na	110	41
Somerville city	6,386	825	5,618	796	112	8	254	7	na	na	310	14
Springfield city	16,969	2,477	10,341	2,038	3,189	195	457	0	282	0	2,834	207
Worcester city	22,688	4,556	19,066	4,369	757	72	887	71	228	0	1,789	87

Table C-3: Places—Older Population by Race and Hispanic Origin—*Continued*

	Total Population		White, Non-Hispanic		Black, Alone		Asian, Alone		Multi-race, Alone		Hispanic	
	65 Years and Over	85 Years and Over	65 Years and Over	85 Years and Over	65 Years and Over	85 Years and Over	65 Years and Over	85 Years and Over	65 Years and Over	85 Years and Over	65 Years and Over	85 Years and Over
Michigan												
Ann Arbor city	11,510	1,678	9,354	1,470	956	170	807	18	138	20	374	20
Dearborn city	10,963	2,226	9,874	2,017	443	132	195	26	154	9	290	42
Detroit city	83,776	12,635	11,362	1,914	68,303	10,251	658	133	1,028	100	2,280	225
Farmington Hills city	13,051	1,935	11,073	1,767	1,288	160	375	8	146	0	140	0
Flint city	11,621	1,276	5,028	593	6,053	677	na	na	187	0	333	6
Grand Rapids city	20,717	4,314	16,480	3,778	2,789	359	224	0	364	19	931	158
Kalamazoo city	7,034	1,813	5,729	1,537	1,055	158	na	na	na	na	74	39
Lansing city	11,568	1,368	8,386	1,210	1,829	69	247	19	219	41	855	29
Livonia city	17,210	2,586	16,129	2,479	436	41	362	16	54	0	178	31
Rochester Hills city	9,690	1,926	8,919	1,870	143	0	439	38	na	na	100	18
Southfield city	12,822	2,761	5,076	1,845	7,234	879	na	na	331	23	na	na
Sterling Heights city	20,459	3,104	19,002	3,050	163	0	771	47	293	7	174	0
Troy city	11,601	1,321	10,012	1,253	144	18	1,251	50	94	0	na	na
Warren city	20,880	3,745	19,573	3,600	696	84	350	24	67	6	160	31
Westland city	12,300	1,989	10,702	1,875	899	83	275	0	na	na	212	0
Wyoming city	6,393	725	5,623	725	172	0	252	0	na	na	289	0
Minnesota												
Bloomington city	15,767	2,109	14,991	2,032	229	0	326	34	30	0	187	27
Brooklyn Park city	6,201	716	5,084	657	486	0	541	59	na	na	108	0
Duluth city	12,126	2,298	11,726	2,274	24	0	na	na	53	12	na	na
Minneapolis city	33,141	5,755	26,520	5,093	4,305	368	1,103	142	366	51	645	94
Plymouth city	9,006	941	8,605	902	132	23	111	0	na	na	na	na
Rochester city	14,063	2,346	13,102	2,180	198	74	509	60	121	26	163	6
St. Cloud city	7,113	1,228	6,916	1,157	39	0	na	na	na	na	na	na
St. Paul city	25,859	3,992	20,678	3,397	2,088	93	1,737	342	300	16	1,043	126
Mississippi												
Gulfport city	8,328	1,048	5,815	714	2,190	318	na	na	na	na	175	16
Jackson city	17,946	2,733	7,352	1,335	10,300	1,321	na	na	na	na	na	na
Missouri												
Columbia city	9,767	1,597	8,668	1,549	647	23	334	2	96	23	22	0
Independence city	19,094	3,373	17,879	3,203	508	69	na	na	217	51	312	37
Kansas City city	51,827	7,534	34,511	5,711	13,283	1,468	1,008	36	566	39	2,469	286
Lee's Summit city	10,904	1,814	10,251	1,706	372	82	na	na	na	na	103	0
O'Fallon city	7,534	1,035	7,217	1,035	149	0	na	na	na	na	na	na
St. Charles city	8,779	1,458	8,494	1,407	170	39	na	na	na	na	na	na
St. Joseph city	10,467	1,840	10,028	1,697	236	95	na	na	59	0	121	34
St. Louis city	35,423	4,963	17,044	2,806	16,665	1,950	721	51	328	57	705	99
Springfield city	23,361	4,624	22,504	4,447	336	45	139	23	232	86	117	17
Montana												
Billings city	15,711	2,656	15,154	2,609	na	na	na	na	na	na	249	22
Missoula city	7,567	1,522	7,443	1,499	na	na	na	na	na	na	na	na
Nebraska												
Lincoln city	28,702	4,577	27,148	4,429	246	17	622	77	147	24	501	20
Omaha city	47,588	7,789	41,138	7,220	4,442	439	437	33	193	16	1,413	86
Nevada												
Henderson city	39,860	3,196	31,875	2,585	1,874	150	3,131	162	334	0	2,433	298
Las Vegas city	76,125	7,863	53,052	6,323	7,732	542	5,414	352	1,322	95	8,675	567
North Las Vegas city	16,146	1,206	9,130	924	3,324	153	957	17	344	8	2,352	91
Reno city	27,363	3,568	22,930	3,265	452	74	1,331	56	316	14	2,183	152
Sparks city	11,064	1,156	9,017	988	na	na	643	59	370	78	862	30
New Hampshire												
Manchester city	13,356	2,382	12,445	2,335	106	34	352	0	100	13	345	0
Nashua city	11,070	1,679	10,316	1,635	na	na	246	0	na	na	301	22
New Jersey												
Camden city	6,136	734	586	153	3,477	423	na	na	189	24	2,005	134
Clifton city	10,870	2,039	7,783	1,773	110	6	1,001	59	154	0	1,768	151
Elizabeth city	11,610	1,772	4,138	939	2,413	370	277	0	na	na	4,865	558
Jersey City city	23,305	2,378	7,168	1,153	6,137	431	4,073	348	474	25	5,644	497
Newark city	23,183	2,822	4,373	973	12,789	1,346	275	14	574	51	5,880	489
Passaic city	5,511	919	1,959	513	1,036	204	na	na	na	na	2,335	145
Paterson city	13,595	1,163	2,675	380	4,762	311	224	0	749	85	6,395	504
Trenton city	7,408	975	2,393	611	4,185	338	na	na	na	na	844	58
Union City city	6,546	972	950	285	na	na	na	na	na	na	5,394	666
New Mexico												
Albuquerque city	68,343	9,424	43,994	6,657	1,551	116	1,426	226	789	47	19,891	2,279
Las Cruces city	12,947	1,714	8,035	1,238	na	na	na	na	274	0	4,342	439
Rio Rancho city	10,191	1,465	7,737	1,088	131	48	na	na	239	31	2,010	298
Santa Fe city	13,122	1,715	8,252	1,175	na	na	na	na	260	20	4,456	457

Table C-3: Places—Older Population by Race and Hispanic Origin—*Continued*

	Total Population		White, Non-Hispanic		Black, Alone		Asian, Alone		Multi-race, Alone		Hispanic	
	65 Years and Over	85 Years and Over	65 Years and Over	85 Years and Over	65 Years and Over	85 Years and Over	65 Years and Over	85 Years and Over	65 Years and Over	85 Years and Over	65 Years and Over	85 Years and Over
New York												
Albany city	11,910	2,253	9,110	1,953	2,332	219	278	31	70	0	144	50
Buffalo city	30,087	4,041	17,853	2,923	10,078	980	500	3	389	61	1,209	100
Mount Vernon city	9,071	1,565	2,992	944	5,472	582	na	na	84	0	395	63
New Rochelle city	11,017	2,116	7,671	1,682	2,000	309	262	0	229	14	956	111
New York city	1,019,436	145,568	471,129	85,553	237,167	29,377	105,790	10,563	19,163	2,073	207,263	20,425
Rochester city	19,383	3,264	11,028	2,422	6,136	584	349	66	209	15	1,834	188
Schenectady city	7,846	1,514	6,549	1,438	855	37	87	8	154	31	192	0
Syracuse city	15,206	3,069	11,197	2,653	2,920	354	385	0	287	55	317	30
Yonkers city	29,033	4,688	19,257	3,821	3,118	317	1,652	90	408	78	5,228	444
North Carolina												
Asheville city	13,344	2,661	11,696	2,317	1,417	313	na	na	na	na	150	4
Charlotte city	66,451	8,959	43,778	7,177	17,811	1,692	1,934	37	515	0	2,454	76
Concord city	8,978	923	7,647	815	1,007	85	na	na	na	na	145	0
Durham city	21,670	3,571	12,131	2,672	8,169	872	699	0	310	11	352	16
Fayetteville city	20,201	2,112	10,884	1,281	7,772	628	628	64	240	15	635	54
Gastonia city	8,484	1,366	6,781	966	1,647	400	na	na	na	na	12	0
Greensboro city	32,361	4,244	22,350	3,258	8,492	895	863	59	150	0	385	52
Greenville city	6,505	1,372	4,275	1,021	1,971	326	122	0	na	na	49	0
High Point city	12,556	1,833	9,554	1,572	2,536	235	167	18	na	na	243	0
Jacksonville city	4,449	617	3,146	346	787	185	na	na	na	na	288	86
Raleigh city	35,242	4,879	25,763	4,105	7,165	663	1,242	51	123	27	946	33
Wilmington city	14,784	2,122	11,957	1,708	2,471	363	na	na	na	na	80	10
Winston-Salem city	29,362	4,301	20,741	3,484	7,878	752	223	37	94	13	403	15
North Dakota												
Fargo city	10,971	1,612	10,576	1,612	20	0	na	na	na	na	47	0
Ohio												
Akron city	25,344	4,112	18,375	3,259	6,320	769	231	14	169	50	204	20
Canton city	9,790	1,909	7,846	1,627	1,683	183	na	na	90	47	na	na
Cincinnati city	32,832	5,547	18,949	3,720	13,154	1,740	229	72	189	15	260	0
Cleveland city	48,737	7,009	21,124	3,853	24,437	2,852	676	64	427	79	2,133	171
Columbus city	70,515	9,546	50,264	7,524	16,829	1,815	1,856	132	684	44	974	31
Dayton city	16,744	2,689	9,167	1,405	7,209	1,222	na	na	139	42	173	20
Parma city	14,696	2,824	14,124	2,749	na	na	na	na	na	na	191	44
Toledo city	34,360	4,929	26,095	4,234	6,709	597	335	14	354	10	941	74
Youngstown city	10,353	1,921	6,087	1,308	3,813	532	na	na	52	11	425	70
Oklahoma												
Broken Arrow city	10,776	1,328	9,693	1,251	172	23	177	0	296	46	238	3
Edmond city	9,480	1,028	8,792	975	119	23	209	5	178	25	132	0
Lawton city	9,600	1,093	7,015	941	1,270	40	na	na	257	0	448	69
Norman city	12,427	1,495	11,310	1,421	227	0	91	14	290	20	260	30
Oklahoma City city	66,315	8,999	51,612	7,587	7,373	841	1,966	98	1,601	183	2,815	273
Tulsa city	49,615	7,746	40,251	6,711	4,950	539	717	54	1,252	165	1,262	139
Oregon												
Beaverton city	9,789	1,565	8,232	1,391	57	0	1,191	148	84	26	238	0
Bend city	11,329	1,938	10,870	1,885	na	na	na	na	na	na	265	0
Eugene city	20,946	3,549	19,634	3,500	na	na	326	0	303	31	583	49
Gresham city	12,008	1,923	10,653	1,810	207	1	603	108	107	4	378	0
Hillsboro city	7,310	955	6,273	907	na	na	473	20	97	0	385	28
Medford city	12,388	2,162	11,746	2,133	na	na	na	na	na	na	285	0
Portland city	63,475	11,012	53,185	9,957	3,264	465	4,504	495	645	25	1,522	65
Salem city	20,075	2,983	18,353	2,843	na	na	489	79	146	18	912	43
Pennsylvania												
Allentown city	13,948	2,574	11,132	2,283	675	42	na	na	119	37	1,949	176
Bethlehem city	11,027	2,310	9,754	2,204	242	0	126	30	54	0	915	76
Erie city	13,250	2,516	11,830	2,333	1,020	122	25	0	116	0	199	61
Philadelphia city	186,585	28,788	94,380	17,880	74,099	9,404	7,625	536	1,845	370	9,543	716
Pittsburgh city	43,053	8,472	32,352	6,897	9,429	1,396	569	86	295	21	395	56
Reading city	8,356	1,112	5,681	1,021	901	91	na	na	98	0	1,934	0
Scranton city	12,784	2,973	11,953	2,928	172	0	245	8	na	na	307	37
Rhode Island												
Cranston city	12,207	2,483	11,230	2,386	203	54	232	17	na	na	479	0
Pawtucket city	9,112	1,321	7,309	1,175	704	73	na	na	260	29	607	10
Providence city	15,087	2,734	9,379	2,321	1,582	128	769	26	317	37	3,054	234
Warwick city	14,573	2,293	14,096	2,287	na	na	80	0	na	na	115	0
South Carolina												
Charleston city	15,068	1,963	10,486	1,449	4,185	471	na	na	na	na	206	0
Columbia city	11,764	2,258	7,072	1,380	4,535	851	26	0	na	na	88	11
North Charleston city	8,550	978	5,162	633	3,007	322	na	na	na	na	135	23
Rock Hill city	6,790	1,201	4,563	887	2,000	286	na	na	na	na	110	28
South Dakota												
Rapid City city	10,066	1,909	9,357	1,879	na	na	na	na	124	0	130	0
Sioux Falls city	17,766	2,744	17,302	2,672	93	38	186	0	0	0	55	0

Table C-3: Places—Older Population by Race and Hispanic Origin—*Continued*

	Total Population		White, Non-Hispanic		Black, Alone		Asian, Alone		Multi-race, Alone		Hispanic	
	65 Years and Over	85 Years and Over	65 Years and Over	85 Years and Over	65 Years and Over	85 Years and Over	65 Years and Over	85 Years and Over	65 Years and Over	85 Years and Over	65 Years and Over	85 Years and Over
Tennessee												
Chattanooga city	25,216	3,600	18,481	2,733	6,002	819	310	31	114	17	171	17
Clarksville city	9,977	1,093	7,662	818	1,722	223	308	0	74	0	204	52
Jackson city	8,959	1,311	6,537	1,091	2,250	220	na	na	na	na	144	0
Knoxville city	25,921	3,684	22,386	3,323	3,093	331	na	na	159	13	185	17
Memphis city	68,321	8,936	32,226	5,318	33,648	3,447	934	35	541	28	1,012	108
Murfreesboro city	9,804	1,400	8,544	1,283	707	117	259	0	na	na	212	90
Nashville-Davidson metropolitan government (bal)	63,509	8,725	47,901	7,221	12,753	1,276	1,217	73	500	113	1,108	33
Texas												
Abilene city	14,982	2,231	12,401	2,053	619	13	270	16	58	0	1,581	149
Allen city	5,380	382	3,982	351	212	0	752	0	na	na	420	31
Amarillo city	23,214	3,250	19,571	3,049	780	45	419	34	424	20	2,127	102
Arlington city	30,493	3,448	23,668	2,846	1,890	221	1,899	237	227	0	2,746	144
Austin city	58,305	7,986	39,901	6,161	5,497	607	2,242	230	565	0	10,034	988
Baytown city	6,803	1,085	4,418	842	744	90	na	na	na	na	1,467	134
Beaumont city	14,876	2,187	7,908	1,504	5,808	578	238	27	na	na	780	70
Brownsville city	17,446	2,095	2,739	464	na	na	na	na	na	na	14,642	1,621
Bryan city	7,456	864	5,082	643	1,149	72	na	na	na	na	1,202	157
Carrollton city	10,350	1,141	6,789	761	467	44	1,793	204	148	7	1,138	132
College Station city	4,785	402	3,998	398	153	0	313	0	na	na	281	4
Corpus Christi city	36,661	4,763	17,886	2,751	1,515	223	553	12	420	34	16,507	1,757
Dallas city	111,981	15,720	60,082	11,091	29,023	2,875	2,938	134	1,524	196	18,642	1,448
Denton city	10,075	1,283	8,774	1,248	326	23	163	0	296	12	763	0
Edinburg city	5,699	588	1,054	81	na	na	na	na	na	na	4,380	507
El Paso city	75,109	9,495	17,370	2,599	1,670	222	917	60	1,266	115	54,735	6,577
Fort Worth city	63,187	8,379	39,398	6,136	11,422	1,220	1,859	110	582	88	9,924	849
Frisco city	7,694	622	6,179	412	343	203	472	7	na	na	624	0
Garland city	20,891	2,381	14,850	1,959	1,739	107	1,977	139	386	0	2,029	156
Grand Prairie city	12,493	1,037	7,350	774	1,467	162	1,050	0	125	9	2,406	92
Harlingen city	8,769	1,021	3,867	432	na	na	na	na	na	na	4,632	568
Houston city	196,834	25,014	96,266	15,598	48,075	4,849	11,062	726	2,290	271	39,689	3,500
Irving city	14,627	1,479	10,578	1,216	658	92	1,256	44	215	39	1,904	88
Killeen city	6,656	430	3,155	251	1,700	15	537	0	166	0	1,044	164
Laredo city	19,332	2,599	1,044	110	na	na	na	na	na	na	18,262	2,489
League City city	7,289	1,038	5,818	877	209	25	456	28	na	na	686	108
Lewisville city	7,092	707	5,504	675	296	32	266	0	146	0	869	0
Longview city	11,140	1,918	9,181	1,531	1,454	322	na	na	na	na	257	30
Lubbock city	25,969	3,159	19,729	2,713	1,494	180	304	0	257	17	4,321	299
McAllen city	14,299	1,981	3,126	395	na	na	238	8	na	na	10,774	1,578
McKinney city	10,073	1,080	8,484	862	573	174	324	0	na	na	568	39
Mesquite city	12,312	1,510	9,609	1,127	872	51	186	36	37	15	1,541	296
Midland city	12,902	1,698	9,600	1,506	926	57	na	na	na	na	2,112	135
Mission city	8,322	679	3,760	376	na	na	na	na	na	na	4,534	303
Missouri City city	7,079	488	3,027	271	2,109	186	986	31	na	na	642	0
Odessa city	10,557	1,386	7,008	1,096	540	57	na	na	151	17	2,818	219
Pasadena city	13,239	1,540	9,252	1,341	220	6	194	0	93	13	3,329	144
Pearland city	7,289	1,154	4,888	757	667	119	905	92	na	na	749	173
Pharr city	7,929	1,175	2,016	257	na	na	na	na	na	na	5,894	918
Plano city	25,850	3,105	20,428	2,699	1,027	79	2,663	249	333	20	1,365	85
Richardson city	12,547	1,673	10,442	1,464	296	36	1,158	173	201	0	494	0
Round Rock city	6,708	863	4,685	444	492	170	347	32	47	0	1,167	217
San Angelo city	12,983	1,425	9,709	920	419	36	na	na	na	na	2,729	427
San Antonio city	146,523	19,658	61,839	10,466	8,915	1,148	2,443	123	2,029	311	72,394	7,810
Sugar Land city	8,849	890	4,974	544	387	0	2,785	201	na	na	665	130
Temple city	10,083	1,627	8,166	1,387	961	108	na	na	na	na	824	93
Tyler city	14,596	2,818	10,930	2,285	2,377	422	na	na	na	na	831	111
Waco city	14,200	2,658	9,672	2,078	2,429	339	na	na	152	40	1,859	199
Wichita Falls city	12,592	2,046	10,355	1,879	1,031	99	192	0	75	0	946	68
Utah												
Layton city	5,210	397	4,428	313	na	na	na	na	na	na	389	59
Ogden city	7,746	1,259	6,285	1,115	na	na	na	na	na	na	869	79
Orem city	7,523	858	7,046	810	na	na	na	na	94	16	364	32
Provo city	6,809	1,411	5,967	1,340	na	na	171	56	25	0	517	15
St. George city	13,140	2,204	12,595	2,128	na	na	na	na	na	na	415	30
Salt Lake City city	17,812	2,899	14,941	2,620	203	33	871	66	193	43	1,241	148
Sandy city	8,741	904	8,070	890	na	na	285	0	64	10	359	10
West Jordan city	5,172	522	4,254	448	na	na	100	0	83	0	735	74
West Valley City city	9,486	719	7,332	499	21	0	457	80	209	24	1,406	71
Virginia												
Alexandria city	13,405	2,086	9,366	1,611	2,308	383	698	0	283	25	823	67
Chesapeake city	24,382	2,609	16,571	1,779	6,617	768	697	0	156	34	484	50
Hampton city	17,308	2,133	9,076	1,311	7,400	806	556	0	88	16	125	11
Lynchburg city	10,473	1,946	8,103	1,629	2,169	305	na	na	na	na	na	na
Newport News city	19,477	2,941	12,713	2,224	5,800	717	585	0	164	0	217	0
Norfolk city	23,063	3,234	13,021	2,037	8,441	1,066	879	37	338	39	400	55
Portsmouth city	12,762	1,931	6,708	1,031	5,616	865	na	na	217	35	97	0
Richmond city	23,264	3,875	10,712	2,006	11,524	1,769	265	69	454	21	341	10
Roanoke city	13,764	2,778	10,713	2,390	2,753	381	106	0	126	7	66	0
Suffolk city	10,000	1,309	6,203	689	3,519	533	na	na	na	na	na	na
Virginia Beach city	48,496	5,635	37,721	4,550	5,996	706	3,370	287	320	0	1,130	137

Table C-3: Places—Older Population by Race and Hispanic Origin—*Continued*

	Total Population		White, Non-Hispanic		Black, Alone		Asian, Alone		Multi-race, Alone		Hispanic	
	65 Years and Over	85 Years and Over	65 Years and Over	85 Years and Over	65 Years and Over	85 Years and Over	65 Years and Over	85 Years and Over	65 Years and Over	85 Years and Over	65 Years and Over	85 Years and Over
Washington												
Auburn city	8,058	1,036	7,384	1,023	98	4	436	9	51	0	41	0
Bellevue city	17,127	3,089	14,217	2,785	319	45	2,130	233	190	12	251	14
Bellingham city	10,535	1,777	10,036	1,763	na	na	na	na	25	0	50	14
Everett city	10,795	1,754	9,359	1,486	63	20	765	136	165	20	333	92
Federal Way city	9,751	1,575	7,298	1,271	487	43	1,331	187	109	0	409	37
Kennewick city	8,424	1,301	7,750	1,283	na	na	na	na	na	na	377	18
Kent city	11,529	1,588	8,805	1,324	345	14	1,704	219	279	13	399	0
Renton city	9,369	1,546	7,135	1,248	685	85	1,192	184	167	0	110	0
Seattle city	68,854	11,819	50,258	9,259	4,694	556	11,235	1,558	840	160	1,381	370
Spokane city	28,661	4,435	26,792	4,289	241	0	687	60	342	51	450	48
Spokane Valley city	12,971	1,794	12,506	1,767	na	na	na	na	na	na	126	0
Tacoma city	23,185	4,201	17,927	3,658	1,509	169	2,276	228	479	73	691	84
Vancouver city	21,672	2,988	19,531	2,850	474	15	1,101	86	50	0	372	37
Yakima city	12,729	2,450	10,766	2,178	na	na	na	na	227	115	1,538	92
Wisconsin												
Appleton city	8,151	1,350	7,868	1,317	na	na	88	13	na	na	139	20
Eau Claire city	7,424	1,179	7,350	1,179	na	na	55	0	na	na	na	na
Green Bay city	12,289	2,485	11,804	2,457	30	0	114	0	70	0	182	28
Kenosha city	10,911	1,914	9,828	1,892	503	5	na	na	na	na	470	17
Madison city	22,627	3,632	20,997	3,562	601	53	581	0	29	0	395	0
Milwaukee city	54,186	7,929	33,345	6,216	15,988	1,422	935	44	319	28	3,390	168
Oshkosh city	8,277	1,546	8,142	1,546	na	na	na	na	na	na	na	na
Racine city	8,651	1,209	6,746	1,073	1,264	118	na	na	58	0	602	18
Waukesha city	7,677	1,222	7,284	1,210	na	na	109	0	na	na	221	12

Table C-4: Metropolitan Statistical Areas—Older Population by Race and Hispanic Origin

	Total Population		White, Non-Hispanic		Black, Alone		Asian, Alone		Multi-race, Alone		Hispanic	
	65 Years and Over	85 Years and Over	65 Years and Over	85 Years and Over	65 Years and Over	85 Years and Over	65 Years and Over	85 Years and Over	65 Years and Over	85 Years and Over	65 Years and Over	85 Years and Over
Abilene, TX	23,098	2,933	19,697	2,709	770	38	295	16	208	0	2,066	170
Akron, OH	102,273	14,740	91,514	13,534	8,664	1,021	947	48	572	50	470	126
Albany, GA	19,813	2,338	12,187	1,525	7,057	795	na	na	158	0	259	18
Albany-Schenectady-Troy, NY	125,011	20,533	116,516	19,731	4,757	416	1,552	72	666	107	1,338	216
Albuquerque, NM	114,446	14,316	70,879	9,429	1,966	220	1,829	226	1,655	225	35,698	3,984
Alexandria, LA	21,281	2,536	16,392	2,007	4,157	469	na	na	185	0	288	60
Allentown-Bethlehem-Easton, PA-NJ	127,577	20,428	118,340	19,644	2,255	133	1,581	119	590	76	4,813	358
Altoona, PA	22,825	3,637	22,536	3,609	136	28	na	na	na	na	na	na
Amarillo, TX	30,343	4,035	26,127	3,819	828	48	419	34	500	29	2,584	105
Ames, IA	9,096	1,547	8,886	1,533	23	0	151	13	na	na	na	na
Anchorage, AK	30,422	2,300	23,495	1,704	937	95	2,350	313	732	0	980	87
Anderson, IN	20,715	2,915	19,371	2,857	827	30	na	na	206	2	220	26
Anderson, SC	29,491	3,431	25,742	3,083	3,216	273	na	na	na	na	229	0
Ann Arbor, MI	37,073	5,501	31,163	4,912	3,239	442	1,646	70	464	32	635	48
Anniston-Oxford, AL	17,423	1,905	14,794	1,554	2,161	251	na	na	152	100	246	0
Appleton, WI	27,293	4,032	26,522	3,980	27	0	191	13	99	20	235	28
Asheville, NC	80,896	11,076	76,841	10,437	2,411	492	343	27	391	5	892	115
Athens-Clarke County, GA	20,460	2,385	16,363	1,988	3,169	294	291	0	64	0	560	103
Atlanta-Sandy Springs-Marietta, GA	503,523	53,291	356,482	40,251	112,548	10,691	16,912	1,060	3,823	377	14,470	1,022
Atlantic City-Hammonton, NJ	40,020	5,176	30,796	4,253	4,935	515	1,888	173	331	28	2,162	219
Auburn-Opelika, AL	13,450	1,511	10,548	1,296	2,522	209	114	0	na	na	170	6
Augusta-Richmond County, GA-SC	72,402	6,648	51,693	5,213	17,789	1,309	1,173	17	612	45	1,195	48
Austin-Round Rock-San Marcos, TX	149,824	17,619	112,955	13,732	9,081	1,493	4,435	351	1,172	110	22,114	2,047
Bakersfield-Delano, CA	77,955	8,418	51,707	6,076	3,337	405	3,743	411	850	19	17,702	1,481
Baltimore-Towson, MD	353,937	50,307	259,678	40,310	76,995	8,425	10,453	691	2,079	281	4,513	444
Bangor, ME	22,900	2,858	22,428	2,823	na	na	na	na	103	0	na	na
Barnstable Town, MA	55,418	7,009	53,571	6,789	487	52	226	49	266	14	357	74
Baton Rouge, LA	90,143	11,004	63,896	7,869	23,267	2,908	822	87	638	43	1,589	97
Battle Creek, MI	20,385	3,063	18,054	2,733	1,771	308	107	0	71	6	305	16
Bay City, MI	17,937	2,872	17,343	2,818	na	na	na	na	137	0	313	11
Beaumont-Port Arthur, TX	51,432	6,613	38,464	5,316	9,627	937	719	38	316	22	2,390	310
Bellingham, WA	27,966	3,710	26,080	3,620	na	na	715	40	300	28	491	28
Bend, OR	25,290	3,476	24,336	3,402	na	na	na	na	326	66	444	1
Billings, MT	23,429	3,482	22,486	3,418	na	na	na	na	41	0	405	39
Binghamton, NY	41,571	6,631	39,904	6,516	448	35	402	45	221	9	501	39
Birmingham-Hoover, AL	150,337	18,963	117,759	14,989	29,798	3,840	876	3	784	79	1,102	79
Bismarck, ND	15,567	2,544	15,263	2,544	na	na	na	na	na	na	na	na
Blacksburg-Christiansburg-Radford, VA	20,766	2,710	19,567	2,549	820	142	108	0	na	na	167	19
Bloomington, IN	23,319	3,030	22,642	2,953	150	7	173	12	90	16	234	42
Bloomington-Normal, IL	17,918	2,724	16,843	2,645	420	57	210	11	130	0	299	11
Boise City-Nampa, ID	71,521	9,522	66,759	8,983	82	47	985	74	777	192	2,680	196
Boston-Cambridge-Quincy, MA-NH	615,598	95,934	538,947	87,577	29,160	3,392	22,518	2,438	5,940	585	20,025	2,001
Boulder, CO	31,696	4,426	28,892	4,151	na	na	644	27	271	28	1,670	170
Bowling Green, KY	14,943	1,843	13,803	1,797	694	28	na	na	179	0	61	0
Bremerton-Silverdale, WA	35,096	4,247	31,699	3,985	227	0	1,668	192	425	21	647	46
Bridgeport-Stamford-Norwalk, CT	127,386	20,420	106,124	18,600	9,856	936	3,089	154	621	53	8,188	713
Brownsville-Harlingen, TX	46,553	4,957	14,276	1,949	na	na	245	21	254	71	31,829	2,977
Brunswick, GA	17,681	1,796	14,718	1,514	2,603	277	na	na	na	na	138	5
Buffalo-Niagara Falls, NY	180,506	27,652	161,182	25,830	13,680	1,427	1,535	34	1,051	129	2,396	197
Burlington, NC	22,781	3,757	18,797	3,321	3,287	381	na	na	324	3	477	56
Burlington-South Burlington, VT	25,657	3,436	24,821	3,350	115	3	371	40	103	14	182	0
Canton-Massillon, OH	66,876	10,364	62,765	9,878	2,949	316	248	0	355	68	476	38
Cape Coral-Fort Myers, FL	153,513	19,743	139,378	18,381	4,404	415	1,387	29	789	104	7,358	868
Cape Girardeau-Jackson, MO-IL	14,653	2,521	13,860	2,442	661	56	na	na	na	na	18	8
Casper, WY	9,606	1,300	9,048	1,250	na	na	na	na	77	4	352	50
Cedar Rapids, IA	36,006	5,073	35,177	4,891	248	31	215	91	45	0	222	60
Champaign-Urbana, IL	26,270	3,814	23,744	3,547	1,475	193	518	31	232	32	281	11
Charleston, WV	49,372	6,148	46,972	5,988	1,014	94	na	na	851	44	240	18
Charleston-North Charleston-Summerville, SC	81,392	8,810	59,268	6,397	19,230	2,204	1,226	28	560	50	876	67
Charlotte-Gastonia-Rock Hill, NC-SC	186,428	22,466	147,062	18,610	30,881	3,378	2,859	37	839	0	4,438	420
Charlottesville, VA	28,772	3,871	25,153	3,376	2,712	398	396	25	292	0	184	72
Chattanooga, TN-GA	80,270	10,116	70,502	9,027	7,475	1,041	617	31	468	17	1,016	17
Cheyenne, WY	12,078	1,489	10,518	1,387	na	na	na	na	132	0	1,005	77
Chicago-Joliet-Naperville, IL-IN-WI	1,111,994	160,222	789,624	128,404	174,406	19,840	53,148	4,318	8,097	665	87,954	7,015
Chico, CA	34,534	5,476	31,225	5,004	na	na	549	85	830	51	1,766	279
Cincinnati-Middletown, OH-KY-IN	266,872	36,855	238,220	33,267	22,927	3,103	2,378	226	1,202	32	1,816	127
Clarksville, TN-KY	26,730	2,701	22,638	2,315	3,162	334	380	0	199	0	348	52
Cleveland, TN	17,731	1,712	16,728	1,685	411	27	na	na	na	na	315	0
Cleveland-Elyria-Mentor, OH	320,469	50,729	260,560	43,707	48,690	6,091	4,011	239	1,799	210	5,671	495
Coeur d'Alene, ID	21,061	2,369	20,435	2,349	na	na	na	na	166	0	234	20
College Station-Bryan, TX	21,025	2,321	16,107	1,915	2,282	169	336	0	81	0	2,227	237
Colorado Springs, CO	68,685	7,696	58,837	7,118	2,654	174	1,856	135	967	81	4,535	228
Columbia, MO	17,389	2,573	15,797	2,454	880	94	365	2	231	23	91	0
Columbia, SC	92,075	11,127	67,986	8,769	21,390	2,142	850	76	478	32	1,212	58
Columbus, GA-AL	35,039	4,181	22,797	2,870	10,948	1,219	480	30	289	23	493	39
Columbus, IN	11,140	1,338	10,757	1,324	na	na	75	0	na	na	30	0
Columbus, OH	201,981	25,363	175,409	22,577	20,181	2,288	3,354	285	1,550	118	1,602	107
Corpus Christi, TX	56,786	6,768	30,171	3,888	1,621	223	637	12	658	34	24,049	2,625
Corvallis, OR	10,787	1,929	10,155	1,828	na	na	257	93	152	0	152	0
Crestview-Fort Walton Beach-Destin, FL	25,929	2,704	23,432	2,470	1,192	91	596	39	138	11	583	93

Table C-4: Metropolitan Statistical Areas—Older Population by Race and Hispanic Origin—*Continued*

	Total Population		White, Non-Hispanic		Black, Alone		Asian, Alone		Multi-race, Alone		Hispanic	
	65 Years and Over	85 Years and Over	65 Years and Over	85 Years and Over	65 Years and Over	85 Years and Over	65 Years and Over	85 Years and Over	65 Years and Over	85 Years and Over	65 Years and Over	85 Years and Over
Cumberland, MD-WV	18,568	2,886	17,923	2,821	413	36	na	na	na	na	na	na
Dallas-Fort Worth-Arlington, TX	594,373	67,366	440,664	54,487	64,454	6,407	23,009	1,545	6,782	463	59,584	4,524
Dalton, GA	16,183	1,634	15,047	1,438	390	112	na	na	146	0	492	57
Danville, IL	13,249	1,936	12,316	1,895	739	26	na	na	na	na	23	2
Danville, VA	19,469	2,450	14,619	2,062	4,608	388	na	na	na	na	36	0
Davenport-Moline-Rock Island, IA-IL	58,709	8,903	54,422	8,508	1,953	155	487	28	332	14	1,595	198
Dayton, OH	128,726	17,788	111,090	15,578	14,515	1,888	1,452	142	810	80	842	83
Decatur, AL	22,420	2,295	20,209	1,994	1,662	219	na	na	265	38	234	29
Decatur, IL	18,335	2,852	16,532	2,732	1,592	110	na	na	59	0	103	9
Deltona-Daytona Beach-Ormond Beach, FL	107,097	14,807	94,468	13,214	5,402	723	881	134	546	74	5,901	662
Denver-Aurora-Broomfield, CO	271,402	35,419	220,209	30,428	11,540	1,296	8,120	869	2,750	301	28,814	2,597
Des Moines-West Des Moines, IA	65,905	9,308	61,963	9,095	1,590	114	1,005	63	243	1	997	49
Detroit-Warren-Livonia, MI	581,383	86,465	452,768	69,861	102,311	14,228	11,250	962	4,948	424	8,849	911
Dothan, AL	23,272	2,316	19,199	1,839	3,548	444	na	na	164	15	219	14
Dover, DE	23,105	2,511	18,049	1,978	3,875	432	539	44	100	26	497	85
Dubuque, IA	14,434	2,116	14,341	2,099	na	na	na	na	28	0	21	0
Duluth, MN-WI	44,189	6,820	42,993	6,775	85	0	206	12	267	15	186	7
Durham-Chapel Hill, NC	60,480	8,124	44,168	6,613	13,543	1,484	1,231	0	399	11	911	16
Eau Claire, WI	21,987	3,495	21,690	3,493	na	na	137	0	38	0	95	0
El Centro, CA	18,894	2,533	5,142	503	261	22	386	121	489	47	12,735	1,880
Elizabethtown, KY	13,919	1,625	12,789	1,515	759	110	306	0	17	0	48	0
Elkhart-Goshen, IN	24,447	3,734	23,164	3,601	701	133	na	na	122	0	480	0
Elmira, NY	13,656	2,356	13,331	2,311	270	33	na	na	14	12	na	na
El Paso, TX	84,785	10,499	18,438	2,700	1,751	222	927	60	1,519	115	63,184	7,480
Erie, PA	41,308	6,441	39,346	6,244	1,190	122	137	0	181	0	357	75
Eugene-Springfield, OR	54,955	7,297	52,107	7,083	126	0	640	13	734	78	1,034	154
Evansville, IN-KY	52,215	7,683	49,536	7,279	2,026	346	200	20	208	28	214	10
Fairbanks, AK	6,666	741	5,733	622	216	0	na	na	0	0	80	0
Fargo, ND-MN	22,428	3,259	21,900	3,254	21	0	245	0	123	5	76	0
Farmington, NM	14,445	1,702	8,994	1,338	na	na	na	na	221	0	1,596	51
Fayetteville, NC	34,763	3,611	20,553	2,271	11,591	1,086	880	69	378	15	1,056	59
Fayetteville-Springdale-Rogers, AR-MO	53,554	7,506	51,300	7,265	328	39	309	0	613	37	833	148
Flagstaff, AZ	12,670	1,382	8,612	979	na	na	na	na	119	0	952	56
Flint, MI	59,719	7,641	48,776	6,620	9,044	945	379	14	611	9	795	41
Florence, SC	28,752	3,199	19,429	2,073	8,875	1,055	na	na	224	43	80	28
Florence-Muscle Shoals, AL	25,398	3,270	22,776	2,995	2,180	249	na	na	na	na	14	0
Fond du Lac, WI	15,621	2,830	15,345	2,778	na	na	na	na	na	na	122	27
Fort Collins-Loveland, CO	37,722	5,129	35,533	4,968	75	0	400	18	177	46	1,535	133
Fort Smith, AR-OK	42,570	4,459	38,199	4,134	928	95	463	14	1,438	132	468	22
Fort Wayne, IN	52,845	7,636	47,778	7,217	3,199	221	530	46	354	70	789	82
Fresno, CA	96,924	14,407	57,441	9,746	3,674	391	8,284	1,216	2,006	371	25,954	2,825
Gadsden, AL	16,754	2,400	14,868	2,032	1,560	359	na	na	na	na	74	0
Gainesville, FL	30,406	3,928	24,723	3,345	4,034	485	389	0	228	7	1,094	91
Gainesville, GA	21,659	2,307	19,328	2,068	1,038	90	247	0	112	0	900	149
Glens Falls, NY	21,670	2,975	21,122	2,872	na	na	na	na	na	na	175	33
Goldsboro, NC	16,464	1,992	11,383	1,348	4,656	644	na	na	240	0	25	0
Grand Forks, ND-MN	12,461	1,991	11,998	1,972	na	na	na	na	43	8	85	11
Grand Junction, CO	22,644	3,281	20,977	3,108	na	na	na	na	278	39	1,192	131
Grand Rapids-Wyoming, MI	93,323	14,012	85,694	13,306	3,931	380	967	27	833	29	2,038	273
Great Falls, MT	12,936	1,797	12,325	1,695	na	na	na	na	107	0	107	55
Greeley, CO	25,925	2,876	21,750	2,512	87	0	277	54	309	40	3,597	270
Green Bay, WI	39,452	5,960	38,252	5,844	34	0	293	44	230	33	395	51
Greensboro-High Point, NC	98,900	11,311	79,448	9,556	16,280	1,590	1,245	91	561	36	1,189	71
Greenville, NC	20,184	2,747	13,873	1,942	5,744	756	175	16	113	25	281	8
Greenville-Mauldin-Easley, SC	87,079	10,796	74,513	9,831	9,953	879	719	13	489	33	1,386	40
Gulfport-Biloxi, MS	32,408	3,227	27,119	2,624	4,011	544	605	28	251	15	505	63
Hagerstown-Martinsburg, MD-WV	37,326	4,480	35,537	4,317	1,014	38	265	8	104	19	358	96
Hanford-Corcoran, CA	12,328	1,452	7,411	981	468	0	570	107	270	0	3,712	364
Harrisburg-Carlisle, PA	81,808	12,914	74,598	12,165	4,914	504	1,081	53	464	31	916	218
Harrisonburg, VA	16,371	2,448	15,865	2,340	270	65	na	na	na	na	140	43
Hartford-West Hartford-East Hartford, CT	177,974	30,284	154,807	28,046	11,248	1,344	2,951	173	1,291	76	7,978	652
Hattiesburg, MS	16,933	2,043	14,046	1,623	2,655	368	na	na	na	na	91	26
Hickory-Lenoir-Morganton, NC	57,276	6,354	52,918	5,782	2,980	359	649	105	95	20	539	88
Hinesville-Fort Stewart, GA	5,458	477	3,342	198	1,778	279	na	na	61	0	147	0
Holland-Grand Haven, MI	32,067	4,818	30,773	4,671	87	25	215	0	205	23	829	116
Honolulu, HI	143,047	24,044	26,364	3,481	809	130	93,897	18,351	12,747	1,406	3,892	330
Hot Springs, AR	20,125	2,966	19,041	2,824	527	142	na	na	na	na	269	0
Houma-Bayou Cane-Thibodaux, LA	25,190	2,744	21,526	2,374	2,725	279	na	na	62	19	425	0
Houston-Sugar Land-Baytown, TX	543,484	60,514	337,062	43,138	79,067	7,832	33,892	2,137	5,670	437	88,011	6,845
Huntington-Ashland, WV-KY-OH	47,322	5,742	45,830	5,523	814	129	na	na	361	72	130	18
Huntsville, AL	53,167	6,244	44,502	5,498	6,951	666	684	37	273	7	559	36
Idaho Falls, ID	14,364	2,065	13,784	2,035	na	na	na	na	46	0	446	26
Indianapolis-Carmel, IN	197,975	26,228	170,247	23,356	21,063	2,396	2,455	64	1,536	149	2,440	261
Iowa City, IA	15,517	2,461	15,082	2,418	141	43	199	0	27	0	55	0
Ithaca, NY	11,365	1,751	10,683	1,691	226	23	305	37	43	0	87	0
Jackson, MI	23,197	3,605	21,879	3,458	902	147	na	na	131	0	156	0
Jackson, MS	62,882	8,181	41,819	5,435	19,936	2,615	233	6	419	38	458	87
Jackson, TN	15,792	2,256	12,605	1,831	2,957	425	na	na	na	na	190	0
Jacksonville, FL	171,792	21,519	137,107	18,013	23,137	2,528	4,372	210	1,444	172	5,917	581
Jacksonville, NC	13,878	1,317	10,992	988	2,012	222	361	0	76	0	364	86

Table C-4: Metropolitan Statistical Areas—Older Population by Race and Hispanic Origin—*Continued*

	Total Population		White, Non-Hispanic		Black, Alone		Asian, Alone		Multi-race, Alone		Hispanic	
	65 Years and Over	85 Years and Over	65 Years and Over	85 Years and Over	65 Years and Over	85 Years and Over	65 Years and Over	85 Years and Over	65 Years and Over	85 Years and Over	65 Years and Over	85 Years and Over
Janesville, WI	22,209	2,999	21,235	2,919	615	80	142	0	102	0	115	0
Jefferson City, MO	19,780	2,455	18,813	2,412	504	25	na	na	166	3	204	0
Johnson City, TN	33,365	3,955	32,197	3,765	414	66	na	na	na	na	345	59
Johnstown, PA	27,189	4,525	26,385	4,460	497	38	na	na	46	8	200	19
Jonesboro, AR	15,824	1,944	15,234	1,928	357	13	na	na	na	na	37	0
Joplin, MO	25,081	3,393	23,792	3,215	183	57	na	na	265	46	276	50
Kalamazoo-Portage, MI	42,363	5,966	38,712	5,428	2,427	220	425	165	186	53	519	100
Kankakee-Bradley, IL	15,361	2,270	13,558	2,128	1,495	129	na	na	na	na	179	0
Kansas City, MO-KS	252,245	36,648	216,774	32,634	22,929	2,695	3,206	177	2,242	314	6,754	802
Kennewick-Pasco-Richland, WA	27,682	3,250	24,363	3,188	na	na	700	0	315	0	2,009	48
Killeen-Temple-Fort Hood, TX	37,782	3,992	28,847	3,161	3,621	240	1,218	74	451	11	3,508	506
Kingsport-Bristol-Bristol, TN-VA	57,907	7,019	56,238	6,819	788	137	na	na	261	0	199	32
Kingston, NY	28,178	4,304	25,859	3,957	819	131	274	48	267	45	943	122
Knoxville, TN	106,237	13,195	99,678	12,564	4,210	548	959	0	484	24	757	59
Kokomo, IN	16,797	2,199	15,752	2,141	618	0	na	na	69	12	197	17
La Crosse, WI-MN	19,095	3,199	18,759	3,180	na	na	159	19	30	0	na	na
Lafayette, IN	21,369	3,184	20,669	3,114	201	40	209	18	110	0	250	20
Lafayette, LA	29,895	3,568	23,449	2,948	5,556	561	217	0	154	5	498	54
Lake Charles, LA	25,751	2,803	20,231	2,326	4,489	388	177	0	285	21	313	14
Lake Havasu City-Kingman, AZ	48,584	4,700	44,459	4,403	na	na	na	na	832	85	2,698	174
Lakeland-Winter Haven, FL	111,849	13,506	94,882	11,805	8,255	752	1,392	50	678	113	6,782	764
Lancaster, PA	80,119	13,886	75,957	13,251	1,102	155	809	153	319	137	1,986	190
Lansing-East Lansing, MI	56,354	7,681	50,773	7,345	2,849	118	870	45	399	53	1,400	120
Laredo, TX	20,230	2,711	1,116	110	na	na	na	na	na	na	19,088	2,601
Las Cruces, NM	26,999	2,973	14,236	1,638	na	na	276	18	435	0	11,910	1,255
Las Vegas-Paradise, NV	233,408	21,844	164,439	16,878	19,020	1,618	20,610	1,519	3,764	179	24,622	1,657
Lawrence, KS	10,285	1,500	9,567	1,401	238	22	184	45	74	0	53	5
Lawton, OK	12,964	1,427	10,033	1,273	1,286	40	na	na	313	2	496	69
Lebanon, PA	22,939	3,413	22,272	3,398	141	0	na	na	3	0	350	15
Lewiston-Auburn, ME	15,552	2,190	15,214	2,173	32	5	na	na	197	12	na	na
Lexington-Fayette, KY	54,619	6,617	48,520	6,063	4,629	493	534	22	241	0	631	21
Lima, OH	15,696	2,573	14,368	2,459	1,098	32	na	na	na	na	115	15
Lincoln, NE	34,665	5,190	33,091	5,042	246	17	622	77	150	24	518	20
Little Rock-North Little Rock-Conway, AR	88,696	9,948	75,449	8,607	10,646	1,225	677	0	811	57	869	7
Logan, UT-ID	10,763	1,449	10,384	1,446	na	na	52	0	29	3	281	0
Longview, TX	30,550	4,485	25,527	3,605	3,902	772	na	na	198	27	687	51
Longview, WA	16,595	2,221	15,733	2,154	na	na	na	na	389	54	248	4
Los Angeles-Long Beach-Santa Ana, CA	1,472,725	212,830	742,921	129,007	105,012	12,585	256,185	31,666	26,524	2,697	346,409	37,600
Louisville/Jefferson County, KY-IN	169,533	21,639	150,092	19,651	15,223	1,590	1,423	187	1,126	107	1,524	99
Lubbock, TX	32,716	4,004	25,047	3,369	1,724	199	304	0	321	17	5,474	469
Lynchburg, VA	41,173	5,584	34,756	4,832	5,603	720	90	14	237	12	397	0
Macon, GA	31,201	3,513	20,657	2,614	9,921	899	298	0	na	na	240	0
Madera-Chowchilla, CA	17,912	1,882	12,525	1,461	414	48	438	37	201	33	4,028	336
Madison, WI	64,781	9,071	61,977	8,924	832	71	985	10	199	19	713	30
Manchester-Nashua, NH	49,471	6,877	47,321	6,786	360	34	760	0	297	35	782	22
Manhattan, KS	10,509	1,607	9,718	1,577	481	30	110	0	49	0	140	0
Mankato-North Mankato, MN	11,806	2,216	11,615	2,216	2	0	na	na	na	na	68	0
Mansfield, OH	20,768	2,656	19,200	2,535	1,052	99	na	na	111	10	na	na
McAllen-Edinburg-Mission, TX	75,801	8,386	22,201	2,505	224	42	498	8	565	94	52,718	5,873
Medford, OR	37,277	5,744	35,389	5,482	na	na	na	na	396	101	933	101
Memphis, TN-MS-AR	143,766	16,331	92,623	11,460	46,956	4,626	1,803	35	865	95	1,587	124
Merced, CA	25,198	3,093	14,720	1,977	1,013	79	1,652	208	452	0	7,245	825
Miami-Fort Lauderdale-Pompano Beach, FL	915,028	144,234	489,744	94,436	103,879	10,282	12,538	763	7,853	584	309,349	39,059
Michigan City-La Porte, IN	16,122	2,008	14,919	1,897	845	77	na	na	45	0	218	34
Midland, TX	15,298	1,851	11,543	1,659	926	57	na	na	na	na	2,529	135
Milwaukee-Waukesha-West Allis, WI	199,855	31,013	173,187	28,649	17,666	1,596	2,523	135	856	131	5,183	437
Minneapolis-St. Paul-Bloomington, MN-WI	365,949	52,919	338,736	50,081	10,435	740	9,587	1,127	2,283	331	4,271	582
Missoula, MT	12,935	1,945	12,674	1,922	na	na	na	na	80	0	66	23
Mobile, AL	54,982	6,289	39,041	4,428	14,131	1,673	508	25	483	93	726	95
Modesto, CA	56,938	8,517	40,715	6,558	1,089	167	2,621	179	1,445	169	10,890	1,378
Monroe, LA	23,289	2,916	17,915	2,333	4,852	530	na	na	na	na	292	53
Monroe, MI	21,131	2,455	20,450	2,404	197	4	na	na	100	29	300	18
Montgomery, AL	46,361	5,240	32,140	3,741	13,070	1,393	480	0	217	20	368	86
Morgantown, WV	15,359	1,933	14,963	1,878	184	45	23	0	na	na	55	7
Morristown, TN	22,818	2,169	21,867	2,022	620	135	na	na	206	12	55	0
Mount Vernon-Anacortes, WA	19,708	2,652	18,550	2,581	na	na	202	44	247	18	574	0
Muncie, IN	17,592	1,931	16,585	1,852	653	60	na	na	180	14	132	0
Muskegon-Norton Shores, MI	23,796	3,325	21,153	3,095	2,072	174	na	na	157	18	356	38
Myrtle Beach-North Myrtle Beach-Conway, SC	49,069	4,537	44,682	4,168	3,453	280	295	0	144	76	503	13
Napa, CA	21,451	3,557	17,649	3,113	277	48	1,117	105	280	0	2,047	295
Naples-Marco Island, FL	89,552	11,345	81,802	10,666	1,808	128	489	59	440	83	5,023	409
Nashville-Davidson--Murfreesboro--Franklin, TN	178,446	21,653	154,334	19,916	18,228	1,826	2,064	84	1,156	206	2,599	291
New Haven-Milford, CT	126,344	23,684	108,316	22,243	9,309	898	1,733	16	881	28	5,966	488
New Orleans-Metairie-Kenner, LA	148,551	19,252	99,949	14,041	37,063	4,162	2,708	195	1,086	138	7,499	728
New York-Northern New Jersey-Long Island, NY-NJ-PA.	2,539,430	380,351	1,650,643	287,957	367,248	42,804	180,376	16,381	33,624	3,367	334,991	33,124
Niles-Benton Harbor, MI	25,836	3,931	22,831	3,513	2,291	330	196	0	187	51	300	37
North Port-Bradenton-Sarasota, FL	200,092	29,718	188,239	28,452	4,539	473	1,500	111	822	102	4,967	580
Norwich-New London, CT	40,149	5,336	36,767	5,053	1,204	146	757	14	378	61	919	38
Ocala, FL	87,503	9,397	77,153	8,487	5,046	567	722	0	635	19	4,001	304
Ocean City, NJ	21,534	2,730	20,344	2,502	681	208	na	na	na	na	287	7

Table C-4: Metropolitan Statistical Areas—Older Population by Race and Hispanic Origin—*Continued*

	Total Population		White, Non-Hispanic		Black, Alone		Asian, Alone		Multi-race, Alone		Hispanic	
	65 Years and Over	85 Years and Over	65 Years and Over	85 Years and Over	65 Years and Over	85 Years and Over	65 Years and Over	85 Years and Over	65 Years and Over	85 Years and Over	65 Years and Over	85 Years and Over
Odessa, TX	14,068	1,576	9,281	1,181	564	57	na	na	182	17	4,012	324
Ogden-Clearfield, UT	51,625	6,223	47,442	5,746	555	11	829	85	264	53	2,440	294
Oklahoma City, OK	152,609	18,977	128,631	16,656	10,145	1,159	2,860	206	3,837	394	4,255	369
Olympia, WA	34,479	4,483	31,316	4,275	362	17	1,524	21	415	85	661	86
Omaha-Council Bluffs, NE-IA	98,887	14,717	90,324	14,054	5,206	453	798	33	346	24	2,229	158
Orlando-Kissimmee-Sanford, FL	276,326	34,090	194,986	27,020	27,850	2,312	7,966	553	3,232	250	43,822	4,114
Oshkosh-Neenah, WI	22,787	3,956	22,448	3,896	na	na	87	0	50	0	123	60
Owensboro, KY	17,367	2,264	16,764	2,218	390	46	na	na	na	na	79	0
Oxnard-Thousand Oaks-Ventura, CA	100,859	14,468	71,743	11,318	1,459	89	7,290	697	1,621	150	19,203	2,210
Palm Bay-Melbourne-Titusville, FL	114,082	14,013	99,896	12,922	7,165	731	1,464	79	978	86	4,939	215
Palm Coast, FL	25,015	2,962	20,395	2,334	2,545	502	na	na	na	na	1,403	103
Panama City-Lynn Haven-Panama City Beach, FL	25,463	2,599	22,750	2,334	1,587	210	280	0	348	17	415	38
Parkersburg-Marietta-Vienna, WV-OH	27,828	3,291	27,244	3,247	na	na	na	na	167	15	na	na
Pascagoula, MS	20,935	1,646	17,857	1,430	2,508	112	114	0	na	na	193	85
Pensacola-Ferry Pass-Brent, FL	64,585	7,515	53,961	6,507	7,036	741	1,274	0	959	133	1,121	98
Peoria, IL	57,552	8,522	54,160	8,183	2,328	216	417	26	187	38	396	59
Philadelphia-Camden-Wilmington, PA-NJ-DE-MD	811,495	125,351	632,345	105,593	128,511	15,641	24,695	1,483	5,570	782	21,414	1,981
Phoenix-Mesa-Glendale, AZ	543,706	64,503	458,689	57,490	14,008	1,301	11,459	815	3,892	303	53,009	4,527
Pine Bluff, AR	13,696	1,836	9,247	1,325	4,241	511	na	na	na	na	26	0
Pittsburgh, PA	410,509	68,432	381,948	64,943	21,981	2,813	2,749	267	1,726	242	2,068	161
Pittsfield, MA	25,072	4,486	24,146	4,291	334	124	na	na	156	0	270	51
Pocatello, ID	10,500	1,119	9,893	1,077	na	na	na	na	73	15	239	15
Portland-South Portland-Biddeford, ME	79,499	11,021	77,525	10,947	248	0	682	8	350	46	521	35
Portland-Vancouver-Hillsboro, OR-WA	266,798	39,516	239,892	37,116	5,035	569	11,558	1,114	2,469	154	6,349	531
Port St. Lucie, FL	99,068	13,827	86,740	13,001	6,413	333	726	17	612	53	4,676	435
Poughkeepsie-Newburgh-Middletown, NY	84,059	11,706	71,714	10,788	5,394	522	1,666	36	717	42	4,815	337
Prescott, AZ	53,313	7,010	49,851	6,536	na	na	na	na	314	11	2,307	376
Providence-New Bedford-Fall River, RI-MA	234,456	40,696	216,052	38,832	5,047	575	2,533	168	2,204	269	7,165	500
Provo-Orem, UT	36,447	4,530	34,116	4,362	103	0	456	69	176	27	1,494	83
Pueblo, CO	25,026	3,150	17,510	2,364	430	86	na	na	383	0	6,819	627
Punta Gorda, FL	56,719	8,101	52,535	7,574	1,966	332	na	na	na	na	1,403	109
Racine, WI	26,333	3,575	23,544	3,366	1,606	191	197	0	76	0	901	18
Raleigh-Cary, NC	108,919	12,101	85,336	9,840	17,473	1,820	2,873	274	683	81	2,579	74
Rapid City, SD	17,359	2,639	16,433	2,584	na	na	na	na	171	0	208	25
Reading, PA	60,772	9,371	56,222	9,119	1,561	109	352	50	298	3	2,616	90
Redding, CA	31,209	4,189	28,753	3,930	na	na	455	59	690	52	940	145
Reno-Sparks, NV	54,704	6,177	46,623	5,578	762	74	2,311	174	845	92	3,761	235
Richmond, VA	160,152	22,140	114,874	16,939	38,982	4,490	2,632	334	1,203	138	2,043	143
Riverside-San Bernardino-Ontario, CA	460,667	54,619	295,889	39,318	26,375	2,085	28,108	2,353	7,976	584	103,309	10,427
Roanoke, VA	51,554	7,090	46,382	6,423	4,349	643	309	17	321	7	222	22
Rochester, MN	25,206	3,764	24,037	3,585	198	74	535	60	162	39	287	6
Rochester, NY	153,409	24,840	137,552	23,391	9,817	884	1,971	196	735	44	3,285	353
Rockford, IL	48,379	6,539	43,501	6,251	2,623	148	661	38	226	48	1,333	54
Rocky Mount, NC	22,437	2,791	14,075	1,890	7,805	888	na	na	196	13	149	0
Rome, GA	13,894	1,741	12,337	1,608	1,265	60	na	na	na	na	138	73
Sacramento--Arden-Arcade--Roseville, CA	271,120	39,322	201,350	31,009	12,790	1,448	27,166	3,185	5,426	577	23,681	3,013
Saginaw-Saginaw Township North, MI	31,123	4,628	25,671	4,017	3,905	425	143	4	225	26	1,277	170
St. Cloud, MN	23,516	3,504	23,026	3,381	64	15	na	na	na	na	169	21
St. George, UT	25,428	3,421	24,298	3,298	na	na	na	na	na	na	813	77
St. Joseph, MO-KS	18,214	3,036	17,576	2,875	269	95	na	na	137	4	168	48
St. Louis, MO-IL	385,344	55,390	324,830	48,797	49,499	5,583	5,046	313	2,320	242	3,735	474
Salem, OR	53,770	8,274	49,427	7,795	140	29	749	110	751	110	2,439	208
Salinas, CA	46,040	7,052	29,640	5,108	1,331	169	4,250	638	566	27	10,296	1,155
Salisbury, MD	17,045	2,191	13,386	1,734	3,140	457	na	na	93	0	267	0
Salt Lake City, UT	100,283	12,192	89,833	11,162	383	33	2,671	319	879	77	6,056	542
San Angelo, TX	15,710	1,642	12,094	1,133	419	36	na	na	na	na	2,996	431
San Antonio-New Braunfels, TX	246,536	31,051	133,436	19,622	12,445	1,440	3,816	172	3,264	499	94,846	9,655
San Diego-Carlsbad-San Marcos, CA	365,780	57,661	251,652	44,625	12,332	1,527	38,700	3,882	5,400	603	57,994	7,232
Sandusky, OH	13,703	1,779	12,601	1,715	783	39	na	na	na	na	164	25
San Francisco-Oakland-Fremont, CA	570,451	86,927	325,573	56,195	42,973	6,475	133,772	16,682	10,949	1,039	56,631	6,987
San Jose-Sunnyvale-Santa Clara, CA	211,534	29,018	117,011	18,511	3,852	409	57,734	6,514	4,065	429	29,396	3,106
San Luis Obispo-Paso Robles, CA	42,727	6,712	37,755	6,123	343	3	1,082	278	355	28	3,078	275
Santa Barbara-Santa Maria-Goleta, CA	56,046	10,019	42,229	8,263	891	76	2,157	392	844	100	9,754	1,098
Santa Cruz-Watsonville, CA	30,785	4,892	25,006	4,174	283	0	1,263	184	436	16	3,954	534
Santa Fe, NM	23,581	2,518	15,044	1,622	na	na	na	na	410	28	7,767	799
Santa Rosa-Petaluma, CA	70,993	11,383	62,054	10,339	621	97	2,168	142	1,003	106	5,042	626
Savannah, GA	42,188	5,427	29,955	3,805	10,618	1,424	657	51	301	100	659	47
Scranton--Wilkes-Barre, PA	101,721	17,073	98,510	16,932	617	26	613	8	373	8	1,133	83
Seattle-Tacoma-Bellevue, WA	391,481	57,323	322,590	50,188	13,467	1,425	39,343	4,211	4,769	482	8,978	1,089
Sebastian-Vero Beach, FL	39,107	6,497	36,113	6,065	1,359	57	na	na	na	na	1,191	172
Sheboygan, WI	17,184	2,993	16,763	2,935	na	na	160	14	na	na	202	44
Sherman-Denison, TX	19,174	2,535	17,723	2,311	633	190	na	na	286	0	373	34
Shreveport-Bossier City, LA	53,345	6,445	37,277	4,684	14,592	1,660	334	23	452	6	562	69
Sioux City, IA-NE-SD	18,956	3,009	17,805	2,930	99	31	430	0	71	0	444	48
Sioux Falls, SD	26,322	4,042	25,799	3,940	93	38	186	0	16	0	98	30
South Bend-Mishawaka, IN-MI	44,942	6,767	40,402	6,356	3,126	323	351	24	381	39	586	25
Spartanburg, SC	39,447	3,986	33,122	3,352	5,539	634	331	0	136	0	344	0
Spokane, WA	63,283	8,679	59,931	8,499	364	0	1,089	87	851	51	836	48
Springfield, IL	30,049	4,697	27,984	4,492	1,533	124	185	16	165	26	172	65
Springfield, MA	99,398	16,728	88,638	15,874	3,962	248	1,142	76	708	21	5,015	468

Table C-4: Metropolitan Statistical Areas—Older Population by Race and Hispanic Origin—*Continued*

	Total Population		White, Non-Hispanic		Black, Alone		Asian, Alone		Multi-race, Alone		Hispanic	
	65 Years and Over	85 Years and Over	65 Years and Over	85 Years and Over	65 Years and Over	85 Years and Over	65 Years and Over	85 Years and Over	65 Years and Over	85 Years and Over	65 Years and Over	85 Years and Over
Springfield, MO	63,006	8,591	60,862	8,182	567	94	201	49	563	167	654	78
Springfield, OH	22,620	3,490	20,780	3,169	1,616	285	na	na	102	0	47	8
State College, PA	17,752	2,566	17,413	2,505	33	0	137	0	26	0	97	24
Steubenville-Weirton, OH-WV	23,117	3,201	22,146	3,110	706	44	na	na	88	19	na	na
Stockton, CA	74,322	10,314	44,246	7,214	4,095	477	10,061	1,054	2,449	223	14,006	1,416
Sumter, SC	14,136	1,694	8,173	955	5,733	719	na	na	na	na	na	na
Syracuse, NY	93,016	14,779	86,695	14,173	3,531	376	899	31	624	88	884	134
Tallahassee, FL	39,930	5,073	29,213	4,147	9,075	726	518	11	178	35	968	154
Tampa-St. Petersburg-Clearwater, FL	494,529	72,286	416,386	63,819	27,549	2,931	7,815	627	4,264	384	39,710	4,407
Terre Haute, IN	24,812	3,738	23,917	3,692	533	41	na	na	162	0	90	5
Texarkana, TX-Texarkana, AR	19,682	2,524	15,927	1,890	3,181	510	na	na	204	34	246	87
Toledo, OH	89,540	12,782	78,337	11,836	7,919	704	746	43	605	24	2,016	175
Topeka, KS	35,398	4,937	32,009	4,545	1,428	169	194	0	434	15	1,108	196
Trenton-Ewing, NJ	47,385	7,261	34,929	6,172	7,316	704	2,586	256	389	25	2,176	136
Tucson, AZ	157,849	21,477	125,224	18,139	3,045	268	2,603	168	1,455	70	24,511	2,787
Tulsa, OK	124,949	16,103	105,114	14,249	6,763	694	1,118	62	4,919	447	2,241	146
Tuscaloosa, AL	25,545	3,033	18,168	2,097	6,858	824	115	20	na	na	250	76
Tyler, TX	30,979	4,509	25,302	3,794	3,910	515	na	na	308	0	1,123	173
Utica-Rome, NY	49,761	9,381	47,534	9,139	934	169	469	42	310	12	532	28
Valdosta, GA	15,000	1,813	10,891	1,420	3,620	387	na	na	172	0	342	6
Vallejo-Fairfield, CA	49,340	5,922	28,360	3,898	5,869	565	8,836	935	1,018	58	5,213	498
Victoria, TX	16,937	1,894	11,720	1,371	779	179	na	na	314	14	4,271	348
Vineland-Millville-Bridgeton, NJ	20,154	2,843	15,279	2,244	2,280	271	na	na	217	10	2,161	216
Virginia Beach-Norfolk-Newport News, VA-NC	200,048	24,444	139,900	17,820	48,959	5,855	6,750	396	1,743	183	2,880	268
Visalia-Porterville, CA	43,156	5,689	27,077	4,101	526	57	1,524	253	1,171	65	13,141	1,212
Waco, TX	30,023	4,469	23,498	3,698	3,384	432	188	31	224	64	2,674	273
Warner Robins, GA	15,075	1,539	12,131	1,157	2,440	382	na	na	91	0	234	0
Washington-Arlington-Alexandria, DC-VA-MD-WV	588,571	75,781	366,582	53,924	137,467	14,436	47,104	4,028	8,521	827	30,038	2,684
Waterloo-Cedar Falls, IA	24,946	4,039	23,760	3,872	947	139	84	12	51	0	81	16
Wausau, WI	19,728	3,252	19,228	3,215	na	na	321	6	97	9	105	22
Wenatchee-East Wenatchee, WA	16,803	2,539	16,175	2,507	na	na	na	na	188	20	302	6
Wheeling, WV-OH	26,465	3,997	25,852	3,917	273	36	na	na	128	18	na	na
Wichita, KS	76,821	11,698	67,865	10,980	3,893	319	1,528	0	841	143	2,479	252
Wichita Falls, TX	20,708	2,716	18,048	2,516	1,134	99	220	0	151	0	1,161	101
Williamsport, PA	19,304	3,409	18,903	3,324	166	43	na	na	32	0	na	na
Wilmington, NC	62,904	6,054	55,194	5,187	6,563	774	364	60	275	0	429	33
Winchester, VA-WV	17,958	2,115	17,392	2,076	341	39	na	na	na	na	77	0
Winston-Salem, NC	68,307	8,563	57,195	7,494	9,653	976	369	37	196	13	873	43
Worcester, MA	104,748	17,839	97,694	17,305	1,406	168	1,817	135	568	31	3,203	253
Yakima, WA	29,016	4,420	23,317	3,934	na	na	287	68	612	125	4,190	245
York-Hanover, PA	63,155	8,678	60,120	8,478	1,524	114	459	0	170	29	838	57
Youngstown-Warren-Boardman, OH-PA	101,541	16,434	92,525	15,355	7,454	912	247	0	332	33	1,028	156
Yuba City, CA	19,873	2,119	14,623	1,670	389	111	2,277	187	430	8	2,171	171
Yuma, AZ	31,751	2,635	23,283	1,865	151	4	357	0	210	52	7,547	664

Table C-5: 113th Congressional Districts—Older Population by Race and Hispanic Origin

	Total Population		White, Non-Hispanic		Black, Alone		Asian, Alone		Multi-race, Alone		Hispanic	
	65 Years and Over	85 Years and Over	65 Years and Over	85 Years and Over	65 Years and Over	85 Years and Over	65 Years and Over	85 Years and Over	65 Years and Over	85 Years and Over	65 Years and Over	85 Years and Over
Alabama												
Congressional District 1................	100,507	11,152	78,891	8,709	18,883	2,210	584	25	690	96	1,025	95
Congressional District 2................	98,176	11,112	78,180	8,785	17,483	2,164	808	20	823	100	728	39
Congressional District 3................	94,315	10,395	75,013	8,273	17,496	1,978	287	3	461	135	963	6
Congressional District 4................	109,146	11,970	101,621	11,062	5,352	753	319	35	988	68	572	30
Congressional District 5................	95,320	10,982	83,554	9,804	9,332	995	812	40	495	45	798	65
Congressional District 6................	91,264	11,721	83,665	10,819	5,597	803	709	0	478	52	776	36
Congressional District 7................	88,397	11,465	40,139	5,158	47,004	6,084	189	20	431	46	703	179
Alaska												
Congressional District (at Large)	58,586	4,909	43,585	3,664	1,279	95	3,353	342	1,238	50	1,300	105
Arizona												
Congressional District 1................	102,031	10,681	73,969	8,196	1,373	116	1,084	20	793	57	10,861	984
Congressional District 2................	129,414	18,304	109,145	16,437	2,175	127	2,665	128	1,136	61	14,342	1,546
Congressional District 3................	66,560	6,933	33,215	3,779	1,959	197	866	67	937	67	28,553	2,826
Congressional District 4................	161,536	16,496	149,812	15,174	554	35	897	150	1,593	136	7,919	901
Congressional District 5................	109,142	11,476	99,171	10,928	1,607	73	2,079	110	512	25	5,343	277
Congressional District 6................	106,142	12,710	97,557	11,853	1,049	132	2,196	144	438	27	4,410	551
Congressional District 7................	46,883	4,831	21,309	2,766	5,471	500	1,489	69	704	71	17,651	1,381
Congressional District 8................	134,799	17,938	121,410	16,652	2,290	244	2,642	209	765	71	7,450	762
Congressional District 9................	70,519	10,592	57,918	9,574	1,954	264	2,219	133	625	34	7,358	557
Arkansas												
Congressional District 1................	117,546	13,979	103,682	12,042	11,748	1,812	272	3	1,078	54	568	44
Congressional District 2................	97,003	11,360	83,360	9,875	10,845	1,359	644	0	928	74	968	0
Congressional District 3................	93,618	12,134	89,257	11,776	1,042	110	722	0	1,027	34	1,324	193
Congressional District 4................	121,518	14,637	103,131	12,603	15,209	1,906	285	0	1,189	86	1,242	14
California												
Congressional District 1................	124,506	17,142	113,767	16,036	789	26	1,705	209	2,403	163	5,123	633
Congressional District 2................	113,154	15,495	100,510	14,297	1,128	141	3,151	229	2,173	157	5,265	518
Congressional District 3................	82,747	10,398	58,596	8,222	4,402	470	7,741	822	1,820	78	9,974	881
Congressional District 4................	119,427	14,360	106,704	13,116	822	42	3,300	296	1,556	117	6,015	790
Congressional District 5................	99,389	15,649	75,066	12,871	4,143	552	9,899	1,048	1,510	96	8,637	1,011
Congressional District 6................	75,852	11,529	43,949	7,780	7,972	795	12,603	1,727	1,884	177	9,117	1,079
Congressional District 7................	87,722	13,236	65,243	10,352	3,924	574	9,841	890	2,035	310	6,558	978
Congressional District 8................	80,982	8,481	60,244	6,916	4,061	273	1,936	107	1,238	122	12,818	1,018
Congressional District 9................	79,074	10,396	47,565	7,334	4,640	533	10,682	980	2,569	215	14,401	1,405
Congressional District 10................	75,228	10,706	52,909	8,317	1,755	191	3,907	294	2,108	177	14,252	1,681
Congressional District 11................	99,443	15,865	69,435	12,392	7,669	1,100	11,726	1,357	1,548	24	8,762	1,044
Congressional District 12................	95,959	15,796	39,783	7,069	5,953	761	40,373	6,462	1,755	181	8,394	1,491
Congressional District 13................	86,267	13,745	39,074	6,689	18,148	3,263	19,955	2,596	1,838	364	7,301	897
Congressional District 14................	99,646	15,777	52,196	10,628	4,597	690	28,320	3,058	1,942	144	12,364	1,294
Congressional District 15................	75,584	10,630	42,071	7,134	3,132	294	18,692	1,949	1,766	175	9,654	1,204
Congressional District 16................	63,335	8,416	32,221	4,906	3,671	419	5,142	648	1,579	248	20,963	2,294
Congressional District 17................	76,662	11,408	36,311	6,104	1,755	168	29,539	2,801	1,263	78	7,981	1,009
Congressional District 18................	96,943	15,986	73,470	12,976	1,101	194	14,555	1,974	1,468	232	6,317	553
Congressional District 19................	73,386	8,359	32,050	3,906	1,660	131	22,223	2,546	1,709	227	15,966	1,573
Congressional District 20................	78,515	12,138	53,149	9,083	1,633	176	5,570	805	1,198	43	17,127	2,092
Congressional District 21................	53,389	6,444	23,812	3,102	2,015	283	3,303	804	1,103	12	23,652	2,262
Congressional District 22................	77,990	11,408	54,166	9,052	1,590	96	4,600	504	1,370	160	16,454	1,633
Congressional District 23................	78,393	9,188	58,088	7,560	2,885	288	3,550	330	1,048	60	12,003	911
Congressional District 24................	99,867	16,788	80,813	14,414	1,249	79	3,258	670	1,227	128	13,035	1,402
Congressional District 25................	64,992	7,351	42,829	5,479	3,661	173	5,361	485	1,414	170	11,756	1,056
Congressional District 26................	88,218	13,121	61,880	10,217	1,317	61	6,333	635	1,227	104	17,867	2,100
Congressional District 27................	105,407	18,467	43,894	8,824	4,940	673	35,985	5,858	1,578	342	19,394	2,887
Congressional District 28................	98,991	14,237	67,499	10,626	1,714	373	13,854	1,376	1,918	162	14,200	1,708
Congressional District 29................	61,633	8,068	23,715	4,247	3,247	338	8,940	1,029	1,380	58	24,846	2,438
Congressional District 30................	96,711	15,094	70,646	12,520	2,053	345	10,821	1,153	2,083	238	11,214	942
Congressional District 31................	61,985	8,369	31,278	4,446	5,801	688	5,961	492	1,227	62	18,215	2,717
Congressional District 32................	79,081	10,899	26,132	4,917	2,265	262	16,758	2,020	1,555	195	33,000	3,535
Congressional District 33................	107,873	16,847	88,092	14,704	2,296	248	8,580	855	2,065	113	6,725	931
Congressional District 34................	70,206	9,832	9,941	1,821	2,579	284	25,082	3,877	1,492	83	31,835	3,800
Congressional District 35................	53,148	6,497	17,355	3,211	5,431	308	5,381	626	1,184	130	24,107	2,331
Congressional District 36................	136,193	18,014	109,414	15,491	2,860	286	3,330	459	1,622	103	19,108	1,642
Congressional District 37................	80,365	13,479	26,906	5,508	30,110	4,519	7,973	1,351	1,573	204	13,934	1,966
Congressional District 38................	85,926	12,203	31,083	5,978	2,372	256	15,721	1,884	1,365	57	35,764	4,027
Congressional District 39................	86,941	11,487	43,364	6,763	1,466	176	25,911	3,038	1,212	165	14,832	1,343
Congressional District 40................	50,219	6,144	8,924	1,742	4,282	543	2,841	469	944	57	34,090	3,358
Congressional District 41................	56,226	6,812	28,433	4,333	5,818	551	3,800	483	1,226	32	17,305	1,418
Congressional District 42................	71,724	7,284	47,077	5,151	3,782	148	6,348	344	1,349	276	13,196	1,496
Congressional District 43................	72,981	9,666	20,753	3,807	20,306	2,061	13,675	1,956	1,408	107	17,120	1,694
Congressional District 44................	59,613	6,189	11,275	1,820	14,985	1,534	5,733	360	1,806	200	26,382	2,437
Congressional District 45................	90,423	13,482	66,244	11,400	1,028	91	13,645	1,264	1,203	50	8,203	681
Congressional District 46................	55,849	8,457	25,641	5,461	1,104	122	10,231	757	1,037	87	18,178	2,062
Congressional District 47................	81,363	11,492	46,625	8,122	3,835	313	17,908	1,735	1,353	117	11,475	1,247
Congressional District 48................	104,415	14,882	76,577	11,933	700	20	17,864	1,924	1,084	160	8,034	823
Congressional District 49................	87,886	14,406	70,900	12,402	862	179	5,174	399	1,165	187	9,679	1,245
Congressional District 50................	87,196	13,934	71,834	11,952	775	140	3,373	386	1,241	181	10,041	1,351

Table C-5: 113th Congressional Districts—Older Population by Race and Hispanic Origin—*Continued*

	Total Population		White, Non-Hispanic		Black, Alone		Asian, Alone		Multi-race, Alone		Hispanic	
	65 Years and Over	85 Years and Over	65 Years and Over	85 Years and Over	65 Years and Over	85 Years and Over	65 Years and Over	85 Years and Over	65 Years and Over	85 Years and Over	65 Years and Over	85 Years and Over
California—Cont.												
Congressional District 51	70,177	9,366	19,538	3,015	4,631	627	8,400	851	1,315	195	36,675	4,825
Congressional District 52	86,263	13,672	65,614	11,162	1,386	205	12,635	1,382	1,162	130	5,382	820
Congressional District 53	81,436	13,349	51,734	10,442	5,015	415	10,732	1,110	1,427	57	12,757	1,335
Colorado												
Congressional District 1	78,341	12,655	55,816	10,321	7,229	956	2,176	173	868	161	12,356	1,100
Congressional District 2	82,009	9,982	76,559	9,610	294	63	1,315	61	470	66	3,378	270
Congressional District 3	103,649	12,465	87,212	10,550	625	118	425	42	1,442	152	13,934	1,526
Congressional District 4	80,065	9,789	69,996	8,641	310	43	677	109	779	94	8,326	918
Congressional District 5	81,970	9,168	71,194	8,515	2,674	174	1,878	135	1,091	81	5,207	303
Congressional District 6	70,735	8,623	58,071	7,560	3,707	258	2,974	264	887	30	4,995	495
Congressional District 7	84,546	10,969	70,912	9,474	497	80	2,382	379	803	107	10,061	970
Connecticut												
Congressional District 1	107,707	19,343	89,176	17,487	9,651	1,186	2,268	130	909	50	6,027	491
Congressional District 2	102,946	14,517	97,169	13,961	1,773	175	1,277	44	736	87	1,841	232
Congressional District 3	104,522	19,023	89,809	17,950	8,051	805	1,628	16	755	28	4,072	246
Congressional District 4	99,387	16,067	81,628	14,478	8,490	821	2,562	113	375	53	6,719	638
Congressional District 5	104,177	18,088	93,515	17,207	3,992	351	1,036	54	612	26	5,216	443
Delaware												
Congressional District (at Large)	134,601	16,505	110,758	14,208	17,398	1,827	2,592	153	884	100	2,707	308
District of Columbia												
Delegate District (at Large)	70,302	10,229	21,878	3,347	43,449	6,305	1,386	253	884	120	3,032	253
Florida												
Congressional District 1	101,989	11,437	88,085	10,138	8,608	865	1,964	63	1,235	144	1,808	191
Congressional District 2	91,094	10,587	73,885	9,023	13,588	1,233	834	11	736	84	1,877	209
Congressional District 3	106,220	12,529	93,739	11,149	7,271	926	1,108	12	810	15	3,165	427
Congressional District 4	87,437	11,340	75,297	10,272	5,358	592	2,761	73	720	122	3,359	266
Congressional District 5	74,854	8,645	35,745	4,839	31,555	3,061	1,699	137	1,239	132	5,383	623
Congressional District 6	151,827	18,834	136,839	17,377	8,269	989	1,666	38	656	23	4,412	376
Congressional District 7	92,573	14,425	72,624	12,094	5,210	596	2,021	344	1,036	126	11,994	1,268
Congressional District 8	154,853	20,529	137,235	19,006	8,579	788	1,669	237	1,342	131	6,469	387
Congressional District 9	77,152	8,085	41,273	4,817	7,300	587	2,684	151	1,168	128	25,765	2,459
Congressional District 10	123,374	14,143	103,234	12,437	7,576	719	3,224	154	650	52	8,603	781
Congressional District 11	213,186	22,913	195,402	21,165	6,965	821	1,397	0	1,215	73	8,323	801
Congressional District 12	142,428	21,604	129,759	20,394	2,667	269	1,752	127	1,205	42	7,149	744
Congressional District 13	155,143	25,177	143,573	23,741	3,209	404	2,333	179	877	126	5,093	646
Congressional District 14	82,835	10,271	45,620	6,288	16,140	1,411	1,917	130	1,132	118	18,826	2,340
Congressional District 15	95,091	12,091	78,088	10,395	7,079	848	2,108	241	859	101	7,121	424
Congressional District 16	199,378	29,680	187,758	28,414	4,539	473	1,500	111	822	102	4,734	580
Congressional District 17	178,647	24,434	161,513	22,451	6,769	1,041	1,121	69	1,186	187	8,087	732
Congressional District 18	159,903	23,084	141,450	21,648	8,640	604	1,448	105	752	67	7,601	686
Congressional District 19	188,998	25,009	174,387	23,639	4,389	220	1,507	88	820	80	7,714	1,036
Congressional District 20	94,585	16,477	49,236	11,970	32,399	2,974	1,658	90	1,309	270	10,998	1,437
Congressional District 21	156,557	30,258	135,814	27,936	5,450	801	2,100	0	827	66	12,384	1,473
Congressional District 22	145,605	26,428	125,539	24,196	6,477	937	928	97	705	39	12,133	1,240
Congressional District 23	110,125	16,703	69,163	12,291	5,627	496	2,438	162	1,206	71	32,752	3,729
Congressional District 24	75,707	8,460	14,691	2,569	37,132	3,567	885	74	987	26	23,743	2,419
Congressional District 25	103,432	11,936	34,807	4,329	4,596	329	1,130	19	1,154	72	63,333	7,273
Congressional District 26	102,763	12,845	24,398	3,198	7,094	703	1,605	207	921	33	69,393	8,830
Congressional District 27	115,743	17,109	23,192	3,816	4,623	397	1,392	26	999	65	87,794	12,865
Georgia												
Congressional District 1	84,613	9,572	63,909	7,077	18,262	2,246	888	51	475	105	922	93
Congressional District 2	87,496	9,903	51,964	6,503	33,255	3,274	692	0	483	1	952	125
Congressional District 3	85,613	9,089	69,986	7,176	13,502	1,666	595	57	391	19	1,232	171
Congressional District 4	62,191	6,855	33,320	4,613	23,872	1,796	2,953	300	530	30	1,733	196
Congressional District 5	63,743	9,405	20,519	4,469	40,250	4,847	1,534	13	444	11	1,322	65
Congressional District 6	70,512	8,231	59,580	7,256	4,319	357	3,607	323	666	70	2,442	264
Congressional District 7	54,609	5,301	41,020	4,487	4,783	333	5,409	235	388	105	2,963	141
Congressional District 8	89,986	10,494	69,942	8,167	17,945	2,249	384	25	403	6	1,296	47
Congressional District 9	106,151	10,052	98,466	9,276	4,561	508	465	0	683	0	1,897	264
Congressional District 10	82,935	8,330	63,844	6,371	16,581	1,639	674	102	380	43	1,511	175
Congressional District 11	66,643	5,843	58,126	5,187	4,844	316	1,244	60	474	111	1,765	160
Congressional District 12	83,361	8,495	59,674	6,611	20,407	1,793	1,185	17	488	74	1,592	24
Congressional District 13	60,842	6,288	37,792	4,618	19,281	1,618	1,403	0	692	31	1,795	21
Congressional District 14	84,707	8,982	78,454	8,334	4,123	477	487	0	449	14	1,157	130
Hawaii												
Congressional District 1	110,613	19,581	17,839	2,335	622	111	78,230	15,624	8,652	1,078	2,485	280
Congressional District 2	92,582	14,180	32,382	4,274	321	19	40,234	8,118	10,550	980	4,106	434
Idaho												
Congressional District 1	107,237	12,490	101,995	11,933	60	47	547	35	1,166	137	2,770	288
Congressional District 2	95,973	13,129	90,297	12,545	164	3	1,039	164	790	183	2,959	229

Table C-5: 113th Congressional Districts—Older Population by Race and Hispanic Origin—*Continued*

	Total Population		White, Non-Hispanic		Black, Alone		Asian, Alone		Multi-race, Alone		Hispanic	
	65 Years and Over	85 Years and Over	65 Years and Over	85 Years and Over	65 Years and Over	85 Years and Over	65 Years and Over	85 Years and Over	65 Years and Over	85 Years and Over	65 Years and Over	85 Years and Over
Illinois												
Congressional District 1	96,833	13,576	38,931	6,716	52,553	6,467	1,280	115	715	87	3,262	199
Congressional District 2	93,931	13,786	43,840	8,296	43,703	4,904	711	117	754	79	4,996	390
Congressional District 3	89,539	14,928	74,954	13,090	2,650	484	2,250	264	540	44	9,141	1,052
Congressional District 4	54,981	6,557	26,649	4,813	2,090	230	2,232	197	518	0	23,967	1,317
Congressional District 5	84,617	14,485	67,944	12,512	1,464	297	5,145	669	645	30	9,706	990
Congressional District 6	89,670	12,538	79,531	11,878	1,653	247	5,326	216	459	36	2,627	145
Congressional District 7	74,370	8,504	24,717	3,811	40,827	3,948	4,255	493	622	0	4,131	263
Congressional District 8	72,496	10,752	59,038	9,829	1,187	14	6,760	322	380	61	5,106	533
Congressional District 9	111,895	19,467	88,938	17,012	5,738	853	11,514	1,107	1,115	123	4,505	350
Congressional District 10	86,278	13,014	71,248	11,966	3,597	283	5,934	322	718	86	5,026	427
Congressional District 11	70,597	9,352	53,978	8,017	5,108	503	4,560	372	707	60	6,376	376
Congressional District 12	103,683	14,314	90,610	12,874	10,369	1,311	763	0	776	68	1,057	44
Congressional District 13	97,989	15,007	90,941	14,278	4,850	535	837	64	545	53	789	111
Congressional District 14	72,531	7,754	67,306	7,463	638	0	2,004	87	399	49	2,239	122
Congressional District 15	117,440	17,472	113,879	17,028	1,682	240	541	0	454	80	750	65
Congressional District 16	106,334	14,952	102,143	14,702	967	119	810	30	419	36	2,082	67
Congressional District 17	114,419	17,414	104,274	16,409	5,889	507	833	70	672	53	2,762	331
Congressional District 18	112,449	17,348	109,563	17,067	1,314	146	665	42	414	37	396	56
Indiana												
Congressional District 1	96,735	12,987	74,141	10,298	14,932	1,774	838	37	554	23	6,339	855
Congressional District 2	99,749	14,467	93,820	13,959	3,530	436	421	0	599	47	1,252	25
Congressional District 3	94,945	13,374	89,313	12,900	3,266	251	538	46	509	78	1,064	99
Congressional District 4	95,509	12,365	92,492	12,110	1,187	85	652	47	397	50	771	57
Congressional District 5	89,604	13,443	81,112	12,495	5,368	780	1,456	33	568	28	997	107
Congressional District 6	107,554	13,060	104,439	12,762	1,468	145	250	14	739	85	520	43
Congressional District 7	75,109	9,648	55,556	7,737	16,835	1,706	742	31	622	65	1,311	109
Congressional District 8	107,489	15,132	103,693	14,649	2,300	390	332	20	468	66	618	7
Congressional District 9	96,285	11,648	92,949	11,398	1,365	79	449	35	710	15	694	119
Iowa												
Congressional District 1	118,999	18,405	116,226	17,989	1,266	187	358	139	255	5	616	83
Congressional District 2	112,960	18,033	109,077	17,665	1,369	80	758	28	322	11	1,515	249
Congressional District 3	98,424	14,786	93,896	14,492	1,607	114	1,009	63	436	48	1,333	83
Congressional District 4	129,642	23,902	127,063	23,739	241	31	738	13	270	4	1,080	106
Kansas												
Congressional District 1	105,616	17,455	99,611	16,853	1,355	204	556	35	810	176	3,239	204
Congressional District 2	103,262	15,351	95,924	14,545	2,783	360	580	45	1,263	55	1,901	285
Congressional District 3	81,186	13,083	70,371	11,795	5,653	751	1,632	120	782	151	2,663	299
Congressional District 4	94,113	14,313	84,464	13,557	3,955	319	1,573	0	1,098	146	2,725	261
Kentucky												
Congressional District 1	114,216	13,500	108,388	12,992	4,359	442	126	0	640	38	614	28
Congressional District 2	98,109	11,845	92,858	11,306	3,387	427	534	18	746	49	458	29
Congressional District 3	98,854	14,465	82,808	12,736	13,048	1,425	1,184	156	653	61	1,115	87
Congressional District 4	89,547	10,917	86,680	10,766	1,555	116	225	8	367	17	587	10
Congressional District 5	105,071	10,659	102,752	10,417	841	157	124	20	754	33	535	32
Congressional District 6	88,423	10,416	80,890	9,707	5,757	637	587	22	376	22	741	21
Louisiana												
Congressional District 1	102,412	13,295	88,598	11,989	6,936	771	956	73	473	84	4,667	331
Congressional District 2	85,924	11,031	34,513	5,102	45,643	5,342	1,703	132	758	78	3,515	398
Congressional District 3	92,733	10,603	73,215	8,996	16,457	1,413	588	0	757	39	1,405	92
Congressional District 4	103,953	11,891	75,861	8,763	25,114	2,866	513	26	981	75	1,043	150
Congressional District 5	104,506	12,938	77,887	9,876	24,373	2,887	313	0	622	5	1,001	170
Congressional District 6	86,017	9,420	70,812	7,683	12,171	1,487	949	111	562	43	1,542	96
Maine												
Congressional District 1	107,561	15,149	105,135	15,023	292	0	726	8	557	79	651	48
Congressional District 2	110,770	13,955	108,716	13,813	178	5	360	0	729	48	435	84
Maryland												
Congressional District 1	113,441	13,533	101,235	11,855	9,729	1,472	1,037	47	449	46	907	40
Congressional District 2	84,857	13,043	65,088	11,283	14,473	1,326	3,456	227	452	45	1,330	115
Congressional District 3	95,451	15,625	76,397	13,512	12,265	1,375	4,406	420	752	182	1,667	136
Congressional District 4	76,158	8,559	31,884	4,828	38,086	3,116	2,577	271	970	140	2,849	147
Congressional District 5	78,778	8,793	51,134	6,374	22,791	1,997	2,565	234	565	22	1,619	223
Congressional District 6	90,332	12,219	74,316	11,035	4,832	209	7,149	555	831	30	3,354	388
Congressional District 7	94,368	12,974	40,803	7,006	49,002	5,446	2,710	188	837	124	953	174
Congressional District 8	101,790	16,885	78,021	14,044	9,360	1,249	7,673	893	1,467	103	5,534	628
Massachusetts												
Congressional District 1	111,910	18,995	100,943	17,948	4,051	359	1,062	76	722	21	5,220	530
Congressional District 2	96,124	16,590	89,590	16,185	1,354	115	1,837	116	587	8	2,707	209
Congressional District 3	90,463	13,989	79,812	13,057	1,528	25	3,300	319	623	104	5,544	513
Congressional District 4	99,335	16,410	93,244	15,761	1,438	193	2,298	217	722	71	1,438	168
Congressional District 5	104,791	17,321	94,747	15,973	2,373	414	4,727	648	764	11	2,071	261
Congressional District 6	111,694	17,866	105,256	17,322	1,420	172	1,783	119	751	76	2,889	261
Congressional District 7	73,035	10,518	40,708	6,778	18,151	2,113	6,479	887	2,035	167	6,564	639
Congressional District 8	107,611	18,840	95,769	17,651	4,615	529	4,020	195	1,082	176	2,012	220
Congressional District 9	134,965	19,330	128,725	18,535	1,675	245	602	89	865	106	1,452	136

Table C-5: 113th Congressional Districts—Older Population by Race and Hispanic Origin—*Continued*

	Total Population		White, Non-Hispanic		Black, Alone		Asian, Alone		Multi-race, Alone		Hispanic	
	65 Years and Over	85 Years and Over	65 Years and Over	85 Years and Over	65 Years and Over	85 Years and Over	65 Years and Over	85 Years and Over	65 Years and Over	85 Years and Over	65 Years and Over	85 Years and Over
Michigan												
Congressional District 1	135,818	17,061	132,239	16,713	392	54	235	19	968	137	655	74
Congressional District 2	92,958	12,877	86,259	12,355	3,207	243	829	0	719	41	2,037	250
Congressional District 3	89,195	13,751	81,521	12,806	4,867	688	512	27	663	35	1,595	198
Congressional District 4	112,216	13,470	109,448	13,167	578	100	369	22	477	49	1,043	97
Congressional District 5	107,406	14,713	90,631	13,065	12,995	1,418	493	14	960	31	2,252	195
Congressional District 6	100,920	14,053	92,644	12,903	5,596	677	711	189	617	137	1,168	147
Congressional District 7	101,761	14,073	97,133	13,643	1,938	191	496	25	534	50	1,456	158
Congressional District 8	82,972	9,830	76,648	9,445	2,684	134	1,450	84	553	41	1,564	126
Congressional District 9	109,625	18,728	100,877	17,768	4,404	484	2,526	284	646	21	877	147
Congressional District 10	102,115	13,274	98,176	12,884	1,008	172	890	43	780	119	1,010	42
Congressional District 11	95,496	13,582	87,783	12,946	2,235	205	3,617	219	523	0	1,135	193
Congressional District 12	83,608	12,375	72,800	11,237	5,717	735	2,237	111	824	90	1,966	199
Congressional District 13	87,355	13,708	37,994	6,671	44,861	6,609	890	161	1,120	113	2,258	141
Congressional District 14	96,543	15,713	44,504	8,786	46,780	6,436	2,086	172	1,342	142	1,735	160
Minnesota												
Congressional District 1	101,113	17,592	98,579	17,305	368	108	1,028	83	260	63	808	15
Congressional District 2	71,429	9,686	67,893	9,368	830	97	1,339	77	487	84	747	60
Congressional District 3	81,795	10,728	77,210	10,234	1,503	48	1,891	153	455	152	667	125
Congressional District 4	80,444	12,082	72,371	11,149	2,542	106	3,478	552	534	48	1,430	191
Congressional District 5	74,161	14,337	64,360	13,322	5,483	484	2,279	289	671	51	1,128	201
Congressional District 6	66,245	8,231	64,745	8,037	118	20	696	107	207	9	344	27
Congressional District 7	116,871	19,815	114,469	19,590	147	28	304	42	466	34	517	42
Congressional District 8	113,557	15,059	110,788	14,900	227	15	408	12	542	22	432	15
Mississippi												
Congressional District 1	100,583	11,482	82,954	9,759	16,304	1,631	371	20	328	63	574	9
Congressional District 2	90,999	12,333	48,562	6,218	41,298	5,961	399	56	297	25	311	61
Congressional District 3	101,570	11,716	75,817	9,135	23,886	2,386	269	6	707	92	686	97
Congressional District 4	97,649	9,623	81,509	7,919	13,939	1,489	734	28	613	60	821	174
Missouri												
Congressional District 1	89,830	14,157	50,517	9,753	36,122	3,863	1,364	187	730	125	1,237	290
Congressional District 2	118,892	19,338	111,731	18,661	3,377	396	2,369	126	604	29	970	126
Congressional District 3	99,071	10,941	95,768	10,690	1,360	191	441	0	617	6	691	30
Congressional District 4	108,676	13,894	103,846	13,473	2,254	259	674	54	896	61	612	31
Congressional District 5	100,542	14,711	79,617	12,318	16,063	1,886	926	4	936	155	2,928	339
Congressional District 6	106,475	15,515	102,200	14,927	1,735	263	654	53	504	22	1,198	190
Congressional District 7	114,802	15,126	110,526	14,490	789	176	406	80	1,166	226	1,237	133
Congressional District 8	121,289	14,980	116,941	14,594	2,156	183	228	0	988	148	510	31
Montana												
Congressional District (at Large)	151,961	20,461	144,644	19,823	155	0	615	120	1,103	27	1,496	258
Nebraska												
Congressional District 1	80,879	12,535	77,751	12,207	646	69	786	77	369	64	1,060	85
Congressional District 2	63,721	9,610	56,307	9,041	4,827	439	695	33	206	16	1,729	86
Congressional District 3	105,955	17,016	103,016	16,790	114	11	265	26	470	36	1,884	157
Nevada												
Congressional District 1	81,313	8,168	53,869	5,971	5,210	597	7,424	481	1,281	126	13,166	1,004
Congressional District 2	92,739	9,999	80,849	9,160	920	83	2,851	179	998	106	5,769	406
Congressional District 3	87,495	8,066	65,667	6,041	4,950	647	9,530	900	1,364	10	5,502	442
Congressional District 4	81,157	6,767	59,477	5,852	9,151	374	3,877	164	1,240	43	6,734	250
New Hampshire												
Congressional District 1	91,778	12,241	89,162	12,112	339	34	897	50	527	26	763	0
Congressional District 2	93,662	12,035	91,520	11,856	302	6	512	31	553	75	749	32
New Jersey												
Congressional District 1	97,197	14,905	77,243	12,648	11,813	1,692	3,413	249	974	68	3,885	239
Congressional District 2	113,956	14,669	95,608	12,665	10,000	1,148	2,526	281	775	38	5,083	523
Congressional District 3	125,859	18,925	111,388	17,776	8,642	710	2,448	63	500	40	3,004	345
Congressional District 4	123,238	19,632	110,231	18,235	5,649	597	2,793	257	811	123	3,774	407
Congressional District 5	108,929	17,576	91,513	15,836	4,045	459	6,514	603	872	63	6,201	650
Congressional District 6	87,231	12,308	62,509	10,154	6,732	463	9,498	907	1,025	88	7,890	736
Congressional District 7	98,051	15,510	85,611	14,430	2,703	390	5,096	235	412	136	4,374	461
Congressional District 8	70,575	9,573	28,060	5,353	5,727	757	3,919	229	1,670	86	33,190	3,359
Congressional District 9	96,868	15,070	64,205	12,276	8,645	889	7,840	568	1,458	121	16,160	1,270
Congressional District 10	82,333	10,884	28,088	5,752	39,759	3,830	4,355	352	1,388	105	9,078	1,059
Congressional District 11	115,572	19,838	102,577	18,482	2,667	389	6,145	543	580	0	3,810	441
Congressional District 12	96,620	15,464	70,369	13,100	13,168	1,292	8,147	559	709	17	4,212	528
New Mexico												
Congressional District 1	89,553	11,488	55,365	7,667	1,716	128	1,569	226	1,174	115	28,755	3,250
Congressional District 2	101,911	11,506	63,308	7,440	1,412	194	425	18	1,573	127	32,832	3,481
Congressional District 3	92,075	10,531	52,798	6,572	668	99	597	39	1,499	88	27,551	2,918

Table C-5: 113th Congressional Districts—Older Population by Race and Hispanic Origin—*Continued*

	Total Population		White, Non-Hispanic		Black, Alone		Asian, Alone		Multi-race, Alone		Hispanic	
	65 Years and Over	85 Years and Over	65 Years and Over	85 Years and Over	65 Years and Over	85 Years and Over	65 Years and Over	85 Years and Over	65 Years and Over	85 Years and Over	65 Years and Over	85 Years and Over
New York												
Congressional District 1..................	105,187	13,772	95,292	12,763	3,145	288	1,529	56	842	109	4,474	526
Congressional District 2..................	95,262	14,253	78,542	12,923	6,163	450	2,033	282	658	58	8,091	611
Congressional District 3..................	126,715	21,897	108,200	19,988	2,792	391	9,116	797	1,029	144	5,437	544
Congressional District 4..................	105,114	18,477	81,132	16,167	12,267	1,135	4,076	367	934	62	7,039	756
Congressional District 5..................	89,569	11,771	21,096	4,146	44,044	5,447	8,787	784	2,889	297	11,613	964
Congressional District 6..................	109,100	17,342	61,438	12,818	4,117	404	29,651	2,953	1,460	243	12,630	955
Congressional District 7..................	67,061	9,154	17,189	3,623	7,136	1,070	16,302	2,093	1,609	94	26,624	2,413
Congressional District 8..................	90,816	11,653	33,696	6,117	43,896	4,357	2,797	259	1,435	153	11,504	898
Congressional District 9..................	85,664	11,479	29,026	5,580	46,542	5,197	4,118	240	916	93	7,218	610
Congressional District 10..............	95,392	14,939	70,068	12,234	5,980	912	9,963	673	1,214	103	9,646	1,112
Congressional District 11..............	104,186	15,646	84,365	13,612	3,995	354	8,990	929	725	41	6,275	742
Congressional District 12..............	97,919	12,687	73,985	9,833	4,351	495	8,018	1,180	897	105	11,264	1,130
Congressional District 13..............	82,276	12,939	11,347	2,665	30,183	5,424	2,841	335	4,065	364	40,244	5,035
Congressional District 14..............	83,707	11,886	39,564	7,718	10,024	1,229	9,698	856	1,387	179	24,419	2,136
Congressional District 15..............	61,125	6,274	2,580	441	20,998	2,460	1,316	65	2,241	382	38,566	3,441
Congressional District 16..............	108,448	17,980	61,720	12,817	29,286	3,577	4,047	138	1,243	140	13,852	1,630
Congressional District 17..............	104,140	15,770	82,658	13,795	9,366	1,070	4,643	378	927	63	7,070	505
Congressional District 18..............	91,399	12,898	78,608	11,801	5,335	545	1,578	36	879	62	5,227	427
Congressional District 19..............	115,575	15,662	108,832	15,014	2,189	302	842	54	932	98	2,857	187
Congressional District 20..............	103,746	18,159	95,282	17,406	4,756	388	1,515	72	540	86	1,511	216
Congressional District 21..............	105,185	14,086	102,259	13,747	462	157	737	50	613	50	598	70
Congressional District 22..............	114,501	19,126	110,243	18,785	1,475	208	886	61	748	39	1,094	50
Congressional District 23..............	110,106	16,438	106,882	15,980	1,259	179	586	88	280	31	732	115
Congressional District 24..............	102,817	16,229	95,836	15,656	3,849	361	906	31	696	70	1,129	134
Congressional District 25..............	103,104	17,768	89,349	16,508	8,949	773	1,706	168	407	44	2,791	308
Congressional District 26..............	111,987	17,711	95,099	16,139	12,839	1,315	1,117	3	890	122	1,877	134
Congressional District 27..............	113,794	16,885	109,605	16,438	1,590	227	725	59	342	7	751	84
North Carolina												
Congressional District 1..................	103,676	13,520	53,050	7,326	47,447	6,001	359	11	1,130	130	1,131	39
Congressional District 2..................	90,819	10,558	75,967	8,992	10,921	1,313	1,383	100	506	8	1,823	88
Congressional District 3..................	98,780	11,191	81,024	8,980	15,111	1,988	623	16	367	25	1,401	148
Congressional District 4..................	71,250	8,396	47,355	6,451	19,095	1,612	2,751	147	419	34	1,504	61
Congressional District 5..................	112,466	13,691	101,459	12,481	8,755	1,079	590	53	240	12	1,332	66
Congressional District 6..................	114,690	14,568	99,094	12,817	12,387	1,614	951	18	742	28	1,397	110
Congressional District 7..................	112,736	10,490	92,963	8,361	16,493	1,805	419	78	655	66	1,052	97
Congressional District 8..................	98,166	10,823	77,442	8,949	13,460	1,524	554	0	478	21	1,266	43
Congressional District 9..................	80,611	9,893	70,360	8,902	5,424	688	1,804	20	518	0	2,390	279
Congressional District 10..............	112,143	14,385	100,559	12,693	9,038	1,344	1,117	138	250	35	1,021	190
Congressional District 11..............	143,435	16,735	137,006	16,140	2,917	404	517	23	937	30	1,241	94
Congressional District 12..............	64,378	7,832	30,892	4,992	30,395	2,629	1,088	96	474	6	1,555	129
Congressional District 13..............	85,748	9,934	71,223	8,535	11,594	1,240	1,067	144	573	15	1,202	0
North Dakota												
Congressional District (at Large)	99,040	16,737	95,731	16,650	123	0	443	0	445	8	397	15
Ohio												
Congressional District 1..................	88,952	12,491	73,071	10,743	13,762	1,545	1,188	166	370	7	487	37
Congressional District 2..................	102,327	14,717	93,197	13,244	7,119	1,333	486	0	704	25	727	71
Congressional District 3..................	66,582	8,461	45,897	6,485	17,873	1,817	1,264	60	794	64	801	35
Congressional District 4..................	106,000	15,025	100,912	14,372	2,947	270	285	23	638	150	1,073	195
Congressional District 5..................	108,969	15,598	104,092	15,275	1,768	130	821	67	468	43	1,752	83
Congressional District 6..................	123,125	16,616	119,477	16,167	1,782	319	398	0	778	35	522	84
Congressional District 7..................	111,120	15,316	106,086	14,766	3,194	357	407	24	396	70	759	17
Congressional District 8..................	100,698	13,413	95,218	12,746	3,793	489	658	74	467	0	387	42
Congressional District 9..................	97,460	15,149	82,397	13,928	9,842	894	920	62	636	37	3,869	231
Congressional District 10..............	109,825	15,561	92,566	13,345	14,316	1,914	1,439	142	728	80	787	63
Congressional District 11..............	103,702	17,730	53,030	11,514	47,131	5,789	1,123	102	870	101	1,719	234
Congressional District 12..............	91,781	11,607	86,743	11,069	2,550	345	1,416	56	553	63	519	74
Congressional District 13..............	115,537	18,243	104,479	17,027	8,962	1,008	543	10	561	54	1,043	157
Congressional District 14..............	117,668	17,270	112,113	16,638	3,332	436	1,046	79	410	26	709	109
Congressional District 15..............	92,347	11,763	89,025	11,274	1,306	275	959	152	634	29	458	45
Congressional District 16..............	122,006	17,984	117,231	17,467	1,738	309	1,677	57	463	16	779	113
Oklahoma												
Congressional District 1..................	96,729	13,263	82,338	11,974	5,032	464	1,127	62	3,237	307	1,990	142
Congressional District 2..................	123,553	13,031	101,011	10,841	3,283	349	295	43	8,102	724	1,105	47
Congressional District 3..................	109,325	13,745	97,956	12,640	2,852	399	509	13	2,740	232	2,153	155
Congressional District 4..................	96,840	10,963	84,652	9,961	2,930	230	1,350	141	2,983	195	2,103	187
Congressional District 5..................	93,834	12,314	75,491	10,587	8,737	1,000	1,804	63	2,445	278	3,249	260
Oregon												
Congressional District 1..................	91,190	13,823	82,749	13,031	591	40	3,646	304	989	57	2,623	386
Congressional District 2..................	133,691	18,806	125,908	18,085	310	3	790	115	1,611	245	3,949	268
Congressional District 3..................	86,085	13,185	73,932	11,975	3,563	469	5,257	591	767	51	1,988	70
Congressional District 4..................	133,488	17,292	126,160	16,605	386	8	1,405	201	2,017	147	2,461	371
Congressional District 5..................	113,213	16,750	105,646	16,054	333	52	1,906	194	1,353	132	3,521	277

Table C-5: 113th Congressional Districts—Older Population by Race and Hispanic Origin—*Continued*

	Total Population		White, Non-Hispanic		Black, Alone		Asian, Alone		Multi-race, Alone		Hispanic	
	65 Years and Over	85 Years and Over	65 Years and Over	85 Years and Over	65 Years and Over	85 Years and Over	65 Years and Over	85 Years and Over	65 Years and Over	85 Years and Over	65 Years and Over	85 Years and Over
Pennsylvania												
Congressional District 1	77,108	10,990	48,737	7,954	19,920	2,445	3,397	293	600	71	4,855	285
Congressional District 2	92,431	12,825	29,683	4,995	57,262	7,234	2,358	153	1,169	277	2,206	179
Congressional District 3	117,141	18,254	112,914	17,863	2,598	294	401	6	426	9	612	88
Congressional District 4	105,387	15,491	98,604	14,873	3,936	404	995	39	501	48	1,403	148
Congressional District 5	114,028	16,604	112,334	16,420	422	40	349	0	314	31	418	75
Congressional District 6	102,208	15,249	96,206	14,808	2,590	257	1,623	85	428	37	1,343	62
Congressional District 7	111,067	19,679	103,543	18,663	3,808	644	2,240	190	411	59	1,040	118
Congressional District 8	106,568	16,449	100,154	15,717	1,947	201	2,603	104	494	111	1,362	294
Congressional District 9	124,178	18,910	120,690	18,526	2,029	259	365	16	443	16	742	97
Congressional District 10	120,737	16,598	117,015	16,104	1,556	131	436	70	613	137	1,110	214
Congressional District 11	115,375	17,421	110,464	17,004	2,878	214	609	16	439	20	1,123	187
Congressional District 12	130,893	21,688	126,089	21,180	2,896	349	920	47	404	73	625	52
Congressional District 13	104,076	19,620	85,285	17,694	9,306	1,206	5,390	274	694	50	3,664	443
Congressional District 14	115,723	21,098	96,809	18,610	16,596	2,163	959	115	654	117	621	77
Congressional District 15	109,042	17,780	101,619	17,105	1,608	114	1,390	98	376	61	3,962	328
Congressional District 16	101,501	17,345	93,021	16,385	3,211	382	855	166	489	137	4,263	275
Congressional District 17	120,694	19,954	114,929	19,546	2,062	200	1,015	39	594	3	2,097	175
Congressional District 18	125,796	20,065	122,351	19,676	1,558	193	698	97	461	54	719	45
Rhode Island												
Congressional District 1	78,453	14,295	69,849	13,264	2,822	353	1,014	47	961	122	3,459	324
Congressional District 2	76,063	12,663	71,065	12,283	1,029	106	906	103	459	33	2,314	86
South Carolina												
Congressional District 1	98,295	10,409	81,664	8,625	13,209	1,611	1,442	28	461	20	1,348	95
Congressional District 2	86,215	9,692	71,545	8,382	11,945	1,142	944	76	369	0	1,204	52
Congressional District 3	103,371	12,030	87,974	10,488	13,725	1,341	403	13	509	137	737	51
Congressional District 4	90,379	10,490	76,094	9,320	11,418	1,134	913	0	548	17	1,419	19
Congressional District 5	91,728	9,355	71,820	7,523	17,982	1,718	221	0	319	11	994	48
Congressional District 6	84,860	9,700	41,194	4,607	42,275	4,960	276	0	441	46	590	53
Congressional District 7	107,661	10,475	84,792	7,934	21,022	2,351	475	0	568	134	697	83
South Dakota												
Congressional District (at Large)	119,198	19,915	113,210	19,411	163	38	358	0	716	43	795	118
Tennessee												
Congressional District 1	122,602	13,072	118,618	12,518	1,733	335	428	11	868	65	743	91
Congressional District 2	107,335	11,713	100,893	11,126	4,149	503	923	0	560	25	696	59
Congressional District 3	114,531	14,558	103,314	13,239	8,037	1,208	790	31	876	55	1,171	42
Congressional District 4	92,771	10,037	84,851	9,228	4,606	487	624	11	1,596	217	940	144
Congressional District 5	77,457	10,451	61,009	8,803	13,291	1,395	1,258	73	558	113	1,284	33
Congressional District 6	109,705	11,560	104,668	11,000	2,979	294	381	0	593	43	977	177
Congressional District 7	91,180	10,444	83,512	9,625	5,651	650	732	0	483	51	814	100
Congressional District 8	101,575	11,841	87,912	10,433	12,015	1,359	666	7	372	42	656	23
Congressional District 9	68,860	8,501	30,231	4,613	36,034	3,717	1,012	35	597	28	1,026	108
Texas												
Congressional District 1	102,140	13,987	84,468	11,436	13,066	2,039	818	101	601	59	3,126	352
Congressional District 2	63,387	6,548	48,530	5,373	2,911	333	3,951	218	461	0	7,568	552
Congressional District 3	60,135	5,431	48,842	4,606	2,405	281	4,951	326	616	20	3,339	220
Congressional District 4	105,905	12,619	93,173	10,889	8,353	1,345	352	36	955	76	2,526	241
Congressional District 5	86,856	10,546	74,120	9,283	5,677	715	1,160	70	705	109	4,906	351
Congressional District 6	67,250	7,649	53,766	6,439	5,340	672	2,756	237	608	15	4,727	286
Congressional District 7	65,396	9,279	49,701	8,553	2,122	145	5,611	236	650	3	7,375	342
Congressional District 8	83,388	8,866	71,728	7,761	4,930	642	855	74	685	56	5,110	319
Congressional District 9	56,277	5,710	16,810	2,550	21,745	1,761	7,795	633	907	100	9,065	580
Congressional District 10	74,339	9,931	59,313	8,218	5,892	996	2,019	187	500	0	6,744	553
Congressional District 11	105,354	12,153	87,142	10,470	2,674	288	430	0	1,074	141	13,913	1,291
Congressional District 12	78,330	10,066	68,173	9,069	3,187	443	1,238	110	735	27	4,893	438
Congressional District 13	96,369	12,089	83,652	11,233	2,952	301	861	34	1,184	46	7,560	372
Congressional District 14	84,102	10,236	59,364	7,828	14,280	1,328	1,451	66	692	56	8,247	968
Congressional District 15	70,806	7,726	24,450	2,643	947	127	520	8	562	127	44,668	4,957
Congressional District 16	77,803	9,581	18,154	2,691	1,729	222	923	60	1,411	115	56,584	6,571
Congressional District 17	76,778	9,977	59,711	8,292	8,263	1,000	1,365	48	499	64	6,943	602
Congressional District 18	59,824	6,419	17,032	2,035	29,014	3,150	2,464	158	519	90	11,096	1,045
Congressional District 19	90,031	11,482	70,659	9,891	3,359	324	671	16	765	40	14,788	1,284
Congressional District 20	71,347	9,277	24,852	4,538	2,351	212	1,037	6	1,239	137	42,668	4,555
Congressional District 21	97,884	13,841	82,048	12,415	1,467	151	1,157	39	1,089	98	12,184	1,160
Congressional District 22	60,816	6,644	37,241	4,600	4,720	680	9,114	573	746	64	9,030	774
Congressional District 23	77,355	8,494	31,453	3,456	2,114	317	748	59	979	102	42,561	4,662
Congressional District 24	63,840	7,720	51,266	6,889	2,288	155	4,455	280	784	96	5,010	307
Congressional District 25	84,759	8,601	72,567	7,599	4,793	468	1,225	99	866	36	5,057	405
Congressional District 26	54,122	4,823	46,547	4,040	1,780	416	1,684	35	713	53	3,583	279
Congressional District 27	96,292	11,707	59,580	7,649	5,116	939	786	50	919	54	30,475	3,088
Congressional District 28	70,871	8,074	25,628	3,439	2,169	190	516	26	727	137	42,197	4,401
Congressional District 29	49,961	5,270	17,560	2,894	4,376	173	1,363	163	737	50	25,976	1,937
Congressional District 30	61,775	6,835	22,196	3,043	29,649	2,925	1,156	23	682	71	8,198	788

Table C-5: 113th Congressional Districts—Older Population by Race and Hispanic Origin—*Continued*

	Total Population		White, Non-Hispanic		Black, Alone		Asian, Alone		Multi-race, Alone		Hispanic	
	65 Years and Over	85 Years and Over	65 Years and Over	85 Years and Over	65 Years and Over	85 Years and Over	65 Years and Over	85 Years and Over	65 Years and Over	85 Years and Over	65 Years and Over	85 Years and Over
Texas—Cont.												
Congressional District 31	69,024	7,569	55,807	6,270	3,962	358	2,025	126	583	11	6,432	792
Congressional District 32	74,688	10,696	59,270	9,347	3,581	182	4,198	375	1,221	67	6,528	697
Congressional District 33	53,174	5,308	21,502	3,046	12,383	1,075	1,235	53	697	29	17,559	1,105
Congressional District 34	85,222	9,861	31,579	4,430	816	194	349	23	587	71	52,376	5,191
Congressional District 35	60,611	7,641	22,680	3,130	6,462	816	1,217	93	876	223	29,873	3,497
Congressional District 36	86,309	9,161	71,942	7,834	6,664	708	1,085	59	682	60	5,644	486
Utah												
Congressional District 1	62,491	6,812	57,577	6,341	602	18	867	113	330	12	2,804	294
Congressional District 2	79,681	10,522	73,614	9,909	258	33	1,366	214	770	107	3,280	248
Congressional District 3	61,532	6,832	57,019	6,501	147	12	894	127	325	27	2,338	137
Congressional District 4	56,935	7,275	51,595	6,721	74	0	1,182	121	353	34	3,597	374
Vermont												
Congressional District (at Large)	94,567	12,631	92,627	12,441	199	12	618	40	390	68	538	10
Virginia												
Congressional District 1	93,300	10,301	76,583	8,996	12,782	1,119	1,626	64	684	55	1,286	47
Congressional District 2	85,639	10,498	66,907	8,760	12,111	1,284	4,491	310	597	40	1,566	149
Congressional District 3	81,173	11,251	33,437	5,229	44,291	5,752	1,351	117	1,078	88	843	64
Congressional District 4	88,230	10,109	62,083	7,424	22,949	2,308	1,491	219	699	98	1,234	65
Congressional District 5	122,713	14,846	98,853	11,847	21,382	2,806	650	39	967	14	738	134
Congressional District 6	115,830	16,068	105,310	14,746	8,589	1,143	441	9	538	58	807	144
Congressional District 7	96,737	13,478	82,443	12,004	10,671	1,123	1,803	94	368	57	1,172	153
Congressional District 8	71,280	10,058	51,239	8,409	7,173	715	7,076	523	1,141	103	4,948	328
Congressional District 9	123,793	15,735	117,331	14,578	4,989	980	288	45	721	77	513	90
Congressional District 10	68,407	6,750	55,016	5,935	3,818	260	6,034	362	1,023	110	2,478	83
Congressional District 11	71,813	8,110	49,743	6,381	4,582	283	10,883	693	1,362	143	5,509	627
Washington												
Congressional District 1	74,820	9,380	67,570	8,886	216	28	4,370	261	964	100	1,395	153
Congressional District 2	89,548	12,954	80,857	12,220	630	129	4,707	435	827	47	1,792	167
Congressional District 3	95,521	12,295	89,484	11,841	766	38	2,030	149	1,139	127	1,648	134
Congressional District 4	80,656	10,928	68,456	10,082	511	15	1,274	90	1,329	184	8,103	452
Congressional District 5	96,015	13,385	90,992	13,017	408	0	1,225	120	1,227	93	1,504	138
Congressional District 6	110,213	14,251	100,620	13,406	1,528	151	3,636	399	1,464	104	1,531	160
Congressional District 7	84,802	14,108	72,011	12,789	2,196	152	7,364	656	752	178	2,153	347
Congressional District 8	71,324	9,014	64,745	8,539	559	65	3,771	280	657	19	1,258	94
Congressional District 9	81,270	13,577	55,993	10,241	6,414	792	15,026	2,198	1,304	100	1,977	232
Congressional District 10	82,879	10,417	70,752	9,611	2,730	135	5,565	368	1,134	115	1,975	169
West Virginia												
Congressional District 1	100,993	13,399	98,569	13,048	1,053	191	202	13	601	71	441	62
Congressional District 2	98,893	11,750	94,555	11,345	2,107	293	443	14	1,139	90	598	18
Congressional District 3	103,424	12,295	98,751	11,723	3,180	408	380	18	653	124	370	22
Wisconsin												
Congressional District 1	93,940	12,784	88,797	12,494	2,197	196	791	21	191	0	1,924	62
Congressional District 2	86,057	12,616	82,280	12,347	1,453	151	1,068	10	302	19	861	72
Congressional District 3	105,860	15,396	104,147	15,276	81	5	490	29	358	11	537	30
Congressional District 4	72,913	10,881	50,340	8,927	16,801	1,547	1,332	63	426	74	3,753	219
Congressional District 5	106,286	17,907	103,154	17,532	806	49	679	51	398	69	1,163	192
Congressional District 6	110,401	18,061	108,266	17,874	231	0	638	14	302	8	782	146
Congressional District 7	121,384	16,775	118,591	16,598	71	10	524	17	659	22	486	43
Congressional District 8	101,546	15,066	98,493	14,762	104	0	662	67	476	78	792	128
Wyoming												
Congressional District (at Large)	72,274	8,656	67,423	8,196	533	84	416	78	637	30	2,710	235

PART D

HOUSEHOLD RELATIONSHIP

HOUSEHOLD RELATIONSHIP

Though people live in a multitude of different living arrangements, the Census classifies everyone as living in either households or group quarters facilities. Those living in households live in either family or non-family households. A family household is comprised of two or more individuals related by blood, marriage, or adoption to the householder. Non-family households are ones where all of the individuals are unrelated or it is occupied by a single person living alone. There are no other household types. All households have a single householder which is generally the person who owns or rents the unit. Group quarters facilities can be either institutional or non-institutional. Examples of institutional facilities include correctional facilities, nursing homes and other institutional health facilities. Non-institutional group quarters include college student housing, military and other group home situations. For the older population described here, the group quarters total will be predominantly nursing home facilities.

A slight majority (53.8 percent) of U.S. households, where the householder is age 60 or over, are family households – those that include related family members. Only 2.4 percent are in non-family households and nearly 44 percent are older householders living alone. About 3.8 percent of the 65 and over population lives in group quarters, a total of 1.5 million people. By state, the percent of non-family householders varies only slightly between 1.2 and 4.3 percent. However, the percent of 65 and over living alone ranges from a low of 33.3 percent in Hawaii to a high of 56.1 percent in the District of Columbia. The complementary totals for family householders are the opposite with the District of Columbia having the lowest percent at 40.4 and Hawaii the highest at 63.5 percent. South Dakota has the highest percent of group quarters population at 7.4 percent while at 1.7 percent, Nevada is the lowest.

The aging Baby Boom population is faced with care of older parents as well as care for younger grandchildren. Nationally, 3.2 million people over the age of 60 are grandparents living with their grandchildren. Not only

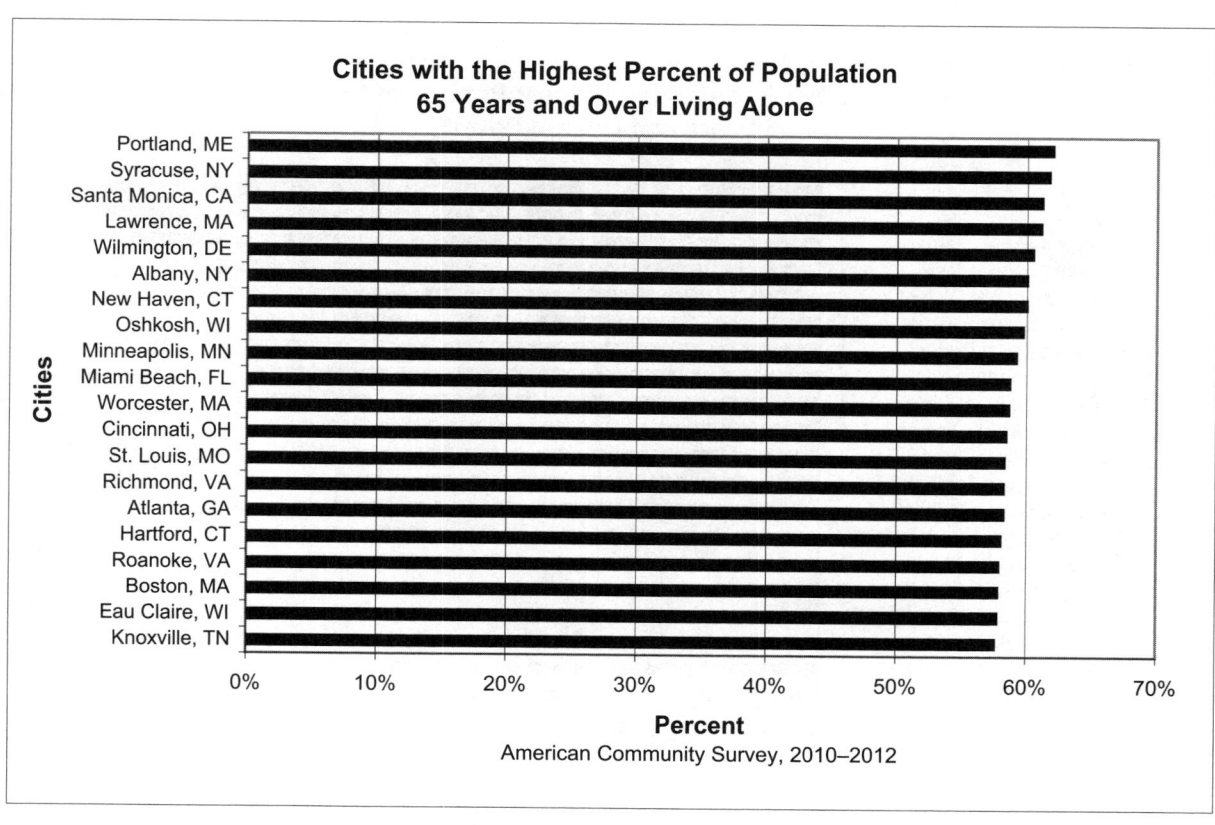

are they living with their grandchildren but an increasingly important responsibility is care for their grandchildren. In the Census data, a "responsible grandparent" is defined as being financially responsible for such needs as food, shelter, clothing, day care, etc. Nearly a million grandparents (28.9 percent) 60 and over are responsible for their grandchildren. That percent varies from a low of 17.5 percent in Hawaii to 49.4 percent in Kentucky. Of those responsible, many have incomes below the poverty level. Nationwide, 18.5 percent of grandparents responsible for grandchildren are in poverty. Vermont has the lowest percent at 8.2 while South Dakota is the highest at 27.0 percent. Fifteen states have 20 percent or more of responsible grandparents below the poverty level. While mortality and divorce take a toll on couple's relationships, nearly two-thirds of the population 60 and over (62.7 percent) are currently married. The District of Columbia has the lowest percent (48.8 percent) while Utah is highest at 70.3 percent.

More than half of the 814 counties have a higher percent of the 60 and over population that are family householders than the U.S. average. Sumter County, Florida has the highest percent (68.5 percent) while New York County (Manhattan), New York has the lowest at 36.2 percent. The percentage of persons 60 and over living alone varies from a low of 28.8 percent to a high of 60.6 percent with 352 counties above the national average. Nearly 60 percent of all counties have a higher percentage of

grandparents responsible for their grandchildren than the U.S. as a whole. Bullock County, Georgia is the highest at 78.9 percent while the lowest (3.1 percent) is also in Georgia in Forsyth County. More than two-thirds of the grandparents responsible for grandchildren are in poverty in Albemarle County, Virginia which is the nation's highest rate and one-third of all counties (266) are above the national rate. Sumter County, Georgia with the highest percent of family householders also has the highest percent of married persons in the nation at 78.7 percent. Only two counties have less than 50 percent who are married – Orleans Parish, Louisiana and Philadelphia County, Pennsylvania. Cape Girardeau County, Missouri has the highest percentage of group quarters population at 8.7 percent.

Perris City, California is one of only a few cities with less than 2,000 family householders over the age of 65 but at 76.3 percent, it has the highest percentage of such households and very nearly the lowest percent of persons living alone. Wilmington, Delaware has the lowest percent of family households with only one out of three households occupied by a family. Portland, Maine is the city with the highest percentage of persons 65 and over living alone at 62.0 percent while Goodyear, Arizona is the lowest with 21.2 percent. There are 326 cities where the percent of persons living alone is above the national average of 43.8 percent. The percentage of grandparents responsible for grandchildren is more than twice the national average in

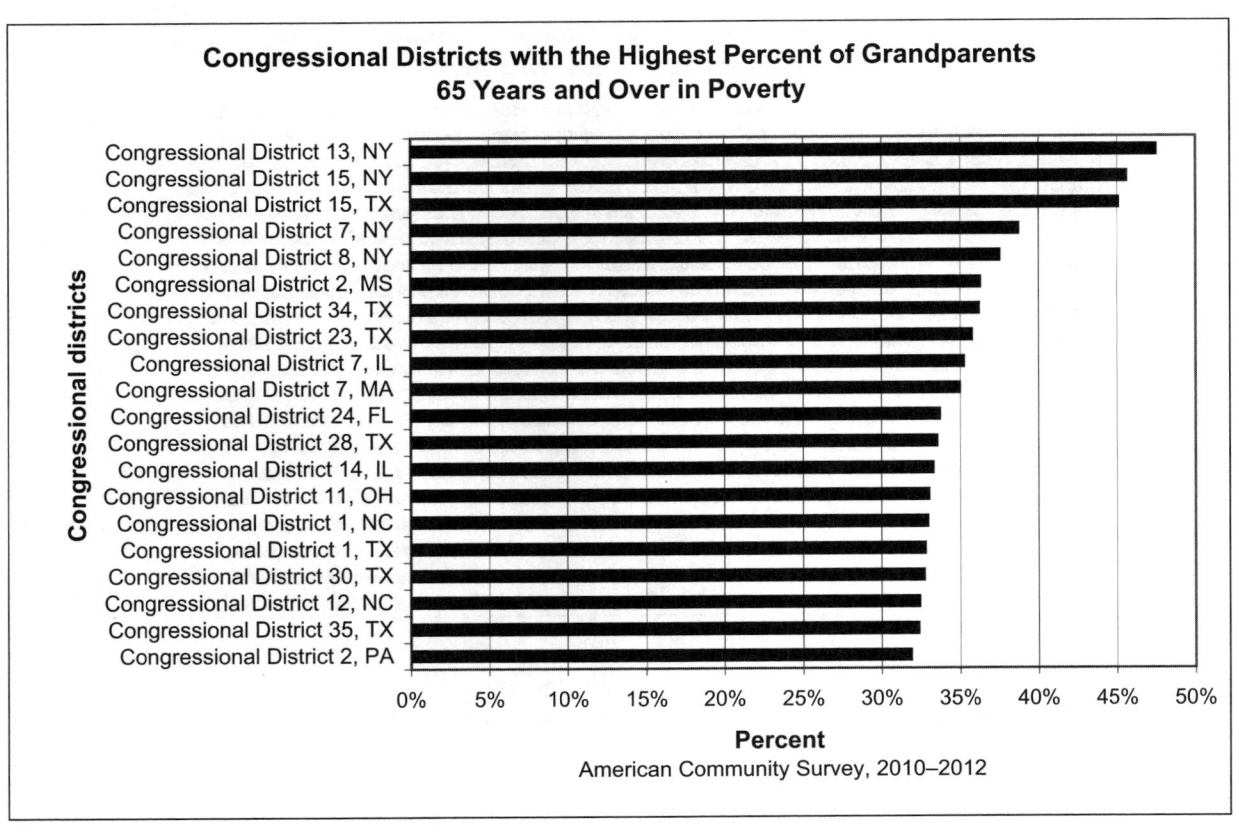

Congressional Districts with the Highest Percent of Grandparents 65 Years and Over in Poverty

American Community Survey, 2010–2012

Pueblo, Colorado (65.6 percent), the highest of all cities. Two hundred and five cities exceed the national rate while Stamford, Connecticut (2.9 percent) is the lowest in the nation. Nearly two-thirds (64.9 percent) of grandparents responsible for grandchildren are in poverty in Erie, Pennsylvania, the highest in the nation. With 12.9 percent of the 65 and over population in group quarters, the city of Syracuse, New York has the highest proportion.

Householders over the age of 65 that head family households ranges from a low of 44.4 percent in the Cumberland, Maryland-West Virginia metro to a high of 67.5 percent in the Madera-Chowchilla, California metro area. Other metropolitan areas with high percentages of family households include: Flagstaff, Arizona (65.4 percent); Laredo, Texas (66.7 percent), McAllen-Edinburg-Mission, Texas (66.2 percent), Provo-Orem, Utah (66.2 percent), St. George, Utah (66.6 percent), and Yuma, Arizona (65.7 percent). As expected, those metros with high percentages of family households have low percentages of persons 65 and over living alone. Two-thirds (68.0 percent) of grandparents in the Decatur, Illinois metropolitan area are responsible for their grandchildren and 21.8 percent of them have incomes below the poverty level. The Champaign-Urbana, Illinois metropolitan area has the highest percent of poverty grandparents responsible for grandchildren at 55.0 percent, three times the national rate of 18.5 percent. It's one of 132 metro areas above the national average.

Congressional District 39 in California has the highest percentage of family households and the lowest percent of persons living alone. The opposite occurs in New York's 12th Congressional District which has the highest percentage of persons living alone and the lowest percent of 65 and over householders of family households. The percent of grandparents responsible for grandchildren is highest in Kentucky's 5th Congressional District at 58.9 percent and nearly a third of them (30.6 percent) are poverty households. The district with the highest poverty percentages is the 13th Congressional District in New York at 47.5 percent. Nearly three-quarters (72.9 percent) of persons 60 and older are married in Utah's 1st Congressional District.

Percent of Grandparents 60 Years and Over Who are Responsible for Grandchildren

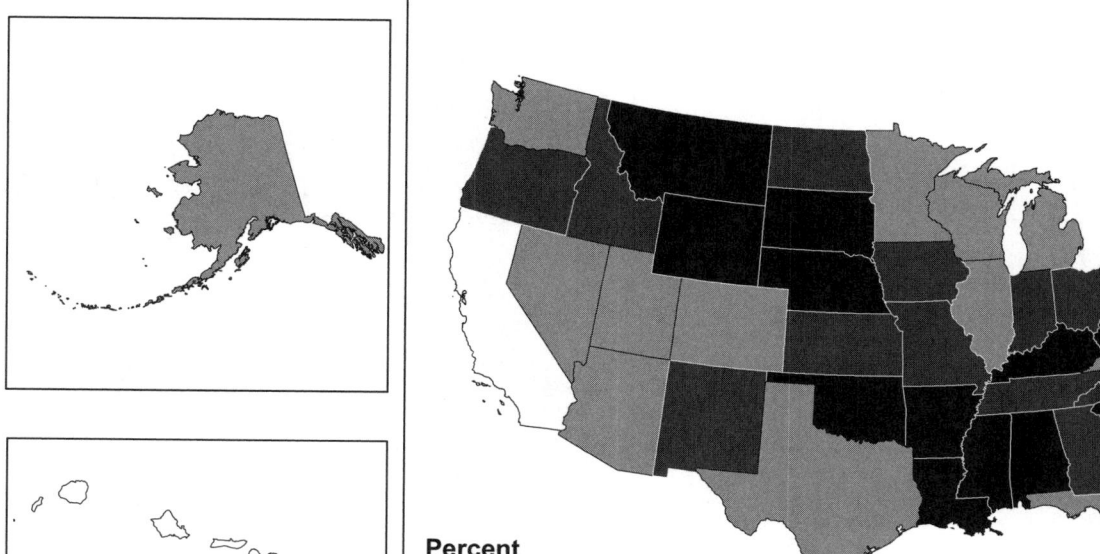

Percent

- 41.0% - 49.9%
- 33.0% - 40.9%
- 26.0% - 32.9%
- 17.0% - 25.9%

Table D-1: States—Household Relationship, Grandparents, and Marital Status

	Total Householders Age 65 Years and Over	Family Householders 65 Years and Over	Non-Family Householders 65 Years and Over		Persons 65 Years and Over Living in Group Quarters	Grandparents 60 Years and Over Living with Grandchildren			Marital Status - Persons 60 Years and Over		
			Male Living Alone	Female Living Alone		Total	Responsible for Grandchildren	Responsible for Grandchildren and In Poverty	Married	Widowed	Divorced
United States	25,624,042	13,792,788	3,266,416	7,945,214	1,513,438	3,241,595	936,507	172,924	35,070,908	12,841,156	8,042,062
Alabama	431,900	240,001	51,511	134,436	21,661	50,512	23,380	5,355	570,598	229,681	126,906
Alaska	35,129	19,247	5,872	8,797	2,218	7,367	2,402	215	58,071	16,158	17,577
Arizona	564,283	322,601	72,666	150,368	17,003	68,086	21,938	4,449	801,272	242,928	191,389
Arkansas	270,357	150,411	33,338	82,166	17,195	26,128	12,770	2,797	364,044	139,768	78,043
California	2,544,599	1,392,899	322,977	738,284	134,493	565,306	114,727	17,171	3,678,898	1,307,053	941,573
Colorado	364,159	194,054	49,154	111,447	17,841	38,321	11,750	1,570	530,474	153,746	141,540
Connecticut	315,972	160,633	41,852	105,037	24,826	35,232	7,654	904	422,730	158,605	98,062
Delaware	81,975	44,938	9,638	24,788	4,315	10,480	3,380	378	113,249	39,907	25,963
District of Columbia	49,026	19,784	8,798	18,720	2,528	5,121	1,536	263	40,493	23,099	19,314
Florida	2,006,651	1,101,762	259,379	578,737	75,316	233,751	61,836	13,240	2,681,467	982,693	669,227
Georgia	659,443	371,940	77,369	197,720	32,881	112,521	39,294	8,444	941,318	355,410	230,294
Hawaii	110,898	70,433	12,142	24,835	6,453	33,817	5,908	684	170,167	60,431	36,956
Idaho	127,817	73,269	15,240	35,890	4,825	10,997	4,083	604	189,642	53,077	41,658
Illinois	1,032,851	540,064	131,693	340,476	69,371	125,366	32,601	6,410	1,360,250	534,876	302,995
Indiana	543,017	291,131	66,882	174,814	39,858	48,708	18,234	2,471	738,232	269,650	166,132
Iowa	289,929	151,774	35,318	98,225	26,469	15,307	5,844	684	405,304	138,972	69,693
Kansas	241,937	126,884	30,623	80,576	19,843	19,477	7,062	784	335,171	116,296	68,945
Kentucky	379,625	202,859	48,816	121,476	26,097	36,195	17,872	3,679	501,557	198,870	117,643
Louisiana	365,758	200,544	45,360	112,693	22,784	49,116	22,243	5,531	466,704	200,444	116,247
Maine	136,326	69,120	18,749	43,882	8,252	7,692	2,059	248	189,686	62,940	45,093
Maryland	447,752	242,745	56,582	137,415	27,603	69,202	17,516	2,007	620,369	235,261	143,199
Massachusetts	576,645	285,292	79,380	197,262	43,971	63,748	12,901	1,871	744,800	287,831	173,293
Michigan	898,838	479,502	117,568	283,711	46,632	77,575	23,902	3,896	1,180,738	433,954	275,001
Minnesota	449,498	232,603	56,747	150,572	34,065	26,562	7,505	1,044	631,407	197,479	118,413
Mississippi	248,897	138,722	29,867	76,312	15,088	33,888	15,866	3,958	321,289	139,701	71,335
Missouri	544,100	292,004	68,417	173,485	41,615	44,773	16,013	2,595	728,897	268,177	159,308
Montana	97,403	50,973	14,728	29,424	5,566	6,303	2,698	570	136,470	42,506	30,926
Nebraska	159,628	82,248	20,360	54,212	13,326	9,189	3,934	665	222,540	75,499	39,484
Nevada	204,680	112,054	32,983	50,788	5,409	33,813	10,019	1,322	288,905	92,954	93,758
New Hampshire	113,302	61,562	14,171	33,821	8,181	9,212	1,968	184	168,933	51,680	38,029
New Jersey	733,601	386,858	89,983	240,396	44,313	111,184	20,437	2,624	984,234	402,030	201,684
New Mexico	177,448	97,934	24,974	49,789	6,606	22,514	8,991	2,114	239,808	78,687	67,000
New York	1,639,609	825,988	218,616	553,524	124,777	235,992	49,839	11,073	2,106,674	861,940	458,970
North Carolina	808,175	443,565	94,782	254,208	46,426	84,944	33,188	7,995	1,121,992	411,074	232,325
North Dakota	62,826	31,015	8,974	21,861	6,736	2,707	991	166	87,172	30,588	13,497
Ohio	1,060,964	550,735	137,534	351,343	73,695	89,840	31,649	5,041	1,373,272	532,787	327,201
Oklahoma	331,413	177,874	44,540	103,195	20,264	32,477	14,620	2,907	440,429	164,560	104,212
Oregon	351,883	186,415	44,788	108,908	15,154	30,871	10,322	1,418	485,799	150,716	137,735
Pennsylvania	1,248,228	640,698	164,069	416,425	91,717	107,386	27,392	4,333	1,601,937	662,803	310,744
Rhode Island	96,289	46,658	12,923	34,241	7,975	9,000	2,286	353	119,840	50,804	30,573
South Carolina	416,443	237,384	49,771	122,617	19,101	48,819	20,128	4,688	584,604	215,337	109,177
South Dakota	74,354	38,043	10,505	24,164	8,575	4,207	1,988	537	102,538	35,851	18,425
Tennessee	555,184	308,664	67,427	169,055	30,415	63,483	25,073	4,510	759,809	286,092	174,967
Texas	1,628,989	938,537	196,143	461,994	90,222	303,967	94,430	22,422	2,411,189	844,060	552,414
Utah	160,392	99,347	17,312	41,837	4,631	25,860	7,366	697	255,751	64,147	43,864
Vermont	60,018	30,812	8,035	19,074	3,912	3,130	853	70	84,315	25,310	20,094
Virginia	631,149	353,494	74,123	190,604	28,488	87,172	26,321	3,629	911,865	314,263	186,505
Washington	541,768	286,698	72,408	165,446	28,569	57,776	15,029	1,900	778,432	236,800	204,633
West Virginia	196,951	103,572	27,500	62,392	9,327	15,471	6,915	1,253	253,094	105,708	52,434
Wisconsin	510,565	262,052	67,385	170,087	34,426	27,428	8,050	1,003	697,135	238,217	132,800
Wyoming	45,398	24,392	6,444	13,685	2,424	3,602	1,744	198	67,344	19,736	14,812

Table D-2: Counties—Household Relationship, Grandparents, and Marital Status

	Total Householders Age 65 Years and Over	Family Householders 65 Years and Over	Non-Family Householders 65 Years and Over		Persons 65 Years and Over Living in Group Quarters	Grandparents 60 Years and Over Living with Grandchildren			Marital Status - Persons 60 Years and Over		
			Male Living Alone	Female Living Alone		Total	Responsible for Grandchildren	Responsible for Grandchildren and In Poverty	Married	Widowed	Divorced
Alabama											
Baldwin County	19,751	12,961	1,761	4,839	563	1,813	633	83	31,004	7,920	4,870
Calhoun County	11,127	6,222	1,222	3,434	399	1,501	611	132	14,504	5,994	3,131
Cullman County	8,672	4,836	1,054	2,602	428	884	350	17	11,374	4,571	2,346
DeKalb County	6,209	3,415	829	1,877	354	569	301	140	9,232	3,266	1,720
Elmore County	5,647	3,390	604	1,585	408	848	369	15	8,662	3,520	1,322
Etowah County	10,485	5,592	1,272	3,536	587	1,119	608	66	13,508	6,516	3,020
Houston County	9,594	5,234	1,158	3,033	444	1,083	372	101	12,376	4,975	3,068
Jefferson County	56,890	30,521	6,723	18,712	3,026	6,497	2,887	603	67,820	31,583	18,631
Lauderdale County	10,481	5,658	1,072	3,569	529	693	288	13	13,825	5,187	2,562
Lee County	8,548	5,021	997	2,417	265	1,071	514	124	12,864	4,050	2,562
Limestone County	7,086	3,789	667	2,533	303	654	277	8	10,346	3,338	1,609
Madison County	26,641	15,441	2,897	7,997	1,157	3,239	1,719	307	38,143	13,128	8,300
Marshall County	9,209	4,939	1,034	3,086	493	1,006	437	123	11,447	5,275	2,358
Mobile County	34,830	19,716	4,165	10,402	1,611	5,292	2,748	514	45,115	18,593	11,838
Montgomery County	18,557	9,603	2,425	6,241	1,065	1,944	748	157	21,994	9,899	6,639
Morgan County	10,798	6,248	1,168	3,291	643	1,148	566	89	15,807	5,085	3,700
St. Clair County	7,275	4,154	842	2,169	286	1,210	742	93	na	na	na
Shelby County	13,741	8,276	1,414	3,927	410	1,689	632	99	22,175	6,510	3,890
Talladega County	7,542	4,084	929	2,366	411	903	547	90	9,873	4,280	2,415
Tuscaloosa County	12,736	7,076	1,389	4,156	743	1,621	734	149	18,297	7,327	4,564
Walker County	7,241	4,339	801	1,964	370	942	438	68	10,195	3,638	2,029
Alaska											
Fairbanks North Star Borough	4,117	2,263	722	1,030	84	701	193	0	7,430	1,746	1,634
Matanuska-Susitna Borough	4,302	2,470	703	987	137	784	202	6	7,884	1,840	2,280
Arizona											
Apache County	5,401	3,173	830	1,171	98	1,352	649	259	6,722	2,850	1,842
Cochise County	15,260	8,368	2,277	4,138	435	1,464	728	163	19,950	6,878	4,611
Coconino County	7,670	5,016	770	1,726	194	1,940	949	215	12,818	2,740	2,755
Maricopa County	293,480	166,267	35,035	82,785	9,422	37,051	9,453	1,241	420,148	129,399	103,645
Mohave County	30,103	17,389	4,800	6,295	580	2,547	1,292	543	40,733	12,487	10,264
Navajo County	9,553	5,792	1,372	2,152	160	1,863	888	375	13,090	4,188	2,877
Pima County	97,843	52,812	13,748	28,186	3,593	10,925	3,740	836	130,527	43,192	33,823
Pinal County	33,042	20,636	4,104	7,269	704	4,550	1,759	305	53,607	13,567	10,431
Yavapai County	34,015	19,436	4,720	8,809	874	1,996	1,291	266	46,337	12,435	11,611
Yuma County	18,834	12,372	1,984	3,657	481	2,081	500	97	29,621	7,123	3,872
Arkansas											
Benton County	16,868	10,677	1,572	4,179	788	1,336	585	59	26,130	7,643	4,902
Craighead County	7,167	4,136	677	2,344	667	802	200	11	10,673	4,166	2,156
Faulkner County	7,091	4,316	715	2,029	330	907	377	6	10,901	3,702	1,800
Garland County	12,591	7,237	1,645	3,489	727	999	601	91	16,354	6,310	3,638
Jefferson County	6,807	3,598	999	2,104	568	1,114	497	192	8,572	3,639	2,456
Lonoke County	4,849	2,799	666	1,329	416	652	377	87	6,877	2,852	1,193
Pulaski County	29,549	16,316	3,553	9,070	1,717	3,322	1,069	150	39,215	15,005	11,239
Saline County	10,363	6,360	1,060	2,729	457	1,173	521	93	15,620	4,478	2,706
Sebastian County	10,599	5,525	1,140	3,802	740	1,091	510	169	14,082	5,511	3,317
Washington County	13,001	6,771	1,540	4,377	622	1,123	443	66	16,607	7,765	4,183
White County	7,476	4,064	725	2,673	441	717	402	42	9,491	3,720	1,561
California											
Alameda County	101,384	52,408	14,579	30,538	6,406	24,367	4,820	556	144,255	54,052	39,497
Butte County	22,252	11,662	2,712	7,167	1,004	2,328	927	173	28,025	10,277	9,122
Contra Costa County	81,300	44,991	9,827	24,220	3,719	14,397	3,117	294	120,568	39,511	29,869
El Dorado County	16,779	10,363	2,152	3,696	307	1,984	375	0	28,542	6,347	5,500
Fresno County	56,190	31,349	6,810	16,353	3,432	13,408	2,834	679	81,552	30,272	20,242
Humboldt County	11,281	5,819	1,731	3,434	397	853	465	2	15,516	5,157	4,679
Imperial County	10,086	5,804	1,511	2,530	398	3,576	863	224	15,528	5,535	3,007
Kern County	45,718	25,583	6,612	12,338	1,451	11,878	3,174	744	68,816	24,488	15,953
Kings County	6,842	3,804	809	2,073	958	1,949	697	234	10,887	3,809	2,249
Lake County	7,633	3,498	1,444	1,925	342	327	213	37	9,120	3,501	3,651
Los Angeles County	615,860	336,433	79,932	176,634	36,280	163,881	31,421	4,785	870,896	336,360	226,652
Madera County	9,464	6,391	1,011	1,813	691	2,043	902	102	16,521	4,695	3,084
Marin County	28,524	14,028	3,448	9,642	1,104	1,406	210	0	37,617	9,892	12,261
Mendocino County	8,852	4,280	1,382	2,726	476	1,361	492	49	11,533	3,904	4,491
Merced County	13,739	8,109	1,709	3,405	784	3,635	534	52	22,006	7,483	4,856
Monterey County	25,539	14,516	2,601	7,420	1,560	6,484	1,277	107	41,128	12,310	9,213
Napa County	12,918	6,832	1,595	3,950	1,383	1,282	255	24	17,506	6,062	4,633
Nevada County	12,646	7,186	1,412	3,516	454	503	141	44	18,824	4,422	4,676
Orange County	206,912	119,086	21,488	59,507	11,546	45,790	7,779	738	317,727	104,419	72,809
Placer County	34,439	19,486	3,652	10,408	1,239	3,890	622	27	50,949	14,532	11,042
Riverside County	155,054	84,849	20,152	42,832	4,440	34,507	7,619	1,143	219,076	75,109	57,134
Sacramento County	99,171	50,808	13,615	31,977	5,701	19,016	3,605	780	131,704	52,384	42,654
San Bernardino County	103,717	58,943	13,406	28,138	4,644	36,081	7,575	1,386	163,325	62,404	43,753
San Diego County	209,064	113,837	26,839	60,791	11,546	46,186	9,386	1,264	301,500	109,842	80,116
San Francisco County	68,503	30,289	12,114	22,770	2,836	11,623	1,640	372	81,171	34,251	21,782
San Joaquin County	41,585	23,896	4,614	11,808	2,714	10,998	2,447	516	60,203	24,380	15,794
San Luis Obispo County	25,629	14,357	2,912	7,511	1,435	2,187	528	44	37,797	11,602	8,997
San Mateo County	56,479	29,928	7,209	17,325	3,116	11,707	2,203	150	82,444	29,026	20,630
Santa Barbara County	33,861	18,158	4,203	10,356	2,056	4,947	868	175	45,594	16,642	10,664
Santa Clara County	112,271	66,118	12,340	30,338	6,687	31,289	4,586	240	181,290	57,162	37,503

Table D-2: Counties—Household Relationship, Grandparents, and Marital Status—*Continued*

	Total Householders Age 65 Years and Over	Family Householders 65 Years and Over	Non-Family Householders 65 Years and Over		Persons 65 Years and Over Living in Group Quarters	Grandparents 60 Years and Over Living with Grandchildren			Marital Status - Persons 60 Years and Over		
			Male Living Alone	Female Living Alone		Total	Responsible for Grandchildren	Responsible for Grandchildren and In Poverty	Married	Widowed	Divorced
California—Cont.											
Santa Cruz County	19,970	9,948	2,688	6,433	896	2,608	593	87	26,862	7,863	9,487
Shasta County	19,897	10,653	2,819	5,858	776	1,357	727	83	26,701	9,047	6,504
Solano County	28,831	16,346	3,294	8,246	1,901	6,997	1,501	56	44,867	15,085	11,226
Sonoma County	44,296	22,074	5,496	14,779	2,253	3,581	805	62	59,701	18,648	19,960
Stanislaus County	33,059	18,540	3,917	9,788	2,138	7,565	1,795	628	48,418	17,845	11,599
Sutter County	7,275	3,889	1,051	2,086	407	1,888	302	96	10,863	3,838	2,478
Tulare County	24,691	14,432	3,149	6,569	1,819	7,150	2,232	461	37,977	13,651	7,561
Ventura County	59,887	34,482	6,164	17,171	2,346	11,991	2,333	210	89,254	28,476	21,461
Yolo County	12,783	6,297	1,857	4,091	652	2,005	594	63	17,763	6,240	4,582
Yuba County	4,379	2,622	509	1,080	130	907	221	34	6,526	2,346	2,345
Colorado											
Adams County	23,266	13,032	2,951	6,745	809	5,229	1,442	205	33,560	12,033	9,900
Arapahoe County	38,061	20,711	4,297	12,102	2,168	5,262	1,044	160	56,433	16,786	16,347
Boulder County	19,981	10,712	2,439	6,279	1,346	1,288	385	63	29,937	7,219	8,098
Denver County	43,278	18,463	7,658	16,090	2,238	4,892	1,098	150	45,479	18,965	20,714
Douglas County	13,496	8,881	1,069	3,159	172	1,835	251	13	25,884	4,320	5,277
El Paso County	40,618	22,440	4,961	12,338	1,577	4,142	1,068	188	61,433	18,087	15,177
Jefferson County	44,554	24,231	5,756	13,250	2,228	3,834	1,152	212	66,346	18,392	17,604
Larimer County	23,052	12,921	2,572	6,921	1,147	1,648	835	20	36,391	9,128	8,201
Mesa County	14,901	7,429	2,070	4,998	607	1,150	575	10	19,348	6,656	4,420
Pueblo County	15,828	8,255	2,237	4,889	1,011	1,465	841	148	21,101	7,007	5,300
Weld County	15,559	8,895	1,879	4,503	653	2,505	1,030	113	25,087	6,995	5,166
Connecticut											
Fairfield County	76,458	40,522	9,515	24,416	5,639	10,352	1,548	156	104,900	39,090	22,487
Hartford County	81,908	40,294	10,947	28,408	6,923	8,270	1,955	264	103,416	40,899	25,605
Litchfield County	19,301	9,822	2,542	6,325	1,380	1,536	252	31	26,385	9,248	5,625
Middlesex County	15,872	8,652	2,077	4,863	1,386	1,188	146	na	23,616	7,415	5,098
New Haven County	77,105	37,746	10,341	26,996	6,349	9,104	2,379	329	97,665	40,196	25,046
New London County	24,579	12,359	3,639	7,916	1,687	2,709	768	7	34,164	12,429	7,905
Tolland County	11,494	6,427	1,628	3,178	584	1,087	296	23	18,684	4,883	3,315
Windham County	9,255	4,811	1,163	2,935	878	986	310	50	13,900	4,445	2,981
Delaware											
Kent County	13,607	7,879	1,448	3,834	712	2,541	702	34	19,595	7,053	4,446
New Castle County	42,316	22,155	5,164	13,849	2,460	5,734	1,677	190	56,224	20,559	14,566
Sussex County	26,052	14,904	3,026	7,105	1,143	2,205	1,001	154	37,430	12,295	6,951
Florida											
Alachua County	16,705	9,196	1,897	5,119	881	1,739	497	153	23,205	8,346	6,475
Bay County	16,502	9,263	2,082	4,735	879	1,154	402	26	21,525	7,658	5,240
Brevard County	70,245	38,596	9,825	19,636	2,456	6,977	2,726	247	89,448	33,129	22,720
Broward County	154,109	71,970	23,269	52,314	4,324	25,506	5,593	939	184,326	83,904	62,656
Charlotte County	34,687	20,274	4,376	8,504	996	1,514	639	62	48,041	14,873	6,982
Citrus County	27,506	15,663	3,618	6,732	994	1,838	466	165	37,638	12,311	7,644
Clay County	13,066	8,056	1,790	2,807	678	2,274	879	66	22,957	6,859	4,674
Collier County	52,578	31,644	6,189	13,195	757	3,767	726	243	77,248	18,937	12,807
Columbia County	6,336	3,602	777	1,745	458	648	152	0	9,586	2,784	2,261
Duval County	62,242	32,364	8,090	20,499	3,061	8,191	2,555	451	80,173	35,390	26,516
Escambia County	28,334	15,405	4,104	8,267	1,301	3,534	1,694	407	34,795	15,604	9,604
Flagler County	13,858	8,879	1,168	3,315	242	1,155	229	0	22,614	6,177	3,405
Hernando County	27,698	16,076	3,717	7,263	614	2,040	919	70	37,807	12,885	5,984
Highlands County	19,350	11,277	2,557	4,760	652	1,092	322	34	24,465	8,171	4,363
Hillsborough County	90,712	49,095	11,377	27,776	3,283	13,418	3,777	866	123,821	47,791	36,407
Indian River County	24,390	12,681	3,322	7,710	384	1,273	141	0	29,264	11,420	6,538
Lake County	44,524	26,959	4,987	11,508	1,177	3,896	1,092	154	64,740	18,750	9,083
Lee County	87,499	51,560	11,711	21,148	2,255	6,961	1,292	505	128,878	39,624	24,318
Leon County	17,555	8,968	2,364	5,699	833	1,608	445	92	24,821	7,859	6,827
Manatee County	48,208	26,742	5,564	13,791	1,267	2,820	1,017	170	64,998	21,009	12,081
Marion County	53,390	32,450	6,356	13,169	1,074	3,116	1,079	290	73,725	22,204	13,666
Martin County	24,833	13,881	3,538	6,784	607	1,229	497	126	31,878	10,314	7,413
Miami-Dade County	185,793	103,414	23,279	52,645	9,527	51,129	8,017	2,543	254,367	113,723	86,564
Monroe County	8,057	4,358	1,559	1,620	205	981	188	na	11,985	3,231	3,590
Nassau County	7,596	5,043	867	1,580	328	1,153	508	96	11,993	2,963	2,396
Okaloosa County	15,915	9,370	1,977	4,230	506	1,656	414	0	23,103	6,886	5,394
Orange County	65,171	37,592	7,497	18,179	3,728	13,593	3,583	900	97,594	36,763	27,055
Osceola County	17,294	10,255	1,809	4,619	673	5,105	886	154	28,771	9,354	7,414
Palm Beach County	177,102	91,155	21,838	57,485	5,517	15,356	3,486	784	217,357	85,791	50,816
Pasco County	60,399	33,479	7,636	17,151	2,159	4,937	1,402	234	79,315	30,426	17,637
Pinellas County	126,874	59,034	20,131	43,745	6,701	8,091	2,364	374	141,412	61,580	48,440
Polk County	67,040	38,810	7,932	18,319	2,235	7,204	2,403	561	96,031	31,200	17,198
Putnam County	8,909	5,199	1,126	2,195	355	1,037	788	236	11,273	4,700	3,087
St. Johns County	19,214	10,771	2,400	5,193	682	1,820	634	141	28,006	8,430	7,018
St. Lucie County	34,902	20,282	4,159	9,018	843	2,984	1,049	160	47,031	16,689	9,138
Santa Rosa County	12,360	7,899	1,285	2,910	400	1,290	545	186	19,753	5,375	3,588
Sarasota County	75,984	41,395	9,579	21,950	2,613	2,743	880	275	94,306	30,759	19,374
Seminole County	29,449	17,203	3,093	8,227	1,176	5,643	1,207	178	43,886	17,218	14,589
Sumter County	27,991	19,167	2,534	5,712	541	na	na	na	44,148	7,927	4,057
Volusia County	65,197	34,670	8,815	19,535	2,849	4,546	1,912	429	84,217	30,180	21,887

Table D-2: Counties—Household Relationship, Grandparents, and Marital Status—*Continued*

	Total Householders Age 65 Years and Over	Family Householders 65 Years and Over	Non-Family Householders 65 Years and Over		Persons 65 Years and Over Living in Group Quarters	Grandparents 60 Years and Over Living with Grandchildren			Marital Status - Persons 60 Years and Over		
			Male Living Alone	Female Living Alone		Total	Responsible for Grandchildren	Responsible for Grandchildren and In Poverty	Married	Widowed	Divorced
Georgia											
Barrow County	3,742	2,389	335	913	134	1,001	436	71	na	na	na
Bartow County	6,660	3,919	734	1,839	344	1,345	298	23	na	na	na
Bibb County	12,547	6,780	1,282	4,318	746	1,518	660	74	15,375	7,098	4,149
Bulloch County	4,231	2,407	415	1,315	222	659	520	138	5,320	2,244	1,356
Carroll County	7,632	4,109	857	2,388	341	1,276	323	62	10,217	3,863	2,900
Catoosa County	5,795	3,602	358	1,654	195	744	396	82	na	na	na
Chatham County	21,924	11,331	3,041	6,928	1,197	2,892	857	133	25,563	11,745	8,563
Cherokee County	12,997	8,040	1,502	3,303	202	1,466	606	217	20,824	6,588	4,414
Clarke County	6,367	3,621	605	2,082	349	707	197	71	8,507	3,406	2,297
Clayton County	9,931	5,726	1,387	2,658	372	3,048	1,118	257	15,461	6,684	6,479
Cobb County	39,393	23,080	3,686	11,747	1,615	7,452	2,005	271	63,743	17,794	14,743
Columbia County	7,634	4,685	1,023	1,764	402	1,295	452	12	13,493	3,784	2,744
Coweta County	8,188	5,070	997	1,921	167	1,755	550	0	14,428	4,444	2,408
DeKalb County	40,015	20,908	4,792	13,431	2,076	7,624	2,660	582	51,712	21,094	19,122
Dougherty County	7,852	4,539	760	2,502	224	1,277	804	152	9,091	4,091	2,646
Douglas County	6,597	3,938	777	1,844	220	1,582	539	93	11,440	3,935	3,011
Fayette County	8,868	5,402	912	2,515	281	1,185	370	53	14,509	3,802	2,303
Floyd County	9,051	4,519	1,213	3,090	480	1,337	708	254	11,449	4,719	2,949
Forsyth County	8,366	5,303	756	2,225	259	2,986	92	na	na	na	na
Fulton County	56,248	26,560	8,188	20,455	2,363	8,926	2,099	498	68,293	29,941	25,728
Glynn County	8,374	5,092	837	2,424	295	974	586	88	12,514	3,263	2,525
Gwinnett County	30,096	19,237	2,548	7,483	1,252	12,218	2,085	211	62,942	17,852	12,977
Hall County	12,796	7,854	1,143	3,588	505	2,352	751	115	19,696	6,709	3,645
Henry County	9,972	6,185	1,301	2,427	199	2,873	986	188	16,618	5,462	3,650
Houston County	8,976	5,010	1,011	2,824	429	1,463	492	53	13,345	4,316	3,335
Liberty County	2,671	1,762	168	688	92	421	232	0	3,759	1,463	819
Lowndes County	6,975	4,049	638	2,125	299	1,180	404	100	9,396	3,507	2,653
Muscogee County	15,015	7,478	1,981	5,342	859	1,596	544	99	16,178	8,767	5,401
Newton County	5,917	3,485	847	1,525	278	1,034	250	42	8,711	3,528	2,065
Paulding County	6,247	3,990	454	1,609	181	1,249	324	14	na	na	na
Richmond County	14,145	7,456	1,901	4,455	1,206	2,124	974	202	17,422	8,527	5,146
Rockdale County	5,647	3,331	553	1,616	257	1,491	659	158	8,619	3,497	1,806
Troup County	5,337	2,982	486	1,761	351	786	295	128	6,801	3,396	1,511
Walker County	6,583	3,693	916	1,895	334	701	438	49	na	na	na
Walton County	5,978	3,980	427	1,553	259	1,426	471	57	na	na	na
Whitfield County	6,887	4,251	775	1,826	411	1,441	538	154	9,770	4,205	2,011
Hawaii											
Hawaii County	16,222	9,550	2,373	3,658	835	3,245	837	273	24,352	8,825	6,513
Honolulu County	77,959	50,128	7,983	17,520	4,742	25,167	4,258	368	116,555	43,269	23,752
Kauai County	5,565	3,697	563	1,038	362	1,625	346	8	9,722	2,744	2,106
Maui County	11,138	7,055	1,223	2,608	512	3,780	467	35	19,524	5,588	4,578
Idaho											
Ada County	27,658	15,318	2,742	9,041	1,169	2,617	696	41	41,316	11,840	10,432
Bannock County	5,794	3,486	650	1,591	204	437	237	22	8,692	2,356	2,012
Bonneville County	7,600	4,388	694	2,332	239	708	86	16	10,789	3,486	2,711
Canyon County	13,265	7,929	1,264	3,824	511	1,613	601	56	19,941	5,731	4,008
Kootenai County	13,114	7,833	1,377	3,327	388	1,090	393	42	20,160	4,534	5,398
Twin Falls County	6,465	3,738	648	1,808	366	655	231	0	10,041	3,566	1,574
Illinois											
Adams County	7,170	3,926	842	2,271	962	460	32	0	10,045	3,583	1,734
Champaign County	13,396	7,318	1,464	4,391	810	786	225	153	18,853	5,483	4,321
Cook County	399,022	199,445	54,681	135,959	22,493	65,643	15,988	3,693	465,638	219,571	128,195
DeKalb County	6,674	3,108	1,067	2,357	586	675	167	29	8,896	3,684	2,101
DuPage County	66,279	37,359	7,001	20,792	4,411	8,649	1,213	102	103,983	32,883	19,601
Kane County	31,517	18,420	3,128	9,524	1,758	5,266	776	33	51,354	16,197	9,477
Kankakee County	9,408	4,918	1,208	3,190	1,203	1,057	233	47	12,367	5,290	2,682
Kendall County	5,443	3,309	685	1,424	113	1,140	65	na	na	na	na
Lake County	45,604	25,858	5,199	13,826	2,930	6,047	772	82	72,637	22,639	13,615
LaSalle County	11,928	6,316	1,448	3,962	1,170	647	302	40	15,383	6,052	2,840
McHenry County	19,867	11,631	2,452	5,340	882	2,555	397	169	31,771	9,624	6,193
McLean County	11,076	5,989	1,448	3,364	816	689	156	6	16,405	5,390	3,605
Macon County	11,817	6,219	1,672	3,750	1,096	1,046	711	155	15,439	5,520	3,538
Madison County	25,080	13,002	3,370	8,222	1,808	1,876	473	174	31,785	12,370	7,413
Peoria County	17,184	8,685	2,219	5,909	1,165	1,069	529	134	21,759	8,014	4,902
Rock Island County	16,222	7,596	2,473	5,920	890	1,290	593	94	19,930	8,119	4,688
St. Clair County	22,614	10,745	3,536	7,950	1,698	2,524	1,080	271	26,055	12,376	6,927
Sangamon County	18,562	8,955	2,342	6,822	1,131	1,290	599	98	23,748	8,831	5,836
Tazewell County	13,854	7,680	1,505	4,477	1,015	777	412	61	19,418	6,438	3,399
Vermilion County	8,899	4,253	1,454	2,983	560	514	170	20	9,935	4,687	2,770
Will County	39,421	22,881	4,204	11,322	1,747	7,368	1,746	167	62,933	20,806	10,961
Williamson County	6,960	3,613	833	2,350	518	377	100	27	9,509	3,307	2,204
Winnebago County	25,799	13,745	3,540	7,931	1,786	2,882	898	52	34,522	13,024	8,788

Table D-2: Counties—Household Relationship, Grandparents, and Marital Status—*Continued*

	Total Householders Age 65 Years and Over	Family Householders 65 Years and Over	Non-Family Householders 65 Years and Over		Persons 65 Years and Over Living in Group Quarters	Grandparents 60 Years and Over Living with Grandchildren			Marital Status - Persons 60 Years and Over		
			Male Living Alone	Female Living Alone		Total	Responsible for Grandchildren	Responsible for Grandchildren and In Poverty	Married	Widowed	Divorced
Indiana											
Allen County	27,935	14,292	3,755	9,220	2,085	2,118	843	128	37,229	13,547	9,254
Bartholomew County	6,948	3,555	981	2,330	564	397	223	34	na	na	na
Clark County	9,165	4,883	1,020	2,924	481	815	349	0	12,068	4,704	3,618
Delaware County	11,532	6,260	1,076	4,078	798	822	383	17	14,710	4,973	3,750
Elkhart County	15,273	8,569	1,660	4,765	1,256	1,803	633	179	22,322	7,080	4,231
Floyd County	6,332	3,242	859	2,136	699	360	137	49	8,282	3,197	2,174
Grant County	7,615	4,033	931	2,560	539	436	132	82	9,682	3,598	2,007
Hamilton County	14,779	8,886	1,403	4,179	911	2,031	463	0	27,217	6,071	5,365
Hancock County	5,619	3,292	541	1,738	259	471	130	na	na	na	na
Hendricks County	10,047	5,606	1,130	3,211	724	845	232	na	14,799	5,301	2,795
Howard County	9,030	4,561	1,009	3,309	530	372	275	24	11,637	4,438	2,491
Johnson County	11,086	5,755	1,519	3,692	919	1,259	521	128	16,527	5,343	3,383
Kosciusko County	6,939	3,780	844	2,210	430	689	240	32	9,497	3,509	1,391
Lake County	41,018	22,104	5,444	12,502	2,188	5,431	1,607	149	52,501	23,986	12,909
LaPorte County	10,456	5,538	1,374	3,369	585	832	259	32	14,161	4,847	3,126
Madison County	13,929	6,963	1,907	4,803	894	813	452	91	16,587	6,962	4,105
Marion County	63,430	31,450	8,681	21,982	4,514	7,101	2,485	452	71,662	33,223	26,445
Monroe County	9,410	4,695	1,407	3,097	571	456	75	na	12,520	4,273	3,482
Morgan County	5,550	3,359	462	1,624	247	813	252	11	na	na	na
Porter County	12,514	7,432	1,193	3,587	806	1,916	598	0	19,311	6,489	4,308
St. Joseph County	22,588	11,916	2,578	7,539	1,848	1,776	573	53	29,608	11,276	6,774
Tippecanoe County	10,609	5,605	1,121	3,713	813	992	250	66	14,696	5,437	3,250
Vanderburgh County	16,819	8,148	2,462	5,861	1,551	1,035	345	21	19,674	8,679	5,753
Vigo County	8,907	4,542	1,012	3,136	911	784	369	22	11,649	4,945	2,726
Wayne County	7,535	3,777	1,039	2,597	486	455	210	52	9,022	3,365	2,184
Iowa											
Black Hawk County	11,863	5,928	1,619	4,090	797	621	287	7	16,303	5,397	3,210
Dallas County	4,323	2,378	472	1,382	364	na	na	na	na	na	na
Dubuque County	8,939	4,734	1,161	2,893	1,187	266	144	18	12,544	4,030	1,965
Johnson County	7,794	3,907	912	2,745	468	369	194	26	11,748	2,733	2,856
Linn County	18,216	9,513	2,251	6,135	1,131	1,447	517	15	24,562	8,192	5,063
Polk County	30,000	15,712	3,438	10,393	2,170	3,119	1,041	239	43,467	14,699	9,915
Pottawattamie County	8,432	4,625	1,001	2,662	548	727	316	52	11,442	4,372	2,734
Scott County	14,428	7,488	1,998	4,732	852	1,008	249	32	20,046	6,943	4,068
Story County	5,780	3,248	571	1,829	343	na	na	na	9,050	2,237	1,345
Woodbury County	8,837	3,977	1,283	3,441	523	640	192	33	10,103	4,759	2,629
Kansas											
Butler County	5,372	2,768	667	1,901	447	508	219	0	7,330	2,874	1,467
Douglas County	6,461	3,259	930	2,160	323	839	329	40	9,500	2,927	2,314
Johnson County	39,101	21,406	4,360	12,787	2,268	3,377	749	84	60,090	17,468	11,997
Leavenworth County	5,331	3,122	481	1,603	455	489	236	26	8,207	2,408	1,761
Riley County	3,449	1,701	430	1,237	310	na	na	na	4,670	1,559	872
Sedgwick County	37,312	18,774	5,182	12,524	1,848	4,093	1,262	237	49,281	18,431	12,939
Shawnee County	16,495	9,046	1,706	5,552	1,541	1,386	523	30	22,800	7,412	5,822
Wyandotte County	10,853	5,595	1,502	3,419	595	1,866	719	125	12,246	6,592	4,566
Kentucky											
Boone County	7,509	4,457	725	2,111	285	1,035	422	14	12,033	3,595	2,620
Bullitt County	5,983	3,540	771	1,525	42	547	202	34	8,423	2,556	1,729
Campbell County	7,577	4,191	950	2,325	588	621	304	31	9,723	3,924	2,284
Christian County	4,833	2,533	482	1,688	356	366	238	11	6,172	2,922	1,303
Daviess County	9,372	4,800	1,211	3,146	761	782	388	80	11,986	4,770	2,512
Fayette County	20,954	10,377	2,550	7,547	1,447	1,675	773	124	26,282	9,485	9,189
Hardin County	7,210	4,263	716	2,184	453	927	444	76	10,887	3,883	2,110
Jefferson County	65,238	32,682	8,595	22,741	4,671	5,469	2,330	426	79,054	33,632	23,005
Kenton County	11,711	5,885	1,797	3,860	850	1,429	543	11	14,521	6,671	4,030
McCracken County	6,928	3,492	836	2,506	543	309	212	18	8,787	3,629	2,028
Madison County	6,097	3,307	670	2,005	350	529	314	40	8,348	3,298	1,736
Pike County	6,227	3,267	793	2,099	345	871	430	52	7,848	4,079	1,616
Warren County	8,312	4,212	1,309	2,581	401	1,031	291	14	10,016	4,331	2,736
Louisiana											
Ascension Parish	6,304	3,790	621	1,716	263	1,072	697	78	10,296	2,639	2,270
Bossier Parish	9,301	5,021	939	3,190	602	1,427	594	97	11,354	4,359	3,413
Caddo Parish	22,588	12,132	2,908	7,163	1,549	2,983	1,391	359	26,006	12,607	7,625
Calcasieu Parish	15,754	8,697	1,825	4,910	786	1,892	941	256	21,952	8,331	5,232
East Baton Rouge Parish	30,978	17,089	4,016	9,505	1,557	4,385	1,987	766	40,813	17,413	10,815
Iberia Parish	6,097	3,368	720	1,898	323	769	469	15	7,601	2,969	1,673
Jefferson Parish	38,072	19,928	5,360	11,751	1,362	5,410	1,522	137	46,920	21,506	13,205
Lafayette Parish	14,646	8,117	1,439	4,667	1,279	1,375	579	171	19,920	7,678	4,287
Lafourche Parish	7,842	4,509	736	2,559	483	1,034	423	47	10,862	4,310	1,332
Livingston Parish	8,216	4,753	967	2,366	301	1,521	654	225	12,648	3,904	3,295
Orleans Parish	26,272	12,403	4,446	8,635	1,503	3,758	1,629	567	26,275	15,320	12,454
Ouachita Parish	12,544	6,594	1,104	4,638	994	1,690	931	308	14,953	6,376	4,398
Rapides Parish	11,646	5,893	1,515	3,970	1,026	1,143	413	82	13,752	6,733	3,523
St. Landry Parish	7,576	4,150	920	2,389	519	770	359	94	9,367	4,385	1,743
St. Tammany Parish	18,763	11,115	2,236	5,062	668	2,469	823	117	28,010	9,564	6,802
Tangipahoa Parish	9,082	5,307	777	2,657	543	1,286	741	174	12,210	5,220	2,810
Terrebonne Parish	8,315	4,841	1,007	2,159	429	1,243	684	180	10,732	4,721	1,970

Table D-2: Counties—Household Relationship, Grandparents, and Marital Status—*Continued*

	Total Householders Age 65 Years and Over	Family Householders 65 Years and Over	Non-Family Householders 65 Years and Over		Persons 65 Years and Over Living in Group Quarters	Grandparents 60 Years and Over Living with Grandchildren			Marital Status - Persons 60 Years and Over		
			Male Living Alone	Female Living Alone		Total	Responsible for Grandchildren	Responsible for Grandchildren and In Poverty	Married	Widowed	Divorced
Maine											
Androscoggin County	9,997	5,089	1,265	3,262	705	738	162	0	13,578	4,432	3,316
Aroostook County	8,899	4,402	1,398	2,955	705	401	113	10	11,776	4,420	2,130
Cumberland County	25,922	12,388	3,531	9,372	1,830	1,757	328	29	34,791	12,546	9,108
Kennebec County	12,060	5,912	1,800	3,920	1,044	456	204	67	16,295	5,816	4,406
Penobscot County	14,088	7,203	2,174	4,083	994	783	177	46	20,315	7,061	4,689
York County	20,159	10,556	2,579	6,543	889	1,360	429	48	28,446	8,799	6,495
Maryland											
Allegany County	8,459	4,052	1,316	2,865	835	599	201	24	10,268	4,751	2,458
Anne Arundel County	40,034	22,802	4,417	11,552	1,781	5,610	1,266	27	61,359	20,334	12,841
Baltimore County	74,636	38,169	9,893	25,003	5,021	9,122	2,836	343	96,277	40,603	21,270
Calvert County	5,903	3,536	771	1,451	315	1,317	197	0	9,245	3,680	1,925
Carroll County	13,690	7,801	1,401	4,176	1,155	1,991	223	31	21,770	7,182	3,885
Cecil County	7,182	4,215	824	1,953	473	1,252	341	0	11,485	3,643	2,919
Charles County	7,861	4,686	759	2,181	475	1,976	611	106	13,237	4,829	3,388
Frederick County	16,698	9,261	1,963	5,256	1,068	2,429	655	15	25,879	7,798	5,422
Harford County	19,247	11,343	2,341	5,236	808	2,483	770	26	29,479	9,876	5,189
Howard County	17,728	10,676	1,978	4,603	619	3,663	462	55	31,225	7,691	5,508
Montgomery County	73,571	39,948	8,104	23,809	4,893	12,260	2,242	73	113,991	35,175	21,346
Prince George's County	50,886	29,629	6,370	13,724	2,709	13,309	3,064	195	70,034	28,932	21,895
St. Mary's County	6,787	4,208	699	1,692	576	1,040	303	na	10,862	3,349	1,495
Washington County	13,680	7,060	1,867	4,419	1,132	845	294	39	17,750	7,405	3,739
Wicomico County	8,249	4,513	1,175	2,387	575	852	286	33	10,065	4,876	2,403
Massachusetts											
Barnstable County	34,374	18,504	4,061	10,641	1,577	1,303	67	15	46,118	14,136	8,519
Berkshire County	16,435	7,468	2,577	6,073	1,242	1,038	455	41	18,581	8,225	5,543
Bristol County	48,386	24,717	6,438	16,021	4,404	5,133	1,123	132	63,490	27,481	13,946
Essex County	66,454	32,320	9,022	23,359	5,140	7,586	1,702	223	88,137	33,609	21,712
Franklin County	6,942	3,449	907	2,247	487	767	123	0	9,937	3,277	2,894
Hampden County	41,761	20,163	5,478	15,003	3,640	3,993	1,014	168	53,122	22,150	11,975
Hampshire County	13,699	6,422	1,968	4,754	955	972	119	0	17,266	6,427	4,894
Middlesex County	125,401	64,129	16,865	41,730	8,629	14,807	2,453	342	166,744	60,947	35,882
Norfolk County	62,632	31,001	8,405	21,808	4,237	7,421	992	97	80,771	30,310	15,986
Plymouth County	43,633	24,204	4,958	13,142	3,554	6,705	1,443	197	62,361	22,394	13,216
Suffolk County	51,273	20,632	9,296	20,144	4,104	6,509	1,584	506	51,100	22,982	18,512
Worcester County	63,136	30,946	9,132	21,530	5,742	7,473	1,813	150	83,497	34,890	19,265
Michigan											
Allegan County	9,407	5,545	1,111	2,585	534	856	211	18	13,883	4,397	2,818
Bay County	11,597	6,497	1,207	3,748	854	820	385	60	16,020	5,798	2,367
Berrien County	16,237	8,744	2,228	4,893	1,069	1,189	444	43	20,970	8,067	5,006
Calhoun County	13,077	7,014	1,678	4,087	888	990	323	29	17,327	6,120	4,704
Clinton County	6,360	3,844	773	1,648	338	458	133	0	9,318	2,977	1,792
Eaton County	9,751	5,483	1,090	3,004	527	752	188	4	14,409	4,189	2,789
Genesee County	39,113	20,902	5,271	12,100	1,778	3,792	1,492	187	48,178	19,816	13,108
Grand Traverse County	8,457	4,504	885	2,820	539	463	129	27	12,490	3,568	2,507
Ingham County	19,912	9,568	3,053	6,921	846	1,590	455	32	25,876	8,612	8,017
Isabella County	4,332	2,280	400	1,567	246	273	81	23	6,181	1,970	1,189
Jackson County	14,626	8,166	1,678	4,395	1,089	1,207	575	151	20,114	7,186	5,059
Kalamazoo County	20,203	10,350	2,293	7,081	1,116	1,413	512	68	26,950	9,241	7,216
Kent County	43,911	23,561	4,954	14,596	2,983	3,995	936	121	62,446	19,616	12,913
Lapeer County	7,587	4,765	649	2,073	477	991	242	35	12,154	3,225	1,723
Lenawee County	9,461	5,278	1,238	2,733	916	713	150	6	13,005	4,366	2,594
Livingston County	14,436	9,219	1,640	3,332	434	1,360	343	20	23,069	6,169	3,971
Macomb County	79,675	40,352	10,315	27,686	3,737	7,060	1,328	176	99,255	43,251	22,043
Marquette County	6,460	3,311	963	2,056	511	240	126	na	9,158	2,924	1,786
Midland County	8,123	4,583	647	2,637	427	401	56	5	11,903	3,393	1,783
Monroe County	13,592	7,563	1,592	4,211	776	1,406	524	55	18,936	6,505	3,915
Muskegon County	15,242	8,310	1,885	4,728	929	1,012	249	58	19,475	7,615	5,248
Oakland County	106,767	55,784	13,416	35,393	4,061	9,581	2,181	95	143,891	49,020	35,059
Ottawa County	19,807	12,117	1,644	5,818	983	1,454	481	78	31,828	8,784	3,839
Saginaw County	20,511	10,259	2,718	7,011	1,263	1,439	530	196	25,557	9,821	5,411
St. Clair County	15,532	8,475	1,976	4,752	871	1,033	285	13	22,513	7,193	4,374
Shiawassee County	6,427	3,859	664	1,781	242	431	14	0	9,960	3,099	1,321
Van Buren County	6,789	3,682	887	2,045	286	557	183	84	9,628	3,430	1,893
Washtenaw County	24,398	12,456	3,310	7,992	1,151	2,496	971	18	32,720	10,491	8,673
Wayne County	154,962	76,075	23,348	52,421	6,922	20,798	6,685	1,623	158,415	87,138	58,284
Minnesota											
Anoka County	21,874	12,208	2,451	6,907	552	2,669	577	71	33,688	8,687	7,082
Blue Earth County	4,944	2,380	609	1,897	603	na	na	na	6,663	2,291	1,139
Carver County	5,237	2,822	593	1,753	213	296	36	na	na	na	na
Dakota County	26,628	14,854	2,723	8,667	1,205	1,529	423	25	42,223	11,516	7,842
Hennepin County	87,965	41,583	12,090	31,845	6,084	5,743	1,534	345	114,088	37,188	30,562
Olmsted County	11,322	6,147	1,179	3,714	1,143	793	144	10	17,238	4,770	3,057
Ramsey County	40,715	19,265	5,345	15,110	3,084	3,284	876	174	50,960	18,389	13,636
St. Louis County	20,875	9,815	3,048	7,623	1,961	700	317	35	27,009	9,854	6,552
Scott County	6,480	3,632	760	1,922	426	962	165	na	11,223	2,664	1,875
Sherburne County	4,524	2,361	599	1,427	517	na	na	na	na	na	na

Table D-2: Counties—Household Relationship, Grandparents, and Marital Status—*Continued*

| | Total Householders Age 65 Years and Over | Family Householders 65 Years and Over | Non-Family Householders 65 Years and Over | | Persons 65 Years and Over Living in Group Quarters | Grandparents 60 Years and Over Living with Grandchildren | | | Marital Status - Persons 60 Years and Over | | |
			Male Living Alone	Female Living Alone		Total	Responsible for Grandchildren	Responsible for Grandchildren and In Poverty	Married	Widowed	Divorced
Minnesota—Cont.											
Stearns County	11,817	6,519	1,262	3,902	997	305	89	0	18,044	5,136	2,185
Washington County	16,953	9,676	1,897	4,995	683	1,796	332	43	27,790	6,695	4,508
Wright County	7,685	4,409	816	2,364	608	857	206	na	12,576	3,208	1,662
Mississippi											
DeSoto County	10,554	6,777	1,053	2,665	258	1,747	731	46	16,382	5,184	3,257
Forrest County	5,577	2,988	808	1,756	418	878	477	212	6,799	3,323	2,082
Harrison County	14,816	8,271	1,545	4,455	566	2,415	1,202	302	17,715	7,788	5,586
Hinds County	17,118	9,617	1,968	5,241	1,168	2,494	972	258	20,601	10,344	6,157
Jackson County	11,224	6,706	1,428	2,799	302	1,689	601	33	15,313	5,537	3,962
Jones County	6,240	3,726	407	1,936	504	820	550	149	8,353	3,458	1,485
Lauderdale County	7,316	3,928	1,022	2,198	473	867	345	49	8,891	4,177	2,202
Lee County	7,122	3,810	1,020	2,174	521	1,346	540	32	9,033	4,268	2,175
Madison County	6,612	3,793	620	2,114	424	983	237	14	9,429	3,565	1,681
Rankin County	10,708	6,774	991	2,849	674	1,372	446	49	14,720	5,577	3,582
Missouri											
Boone County	9,695	5,350	927	3,340	714	855	109	37	13,626	4,662	3,692
Buchanan County	7,777	3,905	996	2,754	653	650	92	0	9,690	3,971	2,432
Cape Girardeau County	6,487	3,701	743	1,995	963	472	208	0	9,916	3,295	1,326
Cass County	8,700	4,962	1,127	2,432	631	604	191	30	12,939	3,601	2,188
Christian County	6,348	3,825	595	1,730	304	732	339	0	na	na	na
Clay County	16,195	9,396	1,708	4,747	831	1,520	458	50	23,382	8,042	5,630
Cole County	6,589	3,550	677	2,197	625	529	251	85	9,146	3,044	1,748
Franklin County	8,825	5,031	889	2,803	581	796	301	0	12,688	4,970	1,829
Greene County	25,202	13,034	2,832	8,979	1,879	1,524	483	216	33,181	12,752	7,719
Jackson County	56,156	28,146	7,733	19,041	3,576	5,556	1,658	270	66,222	27,147	21,701
Jasper County	9,733	5,013	1,338	3,059	600	708	338	48	12,773	4,982	2,990
Jefferson County	15,780	9,654	1,692	4,030	1,094	2,423	915	0	24,930	7,510	4,813
Platte County	6,619	3,630	911	1,960	279	759	156	0	10,334	3,178	1,841
St. Charles County	27,199	16,041	2,714	7,915	1,049	2,706	549	28	42,544	12,280	6,125
St. Francois County	6,033	3,056	851	1,997	711	290	199	44	7,641	3,018	1,781
St. Louis County	96,508	51,326	11,063	32,563	8,401	7,155	2,065	367	126,020	47,997	28,304
Montana											
Cascade County	8,117	4,297	1,234	2,433	509	530	166	0	10,481	4,009	2,825
Flathead County	8,779	4,764	1,274	2,535	413	478	46	6	13,105	3,147	2,816
Gallatin County	5,808	3,457	561	1,673	242	na	na	na	9,212	2,244	1,640
Missoula County	8,036	4,506	916	2,402	309	465	195	77	12,099	3,243	3,367
Yellowstone County	14,161	7,196	1,702	4,899	791	1,017	388	105	18,390	6,572	4,545
Nebraska											
Douglas County	37,242	18,621	4,633	13,326	2,442	3,376	1,232	337	47,770	18,604	11,666
Lancaster County	20,392	10,768	2,447	6,903	1,103	1,308	494	55	30,749	8,325	6,142
Sarpy County	8,953	5,258	740	2,792	456	710	298	54	14,818	3,678	2,637
Nevada											
Clark County	137,213	73,947	22,599	34,581	3,413	25,797	7,082	1,001	191,036	66,005	64,738
Washoe County	32,880	17,616	5,333	8,617	1,033	4,516	1,359	194	47,214	13,337	16,267
New Hampshire											
Cheshire County	7,472	3,905	1,155	2,229	546	548	139	na	10,428	3,330	2,534
Grafton County	8,927	4,798	1,139	2,755	420	432	124	46	12,745	3,658	2,819
Hillsborough County	29,700	16,234	3,637	8,985	2,502	3,159	548	84	45,538	14,396	9,868
Merrimack County	12,436	6,624	1,382	3,922	1,484	1,221	484	0	18,179	5,772	4,859
Rockingham County	24,103	13,804	2,852	6,646	1,055	2,226	368	0	38,646	10,429	7,313
Strafford County	9,381	4,693	960	3,379	616	741	88	0	11,661	5,072	3,466
New Jersey											
Atlantic County	24,270	12,541	3,633	7,412	1,438	4,245	957	245	31,319	13,835	7,727
Bergen County	83,020	45,625	9,248	26,297	4,355	12,122	1,957	300	114,492	44,640	19,938
Burlington County	39,411	21,726	4,100	12,676	2,196	5,412	1,185	88	53,825	20,834	11,824
Camden County	41,664	21,218	5,245	14,426	2,452	7,022	1,413	189	52,749	24,308	11,813
Cape May County	13,676	7,329	1,643	4,249	638	858	234	47	18,800	6,141	2,896
Cumberland County	12,301	5,980	1,693	4,222	1,267	1,691	420	22	14,546	7,163	4,087
Essex County	55,719	26,711	8,329	19,234	3,788	9,326	1,891	386	66,330	32,317	17,711
Gloucester County	22,640	12,358	2,613	7,106	1,143	3,001	655	61	31,716	12,578	6,544
Hudson County	40,421	19,950	5,709	13,731	2,244	8,858	1,898	405	50,490	22,660	13,132
Hunterdon County	10,475	6,271	1,043	2,909	680	992	108	na	16,785	4,055	3,138
Mercer County	29,042	14,820	3,727	9,871	1,890	4,121	588	59	37,891	15,750	8,717
Middlesex County	58,029	32,177	6,900	17,883	3,637	12,172	1,318	25	84,604	35,207	16,109
Monmouth County	56,213	29,670	6,768	18,876	2,551	6,831	1,287	147	75,790	29,029	15,470
Morris County	41,827	22,977	4,657	13,417	2,902	5,524	850	26	62,396	20,723	10,814
Ocean County	79,232	39,995	9,706	27,714	3,939	4,874	1,499	242	97,098	40,467	16,017
Passaic County	34,527	18,097	4,651	11,090	2,684	8,122	1,483	165	46,967	21,145	10,496
Salem County	6,556	3,316	960	2,112	527	759	188	43	7,963	3,733	1,510
Somerset County	24,470	13,671	2,393	8,058	1,796	4,875	615	121	35,529	14,047	6,562
Sussex County	11,022	6,687	1,306	2,827	836	1,526	391	0	18,492	5,204	2,992
Union County	40,075	20,798	4,675	13,469	2,614	7,968	1,398	32	53,260	23,077	11,480
Warren County	9,011	4,941	984	2,817	736	885	102	na	13,192	5,117	2,707

Table D-2: Counties—Household Relationship, Grandparents, and Marital Status—*Continued*

	Total Householders Age 65 Years and Over	Family Householders 65 Years and Over	Non-Family Householders 65 Years and Over		Persons 65 Years and Over Living in Group Quarters	Grandparents 60 Years and Over Living with Grandchildren			Marital Status - Persons 60 Years and Over		
			Male Living Alone	Female Living Alone		Total	Responsible for Grandchildren	Responsible for Grandchildren and In Poverty	Married	Widowed	Divorced
New Mexico											
Bernalillo County	53,537	27,607	7,700	16,649	1,839	7,132	2,343	488	69,275	22,520	24,163
Chaves County	5,676	2,994	909	1,711	309	769	379	124	7,424	3,081	1,809
Doña Ana County	16,964	10,738	1,900	4,080	416	2,491	721	79	24,022	7,128	4,719
Lea County	4,453	2,649	542	1,178	248	600	292	55	6,591	1,841	1,157
McKinley County	4,378	2,448	732	1,118	200	1,309	807	381	4,938	2,826	1,372
Otero County	6,175	3,392	998	1,726	279	473	244	59	8,976	2,811	1,858
Sandoval County	10,240	5,820	1,356	2,725	238	1,535	429	85	15,596	4,747	3,424
San Juan County	8,792	5,426	1,024	2,049	402	1,827	725	394	12,527	4,476	2,462
Santa Fe County	15,667	7,393	2,393	5,165	316	1,307	460	54	19,943	5,243	8,101
Valencia County	6,177	3,543	808	1,606	169	592	266	63	9,435	2,937	2,050
New York											
Albany County	26,694	12,147	3,996	9,596	3,016	1,748	470	77	32,645	14,604	7,222
Bronx County	89,776	39,129	14,900	33,675	9,787	20,634	4,717	1,716	94,846	49,099	33,559
Broome County	20,716	10,088	2,895	7,296	2,043	1,361	184	0	25,865	10,342	6,284
Cattaraugus County	7,955	4,006	1,205	2,515	651	463	206	12	10,765	4,078	1,949
Cayuga County	8,022	4,064	909	2,765	513	582	181	9	10,372	4,214	2,325
Chautauqua County	14,404	7,208	2,044	4,828	1,263	869	259	24	19,043	6,969	4,162
Chemung County	8,794	4,030	1,257	3,312	957	414	117	10	10,938	5,192	2,341
Clinton County	7,230	3,741	1,147	2,173	530	420	141	40	10,213	3,204	1,748
Dutchess County	25,133	13,675	3,088	7,644	2,344	3,496	788	13	36,194	12,338	6,674
Erie County	94,461	45,619	12,500	34,399	7,046	5,490	1,609	275	108,920	49,861	24,870
Jefferson County	8,655	4,146	1,149	3,108	604	809	252	33	11,674	4,505	2,063
Kings County	180,377	86,280	24,458	65,255	11,485	37,865	11,167	3,573	215,167	102,791	50,607
Livingston County	5,743	3,200	744	1,721	512	443	115	25	8,719	2,738	1,362
Madison County	6,509	3,736	768	1,839	379	584	175	na	9,092	2,980	1,784
Monroe County	68,181	34,452	8,637	23,350	5,210	4,975	1,446	193	85,102	32,949	18,725
Nassau County	118,422	70,823	10,786	34,163	6,988	23,290	2,590	92	180,702	67,372	26,797
New York County	153,315	55,514	28,814	64,105	7,644	14,306	3,435	1,563	132,748	59,121	55,260
Niagara County	22,254	11,326	2,864	7,800	1,640	1,443	232	81	27,865	11,595	5,929
Oneida County	23,948	11,346	3,518	8,422	2,833	1,507	336	120	29,899	13,493	6,746
Onondaga County	42,609	20,083	6,611	14,948	3,494	3,283	790	89	52,586	20,940	11,906
Ontario County	10,730	5,654	1,223	3,610	876	719	183	4	15,792	5,521	3,041
Orange County	25,451	13,658	3,392	7,726	1,988	4,114	682	10	37,171	13,433	7,869
Oswego County	9,931	5,384	1,226	2,901	641	849	250	51	14,175	4,804	2,990
Putnam County	7,531	4,515	924	1,916	554	1,604	52	na	12,318	3,960	1,408
Queens County	164,595	87,894	19,385	53,435	10,832	42,578	7,658	1,392	227,860	97,926	46,693
Rensselaer County	13,772	6,544	2,031	4,738	1,300	1,237	455	0	18,099	7,720	4,050
Richmond County	35,919	20,365	3,969	11,231	3,414	7,011	1,645	292	53,959	22,729	8,094
Rockland County	24,214	14,748	2,228	6,672	2,270	5,338	655	35	38,784	12,559	4,924
St. Lawrence County	10,195	5,125	1,229	3,457	886	644	338	130	13,529	5,419	2,340
Saratoga County	19,879	10,804	2,389	6,101	1,079	1,109	323	0	27,983	8,991	5,884
Schenectady County	14,296	6,836	2,145	4,973	1,214	1,439	266	37	16,848	8,927	4,013
Steuben County	10,147	5,076	1,447	3,339	729	773	313	19	13,813	4,930	2,848
Suffolk County	120,129	70,712	12,385	33,727	10,123	21,936	2,729	468	176,715	68,142	30,598
Sullivan County	7,407	3,822	1,282	1,974	756	631	241	55	9,634	3,478	2,215
Tompkins County	7,172	3,504	1,002	2,420	402	382	122	na	10,359	2,967	2,329
Ulster County	17,228	8,023	2,582	5,796	1,593	1,283	289	0	22,593	9,259	5,893
Warren County	7,525	4,049	879	2,408	383	618	267	30	10,420	3,371	2,049
Wayne County	8,545	4,849	1,101	2,331	702	642	199	0	12,688	3,862	2,212
Westchester County	85,012	44,678	10,264	28,799	7,248	11,576	1,496	105	115,794	42,948	20,415
North Carolina											
Alamance County	15,143	7,582	1,411	5,932	755	839	307	52	18,045	7,973	3,898
Brunswick County	15,532	10,218	1,414	3,535	444	873	425	32	25,580	5,679	4,166
Buncombe County	24,525	12,930	3,288	7,729	2,114	1,897	809	202	32,259	11,616	9,315
Burke County	9,550	4,841	1,425	3,167	676	753	228	16	12,156	5,017	2,612
Cabarrus County	12,266	6,893	1,468	3,714	610	1,910	539	141	18,553	6,096	3,712
Caldwell County	8,715	4,572	1,163	2,962	341	686	286	79	11,179	5,073	2,522
Carteret County	8,027	4,542	1,021	2,267	327	402	201	34	12,213	3,565	2,314
Catawba County	13,927	7,628	1,697	4,238	853	1,361	287	33	19,169	8,422	3,917
Chatham County	7,609	4,171	963	2,419	488	450	266	na	na	na	na
Cleveland County	10,113	4,957	1,320	3,603	329	791	473	39	12,416	5,208	2,602
Craven County	10,411	6,332	722	3,156	394	1,055	525	80	15,788	4,440	2,023
Cumberland County	20,132	10,884	2,241	6,591	1,048	2,877	1,069	259	25,751	11,652	6,404
Davidson County	15,360	9,019	1,558	4,611	787	1,049	579	150	22,353	7,290	4,302
Durham County	17,478	9,278	2,060	5,706	1,776	1,918	1,044	317	22,571	8,970	6,654
Forsyth County	29,928	15,424	3,747	10,273	1,755	2,796	999	225	39,142	14,658	9,497
Gaston County	17,191	9,778	2,262	4,922	1,159	1,970	891	285	23,298	10,339	5,172
Guilford County	40,114	21,553	4,245	13,550	2,072	4,026	1,162	160	54,098	18,783	12,283
Harnett County	7,745	4,043	1,085	2,398	414	1,015	257	10	10,474	4,639	1,996
Henderson County	15,045	8,746	1,893	3,934	1,012	1,050	498	26	21,641	6,677	3,642
Iredell County	12,673	7,424	1,540	3,564	572	1,154	374	13	19,988	6,192	3,665

Table D-2: Counties—Household Relationship, Grandparents, and Marital Status—*Continued*

	Total Householders Age 65 Years and Over	Family Householders 65 Years and Over	Non-Family Householders 65 Years and Over		Persons 65 Years and Over Living in Group Quarters	Grandparents 60 Years and Over Living with Grandchildren			Marital Status - Persons 60 Years and Over		
			Male Living Alone	Female Living Alone		Total	Responsible for Grandchildren	Responsible for Grandchildren and In Poverty	Married	Widowed	Divorced
North Carolina—Cont.											
Johnston County	11,292	6,346	964	3,693	675	1,022	431	92	17,749	5,814	3,394
Lincoln County	6,568	3,663	846	1,869	377	774	268	173	10,459	3,213	1,766
Mecklenburg County	52,955	29,302	5,457	17,138	2,776	7,905	1,943	576	76,239	28,404	18,894
Moore County	12,681	7,085	1,372	3,953	658	608	259	26	17,855	5,841	2,492
Nash County	9,311	4,450	1,329	3,288	579	831	215	54	11,342	5,244	2,660
New Hanover County	18,801	9,969	2,033	6,401	868	1,264	409	83	25,783	8,052	5,936
Onslow County	8,668	4,726	1,176	2,637	416	1,432	513	130	11,810	4,447	2,810
Orange County	8,516	4,733	946	2,609	380	771	421	na	12,887	3,540	2,796
Pitt County	11,087	5,921	1,444	3,611	619	1,362	511	213	15,344	5,792	3,106
Randolph County	12,944	7,067	1,826	3,831	578	1,274	499	81	19,010	6,605	3,552
Robeson County	9,833	5,716	1,119	2,745	634	2,677	1,413	420	12,924	6,251	2,632
Rockingham County	9,877	5,172	1,179	3,438	634	1,105	416	105	12,663	5,340	2,766
Rowan County	13,295	7,317	1,713	4,064	1,006	818	392	106	17,271	7,338	3,272
Rutherford County	7,588	4,142	845	2,530	545	1,032	569	119	10,504	3,957	1,926
Surry County	8,442	4,446	859	3,023	511	809	451	122	10,892	4,016	1,899
Union County	11,867	7,726	949	2,925	563	1,746	584	86	21,255	6,199	2,725
Wake County	50,571	27,596	5,357	16,624	2,509	7,085	1,558	154	77,538	25,044	17,160
Wayne County	10,404	5,289	1,260	3,628	727	1,187	571	174	13,967	5,488	3,094
Wilkes County	7,838	4,569	698	2,528	458	627	360	145	10,984	3,601	1,529
Wilson County	7,792	3,820	1,086	2,801	673	457	205	50	9,642	4,069	2,116
North Dakota											
Burleigh County	7,417	3,717	846	2,703	582	293	65	na	10,588	3,536	1,603
Cass County	9,923	4,446	1,419	3,816	824	432	149	na	14,385	4,357	2,794
Grand Forks County	4,748	2,286	608	1,795	438	302	113	na	na	na	na
Ohio											
Allen County	9,963	5,130	1,253	3,400	763	447	228	58	12,882	4,766	2,858
Ashtabula County	10,295	4,979	1,631	3,361	833	839	234	0	12,488	5,682	3,417
Belmont County	7,881	3,988	976	2,839	780	487	155	0	10,202	4,463	1,951
Butler County	27,637	15,215	3,314	8,674	1,681	3,223	1,224	140	40,829	14,818	7,671
Clark County	14,890	7,961	1,799	4,907	1,161	1,095	394	115	18,879	7,220	4,731
Clermont County	15,326	8,549	1,916	4,599	711	1,702	285	0	22,225	7,353	4,471
Columbiana County	11,225	6,307	1,190	3,490	891	961	476	104	15,851	5,987	3,065
Cuyahoga County	131,447	60,123	19,078	49,421	9,161	11,662	3,678	1,034	137,719	69,466	45,362
Delaware County	10,771	6,706	1,040	2,937	499	1,342	283	28	19,792	4,276	3,167
Erie County	8,524	4,666	1,175	2,582	869	487	243	39	12,069	4,217	2,357
Fairfield County	11,630	7,088	1,075	3,270	587	1,366	270	30	17,501	5,518	2,742
Franklin County	76,037	37,172	10,367	26,637	3,910	10,044	3,077	389	94,803	38,676	32,172
Geauga County	8,947	5,604	805	2,362	561	578	134	18	14,579	4,165	1,955
Greene County	14,111	8,161	1,582	4,201	946	1,524	370	83	21,922	6,511	3,545
Hamilton County	70,311	33,835	9,251	26,109	5,646	5,393	1,946	493	84,648	35,141	22,411
Hancock County	6,948	3,712	906	2,228	559	63	11	na	na	na	na
Jefferson County	8,400	4,250	1,034	2,928	443	527	290	47	10,376	4,141	2,021
Lake County	24,006	12,896	2,775	7,854	1,385	1,638	506	16	31,767	11,702	7,017
Licking County	14,450	7,690	1,816	4,452	601	1,091	339	9	20,031	6,723	4,968
Lorain County	27,906	16,088	2,831	8,549	2,146	3,051	1,128	155	40,431	13,161	8,178
Lucas County	38,251	19,013	5,509	12,932	3,018	2,641	987	167	46,003	19,102	13,044
Mahoning County	28,479	14,394	3,669	9,796	2,203	2,073	592	118	31,657	16,332	7,800
Marion County	6,414	3,419	705	2,173	372	444	261	34	8,698	3,093	1,874
Medina County	14,720	8,091	1,951	4,274	823	1,123	312	0	21,969	7,016	4,401
Miami County	10,437	5,914	1,237	3,076	590	615	157	0	14,397	5,082	2,243
Montgomery County	55,283	26,134	8,471	19,372	3,882	4,080	1,644	258	62,069	27,262	20,871
Muskingum County	8,262	4,268	1,005	2,860	604	485	159	14	11,051	4,717	2,461
Portage County	13,015	7,620	1,616	3,300	671	1,496	825	10	19,178	5,744	4,530
Richland County	13,532	7,034	1,825	4,481	963	631	310	143	17,163	7,135	3,731
Ross County	6,824	3,474	1,121	2,136	593	475	186	53	8,774	3,358	1,987
Scioto County	8,017	4,048	1,229	2,620	707	1,186	630	206	9,679	4,459	2,552
Stark County	38,956	20,915	5,036	11,982	3,313	3,199	1,307	105	50,635	19,897	11,050
Summit County	51,983	26,327	7,126	17,468	2,991	4,295	1,377	70	64,634	26,724	16,260
Trumbull County	23,974	12,197	3,613	7,751	1,376	1,894	446	75	30,073	12,528	7,314
Tuscarawas County	9,621	5,213	1,101	3,209	856	579	270	56	13,489	4,749	2,449
Warren County	14,338	8,545	1,319	4,161	906	1,639	575	0	24,346	6,362	4,655
Wayne County	10,462	6,198	1,209	2,870	815	1,016	229	0	15,512	5,078	2,722
Wood County	10,464	5,456	1,029	3,631	665	647	293	10	14,199	5,056	2,930
Oklahoma											
Canadian County	8,051	4,662	882	2,360	408	967	351	25	13,010	4,036	2,354
Cleveland County	16,651	9,449	2,008	5,016	1,184	1,775	545	77	25,923	8,397	5,728
Comanche County	8,725	4,582	1,243	2,765	603	953	463	53	10,506	4,489	2,739
Creek County	6,708	3,640	934	1,987	373	703	373	53	9,273	3,934	1,565
Muskogee County	6,568	3,659	751	2,074	556	574	192	53	9,047	3,307	1,959
Oklahoma County	57,340	28,687	8,235	19,262	2,899	6,430	2,770	738	70,189	28,793	21,988
Payne County	5,209	2,858	673	1,541	203	248	124	14	7,828	2,203	1,313
Pottawatomie County	6,421	3,525	849	1,962	472	731	450	71	8,781	2,915	2,080
Rogers County	7,325	4,795	722	1,736	587	716	215	18	12,290	2,866	1,838
Tulsa County	48,412	25,136	6,112	16,432	2,578	4,693	1,840	336	61,274	23,925	17,395
Wagoner County	6,146	3,823	982	1,286	142	828	248	54	10,186	2,585	1,922

Table D-2: Counties—Household Relationship, Grandparents, and Marital Status—*Continued*

	Total Householders Age 65 Years and Over	Family Householders 65 Years and Over	Non-Family Householders 65 Years and Over		Persons 65 Years and Over Living in Group Quarters	Grandparents 60 Years and Over Living with Grandchildren			Marital Status - Persons 60 Years and Over		
			Male Living Alone	Female Living Alone		Total	Responsible for Grandchildren	Responsible for Grandchildren and In Poverty	Married	Widowed	Divorced
Oregon											
Benton County	6,771	3,527	1,112	1,906	122	464	85	na	9,939	2,209	2,854
Clackamas County	33,314	18,654	3,425	10,139	1,353	3,754	899	46	52,954	13,891	12,740
Deschutes County	15,950	9,040	1,858	4,578	400	1,160	485	26	23,616	6,410	5,772
Douglas County	14,506	8,178	2,077	3,683	433	1,117	540	130	20,712	6,738	4,362
Jackson County	23,740	12,502	3,042	7,365	829	1,495	544	0	31,402	9,167	9,526
Josephine County	11,849	6,305	1,550	3,693	368	839	184	48	15,668	4,776	4,491
Klamath County	7,609	4,547	989	1,721	135	655	362	50	10,800	3,026	2,515
Lane County	34,894	17,975	4,454	11,083	1,663	2,360	1,004	143	46,307	14,742	14,800
Linn County	12,108	6,736	1,473	3,516	346	946	251	36	17,254	5,026	4,173
Marion County	26,123	13,839	3,159	8,680	1,710	2,540	908	195	36,034	11,447	9,280
Multnomah County	52,357	24,212	7,890	18,190	3,293	5,705	1,409	200	63,089	24,868	25,585
Polk County	7,109	4,147	743	1,912	334	409	189	0	na	na	na
Umatilla County	6,242	3,431	943	1,771	374	732	338	na	8,659	2,738	2,627
Washington County	35,955	18,277	4,069	12,540	995	4,144	1,119	229	49,389	16,257	15,136
Yamhill County	8,356	4,907	850	2,365	483	943	392	22	11,803	3,752	2,687
Pennsylvania											
Adams County	9,970	5,508	1,292	2,863	866	760	226	95	14,720	5,125	2,165
Allegheny County	135,087	63,904	18,820	50,180	9,254	9,137	3,061	390	151,769	72,445	34,582
Armstrong County	8,268	4,041	1,104	2,993	523	451	205	104	10,721	4,410	1,630
Beaver County	20,859	10,769	2,592	7,191	812	1,476	595	73	25,290	11,270	4,481
Berks County	37,479	19,879	4,728	11,617	2,812	3,196	793	245	50,515	18,598	10,176
Blair County	14,484	7,389	1,675	5,137	1,645	828	258	4	18,011	8,364	3,797
Bucks County	56,346	32,106	6,507	16,134	3,595	7,173	1,207	21	84,838	30,590	13,476
Butler County	17,817	9,673	2,230	5,477	1,212	685	297	8	25,808	8,699	3,788
Cambria County	17,817	8,663	2,561	6,312	1,122	796	227	27	21,234	9,423	3,700
Carbon County	7,076	3,794	845	2,184	404	636	167	0	10,120	3,733	1,491
Centre County	11,231	5,898	1,484	3,631	720	454	67	0	15,768	4,997	2,839
Chester County	39,824	22,600	4,552	11,770	2,963	4,447	810	46	61,829	18,962	9,945
Clearfield County	9,071	4,747	1,121	3,064	779	516	177	26	11,892	5,172	1,919
Columbia County	7,062	3,403	912	2,583	450	385	53	0	9,046	3,515	1,595
Crawford County	9,560	5,215	1,396	2,702	539	632	232	65	12,772	4,377	2,712
Cumberland County	23,269	12,281	2,590	7,763	1,908	1,232	411	0	33,321	11,266	5,572
Dauphin County	24,168	12,109	3,279	8,206	1,389	1,988	480	111	30,676	13,398	6,394
Delaware County	50,131	25,356	6,160	17,788	4,223	5,803	1,082	135	60,598	29,104	12,997
Erie County	25,679	12,970	3,197	8,840	2,351	1,919	417	41	33,222	14,069	6,990
Fayette County	15,556	7,797	2,235	5,263	1,291	1,311	475	113	18,802	9,433	3,373
Franklin County	15,592	8,816	1,761	4,775	764	909	197	0	22,547	7,147	3,090
Indiana County	8,758	4,834	1,128	2,552	555	512	130	9	11,917	4,393	1,490
Lackawanna County	23,796	11,803	3,420	8,087	2,591	1,960	358	37	28,026	13,945	5,591
Lancaster County	47,590	26,185	5,486	14,661	4,576	3,816	924	122	70,610	22,813	9,815
Lawrence County	10,927	5,602	1,443	3,703	740	811	276	0	13,935	5,353	2,637
Lebanon County	14,277	7,773	1,433	4,771	1,244	811	216	88	19,416	7,076	3,400
Lehigh County	31,004	16,145	4,301	9,830	3,017	3,592	522	110	42,364	16,758	8,553
Luzerne County	36,834	17,623	5,527	13,136	2,890	2,576	725	78	43,315	20,418	8,601
Lycoming County	11,867	6,428	1,201	3,926	971	665	168	64	16,045	6,449	2,708
Mercer County	14,049	7,355	1,718	4,787	1,254	658	265	20	17,125	7,571	3,156
Monroe County	11,953	7,150	1,249	3,050	602	2,165	535	37	20,442	7,024	3,733
Montgomery County	74,581	39,901	8,471	24,610	7,191	7,470	1,111	157	103,694	38,519	17,671
Northampton County	29,061	15,283	3,767	9,348	2,054	3,248	668	120	38,909	15,524	6,656
Northumberland County	11,300	5,872	1,441	3,786	989	482	103	9	14,364	5,713	2,824
Philadelphia County	122,082	51,736	20,902	46,671	8,134	17,444	4,593	1,292	110,021	73,451	41,544
Schuylkill County	17,174	9,050	2,403	5,436	1,619	1,103	397	42	21,221	9,494	3,636
Somerset County	9,121	4,738	1,127	3,057	760	379	103	0	11,874	5,026	1,786
Washington County	23,892	11,846	3,032	8,405	1,319	1,811	729	68	29,621	13,521	5,703
Westmoreland County	45,195	23,546	5,685	15,016	2,282	2,332	744	93	56,731	23,906	9,991
York County	39,794	21,676	5,011	12,341	2,074	3,251	1,076	272	56,877	18,799	10,937
Rhode Island											
Kent County	17,045	7,970	2,501	6,108	1,058	1,416	275	0	20,358	9,340	5,746
Newport County	9,167	4,588	1,050	3,156	507	811	245	12	11,910	3,710	3,234
Providence County	52,402	24,325	7,486	19,409	5,047	5,729	1,380	341	62,407	29,412	16,621
Washington County	12,599	6,904	1,411	3,986	780	683	242	na	18,193	5,725	3,801
South Carolina											
Aiken County	16,110	9,556	1,649	4,723	704	2,249	1,105	462	22,815	8,415	3,779
Anderson County	18,798	10,479	2,394	5,597	1,068	2,664	1,053	301	25,315	10,015	4,253
Beaufort County	22,118	14,366	2,002	5,315	390	1,754	408	8	34,701	8,068	4,800
Berkeley County	11,717	7,472	1,325	2,703	331	1,920	849	75	18,914	5,868	3,246
Charleston County	30,038	16,346	3,416	9,817	1,290	3,402	1,185	389	39,709	15,252	9,055
Darlington County	6,784	3,773	845	2,102	398	982	348	18	8,663	3,667	1,576
Dorchester County	8,916	5,205	1,024	2,608	297	1,582	773	32	13,463	4,701	3,236
Florence County	11,261	6,748	1,128	3,196	788	2,001	560	120	15,669	6,700	3,293
Greenville County	37,562	20,901	4,356	11,805	1,424	3,756	1,178	257	52,179	19,038	10,111
Greenwood County	7,065	3,675	821	2,532	503	936	493	209	9,017	3,794	1,653

Table D-2: Counties—Household Relationship, Grandparents, and Marital Status—*Continued*

	Total Householders Age 65 Years and Over	Family Householders 65 Years and Over	Non-Family Householders 65 Years and Over		Persons 65 Years and Over Living in Group Quarters	Grandparents 60 Years and Over Living with Grandchildren			Marital Status - Persons 60 Years and Over		
			Male Living Alone	Female Living Alone		Total	Responsible for Grandchildren	Responsible for Grandchildren and In Poverty	Married	Widowed	Divorced
South Carolina—Cont.											
Horry County	31,520	17,497	4,133	9,069	747	3,004	889	135	45,244	15,033	8,595
Lancaster County	7,703	4,879	675	2,056	390	702	278	92	12,127	3,769	1,640
Laurens County	6,158	3,446	578	2,041	671	775	286	72	9,206	3,366	1,333
Lexington County	20,450	11,935	2,542	5,694	1,017	1,916	894	161	31,247	10,732	6,310
Oconee County	9,024	5,609	1,124	2,211	200	327	94	25	13,744	3,847	1,882
Orangeburg County	8,962	4,808	1,347	2,645	327	1,451	887	226	11,593	5,240	1,754
Pickens County	10,102	5,872	1,036	2,994	473	1,112	553	210	14,377	4,858	2,758
Richland County	24,800	13,070	3,016	8,251	1,577	2,938	1,209	131	33,007	13,787	8,626
Spartanburg County	24,662	13,847	2,964	7,522	1,230	3,661	1,711	620	34,938	13,483	6,399
Sumter County	9,106	5,148	1,186	2,620	505	1,441	701	106	11,866	5,436	1,902
York County	17,045	10,221	1,835	4,727	720	1,696	669	140	25,515	7,481	5,212
South Dakota											
Minnehaha County	12,106	6,348	1,520	3,933	968	882	298	45	17,076	6,017	3,817
Pennington County	8,758	4,685	1,246	2,597	809	628	275	na	12,538	3,943	2,808
Tennessee											
Anderson County	8,590	4,748	1,214	2,568	539	962	425	81	10,814	4,142	2,499
Blount County	12,826	7,218	1,426	3,863	563	1,561	697	92	18,267	6,131	3,645
Bradley County	9,145	5,110	1,253	2,740	435	1,010	294	71	12,459	4,921	2,477
Davidson County	42,599	21,271	5,857	14,388	2,363	5,260	1,637	280	52,512	21,708	17,808
Greene County	7,888	4,304	1,011	2,423	433	621	314	124	10,962	3,765	2,368
Hamilton County	32,214	17,275	3,767	10,797	1,481	3,190	1,343	204	41,418	16,567	11,205
Knox County	37,182	18,477	5,423	12,817	1,730	3,220	1,348	142	49,056	19,502	11,484
Madison County	8,034	4,430	1,055	2,447	577	961	321	44	10,433	4,519	3,130
Maury County	6,547	3,509	641	2,216	466	894	374	12	9,806	3,615	2,471
Montgomery County	8,609	4,982	1,081	2,263	397	1,173	454	52	13,224	4,692	2,708
Putnam County	6,939	4,172	536	2,113	413	600	137	28	8,945	3,722	1,833
Robertson County	5,220	2,982	556	1,567	239	624	287	0	7,474	2,675	1,395
Rutherford County	14,063	8,341	1,339	3,951	760	2,128	869	64	22,015	7,571	5,222
Sevier County	8,874	5,629	937	2,190	284	687	436	0	13,708	4,367	2,241
Shelby County	61,462	32,610	7,808	19,733	3,071	9,890	3,425	923	76,695	35,768	25,640
Sullivan County	20,031	11,292	2,120	6,236	1,063	2,070	1,061	153	25,564	9,362	5,234
Sumner County	12,748	7,686	1,014	3,800	636	1,842	693	88	20,435	6,690	3,626
Washington County	12,311	6,797	1,459	3,873	870	1,199	558	106	16,984	5,996	3,395
Williamson County	11,552	7,168	910	3,409	473	1,538	308	29	21,174	5,154	2,895
Wilson County	9,111	5,851	943	2,157	467	1,615	372	23	14,455	4,515	2,914
Texas											
Angelina County	7,547	4,480	643	2,269	677	864	329	119	10,658	3,822	2,104
Bastrop County	4,902	2,782	555	1,515	367	994	354	0	na	na	na
Bell County	16,529	9,653	1,837	4,632	1,181	2,708	822	203	25,052	9,316	5,155
Bexar County	110,503	62,907	13,205	31,907	5,596	24,364	6,588	1,457	152,449	57,287	42,163
Bowie County	8,732	4,571	1,304	2,754	694	764	425	135	10,508	4,795	2,648
Brazoria County	18,734	11,230	2,346	4,575	1,226	3,348	1,191	164	28,629	10,785	5,987
Brazos County	9,419	5,244	1,117	2,864	519	1,042	334	58	13,972	4,846	2,485
Cameron County	25,830	16,236	2,636	6,435	1,106	7,562	1,782	639	40,010	13,665	5,829
Collin County	36,949	23,034	3,393	10,013	1,246	8,318	983	107	69,167	17,289	13,337
Comal County	10,803	6,818	1,167	2,583	458	1,402	594	76	17,951	3,963	3,167
Coryell County	3,511	2,340	356	793	185	733	85	12	5,354	1,710	1,466
Dallas County	131,881	71,873	16,086	40,326	6,825	27,289	8,387	2,212	181,759	69,740	54,634
Denton County	28,022	16,668	3,110	7,656	1,169	7,154	1,614	237	50,880	14,739	10,999
Ector County	9,061	4,755	1,191	2,947	368	1,376	558	167	11,661	4,912	2,815
Ellis County	9,565	5,991	820	2,553	516	2,124	1,036	42	15,879	4,809	2,738
El Paso County	49,572	29,786	5,612	12,962	1,564	14,774	4,336	1,547	69,261	28,190	16,316
Fort Bend County	24,655	16,337	2,000	5,835	1,018	8,895	1,756	153	50,612	14,888	9,354
Galveston County	20,486	11,712	3,209	5,232	983	3,262	927	161	30,039	11,405	8,650
Grayson County	11,431	6,215	1,422	3,539	818	1,289	437	54	15,961	6,047	4,291
Gregg County	10,619	5,387	1,433	3,691	900	1,015	481	142	13,107	6,248	3,228
Guadalupe County	10,201	5,904	1,103	3,043	439	1,473	461	110	14,830	4,867	3,254
Harris County	205,093	116,154	27,166	57,432	8,521	49,416	12,226	2,898	312,616	112,014	82,971
Harrison County	5,890	3,103	942	1,798	272	661	392	82	7,631	3,224	1,807
Hays County	8,277	4,857	869	2,284	384	2,295	481	60	13,967	3,952	3,688
Henderson County	9,403	5,504	1,307	2,349	566	1,047	656	151	13,207	4,653	2,834
Hidalgo County	41,006	27,135	4,463	8,690	1,706	14,165	3,639	1,644	70,680	22,506	8,246
Hunt County	7,492	4,322	960	2,090	487	1,527	436	114	10,581	4,282	2,508
Jefferson County	21,674	10,824	3,315	7,216	1,138	2,271	1,095	112	25,149	11,979	7,134
Johnson County	10,832	7,251	904	2,482	631	1,809	937	56	16,979	4,692	3,548
Kaufman County	6,669	4,043	622	1,874	486	1,560	557	94	10,792	3,387	2,322
Liberty County	5,552	3,402	553	1,483	304	816	490	45	7,969	2,591	1,945
Lubbock County	20,165	11,068	2,330	6,452	1,215	2,239	996	212	25,688	10,640	5,820
McLennan County	18,149	9,719	2,229	5,866	1,786	2,012	765	78	23,986	9,719	6,036
Midland County	9,229	4,896	1,274	2,906	581	1,311	547	169	13,822	4,684	3,135
Montgomery County	30,909	19,023	2,504	8,813	943	4,775	1,450	355	49,999	15,298	10,150
Nacogdoches County	4,957	2,441	720	1,732	380	404	186	22	6,500	2,535	1,346
Nueces County	25,772	15,416	3,069	6,775	1,353	5,038	1,918	225	35,229	13,083	10,287
Orange County	7,230	4,111	1,005	1,981	322	751	353	72	10,178	3,928	1,847
Parker County	9,609	5,996	981	2,461	413	1,033	314	20	15,286	4,475	2,536
Potter County	8,181	4,071	1,189	2,694	1,071	1,353	742	187	10,516	4,999	3,254

Table D-2: Counties—Household Relationship, Grandparents, and Marital Status—*Continued*

	Total Householders Age 65 Years and Over	Family Householders 65 Years and Over	Non-Family Householders 65 Years and Over		Persons 65 Years and Over Living in Group Quarters	Grandparents 60 Years and Over Living with Grandchildren			Marital Status - Persons 60 Years and Over		
			Male Living Alone	Female Living Alone		Total	Responsible for Grandchildren	Responsible for Grandchildren and In Poverty	Married	Widowed	Divorced
Texas—Cont.											
Randall County	10,099	5,724	929	3,285	205	911	443	89	14,507	4,340	3,034
Rockwall County	4,518	2,898	393	1,053	368	701	61	na	na	na	na
San Patricio County	5,198	3,204	516	1,349	272	862	237	114	7,554	2,913	1,446
Smith County	19,347	10,996	2,264	5,718	971	2,293	789	389	26,700	10,023	4,492
Tarrant County	103,760	57,599	12,544	32,002	5,943	19,353	5,767	1,092	155,654	53,486	41,985
Taylor County	11,015	6,160	1,294	3,441	869	1,362	766	289	14,284	5,985	2,942
Tom Green County	10,089	5,706	1,241	3,013	457	1,057	375	123	13,226	4,354	2,950
Travis County	49,015	27,780	5,086	14,746	2,462	8,178	2,163	644	74,423	22,828	22,376
Victoria County	7,265	4,207	917	2,089	531	1,152	387	50	10,527	3,337	2,059
Walker County	4,461	2,378	666	1,316	549	575	420	na	5,884	2,159	1,604
Webb County	10,908	7,277	1,063	2,534	425	5,401	1,331	616	17,625	6,881	2,829
Wichita County	11,069	6,010	1,125	3,725	952	1,066	565	104	14,398	5,700	2,982
Williamson County	23,368	14,244	2,504	6,227	1,035	4,499	922	60	41,837	9,268	8,459
Utah											
Cache County	5,564	3,543	523	1,463	122	803	265	0	9,170	2,150	987
Davis County	15,780	10,663	1,393	3,560	410	2,735	912	69	28,306	5,677	3,393
Salt Lake County	57,796	33,474	7,008	16,558	1,803	10,893	2,443	272	87,067	26,363	19,961
Utah County	20,809	13,784	1,564	5,228	593	5,248	1,407	121	35,851	7,957	4,813
Washington County	15,283	10,186	1,581	3,235	334	659	156	18	24,194	4,684	2,896
Weber County	15,399	9,236	1,681	4,386	560	1,895	593	3	23,459	5,568	4,568
Vermont											
Chittenden County	11,803	5,881	1,368	4,091	739	963	249	0	16,520	4,949	4,301
Virginia											
Albemarle County	9,195	4,999	923	3,128	580	811	359	246	12,851	4,296	2,707
Arlington County	12,176	5,349	2,137	4,292	464	1,152	264	na	15,407	4,423	4,807
Augusta County	7,768	4,989	805	1,888	208	999	328	32	12,115	3,540	1,361
Bedford County	7,426	4,585	804	1,964	113	626	156	na	na	na	na
Chesterfield County	21,476	12,429	2,144	6,305	498	3,526	1,143	30	33,200	10,974	7,454
Fairfax County	64,675	39,131	6,734	17,034	1,492	13,128	2,172	249	119,029	29,870	19,515
Fauquier County	5,124	3,108	627	1,248	218	805	193	4	na	na	na
Frederick County	6,175	3,688	747	1,418	137	1,010	306	na	na	na	na
Hanover County	8,435	5,417	611	2,232	273	964	319	41	13,213	4,048	2,098
Henrico County	25,135	12,652	2,870	9,110	1,542	3,399	1,112	127	32,371	13,269	8,934
James City County	8,682	5,492	1,031	2,094	287	812	77	0	na	na	na
Loudoun County	11,937	7,356	986	3,426	327	3,994	934	49	23,213	6,281	3,955
Montgomery County	5,998	3,560	488	1,838	296	384	17	0	8,942	2,775	1,548
Prince William County	15,513	9,807	1,406	3,781	465	6,178	1,050	32	31,627	8,729	6,621
Roanoke County	10,426	5,793	1,089	3,429	1,031	932	350	66	14,465	5,311	2,429
Rockingham County	7,980	4,757	878	2,224	301	635	255	0	11,583	3,769	1,445
Spotsylvania County	7,813	5,051	612	2,025	296	1,542	791	87	13,780	3,844	1,708
Stafford County	5,781	3,791	524	1,355	171	1,299	384	0	10,223	2,744	1,920
York County	4,985	3,305	376	1,178	43	529	118	na	na	na	na
Washington											
Benton County	13,851	8,053	1,671	3,973	548	1,597	566	137	21,514	5,775	4,145
Chelan County	7,294	3,793	815	2,308	256	468	150	na	na	na	na
Clallam County	10,954	6,172	1,411	2,910	420	409	182	15	15,000	3,847	4,032
Clark County	32,636	18,586	3,697	9,373	909	4,271	1,187	95	50,112	13,862	11,950
Cowlitz County	10,586	5,626	1,401	3,250	592	721	316	0	14,421	4,685	3,885
Franklin County	3,448	1,796	460	1,091	137	1,145	141	42	6,298	1,768	1,280
Grant County	7,157	4,049	985	1,921	294	853	171	7	9,720	3,150	1,965
Grays Harbor County	7,566	3,909	1,340	2,091	283	723	283	44	10,720	3,133	2,905
Island County	9,195	5,466	1,058	2,461	228	503	215	26	14,812	3,388	2,451
King County	139,478	67,444	20,145	47,150	8,544	17,534	3,078	425	188,686	60,727	57,937
Kitsap County	21,257	11,940	2,582	6,103	1,592	1,889	571	92	33,462	9,574	7,873
Lewis County	8,882	4,938	1,188	2,664	444	641	293	92	12,160	3,795	2,262
Pierce County	56,645	30,110	7,496	16,938	3,134	7,459	1,691	185	81,312	26,682	23,474
Skagit County	12,155	6,719	1,613	3,322	465	854	221	13	17,666	5,257	4,007
Snohomish County	47,824	26,151	5,702	14,485	2,477	6,510	1,653	147	72,546	22,095	20,224
Spokane County	40,702	20,550	5,779	13,328	2,610	2,893	831	35	55,343	18,315	15,445
Thurston County	21,508	11,258	2,566	6,922	982	1,539	398	0	32,633	9,328	7,761
Whatcom County	17,606	9,768	2,281	5,247	617	1,509	705	93	26,285	7,291	6,064
Yakima County	16,886	9,205	1,847	5,225	1,317	2,715	762	212	24,299	9,155	5,697
West Virginia											
Berkeley County	7,552	4,352	923	2,011	269	758	214	45	11,830	3,937	2,601
Cabell County	10,095	5,423	1,200	3,293	560	537	216	76	12,168	5,495	3,038
Harrison County	7,720	4,018	1,087	2,502	435	466	172	12	9,232	4,626	1,743
Kanawha County	22,134	11,552	2,941	7,240	758	1,583	934	156	25,265	11,366	6,669
Monongalia County	5,975	3,057	696	2,129	311	184	45	na	8,394	3,258	2,112
Raleigh County	8,358	4,214	1,037	2,973	430	510	203	67	11,036	4,690	1,924
Wood County	9,880	4,821	1,426	3,422	438	887	344	53	12,327	4,952	2,657

Table D-2: Counties—Household Relationship, Grandparents, and Marital Status—*Continued*

	Total Householders Age 65 Years and Over	Family Householders 65 Years and Over	Non-Family Householders 65 Years and Over		Persons 65 Years and Over Living in Group Quarters	Grandparents 60 Years and Over Living with Grandchildren			Marital Status - Persons 60 Years and Over		
			Male Living Alone	Female Living Alone		Total	Responsible for Grandchildren	Responsible for Grandchildren and In Poverty	Married	Widowed	Divorced
Wisconsin											
Brown County	18,977	9,746	2,283	6,582	1,314	1,143	447	67	26,295	8,943	5,130
Dane County	34,303	17,918	3,724	11,658	1,729	1,758	323	60	50,099	13,700	11,476
Dodge County	8,083	4,351	1,143	2,422	1,026	163	54	0	11,519	4,081	1,965
Eau Claire County.........	8,546	4,003	1,218	3,137	456	345	59	na	11,331	3,858	2,292
Fond du Lac County	9,918	5,368	1,179	3,274	888	327	94	7	13,779	4,848	2,315
Jefferson County..........	7,181	3,665	962	2,430	376	341	68	0	10,258	3,371	1,779
Kenosha County............	12,001	5,812	1,485	4,336	686	1,188	460	29	14,862	6,639	3,975
La Crosse County..........	10,188	5,166	1,422	3,382	815	440	118	na	14,082	4,589	2,008
Manitowoc County	8,800	4,390	1,231	2,992	825	361	199	39	12,169	4,265	1,527
Marathon County	11,818	6,643	1,443	3,513	943	662	118	9	18,869	5,195	2,679
Milwaukee County.........	73,522	30,835	11,790	28,763	4,796	6,660	1,822	405	75,901	38,069	26,044
Outagamie County.........	13,975	7,317	1,428	5,041	793	831	147	na	20,199	6,207	3,137
Ozaukee County	8,761	5,066	938	2,646	288	na	na	na	13,332	4,044	1,122
Portage County............	6,118	3,356	633	2,065	242	247	48	na	8,828	2,868	1,435
Racine County..............	17,221	8,900	2,252	5,774	622	1,437	390	31	22,785	8,109	4,771
Rock County................	14,192	7,437	1,864	4,679	867	1,195	320	34	19,281	6,878	3,587
St. Croix County...........	5,266	3,178	490	1,529	514	409	50	0	na	na	na
Sheboygan County........	10,784	5,785	1,203	3,547	837	341	125	10	14,985	5,227	2,385
Walworth County	8,640	4,730	1,116	2,607	588	645	174	0	12,389	4,485	2,306
Washington County........	11,986	6,774	1,061	3,969	706	346	83	na	18,086	5,340	2,364
Waukesha County	36,335	19,789	4,013	12,062	1,917	1,485	429	8	55,530	16,846	7,672
Winnebago County.........	14,435	6,904	2,226	5,094	1,225	593	165	0	19,656	7,075	4,137
Wood County	8,541	4,437	1,038	2,897	588	491	179	7	11,178	3,847	1,896
Wyoming											
Laramie County............	7,710	3,825	1,074	2,662	332	714	353	41	10,112	3,571	2,885
Natrona County............	6,257	3,440	825	1,847	406	409	121	0	8,578	2,945	2,126

Table D-3: Places—Household Relationship, Grandparents, and Marital Status

	Total Householders Age 65 Years and Over	Family Householders 65 Years and Over	Non-Family Householders 65 Years and Over		Persons 65 Years and Over Living in Group Quarters	Grandparents 60 Years and Over Living with Grandchildren			Marital Status - Persons 60 Years and Over		
			Male Living Alone	Female Living Alone		Total	Responsible for Grandchildren	Responsible for Grandchildren and In Poverty	Married	Widowed	Divorced
Alabama											
Birmingham city	18,290	9,154	2,499	6,295	1,434	2,064	1,090	380	15,745	11,337	7,734
Dothan city	6,154	3,378	737	1,933	433	553	170	50	8,042	3,077	2,057
Hoover city	6,100	3,713	397	1,922	333	941	168	na	na	na	na
Huntsville city	16,524	9,092	1,776	5,471	842	1,488	732	184	21,142	7,573	5,488
Mobile city	17,863	9,263	2,244	6,084	1,269	2,395	1,244	182	19,188	10,035	6,082
Montgomery city	16,232	8,038	2,113	5,793	989	1,665	575	95	18,327	8,613	6,120
Tuscaloosa city	5,512	2,719	612	2,122	270	799	311	121	6,707	3,508	2,130
Alaska											
Anchorage Municipality	13,374	6,778	2,153	3,834	1,132	2,990	755	55	21,256	6,881	7,652
Arizona											
Avondale city	2,137	1,579	182	348	107	1,244	281	104	na	na	na
Chandler city	12,219	7,287	1,313	3,276	294	2,904	574	43	20,169	5,656	4,798
Flagstaff city	2,804	1,728	235	786	120	353	149	na	na	na	na
Glendale city	12,528	6,705	1,479	3,933	843	2,483	903	119	18,956	6,399	5,340
Goodyear city	3,868	2,948	205	615	135	454	101	na	na	na	na
Mesa city	41,346	22,848	4,609	12,663	1,393	3,314	866	92	57,244	18,665	13,388
Peoria city	13,410	7,598	1,442	4,130	832	1,955	579	78	18,810	6,467	4,004
Phoenix city	77,061	41,275	11,152	21,779	3,290	14,494	3,944	591	107,193	38,775	36,318
Scottsdale city	28,373	15,786	3,131	8,424	916	1,120	454	65	38,497	10,467	9,501
Surprise city	13,145	8,859	1,119	2,759	135	1,029	279	0	na	na	na
Tempe city	8,421	4,869	950	2,412	325	1,215	268	0	12,555	3,774	3,951
Tucson city	41,664	19,783	6,901	13,680	2,183	5,653	1,889	449	45,573	20,362	18,275
Yuma city	7,471	4,478	680	2,019	417	542	145	13	10,044	3,293	2,091
Arkansas											
Fayetteville city	4,228	1,877	592	1,684	271	na	na	0	na	na	na
Fort Smith city	7,098	3,349	777	2,865	535	615	397	150	8,484	3,877	2,432
Jonesboro city	4,751	2,747	372	1,632	544	371	148	0	na	na	na
Little Rock city	14,384	7,593	1,540	5,046	1,103	1,697	600	92	17,814	7,734	5,649
Springdale city	3,706	2,213	247	1,196	401	264	105	17	na	na	na
California											
Alameda city	5,614	2,981	665	1,772	509	933	177	na	8,201	2,530	2,381
Alhambra city	6,093	3,691	627	1,606	403	1,705	168	0	10,243	3,869	1,695
Anaheim city	17,509	10,489	1,421	5,053	1,930	6,412	862	135	29,075	10,642	6,550
Antioch city	5,280	3,122	577	1,351	291	1,803	464	116	10,012	2,940	2,061
Bakersfield city	17,566	9,854	2,177	5,041	710	5,208	1,018	182	27,103	9,493	6,809
Baldwin Park city	2,679	1,886	127	599	294	2,334	388	41	5,662	2,763	1,084
Bellflower city	3,456	1,620	382	1,330	323	830	95	0	4,759	2,440	1,868
Berkeley city	9,832	4,031	2,013	3,120	353	657	109	na	10,547	3,129	4,039
Buena Park city	4,317	2,888	357	906	541	1,542	133	0	7,460	3,376	1,496
Burbank city	9,097	4,256	1,262	3,394	347	1,369	224	na	9,880	4,917	3,850
Camarillo city	7,463	3,901	656	2,592	211	823	196	na	8,900	3,564	2,270
Carlsbad city	9,689	5,354	1,265	2,661	350	na	na	na	13,793	4,065	3,449
Carson city	6,307	4,248	671	1,202	94	2,913	600	50	10,632	4,259	2,112
Chico city	5,979	2,655	785	2,445	473	695	369	97	6,523	3,335	2,928
Chino city	3,383	1,919	432	951	213	1,587	251	122	5,856	2,676	1,566
Chino Hills city	2,412	1,628	117	658	0	1,642	193	26	na	na	na
Chula Vista city	13,541	7,379	1,721	3,906	496	5,416	1,094	152	20,699	7,733	5,531
Citrus Heights city	7,453	3,696	1,077	2,546	306	887	258	22	9,319	3,030	3,168
Clovis city	6,390	3,580	689	1,999	215	1,329	278	133	9,560	3,226	2,208
Compton city	4,257	2,550	394	1,130	133	2,198	672	83	5,304	2,583	1,771
Concord city	9,029	5,220	1,062	2,517	696	1,341	229	na	12,650	4,641	3,019
Corona city	5,416	3,305	472	1,465	182	2,798	460	46	11,183	3,956	2,208
Costa Mesa city	6,028	3,239	722	1,874	445	1,269	303	0	7,438	3,332	3,119
Daly City city	6,493	3,892	923	1,497	543	3,421	711	20	11,937	4,320	2,389
Davis city	3,625	1,526	586	1,386	224	na	na	na	na	na	na
Downey city	6,050	3,871	683	1,353	385	1,975	389	47	9,223	3,614	2,675
El Cajon city	5,866	3,053	709	1,981	1,340	1,247	340	156	7,821	3,966	2,313
Elk Grove city	6,438	4,227	524	1,501	344	3,542	559	23	13,510	4,280	2,764
El Monte city	4,959	3,492	418	954	535	2,922	858	97	10,288	4,163	1,476
Escondido city	7,965	3,947	879	2,814	939	1,837	297	18	11,755	5,576	2,773
Fairfield city	6,404	3,733	624	1,825	387	1,498	366	0	9,004	4,046	2,125
Folsom city	4,582	1,977	805	1,705	275	na	na	na	6,022	1,814	1,851
Fontana city	4,711	2,911	547	1,138	182	3,860	554	140	10,909	4,349	2,498
Fremont city	11,261	6,908	1,535	2,558	983	5,329	1,279	37	22,016	6,472	3,901
Fresno city	28,015	14,897	3,759	8,526	1,819	6,283	1,112	429	36,486	15,031	12,214
Fullerton city	8,634	5,645	890	2,041	847	2,298	428	16	14,381	4,615	2,805
Garden Grove city	9,097	5,739	799	2,130	1,033	4,312	330	34	15,109	7,125	3,667
Glendale city	16,471	8,830	2,015	5,065	998	3,199	287	41	24,737	8,957	4,807
Hawthorne city	3,391	1,538	639	1,046	341	1,383	383	13	4,092	2,086	2,152
Hayward city	7,670	4,303	1,002	2,214	812	3,024	249	45	12,597	5,146	2,829
Hemet city	12,189	5,097	2,328	4,527	511	1,144	404	24	11,328	6,182	4,220
Hesperia city	5,067	3,010	494	1,411	38	2,007	442	135	7,529	3,147	2,225
Huntington Beach city	17,239	9,907	1,918	4,715	499	1,943	600	7	25,155	7,633	5,412
Indio city	5,756	3,436	714	1,469	200	1,102	174	75	9,448	2,463	1,742
Inglewood city	6,548	2,996	1,233	1,993	431	1,663	437	46	6,997	3,498	2,930
Irvine city	10,385	6,314	1,206	2,542	151	3,066	544	33	19,374	4,251	4,547
Jurupa Valley city[1]	3,998	2,192	502	1,179	357	1,573	326	111	6,881	2,290	1,469

[1] Jurupa Valley city was incorporated in 2011. The 2010 population is the U.S. Census Bureau's estimates base figure.

Table D-3: Places—Household Relationship, Grandparents, and Marital Status—*Continued*

	Total Householders Age 65 Years and Over	Family Householders 65 Years and Over	Non-Family Householders 65 Years and Over - Male Living Alone	Non-Family Householders 65 Years and Over - Female Living Alone	Persons 65 Years and Over Living in Group Quarters	Grandparents 60 Years and Over Living with Grandchildren - Total	Responsible for Grandchildren	Responsible for Grandchildren and In Poverty	Marital Status - Persons 60 Years and Over - Married	Widowed	Divorced
California—Cont.											
Lake Forest city	4,442	2,478	395	1,420	259	na	na	na	na	na	na
Lakewood city	5,434	2,932	644	1,697	5	1,670	188	30	7,708	3,406	2,157
Lancaster city	7,390	4,057	972	2,042	633	2,475	557	148	11,196	4,552	3,617
Livermore city	5,198	3,024	506	1,509	180	915	356	na	na	na	na
Long Beach city	25,039	12,439	4,369	7,257	2,340	7,070	1,879	286	33,402	14,028	11,801
Los Angeles city	237,046	119,370	35,448	72,175	14,252	48,669	8,796	1,881	303,814	122,339	87,874
Lynwood city	1,648	1,219	124	275	426	1,933	337	12	3,615	1,627	747
Manteca city	4,198	2,595	390	1,202	266	1,121	206	22	6,518	2,382	1,313
Menifee city	8,860	4,650	1,174	2,674	150	1,123	217	0	10,451	3,604	3,563
Merced city	4,060	2,085	611	1,210	479	968	163	25	5,971	2,345	2,158
Milpitas city	2,848	1,909	268	618	58	1,775	255	0	6,702	2,131	987
Mission Viejo city	8,517	5,096	485	2,679	649	1,198	289	na	13,514	4,356	2,455
Modesto city	14,085	7,489	1,605	4,653	1,284	2,510	716	270	19,226	7,643	5,415
Moreno Valley city	6,104	4,390	295	1,086	122	3,886	827	86	12,783	4,474	2,553
Mountain View city	5,174	2,434	645	1,827	270	na	na	na	6,476	1,969	2,120
Murrieta city	6,159	2,962	430	2,619	79	1,645	261	0	na	na	na
Napa city	6,718	3,387	870	2,294	493	531	156	na	8,717	2,992	2,699
Newport Beach city	10,180	5,953	1,083	2,983	372	na	na	na	14,937	3,405	3,268
Norwalk city	5,292	3,519	530	1,127	434	2,661	489	119	8,387	3,555	2,106
Oakland city	29,723	13,260	4,887	10,199	1,721	4,700	948	215	30,625	16,092	12,719
Oceanside city	12,722	6,465	1,805	4,042	142	2,786	618	42	17,033	6,252	4,460
Ontario city	6,048	3,596	604	1,672	316	3,398	717	238	10,400	4,558	3,150
Orange city	8,077	4,967	736	2,046	638	2,103	578	14	13,425	4,445	2,892
Oxnard city	8,338	5,267	892	1,872	537	3,875	751	68	14,068	5,495	3,497
Palmdale city	5,191	3,214	749	1,133	13	2,552	765	140	9,132	2,880	2,497
Palo Alto city	7,239	3,495	994	2,497	357	na	na	na	na	na	na
Pasadena city	11,195	5,471	1,515	3,894	1,246	1,937	302	15	13,418	6,192	3,933
Perris city	1,558	1,188	147	195	103	1,133	269	109	na	na	na
Pleasanton city	4,777	2,801	363	1,567	192	819	144	na	na	na	na
Pomona city	6,121	3,536	653	1,720	976	2,981	586	206	10,009	4,043	2,719
Rancho Cordova city	4,373	2,310	552	1,306	244	758	117	55	5,716	2,401	2,129
Rancho Cucamonga city	7,504	4,268	978	2,055	103	2,857	486	22	13,687	4,701	2,690
Redding city	9,678	4,796	1,442	3,144	589	404	165	0	11,932	4,345	3,506
Redlands city	5,345	2,801	559	1,908	435	528	95	0	na	na	na
Redondo Beach city	4,936	2,400	602	1,714	58	na	na	na	na	na	na
Redwood City city	5,268	2,214	866	1,983	170	761	79	na	6,295	2,730	1,924
Rialto city	3,995	2,256	493	1,004	149	2,408	524	166	5,744	2,912	1,760
Richmond city	6,393	3,413	1,062	1,792	182	1,720	284	0	8,527	2,900	3,213
Riverside city	15,759	8,519	2,243	4,454	1,209	4,459	1,009	197	21,882	9,157	7,076
Roseville city	10,180	5,201	1,159	3,613	458	1,435	117	na	12,600	5,061	3,649
Sacramento city	32,016	15,171	5,211	10,774	2,021	6,633	1,388	493	38,888	16,912	14,379
Salinas city	5,951	3,004	740	1,913	586	2,938	583	89	10,015	3,424	2,563
San Bernardino city	9,607	5,047	1,460	2,757	827	3,142	499	82	11,927	6,053	4,662
San Buenaventura (Ventura) city	10,104	4,883	1,522	3,327	485	1,059	164	16	11,638	4,762	4,154
San Diego city	84,219	43,690	12,085	25,362	4,116	20,454	4,043	527	114,753	43,810	34,250
San Francisco city	68,503	30,289	12,114	22,770	2,836	11,623	1,640	372	81,171	34,251	21,782
San Jose city	52,773	32,296	5,513	13,140	3,468	19,486	2,920	210	89,869	29,628	19,980
San Leandro city	6,252	2,924	994	2,054	415	1,821	412	0	9,628	3,744	2,510
San Marcos city	5,474	2,543	564	1,979	100	915	110	57	na	na	na
San Mateo city	8,714	3,913	1,111	3,394	406	na	na	na	10,700	4,067	3,314
San Ramon city	2,920	1,651	300	927	28	na	na	na	na	na	na
Santa Ana city	9,878	6,316	962	2,223	1,194	6,735	1,028	255	18,447	7,187	3,761
Santa Barbara city	7,921	3,667	1,303	2,739	637	696	107	43	9,344	3,391	2,961
Santa Clara city	6,487	3,414	879	1,992	337	1,406	259	na	9,240	3,293	1,706
Santa Clarita city	10,565	5,930	1,174	3,097	206	2,097	388	0	15,694	5,115	4,671
Santa Maria city	5,330	3,058	598	1,491	428	1,959	273	74	7,810	3,112	1,489
Santa Monica city	9,500	3,228	1,880	3,929	669	na	na	na	8,046	3,383	4,606
Santa Rosa city	14,615	6,640	1,798	5,604	829	1,234	166	18	17,364	6,322	6,100
Simi Valley city	8,012	5,064	705	2,106	329	1,482	299	28	13,336	3,657	3,025
South Gate city	3,404	2,219	244	905	69	1,972	200	13	7,045	1,973	846
Stockton city	16,456	8,875	2,232	4,787	1,271	5,114	1,120	270	23,018	9,673	6,897
Sunnyvale city	9,181	5,174	1,154	2,527	451	1,527	172	0	13,213	3,928	2,753
Temecula city	4,246	2,636	337	1,113	12	1,231	210	29	na	na	na
Thousand Oaks city	11,638	6,773	946	3,424	361	1,286	258	na	19,151	4,791	3,129
Torrance city	14,053	7,997	1,335	4,252	524	1,719	464	13	17,230	6,779	4,737
Tracy city	2,799	1,684	259	744	142	2,038	179	83	na	na	na
Turlock city	4,676	2,477	544	1,623	470	521	150	16	6,463	2,603	1,320
Tustin city	3,721	1,802	541	1,279	166	1,109	151	15	5,841	1,646	1,540
Union City city	3,817	2,357	445	903	153	2,136	152	0	7,528	2,651	1,303
Upland city	5,168	3,539	486	1,040	344	1,490	367	53	8,726	2,603	2,047
Vacaville city	6,089	3,229	730	1,876	968	1,084	118	0	8,744	2,465	2,966
Vallejo city	7,994	4,206	989	2,526	496	2,621	561	21	12,218	5,104	3,691
Victorville city	5,023	2,735	677	1,304	319	2,284	580	91	6,970	2,701	2,383
Visalia city	8,055	4,114	1,239	2,615	600	1,629	576	91	11,414	4,647	2,954
Vista city	4,814	2,604	662	1,380	763	1,162	265	19	7,176	2,900	2,221
West Covina city	6,441	4,045	592	1,731	314	3,026	618	94	11,486	4,262	2,108
Westminster city	6,777	4,194	892	1,472	355	2,431	285	21	11,432	3,894	2,434
Whittier city	5,730	3,401	655	1,472	526	1,207	268	30	7,008	3,263	2,243
Yorba Linda city	4,885	2,949	490	1,389	137	na	na	na	na	na	na
Yuba City city	4,648	2,207	754	1,477	305	1,578	224	96	6,814	2,612	1,822

Table D-3: Places—Household Relationship, Grandparents, and Marital Status—*Continued*

	Total Householders Age 65 Years and Over	Family Householders 65 Years and Over	Non-Family Householders 65 Years and Over		Persons 65 Years and Over Living in Group Quarters	Grandparents 60 Years and Over Living with Grandchildren			Marital Status - Persons 60 Years and Over		
			Male Living Alone	Female Living Alone		Total	Responsible for Grandchildren	Responsible for Grandchildren and In Poverty	Married	Widowed	Divorced
Colorado											
Arvada city	10,077	5,430	1,376	3,140	325	951	372	8	14,613	3,880	3,660
Aurora city	19,195	9,872	2,335	6,396	1,095	3,692	660	157	26,474	9,366	9,380
Boulder city	5,772	2,841	758	1,998	694	na	na	na	7,827	1,976	2,570
Centennial city	7,538	4,525	757	2,136	370	743	272	31	13,795	2,889	2,542
Colorado Springs city	29,663	15,683	3,536	9,806	1,510	2,569	686	116	41,730	13,344	11,709
Denver city	43,278	18,463	7,658	16,090	2,238	4,892	1,098	150	45,479	18,965	20,714
Fort Collins city	7,907	3,810	825	3,075	567	706	346	0	11,318	3,504	3,534
Greeley city	6,143	3,308	695	2,108	508	727	316	105	8,982	3,054	2,222
Lakewood city	13,204	6,636	1,818	4,309	1,132	954	365	165	16,565	6,153	5,326
Longmont city	6,145	3,176	766	1,998	476	700	295	63	8,190	2,891	2,336
Loveland city	6,163	2,937	595	2,461	404	322	128	0	na	na	na
Pueblo city	10,932	5,105	1,660	3,944	997	844	554	121	12,820	5,012	3,743
Thornton city	4,526	2,819	398	1,246	219	1,531	365	50	8,123	2,364	2,151
Westminster city	6,626	3,305	816	2,266	176	1,183	211	53	9,531	3,164	2,635
Connecticut											
Bridgeport city	8,915	3,701	1,664	3,267	710	2,143	475	76	8,933	5,715	3,709
Danbury city	5,770	2,471	881	2,258	539	836	210	0	7,424	3,443	1,866
Hartford city	8,305	3,242	1,799	3,023	598	1,327	480	99	6,802	3,746	3,681
New Britain city	5,395	2,467	682	2,131	576	625	225	92	5,735	2,949	2,154
New Haven city	8,430	3,106	1,697	3,361	636	1,042	342	76	7,002	4,437	3,798
Norwalk city	8,293	4,222	1,139	2,599	336	na	na	na	10,510	4,031	3,124
Stamford city	9,437	4,594	903	3,721	578	1,227	36	na	12,003	4,828	2,515
Waterbury city	8,254	3,880	1,205	2,921	925	1,196	653	203	9,130	4,462	2,786
Delaware											
Wilmington city	6,344	2,143	991	2,845	535	762	336	101	3,985	3,054	2,539
District of Columbia											
Washington city	49,026	19,784	8,798	18,720	2,528	5,121	1,536	263	40,493	23,099	19,314
Florida											
Boca Raton city	10,681	5,741	1,444	3,147	523	na	na	na	15,192	4,191	3,670
Boynton Beach city	9,779	4,330	1,474	3,492	580	465	162	17	9,424	4,893	2,645
Cape Coral city	14,963	9,076	2,060	3,144	369	2,437	409	185	24,705	7,552	5,330
Clearwater city	14,824	6,697	2,510	5,298	847	734	274	30	16,351	6,881	5,865
Coral Springs city	6,257	4,102	424	1,648	201	1,381	249	0	11,629	3,303	2,391
Deerfield Beach city	10,330	4,218	1,554	4,268	301	682	257	160	10,292	5,076	3,587
Deltona city	6,715	4,469	562	1,613	107	1,308	679	252	na	na	na
Fort Lauderdale city	17,008	7,074	4,113	4,467	445	2,220	597	90	16,970	7,021	8,580
Gainesville city	6,416	3,163	758	2,274	766	650	93	20	7,653	3,745	2,846
Hialeah city	20,913	12,396	2,146	5,518	1,218	5,630	1,162	284	29,157	14,295	7,359
Hollywood city	12,296	5,821	1,741	4,080	600	1,802	373	67	15,456	6,450	5,973
Jacksonville city	57,872	30,156	7,399	19,153	2,938	7,959	2,474	451	74,659	33,377	25,009
Lakeland city	12,731	6,012	1,764	4,537	935	957	352	212	14,902	6,299	4,014
Largo city	12,557	5,723	2,258	4,307	683	na	na	na	13,087	5,988	3,859
Lauderhill city	5,317	2,619	762	1,688	270	981	175	79	5,227	3,016	2,651
Melbourne city	10,003	4,420	1,653	3,590	669	1,259	363	26	9,791	5,405	3,810
Miami city	35,694	15,986	6,402	11,758	2,082	6,096	1,144	521	35,242	20,492	18,470
Miami Beach city	9,362	3,632	2,073	3,423	435	na	na	na	8,726	3,459	4,255
Miami Gardens city	6,720	4,344	557	1,568	91	2,567	482	106	9,500	3,993	2,855
Miramar city	3,210	2,322	280	545	40	3,013	396	52	8,044	3,511	1,818
Orlando city	13,677	6,379	2,204	4,658	925	2,263	768	351	14,719	8,238	6,650
Palm Bay city	9,483	5,000	1,316	2,764	390	1,616	530	77	13,402	5,911	3,671
Palm Coast city	10,098	6,453	781	2,503	155	1,038	197	0	na	na	na
Pembroke Pines city	13,710	6,592	1,729	5,187	117	3,156	446	0	17,861	8,315	4,837
Plantation city	6,926	3,924	720	2,029	306	1,107	230	125	10,797	3,712	2,508
Pompano Beach city	12,414	5,038	2,209	4,596	452	804	339	101	10,928	6,512	4,699
Port St. Lucie city	15,429	9,665	1,658	3,491	368	2,145	818	121	22,895	7,795	4,439
St. Petersburg city	24,354	11,342	4,149	8,104	2,009	2,756	759	138	27,449	12,046	12,083
Sunrise city	8,033	3,477	830	3,491	406	1,198	236	0	8,798	4,927	2,943
Tallahassee city	9,945	4,487	1,545	3,637	688	350	105	38	11,820	4,850	3,821
Tampa city	24,456	11,330	4,018	8,546	897	2,994	1,151	431	26,892	13,146	10,312
Weston city	2,607	1,605	204	731	0	na	na	na	na	na	na
West Palm Beach city	10,164	4,777	1,367	3,359	1,062	958	148	0	12,550	5,673	3,821
Georgia											
Albany city	6,083	3,322	629	2,097	221	882	494	69	6,492	3,262	2,031
Athens-Clarke County unified govt (bal)	6,218	3,517	586	2,056	349	701	191	71	8,272	3,313	2,273
Atlanta city	28,912	11,330	5,250	11,596	1,471	2,838	941	368	25,065	16,252	12,811
Augusta-Richmond County consolidated govt (bal)	13,732	7,260	1,837	4,332	1,206	2,045	963	202	17,042	8,265	5,074
Columbus city	15,015	7,478	1,981	5,342	859	1,596	544	99	16,178	8,767	5,401
Johns Creek city	3,200	1,941	304	928	46	na	na	na	na	na	na
Macon city	6,957	3,246	814	2,796	489	748	317	74	6,714	4,374	2,696
Roswell city	6,430	3,608	604	2,169	275	na	na	na	na	na	na
Sandy Springs city	6,708	3,730	700	2,208	267	na	na	na	9,995	2,765	2,311
Savannah city	10,862	5,082	1,819	3,618	656	1,729	473	112	10,003	6,660	4,400
Warner Robins city	4,253	1,937	589	1,648	224	663	215	53	na	na	na

Table D-3: Places—Household Relationship, Grandparents, and Marital Status—*Continued*

	Total Householders Age 65 Years and Over	Family Householders 65 Years and Over	Non-Family Householders 65 Years and Over		Persons 65 Years and Over Living in Group Quarters	Grandparents 60 Years and Over Living with Grandchildren			Marital Status - Persons 60 Years and Over		
			Male Living Alone	Female Living Alone		Total	Responsible for Grandchildren	Responsible for Grandchildren and In Poverty	Married	Widowed	Divorced
Hawaii											
Urban Honolulu CDP	35,645	19,188	4,808	10,412	2,587	7,362	1,162	95	42,890	19,720	11,236
Idaho											
Boise City city	16,553	8,540	2,038	5,632	737	1,377	308	16	21,698	7,264	6,884
Meridian city	4,565	2,555	365	1,625	212	317	149	na	na	na	na
Nampa city	5,623	3,321	313	1,830	350	686	296	28	na	na	na
Illinois											
Aurora city	7,685	3,956	1,342	2,286	558	2,073	408	0	11,716	3,988	3,279
Bloomington city	5,079	2,352	796	1,784	302	274	98	0	6,763	2,671	2,040
Champaign city	4,507	2,428	447	1,561	262	na	na	na	6,189	1,613	1,919
Chicago city	182,180	86,831	28,159	62,598	9,682	34,198	9,787	2,897	184,161	102,185	66,335
Decatur city	8,228	4,073	1,177	2,844	1,008	702	435	155	9,628	4,137	2,877
Elgin city	5,952	3,230	398	2,245	639	1,095	189	21	8,492	3,874	1,862
Evanston city	5,710	2,616	833	2,111	385	623	160	na	6,555	2,507	2,001
Joliet city	7,585	3,592	1,095	2,630	1,019	1,740	396	79	9,748	4,633	2,746
Naperville city	7,421	4,527	653	2,073	1,000	1,031	255	0	14,987	3,651	2,372
Peoria city	10,009	4,666	1,312	3,802	719	680	329	134	11,030	4,961	3,058
Rockford city	13,412	6,195	2,156	4,771	1,538	1,606	379	41	14,123	7,652	5,285
Springfield city	11,949	5,147	1,620	4,798	794	741	422	17	13,252	5,454	4,387
Waukegan city	3,931	1,891	797	1,178	613	818	120	65	5,879	2,402	1,690
Indiana											
Bloomington city	4,483	1,825	717	1,838	315	na	na	na	na	na	na
Carmel city	4,936	3,180	336	1,397	375	394	62	na	na	na	na
Evansville city	11,492	5,004	1,862	4,402	1,316	759	303	21	11,233	6,510	4,041
Fort Wayne city	20,604	9,842	2,915	7,456	1,756	1,331	588	128	24,107	10,472	7,779
Gary city	7,903	3,884	1,390	2,377	353	1,058	537	133	6,884	5,173	3,076
Hammond city	5,621	2,940	846	1,741	121	1,052	262	16	6,619	3,289	1,630
Indianapolis city (bal)	56,836	27,990	7,810	19,821	4,090	6,298	2,214	418	63,923	29,951	24,000
Lafayette city	5,001	2,446	702	1,772	384	441	153	66	na	na	na
Muncie city	6,280	2,877	697	2,634	579	421	151	17	6,473	2,852	2,650
South Bend city	8,609	3,919	1,248	3,175	962	751	272	31	8,759	4,737	3,180
Iowa											
Cedar Rapids city	10,513	5,291	1,467	3,607	739	1,005	397	na	13,556	4,995	3,288
Davenport city	8,009	3,835	1,269	2,735	674	639	115	0	10,054	4,270	2,522
Des Moines city	14,491	6,807	2,067	5,317	1,206	1,884	763	239	16,343	8,108	5,788
Iowa City city	3,932	1,711	518	1,569	205	na	na	na	na	na	na
Sioux City city	7,036	3,178	970	2,770	469	551	178	33	7,710	3,827	2,200
Waterloo city	6,487	2,888	1,167	2,297	436	362	201	7	7,863	3,261	2,001
Kansas											
Kansas City city	10,001	5,163	1,364	3,137	429	1,719	719	125	11,102	5,974	4,195
Lawrence city	4,360	1,971	598	1,679	213	589	310	40	5,804	2,193	1,637
Olathe city	5,755	3,300	622	1,804	461	814	206	35	10,214	2,667	2,071
Overland Park city	14,305	7,129	1,875	5,114	813	1,027	206	na	20,094	6,734	4,510
Topeka city	11,733	5,477	1,242	4,866	1,239	885	362	30	13,185	6,010	4,808
Wichita city	28,688	13,811	4,311	9,866	1,414	3,489	1,103	237	36,676	14,283	10,903
Kentucky											
Lexington-Fayette urban county	20,954	10,377	2,550	7,547	1,447	1,675	773	124	26,282	9,485	9,189
Louisville/Jefferson County metro govt (bal)	49,976	24,771	6,878	17,348	3,413	4,552	1,936	408	58,721	26,748	19,122
Louisiana											
Baton Rouge city	16,907	8,935	2,220	5,505	804	2,752	1,386	570	17,988	9,640	5,924
Kenner city	5,491	2,928	681	1,737	301	1,233	359	50	7,216	2,941	2,152
Lafayette city	9,626	5,144	1,114	3,070	665	894	385	112	12,153	4,723	2,888
Lake Charles city	6,613	3,049	838	2,577	488	836	296	69	7,750	3,486	2,806
New Orleans city	26,272	12,403	4,446	8,635	1,503	3,758	1,629	567	26,275	15,320	12,454
Shreveport city	16,617	8,674	2,219	5,449	1,507	1,994	1,017	211	17,411	9,673	6,285
Maine											
Portland city	5,304	1,913	724	2,563	590	332	108	na	4,996	2,860	2,628
Maryland											
Baltimore city	50,955	22,400	8,546	18,354	3,132	7,833	2,843	826	41,337	30,060	19,720
Frederick city	4,734	2,043	599	1,972	698	415	82	na	6,353	2,093	2,191
Massachusetts											
Boston city	42,931	17,112	7,948	16,874	3,447	5,313	1,357	506	41,815	18,794	15,842
Brockton city	7,041	3,292	1,223	2,378	845	1,673	259	90	8,116	4,273	2,210
Cambridge city	7,952	3,212	1,191	3,262	459	na	na	na	8,760	5,376	2,803
Fall River city	8,833	3,889	1,468	3,347	1,108	714	266	na	4,566	2,194	2,403
Lawrence city	3,597	1,328	855	1,342	386	1,167	221	75	8,022	4,582	1,407
Lowell city	6,538	2,944	1,213	2,270	994	1,475	175	25	6,201	3,630	2,337
Lynn city	6,702	2,850	1,116	2,564	397	993	219	54	9,764	5,099	2,468
New Bedford city	9,128	4,000	1,419	3,450	1,100	423	158	49	9,764	5,099	2,931
Newton city	8,380	4,296	807	3,034	428	na	na	na	na	na	na
Quincy city	8,459	3,547	1,474	3,193	403	1,239	302	na	9,668	4,185	2,405

Table D-3: Places—Household Relationship, Grandparents, and Marital Status—*Continued*

	Total Householders Age 65 Years and Over	Family Householders 65 Years and Over	Non-Family Householders 65 Years and Over		Persons 65 Years and Over Living in Group Quarters	Grandparents 60 Years and Over Living with Grandchildren			Marital Status - Persons 60 Years and Over		
			Male Living Alone	Female Living Alone		Total	Responsible for Grandchildren	Responsible for Grandchildren and In Poverty	Married	Widowed	Divorced
Massachusetts—Cont.											
Somerville city	4,585	2,248	795	1,529	51	na	na	na	4,685	1,932	1,139
Springfield city	11,110	5,195	1,859	3,693	546	1,259	339	168	12,006	5,250	3,799
Worcester city	13,292	5,131	2,046	5,750	1,873	1,730	510	136	14,059	8,432	4,686
Michigan											
Ann Arbor city	8,021	3,320	1,287	3,159	266	na	na	na	8,511	3,176	3,162
Dearborn city	7,528	3,336	1,409	2,666	158	1,062	253	90	8,162	4,307	2,250
Detroit city	57,719	27,497	9,553	19,347	2,750	10,711	3,479	1,147	41,922	36,036	26,843
Farmington Hills city	8,126	4,048	972	2,987	354	630	140	0	11,554	4,015	2,315
Flint city	8,223	3,622	1,500	2,862	174	1,288	647	109	7,038	3,991	4,461
Grand Rapids city	13,491	6,174	1,921	5,024	1,730	1,004	291	103	14,745	7,072	4,400
Kalamazoo city	4,671	1,961	543	1,975	445	217	118	25	4,283	2,509	2,199
Lansing city	7,855	3,327	1,384	3,045	232	842	307	24	8,428	3,555	4,291
Livonia city	11,070	5,911	1,569	3,428	696	713	196	0	14,102	5,088	2,821
Rochester Hills city	6,177	3,096	593	2,392	326	603	110	0	na	na	na
Southfield city	8,403	3,908	1,482	2,897	573	896	374	0	9,105	4,449	3,487
Sterling Heights city	12,444	6,559	1,405	4,358	679	1,603	112	0	17,117	7,353	2,565
Troy city	7,155	4,076	887	2,105	96	na	na	0	11,847	2,832	1,981
Warren city	13,385	6,514	1,954	4,650	876	1,078	344	78	14,592	8,025	3,503
Westland city	7,783	3,412	864	3,307	592	486	90	33	8,306	4,243	3,204
Wyoming city	4,208	2,116	651	1,363	143	659	68	18	5,893	2,096	1,550
Minnesota											
Bloomington city	10,075	5,159	1,352	3,351	464	676	48	0	12,409	4,505	3,088
Brooklyn Park city	3,527	2,184	298	996	21	683	73	21	6,050	1,626	1,332
Duluth city	7,817	3,323	1,066	3,265	1,037	264	103	7	8,959	3,940	2,625
Minneapolis city	22,268	8,052	4,709	8,474	2,600	1,659	723	236	22,638	8,868	10,468
Plymouth city	5,630	3,249	517	1,795	123	na	na	na	na	na	na
Rochester city	8,501	4,468	935	2,840	1,046	na	na	na	12,155	3,618	2,509
St. Cloud city	4,355	2,171	387	1,599	638	197	52	na	6,192	2,224	947
St. Paul city	16,768	7,165	2,547	6,570	1,662	2,070	590	174	18,641	8,151	7,112
Mississippi											
Gulfport city	5,444	2,615	696	1,856	253	684	385	49	5,324	3,027	2,197
Jackson city	11,246	6,234	1,298	3,535	955	1,864	796	229	11,922	7,247	5,010
Missouri											
Columbia city	5,933	3,141	494	2,248	623	555	68	0	na	na	na
Independence city	12,340	6,063	1,763	4,258	849	963	355	60	13,931	6,558	3,838
Kansas City city	34,840	16,880	5,158	11,906	1,892	3,253	1,115	236	38,384	16,887	14,841
Lee's Summit city	6,916	3,603	540	2,681	437	734	176	0	na	na	na
O'Fallon city	4,802	2,788	411	1,532	220	885	150	na	na	na	na
St. Charles city	5,909	2,862	869	2,087	422	323	123	0	na	na	na
St. Joseph city	6,601	3,092	889	2,512	651	498	36	0	7,821	3,424	2,235
St. Louis city	25,167	9,866	4,608	10,067	1,667	2,665	1,122	155	20,505	13,496	10,327
Springfield city	15,397	6,763	1,970	6,343	1,492	717	263	148	15,783	8,334	5,546
Montana											
Billings city	10,499	5,130	1,278	3,864	705	699	279	105	13,276	5,043	3,149
Missoula city	4,841	2,378	487	1,783	309	na	na	na	na	na	na
Nebraska											
Lincoln city	18,487	9,406	2,296	6,547	999	1,104	444	55	26,352	7,781	5,626
Omaha city	31,656	15,358	4,218	11,458	2,228	2,902	1,121	337	37,827	16,206	10,229
Nevada											
Henderson city	23,115	13,973	2,768	5,426	551	2,998	668	65	36,412	10,028	9,036
Las Vegas city	45,369	23,791	7,669	12,018	1,593	7,026	2,525	455	58,433	21,630	21,796
North Las Vegas city	8,880	4,783	1,637	2,124	372	2,879	840	185	13,055	5,259	5,035
Reno city	17,420	8,256	3,225	5,238	639	1,915	642	100	21,462	7,228	9,152
Sparks city	6,451	3,517	917	1,718	236	972	271	32	9,420	2,774	3,468
New Hampshire											
Manchester city	8,305	3,914	1,356	2,794	798	818	219	55	10,717	4,246	3,215
Nashua city	6,921	3,528	873	2,313	488	652	93	na	9,145	3,338	2,235
New Jersey											
Camden city	4,296	2,114	655	1,395	226	840	309	59	3,617	2,554	1,615
Clifton city	6,499	3,314	987	2,055	202	1,109	98	0	8,195	3,907	1,591
Elizabeth city	6,269	2,948	1,085	2,002	563	2,281	309	32	8,150	3,761	2,518
Jersey City city	13,793	6,998	1,915	4,576	965	3,569	906	209	17,309	8,406	4,940
Newark city	14,658	6,360	2,654	5,191	793	2,553	825	232	14,241	9,006	5,418
Passaic city	3,248	1,404	636	1,134	229	1,075	248	13	na	na	na
Paterson city	7,259	3,737	1,165	2,279	309	3,002	578	136	9,291	4,671	2,359
Trenton city	4,865	2,029	875	1,856	518	929	184	59	4,208	2,796	2,388
Union City city	3,789	1,970	674	1,043	259	1,141	416	133	4,897	2,014	1,568

Table D-3: Places—Household Relationship, Grandparents, and Marital Status—*Continued*

	Total Householders Age 65 Years and Over	Family Householders 65 Years and Over	Non-Family Householders 65 Years and Over		Persons 65 Years and Over Living in Group Quarters	Grandparents 60 Years and Over Living with Grandchildren			Marital Status - Persons 60 Years and Over		
			Male Living Alone	Female Living Alone		Total	Responsible for Grandchildren	Responsible for Grandchildren and In Poverty	Married	Widowed	Divorced
New Mexico											
Albuquerque city	44,318	21,705	6,622	14,689	1,640	5,116	1,543	361	53,846	18,626	20,212
Las Cruces city	8,434	4,446	1,257	2,591	296	1,061	246	50	10,348	3,889	2,990
Rio Rancho city	6,090	3,149	758	1,976	181	700	133	0	8,697	3,042	2,136
Santa Fe city	9,110	3,813	1,471	3,426	257	643	189	9	9,389	3,268	4,683
New York											
Albany city	7,417	2,772	1,468	2,984	1,384	450	193	na	6,579	4,407	2,065
Buffalo city	20,530	8,764	3,370	7,970	1,688	1,662	675	125	17,822	11,273	7,229
Mount Vernon city	5,674	2,600	873	2,153	407	1,285	111	10	5,477	3,510	1,640
New Rochelle city	6,474	3,163	959	2,277	957	709	155	37	8,332	3,618	1,515
New York city	623,982	289,182	91,526	227,701	43,162	122,394	28,622	8,536	724,580	331,666	194,213
Rochester city	12,766	5,298	2,353	4,711	1,969	1,601	564	115	11,607	7,100	5,614
Schenectady city	4,988	2,119	849	1,900	544	423	130	27	4,665	3,193	1,810
Syracuse city	9,764	3,519	2,219	3,804	1,956	1,023	223	60	9,200	5,364	3,989
Yonkers city	17,880	8,601	2,522	6,507	871	3,178	613	58	22,793	9,699	4,354
North Carolina											
Asheville city	8,896	3,750	1,451	3,418	1,198	470	232	141	8,451	4,420	4,166
Charlotte city	41,262	22,230	4,577	13,524	2,108	6,248	1,541	553	56,965	22,637	15,388
Concord city	5,328	2,954	443	1,879	379	910	182	52	na	na	na
Durham city	13,814	7,025	1,715	4,683	1,386	1,692	878	241	16,917	7,339	5,677
Fayetteville city	13,108	6,924	1,422	4,445	829	1,516	664	205	15,946	7,438	4,066
Gastonia city	4,942	2,883	502	1,469	621	824	406	105	6,952	3,090	1,755
Greensboro city	20,939	10,540	2,454	7,433	1,305	2,038	499	60	26,031	10,133	7,574
Greenville city	4,084	2,072	632	1,380	448	645	90	39	5,382	2,257	1,368
High Point city	8,258	4,069	920	3,099	550	548	155	67	9,515	4,272	2,278
Jacksonville city	2,617	1,136	456	1,010	371	464	199	na	na	na	na
Raleigh city	22,166	10,802	2,570	8,322	1,550	2,459	775	62	28,510	11,413	9,387
Wilmington city	9,696	4,835	1,264	3,337	430	423	109	65	12,315	4,108	3,307
Winston-Salem city	19,117	8,954	2,720	7,140	1,381	1,552	566	178	21,147	10,112	6,721
North Dakota											
Fargo city	7,064	2,945	978	2,950	793	388	117	na	9,706	3,368	2,066
Ohio											
Akron city	17,030	7,767	2,813	6,170	847	1,508	648	44	17,075	8,936	6,924
Canton city	6,425	3,100	1,018	2,150	646	684	235	58	6,669	3,238	2,598
Cincinnati city	22,599	9,009	3,936	9,273	2,155	1,799	699	186	20,185	11,818	9,698
Cleveland city	33,934	13,867	6,162	12,889	2,328	3,606	1,695	669	25,328	19,288	15,647
Columbus city	46,612	20,786	7,287	17,082	2,300	7,174	2,087	293	50,075	23,970	22,616
Dayton city	11,844	5,139	2,244	4,219	836	1,046	505	159	9,006	6,067	6,547
Parma city	9,135	4,914	1,078	3,069	729	913	88	na	10,942	5,119	2,587
Toledo city	23,528	11,030	3,723	8,290	1,367	1,818	763	145	23,663	11,763	8,922
Youngstown city	7,091	3,516	1,144	2,242	601	639	280	107	5,797	4,238	3,000
Oklahoma											
Broken Arrow city	6,693	3,889	878	1,832	373	929	319	35	10,394	3,185	2,306
Edmond city	5,833	3,288	593	1,922	268	569	103	0	na	na	na
Lawton city	6,506	3,406	820	2,163	570	786	383	51	7,295	3,565	2,126
Norman city	7,900	4,273	1,002	2,515	588	432	178	na	10,615	3,791	3,124
Oklahoma City city	42,365	21,344	5,972	14,230	2,094	5,124	2,074	613	55,726	20,772	16,909
Tulsa city	33,014	15,955	4,644	11,963	1,665	2,775	1,090	290	37,801	16,180	13,063
Oregon											
Beaverton city	6,308	2,785	1,021	2,260	164	na	na	na	7,748	2,652	3,304
Bend city	7,490	3,510	861	2,916	271	na	na	na	na	na	na
Eugene city	13,664	6,212	1,667	5,216	901	596	203	31	16,343	6,133	5,924
Gresham city	7,368	3,798	927	2,415	603	858	253	15	9,553	3,856	3,104
Hillsboro city	4,410	2,152	369	1,723	217	693	87	na	6,079	2,123	2,321
Medford city	8,144	4,035	1,256	2,639	457	555	268	0	9,497	3,485	2,934
Portland city	41,715	18,311	6,581	15,116	2,634	4,389	1,124	185	47,640	19,755	21,046
Salem city	12,607	6,281	1,297	4,746	1,059	1,169	462	126	16,117	5,600	5,331
Pennsylvania											
Allentown city	8,216	3,810	1,188	3,027	929	1,476	176	67	9,556	4,586	3,425
Bethlehem city	7,150	2,993	1,264	2,739	770	394	149	56	7,410	3,860	1,871
Erie city	8,364	3,510	1,327	3,201	948	534	57	37	8,280	4,732	2,883
Philadelphia city	122,082	51,736	20,902	46,671	8,134	17,444	4,593	1,292	110,021	73,451	41,544
Pittsburgh city	29,182	11,893	4,428	12,325	2,637	2,057	678	115	26,066	16,126	9,019
Reading city	5,553	2,293	1,118	1,793	270	1,244	385	221	4,915	2,963	2,460
Scranton city	7,982	3,242	1,455	3,134	1,332	579	182	32	7,423	5,163	2,231
Rhode Island											
Cranston city	7,475	3,681	843	2,803	268	857	186	na	9,782	3,703	2,286
Pawtucket city	6,078	2,732	914	2,350	325	755	238	33	6,450	2,926	2,120
Providence city	9,006	3,953	1,795	2,954	1,058	1,539	347	185	10,463	5,726	3,336
Warwick city	9,705	4,309	1,343	3,832	517	726	150	0	10,673	5,277	2,994
South Carolina											
Charleston city	9,715	4,732	1,234	3,614	325	918	358	134	12,029	5,405	3,139
Columbia city	7,637	3,522	1,174	2,759	880	522	199	72	7,999	4,408	2,649
North Charleston city	5,604	2,964	703	1,835	428	949	435	117	6,642	3,117	2,239
Rock Hill city	4,457	2,041	581	1,726	504	583	251	18	5,069	2,748	1,778

Table D-3: Places—Household Relationship, Grandparents, and Marital Status—*Continued*

	Total Householders Age 65 Years and Over	Family Householders 65 Years and Over	Non-Family Householders 65 Years and Over		Persons 65 Years and Over Living in Group Quarters	Grandparents 60 Years and Over Living with Grandchildren			Marital Status - Persons 60 Years and Over		
			Male Living Alone	Female Living Alone		Total	Responsible for Grandchildren	Responsible for Grandchildren and In Poverty	Married	Widowed	Divorced
South Dakota											
Rapid City city	6,316	2,991	971	2,161	751	na	na	na	8,043	3,000	2,486
Sioux Falls city	11,068	5,735	1,386	3,612	860	748	252	45	15,641	5,269	3,620
Tennessee											
Chattanooga city	16,679	8,151	2,288	5,973	911	1,253	593	126	17,514	9,234	6,535
Clarksville city	6,113	3,485	724	1,732	354	923	268	52	8,903	3,351	2,035
Jackson city	5,420	2,713	664	1,965	573	665	156	24	6,256	3,114	2,168
Knoxville city	17,327	7,066	3,301	6,682	1,154	989	422	46	16,231	10,288	5,972
Memphis city	44,272	21,844	6,237	15,133	2,458	6,426	2,769	818	46,555	26,767	20,119
Murfreesboro city	5,957	3,132	539	1,958	438	651	116	0	8,853	3,119	2,609
Nashville-Davidson metropolitan government (bal)	40,491	19,820	5,685	13,988	2,311	5,112	1,603	280	48,965	20,821	17,150
Texas											
Abilene city	9,307	5,044	1,066	3,087	908	1,258	745	289	11,622	5,356	2,655
Allen city	2,485	1,780	101	580	103	na	na	na	na	na	na
Amarillo city	15,039	7,880	1,817	5,095	1,113	1,595	984	210	19,084	7,711	4,888
Arlington city	18,636	10,650	2,165	5,523	916	4,070	1,182	119	29,661	9,224	7,325
Austin city	36,373	18,885	4,163	12,158	1,988	5,871	1,595	485	48,799	17,664	19,130
Baytown city	4,056	2,253	403	1,302	427	1,328	616	211	5,727	2,785	1,856
Beaumont city	10,218	4,533	1,864	3,670	461	1,195	613	41	11,397	5,772	3,793
Brownsville city	9,563	5,702	1,038	2,713	607	3,710	767	310	14,271	6,034	2,125
Bryan city	4,904	2,493	822	1,488	330	638	141	20	5,752	2,647	1,671
Carrollton city	5,410	3,367	425	1,503	323	1,047	200	31	9,721	3,171	2,042
College Station city	2,918	1,742	164	1,000	188	183	106	na	na	na	na
Corpus Christi city	22,401	13,096	2,831	6,053	1,226	4,484	1,722	225	30,533	11,409	9,103
Dallas city	69,999	34,953	10,605	22,563	3,776	12,574	3,623	1,412	84,476	37,807	30,244
Denton city	6,081	3,431	546	1,960	371	1,092	242	19	9,278	2,873	2,014
Edinburg city	3,062	1,888	467	684	181	1,012	139	49	na	na	na
El Paso city	44,679	26,466	5,004	12,049	1,446	11,650	3,554	1,150	59,442	24,734	14,637
Fort Worth city	38,727	19,940	5,231	12,810	2,329	7,870	2,342	548	50,318	21,391	18,212
Frisco city	4,119	2,636	260	1,159	141	1,019	74	na	na	na	na
Garland city	12,289	7,526	1,096	3,185	332	3,510	952	209	18,696	6,704	4,645
Grand Prairie city	7,005	4,238	801	1,764	220	2,720	726	144	12,420	3,346	3,352
Harlingen city	5,079	2,875	582	1,545	448	808	147	0	6,622	3,225	991
Houston city	122,402	64,592	17,896	36,997	5,463	23,306	6,742	1,718	152,633	64,891	48,382
Irving city	8,690	5,046	991	2,374	316	2,186	870	113	13,896	4,580	3,323
Killeen city	4,053	2,247	558	1,154	39	1,072	224	7	6,250	2,147	1,352
Laredo city	10,430	6,980	932	2,494	425	5,122	1,274	599	16,797	6,587	2,763
League City city	3,994	2,613	476	905	321	555	23	na	na	na	na
Lewisville city	4,234	1,933	806	1,444	208	1,182	111	0	6,359	2,169	1,760
Longview city	7,090	3,557	1,056	2,456	707	617	203	83	8,287	4,397	2,081
Lubbock city	16,713	8,820	2,092	5,523	1,063	1,827	762	203	20,349	8,894	5,169
McAllen city	7,802	4,632	1,066	2,029	822	2,426	735	341	12,179	5,150	2,268
McKinney city	5,682	3,537	489	1,553	352	1,226	193	na	10,403	2,169	2,230
Mesquite city	7,112	4,214	409	2,363	529	1,893	750	172	10,934	3,900	2,821
Midland city	7,578	4,213	963	2,249	536	1,146	416	169	11,561	3,980	2,588
Mission city	4,644	2,691	442	1,285	148	1,241	266	69	na	na	na
Missouri City city	3,585	2,326	255	953	159	1,148	137	0	na	na	na
Odessa city	6,972	3,563	884	2,438	411	949	468	137	8,886	4,014	1,843
Pasadena city	7,980	4,102	1,066	2,598	504	1,959	456	235	10,850	4,933	3,726
Pearland city	4,038	2,592	315	1,050	225	1,351	219	0	na	na	na
Pharr city	4,435	3,124	302	978	0	1,264	155	89	na	na	na
Plano city	14,766	8,943	1,613	4,022	553	2,700	274	92	25,806	7,373	5,698
Richardson city	7,359	4,483	648	2,066	380	851	209	19	11,757	3,174	2,329
Round Rock city	3,438	2,128	260	969	272	1,199	206	na	na	na	na
San Angelo city	8,590	4,657	1,065	2,739	455	851	299	123	10,440	3,828	2,587
San Antonio city	89,493	49,332	11,429	26,644	5,049	20,049	5,518	1,305	113,930	46,653	35,476
Sugar Land city	4,077	2,823	203	946	227	1,692	281	0	na	na	na
Temple city	6,009	3,241	725	1,941	796	683	331	102	7,709	3,845	1,626
Tyler city	9,052	4,381	1,113	3,355	804	1,116	329	182	11,210	5,157	2,389
Waco city	8,666	3,817	1,324	3,353	1,283	815	281	41	9,339	5,406	3,470
Wichita Falls city	8,174	4,296	990	2,703	840	781	397	98	10,226	4,482	2,381
Utah											
Layton city	3,023	2,171	241	599	1	764	222	0	na	na	na
Ogden city	4,975	2,716	772	1,457	279	447	190	3	6,225	2,129	2,040
Orem city	4,539	2,931	286	1,290	159	1,333	363	0	7,642	1,844	1,224
Provo city	4,068	2,558	342	1,092	259	1,182	417	na	6,356	1,712	1,150
St. George city	8,087	5,204	691	2,031	294	400	90	na	na	na	na
Salt Lake City city	12,225	5,026	2,337	4,694	476	1,698	519	143	13,710	5,798	4,654
Sandy city	5,012	3,449	358	1,178	203	1,079	181	15	9,944	2,111	1,384
West Jordan city	3,049	1,930	425	653	60	965	206	0	6,669	1,522	1,063
West Valley City city	5,708	3,799	705	1,127	32	2,086	414	114	9,076	2,551	2,328

Table D-3: Places—Household Relationship, Grandparents, and Marital Status—*Continued*

	Total Householders Age 65 Years and Over	Family Householders 65 Years and Over	Non-Family Householders 65 Years and Over		Persons 65 Years and Over Living in Group Quarters	Grandparents 60 Years and Over Living with Grandchildren			Marital Status - Persons 60 Years and Over		
			Male Living Alone	Female Living Alone		Total	Responsible for Grandchildren	Responsible for Grandchildren and In Poverty	Married	Widowed	Divorced
Virginia											
Alexandria city	8,939	3,860	1,455	3,303	427	566	309	27	10,493	3,329	3,789
Chesapeake city	14,794	8,892	1,525	4,141	647	2,905	836	61	22,784	7,842	4,253
Hampton city	11,080	5,708	1,484	3,646	299	1,731	451	51	13,771	5,831	3,593
Lynchburg city	6,872	2,996	878	2,795	711	633	244	30	7,582	3,539	2,114
Newport News city	12,796	6,775	1,537	4,344	679	1,337	535	42	15,397	6,693	4,342
Norfolk city	15,010	7,137	2,101	5,414	753	1,884	687	163	16,002	8,518	6,211
Portsmouth city	8,147	4,511	798	2,730	374	1,396	599	110	9,463	5,319	2,479
Richmond city	15,786	6,295	2,647	6,551	915	1,569	497	111	13,505	8,566	7,523
Roanoke city	9,667	3,934	1,508	4,090	675	1,053	679	162	9,410	4,956	4,119
Suffolk city	6,001	3,631	687	1,529	279	1,118	207	40	8,753	3,445	1,614
Virginia Beach city	30,003	17,347	2,852	9,081	1,193	4,648	1,342	142	44,427	14,435	9,808
Washington											
Auburn city	4,927	2,685	800	1,243	286	798	168	2	6,753	2,466	2,194
Bellevue city	10,203	5,677	1,094	2,922	321	1,060	115	0	15,576	3,829	3,652
Bellingham city	7,002	3,090	982	2,709	464	na	na	na	8,163	3,259	3,031
Everett city	7,347	3,017	943	3,102	540	760	143	0	7,843	4,124	3,786
Federal Way city	6,032	3,146	881	1,940	312	866	329	54	8,155	2,778	2,793
Kennewick city	5,717	2,725	859	2,062	326	547	316	na	na	na	na
Kent city	6,667	3,202	961	2,319	311	1,983	103	0	9,992	3,168	3,293
Renton city	5,793	2,450	898	2,228	273	1,211	306	42	7,133	2,807	2,832
Seattle city	46,319	17,732	8,096	18,450	4,061	3,921	686	179	50,151	19,839	21,707
Spokane city	19,055	8,476	2,755	7,421	1,354	1,364	372	28	21,513	9,169	7,481
Spokane Valley city	8,182	3,956	1,218	2,679	631	566	221	0	11,216	3,701	3,459
Tacoma city	14,668	6,428	2,305	5,529	1,459	1,631	480	34	17,070	7,713	7,138
Vancouver city	14,025	6,748	1,979	4,896	576	1,427	401	83	17,549	6,369	5,972
Yakima city	7,758	3,559	1,057	2,928	813	872	346	71	8,919	4,653	2,632
Wisconsin											
Appleton city	5,622	2,570	793	2,155	396	473	146	32	7,552	2,828	1,588
Eau Claire city	5,188	2,068	720	2,277	319	na	na	na	na	na	na
Green Bay city	8,094	3,723	1,250	2,944	723	470	199	18	9,176	4,017	2,782
Kenosha city	6,898	3,005	918	2,765	544	901	393	29	7,595	4,030	2,477
Madison city	14,802	7,330	1,744	5,305	932	489	87	na	19,488	5,721	5,932
Milwaukee city	35,948	14,740	6,279	13,694	2,479	4,498	1,274	346	34,543	19,650	15,538
Oshkosh city	5,265	2,081	953	2,191	795	98	50	0	5,914	2,856	1,858
Racine city	5,985	2,799	945	2,132	84	616	151	14	6,595	2,442	2,356
Waukesha city	5,269	2,470	654	2,083	338	na	na	na	7,015	2,837	1,543

Table D-4: Metropolitan Statistical Areas—Household Relationship, Grandparents, and Marital Status

	Total Householders Age 65 Years and Over	Family Householders 65 Years and Over	Non-Family Householders 65 Years and Over — Male Living Alone	Non-Family Householders 65 Years and Over — Female Living Alone	Persons 65 Years and Over Living in Group Quarters	Grandparents 60 Years and Over Living with Grandchildren — Total	Grandparents 60 Years and Over Living with Grandchildren — Responsible for Grandchildren	Grandparents 60 Years and Over Living with Grandchildren — Responsible for Grandchildren and In Poverty	Marital Status - Persons 60 Years and Over — Married	Marital Status - Persons 60 Years and Over — Widowed	Marital Status - Persons 60 Years and Over — Divorced
Abilene, TX	14,532	7,783	1,930	4,620	1,139	1,569	879	316	18,739	7,890	3,955
Akron, OH	64,998	33,947	8,742	20,768	3,662	5,791	2,202	80	83,812	32,468	20,790
Albany, GA	12,989	7,423	1,332	4,127	416	2,023	1,150	325	16,019	6,955	4,083
Albany-Schenectady-Troy, NY	78,336	38,021	11,219	26,657	6,672	5,899	1,649	114	100,531	42,179	22,019
Albuquerque, NM	71,559	38,048	10,035	21,318	2,249	9,582	3,246	641	96,940	30,726	30,374
Alexandria, LA	13,393	6,759	1,809	4,489	1,148	1,331	493	82	15,906	7,647	3,968
Allentown-Bethlehem-Easton, PA-NJ	76,152	40,163	9,897	24,179	6,211	8,361	1,459	251	104,585	41,132	19,407
Altoona, PA	14,484	7,389	1,675	5,137	1,645	828	258	4	18,011	8,364	3,797
Amarillo, TX	19,059	10,293	2,241	6,134	1,397	2,299	1,203	276	26,421	9,742	6,490
Ames, IA	5,780	3,248	571	1,829	343	na	na	na	9,050	2,237	1,345
Anchorage, AK	17,676	9,248	2,856	4,821	1,269	3,774	957	61	29,140	8,721	9,932
Anderson, IN	13,929	6,963	1,907	4,803	894	813	452	91	16,587	6,962	4,105
Anderson, SC	18,798	10,479	2,394	5,597	1,068	2,664	1,053	301	25,315	10,015	4,253
Ann Arbor, MI	24,398	12,456	3,310	7,992	1,151	2,496	971	18	32,720	10,491	8,673
Anniston-Oxford, AL	11,127	6,222	1,222	3,434	399	1,501	611	132	14,504	5,994	3,131
Appleton, WI	17,635	9,364	1,844	6,101	956	1,006	229	41	26,155	7,738	3,804
Asheville, NC	50,318	27,773	6,346	14,855	3,757	3,587	1,615	369	68,677	23,128	15,452
Athens-Clarke County, GA	12,485	7,225	1,405	3,673	630	1,556	662	158	17,931	6,558	3,961
Atlanta-Sandy Springs-Marietta, GA	295,043	167,354	33,994	87,929	12,033	63,396	17,238	3,049	452,933	159,215	119,854
Atlantic City-Hammonton, NJ	24,270	12,541	3,633	7,412	1,438	4,245	957	245	31,319	13,835	7,727
Auburn-Opelika, AL	8,548	5,021	997	2,417	265	1,071	514	124	12,864	4,050	2,562
Augusta-Richmond County, GA-SC	43,944	25,215	5,334	12,653	2,702	6,445	2,909	806	62,518	24,058	13,120
Austin-Round Rock-San Marcos, TX	88,351	51,254	9,323	25,522	4,579	16,689	4,175	899	142,664	40,336	37,387
Bakersfield-Delano, CA	45,718	25,583	6,612	12,338	1,451	11,878	3,174	744	68,816	24,489	15,953
Baltimore-Towson, MD	220,901	116,136	29,082	69,998	12,611	31,152	8,534	1,360	289,008	117,611	69,292
Bangor, ME	14,088	7,203	2,174	4,083	994	783	177	46	20,315	7,061	4,689
Barnstable Town, MA	34,374	18,504	4,061	10,641	1,577	1,303	67	15	46,118	14,136	8,519
Baton Rouge, LA	56,292	31,724	6,918	16,726	3,228	8,496	4,366	1,187	77,112	30,019	19,990
Battle Creek, MI	13,077	7,014	1,678	4,087	888	990	323	29	17,327	6,120	4,704
Bay City, MI	11,597	6,497	1,207	3,748	854	820	385	60	16,020	5,798	2,367
Beaumont-Port Arthur, TX	33,882	17,977	4,712	10,642	1,724	3,453	1,628	227	41,908	18,886	10,347
Bellingham, WA	17,606	9,768	2,281	5,247	617	1,509	705	93	26,285	7,291	6,064
Bend, OR	15,950	9,040	1,858	4,578	400	1,160	485	26	23,616	6,410	5,772
Billings, MT	15,467	7,883	1,939	5,277	839	1,064	388	105	20,361	7,147	4,812
Binghamton, NY	25,935	13,174	3,405	8,830	2,280	1,746	280	42	33,816	12,431	7,842
Birmingham-Hoover, AL	96,165	53,438	11,383	29,962	4,578	12,337	5,425	1,080	126,271	52,204	29,474
Bismarck, ND	9,938	5,020	1,322	3,445	865	329	89	na	14,660	4,673	2,171
Blacksburg-Christiansburg-Radford, VA	13,742	7,894	1,470	4,134	678	807	262	20	18,141	7,044	3,146
Bloomington, IN	15,036	7,984	2,129	4,580	804	951	329	88	20,831	6,734	5,076
Bloomington-Normal, IL	11,076	5,989	1,448	3,364	816	689	156	6	16,405	5,390	3,605
Boise City-Nampa, ID	44,817	25,529	4,663	13,687	1,784	4,551	1,492	109	66,979	18,893	15,661
Boston-Cambridge-Quincy, MA-NH	382,877	190,783	52,358	130,208	27,335	45,995	8,630	1,365	499,420	185,743	116,087
Boulder, CO	19,981	10,712	2,439	6,279	1,346	1,288	385	63	29,937	7,219	8,098
Bowling Green, KY	9,560	4,993	1,452	2,885	483	1,107	356	17	12,036	4,998	2,960
Bremerton-Silverdale, WA	21,257	11,940	2,582	6,103	1,592	1,889	571	92	33,462	9,574	7,873
Bridgeport-Stamford-Norwalk, CT	76,458	40,522	9,515	24,416	5,639	10,352	1,548	156	104,900	39,090	22,487
Brownsville-Harlingen, TX	25,830	16,236	2,636	6,435	1,106	7,562	1,782	639	40,010	13,665	5,829
Brunswick, GA	11,839	6,915	1,417	3,336	359	1,623	883	88	16,926	5,354	3,618
Buffalo-Niagara Falls, NY	116,715	56,945	15,364	42,199	8,686	6,933	1,841	356	136,785	61,456	30,799
Burlington, NC	15,143	7,582	1,411	5,932	755	839	307	52	18,045	7,973	3,898
Burlington-South Burlington, VT	16,287	8,380	1,835	5,459	1,024	1,183	295	5	23,132	7,000	5,784
Canton-Massillon, OH	41,933	22,692	5,484	12,668	3,532	3,415	1,413	188	55,275	21,174	11,989
Cape Coral-Fort Myers, FL	87,499	51,560	11,711	21,148	2,255	6,961	1,292	505	128,878	39,624	24,318
Cape Girardeau-Jackson, MO-IL	8,706	4,803	1,042	2,761	1,148	577	250	6	12,748	4,679	1,939
Casper, WY	6,257	3,440	825	1,847	406	409	121	0	8,578	2,945	2,126
Cedar Rapids, IA	23,070	11,982	3,071	7,657	1,568	1,573	540	23	31,486	10,534	6,334
Champaign-Urbana, IL	16,746	9,068	1,831	5,591	1,179	918	278	153	23,786	7,334	4,884
Charleston, WV	32,508	17,751	4,070	10,100	1,133	2,555	1,433	217	40,440	17,197	8,970
Charleston-North Charleston-Summerville, SC	50,671	29,023	5,765	15,128	1,918	6,904	2,807	496	72,086	25,821	15,537
Charlotte-Gastonia-Rock Hill, NC-SC	113,854	65,337	12,246	34,250	5,981	15,334	4,648	1,246	167,809	59,772	36,728
Charlottesville, VA	17,931	9,649	2,372	5,715	955	1,892	645	263	25,012	8,594	5,403
Chattanooga, TN-GA	50,496	28,185	5,715	15,847	2,280	5,159	2,576	465	67,088	26,303	16,121
Cheyenne, WY	7,710	3,825	1,074	2,662	332	714	353	41	10,112	3,571	2,885
Chicago-Joliet-Naperville, IL-IN-WI	687,259	361,913	87,284	223,444	39,099	106,716	24,300	4,494	905,294	368,705	214,786
Chico, CA	22,252	11,662	2,712	7,167	1,004	2,328	927	173	28,025	10,277	9,122
Cincinnati-Middletown, OH-KY-IN	169,699	89,201	21,457	56,080	11,856	16,717	6,042	884	230,280	85,565	52,523
Clarksville, TN-KY	16,678	9,523	1,919	4,779	877	1,871	889	92	23,609	9,024	4,631
Cleveland, TN	11,151	6,147	1,585	3,308	531	1,276	351	71	15,094	5,867	2,969
Cleveland-Elyria-Mentor, OH	207,026	102,802	27,440	72,460	14,076	18,052	5,758	1,223	246,465	105,510	66,913
Coeur d'Alene, ID	13,114	7,833	1,377	3,327	388	1,090	393	42	20,160	4,534	5,398

Table D-4: Metropolitan Statistical Areas—Household Relationship, Grandparents, and Marital Status—*Continued*

	Total Householders Age 65 Years and Over	Family Householders 65 Years and Over	Non-Family Householders 65 Years and Over — Male Living Alone	Non-Family Householders 65 Years and Over — Female Living Alone	Persons 65 Years and Over Living in Group Quarters	Grandparents 60 Years and Over Living with Grandchildren — Total	Grandparents — Responsible for Grandchildren	Grandparents — Responsible for Grandchildren and In Poverty	Marital Status — Persons 60 Years and Over — Married	Widowed	Divorced
College Station-Bryan, TX	12,943	7,343	1,516	3,841	759	1,394	375	58	19,402	6,477	3,369
Colorado Springs, CO	42,773	23,704	5,199	12,926	1,591	4,285	1,189	219	65,600	18,651	16,192
Columbia, MO	10,703	5,898	1,071	3,643	832	886	109	37	14,961	5,180	3,952
Columbia, SC	57,244	32,150	7,023	17,123	3,253	6,368	2,743	336	80,676	30,681	18,464
Columbus, GA-AL	23,214	11,787	3,136	7,951	1,220	2,857	989	182	25,923	13,719	8,054
Columbus, IN	6,948	3,555	981	2,330	564	397	223	34	na	na	na
Columbus, OH	127,255	66,503	16,103	41,721	6,647	15,712	4,772	593	173,693	61,877	47,070
Corpus Christi, TX	34,267	20,699	3,973	8,908	1,839	6,088	2,238	339	47,983	17,121	12,940
Corvallis, OR	6,771	3,527	1,112	1,906	122	464	85	na	9,939	2,209	2,854
Crestview-Fort Walton Beach-Destin, FL	15,915	9,370	1,977	4,230	506	1,656	414	0	23,103	6,886	5,394
Cumberland, MD-WV	11,888	5,276	2,214	4,134	977	854	250	24	13,783	6,480	3,186
Dallas-Fort Worth-Arlington, TX	354,325	203,056	40,421	103,448	18,372	71,665	20,325	4,052	544,311	181,256	137,961
Dalton, GA	9,721	5,975	997	2,670	491	1,844	604	206	13,594	5,616	3,398
Danville, IL	8,899	4,253	1,454	2,983	560	514	170	20	9,935	4,687	2,770
Danville, VA	13,120	7,316	1,446	4,102	749	1,323	635	211	16,087	6,403	3,164
Davenport-Moline-Rock Island, IA-IL	38,299	19,469	5,484	12,811	2,242	2,658	989	126	50,851	18,425	10,219
Dayton, OH	84,112	42,759	11,707	27,891	5,673	6,613	2,217	341	104,516	41,132	27,730
Decatur, AL	14,058	8,025	1,603	4,282	757	1,426	651	105	20,035	6,910	4,505
Decatur, IL	11,817	6,219	1,672	3,750	1,096	1,046	711	155	15,439	5,520	3,538
Deltona-Daytona Beach-Ormond Beach, FL	65,197	34,670	8,815	19,535	2,849	4,546	1,912	429	84,217	30,180	21,887
Denver-Aurora-Broomfield, CO	170,199	89,396	23,022	53,302	7,775	21,981	5,128	740	239,901	73,325	73,160
Des Moines-West Des Moines, IA	41,036	21,809	4,745	13,865	3,185	3,703	1,255	256	61,117	19,833	12,370
Detroit-Warren-Livonia, MI	378,959	194,670	51,344	125,657	16,502	40,823	11,064	1,962	459,297	195,996	125,454
Dothan, AL	14,793	8,290	1,613	4,661	712	1,413	500	200	19,227	7,302	4,648
Dover, DE	13,607	7,879	1,448	3,834	712	2,541	702	34	19,595	7,053	4,446
Dubuque, IA	8,939	4,734	1,161	2,893	1,187	266	144	18	12,544	4,030	1,965
Duluth, MN-WI	28,720	13,725	4,170	10,285	2,607	1,132	440	35	37,471	13,345	8,731
Durham-Chapel Hill, NC	37,470	20,560	4,293	11,801	2,906	3,330	1,763	644	53,041	17,964	12,607
Eau Claire, WI	14,520	7,039	2,007	5,181	757	570	138	30	19,626	6,440	3,801
El Centro, CA	10,086	5,804	1,511	2,530	398	3,576	863	224	15,528	5,535	3,007
Elizabethtown, KY	8,592	5,021	867	2,623	571	1,042	537	93	12,668	4,684	2,438
Elkhart-Goshen, IN	15,273	8,569	1,660	4,765	1,256	1,803	633	179	22,322	7,080	4,231
Elmira, NY	8,794	4,030	1,257	3,312	957	414	117	10	10,938	5,192	2,341
El Paso, TX	49,572	29,786	5,612	12,962	1,564	14,774	4,336	1,547	69,261	28,190	16,316
Erie, PA	25,679	12,970	3,197	8,840	2,351	1,919	417	41	33,222	14,069	6,990
Eugene-Springfield, OR	34,894	17,975	4,454	11,083	1,663	2,360	1,004	143	46,307	14,742	14,800
Evansville, IN-KY	32,970	17,524	4,496	10,423	2,882	2,951	1,445	112	44,210	16,508	9,908
Fairbanks, AK	4,117	2,263	722	1,030	84	701	193	0	7,430	1,746	1,634
Fargo, ND-MN	14,513	6,800	2,082	5,259	1,189	721	258	0	20,399	6,565	4,096
Farmington, NM	8,792	5,426	1,024	2,049	402	1,827	725	394	12,527	4,476	2,462
Fayetteville, NC	22,266	12,046	2,669	7,135	1,165	3,409	1,340	259	28,796	13,085	7,125
Fayetteville-Springdale-Rogers, AR-MO	33,426	18,967	3,918	9,763	1,566	2,877	1,172	167	47,121	17,252	10,308
Flagstaff, AZ	7,670	5,016	770	1,726	194	1,940	949	215	12,818	2,740	2,755
Flint, MI	39,113	20,902	5,271	12,100	1,778	3,792	1,492	187	48,178	19,816	13,108
Florence, SC	18,045	10,521	1,973	5,298	1,186	2,983	908	138	24,332	10,367	4,869
Florence-Muscle Shoals, AL	16,800	9,348	1,751	5,433	848	1,225	687	123	22,259	8,041	4,331
Fond du Lac, WI	9,918	5,368	1,179	3,274	888	327	94	7	13,779	4,848	2,315
Fort Collins-Loveland, CO	23,052	12,921	2,572	6,921	1,147	1,648	835	20	36,391	9,128	8,201
Fort Smith, AR-OK	26,464	14,602	3,141	8,244	1,840	2,532	1,172	298	36,732	13,820	7,692
Fort Wayne, IN	33,792	17,518	4,529	11,041	2,668	2,331	906	128	45,515	16,190	10,979
Fresno, CA	56,190	31,349	6,810	16,353	3,432	13,408	2,834	679	81,552	30,272	20,242
Gadsden, AL	10,485	5,592	1,272	3,536	587	1,119	608	66	13,508	6,516	3,020
Gainesville, FL	18,310	10,129	2,076	5,550	1,046	1,888	502	153	25,718	9,187	7,039
Gainesville, GA	12,796	7,854	1,143	3,588	505	2,352	751	115	19,696	6,709	3,645
Glens Falls, NY	13,773	7,215	1,822	4,309	927	926	360	60	18,582	6,784	3,758
Goldsboro, NC	10,404	5,289	1,260	3,628	727	1,187	571	174	13,967	5,488	3,094
Grand Forks, ND-MN	8,067	3,890	1,154	2,890	1,007	462	184	na	10,522	4,065	1,625
Grand Junction, CO	14,901	7,429	2,070	4,998	607	1,150	575	10	19,348	6,656	4,420
Grand Rapids-Wyoming, MI	58,937	32,287	6,854	18,693	3,535	5,127	1,252	161	85,756	26,324	16,886
Great Falls, MT	8,117	4,297	1,234	2,433	509	530	166	0	10,481	4,009	2,825
Greeley, CO	15,559	8,895	1,879	4,503	653	2,505	1,030	113	25,087	6,995	5,166
Green Bay, WI	25,021	13,110	3,140	8,288	1,605	1,339	495	94	35,498	11,618	6,319
Greensboro-High Point, NC	62,935	33,792	7,250	20,819	3,284	6,405	2,077	346	85,771	30,728	18,601
Greenville, NC	12,947	6,827	1,672	4,318	771	1,623	589	246	17,392	6,875	3,559
Greenville-Mauldin-Easley, SC	53,822	30,219	5,970	16,840	2,568	5,643	2,017	539	75,762	27,262	14,202
Gulfport-Biloxi, MS	20,264	11,722	2,093	5,832	976	3,214	1,723	400	25,546	10,518	7,287
Hagerstown-Martinsburg, MD-WV	23,320	12,179	3,470	7,023	1,487	1,611	516	84	31,637	12,596	6,869
Hanford-Corcoran, CA	6,842	3,804	809	2,073	958	1,949	697	234	10,887	3,809	2,249
Harrisburg-Carlisle, PA	51,597	26,820	6,303	17,138	3,531	3,447	963	115	70,500	26,551	12,941
Harrisonburg, VA	10,301	5,873	1,097	3,111	620	703	310	12	14,719	4,890	2,022
Hartford-West Hartford-East Hartford, CT	109,274	55,373	14,652	36,449	8,893	10,545	2,397	331	145,716	53,197	34,018
Hattiesburg, MS	10,789	5,671	1,578	3,453	580	1,657	833	260	13,709	5,860	3,418
Hickory-Lenoir-Morganton, NC	35,767	19,144	4,532	11,521	2,070	3,289	920	128	48,040	20,397	9,825
Hinesville-Fort Stewart, GA	3,535	2,232	250	973	158	750	345	0	4,906	1,993	1,269
Holland-Grand Haven, MI	19,807	12,117	1,644	5,818	983	1,454	481	78	31,828	8,784	3,839
Honolulu, HI	77,959	50,128	7,983	17,520	4,742	25,167	4,258	368	116,555	43,269	23,752
Hot Springs, AR	12,591	7,237	1,645	3,489	727	999	601	91	16,354	6,310	3,638
Houma-Bayou Cane-Thibodaux, LA	16,157	9,350	1,743	4,718	912	2,277	1,107	227	21,594	9,031	3,302
Houston-Sugar Land-Baytown, TX	315,707	184,420	38,790	85,717	13,442	71,892	18,751	3,917	497,717	171,527	121,695
Huntington-Ashland, WV-KY-OH	30,945	16,665	3,732	10,137	1,665	3,331	1,520	197	38,724	17,397	9,136

Table D-4: Metropolitan Statistical Areas—Household Relationship, Grandparents, and Marital Status—*Continued*

	Total Householders Age 65 Years and Over	Family Householders 65 Years and Over	Non-Family Householders 65 Years and Over		Persons 65 Years and Over Living in Group Quarters	Grandparents 60 Years and Over Living with Grandchildren			Marital Status - Persons 60 Years and Over		
			Male Living Alone	Female Living Alone		Total	Responsible for Grandchildren	Responsible for Grandchildren and In Poverty	Married	Widowed	Divorced
Huntsville, AL	33,727	19,230	3,564	10,530	1,460	3,893	1,996	315	48,489	16,466	9,909
Idaho Falls, ID	9,202	5,431	905	2,675	247	838	115	16	13,598	4,062	2,976
Indianapolis-Carmel, IN	123,762	65,933	15,335	40,384	8,621	13,455	4,364	612	168,218	61,451	44,518
Iowa City, IA	10,229	5,126	1,213	3,594	707	461	232	41	15,009	3,845	3,394
Ithaca, NY	7,172	3,504	1,002	2,420	402	382	122	na	10,359	2,967	2,329
Jackson, MI	14,626	8,166	1,678	4,395	1,089	1,207	575	151	20,114	7,186	5,059
Jackson, MS	39,518	22,897	4,230	11,872	2,677	5,604	1,887	430	51,540	22,568	12,485
Jackson, TN	9,460	5,194	1,209	2,924	708	1,082	356	44	12,319	5,467	3,478
Jacksonville, FL	103,893	57,285	13,413	30,537	5,085	13,927	4,953	754	145,948	54,577	41,179
Jacksonville, NC	8,668	4,726	1,176	2,637	416	1,432	513	130	11,810	4,447	2,810
Janesville, WI	14,192	7,437	1,864	4,679	867	1,195	320	34	19,281	6,878	3,587
Jefferson City, MO	12,941	7,075	1,317	4,276	1,114	1,164	635	161	18,443	6,397	2,913
Johnson City, TN	21,283	11,510	2,689	6,759	1,523	1,779	831	140	28,861	10,552	5,829
Johnstown, PA	17,817	8,663	2,561	6,312	1,122	796	227	27	21,234	9,423	3,700
Jonesboro, AR	9,827	5,436	1,031	3,350	870	1,089	357	86	13,475	5,918	2,767
Joplin, MO	15,510	8,597	1,852	4,562	1,044	1,074	472	48	21,379	7,504	4,329
Kalamazoo-Portage, MI	26,992	14,032	3,180	9,126	1,402	1,970	695	152	36,578	12,671	9,109
Kankakee-Bradley, IL	9,408	4,918	1,208	3,190	1,203	1,057	233	47	12,367	5,290	2,682
Kansas City, MO-KS	160,004	85,649	20,308	50,908	10,353	15,333	4,566	651	218,792	76,617	53,283
Kennewick-Pasco-Richland, WA	17,299	9,849	2,131	5,064	685	2,742	707	179	27,812	7,543	5,425
Killeen-Temple-Fort Hood, TX	22,199	13,192	2,477	5,987	1,515	3,604	999	238	33,285	12,189	7,156
Kingsport-Bristol-Bristol, TN-VA	37,875	21,169	4,145	11,589	1,728	3,462	1,664	241	49,687	18,798	9,269
Kingston, NY	17,228	8,023	2,582	5,796	1,593	1,283	289	0	22,593	9,259	5,893
Knoxville, TN	67,028	35,951	9,020	21,025	3,194	6,490	2,684	352	91,919	33,079	19,397
Kokomo, IN	10,870	5,583	1,204	3,896	693	466	305	24	14,160	5,207	2,837
La Crosse, WI-MN	12,377	6,305	1,639	4,199	1,012	488	145	na	17,117	5,673	2,276
Lafayette, IN	13,741	7,159	1,618	4,750	962	1,094	278	66	18,593	6,914	3,924
Lafayette, LA	18,765	10,401	1,975	5,898	1,478	2,006	821	219	25,278	10,094	5,456
Lake Charles, LA	16,269	8,954	1,868	5,125	791	1,964	959	256	22,668	8,517	5,352
Lake Havasu City-Kingman, AZ	30,103	17,389	4,800	6,295	580	2,547	1,292	543	40,733	12,487	10,264
Lakeland-Winter Haven, FL	67,040	38,810	7,932	18,319	2,235	7,204	2,403	561	96,031	31,200	17,198
Lancaster, PA	47,590	26,185	5,486	14,661	4,576	3,816	924	122	70,610	22,813	9,815
Lansing-East Lansing, MI	36,023	18,895	4,916	11,573	1,711	2,800	776	36	49,603	15,778	12,598
Laredo, TX	10,908	7,277	1,063	2,534	425	5,401	1,331	616	17,625	6,881	2,829
Las Cruces, NM	16,964	10,738	1,900	4,080	416	2,491	721	79	24,022	7,128	4,719
Las Vegas-Paradise, NV	137,213	73,947	22,599	34,581	3,413	25,797	7,082	1,001	191,036	66,005	64,738
Lawrence, KS	6,461	3,259	930	2,160	323	839	329	40	9,500	2,927	2,314
Lawton, OK	8,725	4,582	1,243	2,765	603	953	463	53	10,506	4,489	2,739
Lebanon, PA	14,277	7,773	1,433	4,771	1,244	811	216	88	19,416	7,076	3,400
Lewiston-Auburn, ME	9,997	5,089	1,265	3,262	705	738	162	0	13,578	4,432	3,316
Lexington-Fayette, KY	34,928	18,403	3,875	11,984	2,249	3,020	1,495	245	47,161	16,051	13,987
Lima, OH	9,963	5,130	1,253	3,400	763	447	228	58	12,882	4,766	2,858
Lincoln, NE	21,994	11,653	2,692	7,368	1,264	1,351	517	68	33,194	8,963	6,419
Little Rock-North Little Rock-Conway, AR	54,676	31,417	6,318	15,990	3,044	6,354	2,516	336	76,822	27,509	17,488
Logan, UT-ID	6,708	4,200	642	1,827	152	835	265	0	10,624	2,479	1,307
Longview, TX	18,937	9,942	2,708	6,046	1,573	1,786	983	171	24,670	11,223	6,000
Longview, WA	10,586	5,626	1,401	3,250	592	721	316	0	14,421	4,685	3,885
Los Angeles-Long Beach-Santa Ana, CA	822,772	455,519	101,420	236,141	47,826	209,671	39,200	5,523	1,188,623	440,779	299,461
Louisville/Jefferson County, KY-IN	108,380	57,455	13,643	35,232	7,251	9,636	3,887	606	141,990	54,430	36,427
Lubbock, TX	20,867	11,498	2,373	6,681	1,281	2,396	1,069	230	26,841	10,937	5,900
Lynchburg, VA	25,581	14,257	3,144	7,657	1,256	2,655	816	83	36,315	12,119	6,843
Macon, GA	19,230	10,948	2,016	6,032	1,175	2,392	916	74	25,989	10,066	6,030
Madera-Chowchilla, CA	9,464	6,391	1,011	1,813	691	2,043	902	102	16,521	4,695	3,084
Madison, WI	41,825	21,823	4,759	14,059	2,257	2,129	476	63	60,762	17,095	13,692
Manchester-Nashua, NH	29,700	16,234	3,637	8,985	2,502	3,159	548	84	45,538	14,396	9,868
Manhattan, KS	6,642	3,363	872	2,322	603	533	110	3	9,814	3,344	1,675
Mankato-North Mankato, MN	7,670	3,844	881	2,776	714	228	53	na	10,340	3,606	1,588
Mansfield, OH	13,532	7,034	1,825	4,481	963	631	310	143	17,163	7,135	3,731
McAllen-Edinburg-Mission, TX	41,006	27,135	4,463	8,690	1,706	14,165	3,639	1,644	70,600	22,506	8,246
Medford, OR	23,740	12,502	3,042	7,365	829	1,495	544	0	31,402	9,167	9,526
Memphis, TN-MS-AR	89,448	50,102	11,061	26,695	4,307	14,295	5,373	1,146	118,588	50,570	34,273
Merced, CA	13,739	8,109	1,709	3,405	784	3,635	534	52	22,006	7,483	4,856
Miami-Fort Lauderdale-Pompano Beach, FL	517,004	266,539	68,386	162,444	19,368	91,991	17,096	4,266	656,050	283,418	200,036
Michigan City-La Porte, IN	10,456	5,538	1,374	3,369	585	832	259	32	14,161	4,847	3,126
Midland, TX	9,229	4,896	1,274	2,906	581	1,311	547	169	13,822	4,684	3,135
Milwaukee-Waukesha-West Allis, WI	130,604	62,464	17,802	47,440	7,707	8,781	2,447	413	162,849	64,299	37,202
Minneapolis-St. Paul-Bloomington, MN-WI	233,272	119,819	28,997	79,255	14,543	18,817	4,451	722	332,975	99,425	73,042
Missoula, MT	8,036	4,506	916	2,402	309	465	195	77	12,099	3,243	3,367
Mobile, AL	34,830	19,716	4,165	10,402	1,611	5,292	2,748	514	45,115	18,593	11,838
Modesto, CA	33,059	18,540	3,917	9,788	2,138	7,565	1,795	628	48,418	17,845	11,599
Monroe, LA	14,969	7,855	1,434	5,427	1,070	1,881	1,044	350	18,262	7,659	5,010
Monroe, MI	13,592	7,563	1,592	4,211	776	1,406	524	55	18,936	6,505	3,915
Montgomery, AL	29,334	15,790	3,636	9,542	1,671	3,657	1,438	299	37,227	16,245	9,581
Morgantown, WV	9,332	4,837	1,220	3,127	576	541	319	6	13,435	5,064	2,868
Morristown, TN	14,596	7,931	1,951	4,464	798	1,753	790	194	19,459	6,952	4,375
Mount Vernon-Anacortes, WA	12,155	6,719	1,613	3,322	465	854	221	13	17,666	5,257	4,007
Muncie, IN	11,532	6,260	1,076	4,078	798	822	383	17	14,710	4,973	3,750
Muskegon-Norton Shores, MI	15,242	8,310	1,885	4,728	929	1,012	249	58	19,475	7,615	5,248
Myrtle Beach-North Myrtle Beach-Conway, SC	31,520	17,497	4,133	9,069	747	3,004	889	135	45,244	15,033	8,595
Napa, CA	12,918	6,832	1,595	3,950	1,383	1,282	255	24	17,506	6,062	4,633

Table D-4: Metropolitan Statistical Areas—Household Relationship, Grandparents, and Marital Status—*Continued*

	Total Householders Age 65 Years and Over	Family Householders 65 Years and Over	Non-Family Householders 65 Years and Over Male Living Alone	Non-Family Householders 65 Years and Over Female Living Alone	Persons 65 Years and Over Living in Group Quarters	Grandparents 60 Years and Over Living with Grandchildren Total	Grandparents 60 Years and Over Living with Grandchildren Responsible for Grandchildren	Grandparents 60 Years and Over Living with Grandchildren Responsible for Grandchildren and In Poverty	Marital Status - Persons 60 Years and Over Married	Widowed	Divorced
Naples-Marco Island, FL	52,578	31,644	6,189	13,195	757	3,767	726	243	77,248	18,937	12,807
Nashville-Davidson--Murfreesboro--Franklin, TN	110,342	62,171	12,183	33,475	5,694	14,898	4,996	609	159,516	56,322	38,130
New Haven-Milford, CT	77,105	37,746	10,341	26,996	6,349	9,104	2,379	329	97,665	40,196	25,046
New Orleans-Metairie-Kenner, LA	93,431	49,372	13,613	28,084	3,936	13,338	4,626	1,112	115,212	52,585	35,993
New York-Northern New Jersey-Long Island, NY-NJ-PA	1,520,309	781,116	194,233	509,813	102,449	270,087	50,960	11,085	1,980,536	821,677	423,765
Niles-Benton Harbor, MI	16,237	8,744	2,228	4,893	1,069	1,189	444	43	20,970	8,067	5,006
North Port-Bradenton-Sarasota, FL	124,192	68,137	15,143	35,741	3,880	5,563	1,897	445	159,304	51,768	31,455
Norwich-New London, CT	24,579	12,359	3,639	7,916	1,687	2,709	768	7	34,164	12,429	7,905
Ocala, FL	53,390	32,450	6,356	13,169	1,074	3,116	1,079	290	73,725	22,204	13,666
Ocean City, NJ	13,676	7,329	1,643	4,249	638	858	234	47	18,800	6,141	2,896
Odessa, TX	9,061	4,755	1,191	2,947	368	1,376	558	167	11,661	4,912	2,815
Ogden-Clearfield, UT	31,825	20,422	3,107	8,036	970	4,694	1,512	72	53,004	11,362	8,116
Oklahoma City, OK	97,069	51,697	12,857	30,852	5,350	10,876	4,349	875	130,828	48,555	33,780
Olympia, WA	21,508	11,258	2,566	6,922	982	1,539	398	0	32,633	9,328	7,761
Omaha-Council Bluffs, NE-IA	63,409	33,382	7,526	21,406	4,543	5,381	2,148	476	88,685	30,822	19,103
Orlando-Kissimmee-Sanford, FL	156,438	92,009	17,386	42,533	6,754	28,237	6,768	1,386	234,991	82,085	58,141
Oshkosh-Neenah, WI	14,435	6,904	2,226	5,094	1,225	593	165	0	19,656	7,075	4,137
Owensboro, KY	11,161	5,942	1,371	3,609	893	879	429	86	14,840	5,501	2,900
Oxnard-Thousand Oaks-Ventura, CA	59,887	34,482	6,164	17,171	2,346	11,991	2,333	210	89,254	28,476	21,461
Palm Bay-Melbourne-Titusville, FL	70,245	38,596	9,825	19,636	2,456	6,977	2,726	247	89,448	33,129	22,720
Palm Coast, FL	13,858	8,879	1,168	3,315	242	1,155	229	0	22,614	6,177	3,405
Panama City-Lynn Haven-Panama City Beach, FL	16,502	9,263	2,082	4,735	879	1,154	402	26	21,525	7,658	5,240
Parkersburg-Marietta-Vienna, WV-OH	18,054	9,376	2,447	5,786	1,078	1,527	524	159	23,274	8,834	4,949
Pascagoula, MS	13,309	7,972	1,599	3,412	365	1,917	721	69	18,177	6,407	4,450
Pensacola-Ferry Pass-Brent, FL	40,694	23,304	5,389	11,177	1,701	4,824	2,239	593	54,548	20,979	13,192
Peoria, IL	36,912	19,874	4,235	12,122	3,052	2,123	1,109	227	49,894	17,183	9,560
Philadelphia-Camden-Wilmington, PA-NJ-DE-MD	502,733	256,687	65,498	169,095	35,357	65,517	14,262	2,222	634,942	276,281	144,809
Phoenix-Mesa-Glendale, AZ	326,522	186,903	39,139	90,054	10,126	41,601	11,212	1,546	473,755	142,966	114,076
Pine Bluff, AR	8,567	4,662	1,150	2,590	856	1,386	637	223	11,602	4,647	2,917
Pittsburgh, PA	266,674	131,576	35,698	94,525	16,693	17,203	6,106	849	318,742	143,684	63,548
Pittsfield, MA	16,435	7,468	2,577	6,073	1,242	1,038	455	41	18,581	8,225	5,543
Pocatello, ID	6,496	3,915	717	1,735	214	445	237	22	9,735	2,632	2,208
Portland-South Portland-Biddeford, ME	49,863	25,092	6,463	17,071	2,883	3,423	851	77	68,653	23,010	16,772
Portland-Vancouver-Hillsboro, OR-WA	168,214	87,954	20,611	54,023	7,181	19,330	5,295	633	236,006	74,926	69,964
Port St. Lucie, FL	59,735	34,163	7,697	15,802	1,450	4,213	1,546	286	78,909	27,003	16,551
Poughkeepsie-Newburgh-Middletown, NY	50,584	27,333	6,480	15,370	4,332	7,610	1,470	23	73,365	25,771	14,543
Prescott, AZ	34,015	19,436	4,720	8,809	874	1,996	1,291	266	46,337	12,435	11,611
Providence-New Bedford-Fall River, RI-MA	144,675	71,375	19,361	50,262	12,379	14,133	3,409	485	183,330	78,285	44,519
Provo-Orem, UT	21,416	14,188	1,602	5,393	628	5,341	1,435	121	36,950	8,187	5,008
Pueblo, CO	15,828	8,255	2,237	4,889	1,011	1,465	841	148	21,101	7,007	5,300
Punta Gorda, FL	34,637	20,274	4,376	8,504	996	1,514	639	62	48,041	14,873	6,982
Racine, WI	17,221	8,900	2,252	5,774	622	1,437	390	31	22,785	8,109	4,771
Raleigh-Cary, NC	67,021	36,517	6,992	22,098	3,516	8,783	2,272	246	102,349	33,266	21,780
Rapid City, SD	10,675	5,651	1,489	3,209	904	727	309	72	15,630	4,643	3,485
Reading, PA	37,479	19,879	4,728	11,617	2,812	3,196	793	245	50,515	18,598	10,176
Redding, CA	19,897	10,653	2,819	5,858	776	1,357	727	83	26,701	9,047	6,504
Reno-Sparks, NV	33,271	17,834	5,406	8,717	1,033	4,516	1,359	194	48,074	13,486	16,573
Richmond, VA	100,701	54,857	11,532	32,163	4,636	13,725	4,711	407	136,217	51,548	34,025
Riverside-San Bernardino-Ontario, CA	258,771	143,792	33,558	70,970	9,084	70,588	15,194	2,529	382,401	137,513	100,887
Roanoke, VA	33,552	17,846	4,160	11,176	2,241	3,325	1,566	249	44,106	15,957	10,208
Rochester, MN	15,468	8,459	1,712	4,982	1,391	965	217	10	22,989	6,483	3,759
Rochester, NY	97,083	50,256	12,179	32,218	7,652	7,343	2,186	289	127,974	47,082	26,285
Rockford, IL	29,690	16,377	3,924	8,700	1,949	3,366	967	85	40,944	14,840	9,598
Rocky Mount, NC	14,820	7,349	2,089	5,001	921	1,631	668	147	17,796	8,430	4,338
Rome, GA	9,051	4,519	1,213	3,090	480	1,337	708	254	11,449	4,719	2,949
Sacramento--Arden-Arcade--Roseville, CA	163,172	86,954	21,276	50,172	7,899	26,895	5,196	870	228,958	79,503	63,778
Saginaw-Saginaw Township North, MI	20,511	10,259	2,718	7,011	1,263	1,439	530	196	25,557	9,821	5,411
St. Cloud, MN	14,791	7,825	1,689	4,951	1,379	442	172	0	21,809	6,952	2,884
St. George, UT	15,283	10,186	1,581	3,235	334	659	156	18	24,194	4,684	2,896
St. Joseph, MO-KS	11,423	5,758	1,562	3,941	1,115	931	285	18	14,714	5,868	3,425
St. Louis, MO-IL	246,259	129,475	30,741	81,610	18,429	22,023	7,334	1,133	320,222	123,473	71,630
Salem, OR	33,232	17,986	3,902	10,592	2,044	2,949	1,097	195	47,008	14,362	11,616
Salinas, CA	25,539	14,516	2,601	7,420	1,560	6,484	1,277	107	41,128	12,310	9,213
Salisbury, MD	10,516	5,643	1,443	3,154	948	1,013	323	47	13,108	6,109	3,191
Salt Lake City, UT	62,577	36,687	7,502	17,553	1,886	11,865	2,749	272	96,286	28,081	21,310
San Angelo, TX	10,206	5,771	1,251	3,050	459	1,081	375	123	13,409	4,434	2,960
San Antonio-New Braunfels, TX	148,360	86,604	17,408	41,054	7,628	30,006	8,775	1,814	214,985	72,981	52,718
San Diego-Carlsbad-San Marcos, CA	209,064	113,837	26,839	60,791	11,546	46,186	9,386	1,264	301,500	109,842	80,116
Sandusky, OH	8,524	4,666	1,175	2,582	869	487	243	39	12,069	4,217	2,357
San Francisco-Oakland-Fremont, CA	336,190	171,644	47,177	104,495	17,181	63,500	11,990	1,372	466,055	166,732	124,039

Table D-4: Metropolitan Statistical Areas—Household Relationship, Grandparents, and Marital Status—*Continued*

	Total Householders Age 65 Years and Over	Family Householders 65 Years and Over	Non-Family Householders 65 Years and Over		Persons 65 Years and Over Living in Group Quarters	Grandparents 60 Years and Over Living with Grandchildren			Marital Status - Persons 60 Years and Over		
			Male Living Alone	Female Living Alone		Total	Responsible for Grandchildren	Responsible for Grandchildren and In Poverty	Married	Widowed	Divorced
San Jose-Sunnyvale-Santa Clara, CA	115,635	68,060	12,699	31,344	6,873	32,253	4,739	303	186,561	58,878	38,661
San Luis Obispo-Paso Robles, CA	25,629	14,357	2,912	7,511	1,435	2,187	528	44	37,797	11,602	8,997
Santa Barbara-Santa Maria-Goleta, CA	33,861	18,158	4,203	10,356	2,056	4,947	868	175	45,594	16,642	10,664
Santa Cruz-Watsonville, CA	19,970	9,948	2,688	6,433	896	2,608	593	87	26,862	7,863	9,487
Santa Fe, NM	15,667	7,393	2,393	5,165	316	1,307	460	54	19,943	5,243	8,101
Santa Rosa-Petaluma, CA	44,296	22,074	5,496	14,779	2,253	3,581	805	62	59,701	18,648	19,960
Savannah, GA	26,733	14,043	3,734	8,296	1,357	4,065	1,353	314	33,571	14,532	10,100
Scranton--Wilkes-Barre, PA	63,550	31,145	9,296	22,014	5,623	4,743	1,114	115	75,724	35,740	14,889
Seattle-Tacoma-Bellevue, WA	243,947	123,705	33,343	78,573	14,155	31,503	6,422	757	342,544	109,504	101,635
Sebastian-Vero Beach, FL	24,390	12,681	3,322	7,710	384	1,273	141	0	29,264	11,420	6,538
Sheboygan, WI	10,784	5,785	1,203	3,547	837	341	125	10	14,985	5,227	2,385
Sherman-Denison, TX	11,431	6,215	1,422	3,539	818	1,289	437	54	15,961	6,047	4,291
Shreveport-Bossier City, LA	34,799	18,833	4,219	11,075	2,284	4,883	2,294	472	40,629	18,335	11,662
Sioux City, IA-NE-SD	12,252	5,733	1,785	4,541	822	999	258	33	15,483	6,334	3,447
Sioux Falls, SD	16,138	8,580	1,975	5,124	1,538	984	327	45	23,983	8,009	4,374
South Bend-Mishawaka, IN-MI	28,220	15,357	3,435	8,835	1,990	2,220	768	87	37,536	13,573	8,612
Spartanburg, SC	24,662	13,847	2,964	7,522	1,230	3,661	1,711	620	34,938	13,483	6,399
Spokane, WA	40,702	20,550	5,779	13,328	2,610	2,893	831	35	55,343	18,315	15,445
Springfield, IL	19,890	9,639	2,495	7,297	1,211	1,330	616	109	25,597	9,711	6,035
Springfield, MA	62,402	30,034	8,353	22,004	5,082	5,732	1,256	168	80,325	31,854	19,763
Springfield, MO	39,922	21,544	4,590	13,100	2,748	2,784	952	238	54,524	19,888	11,556
Springfield, OH	14,890	7,961	1,799	4,907	1,161	1,095	394	115	18,879	7,220	4,731
State College, PA	11,231	5,898	1,484	3,631	720	454	67	0	15,768	4,997	2,839
Steubenville-Weirton, OH-WV	15,188	7,871	1,845	5,235	821	901	357	47	18,949	7,842	3,892
Stockton, CA	41,585	23,896	4,614	11,808	2,714	10,998	2,447	516	60,203	24,380	15,794
Sumter, SC	9,106	5,148	1,186	2,620	505	1,441	701	106	11,886	5,436	1,902
Syracuse, NY	59,049	29,203	8,605	19,688	4,514	4,716	1,215	155	75,853	28,724	16,680
Tallahassee, FL	25,354	13,536	3,377	7,799	1,250	2,760	986	220	36,054	11,555	9,624
Tampa-St. Petersburg-Clearwater, FL	305,683	157,684	42,861	95,935	12,757	28,486	8,462	1,544	382,355	152,682	108,468
Terre Haute, IN	15,187	8,124	1,876	4,907	1,384	1,053	548	58	20,556	8,312	4,538
Texarkana, TX-Texarkana, AR	12,536	6,570	1,961	3,820	905	1,093	598	221	15,102	7,414	3,609
Toledo, OH	57,899	29,563	7,706	19,315	4,321	3,685	1,522	249	73,868	28,482	17,756
Topeka, KS	22,190	12,188	2,487	7,274	2,057	1,751	699	48	31,063	10,037	7,357
Trenton-Ewing, NJ	29,042	14,820	3,727	9,871	1,890	4,121	588	59	37,891	15,750	8,717
Tucson, AZ	97,843	52,812	13,748	28,186	3,593	10,925	3,740	836	130,527	43,192	33,823
Tulsa, OK	79,539	43,232	10,426	24,712	4,267	8,142	3,161	583	106,914	39,074	26,407
Tuscaloosa, AL	15,326	8,216	1,925	5,002	909	1,904	833	197	21,027	8,882	5,308
Tyler, TX	19,347	10,996	2,264	5,718	971	2,293	789	389	26,700	10,023	4,492
Utica-Rome, NY	31,249	14,655	4,815	10,867	3,417	1,820	455	137	38,633	17,199	8,768
Valdosta, GA	9,597	5,647	902	2,865	399	1,680	678	129	12,756	4,785	3,285
Vallejo-Fairfield, CA	28,831	16,346	3,294	8,246	1,901	6,997	1,501	56	44,867	15,085	11,226
Victoria, TX	10,442	6,094	1,328	2,849	676	1,628	601	80	15,504	4,638	2,672
Vineland-Millville-Bridgeton, NJ	12,301	5,980	1,693	4,222	1,267	1,691	420	22	14,546	7,163	4,087
Virginia Beach-Norfolk-Newport News, VA-NC	125,196	71,376	13,789	37,623	5,122	17,866	5,072	657	174,403	63,592	38,838
Visalia-Porterville, CA	24,691	14,432	3,149	6,569	1,819	7,150	2,232	461	37,977	13,651	7,561
Waco, TX	18,149	9,719	2,229	5,866	1,786	2,012	765	78	23,986	9,719	6,036
Warner Robins, GA	8,976	5,010	1,011	2,824	429	1,463	492	53	13,345	4,316	3,335
Washington-Arlington-Alexandria, DC-VA-MD-WV	350,684	192,755	43,176	105,710	16,615	67,517	15,020	1,308	528,307	173,007	121,626
Waterloo-Cedar Falls, IA	16,019	8,195	2,087	5,458	1,165	735	321	25	22,250	7,458	3,836
Wausau, WI	11,818	6,643	1,443	3,513	943	662	118	9	18,869	5,195	2,679
Wenatchee-East Wenatchee, WA	10,713	5,920	1,161	3,097	401	729	278	32	15,844	3,973	3,610
Wheeling, WV-OH	17,078	8,513	2,231	6,083	1,361	831	220	7	21,787	9,564	4,156
Wichita, KS	48,651	24,744	6,464	16,557	3,112	5,191	1,725	246	64,582	24,082	15,892
Wichita Falls, TX	13,139	7,275	1,420	4,206	1,050	1,298	657	144	17,549	6,692	3,405
Williamsport, PA	11,867	6,428	1,201	3,926	971	665	168	64	16,045	6,449	2,708
Wilmington, NC	39,482	23,163	4,196	11,146	1,508	2,584	1,000	164	58,987	16,066	11,703
Winchester, VA-WV	11,457	5,794	1,826	3,384	342	1,452	435	38	16,291	5,216	2,869
Winston-Salem, NC	43,386	23,033	5,299	14,456	2,520	4,192	1,777	428	58,887	21,319	12,162
Worcester, MA	63,136	30,946	9,132	21,530	5,742	7,473	1,813	150	83,497	34,890	19,265
Yakima, WA	16,886	9,205	1,847	5,225	1,317	2,715	762	212	24,299	9,155	5,697
York-Hanover, PA	39,794	21,676	5,011	12,341	2,074	3,251	1,076	272	56,877	18,799	10,937
Youngstown-Warren-Boardman, OH-PA	66,502	33,946	9,000	22,334	4,833	4,625	1,303	213	78,855	36,431	18,270
Yuba City, CA	11,654	6,511	1,560	3,166	537	2,795	523	130	17,389	6,184	4,823
Yuma, AZ	18,834	12,372	1,984	3,657	481	2,081	500	97	29,621	7,123	3,872

Table D-5: 113th Congressional Districts—Household Relationship, Grandparents, and Marital Status

	Total Householders Age 65 Years and Over	Family Householders 65 Years and Over	Non-Family Householders 65 Years and Over		Persons 65 Years and Over Living in Group Quarters	Grandparents 60 Years and Over Living with Grandchildren			Marital Status - Persons 60 Years and Over		
			Male Living Alone	Female Living Alone		Total	Responsible for Grandchildren	Responsible for Grandchildren and In Poverty	Married	Widowed	Divorced
Alabama											
Congressional District 1.............	63,296	37,354	7,063	18,032	2,579	8,409	4,102	891	86,825	31,174	19,163
Congressional District 2.............	62,194	33,860	7,391	20,214	3,477	6,337	2,679	655	80,368	33,551	18,127
Congressional District 3.............	60,439	33,607	7,602	18,227	3,093	7,177	3,500	768	80,452	32,224	17,724
Congressional District 4.............	70,393	39,312	8,111	22,018	3,590	7,213	3,445	774	94,351	37,780	18,397
Congressional District 5.............	61,062	34,404	6,542	19,375	2,856	6,277	3,134	543	85,850	29,874	17,531
Congressional District 6.............	57,022	32,302	6,505	17,322	2,425	7,305	2,764	571	81,531	29,492	15,556
Congressional District 7.............	57,494	29,162	8,297	19,248	3,641	7,794	3,756	1,153	61,221	35,586	20,408
Alaska											
Congressional District (at Large)....	35,129	19,247	5,872	8,797	2,218	7,367	2,402	215	58,071	16,158	17,577
Arizona											
Congressional District 1.............	61,895	38,253	8,223	13,968	1,098	10,583	4,676	1,388	92,901	25,904	19,674
Congressional District 2.............	82,408	42,319	12,228	25,374	3,381	6,201	2,221	430	104,873	36,137	27,760
Congressional District 3.............	38,254	23,233	4,866	8,803	1,278	10,727	2,959	702	59,971	18,572	14,375
Congressional District 4.............	98,872	59,213	13,684	21,736	2,036	7,097	3,306	875	144,082	38,305	30,626
Congressional District 5.............	65,598	38,188	6,820	18,514	1,363	7,073	1,313	201	96,263	26,825	20,055
Congressional District 6.............	64,829	37,408	7,073	18,251	1,956	5,865	1,922	192	95,690	26,609	24,299
Congressional District 7.............	27,728	14,340	4,767	7,595	1,138	8,471	2,353	494	35,280	16,035	13,415
Congressional District 8.............	80,030	47,155	8,253	22,174	2,597	7,166	1,970	144	115,249	32,984	20,913
Congressional District 9.............	44,669	22,492	6,752	13,953	2,156	4,903	1,218	23	56,963	21,557	20,272
Arkansas											
Congressional District 1.............	74,629	39,983	9,878	23,480	5,504	6,895	3,590	983	96,508	39,910	21,061
Congressional District 2.............	60,603	34,429	7,017	18,258	3,303	6,532	2,555	296	83,168	29,934	18,750
Congressional District 3.............	58,181	33,589	6,056	17,404	3,180	5,046	2,416	406	82,992	29,570	17,060
Congressional District 4.............	76,944	42,410	10,387	23,024	5,208	7,655	4,209	1,112	101,376	40,354	21,172
California											
Congressional District 1.............	78,841	42,555	10,205	23,495	3,457	6,183	2,622	404	107,457	34,379	27,609
Congressional District 2.............	71,143	35,935	9,569	22,370	2,945	5,739	1,826	78	96,453	28,634	30,506
Congressional District 3.............	50,081	27,158	6,759	14,096	2,745	9,441	2,187	383	73,495	24,480	18,900
Congressional District 4.............	73,173	43,080	8,687	19,278	1,919	7,417	1,941	162	110,926	29,688	23,066
Congressional District 5.............	59,631	30,207	7,284	19,742	3,747	8,384	1,717	211	83,128	28,858	26,255
Congressional District 6.............	46,049	22,173	7,222	15,289	2,678	9,069	2,008	515	55,372	25,227	20,375
Congressional District 7.............	52,070	27,890	6,403	16,367	2,949	9,876	1,601	201	73,204	26,908	21,782
Congressional District 8.............	49,070	27,135	7,698	12,689	1,381	10,163	2,957	386	69,374	24,662	19,849
Congressional District 9.............	44,298	25,258	5,406	12,360	2,685	10,864	2,907	528	65,012	24,916	16,929
Congressional District 10.............	42,739	24,515	4,652	12,531	2,635	11,076	2,410	763	64,620	23,849	15,352
Congressional District 11.............	60,723	33,311	7,485	18,150	3,236	8,416	1,685	96	86,043	28,278	21,549
Congressional District 12.............	60,556	25,643	11,273	20,664	2,648	8,499	1,189	372	65,885	29,852	19,342
Congressional District 13.............	54,816	24,737	9,210	18,307	3,017	8,400	1,773	224	63,353	26,871	22,917
Congressional District 14.............	54,105	29,217	6,576	16,441	2,697	13,903	2,481	150	83,330	29,514	19,408
Congressional District 15.............	40,607	23,733	4,529	11,169	2,571	12,757	1,921	332	69,212	22,796	14,905
Congressional District 16.............	35,459	20,318	4,968	8,836	2,749	9,692	2,089	521	51,605	19,965	14,188
Congressional District 17.............	38,926	23,579	4,691	9,627	2,319	14,332	2,511	10	68,472	22,519	11,797
Congressional District 18.............	57,686	31,923	6,666	17,098	3,625	7,732	1,065	16	84,961	24,961	18,784
Congressional District 19.............	38,425	23,466	4,070	9,596	1,988	14,470	2,277	214	64,963	20,298	14,999
Congressional District 20.............	45,790	24,710	5,196	14,080	2,850	9,955	2,114	257	68,217	21,152	18,429
Congressional District 21.............	28,615	17,290	3,408	7,174	2,373	11,645	3,100	793	47,926	17,243	9,492
Congressional District 22.............	45,926	26,191	4,947	13,821	2,055	9,756	2,278	453	68,798	23,697	14,700
Congressional District 23.............	46,736	25,037	7,253	12,989	2,235	9,471	2,801	569	67,351	23,807	16,858
Congressional District 24.............	60,205	32,832	7,226	18,127	3,491	7,273	1,396	219	84,197	28,531	20,029
Congressional District 25.............	35,311	21,510	3,802	8,951	888	10,188	2,147	252	59,666	18,294	14,908
Congressional District 26.............	52,466	29,856	5,384	15,307	2,034	10,525	2,069	182	76,631	24,960	18,604
Congressional District 27.............	55,033	31,802	6,025	15,254	4,144	14,668	2,881	505	87,620	31,610	17,457
Congressional District 28.............	58,144	27,208	9,377	18,999	3,521	7,842	1,074	204	72,509	29,437	18,840
Congressional District 29.............	30,344	17,088	4,554	7,558	2,663	13,158	2,122	428	49,748	18,613	12,092
Congressional District 30.............	54,729	29,663	6,651	16,476	3,192	9,680	1,676	208	77,276	27,803	21,942
Congressional District 31.............	33,895	18,306	4,233	10,292	2,317	11,375	2,070	383	50,773	21,766	13,997
Congressional District 32.............	39,516	24,294	3,937	10,294	2,772	18,520	4,059	416	66,808	26,568	14,043
Congressional District 33.............	67,969	35,607	8,874	20,563	1,958	4,369	858	49	86,094	26,142	23,963
Congressional District 34.............	38,587	19,461	6,153	11,273	3,386	9,860	1,943	455	52,208	21,433	12,582
Congressional District 35.............	24,732	14,702	2,637	6,507	2,097	15,375	2,853	758	45,329	18,113	12,126
Congressional District 36.............	84,960	42,717	12,775	24,799	2,076	8,902	2,466	424	100,198	34,845	27,629
Congressional District 37.............	52,754	23,026	8,270	18,974	2,070	7,121	1,533	344	49,873	25,266	21,360
Congressional District 38.............	46,143	29,241	3,963	11,497	2,639	15,101	2,653	314	68,650	27,589	15,443
Congressional District 39.............	44,798	29,774	3,689	10,349	1,994	15,111	2,254	207	83,574	25,598	12,812
Congressional District 40.............	24,055	14,922	2,695	5,753	1,405	13,668	1,815	355	40,414	16,569	8,849
Congressional District 41.............	29,365	17,547	3,467	7,299	1,807	12,344	2,782	636	47,867	18,377	12,646
Congressional District 42.............	37,443	22,417	3,652	9,994	547	12,217	2,161	54	64,324	20,436	15,397
Congressional District 43.............	43,125	22,605	6,031	13,032	2,602	10,640	2,738	353	53,536	23,903	17,626
Congressional District 44.............	31,432	19,045	3,836	7,596	1,594	15,367	3,551	491	48,144	20,206	11,868
Congressional District 45.............	52,624	29,507	4,846	16,482	2,040	9,375	1,605	62	83,339	23,966	17,915
Congressional District 46.............	27,832	16,573	2,707	7,686	3,876	13,261	2,021	300	45,727	18,987	11,245
Congressional District 47.............	45,252	24,244	6,685	12,510	3,368	11,241	1,923	248	62,294	25,202	18,743
Congressional District 48.............	62,120	34,685	7,060	18,119	2,240	9,023	1,708	124	88,930	28,210	21,682
Congressional District 49.............	51,672	28,538	6,248	15,103	1,901	7,863	1,594	106	77,470	22,501	18,650
Congressional District 50.............	49,651	28,651	5,434	13,641	2,756	9,166	1,900	216	77,073	26,657	17,468

Table D-5: 113th Congressional Districts—Household Relationship, Grandparents, and Marital Status—Continued

	Total Householders Age 65 Years and Over	Family Householders 65 Years and Over	Non-Family Householders 65 Years and Over		Persons 65 Years and Over Living in Group Quarters	Grandparents 60 Years and Over Living with Grandchildren			Marital Status - Persons 60 Years and Over		
			Male Living Alone	Female Living Alone		Total	Responsible for Grandchildren	Responsible for Grandchildren and In Poverty	Married	Widowed	Divorced
California—Cont.											
Congressional District 51	37,498	21,502	4,980	10,024	1,685	14,443	2,984	714	53,976	23,024	13,822
Congressional District 52	51,293	26,571	7,126	15,924	2,135	9,586	1,760	56	73,939	23,663	19,597
Congressional District 53	46,186	23,944	6,503	13,732	3,791	10,804	2,671	470	61,554	26,230	20,247
Colorado											
Congressional District 1	52,387	23,192	8,977	18,983	2,568	5,530	1,320	150	58,249	22,856	24,556
Congressional District 2	50,240	28,406	6,265	14,098	2,435	3,671	1,189	22	83,341	18,209	19,729
Congressional District 3	66,323	34,609	10,118	19,481	3,345	4,990	2,327	315	95,480	26,709	22,889
Congressional District 4	48,484	27,711	5,849	13,940	2,755	5,864	2,168	227	76,823	20,847	16,042
Congressional District 5	51,265	28,012	6,677	15,428	2,126	4,744	1,430	266	77,602	22,312	18,586
Congressional District 6	42,773	23,900	4,464	13,387	2,073	6,952	1,286	201	66,314	19,126	18,490
Congressional District 7	52,687	28,224	6,804	16,130	2,539	6,570	2,030	389	72,665	23,687	21,248
Connecticut											
Congressional District 1	66,372	32,670	8,755	23,110	5,950	6,738	1,631	155	83,636	34,114	21,095
Congressional District 2	62,012	33,033	8,368	18,936	4,296	6,281	1,537	124	92,336	29,169	18,968
Congressional District 3	64,640	31,598	9,372	22,022	4,679	7,431	1,685	76	80,467	33,941	21,022
Congressional District 4	59,564	32,147	7,022	18,888	4,484	8,182	1,211	206	82,524	30,087	17,556
Congressional District 5	63,384	31,185	8,335	22,081	5,417	6,600	1,590	343	83,767	31,294	19,421
Delaware											
Congressional District (at Large)	81,975	44,938	9,638	24,788	4,315	10,480	3,380	378	113,249	39,907	25,963
District of Columbia											
Delegate District ((at Large)	49,026	19,784	8,798	18,720	2,528	5,121	1,536	263	40,493	23,099	19,314
Florida											
Congressional District 1	63,862	36,753	8,329	17,540	2,387	6,940	2,901	674	87,705	30,892	21,117
Congressional District 2	57,302	31,640	7,419	16,807	3,663	5,461	2,147	298	78,020	27,015	20,288
Congressional District 3	62,566	35,845	7,927	16,853	3,479	7,285	2,883	605	92,319	30,939	21,507
Congressional District 4	53,158	29,346	6,368	16,420	2,761	6,892	2,320	258	76,318	27,927	20,959
Congressional District 5	45,734	23,967	6,144	14,325	2,512	8,690	2,918	773	54,486	26,127	20,801
Congressional District 6	91,244	50,497	11,557	25,641	3,443	6,611	2,621	492	124,331	41,742	30,231
Congressional District 7	52,401	30,031	5,931	15,144	2,571	7,925	2,102	476	76,184	28,459	22,200
Congressional District 8	95,706	52,071	13,193	27,500	2,840	8,381	2,867	247	120,619	44,997	29,428
Congressional District 9	42,093	25,389	4,437	10,828	1,445	10,193	2,127	492	69,368	23,184	16,434
Congressional District 10	72,215	43,348	8,282	18,832	2,615	9,374	2,690	405	107,998	33,179	18,422
Congressional District 11	130,399	79,426	15,573	31,429	3,185	6,989	2,432	484	182,924	52,828	29,008
Congressional District 12	86,993	47,786	11,062	25,563	3,235	7,158	1,901	312	115,272	43,592	26,731
Congressional District 13	99,789	45,468	15,897	35,058	5,016	6,017	1,787	168	109,238	48,297	37,659
Congressional District 14	50,835	25,264	7,866	16,153	2,650	7,762	2,637	779	60,330	26,856	24,263
Congressional District 15	56,084	31,444	6,434	16,511	2,134	8,119	2,424	578	81,153	29,399	19,870
Congressional District 16	123,819	67,919	15,029	35,725	3,880	5,373	1,793	365	158,459	51,647	31,333
Congressional District 17	107,005	62,960	13,519	26,380	3,425	7,399	2,347	673	146,272	48,120	24,532
Congressional District 18	96,368	53,944	12,027	27,321	1,953	7,482	1,963	331	127,646	44,532	26,037
Congressional District 19	109,884	64,118	14,506	27,766	2,843	7,040	1,227	355	160,532	45,838	28,008
Congressional District 20	57,393	26,548	9,076	19,066	3,509	11,118	3,368	723	61,022	33,705	23,080
Congressional District 21	96,018	49,412	10,491	32,587	1,402	7,833	1,712	262	118,035	48,061	23,734
Congressional District 22	90,806	41,958	14,903	29,886	3,542	6,138	1,417	431	102,012	40,936	34,743
Congressional District 23	66,819	31,171	9,550	23,631	1,450	8,388	1,971	336	80,724	33,867	26,097
Congressional District 24	41,211	22,020	6,164	11,355	3,204	13,265	3,428	1,155	51,299	25,368	20,462
Congressional District 25	49,231	31,620	4,578	11,440	1,209	16,545	2,569	669	81,908	29,490	20,027
Congressional District 26	47,260	29,339	4,648	11,539	2,032	17,647	1,678	420	78,039	31,910	23,921
Congressional District 27	60,456	32,478	8,469	17,437	2,931	11,726	1,606	479	79,254	33,786	28,335
Georgia											
Congressional District 1	54,470	30,087	7,081	16,278	2,677	8,150	3,662	611	72,219	28,070	18,947
Congressional District 2	57,264	30,813	7,180	18,317	3,151	7,084	3,397	1,008	66,818	33,025	17,440
Congressional District 3	52,125	29,519	5,773	15,683	2,622	8,716	2,839	474	75,015	28,707	16,134
Congressional District 4	35,772	20,882	3,837	10,421	1,658	8,755	2,513	470	54,244	20,893	17,546
Congressional District 5	42,195	17,966	7,546	15,559	2,470	6,541	2,592	627	39,819	24,300	21,879
Congressional District 6	42,234	24,300	4,305	12,952	1,129	6,584	1,020	125	71,332	19,173	13,938
Congressional District 7	27,528	17,001	2,336	7,465	1,267	10,355	1,694	152	55,936	16,161	10,687
Congressional District 8	55,875	31,050	6,324	17,443	3,535	7,600	2,999	684	75,883	29,765	16,551
Congressional District 9	63,534	38,624	7,291	16,358	2,189	8,536	2,869	673	96,759	31,066	17,808
Congressional District 10	48,726	29,751	5,082	13,103	2,966	8,722	3,030	598	75,255	25,744	15,089
Congressional District 11	41,487	23,974	4,202	12,464	1,386	6,109	1,866	464	61,744	19,504	15,508
Congressional District 12	51,734	27,609	6,491	16,825	3,934	8,125	4,268	1,090	69,520	29,712	15,946
Congressional District 13	34,488	20,127	4,239	9,762	1,336	9,525	3,088	529	54,075	19,739	16,173
Congressional District 14	52,011	30,237	5,682	15,090	2,561	7,719	3,457	939	72,699	29,551	16,648
Hawaii											
Congressional District 1	60,659	37,464	6,455	14,780	3,942	17,860	2,819	181	87,670	33,422	18,561
Congressional District 2	50,239	32,969	5,687	10,055	2,511	15,957	3,089	503	82,497	27,009	18,395
Idaho											
Congressional District 1	66,692	39,108	7,802	17,694	2,568	5,941	2,284	241	102,609	26,472	22,134
Congressional District 2	61,125	34,161	7,438	18,196	2,257	5,056	1,799	363	87,033	26,605	19,524

Table D-5: 113th Congressional Districts—Household Relationship, Grandparents, and Marital Status—*Continued*

	Total Householders Age 65 Years and Over	Family Householders 65 Years and Over	Non-Family Householders 65 Years and Over		Persons 65 Years and Over Living in Group Quarters	Grandparents 60 Years and Over Living with Grandchildren			Marital Status - Persons 60 Years and Over		
			Male Living Alone	Female Living Alone		Total	Responsible for Grandchildren	Responsible for Grandchildren and In Poverty	Married	Widowed	Divorced
Illinois											
Congressional District 1	63,639	33,172	8,599	20,434	2,783	10,318	4,216	893	65,540	36,186	21,461
Congressional District 2	60,904	31,493	7,862	20,009	3,267	9,262	3,492	746	64,695	34,000	21,696
Congressional District 3	53,766	28,295	6,987	17,647	2,683	9,089	1,245	189	70,240	32,172	14,229
Congressional District 4	32,366	16,981	4,549	9,981	1,281	10,363	1,671	314	40,584	20,991	10,432
Congressional District 5	52,736	24,919	8,257	18,073	3,146	7,584	959	81	63,882	28,099	15,563
Congressional District 6	53,412	30,701	5,125	16,824	3,426	6,165	901	83	86,168	25,628	14,051
Congressional District 7	49,877	23,286	7,965	17,455	2,373	8,817	3,626	1,277	48,949	25,659	18,866
Congressional District 8	44,160	23,817	5,196	14,354	2,350	8,351	1,023	77	67,305	23,393	15,283
Congressional District 9	69,300	34,157	8,390	25,532	5,677	7,287	868	230	88,034	34,987	18,108
Congressional District 10	51,370	28,167	5,466	16,713	4,375	7,002	808	82	77,361	26,291	15,847
Congressional District 11	42,364	23,040	5,291	13,237	2,540	8,244	1,820	141	64,082	21,738	14,656
Congressional District 12	67,007	33,286	9,322	23,096	5,036	5,449	2,204	489	81,474	35,341	18,981
Congressional District 13	62,715	32,260	8,054	21,011	5,829	4,137	2,077	348	81,915	29,926	19,465
Congressional District 14	43,461	25,953	5,037	11,562	1,683	5,309	595	198	73,641	20,765	12,312
Congressional District 15	75,149	38,320	9,520	26,134	6,068	4,438	2,009	553	97,516	38,858	17,246
Congressional District 16	65,819	35,478	8,249	20,747	5,696	4,716	1,535	121	93,448	32,800	16,869
Congressional District 17	74,168	38,286	9,709	24,889	5,057	5,466	2,324	231	93,633	35,654	21,012
Congressional District 18	70,638	38,453	8,115	22,778	6,101	3,369	1,228	357	101,783	32,388	16,918
Indiana											
Congressional District 1	59,248	32,429	7,551	17,906	3,339	7,787	2,327	181	78,837	33,205	19,083
Congressional District 2	62,647	34,491	7,172	19,802	5,072	5,365	1,968	342	87,607	29,586	16,969
Congressional District 3	60,316	32,238	7,519	19,351	4,748	4,153	1,589	223	84,519	28,929	16,772
Congressional District 4	59,975	32,830	6,715	19,490	4,403	4,809	1,860	125	84,116	30,014	15,568
Congressional District 5	56,560	30,406	6,429	18,800	4,043	4,873	1,413	231	80,449	26,476	17,854
Congressional District 6	68,201	36,030	8,441	22,659	4,957	5,618	2,646	306	92,918	32,548	19,851
Congressional District 7	48,994	24,363	6,968	16,498	3,195	5,933	2,315	418	53,089	25,804	21,546
Congressional District 8	66,676	36,223	8,482	20,780	5,912	5,031	2,390	287	92,746	33,181	19,336
Congressional District 9	60,400	32,121	7,605	19,528	4,189	5,139	1,726	358	83,951	29,907	19,153
Iowa											
Congressional District 1	74,800	39,548	9,591	24,407	7,187	3,663	1,499	88	104,886	34,411	17,543
Congressional District 2	71,833	37,260	8,958	24,268	5,723	4,126	1,648	216	100,299	34,197	18,850
Congressional District 3	61,362	32,533	7,099	20,719	5,228	4,831	1,743	318	88,968	30,192	17,432
Congressional District 4	81,934	42,433	9,670	28,831	8,331	2,687	954	62	111,151	40,172	15,868
Kansas											
Congressional District 1	66,555	33,730	9,034	22,818	6,640	3,401	1,440	93	91,711	32,342	15,120
Congressional District 2	65,186	35,169	7,665	21,458	6,037	4,936	2,062	197	90,250	30,228	18,905
Congressional District 3	50,782	27,476	5,911	16,480	2,939	5,366	1,498	209	73,865	24,512	16,727
Congressional District 4	59,414	30,509	8,013	19,820	4,227	5,774	2,062	285	79,345	29,214	18,193
Kentucky											
Congressional District 1	73,165	38,734	9,508	23,942	5,284	5,419	2,787	649	96,798	38,196	19,515
Congressional District 2	62,186	34,365	7,716	18,903	4,114	5,326	2,434	449	84,516	31,958	17,251
Congressional District 3	63,933	31,711	8,577	22,452	4,599	5,223	2,272	426	75,893	33,300	22,801
Congressional District 4	56,281	31,720	6,809	16,919	4,029	6,925	2,772	256	81,090	29,215	18,129
Congressional District 5	67,095	36,129	9,349	20,528	4,593	8,069	4,753	1,456	88,190	38,919	18,969
Congressional District 6	56,965	30,200	6,857	18,732	3,478	5,233	2,854	443	75,070	27,282	20,978
Louisiana											
Congressional District 1	64,336	34,827	8,155	19,732	2,523	7,590	2,726	494	85,290	34,479	20,422
Congressional District 2	55,094	29,276	8,194	16,497	3,048	10,705	4,876	1,514	60,188	33,916	23,473
Congressional District 3	58,991	32,592	6,605	18,563	4,035	7,389	3,285	687	77,740	31,014	17,831
Congressional District 4	67,450	36,776	8,346	21,291	4,528	8,717	4,313	1,088	83,145	36,685	19,354
Congressional District 5	66,226	36,443	7,609	21,118	6,247	8,094	3,958	966	82,548	37,254	18,401
Congressional District 6	53,661	30,630	6,451	15,492	2,403	6,621	3,085	782	77,793	27,096	16,766
Maine											
Congressional District 1	67,165	33,868	8,739	22,599	4,171	4,072	1,073	126	92,337	31,115	22,849
Congressional District 2	69,161	35,252	10,010	21,283	4,081	3,620	986	122	97,349	31,825	22,244
Maryland											
Congressional District 1	67,990	40,548	7,985	17,916	3,493	8,042	2,182	232	101,826	33,637	18,081
Congressional District 2	52,049	27,218	6,851	16,552	3,143	8,405	2,607	461	67,574	30,752	17,865
Congressional District 3	60,493	29,248	7,457	22,260	3,478	7,553	1,526	192	77,401	31,108	19,286
Congressional District 4	45,816	26,075	5,741	13,005	2,222	10,326	2,320	183	63,033	24,983	17,864
Congressional District 5	44,843	27,727	5,104	10,804	2,700	9,919	2,405	159	72,587	24,548	16,470
Congressional District 6	53,783	28,447	6,816	17,491	3,786	7,826	1,701	77	80,680	27,338	16,082
Congressional District 7	61,093	30,406	9,648	19,362	4,161	9,078	3,024	644	66,632	32,944	20,139
Congressional District 8	61,685	33,076	6,980	20,025	4,620	8,053	1,751	59	90,636	29,951	17,412
Massachusetts											
Congressional District 1	70,654	33,564	9,728	25,375	5,295	6,098	1,846	209	88,322	37,246	21,430
Congressional District 2	58,359	28,026	8,624	20,046	5,694	6,754	1,427	150	76,478	30,966	18,981
Congressional District 3	54,213	27,381	7,862	17,760	4,353	7,768	1,164	133	75,516	28,802	17,814
Congressional District 4	59,690	32,217	6,733	19,445	4,949	6,700	866	69	86,632	29,129	16,331
Congressional District 5	65,582	32,887	8,972	22,303	4,617	7,611	1,260	105	92,199	34,033	18,929
Congressional District 6	68,756	34,740	8,701	23,437	5,121	7,500	1,650	164	92,199	34,033	21,423
Congressional District 7	48,752	20,235	8,538	19,018	2,833	6,761	1,679	587	49,342	21,612	16,394
Congressional District 8	66,721	32,082	9,884	23,364	5,775	8,211	1,494	215	80,463	34,815	18,382
Congressional District 9	83,918	44,160	10,338	26,514	5,334	6,345	1,515	239	111,424	39,913	23,609

Table D-5: 113th Congressional Districts—Household Relationship, Grandparents, and Marital Status—*Continued*

	Total Householders Age 65 Years and Over	Family Householders 65 Years and Over	Non-Family Householders 65 Years and Over		Persons 65 Years and Over Living in Group Quarters	Grandparents 60 Years and Over Living with Grandchildren			Marital Status - Persons 60 Years and Over		
			Male Living Alone	Female Living Alone		Total	Responsible for Grandchildren	Responsible for Grandchildren and In Poverty	Married	Widowed	Divorced
Michigan											
Congressional District 1	86,476	47,908	12,432	24,342	5,353	3,598	1,628	231	122,751	36,479	21,251
Congressional District 2	58,368	32,871	6,787	17,631	3,354	4,776	1,268	208	83,409	27,525	16,181
Congressional District 3	56,348	31,260	6,285	17,761	3,543	4,225	1,262	146	81,964	24,913	16,629
Congressional District 4	70,829	40,051	8,356	20,888	3,950	3,971	1,202	248	103,041	31,790	17,349
Congressional District 5	70,085	37,168	9,393	22,014	3,762	5,865	2,440	473	87,238	35,066	21,435
Congressional District 6	63,960	34,979	8,118	19,616	3,359	4,788	1,632	282	86,890	30,242	20,129
Congressional District 7	63,933	36,112	7,589	18,841	4,191	5,458	1,975	252	92,308	29,630	18,816
Congressional District 8	52,661	29,551	6,559	15,634	1,904	4,544	1,136	52	78,293	22,764	17,655
Congressional District 9	72,707	34,561	10,264	26,378	3,388	5,896	1,140	110	80,053	38,445	22,545
Congressional District 10	63,850	35,846	7,369	19,462	3,264	5,483	1,221	172	95,807	30,824	15,585
Congressional District 11	60,804	32,825	7,445	19,450	2,341	5,620	1,212	81	86,353	27,329	17,479
Congressional District 12	55,781	27,029	8,151	19,343	2,349	6,295	2,124	283	66,035	28,382	19,373
Congressional District 13	59,820	27,932	9,935	20,720	2,650	8,546	2,932	762	50,443	35,340	26,119
Congressional District 14	63,216	31,409	8,885	21,631	3,224	8,510	2,730	596	66,153	35,225	24,455
Minnesota											
Congressional District 1	64,269	33,531	7,449	22,116	5,898	2,567	778	124	88,944	29,521	12,738
Congressional District 2	44,625	24,875	4,847	14,095	2,628	3,183	760	54	70,636	19,152	12,043
Congressional District 3	52,318	28,282	5,693	17,471	1,647	3,251	566	58	79,528	20,596	15,632
Congressional District 4	52,030	25,585	6,637	18,619	3,536	4,382	1,006	174	69,018	22,742	16,716
Congressional District 5	49,190	20,274	8,043	19,151	4,892	3,403	1,143	302	52,326	22,116	19,370
Congressional District 6	40,864	22,981	4,466	12,564	2,620	4,167	967	74	67,666	17,626	10,050
Congressional District 7	73,648	38,668	9,462	24,056	7,388	2,399	1,029	154	102,079	34,645	13,336
Congressional District 8	72,554	38,407	10,150	22,500	5,456	3,210	1,256	104	101,210	31,081	18,528
Mississippi											
Congressional District 1	63,562	36,236	7,100	19,546	3,732	8,100	3,729	598	86,804	34,889	17,579
Congressional District 2	58,279	31,106	7,568	18,480	3,866	8,935	4,052	1,470	67,501	36,689	16,986
Congressional District 3	65,405	36,690	7,790	20,166	4,360	8,270	3,905	909	86,214	35,856	17,458
Congressional District 4	61,651	34,690	7,409	18,120	3,130	8,583	4,180	981	80,770	32,267	19,312
Missouri											
Congressional District 1	61,438	27,594	9,375	23,070	4,120	6,460	2,468	466	60,224	32,502	23,919
Congressional District 2	73,521	40,941	7,593	23,874	6,793	4,850	1,111	56	105,696	35,408	18,087
Congressional District 3	62,537	36,530	6,823	17,986	3,428	6,444	2,273	280	94,070	29,472	15,229
Congressional District 4	67,398	37,914	8,229	20,236	4,963	4,753	1,720	333	94,970	31,833	18,688
Congressional District 5	66,508	32,479	9,466	23,114	4,376	5,844	1,884	297	76,165	32,861	24,809
Congressional District 6	65,556	35,834	8,293	20,263	6,271	5,158	1,699	231	93,721	32,901	17,875
Congressional District 7	71,462	39,644	8,823	21,454	4,759	5,148	1,968	353	99,843	34,538	21,045
Congressional District 8	75,680	41,068	9,815	23,488	6,905	6,116	2,890	579	104,208	38,662	19,656
Montana											
Congressional District (at Large)	97,403	50,973	14,728	29,424	5,566	6,303	2,698	570	136,470	42,506	30,926
Nebraska											
Congressional District 1	50,998	27,056	6,481	16,664	3,972	2,750	1,208	185	74,834	22,799	12,213
Congressional District 2	41,658	21,330	4,870	14,700	2,842	3,750	1,384	367	55,738	20,472	13,120
Congressional District 3	66,972	33,862	9,009	22,848	6,512	2,689	1,342	113	91,968	32,228	14,151
Nevada											
Congressional District 1	49,790	22,655	10,399	14,185	1,302	9,061	3,066	503	54,736	25,685	26,247
Congressional District 2	57,060	32,065	8,830	14,062	1,822	7,252	2,542	247	83,749	23,063	25,799
Congressional District 3	49,698	29,379	6,930	11,138	937	9,040	1,759	138	80,141	22,214	21,291
Congressional District 4	48,132	27,955	6,824	11,403	1,348	8,460	2,652	434	70,279	21,992	20,421
New Hampshire											
Congressional District 1	55,685	30,521	6,608	16,605	3,993	4,692	972	79	83,564	25,474	18,619
Congressional District 2	57,617	31,041	7,563	17,216	4,188	4,520	996	105	85,369	26,206	19,410
New Jersey											
Congressional District 1	60,165	30,891	7,518	20,603	3,614	9,296	1,910	237	76,455	34,773	17,579
Congressional District 2	70,540	37,326	9,244	21,881	4,229	9,045	2,287	484	93,592	37,363	19,268
Congressional District 3	78,363	41,498	9,170	25,796	4,005	7,855	2,029	190	103,710	41,717	19,360
Congressional District 4	78,391	40,028	8,918	27,934	4,195	7,876	1,407	132	97,998	40,407	18,740
Congressional District 5	62,712	36,383	6,446	18,459	5,262	8,775	1,472	204	94,360	33,865	15,167
Congressional District 6	49,969	27,322	6,180	15,539	3,122	10,382	1,383	66	72,541	29,769	15,682
Congressional District 7	58,088	32,165	5,991	18,905	3,970	8,796	1,165	53	87,400	30,000	14,857
Congressional District 8	41,136	19,864	6,244	13,755	2,387	10,176	2,019	444	51,861	23,053	14,340
Congressional District 9	58,242	29,841	8,209	19,033	1,440	11,317	1,792	211	73,175	32,906	15,501
Congressional District 10	51,555	23,804	7,664	18,752	2,602	10,509	2,409	450	55,342	30,365	18,023
Congressional District 11	66,166	36,144	7,268	21,341	6,022	8,441	1,397	26	99,391	35,533	16,951
Congressional District 12	58,274	31,592	7,131	18,398	3,465	8,716	1,167	127	78,409	32,279	16,216
New Mexico											
Congressional District 1	56,382	29,506	8,063	17,144	1,844	7,690	2,655	505	74,447	23,690	25,313
Congressional District 2	63,242	36,759	8,839	16,586	2,653	7,410	3,311	754	86,547	29,122	19,771
Congressional District 3	57,824	31,669	8,072	16,059	2,109	7,414	3,025	855	78,814	25,875	21,916

Table D-5: 113th Congressional Districts—Household Relationship, Grandparents, and Marital Status—*Continued*

	Total Householders Age 65 Years and Over	Family Householders 65 Years and Over	Non-Family Householders 65 Years and Over		Persons 65 Years and Over Living in Group Quarters	Grandparents 60 Years and Over Living with Grandchildren			Marital Status - Persons 60 Years and Over		
			Male Living Alone	Female Living Alone		Total	Responsible for Grandchildren	Responsible for Grandchildren and In Poverty	Married	Widowed	Divorced
New York											
Congressional District 1................	61,352	35,532	6,780	16,978	5,095	9,171	1,277	329	90,337	32,980	16,207
Congressional District 2................	53,807	32,215	5,426	14,910	3,540	13,837	1,346	121	76,228	34,233	13,767
Congressional District 3................	72,842	44,043	5,880	21,533	5,406	9,696	1,316	51	111,965	38,532	14,765
Congressional District 4................	60,479	34,666	6,066	18,401	3,751	12,504	1,550	92	88,966	35,003	14,244
Congressional District 5................	46,869	28,164	4,431	12,967	4,477	17,455	3,282	513	68,067	31,291	16,735
Congressional District 6................	61,218	31,573	7,784	20,649	3,799	13,673	2,081	463	89,044	35,960	13,814
Congressional District 7................	40,174	19,709	5,485	13,810	1,732	10,155	2,878	1,114	50,062	22,625	12,422
Congressional District 8................	57,410	26,920	8,217	20,924	4,724	12,555	3,263	1,224	59,691	33,941	16,856
Congressional District 9................	52,588	25,732	6,679	18,884	3,210	11,672	3,668	958	62,430	28,826	17,194
Congressional District 10..............	63,915	24,834	11,668	25,434	2,693	6,883	1,824	476	71,487	24,971	19,504
Congressional District 11..............	61,466	32,268	7,765	20,724	4,383	10,571	2,255	558	85,716	37,135	13,493
Congressional District 12..............	69,281	23,759	13,278	30,140	2,964	2,671	443	61	59,105	24,882	22,174
Congressional District 13..............	51,805	21,145	8,593	20,551	4,766	11,295	2,784	1,322	45,426	27,814	22,115
Congressional District 14..............	47,181	23,268	6,180	16,090	4,313	10,992	1,880	275	60,584	26,854	15,688
Congressional District 15..............	39,856	16,807	7,000	15,224	1,620	10,337	2,967	1,353	38,293	19,621	15,450
Congressional District 16..............	65,395	31,665	9,229	23,506	6,808	10,734	2,096	291	79,654	35,303	17,403
Congressional District 17..............	59,751	33,656	6,102	18,877	5,862	9,858	1,182	35	88,751	30,178	13,672
Congressional District 18..............	54,771	30,513	6,794	16,016	4,441	8,597	1,365	23	80,192	27,860	14,523
Congressional District 19..............	71,306	36,610	10,424	21,602	6,212	6,008	1,685	161	98,829	35,239	20,078
Congressional District 20..............	64,691	30,620	9,503	22,678	6,410	4,390	1,136	114	79,657	35,627	18,318
Congressional District 21..............	66,841	34,497	8,988	21,144	4,772	4,492	1,679	288	90,923	32,914	16,607
Congressional District 22..............	71,222	35,094	10,222	23,954	6,666	4,856	1,037	200	92,080	37,116	20,380
Congressional District 23..............	69,521	35,182	9,674	22,768	5,721	4,660	1,608	187	94,772	34,151	19,285
Congressional District 24..............	65,266	32,355	9,295	21,947	5,304	5,019	1,310	138	84,512	31,928	18,396
Congressional District 25..............	65,975	33,334	8,292	22,734	5,180	4,953	1,446	193	81,651	31,852	18,112
Congressional District 26..............	74,605	34,125	10,557	28,656	4,750	4,164	1,156	258	77,113	40,403	20,633
Congressional District 27..............	70,022	37,702	8,304	22,423	6,178	4,794	1,325	275	101,139	34,701	17,125
North Carolina											
Congressional District 1................	66,554	32,651	8,680	23,677	6,487	9,060	4,355	1,434	72,935	39,952	20,600
Congressional District 2................	55,632	30,446	6,815	17,357	2,801	6,027	1,948	365	81,465	29,045	14,966
Congressional District 3................	62,436	35,506	7,863	17,826	2,387	6,487	2,861	741	89,707	29,272	17,493
Congressional District 4................	45,224	22,749	5,307	16,179	2,726	5,735	2,218	514	59,161	22,778	17,083
Congressional District 5................	70,921	39,729	7,993	22,292	3,918	5,972	2,548	560	100,522	33,945	17,821
Congressional District 6................	72,716	40,257	7,421	24,017	4,074	5,898	2,124	369	101,865	34,850	18,227
Congressional District 7................	71,476	40,456	7,778	21,806	3,185	6,415	2,959	619	102,699	34,506	18,666
Congressional District 8................	62,266	35,134	7,084	18,692	3,411	9,019	3,904	977	84,931	32,899	17,196
Congressional District 9................	48,157	27,714	4,649	15,029	2,038	5,546	978	109	77,977	24,230	14,875
Congressional District 10..............	69,278	37,712	8,662	21,479	5,088	7,125	2,914	791	94,146	37,782	21,079
Congressional District 11..............	89,001	49,638	11,254	26,169	5,121	6,020	2,689	539	124,914	41,809	23,487
Congressional District 12..............	41,118	21,172	5,419	13,613	2,873	6,415	2,559	829	47,899	24,212	16,290
Congressional District 13..............	53,396	30,401	5,857	16,072	2,317	5,225	1,131	148	83,771	25,794	14,542
North Dakota											
Congressional District (at Large) ..	62,826	31,015	8,974	21,861	6,736	2,707	991	166	87,172	30,588	13,497
Ohio											
Congressional District 1................	56,278	29,211	7,140	18,875	4,042	5,350	2,085	337	74,366	26,926	18,610
Congressional District 2................	65,963	33,114	8,778	22,963	5,169	5,472	1,663	503	85,165	34,001	19,689
Congressional District 3................	43,825	20,297	6,990	15,540	2,167	6,993	2,186	333	46,212	23,529	20,981
Congressional District 4................	67,395	37,100	7,504	21,719	4,890	4,419	1,680	155	94,705	31,976	17,408
Congressional District 5................	69,228	37,251	8,143	22,461	5,387	3,292	1,522	128	96,421	33,402	16,620
Congressional District 6................	77,660	41,743	9,575	24,781	5,738	6,498	2,839	473	104,783	40,593	21,177
Congressional District 7................	68,916	38,558	8,603	20,449	5,980	5,422	1,901	176	98,553	34,284	18,359
Congressional District 8................	64,548	35,718	7,668	20,178	4,309	5,605	2,013	267	90,044	32,905	17,023
Congressional District 9................	64,955	30,977	9,461	23,131	4,270	5,574	2,177	560	71,642	33,578	23,081
Congressional District 10..............	71,934	35,444	10,460	24,489	5,058	5,797	2,089	344	86,723	35,079	25,426
Congressional District 11..............	69,855	30,473	11,084	26,473	5,230	6,745	2,530	835	63,806	38,393	27,907
Congressional District 12..............	57,210	31,301	6,431	18,183	3,327	4,806	1,516	310	86,502	26,324	18,948
Congressional District 13..............	75,629	37,729	10,760	25,455	4,703	6,138	2,261	314	86,916	40,447	24,842
Congressional District 14..............	73,757	39,852	8,881	23,533	4,528	5,678	1,453	34	101,657	36,328	19,990
Congressional District 15..............	57,635	31,070	6,705	18,704	3,568	6,050	2,143	272	81,261	27,790	17,099
Congressional District 16..............	76,176	40,897	9,351	24,409	5,329	6,001	1,591	0	104,516	37,232	20,041
Oklahoma											
Congressional District 1................	62,489	33,136	7,955	20,516	2,995	6,140	2,433	485	82,042	30,080	21,498
Congressional District 2................	77,562	42,838	10,639	22,567	5,459	7,583	3,921	830	104,300	38,275	22,697
Congressional District 3................	68,953	37,794	9,275	20,613	4,629	5,979	2,632	436	95,505	34,421	18,161
Congressional District 4................	61,389	33,184	8,019	19,209	3,865	5,846	2,465	347	83,307	31,343	19,053
Congressional District 5................	61,020	30,922	8,652	20,290	3,316	6,929	3,169	809	75,275	30,441	22,803
Oregon											
Congressional District 1................	57,497	29,729	6,701	19,353	1,954	6,083	2,086	404	80,308	25,749	22,604
Congressional District 2................	84,449	46,096	11,035	24,653	3,524	5,831	2,365	178	116,982	34,448	30,767
Congressional District 3................	54,792	27,522	7,575	17,564	3,089	6,490	1,506	212	70,731	25,362	25,826
Congressional District 4................	84,442	45,341	11,188	24,701	2,987	5,978	2,218	350	115,764	35,693	32,319
Congressional District 5................	70,703	37,727	8,289	22,637	3,600	6,489	2,147	274	102,014	29,464	26,219

Table D-5: 113th Congressional Districts—Household Relationship, Grandparents, and Marital Status—*Continued*

	Total Householders Age 65 Years and Over	Family Householders 65 Years and Over	Non-Family Householders 65 Years and Over		Persons 65 Years and Over Living in Group Quarters	Grandparents 60 Years and Over Living with Grandchildren			Marital Status - Persons 60 Years and Over		
			Male Living Alone	Female Living Alone		Total	Responsible for Grandchildren	Responsible for Grandchildren and In Poverty	Married	Widowed	Divorced
Pennsylvania											
Congressional District 1	49,999	22,156	8,628	18,058	2,490	7,569	1,902	340	48,448	30,541	16,667
Congressional District 2	63,296	26,283	10,263	25,067	4,890	7,333	2,103	670	51,231	34,477	22,854
Congressional District 3	73,915	38,353	9,753	24,222	5,815	4,090	1,411	238	96,567	37,710	17,737
Congressional District 4	66,376	35,300	8,239	21,208	3,941	5,021	1,654	473	91,978	32,337	17,524
Congressional District 5	72,084	37,546	9,348	23,795	5,153	4,493	1,639	89	96,533	36,464	16,296
Congressional District 6	62,853	34,191	7,121	19,991	4,674	5,487	960	112	88,795	31,145	15,612
Congressional District 7	66,840	36,267	7,567	21,792	5,217	6,349	1,123	95	95,257	35,749	13,961
Congressional District 8	63,106	36,469	7,120	17,798	3,917	8,018	1,378	21	96,948	33,642	14,669
Congressional District 9	78,422	41,019	9,960	26,006	5,514	5,109	1,615	154	101,156	42,257	16,962
Congressional District 10	72,892	41,295	8,358	21,290	5,005	6,008	1,216	210	107,245	36,421	16,813
Congressional District 11	72,457	37,390	9,500	24,118	5,788	4,528	1,009	51	96,257	37,995	17,520
Congressional District 12	83,948	43,273	10,455	28,853	4,652	5,494	1,741	184	106,956	44,094	16,617
Congressional District 13	62,168	30,755	8,487	21,929	6,813	8,755	1,629	462	77,181	37,589	17,043
Congressional District 14	78,595	33,647	12,554	30,915	4,955	5,097	1,890	276	75,675	43,148	22,977
Congressional District 15	65,964	35,081	8,877	20,458	5,060	6,377	1,124	198	91,009	34,230	16,402
Congressional District 16	61,178	32,242	7,627	19,444	5,791	5,890	1,467	384	84,908	30,053	14,908
Congressional District 17	73,422	36,941	10,453	24,519	6,644	7,050	1,943	193	91,213	42,405	17,308
Congressional District 18	80,713	42,490	9,759	26,962	5,398	4,718	1,588	183	104,580	42,546	18,874
Rhode Island											
Congressional District 1	48,757	22,902	6,655	18,015	4,737	4,455	1,299	195	58,588	25,722	15,165
Congressional District 2	47,532	23,756	6,268	16,226	3,238	4,545	987	158	61,252	25,082	15,408
South Carolina											
Congressional District 1	60,335	36,454	6,192	16,688	1,740	6,797	2,314	261	91,985	27,576	16,218
Congressional District 2	53,496	30,921	5,973	15,833	2,329	6,244	2,894	772	78,012	27,724	15,399
Congressional District 3	64,787	36,694	7,785	19,486	3,524	7,283	3,117	912	91,905	32,686	15,192
Congressional District 4	56,127	31,554	6,360	17,404	2,578	6,460	2,352	727	78,265	29,733	14,667
Congressional District 5	58,130	34,354	6,883	16,142	2,808	6,789	3,198	758	82,129	29,570	15,309
Congressional District 6	54,028	28,871	7,632	16,383	3,242	7,454	3,685	936	66,847	31,533	14,851
Congressional District 7	69,540	38,536	8,946	20,681	2,880	7,792	2,568	322	95,461	36,515	17,541
South Dakota											
Congressional District (at Large)	74,354	38,043	10,505	24,164	8,575	4,207	1,988	537	102,538	35,851	18,425
Tennessee											
Congressional District 1	78,559	44,003	9,192	23,770	4,318	7,070	3,484	626	106,763	38,784	21,041
Congressional District 2	67,244	36,257	8,875	21,144	3,257	6,433	2,608	332	93,336	33,266	19,617
Congressional District 3	71,872	40,089	9,039	21,819	3,642	7,701	3,420	541	96,840	35,891	22,290
Congressional District 4	57,673	33,520	6,459	16,531	3,295	6,460	2,340	441	82,312	30,023	18,022
Congressional District 5	48,840	24,879	6,560	16,059	2,656	6,196	2,090	342	61,531	25,165	19,828
Congressional District 6	67,865	40,459	6,982	19,383	3,416	7,635	2,653	474	98,460	33,936	18,212
Congressional District 7	56,764	31,674	7,152	16,993	3,384	6,392	2,645	437	82,525	29,474	16,414
Congressional District 8	61,894	35,988	6,693	18,220	3,895	8,304	2,996	481	90,489	31,928	18,311
Congressional District 9	44,473	21,795	6,475	15,136	2,552	7,292	2,837	836	47,553	27,625	21,232
Texas											
Congressional District 1	63,924	35,004	8,357	19,603	4,330	6,605	3,040	996	86,563	33,984	17,865
Congressional District 2	35,897	21,919	4,810	8,522	1,730	6,561	1,351	92	64,923	16,945	13,562
Congressional District 3	33,448	20,829	3,092	9,037	1,014	7,286	801	107	62,032	15,328	12,036
Congressional District 4	64,787	37,052	8,209	18,368	4,837	8,027	3,271	758	92,551	32,762	19,933
Congressional District 5	53,103	29,427	6,754	15,860	3,907	8,272	3,355	865	73,772	28,956	18,152
Congressional District 6	40,426	23,609	4,403	11,763	2,112	8,122	3,008	243	65,545	20,128	15,144
Congressional District 7	40,123	20,664	5,413	13,427	753	5,895	822	40	60,249	19,251	14,155
Congressional District 8	49,965	30,247	5,145	13,630	2,403	8,030	2,618	526	77,849	24,810	16,377
Congressional District 9	31,161	17,235	4,082	9,113	1,655	10,591	2,878	817	47,404	20,270	13,960
Congressional District 10	43,255	24,330	4,984	12,953	3,040	6,257	1,613	319	67,928	23,070	14,301
Congressional District 11	65,403	35,569	9,244	19,383	4,007	6,967	3,020	622	89,443	32,203	18,793
Congressional District 12	48,788	27,311	5,875	14,944	3,311	5,964	2,043	395	69,441	23,698	18,497
Congressional District 13	60,794	33,301	7,637	18,673	4,363	6,805	3,362	609	84,136	30,325	17,256
Congressional District 14	52,832	28,820	8,070	14,993	3,071	6,863	2,726	353	71,050	29,526	18,956
Congressional District 15	40,468	25,409	4,838	9,686	1,877	11,530	2,870	1,294	63,338	22,708	9,391
Congressional District 16	45,848	27,415	5,042	12,211	1,530	12,218	3,642	1,103	61,917	25,547	14,977
Congressional District 17	46,729	25,590	5,584	14,644	3,556	5,230	1,812	337	65,207	24,026	15,405
Congressional District 18	36,168	19,986	5,141	10,167	1,704	9,076	2,843	773	44,342	21,920	16,606
Congressional District 19	56,285	30,880	6,748	17,786	4,086	7,133	3,361	828	74,007	30,112	15,273
Congressional District 20	43,172	25,117	4,944	11,902	2,037	10,145	2,444	667	56,893	23,253	16,693
Congressional District 21	60,200	34,202	7,051	17,679	3,085	6,777	2,099	227	88,998	24,911	20,870
Congressional District 22	32,218	20,639	2,973	7,926	1,427	9,868	1,765	166	61,314	18,158	11,508
Congressional District 23	45,265	28,898	5,232	10,731	1,701	11,219	3,857	1,378	73,381	23,846	11,867
Congressional District 24	38,054	20,886	4,831	11,424	1,679	6,774	1,625	299	60,276	19,674	14,731
Congressional District 25	50,768	31,172	5,150	13,206	3,038	6,767	2,248	157	78,869	22,983	16,018
Congressional District 26	30,049	18,264	3,007	8,227	1,300	7,735	1,709	225	56,258	14,639	11,291
Congressional District 27	58,692	33,917	7,133	16,525	3,894	9,041	3,414	542	82,461	29,565	19,321
Congressional District 28	38,665	25,134	3,931	8,932	1,698	13,099	3,753	1,258	67,588	20,028	10,093
Congressional District 29	28,978	16,666	3,749	7,731	979	10,637	2,657	720	40,268	17,785	12,438
Congressional District 30	38,028	20,364	4,872	11,614	2,308	9,243	2,979	974	47,727	22,688	18,164

Table D-5: 113th Congressional Districts—Household Relationship, Grandparents, and Marital Status—*Continued*

	Total Householders Age 65 Years and Over	Family Householders 65 Years and Over	Non-Family Householders 65 Years and Over		Persons 65 Years and Over Living in Group Quarters	Grandparents 60 Years and Over Living with Grandchildren			Marital Status - Persons 60 Years and Over		
			Male Living Alone	Female Living Alone		Total	Responsible for Grandchildren	Responsible for Grandchildren and In Poverty	Married	Widowed	Divorced
Texas—Cont.											
Congressional District 31.............	39,647	23,722	4,341	10,820	2,216	7,076	1,744	263	65,952	18,370	13,495
Congressional District 32.............	44,912	25,523	4,831	13,355	1,938	7,285	2,180	352	66,798	20,639	16,465
Congressional District 33.............	32,269	17,587	4,205	9,701	1,548	9,429	2,819	806	41,708	18,730	13,709
Congressional District 34.............	48,254	30,534	5,178	11,623	2,810	13,219	4,042	1,463	75,552	25,663	11,023
Congressional District 35.............	37,093	19,351	5,238	11,501	2,446	10,563	3,043	984	45,459	20,802	17,643
Congressional District 36.............	53,321	31,964	6,049	14,388	2,832	7,658	3,616	864	79,990	26,757	16,446
Utah											
Congressional District 1...............	39,016	24,690	3,897	10,131	984	5,527	1,749	79	64,610	14,317	9,760
Congressional District 2...............	49,485	29,852	6,284	12,664	1,491	5,888	1,885	175	74,448	19,345	12,644
Congressional District 3...............	36,967	24,328	3,123	9,123	1,035	7,227	2,191	323	63,549	14,445	9,281
Congressional District 4...............	34,924	20,477	4,008	9,919	1,121	7,218	1,541	120	53,144	16,040	12,179
Vermont											
Congressional District (at Large) ..	60,018	30,812	8,035	19,074	3,912	3,130	853	70	84,315	25,310	20,094
Virginia											
Congressional District 1...............	56,291	34,333	6,011	14,505	1,994	8,879	2,220	44	88,937	25,347	15,691
Congressional District 2...............	54,078	29,983	5,799	17,103	2,197	7,039	2,143	206	75,024	26,705	16,851
Congressional District 3...............	53,307	25,978	7,499	18,684	2,754	7,787	2,810	492	55,284	31,396	21,560
Congressional District 4...............	53,177	31,591	5,496	14,991	2,990	9,200	2,444	167	79,425	28,915	16,127
Congressional District 5...............	77,295	43,275	9,960	22,830	3,981	7,936	3,019	733	107,542	37,218	20,551
Congressional District 6...............	74,617	39,933	9,506	23,927	4,270	6,881	2,589	378	98,944	36,275	19,126
Congressional District 7...............	59,890	34,420	5,953	18,340	2,459	7,276	2,567	326	90,238	28,315	17,529
Congressional District 8...............	44,714	22,183	6,566	14,620	1,704	6,008	1,457	336	61,271	19,495	16,163
Congressional District 9...............	80,517	43,929	10,036	25,506	4,135	6,896	3,463	801	104,305	42,487	19,592
Congressional District 10.............	38,090	23,880	3,263	9,896	971	9,358	1,968	49	75,506	18,724	9,999
Congressional District 11.............	39,173	23,989	4,034	10,202	1,033	9,912	1,641	97	75,389	19,386	13,316
Washington											
Congressional District 1...............	45,144	25,876	5,022	13,047	1,766	6,113	1,800	154	75,090	19,721	16,709
Congressional District 2...............	56,310	30,144	7,074	17,436	2,541	4,935	1,354	125	80,110	24,595	22,118
Congressional District 3...............	60,556	33,859	7,847	17,160	2,158	6,069	1,986	196	88,876	25,782	21,004
Congressional District 4...............	49,062	27,427	6,357	14,103	3,073	7,045	2,095	478	73,421	23,183	15,583
Congressional District 5...............	61,573	31,733	8,879	19,186	3,785	4,213	1,394	154	84,622	27,306	22,199
Congressional District 6...............	68,148	37,113	9,328	19,349	3,860	4,926	1,560	176	99,045	28,725	25,496
Congressional District 7...............	56,152	24,075	8,899	20,910	4,014	4,006	709	102	66,930	21,906	24,932
Congressional District 8...............	43,636	24,763	5,118	12,067	1,536	6,693	1,387	162	71,065	18,423	16,072
Congressional District 9...............	49,636	24,450	7,563	16,068	3,338	8,507	1,510	246	65,321	23,715	20,771
Congressional District 10.............	51,551	27,258	6,321	16,120	2,498	5,269	1,234	107	73,952	23,444	19,749
West Virginia											
Congressional District 1...............	66,039	33,356	9,342	22,285	3,608	4,305	1,542	140	83,609	34,942	16,440
Congressional District 2...............	63,481	33,953	9,305	19,020	2,560	5,029	2,308	465	82,819	32,631	18,163
Congressional District 3...............	67,431	36,263	8,853	21,087	3,159	6,137	3,065	648	86,666	38,135	17,831
Wisconsin											
Congressional District 1...............	59,452	31,511	7,580	19,106	2,667	4,965	1,377	90	83,413	28,728	16,753
Congressional District 2...............	55,307	28,832	6,337	18,650	3,132	2,932	730	93	79,363	23,698	16,985
Congressional District 3...............	67,859	34,927	9,387	22,132	4,909	3,166	900	123	93,628	31,098	16,134
Congressional District 4...............	48,766	20,295	8,280	18,589	3,033	5,412	1,595	391	48,126	25,802	19,176
Congressional District 5...............	68,769	34,162	8,064	25,502	4,852	2,381	596	22	92,700	33,033	15,665
Congressional District 6...............	69,461	36,422	9,328	22,464	5,497	2,447	866	59	96,746	33,425	15,671
Congressional District 7...............	76,850	41,754	10,650	22,688	5,600	3,016	909	65	110,604	33,661	17,156
Congressional District 8...............	64,101	34,149	7,759	20,956	4,736	3,109	1,077	160	92,555	28,772	15,260
Wyoming											
Congressional District (at Large) ..	45,398	24,392	6,444	13,685	2,424	3,602	1,744	198	67,344	19,736	14,812

PART E

EDUCATION AND LANGUAGE SPOKEN AT HOME

EDUCATION AND LANGUAGE SPOKEN AT HOME

Today's population age 65 and over was mostly born before 1950. It includes generations born at a time when college, and even high school educations, weren't as universally accepted or expected as they are today. This factor is reflected in the educational attainment levels of the older population and also across geographic areas. Also, the nation wasn't as racially and ethnically diverse as today and while European languages would often be a primary language at home, English was spoken by most. Today, immigration from many different origin countries has added to the mix of languages spoken and immigration has even impacted the older population through family unification. These differences are shown in the data on education and language spoken.

Education

Nationally, 33.9 percent of the population over 65 years has a high school or equivalent education but less than one in four (22.2 percent) have a bachelor's degree or higher. Among the states, California has the lowest percent of people with only a high school education at 23.3 percent while nearly half of Iowa's older population (46.0 percent) have not gone beyond high school. In the District of Columbia, 36.9 percent of residents 65 and over have a bachelor's degree or higher (the nation's highest) compared to only 12.3 percent in West Virginia. Colorado is the only other state where 30 percent or more of its older residents have a college education. In 465 counties the percent of 65 and over with a high school education exceeds that of the nation and in 24 counties it's greater than 50 percent. Armstrong County, Pennsylvania has the highest rate at 56.7 percent while at 13.9 percent Webb County, Texas is lowest. More than 50 percent (52.5) of Marin County, California residents 65 and over have bachelor's degrees which is two and a half times the national rate of 22.2 percent. More than 300 counties are above the national average but in 26 counties, less than 10 percent of the population has a college education. The lowest is Bullit County, Kentucky with 6.2 percent.

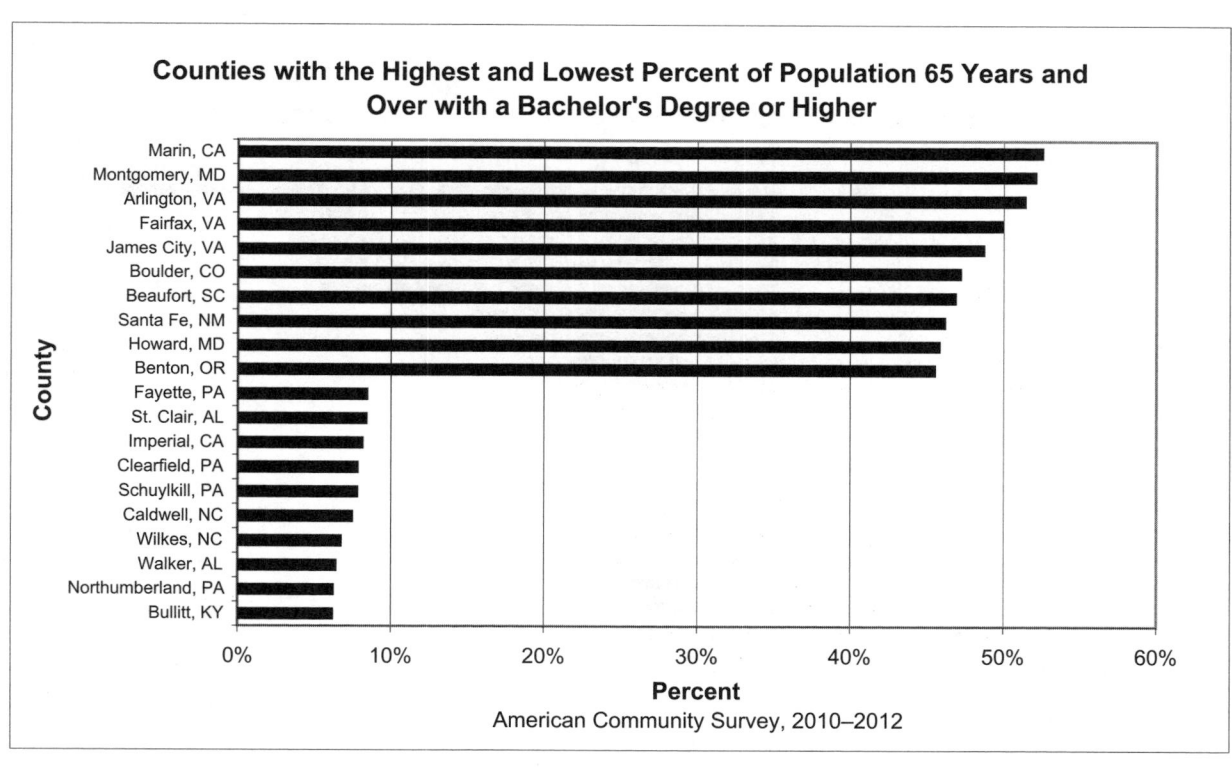

American Community Survey, 2010–2012

In 130 cities, the percent of older residents with only a high school education is above the national rate and Hammond, Indiana at 48.6 percent is the highest. Palo Alto, California is the city with the lowest percent of persons with only a high school education and it's also the city with the highest percent (68.4 percent) of residents with a bachelor's degree or higher. In only 10 cities is the percent of older residents with a bachelor's degree over 50 percent. South Gate, California is the lowest at 2.2 percent. Linwood, California and Camden, New Jersey are also among the cities with the lowest percent of bachelor's degree holders. The Altoona, Pennsylvania metropolitan area has the highest percent (55.9 percent) of persons with only a high school education and, while not the lowest, only 9.4 percent have a bachelor's degree or higher. The Laredo, Texas metro area has the lowest percent of high school diploma holders at 13.9 percent. Only six metropolitan areas have greater than 40 percent of their senior population with bachelor's degrees or higher: Ann Arbor, Michigan (40.4 percent), Barnstable Town, Massachusetts (40.2 percent), Boulder, Colorado (47.2 percent), Corvalis, Oregon (45.5 percent), Ithaca, New York (42.9 percent) and Santa Fe, New Mexico (46.2 percent). Residents of Congressional District 9 in Pennsylvania have the highest percent of high school only education and only 11.4 percent hold bachelor's degrees or higher. But New York's 15th Congressional District has the lowest percent of college degree holders at 6.0 percent. A total of 189 congressional districts have greater than the national average of college degree holders, but only 14 have greater than 40 percent.

Language Spoken

Not surprisingly, nationwide, more than 85 percent of the population over age 65 speaks English at home while 6.6 percent speak Spanish at home, 4.5 percent speak an Indo-European language, and 2.8 percent speak an Asian language. Many states have very low percentages of residents speaking a language other than English: 21 have less than 1 percent Spanish speakers, 11 have less than 1 percent Indo-European speakers, and 33 have less than 1 percent Asian language speakers. New Mexico and California have the lowest percent of English speaking seniors at 63.3 percent and 65.7 percent, respectively. They also have high percentages of Spanish speaking population at 29.5 percent in New Mexico and 15.7 percent in California. Texas also has a high percentage of Spanish language speakers at 20.0 percent. Twenty-eight percent of the Hawaiian senior population speaks an Asian language at home and California is a distant second with 11.5 percent Asian speakers. Forty-three states have less than the national average of Asian speakers while 37 states are less than the national figure for Indo-European languages.

Webb County, Texas has the highest percent of older residents who speak Spanish at home with 92.4 percent. Imperial County, California, Miami-Dade County, Florida, El Paso and Hidalgo County, Texas are all primary

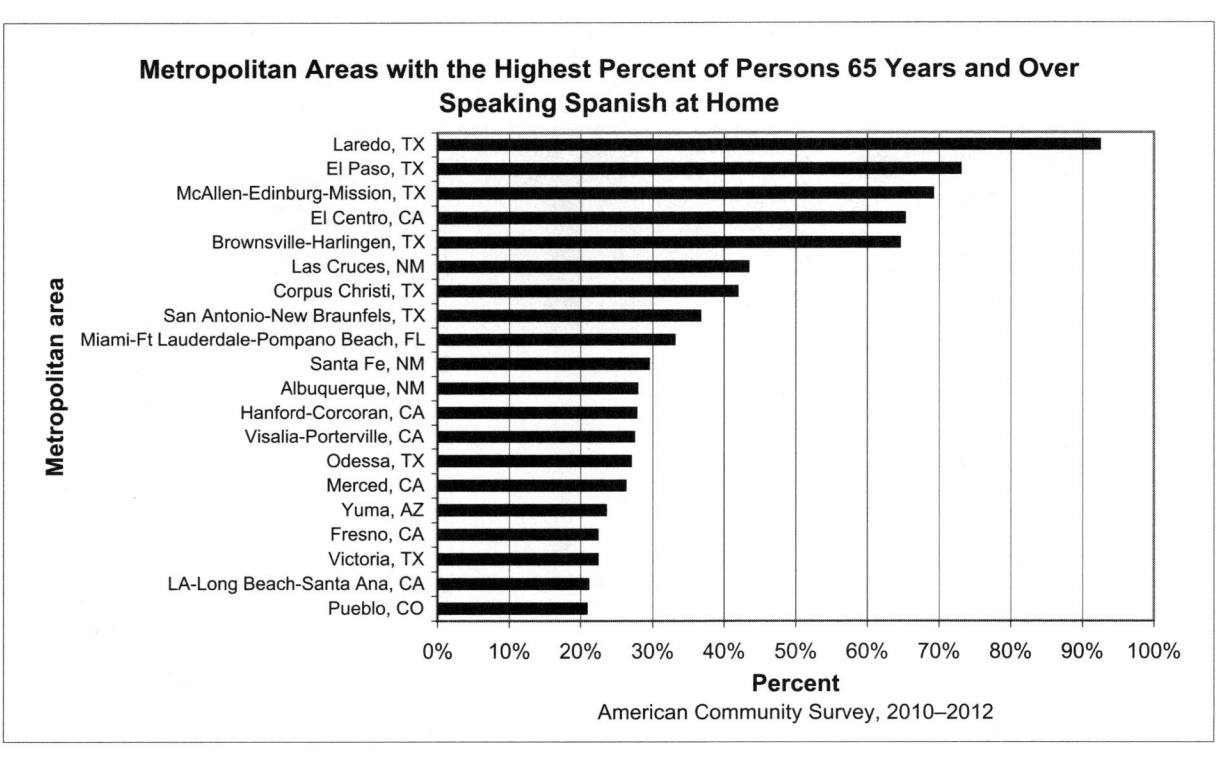

Metropolitan Areas with the Highest Percent of Persons 65 Years and Over Speaking Spanish at Home

American Community Survey, 2010–2012

Spanish language counties with more than 65 percent of the population speaking the language at home. Lafourche Parish, Louisiana (38.2 percent) has the highest percent of Indo-European language speakers followed by St. Landry and Lafeyette, Parish, Louisiana at 31.1 percent and 35.5 percent, respectively. San Francisco County, California (39.1 percent) and Honolulu County, Hawaii (31.1 percent) have the highest percent of Asian speaking residents. There are more than 500 counties where less than 1.0 percent of the older population speaks an Asian language. Laredo, Texas is the city with the highest percentage of Spanish speaking persons 65 and over at 92.0 percent.

CITIES WITH HIGHEST PERCENTAGE OF SPANISH LANGUAGE SPOKEN AT HOME

Glendale, California has the largest proportion of Indo-European language speakers at 47.2 percent followed by New Bedford, Massachusetts. More than 200 cities are above the national rate of 4.5 percent. Milpitas, California has the largest percentage of Asian speaking 65 and over population (58.5 percent) and 18 cities have more than 25 percent Asian speaking and 16 of them are in California.

As with Laredo city, the Laredo, Texas metropolitan area as a whole has the highest percent of Spanish speaking residents over 65. Four metro areas are between 50 and 75 percent Spanish speaking: Brownsville-Harlingen, Texas (64.5 percent), El Centro, California (65.2 percent), El Paso, Texas (72.9 percent) and McAllen-Edinburg-Mission, Texas (69.1 percent). Hawaii and California are the only states with metropolitan areas having more than 20 percent Asian speaking seniors: Honolulu (31.1 percent), San Francisco-Oakland-Fremont (20.1 percent) and San Jose-Sunnyvale-Santa Clara (22.7 percent). Asian speaking seniors are less than one percent of the population in 210 congressional districts and greater than 10 percent in only 31 districts. California's 12th Congressional District is the highest at 38.6 percent.

Percent of the Population 65 Years and Over With a Bachelor's Degree or Greater

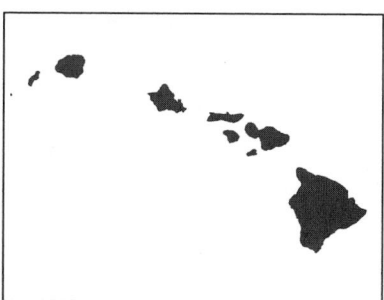

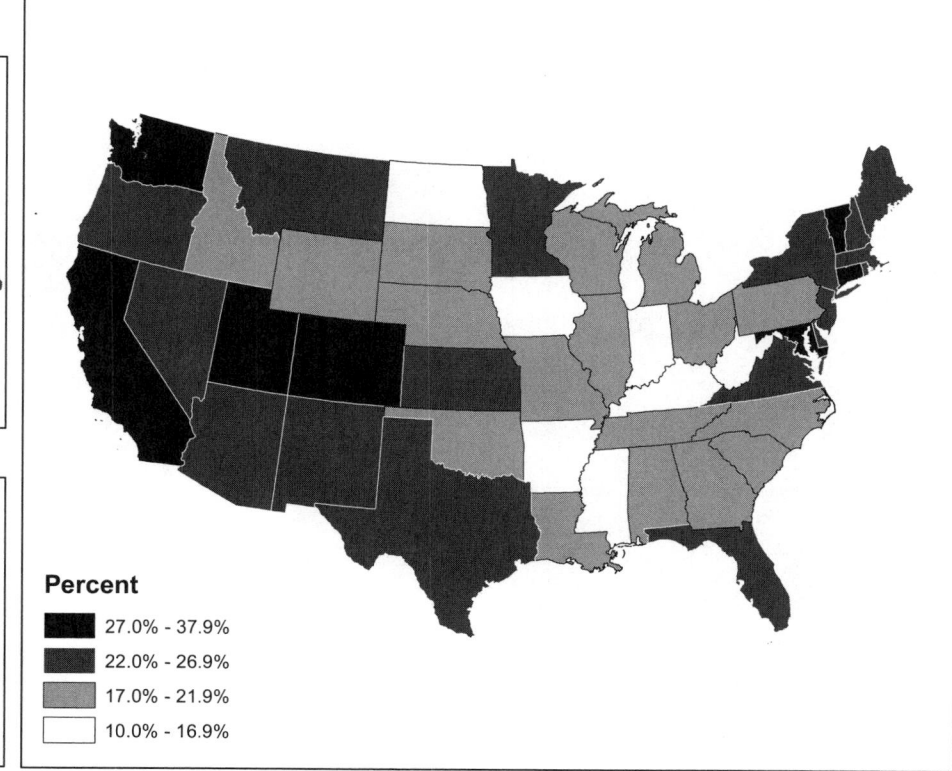

Percent

- 27.0% - 37.9%
- 22.0% - 26.9%
- 17.0% - 21.9%
- 10.0% - 16.9%

Cities with Highest Percentage of Spanish Language Spoken at Home			
50 to 74.9 Percent		**75 Percent or Greater**	
Baldwin Park CA	54.6	South Gate CA	80.3
Lynwood CA	65.1	Hialeah FL	90.1
Miami Beach FL	61.3	Miami FL	75.5
El Paso TX	71.2	Union City NJ	80.7
Mission TX	54.4	Brownsville TX	81.0
		Laredo TX	92.0
		McAllen TX	76.4

Table E-1: States—Educational Attainment and Language Spoken at Home, Persons 65 Years and Over

	High School or Equivalent	Some College or Associates Degree	Bachelor's Degree or Higher	Speaks English at Home	Speaks Spanish at Home		Speaks Indo-European at Home		Speaks Asian at Home	
				Total	Total	Speaks English Less Than Very Well	Total	Speaks English Less Than Very Well	Total	Speaks English Less Than Very Well
United States	14,129,175	9,453,544	9,254,187	35,647,700	2,733,087	1,732,760	1,885,627	857,719	1,151,104	832,865
Alabama	235,890	144,532	118,928	663,846	5,048	2,273	5,643	1,290	2,379	1,314
Alaska	16,068	17,513	14,952	48,234	1,153	551	1,489	334	3,445	2,451
Arizona	262,070	278,699	237,471	773,446	96,925	48,790	26,737	7,907	11,780	7,408
Arkansas	162,268	91,832	67,648	420,155	3,814	1,762	4,113	1,302	1,239	876
California	1,032,741	1,181,073	1,202,271	2,907,166	694,973	461,453	279,940	150,413	507,019	377,792
Colorado	167,408	156,877	180,265	508,353	44,556	17,414	17,621	5,836	8,775	6,578
Connecticut	178,686	99,142	142,036	434,935	22,933	17,142	52,506	24,589	5,869	4,232
Delaware	47,787	29,666	31,761	124,724	2,598	990	5,329	2,119	1,620	775
District of Columbia	16,523	12,484	25,938	63,373	2,582	1,100	2,769	527	734	468
Florida	1,112,875	825,949	793,091	2,707,977	447,267	331,602	179,550	81,854	32,470	20,129
Georgia	363,022	229,747	222,222	1,018,446	21,767	11,742	23,825	9,762	15,766	12,275
Hawaii	67,388	45,225	51,019	141,805	1,671	344	2,735	759	56,842	37,559
Idaho	66,409	61,522	43,397	193,474	4,987	2,518	2,978	766	959	553
Illinois	597,166	372,361	341,142	1,408,018	83,584	59,101	108,128	57,182	39,821	26,215
Indiana	382,976	171,208	138,186	827,834	12,422	6,210	17,471	6,362	3,697	2,210
Iowa	211,631	100,933	76,409	446,559	4,467	1,890	5,875	1,534	2,616	1,873
Kansas	144,308	99,897	84,737	364,289	8,550	4,481	7,275	1,701	3,386	2,610
Kentucky	210,208	110,909	86,293	582,832	3,593	1,656	5,304	1,780	2,142	1,220
Louisiana	209,256	110,123	100,382	503,549	10,283	5,379	56,776	11,555	4,221	3,042
Maine	82,102	46,309	50,867	195,126	913	109	20,880	4,585	935	742
Maryland	229,177	149,344	213,478	655,110	17,423	10,129	33,581	14,106	23,405	15,734
Massachusetts	317,076	185,413	248,252	771,371	28,615	21,603	102,223	53,199	22,003	18,398
Michigan	530,356	334,482	269,544	1,300,800	17,099	6,980	52,367	20,734	11,689	6,970
Minnesota	274,089	166,874	160,342	664,751	5,709	2,818	20,023	5,896	8,903	6,761
Mississippi	129,733	84,220	64,818	384,456	2,152	735	2,462	672	1,228	887
Missouri	334,834	194,077	154,409	831,334	7,674	3,051	13,264	4,864	5,804	4,063
Montana	54,252	41,678	35,663	146,441	1,285	383	2,732	612	419	291
Nebraska	104,518	65,250	46,161	239,253	3,786	2,123	5,738	1,474	1,295	1,040
Nevada	107,793	100,434	75,696	283,426	25,695	15,240	11,792	4,153	19,678	11,074
New Hampshire	66,876	41,222	48,786	169,453	1,413	737	13,226	3,428	986	687
New Jersey	455,341	210,195	293,281	950,081	96,795	74,950	117,429	62,961	41,014	26,846
New Mexico	77,490	69,077	73,382	179,611	83,708	27,498	5,620	1,069	1,890	1,089
New York	933,032	485,675	633,400	2,010,450	251,952	178,047	290,714	167,274	106,621	85,981
North Carolina	415,127	295,545	266,528	1,239,401	17,202	9,422	21,036	6,546	9,244	5,955
North Dakota	34,746	25,397	15,434	91,898	258	25	6,145	1,536	303	269
Ohio	700,631	332,384	288,684	1,577,002	14,037	6,324	50,178	19,806	9,998	5,516
Oklahoma	184,302	133,082	99,508	498,510	9,056	4,747	4,944	1,317	4,582	3,317
Oregon	172,237	170,276	142,205	518,809	13,286	6,403	13,555	4,638	10,268	8,201
Pennsylvania	900,936	324,999	353,525	1,853,359	29,803	18,477	85,866	35,229	19,204	14,407
Rhode Island	50,187	29,066	34,514	126,854	5,467	4,441	20,007	9,224	1,592	1,139
South Carolina	211,565	143,221	141,114	640,982	7,544	3,459	9,637	2,851	3,588	2,102
South Dakota	46,427	27,348	23,372	112,784	729	120	3,770	967	276	178
Tennessee	304,708	183,896	151,565	863,126	7,471	3,562	8,726	2,864	5,193	3,597
Texas	762,113	655,776	601,868	2,048,659	545,652	322,689	62,870	22,474	55,447	40,343
Utah	75,617	84,252	71,444	238,014	10,114	5,227	7,322	2,120	3,866	2,596
Vermont	32,165	19,440	27,589	88,938	485	132	4,498	1,102	436	361
Virginia	307,768	217,280	263,549	935,140	20,108	10,419	30,130	11,739	28,348	19,418
Washington	248,391	261,487	242,031	767,737	21,188	10,537	32,421	14,721	42,230	31,521
West Virginia	130,485	51,134	37,281	298,305	1,090	349	2,641	710	903	361
Wisconsin	343,949	164,596	152,511	759,423	9,489	5,038	22,833	7,150	4,732	3,302
Wyoming	26,472	20,441	15,238	68,081	2,716	588	933	126	244	139

Table E-2: Counties—Educational Attainment and Language Spoken at Home, Persons 65 Years and Over

	High School or Equivalent	Some College or Associates Degree	Bachelor's Degree or Higher	Speaks English at Home Total	Speaks Spanish at Home Total	Speaks English Less Than Very Well	Speaks Indo-European at Home Total	Speaks English Less Than Very Well	Speaks Asian at Home Total	Speaks English Less Than Very Well
Alabama										
Baldwin County	10,523	8,749	8,521	31,269	324	na	383	na	62	na
Calhoun County	5,832	3,441	2,801	16,905	272	na	215	na	31	na
Cullman County	5,046	2,353	1,656	13,031	87	na	89	na	54	na
DeKalb County	3,468	1,690	1,019	9,989	9	na	0	na	0	na
Elmore County	3,874	2,222	1,756	9,726	12	na	56	na	0	na
Etowah County	6,189	4,158	2,064	16,654	21	na	60	na	19	na
Houston County	5,867	3,440	2,032	14,901	127	na	140	na	23	na
Jefferson County	30,348	19,976	18,832	85,713	529	176	1,013	416	156	109
Lauderdale County	5,403	3,346	3,396	15,713	52	na	31	na	21	na
Lee County	3,331	3,374	3,263	13,124	162	na	37	na	127	na
Limestone County	3,818	2,395	1,800	10,504	99	na	122	na	21	na
Madison County	11,701	10,654	13,731	40,930	387	85	682	159	415	284
Marshall County	5,249	2,826	1,765	13,962	175	na	99	na	0	na
Mobile County	20,721	11,797	9,253	53,312	651	319	572	98	420	189
Montgomery County	8,140	6,226	7,781	27,360	197	58	320	75	258	118
Morgan County	6,298	4,437	2,571	17,095	189	na	81	na	0	na
St. Clair County	4,248	2,679	950	na	na	na	na	na	na	na
Shelby County	6,994	5,665	6,415	21,317	395	na	495	na	127	na
Talladega County	4,535	2,155	1,347	11,819	89	na	48	na	0	na
Tuscaloosa County	7,592	4,311	4,556	21,278	160	na	125	na	50	na
Walker County	4,600	2,247	710	na	na	na	na	na	na	na
Alaska										
Fairbanks North Star Borough	1,827	1,918	1,866	6,303	69	na	68	na	185	na
Matanuska-Susitna Borough	2,653	2,632	1,283	7,098	106	na	202	na	160	na
Arizona										
Apache County	1,892	1,843	1,057	3,162	507	na	52	na	110	na
Cochise County	5,984	7,578	5,429	18,436	3,786	na	785	na	500	na
Coconino County	2,296	3,644	3,871	8,854	1,063	161	136	32	151	13
Maricopa County	139,775	147,228	131,819	415,399	43,517	22,251	16,612	5,758	8,135	5,182
Mohave County	18,523	16,399	5,662	44,987	2,114	na	955	na	229	na
Navajo County	3,330	4,653	2,722	10,183	899	na	77	na	65	na
Pima County	39,254	43,830	50,042	126,919	23,476	10,696	4,535	1,158	1,781	1,281
Pinal County	17,483	17,491	12,559	48,732	5,441	2,487	1,289	96	428	227
Yavapai County	13,736	19,101	15,655	50,031	1,640	na	1,502	na	61	na
Yuma County	10,093	8,263	3,446	23,338	7,447	5,653	554	300	246	61
Arkansas										
Benton County	9,340	7,349	6,579	26,449	496	na	606	na	29	na
Craighead County	4,497	2,411	1,927	11,576	8	na	161	na	74	na
Faulkner County	4,527	2,808	2,155	11,585	140	na	73	na	15	na
Garland County	7,028	5,177	4,341	19,385	212	na	459	na	59	na
Jefferson County	3,610	1,651	1,825	10,315	17	na	92	na	10	na
Lonoke County	3,187	1,676	998	7,792	76	na	18	na	0	na
Pulaski County	14,908	10,434	12,631	45,795	578	327	767	446	185	124
Saline County	6,868	4,319	3,174	16,802	112	na	185	na	42	na
Sebastian County	6,178	4,246	3,106	16,008	137	na	227	na	215	na
Washington County	7,810	4,308	4,041	19,883	331	na	70	na	196	na
White County	4,121	2,868	1,351	11,056	99	na	64	na	0	na
California										
Alameda County	41,443	41,483	54,903	110,565	15,148	9,308	12,689	6,647	36,448	28,420
Butte County	9,838	11,888	7,915	32,136	1,304	793	756	298	338	252
Contra Costa County	30,775	38,338	50,194	102,161	11,459	6,559	9,407	4,718	13,309	8,343
El Dorado County	7,380	9,930	8,354	25,186	973	482	1,139	429	495	328
Fresno County	23,015	26,081	17,697	64,140	21,614	12,113	5,569	3,096	5,055	3,793
Humboldt County	5,875	5,690	4,228	17,180	403	na	540	na	150	na
Imperial County	3,069	2,814	1,533	6,016	12,313	na	223	na	295	na
Kern County	20,831	21,843	12,411	57,592	15,403	11,165	2,195	1,133	2,273	1,437
Kings County	3,779	2,938	1,526	7,588	3,413	1,866	704	132	520	276
Lake County	2,786	4,297	2,647	10,886	390	na	266	na	75	na
Los Angeles County	246,257	254,232	278,962	565,268	265,932	192,175	97,657	64,927	166,602	127,563
Madera County	4,561	5,304	2,632	13,605	3,460	2,135	595	288	168	98
Marin County	6,724	11,917	23,407	37,227	1,712	735	4,245	1,164	1,170	581
Mendocino County	3,875	4,539	3,458	13,012	589	na	443	na	189	na
Merced County	5,750	6,072	3,282	15,513	6,599	4,381	2,060	1,377	1,014	954
Monterey County	8,995	11,769	14,047	31,243	9,251	6,350	2,019	624	3,131	1,781
Napa County	4,664	6,656	7,104	17,644	1,854	1,174	926	312	939	660
Nevada County	5,125	7,674	6,067	19,096	242	na	596	na	134	na
Orange County	80,457	101,120	119,126	242,924	43,386	26,989	22,567	10,232	53,924	42,754
Placer County	14,191	20,730	16,440	49,765	2,099	995	2,753	1,151	2,070	1,290
Riverside County	70,301	82,346	60,910	201,935	44,932	28,478	10,482	3,532	10,891	7,206
Sacramento County	42,763	49,812	40,904	123,240	12,356	6,964	12,207	7,517	17,102	12,854
San Bernardino County	52,475	51,777	32,129	125,510	44,287	28,353	6,059	2,319	12,542	8,399
San Diego County	78,700	101,742	114,759	255,433	52,216	35,029	18,195	7,815	35,181	24,001
San Francisco County	21,247	22,344	36,224	48,943	8,727	5,922	10,387	6,450	44,006	36,072
San Joaquin County	19,537	20,507	12,498	50,839	10,791	7,041	3,949	2,346	8,155	6,006
San Luis Obispo County	10,213	13,651	15,006	38,314	2,240	1,088	1,381	379	703	277
San Mateo County	24,376	25,336	34,613	60,048	10,134	6,573	8,754	3,836	19,561	12,283
Santa Barbara County	11,929	15,843	18,312	42,804	8,231	4,913	3,149	639	1,671	1,162
Santa Clara County	41,108	46,123	76,702	117,108	22,155	12,249	16,757	9,321	47,835	37,764

Table E-2: Counties—Educational Attainment and Language Spoken at Home, Persons 65 Years and Over—*Continued*

	High School or Equivalent	Some College or Associates Degree	Bachelor's Degree or Higher	Speaks English at Home Total	Speaks Spanish at Home Total	Speaks English Less Than Very Well	Speaks Indo-European at Home Total	Speaks English Less Than Very Well	Speaks Asian at Home Total	Speaks English Less Than Very Well
California—Cont.										
Santa Cruz County	5,522	8,765	11,867	24,613	3,807	2,548	1,464	530	800	592
Shasta County	9,699	12,061	4,947	29,407	685	na	693	na	368	na
Solano County	13,280	15,918	11,608	34,883	4,583	2,245	2,130	894	7,552	3,975
Sonoma County	17,077	20,720	24,810	61,774	4,219	2,547	2,930	1,024	1,753	910
Stanislaus County	16,859	14,427	8,229	40,445	9,304	6,081	3,292	1,911	1,493	1,134
Sutter County	3,280	3,804	2,046	9,008	1,390	916	1,780	1,353	286	132
Tulare County	9,974	11,457	6,382	28,770	11,811	7,176	1,192	415	1,324	937
Ventura County	21,737	30,954	29,335	73,024	16,761	10,821	4,231	1,446	5,854	4,021
Yolo County	5,259	4,622	6,177	15,304	3,157	1,973	1,494	730	628	481
Yuba County	2,197	2,305	1,108	6,393	530	430	104	32	367	211
Colorado										
Adams County	13,978	10,157	5,688	30,835	5,966	2,838	1,393	505	816	639
Arapahoe County	16,395	17,596	21,859	53,577	3,015	1,384	2,685	1,016	2,159	1,781
Boulder County	6,791	7,979	14,958	28,795	1,325	615	1,120	241	361	191
Denver County	16,503	13,072	21,406	51,187	8,401	4,227	2,917	1,572	1,519	1,287
Douglas County	5,573	6,687	9,767	21,108	623	166	679	200	494	300
El Paso County	18,462	20,236	20,314	57,321	3,592	812	2,847	622	1,442	1,013
Jefferson County	20,630	18,991	24,392	64,347	3,060	857	1,906	798	1,087	881
Larimer County	9,989	10,540	13,807	35,573	984	na	804	na	322	na
Mesa County	7,525	7,468	4,918	21,379	1,029	na	153	na	53	na
Pueblo County	8,188	6,268	4,866	19,231	5,198	na	452	na	83	na
Weld County	8,837	6,876	5,323	22,476	2,750	1,534	574	168	101	42
Connecticut										
Fairfield County	38,666	22,508	43,919	102,511	7,718	5,850	14,381	7,309	1,889	1,253
Hartford County	45,795	25,308	33,607	106,137	7,270	5,914	17,005	9,140	1,375	914
Litchfield County	10,588	5,920	9,048	28,282	319	139	2,377	694	158	68
Middlesex County	9,078	5,921	7,797	24,257	390	na	1,613	na	273	na
New Haven County	47,424	23,447	29,531	107,123	5,849	4,290	11,346	5,017	1,487	1,269
New London County	14,892	8,581	9,887	36,130	786	539	2,494	1,069	632	509
Tolland County	6,238	4,430	5,318	17,141	155	na	1,469	na	55	na
Windham County	6,005	3,027	2,929	13,354	446	na	1,821	na	0	na
Delaware										
Kent County	8,415	4,950	4,306	21,328	389	12	967	321	393	206
New Castle County	23,240	15,180	17,295	61,852	1,832	844	3,202	1,204	1,133	531
Sussex County	16,132	9,536	10,160	41,544	377	134	1,160	594	94	38
Florida										
Alachua County	6,819	6,921	10,026	25,401	939	350	863	299	148	130
Bay County	9,109	7,449	4,972	24,129	353	na	539	na	298	na
Brevard County	39,960	31,867	25,533	103,275	4,937	2,407	4,533	1,501	892	639
Broward County	88,167	58,576	57,024	179,425	40,985	28,936	31,828	17,448	2,938	2,090
Charlotte County	21,471	16,439	12,259	51,631	1,403	na	3,232	na	304	na
Citrus County	18,467	12,398	7,086	43,003	981	na	1,618	na	159	na
Clay County	7,492	6,186	5,344	21,852	786	na	518	na	585	na
Collier County	22,222	23,807	34,006	77,769	5,198	4,203	5,984	2,683	468	319
Columbia County	3,881	3,125	1,046	10,185	277	na	185	na	48	na
Duval County	31,639	25,981	23,193	90,245	3,591	2,167	2,877	1,394	2,956	1,920
Escambia County	13,785	13,006	8,784	41,463	592	308	1,198	412	778	507
Flagler County	8,240	6,853	6,216	21,337	1,237	na	1,864	na	488	na
Hernando County	18,528	11,646	7,343	40,753	2,298	1,179	2,082	801	191	170
Highlands County	12,003	9,262	4,892	29,087	1,971	na	668	na	188	na
Hillsborough County	51,780	34,968	33,755	118,747	24,295	14,696	5,339	1,900	3,053	2,062
Indian River County	11,952	10,662	11,405	36,070	1,452	na	1,358	na	136	na
Lake County	27,060	19,818	15,636	68,321	2,733	1,651	2,191	697	671	443
Lee County	51,790	41,094	41,317	137,644	7,413	5,833	6,998	2,680	865	357
Leon County	7,178	5,935	10,542	25,152	955	404	968	212	348	232
Manatee County	27,916	21,146	19,998	71,348	2,382	1,375	4,142	1,294	287	126
Marion County	33,913	24,178	14,883	81,395	3,570	na	2,042	na	297	na
Martin County	11,579	11,892	12,725	38,505	1,020	na	1,310	na	68	na
Miami-Dade County	90,208	55,636	68,625	97,842	239,659	197,172	23,890	16,160	2,334	1,690
Monroe County	3,675	3,772	4,193	11,291	1,721	na	219	na	9	na
Nassau County	4,363	2,873	3,057	12,302	188	na	194	na	61	na
Okaloosa County	7,632	7,930	7,717	24,281	488	na	718	na	427	na
Orange County	38,579	27,004	25,739	82,682	23,051	16,708	7,347	4,176	3,011	1,977
Osceola County	12,026	6,595	3,931	19,607	10,518	8,141	1,332	423	492	292
Palm Beach County	87,643	70,081	94,764	243,486	21,378	15,169	22,017	9,247	2,450	1,804
Pasco County	41,447	23,648	14,752	87,777	4,600	2,638	5,662	2,110	472	241
Pinellas County	68,724	52,392	47,274	176,462	6,382	3,670	12,427	5,234	2,263	1,537
Polk County	42,903	27,994	18,914	101,890	6,135	3,951	2,577	866	1,187	533
Putnam County	5,902	2,916	1,692	13,669	388	na	286	na	72	na
St. Johns County	7,431	9,095	12,039	29,722	931	na	1,099	na	165	na
St. Lucie County	21,036	14,836	12,652	50,384	3,972	1,928	3,151	1,743	546	368
Santa Rosa County	7,087	5,671	4,817	19,475	264	na	273	na	279	na
Sarasota County	37,430	33,210	40,316	111,189	2,460	1,203	6,571	2,140	568	140
Seminole County	17,719	12,870	14,947	44,777	5,603	3,226	2,406	1,119	780	497
Sumter County	14,242	13,733	12,566	43,268	798	na	1,176	na	69	na
Volusia County	39,239	27,834	22,139	96,031	5,869	2,480	4,120	1,236	743	414

Table E-2: Counties—Educational Attainment and Language Spoken at Home, Persons 65 Years and Over—*Continued*

	High School or Equivalent	Some College or Associates Degree	Bachelor's Degree or Higher	Speaks English at Home — Total	Speaks Spanish at Home — Total	Speaks Spanish at Home — Speaks English Less Than Very Well	Speaks Indo-European at Home — Total	Speaks Indo-European at Home — Speaks English Less Than Very Well	Speaks Asian at Home — Total	Speaks Asian at Home — Speaks English Less Than Very Well
Georgia										
Barrow County	2,809	1,126	679	6,441	241	na	34	na	0	na
Bartow County	4,171	2,507	1,280	10,855	312	na	47	na	0	na
Bibb County	7,376	3,633	3,757	19,511	119	na	196	na	178	na
Bulloch County	2,210	1,383	1,421	6,386	44	na	30	na	27	na
Carroll County	4,344	2,309	1,980	12,125	219	na	91	na	0	na
Catoosa County	3,290	2,396	1,125	9,148	57	na	27	na	34	na
Chatham County	10,716	7,633	9,447	32,850	288	na	708	na	330	na
Cherokee County	6,912	5,544	4,997	20,036	482	na	596	na	88	na
Clarke County	2,769	1,619	4,127	9,718	303	na	223	na	223	na
Clayton County	6,419	4,052	2,112	15,979	699	651	493	300	1,218	1,090
Cobb County	19,163	16,239	20,064	58,565	2,132	1,375	2,317	1,013	1,116	852
Columbia County	4,156	2,874	3,920	12,286	241	na	562	na	434	na
Coweta County	5,095	3,686	1,877	13,512	198	na	87	na	83	na
DeKalb County	16,730	15,111	20,526	57,933	1,700	1,099	2,201	1,219	1,947	1,780
Dougherty County	3,701	2,561	2,111	11,478	68	na	94	na	94	na
Douglas County	4,976	2,575	1,796	11,389	245	na	295	na	112	na
Fayette County	4,578	3,730	4,665	13,772	262	95	307	111	205	62
Floyd County	4,980	2,929	2,256	13,729	88	na	43	na	34	na
Forsyth County	6,449	4,721	3,903	15,335	953	562	872	634	337	241
Fulton County	21,795	19,014	32,683	80,258	2,237	1,047	3,831	1,742	2,001	1,471
Glynn County	3,134	3,461	3,602	11,984	213	na	289	na	78	na
Gwinnett County	19,798	14,583	14,491	47,715	3,660	2,145	4,050	1,759	4,558	4,021
Hall County	6,022	5,386	4,869	20,276	911	na	165	na	269	na
Henry County	6,997	4,733	2,477	16,814	289	na	498	na	230	na
Houston County	5,635	3,435	2,684	14,477	245	na	212	na	141	na
Liberty County	1,637	823	444	3,725	191	na	83	na	53	na
Lowndes County	4,260	1,965	2,114	10,819	64	na	55	na	44	na
Muscogee County	7,022	5,237	4,217	20,814	389	na	646	na	422	na
Newton County	3,999	2,289	1,478	9,943	267	na	243	na	11	na
Paulding County	4,400	2,384	1,291	10,676	251	na	188	na	33	na
Richmond County	8,291	5,071	3,983	22,018	454	na	625	na	274	na
Rockdale County	3,261	2,572	1,808	9,117	126	na	197	na	96	na
Troup County	3,555	1,404	1,286	8,406	73	na	125	na	17	na
Walker County	3,985	2,023	1,397	10,351	101	na	20	na	24	na
Walton County	3,777	2,281	1,236	10,147	85	na	279	na	0	na
Whitfield County	4,373	2,137	1,450	11,141	445	na	43	na	57	na
Hawaii										
Hawaii County	9,260	7,055	7,588	22,821	278	na	441	na	5,107	na
Honolulu County	48,622	30,446	35,919	95,955	972	222	1,528	441	44,506	30,034
Kauai County	3,150	2,622	2,594	7,692	211	na	235	na	2,339	na
Maui County	6,339	5,102	4,918	15,331	210	79	531	145	4,875	3,362
Idaho										
Ada County	12,644	14,368	12,484	41,618	845	254	673	301	455	284
Bannock County	2,910	2,946	2,046	8,990	150	na	160	na	106	na
Bonneville County	3,766	4,056	2,716	11,079	328	na	272	na	19	na
Canyon County	7,318	6,473	2,881	20,174	1,071	na	291	na	81	na
Kootenai County	6,379	6,766	4,895	20,433	128	na	361	na	109	na
Twin Falls County	3,674	3,818	1,620	10,265	282	na	276	na	128	na
Illinois										
Adams County	5,756	2,854	1,244	11,691	36	na	130	na	35	na
Champaign County	6,889	5,121	6,357	19,401	367	92	507	145	495	435
Cook County	192,325	137,992	143,468	471,039	58,961	43,796	70,074	41,754	25,543	17,659
DeKalb County	4,166	2,382	2,311	9,888	192	na	353	na	84	na
DuPage County	34,119	27,607	35,167	88,456	4,355	2,719	12,166	5,376	5,425	3,104
Kane County	17,438	13,691	12,659	45,113	4,562	3,545	2,104	787	1,105	598
Kankakee County	6,853	3,128	1,837	14,798	143	na	392	na	14	na
Kendall County	4,007	1,708	1,674	8,000	261	na	210	na	26	na
Lake County	22,885	17,487	24,779	62,076	3,978	2,750	6,803	3,122	2,736	1,858
LaSalle County	8,949	4,660	1,759	18,325	277	na	208	na	26	na
McHenry County	12,983	8,171	6,742	29,479	849	479	1,810	958	441	258
McLean County	6,563	4,238	5,001	17,287	257	na	306	na	68	na
Macon County	7,803	4,219	3,105	18,085	75	na	160	na	10	na
Madison County	17,859	7,873	6,335	38,377	264	na	434	na	251	na
Peoria County	10,377	6,346	5,251	25,115	317	170	653	249	224	121
Rock Island County	10,012	6,016	3,882	22,797	736	510	709	265	92	37
St. Clair County	12,453	8,709	5,992	33,261	517	na	293	na	350	na
Sangamon County	11,295	6,784	6,503	27,004	148	na	699	na	97	na
Tazewell County	9,754	5,104	2,972	21,159	44	na	212	na	39	na
Vermilion County	5,941	3,013	1,611	12,947	21	na	144	na	72	na
Will County	25,359	16,249	13,083	56,929	3,398	2,068	3,902	1,922	1,435	871
Williamson County	4,097	2,757	1,745	10,911	59	na	143	na	18	na
Winnebago County	15,962	9,552	7,654	38,866	1,068	784	1,480	723	372	303

Table E-2: Counties—Educational Attainment and Language Spoken at Home, Persons 65 Years and Over—*Continued*

	High School or Equivalent	Some College or Associates Degree	Bachelor's Degree or Higher	Speaks English at Home Total	Speaks Spanish at Home Total	Speaks Spanish at Home Speaks English Less Than Very Well	Speaks Indo-European at Home Total	Speaks Indo-European at Home Speaks English Less Than Very Well	Speaks Asian at Home Total	Speaks Asian at Home Speaks English Less Than Very Well
Indiana										
Allen County	17,173	10,724	8,679	41,587	452	123	969	355	362	232
Bartholomew County	5,136	2,144	1,777	11,083	0	na	57	na	0	na
Clark County	5,774	3,213	1,955	14,323	42	na	82	na	113	na
Delaware County	7,493	3,263	2,878	17,361	154	na	51	na	10	na
Elkhart County	10,294	4,410	4,329	22,982	449	361	951	290	4	0
Floyd County	3,957	2,361	1,372	9,836	87	na	68	na	11	na
Grant County	5,078	2,091	1,610	11,285	124	na	68	na	27	na
Hamilton County	8,095	6,408	9,007	23,914	160	47	784	131	456	256
Hancock County	5,003	1,786	1,330	na	na	na	na	na	na	na
Hendricks County	7,629	4,054	2,707	16,030	110	na	329	na	83	na
Howard County	6,306	3,086	2,013	13,403	164	na	288	na	95	na
Johnson County	8,737	3,400	2,904	17,491	192	na	197	na	22	na
Kosciusko County	4,867	2,119	1,864	10,285	161	na	211	na	0	na
Lake County	29,813	13,303	8,824	57,148	4,177	2,179	4,698	2,351	508	260
LaPorte County	7,556	2,929	2,465	15,543	232	na	333	na	0	na
Madison County	9,625	4,187	2,684	20,209	260	na	153	na	52	na
Marion County	34,863	21,972	20,082	93,250	1,755	1,151	1,759	785	666	495
Monroe County	4,549	2,721	5,101	13,995	249	na	227	na	37	na
Morgan County	4,585	2,035	1,143	9,282	55	na	173	na	0	na
Porter County	9,233	4,251	4,261	20,095	421	na	459	na	226	na
St. Joseph County	15,499	6,884	7,345	33,868	596	365	1,229	411	186	98
Tippecanoe County	7,062	3,428	4,022	16,059	252	na	265	na	148	na
Vanderburgh County	11,429	5,910	4,213	25,684	135	na	258	na	24	na
Vigo County	6,204	2,845	2,722	14,225	136	na	209	na	60	na
Wayne County	5,375	1,779	1,472	11,147	76	na	154	na	0	na
Iowa										
Black Hawk County	8,156	3,686	3,760	17,829	137	na	328	na	39	na
Dallas County	3,347	1,723	1,038	6,622	101	na	203	na	0	na
Dubuque County	6,591	2,482	2,552	14,248	37	na	117	na	17	na
Johnson County	3,311	3,005	4,325	10,985	112	18	303	53	248	123
Linn County	12,093	6,935	6,029	27,197	230	na	699	na	169	na
Polk County	18,768	11,459	11,374	45,120	857	328	872	271	1,040	643
Pottawattamie County	6,300	3,015	1,856	13,176	223	na	60	na	3	na
Scott County	8,945	5,195	5,254	21,624	225	na	207	na	250	na
Story County	2,928	1,944	3,347	8,792	40	na	156	na	92	na
Woodbury County	5,858	3,033	1,765	12,726	275	na	93	na	253	na
Kansas										
Butler County	3,738	2,505	1,063	8,335	36	na	98	na	0	na
Douglas County	2,993	2,180	4,032	9,818	117	na	210	na	116	na
Johnson County	16,203	17,267	24,478	58,765	1,057	491	1,503	601	971	659
Leavenworth County	3,816	1,753	1,924	8,460	91	na	109	na	73	na
Riley County	1,537	1,179	2,082	5,157	4	na	93	na	27	na
Sedgwick County	20,389	15,918	12,884	54,547	1,705	1,045	1,067	274	1,168	1,023
Shawnee County	11,143	6,355	5,908	24,978	804	na	387	na	119	na
Wyandotte County	6,499	3,941	1,961	15,345	1,148	695	394	115	254	232
Kentucky										
Boone County	4,805	2,682	2,106	11,712	45	na	55	na	125	na
Bullitt County	4,283	1,229	555	8,912	47	na	27	na	0	na
Campbell County	4,415	2,865	1,705	11,537	50	na	145	na	0	na
Christian County	3,026	1,748	953	7,540	83	na	89	na	0	na
Daviess County	6,086	2,932	2,213	14,297	49	na	96	na	22	na
Fayette County	9,080	7,712	9,657	30,987	317	108	480	203	338	251
Hardin County	4,754	2,441	1,311	11,093	20	na	425	na	178	na
Jefferson County	34,461	23,106	21,493	97,451	1,124	715	1,350	527	1,034	517
Kenton County	6,815	3,709	3,771	17,911	221	na	84	na	0	na
McCracken County	4,133	3,310	1,571	10,950	0	na	129	na	34	na
Madison County	2,983	1,300	2,102	9,387	74	na	162	na	20	na
Pike County	2,744	1,121	863	na	na	na	na	na	na	na
Warren County	4,572	2,917	2,372	12,419	74	50	214	142	117	78
Louisiana										
Ascension Parish	4,858	1,756	1,626	9,056	211	na	770	na	74	na
Bossier Parish	5,632	3,649	2,501	13,918	143	na	161	na	17	na
Caddo Parish	12,113	8,171	7,224	34,064	151	na	621	na	195	na
Calcasieu Parish	10,351	4,859	3,571	20,930	169	na	3,768	na	177	na
East Baton Rouge Parish	14,506	11,469	15,016	46,599	753	460	1,623	279	618	352
Iberia Parish	3,323	1,226	1,357	6,580	91	na	2,439	na	105	na
Jefferson Parish	23,397	12,802	10,142	52,587	4,307	2,615	2,241	514	1,341	1,152
Lafayette Parish	6,374	4,820	5,697	15,684	382	190	7,318	1,416	106	106
Lafourche Parish	4,777	1,230	1,277	7,497	97	na	4,751	na	81	na
Livingston Parish	6,129	2,176	1,564	13,073	255	na	230	na	0	na
Orleans Parish	10,704	7,684	10,361	37,021	1,167	676	1,175	146	737	573
Ouachita Parish	7,057	3,804	3,932	19,149	138	na	73	na	42	na
Rapides Parish	6,780	4,117	3,266	17,372	166	na	852	na	133	na
St. Landry Parish	3,996	1,642	1,677	7,437	14	na	4,100	na	0	na
St. Tammany Parish	11,533	7,496	7,272	29,796	680	na	697	na	154	na
Tangipahoa Parish	5,646	2,586	2,310	13,615	300	na	464	na	0	na
Terrebonne Parish	4,840	1,903	1,603	9,561	225	na	2,928	na	0	na

Table E-2: Counties—Educational Attainment and Language Spoken at Home, Persons 65 Years and Over—*Continued*

	High School or Equivalent	Some College or Associates Degree	Bachelor's Degree or Higher	Speaks English at Home Total	Speaks Spanish at Home Total	Speaks English Less Than Very Well	Speaks Indo-European at Home Total	Speaks English Less Than Very Well	Speaks Asian at Home Total	Speaks English Less Than Very Well
Maine										
Androscoggin County	6,348	2,912	1,696	10,889	36	na	4,464	na	77	na
Aroostook County	5,658	2,496	1,551	9,874	4	na	3,954	na	59	na
Cumberland County	13,141	10,543	13,078	38,564	282	44	2,301	520	485	476
Kennebec County	7,965	4,262	3,966	17,416	82	na	2,073	na	0	na
Penobscot County	10,065	4,634	3,731	21,670	48	na	1,119	na	47	na
York County	11,263	7,288	7,823	26,956	215	na	4,370	na	134	na
Maryland										
Allegany County	6,296	2,769	1,402	13,278	65	na	158	na	92	na
Anne Arundel County	21,889	14,536	19,028	62,411	727	312	2,161	532	1,367	942
Baltimore County	41,016	24,289	31,885	110,436	1,147	456	5,405	2,666	2,736	1,672
Calvert County	3,707	2,312	2,217	9,660	135	na	271	na	25	na
Carroll County	9,941	4,737	4,316	22,215	297	na	374	na	127	na
Cecil County	5,006	2,284	1,886	11,923	102	na	238	na	132	na
Charles County	5,612	3,076	2,490	14,075	208	na	260	na	181	na
Frederick County	9,000	6,680	6,742	25,740	348	208	791	157	397	315
Harford County	12,314	7,316	6,615	30,206	336	na	1,020	na	365	na
Howard County	6,911	6,290	14,347	26,366	730	332	1,303	482	2,647	1,963
Montgomery County	22,802	22,779	65,005	88,284	8,595	5,756	13,702	6,414	11,666	8,227
Prince George's County	27,460	19,975	21,750	75,913	2,967	2,011	3,223	1,351	2,524	1,365
St. Mary's County	4,331	2,343	2,741	10,804	119	na	378	na	116	na
Washington County	9,340	4,203	2,813	20,815	233	na	415	na	102	na
Wicomico County	4,607	2,245	3,411	12,742	197	na	194	na	82	na
Massachusetts										
Barnstable County	14,970	14,809	22,295	51,989	408	98	2,608	555	228	97
Berkshire County	9,108	4,992	6,899	23,199	330	na	1,410	na	67	na
Bristol County	27,374	12,032	12,915	61,044	1,158	670	16,903	9,920	490	418
Essex County	39,528	22,998	27,264	89,825	5,926	4,887	10,251	4,439	1,488	1,232
Franklin County	3,760	2,816	2,994	10,687	66	na	462	na	22	na
Hampden County	25,422	12,946	11,855	54,513	4,422	3,726	7,543	3,969	586	530
Hampshire County	7,114	4,520	6,637	19,426	187	130	1,222	422	161	121
Middlesex County	64,714	38,342	66,005	163,811	4,132	2,763	25,793	13,069	7,110	5,506
Norfolk County	34,283	21,782	30,957	84,460	1,069	498	9,179	4,683	4,471	3,646
Plymouth County	26,791	16,625	18,089	65,261	952	521	5,413	2,781	408	342
Suffolk County	25,166	11,507	17,530	52,924	6,843	5,631	12,007	8,593	5,410	5,104
Worcester County	37,866	21,389	22,792	90,078	3,120	2,544	9,309	4,103	1,546	1,337
Michigan										
Allegan County	5,991	3,234	2,945	14,642	191	na	288	na	18	na
Bay County	7,658	4,271	2,225	17,403	200	na	334	na	0	na
Berrien County	9,417	6,277	5,368	24,543	301	120	767	354	111	31
Calhoun County	8,521	5,175	2,925	19,705	207	na	351	na	100	na
Clinton County	4,662	2,556	1,716	9,984	104	na	237	na	3	na
Eaton County	6,372	4,396	3,230	15,066	233	na	222	na	57	na
Genesee County	24,080	15,137	8,686	57,262	588	220	1,110	341	334	193
Grand Traverse County	4,445	3,612	4,180	13,260	24	na	72	na	0	na
Ingham County	8,930	7,405	9,299	27,750	953	434	874	328	636	450
Isabella County	2,847	1,387	1,483	6,734	30	na	127	na	52	na
Jackson County	9,392	6,356	3,331	22,415	115	na	586	na	81	na
Kalamazoo County	11,168	7,651	8,858	30,257	171	0	796	238	228	98
Kent County	24,839	18,661	14,933	64,488	1,624	972	1,960	704	814	689
Lapeer County	5,654	3,306	1,506	11,882	126	na	302	na	16	na
Lenawee County	6,435	3,212	2,656	14,354	514	na	215	na	37	na
Livingston County	8,236	6,834	5,128	22,405	228	na	473	na	10	na
Macomb County	50,419	28,457	16,419	105,685	680	244	12,732	6,594	1,515	998
Marquette County	4,321	2,400	2,149	9,516	32	na	122	na	36	na
Midland County	4,952	3,032	2,848	12,368	76	na	111	na	38	na
Monroe County	9,223	4,748	3,044	20,389	195	na	442	na	29	na
Muskegon County	9,060	6,126	3,630	22,848	358	na	545	na	29	na
Oakland County	48,957	40,837	53,074	145,239	1,675	596	10,405	4,659	3,441	1,841
Ottawa County	11,745	6,717	7,141	30,248	788	476	773	153	188	173
Saginaw County	13,776	6,569	3,789	29,223	910	na	835	na	101	na
St. Clair County	10,902	6,263	3,095	23,548	108	na	526	na	116	na
Shiawassee County	4,990	2,383	1,139	10,114	63	na	182	na	36	na
Van Buren County	4,552	2,496	1,550	10,451	242	na	148	na	0	na
Washtenaw County	8,548	8,440	14,975	33,262	507	108	1,825	856	1,131	610
Wayne County	82,876	53,412	36,427	211,597	3,898	1,801	10,361	4,199	2,054	1,260
Minnesota										
Anoka County	14,985	8,995	6,213	32,166	416	289	1,028	368	397	302
Blue Earth County	2,948	1,786	2,129	7,382	54	na	217	na	13	na
Carver County	3,087	2,119	2,040	7,669	35	na	437	na	108	na
Dakota County	14,389	11,867	12,072	39,688	410	251	1,361	405	645	289
Hennepin County	40,984	34,556	45,311	122,722	1,407	658	5,257	1,877	3,244	2,735
Olmsted County	7,225	4,695	5,095	17,764	147	88	383	121	440	404
Ramsey County	21,462	14,443	18,516	56,625	1,147	615	2,026	987	2,156	1,745
St. Louis County	12,897	7,833	7,063	30,803	230	na	698	na	114	na
Scott County	4,253	2,786	2,536	9,824	154	102	620	366	368	170
Sherburne County	3,249	1,966	1,606	7,558	0	na	95	na	52	na

Table E-2: Counties—Educational Attainment and Language Spoken at Home, Persons 65 Years and Over—*Continued*

	High School or Equivalent	Some College or Associates Degree	Bachelor's Degree or Higher	Speaks English at Home Total	Speaks Spanish at Home Total	Speaks English Less Than Very Well	Speaks Indo-European at Home Total	Speaks English Less Than Very Well	Speaks Asian at Home Total	Speaks English Less Than Very Well
Minnesota—Cont.										
Stearns County	7,965	3,356	3,242	17,434	44	na	1,147	na	67	na
Washington County	9,567	7,108	7,397	25,476	204	72	573	68	410	371
Wright County	5,849	2,593	2,043	12,051	151	na	198	na	34	na
Mississippi										
DeSoto County	6,876	4,959	2,279	16,887	283	na	79	na	27	na
Forrest County	2,648	1,760	1,973	8,830	28	na	13	na	0	na
Harrison County	7,934	6,281	4,539	22,072	249	na	307	na	337	na
Hinds County	6,367	5,914	7,464	26,751	218	na	151	na	43	na
Jackson County	6,725	4,370	3,539	17,302	139	na	315	na	137	na
Jones County	3,450	2,091	1,481	na	na	na	na	na	na	na
Lauderdale County	3,081	3,441	2,066	11,176	23	na	124	na	0	na
Lee County	3,970	2,644	1,863	11,019	17	na	0	na	129	na
Madison County	3,008	2,292	3,364	10,258	89	na	111	na	92	na
Rankin County	6,718	4,395	2,748	17,027	65	na	0	na	0	na
Missouri										
Boone County	4,338	3,844	5,371	14,941	154	na	346	na	301	na
Buchanan County	4,971	2,931	1,979	12,099	52	na	136	na	22	na
Cape Girardeau County	4,283	2,077	1,912	10,727	0	na	263	na	43	na
Cass County	6,167	3,833	2,408	13,855	125	na	68	na	52	na
Christian County	4,267	2,735	1,484	9,871	105	na	117	na	0	na
Clay County	11,000	6,665	4,595	25,087	560	353	202	36	209	133
Cole County	3,860	2,200	2,052	9,679	168	na	20	na	0	na
Franklin County	5,999	2,696	1,861	14,252	25	na	89	na	0	na
Greene County	13,787	11,332	8,747	39,038	207	na	335	na	163	na
Jackson County	32,446	21,651	17,264	81,994	1,679	849	908	290	855	672
Jasper County	6,388	3,635	2,243	15,272	172	na	96	na	90	na
Jefferson County	11,120	5,852	2,247	25,321	75	na	255	na	56	na
Platte County	4,039	2,598	2,772	9,982	220	na	157	na	164	na
St. Charles County	16,774	10,958	8,665	41,361	374	na	589	na	271	na
St. Francois County	3,221	2,224	1,376	9,319	27	na	20	na	0	na
St. Louis County	49,200	36,145	45,187	143,641	1,437	384	4,723	2,042	2,224	1,491
Montana										
Cascade County	4,788	3,475	2,374	12,469	98	na	267	na	79	na
Flathead County	3,925	3,655	4,579	13,334	128	na	169	na	50	na
Gallatin County	2,402	2,241	3,317	8,852	52	na	83	na	21	na
Missoula County	4,390	2,975	4,414	12,307	114	na	412	na	48	na
Yellowstone County	8,054	6,306	4,333	20,515	251	na	480	na	94	na
Nebraska										
Douglas County	19,631	14,781	14,045	52,960	1,105	745	1,750	563	375	244
Lancaster County	11,499	9,076	8,815	29,910	387	135	1,102	446	542	505
Sarpy County	5,375	4,334	3,022	13,704	260	na	250	na	117	na
Nevada										
Clark County	73,261	65,788	51,792	185,002	20,956	12,847	8,720	3,268	17,342	9,565
Washoe County	16,687	16,065	14,237	47,283	2,840	1,654	1,741	485	1,814	1,242
New Hampshire										
Cheshire County	4,653	1,922	3,128	11,529	11	na	140	na	0	na
Grafton County	4,348	2,958	5,179	13,691	85	na	452	na	59	na
Hillsborough County	17,759	11,089	12,283	42,375	663	425	5,727	1,752	524	424
Merrimack County	7,517	4,745	5,865	19,801	126	na	826	na	73	na
Rockingham County	14,428	9,691	10,016	36,942	296	166	1,912	427	95	83
Strafford County	5,808	3,530	3,209	13,778	148	na	1,098	na	156	na
New Jersey										
Atlantic County	15,340	8,242	7,658	34,214	2,108	1,474	2,275	1,337	1,244	754
Bergen County	48,494	23,633	43,107	97,837	9,983	7,266	19,928	10,933	10,316	7,915
Burlington County	24,965	13,410	15,025	57,180	1,246	480	4,025	1,386	1,238	966
Camden County	25,809	11,530	14,007	57,818	3,525	2,516	3,773	1,729	2,183	1,413
Cape May County	8,849	4,554	5,183	19,952	236	na	1,189	na	120	na
Cumberland County	8,085	2,913	2,001	17,247	2,084	na	636	na	105	na
Essex County	30,946	14,214	21,832	68,193	9,889	7,999	10,496	6,859	2,660	1,551
Gloucester County	16,245	6,272	6,231	34,692	500	208	1,084	421	570	194
Hudson County	21,283	8,478	10,548	28,658	25,098	21,099	9,112	5,864	3,554	2,172
Hunterdon County	5,706	3,440	5,803	15,554	359	232	1,020	433	223	128
Mercer County	15,965	8,273	13,913	38,670	2,054	1,326	4,990	2,114	1,245	665
Middlesex County	37,587	15,668	26,455	71,924	7,935	6,035	14,197	8,855	6,521	4,080
Monmouth County	32,491	17,902	25,373	78,301	2,514	1,448	5,667	2,614	2,396	1,699
Morris County	24,864	12,049	24,598	58,665	2,741	2,060	6,881	3,215	2,201	1,413
Ocean County	56,712	24,496	22,190	110,799	2,647	1,349	7,964	3,020	926	534
Passaic County	23,107	9,382	10,820	39,664	11,762	9,849	7,747	4,535	1,411	965
Salem County	4,311	1,789	1,505	9,688	181	na	277	na	29	na
Somerset County	14,156	6,628	14,890	32,892	1,706	1,218	4,807	2,146	1,967	1,259
Sussex County	7,528	3,669	4,733	16,755	476	332	1,037	397	127	95
Union County	26,014	10,949	14,805	47,375	9,434	7,951	9,424	6,095	1,848	784
Warren County	6,884	2,704	2,604	14,003	317	na	900	na	130	na

Table E-2: Counties—Educational Attainment and Language Spoken at Home, Persons 65 Years and Over—*Continued*

	High School or Equivalent	Some College or Associates Degree	Bachelor's Degree or Higher	Speaks English at Home	Speaks Spanish at Home		Speaks Indo-European at Home		Speaks Asian at Home	
				Total	Total	Speaks English Less Than Very Well	Total	Speaks English Less Than Very Well	Total	Speaks English Less Than Very Well
New Mexico										
Bernalillo County	22,887	21,993	25,800	56,278	23,727	6,347	2,204	402	1,293	754
Chaves County	2,293	2,609	1,728	6,516	2,540	na	193	na	0	na
Doña Ana County	5,577	5,936	6,732	14,602	11,705	6,898	449	129	168	68
Lea County	1,910	1,804	868	5,192	1,686	na	202	na	26	na
McKinley County	1,355	1,187	886	2,009	758	na	104	na	0	na
Otero County	2,932	3,352	1,627	7,284	1,970	na	231	na	40	na
Sandoval County	5,188	4,307	5,325	12,172	3,124	714	536	93	17	0
San Juan County	4,799	2,881	2,481	9,203	1,540	429	160	79	0	0
Santa Fe County	5,027	5,038	10,888	15,745	6,942	1,588	581	21	100	78
Valencia County	3,396	2,868	1,712	5,616	4,349	na	146	na	35	na
New York										
Albany County	16,439	8,172	12,346	39,513	533	327	2,605	1,053	416	205
Bronx County	46,288	17,871	17,933	74,961	58,308	43,782	11,352	6,807	3,205	2,635
Broome County	14,117	7,257	6,170	31,002	422	184	1,464	590	264	200
Cattaraugus County	5,930	2,441	1,725	12,100	60	na	263	na	0	na
Cayuga County	5,264	3,018	1,868	11,938	57	na	445	na	19	na
Chautauqua County	9,647	4,982	3,725	21,476	271	na	700	na	32	na
Chemung County	5,535	2,966	2,527	13,339	2	na	287	na	26	na
Clinton County	4,372	2,193	1,867	10,329	30	na	668	na	91	na
Dutchess County	14,395	8,544	11,198	35,916	1,440	778	3,391	1,471	648	413
Erie County	56,125	32,001	29,433	131,825	2,048	1,185	9,880	3,349	1,071	695
Jefferson County	5,916	2,532	2,238	12,647	77	na	400	na	121	na
Kings County	98,906	40,253	50,887	154,205	40,924	28,198	71,590	58,091	21,187	19,799
Livingston County	3,537	1,901	2,144	9,002	58	na	302	na	40	na
Madison County	4,457	2,033	2,052	10,192	93	na	225	na	10	na
Monroe County	35,129	23,835	28,285	94,816	2,857	2,049	6,989	3,174	1,392	852
Nassau County	76,778	38,557	59,366	162,479	11,459	7,613	26,290	14,259	6,467	4,615
New York County	37,563	32,650	91,442	133,328	48,283	37,116	17,456	6,586	18,313	14,949
Niagara County	15,796	6,981	5,227	32,972	269	na	1,492	na	40	na
Oneida County	15,404	8,343	6,894	35,168	522	389	2,364	942	315	300
Onondaga County	24,498	14,829	15,802	60,671	803	304	4,277	1,914	745	461
Ontario County	6,184	4,060	4,131	16,650	138	na	451	na	24	na
Orange County	17,164	8,149	8,373	36,165	3,020	1,469	2,671	998	385	157
Oswego County	7,142	3,030	1,936	15,274	73	na	315	na	4	na
Putnam County	4,842	2,524	3,732	11,138	624	na	1,130	na	32	na
Queens County	95,501	45,978	60,671	147,142	45,535	34,055	58,129	36,969	38,625	32,345
Rensselaer County	8,660	4,868	4,278	21,019	180	99	844	350	71	65
Richmond County	25,342	10,845	11,180	45,247	3,584	1,933	9,359	5,491	2,996	1,927
Rockland County	13,455	8,373	14,368	31,800	2,558	1,287	6,669	3,705	2,016	1,005
St. Lawrence County	6,022	3,375	2,876	15,115	97	na	590	na	97	na
Saratoga County	12,072	7,148	7,976	29,579	113	32	1,381	395	143	90
Schenectady County	9,786	4,872	4,987	20,844	380	137	1,772	694	145	100
Steuben County	6,509	3,662	2,527	15,538	121	na	300	na	79	na
Suffolk County	82,007	42,495	52,240	177,765	11,478	6,814	16,207	6,666	2,817	1,830
Sullivan County	4,534	2,371	2,434	10,279	715	404	833	310	55	11
Tompkins County	3,225	1,830	4,878	10,201	106	na	795	na	161	na
Ulster County	9,656	6,246	7,432	25,208	861	390	1,853	454	146	70
Warren County	4,228	2,530	3,156	11,084	171	na	347	na	62	na
Wayne County	5,766	3,393	2,307	13,358	121	na	328	na	29	na
Westchester County	42,856	23,769	50,849	106,645	12,055	7,797	18,237	8,612	3,821	2,532
North Carolina										
Alamance County	7,376	5,879	4,070	22,202	288	na	209	na	82	na
Brunswick County	7,453	6,714	7,401	24,254	173	na	596	na	44	na
Buncombe County	12,539	8,431	11,938	38,388	417	na	531	na	169	na
Burke County	4,770	3,071	2,179	14,651	79	na	107	na	146	na
Cabarrus County	7,227	4,273	3,090	19,976	326	na	394	na	69	na
Caldwell County	4,466	2,597	992	na	na	na	na	na	0	na
Carteret County	4,053	3,898	2,980	12,823	123	na	136	na	359	na
Catawba County	8,226	4,552	4,101	21,888	432	na	319	na	31	na
Chatham County	3,548	2,306	4,477	12,496	93	na	277	na	35	na
Cleveland County	5,126	3,202	1,895	14,871	172	na	99	na	35	na
Craven County	4,969	4,616	4,156	15,930	190	na	262	na	104	na
Cumberland County	10,331	8,294	5,865	28,513	811	302	1,490	363	562	333
Davidson County	9,209	5,489	2,518	24,239	257	na	79	na	109	na
Durham County	7,657	6,020	9,079	25,682	656	264	920	296	426	189
Forsyth County	16,351	11,086	11,228	44,959	905	517	818	490	183	94
Gaston County	7,798	7,302	3,830	27,478	176	na	345	na	147	na
Guilford County	20,466	13,780	16,041	59,315	877	585	1,171	366	1,041	716
Harnett County	4,502	2,538	1,501	12,146	167	na	39	na	65	na
Henderson County	7,159	6,738	7,445	23,744	398	na	466	na	82	na
Iredell County	7,674	5,185	3,307	20,894	298	na	86	na	64	na

Table E-2: Counties—Educational Attainment and Language Spoken at Home, Persons 65 Years and Over—*Continued*

	High School or Equivalent	Some College or Associates Degree	Bachelor's Degree or Higher	Speaks English at Home — Total	Speaks Spanish at Home — Total	Speaks Spanish at Home — Speaks English Less Than Very Well	Speaks Indo-European at Home — Total	Speaks Indo-European at Home — Speaks English Less Than Very Well	Speaks Asian at Home — Total	Speaks Asian at Home — Speaks English Less Than Very Well
North Carolina—Cont.										
Johnston County	6,405	4,019	2,681	18,005	375	na	148	na	93	na
Lincoln County	3,872	2,627	1,555	10,589	60	na	97	na	202	na
Mecklenburg County	23,346	24,363	24,563	77,646	2,657	1,774	3,380	1,367	1,914	1,309
Moore County	5,402	5,682	6,537	19,893	226	na	342	na	0	na
Nash County	5,184	2,681	2,204	13,723	100	na	51	na	101	na
New Hanover County	8,284	7,705	9,625	28,339	256	na	749	na	115	na
Onslow County	4,957	3,904	2,093	13,074	354	na	165	na	248	na
Orange County	2,949	2,472	6,213	12,372	337	49	682	92	195	162
Pitt County	5,215	3,616	3,713	16,853	279	na	196	na	77	na
Randolph County	7,796	4,105	2,299	20,265	163	na	226	na	0	na
Robeson County	4,121	2,601	1,829	15,279	295	na	115	na	44	na
Rockingham County	5,943	3,046	1,523	15,427	87	na	106	na	43	na
Rowan County	8,166	4,542	2,538	20,376	34	na	129	na	50	na
Rutherford County	4,016	2,634	1,810	11,799	54	na	145	na	49	na
Surry County	3,927	2,411	1,557	12,376	113	na	8	na	0	na
Union County	8,037	5,372	3,256	19,547	491	na	387	na	117	na
Wake County	22,012	21,376	28,148	75,524	1,731	1,107	2,901	1,090	1,577	1,133
Wayne County	6,001	3,743	2,063	15,963	198	na	190	na	113	na
Wilkes County	3,718	2,898	829	na	na	na	na	na	na	na
Wilson County	3,976	2,182	1,838	11,795	144	na	55	na	0	na
North Dakota										
Burleigh County	3,388	2,993	2,473	10,401	3	na	1,070	na	11	na
Cass County	4,947	4,582	3,873	14,529	53	0	452	116	197	182
Grand Forks County	2,303	1,979	1,446	6,882	47	na	159	na	34	na
Ohio										
Allen County	7,639	2,777	2,108	15,500	112	na	66	na	7	na
Ashtabula County	7,756	2,795	1,935	15,584	191	na	196	na	15	na
Belmont County	6,997	1,963	1,130	12,093	52	na	211	na	84	na
Butler County	17,661	8,280	8,380	42,227	294	61	772	389	370	107
Clark County	9,576	5,234	3,271	22,256	104	na	201	na	47	na
Clermont County	8,947	4,816	4,174	23,735	103	na	338	na	124	na
Columbiana County	8,903	3,002	2,079	17,814	76	na	214	na	27	na
Cuyahoga County	71,660	43,847	40,156	177,037	3,013	1,907	14,968	7,912	2,145	1,242
Delaware County	5,714	3,692	6,116	16,946	38	na	642	na	267	na
Erie County	6,076	2,756	2,406	13,359	143	na	137	na	60	na
Fairfield County	9,118	3,880	3,009	18,197	184	na	163	na	97	na
Franklin County	42,527	26,305	30,115	111,601	1,139	693	3,500	1,256	2,136	1,254
Geauga County	5,696	3,406	3,747	13,463	61	na	1,360	na	7	na
Greene County	8,020	5,203	6,192	21,987	243	na	388	na	302	na
Hamilton County	34,928	23,578	28,223	102,971	550	158	2,911	1,095	926	378
Hancock County	5,353	2,350	1,891	10,928	99	na	44	na	58	na
Jefferson County	6,731	2,121	1,514	12,241	170	na	330	na	42	na
Lake County	15,766	9,017	6,148	35,155	308	163	2,267	1,138	160	26
Licking County	10,510	4,582	3,454	22,434	46	na	310	na	66	na
Lorain County	18,730	9,489	7,192	41,059	1,548	885	1,410	531	243	95
Lucas County	24,064	13,097	10,795	55,878	981	273	1,347	217	423	186
Mahoning County	20,334	7,901	5,782	40,134	488	272	1,657	429	127	38
Marion County	4,821	1,700	849	9,419	35	na	81	na	0	na
Medina County	9,824	5,615	4,330	22,145	89	na	1,191	na	52	na
Miami County	7,466	3,267	2,592	16,055	20	na	123	na	0	na
Montgomery County	30,268	20,248	16,776	80,273	494	214	1,444	488	611	452
Muskingum County	7,349	2,116	1,149	13,110	70	na	53	na	28	na
Portage County	9,423	4,232	4,271	20,904	65	na	398	na	56	na
Richland County	10,109	3,624	2,717	20,154	0	na	468	na	129	na
Ross County	4,903	1,720	1,100	10,604	8	na	28	na	73	na
Scioto County	5,167	1,895	1,183	12,279	13	na	23	na	12	na
Stark County	29,910	11,880	8,526	59,422	286	136	1,896	675	88	58
Summit County	31,962	17,496	16,742	76,917	324	168	2,756	1,049	516	217
Trumbull County	18,385	6,427	4,187	34,679	99	na	2,138	na	110	na
Tuscarawas County	8,364	2,315	1,566	14,975	26	na	325	na	0	na
Warren County	9,006	4,895	5,441	23,229	136	na	606	na	153	na
Wayne County	8,288	2,951	2,708	16,294	82	na	794	na	77	na
Wood County	6,986	3,580	3,144	15,455	182	na	228	na	30	na
Oklahoma										
Canadian County	4,678	4,063	2,662	12,745	196	na	161	na	278	na
Cleveland County	9,151	7,223	7,467	26,059	567	225	272	16	650	473
Comanche County	4,521	3,281	2,386	11,446	307	177	660	186	396	234
Creek County	4,115	2,551	1,490	10,699	40	na	48	na	27	na
Muskogee County	3,482	2,643	1,932	10,282	87	na	80	na	27	na
Oklahoma County	26,180	24,937	22,649	82,130	2,704	1,555	1,043	292	1,767	1,446
Payne County	2,479	2,038	2,350	7,909	45	na	80	na	5	na
Pottawatomie County	4,145	2,752	1,272	9,946	61	na	111	na	28	na
Rogers County	4,736	3,127	2,098	11,903	154	na	72	na	0	na
Tulsa County	23,829	20,712	18,224	71,014	1,526	802	1,191	349	694	502
Wagoner County	3,959	2,443	1,571	9,477	235	na	102	na	104	na

Table E-2: Counties—Educational Attainment and Language Spoken at Home, Persons 65 Years and Over—*Continued*

	High School or Equivalent	Some College or Associates Degree	Bachelor's Degree or Higher	Speaks English at Home — Total	Speaks Spanish at Home — Total	Speaks Spanish at Home — Speaks English Less Than Very Well	Speaks Indo-European at Home — Total	Speaks Indo-European at Home — Speaks English Less Than Very Well	Speaks Asian at Home — Total	Speaks Asian at Home — Speaks English Less Than Very Well
Oregon										
Benton County	2,042	2,939	4,911	10,114	230	na	303	na	90	na
Clackamas County	16,648	17,581	14,843	50,993	937	290	1,208	533	914	757
Deschutes County	7,091	8,472	7,421	24,377	341	na	460	na	81	na
Douglas County	8,418	7,394	3,196	22,430	277	na	374	na	104	na
Jackson County	11,297	11,591	9,519	35,436	830	na	778	na	174	na
Josephine County	6,120	6,787	3,214	18,319	229	na	195	na	99	na
Klamath County	4,383	3,744	1,997	10,918	579	na	247	na	42	na
Lane County	17,270	16,294	15,066	52,593	904	295	858	170	512	411
Linn County	7,139	5,483	2,899	18,243	255	na	225	na	47	na
Marion County	13,950	13,054	9,539	38,486	1,693	1,065	1,281	507	499	376
Multnomah County	21,642	22,100	25,664	70,216	1,878	839	3,914	2,030	4,467	3,788
Polk County	3,406	3,740	2,977	10,925	542	na	222	na	75	na
Umatilla County	3,228	3,437	1,493	9,222	390	na	172	na	22	na
Washington County	14,903	16,906	18,488	49,432	1,991	1,189	2,165	717	2,700	2,264
Yamhill County	5,404	3,789	2,632	13,210	433	na	171	na	86	na
Pennsylvania										
Adams County	6,977	2,458	2,992	16,166	186	na	223	na	55	na
Allegheny County	93,751	37,109	42,716	193,483	1,205	265	9,066	3,341	1,203	791
Armstrong County	7,324	1,461	1,252	12,598	47	na	251	na	20	na
Beaver County	15,821	5,749	4,091	30,495	233	na	1,082	na	26	na
Berks County	27,826	8,362	8,718	54,479	2,291	1,832	3,524	947	358	257
Blair County	12,751	3,311	2,152	22,256	49	na	482	na	38	na
Bucks County	38,145	18,183	23,323	85,806	999	513	6,087	3,079	1,423	873
Butler County	14,120	5,167	5,173	28,000	140	na	512	na	88	na
Cambria County	14,807	3,272	2,831	26,202	171	na	760	na	22	na
Carbon County	6,325	1,848	1,015	11,154	27	na	607	na	10	na
Centre County	7,291	2,659	5,251	17,143	78	6	388	51	143	63
Chester County	21,961	12,774	23,084	62,369	959	421	2,518	1,097	774	492
Clearfield County	7,736	1,896	1,126	14,215	13	na	185	na	15	na
Columbia County	5,482	1,453	1,234	10,626	25	na	187	na	11	na
Crawford County	7,586	2,379	2,017	14,454	7	na	493	na	23	na
Cumberland County	16,373	6,780	8,306	35,680	320	170	1,420	464	338	122
Dauphin County	16,931	6,108	6,802	35,282	630	330	1,272	541	253	134
Delaware County	33,583	13,917	20,211	72,462	766	281	5,314	2,182	1,762	1,314
Erie County	19,913	7,393	7,253	39,302	303	113	1,618	458	68	39
Fayette County	13,195	3,100	2,075	24,013	52	na	529	na	12	na
Franklin County	12,199	3,420	4,223	24,625	270	na	529	na	0	na
Indiana County	6,894	1,544	2,062	13,688	7	na	243	na	93	na
Lackawanna County	18,576	7,071	4,644	35,456	385	231	2,476	919	136	114
Lancaster County	33,949	12,741	14,534	73,877	1,755	1,047	3,767	1,569	678	570
Lawrence County	9,024	2,417	2,304	16,069	26	na	1,040	na	34	na
Lebanon County	11,440	3,098	3,142	21,644	350	294	846	311	99	65
Lehigh County	21,919	9,113	8,576	45,411	2,640	2,007	3,443	1,356	440	363
Luzerne County	29,475	10,270	7,020	54,889	679	496	2,308	536	84	84
Lycoming County	9,504	3,023	2,414	18,816	73	na	334	na	15	na
Mercer County	11,335	3,190	2,993	21,127	19	na	564	na	15	na
Monroe County	9,684	4,230	3,943	19,738	781	589	1,158	597	186	102
Montgomery County	43,269	23,519	38,840	112,842	1,292	583	6,233	2,771	3,191	2,338
Northampton County	20,377	8,299	8,089	43,102	1,494	1,081	2,325	1,098	309	242
Northumberland County	9,698	1,994	1,091	17,068	9	na	460	na	14	na
Philadelphia County	71,433	27,389	27,911	156,247	9,256	6,588	13,844	9,310	6,262	5,555
Schuylkill County	15,284	3,535	2,103	25,608	87	na	1,202	na	48	na
Somerset County	7,761	1,863	1,243	14,184	28	na	428	na	41	na
Washington County	19,304	5,801	4,999	35,365	145	na	1,364	na	142	na
Westmoreland County	34,273	11,359	11,141	67,432	226	88	1,614	370	149	87
York County	29,455	9,891	8,641	60,970	674	466	1,124	247	332	243
Rhode Island										
Kent County	9,794	5,610	5,609	24,308	271	na	1,819	na	153	na
Newport County	4,226	3,453	4,839	13,225	100	na	953	na	202	na
Providence County	27,947	14,326	14,508	64,144	4,808	4,167	14,611	6,883	1,070	874
Washington County	5,880	4,165	6,691	18,360	113	na	1,154	na	154	na
South Carolina										
Aiken County	7,770	6,649	5,519	25,164	257	na	288	na	88	na
Anderson County	9,715	6,548	4,445	28,725	309	na	420	na	13	na
Beaufort County	7,452	8,354	16,657	33,864	712	na	776	na	197	na
Berkeley County	7,071	4,408	2,590	18,474	201	na	250	na	575	na
Charleston County	11,426	11,875	14,521	45,613	421	199	811	349	292	195
Darlington County	3,563	1,821	1,580	10,025	71	na	88	na	0	na
Dorchester County	5,599	3,343	2,754	13,541	560	na	316	na	270	na
Florence County	6,479	3,364	2,986	18,247	148	na	157	na	16	na
Greenville County	18,984	12,970	14,069	57,527	1,230	810	967	188	445	261
Greenwood County	3,203	1,654	2,431	na	na	na	na	na	na	na

Table E-2: Counties—Educational Attainment and Language Spoken at Home, Persons 65 Years and Over—*Continued*

	High School or Equivalent	Some College or Associates Degree	Bachelor's Degree or Higher	Speaks English at Home Total	Speaks Spanish at Home Total	Speaks English Less Than Very Well	Speaks Indo-European at Home Total	Speaks English Less Than Very Well	Speaks Asian at Home Total	Speaks English Less Than Very Well
South Carolina—Cont.										
Horry County	17,762	13,008	10,694	46,896	560	152	1,314	620	239	165
Lancaster County	4,602	2,862	2,344	12,406	157	na	240	na	0	na
Laurens County	3,823	1,780	1,400	na	na	na	na	na	na	na
Lexington County	11,473	8,253	7,552	32,560	437	na	507	na	216	na
Oconee County	4,495	3,562	3,070	14,102	222	na	285	na	25	na
Orangeburg County	5,354	1,918	2,220	13,971	68	na	59	na	49	na
Pickens County	4,710	2,915	3,383	15,951	218	na	152	na	129	na
Richland County	10,902	9,361	11,540	37,261	648	335	1,037	306	335	202
Spartanburg County	12,526	8,766	6,454	38,256	316	161	523	190	307	162
Sumter County	4,035	3,453	2,211	13,873	82	na	59	na	97	na
York County	8,809	6,011	5,510	26,355	285	na	336	na	39	na
South Dakota										
Minnehaha County	7,501	4,665	3,919	18,406	51	0	705	359	109	105
Pennington County	4,724	3,643	3,743	13,543	174	na	333	na	23	na
Tennessee										
Anderson County	4,059	2,933	3,246	13,026	88	na	77	na	58	na
Blount County	7,114	4,943	3,885	20,089	119	na	321	na	40	na
Bradley County	5,188	3,341	1,709	14,272	284	na	91	na	12	na
Davidson County	21,449	15,026	17,167	63,205	1,117	567	1,427	612	852	671
Greene County	3,959	2,918	1,483	na	na	na	na	na	na	na
Hamilton County	15,897	12,993	10,647	49,480	695	496	478	136	421	269
Knox County	18,828	15,462	13,152	56,460	373	146	893	445	567	358
Madison County	4,497	3,115	2,573	13,188	28	na	55	na	0	na
Maury County	4,146	2,297	1,480	10,750	0	na	166	na	77	na
Montgomery County	5,255	3,124	2,813	13,061	363	na	489	na	314	na
Putnam County	3,466	1,536	2,035	10,604	51	na	133	na	48	na
Robertson County	3,679	1,745	1,006	na	na	na	na	na	na	na
Rutherford County	8,432	5,647	4,316	22,106	406	na	368	na	240	na
Sevier County	4,879	3,119	1,808	14,211	140	na	132	na	57	na
Shelby County	30,174	22,514	22,192	94,382	1,130	531	1,116	430	1,246	949
Sullivan County	11,158	6,095	5,678	29,662	73	na	178	na	123	na
Sumner County	7,781	5,248	3,254	21,115	393	na	208	na	0	na
Washington County	6,571	3,815	4,187	18,859	172	na	214	na	73	na
Williamson County	5,353	4,708	6,487	18,398	214	na	249	na	150	na
Wilson County	5,396	3,388	2,381	14,627	123	na	159	na	93	na
Texas										
Angelina County	4,100	2,875	2,078	11,209	659	na	326	na	21	na
Bastrop County	2,677	2,101	1,656	7,771	1,028	na	57	na	0	na
Bell County	8,616	7,855	5,860	23,949	2,497	1,852	914	208	907	592
Bexar County	44,868	45,214	40,386	98,292	77,684	33,805	4,578	1,309	2,754	1,574
Bowie County	4,576	3,587	2,607	13,224	163	na	56	na	48	na
Brazoria County	9,436	9,296	6,245	25,969	3,843	1,913	618	169	1,104	602
Brazos County	3,799	3,286	5,096	12,802	1,375	712	440	128	186	141
Cameron County	9,592	6,832	5,586	15,872	30,010	20,509	394	113	211	163
Collin County	16,007	18,237	24,908	55,449	3,125	1,436	4,381	2,616	3,485	2,405
Comal County	5,503	4,268	5,550	14,916	2,063	na	987	na	0	na
Coryell County	1,828	1,828	1,050	5,278	340	na	309	na	200	na
Dallas County	56,299	51,306	59,362	173,573	29,244	18,654	5,839	2,510	6,351	5,125
Denton County	13,876	14,497	15,350	43,429	3,215	1,854	1,883	878	1,758	1,107
Ector County	3,832	3,217	1,784	10,082	3,787	na	84	na	68	na
Ellis County	5,471	4,257	2,629	14,219	1,397	na	254	na	33	na
El Paso County	18,226	13,720	11,117	20,499	61,831	41,771	1,451	476	822	512
Fort Bend County	11,086	12,554	14,551	31,896	6,589	3,016	3,354	1,706	5,106	3,361
Galveston County	11,186	9,199	8,046	29,818	3,177	1,083	534	106	664	216
Grayson County	6,286	5,892	3,426	18,758	348	na	68	na	0	na
Gregg County	4,931	4,779	3,597	15,734	446	na	276	na	120	na
Guadalupe County	5,131	3,894	3,460	12,172	3,309	na	634	na	82	na
Harris County	88,398	82,573	91,443	252,718	65,964	42,589	12,049	5,145	18,638	14,375
Harrison County	3,644	2,283	1,334	na	na	na	na	na	na	na
Hays County	3,795	3,203	5,583	11,539	2,632	na	172	na	109	na
Henderson County	5,470	4,222	2,497	14,915	402	na	36	na	0	na
Hidalgo County	14,936	9,897	8,515	22,204	52,370	38,847	807	402	400	147
Hunt County	3,839	2,567	2,549	11,704	301	na	50	na	0	na
Jefferson County	10,989	8,304	5,879	28,601	1,808	827	1,225	248	490	351
Johnson County	6,324	5,136	2,843	17,068	954	na	71	na	114	na
Kaufman County	4,137	3,105	1,484	10,481	482	na	200	na	30	na
Liberty County	3,560	1,882	894	8,045	287	na	399	na	0	na
Lubbock County	8,528	7,672	7,811	26,055	4,982	2,588	157	15	241	197
McLennan County	9,463	7,870	6,199	26,716	2,589	1,298	438	88	160	160
Midland County	4,098	4,096	3,366	12,151	2,646	na	190	na	180	na
Montgomery County	15,461	14,331	13,253	46,308	3,211	1,382	949	109	628	592
Nacogdoches County	2,468	1,219	2,160	7,431	269	na	22	na	30	na
Nueces County	10,026	8,996	8,653	21,350	19,728	9,200	720	241	497	348
Orange County	5,264	2,898	1,111	10,877	278	na	366	na	81	na
Parker County	4,940	4,579	3,216	14,774	474	na	91	na	0	na
Potter County	3,497	3,679	2,269	11,335	1,709	888	52	9	340	309

Table E-2: Counties—Educational Attainment and Language Spoken at Home, Persons 65 Years and Over—*Continued*

	High School or Equivalent	Some College or Associates Degree	Bachelor's Degree or Higher	Speaks English at Home Total	Speaks Spanish at Home Total	Speaks English Less Than Very Well	Speaks Indo-European at Home Total	Speaks English Less Than Very Well	Speaks Asian at Home Total	Speaks English Less Than Very Well
Texas—Cont.										
Randall County	4,621	4,990	4,007	14,682	636	na	131	na	0	na
Rockwall County	2,307	2,558	2,200	7,406	441	na	183	na	123	na
San Patricio County	2,357	1,816	1,172	5,112	3,225	na	119	na	28	na
Smith County	8,624	10,169	7,181	29,275	1,189	na	344	na	171	na
Tarrant County	49,287	46,267	41,315	144,687	16,477	9,596	3,920	1,641	4,524	3,610
Taylor County	5,073	4,926	4,468	15,529	1,595	na	288	na	190	na
Tom Green County	4,893	3,634	3,312	12,460	2,958	na	95	na	28	na
Travis County	16,672	19,945	31,036	63,464	12,035	6,116	2,039	668	2,505	1,918
Victoria County	3,562	3,106	1,685	8,888	2,677	na	186	na	16	na
Walker County	2,355	1,645	1,941	6,868	281	na	13	na	0	na
Webb County	2,822	2,786	1,818	1,470	18,684	na	76	na	0	na
Wichita County	6,430	4,494	3,017	16,003	941	433	143	93	148	103
Williamson County	10,694	10,885	14,339	35,971	2,820	1,496	1,765	825	470	325
Utah										
Cache County	2,014	2,981	3,055	8,546	302	na	147	na	32	na
Davis County	8,066	9,016	7,337	24,515	701	267	670	122	345	286
Salt Lake County	26,292	28,608	26,037	81,510	4,449	2,438	3,989	1,586	2,560	1,718
Utah County	8,540	12,036	12,479	32,364	1,744	1,018	816	96	424	247
Washington County	7,709	8,557	7,050	24,140	753	na	425	na	103	na
Weber County	6,793	8,908	5,302	22,348	1,045	671	658	98	228	161
Vermont										
Chittenden County	5,527	3,812	7,022	16,944	109	21	1,140	190	267	258
Virginia										
Albemarle County	3,356	3,095	6,538	13,997	177	na	599	na	215	na
Arlington County	3,516	3,238	9,688	14,390	1,515	759	1,509	628	1,090	706
Augusta County	5,082	2,255	1,974	12,229	53	na	113	na	0	na
Bedford County	3,860	2,614	2,385	11,604	154	na	92	na	27	na
Chesterfield County	11,304	8,360	9,755	33,270	534	224	723	221	652	438
Fairfax County	23,056	21,592	56,435	80,822	7,245	4,160	9,314	4,082	13,325	9,644
Fauquier County	2,660	2,671	2,450	8,855	101	na	44	na	29	na
Frederick County	3,771	2,041	1,886	10,188	21	na	143	na	0	na
Hanover County	5,481	3,070	2,981	13,193	79	na	372	na	9	na
Henrico County	12,152	9,609	10,634	36,316	583	199	1,332	773	943	640
James City County	3,191	3,270	7,058	13,829	135	na	362	na	146	na
Loudoun County	5,988	5,409	8,894	17,488	1,207	856	2,142	1,093	1,747	1,361
Montgomery County	2,465	1,662	3,071	9,253	63	na	141	na	50	na
Prince William County	8,565	7,137	9,134	23,583	1,966	1,349	2,038	795	1,900	1,343
Roanoke County	5,207	5,033	3,286	16,031	131	na	371	na	14	na
Rockingham County	4,256	1,975	2,311	12,381	60	na	112	na	0	na
Spotsylvania County	4,169	3,136	2,848	12,375	157	na	298	na	59	na
Stafford County	3,289	2,231	2,796	9,285	257	95	397	142	219	75
York County	2,101	2,252	2,724	7,715	45	na	265	na	150	na
Washington										
Benton County	6,492	5,797	6,655	19,595	899	313	849	336	362	203
Chelan County	3,875	3,139	2,776	10,917	167	na	135	na	59	na
Clallam County	4,835	5,639	5,503	16,862	176	na	458	na	56	na
Clark County	15,803	17,365	12,538	47,017	862	405	2,541	1,580	1,565	1,091
Cowlitz County	5,447	5,674	2,721	16,034	112	na	283	na	109	na
Franklin County	1,703	1,584	1,031	4,652	998	na	203	na	95	na
Grant County	3,687	3,387	1,497	9,627	1,069	na	185	na	126	na
Grays Harbor County	4,415	4,196	1,483	11,689	100	na	154	na	116	na
Island County	3,478	5,124	5,577	13,966	230	na	425	na	423	na
King County	52,374	61,554	81,252	179,468	4,246	1,566	12,702	6,655	23,443	17,749
Kitsap County	9,444	12,190	10,403	32,150	577	355	774	240	1,587	904
Lewis County	4,912	3,885	2,459	12,936	220	na	186	na	17	na
Pierce County	31,114	26,917	20,820	80,887	1,577	633	3,565	1,254	5,702	4,172
Skagit County	5,441	6,452	5,157	18,480	546	265	493	219	184	115
Snohomish County	23,127	24,045	20,630	67,710	1,316	655	3,369	1,638	5,242	4,564
Spokane County	19,716	19,445	15,882	59,319	833	215	2,180	1,054	867	692
Thurston County	8,912	10,847	11,029	31,799	716	317	558	72	1,225	841
Whatcom County	7,856	8,679	8,123	25,350	437	174	1,582	841	370	87
Yakima County	7,692	7,635	4,695	24,280	3,973	2,869	434	178	284	275
West Virginia										
Berkeley County	4,976	2,674	2,008	12,001	83	na	289	na	101	na
Cabell County	5,936	2,922	2,737	15,157	50	na	176	na	44	na
Harrison County	5,533	2,160	1,586	11,364	42	na	169	na	17	na
Kanawha County	14,028	5,793	5,655	32,073	73	na	284	na	195	na
Monongalia County	3,879	1,544	2,294	9,739	15	na	164	na	16	na
Raleigh County	5,095	2,494	1,551	12,648	16	na	171	na	76	na
Wood County	6,169	3,626	1,835	14,629	118	na	63	na	91	na

Table E-2: Counties—Educational Attainment and Language Spoken at Home, Persons 65 Years and Over—*Continued*

	High School or Equivalent	Some College or Associates Degree	Bachelor's Degree or Higher	Speaks English at Home Total	Speaks Spanish at Home Total	Speaks English Less Than Very Well	Speaks Indo-European at Home Total	Speaks English Less Than Very Well	Speaks Asian at Home Total	Speaks English Less Than Very Well
Wisconsin										
Brown County	13,381	6,371	4,937	28,365	354	277	653	174	136	130
Dane County	17,661	10,657	19,753	49,785	530	292	1,612	467	701	510
Dodge County	5,845	2,309	1,684	13,068	61	na	295	na	0	na
Eau Claire County	5,220	3,055	2,911	12,532	64	na	117	na	38	na
Fond du Lac County	7,288	2,976	2,228	15,125	120	na	331	na	45	na
Jefferson County	5,418	2,068	2,094	11,022	38	na	267	na	0	na
Kenosha County	8,533	3,703	2,598	17,437	474	na	1,013	na	82	na
La Crosse County	6,505	3,863	3,333	15,284	39	na	194	na	152	na
Manitowoc County	7,183	2,396	1,996	13,599	121	na	253	na	93	na
Marathon County	8,828	3,301	2,898	18,827	104	18	563	189	183	103
Milwaukee County	41,665	23,545	21,907	97,812	4,150	2,841	5,870	2,785	1,600	1,187
Outagamie County	10,442	3,990	3,659	20,702	262	146	233	51	151	151
Ozaukee County	4,506	3,455	4,338	12,943	43	na	553	na	69	na
Portage County	4,218	1,547	1,585	8,770	38	na	389	na	57	na
Racine County	10,783	5,529	4,806	24,486	824	366	867	218	65	44
Rock County	10,390	5,001	3,123	21,311	168	na	582	na	80	na
St. Croix County	4,093	1,403	2,390	8,757	27	na	76	na	32	na
Sheboygan County	9,047	2,765	2,379	16,360	201	109	532	175	91	91
Walworth County	5,510	3,243	3,285	13,498	160	na	355	na	20	na
Washington County	7,506	4,073	3,204	17,576	103	na	664	na	0	na
Waukesha County	22,662	14,538	15,077	54,632	487	203	2,324	562	401	268
Winnebago County	10,614	4,612	4,726	22,232	109	na	329	na	104	na
Wood County	6,614	2,279	1,412	12,635	26	na	215	na	65	na
Wyoming										
Laramie County	4,571	3,406	2,342	10,867	924	na	117	na	165	na
Natrona County	3,253	3,282	1,765	9,158	292	na	101	na	34	na

Table E-3: Places—Educational Attainment and Language Spoken at Home, Persons 65 Years and Over

	High School or Equivalent	Some College or Associates Degree	Bachelor's Degree or Higher	Speaks English at Home Total	Speaks Spanish at Home Total	Speaks Spanish at Home Speaks English Less Than Very Well	Speaks Indo-European at Home Total	Speaks Indo-European at Home Speaks English Less Than Very Well	Speaks Asian at Home Total	Speaks Asian at Home Speaks English Less Than Very Well
Alabama										
Birmingham city	8,728	5,840	4,833	26,527	106	na	373	na	49	na
Dothan city	3,386	2,533	1,635	9,592	117	na	84	na	19	na
Hoover city	2,151	2,792	4,492	9,634	49	na	194	na	87	na
Huntsville city	6,522	6,542	9,548	24,642	226	na	404	na	218	na
Mobile city	9,235	6,244	6,207	26,253	286	na	333	na	87	na
Montgomery city	6,888	5,652	7,203	23,800	197	na	272	na	258	na
Tuscaloosa city	2,769	1,789	3,063	9,276	84	na	73	na	39	na
Alaska										
Anchorage Municipality	5,695	7,264	6,459	18,198	719	402	769	177	2,337	1,727
Arizona										
Avondale city	968	1,158	433	2,541	1,725	na	132	na	24	na
Chandler city	5,035	6,689	5,685	16,941	1,448	635	961	239	886	510
Flagstaff city	687	1,127	2,146	3,648	625	na	84	na	34	na
Glendale city	6,284	6,121	4,218	17,115	2,189	1,226	595	312	807	433
Goodyear city	1,624	2,934	2,385	6,466	804	na	48	na	331	na
Mesa city	24,951	20,693	14,152	60,979	4,284	2,004	1,823	518	789	512
Peoria city	7,074	7,303	5,050	19,589	1,297	500	619	137	625	504
Phoenix city	34,399	37,221	30,614	99,984	19,706	10,939	4,976	1,939	2,670	1,953
Scottsdale city	9,921	13,706	19,365	40,863	1,144	255	2,662	822	425	159
Surprise city	6,536	7,331	7,467	21,339	912	na	585	na	175	na
Tempe city	3,728	3,463	5,050	11,141	1,390	426	702	278	519	300
Tucson city	16,982	18,106	15,166	45,748	15,425	7,470	2,081	554	1,014	857
Yuma city	3,821	3,122	1,543	8,734	2,910	na	348	na	165	na
Arkansas										
Fayetteville city	1,958	1,491	2,109	6,221	28	na	0	na	30	na
Fort Smith city	3,802	2,710	2,495	10,410	95	na	121	na	147	na
Jonesboro city	2,611	1,779	1,556	7,392	0	na	122	na	71	na
Little Rock city	6,061	5,002	7,924	22,040	281	na	487	na	74	na
Springdale city	2,433	1,280	1,023	6,077	59	na	14	na	29	na
California										
Alameda city	1,615	2,734	3,865	6,008	367	200	716	330	2,314	1,613
Alhambra city	2,658	2,592	2,967	2,806	2,810	1,275	529	260	6,239	5,259
Anaheim city	8,812	8,020	7,077	18,144	6,642	4,608	2,349	1,186	5,097	3,877
Antioch city	3,329	3,069	1,572	6,730	1,247	777	449	233	1,012	728
Bakersfield city	8,034	8,896	5,694	22,183	6,060	4,179	1,676	1,028	991	584
Baldwin Park city	1,338	801	825	1,278	3,788	na	38	na	1,746	na
Bellflower city	2,396	1,541	696	3,768	1,650	1,076	303	132	922	567
Berkeley city	1,728	2,484	8,997	11,370	777	420	1,000	273	1,130	603
Buena Park city	2,524	2,323	2,189	4,395	1,427	776	747	447	2,573	2,162
Burbank city	3,590	3,720	3,326	6,847	1,986	1,083	3,833	3,183	1,500	1,092
Camarillo city	2,694	3,680	3,768	9,382	1,103	588	443	108	605	434
Carlsbad city	2,893	5,062	7,096	12,938	1,168	431	959	287	925	786
Carson city	3,392	3,035	2,385	6,458	2,336	1,506	201	63	3,643	2,553
Chico city	2,589	2,863	2,664	8,566	396	na	319	na	105	na
Chino city	2,260	1,553	1,555	3,089	2,059	997	512	280	1,336	740
Chino Hills city	1,338	1,549	1,736	2,431	896	656	400	98	1,631	1,187
Chula Vista city	5,561	5,739	5,208	11,556	9,471	6,790	546	256	3,762	1,911
Citrus Heights city	3,368	4,007	2,529	10,155	496	209	607	504	406	254
Clovis city	3,023	3,338	2,693	8,434	1,027	456	543	226	597	438
Compton city	1,865	1,818	532	5,011	2,221	na	17	na	94	na
Concord city	4,053	4,847	4,480	11,287	1,104	621	966	592	1,362	806
Corona city	3,353	2,924	2,511	7,030	2,385	1,701	676	383	1,633	1,194
Costa Mesa city	2,231	3,153	3,178	7,706	948	709	566	182	567	378
Daly City city	3,610	3,221	3,765	4,080	1,655	1,046	944	437	7,006	4,682
Davis city	717	941	3,352	4,511	262	na	330	na	274	na
Downey city	3,177	2,529	1,844	5,124	4,819	3,650	329	111	1,152	741
El Cajon city	3,071	2,832	2,158	7,784	786	534	514	244	366	256
Elk Grove city	3,903	4,480	3,024	8,554	1,307	920	1,460	729	2,972	2,092
El Monte city	2,996	1,285	850	2,515	4,880	3,632	100	51	4,251	3,863
Escondido city	3,518	4,300	3,769	10,586	2,608	1,906	589	177	976	675
Fairfield city	3,138	3,618	2,168	7,840	915	488	514	228	1,997	1,192
Folsom city	1,853	1,984	2,281	5,800	191	na	513	na	269	na
Fontana city	2,704	2,415	914	5,375	5,123	4,121	124	53	1,297	779
Fremont city	6,715	4,601	7,638	11,610	1,653	742	3,382	2,184	7,271	5,718
Fresno city	10,809	12,578	8,534	30,177	9,736	5,386	2,819	1,635	3,623	2,904
Fullerton city	3,976	4,130	5,697	10,048	2,126	1,030	1,316	680	3,017	2,023
Garden Grove city	4,707	4,926	3,193	9,083	2,404	1,681	447	253	7,301	6,853
Glendale city	6,094	5,339	8,467	9,526	2,554	1,859	14,377	12,737	3,640	2,323
Hawthorne city	1,535	1,499	887	3,399	2,080	1,676	252	99	553	368
Hayward city	4,654	3,510	2,872	8,162	2,734	1,862	950	542	3,347	2,666

Table E-3: Places—Educational Attainment and Language Spoken at Home, Persons 65 Years and Over—*Continued*

	High School or Equivalent	Some College or Associates Degree	Bachelor's Degree or Higher	Speaks English at Home	Speaks Spanish at Home		Speaks Indo-European at Home		Speaks Asian at Home	
				Total	Total	Speaks English Less Than Very Well	Total	Speaks English Less Than Very Well	Total	Speaks English Less Than Very Well
California—Cont.										
Hemet city	5,738	6,372	2,308	15,104	2,092	na	442	na	393	na
Hesperia city	2,960	2,495	732	6,760	1,864	na	252	na	167	na
Huntington Beach city	6,693	9,092	9,839	21,950	1,814	812	1,730	445	2,388	1,775
Indio city	1,909	3,743	2,093	7,285	2,962	na	157	na	77	na
Inglewood city	1,981	3,162	1,997	7,472	2,444	na	212	na	131	na
Irvine city	3,113	4,233	9,480	10,506	913	350	3,412	2,123	4,144	3,076
Jurupa Valley city[1]	2,124	1,921	659	4,643	2,311	na	103	na	277	na
Lake Forest city	1,783	2,679	2,534	5,655	1,122	675	305	209	808	588
Lakewood city	3,123	2,577	1,691	6,393	1,136	789	437	132	1,671	1,188
Lancaster city	3,335	4,596	2,144	10,082	2,227	1,713	532	337	609	325
Livermore city	1,694	3,141	2,839	7,323	492	na	365	na	438	na
Long Beach city	9,060	11,462	12,252	28,817	6,228	4,526	1,542	473	7,253	5,570
Los Angeles city	87,985	91,845	109,566	205,969	95,072	74,789	47,449	31,637	55,136	41,465
Lynwood city	700	736	149	1,493	2,972	na	48	na	53	na
Manteca city	2,625	1,850	933	5,323	854	346	375	271	395	295
Menifee city	4,170	5,458	2,333	12,312	1,586	na	262	na	285	na
Merced city	1,719	2,011	1,117	4,927	1,691	1,131	261	132	402	402
Milpitas city	1,105	1,369	2,085	1,552	725	558	414	241	3,931	2,866
Mission Viejo city	2,832	4,946	5,160	11,400	846	278	1,244	415	534	257
Modesto city	6,995	6,717	4,164	17,764	2,722	1,543	1,263	624	809	550
Moreno Valley city	3,252	3,302	1,891	6,981	4,331	3,157	596	167	1,064	623
Mountain View city	1,710	1,931	3,587	4,881	701	324	1,194	728	1,339	1,069
Murrieta city	2,878	3,092	2,697	8,037	1,238	552	349	135	854	423
Napa city	2,761	3,383	3,124	9,085	696	na	569	na	207	na
Newport Beach city	2,354	3,879	9,394	14,343	696	na	703	na	360	na
Norwalk city	2,467	2,781	893	4,063	4,360	2,913	380	285	1,777	1,434
Oakland city	8,883	10,370	13,877	30,095	3,774	2,485	1,269	390	10,377	8,932
Oceanside city	4,868	6,364	5,792	15,782	2,700	1,903	933	169	1,416	1,086
Ontario city	3,179	2,546	1,269	6,508	4,759	3,729	322	118	635	493
Orange city	3,388	4,814	4,872	10,686	1,748	1,112	737	459	1,998	1,452
Oxnard city	3,198	3,735	3,145	7,446	6,564	4,850	333	92	2,322	1,401
Palmdale city	2,763	2,896	1,956	6,968	2,665	2,097	418	320	553	282
Palo Alto city	1,002	2,007	7,722	8,627	380	na	970	na	1,292	na
Pasadena city	3,778	4,197	7,798	12,432	3,315	2,148	1,182	698	2,228	1,720
Perris city	694	701	214	1,619	1,322	na	57	na	128	na
Pleasanton city	2,160	2,366	2,715	6,721	264	152	335	160	707	564
Pomona city	2,703	2,451	1,791	5,605	4,570	3,595	328	192	1,435	1,103
Rancho Cordova city	2,721	1,823	1,309	4,990	434	255	996	665	715	527
Rancho Cucamonga city	4,429	3,751	2,669	7,940	3,586	1,870	365	111	1,628	1,183
Redding city	4,422	5,673	2,818	13,924	361	na	432	na	242	na
Redlands city	1,947	2,239	3,329	6,962	1,250	632	316	121	267	140
Redondo Beach city	1,042	2,552	3,053	5,791	900	321	413	300	448	374
Redwood City city	1,981	2,263	2,791	6,003	1,233	940	722	225	612	400
Rialto city	2,048	2,042	781	4,701	2,344	na	175	na	208	na
Richmond city	1,893	2,829	3,129	7,343	963	696	404	113	1,483	978
Riverside city	7,318	7,947	6,542	19,612	6,490	3,951	822	275	1,282	860
Roseville city	4,277	5,793	4,756	14,038	846	370	745	354	668	584
Sacramento city	12,010	13,775	13,465	35,733	5,440	3,152	3,259	1,914	7,947	6,098
Salinas city	2,875	2,346	2,122	5,838	4,119	2,932	392	115	1,148	657
San Bernardino city	4,558	4,119	2,160	9,992	5,524	3,290	406	142	1,081	740
San Buenaventura (Ventura) city	3,118	5,170	4,809	12,147	2,003	905	672	160	298	216
San Diego city	28,677	36,337	50,260	93,784	21,010	14,456	8,124	4,038	21,008	14,771
San Francisco city	21,247	22,344	36,249	48,943	8,727	5,922	10,387	6,450	44,006	36,072
San Jose city	22,321	23,134	28,664	49,284	13,974	8,020	7,999	4,722	29,273	24,321
San Leandro city	3,753	2,623	2,046	6,887	989	611	736	236	2,901	2,349
San Marcos city	1,809	3,643	2,466	7,448	853	690	658	370	500	345
San Mateo city	3,566	3,846	4,792	8,533	1,281	1,046	1,686	688	2,735	1,643
San Ramon city	1,217	1,480	2,375	3,572	247	53	451	337	1,132	765
Santa Ana city	4,171	3,437	2,547	7,246	9,875	7,956	253	141	4,498	3,901
Santa Barbara city	1,699	3,224	5,177	9,045	2,105	1,235	1,007	146	290	155
Santa Clara city	2,965	3,009	2,988	6,791	1,014	587	1,034	755	2,011	1,428
Santa Clarita city	4,509	6,198	4,000	13,103	2,428	1,309	827	502	1,167	717
Santa Maria city	2,597	2,415	1,727	6,066	2,477	1,612	361	94	704	675
Santa Monica city	2,245	3,252	6,354	9,052	1,191	647	2,564	1,669	677	382
Santa Rosa city	5,053	6,600	8,353	19,615	1,425	903	630	262	507	270
Simi Valley city	3,738	4,652	3,609	10,847	977	601	786	261	889	672
South Gate city	1,493	513	164	1,222	5,949	na	112	na	119	na
Stockton city	6,813	7,970	5,320	17,743	4,671	2,720	1,068	694	5,785	4,352
Sunnyvale city	3,212	3,797	6,474	10,085	908	333	1,131	558	3,558	2,514
Temecula city	1,818	2,227	2,002	5,264	1,528	813	348	122	518	388

[1] Jurupa Valley city was incorporated in 2011. The 2010 population is the U.S. Census Bureau's estimates base figure.

Table E-3: Places—Educational Attainment and Language Spoken at Home, Persons 65 Years and Over—*Continued*

	High School or Equivalent	Some College or Associates Degree	Bachelor's Degree or Higher	Speaks English at Home Total	Speaks Spanish at Home Total	Speaks Spanish Speaks English Less Than Very Well	Speaks Indo-European at Home Total	Speaks Indo-European Speaks English Less Than Very Well	Speaks Asian at Home Total	Speaks Asian Speaks English Less Than Very Well
California—Cont.										
Thousand Oaks city	4,092	6,363	7,070	15,453	1,195	616	1,138	421	1,073	800
Torrance city	6,561	6,272	7,073	15,707	1,715	993	1,345	592	4,006	3,045
Tracy city	1,506	1,349	1,050	3,053	1,665	1,357	578	447	966	570
Turlock city	2,756	1,724	1,247	5,296	810	413	811	651	46	34
Tustin city	1,215	1,871	2,298	4,365	821	588	428	240	797	595
Union City city	2,107	1,763	1,665	2,667	1,135	689	1,279	901	3,010	2,137
Upland city	2,217	2,809	2,934	6,674	1,337	759	535	190	1,105	705
Vacaville city	2,870	3,462	2,040	7,911	1,441	na	372	na	258	na
Vallejo city	3,834	4,145	3,423	8,259	1,229	803	713	285	3,973	1,999
Victorville city	2,432	2,555	794	5,794	2,224	na	290	na	362	na
Visalia city	3,718	4,104	2,505	10,231	2,602	1,112	167	31	592	410
Vista city	2,035	3,066	2,324	6,652	1,384	971	406	151	710	568
West Covina city	3,645	3,203	2,705	6,017	3,091	1,752	251	108	3,637	2,613
Westminster city	3,270	3,510	2,348	6,235	1,263	529	550	277	5,588	5,186
Whittier city	2,656	2,710	2,164	6,292	2,811	na	593	na	300	na
Yorba Linda city	1,886	2,551	2,799	6,223	475	285	655	237	816	565
Yuba City city	2,202	2,402	1,374	5,667	784	518	1,562	1,186	245	120
Colorado										
Arvada city	5,282	4,463	4,652	14,293	855	na	535	na	114	na
Aurora city	9,433	9,605	8,227	25,584	2,305	1,350	1,619	709	1,338	1,045
Boulder city	1,321	1,811	5,735	8,526	239	na	336	na	112	na
Centennial city	2,345	3,738	5,962	11,603	340	131	369	133	347	315
Colorado Springs city	12,949	14,293	14,906	40,863	2,849	658	2,067	492	1,052	782
Denver city	16,503	13,072	21,406	51,187	8,401	4,227	2,917	1,572	1,519	1,287
Fort Collins city	3,103	3,571	5,039	11,710	484	na	256	na	171	na
Greeley city	3,311	2,383	2,743	8,694	1,154	na	410	na	42	na
Lakewood city	6,331	5,932	6,668	19,017	943	251	374	138	418	279
Longmont city	2,725	2,978	3,040	8,863	688	372	273	22	52	52
Loveland city	3,352	2,875	2,417	9,374	174	na	235	na	73	na
Pueblo city	5,379	3,866	3,125	11,992	4,321	na	300	na	83	na
Thornton city	2,858	2,460	1,612	6,277	1,427	480	669	264	209	87
Westminster city	3,459	2,823	2,982	9,018	605	194	271	102	562	533
Connecticut										
Bridgeport city	4,784	2,213	1,730	9,365	2,732	2,431	1,968	1,461	164	157
Danbury city	3,047	1,471	2,519	7,015	947	825	1,330	748	249	231
Hartford city	2,764	1,588	1,539	6,882	3,537	3,121	1,143	756	111	84
New Britain city	3,343	1,258	1,051	5,222	1,236	1,051	2,376	1,600	25	25
New Haven city	4,240	1,507	2,749	9,817	1,655	1,438	970	468	235	168
Norwalk city	4,673	2,365	3,816	10,503	778	671	1,450	799	192	89
Stamford city	4,084	2,606	5,543	10,819	1,665	1,148	2,608	1,614	527	352
Waterbury city	5,036	2,277	1,530	10,018	1,340	949	1,763	875	0	0
Delaware										
Wilmington city	3,190	1,501	1,464	7,898	389	na	255	na	37	na
District of Columbia										
Washington city	16,523	12,484	25,938	63,373	2,582	1,100	2,769	527	734	468
Florida										
Boca Raton city	3,712	4,256	8,712	15,404	1,150	na	1,460	na	97	na
Boynton Beach city	5,275	3,577	3,432	12,544	775	na	1,547	na	70	na
Cape Coral city	10,892	7,582	5,366	23,972	2,410	2,031	1,663	754	264	211
Clearwater city	7,785	5,386	6,173	19,699	916	490	1,642	685	273	183
Coral Springs city	3,407	3,084	2,636	7,652	2,078	1,515	1,254	770	130	63
Deerfield Beach city	6,172	2,670	3,666	11,956	701	na	3,337	na	78	na
Deltona city	4,541	2,590	1,514	8,393	2,910	na	403	na	88	na
Fort Lauderdale city	7,300	5,633	8,944	21,280	2,173	1,212	2,972	1,630	329	167
Gainesville city	2,124	2,684	4,028	9,704	263	na	327	na	85	na
Hialeah city	10,675	3,788	3,335	3,940	39,715	na	316	na	93	na
Hollywood city	6,851	4,534	4,741	13,889	4,904	3,842	2,250	1,073	122	84
Jacksonville city	30,191	23,941	21,045	83,952	3,527	2,154	2,725	1,347	2,929	1,920
Lakeland city	7,518	5,060	4,027	18,804	996	na	302	na	109	na
Largo city	7,849	4,971	3,566	17,898	492	na	786	na	163	na
Lauderhill city	2,490	1,929	1,767	6,826	323	na	1,092	na	91	na
Melbourne city	6,094	4,398	2,955	14,286	761	na	618	na	223	na
Miami city	13,015	7,881	8,469	11,265	48,205	42,065	3,717	2,824	450	450
Miami Beach city	3,061	2,436	4,173	3,779	8,356	6,447	1,314	630	22	0
Miami Gardens city	3,760	1,734	1,047	8,151	3,044	na	1,028	na	15	na
Miramar city	3,547	1,523	1,348	4,508	3,436	2,912	1,134	1,005	232	148
Orlando city	7,149	5,443	5,031	15,343	5,569	3,862	1,614	921	443	341
Palm Bay city	6,890	4,004	1,860	14,236	1,898	na	604	na	129	na
Palm Coast city	6,265	5,475	3,899	15,359	1,067	na	1,605	na	488	na
Pembroke Pines city	9,453	5,776	3,801	12,402	8,048	6,445	2,758	1,390	325	264
Plantation city	4,195	3,056	3,853	9,884	1,543	na	963	na	24	na
Pompano Beach city	6,209	4,146	4,627	14,547	1,127	708	2,958	1,241	196	106
Port St. Lucie city	10,731	6,869	5,524	22,159	2,970	1,642	1,587	811	394	292
St. Petersburg city	11,337	9,889	10,476	34,236	1,960	1,275	2,161	1,153	739	503
Sunrise city	4,594	2,833	2,428	8,818	2,448	1,626	1,521	909	138	103
Tallahassee city	3,358	3,277	6,376	13,804	527	199	505	121	198	152

Table E-3: Places—Educational Attainment and Language Spoken at Home, Persons 65 Years and Over—*Continued*

	High School or Equivalent	Some College or Associates Degree	Bachelor's Degree or Higher	Speaks English at Home Total	Speaks Spanish at Home Total	Speaks Spanish at Home Speaks English Less Than Very Well	Speaks Indo-European at Home Total	Speaks Indo-European at Home Speaks English Less Than Very Well	Speaks Asian at Home Total	Speaks Asian at Home Speaks English Less Than Very Well
Florida—Cont.										
Tampa city	12,419	7,176	8,001	27,294	7,834	4,985	1,271	550	850	672
Weston city	1,207	1,542	1,733	2,845	1,828	na	296	na	20	na
West Palm Beach city	4,863	4,028	4,897	13,919	1,820	na	1,493	na	82	na
Georgia										
Albany city	2,651	1,885	1,808	8,859	68	na	50	na	94	na
Athens-Clarke County unified govt (bal)	2,673	1,556	4,063	9,463	303	na	223	na	223	na
Atlanta city	10,689	7,286	14,011	39,894	685	238	1,069	351	424	363
Augusta-Richmond County consolidated govt (bal)	8,090	4,961	3,964	21,433	454	na	615	na	274	na
Columbus city	7,022	5,237	4,217	20,814	389	na	646	na	422	na
Johns Creek city	1,081	1,764	2,405	4,092	336	na	705	na	856	na
Macon city	3,836	1,607	1,815	10,714	98	na	67	na	0	na
Roswell city	2,223	2,761	4,840	9,716	169	na	531	na	260	na
Sandy Springs city	1,928	2,271	6,069	9,648	204	na	493	na	334	na
Savannah city	6,049	3,428	3,143	15,832	153	na	336	na	161	na
Warner Robins city	2,734	1,531	1,051	6,538	146	na	25	na	85	na
Hawaii										
Urban Honolulu CDP	20,759	12,905	15,183	37,911	303	112	663	231	22,571	16,037
Idaho										
Boise City city	6,492	8,540	7,841	23,735	474	213	377	137	421	250
Meridian city	2,832	2,360	1,489	6,909	118	na	94	na	34	na
Nampa city	3,041	2,803	1,261	8,373	510	na	164	na	60	na
Illinois										
Aurora city	3,193	2,903	2,884	9,600	2,697	2,030	443	128	457	179
Bloomington city	2,405	2,090	2,420	7,572	125	na	149	na	46	na
Champaign city	1,683	1,826	2,586	6,233	188	na	143	na	304	na
Chicago city	79,137	55,973	54,126	201,072	39,107	30,144	27,061	18,142	12,753	9,499
Decatur city	5,498	2,872	2,062	12,540	48	na	140	na	10	na
Elgin city	3,201	2,702	1,871	8,316	931	635	426	186	226	200
Evanston city	1,138	1,751	4,806	7,601	223	na	582	na	52	na
Joliet city	3,964	3,033	2,350	10,705	1,092	666	770	320	263	161
Naperville city	3,466	2,941	5,963	10,574	195	93	1,812	816	1,052	674
Peoria city	5,258	3,562	3,963	14,213	219	na	519	na	159	na
Rockford city	7,531	4,706	4,077	19,382	780	651	770	308	282	233
Springfield city	6,283	4,207	4,448	16,533	116	na	560	na	46	na
Waukegan city	2,391	1,312	897	4,838	1,413	1,020	293	108	256	177
Indiana										
Bloomington city	1,423	1,351	3,222	6,231	108	na	161	na	37	na
Carmel city	1,748	2,225	4,372	8,096	37	na	298	na	312	na
Evansville city	7,735	3,659	2,533	17,216	115	na	104	na	0	na
Fort Wayne city	11,973	7,746	6,524	30,004	349	116	749	319	254	232
Gary city	4,974	2,318	1,227	11,329	384	na	120	na	35	na
Hammond city	4,109	1,229	600	6,951	926	na	556	na	30	na
Indianapolis city (bal)	31,112	19,219	17,857	83,157	1,551	1,021	1,595	722	599	431
Lafayette city	3,555	1,625	1,253	7,444	132	na	26	na	48	na
Muncie city	3,578	1,744	1,575	9,084	79	na	36	na	10	na
South Bend city	5,310	2,587	2,692	12,206	356	256	378	84	105	34
Iowa										
Cedar Rapids city	6,978	3,992	3,508	15,772	142	na	503	na	94	na
Davenport city	5,393	2,636	2,422	11,965	192	na	183	na	201	na
Des Moines city	9,033	4,629	4,474	20,553	541	229	456	146	666	428
Iowa City city	1,428	1,137	2,617	5,278	94	na	212	na	130	na
Sioux City city	4,581	2,410	1,495	10,053	275	na	64	na	251	na
Waterloo city	4,182	2,117	1,436	9,169	137	na	234	na	0	na
Kansas										
Kansas City city	5,960	3,600	1,727	13,983	1,048	610	375	115	254	232
Lawrence city	1,457	1,534	3,160	6,427	96	na	197	na	116	na
Olathe city	2,979	2,749	2,524	8,652	168	63	230	83	249	161
Overland Park city	5,039	6,357	9,871	20,885	545	297	791	360	373	331
Topeka city	7,328	4,285	4,177	16,993	664	na	304	na	119	na
Wichita city	14,991	11,932	10,277	41,199	1,554	1,000	783	252	1,115	986
Kentucky										
Lexington-Fayette urban county	9,080	7,712	9,657	30,987	317	108	480	203	338	251
Louisville/Jefferson County metro govt (bal)	27,656	16,423	13,685	74,023	868	623	1,040	420	706	452
Louisiana										
Baton Rouge city	6,374	5,901	8,466	24,328	457	294	859	181	276	234
Kenner city	3,831	1,991	1,196	7,132	1,317	na	317	na	196	na
Lafayette city	3,555	3,227	4,634	10,759	303	na	3,905	na	70	na
Lake Charles city	3,528	1,969	1,961	8,477	86	na	1,462	na	91	na
New Orleans city	10,704	7,684	10,361	37,021	1,167	676	1,175	146	737	573
Shreveport city	8,668	5,825	5,724	25,185	83	na	370	na	188	na
Maine										
Portland city	2,401	2,017	2,399	7,084	63	na	545	na	124	na

Table E-3: Places—Educational Attainment and Language Spoken at Home, Persons 65 Years and Over—*Continued*

	High School or Equivalent	Some College or Associates Degree	Bachelor's Degree or Higher	Speaks English at Home Total	Speaks Spanish at Home Total	Speaks Spanish at Home Speaks English Less Than Very Well	Speaks Indo-European at Home Total	Speaks Indo-European at Home Speaks English Less Than Very Well	Speaks Asian at Home Total	Speaks Asian at Home Speaks English Less Than Very Well
Maryland										
Baltimore city	19,732	13,131	12,914	69,051	768	192	2,430	1,170	705	464
Frederick city	1,927	1,936	2,084	6,713	194	na	248	na	174	na
Massachusetts										
Boston city	19,783	9,402	15,505	42,654	5,793	4,704	10,688	7,804	5,180	4,874
Brockton city	4,123	2,311	1,536	8,658	494	424	2,658	2,000	202	177
Cambridge city	2,299	1,538	5,679	8,389	344	185	2,183	1,119	512	319
Fall River city	3,581	1,700	998	8,618	165	na	4,427	na	179	na
Lawrence city	1,861	728	733	2,865	2,749	2,624	474	91	176	167
Lowell city	3,683	1,835	1,707	7,721	650	405	2,199	1,215	853	796
Lynn city	4,052	1,920	1,646	7,053	1,227	941	1,711	1,249	193	193
New Bedford city	4,311	1,744	1,447	8,653	609	298	5,037	3,303	46	46
Newton city	2,595	2,049	7,759	10,379	184	66	2,255	1,168	413	291
Quincy city	5,011	2,833	2,747	9,941	97	1	1,198	728	2,023	1,702
Somerville city	2,658	786	1,049	4,446	385	na	1,305	na	230	na
Springfield city	5,799	3,105	2,265	11,964	2,714	2,284	1,752	805	457	420
Worcester city	7,913	4,152	4,717	17,138	1,703	1,511	2,730	1,423	866	826
Michigan										
Ann Arbor city	1,502	2,316	6,773	9,825	273	92	726	359	534	379
Dearborn city	3,531	2,643	2,238	8,187	202	90	800	394	122	83
Detroit city	27,067	18,481	9,857	79,160	2,032	1,057	1,577	540	282	144
Farmington Hills city	3,535	2,940	5,097	10,889	154	32	859	406	304	143
Flint city	4,299	2,736	1,304	11,201	197	na	127	na	67	na
Grand Rapids city	6,897	5,409	4,463	18,835	830	532	687	303	266	174
Kalamazoo city	2,235	1,579	2,304	6,730	14	na	152	na	88	na
Lansing city	3,804	2,979	1,875	10,201	842	386	312	172	140	105
Livonia city	6,075	4,836	3,523	15,034	90	57	1,416	519	260	166
Rochester Hills city	2,765	2,716	3,288	8,148	36	18	1,130	609	209	123
Southfield city	3,431	3,556	4,058	10,976	70	34	912	408	64	37
Sterling Heights city	7,970	4,782	2,995	15,127	86	0	3,126	1,848	538	353
Troy city	2,932	2,457	4,415	8,808	74	49	1,200	664	775	395
Warren city	8,648	4,174	2,103	17,736	134	42	2,339	1,146	177	109
Westland city	5,034	3,626	1,176	11,327	121	na	641	na	177	na
Wyoming city	2,355	1,754	747	5,705	275	na	126	na	252	na
Minnesota										
Bloomington city	4,940	4,076	5,420	14,549	156	95	643	177	309	285
Brooklyn Park city	2,561	1,641	1,060	5,174	138	41	160	34	492	472
Duluth city	4,544	2,996	3,149	11,531	124	na	249	na	104	na
Minneapolis city	9,130	7,549	10,264	28,318	582	333	1,574	479	988	824
Plymouth city	2,654	2,384	3,558	8,351	69	na	326	na	47	na
Rochester city	5,127	3,683	3,951	13,041	139	88	348	121	426	390
St. Cloud city	2,404	1,583	2,033	6,692	0	na	335	na	47	na
St. Paul city	8,463	4,724	7,572	21,939	855	492	1,016	635	1,453	1,315
Mississippi										
Gulfport city	2,649	2,213	1,755	8,003	109	na	144	na	72	na
Jackson city	3,654	3,721	5,249	17,708	122	na	88	na	0	na
Missouri										
Columbia city	2,211	2,252	4,034	9,068	126	na	286	na	253	na
Independence city	8,602	4,356	2,973	18,472	201	na	262	na	152	na
Kansas City city	17,853	12,973	11,256	48,430	1,779	938	557	183	847	732
Lee's Summit city	4,179	2,939	3,027	10,678	97	na	14	na	115	na
O'Fallon city	3,102	1,858	1,401	7,384	71	na	79	na	0	na
St. Charles city	3,765	1,925	1,816	8,594	30	na	111	na	36	na
St. Joseph city	4,055	2,468	1,793	10,259	52	na	136	na	20	na
St. Louis city	11,063	7,254	6,021	33,100	501	264	1,036	577	601	539
Springfield city	7,795	6,575	5,363	22,960	110	na	185	na	101	na
Montana										
Billings city	5,731	4,917	3,475	15,075	223	na	288	na	81	na
Missoula city	2,289	1,855	2,712	7,162	69	na	276	na	27	na
Nebraska										
Lincoln city	10,211	8,139	7,935	26,689	370	124	977	446	542	505
Omaha city	16,402	12,548	11,368	44,558	1,034	745	1,566	508	232	129
Nevada										
Henderson city	12,400	11,515	11,364	33,165	2,398	845	1,658	547	2,427	1,014
Las Vegas city	23,058	22,071	16,026	61,481	6,734	4,320	2,963	956	4,425	2,650
North Las Vegas city	5,405	4,585	2,127	12,249	2,523	1,711	386	73	976	388
Reno city	7,480	8,382	7,911	23,759	1,582	785	945	252	901	643
Sparks city	4,401	3,056	1,867	9,606	637	na	118	na	668	na
New Hampshire										
Manchester city	5,356	2,823	2,273	10,127	323	181	2,620	1,131	263	263
Nashua city	3,539	2,451	2,792	9,083	259	na	1,469	na	134	na

Table E-3: Places—Educational Attainment and Language Spoken at Home, Persons 65 Years and Over—*Continued*

	High School or Equivalent	Some College or Associates Degree	Bachelor's Degree or Higher	Speaks English at Home Total	Speaks Spanish at Home Total	Speaks Spanish at Home Speaks English Less Than Very Well	Speaks Indo-European at Home Total	Speaks Indo-European at Home Speaks English Less Than Very Well	Speaks Asian at Home Total	Speaks Asian at Home Speaks English Less Than Very Well
New Jersey										
Camden city	1,938	801	291	3,981	1,951	na	77	na	111	na
Clifton city	4,431	2,032	1,485	6,517	1,828	1,372	1,834	1,130	503	242
Elizabeth city	3,996	1,522	1,339	4,459	4,713	4,286	2,129	1,724	258	168
Jersey City city	6,710	3,284	4,208	11,582	5,440	4,587	3,133	2,279	2,672	1,624
Newark city	7,270	2,664	1,935	13,861	6,099	5,182	2,695	2,257	237	176
Passaic city	1,769	620	691	2,293	2,296	na	738	na	102	na
Paterson city	4,395	1,530	962	6,160	6,217	5,621	779	624	190	147
Trenton city	2,907	1,024	456	6,144	686	na	527	na	9	na
Union City city	1,791	571	521	908	5,282	na	266	na	70	na
New Mexico										
Albuquerque city	18,717	18,423	21,451	47,444	17,245	4,405	1,890	371	1,155	682
Las Cruces city	3,014	3,697	3,533	8,312	4,129	na	294	na	168	na
Rio Rancho city	3,570	2,816	2,881	8,213	1,567	na	393	na	5	na
Santa Fe city	2,562	2,717	6,411	8,646	4,035	na	301	na	100	na
New York										
Albany city	4,244	1,899	3,356	10,775	127	na	887	na	121	na
Buffalo city	10,181	5,650	4,680	26,389	1,340	919	1,777	606	386	334
Mount Vernon city	3,540	1,415	1,616	7,622	476	na	822	na	95	na
New Rochelle city	3,760	1,842	3,352	8,203	955	685	1,539	899	233	232
New York city	303,600	147,597	232,113	554,883	196,634	145,084	167,886	113,944	84,326	71,655
Rochester city	5,520	3,607	3,391	16,092	1,834	1,515	1,162	681	244	237
Schenectady city	3,179	1,519	1,218	6,685	175	na	967	na	19	na
Syracuse city	5,154	2,927	3,006	13,284	388	67	1,201	646	251	231
Yonkers city	9,896	4,779	6,345	17,549	5,180	3,703	4,474	2,563	1,234	895
North Carolina										
Asheville city	3,585	2,992	4,683	12,865	174	na	278	na	27	na
Charlotte city	17,675	18,520	19,003	59,239	2,282	1,599	2,982	1,197	1,579	1,068
Concord city	3,034	1,693	1,680	8,597	144	na	168	na	69	na
Durham city	5,672	4,540	7,499	19,988	470	194	815	296	393	170
Fayetteville city	6,522	5,298	4,465	18,081	585	180	1,112	337	423	242
Gastonia city	2,145	2,227	1,709	8,204	85	na	128	na	59	na
Greensboro city	9,765	6,785	9,821	30,417	411	284	699	209	707	505
Greenville city	2,044	1,212	2,103	6,257	89	na	92	na	67	na
High Point city	3,614	3,283	2,528	11,949	280	na	193	na	114	na
Jacksonville city	1,227	1,299	648	3,918	256	na	89	na	149	na
Raleigh city	8,299	8,818	13,752	31,959	884	566	1,270	344	824	669
Wilmington city	3,661	3,719	5,314	14,197	80	na	413	na	68	na
Winston-Salem city	9,288	7,233	7,797	28,033	491	225	577	301	183	94
North Dakota										
Fargo city	3,488	3,130	3,241	10,351	53	na	321	na	197	na
Ohio										
Akron city	9,455	4,855	4,712	24,212	126	65	711	341	162	82
Canton city	4,676	1,660	841	9,234	37	na	420	na	26	na
Cincinnati city	9,545	6,712	8,134	31,634	321	28	658	197	156	34
Cleveland city	17,847	8,823	4,074	43,648	1,876	1,280	2,225	1,100	588	356
Columbus city	25,796	15,381	15,559	65,356	797	513	2,073	760	1,446	930
Dayton city	6,643	3,321	2,332	16,318	127	na	163	na	82	na
Parma city	6,397	3,262	1,850	12,141	115	67	2,136	1,328	154	109
Toledo city	14,264	7,340	5,180	32,237	710	197	855	191	296	136
Youngstown city	4,664	1,649	819	9,543	329	na	444	na	23	na
Oklahoma										
Broken Arrow city	3,903	3,370	2,203	10,258	200	na	161	na	157	na
Edmond city	2,480	2,404	3,727	9,167	80	na	108	na	110	na
Lawton city	3,330	2,313	1,772	8,235	307	177	655	186	396	234
Norman city	3,416	2,934	4,707	11,953	138	na	151	na	77	na
Oklahoma City city	19,241	19,405	16,965	60,964	2,536	1,523	700	250	1,892	1,577
Tulsa city	14,607	13,652	13,811	46,902	1,149	728	880	268	482	322
Oregon										
Beaverton city	2,173	2,828	3,477	8,099	254	166	618	406	794	715
Bend city	2,772	4,119	3,733	10,930	217	na	147	na	35	na
Eugene city	5,325	6,033	7,659	19,715	509	159	345	65	317	280
Gresham city	4,075	3,890	2,105	10,714	298	176	546	298	398	258
Hillsboro city	2,431	2,157	1,854	6,153	582	na	144	na	412	na
Medford city	3,958	3,926	3,149	11,473	354	na	485	na	76	na
Portland city	16,150	16,691	21,359	54,445	1,545	646	2,982	1,565	4,039	3,535
Salem city	6,292	6,079	5,477	18,344	726	496	660	283	311	206

Table E-3: Places—Educational Attainment and Language Spoken at Home, Persons 65 Years and Over—*Continued*

	High School or Equivalent	Some College or Associates Degree	Bachelor's Degree or Higher	Speaks English at Home Total	Speaks Spanish at Home Total	Speaks English Less Than Very Well	Speaks Indo-European at Home Total	Speaks English Less Than Very Well	Speaks Asian at Home Total	Speaks English Less Than Very Well
Pennsylvania										
Allentown city	5,578	2,290	1,592	10,967	1,896	1,521	538	239	174	174
Bethlehem city	4,351	1,867	2,281	9,413	857	732	502	109	100	86
Erie city	6,185	2,224	2,052	12,382	151	108	700	317	0	0
Philadelphia city	71,433	27,389	27,911	156,247	9,256	6,588	13,844	9,310	6,262	5,555
Pittsburgh city	17,996	6,878	9,200	39,745	415	92	2,399	863	284	189
Reading city	3,706	814	648	6,340	1,736	na	241	na	16	na
Scranton city	6,129	2,257	1,336	11,660	274	na	727	na	106	na
Rhode Island										
Cranston city	4,488	2,582	1,900	10,114	436	336	1,374	606	221	167
Pawtucket city	2,790	1,373	1,221	5,945	598	482	2,457	1,772	50	28
Providence city	3,037	2,087	3,464	9,246	2,834	2,583	2,269	1,224	552	432
Warwick city	5,471	3,170	3,130	13,523	182	na	775	na	80	na
South Carolina										
Charleston city	3,601	3,393	5,364	14,591	145	na	192	na	87	na
Columbia city	3,032	2,244	3,938	11,427	127	na	188	na	15	na
North Charleston city	2,873	2,281	1,131	8,107	142	na	109	na	192	na
Rock Hill city	2,004	1,255	1,694	6,520	93	na	138	na	39	na
South Dakota										
Rapid City city	3,577	2,605	2,581	9,627	147	na	184	na	23	na
Sioux Falls city	6,090	4,631	4,185	16,884	51	0	599	329	105	105
Tennessee										
Chattanooga city	7,338	6,208	5,146	24,575	201	na	226	na	196	na
Clarksville city	3,636	2,086	2,095	8,958	280	na	381	na	314	na
Jackson city	2,838	2,252	2,062	8,892	20	na	47	na	0	na
Knoxville city	8,300	7,592	4,997	25,130	139	na	423	na	148	na
Memphis city	20,553	14,577	13,798	65,749	914	449	708	313	770	629
Murfreesboro city	2,790	2,698	2,411	9,198	225	na	199	na	129	na
Nashville-Davidson metropolitan government (bal)	20,700	14,359	15,301	59,661	1,091	567	1,411	612	834	661
Texas										
Abilene city	4,107	4,207	3,879	12,949	1,555	na	288	na	190	na
Allen city	1,120	1,572	2,104	4,038	373	na	431	na	493	na
Amarillo city	6,331	7,204	4,934	20,665	2,002	947	180	24	340	309
Arlington city	8,236	7,942	8,532	24,747	2,725	1,580	932	325	1,632	1,373
Austin city	11,816	13,694	22,482	45,443	9,327	4,944	1,287	409	1,962	1,507
Baytown city	2,072	1,742	941	5,122	1,436	na	215	na	30	na
Beaumont city	4,349	3,834	3,229	13,109	909	na	530	na	225	na
Brownsville city	3,135	2,029	1,788	3,044	14,136	na	255	na	11	na
Bryan city	2,298	1,646	1,830	6,308	981	na	144	na	23	na
Carrollton city	3,169	2,767	2,903	7,537	1,044	632	562	450	1,175	847
College Station city	782	1,013	2,486	4,076	296	na	226	na	163	na
Corpus Christi city	9,238	7,910	7,797	19,151	16,340	7,034	659	241	497	348
Dallas city	25,671	23,694	33,697	88,328	17,913	12,079	2,906	1,254	2,252	1,732
Denton city	2,294	2,810	3,766	9,104	746	na	105	na	98	na
Edinburg city	911	945	1,158	909	4,454	na	132	na	204	na
El Paso city	16,546	12,954	10,498	19,242	53,471	34,909	1,430	476	784	502
Fort Worth city	17,259	14,751	14,694	50,971	9,356	5,776	1,249	528	1,332	1,160
Frisco city	1,704	2,137	3,010	6,296	602	na	605	na	176	na
Garland city	6,591	5,525	4,689	16,413	1,918	1,077	512	241	1,565	1,426
Grand Prairie city	3,569	3,554	1,684	8,796	2,433	1,641	389	126	804	579
Harlingen city	1,797	1,764	1,407	4,209	4,338	na	37	na	185	na
Houston city	46,147	43,567	53,908	141,290	38,595	24,461	6,058	2,961	9,361	7,654
Irving city	4,125	3,787	3,688	11,398	1,796	1,227	687	178	650	566
Killeen city	1,644	2,332	946	4,563	1,027	na	472	na	594	na
Laredo city	2,712	2,697	1,785	1,461	17,795	na	76	na	0	na
League City city	2,426	1,988	2,145	6,264	433	na	22	na	380	na
Lewisville city	2,454	1,960	1,463	5,947	740	529	208	111	197	95
Longview city	3,054	3,290	2,696	10,468	365	na	187	na	120	na
Lubbock city	6,774	6,578	6,915	21,449	4,082	2,178	131	15	241	197
McAllen city	2,572	2,331	2,259	3,077	10,929	na	115	na	158	na
McKinney city	2,558	2,727	3,558	9,192	398	na	264	na	152	na
Mesquite city	3,917	3,268	2,236	10,408	1,337	763	268	37	157	144
Midland city	3,379	3,420	2,933	10,278	2,194	na	152	na	147	na
Mission city	2,311	1,286	1,336	3,708	4,531	na	82	na	1	na
Missouri City city	1,405	2,033	2,654	4,963	637	334	312	78	916	451
Odessa city	2,867	2,539	1,685	7,656	2,702	na	84	na	68	na
Pasadena city	4,365	2,691	1,663	9,671	3,105	2,060	283	32	167	138
Pearland city	1,764	2,053	2,437	5,479	700	na	259	na	784	na
Pharr city	1,446	962	716	#N/A	#N/A	na	#N/A	na	#N/A	na
Plano city	5,236	6,700	10,476	20,254	1,254	505	2,068	1,390	2,197	1,472

Table E-3: Places—Educational Attainment and Language Spoken at Home, Persons 65 Years and Over—*Continued*

	High School or Equivalent	Some College or Associates Degree	Bachelor's Degree or Higher	Speaks English at Home Total	Speaks Spanish at Home Total	Speaks Spanish at Home Speaks English Less Than Very Well	Speaks Indo-European at Home Total	Speaks Indo-European at Home Speaks English Less Than Very Well	Speaks Asian at Home Total	Speaks Asian at Home Speaks English Less Than Very Well
Texas—Cont.										
Richardson city	2,509	3,184	5,744	10,732	479	157	631	238	684	532
Round Rock city	1,831	1,650	2,176	5,316	757	na	381	na	127	na
San Angelo city	3,989	2,871	2,869	10,119	2,768	na	68	na	28	na
San Antonio city	35,432	35,458	29,342	72,194	68,549	30,002	3,389	864	2,075	1,234
Sugar Land city	1,799	2,132	3,546	5,493	495	301	1,069	891	1,505	960
Temple city	3,283	2,475	2,249	9,101	688	na	183	na	48	na
Tyler city	3,699	4,624	4,066	13,457	809	na	216	na	114	na
Waco city	4,021	3,422	3,245	12,102	1,688	na	231	na	59	na
Wichita Falls city	4,796	3,058	2,345	11,487	799	352	143	93	148	103
Utah										
Layton city	1,813	1,754	1,076	4,671	276	na	97	na	166	na
Ogden city	1,999	2,835	1,439	6,731	693	na	166	na	125	na
Orem city	1,727	2,428	2,872	6,883	416	na	161	na	63	na
Provo city	1,176	2,059	2,917	5,778	652	na	193	na	153	na
St. George city	3,992	4,787	3,272	12,640	290	na	171	na	39	na
Salt Lake City city	3,944	4,728	6,514	14,396	966	473	1,328	643	986	643
Sandy city	2,737	2,802	2,420	7,715	275	na	547	na	192	na
West Jordan city	1,564	1,714	1,082	4,484	508	na	82	na	84	na
West Valley City city	3,258	2,707	1,239	7,667	951	719	294	92	528	476
Virginia										
Alexandria city	2,528	2,550	6,692	10,851	732	375	982	429	485	266
Chesapeake city	8,100	6,895	4,217	22,841	400	124	682	195	383	261
Hampton city	5,655	4,836	2,760	16,404	168	na	273	na	441	na
Lynchburg city	3,153	2,231	2,870	10,260	86	na	93	na	34	na
Newport News city	6,922	5,374	3,802	18,240	251	101	422	167	491	437
Norfolk city	6,649	5,703	5,016	21,174	278	132	629	227	909	390
Portsmouth city	4,635	2,701	1,606	12,380	50	na	222	na	110	na
Richmond city	5,824	4,726	6,428	22,516	305	na	180	na	234	na
Roanoke city	3,906	3,456	3,031	13,403	81	na	210	na	70	na
Suffolk city	3,203	2,085	1,916	9,796	21	na	71	na	93	na
Virginia Beach city	14,448	13,174	14,078	42,878	922	436	1,515	503	2,974	1,674
Washington										
Auburn city	2,650	2,502	1,359	7,178	15	11	480	354	385	200
Bellevue city	2,519	4,925	8,539	13,674	251	25	1,493	831	1,709	1,312
Bellingham city	2,760	3,397	3,355	9,419	90	na	685	na	181	na
Everett city	3,232	3,627	2,027	9,058	264	228	708	495	700	616
Federal Way city	2,965	2,930	2,715	7,498	327	212	590	449	1,271	985
Kennewick city	2,685	2,470	2,314	7,933	273	na	124	na	94	na
Kent city	3,636	3,373	2,550	9,002	245	188	1,007	776	1,244	1,012
Renton city	2,949	2,587	1,885	7,378	122	0	684	513	1,163	751
Seattle city	13,158	16,514	29,972	53,424	1,135	319	3,393	1,324	10,247	8,005
Spokane city	8,819	8,544	7,263	26,140	439	148	1,432	750	580	484
Spokane Valley city	4,298	4,500	2,164	12,373	85	na	387	na	126	na
Tacoma city	8,291	5,807	5,146	19,144	532	182	1,272	543	2,127	1,665
Vancouver city	6,692	6,927	5,065	18,635	428	133	1,523	1,167	938	768
Yakima city	3,327	3,690	2,359	11,154	1,431	na	89	na	55	na
Wisconsin										
Appleton city	3,456	1,756	1,968	7,879	101	na	70	na	88	na
Eau Claire city	3,059	1,744	1,851	7,315	45	na	45	na	19	na
Green Bay city	5,572	2,417	2,073	11,578	202	na	297	na	114	na
Kenosha city	4,898	2,007	1,430	9,810	407	na	589	na	75	na
Madison city	6,411	4,803	9,903	21,057	197	104	887	299	339	184
Milwaukee city	20,323	10,586	8,646	47,299	3,208	2,348	2,530	1,135	890	614
Oshkosh city	3,946	1,624	1,629	8,061	41	na	136	na	39	na
Racine city	3,276	1,577	1,374	7,817	465	na	342	na	0	na
Waukesha city	2,779	1,863	1,953	7,132	180	na	256	na	109	na

Table E-4: Metropolitan Statistical Areas—Educational Attainment and Language Spoken at Home, Persons 65 Years and Over

	High School or Equivalent	Some College or Associates Degree	Bachelor's Degree or Higher	Speaks English at Home Total	Speaks Spanish at Home Total	Speaks Spanish at Home Speaks English Less Than Very Well	Speaks Indo-European at Home Total	Speaks Indo-European at Home Speaks English Less Than Very Well	Speaks Asian at Home Total	Speaks Asian at Home Speaks English Less Than Very Well
Abilene, TX	7,383	6,294	5,053	20,558	1,987	na	326	na	215	na
Akron, OH	41,385	21,728	21,013	97,821	389	195	3,154	1,086	572	254
Albany, GA	6,772	3,642	2,843	19,350	234	na	122	na	107	na
Albany-Schenectady-Troy, NY	49,294	26,207	30,370	116,115	1,244	602	6,702	2,539	775	460
Albuquerque, NM	32,528	29,741	33,257	75,846	31,871	8,134	2,886	543	1,345	754
Alexandria, LA	7,891	4,469	3,657	20,025	166	na	939	na	133	na
Allentown-Bethlehem-Easton, PA-NJ	55,505	21,964	20,284	113,670	4,478	3,158	7,275	2,722	889	702
Altoona, PA	12,751	3,311	2,152	22,256	49	na	482	na	38	na
Amarillo, TX	8,522	9,006	6,608	27,406	2,379	1,075	188	24	343	309
Ames, IA	2,928	1,944	3,347	8,792	40	na	156	na	92	na
Anchorage, AK	8,348	9,896	7,742	25,296	825	407	971	229	2,497	1,761
Anderson, IN	9,625	4,187	2,684	20,209	260	na	153	na	52	na
Anderson, SC	9,715	6,548	4,445	28,725	309	na	420	na	13	na
Ann Arbor, MI	8,548	8,440	14,975	33,262	507	108	1,825	856	1,131	610
Anniston-Oxford, AL	5,832	3,441	2,801	16,905	272	na	215	na	31	na
Appleton, WI	13,458	4,640	4,527	26,493	268	146	265	79	191	191
Asheville, NC	24,719	19,137	23,028	78,426	888	439	1,144	339	317	128
Athens-Clarke County, GA	6,754	3,462	6,075	19,307	458	189	362	160	296	208
Atlanta-Sandy Springs-Marietta, GA	158,501	115,976	125,388	456,804	14,475	8,062	16,888	7,847	12,210	9,951
Atlantic City-Hammonton, NJ	15,340	8,242	7,658	34,214	2,108	1,474	2,275	1,337	1,244	754
Auburn-Opelika, AL	3,331	3,374	3,263	13,124	162	na	37	na	127	na
Augusta-Richmond County, GA-SC	23,310	16,152	15,083	68,808	1,023	415	1,617	465	838	561
Austin-Round Rock-San Marcos, TX	35,273	37,103	53,451	122,339	19,649	9,903	4,060	1,559	3,095	2,310
Bakersfield-Delano, CA	20,831	21,843	12,411	57,592	15,403	11,165	2,195	1,133	2,273	1,437
Baltimore-Towson, MD	114,099	71,719	91,826	327,934	4,071	1,551	12,787	5,286	8,044	5,427
Bangor, ME	10,065	4,634	3,731	21,670	48	na	1,119	na	47	na
Barnstable Town, MA	14,970	14,809	22,295	51,989	408	98	2,608	555	228	97
Baton Rouge, LA	32,449	18,759	19,986	84,776	1,284	644	3,211	508	715	369
Battle Creek, MI	8,521	5,175	2,925	19,705	207	na	351	na	100	na
Bay City, MI	7,658	4,271	2,225	17,403	200	na	334	na	0	na
Beaumont-Port Arthur, TX	19,477	13,149	7,755	46,791	2,278	953	1,647	341	598	392
Bellingham, WA	7,856	8,679	8,123	25,350	437	174	1,582	841	370	87
Bend, OR	7,091	8,472	7,421	24,377	341	na	460	na	81	na
Billings, MT	8,881	6,837	4,749	22,441	264	na	504	na	94	na
Binghamton, NY	17,608	9,363	7,633	38,976	501	223	1,760	639	301	211
Birmingham-Hoover, AL	52,801	33,632	28,495	146,998	1,185	592	1,698	537	406	255
Bismarck, ND	4,860	3,946	2,969	14,000	3	na	1,541	na	11	na
Blacksburg-Christiansburg-Radford, VA	6,163	3,949	4,706	20,330	85	na	211	na	69	na
Bloomington, IN	8,848	4,024	5,846	22,710	296	na	238	na	44	na
Bloomington-Normal, IL	6,563	4,238	5,001	17,287	257	na	306	na	68	na
Boise City-Nampa, ID	22,337	22,448	16,156	67,511	2,121	1,063	1,066	356	547	335
Boston-Cambridge-Quincy, MA-NH	210,718	124,475	173,070	507,001	19,366	14,539	65,653	34,207	19,138	16,015
Boulder, CO	6,791	7,979	14,958	28,795	1,325	615	1,120	241	361	191
Bowling Green, KY	5,540	3,137	2,401	14,465	85	61	259	142	117	78
Bremerton-Silverdale, WA	9,444	12,190	10,403	32,150	577	355	774	240	1,587	904
Bridgeport-Stamford-Norwalk, CT	38,666	22,508	43,919	102,511	7,718	5,850	14,381	7,309	1,889	1,253
Brownsville-Harlingen, TX	9,592	6,832	5,586	15,872	30,010	20,509	394	113	211	163
Brunswick, GA	4,646	4,625	4,314	16,978	213	na	412	na	78	na
Buffalo-Niagara Falls, NY	71,921	38,982	34,660	164,797	2,317	1,329	11,372	3,853	1,111	713
Burlington, NC	7,376	5,879	4,070	22,202	288	na	209	na	82	na
Burlington-South Burlington, VT	8,205	5,297	8,242	23,420	168	49	1,744	302	267	258
Canton-Massillon, OH	32,325	12,717	8,972	64,309	335	185	1,936	675	91	61
Cape Coral-Fort Myers, FL	51,790	41,094	41,317	137,644	7,413	5,833	6,998	2,680	865	357
Cape Girardeau-Jackson, MO-IL	5,286	2,776	2,257	14,307	17	na	281	na	48	na
Casper, WY	3,253	3,282	1,765	9,158	292	na	101	na	34	na
Cedar Rapids, IA	16,326	8,316	6,848	34,765	235	na	791	na	169	na
Champaign-Urbana, IL	9,386	6,254	7,085	24,806	388	92	549	147	510	450
Charleston, WV	20,906	8,484	7,200	48,660	104	na	320	na	208	na
Charleston-North Charleston-Summerville, SC	24,096	19,626	19,865	77,628	1,182	434	1,377	467	1,137	614
Charlotte-Gastonia-Rock Hill, NC-SC	56,816	48,007	40,618	174,883	3,935	2,546	4,842	1,760	2,286	1,604
Charlottesville, VA	7,744	5,382	10,716	27,093	304	73	1,025	464	317	238
Chattanooga, TN-GA	26,151	19,213	14,356	78,359	866	539	532	147	479	303
Cheyenne, WY	4,571	3,406	2,342	10,867	924	na	117	na	165	na
Chicago-Joliet-Naperville, IL-IN-WI	367,756	248,825	256,785	878,144	81,756	58,286	103,827	57,054	37,698	24,850
Chico, CA	9,838	11,888	7,915	32,136	1,304	793	756	298	338	252
Cincinnati-Middletown, OH-KY-IN	97,922	54,963	56,168	257,729	1,511	470	5,078	2,019	1,701	721
Clarksville, TN-KY	10,046	6,174	4,274	25,245	462	221	651	133	328	234
Cleveland, TN	6,373	3,714	2,063	17,174	290	na	146	na	12	na
Cleveland-Elyria-Mentor, OH	121,676	71,374	61,573	288,859	5,019	2,955	21,196	10,576	2,607	1,393
Coeur d'Alene, ID	6,379	6,766	4,895	20,433	128	na	361	na	109	na
College Station-Bryan, TX	6,040	4,335	6,116	18,270	1,982	1,051	532	131	217	141
Colorado Springs, CO	19,521	21,056	21,568	60,492	3,634	812	2,933	622	1,468	1,030
Columbia, MO	4,933	4,110	5,682	16,531	168	na	350	na	301	na
Columbia, SC	29,780	20,894	21,933	88,403	1,184	668	1,732	468	551	339
Columbus, GA-AL	11,323	7,558	6,137	33,135	545	315	872	187	466	196
Columbus, IN	5,136	2,144	1,777	11,083	0	na	57	na	0	na
Columbus, OH	79,420	42,411	45,410	191,841	1,469	762	4,936	1,715	2,566	1,577
Corpus Christi, TX	13,864	12,731	11,213	31,613	23,758	11,692	856	277	525	367
Corvallis, OR	2,042	2,939	4,911	10,114	230	na	303	na	90	na
Crestview-Fort Walton Beach-Destin, FL	7,632	7,930	7,717	24,281	488	na	718	na	427	na

Table E-4: Metropolitan Statistical Areas—Educational Attainment and Language Spoken at Home, Persons 65 Years and Over—*Continued*

	High School or Equivalent	Some College or Associates Degree	Bachelor's Degree or Higher	Speaks English at Home	Speaks Spanish at Home		Speaks Indo-European at Home		Speaks Asian at Home	
				Total	Total	Speaks English Less Than Very Well	Total	Speaks English Less Than Very Well	Total	Speaks English Less Than Very Well
Cumberland, MD-WV	8,515	3,455	1,933	18,194	115	na	158	na	101	na
Dallas-Fort Worth-Arlington, TX	166,046	154,661	156,835	501,201	56,540	33,893	16,886	7,931	16,420	12,521
Dalton, GA	5,848	2,705	1,778	15,535	445	na	65	na	86	na
Danville, IL	5,941	3,013	1,611	12,947	21	na	144	na	72	na
Danville, VA	6,478	3,210	2,161	19,257	30	na	127	na	55	na
Davenport-Moline-Rock Island, IA-IL	24,812	14,047	10,372	56,208	1,101	783	1,004	344	352	270
Dayton, OH	48,660	29,817	26,298	124,814	777	237	1,995	591	913	638
Decatur, AL	8,525	5,041	2,974	22,130	198	na	92	na	0	na
Decatur, IL	7,803	4,219	3,105	18,085	75	na	160	na	10	na
Deltona-Daytona Beach-Ormond Beach, FL	39,239	27,834	22,139	96,031	5,869	2,480	4,120	1,236	743	414
Denver-Aurora-Broomfield, CO	76,706	70,171	87,082	232,731	21,318	9,595	9,800	4,175	6,231	4,974
Des Moines-West Des Moines, IA	27,821	15,912	13,892	62,667	1,004	390	1,099	384	1,040	643
Detroit-Warren-Livonia, MI	207,044	139,109	115,649	520,356	6,715	2,742	34,799	15,764	7,152	4,167
Dothan, AL	9,065	4,924	2,684	22,791	222	na	183	na	45	na
Dover, DE	8,415	4,950	4,306	21,328	389	12	967	321	393	206
Dubuque, IA	6,591	2,482	2,552	14,248	37	na	117	na	17	na
Duluth, MN-WI	18,078	10,783	9,117	42,316	240	92	790	200	141	12
Durham-Chapel Hill, NC	16,316	12,061	20,413	56,643	1,157	335	1,879	388	654	353
Eau Claire, WI	9,754	4,885	3,975	21,603	64	na	217	na	96	na
El Centro, CA	3,069	2,814	1,533	6,016	12,313	na	223	na	295	na
Elizabethtown, KY	5,797	2,693	1,418	13,226	20	na	479	na	178	na
Elkhart-Goshen, IN	10,294	4,410	4,329	22,982	449	361	951	290	4	0
Elmira, NY	5,535	2,966	2,527	13,339	2	na	287	na	26	na
El Paso, TX	18,226	13,720	11,117	20,499	61,831	41,771	1,451	476	822	512
Erie, PA	19,913	7,393	7,253	39,302	303	113	1,618	458	68	39
Eugene-Springfield, OR	17,270	16,294	15,066	52,593	904	295	858	170	512	411
Evansville, IN-KY	24,050	11,367	7,202	51,467	172	na	461	na	104	na
Fairbanks, AK	1,827	1,918	1,866	6,303	69	na	68	na	185	na
Fargo, ND-MN	7,864	6,433	5,064	21,370	63	0	738	180	208	182
Farmington, NM	4,799	2,881	2,481	9,203	1,540	429	160	79	0	0
Fayetteville, NC	11,568	9,054	6,238	31,819	822	313	1,549	363	573	333
Fayetteville-Springdale-Rogers, AR-MO	19,455	12,660	11,187	51,708	875	465	731	186	225	170
Flagstaff, AZ	2,296	3,644	3,871	8,854	1,063	161	136	32	151	13
Flint, MI	24,080	15,137	8,686	57,262	588	220	1,110	341	334	193
Florence, SC	10,042	5,185	4,566	28,272	219	na	245	na	16	na
Florence-Muscle Shoals, AL	9,023	5,407	4,747	25,142	77	na	131	na	36	na
Fond du Lac, WI	7,288	2,976	2,228	15,125	120	na	331	na	45	na
Fort Collins-Loveland, CO	9,989	10,540	13,807	35,573	984	na	804	na	322	na
Fort Smith, AR-OK	16,615	9,780	5,522	41,409	295	152	324	109	347	331
Fort Wayne, IN	21,973	12,566	9,951	50,853	452	123	1,036	389	362	232
Fresno, CA	23,015	26,081	17,697	64,140	21,614	12,113	5,569	3,096	5,055	3,793
Gadsden, AL	6,189	4,158	2,064	16,654	21	na	60	na	19	na
Gainesville, FL	8,199	7,471	10,340	28,355	964	367	863	299	148	130
Gainesville, GA	6,022	5,386	4,869	20,276	911	na	165	na	269	na
Glens Falls, NY	9,221	4,195	4,701	20,918	192	na	427	na	70	na
Goldsboro, NC	6,001	3,743	2,063	15,963	198	na	190	na	113	na
Grand Forks, ND-MN	4,270	3,203	2,352	11,841	92	na	365	na	69	na
Grand Junction, CO	7,525	7,468	4,918	21,379	1,029	na	153	na	53	na
Grand Rapids-Wyoming, MI	36,239	24,128	17,853	88,278	1,915	1,037	2,036	719	876	689
Great Falls, MT	4,788	3,475	2,374	12,469	98	na	267	na	79	na
Greeley, CO	8,837	6,876	5,323	22,476	2,750	1,534	574	168	101	42
Green Bay, WI	18,542	8,141	5,816	37,845	404	277	853	210	211	130
Greensboro-High Point, NC	34,205	20,931	19,863	95,007	1,127	757	1,503	429	1,084	741
Greenville, NC	6,513	4,070	3,929	19,577	311	na	203	na	93	na
Greenville-Mauldin-Easley, SC	27,517	17,665	18,852	83,635	1,448	943	1,164	243	574	306
Gulfport-Biloxi, MS	11,068	8,626	6,818	31,145	399	na	402	na	413	na
Hagerstown-Martinsburg, MD-WV	15,681	7,238	5,362	36,037	343	193	726	165	203	138
Hanford-Corcoran, CA	3,779	2,938	1,526	7,588	3,413	1,866	704	132	520	276
Harrisburg-Carlisle, PA	36,616	13,904	15,705	77,332	956	500	2,773	1,015	591	256
Harrisonburg, VA	5,631	2,639	3,422	15,979	79	na	244	na	55	na
Hartford-West Hartford-East Hartford, CT	61,111	35,659	46,722	147,535	7,815	6,078	20,087	10,070	1,703	1,133
Hattiesburg, MS	5,319	3,785	3,816	16,622	182	na	106	na	23	na
Hickory-Lenoir-Morganton, NC	19,826	11,153	7,768	55,529	556	439	607	176	505	461
Hinesville-Fort Stewart, GA	2,189	1,157	537	5,087	191	na	95	na	76	na
Holland-Grand Haven, MI	11,745	6,717	7,141	30,248	788	476	773	153	188	173
Honolulu, HI	48,622	30,446	35,919	95,955	972	222	1,528	441	44,506	30,034
Hot Springs, AR	7,028	5,177	4,341	19,385	212	na	459	na	59	na
Houma-Bayou Cane-Thibodaux, LA	9,617	3,133	2,880	17,058	322	196	7,679	1,568	81	81
Houston-Sugar Land-Baytown, TX	145,463	134,316	137,508	411,097	83,718	50,441	18,399	7,388	26,165	19,146
Huntington-Ashland, WV-KY-OH	19,551	8,789	5,799	46,790	127	na	293	na	65	na
Huntsville, AL	15,519	13,049	15,531	51,434	486	121	804	159	436	284
Idaho Falls, ID	4,826	4,742	3,234	13,456	482	na	393	na	25	na
Indianapolis-Carmel, IN	79,063	43,554	40,580	189,961	2,643	1,371	3,471	1,402	1,289	856
Iowa City, IA	4,755	3,858	5,078	14,700	136	30	344	68	248	123
Ithaca, NY	3,225	1,830	4,878	10,201	106	na	795	na	161	na
Jackson, MI	9,392	6,356	3,331	22,415	115	na	586	na	81	na
Jackson, MS	18,517	14,301	14,759	61,929	392	na	366	na	135	na
Jackson, TN	5,262	3,756	2,715	15,709	28	na	55	na	0	na
Jacksonville, FL	52,218	44,680	43,869	157,045	5,539	3,396	4,697	1,819	3,888	2,144
Jacksonville, NC	4,957	3,904	2,093	13,074	354	na	165	na	248	na

Table E-4: Metropolitan Statistical Areas—Educational Attainment and Language Spoken at Home, Persons 65 Years and Over—*Continued*

	High School or Equivalent	Some College or Associates Degree	Bachelor's Degree or Higher	Speaks English at Home Total	Speaks Spanish at Home Total	Speaks English Less Than Very Well	Speaks Indo-European at Home Total	Speaks English Less Than Very Well	Speaks Asian at Home Total	Speaks English Less Than Very Well
Janesville, WI	10,390	5,001	3,123	21,311	168	na	582	na	80	na
Jefferson City, MO	8,458	4,000	3,464	19,453	197	na	123	na	0	na
Johnson City, TN	11,084	6,611	5,744	32,620	218	na	290	na	220	na
Johnstown, PA	14,807	3,272	2,831	26,202	171	na	760	na	22	na
Jonesboro, AR	5,866	2,893	2,123	15,552	18	na	168	na	74	na
Joplin, MO	9,711	6,006	3,672	24,417	293	na	182	na	149	na
Kalamazoo-Portage, MI	15,720	10,147	10,408	40,708	413	125	944	277	228	98
Kankakee-Bradley, IL	6,853	3,128	1,837	14,798	143	na	392	na	14	na
Kansas City, MO-KS	93,723	63,653	58,598	240,517	5,006	2,577	3,459	1,162	2,628	1,929
Kennewick-Pasco-Richland, WA	8,195	7,381	7,686	24,247	1,897	1,085	1,052	460	457	273
Killeen-Temple-Fort Hood, TX	11,491	10,622	7,589	32,410	2,979	2,173	1,223	291	1,107	730
Kingsport-Bristol-Bristol, TN-VA	20,665	10,706	8,764	57,326	127	na	272	na	179	na
Kingston, NY	9,656	6,246	7,432	25,208	861	390	1,853	454	146	70
Knoxville, TN	34,382	25,997	24,057	103,324	681	222	1,326	516	665	430
Kokomo, IN	7,620	3,598	2,347	16,154	230	na	288	na	125	na
La Crosse, WI-MN	8,043	4,552	3,819	18,633	45	na	252	na	154	na
Lafayette, IN	9,297	4,260	4,498	20,579	310	na	315	na	148	na
Lafayette, LA	8,571	5,464	6,315	18,739	426	200	10,540	2,299	156	154
Lake Charles, LA	10,695	4,929	3,696	21,474	169	na	3,931	na	177	na
Lake Havasu City-Kingman, AZ	18,523	16,399	5,662	44,987	2,114	na	955	na	229	na
Lakeland-Winter Haven, FL	42,903	27,994	18,914	101,890	6,135	3,951	2,577	866	1,187	533
Lancaster, PA	33,949	12,741	14,534	73,877	1,755	1,047	3,767	1,569	678	570
Lansing-East Lansing, MI	19,964	14,357	14,245	52,800	1,290	552	1,333	439	696	479
Laredo, TX	2,822	2,786	1,818	1,470	18,684	na	76	na	0	na
Las Cruces, NM	5,577	5,936	6,732	14,602	11,705	6,898	449	129	168	68
Las Vegas-Paradise, NV	73,261	65,788	51,792	185,002	20,956	12,847	8,720	3,268	17,342	9,565
Lawrence, KS	2,993	2,180	4,032	9,818	117	na	210	na	116	na
Lawton, OK	4,521	3,281	2,386	11,446	307	177	660	186	396	234
Lebanon, PA	11,440	3,098	3,142	21,644	350	294	846	311	99	65
Lewiston-Auburn, ME	6,348	2,912	1,696	10,889	36	na	4,464	na	77	na
Lexington-Fayette, KY	17,109	12,160	13,499	53,081	578	267	574	232	366	251
Lima, OH	7,639	2,777	2,108	15,500	112	na	66	na	7	na
Lincoln, NE	12,680	9,642	9,241	32,419	405	135	1,175	469	542	505
Little Rock-North Little Rock-Conway, AR	31,318	20,057	19,394	86,333	967	472	1,043	487	242	172
Logan, UT-ID	2,717	3,637	3,273	10,248	302	na	166	na	32	na
Longview, TX	10,520	8,231	5,220	29,425	592	na	355	na	178	na
Longview, WA	5,447	5,674	2,721	16,034	112	na	283	na	109	na
Los Angeles-Long Beach-Santa Ana, CA	326,714	355,352	398,088	808,192	309,318	219,164	120,224	75,159	220,526	170,317
Louisville/Jefferson County, KY-IN	62,535	36,519	30,555	164,664	1,599	808	1,820	687	1,241	655
Lubbock, TX	8,796	7,975	7,982	26,908	5,344	2,790	157	15	241	197
Lynchburg, VA	14,168	8,511	7,428	40,369	351	na	323	na	75	na
Macon, GA	11,139	5,451	5,258	30,619	157	na	196	na	186	na
Madera-Chowchilla, CA	4,561	5,304	2,632	13,605	3,460	2,135	595	288	168	98
Madison, WI	22,855	13,499	21,727	61,538	628	311	1,730	497	715	510
Manchester-Nashua, NH	17,759	11,089	12,283	42,375	663	425	5,727	1,752	524	424
Manhattan, KS	3,906	2,381	2,971	10,086	61	na	280	na	82	na
Mankato-North Mankato, MN	4,328	2,624	3,395	11,316	70	na	326	na	94	na
Mansfield, OH	10,109	3,624	2,717	20,154	0	na	468	na	129	na
McAllen-Edinburg-Mission, TX	14,936	9,897	8,515	22,204	52,370	38,847	807	402	400	147
Medford, OR	11,297	11,591	9,519	35,436	830	na	778	na	174	na
Memphis, TN-MS-AR	47,122	33,318	27,741	139,305	1,552	650	1,312	471	1,319	980
Merced, CA	5,750	6,072	3,282	15,513	6,599	4,381	2,060	1,377	1,014	954
Miami-Fort Lauderdale-Pompano Beach, FL	266,018	184,293	220,413	520,753	302,022	241,277	77,735	42,855	7,722	5,584
Michigan City-La Porte, IN	7,556	2,929	2,465	15,543	232	na	333	na	0	na
Midland, TX	4,098	4,096	3,366	12,151	2,646	na	190	na	180	na
Milwaukee-Waukesha-West Allis, WI	76,339	45,611	44,526	182,963	4,783	3,080	9,411	3,595	2,070	1,455
Minneapolis-St. Paul-Bloomington, MN-WI	129,385	91,585	102,556	338,129	3,983	2,074	11,996	4,257	7,503	5,812
Missoula, MT	4,390	2,975	4,414	12,307	114	na	412	na	48	na
Mobile, AL	20,721	11,797	9,253	53,312	651	319	572	98	420	189
Modesto, CA	16,859	14,427	8,229	40,445	9,304	6,081	3,292	1,911	1,493	1,134
Monroe, LA	8,758	4,627	4,178	22,990	167	na	73	na	47	na
Monroe, MI	9,223	4,748	3,044	20,389	195	na	442	na	29	na
Montgomery, AL	15,616	10,140	10,622	45,414	271	58	404	131	258	118
Morgantown, WV	6,106	2,544	2,868	15,045	32	na	212	na	30	na
Morristown, TN	8,745	4,095	2,376	22,534	76	na	121	na	66	na
Mount Vernon-Anacortes, WA	5,441	6,452	5,157	18,480	546	265	493	219	184	115
Muncie, IN	7,493	3,263	2,878	17,361	154	na	51	na	10	na
Muskegon-Norton Shores, MI	9,060	6,126	3,630	22,848	358	na	545	na	29	na
Myrtle Beach-North Myrtle Beach-Conway, SC	17,762	13,008	10,694	46,896	560	152	1,314	620	239	165
Napa, CA	4,664	6,656	7,104	17,644	1,854	1,174	926	312	939	660

Table E-4: Metropolitan Statistical Areas—Educational Attainment and Language Spoken at Home, Persons 65 Years and Over—*Continued*

	High School or Equivalent	Some College or Associates Degree	Bachelor's Degree or Higher	Speaks English at Home	Speaks Spanish at Home		Speaks Indo-European at Home		Speaks Asian at Home	
				Total	Total	Speaks English Less Than Very Well	Total	Speaks English Less Than Very Well	Total	Speaks English Less Than Very Well
Naples-Marco Island, FL	22,222	23,807	34,006	77,769	5,198	4,203	5,984	2,683	468	319
Nashville-Davidson--Murfreesboro--Franklin, TN	61,652	39,586	36,993	171,276	2,405	1,323	2,733	924	1,370	1,106
New Haven-Milford, CT	47,424	23,447	29,531	107,123	5,849	4,290	11,346	5,017	1,487	1,269
New Orleans-Metairie-Kenner, LA	52,916	30,873	29,583	134,677	6,444	3,598	4,975	1,189	2,320	1,881
New York-Northern New Jersey-Long Island, NY-NJ-PA	856,266	416,391	639,957	1,720,396	319,589	235,779	335,380	203,031	133,651	104,249
Niles-Benton Harbor, MI	9,417	6,277	5,368	24,543	301	120	767	354	111	31
North Port-Bradenton-Sarasota, FL	65,346	54,356	60,314	182,537	4,842	2,578	10,713	3,434	855	266
Norwich-New London, CT	14,892	8,581	9,887	36,130	786	539	2,494	1,069	632	509
Ocala, FL	33,913	24,178	14,883	81,395	3,570	na	2,042	na	297	na
Ocean City, NJ	8,849	4,554	5,183	19,952	236	na	1,189	na	120	na
Odessa, TX	3,832	3,217	1,784	10,082	3,787	na	84	na	68	na
Ogden-Clearfield, UT	15,159	18,340	12,922	47,871	1,756	938	1,328	220	573	447
Oklahoma City, OK	49,623	42,156	36,079	144,251	3,618	1,939	1,524	379	2,708	2,140
Olympia, WA	8,912	10,847	11,029	31,799	716	317	558	72	1,225	841
Omaha-Council Bluffs, NE-IA	38,347	25,637	21,183	94,047	1,705	1,068	2,397	627	495	341
Orlando-Kissimmee-Sanford, FL	95,384	66,287	60,253	215,387	41,905	29,726	13,276	6,415	4,954	3,209
Oshkosh-Neenah, WI	10,614	4,612	4,726	22,232	109	na	329	na	104	na
Owensboro, KY	7,291	3,494	2,451	17,158	79	na	108	na	22	na
Oxnard-Thousand Oaks-Ventura, CA	21,737	30,954	29,335	73,024	16,761	10,821	4,231	1,446	5,854	4,021
Palm Bay-Melbourne-Titusville, FL	39,960	31,867	25,533	103,275	4,937	2,407	4,533	1,501	892	639
Palm Coast, FL	8,240	6,853	6,216	21,337	1,237	na	1,864	na	488	na
Panama City-Lynn Haven-Panama City Beach, FL	9,109	7,449	4,972	24,129	353	na	539	na	298	na
Parkersburg-Marietta-Vienna, WV-OH	12,956	6,065	2,960	27,294	192	na	180	na	162	na
Pascagoula, MS	8,299	4,792	3,753	20,264	164	na	347	na	137	na
Pensacola-Ferry Pass-Brent, FL	20,872	18,677	13,601	60,938	856	392	1,471	445	1,057	705
Peoria, IL	24,596	13,554	9,810	55,909	401	183	945	324	273	135
Philadelphia-Camden-Wilmington, PA-NJ-DE-MD	307,967	146,247	189,318	722,879	20,658	12,603	46,595	23,344	18,697	13,706
Phoenix-Mesa-Glendale, AZ	157,258	164,719	144,378	464,131	48,958	24,738	17,901	5,854	8,563	5,409
Pine Bluff, AR	5,113	2,034	2,101	13,561	33	na	92	na	10	na
Pittsburgh, PA	197,788	69,746	71,447	391,386	2,048	647	14,418	4,635	1,640	1,089
Pittsfield, MA	9,108	4,992	6,899	23,199	330	na	1,410	na	67	na
Pocatello, ID	3,328	3,215	2,188	9,987	198	na	160	na	106	na
Portland-South Portland-Biddeford, ME	26,634	19,136	22,560	71,289	497	44	6,905	1,251	639	584
Portland-Vancouver-Hillsboro, OR-WA	77,888	80,440	75,340	239,307	6,314	3,051	10,097	4,898	9,779	7,932
Port St. Lucie, FL	32,615	26,728	25,377	88,889	4,992	2,355	4,461	2,035	614	368
Poughkeepsie-Newburgh-Middletown, NY	31,559	16,693	19,571	72,081	4,460	2,247	6,062	2,469	1,033	570
Prescott, AZ	13,736	19,101	15,655	50,031	1,640	na	1,502	na	61	na
Providence-New Bedford-Fall River, RI-MA	77,561	41,098	47,429	187,898	6,625	5,111	36,910	19,144	2,082	1,557
Provo-Orem, UT	8,983	12,322	12,589	33,352	1,744	1,018	881	103	437	254
Pueblo, CO	8,188	6,268	4,866	19,231	5,198	na	452	na	83	na
Punta Gorda, FL	21,471	16,439	12,259	51,631	1,403	na	3,232	na	304	na
Racine, WI	10,783	5,529	4,806	24,486	824	366	867	218	65	44
Raleigh-Cary, NC	31,670	26,873	31,631	101,539	2,106	1,477	3,119	1,167	1,670	1,190
Rapid City, SD	5,924	4,692	4,235	16,693	202	na	351	na	23	na
Reading, PA	27,826	8,362	8,718	54,479	2,291	1,832	3,524	947	358	257
Redding, CA	9,699	12,061	4,947	29,407	685	na	693	na	368	na
Reno-Sparks, NV	16,954	16,220	14,369	47,890	2,840	1,654	1,777	485	1,826	1,242
Richmond, VA	50,998	35,673	37,740	152,334	1,788	691	3,399	1,501	2,036	1,304
Riverside-San Bernardino-Ontario, CA	122,776	134,123	93,039	327,445	89,219	56,831	16,541	5,851	23,433	15,605
Roanoke, VA	16,557	13,025	10,123	50,302	236	134	837	293	140	65
Rochester, MN	10,626	5,840	5,915	24,044	172	88	441	139	440	404
Rochester, NY	53,453	34,312	37,792	140,058	3,188	2,257	8,162	3,389	1,500	919
Rockford, IL	18,989	11,144	8,443	44,831	1,284	914	1,781	803	466	362
Rocky Mount, NC	8,299	4,393	2,852	22,106	150	na	68	na	113	na
Rome, GA	4,980	2,929	2,256	13,729	88	na	43	na	34	na
Sacramento--Arden-Arcade--Roseville, CA	69,593	85,094	71,875	213,495	18,585	10,414	17,593	9,827	20,295	14,953
Saginaw-Saginaw Township North, MI	13,776	6,569	3,789	29,223	910	na	835	na	101	na
St. Cloud, MN	10,090	4,107	4,000	22,071	75	24	1,203	370	111	107
St. George, UT	7,709	8,557	7,050	24,140	753	na	425	na	103	na
St. Joseph, MO-KS	7,660	4,023	2,755	17,928	92	na	141	na	49	na
St. Louis, MO-IL	142,242	87,575	80,429	368,948	3,404	1,083	8,056	3,239	3,944	2,710
Salem, OR	17,356	16,794	12,516	49,411	2,235	1,415	1,503	527	574	382
Salinas, CA	8,995	11,769	14,047	31,243	9,251	6,350	2,019	624	3,131	1,781
Salisbury, MD	6,102	2,943	4,136	16,384	266	na	239	na	82	na
Salt Lake City, UT	28,768	30,563	28,106	88,586	4,647	2,517	4,152	1,616	2,580	1,718
San Angelo, TX	4,936	3,676	3,326	12,591	2,996	na	95	na	28	na
San Antonio-New Braunfels, TX	63,606	60,114	55,291	146,226	90,221	39,562	6,758	1,612	2,884	1,656
San Diego-Carlsbad-San Marcos, CA	78,700	101,742	114,759	255,433	52,216	35,029	18,195	7,815	35,181	24,001
Sandusky, OH	6,076	2,756	2,406	13,359	143	na	137	na	60	na
San Francisco-Oakland-Fremont, CA	124,565	139,418	199,366	358,944	47,180	29,097	45,482	22,815	114,494	85,699

Table E-4: Metropolitan Statistical Areas—Educational Attainment and Language Spoken at Home, Persons 65 Years and Over—*Continued*

	High School or Equivalent	Some College or Associates Degree	Bachelor's Degree or Higher	Speaks English at Home	Speaks Spanish at Home		Speaks Indo-European at Home		Speaks Asian at Home	
				Total	Total	Speaks English Less Than Very Well	Total	Speaks English Less Than Very Well	Total	Speaks English Less Than Very Well
San Jose-Sunnyvale-Santa Clara, CA	42,176	47,953	77,841	120,903	23,779	13,201	16,931	9,375	48,021	37,817
San Luis Obispo-Paso Robles, CA	10,213	13,651	15,006	38,314	2,240	1,088	1,381	379	703	277
Santa Barbara-Santa Maria-Goleta, CA	11,929	15,843	18,312	42,804	8,231	4,913	3,149	639	1,671	1,162
Santa Cruz-Watsonville, CA	5,522	8,765	11,867	24,613	3,807	2,548	1,464	530	800	592
Santa Fe, NM	5,027	5,038	10,888	15,745	6,942	1,588	581	21	100	78
Santa Rosa-Petaluma, CA	17,077	20,720	24,810	61,774	4,219	2,547	2,930	1,024	1,753	910
Savannah, GA	13,983	9,034	10,486	40,455	490	92	854	277	378	368
Scranton--Wilkes-Barre, PA	50,543	18,201	12,296	94,953	1,083	733	4,810	1,467	222	200
Seattle-Tacoma-Bellevue, WA	106,615	112,516	122,702	328,065	7,139	2,854	19,636	9,547	34,387	26,485
Sebastian-Vero Beach, FL	11,952	10,662	11,405	36,070	1,452	na	1,358	na	136	na
Sheboygan, WI	9,047	2,765	2,379	16,360	201	109	532	175	91	91
Sherman-Denison, TX	6,286	5,892	3,426	18,758	348	na	68	na	0	na
Shreveport-Bossier City, LA	19,356	12,423	10,110	51,848	310	na	826	na	241	na
Sioux City, IA-NE-SD	8,344	4,343	2,534	18,017	435	335	198	88	294	282
Sioux Falls, SD	10,268	6,236	5,419	25,177	56	0	849	376	113	105
South Bend-Mishawaka, IN-MI	19,333	9,078	8,608	42,443	665	383	1,365	411	255	122
Spartanburg, SC	12,526	8,766	6,454	38,256	316	161	523	190	307	162
Spokane, WA	19,716	19,445	15,882	59,319	833	215	2,180	1,054	867	692
Springfield, IL	12,427	7,184	6,767	29,048	148	na	711	na	97	na
Springfield, MA	36,296	20,282	21,486	84,626	4,675	3,886	9,227	4,580	769	665
Springfield, MO	23,754	16,640	11,936	61,718	341	38	718	170	213	189
Springfield, OH	9,576	5,234	3,271	22,256	104	na	201	na	47	na
State College, PA	7,291	2,659	5,251	17,143	78	6	388	51	143	63
Steubenville-Weirton, OH-WV	12,341	3,835	2,385	22,279	207	na	579	na	42	na
Stockton, CA	19,537	20,507	12,498	50,839	10,791	7,041	3,949	2,346	8,155	6,006
Sumter, SC	4,035	3,453	2,211	13,873	82	na	59	na	97	na
Syracuse, NY	36,097	19,892	19,790	86,137	969	304	4,817	2,019	759	468
Tallahassee, FL	11,681	8,328	12,385	37,276	1,094	525	1,103	227	378	245
Tampa-St. Petersburg-Clearwater, FL	180,479	122,654	103,124	423,739	37,575	22,183	25,510	10,045	5,979	4,010
Terre Haute, IN	11,188	4,614	3,920	24,178	185	na	349	na	86	na
Texarkana, TX-Texarkana, AR	7,128	5,112	3,210	19,372	193	na	69	na	48	na
Toledo, OH	38,002	19,306	16,096	85,187	1,543	477	1,734	252	456	195
Topeka, KS	16,091	8,101	7,064	33,950	847	254	442	124	128	39
Trenton-Ewing, NJ	15,965	8,273	13,913	38,670	2,054	1,326	4,990	2,114	1,245	665
Tucson, AZ	39,254	43,830	50,042	126,919	23,476	10,696	4,535	1,158	1,781	1,281
Tulsa, OK	43,771	32,848	25,525	120,007	2,109	1,078	1,482	458	838	609
Tuscaloosa, AL	8,714	4,892	5,180	25,155	196	na	125	na	69	na
Tyler, TX	8,624	10,169	7,181	29,275	1,189	na	344	na	171	na
Utica-Rome, NY	19,554	10,813	8,916	45,800	618	420	2,804	1,116	317	302
Valdosta, GA	5,771	2,621	2,449	14,757	96	na	91	na	44	na
Vallejo-Fairfield, CA	13,280	15,918	11,608	34,883	4,583	2,245	2,130	894	7,552	3,975
Victoria, TX	5,170	4,335	2,528	12,693	3,775	na	249	na	72	na
Vineland-Millville-Bridgeton, NJ	8,085	2,913	2,001	17,247	2,084	na	636	na	105	na
Virginia Beach-Norfolk-Newport News, VA-NC	62,315	50,981	48,645	186,718	2,343	953	4,727	1,356	5,750	3,442
Visalia-Porterville, CA	9,974	11,457	6,382	28,770	11,811	7,176	1,192	415	1,324	937
Waco, TX	9,463	7,870	6,199	26,716	2,589	1,298	438	88	160	160
Warner Robins, GA	5,635	3,435	2,684	14,477	245	na	212	na	141	na
Washington-Arlington-Alexandria, DC-VA-MD-WV	146,579	120,958	229,823	477,316	28,729	17,359	38,563	15,973	35,027	24,545
Waterloo-Cedar Falls, IA	11,486	5,043	4,754	24,262	143	na	495	na	46	na
Wausau, WI	8,828	3,301	2,898	18,827	104	18	563	189	183	103
Wenatchee-East Wenatchee, WA	5,684	5,190	3,697	16,190	356	na	192	na	65	na
Wheeling, WV-OH	14,587	4,162	3,167	25,812	62	na	405	na	99	na
Wichita, KS	27,959	20,780	15,864	72,102	1,969	1,164	1,357	357	1,179	1,034
Wichita Falls, TX	7,770	5,301	3,420	19,382	986	446	149	97	176	131
Williamsport, PA	9,504	3,023	2,414	18,816	73	na	334	na	15	na
Wilmington, NC	18,934	16,194	18,746	60,860	478	na	1,370	na	159	na
Winchester, VA-WV	6,763	3,117	3,034	17,527	21	na	372	na	21	na
Winston-Salem, NC	24,501	14,330	14,350	66,052	986	570	991	542	183	94
Worcester, MA	37,866	21,389	22,792	90,078	3,120	2,544	9,309	4,103	1,546	1,337
Yakima, WA	7,692	7,635	4,695	24,280	3,973	2,869	434	178	284	275
York-Hanover, PA	29,455	9,891	8,641	60,970	674	466	1,124	247	332	243
Youngstown-Warren-Boardman, OH-PA	50,054	17,518	12,962	95,940	606	307	4,359	1,288	252	93
Yuba City, CA	5,477	6,109	3,154	15,401	1,920	1,346	1,884	1,385	653	343
Yuma, AZ	10,093	8,263	3,446	23,338	7,447	5,653	554	300	246	61

Table E-5: 113th Congressional Districts—Educational Attainment and Language Spoken at Home, Persons 65 Years and Over

	High School or Equivalent	Some College or Associates Degree	Bachelor's Degree or Higher	Speaks English at Home	Speaks Spanish at Home		Speaks Indo-European at Home		Speaks Asian at Home	
				Total	Total	Speaks English Less Than Very Well	Total	Speaks English Less Than Very Well	Total	Speaks English Less Than Very Well
Alabama										
Congressional District 1	36,782	22,843	19,321	97,995	1,026	427	955	98	482	189
Congressional District 2	34,684	21,211	15,942	96,062	764	350	761	207	544	365
Congressional District 3	31,848	19,017	14,151	92,666	702	330	628	37	297	128
Congressional District 4	39,818	21,374	12,577	108,008	433	263	547	204	142	96
Congressional District 5	30,401	22,742	22,400	93,052	747	272	1,034	177	469	317
Congressional District 6	30,689	21,323	21,534	88,693	1,017	527	1,209	335	295	183
Congressional District 7	31,668	16,022	13,003	87,370	359	na	509	na	150	na
Alaska										
Congressional District (at Large)	16,068	17,513	14,952	48,234	1,153	551	1,489	334	3,445	2,451
Arizona										
Congressional District 1	25,086	29,105	27,244	75,744	11,139	3,411	1,638	224	767	291
Congressional District 2	32,809	37,778	42,554	109,431	13,346	5,722	4,226	1,000	2,020	1,458
Congressional District 3	15,956	15,397	9,449	36,560	27,413	17,469	1,089	440	485	249
Congressional District 4	54,078	54,709	29,742	150,335	6,280	2,993	3,565	801	638	401
Congressional District 5	37,048	33,893	26,517	98,951	5,209	2,382	3,306	948	1,367	827
Congressional District 6	26,689	31,523	38,600	93,337	4,630	1,938	5,323	1,901	1,625	975
Congressional District 7	11,162	11,177	6,093	27,946	16,301	8,925	1,026	328	1,249	982
Congressional District 8	40,108	44,550	35,537	121,975	6,137	2,995	3,596	1,252	2,058	1,265
Congressional District 9	19,134	20,567	21,735	59,167	6,470	2,955	2,968	1,013	1,571	960
Arkansas										
Congressional District 1	45,497	21,446	13,645	115,852	468	158	952	187	225	91
Congressional District 2	34,098	22,431	20,599	94,473	996	502	1,112	487	242	172
Congressional District 3	34,429	22,562	17,443	90,536	1,203	607	1,232	295	545	458
Congressional District 4	48,244	25,393	15,961	119,294	1,147	495	817	333	227	155
California										
Congressional District 1	36,749	45,443	26,032	116,153	3,863	1,917	3,117	1,075	1,261	684
Congressional District 2	26,058	32,591	42,165	99,514	4,490	2,175	6,407	1,755	2,328	1,061
Congressional District 3	22,113	25,332	17,844	64,840	8,760	4,783	4,232	2,293	4,756	2,521
Congressional District 4	31,145	43,438	33,406	108,193	3,769	1,624	4,493	1,732	2,556	1,609
Congressional District 5	23,901	30,182	31,518	78,530	7,477	4,655	4,472	1,783	8,377	4,708
Congressional District 6	19,176	20,298	17,161	51,729	7,485	4,290	6,886	4,623	9,312	7,182
Congressional District 7	23,173	28,409	23,211	69,193	4,733	2,741	5,756	3,353	7,605	5,662
Congressional District 8	24,923	26,073	12,377	66,282	10,359	5,580	2,600	964	1,379	934
Congressional District 9	20,467	22,846	14,676	55,442	10,958	6,467	3,971	2,054	8,094	5,937
Congressional District 10	22,464	19,128	10,854	52,842	12,141	8,071	4,652	2,831	2,913	2,058
Congressional District 11	20,100	27,102	40,376	75,355	7,558	4,600	7,098	3,428	8,722	5,535
Congressional District 12	17,838	19,124	30,748	42,192	6,928	4,646	9,248	5,840	37,087	30,697
Congressional District 13	16,391	19,434	31,809	58,327	6,153	3,865	4,024	1,358	17,237	13,870
Congressional District 14	24,883	24,821	31,443	53,182	10,654	6,980	8,532	3,919	25,781	17,284
Congressional District 15	20,725	19,615	19,779	46,714	7,533	4,533	6,028	3,829	15,003	11,108
Congressional District 16	14,293	14,865	7,455	37,650	18,315	11,175	3,575	2,296	3,682	3,154
Congressional District 17	17,319	17,595	26,000	38,149	6,200	3,230	7,652	4,642	24,199	18,608
Congressional District 18	16,543	22,555	48,823	72,420	5,079	2,679	8,417	4,085	10,016	7,357
Congressional District 19	16,652	15,653	18,583	34,614	13,182	7,616	5,326	3,024	19,576	16,319
Congressional District 20	14,750	20,636	24,960	54,939	15,419	10,406	3,468	1,102	4,200	2,487
Congressional District 21	12,619	10,218	4,748	27,883	21,253	14,628	2,270	1,049	1,833	1,192
Congressional District 22	19,579	22,997	16,529	56,268	13,914	8,071	4,142	1,823	3,181	2,274
Congressional District 23	21,390	25,086	14,818	63,183	10,188	6,087	2,502	1,321	2,012	1,093
Congressional District 24	22,359	29,731	33,807	81,998	10,650	6,080	4,546	1,034	2,393	1,439
Congressional District 25	16,468	21,034	14,405	47,135	9,504	6,539	3,045	1,687	4,565	2,948
Congressional District 26	18,185	26,597	26,219	62,997	15,714	10,197	3,498	1,201	5,110	3,442
Congressional District 27	21,956	24,318	32,111	50,356	16,776	8,887	4,744	2,572	32,983	28,517
Congressional District 28	20,262	20,983	30,750	40,624	13,417	9,461	31,184	26,524	12,048	7,789
Congressional District 29	13,779	12,507	10,586	22,524	23,040	18,391	7,198	5,604	7,844	5,036
Congressional District 30	21,965	27,064	32,806	59,979	10,538	6,966	15,327	10,158	8,955	6,218
Congressional District 31	16,690	15,558	12,577	38,117	15,574	9,158	1,780	658	5,396	3,808
Congressional District 32	20,430	16,463	13,005	33,133	28,495	18,800	2,041	916	14,934	11,583
Congressional District 33	17,760	26,645	54,334	79,760	5,850	2,820	14,229	7,257	6,769	4,475
Congressional District 34	14,616	10,276	11,750	15,203	29,805	24,144	1,892	1,044	23,078	19,751
Congressional District 35	12,731	10,891	6,129	25,021	21,341	16,105	1,416	735	4,945	3,290
Congressional District 36	34,669	44,259	34,427	109,893	17,821	11,226	4,803	1,028	2,934	2,081
Congressional District 37	17,638	20,168	22,132	53,177	13,671	10,311	6,692	4,095	5,665	4,163
Congressional District 38	22,519	19,935	13,928	37,323	30,540	18,244	4,164	2,227	13,092	9,141
Congressional District 39	20,681	23,281	27,161	46,967	11,700	6,564	5,078	2,292	22,355	16,926
Congressional District 40	10,407	6,208	3,330	15,065	31,594	26,704	812	400	2,489	1,746
Congressional District 41	14,430	14,790	9,909	35,351	15,592	10,320	1,741	588	2,873	1,828
Congressional District 42	19,728	21,460	14,975	52,686	10,258	6,253	3,628	1,811	4,620	2,948
Congressional District 43	19,159	19,232	14,047	44,735	15,692	12,129	2,390	945	9,523	7,036
Congressional District 44	14,004	11,818	5,915	28,816	23,518	19,644	1,616	536	5,467	3,975
Congressional District 45	18,415	26,817	35,721	63,766	6,658	3,315	8,626	4,293	10,536	7,352
Congressional District 46	13,041	11,771	9,463	27,198	16,965	13,001	1,690	877	9,167	7,606
Congressional District 47	18,738	21,870	21,244	51,222	9,589	5,946	3,021	1,203	17,046	14,344
Congressional District 48	21,589	30,291	39,030	76,072	6,815	3,365	6,153	2,403	14,876	12,285
Congressional District 49	16,896	26,188	34,752	69,843	8,391	4,839	5,177	1,510	3,862	2,891
Congressional District 50	20,864	29,508	23,108	69,587	8,640	5,305	4,129	1,652	2,993	1,854

Table E-5: 113th Congressional Districts—Educational Attainment and Language Spoken at Home, Persons 65 Years and Over—*Continued*

	High School or Equivalent	Some College or Associates Degree	Bachelor's Degree or Higher	Speaks English at Home Total	Speaks Spanish at Home Total	Speaks Spanish at Home Speaks English Less Than Very Well	Speaks Indo-European at Home Total	Speaks Indo-European at Home Speaks English Less Than Very Well	Speaks Asian at Home Total	Speaks Asian at Home Speaks English Less Than Very Well
California—Cont.										
Congressional District 51	13,455	13,167	7,433	26,469	34,740	26,926	760	154	7,878	5,645
Congressional District 52	16,678	21,933	38,534	63,924	4,456	2,049	5,816	3,082	11,182	7,857
Congressional District 53	19,378	22,869	23,368	54,631	11,218	6,945	3,876	1,748	10,331	6,484
Colorado										
Congressional District 1	20,551	16,768	26,171	63,828	9,112	4,565	3,277	1,767	1,641	1,384
Congressional District 2	18,696	21,602	35,913	76,423	2,391	676	2,139	488	945	602
Congressional District 3	30,669	28,853	28,594	89,644	11,552	3,536	1,900	407	217	90
Congressional District 4	27,267	22,135	18,308	71,840	6,205	3,015	1,572	428	359	180
Congressional District 5	24,081	24,729	25,104	73,229	3,995	846	3,086	622	1,488	1,030
Congressional District 6	18,526	20,916	24,260	60,420	4,282	2,117	3,003	1,117	2,528	2,023
Congressional District 7	27,618	21,874	21,915	72,969	7,019	2,659	2,644	1,007	1,597	1,269
Connecticut										
Congressional District 1	37,296	20,778	25,885	87,063	5,863	4,670	12,983	6,951	1,247	832
Congressional District 2	36,655	22,466	27,319	92,413	1,660	987	7,635	2,462	899	691
Congressional District 3	39,972	19,103	24,687	89,889	4,110	3,024	8,749	3,937	1,389	1,135
Congressional District 4	28,928	17,140	36,192	79,353	6,210	4,671	11,672	5,896	1,462	903
Congressional District 5	35,835	19,655	27,953	86,217	5,090	3,790	11,467	5,343	872	671
Delaware										
Congressional District (at Large)	47,787	29,666	31,761	124,724	2,598	990	5,329	2,119	1,620	775
District of Columbia										
Delegate District (at Large)	16,523	12,484	25,938	63,373	2,582	1,100	2,769	527	734	468
Florida										
Congressional District 1	32,149	29,571	24,147	96,256	1,509	580	2,418	818	1,528	965
Congressional District 2	29,683	21,659	21,080	86,002	2,012	952	2,135	737	697	381
Congressional District 3	35,987	27,239	22,343	100,102	2,858	1,572	2,268	693	735	263
Congressional District 4	27,602	22,927	22,118	78,985	2,991	1,645	2,530	1,223	2,457	1,475
Congressional District 5	26,153	16,902	10,556	65,119	5,102	3,477	3,236	1,848	1,244	861
Congressional District 6	50,735	40,268	38,300	139,147	4,379	2,313	6,583	2,183	1,356	762
Congressional District 7	31,436	22,452	23,594	76,417	11,282	6,357	3,232	1,427	1,159	752
Congressional District 8	52,387	42,659	37,421	140,715	6,592	3,207	5,960	1,936	1,050	639
Congressional District 9	27,013	16,951	12,479	46,976	24,760	18,714	3,606	1,677	1,596	654
Congressional District 10	43,547	32,412	27,495	107,343	8,271	5,387	5,264	2,296	2,280	1,574
Congressional District 11	80,822	58,732	40,112	197,894	7,322	3,963	6,916	2,096	716	378
Congressional District 12	55,587	36,408	26,316	124,548	7,189	3,891	9,183	3,296	942	468
Congressional District 13	54,934	40,738	36,776	138,374	4,827	2,688	9,264	3,938	1,991	1,461
Congressional District 14	26,993	17,274	15,963	60,508	17,791	11,989	2,741	1,365	1,461	1,230
Congressional District 15	35,085	22,913	19,459	84,307	6,659	3,190	2,292	705	1,824	955
Congressional District 16	64,967	54,251	60,243	182,074	4,609	2,345	10,713	3,434	855	266
Congressional District 17	68,360	47,843	32,382	162,854	8,073	4,936	6,483	2,248	882	370
Congressional District 18	50,340	41,672	47,424	141,830	7,993	4,158	8,320	3,186	1,172	821
Congressional District 19	56,917	50,058	62,494	169,050	8,028	6,265	10,245	4,012	1,016	431
Congressional District 20	33,278	19,045	14,616	70,021	11,024	7,776	12,159	7,773	795	683
Congressional District 21	51,287	38,558	46,922	129,046	12,509	8,620	11,905	4,703	1,538	1,078
Congressional District 22	41,596	34,903	49,633	116,571	12,049	8,047	14,805	6,521	966	485
Congressional District 23	35,342	26,290	25,770	60,778	32,841	23,824	13,421	7,134	1,345	1,071
Congressional District 24	20,538	11,445	10,289	37,003	23,159	18,631	14,399	11,875	495	248
Congressional District 25	26,851	17,960	18,586	38,634	60,377	53,043	3,651	2,122	636	493
Congressional District 26	28,748	17,905	22,428	30,780	67,922	53,159	3,178	1,685	773	608
Congressional District 27	24,538	16,914	24,145	26,643	85,139	70,873	2,643	923	961	757
Georgia										
Congressional District 1	27,525	18,786	18,073	81,578	847	378	1,586	380	582	471
Congressional District 2	31,044	15,942	11,782	85,173	803	391	869	248	568	406
Congressional District 3	30,197	18,678	15,032	82,621	1,050	434	1,112	261	583	125
Congressional District 4	19,118	15,743	14,254	55,389	1,872	968	2,468	1,069	1,557	1,407
Congressional District 5	17,850	11,616	16,830	59,517	1,441	839	1,240	504	1,342	1,271
Congressional District 6	15,303	17,609	32,243	60,226	2,488	1,414	4,478	2,410	2,929	2,285
Congressional District 7	17,455	13,483	14,062	43,673	2,868	1,585	3,272	1,795	4,105	3,538
Congressional District 8	31,883	17,025	13,265	87,875	1,009	430	702	193	345	259
Congressional District 9	36,628	23,557	19,588	102,521	1,910	1,217	1,196	296	439	305
Congressional District 10	29,698	15,068	15,322	79,481	1,576	671	1,137	374	668	508
Congressional District 11	20,641	16,596	18,560	62,032	1,805	999	1,889	641	754	564
Congressional District 12	31,631	15,547	13,137	79,487	1,425	606	1,466	440	816	470
Congressional District 13	22,604	14,352	9,704	56,179	1,679	1,090	1,778	815	789	546
Congressional District 14	31,445	15,745	10,370	82,694	994	720	632	336	289	120
Hawaii										
Congressional District 1	37,699	23,170	28,016	71,104	599	180	1,097	339	37,727	25,719
Congressional District 2	29,689	22,055	23,003	70,701	1,072	164	1,638	420	19,115	11,840
Idaho										
Congressional District 1	36,189	31,894	21,150	102,987	2,325	1,045	1,381	278	272	108
Congressional District 2	30,220	29,628	22,247	90,487	2,662	1,473	1,597	488	687	445

Table E-5: 113th Congressional Districts—Educational Attainment and Language Spoken at Home, Persons 65 Years and Over—*Continued*

	High School or Equivalent	Some College or Associates Degree	Bachelor's Degree or Higher	Speaks English at Home Total	Speaks Spanish at Home Total	Speaks Spanish at Home Speaks English Less Than Very Well	Speaks Indo-European at Home Total	Speaks Indo-European at Home Speaks English Less Than Very Well	Speaks Asian at Home Total	Speaks Asian at Home Speaks English Less Than Very Well
Illinois										
Congressional District 1	33,369	25,242	16,226	88,937	3,229	1,896	2,865	985	1,078	499
Congressional District 2	31,716	23,839	15,807	85,073	4,768	2,921	3,330	1,011	480	180
Congressional District 3	35,177	18,905	13,592	67,158	8,460	6,477	10,630	6,472	1,930	1,387
Congressional District 4	16,310	7,533	6,157	24,066	22,637	19,131	6,059	3,974	1,894	1,366
Congressional District 5	26,102	16,677	21,471	55,584	9,287	6,666	14,568	9,708	4,086	2,582
Congressional District 6	26,932	22,248	31,175	74,637	2,581	1,711	8,499	3,211	3,344	2,198
Congressional District 7	19,377	13,767	15,837	62,527	3,938	2,537	3,907	1,880	3,757	2,963
Congressional District 8	25,048	18,473	15,142	54,837	4,361	2,952	8,805	5,129	4,000	2,751
Congressional District 9	27,593	25,414	40,839	77,764	4,368	2,587	18,852	11,260	7,857	5,275
Congressional District 10	24,513	19,414	29,079	64,875	4,841	3,497	11,110	6,220	4,476	3,065
Congressional District 11	23,195	16,529	16,531	55,957	5,962	4,007	5,480	2,384	2,740	1,634
Congressional District 12	42,202	23,164	14,709	100,594	1,003	267	1,325	344	708	377
Congressional District 13	41,276	21,708	18,666	94,762	904	329	1,540	481	697	529
Congressional District 14	26,748	18,448	18,163	65,420	2,106	1,218	3,424	1,757	1,083	474
Congressional District 15	51,347	25,207	15,241	115,093	557	149	1,434	269	241	117
Congressional District 16	48,155	24,069	15,167	101,350	1,844	1,232	2,565	981	537	265
Congressional District 17	49,456	25,406	15,954	109,571	2,168	1,320	2,101	566	534	336
Congressional District 18	48,650	26,318	21,386	109,813	570	204	1,634	550	379	217
Indiana										
Congressional District 1	42,759	19,179	14,698	85,548	4,803	2,531	5,376	2,477	734	434
Congressional District 2	45,530	18,324	16,405	94,959	1,366	840	2,901	870	271	139
Congressional District 3	42,347	20,533	15,397	91,781	709	255	1,858	788	421	251
Congressional District 4	46,319	19,140	13,505	92,827	857	403	1,403	484	364	240
Congressional District 5	32,049	20,440	24,668	85,286	1,136	504	1,899	527	901	646
Congressional District 6	51,975	18,373	13,167	106,141	563	162	613	111	177	35
Congressional District 7	29,407	16,196	10,625	72,184	1,400	962	1,027	453	351	214
Congressional District 8	51,111	20,648	13,927	104,923	749	388	1,517	396	251	97
Congressional District 9	41,479	18,375	15,794	94,185	839	165	877	256	227	154
Iowa										
Congressional District 1	55,651	24,580	20,309	115,987	701	282	1,893	501	261	233
Congressional District 2	51,268	24,230	18,992	109,775	1,232	493	1,107	316	683	471
Congressional District 3	43,739	23,188	18,242	94,662	1,324	538	1,296	403	1,047	643
Congressional District 4	60,973	28,935	18,866	126,135	1,210	577	1,579	314	625	526
Kansas										
Congressional District 1	42,147	28,284	18,976	99,583	2,747	1,674	2,771	359	494	359
Congressional District 2	44,059	24,111	20,282	100,165	1,373	315	1,138	260	447	285
Congressional District 3	23,343	21,622	26,673	75,560	2,205	1,186	1,903	716	1,225	891
Congressional District 4	34,759	25,880	18,806	88,981	2,225	1,306	1,463	366	1,220	1,075
Kentucky										
Congressional District 1	43,831	22,338	11,622	112,640	453	208	993	355	113	56
Congressional District 2	38,024	16,826	12,013	96,136	408	179	1,161	346	371	215
Congressional District 3	33,825	22,532	20,545	95,390	1,046	715	1,262	477	1,007	490
Congressional District 4	34,371	18,108	14,197	88,091	551	165	627	236	194	136
Congressional District 5	31,120	14,046	9,594	104,178	290	80	506	108	51	37
Congressional District 6	29,037	17,059	18,322	86,397	845	309	755	258	406	286
Louisiana										
Congressional District 1	37,122	21,847	21,887	88,669	4,036	1,967	8,810	2,010	753	546
Congressional District 2	29,974	14,792	13,105	78,526	2,780	1,798	2,956	561	1,621	1,329
Congressional District 3	33,374	15,436	13,621	64,098	787	401	27,294	5,185	520	370
Congressional District 4	39,123	21,214	16,582	96,377	622	266	6,372	1,348	385	290
Congressional District 5	37,521	19,181	16,086	98,010	695	207	5,435	1,343	223	54
Congressional District 6	32,142	17,653	19,101	77,869	1,363	740	5,909	1,108	719	453
Maine										
Congressional District 1	36,374	25,026	30,937	97,214	661	74	8,861	1,689	639	584
Congressional District 2	45,728	21,283	19,930	97,912	252	35	12,019	2,896	296	158
Maryland										
Congressional District 1	42,584	22,586	27,003	108,873	1,113	294	2,403	839	869	500
Congressional District 2	29,550	17,063	16,244	77,277	1,016	541	3,594	1,527	2,615	1,522
Congressional District 3	26,922	18,282	33,183	83,221	1,704	512	6,421	3,029	3,350	2,502
Congressional District 4	24,795	17,362	19,937	68,601	2,184	1,583	2,570	950	1,766	997
Congressional District 5	26,812	17,526	19,972	72,114	1,673	834	2,732	934	1,456	819
Congressional District 6	28,318	18,397	27,527	75,388	3,346	2,232	5,530	2,528	5,156	3,722
Congressional District 7	25,894	19,103	24,590	89,132	922	432	1,849	546	2,181	1,515
Congressional District 8	24,302	19,025	45,022	80,504	5,465	3,701	8,482	3,753	6,012	4,157
Massachusetts										
Congressional District 1	41,747	22,291	23,247	95,404	5,035	4,078	10,577	4,894	668	580
Congressional District 2	33,754	20,102	23,327	84,297	2,451	2,003	7,346	3,136	1,556	1,343
Congressional District 3	30,551	18,343	22,208	71,402	5,419	4,403	9,946	4,183	2,752	2,394
Congressional District 4	31,342	17,707	32,924	82,810	1,341	609	12,766	6,395	1,856	1,503
Congressional District 5	32,494	18,806	36,503	85,162	1,965	1,500	12,708	6,460	3,985	2,938
Congressional District 6	42,415	24,834	28,935	97,684	2,697	1,839	9,692	4,218	1,148	868
Congressional District 7	23,514	10,600	14,318	46,123	6,287	5,215	14,009	10,398	5,981	5,578
Congressional District 8	39,869	22,799	27,525	90,500	1,923	1,310	10,648	6,097	3,571	2,880
Congressional District 9	41,390	29,931	39,265	117,989	1,497	646	14,531	7,418	486	314

Table E-5: 113th Congressional Districts—Educational Attainment and Language Spoken at Home, Persons 65 Years and Over—*Continued*

	High School or Equivalent	Some College or Associates Degree	Bachelor's Degree or Higher	Speaks English at Home Total	Speaks Spanish at Home Total	Speaks English Less Than Very Well	Speaks Indo-European at Home Total	Speaks English Less Than Very Well	Speaks Asian at Home Total	Speaks English Less Than Very Well
Michigan										
Congressional District 1	54,953	31,902	28,313	130,772	674	165	2,456	527	230	159
Congressional District 2	35,937	22,397	16,203	88,068	1,992	1,053	2,041	568	700	669
Congressional District 3	34,566	23,142	17,175	85,271	1,384	689	1,862	525	497	246
Congressional District 4	49,349	26,244	15,903	109,120	743	142	1,941	398	248	134
Congressional District 5	44,606	25,789	14,571	102,784	1,693	575	2,115	542	376	202
Congressional District 6	38,780	23,569	21,223	96,766	1,065	425	2,386	760	426	171
Congressional District 7	41,476	25,167	17,799	97,894	1,373	624	2,002	516	258	148
Congressional District 8	26,526	22,015	23,028	77,408	1,334	515	2,905	1,190	949	599
Congressional District 9	41,692	23,699	20,567	93,994	657	149	10,174	4,825	1,701	943
Congressional District 10	43,665	25,426	13,907	94,709	618	228	5,746	2,881	648	376
Congressional District 11	31,053	23,863	27,877	84,346	721	374	6,248	2,589	2,301	1,265
Congressional District 12	28,177	18,071	19,441	73,658	1,355	485	4,526	2,088	1,563	904
Congressional District 13	32,652	19,896	8,582	80,849	1,834	885	2,671	925	619	428
Congressional District 14	26,924	23,302	24,955	85,161	1,656	671	5,294	2,400	1,173	726
Minnesota										
Congressional District 1	43,696	21,725	18,524	97,232	724	405	2,101	426	919	664
Congressional District 2	26,586	18,637	17,999	67,254	613	355	2,331	794	1,043	473
Congressional District 3	25,550	21,917	28,276	75,683	684	256	2,929	1,081	1,577	1,379
Congressional District 4	27,302	18,855	24,224	73,247	1,292	687	2,424	1,055	2,546	2,105
Congressional District 5	23,667	18,362	21,287	66,039	954	537	3,137	978	1,979	1,624
Congressional District 6	28,593	15,175	12,390	63,380	438	235	1,764	570	381	277
Congressional District 7	51,076	25,289	16,658	112,359	586	223	3,227	595	228	175
Congressional District 8	47,619	26,914	20,984	109,557	418	120	2,110	397	230	64
Mississippi										
Congressional District 1	35,551	21,020	13,888	99,657	438	na	241	na	235	na
Congressional District 2	25,951	17,274	14,344	89,802	356	157	422	99	205	155
Congressional District 3	33,643	23,058	18,629	100,063	535	157	556	105	211	200
Congressional District 4	34,588	22,850	17,957	94,934	823	289	1,243	401	577	346
Missouri										
Congressional District 1	29,875	19,814	17,183	85,224	1,091	367	1,860	954	1,208	1,045
Congressional District 2	38,560	29,341	37,404	111,452	1,061	427	4,321	1,813	1,681	1,037
Congressional District 3	41,077	21,959	15,539	97,422	559	na	687	na	251	na
Congressional District 4	46,023	24,116	17,699	105,790	495	91	1,727	517	606	347
Congressional District 5	40,006	24,590	17,747	96,395	2,092	1,050	1,019	314	836	665
Congressional District 6	48,371	23,125	16,346	103,996	785	458	978	317	578	406
Congressional District 7	44,727	28,737	19,524	111,892	1,179	394	1,288	464	387	234
Congressional District 8	46,195	22,395	12,967	119,163	412	107	1,384	399	257	119
Montana										
Congressional District (at Large)	54,252	41,678	35,663	146,441	1,285	383	2,732	612	419	291
Nebraska										
Congressional District 1	32,953	22,120	15,932	76,673	911	501	2,416	632	651	597
Congressional District 2	22,852	16,565	15,544	59,978	1,267	848	1,859	590	419	268
Congressional District 3	48,713	26,565	14,685	102,602	1,608	774	1,463	252	225	175
Nevada										
Congressional District 1	26,506	20,938	13,827	60,189	10,913	7,718	3,295	1,400	6,420	4,204
Congressional District 2	29,139	29,409	21,268	83,084	4,146	2,260	2,700	844	2,160	1,411
Congressional District 3	26,106	25,015	24,924	70,845	4,819	2,071	3,348	1,351	7,736	3,650
Congressional District 4	26,042	25,072	15,677	69,308	5,817	3,191	2,449	558	3,362	1,809
New Hampshire										
Congressional District 1	33,762	21,506	22,740	83,331	687	296	6,974	2,003	638	509
Congressional District 2	33,114	19,716	26,046	86,122	726	441	6,252	1,425	348	178
New Jersey										
Congressional District 1	39,406	16,111	18,964	85,578	3,838	2,656	4,856	2,156	2,741	1,667
Congressional District 2	45,904	21,960	20,831	101,907	4,872	3,597	5,017	2,308	1,839	1,110
Congressional District 3	53,587	25,467	25,783	112,719	2,622	1,048	8,449	2,878	1,471	1,109
Congressional District 4	49,651	25,304	29,579	109,229	3,088	1,987	7,789	3,383	2,311	1,477
Congressional District 5	39,177	19,822	34,123	85,792	5,802	3,878	11,046	5,291	5,091	3,690
Congressional District 6	34,281	13,654	19,382	63,019	7,497	5,624	11,427	7,398	4,259	2,750
Congressional District 7	34,593	16,557	32,334	80,412	4,191	3,084	9,742	4,507	3,130	1,809
Congressional District 8	22,184	7,801	8,983	24,470	32,591	28,095	10,715	7,661	2,241	1,407
Congressional District 9	33,947	14,650	19,919	57,617	15,830	13,017	15,642	9,535	6,225	4,900
Congressional District 10	29,906	13,043	13,725	59,840	8,875	6,768	9,004	6,194	3,276	1,750
Congressional District 11	41,468	19,299	38,699	93,715	3,525	2,467	13,417	6,599	3,680	2,535
Congressional District 12	31,237	16,527	30,959	75,783	4,064	2,729	10,325	5,051	4,750	2,642
New Mexico										
Congressional District 1	24,450	22,993	27,148	59,666	25,381	6,591	2,246	402	1,283	744
Congressional District 2	28,060	25,685	19,962	64,522	32,618	14,284	1,645	391	352	175
Congressional District 3	24,980	20,399	26,272	55,423	25,709	6,623	1,729	276	255	170

Table E-5: 113th Congressional Districts—Educational Attainment and Language Spoken at Home, Persons 65 Years and Over—Continued

	High School or Equivalent	Some College or Associates Degree	Bachelor's Degree or Higher	Speaks English at Home Total	Speaks Spanish at Home Total	Speaks Spanish at Home Speaks English Less Than Very Well	Speaks Indo-European at Home Total	Speaks Indo-European at Home Speaks English Less Than Very Well	Speaks Asian at Home Total	Speaks Asian at Home Speaks English Less Than Very Well
New York										
Congressional District 1	40,495	22,730	27,855	92,611	4,221	2,001	6,908	2,382	949	554
Congressional District 2	43,349	17,954	15,844	78,690	7,282	4,868	7,743	3,751	1,144	666
Congressional District 3	39,872	23,663	45,331	95,115	5,483	2,984	19,075	10,059	6,302	4,882
Congressional District 4	39,065	19,744	28,018	83,086	6,514	4,703	11,823	6,025	2,598	1,941
Congressional District 5	29,985	15,818	14,794	60,985	11,268	8,082	12,755	8,609	3,617	2,379
Congressional District 6	34,041	16,574	28,216	46,286	11,925	8,718	23,841	15,339	25,164	21,477
Congressional District 7	16,002	5,981	8,840	20,032	25,944	19,537	6,256	3,625	14,190	13,471
Congressional District 8	32,376	13,530	15,467	55,398	11,148	7,446	20,388	17,065	2,100	1,860
Congressional District 9	28,857	13,735	16,940	55,349	7,189	3,763	18,563	14,839	3,339	3,016
Congressional District 10	19,622	13,081	40,774	56,220	8,510	5,864	18,747	12,267	8,960	7,638
Congressional District 11	42,794	16,338	18,454	65,069	5,226	3,156	24,618	18,430	7,531	6,243
Congressional District 12	17,514	16,865	47,637	65,755	10,645	6,786	13,856	6,726	6,589	4,840
Congressional District 13	20,676	9,828	11,622	35,792	39,007	32,622	4,405	2,604	2,164	1,550
Congressional District 14	29,016	11,147	11,518	35,172	22,694	16,808	17,509	10,882	7,393	6,363
Congressional District 15	16,360	5,302	3,695	21,650	36,369	28,630	1,523	934	769	626
Congressional District 16	34,348	17,518	31,649	78,392	13,606	8,770	11,545	6,198	3,158	2,273
Congressional District 17	32,038	18,615	36,831	78,331	6,959	3,814	14,541	7,119	3,418	1,796
Congressional District 18	32,812	17,976	23,758	77,671	4,862	2,323	7,355	2,957	902	540
Congressional District 19	43,371	24,666	26,913	105,511	2,402	1,149	6,688	1,874	601	225
Congressional District 20	40,811	21,086	25,793	95,171	1,431	780	6,272	2,549	753	453
Congressional District 21	43,157	21,191	19,566	100,018	738	323	3,415	979	587	383
Congressional District 22	47,686	24,492	19,720	107,373	1,195	650	5,015	1,944	640	549
Congressional District 23	44,975	23,138	21,458	105,411	829	340	3,198	690	365	157
Congressional District 24	39,800	23,036	21,282	95,412	1,048	418	5,217	2,209	797	480
Congressional District 25	33,823	23,122	27,335	91,573	2,853	2,045	6,921	3,141	1,327	787
Congressional District 26	42,639	23,944	20,504	100,708	1,827	1,122	7,981	3,005	787	533
Congressional District 27	47,548	24,601	23,586	107,669	777	345	4,556	1,072	477	299
North Carolina										
Congressional District 1	33,256	20,121	13,813	101,428	1,055	540	866	112	312	158
Congressional District 2	29,768	22,016	17,699	86,867	1,460	753	1,688	397	718	398
Congressional District 3	33,949	24,693	20,204	95,669	1,327	414	1,329	307	401	273
Congressional District 4	19,442	15,293	23,920	64,135	1,599	757	3,471	1,284	1,615	1,187
Congressional District 5	38,554	24,737	21,440	109,126	1,553	890	1,283	659	375	247
Congressional District 6	37,784	25,452	23,960	110,965	1,239	693	1,519	356	826	418
Congressional District 7	35,469	26,496	24,698	109,877	998	672	1,544	466	241	86
Congressional District 8	34,853	20,200	11,724	95,897	967	637	942	254	330	211
Congressional District 9	22,451	23,512	24,218	73,502	2,158	1,322	3,227	1,210	1,520	1,011
Congressional District 10	35,643	25,010	21,256	108,516	1,065	613	1,458	407	946	579
Congressional District 11	45,524	32,950	31,167	140,304	1,209	475	1,351	306	338	228
Congressional District 12	22,064	14,585	8,576	60,925	1,497	1,154	713	381	903	769
Congressional District 13	26,370	20,480	23,853	82,190	1,075	502	1,645	407	719	390
North Dakota										
Congressional District (at Large)	34,746	25,397	15,434	91,898	258	25	6,145	1,536	303	269
Ohio										
Congressional District 1	31,173	18,478	20,186	85,321	376	115	2,285	1,073	776	355
Congressional District 2	37,047	20,452	20,929	99,314	446	171	1,764	516	430	164
Congressional District 3	26,486	13,526	11,348	62,005	780	502	1,817	672	1,168	765
Congressional District 4	52,741	19,507	11,989	103,597	838	214	1,107	259	211	97
Congressional District 5	51,953	20,981	17,517	105,135	1,298	490	1,549	139	483	253
Congressional District 6	62,278	20,392	12,819	120,491	594	150	1,520	234	370	186
Congressional District 7	52,550	19,467	14,824	105,914	600	305	4,100	1,738	273	202
Congressional District 8	43,995	19,216	15,881	98,261	514	118	1,228	491	417	137
Congressional District 9	39,753	19,889	15,014	88,230	3,416	1,780	4,453	2,191	635	291
Congressional District 10	40,072	25,912	23,327	106,137	737	214	1,832	512	913	638
Congressional District 11	35,456	21,645	19,556	94,865	1,431	1,030	5,732	2,906	916	587
Congressional District 12	35,989	19,188	22,589	88,124	318	110	2,198	824	897	364
Congressional District 13	53,455	20,972	16,599	109,634	720	352	4,362	1,470	370	148
Congressional District 14	45,974	27,358	24,792	108,668	660	243	6,977	2,937	749	301
Congressional District 15	40,034	17,726	16,933	89,466	575	258	1,474	417	689	551
Congressional District 16	51,675	27,675	24,381	111,840	734	272	7,780	3,427	701	477
Oklahoma										
Congressional District 1	32,512	26,250	22,329	92,270	1,910	982	1,379	394	865	620
Congressional District 2	44,890	30,121	17,022	120,426	947	224	394	82	253	106
Congressional District 3	41,816	27,919	18,530	105,891	1,831	1,132	700	168	510	374
Congressional District 4	36,392	22,753	18,508	91,937	1,725	860	1,412	342	1,356	881
Congressional District 5	28,692	26,039	23,119	87,986	2,643	1,549	1,059	331	1,598	1,336
Oregon										
Congressional District 1	25,998	26,431	28,063	82,155	2,863	1,557	2,797	785	3,063	2,437
Congressional District 2	43,442	42,203	29,254	127,321	3,481	1,597	2,069	332	526	283
Congressional District 3	25,224	24,630	23,483	75,309	1,778	829	3,901	2,092	4,536	3,854
Congressional District 4	43,178	40,943	31,325	128,260	1,926	674	2,174	461	830	620
Congressional District 5	34,395	36,069	30,080	105,764	3,238	1,746	2,614	968	1,313	1,007

Table E-5: 113th Congressional Districts—Educational Attainment and Language Spoken at Home, Persons 65 Years and Over—Continued

	High School or Equivalent	Some College or Associates Degree	Bachelor's Degree or Higher	Speaks English at Home Total	Speaks Spanish at Home Total	Speaks English Less Than Very Well	Speaks Indo-European at Home Total	Speaks English Less Than Very Well	Speaks Asian at Home Total	Speaks English Less Than Very Well
Pennsylvania										
Congressional District 1	29,511	10,824	10,447	63,821	4,523	3,263	5,290	2,871	2,998	2,610
Congressional District 2	30,288	15,768	21,683	85,140	2,144	1,251	2,825	1,200	1,856	1,612
Congressional District 3	59,404	17,986	17,635	112,348	412	151	4,011	1,134	198	99
Congressional District 4	47,165	17,169	17,362	100,949	1,295	814	2,375	687	673	350
Congressional District 5	58,063	17,051	16,695	111,335	450	92	1,885	399	325	166
Congressional District 6	40,367	17,941	25,592	95,331	1,157	555	4,455	1,708	1,140	693
Congressional District 7	44,217	20,192	30,838	101,347	1,127	581	6,482	2,286	1,797	1,318
Congressional District 8	42,996	20,601	25,689	97,019	999	513	6,799	3,498	1,563	994
Congressional District 9	64,757	15,983	14,095	120,570	472	278	2,805	515	220	140
Congressional District 10	57,827	19,715	17,145	114,726	1,099	588	3,877	1,337	279	134
Congressional District 11	56,269	18,639	16,417	110,456	1,083	689	3,321	1,082	299	224
Congressional District 12	63,408	21,265	22,424	125,082	721	271	4,400	1,491	536	355
Congressional District 13	41,421	16,154	23,848	84,721	3,745	2,517	10,871	7,556	4,361	3,566
Congressional District 14	54,786	20,102	18,793	108,446	641	145	5,493	1,980	572	369
Congressional District 15	47,455	17,721	18,134	97,363	3,680	2,767	6,341	2,371	749	540
Congressional District 16	42,516	15,609	19,011	92,798	3,835	2,785	4,043	1,789	733	606
Congressional District 17	60,863	20,018	12,967	111,193	1,735	1,051	6,869	2,143	484	353
Congressional District 18	59,623	22,261	24,750	120,714	685	166	3,724	1,182	421	278
Rhode Island										
Congressional District 1	24,277	13,681	17,761	60,540	3,280	2,668	13,533	6,782	758	553
Congressional District 2	25,910	15,385	16,753	66,314	2,187	1,773	6,474	2,442	834	586
South Carolina										
Congressional District 1	25,327	24,486	34,288	93,259	1,712	691	2,058	518	1,198	674
Congressional District 2	26,231	21,169	21,844	82,872	1,204	727	1,355	434	601	407
Congressional District 3	33,929	20,597	18,057	100,781	965	460	1,257	324	279	195
Congressional District 4	28,390	19,722	19,241	86,650	1,441	879	1,343	358	707	404
Congressional District 5	31,358	17,839	15,487	89,668	839	na	976	na	218	na
Congressional District 6	28,567	15,817	11,769	83,106	520	125	884	246	283	158
Congressional District 7	37,763	23,591	20,428	104,646	863	266	1,764	745	302	212
South Dakota										
Congressional District (at Large)	46,427	27,348	23,372	112,784	729	120	3,770	967	276	178
Tennessee										
Congressional District 1	43,119	23,906	17,212	120,795	506	na	757	na	496	na
Congressional District 2	35,737	25,330	22,143	104,474	599	216	1,346	562	666	444
Congressional District 3	37,784	24,680	18,960	111,720	1,180	750	843	208	645	454
Congressional District 4	33,815	18,893	12,494	90,651	856	533	770	285	404	292
Congressional District 5	25,635	17,095	18,209	73,346	1,161	583	1,579	650	852	671
Congressional District 6	39,988	20,965	15,714	107,576	939	320	882	228	237	190
Congressional District 7	31,821	17,637	14,454	88,541	841	371	1,146	319	551	423
Congressional District 8	35,378	21,060	20,230	99,510	517	136	887	325	519	335
Congressional District 9	21,431	14,330	12,149	66,513	872	449	516	160	823	668
Texas										
Congressional District 1	34,374	27,044	20,119	97,518	3,069	1,928	1,153	225	400	270
Congressional District 2	15,021	17,203	21,554	49,821	7,557	4,623	2,696	747	3,081	2,513
Congressional District 3	13,457	16,240	23,626	49,596	2,838	1,250	4,089	2,342	3,326	2,313
Congressional District 4	37,001	27,705	18,659	102,391	2,543	1,290	575	155	274	191
Congressional District 5	28,515	22,711	15,802	80,049	4,345	2,296	1,092	281	871	702
Congressional District 6	20,240	18,078	15,861	58,557	4,537	2,376	1,629	657	2,137	1,724
Congressional District 7	12,256	15,849	29,813	49,419	7,635	4,328	3,275	1,530	4,242	3,028
Congressional District 8	26,535	22,638	19,531	76,809	4,384	1,792	1,384	254	683	634
Congressional District 9	13,915	13,867	12,806	36,537	9,076	6,134	2,318	1,340	7,087	5,627
Congressional District 10	21,466	18,571	20,478	62,922	6,552	3,202	3,159	926	1,551	861
Congressional District 11	32,402	26,872	19,809	90,646	13,207	8,204	870	193	446	250
Congressional District 12	24,440	22,282	19,213	71,415	4,733	2,096	1,187	413	848	677
Congressional District 13	32,766	25,871	16,509	87,922	7,148	3,983	499	179	744	617
Congressional District 14	28,072	22,523	16,825	73,372	7,104	2,924	2,051	427	1,229	608
Congressional District 15	15,443	10,178	9,226	24,905	44,354	30,334	1,126	206	383	130
Congressional District 16	17,424	13,305	10,841	20,131	55,221	36,230	1,451	476	818	508
Congressional District 17	24,856	18,865	16,924	67,543	6,362	3,302	1,537	381	1,046	859
Congressional District 18	18,408	11,853	9,278	45,600	10,856	7,154	899	226	2,195	1,629
Congressional District 19	26,684	21,699	17,568	74,539	14,250	7,670	644	271	494	401
Congressional District 20	17,229	16,315	11,685	28,041	40,661	17,419	1,673	371	924	448
Congressional District 21	24,038	26,023	36,768	81,672	11,862	4,182	3,315	846	867	556
Congressional District 22	14,370	16,550	17,776	42,364	8,141	3,753	3,673	1,748	5,723	3,863
Congressional District 23	15,874	14,144	13,288	33,738	41,790	26,417	1,167	274	511	364
Congressional District 24	16,464	18,519	20,114	53,193	4,520	2,655	2,691	1,354	2,904	2,140
Congressional District 25	23,502	22,496	24,917	78,006	4,360	2,414	1,443	461	838	591
Congressional District 26	14,806	16,108	16,140	47,477	3,326	1,828	1,868	752	1,104	591
Congressional District 27	27,611	21,601	16,901	63,821	29,408	13,412	2,235	448	643	439
Congressional District 28	16,489	12,714	9,115	27,941	41,369	29,102	1,025	399	472	244
Congressional District 29	12,416	8,281	3,254	23,392	24,385	16,911	879	410	1,198	1,093
Congressional District 30	18,750	14,137	10,531	52,010	7,818	5,077	913	277	919	731
Congressional District 31	19,181	18,550	20,114	59,511	5,100	3,213	2,659	1,033	1,377	917
Congressional District 32	16,558	18,285	29,977	61,879	6,275	3,344	2,799	1,505	3,158	2,614
Congressional District 33	14,674	9,695	5,249	34,149	17,080	12,194	584	227	1,035	920
Congressional District 34	20,270	13,161	9,608	33,828	50,225	32,636	767	183	336	267
Congressional District 35	15,810	13,838	7,928	30,307	27,997	14,079	1,143	269	1,012	675
Congressional District 36	30,796	22,005	14,061	77,638	5,564	2,937	2,402	688	571	348

Table E-5: 113th Congressional Districts—Educational Attainment and Language Spoken at Home, Persons 65 Years and Over—*Continued*

	High School or Equivalent	Some College or Associates Degree	Bachelor's Degree or Higher	Speaks English at Home Total	Speaks Spanish at Home Total	Speaks Spanish at Home Speaks English Less Than Very Well	Speaks Indo-European at Home Total	Speaks Indo-European at Home Speaks English Less Than Very Well	Speaks Asian at Home Total	Speaks Asian at Home Speaks English Less Than Very Well
Utah										
Congressional District 1	18,578	21,193	15,114	58,358	2,148	1,203	1,257	160	565	424
Congressional District 2	23,691	25,060	22,291	72,611	2,766	1,274	2,554	1,018	1,520	1,036
Congressional District 3	14,917	20,128	20,968	55,932	2,361	1,267	1,678	315	797	502
Congressional District 4	18,431	17,871	13,071	51,113	2,839	1,483	1,833	627	984	634
Vermont										
Congressional District (at Large)	32,165	19,440	27,589	88,938	485	132	4,498	1,102	436	361
Virginia										
Congressional District 1	27,315	21,272	28,596	87,700	1,209	512	2,755	709	1,322	854
Congressional District 2	26,898	22,705	22,179	77,830	1,350	580	2,294	751	3,856	2,163
Congressional District 3	26,210	17,655	12,488	77,710	779	293	1,170	333	1,375	846
Congressional District 4	29,765	20,164	14,898	84,853	870	281	1,502	614	800	492
Congressional District 5	39,260	24,148	24,326	119,706	829	227	1,559	636	488	304
Congressional District 6	39,042	23,735	23,136	112,998	689	387	1,747	570	321	234
Congressional District 7	29,845	23,055	28,367	91,383	1,151	403	2,410	1,034	1,461	1,037
Congressional District 8	14,780	13,305	34,399	53,451	4,778	2,714	5,679	2,169	5,528	3,675
Congressional District 9	40,234	22,652	16,072	122,125	544	157	785	171	204	113
Congressional District 10	17,979	14,780	26,975	56,749	2,452	1,515	4,496	2,080	4,103	3,024
Congressional District 11	16,440	13,809	32,113	50,635	5,457	3,350	5,733	2,672	8,890	6,676
Washington										
Congressional District 1	20,374	22,161	24,466	66,002	1,275	566	3,807	1,745	3,433	2,747
Congressional District 2	24,655	28,613	26,072	79,947	1,681	679	3,199	1,618	4,220	3,309
Congressional District 3	31,063	31,672	19,810	88,749	1,437	659	3,208	1,675	1,735	1,203
Congressional District 4	24,216	22,236	15,836	69,985	7,857	5,197	1,741	683	930	728
Congressional District 5	30,764	29,613	23,225	90,786	1,502	507	2,649	1,184	965	744
Congressional District 6	31,561	35,274	31,584	102,400	1,355	505	2,939	741	3,328	2,140
Congressional District 7	16,458	23,318	37,140	71,311	1,399	516	4,938	1,904	6,648	4,987
Congressional District 8	23,350	20,862	17,762	64,198	1,067	527	2,703	1,490	3,180	2,323
Congressional District 9	20,424	22,209	25,704	61,041	1,900	622	4,653	2,844	12,846	9,786
Congressional District 10	25,526	25,529	20,432	73,318	1,715	759	2,584	837	4,945	3,554
West Virginia										
Congressional District 1	46,979	17,771	12,759	99,234	403	97	964	261	267	123
Congressional District 2	42,374	16,954	13,957	97,025	439	na	971	na	337	na
Congressional District 3	41,132	16,409	10,565	102,046	248	121	706	228	299	55
Wisconsin										
Congressional District 1	39,829	21,266	17,160	88,268	1,675	826	3,209	1,198	485	313
Congressional District 2	32,792	17,372	24,566	81,995	713	351	2,415	631	753	536
Congressional District 3	48,554	21,194	17,072	102,780	341	44	2,143	552	413	342
Congressional District 4	26,243	14,885	14,346	63,702	3,562	2,507	4,051	2,029	1,214	869
Congressional District 5	43,720	24,077	23,416	100,068	1,056	444	4,485	1,095	500	347
Congressional District 6	50,517	21,568	19,902	106,583	834	228	2,475	645	435	226
Congressional District 7	54,198	24,519	20,022	117,942	479	131	2,252	568	359	190
Congressional District 8	48,096	19,715	16,027	98,085	829	507	1,803	432	573	479
Wyoming										
Congressional District (at Large)	26,472	20,441	15,238	68,081	2,716	588	933	126	244	139

PART F

EMPLOYMENT AND LABOR FORCE STATUS

EMPLOYMENT AND LABOR FORCE STATUS

U.S. Bureau of Labor Statistics employment data show that between 1980 and 2010, the employment of people age 65 and over doubled (from 3.0 million to 6.2 million) while employment for the civilian non-institutional population 16 and over increased by about 40 percent. The labor force participation rate for seniors was 12.1 in 1980 and increased to 17.4 in 2010.[1] This is not an effect of the Baby Boom generation as the oldest of that age cohort had not entered the 65 and over population. The older population has been working more and working longer in life and that trend can be expected to continue as those numbers swell with the Baby Boomers.

The absolute number of employed persons is important but equally important is the rate at which the population participates in the labor force. Not everyone wants to work, so the older work labor force is comprised of

only those who are employed or unemployed and looking for work. Nationally, of the 59.3 million persons age 60 and over, 16.5 million or 27.8 percent are actively participating in the labor force. Even by age 70 nearly 10 percent of the older population is participating in the labor force. Among the 60 and over population, Alaska has the highest participation rate at 37.0 percent while Idaho (18.7 percent) has the lowest. There's a more narrow range between the highest (the District of Columbia, 13.5 percent) and lowest (West Virginia, 7.2 percent) state for the 70 and over population. In eight states, more than one-third of the 60 and over labor force population is participating in the labor force (either employed or unemployed and looking for work). The unemployment rate for both the 60 and over and the 70 years and over is around 7 percent but varies from a low of 1.5 percent in South Dakota to a high of 14.4 percent in Nevada.

Los Angeles County, California has the largest 60 and over labor force with nearly a half million people and the participation rate is about 30 percent. Arlington County, Virginia has the highest participation rate at 42.7 percent and Sumter County, Florida the lowest at 13.0 percent.

---

1. U.S. Department of Labor, Bureau of Labor Statistics, Labor Force Statistics from the Current Population Survey, 1st quarter data, http://data.bls.gov.

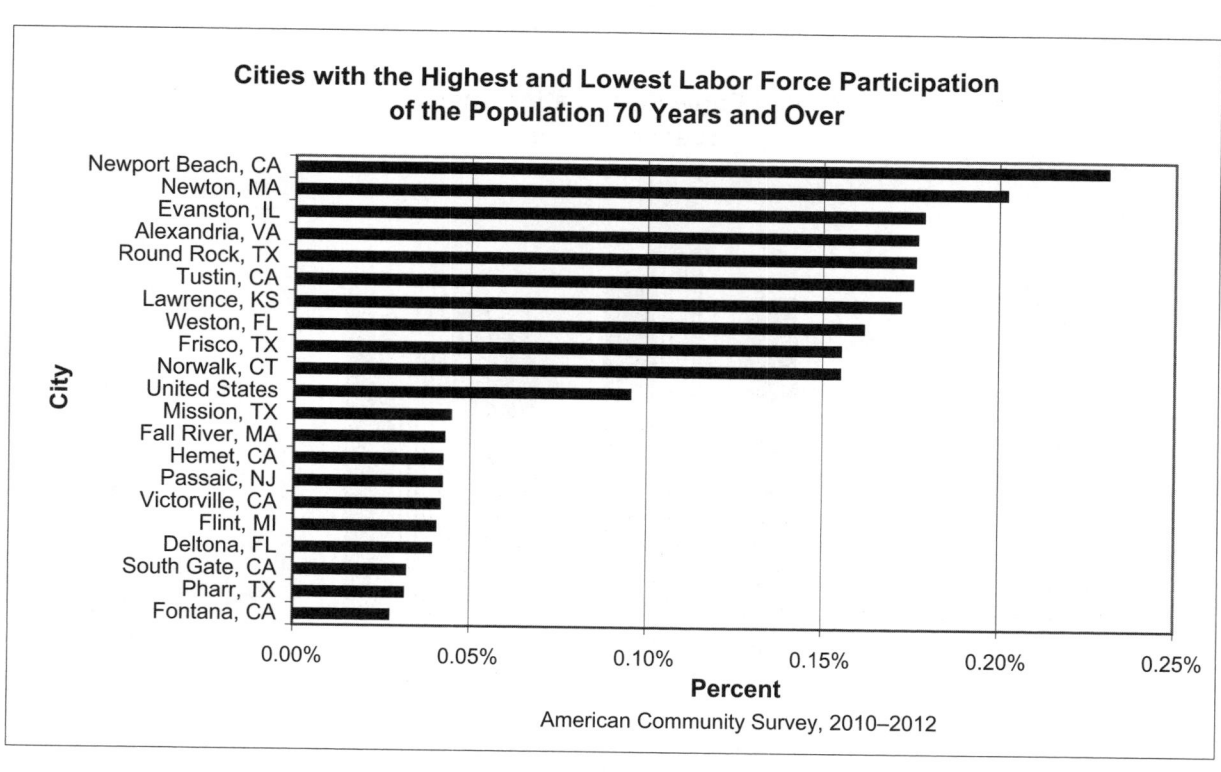

Cities with the Highest and Lowest Labor Force Participation of the Population 70 Years and Over

American Community Survey, 2010–2012

Unemployment is highest in Sutter County, California where more than 20 percent of both the 60 and over and the 70 and over population are unemployed and looking for work. The unemployment rate for persons 70 and over is higher than the national average in 341 counties and over 15 percent in 29 counties. The 60 and over participation rate is higher than the national average in 280 counties but less than 25 percent in 116 counties. Unemployment among the 60 and over population is worse than the national rate in 283 counties and among the 70 and over population it's worse in 243 counties. Among cities, nearly half (44.3 percent) of the Coral Springs, Florida population 60 and over participates in the labor force and, while not the highest, 14.1 percent of the 70 and over population is still participating. Newport Beach, California has the highest percent of the 70 and over population participating in the labor force at 23.1 percent. Perris, California is a relatively small city but more than one-third (36.9 percent) of the labor force 60 and over is unemployed and looking for work.

The New York-Northern New Jersey-Long Island metropolitan area has the largest 60 and over labor force with a population over 1 million and its participation rate at 30.7 percent is just slightly higher than the national rate. The Hinesville-Ft. Stewart metropolitan area in Georgia is the smallest and has a participation rate of 23 percent.

The Washington-Arlington-Alexandria metropolitan area has the highest participation rate at 38.0 percent while the Yuma, Arizona area is lowest at 13.0 percent. Labor force participation among the 60 and over population is above the national rate in 155 metropolitan areas and in 164 metro areas it's above the national rate for the 70 and over population. The Yuba, California metropolitan area has the highest unemployment rate among the 60 and over population at 18.3 percent and is the third highest for the 70 and over population behind Myrtle Beach-North Myrtle Beach-Conway, South Carolina and Redding, California. 139 metropolitan areas have higher unemployment rates than the nation for the 60 and over population and 150 are above the 70 and over rate.

Virginia's 11th Congressional District has the highest labor force participation for the 60 and over population at 41.3 percent while Florida's 11th district has the lowest rate at 15.3 percent. Half of all congressional districts (219) have participation rates above the national average for the 60 and over population and 205 districts are above the national rate for the population 70 and over. At 2.2 percent and 1.5 percent, respectively, unemployment among the 60 and over and 70 and over population is lowest is South Dakota's lone congressional district. California's 36th district has the highest unemployment among the 60 and over while Nevada's 3rd district is highest among the 70 and over population.

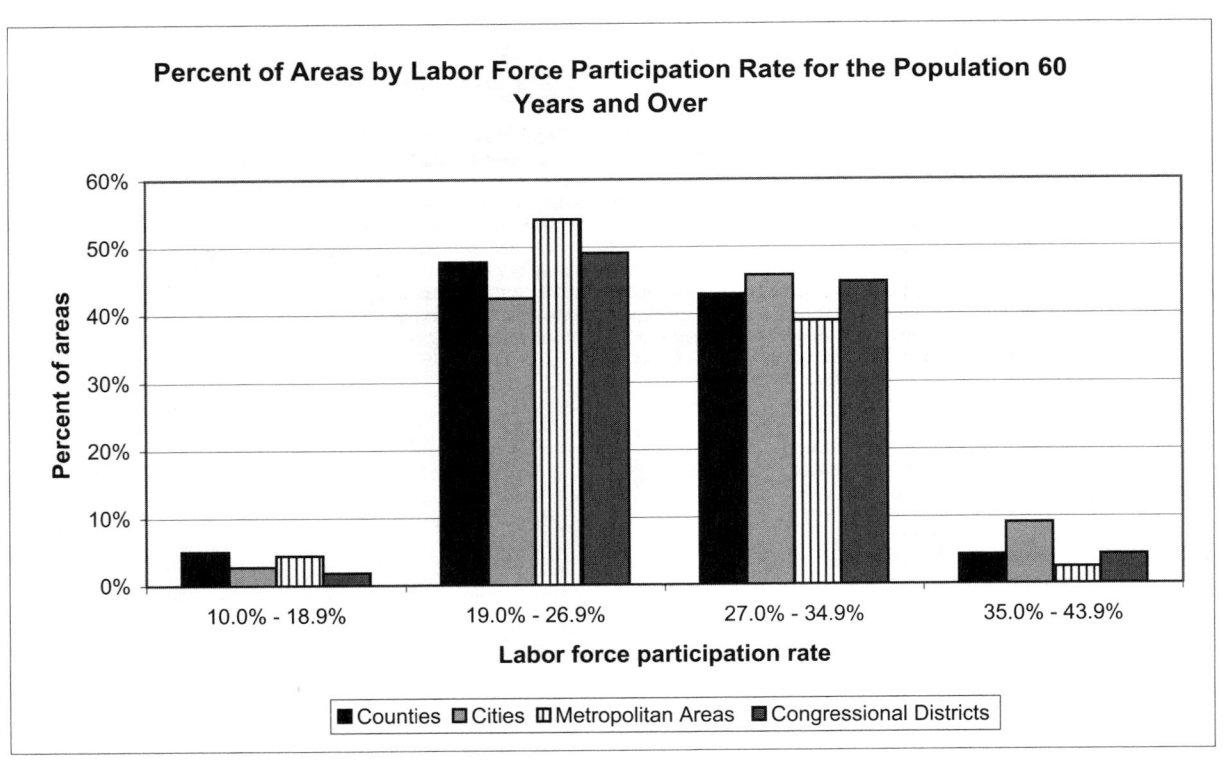

Percent of the Population 60 Years and Over Participating in the Labor Force

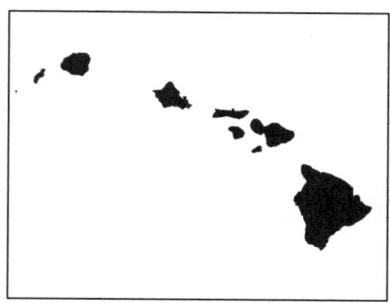

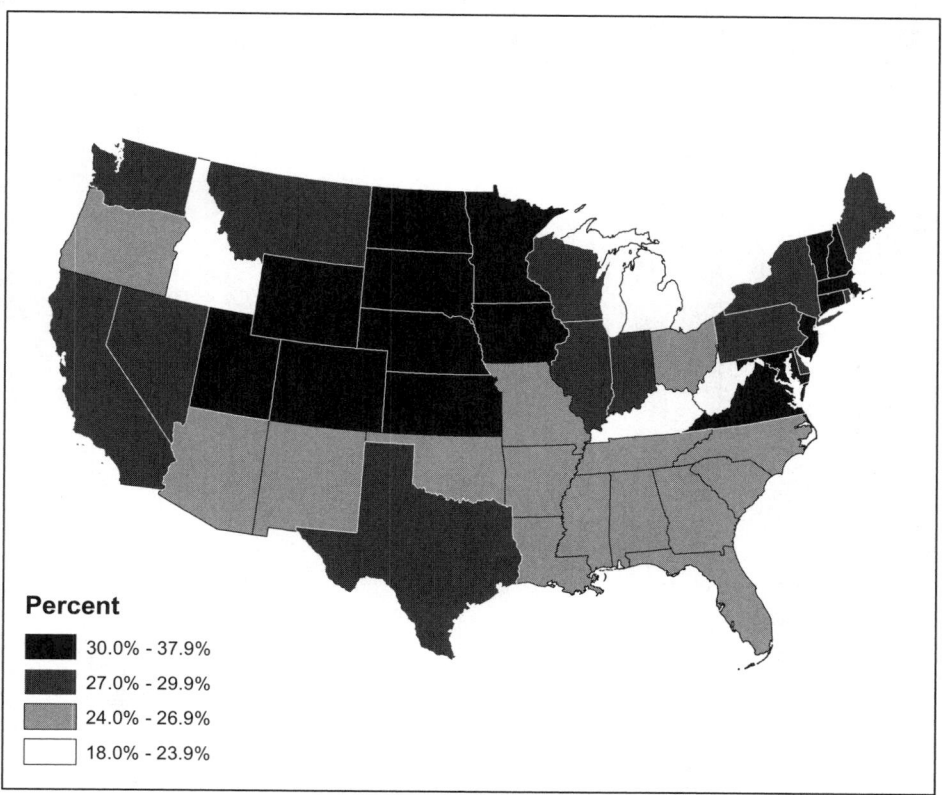

Percent

30.0% - 37.9%
27.0% - 29.9%
24.0% - 26.9%
18.0% - 23.9%

Table F-1: States—Employment and Labor Force Status, Civilian Labor Force

	60 and 61 Years		62 to 64 Years		65 to 69 Years		70 Years And Over		60 Years and Over Not In the Labor Force
	Employed	Unemployed	Employed	Unemployed	Employed	Unemployed	Employed	Unemployed	
United States	4,271,192	354,510	4,674,118	366,550	3,763,260	300,701	2,566,447	184,516	42,806,564
Alabama	62,812	4,162	64,572	3,977	54,914	3,706	36,615	2,156	734,002
Alaska	10,257	502	11,560	450	8,030	292	4,693	181	61,326
Arizona	82,017	8,101	88,312	7,141	70,592	6,651	45,643	3,870	980,236
Arkansas	38,183	2,044	39,288	1,840	35,691	2,143	25,499	960	456,482
California	461,206	51,561	504,792	53,425	408,191	42,744	261,032	24,689	4,545,182
Colorado	74,856	6,329	79,964	5,917	66,286	5,797	36,807	2,991	586,116
Connecticut	57,560	4,758	70,116	6,033	57,312	5,785	37,827	3,450	488,076
Delaware	13,301	941	14,799	812	13,444	970	8,732	649	135,865
District of Columbia	8,027	795	9,675	833	8,554	583	6,230	235	67,194
Florida	256,733	28,201	292,253	31,911	255,490	30,477	179,443	20,576	3,457,012
Georgia	114,145	10,890	126,601	11,517	94,487	7,965	59,620	4,551	1,174,630
Hawaii	24,306	1,313	25,714	1,337	22,634	1,024	14,653	519	199,196
Idaho	22,118	1,345	22,273	1,832	17,593	1,533	11,172	719	213,547
Illinois	174,775	16,321	192,212	15,565	151,819	11,191	104,262	6,722	1,675,423
Indiana	92,787	6,965	95,682	6,345	71,272	4,944	55,066	3,134	892,870
Iowa	52,631	1,802	56,154	2,009	43,187	1,506	34,859	1,269	448,973
Kansas	42,879	2,597	50,680	2,253	41,370	1,618	31,239	1,240	367,621
Kentucky	51,715	3,636	57,006	3,774	45,515	2,716	33,682	1,812	654,477
Louisiana	55,399	4,112	63,714	3,795	52,748	3,238	38,037	1,735	607,933
Maine	24,054	1,358	26,732	1,641	20,633	1,284	14,349	761	222,330
Maryland	92,511	5,798	102,825	5,730	86,947	5,587	56,548	3,854	711,320
Massachusetts	106,088	8,567	120,447	10,522	101,029	8,903	67,455	4,920	888,950
Michigan	126,579	13,611	125,324	13,632	97,567	10,289	65,877	6,294	1,536,566
Minnesota	85,976	5,458	87,157	5,116	65,839	3,533	46,056	2,127	702,483
Mississippi	34,969	2,215	38,296	2,108	31,480	1,525	22,285	1,344	425,225
Missouri	82,503	5,890	92,416	5,768	73,840	4,631	52,130	3,427	888,741
Montana	17,085	1,143	18,231	807	15,753	583	10,980	536	153,503
Nebraska	31,907	1,312	33,855	977	29,109	1,109	22,981	669	231,678
Nevada	38,067	4,403	39,917	5,018	32,317	4,765	21,164	3,573	351,034
New Hampshire	23,916	1,345	28,365	1,582	20,498	1,416	13,601	634	180,090
New Jersey	131,873	13,774	148,159	14,817	125,505	14,336	88,418	8,723	1,167,837
New Mexico	28,681	2,429	30,440	1,984	26,110	1,975	17,306	1,236	299,926
New York	273,618	21,457	298,289	24,774	244,779	20,882	171,833	12,393	2,721,405
North Carolina	125,761	12,481	135,596	13,367	111,598	9,086	75,486	5,692	1,357,398
North Dakota	12,527	261	12,740	279	10,756	318	8,989	238	92,142
Ohio	166,836	13,277	181,504	13,899	137,617	9,320	97,885	4,880	1,733,148
Oklahoma	48,270	2,164	54,790	2,143	46,878	2,138	36,843	1,350	535,576
Oregon	58,491	6,691	63,544	5,889	46,837	4,348	28,449	2,506	591,766
Pennsylvania	194,298	13,693	211,827	15,621	169,550	12,805	126,516	8,272	2,018,630
Rhode Island	16,929	1,642	17,843	1,639	14,323	1,232	10,322	791	151,979
South Carolina	61,137	6,037	68,260	5,121	53,936	4,784	36,510	3,355	712,823
South Dakota	13,973	414	15,424	353	12,971	295	10,921	163	111,955
Tennessee	86,765	6,972	93,568	7,162	72,103	5,581	50,293	3,526	946,865
Texas	305,650	20,219	341,005	20,976	274,980	17,309	181,767	10,838	2,800,783
Utah	29,952	1,904	33,380	1,862	26,700	1,243	16,653	748	261,986
Vermont	12,164	638	14,751	903	11,425	331	7,314	293	89,472
Virginia	120,265	7,088	133,993	6,436	109,088	4,076	70,206	2,821	1,032,128
Washington	100,720	8,163	113,225	7,661	78,793	6,526	43,359	3,602	913,713
West Virginia	26,323	1,366	24,480	1,109	20,095	802	14,321	603	344,445
Wisconsin	87,903	6,183	92,261	6,417	67,275	4,444	48,699	2,735	813,442
Wyoming	9,694	182	10,107	471	7,800	362	5,820	154	71,064

Table F-2: Counties—Employment and Labor Force Status, Civilian Labor Force

	60 and 61 Years		62 to 64 Years		65 to 69 Years		70 Years And Over		60 Years and Over Not In the Labor Force
	Employed	Unemployed	Employed	Unemployed	Employed	Unemployed	Employed	Unemployed	
Alabama									
Baldwin County	2,307	251	3,503	91	2,587	253	1,612	37	34,427
Calhoun County	1,784	0	1,462	98	1,040	0	713	9	19,385
Cullman County	1,081	60	1,114	84	1,247	15	960	13	14,162
DeKalb County	942	63	805	156	666	64	544	72	11,264
Elmore County	876	32	1,014	42	1,029	101	429	0	10,444
Etowah County	1,377	18	1,351	39	1,012	55	820	39	19,071
Houston County	1,468	39	1,221	70	1,297	87	955	27	15,845
Jefferson County	9,198	494	8,352	446	7,294	417	4,992	317	93,884
Lauderdale County	1,551	120	1,239	73	1,223	89	735	0	17,140
Lee County	1,600	33	1,645	0	1,380	115	1,163	38	14,445
Limestone County	1,002	73	1,234	153	820	27	602	40	11,977
Madison County	5,006	229	4,906	183	4,199	271	2,887	260	43,388
Marshall County	1,100	93	1,208	59	902	127	829	32	15,282
Mobile County	5,334	497	5,349	251	4,920	257	2,697	204	59,946
Montgomery County	3,420	57	3,185	129	2,711	124	1,754	115	29,432
Morgan County	1,705	81	1,803	114	1,690	134	1,360	50	18,024
St. Clair County	1,146	36	1,132	199	803	102	588	86	12,582
Shelby County	2,313	259	3,312	256	2,800	176	1,789	105	22,028
Talladega County	1,175	31	783	69	810	79	599	0	13,689
Tuscaloosa County	2,143	167	2,204	90	1,264	50	1,397	124	23,904
Walker County	762	51	928	50	591	58	612	28	13,417
Alaska									
Fairbanks North Star Borough	1,209	48	1,358	29	910	87	521	11	7,384
Matanuska-Susitna Borough	1,109	71	1,379	75	767	50	514	45	8,500
Arizona									
Apache County	873	36	463	29	630	26	331	0	10,384
Cochise County	1,956	171	1,520	290	1,138	112	1,253	85	26,143
Coconino County	1,719	188	1,350	82	1,636	25	819	69	13,335
Maricopa County	46,944	4,444	53,246	3,823	42,454	3,528	25,736	2,302	501,181
Mohave County	2,549	509	3,680	340	2,621	420	1,907	278	53,172
Navajo County	1,616	221	917	83	904	103	610	18	16,715
Pima County	14,647	977	14,544	1,343	12,179	963	7,178	554	167,235
Pinal County	4,333	182	4,487	506	3,001	743	2,425	209	64,893
Yavapai County	3,505	1,013	4,111	253	2,980	372	2,930	231	57,693
Yuma County	1,625	264	1,389	242	1,133	188	899	59	35,506
Arkansas									
Benton County	3,171	134	3,762	166	2,666	193	1,392	0	28,032
Craighead County	1,530	20	1,383	141	994	46	434	36	12,762
Faulkner County	965	19	1,103	94	1,395	80	717	81	12,472
Garland County	1,303	23	1,785	164	1,276	55	1,437	36	21,080
Jefferson County	925	107	881	39	889	44	678	49	11,693
Lonoke County	1,039	5	772	3	831	37	458	49	8,149
Pulaski County	5,373	288	4,985	172	5,023	229	3,232	53	49,535
Saline County	1,402	51	1,255	44	1,538	70	862	124	18,206
Sebastian County	1,325	48	2,017	53	1,336	38	1,055	89	17,691
Washington County	2,398	121	2,332	71	2,114	137	1,523	40	20,728
White County	826	40	866	71	1,217	81	590	13	11,439
California									
Alameda County	22,562	2,266	23,202	2,259	17,681	1,773	9,722	644	179,765
Butte County	2,798	299	3,329	395	2,075	409	1,893	193	38,175
Contra Costa County	15,152	1,190	17,635	1,935	13,790	1,190	9,427	601	139,429
El Dorado County	3,945	192	3,049	311	3,118	330	1,402	123	29,423
Fresno County	9,191	1,378	10,755	927	8,412	983	6,022	546	101,546
Humboldt County	2,087	261	1,885	160	1,449	141	1,260	117	19,771
Imperial County	965	265	1,376	165	940	202	934	28	20,828
Kern County	7,450	736	8,271	766	6,656	596	4,267	619	85,404
Kings County	1,093	137	1,522	129	1,275	51	644	28	13,052
Lake County	769	109	1,204	391	1,108	179	707	136	12,623
Los Angeles County	116,470	13,218	127,180	14,057	105,586	11,718	69,332	6,655	1,116,938
Madera County	1,620	104	1,768	69	1,303	83	791	119	19,726
Marin County	5,781	326	7,211	424	6,616	405	3,972	241	39,413
Mendocino County	1,611	211	2,089	170	1,473	122	900	164	14,525
Merced County	2,417	273	2,407	333	1,975	186	1,099	91	27,175
Monterey County	5,064	259	5,537	722	4,452	372	3,477	267	47,404
Napa County	2,503	130	2,717	181	2,324	133	1,718	82	20,231
Nevada County	2,069	330	2,217	459	1,604	73	866	96	21,565
Orange County	39,028	3,730	45,582	4,514	39,493	3,252	27,100	1,591	355,222
Placer County	5,001	666	5,315	543	3,807	375	2,266	226	60,959
Riverside County	21,779	3,144	23,970	3,385	19,198	3,518	12,880	2,094	283,574
Sacramento County	15,528	2,126	17,164	1,679	12,220	1,352	8,155	1,050	180,499
San Bernardino County	20,871	2,838	19,458	2,211	14,079	2,099	8,608	922	212,153
San Diego County	39,282	4,157	41,215	3,543	33,646	2,777	20,246	1,723	375,411
San Francisco County	12,420	1,356	13,723	1,352	9,500	761	6,302	396	116,358
San Joaquin County	6,480	890	7,871	711	5,881	590	3,416	598	79,304
San Luis Obispo County	4,155	271	4,585	524	3,510	284	2,573	208	44,577
San Mateo County	11,711	904	13,157	1,140	10,269	909	6,163	391	98,123
Santa Barbara County	5,254	374	5,879	674	5,700	414	3,635	282	54,665
Santa Clara County	22,188	3,026	24,535	3,080	20,321	2,188	11,794	1,082	205,084

Table F-2: Counties—Employment and Labor Force Status, Civilian Labor Force—*Continued*

	60 and 61 Years		62 to 64 Years		65 to 69 Years		70 Years And Over		60 Years and Over Not In the Labor Force
	Employed	Unemployed	Employed	Unemployed	Employed	Unemployed	Employed	Unemployed	
California—Cont.									
Santa Cruz County	4,819	433	3,688	290	3,956	326	2,187	137	31,761
Shasta County	2,121	349	2,933	171	2,264	175	1,277	283	34,236
Solano County	5,665	486	7,452	537	4,720	473	2,934	183	52,222
Sonoma County	9,023	1,101	9,604	1,065	7,520	678	4,313	522	71,591
Stanislaus County	5,405	468	5,247	571	4,333	681	2,860	313	61,459
Sutter County	1,037	234	1,118	214	677	246	666	201	13,329
Tulare County	4,111	717	4,667	452	3,763	285	2,445	283	45,260
Ventura County	12,004	1,157	12,873	1,554	11,859	1,066	6,855	531	97,485
Yolo County	2,300	171	2,617	139	1,985	223	1,093	128	21,434
Yuba County	609	172	890	139	797	154	449	40	8,168
Colorado									
Adams County	4,641	452	5,266	347	3,961	659	1,867	309	39,898
Arapahoe County	8,892	745	9,186	764	8,228	747	4,417	390	60,329
Boulder County	5,048	381	4,506	464	4,747	235	1,746	75	30,137
Denver County	8,437	787	8,401	659	6,788	631	4,571	270	64,089
Douglas County	3,682	147	4,828	345	3,106	157	1,783	199	22,162
El Paso County	8,009	747	9,493	882	6,902	545	4,014	419	67,500
Jefferson County	10,567	849	9,434	609	8,149	604	4,798	295	71,192
Larimer County	5,144	402	5,075	348	4,549	322	2,386	76	37,309
Mesa County	1,919	192	2,420	124	1,977	174	1,261	82	23,248
Pueblo County	2,161	214	2,239	214	2,016	95	1,096	95	27,110
Weld County	3,211	127	3,511	232	2,638	408	1,387	187	26,760
Connecticut									
Fairfield County	14,136	1,181	17,601	1,277	15,577	2,088	11,049	926	114,898
Hartford County	13,701	1,271	16,640	1,656	13,924	1,460	8,201	1,004	126,598
Litchfield County	4,257	265	3,814	349	4,018	290	2,642	192	28,287
Middlesex County	2,782	184	4,686	224	2,924	344	1,859	142	25,280
New Haven County	13,625	1,234	16,755	1,645	13,060	973	9,142	739	119,972
New London County	4,753	225	5,491	430	4,355	250	2,544	213	39,199
Tolland County	2,497	112	3,035	263	1,917	294	1,389	80	18,212
Windham County	1,809	286	2,094	189	1,537	86	1,001	154	15,630
Delaware									
Kent County	1,804	64	2,475	82	2,209	169	1,311	98	24,287
New Castle County	7,469	455	8,499	536	7,390	537	4,365	356	67,660
Sussex County	4,028	422	3,825	194	3,845	264	3,056	195	43,918
Florida									
Alachua County	3,552	119	3,725	107	2,488	87	2,063	74	28,395
Bay County	2,399	317	2,227	270	2,204	264	1,620	237	25,836
Brevard County	7,438	980	8,318	1,335	7,550	1,034	6,005	795	117,079
Broward County	24,980	3,416	30,905	2,954	25,472	3,118	16,858	2,249	247,548
Charlotte County	2,661	318	3,124	431	2,717	247	2,747	282	59,137
Citrus County	2,150	295	2,141	185	1,954	426	1,621	188	50,038
Clay County	2,400	259	2,476	222	1,958	291	977	65	26,780
Collier County	6,317	268	5,869	453	6,948	858	5,272	421	87,219
Columbia County	1,007	18	989	7	726	94	216	0	12,149
Duval County	10,818	1,247	12,746	1,511	10,235	951	6,254	521	103,984
Escambia County	3,984	97	4,836	454	3,812	364	2,162	159	46,515
Flagler County	1,692	294	1,489	227	1,208	213	950	53	27,070
Hernando County	2,131	188	2,454	337	1,855	379	1,132	225	49,685
Highlands County	1,244	190	1,294	152	1,428	151	1,178	65	33,069
Hillsborough County	14,928	1,419	16,675	1,885	13,558	1,302	7,616	840	159,639
Indian River County	2,135	573	1,682	618	2,146	318	1,986	265	39,156
Lake County	4,320	434	4,171	418	3,768	472	4,169	168	77,470
Lee County	8,270	982	9,562	1,021	9,794	1,580	8,234	1,243	159,386
Leon County	4,379	104	4,465	153	3,216	256	1,381	62	27,614
Manatee County	3,919	874	5,181	575	5,238	933	3,828	741	80,203
Marion County	4,367	446	5,152	481	4,665	552	3,223	523	94,371
Martin County	2,210	174	2,887	302	2,964	346	2,267	108	40,564
Miami-Dade County	31,736	3,541	37,542	4,937	29,993	3,438	20,672	2,282	365,070
Monroe County	1,942	48	1,812	52	1,795	47	959	108	13,305
Nassau County	740	18	1,361	122	1,113	151	622	0	13,882
Okaloosa County	2,677	104	2,929	111	2,038	105	1,439	271	26,411
Orange County	13,093	1,671	14,935	1,741	11,747	1,283	6,943	742	117,939
Osceola County	3,388	581	3,429	423	3,376	221	1,660	110	33,766
Palm Beach County	19,299	2,007	22,019	2,613	23,310	2,905	18,210	2,289	279,116
Pasco County	5,737	804	6,104	831	5,532	812	3,859	385	107,870
Pinellas County	15,863	1,506	17,743	2,095	14,881	1,828	10,896	1,421	199,810
Polk County	7,873	923	9,274	870	7,016	867	4,972	805	117,332
Putnam County	811	30	917	121	676	75	592	43	16,404
St. Johns County	3,195	569	3,357	186	2,851	285	1,800	183	32,788
St. Lucie County	3,346	287	3,454	581	3,986	683	2,799	393	59,755
Santa Rosa County	1,887	169	2,021	132	1,786	138	897	22	22,252
Sarasota County	6,077	728	7,460	783	7,677	905	6,075	713	121,311
Seminole County	6,781	749	7,399	434	6,119	574	3,343	503	52,867
Sumter County	1,068	164	2,023	189	2,023	151	1,742	78	49,812
Volusia County	6,363	734	7,273	995	7,123	1,153	4,737	541	112,497

Table F-2: Counties—Employment and Labor Force Status, Civilian Labor Force—*Continued*

	60 and 61 Years		62 to 64 Years		65 to 69 Years		70 Years And Over		60 Years and Over Not In the Labor Force
	Employed	Unemployed	Employed	Unemployed	Employed	Unemployed	Employed	Unemployed	
Georgia									
Barrow County	824	57	875	61	713	19	314	42	7,320
Bartow County	1,290	0	960	178	964	6	528	0	12,249
Bibb County	1,540	58	2,056	72	1,640	81	1,342	27	21,737
Bulloch County	710	68	588	15	362	28	460	18	7,021
Carroll County	951	169	1,374	274	902	81	709	63	13,177
Catoosa County	883	75	1,200	69	879	95	827	43	9,366
Chatham County	3,390	201	3,903	183	3,033	252	1,667	65	36,522
Cherokee County	2,634	397	3,166	229	2,345	208	1,055	57	22,558
Clarke County	899	75	1,028	9	911	12	619	110	11,389
Clayton County	3,102	359	2,512	296	1,753	160	1,066	201	21,128
Cobb County	9,205	946	10,228	1,362	8,317	788	4,007	409	65,237
Columbia County	1,695	96	1,803	202	1,178	58	759	0	15,002
Coweta County	2,021	169	2,175	100	1,496	59	788	100	14,875
DeKalb County	7,943	1,199	9,342	934	6,890	697	3,433	347	69,002
Dougherty County	1,033	41	905	8	633	54	463	49	13,702
Douglas County	1,475	74	1,745	134	896	90	516	26	14,074
Fayette County	1,422	159	2,166	158	1,339	164	780	69	15,087
Floyd County	1,196	112	1,334	92	789	166	875	40	15,052
Forsyth County	2,520	173	2,375	134	1,972	91	1,013	84	18,118
Fulton County	10,235	1,267	12,586	1,135	9,118	635	5,356	363	94,672
Glynn County	1,293	0	1,581	145	1,267	131	1,028	36	13,182
Gwinnett County	9,941	924	10,498	1,308	6,588	822	3,984	301	62,163
Hall County	1,668	129	2,777	223	1,683	225	1,266	0	23,100
Henry County	2,083	260	2,069	96	1,309	130	986	220	19,529
Houston County	1,351	30	1,764	113	1,247	87	569	102	16,401
Liberty County	432	38	415	64	437	0	183	8	4,551
Lowndes County	1,118	129	1,435	131	945	61	637	26	11,762
Muscogee County	2,397	96	2,014	156	1,777	120	1,255	57	24,128
Newton County	926	130	949	66	902	70	496	50	11,264
Paulding County	1,236	127	1,272	72	799	115	465	114	12,869
Richmond County	2,526	113	1,858	91	1,793	44	1,106	46	26,141
Rockdale County	1,098	148	932	298	779	27	576	67	10,511
Troup County	771	98	697	42	700	44	273	34	9,654
Walker County	898	37	773	46	835	89	483	48	11,402
Walton County	1,104	38	775	45	722	52	579	36	11,709
Whitfield County	1,046	88	1,058	333	1,143	51	678	51	11,923
Hawaii									
Hawaii County	3,977	239	3,577	448	2,575	334	1,940	154	30,088
Honolulu County	16,065	782	17,458	540	16,433	403	10,298	289	137,728
Kauai County	1,373	37	1,378	104	1,167	25	740	0	10,679
Maui County	2,891	255	3,298	245	2,452	262	1,667	76	20,693
Idaho									
Ada County	6,377	337	5,903	377	3,799	277	2,289	170	46,342
Bannock County	862	10	1,018	45	626	56	588	3	10,248
Bonneville County	1,374	68	1,747	39	1,331	115	679	68	11,893
Canyon County	1,787	92	1,863	400	1,891	228	854	106	23,245
Kootenai County	2,054	149	2,252	328	1,438	128	1,073	75	23,156
Twin Falls County	1,312	120	974	73	1,223	138	820	43	10,808
Illinois									
Adams County	1,041	59	1,009	32	1,149	47	1,148	0	11,485
Champaign County	3,018	107	2,747	27	1,924	105	1,459	60	20,761
Cook County	65,312	6,990	72,748	7,768	57,815	5,110	38,429	3,135	644,238
DeKalb County	1,147	127	1,426	39	850	72	639	37	10,872
DuPage County	15,891	1,431	16,489	1,562	14,449	1,151	7,256	724	105,862
Kane County	6,717	877	8,375	627	5,720	431	3,718	246	52,945
Kankakee County	1,276	115	1,591	167	1,186	64	1,070	47	16,282
Kendall County	1,249	139	1,562	70	1,074	36	840	92	8,708
Lake County	9,969	1,150	12,096	1,101	9,234	831	5,501	395	73,496
LaSalle County	1,630	184	1,955	180	1,601	104	1,248	109	18,437
McHenry County	4,663	570	5,768	408	3,909	399	2,285	171	30,843
McLean County	2,298	108	2,345	81	1,275	111	1,268	19	18,903
Macon County	1,957	114	1,699	53	1,552	101	955	12	19,312
Madison County	3,794	398	3,449	184	3,048	171	2,413	90	40,251
Peoria County	2,705	78	2,705	141	2,243	45	1,800	126	27,071
Rock Island County	2,173	172	2,252	233	1,809	38	1,023	17	26,319
St. Clair County	3,362	195	3,949	140	3,286	182	2,011	98	35,377
Sangamon County	3,215	182	3,345	176	2,544	229	2,076	27	29,117
Tazewell County	2,078	141	1,716	107	1,722	53	1,344	36	22,454
Vermilion County	1,211	62	1,305	55	887	44	643	63	14,017
Will County	7,680	806	9,621	618	6,558	449	4,040	303	69,095
Williamson County	899	81	1,184	32	756	4	484	30	12,148
Winnebago County	4,019	415	4,863	425	3,525	283	2,727	287	42,422

Table F-2: Counties—Employment and Labor Force Status, Civilian Labor Force—Continued

	60 and 61 Years		62 to 64 Years		65 to 69 Years		70 Years And Over		60 Years and Over Not In the Labor Force
	Employed	Unemployed	Employed	Unemployed	Employed	Unemployed	Employed	Unemployed	
Indiana									
Allen County	5,179	515	5,886	354	3,684	213	3,039	159	44,030
Bartholomew County	1,228	41	1,228	56	1,046	7	740	13	11,611
Clark County	1,702	172	1,360	43	1,121	112	853	62	15,991
Delaware County	1,465	86	1,447	125	1,238	97	985	140	18,503
Elkhart County	3,247	385	2,937	260	1,988	336	1,756	50	24,047
Floyd County	921	204	1,102	116	807	44	991	26	10,010
Grant County	927	18	904	55	965	27	659	0	12,287
Hamilton County	4,460	324	4,395	302	3,160	210	2,189	110	24,600
Hancock County	1,188	125	963	32	863	4	497	15	9,964
Hendricks County	2,510	57	2,152	126	1,268	11	729	39	16,975
Howard County	1,023	70	1,100	17	962	43	637	17	15,402
Johnson County	2,112	120	2,462	219	1,625	211	1,073	74	18,019
Kosciusko County	1,029	23	1,129	304	1,190	38	682	21	10,491
Lake County	6,248	512	7,745	391	5,042	322	3,496	347	71,287
LaPorte County	1,817	262	1,746	46	1,499	113	887	59	16,716
Madison County	1,675	93	1,729	133	1,229	55	1,294	110	22,345
Marion County	10,688	922	11,402	915	8,169	696	6,358	653	100,924
Monroe County	1,795	71	1,818	66	1,388	61	1,043	44	14,832
Morgan County	1,223	91	853	7	1,025	41	335	64	10,473
Porter County	2,383	54	2,655	230	2,038	118	934	10	22,967
St. Joseph County	4,727	347	3,806	275	3,145	319	2,557	47	35,664
Tippecanoe County	1,954	117	2,571	87	1,448	125	1,100	76	16,919
Vanderburgh County	2,632	241	2,640	116	2,180	97	2,055	11	26,175
Vigo County	1,505	41	1,491	80	1,036	40	808	56	15,440
Wayne County	1,043	109	879	103	735	56	904	20	11,451
Iowa									
Black Hawk County	1,837	134	2,183	116	1,495	37	1,049	109	19,140
Dallas County	1,061	57	1,095	5	513	36	523	36	7,244
Dubuque County	1,689	42	1,818	125	1,213	29	1,064	115	14,033
Johnson County	2,103	40	2,460	62	1,391	0	921	0	11,643
Linn County	3,036	73	3,632	117	2,891	124	1,606	100	28,041
Polk County	6,239	324	7,144	317	5,098	338	3,918	113	48,073
Pottawattamie County	1,726	78	1,646	95	1,256	30	1,059	36	13,352
Scott County	2,619	115	3,049	256	1,997	97	1,198	61	23,678
Story County	1,046	31	1,403	22	763	32	612	21	9,242
Woodbury County	1,569	26	1,463	23	1,483	0	895	24	13,074
Kansas									
Butler County	774	42	940	53	762	116	498	19	8,802
Douglas County	1,339	74	1,843	27	1,373	22	980	22	9,545
Johnson County	8,579	685	11,149	521	8,270	384	5,110	300	57,586
Leavenworth County	850	108	1,122	50	867	14	569	12	9,505
Riley County	728	0	786	4	856	0	451	0	4,660
Sedgwick County	6,552	635	7,627	459	5,658	301	4,071	122	58,677
Shawnee County	3,327	110	2,980	156	2,744	46	1,796	118	26,276
Wyandotte County	1,590	257	2,114	119	1,130	81	1,357	53	18,401
Kentucky									
Boone County	1,573	45	1,896	100	1,281	69	783	0	12,904
Bullitt County	604	93	798	86	924	104	559	30	9,881
Campbell County	1,331	100	1,511	62	811	38	863	18	12,048
Christian County	635	124	710	43	447	10	703	23	8,099
Daviess County	1,168	38	1,422	68	1,115	0	739	27	15,529
Fayette County	3,821	163	5,237	326	3,363	159	2,610	143	32,488
Hardin County	1,173	128	1,080	109	1,180	59	775	0	12,859
Jefferson County	9,683	1,196	11,640	833	9,183	591	5,615	383	106,487
Kenton County	2,056	133	2,491	166	1,518	134	1,214	133	19,156
McCracken County	724	102	1,129	72	740	33	681	22	11,430
Madison County	734	83	844	92	776	87	405	76	10,830
Pike County	539	3	627	18	709	23	366	0	11,712
Warren County	1,225	121	1,050	113	1,104	59	929	88	13,118
Louisiana									
Ascension Parish	1,299	72	1,524	228	976	93	509	0	10,899
Bossier Parish	1,465	96	1,840	14	1,489	173	1,067	24	13,754
Caddo Parish	3,198	281	3,474	139	2,849	55	2,960	138	36,451
Calcasieu Parish	2,603	225	2,813	288	1,927	192	1,524	54	27,011
East Baton Rouge Parish	5,584	317	5,714	323	5,463	422	3,748	96	51,817
Iberia Parish	772	51	949	63	1,152	42	784	0	8,893
Jefferson Parish	6,291	190	7,766	548	6,195	424	4,062	263	61,182
Lafayette Parish	2,787	116	2,853	109	2,814	80	2,000	42	23,120
Lafourche Parish	814	100	1,186	38	1,310	0	612	16	13,358
Livingston Parish	1,397	189	1,405	27	1,344	129	967	47	14,663
Orleans Parish	4,858	619	5,048	313	3,717	304	2,373	99	43,823
Ouachita Parish	1,693	65	1,869	118	1,948	65	1,349	74	20,108
Rapides Parish	1,309	91	1,452	87	1,716	0	1,439	51	19,384
St. Landry Parish	1,054	58	1,236	27	857	39	821	9	12,467
St. Tammany Parish	3,587	212	3,942	278	3,093	226	2,116	236	32,380
Tangipahoa Parish	1,164	132	1,654	235	1,098	197	964	55	16,124
Terrebonne Parish	1,060	113	1,500	0	1,279	89	1,015	27	13,192

Table F-2: Counties—Employment and Labor Force Status, Civilian Labor Force—*Continued*

	60 and 61 Years		62 to 64 Years		65 to 69 Years		70 Years And Over		60 Years and Over Not In the Labor Force
	Employed	Unemployed	Employed	Unemployed	Employed	Unemployed	Employed	Unemployed	
Maine									
Androscoggin County	1,554	156	2,005	142	1,161	61	1,152	80	16,325
Aroostook County	1,089	69	1,347	65	817	64	842	35	14,831
Cumberland County	5,165	307	5,499	359	4,590	110	2,851	273	40,411
Kennebec County	1,749	189	2,275	102	1,700	228	1,071	13	20,780
Penobscot County	2,584	145	3,005	199	1,644	69	1,410	87	24,199
York County	4,336	128	4,159	254	3,262	211	2,049	22	31,489
Maryland									
Allegany County	695	75	969	22	1,062	45	586	10	15,082
Anne Arundel County	8,631	333	10,511	514	8,154	467	5,226	257	64,991
Baltimore County	14,049	767	15,214	1,083	12,498	970	9,291	662	115,762
Calvert County	1,310	64	1,645	27	1,525	45	580	37	10,136
Carroll County	3,497	205	3,100	190	2,712	95	1,525	84	22,660
Cecil County	1,240	164	2,027	113	1,355	38	935	37	12,766
Charles County	2,022	46	2,268	119	1,459	145	736	66	15,625
Frederick County	3,990	180	4,008	316	3,716	187	1,944	141	26,062
Harford County	3,879	133	4,552	271	3,697	313	2,217	124	31,148
Howard County	4,319	416	5,310	268	4,759	240	2,918	194	28,087
Montgomery County	18,775	938	19,675	1,064	17,296	1,314	12,058	526	110,772
Prince George's County	13,016	921	14,656	744	11,888	537	6,837	589	83,252
St. Mary's County	1,341	78	1,372	126	1,494	0	928	36	11,117
Washington County	2,303	99	2,594	107	1,610	174	1,434	57	22,138
Wicomico County	1,299	180	912	77	1,499	53	784	136	13,617
Massachusetts									
Barnstable County	4,365	390	5,276	448	5,426	598	4,199	498	52,419
Berkshire County	2,541	233	2,845	232	2,224	251	1,894	129	24,330
Bristol County	8,559	836	9,073	847	7,319	751	4,814	491	80,120
Essex County	13,067	854	14,580	1,122	12,191	908	7,608	470	104,153
Franklin County	1,792	184	2,101	138	1,421	67	755	8	10,879
Hampden County	6,924	603	7,439	711	6,296	542	4,401	196	67,731
Hampshire County	2,848	132	3,229	174	2,553	187	1,858	142	19,718
Middlesex County	24,322	2,044	29,447	2,329	24,646	1,860	17,167	941	185,265
Norfolk County	11,203	913	13,230	1,185	11,712	1,119	7,600	600	91,718
Plymouth County	8,426	799	10,019	1,258	8,573	1,034	4,824	435	69,308
Suffolk County	8,732	827	9,838	741	7,681	655	5,293	482	76,759
Worcester County	12,708	752	12,918	1,313	10,618	931	6,481	517	102,268
Michigan									
Allegan County	1,531	59	1,399	211	968	112	651	74	16,895
Bay County	1,458	68	1,216	119	1,039	133	804	134	20,449
Berrien County	2,152	289	2,776	219	2,084	151	1,637	76	26,325
Calhoun County	1,804	288	1,822	117	1,236	146	1,089	51	22,636
Clinton County	931	39	962	42	665	5	516	61	11,535
Eaton County	1,825	125	1,346	157	1,110	166	548	118	16,977
Genesee County	4,044	345	3,998	438	2,926	362	2,186	286	70,555
Grand Traverse County	1,584	38	1,732	150	1,176	67	648	5	13,861
Ingham County	3,888	234	3,668	272	2,707	203	1,862	62	32,490
Isabella County	519	34	726	14	397	40	311	23	7,760
Jackson County	2,176	271	2,040	183	1,492	216	1,290	47	25,762
Kalamazoo County	3,314	298	3,818	297	2,175	60	1,627	257	33,820
Kent County	7,926	877	7,668	643	6,267	518	4,146	239	71,784
Lapeer County	1,156	183	811	123	696	44	457	85	14,221
Lenawee County	1,350	157	1,395	182	914	123	661	44	16,777
Livingston County	2,473	271	2,608	258	2,079	212	1,361	164	24,477
Macomb County	11,065	1,330	11,038	1,609	7,395	1,409	5,319	768	134,021
Marquette County	800	77	646	61	661	31	304	0	11,938
Midland County	942	60	992	67	894	61	437	57	13,998
Monroe County	1,770	242	1,702	309	1,240	65	980	23	24,624
Muskegon County	2,097	244	1,687	230	1,434	159	1,124	91	26,458
Oakland County	18,141	1,830	19,418	2,085	16,762	1,734	9,821	859	169,979
Ottawa County	3,455	514	3,395	366	2,681	168	2,200	167	32,447
Saginaw County	2,297	278	2,011	126	1,750	146	1,375	138	34,995
St. Clair County	2,074	366	2,037	339	1,406	152	994	77	27,949
Shiawassee County	954	53	793	76	693	14	327	70	12,015
Van Buren County	1,036	204	1,126	76	791	60	530	13	11,996
Washtenaw County	5,129	244	5,004	386	3,670	356	2,366	154	38,207
Wayne County	17,788	2,464	18,747	2,335	14,234	1,583	8,736	1,001	267,612
Minnesota									
Anoka County	5,460	328	5,103	385	3,332	242	1,979	208	34,440
Blue Earth County	966	53	894	26	677	9	412	12	7,785
Carver County	1,192	113	1,391	115	995	82	689	4	7,595
Dakota County	6,900	413	6,484	464	4,797	336	2,602	53	42,103
Hennepin County	19,206	1,614	19,346	1,240	14,348	613	9,474	560	132,446
Olmsted County	2,573	4	2,582	35	2,074	106	1,443	21	17,685
Ramsey County	7,741	607	8,466	412	5,769	243	3,302	166	64,401
St. Louis County	2,906	150	2,985	134	2,180	56	1,299	35	36,076
Scott County	1,675	222	1,354	100	1,199	119	822	65	11,027
Sherburne County	1,001	69	1,009	13	435	78	511	44	8,315

Table F-2: Counties—Employment and Labor Force Status, Civilian Labor Force—Continued

	60 and 61 Years		62 to 64 Years		65 to 69 Years		70 Years And Over		60 Years and Over Not In the Labor Force
	Employed	Unemployed	Employed	Unemployed	Employed	Unemployed	Employed	Unemployed	
Minnesota—Cont.									
Stearns County	2,298	96	2,477	111	1,753	132	1,339	57	18,370
Washington County	3,788	275	3,696	299	2,671	112	1,527	32	28,066
Wright County	1,559	123	1,494	236	1,243	125	748	49	12,529
Mississippi									
DeSoto County	2,087	154	2,078	159	2,018	42	1,176	58	17,771
Forrest County	714	61	1,179	25	890	44	567	0	9,390
Harrison County	2,077	128	2,196	216	1,705	43	1,571	88	24,840
Hinds County	2,861	200	3,145	286	2,894	77	1,685	144	28,499
Jackson County	1,629	53	1,608	177	1,127	62	903	75	20,114
Jones County	825	20	794	39	750	58	512	16	10,993
Lauderdale County	1,214	22	942	41	737	30	619	0	12,220
Lee County	1,143	6	1,380	53	1,219	44	748	99	11,146
Madison County	1,177	28	1,361	178	1,344	29	988	62	10,467
Rankin County	1,899	135	2,281	46	1,825	0	1,019	33	17,533
Missouri									
Boone County	1,892	177	1,907	119	2,033	60	1,017	0	15,550
Buchanan County	1,299	236	1,386	36	792	114	686	25	12,758
Cape Girardeau County	1,040	67	1,273	68	822	88	613	19	10,996
Cass County	1,258	78	1,454	62	1,064	68	1,000	126	14,101
Christian County	912	73	1,408	111	867	19	485	3	10,874
Clay County	2,837	142	3,647	105	2,518	232	1,629	73	26,802
Cole County	1,266	0	1,403	47	888	38	721	0	10,200
Franklin County	1,242	48	1,449	84	892	20	781	70	15,374
Greene County	3,538	337	4,530	273	3,455	152	2,534	86	40,802
Jackson County	8,996	575	10,831	727	8,031	614	5,311	326	87,771
Jasper County	1,608	86	1,587	194	1,377	55	826	26	15,688
Jefferson County	2,956	223	3,180	260	2,242	162	1,128	163	28,068
Platte County	1,395	48	1,683	87	975	170	765	44	10,608
St. Charles County	4,768	313	5,982	252	4,190	317	2,015	214	44,577
St. Francois County	575	19	710	15	725	7	335	22	10,449
St. Louis County	15,899	1,163	18,570	1,489	14,414	772	9,896	559	151,186
Montana									
Cascade County	1,185	53	1,453	44	869	5	905	9	13,545
Flathead County	1,908	250	1,356	131	1,412	21	737	109	13,946
Gallatin County	1,077	82	1,373	99	821	47	552	45	9,338
Missoula County	1,572	245	1,802	81	1,556	135	854	4	13,129
Yellowstone County	2,364	140	2,897	98	2,651	91	1,509	22	20,699
Nebraska									
Douglas County	8,206	540	8,591	297	6,474	368	4,504	156	54,364
Lancaster County	4,837	171	5,193	57	3,817	194	2,774	71	30,461
Sarpy County	2,187	103	2,185	78	1,680	45	1,025	34	14,359
Nevada									
Clark County	25,773	3,155	27,104	3,435	22,339	3,509	14,838	2,693	236,550
Washoe County	6,714	726	6,993	845	5,546	606	3,174	512	56,114
New Hampshire									
Cheshire County	1,464	58	2,203	62	1,112	141	1,148	5	11,185
Grafton County	1,720	67	2,048	149	1,685	70	1,085	90	13,294
Hillsborough County	6,700	532	7,794	502	5,500	372	3,523	90	48,224
Merrimack County	2,856	115	3,043	57	2,275	17	1,641	68	20,168
Rockingham County	5,588	216	6,988	389	4,925	551	2,970	288	36,908
Strafford County	1,453	109	1,841	81	1,377	52	1,045	17	15,337
New Jersey									
Atlantic County	4,370	377	5,136	593	4,399	491	3,368	369	38,204
Bergen County	15,325	1,955	17,638	1,412	16,294	1,427	12,694	1,030	124,584
Burlington County	7,056	736	8,432	794	6,208	809	5,360	586	60,964
Camden County	7,000	603	8,745	904	6,928	574	4,466	440	66,385
Cape May County	2,174	246	2,151	212	1,751	178	1,588	245	20,830
Cumberland County	1,763	183	1,895	145	1,544	294	1,204	126	21,102
Essex County	10,103	1,047	11,495	976	9,737	827	6,620	555	90,121
Gloucester County	4,674	348	4,421	508	3,225	699	2,745	328	36,946
Hudson County	7,319	1,051	8,302	632	6,053	617	3,739	551	68,982
Hunterdon County	2,509	196	2,534	327	2,105	99	1,535	51	15,808
Mercer County	5,328	431	5,680	555	4,983	815	3,923	215	45,408
Middlesex County	11,581	1,414	13,268	1,258	10,935	1,154	7,023	809	98,055
Monmouth County	9,666	917	13,042	1,051	9,627	1,313	6,184	819	85,107
Morris County	8,699	656	9,672	1,077	9,329	1,043	6,714	771	61,827
Ocean County	8,646	860	9,489	1,276	8,450	1,324	6,305	507	124,052
Passaic County	7,184	879	6,762	984	6,816	735	3,677	421	60,167
Salem County	1,056	139	1,108	68	770	149	737	88	10,260
Somerset County	4,820	446	5,831	717	4,815	556	2,867	205	39,693
Sussex County	2,730	215	2,821	309	2,645	260	1,323	158	17,768
Union County	8,038	875	7,822	812	7,539	731	5,411	314	65,868
Warren County	1,832	200	1,915	207	1,352	241	935	135	15,706

Table F-2: Counties—Employment and Labor Force Status, Civilian Labor Force—*Continued*

	60 and 61 Years		62 to 64 Years		65 to 69 Years		70 Years And Over		60 Years and Over Not In the Labor Force
	Employed	Unemployed	Employed	Unemployed	Employed	Unemployed	Employed	Unemployed	
New Mexico									
Bernalillo County	9,946	764	10,048	768	8,045	593	5,440	358	87,961
Chaves County	790	0	746	33	1,044	0	806	18	9,160
Doña Ana County	2,661	213	2,063	148	2,226	208	1,743	68	28,015
Lea County	655	45	847	53	782	28	468	48	7,207
McKinley County	860	39	724	2	441	68	499	0	7,766
Otero County	771	176	828	98	492	97	331	21	11,518
Sandoval County	1,556	121	1,823	120	1,399	142	836	176	19,293
San Juan County	1,665	61	1,558	35	1,630	10	833	42	15,145
Santa Fe County	3,318	165	3,388	244	3,300	290	1,631	117	23,275
Valencia County	887	64	1,009	134	596	92	449	0	12,006
New York									
Albany County	4,506	220	5,061	374	3,789	430	2,642	81	44,335
Bronx County	13,302	1,287	13,904	1,378	11,341	1,072	5,676	519	163,616
Broome County	2,967	126	3,302	347	2,486	303	1,640	143	34,038
Cattaraugus County	1,221	71	1,338	60	859	54	871	37	13,306
Cayuga County	1,011	94	1,418	104	1,005	58	762	41	13,470
Chautauqua County	2,275	158	2,242	170	1,503	19	1,618	20	23,714
Chemung County	1,381	124	1,408	76	1,125	40	484	70	14,754
Clinton County	1,051	119	762	84	703	46	478	26	12,650
Dutchess County	4,510	460	4,354	496	3,857	427	3,300	362	41,284
Erie County	12,552	906	13,661	793	11,481	1,114	10,256	774	148,112
Jefferson County	1,555	110	1,433	103	845	152	604	114	14,511
Kings County	33,305	3,126	33,653	3,016	22,343	2,027	11,711	892	314,802
Livingston County	989	11	1,193	83	775	47	671	34	9,596
Madison County	923	43	1,069	106	792	14	821	19	11,151
Monroe County	10,624	564	10,537	859	10,073	621	5,832	373	109,195
Nassau County	23,757	1,664	26,614	1,989	21,640	1,529	18,294	1,330	195,681
New York County	21,021	2,204	25,963	2,040	27,041	2,588	20,291	1,401	204,874
Niagara County	3,162	117	2,734	143	2,156	125	2,120	121	37,650
Oneida County	3,498	99	4,025	427	2,820	112	2,356	159	40,758
Onondaga County	6,887	513	6,957	457	5,878	345	4,005	147	68,067
Ontario County	2,134	140	2,213	53	2,028	108	1,103	66	17,814
Orange County	5,334	462	5,298	428	4,229	450	2,905	209	44,054
Oswego County	1,650	67	1,263	215	1,328	75	741	53	17,382
Putnam County	1,635	106	1,668	115	1,446	115	885	56	12,660
Queens County	27,988	2,930	34,334	3,423	24,499	2,754	16,438	1,036	301,471
Rensselaer County	2,881	171	2,687	314	1,976	52	1,296	108	23,101
Richmond County	6,607	573	6,713	554	5,190	312	2,838	307	67,675
Rockland County	5,370	381	5,073	603	4,980	363	3,957	334	40,017
St. Lawrence County	1,172	19	1,431	184	1,131	59	580	31	18,137
Saratoga County	3,817	205	3,588	132	2,929	151	1,650	243	32,480
Schenectady County	2,089	137	2,636	94	1,674	179	1,182	146	23,721
Steuben County	1,436	199	1,672	149	1,147	63	912	5	17,345
Suffolk County	21,390	1,323	24,422	1,769	21,466	1,806	15,336	1,417	203,482
Sullivan County	1,038	30	1,367	138	1,345	126	1,084	96	11,759
Tompkins County	1,622	16	1,737	93	1,264	87	940	0	11,304
Ulster County	3,581	263	3,532	427	3,166	348	1,887	126	28,044
Warren County	1,113	89	1,364	80	1,050	10	500	50	12,422
Wayne County	1,235	67	1,517	89	1,224	23	805	21	14,842
Westchester County	15,335	1,176	17,817	1,272	16,965	1,267	12,187	854	129,763
North Carolina									
Alamance County	2,027	144	2,237	303	2,209	162	1,303	245	22,427
Brunswick County	2,150	131	1,931	424	1,725	386	1,431	109	27,902
Buncombe County	4,008	487	4,103	242	3,351	131	2,243	246	40,993
Burke County	1,211	141	1,319	79	1,005	90	868	75	16,185
Cabarrus County	2,132	175	2,391	333	1,610	247	1,269	106	21,233
Caldwell County	1,241	170	1,462	146	989	155	657	27	14,558
Carteret County	1,236	32	1,355	166	1,538	143	1,004	60	13,198
Catawba County	2,021	217	2,557	193	1,835	203	1,075	177	24,200
Chatham County	1,592	114	1,172	126	1,417	75	819	40	13,370
Cleveland County	1,059	175	1,267	131	970	44	854	38	16,769
Craven County	1,263	283	1,208	174	967	68	1,066	105	17,672
Cumberland County	3,434	501	3,231	263	2,889	345	1,786	128	33,147
Davidson County	2,082	158	2,270	417	2,285	182	1,154	130	26,006
Durham County	3,623	337	3,968	179	2,973	135	1,846	43	28,164
Forsyth County	5,247	270	5,061	446	4,352	190	2,957	157	48,445
Gaston County	2,048	215	3,124	294	2,433	138	1,201	106	31,021
Guilford County	6,627	904	7,719	658	6,050	556	4,514	331	62,705
Harnett County	1,288	156	1,250	81	877	101	603	24	13,567
Henderson County	1,819	91	1,876	160	1,614	48	1,344	86	25,832
Iredell County	2,405	47	2,431	247	2,120	179	1,160	69	22,299

Table F-2: Counties—Employment and Labor Force Status, Civilian Labor Force—*Continued*

	60 and 61 Years		62 to 64 Years		65 to 69 Years		70 Years And Over		60 Years and Over Not In the Labor Force
	Employed	Unemployed	Employed	Unemployed	Employed	Unemployed	Employed	Unemployed	
North Carolina—Cont.									
Johnston County	1,949	112	2,672	307	1,871	79	815	158	20,120
Lincoln County	1,144	148	1,094	140	1,034	68	670	0	11,589
Mecklenburg County	11,034	1,263	12,061	1,649	9,820	925	6,217	593	86,074
Moore County	1,328	92	1,712	135	1,315	119	1,027	86	21,227
Nash County	1,401	240	1,393	278	868	36	1,016	53	15,269
New Hanover County	2,895	65	2,654	421	2,884	277	1,809	141	30,392
Onslow County	1,536	55	1,486	92	1,352	45	724	15	14,778
Orange County	1,785	139	2,178	91	1,884	46	1,173	7	13,085
Pitt County	2,068	267	1,762	270	1,744	166	1,096	94	18,105
Randolph County	1,941	230	2,899	82	1,997	102	1,089	87	21,523
Robeson County	1,202	113	1,710	54	877	125	895	77	18,135
Rockingham County	1,140	191	1,001	99	1,324	114	594	87	17,200
Rowan County	1,588	141	1,770	394	1,741	95	1,117	81	22,012
Rutherford County	1,052	205	1,155	59	574	69	653	0	13,204
Surry County	912	87	1,130	109	920	122	850	56	13,363
Union County	2,150	500	2,987	167	2,192	233	1,436	139	21,264
Wake County	11,609	733	11,938	902	9,017	707	5,402	319	84,213
Wayne County	1,827	113	1,653	60	1,342	64	1,037	66	17,459
Wilkes County	658	50	734	199	782	40	547	34	13,801
Wilson County	767	179	1,183	168	1,135	88	885	32	12,570
North Dakota									
Burleigh County	1,563	77	1,545	26	1,180	18	995	20	11,053
Cass County	2,393	39	2,673	65	1,951	40	1,489	0	14,120
Grand Forks County	1,051	3	958	47	849	38	532	0	6,760
Ohio									
Allen County	1,550	112	1,310	139	1,115	89	948	12	16,457
Ashtabula County	1,497	112	1,374	125	1,449	24	531	21	17,292
Belmont County	1,005	47	1,291	74	1,076	108	633	18	13,207
Butler County	5,529	571	5,281	464	3,823	234	2,709	77	46,728
Clark County	2,083	193	2,137	117	1,539	91	1,201	103	24,650
Clermont County	2,871	251	2,572	225	2,480	167	1,472	38	25,291
Columbiana County	2,168	180	1,557	165	1,305	92	1,179	122	18,906
Cuyahoga County	19,859	1,716	21,704	1,966	16,526	1,394	12,206	680	201,880
Delaware County	2,386	120	3,173	153	2,065	130	1,427	55	18,418
Erie County	1,361	126	1,739	217	1,274	164	872	17	13,680
Fairfield County	2,161	28	2,142	115	1,643	115	1,048	31	19,912
Franklin County	14,147	913	17,450	1,196	12,358	649	8,026	224	122,014
Geauga County	1,979	179	2,361	106	1,882	27	1,041	98	14,011
Greene County	2,253	119	2,711	180	2,195	121	1,260	95	24,377
Hamilton County	11,951	1,050	12,847	887	10,099	741	7,984	376	107,789
Hancock County	937	83	1,273	85	971	80	657	51	11,254
Jefferson County	999	51	907	102	789	37	647	64	13,984
Lake County	3,945	407	4,417	266	3,611	254	2,308	99	37,418
Licking County	2,260	167	2,741	188	2,158	153	1,082	72	23,834
Lorain County	4,917	448	4,987	499	3,699	107	2,426	144	47,440
Lucas County	5,494	734	5,614	534	4,515	404	3,226	175	63,219
Mahoning County	3,961	439	4,017	265	2,676	276	2,307	257	45,414
Marion County	893	49	1,163	49	720	40	518	8	10,638
Medina County	2,516	213	2,872	230	2,492	161	1,437	55	24,320
Miami County	1,702	13	1,841	72	1,306	142	1,070	28	16,461
Montgomery County	7,709	679	9,276	508	6,891	391	4,671	207	86,831
Muskingum County	1,137	139	1,388	170	770	34	665	32	14,402
Portage County	2,344	187	2,385	385	2,248	33	1,211	62	22,134
Richland County	1,775	278	2,162	66	1,365	187	1,314	63	21,910
Ross County	692	85	766	58	594	39	431	27	12,065
Scioto County	942	49	1,082	45	536	53	566	0	14,116
Stark County	6,067	531	6,307	396	5,091	356	3,697	149	62,993
Summit County	8,225	328	9,213	650	6,121	477	4,699	457	84,509
Trumbull County	3,049	324	3,443	230	1,937	172	1,345	36	42,223
Tuscarawas County	1,650	72	1,563	98	1,130	169	858	50	15,690
Warren County	2,663	321	3,513	256	2,420	176	1,627	85	25,419
Wayne County	1,804	69	1,904	115	1,747	29	1,359	61	17,473
Wood County	2,271	99	1,743	71	1,567	42	1,210	103	16,011
Oklahoma									
Canadian County	1,730	42	1,738	104	1,304	57	941	78	13,852
Cleveland County	3,253	276	3,790	84	2,711	134	2,167	38	28,599
Comanche County	1,250	111	1,535	40	1,157	15	813	51	13,265
Creek County	992	69	985	24	923	93	689	21	11,352
Muskogee County	763	28	971	24	1,007	96	430	17	11,679
Oklahoma County	8,793	277	10,560	361	8,439	466	7,043	314	89,666
Payne County	743	5	1,221	48	900	0	599	5	8,024
Pottawatomie County	768	46	943	15	813	57	643	3	10,841
Rogers County	1,113	22	1,442	74	1,128	59	728	43	12,675
Tulsa County	8,676	482	9,517	400	7,909	488	5,914	292	72,922
Wagoner County	1,363	45	845	35	1,341	31	506	21	10,745

Table F-2: Counties—Employment and Labor Force Status, Civilian Labor Force—*Continued*

	60 and 61 Years		62 to 64 Years		65 to 69 Years		70 Years And Over		60 Years and Over Not In the Labor Force
	Employed	Unemployed	Employed	Unemployed	Employed	Unemployed	Employed	Unemployed	
Oregon									
Benton County	1,319	119	1,607	51	1,241	50	453	31	11,163
Clackamas County	7,095	757	7,270	568	5,910	457	2,916	329	56,671
Deschutes County	2,481	566	2,703	346	1,707	178	804	118	27,729
Douglas County	1,762	218	2,085	67	1,245	232	964	20	26,086
Jackson County	3,409	487	4,125	425	3,175	276	1,915	160	38,305
Josephine County	1,131	176	1,387	151	956	150	823	47	20,897
Klamath County	1,253	151	918	163	749	138	593	99	12,765
Lane County	5,882	474	5,652	438	4,083	400	3,103	223	59,156
Linn County	1,777	297	2,415	43	1,087	40	769	41	20,775
Marion County	3,517	380	4,173	488	3,528	304	1,975	188	44,572
Multnomah County	10,617	1,287	11,041	1,371	7,882	524	4,039	392	86,020
Polk County	1,127	145	1,501	95	870	63	448	0	12,588
Umatilla County	1,003	139	1,488	96	1,038	59	495	37	10,141
Washington County	7,644	705	7,853	627	6,003	664	3,504	378	57,002
Yamhill County	1,172	103	1,545	111	1,249	35	871	0	13,809
Pennsylvania									
Adams County	1,765	64	1,875	103	1,555	141	1,245	91	16,423
Allegheny County	21,103	1,315	21,622	1,857	17,746	1,319	13,565	901	204,115
Armstrong County	1,111	55	1,236	20	717	31	682	134	13,738
Beaver County	2,968	94	3,006	174	2,255	149	1,995	116	32,469
Berks County	5,769	258	6,352	653	5,301	509	3,406	260	61,622
Blair County	2,111	66	1,966	100	1,727	30	1,087	43	24,378
Bucks County	10,692	880	13,425	922	11,033	1,055	7,432	493	88,779
Butler County	3,084	125	2,891	72	2,581	202	1,778	73	29,258
Cambria County	2,244	133	2,269	91	1,659	102	1,292	56	29,185
Carbon County	750	49	1,439	43	676	90	382	0	12,893
Centre County	1,883	41	1,824	190	1,804	48	1,111	42	17,854
Chester County	8,546	709	9,969	701	7,642	593	5,662	455	61,286
Clearfield County	1,282	71	1,214	132	792	23	606	38	15,723
Columbia County	1,088	28	1,179	40	758	69	651	22	11,124
Crawford County	1,475	88	1,121	92	1,265	66	858	53	15,873
Cumberland County	4,276	251	3,713	296	3,283	230	3,444	197	37,006
Dauphin County	3,904	249	4,657	371	3,246	231	2,606	83	39,213
Delaware County	9,606	578	9,541	808	7,841	618	6,601	468	75,944
Erie County	4,520	306	4,289	236	2,795	252	2,441	72	43,432
Fayette County	1,989	138	2,055	120	1,273	121	935	46	27,397
Franklin County	1,900	181	2,465	116	1,947	35	1,382	97	26,418
Indiana County	1,111	88	1,097	98	712	38	537	25	15,493
Lackawanna County	3,099	324	3,957	291	3,001	155	2,302	166	38,610
Lancaster County	8,215	504	9,324	484	8,123	437	7,155	306	74,334
Lawrence County	1,630	109	1,724	63	1,478	49	1,065	67	17,197
Lebanon County	1,897	150	2,836	95	2,002	76	1,596	129	22,521
Lehigh County	5,156	341	5,187	504	3,978	578	3,200	253	53,235
Luzerne County	4,787	450	5,507	264	4,364	363	3,655	132	59,660
Lycoming County	1,775	143	1,739	140	1,723	185	1,024	64	19,812
Mercer County	1,668	77	1,753	124	1,320	57	1,438	136	22,775
Monroe County	2,621	443	2,326	239	1,852	190	1,312	135	23,990
Montgomery County	13,368	813	16,174	1,367	14,744	817	11,153	707	112,689
Northampton County	4,524	288	4,707	365	4,175	621	2,146	231	48,148
Northumberland County	1,536	46	1,886	148	1,173	59	914	119	18,871
Philadelphia County	15,979	1,756	17,632	2,007	13,883	1,333	8,895	954	202,120
Schuylkill County	2,095	161	2,572	95	1,948	122	1,087	61	29,057
Somerset County	1,306	65	1,021	179	798	57	696	37	15,708
Washington County	3,749	304	3,993	218	2,899	275	2,539	70	37,942
Westmoreland County	6,678	456	6,800	289	5,496	273	3,974	205	71,587
York County	7,370	556	7,261	496	6,308	469	4,126	245	63,798
Rhode Island									
Kent County	2,692	341	3,408	190	2,797	363	1,735	184	25,851
Newport County	1,671	104	1,338	116	1,865	16	1,315	41	13,368
Providence County	9,277	986	9,202	1,058	6,229	612	5,493	485	85,532
Washington County	2,260	188	3,192	180	2,427	193	1,234	44	19,180
South Carolina									
Aiken County	1,799	118	2,228	128	1,837	62	1,285	72	28,590
Anderson County	2,039	139	2,675	221	1,778	224	1,717	203	32,067
Beaufort County	2,770	14	3,163	46	3,273	203	1,777	235	37,227
Berkeley County	1,913	149	2,362	130	1,772	164	1,031	172	21,357
Charleston County	5,111	509	5,792	323	4,331	604	3,303	114	48,701
Darlington County	869	253	679	25	927	103	487	45	11,441
Dorchester County	1,526	192	2,029	87	1,237	102	699	104	16,009
Florence County	1,549	138	1,943	144	1,576	76	1,182	90	20,310
Greenville County	5,922	625	6,592	509	5,622	569	3,506	242	61,146
Greenwood County	1,068	69	521	157	932	157	486	87	11,890

Table F-2: Counties—Employment and Labor Force Status, Civilian Labor Force—*Continued*

	60 and 61 Years		62 to 64 Years		65 to 69 Years		70 Years And Over		60 Years and Over Not In the Labor Force
	Employed	Unemployed	Employed	Unemployed	Employed	Unemployed	Employed	Unemployed	
South Carolina—Cont.									
Horry County	4,231	499	5,070	525	4,526	336	2,516	544	52,785
Lancaster County	1,080	146	1,083	197	656	112	519	78	14,422
Laurens County	674	149	1,022	24	790	33	618	40	11,215
Lexington County	4,129	214	4,547	269	3,201	277	2,104	257	34,919
Oconee County	1,063	92	1,069	167	652	11	545	54	16,311
Orangeburg County	1,008	94	1,140	125	811	57	786	148	15,812
Pickens County	1,273	377	1,279	140	1,151	268	804	56	17,681
Richland County	4,693	288	5,808	259	3,921	144	2,674	147	41,010
Spartanburg County	4,254	416	3,802	304	3,204	281	2,155	108	42,715
Sumter County	1,351	86	1,392	134	1,045	96	851	40	15,424
York County	2,693	244	3,977	270	2,148	246	1,578	171	28,090
South Dakota									
Minnehaha County	2,351	116	3,434	136	2,100	14	1,491	10	18,804
Pennington County	1,724	35	1,644	50	1,524	23	1,160	9	14,080
Tennessee									
Anderson County	1,093	42	1,111	63	1,111	47	782	23	14,092
Blount County	1,635	195	2,051	190	1,799	180	1,098	89	21,430
Bradley County	1,156	91	1,202	58	651	107	925	23	16,271
Davidson County	7,997	671	9,326	640	6,817	414	5,215	384	67,224
Greene County	756	92	1,213	77	846	19	486	58	13,982
Hamilton County	5,582	287	5,984	412	4,662	451	3,004	171	52,257
Knox County	6,730	314	7,231	300	4,239	228	2,988	204	62,106
Madison County	837	78	1,527	133	1,191	185	720	72	13,922
Maury County	1,248	96	1,214	81	990	224	514	0	11,997
Montgomery County	1,437	75	1,775	81	1,177	49	817	21	15,745
Putnam County	782	168	1,001	35	1,247	79	584	38	11,129
Robertson County	803	23	983	138	637	89	473	0	8,676
Rutherford County	2,403	410	3,524	316	2,109	115	1,232	58	25,537
Sevier County	1,466	292	1,827	29	1,474	113	934	146	14,569
Shelby County	12,822	965	12,827	1,108	9,668	850	6,854	696	101,911
Sullivan County	2,119	144	2,760	172	1,879	71	2,019	93	32,022
Sumner County	2,517	97	2,525	62	2,106	116	1,522	36	22,583
Washington County	1,635	107	2,021	123	1,367	49	942	76	21,057
Williamson County	3,357	84	3,080	426	2,289	185	1,689	25	19,163
Wilson County	1,611	219	1,784	87	1,680	73	999	50	15,861
Texas									
Angelina County	1,191	11	1,115	43	1,098	38	681	82	13,051
Bastrop County	1,140	72	1,453	74	867	60	872	75	8,763
Bell County	2,625	159	3,055	148	2,538	154	1,627	140	30,896
Bexar County	20,093	896	20,598	955	17,143	669	11,361	599	195,683
Bowie County	1,204	18	1,305	131	1,062	84	931	65	14,282
Brazoria County	3,636	196	4,530	201	3,368	194	1,913	55	32,488
Brazos County	2,235	121	2,617	86	1,793	35	1,212	33	14,159
Cameron County	3,539	296	3,601	261	2,971	261	1,890	145	50,627
Collin County	9,390	593	12,158	673	10,175	705	5,286	230	63,484
Comal County	1,852	85	2,035	145	1,466	15	884	70	19,669
Coryell County	892	10	459	81	418	23	267	0	6,626
Dallas County	27,973	2,106	30,954	2,327	24,763	1,940	15,989	1,268	217,352
Denton County	7,478	718	9,349	430	6,920	677	3,526	207	49,668
Ector County	1,792	35	1,393	35	1,708	85	1,057	82	13,789
Ellis County	1,968	74	2,355	50	1,721	273	1,049	11	16,380
El Paso County	7,791	509	7,727	615	6,492	361	4,011	227	92,496
Fort Bend County	6,989	641	8,667	388	6,958	442	3,082	222	50,364
Galveston County	4,339	468	4,665	193	3,944	315	2,375	231	35,142
Grayson County	1,632	167	1,979	169	1,424	41	1,164	132	20,122
Gregg County	2,070	73	1,695	51	1,636	105	920	40	16,856
Guadalupe County	1,994	54	2,508	71	1,616	98	729	73	16,486
Harris County	49,045	3,504	55,108	4,058	42,737	3,266	25,297	1,934	353,346
Harrison County	1,007	69	976	72	823	17	759	0	9,523
Hays County	1,720	137	2,765	81	1,569	82	618	111	15,271
Henderson County	1,343	128	1,260	70	1,297	68	639	14	16,381
Hidalgo County	5,763	936	5,844	620	4,795	231	2,136	196	84,967
Hunt County	1,059	192	1,451	93	1,063	122	580	5	13,309
Jefferson County	3,086	152	3,633	223	2,270	166	1,813	174	34,455
Johnson County	1,854	165	2,242	72	1,977	169	707	31	18,507
Kaufman County	1,732	66	1,243	80	977	144	921	61	11,807
Liberty County	1,210	73	1,111	9	667	81	416	17	9,283
Lubbock County	3,085	218	4,143	94	3,138	126	2,895	90	30,059
McLennan County	2,759	90	3,541	148	2,440	171	2,031	161	30,108
Midland County	2,115	86	1,788	31	1,467	0	1,478	105	15,233
Montgomery County	6,280	274	6,466	802	5,343	333	3,593	329	53,820
Nacogdoches County	594	83	978	25	564	4	348	15	8,237
Nueces County	4,448	237	5,271	274	4,435	172	2,988	154	43,708
Orange County	775	56	988	0	738	31	660	68	13,023
Parker County	2,084	90	1,946	163	1,302	89	1,164	0	15,775
Potter County	1,452	78	1,660	88	1,049	24	857	27	14,510

Table F-2: Counties—Employment and Labor Force Status, Civilian Labor Force—*Continued*

	60 and 61 Years		62 to 64 Years		65 to 69 Years		70 Years And Over		60 Years and Over Not In the Labor Force
	Employed	Unemployed	Employed	Unemployed	Employed	Unemployed	Employed	Unemployed	
Texas—Cont.									
Randall County	1,817	8	2,037	90	1,311	66	1,393	128	15,493
Rockwall County	1,000	25	1,218	71	875	21	1,087	87	8,330
San Patricio County	866	45	1,147	0	767	9	308	13	9,054
Smith County	3,177	166	3,355	173	2,388	118	2,654	79	30,414
Tarrant County	23,495	1,899	26,519	1,744	20,539	1,458	10,830	714	172,530
Taylor County	1,525	69	1,667	42	1,565	91	1,255	24	17,754
Tom Green County	1,474	10	1,364	63	1,508	24	1,150	0	15,680
Travis County	12,068	789	14,297	709	10,282	479	5,551	401	82,202
Victoria County	774	112	1,685	47	884	76	764	45	12,326
Walker County	580	47	347	26	727	54	605	38	7,615
Webb County	2,360	113	2,084	47	1,936	155	1,107	79	21,497
Wichita County	1,539	49	1,762	83	1,503	75	1,274	59	17,582
Williamson County	5,506	405	5,126	703	3,793	451	2,668	163	42,690
Utah									
Cache County	928	94	1,047	22	841	54	461	8	9,085
Davis County	3,282	180	3,417	203	3,104	73	1,708	143	26,283
Salt Lake County	12,156	720	14,294	757	10,992	595	6,685	243	91,750
Utah County	4,209	311	4,396	389	3,589	250	2,330	112	34,226
Washington County	1,257	212	1,826	137	1,592	160	1,252	31	25,917
Weber County	2,560	179	2,644	93	2,231	20	1,370	29	25,255
Vermont									
Chittenden County	2,796	69	3,234	139	1,972	76	1,609	46	17,440
Virginia									
Albemarle County	1,585	68	1,773	51	1,400	41	1,194	25	14,605
Arlington County	2,881	269	3,455	119	3,049	107	2,225	107	16,388
Augusta County	1,221	25	1,091	108	1,403	59	728	53	12,953
Bedford County	1,230	107	1,404	42	1,089	0	1,128	24	11,974
Chesterfield County	5,062	269	5,251	312	4,235	114	2,028	96	36,279
Fairfax County	19,844	803	23,823	647	17,740	471	10,447	363	103,706
Fauquier County	1,206	77	1,596	13	1,128	22	608	15	8,667
Frederick County	1,545	93	1,558	44	1,210	36	745	72	10,361
Hanover County	1,406	63	2,191	39	1,464	45	1,037	0	13,522
Henrico County	4,817	212	5,574	288	4,441	96	2,625	111	39,497
James City County	1,170	63	1,250	38	1,723	23	710	0	14,484
Loudoun County	4,057	178	3,597	162	4,299	126	2,064	101	20,072
Montgomery County	1,168	17	1,194	0	1,000	16	790	57	9,524
Prince William County	5,421	234	5,876	430	4,648	291	2,175	123	29,596
Roanoke County	1,762	175	2,123	113	1,385	59	1,291	69	16,077
Rockingham County	1,332	65	1,575	16	1,018	13	1,015	19	12,386
Spotsylvania County	2,114	12	1,699	55	1,438	0	715	60	13,794
Stafford County	1,396	95	1,163	33	1,427	73	703	48	10,377
York County	1,171	0	1,128	54	1,023	9	457	15	8,175
Washington									
Benton County	2,688	105	2,878	144	1,835	85	1,416	112	22,954
Chelan County	1,177	85	1,356	93	655	100	761	126	11,645
Clallam County	946	340	1,498	84	770	63	615	78	19,357
Clark County	6,050	494	6,817	647	4,561	576	1,923	254	57,503
Cowlitz County	1,313	151	1,307	144	997	78	616	64	19,194
Franklin County	1,030	21	1,210	74	399	0	391	25	6,711
Grant County	1,136	80	1,168	41	907	151	771	13	10,875
Grays Harbor County	1,165	80	1,255	160	664	96	567	32	13,347
Island County	1,417	69	1,546	93	1,443	99	751	0	15,898
King County	28,883	2,101	32,940	2,341	23,839	1,665	13,063	958	222,587
Kitsap County	4,018	371	4,532	340	2,914	377	1,268	187	38,874
Lewis County	1,273	110	776	57	691	56	563	88	15,197
Pierce County	11,791	831	11,815	559	8,653	797	4,532	343	97,363
Skagit County	1,908	162	2,263	139	1,539	75	884	82	20,945
Snohomish County	11,007	1,001	11,894	950	8,438	690	3,920	419	81,163
Spokane County	7,009	705	8,923	502	5,492	517	2,641	197	66,574
Thurston County	4,109	390	5,056	116	2,820	233	1,655	106	37,333
Whatcom County	3,420	221	3,723	494	2,446	105	1,413	72	29,420
Yakima County	2,863	170	2,945	221	2,770	232	1,266	132	30,086
West Virginia									
Berkeley County	1,637	141	1,377	176	1,239	194	587	105	13,680
Cabell County	1,713	61	1,236	77	1,214	36	699	76	16,573
Harrison County	965	44	753	60	537	27	516	17	13,094
Kanawha County	3,018	224	3,048	36	2,780	31	2,034	21	34,518
Monongalia County	1,037	0	1,056	30	933	0	513	23	11,174
Raleigh County	1,187	38	1,133	17	588	0	699	0	15,125
Wood County	1,241	97	1,049	58	1,062	63	735	39	16,396

Table F-2: Counties—Employment and Labor Force Status, Civilian Labor Force—*Continued*

	60 and 61 Years		62 to 64 Years		65 to 69 Years		70 Years And Over		60 Years and Over Not In the Labor Force
	Employed	Unemployed	Employed	Unemployed	Employed	Unemployed	Employed	Unemployed	
Wisconsin									
Brown County	3,739	230	3,415	184	2,323	139	1,663	62	30,742
Dane County	7,551	235	8,285	607	6,257	268	4,263	150	52,074
Dodge County	1,451	56	1,490	101	940	51	983	23	13,308
Eau Claire County	1,543	139	1,761	48	1,093	96	1,112	114	12,685
Fond du Lac County	1,945	77	1,847	161	1,317	142	855	47	15,834
Jefferson County	1,414	77	1,248	110	936	86	931	59	11,091
Kenosha County	1,977	248	1,572	403	1,847	80	1,059	57	19,643
La Crosse County	1,590	15	2,193	129	1,154	120	1,213	22	15,729
Manitowoc County	1,274	88	1,777	27	927	75	769	10	14,354
Marathon County	2,599	207	2,364	247	1,802	172	1,172	133	19,480
Milwaukee County	11,580	1,414	11,277	709	9,369	694	6,298	528	113,764
Outagamie County	2,672	180	2,641	193	1,616	124	873	27	22,500
Ozaukee County	1,897	94	1,634	123	1,403	57	853	66	13,023
Portage County	1,067	75	1,117	57	626	111	491	24	10,143
Racine County	3,003	102	3,083	378	2,154	231	1,462	207	27,074
Rock County	1,808	141	2,799	115	1,448	113	1,220	46	23,377
St. Croix County	1,462	75	1,133	30	930	39	483	0	9,158
Sheboygan County	1,740	102	2,177	195	1,329	147	1,031	52	17,077
Walworth County	1,764	136	1,694	126	1,501	71	1,067	48	13,696
Washington County	2,725	207	2,468	116	1,514	71	1,119	248	18,202
Waukesha County	6,939	352	8,347	742	5,342	201	3,477	205	57,849
Winnebago County	2,465	113	2,534	147	1,873	131	1,186	34	23,719
Wood County	1,131	95	1,318	58	650	51	565	66	13,705
Wyoming									
Laramie County	1,495	39	1,351	37	1,314	45	606	0	12,195
Natrona County	1,579	91	1,457	78	1,182	39	757	20	8,988

Table F-3: Places—Employment and Labor Force Status, Civilian Labor Force

	60 and 61 Years		62 to 64 Years		65 to 69 Years		70 Years And Over		60 Years and Over Not In the Labor Force
	Employed	Unemployed	Employed	Unemployed	Employed	Unemployed	Employed	Unemployed	
Alabama									
Birmingham city	2,384	217	2,055	66	1,596	110	1,648	106	30,421
Dothan city	1,068	24	775	26	858	59	629	11	10,163
Hoover city	1,601	81	1,564	86	1,130	92	666	56	9,836
Huntsville city	2,585	101	2,709	146	2,346	88	1,956	137	25,420
Mobile city	2,488	259	2,706	185	2,124	124	1,559	92	28,292
Montgomery city	3,037	57	2,492	129	2,456	91	1,572	115	25,379
Tuscaloosa city	863	60	788	55	577	6	894	94	9,758
Alaska									
Anchorage Municipality	4,233	121	4,947	117	3,424	123	1,949	67	22,733
Arizona									
Avondale city	984	43	887	23	413	0	242	35	4,686
Chandler city	3,189	234	3,784	114	2,398	63	998	91	20,811
Flagstaff city	754	16	655	38	701	0	372	19	4,212
Glendale city	3,194	205	2,633	275	2,207	186	844	158	22,374
Goodyear city	769	150	638	89	511	132	288	0	7,907
Mesa city	5,245	680	6,823	461	4,773	232	2,865	429	71,571
Peoria city	2,031	78	2,412	263	1,628	182	1,069	37	22,707
Phoenix city	16,669	1,565	18,395	1,265	13,566	1,122	9,096	746	133,102
Scottsdale city	3,940	452	4,649	252	5,233	266	3,520	185	42,066
Surprise city	940	38	1,132	199	1,442	124	893	105	24,148
Tempe city	1,961	214	2,163	126	1,237	226	900	118	14,233
Tucson city	6,428	610	6,183	712	5,019	410	3,288	311	67,811
Yuma city	592	23	529	99	570	44	492	21	13,349
Arkansas									
Fayetteville city	759	47	786	23	392	69	507	0	6,673
Fort Smith city	905	25	1,419	21	1,044	38	741	50	11,077
Jonesboro city	1,066	14	906	116	581	46	238	36	8,115
Little Rock city	2,879	99	2,305	38	2,388	186	1,895	48	23,441
Springdale city	401	46	806	23	673	42	472	40	6,044
California									
Alameda city	1,270	120	1,017	131	1,188	68	418	0	10,276
Alhambra city	1,122	55	1,002	104	742	114	479	29	13,359
Anaheim city	3,458	476	4,293	364	3,067	405	2,031	73	34,077
Antioch city	1,319	56	1,486	322	795	139	803	112	10,604
Bakersfield city	2,826	264	3,279	268	2,754	218	1,893	175	33,641
Baldwin Park city	903	55	765	69	507	16	307	24	7,666
Bellflower city	710	62	1,113	42	660	60	325	74	6,849
Berkeley city	1,933	95	1,929	118	2,039	273	1,238	29	13,057
Buena Park city	1,109	77	1,018	38	763	84	414	13	9,577
Burbank city	1,671	136	1,480	125	1,407	106	818	43	14,255
Camarillo city	841	135	1,059	304	1,089	21	833	0	10,909
Carlsbad city	1,572	160	1,757	149	1,360	84	918	83	16,039
Carson city	1,324	109	1,484	140	983	245	638	49	13,244
Chico city	997	75	1,073	48	559	113	789	25	9,860
Chino city	1,022	161	721	149	530	61	393	14	7,578
Chino Hills city	1,168	45	1,028	133	702	124	151	16	6,175
Chula Vista city	2,367	298	2,780	316	2,422	251	1,088	89	26,543
Citrus Heights city	893	174	978	136	1,035	153	571	43	12,184
Clovis city	925	165	1,255	37	956	188	539	22	11,526
Compton city	818	95	525	104	442	86	405	50	8,215
Concord city	1,252	189	1,892	304	1,361	119	1,034	92	14,991
Corona city	1,575	68	1,636	194	947	216	564	148	12,560
Costa Mesa city	1,364	112	1,684	139	1,268	81	702	14	9,376
Daly City city	1,359	248	1,988	226	1,058	128	899	39	14,355
Davis city	790	20	860	20	636	23	414	0	5,239
Downey city	1,431	85	1,334	137	940	183	445	118	11,900
El Cajon city	724	278	1,013	141	815	13	454	45	11,399
Elk Grove city	1,596	107	1,575	126	1,038	141	513	47	16,205
El Monte city	1,176	130	1,141	240	816	65	403	103	13,081
Escondido city	1,335	71	1,711	116	921	109	731	216	15,842
Fairfield city	1,062	22	1,214	35	975	45	568	0	11,747
Folsom city	1,026	158	702	167	674	18	480	123	6,700
Fontana city	1,635	125	1,535	176	666	63	182	33	14,230
Fremont city	2,798	300	3,095	251	1,856	244	1,036	90	24,447
Fresno city	4,790	701	5,133	507	3,912	455	2,686	336	49,204
Fullerton city	1,420	143	1,869	254	1,646	159	988	49	16,286
Garden Grove city	2,008	342	1,916	225	1,361	181	932	42	20,658
Glendale city	2,246	363	2,699	268	2,327	113	1,494	57	32,194
Hawthorne city	984	96	718	118	792	12	344	108	6,368
Hayward city	1,859	314	1,936	234	1,298	163	879	142	15,491
Hemet city	780	46	482	156	552	283	461	112	19,831
Hesperia city	848	76	667	121	306	42	341	80	10,929
Huntington Beach city	2,923	320	3,608	358	3,221	189	2,087	144	27,078
Indio city	799	179	853	55	630	327	503	36	10,949
Inglewood city	1,286	71	1,362	145	969	101	521	102	10,764
Irvine city	2,734	97	3,528	342	2,541	102	1,493	136	18,288
Jurupa Valley city[1]	828	83	643	244	550	99	413	57	8,454

[1] Jurupa Valley city was incorporated in 2011. The 2010 population is the U.S. Census Bureau's estimates base figure.

Table F-3: Places—Employment and Labor Force Status, Civilian Labor Force—*Continued*

	60 and 61 Years		62 to 64 Years		65 to 69 Years		70 Years And Over		60 Years and Over Not In the Labor Force
	Employed	Unemployed	Employed	Unemployed	Employed	Unemployed	Employed	Unemployed	
California—Cont.									
Lake Forest city	1,070	156	1,126	93	1,380	86	555	158	7,203
Lakewood city	1,348	92	1,222	146	761	132	564	85	9,835
Lancaster city	1,529	223	1,542	200	1,107	95	642	69	15,213
Livermore city	1,434	74	1,236	65	931	42	505	0	9,010
Long Beach city	5,076	610	5,771	802	3,913	281	2,574	124	47,599
Los Angeles city	43,110	5,688	47,983	5,782	41,417	5,619	29,240	2,996	403,045
Lynwood city	426	74	471	24	423	0	229	0	5,011
Manteca city	646	79	1,004	130	551	34	363	78	7,758
Menifee city	523	97	950	115	975	202	496	122	14,963
Merced city	745	46	757	68	645	45	176	52	8,236
Milpitas city	1,012	171	789	180	806	31	256	8	6,945
Mission Viejo city	1,880	160	1,943	242	1,718	131	1,110	30	13,795
Modesto city	2,487	174	1,945	293	1,598	312	931	81	25,938
Moreno Valley city	1,666	416	1,639	184	1,220	66	518	58	14,840
Mountain View city	945	75	1,024	136	1,038	134	689	125	7,411
Murrieta city	1,447	105	1,388	101	989	94	464	106	10,422
Napa city	1,398	84	1,465	153	944	71	814	66	10,298
Newport Beach city	1,753	161	1,696	92	1,769	112	2,577	130	14,112
Norwalk city	911	60	1,182	121	906	112	339	0	11,505
Oakland city	4,927	637	5,759	664	4,678	367	2,687	163	47,963
Oceanside city	2,356	301	2,127	192	1,900	236	1,003	55	21,038
Ontario city	1,287	226	1,582	394	782	171	734	30	13,749
Orange city	1,807	135	2,088	219	1,814	106	921	28	14,772
Oxnard city	2,174	158	1,954	389	1,361	233	957	151	17,285
Palmdale city	992	179	899	121	822	54	506	15	12,082
Palo Alto city	980	56	870	73	1,208	123	924	23	10,166
Pasadena city	1,631	162	1,956	373	2,434	168	1,266	69	17,981
Perris city	154	41	131	177	102	118	188	0	3,491
Pleasanton city	996	156	1,127	156	798	118	448	51	8,014
Pomona city	1,467	142	1,189	217	1,165	151	578	22	13,280
Rancho Cordova city	594	65	1,029	67	447	85	581	24	7,772
Rancho Cucamonga city	2,477	125	1,521	155	1,300	323	640	142	15,143
Redding city	1,050	154	1,590	87	1,016	67	700	168	15,710
Redlands city	1,125	74	823	50	785	57	719	0	9,053
Redondo Beach city	600	175	967	131	1,098	136	450	24	7,101
Redwood City city	1,019	24	983	69	1,203	50	437	10	8,162
Rialto city	674	153	799	75	920	134	232	85	7,886
Richmond city	1,421	83	1,257	262	1,313	191	556	17	11,269
Riverside city	2,659	303	2,722	456	2,478	390	1,335	210	30,025
Roseville city	1,361	221	1,368	126	972	104	546	147	17,232
Sacramento city	4,708	722	5,281	439	3,632	351	2,692	328	57,647
Salinas city	1,415	51	1,252	104	1,010	167	680	97	12,466
San Bernardino city	1,234	390	1,447	209	1,449	162	812	18	19,276
San Buenaventura (Ventura) city	1,534	63	1,827	147	1,652	220	932	82	15,354
San Diego city	16,624	1,588	16,487	1,125	14,217	1,253	8,129	628	147,926
San Francisco city	12,420	1,356	13,723	1,352	9,500	761	6,302	396	116,358
San Jose city	11,167	1,869	12,660	1,596	9,709	1,187	5,103	444	104,370
San Leandro city	1,650	70	1,515	200	1,107	77	563	13	12,044
San Marcos city	683	27	858	153	923	81	283	64	9,586
San Mateo city	1,465	170	1,555	166	1,323	81	992	65	13,921
San Ramon city	622	55	1,149	79	746	27	493	21	4,907
Santa Ana city	2,283	249	2,338	413	1,964	194	1,201	74	23,149
Santa Barbara city	1,157	65	1,552	96	1,304	83	974	42	11,712
Santa Clara city	1,152	141	1,349	146	848	97	627	125	11,085
Santa Clarita city	2,612	122	2,561	218	2,455	352	861	155	17,113
Santa Maria city	563	107	792	95	909	52	516	0	9,995
Santa Monica city	1,596	103	1,665	210	1,764	74	1,111	128	12,240
Santa Rosa city	3,034	446	2,724	348	1,828	236	1,182	168	22,230
Simi Valley city	1,899	123	2,209	276	2,059	60	1,015	103	12,773
South Gate city	778	158	572	113	585	35	112	42	8,573
Stockton city	2,651	402	2,965	205	2,041	273	1,248	282	32,263
Sunnyvale city	1,764	162	1,868	302	1,589	227	927	69	14,847
Temecula city	1,256	82	1,021	100	590	130	320	19	8,832
Thousand Oaks city	2,788	294	2,747	179	2,426	310	1,371	142	17,386
Torrance city	2,240	50	2,098	194	1,840	97	1,553	99	22,271
Tracy city	578	163	727	48	885	44	266	18	6,666
Turlock city	706	21	838	59	545	20	429	20	8,385
Tustin city	808	72	1,018	82	880	132	633	100	5,657
Union City city	1,101	91	1,099	119	620	143	285	15	8,422
Upland city	1,150	47	1,123	23	1,109	143	655	113	9,562
Vacaville city	1,193	186	1,392	26	1,067	149	637	61	10,326
Vallejo city	1,776	172	2,578	363	1,353	177	907	33	15,052
Victorville city	734	220	825	53	518	81	197	35	10,317

Table F-3: Places—Employment and Labor Force Status, Civilian Labor Force—*Continued*

	60 and 61 Years		62 to 64 Years		65 to 69 Years		70 Years And Over		60 Years and Over Not In the Labor Force
	Employed	Unemployed	Employed	Unemployed	Employed	Unemployed	Employed	Unemployed	
California—Cont.									
Visalia city	1,308	237	1,826	72	1,247	113	913	175	13,770
Vista city	831	221	964	167	1,000	67	456	69	9,444
West Covina city	1,318	254	1,548	206	866	121	441	122	13,876
Westminster city	1,057	175	1,349	137	1,227	70	797	66	13,839
Whittier city	873	71	782	240	855	64	597	0	10,208
Yorba Linda city	1,005	98	1,104	165	1,201	73	720	46	7,743
Yuba City city	806	168	596	114	332	229	444	171	8,839
Colorado									
Arvada city	2,189	224	1,901	154	1,586	76	1,127	93	15,592
Aurora city	4,391	498	4,226	396	3,717	479	2,121	171	31,356
Boulder city	1,483	99	1,240	105	1,079	25	556	12	8,704
Centennial city	2,260	132	2,188	58	2,397	155	864	70	11,677
Colorado Springs city	5,162	639	6,406	639	4,723	274	2,912	235	48,861
Denver city	8,437	787	8,401	659	6,788	631	4,571	270	64,089
Fort Collins city	1,881	145	1,933	187	1,471	124	891	0	12,578
Greeley city	1,041	66	1,127	160	982	167	445	21	10,685
Lakewood city	2,421	169	1,983	125	1,960	179	1,372	126	21,199
Longmont city	1,101	166	933	197	1,093	109	446	23	9,941
Loveland city	1,023	88	1,095	40	959	85	364	35	9,849
Pueblo city	1,372	123	1,272	63	1,334	78	719	47	18,132
Thornton city	1,482	42	1,156	106	722	78	531	122	8,879
Westminster city	1,265	84	1,707	98	1,211	139	655	69	10,557
Connecticut									
Bridgeport city	1,466	289	1,537	183	1,460	257	879	62	14,557
Danbury city	1,039	52	1,455	178	1,004	238	604	45	8,993
Hartford city	819	175	1,163	162	1,157	141	685	92	12,520
New Britain city	986	91	801	119	1,092	31	621	78	8,494
New Haven city	1,337	107	1,665	138	928	89	988	136	12,616
Norwalk city	1,595	120	2,163	145	1,685	334	1,273	125	12,004
Stamford city	1,668	75	1,917	147	1,820	155	1,600	108	13,474
Waterbury city	1,164	108	1,494	132	844	117	862	34	14,122
Delaware									
Wilmington city	563	49	750	52	625	40	550	0	9,318
District of Columbia									
Washington city	8,027	795	9,675	833	8,554	583	6,230	235	67,194
Florida									
Boca Raton city	1,852	68	1,898	140	2,248	283	1,458	55	16,507
Boynton Beach city	525	42	986	259	978	198	708	196	14,172
Cape Coral city	1,822	315	2,194	268	2,207	522	1,866	244	29,467
Clearwater city	1,891	278	2,109	214	2,044	127	1,408	83	22,640
Coral Springs city	1,741	141	2,680	225	1,784	380	852	105	9,941
Deerfield Beach city	1,077	139	879	122	856	103	959	236	15,831
Deltona city	1,122	100	766	190	653	134	258	67	13,288
Fort Lauderdale city	2,923	454	2,825	377	3,140	320	1,803	115	26,311
Gainesville city	1,462	53	1,416	29	1,037	25	999	47	10,754
Hialeah city	2,562	523	2,925	289	2,339	460	1,967	422	44,424
Hollywood city	2,187	416	2,663	388	2,042	291	1,632	190	20,211
Jacksonville city	10,100	1,247	11,936	1,363	9,601	907	5,786	515	97,362
Lakeland city	1,252	163	1,750	165	1,359	207	924	56	20,452
Largo city	1,044	135	896	248	1,365	335	761	198	19,342
Lauderhill city	999	56	1,248	91	720	41	311	0	8,677
Melbourne city	910	181	815	123	996	48	907	53	15,929
Miami city	4,728	734	4,703	694	3,658	489	3,400	489	65,695
Miami Beach city	1,258	149	1,253	38	1,386	87	1,059	48	13,016
Miami Gardens city	1,627	100	1,280	400	899	99	543	78	13,313
Miramar city	1,233	172	1,452	197	1,174	212	449	59	9,172
Orlando city	2,260	307	2,570	524	2,385	291	1,444	147	22,437
Palm Bay city	1,216	332	1,594	182	1,089	237	993	16	17,963
Palm Coast city	1,277	277	1,112	196	901	98	798	22	20,123
Pembroke Pines city	1,812	166	2,715	48	1,883	200	1,384	139	23,803
Plantation city	1,388	128	1,946	168	1,324	168	1,129	78	11,647
Pompano Beach city	1,232	314	1,285	234	1,501	144	1,199	134	18,532
Port St. Lucie city	1,854	158	1,827	323	2,002	400	1,206	275	28,022
St. Petersburg city	3,977	343	4,225	603	3,245	488	2,352	405	39,838
Sunrise city	1,236	156	1,487	138	997	212	818	101	12,755
Tallahassee city	2,304	66	1,673	100	1,428	118	820	47	15,244
Tampa city	3,711	312	4,189	371	3,491	451	1,970	170	39,136
Weston city	872	17	977	48	871	118	368	89	4,786
West Palm Beach city	1,581	212	1,213	314	1,784	64	1,365	230	17,222
Georgia									
Albany city	718	0	611	0	409	37	340	25	10,602
Athens-Clarke County unified govt (bal)	870	75	996	9	901	12	615	110	11,102
Atlanta city	3,936	596	4,501	494	3,455	296	2,437	212	46,551
Augusta-Richmond County consolidated govt (bal)	2,463	113	1,832	91	1,789	20	1,087	42	25,531
Columbus city	2,397	96	2,014	156	1,777	120	1,255	57	24,128
Johns Creek city	1,069	60	1,716	73	532	72	595	25	6,207
Macon city	733	58	904	15	692	45	843	27	12,064
Roswell city	1,205	188	1,496	136	1,636	164	649	12	9,980
Sandy Springs city	1,358	35	1,631	85	1,876	51	751	22	9,982
Savannah city	1,605	145	1,776	112	1,535	66	713	8	17,733
Warner Robins city	674	30	869	43	720	32	202	54	7,083

Table F-3: Places—Employment and Labor Force Status, Civilian Labor Force—*Continued*

	60 and 61 Years		62 to 64 Years		65 to 69 Years		70 Years And Over		60 Years and Over Not In the Labor Force
	Employed	Unemployed	Employed	Unemployed	Employed	Unemployed	Employed	Unemployed	
Hawaii									
Urban Honolulu CDP..........	6,831	384	6,641	204	6,684	201	4,609	186	57,658
Idaho									
Boise City city..........	3,710	242	3,209	258	2,491	193	1,487	38	25,910
Meridian city..........	1,019	79	1,241	28	356	53	325	0	7,652
Nampa city..........	544	47	886	152	573	44	327	67	9,737
Illinois									
Aurora city..........	1,495	380	2,219	261	1,730	21	866	80	13,016
Bloomington city..........	946	59	1,258	62	608	53	544	15	8,462
Champaign city..........	1,158	59	1,098	14	742	69	362	22	6,854
Chicago city..........	27,415	3,329	30,429	3,614	23,829	2,179	15,805	1,326	299,534
Decatur city..........	1,249	82	1,049	26	961	23	778	7	13,501
Elgin city..........	1,430	133	1,334	168	1,198	30	702	54	9,966
Evanston city..........	1,173	77	1,410	137	1,252	67	958	88	7,360
Joliet city..........	1,399	240	1,345	17	1,391	44	793	28	13,214
Naperville city..........	2,104	196	2,920	158	2,056	112	777	140	13,397
Peoria city..........	1,401	11	1,542	57	1,293	18	1,090	80	15,180
Rockford city..........	1,526	280	2,154	347	1,558	81	1,409	180	21,444
Springfield city..........	1,871	74	1,756	146	1,483	178	1,450	23	18,024
Waukegan city..........	985	86	871	109	675	18	264	27	7,707
Indiana									
Bloomington city..........	525	32	774	35	730	21	444	25	6,477
Carmel city..........	1,322	95	1,602	180	1,270	37	700	40	8,406
Evansville city..........	1,653	164	1,523	59	1,363	76	1,284	11	17,216
Fort Wayne city..........	3,289	436	4,017	296	2,595	168	2,279	103	31,806
Gary city..........	758	173	959	86	879	66	538	81	13,083
Hammond city..........	847	111	965	73	389	30	332	48	9,594
Indianapolis city (bal)..........	9,636	885	10,172	774	7,017	578	5,710	612	90,888
Lafayette city..........	639	73	1,012	54	655	88	526	29	7,586
Muncie city..........	813	86	616	78	635	28	400	51	9,820
South Bend city..........	1,511	136	1,616	80	1,175	165	1,091	12	12,703
Iowa									
Cedar Rapids city..........	1,788	49	2,103	101	1,621	31	930	60	16,477
Davenport city..........	1,084	86	1,496	132	1,008	46	619	61	13,772
Des Moines city..........	2,636	180	2,750	209	1,975	132	1,693	21	22,856
Iowa City city..........	961	4	975	0	565	0	446	0	5,630
Sioux City city..........	1,241	24	989	23	1,162	0	676	24	10,373
Waterloo city..........	1,040	134	1,077	88	767	0	536	57	10,243
Kansas									
Kansas City city..........	1,449	257	1,914	119	1,058	81	1,183	53	16,783
Lawrence city..........	927	22	1,147	12	1,007	22	794	22	6,087
Olathe city..........	1,644	245	2,032	86	1,563	71	548	14	9,091
Overland Park city..........	3,012	197	3,594	258	2,939	93	1,767	99	20,583
Topeka city..........	1,946	67	1,806	125	1,746	41	1,330	75	18,134
Wichita city..........	4,954	625	5,826	428	4,428	260	3,206	104	44,797
Kentucky									
Lexington-Fayette urban county..........	3,821	163	5,237	326	3,363	159	2,610	143	32,488
Louisville/Jefferson County metro govt (bal)..........	7,730	1,005	8,621	715	6,308	471	3,926	304	83,570
Louisiana									
Baton Rouge city..........	2,410	140	2,455	125	2,432	250	1,669	0	27,164
Kenner city..........	992	51	1,121	89	915	128	484	54	9,310
Lafayette city..........	1,469	116	1,777	51	1,852	61	1,288	0	14,431
Lake Charles city..........	929	165	1,198	50	704	42	830	23	10,755
New Orleans city..........	4,858	619	5,048	313	3,717	304	2,373	99	43,823
Shreveport city..........	2,458	248	2,424	67	2,186	55	2,207	98	26,606
Maine									
Portland city..........	931	47	1,158	76	754	0	528	11	8,045
Maryland									
Baltimore city..........	7,723	726	8,209	451	6,883	490	4,317	535	77,522
Frederick city..........	1,258	10	1,170	55	821	114	752	23	7,018
Massachusetts									
Boston city..........	7,565	742	8,465	550	6,406	541	4,067	427	64,018
Brockton city..........	1,110	56	1,079	107	1,004	127	683	93	12,174
Cambridge city..........	1,458	100	1,976	145	1,746	122	991	17	10,126
Fall River city..........	1,199	57	943	188	1,013	157	368	40	14,433
Lawrence city..........	830	0	607	36	255	64	287	86	7,357
Lowell city..........	1,022	131	1,183	173	910	89	541	16	12,475
Lynn city..........	697	67	896	57	891	24	514	24	10,753
New Bedford city..........	960	160	1,401	96	1,068	20	943	13	14,942
Newton city..........	1,847	31	1,856	104	2,015	71	1,864	122	10,314
Quincy city..........	1,309	175	1,487	172	1,164	205	869	73	13,057
Somerville city..........	939	159	691	59	590	49	575	16	6,173
Springfield city..........	1,422	131	1,920	68	1,496	84	909	65	18,201
Worcester city..........	1,934	151	2,093	200	2,263	122	1,074	60	22,994

Table F-3: Places—Employment and Labor Force Status, Civilian Labor Force—*Continued*

	60 and 61 Years		62 to 64 Years		65 to 69 Years		70 Years And Over		60 Years and Over Not In the Labor Force
	Employed	Unemployed	Employed	Unemployed	Employed	Unemployed	Employed	Unemployed	
Michigan									
Ann Arbor city	1,554	83	1,497	86	1,181	115	778	41	11,093
Dearborn city	681	108	1,129	205	615	65	438	26	12,799
Detroit city	5,813	1,006	5,255	902	4,126	445	2,545	378	102,050
Farmington Hills city	1,357	83	1,813	139	984	66	862	43	13,415
Flint city	676	34	547	77	516	96	294	18	15,094
Grand Rapids city	1,887	143	1,953	172	1,794	124	1,034	54	21,349
Kalamazoo city	696	63	765	86	353	0	427	26	7,539
Lansing city	1,278	67	1,548	81	1,057	122	571	0	12,994
Livonia city	1,439	162	1,337	123	1,383	110	775	42	18,057
Rochester Hills city	1,008	84	1,204	95	845	112	397	43	10,219
Southfield city	1,044	152	1,190	114	1,237	109	589	57	13,956
Sterling Heights city	1,707	196	2,088	124	1,163	403	766	161	21,684
Troy city	1,738	80	1,528	207	1,215	110	798	17	11,678
Warren city	1,575	207	1,303	259	949	139	885	89	22,664
Westland city	973	78	797	136	573	150	477	45	13,785
Wyoming city	1,106	261	666	115	463	39	355	50	7,298
Minnesota									
Bloomington city	1,466	192	1,826	168	1,815	83	1,215	83	14,402
Brooklyn Park city	970	54	1,022	97	651	27	354	40	6,442
Duluth city	1,284	64	1,087	75	1,063	11	630	16	12,568
Minneapolis city	5,297	609	4,528	334	3,300	160	2,298	78	34,232
Plymouth city	1,282	67	1,424	82	911	58	579	68	8,500
Rochester city	1,794	0	1,901	26	1,448	71	1,020	15	13,245
St. Cloud city	844	26	880	94	433	79	396	23	7,160
St. Paul city	3,421	353	3,873	128	2,387	176	1,311	70	27,235
Mississippi									
Gulfport city	601	15	729	63	450	0	644	23	9,036
Jackson city	2,032	165	1,927	156	1,791	28	1,065	66	18,942
Missouri									
Columbia city	1,068	96	749	46	1,306	53	539	0	9,391
Independence city	1,508	84	1,569	151	1,334	70	1,011	52	19,696
Kansas City city	5,855	390	7,419	423	4,690	482	4,006	147	52,945
Lee's Summit city	1,579	91	1,580	83	1,205	98	498	37	10,691
O'Fallon city	778	67	1,142	46	733	78	414	51	7,885
St. Charles city	862	0	926	8	796	45	332	13	8,841
St. Joseph city	952	236	1,183	13	654	77	527	25	11,021
St. Louis city	4,151	497	3,828	422	2,955	290	2,185	267	37,865
Springfield city	1,840	202	2,324	149	1,753	139	1,439	0	23,314
Montana									
Billings city	1,633	130	2,226	32	1,811	20	1,104	15	15,326
Missoula city	744	169	831	41	812	75	485	0	7,261
Nebraska									
Lincoln city	4,139	168	4,409	54	3,280	174	2,372	43	27,364
Omaha city	6,457	471	6,624	282	4,978	345	3,809	151	46,067
Nevada									
Henderson city	4,058	396	4,785	465	3,856	543	1,836	621	40,884
Las Vegas city	7,662	1,016	7,712	1,093	6,462	952	5,500	715	76,309
North Las Vegas city	2,258	146	2,135	167	1,809	253	1,001	148	16,447
Reno city	2,970	306	3,561	440	3,141	258	1,676	259	27,847
Sparks city	1,217	184	1,124	246	787	119	394	109	12,263
New Hampshire									
Manchester city	1,502	66	1,969	168	1,238	130	1,134	14	13,168
Nashua city	1,270	66	1,448	58	1,279	82	859	35	10,519
New Jersey									
Camden city	589	85	499	28	328	37	278	40	7,343
Clifton city	1,337	256	1,101	237	1,298	125	564	163	10,316
Elizabeth city	1,287	72	1,366	91	1,451	133	593	61	11,496
Jersey City city	2,756	481	2,888	308	2,434	215	1,040	288	24,426
Newark city	2,500	311	2,326	256	1,918	291	1,177	137	25,018
Passaic city	464	42	356	147	501	119	122	24	6,085
Paterson city	1,349	151	1,312	211	1,154	141	774	125	13,996
Trenton city	733	92	613	84	472	110	552	35	8,195
Union City city	512	188	889	8	367	127	407	37	7,157
New Mexico									
Albuquerque city	7,686	555	7,685	566	6,164	474	4,363	238	71,703
Las Cruces city	1,390	96	849	110	943	37	825	29	13,823
Rio Rancho city	847	64	1,057	41	653	80	522	142	11,312
Santa Fe city	1,508	45	1,690	127	1,661	153	921	98	12,672
New York									
Albany city	1,372	46	1,361	97	785	192	504	16	12,267
Buffalo city	2,501	163	2,910	191	2,124	322	1,717	177	32,676
Mount Vernon city	952	80	1,031	109	1,025	71	530	71	8,756
New Rochelle city	906	61	1,462	179	1,151	52	1,199	9	10,157
New York city	102,223	10,120	114,567	10,411	90,414	8,753	56,954	4,155	1,052,438
Rochester city	2,189	116	1,850	219	1,434	169	856	148	22,060
Schenectady city	593	0	732	64	602	79	459	118	7,899
Syracuse city	1,382	124	1,451	150	1,089	81	877	56	16,567
Yonkers city	3,514	215	3,492	254	2,593	356	1,839	156	28,810

Table F-3: Places—Employment and Labor Force Status, Civilian Labor Force—*Continued*

	60 and 61 Years		62 to 64 Years		65 to 69 Years		70 Years And Over		60 Years and Over Not In the Labor Force
	Employed	Unemployed	Employed	Unemployed	Employed	Unemployed	Employed	Unemployed	
North Carolina									
Asheville city	1,367	190	1,223	42	971	77	675	129	13,735
Charlotte city	8,157	1,176	9,159	1,409	7,561	742	5,083	444	66,476
Concord city	881	90	795	150	606	206	736	20	8,821
Durham city	2,931	231	3,525	179	2,480	118	1,376	17	21,881
Fayetteville city	2,291	320	1,870	212	1,904	218	1,288	69	20,412
Gastonia city	685	12	849	58	823	38	362	39	9,641
Greensboro city	3,616	456	4,170	269	2,732	308	2,545	183	32,398
Greenville city	1,016	110	599	124	603	35	404	0	6,656
High Point city	1,127	218	1,315	249	1,287	135	907	94	12,054
Jacksonville city	368	32	380	0	379	18	255	0	4,338
Raleigh city	4,830	399	4,538	427	3,475	368	2,382	179	35,585
Wilmington city	1,191	65	1,303	222	1,386	96	996	67	15,521
Winston-Salem city	2,762	168	2,924	227	2,797	145	1,927	100	29,859
North Dakota									
Fargo city	1,779	18	1,813	65	1,115	40	1,167	0	10,222
Ohio									
Akron city	2,365	103	2,565	142	1,717	149	1,574	92	27,559
Canton city	1,074	93	982	30	807	70	604	41	9,892
Cincinnati city	3,324	443	3,667	401	2,915	294	2,581	147	34,051
Cleveland city	4,511	605	4,274	614	2,603	283	2,378	186	54,722
Columbus city	8,164	708	9,642	921	7,031	466	4,916	153	73,527
Dayton city	1,505	103	1,559	193	904	72	836	0	18,908
Parma city	1,446	63	1,637	128	1,178	55	643	26	14,674
Toledo city	2,924	544	2,832	282	2,319	141	1,520	111	37,806
Youngstown city	684	120	838	60	634	63	432	44	11,569
Oklahoma									
Broken Arrow city	1,462	94	1,617	78	1,297	111	963	56	10,520
Edmond city	1,117	0	1,390	15	1,217	56	775	14	9,095
Lawton city	837	0	1,234	22	892	15	554	17	9,840
Norman city	1,431	57	2,000	41	1,265	84	1,011	21	12,252
Oklahoma City city	7,027	325	8,770	382	6,282	378	5,551	285	68,173
Tulsa city	5,741	338	5,930	352	5,015	300	3,979	141	48,627
Oregon									
Beaverton city	1,403	133	1,356	91	1,167	207	551	32	9,581
Bend city	1,145	237	1,300	131	874	43	301	55	12,050
Eugene city	2,565	150	2,277	185	1,894	88	1,167	88	21,827
Gresham city	1,299	133	1,368	63	964	92	398	38	12,900
Hillsboro city	1,102	47	922	75	736	37	374	93	7,648
Medford city	945	86	1,150	149	800	58	656	132	12,594
Portland city	8,469	1,081	8,683	1,264	6,279	374	3,298	306	67,105
Salem city	1,760	222	2,243	213	1,508	210	658	47	21,640
Pennsylvania									
Allentown city	1,392	135	1,066	75	864	135	787	42	14,922
Bethlehem city	800	83	1,062	37	900	131	441	25	11,378
Erie city	1,200	61	808	104	747	40	835	18	14,108
Philadelphia city	15,979	1,756	17,632	2,007	13,883	1,333	8,895	954	202,120
Pittsburgh city	3,641	360	4,454	479	3,811	335	2,938	102	43,080
Reading city	484	79	551	107	731	23	508	108	9,449
Scranton city	1,104	81	994	99	872	65	704	63	12,821
Rhode Island									
Cranston city	1,335	144	1,485	208	1,039	54	951	70	11,892
Pawtucket city	945	50	982	76	660	115	553	44	9,154
Providence city	1,808	243	1,704	235	1,055	118	832	79	16,335
Warwick city	1,464	115	1,863	106	1,556	186	1,095	127	13,697
South Carolina									
Charleston city	1,876	170	2,136	197	1,259	179	1,152	86	14,855
Columbia city	1,167	26	1,319	29	867	22	1,107	63	12,008
North Charleston city	813	209	1,309	44	851	145	540	15	9,329
Rock Hill city	548	63	1,042	49	528	51	401	56	7,366
South Dakota									
Rapid City city	1,212	10	1,198	12	1,007	23	864	0	10,023
Sioux Falls city	1,940	98	3,395	126	1,951	0	1,373	0	17,093
Tennessee									
Chattanooga city	2,563	141	2,554	277	2,131	180	1,657	102	26,130
Clarksville city	1,101	57	1,190	81	926	42	661	21	10,742
Jackson city	499	73	768	94	745	185	509	58	9,070
Knoxville city	2,011	96	2,691	178	1,783	74	1,367	73	27,316
Memphis city	8,048	718	7,901	864	6,155	535	4,917	427	72,082
Murfreesboro city	929	199	1,418	152	951	59	429	0	10,798
Nashville-Davidson metropolitan government (bal)	7,576	663	8,803	606	6,512	405	4,742	384	63,797

Table F-3: Places—Employment and Labor Force Status, Civilian Labor Force—*Continued*

	60 and 61 Years		62 to 64 Years		65 to 69 Years		70 Years And Over		60 Years and Over Not In the Labor Force
	Employed	Unemployed	Employed	Unemployed	Employed	Unemployed	Employed	Unemployed	
Texas									
Abilene city	1,361	47	1,421	42	1,397	91	1,142	17	14,868
Allen city	877	28	1,103	32	863	156	203	0	5,268
Amarillo city	2,528	86	2,755	135	1,843	79	1,964	126	23,438
Arlington city	4,560	508	5,252	367	3,904	231	2,149	148	30,420
Austin city	9,251	536	10,279	525	7,014	395	4,236	268	59,403
Baytown city	654	10	941	141	553	91	238	0	8,238
Beaumont city	1,417	61	1,798	171	1,142	63	1,026	98	16,236
Brownsville city	1,269	150	1,715	108	1,368	34	518	69	18,826
Bryan city	832	28	1,093	34	734	35	528	24	7,338
Carrollton city	1,549	122	1,932	169	1,940	182	764	94	8,690
College Station city	772	70	847	35	860	0	405	0	4,315
Corpus Christi city	3,973	220	4,824	266	3,982	151	2,527	154	37,673
Dallas city	13,287	1,092	14,432	1,188	12,289	1,160	8,990	470	112,456
Denton city	1,021	167	1,560	71	1,356	179	622	93	9,717
Edinburg city	567	14	513	20	500	41	247	59	6,426
El Paso city	6,647	378	6,682	446	6,045	302	3,638	172	80,416
Fort Worth city	8,300	680	8,626	712	6,488	682	3,428	270	65,336
Frisco city	1,014	117	1,209	67	1,507	106	670	14	6,966
Garland city	3,273	289	2,844	303	2,601	211	1,257	181	20,274
Grand Prairie city	1,739	141	1,933	123	1,615	159	823	41	13,462
Harlingen city	458	52	508	53	356	94	394	0	9,653
Houston city	24,376	1,644	27,469	1,724	23,247	1,723	14,917	1,009	192,866
Irving city	2,088	114	2,306	205	1,888	133	1,154	86	14,499
Killeen city	970	9	663	21	765	16	303	25	7,510
Laredo city	2,318	113	2,012	47	1,878	155	1,044	79	20,497
League City city	1,031	125	1,308	55	843	66	651	50	7,035
Lewisville city	1,304	54	1,094	20	992	72	338	8	6,841
Longview city	1,217	0	1,055	44	904	58	641	35	11,367
Lubbock city	2,396	194	3,488	94	2,620	66	2,581	61	24,399
McAllen city	1,289	139	1,440	261	1,135	99	472	30	15,737
McKinney city	1,241	0	1,644	42	1,209	0	763	22	10,274
Mesquite city	1,536	36	1,692	151	1,457	31	917	92	12,217
Midland city	1,849	29	1,538	31	1,054	0	1,204	105	12,865
Mission city	610	63	753	49	554	0	252	0	9,260
Missouri City city	1,310	60	1,412	46	1,165	52	333	92	7,083
Odessa city	1,504	35	1,172	35	1,217	34	891	40	10,296
Pasadena city	1,614	129	1,563	232	1,076	41	748	104	14,581
Pearland city	916	99	1,318	62	987	53	560	0	7,093
Pharr city	477	117	682	25	647	0	187	0	8,436
Plano city	4,000	194	4,783	407	4,089	248	2,188	177	24,005
Richardson city	1,855	80	1,874	99	1,533	67	1,109	122	11,121
Round Rock city	1,138	42	937	215	848	114	591	81	6,516
San Angelo city	1,301	0	983	63	1,234	24	876	0	13,060
San Antonio city	15,027	600	15,026	800	13,564	621	9,085	411	155,083
Sugar Land city	1,158	84	2,489	78	1,415	57	790	16	8,554
Temple city	618	18	1,028	25	854	66	416	109	10,750
Tyler city	1,260	22	1,746	0	1,062	47	1,182	31	14,279
Waco city	1,354	30	1,638	65	972	66	1,089	113	13,914
Wichita Falls city	1,196	49	1,462	83	1,095	39	1,058	51	12,830
Utah									
Layton city	820	99	661	119	298	11	381	18	5,771
Ogden city	786	158	803	45	735	0	578	0	7,646
Orem city	880	75	1,000	51	852	107	490	7	7,519
Provo city	956	169	681	124	704	19	531	0	6,414
St. George city	602	141	1,175	129	681	90	631	19	13,659
Salt Lake City city	2,095	119	2,585	175	1,754	149	1,489	14	17,741
Sandy city	1,496	49	1,446	101	1,190	56	589	49	8,691
West Jordan city	1,211	128	1,151	82	697	116	411	37	5,648
West Valley City city	1,264	125	1,476	38	1,546	32	575	30	9,248
Virginia									
Alexandria city	2,064	179	2,746	85	2,064	72	1,369	131	11,425
Chesapeake city	2,984	256	3,330	124	2,591	108	1,424	0	25,305
Hampton city	1,776	86	1,546	135	1,642	91	1,132	62	17,797
Lynchburg city	1,162	12	1,071	14	621	19	667	21	10,736
Newport News city	2,248	92	2,376	277	2,008	78	1,191	43	19,761
Norfolk city	2,339	343	2,746	62	1,847	164	1,530	37	24,299
Portsmouth city	1,075	62	1,251	72	742	34	549	45	14,438
Richmond city	2,266	201	2,503	214	2,472	174	1,555	16	23,904
Roanoke city	1,462	41	1,565	112	1,314	41	610	46	14,794
Suffolk city	1,398	43	919	44	1,072	53	548	17	10,640
Virginia Beach city	6,065	361	7,024	273	5,511	146	3,346	124	47,929

Table F-3: Places—Employment and Labor Force Status, Civilian Labor Force—*Continued*

	60 and 61 Years		62 to 64 Years		65 to 69 Years		70 Years And Over		60 Years and Over Not In the Labor Force
	Employed	Unemployed	Employed	Unemployed	Employed	Unemployed	Employed	Unemployed	
Washington									
Auburn city	1,172	90	986	124	641	48	368	45	8,593
Bellevue city	1,874	215	1,989	152	1,559	120	1,334	144	16,383
Bellingham city	1,156	90	1,649	93	1,158	8	420	9	10,679
Everett city	1,452	261	1,573	97	1,581	52	488	49	11,122
Federal Way city	908	238	1,000	211	950	56	562	28	10,186
Kennewick city	1,130	42	1,073	38	794	54	580	58	8,592
Kent city	1,727	232	1,397	136	1,015	112	499	0	12,270
Renton city	1,250	55	1,151	33	788	54	394	39	9,843
Seattle city	8,993	523	11,973	877	7,745	523	4,326	224	68,577
Spokane city	2,813	165	3,493	234	2,383	188	1,124	58	29,851
Spokane Valley city	1,558	256	1,751	219	906	174	579	42	13,541
Tacoma city	3,051	255	2,571	134	1,827	106	1,079	129	24,553
Vancouver city	1,833	214	2,995	305	1,681	253	819	110	23,260
Yakima city	1,161	75	1,058	65	1,123	142	396	44	13,003
Wisconsin									
Appleton city	1,190	107	1,055	79	883	48	319	17	8,915
Eau Claire city	878	50	1,040	47	680	96	642	55	7,145
Green Bay city	1,414	89	1,191	65	882	65	563	10	13,028
Kenosha city	1,059	144	863	183	989	13	653	15	11,236
Madison city	3,418	121	3,162	227	2,394	106	1,936	82	22,307
Milwaukee city	5,641	962	5,262	557	4,370	405	2,985	258	58,840
Oshkosh city	863	56	875	86	505	59	416	16	8,365
Racine city	980	10	1,021	121	711	107	353	109	9,058
Waukesha city	1,089	138	1,202	56	690	20	306	24	8,491

Table F-4: Metropolitan Statistical Areas—Employment and Labor Force Status, Civilian Labor Force

	60 and 61 Years		62 to 64 Years		65 to 69 Years		70 Years And Over		60 Years and Over Not In the Labor Force
	Employed	Unemployed	Employed	Unemployed	Employed	Unemployed	Employed	Unemployed	
Abilene, TX	2,063	77	2,438	74	2,063	93	1,731	44	23,072
Akron, OH	10,569	515	11,598	1,035	8,369	510	5,910	519	106,643
Albany, GA	2,105	188	1,402	22	1,269	83	883	67	22,612
Albany-Schenectady-Troy, NY	13,981	797	14,532	959	10,798	845	7,152	578	129,483
Albuquerque, NM	12,686	966	13,140	1,036	10,260	918	6,873	551	122,137
Alexandria, LA	1,452	112	1,631	87	1,826	38	1,578	55	22,532
Allentown-Bethlehem-Easton, PA-NJ	12,262	878	13,248	1,119	10,181	1,530	6,663	619	129,982
Altoona, PA	2,111	66	1,966	100	1,727	30	1,087	43	24,378
Amarillo, TX	3,474	86	3,862	188	2,467	90	2,419	155	31,367
Ames, IA	1,046	31	1,403	22	763	32	612	21	9,242
Anchorage, AK	5,342	192	6,326	192	4,191	173	2,463	112	31,233
Anderson, IN	1,675	93	1,729	133	1,229	55	1,294	110	22,345
Anderson, SC	2,039	139	2,675	221	1,778	224	1,717	203	32,067
Ann Arbor, MI	5,129	244	5,004	386	3,670	356	2,366	154	38,207
Anniston-Oxford, AL	1,784	0	1,462	98	1,040	0	713	9	19,385
Appleton, WI	3,458	223	3,078	238	2,026	130	1,216	31	28,881
Asheville, NC	6,946	654	7,219	549	6,130	251	4,546	366	84,786
Athens-Clarke County, GA	1,842	183	2,160	38	1,806	84	1,206	133	22,497
Atlanta-Sandy Springs-Marietta, GA	63,103	6,970	70,070	7,185	50,885	4,625	28,179	2,726	536,257
Atlantic City-Hammonton, NJ	4,370	377	5,136	593	4,399	491	3,368	369	38,204
Auburn-Opelika, AL	1,600	33	1,645	0	1,380	115	1,163	38	14,445
Augusta-Richmond County, GA-SC	6,849	430	6,721	462	5,539	221	3,639	118	81,098
Austin-Round Rock-San Marcos, TX	20,901	1,429	23,991	1,644	16,970	1,072	10,077	769	154,051
Bakersfield-Delano, CA	7,450	736	8,271	766	6,656	596	4,267	619	85,404
Baltimore-Towson, MD	42,861	2,603	47,952	2,811	39,788	2,643	26,128	1,887	347,004
Bangor, ME	2,584	145	3,005	199	1,644	69	1,410	87	24,199
Barnstable Town, MA	4,365	390	5,276	448	5,426	598	4,199	498	52,419
Baton Rouge, LA	10,094	769	10,567	786	9,188	721	6,236	188	95,689
Battle Creek, MI	1,804	288	1,822	117	1,236	146	1,089	51	22,636
Bay City, MI	1,458	68	1,216	119	1,039	133	804	134	20,449
Beaumont-Port Arthur, TX	4,521	282	5,148	339	3,441	219	2,853	290	56,285
Bellingham, WA	3,420	221	3,723	494	2,446	105	1,413	72	29,420
Bend, OR	2,481	566	2,703	346	1,707	178	804	118	27,729
Billings, MT	2,647	152	3,077	98	3,088	91	1,646	26	22,518
Binghamton, NY	4,044	193	4,214	519	3,066	396	2,149	143	42,595
Birmingham-Hoover, AL	15,181	917	15,515	1,072	13,089	821	8,810	588	161,836
Bismarck, ND	2,036	77	2,177	30	1,581	66	1,424	44	15,016
Blacksburg-Christiansburg-Radford, VA	2,214	49	2,355	46	1,727	71	1,561	90	21,184
Bloomington, IN	2,744	223	2,489	141	2,112	67	1,546	58	24,527
Bloomington-Normal, IL	2,298	108	2,345	81	1,275	111	1,268	19	18,903
Boise City-Nampa, ID	8,636	497	8,315	777	6,214	594	3,578	280	76,014
Boston-Cambridge-Quincy, MA-NH	72,791	5,762	85,943	7,105	71,105	6,179	46,507	3,233	579,448
Boulder, CO	5,048	381	4,506	464	4,747	235	1,746	75	30,137
Bowling Green, KY	1,375	121	1,196	113	1,208	59	975	88	15,612
Bremerton-Silverdale, WA	4,018	371	4,532	340	2,914	377	1,268	187	38,874
Bridgeport-Stamford-Norwalk, CT	14,136	1,181	17,601	1,277	15,577	2,088	11,049	926	114,898
Brownsville-Harlingen, TX	3,539	296	3,601	261	2,971	261	1,890	145	50,627
Brunswick, GA	1,481	22	2,398	177	1,659	176	1,395	36	19,042
Buffalo-Niagara Falls, NY	15,714	1,023	16,395	936	13,637	1,239	12,376	895	185,762
Burlington, NC	2,027	144	2,237	303	2,209	162	1,303	245	22,427
Burlington-South Burlington, VT	3,762	81	4,393	223	2,843	92	2,038	46	24,461
Canton-Massillon, OH	6,451	531	6,679	416	5,588	368	3,904	197	68,468
Cape Coral-Fort Myers, FL	8,270	982	9,562	1,021	9,794	1,580	8,234	1,243	159,386
Cape Girardeau-Jackson, MO-IL	1,336	73	1,569	113	1,090	88	780	19	15,149
Casper, WY	1,579	91	1,457	78	1,182	39	757	20	8,988
Cedar Rapids, IA	3,936	125	4,583	128	3,631	140	2,191	105	35,648
Champaign-Urbana, IL	3,544	149	3,197	93	2,246	120	1,775	75	26,581
Charleston, WV	4,627	276	4,261	93	3,563	62	2,813	25	54,179
Charleston-North Charleston-Summerville, SC	8,550	850	10,183	540	7,340	870	5,033	390	86,067
Charlotte-Gastonia-Rock Hill, NC-SC	20,358	2,481	25,027	2,753	18,560	1,867	11,814	1,117	191,836
Charlottesville, VA	2,908	148	3,469	180	2,571	69	2,002	60	29,613
Chattanooga, TN-GA	8,544	419	8,687	583	7,351	714	4,780	262	83,154
Cheyenne, WY	1,495	39	1,351	37	1,314	45	606	0	12,195
Chicago-Joliet-Naperville, IL-IN-WI	124,472	13,022	141,209	13,282	109,524	9,055	69,280	5,544	1,123,368
Chico, CA	2,798	299	3,329	395	2,075	409	1,893	193	38,175
Cincinnati-Middletown, OH-KY-IN	30,357	2,643	32,326	2,367	24,219	1,637	18,114	887	276,378
Clarksville, TN-KY	2,303	215	2,708	138	1,856	86	1,637	44	29,407
Cleveland, TN	1,399	91	1,439	86	789	167	1,068	46	19,634
Cleveland-Elyria-Mentor, OH	33,216	2,963	36,341	3,067	28,210	1,943	19,418	1,076	325,069
Coeur d'Alene, ID	2,054	149	2,252	328	1,438	128	1,073	75	23,156
College Station-Bryan, TX	2,669	147	3,288	99	2,326	78	1,662	38	20,239
Colorado Springs, CO	8,611	816	10,289	885	7,675	570	4,043	451	70,982
Columbia, MO	1,996	177	1,981	135	2,209	70	1,126	0	17,303
Columbia, SC	11,140	633	11,790	634	8,416	560	5,577	419	97,226
Columbus, GA-AL	3,479	201	3,399	198	2,784	285	1,905	219	38,082
Columbus, IN	1,228	41	1,228	56	1,046	7	740	13	11,611
Columbus, OH	22,984	1,334	28,113	1,758	20,151	1,179	13,098	443	209,168
Corpus Christi, TX	5,707	282	6,716	274	5,305	253	3,719	172	59,229
Corvallis, OR	1,319	119	1,607	51	1,241	50	453	31	11,163
Crestview-Fort Walton Beach-Destin, FL	2,677	104	2,929	111	2,038	105	1,439	271	26,411

Table F-4: Metropolitan Statistical Areas—Employment and Labor Force Status, Civilian Labor Force—*Continued*

	60 and 61 Years		62 to 64 Years		65 to 69 Years		70 Years And Over		60 Years and Over Not In the Labor Force
	Employed	Unemployed	Employed	Unemployed	Employed	Unemployed	Employed	Unemployed	
Cumberland, MD-WV	1,383	142	1,312	48	1,321	52	673	10	20,924
Dallas-Fort Worth-Arlington, TX	78,989	6,015	90,381	5,789	71,008	5,661	41,573	2,637	596,672
Dalton, GA	1,378	92	1,700	359	1,390	92	885	51	17,102
Danville, IL	1,211	62	1,305	55	887	44	643	63	14,017
Danville, VA	1,901	114	2,011	113	1,517	49	1,424	60	19,837
Davenport-Moline-Rock Island, IA-IL	6,004	342	6,118	555	4,895	158	3,063	89	62,069
Dayton, OH	12,452	934	14,659	806	10,896	687	7,472	359	134,631
Decatur, AL	1,975	170	2,080	127	2,023	177	1,504	73	23,986
Decatur, IL	1,957	114	1,699	53	1,552	101	955	12	19,312
Deltona-Daytona Beach-Ormond Beach, FL	6,363	734	7,273	995	7,123	1,153	4,737	541	112,497
Denver-Aurora-Broomfield, CO	37,596	3,283	39,203	2,911	31,937	2,989	18,060	1,498	270,288
Des Moines-West Des Moines, IA	8,895	383	9,367	419	6,741	447	5,441	182	65,662
Detroit-Warren-Livonia, MI	52,697	6,444	54,659	6,749	42,572	5,134	26,688	2,954	638,259
Dothan, AL	2,141	95	2,066	118	1,859	87	1,373	48	24,395
Dover, DE	1,804	64	2,475	82	2,209	169	1,311	98	24,287
Dubuque, IA	1,689	42	1,818	125	1,213	29	1,064	115	14,033
Duluth, MN-WI	4,202	246	4,078	192	3,047	109	1,816	101	49,129
Durham-Chapel Hill, NC	7,686	769	8,042	396	6,724	296	3,976	111	60,992
Eau Claire, WI	2,430	167	2,656	163	1,747	117	1,581	123	22,444
El Centro, CA	965	265	1,376	165	940	202	934	28	20,828
Elizabethtown, KY	1,367	163	1,255	109	1,361	59	873	39	15,106
Elkhart-Goshen, IN	3,247	385	2,937	260	1,988	336	1,756	50	24,047
Elmira, NY	1,381	124	1,408	76	1,125	40	484	70	14,754
El Paso, TX	7,791	509	7,727	615	6,492	361	4,011	227	92,496
Erie, PA	4,520	306	4,289	236	2,795	252	2,441	72	43,432
Eugene-Springfield, OR	5,882	474	5,652	438	4,083	400	3,103	223	59,156
Evansville, IN-KY	5,595	331	5,525	259	4,314	166	3,684	94	53,952
Fairbanks, AK	1,209	48	1,358	29	910	87	521	11	7,384
Fargo, ND-MN	3,234	41	3,764	175	2,667	85	1,919	7	20,892
Farmington, NM	1,665	61	1,558	35	1,630	10	833	42	15,145
Fayetteville, NC	3,939	533	3,538	263	3,150	408	2,093	128	37,213
Fayetteville-Springdale-Rogers, AR-MO	6,115	297	6,600	319	5,084	358	3,229	82	54,525
Flagstaff, AZ	1,719	188	1,350	82	1,636	25	819	69	13,335
Flint, MI	4,044	345	3,998	438	2,926	362	2,186	286	70,555
Florence, SC	2,418	391	2,622	169	2,503	179	1,669	135	31,751
Florence-Muscle Shoals, AL	2,229	120	1,902	140	1,753	128	992	0	28,216
Fond du Lac, WI	1,945	77	1,847	161	1,317	142	855	47	15,834
Fort Collins-Loveland, CO	5,144	402	5,075	348	4,549	322	2,386	76	37,309
Fort Smith, AR-OK	3,332	191	3,773	126	2,711	119	2,329	111	47,250
Fort Wayne, IN	6,357	630	6,794	414	4,385	242	3,599	200	53,587
Fresno, CA	9,191	1,378	10,755	927	8,412	983	6,022	546	101,546
Gadsden, AL	1,377	18	1,351	39	1,012	55	820	39	19,071
Gainesville, FL	3,671	162	4,036	132	2,689	97	2,186	176	31,520
Gainesville, GA	1,668	129	2,777	223	1,683	225	1,266	0	23,100
Glens Falls, NY	2,078	171	2,409	196	2,162	176	1,095	55	22,310
Goldsboro, NC	1,827	113	1,653	60	1,342	64	1,037	66	17,459
Grand Forks, ND-MN	1,688	22	1,453	82	1,347	46	923	10	11,735
Grand Junction, CO	1,919	192	2,420	124	1,977	174	1,261	82	23,248
Grand Rapids-Wyoming, MI	10,226	1,084	9,498	901	7,943	673	5,311	310	99,241
Great Falls, MT	1,185	53	1,453	44	869	5	905	9	13,545
Greeley, CO	3,211	127	3,511	232	2,638	408	1,387	187	26,760
Green Bay, WI	4,831	301	4,330	249	2,987	190	2,165	105	40,963
Greensboro-High Point, NC	9,708	1,325	11,619	839	9,371	772	6,197	505	101,428
Greenville, NC	2,214	292	2,066	277	1,906	189	1,525	94	20,818
Greenville-Mauldin-Easley, SC	7,869	1,151	8,893	673	7,563	870	4,928	338	90,042
Gulfport-Biloxi, MS	2,793	192	3,083	271	2,436	76	2,142	88	34,834
Hagerstown-Martinsburg, MD-WV	4,324	264	4,265	326	3,018	368	2,195	192	39,527
Hanford-Corcoran, CA	1,093	137	1,522	129	1,275	51	644	28	13,052
Harrisburg-Carlisle, PA	8,829	533	9,209	698	6,974	514	6,448	309	83,347
Harrisonburg, VA	1,670	88	2,056	16	1,390	13	1,315	41	16,026
Hartford-West Hartford-East Hartford, CT	18,980	1,567	24,361	2,143	18,765	2,098	11,449	1,226	170,090
Hattiesburg, MS	1,367	71	1,737	87	1,656	83	1,076	16	17,940
Hickory-Lenoir-Morganton, NC	5,138	584	5,930	445	4,429	550	2,952	290	61,080
Hinesville-Fort Stewart, GA	487	38	541	126	480	0	212	30	6,365
Holland-Grand Haven, MI	3,455	514	3,395	366	2,681	168	2,200	167	32,447
Honolulu, HI	16,065	782	17,458	540	16,433	403	10,298	289	137,728
Hot Springs, AR	1,303	23	1,785	164	1,276	55	1,437	36	21,080
Houma-Bayou Cane-Thibodaux, LA	1,874	213	2,686	38	2,589	89	1,627	43	26,550
Houston-Sugar Land-Baytown, TX	73,159	5,282	82,476	5,734	64,538	4,708	37,805	2,914	553,384
Huntington-Ashland, WV-KY-OH	3,930	129	3,278	154	2,925	143	1,685	189	55,062
Huntsville, AL	6,008	302	6,140	336	5,019	298	3,489	300	55,365
Idaho Falls, ID	1,746	74	2,031	44	1,697	136	824	68	14,387
Indianapolis-Carmel, IN	24,130	1,732	24,443	1,740	17,985	1,355	12,689	1,077	202,475
Iowa City, IA	2,650	40	2,828	62	1,854	6	1,327	2	14,927
Ithaca, NY	1,622	16	1,737	93	1,264	87	940	0	11,304
Jackson, MI	2,176	271	2,040	183	1,492	216	1,290	47	25,762
Jackson, MS	6,617	415	7,276	561	6,687	137	4,179	274	65,591
Jackson, TN	1,013	78	1,748	139	1,341	185	742	102	16,574
Jacksonville, FL	17,492	2,118	20,343	2,041	16,327	1,678	9,714	769	181,062
Jacksonville, NC	1,536	55	1,486	92	1,352	45	724	15	14,778

Table F-4: Metropolitan Statistical Areas—Employment and Labor Force Status, Civilian Labor Force—*Continued*

	60 and 61 Years		62 to 64 Years		65 to 69 Years		70 Years And Over		60 Years and Over Not In the Labor Force
	Employed	Unemployed	Employed	Unemployed	Employed	Unemployed	Employed	Unemployed	
Janesville, WI	1,808	141	2,799	115	1,448	113	1,220	46	23,377
Jefferson City, MO	2,314	105	2,344	125	1,689	101	1,199	55	21,034
Johnson City, TN	2,698	145	3,146	198	2,278	103	1,428	86	37,048
Johnstown, PA	2,244	133	2,269	91	1,659	102	1,292	56	29,185
Jonesboro, AR	1,701	41	1,761	165	1,279	72	703	36	16,953
Joplin, MO	2,321	172	2,400	213	2,178	57	1,431	70	25,388
Kalamazoo-Portage, MI	4,350	502	4,944	373	2,966	120	2,157	270	45,816
Kankakee-Bradley, IL	1,276	115	1,591	167	1,186	64	1,070	47	16,282
Kansas City, MO-KS	28,152	2,063	34,721	1,900	25,473	1,682	17,419	1,011	252,652
Kennewick-Pasco-Richland, WA	3,718	126	4,088	218	2,234	85	1,807	137	29,665
Killeen-Temple-Fort Hood, TX	3,907	169	3,712	229	3,149	177	2,094	140	41,192
Kingsport-Bristol-Bristol, TN-VA	4,501	305	4,449	375	3,562	226	3,377	170	63,256
Kingston, NY	3,581	263	3,532	427	3,166	348	1,887	126	28,044
Knoxville, TN	10,190	628	11,662	612	8,272	460	5,510	357	112,962
Kokomo, IN	1,219	87	1,246	45	1,096	66	774	17	18,617
La Crosse, WI-MN	1,945	32	2,536	129	1,418	139	1,512	35	19,089
Lafayette, IN	2,470	144	3,014	101	1,919	125	1,309	76	21,553
Lafayette, LA	3,204	206	4,112	156	3,481	105	2,337	61	29,820
Lake Charles, LA	2,622	225	2,982	288	2,023	205	1,619	54	27,657
Lake Havasu City-Kingman, AZ	2,549	509	3,680	340	2,621	420	1,907	278	53,172
Lakeland-Winter Haven, FL	7,873	923	9,274	870	7,016	867	4,972	805	117,332
Lancaster, PA	8,215	504	9,324	484	8,123	437	7,155	306	74,334
Lansing-East Lansing, MI	6,644	398	5,976	471	4,482	374	2,926	241	61,002
Laredo, TX	2,360	113	2,084	47	1,936	155	1,107	79	21,497
Las Cruces, NM	2,661	213	2,063	148	2,226	208	1,743	68	28,015
Las Vegas-Paradise, NV	25,773	3,155	27,104	3,435	22,339	3,509	14,838	2,693	236,550
Lawrence, KS	1,339	74	1,843	27	1,373	22	980	22	9,545
Lawton, OK	1,250	111	1,535	40	1,157	15	813	51	13,265
Lebanon, PA	1,897	150	2,836	95	2,002	76	1,596	129	22,521
Lewiston-Auburn, ME	1,554	156	2,005	142	1,161	61	1,152	80	16,325
Lexington-Fayette, KY	6,031	298	7,702	427	5,833	252	4,441	192	56,253
Lima, OH	1,550	112	1,310	139	1,115	89	948	12	16,457
Lincoln, NE	5,150	177	5,500	57	4,025	194	3,130	71	32,849
Little Rock-North Little Rock-Conway, AR	9,033	371	8,448	317	9,128	416	5,469	310	93,609
Logan, UT-ID	971	99	1,172	30	1,095	54	571	8	10,673
Longview, TX	3,397	188	3,201	251	3,023	205	1,947	51	30,970
Longview, WA	1,313	151	1,307	144	997	78	616	64	19,194
Los Angeles-Long Beach-Santa Ana, CA	155,498	16,948	172,762	18,571	145,079	14,970	96,432	8,246	1,472,160
Louisville/Jefferson County, KY-IN	16,758	1,810	19,208	1,421	15,608	1,078	10,034	609	180,083
Lubbock, TX	3,209	218	4,258	94	3,280	126	3,012	95	31,170
Lynchburg, VA	4,030	203	4,347	69	3,168	131	3,091	72	42,728
Macon, GA	2,433	170	2,998	74	2,305	130	1,959	41	34,690
Madera-Chowchilla, CA	1,620	104	1,768	69	1,303	83	791	119	19,726
Madison, WI	8,793	322	9,990	662	7,483	333	5,057	195	64,013
Manchester-Nashua, NH	6,700	532	7,794	502	5,500	372	3,523	90	48,224
Manhattan, KS	1,483	27	1,694	22	1,600	51	857	0	9,691
Mankato-North Mankato, MN	1,628	59	1,350	72	1,084	12	687	66	11,476
Mansfield, OH	1,775	278	2,162	66	1,365	187	1,314	63	21,910
McAllen-Edinburg-Mission, TX	5,763	936	5,844	620	4,795	231	2,136	196	84,967
Medford, OR	3,409	487	4,125	425	3,175	276	1,915	160	38,305
Memphis, TN-MS-AR	17,804	1,353	18,254	1,548	14,152	1,002	9,947	913	150,725
Merced, CA	2,417	273	2,407	333	1,975	186	1,099	91	27,175
Miami-Fort Lauderdale-Pompano Beach, FL	76,015	8,964	90,466	10,504	78,775	9,461	55,740	6,820	891,734
Michigan City-La Porte, IN	1,817	262	1,746	46	1,499	113	887	59	16,716
Midland, TX	2,115	86	1,788	31	1,467	0	1,478	105	15,233
Milwaukee-Waukesha-West Allis, WI	23,141	2,067	23,726	1,690	17,628	1,023	11,747	1,047	202,838
Minneapolis-St. Paul-Bloomington, MN-WI	51,917	3,925	51,085	3,384	37,267	2,066	23,337	1,186	366,000
Missoula, MT	1,572	245	1,802	81	1,556	135	854	4	13,129
Mobile, AL	5,334	497	5,349	251	4,920	257	2,697	204	59,946
Modesto, CA	5,405	468	5,247	571	4,333	681	2,860	313	61,459
Monroe, LA	1,918	78	2,127	118	2,312	80	1,547	74	24,424
Monroe, MI	1,770	242	1,702	309	1,240	65	980	23	24,624
Montgomery, AL	5,131	180	4,805	213	4,260	452	2,751	132	48,712
Morgantown, WV	1,701	10	1,561	47	1,344	0	810	42	17,130
Morristown, TN	1,816	238	1,810	254	1,771	190	1,320	84	24,291
Mount Vernon-Anacortes, WA	1,908	162	2,263	139	1,539	75	884	82	20,945
Muncie, IN	1,465	86	1,447	125	1,238	97	985	140	18,503
Muskegon-Norton Shores, MI	2,097	244	1,687	230	1,434	159	1,124	91	26,458
Myrtle Beach-North Myrtle Beach-Conway, SC	4,231	499	5,070	525	4,526	336	2,516	544	52,785
Napa, CA	2,503	130	2,717	181	2,324	133	1,718	82	20,231
Naples-Marco Island, FL	6,317	268	5,869	453	6,948	858	5,272	421	87,219
Nashville-Davidson--Murfreesboro--Franklin, TN	21,284	1,742	23,520	1,752	17,639	1,067	12,198	595	185,463
New Haven-Milford, CT	13,625	1,234	16,755	1,645	13,060	973	9,142	739	119,972
New Orleans-Metairie-Kenner, LA	16,414	1,069	18,736	1,300	14,381	1,008	9,437	728	155,848
New York-Northern New Jersey-Long Island, NY-NJ-PA	266,982	25,384	299,666	27,096	252,075	24,039	172,081	14,360	2,496,992
Niles-Benton Harbor, MI	2,152	289	2,776	219	2,084	151	1,637	76	26,325
North Port-Bradenton-Sarasota, FL	9,996	1,602	12,641	1,358	12,915	1,838	9,903	1,454	201,514
Norwich-New London, CT	4,753	225	5,491	430	4,355	250	2,544	213	39,199
Ocala, FL	4,367	446	5,152	481	4,665	552	3,223	523	94,371
Ocean City, NJ	2,174	246	2,151	212	1,751	178	1,588	245	20,830

Table F-4: Metropolitan Statistical Areas—Employment and Labor Force Status, Civilian Labor Force—*Continued*

	60 and 61 Years		62 to 64 Years		65 to 69 Years		70 Years And Over		60 Years and Over Not In the Labor Force
	Employed	Unemployed	Employed	Unemployed	Employed	Unemployed	Employed	Unemployed	
Odessa, TX	1,792	35	1,393	35	1,708	85	1,057	82	13,789
Ogden-Clearfield, UT	5,965	359	6,188	296	5,453	93	3,175	172	52,584
Oklahoma City, OK	16,050	630	18,851	607	14,634	701	11,818	479	156,495
Olympia, WA	4,109	390	5,056	116	2,820	233	1,655	106	37,333
Omaha-Council Bluffs, NE-IA	14,336	822	14,449	522	11,084	490	7,715	283	96,345
Orlando-Kissimmee-Sanford, FL	27,582	3,435	29,934	3,016	25,010	2,550	16,115	1,523	282,042
Oshkosh-Neenah, WI	2,465	113	2,534	147	1,873	131	1,186	34	23,719
Owensboro, KY	1,449	51	1,736	68	1,317	4	960	27	18,614
Oxnard-Thousand Oaks-Ventura, CA	12,004	1,157	12,873	1,554	11,859	1,066	6,855	531	97,485
Palm Bay-Melbourne-Titusville, FL	7,438	980	8,318	1,335	7,550	1,034	6,005	795	117,079
Palm Coast, FL	1,692	294	1,489	227	1,208	213	950	53	27,070
Panama City-Lynn Haven-Panama City Beach, FL	2,399	317	2,227	270	2,204	264	1,620	237	25,836
Parkersburg-Marietta-Vienna, WV-OH	2,146	128	2,031	117	2,046	101	1,394	107	30,354
Pascagoula, MS	1,906	53	1,911	177	1,389	68	980	112	23,528
Pensacola-Ferry Pass-Brent, FL	5,871	266	6,857	586	5,598	502	3,059	181	68,767
Peoria, IL	5,544	244	5,244	316	4,846	122	3,820	188	59,285
Philadelphia-Camden-Wilmington, PA-NJ-DE-MD	86,686	7,181	99,973	8,728	81,019	7,222	58,351	4,912	795,799
Phoenix-Mesa-Glendale, AZ	51,277	4,626	57,733	4,329	45,455	4,271	28,161	2,511	566,074
Pine Bluff, AR	1,247	107	1,074	62	1,009	44	1,010	49	15,303
Pittsburgh, PA	40,682	2,487	41,603	2,750	32,967	2,370	25,468	1,545	416,506
Pittsfield, MA	2,541	233	2,845	232	2,224	251	1,894	129	24,330
Pocatello, ID	1,011	10	1,174	45	726	56	662	3	11,286
Portland-South Portland-Biddeford, ME	10,132	466	10,415	645	8,516	368	5,244	310	77,971
Portland-Vancouver-Hillsboro, OR-WA	33,575	3,404	35,457	3,443	26,163	2,329	13,547	1,374	281,224
Port St. Lucie, FL	5,556	461	6,341	883	6,950	1,029	5,066	501	100,319
Poughkeepsie-Newburgh-Middletown, NY	9,844	922	9,652	924	8,086	877	6,205	571	85,338
Prescott, AZ	3,505	1,013	4,111	253	2,980	372	2,930	231	57,693
Providence-New Bedford-Fall River, RI-MA	25,488	2,478	26,916	2,486	21,642	1,983	15,136	1,282	232,099
Provo-Orem, UT	4,363	326	4,526	389	3,749	250	2,372	112	35,259
Pueblo, CO	2,161	214	2,239	214	2,016	95	1,096	95	27,110
Punta Gorda, FL	2,661	318	3,124	431	2,717	247	2,747	282	59,137
Racine, WI	3,003	102	3,083	378	2,154	231	1,462	207	27,074
Raleigh-Cary, NC	14,343	943	15,451	1,231	11,666	913	6,721	491	112,563
Rapid City, SD	2,282	70	1,896	50	1,887	47	1,401	9	17,252
Reading, PA	5,769	258	6,352	653	5,301	509	3,406	260	61,622
Redding, CA	2,121	349	2,933	171	2,264	175	1,277	283	34,236
Reno-Sparks, NV	6,834	726	7,119	845	5,662	606	3,267	527	56,959
Richmond, VA	18,609	1,079	21,328	1,311	16,653	696	10,306	297	165,539
Riverside-San Bernardino-Ontario, CA	42,650	5,982	43,428	5,596	33,277	5,617	21,488	3,016	495,727
Roanoke, VA	5,006	348	6,133	326	4,287	186	3,027	129	53,896
Rochester, MN	3,228	16	3,256	94	2,664	106	1,943	53	23,766
Rochester, NY	15,449	858	16,146	1,126	14,457	843	8,685	578	158,384
Rockford, IL	4,909	453	5,370	491	4,234	452	3,128	304	48,907
Rocky Mount, NC	1,904	302	2,372	278	1,498	113	1,447	78	24,470
Rome, GA	1,196	112	1,334	92	789	166	875	40	15,052
Sacramento--Arden-Arcade--Roseville, CA	26,774	3,155	28,145	2,672	21,130	2,280	12,916	1,527	292,315
Saginaw-Saginaw Township North, MI	2,297	278	2,011	126	1,750	146	1,375	138	34,995
St. Cloud, MN	2,703	120	3,238	192	2,098	132	1,510	78	23,186
St. George, UT	1,257	212	1,826	137	1,592	160	1,252	31	25,917
St. Joseph, MO-KS	1,890	250	1,896	51	1,413	126	1,165	30	18,603
St. Louis, MO-IL	39,734	3,028	43,911	3,080	34,091	2,031	22,854	1,522	395,542
Salem, OR	4,644	525	5,674	583	4,398	367	2,423	188	57,160
Salinas, CA	5,064	259	5,537	722	4,452	372	3,477	267	47,404
Salisbury, MD	1,594	180	1,134	92	1,738	74	1,082	174	17,829
Salt Lake City, UT	13,431	791	16,073	834	12,140	601	7,232	243	99,493
San Angelo, TX	1,483	10	1,381	63	1,510	24	1,172	0	15,905
San Antonio-New Braunfels, TX	26,471	1,208	28,164	1,409	22,785	929	14,455	785	263,458
San Diego-Carlsbad-San Marcos, CA	39,282	4,157	41,215	3,543	33,646	2,777	20,246	1,723	375,411
Sandusky, OH	1,361	126	1,739	217	1,274	164	872	17	13,680
San Francisco-Oakland-Fremont, CA	67,626	6,042	74,928	7,110	57,856	5,038	35,586	2,273	573,088
San Jose-Sunnyvale-Santa Clara, CA	22,910	3,192	25,167	3,203	20,730	2,216	12,138	1,213	211,111
San Luis Obispo-Paso Robles, CA	4,155	271	4,585	524	3,510	284	2,573	208	44,577
Santa Barbara-Santa Maria-Goleta, CA	5,254	374	5,879	674	5,700	414	3,635	282	54,665
Santa Cruz-Watsonville, CA	4,819	433	3,688	290	3,956	326	2,187	137	31,761
Santa Fe, NM	3,318	165	3,388	244	3,300	290	1,631	117	23,275
Santa Rosa-Petaluma, CA	9,023	1,101	9,604	1,065	7,520	678	4,313	522	71,591
Savannah, GA	4,422	249	4,819	232	3,572	304	2,092	77	46,178
Scranton--Wilkes-Barre, PA	8,328	834	9,925	604	7,783	554	6,280	313	103,260
Seattle-Tacoma-Bellevue, WA	51,681	3,933	56,649	3,850	40,930	3,152	21,515	1,720	401,113
Sebastian-Vero Beach, FL	2,135	573	1,682	618	2,146	318	1,986	265	39,156

Table F-4: Metropolitan Statistical Areas—Employment and Labor Force Status, Civilian Labor Force—*Continued*

	60 and 61 Years		62 to 64 Years		65 to 69 Years		70 Years And Over		60 Years and Over Not In the Labor Force
	Employed	Unemployed	Employed	Unemployed	Employed	Unemployed	Employed	Unemployed	
Sheboygan, WI	1,740	102	2,177	195	1,329	147	1,031	52	17,077
Sherman-Denison, TX	1,632	167	1,979	169	1,424	41	1,164	132	20,122
Shreveport-Bossier City, LA	4,921	397	5,727	157	4,623	230	4,246	162	54,748
Sioux City, IA-NE-SD	2,361	44	2,405	32	2,104	25	1,429	69	18,134
Sioux Falls, SD	3,169	116	4,635	154	3,093	17	2,008	11	25,091
South Bend-Mishawaka, IN-MI	5,538	478	4,598	384	4,021	393	3,163	72	44,719
Spartanburg, SC	4,254	416	3,802	304	3,204	281	2,155	108	42,715
Spokane, WA	7,009	705	8,923	502	5,492	517	2,641	197	66,574
Springfield, IL	3,512	190	3,559	180	2,746	229	2,245	31	31,228
Springfield, MA	11,564	919	12,769	1,023	10,270	796	7,014	346	98,328
Springfield, MO	5,538	483	7,141	407	5,086	205	3,618	89	66,096
Springfield, OH	2,083	193	2,137	117	1,539	91	1,201	103	24,650
State College, PA	1,883	41	1,824	190	1,804	48	1,111	42	17,854
Steubenville-Weirton, OH-WV	1,941	95	1,794	102	1,591	111	1,215	115	25,221
Stockton, CA	6,480	890	7,871	711	5,881	590	3,416	598	79,304
Sumter, SC	1,351	86	1,392	134	1,045	96	851	40	15,424
Syracuse, NY	9,460	623	9,289	778	7,998	434	5,567	219	96,600
Tallahassee, FL	5,485	237	6,220	308	4,101	375	2,143	74	41,165
Tampa-St. Petersburg-Clearwater, FL	38,659	3,917	42,976	5,148	35,826	4,321	23,503	2,871	517,004
Terre Haute, IN	2,405	104	2,577	96	1,787	133	1,471	110	26,218
Texarkana, TX-Texarkana, AR	1,676	28	1,803	176	1,522	232	1,433	72	20,454
Toledo, OH	9,219	991	8,862	879	7,529	505	5,203	307	94,122
Topeka, KS	4,574	116	3,686	209	3,751	81	2,464	148	35,300
Trenton-Ewing, NJ	5,328	431	5,680	555	4,983	815	3,923	215	45,408
Tucson, AZ	14,647	977	14,544	1,343	12,179	963	7,178	554	167,235
Tulsa, OK	13,430	721	14,429	666	12,456	735	8,687	393	126,525
Tuscaloosa, AL	2,451	250	2,381	148	1,487	74	1,511	124	28,510
Tyler, TX	3,177	166	3,355	173	2,388	118	2,654	79	30,414
Utica-Rome, NY	4,668	196	4,947	494	3,618	160	3,000	174	52,446
Valdosta, GA	1,422	151	1,803	175	1,284	61	862	26	16,206
Vallejo-Fairfield, CA	5,665	486	7,452	537	4,720	473	2,934	183	52,222
Victoria, TX	1,065	138	2,152	145	1,202	76	1,197	45	17,721
Vineland-Millville-Bridgeton, NJ	1,763	183	1,895	145	1,544	294	1,204	126	21,102
Virginia Beach-Norfolk-Newport News, VA-NC	22,317	1,383	24,504	1,270	20,393	803	12,312	416	205,450
Visalia-Porterville, CA	4,111	717	4,667	452	3,763	285	2,445	283	45,260
Waco, TX	2,759	90	3,541	148	2,440	171	2,031	161	30,108
Warner Robins, GA	1,351	30	1,764	113	1,247	87	569	102	16,401
Washington-Arlington-Alexandria, DC-VA-MD-WV	89,006	5,109	99,837	4,749	82,949	4,141	50,652	2,587	552,121
Waterloo-Cedar Falls, IA	2,428	162	3,132	146	1,976	37	1,438	109	25,615
Wausau, WI	2,599	207	2,364	247	1,802	172	1,172	133	19,480
Wenatchee-East Wenatchee, WA	1,738	87	2,084	96	1,098	124	1,069	146	17,553
Wheeling, WV-OH	2,342	139	2,724	133	2,049	144	1,294	47	28,485
Wichita, KS	8,096	681	9,689	563	7,416	484	5,148	160	76,743
Wichita Falls, TX	1,774	49	2,133	98	1,969	109	1,643	71	20,706
Williamsport, PA	1,775	143	1,739	140	1,723	185	1,024	64	19,812
Wilmington, NC	5,671	310	5,508	845	5,279	687	3,852	294	67,265
Winchester, VA-WV	2,410	136	2,037	54	1,568	36	1,136	99	18,951
Winston-Salem, NC	7,032	436	6,796	590	5,896	308	3,730	245	71,965
Worcester, MA	12,708	752	12,918	1,313	10,618	931	6,481	517	102,268
Yakima, WA	2,863	170	2,945	221	2,770	232	1,266	132	30,086
York-Hanover, PA	7,370	556	7,261	496	6,308	469	4,126	245	63,798
Youngstown-Warren-Boardman, OH-PA	8,678	840	9,213	619	5,933	505	5,090	429	110,412
Yuba City, CA	1,646	406	2,008	353	1,474	400	1,115	241	21,497
Yuma, AZ	1,625	264	1,389	242	1,133	188	899	59	35,506

Table F-5: Congressional Districts—Employment and Labor Force Status, Civilian Labor Force

	60 and 61 Years		62 to 64 Years		65 to 69 Years		70 Years And Over		60 Years and Over Not In the Labor Force
	Employed	Unemployed	Employed	Unemployed	Employed	Unemployed	Employed	Unemployed	
Alabama									
Congressional District 1	8,414	859	10,033	439	8,231	606	5,108	268	109,442
Congressional District 2	9,133	467	8,912	419	8,453	638	5,152	256	104,090
Congressional District 3	8,970	318	8,666	721	7,639	599	4,899	267	103,879
Congressional District 4	8,610	585	9,150	656	7,287	462	5,461	270	122,243
Congressional District 5	9,993	566	10,193	523	8,744	580	5,922	380	100,025
Congressional District 6	9,687	583	10,331	624	9,447	510	5,341	328	93,693
Congressional District 7	8,005	784	7,287	595	5,113	311	4,732	387	100,630
Alaska									
Congressional District (at Large)	10,257	502	11,560	450	8,030	292	4,693	181	61,326
Arizona									
Congressional District 1	9,501	978	8,641	592	7,511	619	5,436	198	112,132
Congressional District 2	11,698	997	11,130	1,058	9,072	728	6,285	508	135,835
Congressional District 3	7,211	564	6,909	758	5,300	658	2,854	223	74,181
Congressional District 4	9,694	1,354	11,036	1,005	8,032	1,397	6,418	686	179,361
Congressional District 5	8,634	799	10,795	646	8,300	760	4,463	515	112,707
Congressional District 6	12,341	815	13,828	859	12,395	741	8,116	564	102,497
Congressional District 7	5,811	613	5,581	393	3,450	361	2,422	243	52,711
Congressional District 8	8,482	802	9,950	1,241	8,890	844	4,868	467	139,685
Congressional District 9	8,645	1,179	10,442	589	7,642	543	4,781	466	71,127
Arkansas									
Congressional District 1	10,100	455	9,895	376	8,680	612	6,611	276	126,035
Congressional District 2	9,247	406	8,711	412	9,785	489	5,758	284	102,241
Congressional District 3	9,445	501	10,838	407	8,313	563	5,431	204	97,827
Congressional District 4	9,391	682	9,844	645	8,913	479	7,699	196	130,379
California									
Congressional District 1	10,052	1,261	11,585	1,458	9,192	834	6,175	846	135,154
Congressional District 2	13,846	1,244	16,007	1,145	13,612	1,006	7,929	871	111,413
Congressional District 3	8,342	1,075	9,943	875	7,419	936	4,474	558	88,157
Congressional District 4	11,385	1,314	11,447	1,162	9,244	1,347	5,203	676	127,642
Congressional District 5	12,248	1,211	13,625	1,582	9,989	1,039	6,896	419	99,861
Congressional District 6	6,380	1,004	7,379	768	5,059	598	3,693	582	83,278
Congressional District 7	8,523	1,020	9,616	949	6,844	741	4,276	532	94,690
Congressional District 8	7,464	1,301	7,352	631	4,898	653	3,259	348	93,199
Congressional District 9	6,987	782	8,181	993	5,752	734	4,117	575	84,770
Congressional District 10	7,145	744	7,464	767	6,255	800	3,658	448	80,759
Congressional District 11	10,785	921	12,295	1,294	10,147	873	6,799	438	100,125
Congressional District 12	10,738	1,242	12,094	1,229	8,121	579	5,159	340	98,772
Congressional District 13	10,489	968	11,073	1,126	9,867	795	5,546	205	87,696
Congressional District 14	11,485	936	12,511	1,043	9,312	959	5,870	432	100,471
Congressional District 15	10,397	1,109	11,126	1,062	6,916	826	3,839	409	77,666
Congressional District 16	5,810	777	6,043	679	4,512	415	2,823	325	70,296
Congressional District 17	8,547	1,120	9,551	1,027	7,258	753	3,518	282	77,362
Congressional District 18	11,375	1,115	11,756	1,052	10,032	953	7,330	500	92,952
Congressional District 19	7,723	1,258	8,670	1,484	7,760	859	3,593	366	74,437
Congressional District 20	9,375	717	9,025	1,044	8,133	660	5,655	535	80,811
Congressional District 21	5,137	670	6,052	724	4,861	434	3,219	316	58,205
Congressional District 22	7,684	1,189	9,560	597	7,067	800	5,166	499	79,056
Congressional District 23	7,364	847	7,541	739	6,816	522	4,038	517	84,628
Congressional District 24	9,561	660	10,592	1,198	9,383	758	6,294	490	100,244
Congressional District 25	8,448	669	8,753	936	7,743	700	3,621	445	66,039
Congressional District 26	9,991	1,055	10,764	1,333	9,865	954	6,122	472	85,233
Congressional District 27	10,891	921	12,268	983	9,541	797	6,183	441	105,466
Congressional District 28	9,166	1,285	10,418	1,047	8,975	931	6,307	527	98,662
Congressional District 29	6,588	1,047	6,532	889	5,325	1,021	2,853	477	64,965
Congressional District 30	11,104	914	12,356	1,303	11,180	1,531	8,317	948	89,037
Congressional District 31	7,397	868	6,241	637	5,341	713	3,363	345	66,923
Congressional District 32	8,371	782	9,195	1,239	6,413	723	3,827	564	83,730
Congressional District 33	11,063	968	13,133	986	14,174	938	11,556	875	93,803
Congressional District 34	7,417	1,263	7,588	1,463	6,014	795	3,378	387	74,562
Congressional District 35	6,027	814	6,049	1,093	3,971	656	2,192	177	59,104
Congressional District 36	7,442	1,220	9,035	1,459	8,411	1,849	6,968	1,130	138,863
Congressional District 37	7,611	1,012	9,394	1,157	7,584	969	6,368	444	78,791
Congressional District 38	7,774	725	8,725	1,029	6,977	784	4,336	252	88,883
Congressional District 39	10,517	928	11,127	1,095	9,987	834	4,976	273	87,038
Congressional District 40	5,771	843	5,516	578	3,690	683	1,843	280	55,727
Congressional District 41	5,855	956	5,560	1,099	4,615	694	2,609	338	61,593
Congressional District 42	7,396	886	8,508	727	5,718	896	3,075	607	76,108
Congressional District 43	8,264	807	8,860	754	7,067	609	4,874	648	72,917
Congressional District 44	6,178	1,000	6,145	728	4,674	680	2,497	226	65,858
Congressional District 45	10,508	639	13,283	1,212	11,296	746	7,304	606	84,302
Congressional District 46	5,894	861	6,310	895	4,828	632	2,857	170	58,722
Congressional District 47	8,300	935	9,167	1,057	7,060	677	4,671	196	84,325
Congressional District 48	10,840	907	12,580	1,001	12,014	877	9,246	553	98,196
Congressional District 49	9,157	1,208	10,762	982	8,787	712	5,686	301	86,594
Congressional District 50	9,434	1,014	10,408	1,098	7,099	589	4,689	518	91,639

Table F-5: Congressional Districts—Employment and Labor Force Status, Civilian Labor Force—*Continued*

	60 and 61 Years		62 to 64 Years		65 to 69 Years		70 Years And Over		60 Years and Over Not In the Labor Force
	Employed	Unemployed	Employed	Unemployed	Employed	Unemployed	Employed	Unemployed	
California—Cont.									
Congressional District 51	5,660	935	5,824	571	4,593	568	3,262	187	76,180
Congressional District 52	10,719	790	10,243	703	9,406	668	5,320	411	85,417
Congressional District 53	8,581	824	9,560	743	7,394	644	4,203	382	84,861
Colorado									
Congressional District 1	10,296	923	11,014	793	8,633	733	5,643	312	77,727
Congressional District 2	13,257	1,044	12,511	891	11,543	795	4,920	254	80,849
Congressional District 3	11,154	1,039	12,911	835	10,498	992	6,012	505	107,468
Congressional District 4	9,645	593	11,098	867	8,851	758	5,445	476	80,071
Congressional District 5	9,393	927	11,664	992	8,785	714	4,678	507	85,621
Congressional District 6	10,459	900	11,006	807	9,160	874	4,952	472	69,415
Congressional District 7	10,652	903	9,760	732	8,816	931	5,157	465	84,965
Connecticut									
Congressional District 1	11,432	1,086	13,836	1,337	11,364	1,373	6,314	831	103,015
Congressional District 2	11,803	789	15,084	1,091	11,109	921	7,113	594	99,268
Congressional District 3	11,458	1,129	14,667	1,440	10,671	855	7,660	828	98,343
Congressional District 4	11,393	1,000	13,880	1,017	12,413	1,495	9,141	711	89,117
Congressional District 5	11,474	754	12,649	1,148	11,755	1,141	7,599	486	98,333
Delaware									
Congressional District (at Large)	13,301	941	14,799	812	13,444	970	8,732	649	135,865
District of Columbia									
Delegate District (at Large)	8,027	795	9,675	833	8,554	583	6,230	235	67,194
Florida									
Congressional District 1	9,792	414	10,490	732	8,463	737	5,270	473	107,400
Congressional District 2	9,603	648	10,255	677	7,717	806	5,146	429	95,069
Congressional District 3	8,814	646	9,886	562	7,339	610	4,882	389	117,022
Congressional District 4	8,690	913	12,016	1,330	9,258	758	5,375	362	90,871
Congressional District 5	8,007	854	7,998	936	6,403	1,014	3,732	499	79,756
Congressional District 6	10,193	1,401	11,341	1,244	10,276	1,464	7,056	753	159,654
Congressional District 7	10,318	1,191	10,612	851	9,257	916	5,635	629	92,534
Congressional District 8	9,778	1,574	10,208	2,009	9,759	1,352	8,063	1,060	158,215
Congressional District 9	7,844	1,330	8,722	1,171	7,411	546	4,054	389	81,514
Congressional District 10	9,320	986	10,435	890	8,433	920	6,918	422	127,414
Congressional District 11	8,989	1,055	10,623	1,116	9,913	1,462	7,586	1,029	230,809
Congressional District 12	9,887	1,188	11,466	1,275	9,183	1,181	6,014	661	151,428
Congressional District 13	12,093	1,108	13,153	1,599	11,906	1,233	8,823	1,139	155,407
Congressional District 14	8,192	714	8,501	1,215	7,824	986	4,252	479	86,786
Congressional District 15	9,504	999	10,524	1,026	7,495	836	4,576	545	100,447
Congressional District 16	9,965	1,602	12,536	1,350	12,772	1,838	9,884	1,454	200,681
Congressional District 17	8,388	953	10,232	1,178	8,824	1,108	8,004	872	186,614
Congressional District 18	9,975	807	11,641	1,193	12,267	1,455	9,173	795	158,506
Congressional District 19	10,252	967	11,587	1,195	13,058	1,697	10,529	1,430	192,096
Congressional District 20	8,804	1,450	9,506	1,364	8,460	1,249	6,208	648	92,761
Congressional District 21	9,626	932	12,327	1,150	11,773	1,848	8,663	1,724	148,528
Congressional District 22	11,900	1,620	13,910	1,605	13,628	1,452	10,171	1,099	137,556
Congressional District 23	9,898	1,041	12,155	1,055	10,780	1,001	7,175	886	105,718
Congressional District 24	7,706	900	8,916	1,570	6,408	881	3,886	334	80,508
Congressional District 25	9,368	823	10,383	1,032	7,891	1,102	5,269	611	104,468
Congressional District 26	9,834	782	11,928	1,240	9,583	1,105	5,746	649	102,021
Congressional District 27	9,993	1,303	10,902	1,346	9,409	920	7,353	816	113,229
Georgia									
Congressional District 1	7,850	327	9,592	631	6,752	559	4,618	207	93,962
Congressional District 2	7,393	779	7,784	459	6,032	434	4,211	229	97,918
Congressional District 3	8,318	917	10,178	623	6,923	510	4,410	562	92,480
Congressional District 4	8,315	1,233	9,532	1,130	5,846	548	3,617	228	67,809
Congressional District 5	6,700	1,116	7,326	973	5,739	466	3,076	496	71,538
Congressional District 6	10,266	616	12,467	776	9,474	711	4,770	351	69,129
Congressional District 7	7,937	848	8,954	1,031	5,923	777	3,355	352	55,731
Congressional District 8	7,553	425	8,928	682	7,312	294	5,273	177	98,279
Congressional District 9	9,275	792	10,377	1,030	8,181	867	5,333	463	113,797
Congressional District 10	7,826	777	7,935	829	6,486	505	4,333	316	92,818
Congressional District 11	8,148	942	9,020	1,043	7,697	631	4,138	247	68,512
Congressional District 12	8,657	569	7,671	530	6,123	280	4,537	278	93,415
Congressional District 13	8,226	879	8,106	977	5,369	471	3,154	265	67,704
Congressional District 14	7,681	670	8,731	803	6,630	912	4,795	380	91,538
Hawaii									
Congressional District 1	12,428	596	12,898	418	12,508	350	8,005	202	105,658
Congressional District 2	11,878	717	12,816	919	10,126	674	6,648	317	93,538
Idaho									
Congressional District 1	10,770	716	10,958	1,125	8,107	769	5,205	437	116,593
Congressional District 2	11,348	629	11,315	707	9,486	764	5,967	282	96,954

Table F-5: Congressional Districts—Employment and Labor Force Status, Civilian Labor Force—*Continued*

	60 and 61 Years		62 to 64 Years		65 to 69 Years		70 Years And Over		60 Years and Over Not In the Labor Force
	Employed	Unemployed	Employed	Unemployed	Employed	Unemployed	Employed	Unemployed	
Illinois									
Congressional District 1	8,420	1,271	9,098	1,152	6,900	639	5,375	568	102,660
Congressional District 2	8,429	1,022	9,756	975	6,736	735	5,677	421	98,751
Congressional District 3	8,401	1,064	10,682	1,046	7,346	674	4,553	585	91,756
Congressional District 4	5,831	1,027	6,449	964	4,631	544	3,133	162	59,496
Congressional District 5	9,606	784	9,956	989	8,998	903	5,042	269	83,080
Congressional District 6	12,531	1,026	14,154	1,202	10,662	807	6,278	492	85,014
Congressional District 7	7,640	632	8,827	825	7,562	407	4,564	456	78,456
Congressional District 8	11,111	1,039	11,533	1,125	7,817	709	4,274	483	73,143
Congressional District 9	11,973	839	13,191	1,400	11,685	972	8,280	424	106,302
Congressional District 10	10,813	1,006	12,382	1,083	10,074	702	6,857	555	81,720
Congressional District 11	8,402	1,167	10,810	851	9,016	546	4,171	390	70,022
Congressional District 12	9,218	698	10,101	350	7,996	299	5,448	217	109,289
Congressional District 13	10,947	715	9,710	421	7,669	557	5,712	105	102,335
Congressional District 14	9,840	1,118	11,611	694	8,301	789	4,998	308	71,928
Congressional District 15	10,055	630	10,732	470	8,759	450	7,268	287	121,148
Congressional District 16	10,205	1,034	11,420	801	9,241	819	7,023	459	107,632
Congressional District 17	10,203	746	10,431	738	8,639	345	7,155	337	118,679
Congressional District 18	11,150	503	11,369	479	9,787	294	8,454	204	114,012
Indiana									
Congressional District 1	9,410	642	11,393	651	7,768	514	4,964	382	103,309
Congressional District 2	11,700	1,231	11,008	763	8,601	801	6,797	232	99,866
Congressional District 3	10,675	938	11,942	959	8,135	543	6,064	254	96,433
Congressional District 4	10,214	485	10,940	493	7,615	452	5,801	210	98,395
Congressional District 5	10,796	661	11,273	645	8,352	388	6,661	455	90,236
Congressional District 6	10,797	758	10,214	713	8,139	530	6,556	476	112,473
Congressional District 7	7,843	762	7,766	817	5,710	657	4,478	454	79,712
Congressional District 8	11,334	688	11,092	500	8,489	515	7,653	383	111,362
Congressional District 9	10,018	800	10,054	804	8,463	544	6,092	288	101,084
Iowa									
Congressional District 1	12,658	458	14,275	482	11,014	344	8,485	460	116,221
Congressional District 2	13,824	509	13,936	614	10,476	387	8,012	274	113,028
Congressional District 3	12,595	551	13,175	586	9,618	507	8,187	278	97,067
Congressional District 4	13,554	284	14,768	327	12,079	268	10,175	257	122,657
Kansas									
Congressional District 1	11,639	373	13,848	418	12,277	353	10,179	288	95,366
Congressional District 2	11,492	545	11,622	573	10,670	264	7,762	348	101,585
Congressional District 3	10,251	977	13,501	652	9,499	465	6,542	353	77,630
Congressional District 4	9,497	702	11,709	610	8,924	536	6,756	251	93,040
Kentucky									
Congressional District 1	9,566	621	9,112	561	7,256	342	6,558	244	125,038
Congressional District 2	8,384	578	8,308	667	8,091	575	5,909	293	105,768
Congressional District 3	9,431	1,174	11,099	792	8,728	591	5,601	383	103,997
Congressional District 4	9,295	523	11,207	799	8,170	523	5,101	377	97,946
Congressional District 5	6,397	266	7,108	372	4,995	294	4,115	198	127,465
Congressional District 6	8,642	474	10,172	583	8,275	391	6,398	317	94,263
Louisiana									
Congressional District 1	10,751	600	12,726	798	10,496	798	7,402	506	103,583
Congressional District 2	9,204	893	9,656	967	7,000	539	4,513	270	95,794
Congressional District 3	8,858	776	10,822	708	8,740	505	6,207	259	95,866
Congressional District 4	8,442	483	10,580	232	8,366	394	7,122	256	110,718
Congressional District 5	9,045	648	9,452	553	9,005	353	6,637	196	111,920
Congressional District 6	9,099	712	10,478	537	9,141	649	6,156	248	90,052
Maine									
Congressional District 1	12,748	631	14,020	782	11,303	591	7,198	370	106,576
Congressional District 2	11,306	727	12,712	859	9,330	693	7,151	391	115,754
Maryland									
Congressional District 1	11,635	930	14,087	780	12,820	772	8,602	614	109,591
Congressional District 2	11,103	594	11,347	792	8,288	780	5,628	626	85,871
Congressional District 3	11,740	678	14,451	665	11,475	758	7,524	530	90,819
Congressional District 4	10,375	657	12,246	711	9,764	463	6,058	396	74,364
Congressional District 5	11,736	616	12,794	682	10,405	444	5,985	439	76,901
Congressional District 6	11,207	528	11,933	662	10,611	1,006	7,193	274	87,386
Congressional District 7	9,898	938	10,800	637	10,294	685	6,276	438	94,362
Congressional District 8	14,817	857	15,167	801	13,290	679	9,282	537	92,026
Massachusetts									
Congressional District 1	12,077	976	13,123	1,153	10,382	971	7,650	458	111,682
Congressional District 2	11,930	802	12,493	1,111	10,930	794	6,333	408	92,321
Congressional District 3	10,333	831	12,743	1,193	8,986	848	6,492	412	89,749
Congressional District 4	12,154	847	14,185	1,415	11,437	1,050	8,234	563	92,139
Congressional District 5	12,768	920	15,909	1,079	13,244	1,114	9,247	531	94,008
Congressional District 6	13,511	1,008	14,525	1,336	13,285	846	8,101	474	105,029
Congressional District 7	8,557	988	9,344	788	7,182	581	4,493	420	72,261
Congressional District 8	11,728	994	13,410	922	11,158	1,201	7,363	688	101,964
Congressional District 9	13,030	1,201	14,715	1,525	14,425	1,498	9,542	966	129,797

Table F-5: Congressional Districts—Employment and Labor Force Status, Civilian Labor Force—*Continued*

	60 and 61 Years		62 to 64 Years		65 to 69 Years		70 Years And Over		60 Years and Over Not In the Labor Force
	Employed	Unemployed	Employed	Unemployed	Employed	Unemployed	Employed	Unemployed	
Michigan									
Congressional District 1	10,841	896	10,166	982	8,119	802	5,639	547	150,366
Congressional District 2	9,270	1,346	8,280	881	6,773	562	5,283	470	99,195
Congressional District 3	9,089	897	8,947	793	7,328	698	5,172	272	95,369
Congressional District 4	8,665	850	8,090	724	6,397	663	4,225	423	127,110
Congressional District 5	7,332	585	6,849	817	5,577	594	4,216	577	124,566
Congressional District 6	9,597	1,055	10,661	933	7,509	508	5,485	483	107,433
Congressional District 7	9,936	969	9,162	1,146	6,910	740	4,757	328	113,500
Congressional District 8	10,021	754	9,744	900	7,643	803	4,599	459	88,751
Congressional District 9	8,705	1,379	10,266	1,517	8,048	1,201	5,401	568	114,311
Congressional District 10	10,348	1,178	8,621	1,103	6,222	841	4,333	566	115,002
Congressional District 11	10,447	867	10,384	1,240	8,978	942	5,182	363	98,706
Congressional District 12	7,844	870	9,115	728	6,162	707	3,749	345	92,270
Congressional District 13	6,276	1,127	5,784	876	4,262	599	2,960	461	103,890
Congressional District 14	8,208	838	9,255	992	7,639	629	4,876	432	106,097
Minnesota									
Congressional District 1	11,728	444	11,791	417	9,699	404	7,655	334	95,574
Congressional District 2	10,925	679	9,832	699	7,556	525	4,988	153	70,895
Congressional District 3	11,895	1,005	12,677	888	9,261	426	5,891	335	78,782
Congressional District 4	10,156	780	10,995	576	7,410	306	4,319	198	82,729
Congressional District 5	10,047	808	9,424	587	6,939	364	4,796	342	73,509
Congressional District 6	9,465	618	9,758	770	6,498	450	4,027	237	67,427
Congressional District 7	11,358	528	12,717	661	10,402	574	8,523	324	112,090
Congressional District 8	10,402	596	9,963	518	8,074	484	5,857	204	121,477
Mississippi									
Congressional District 1	9,214	652	10,329	524	8,553	494	5,927	329	108,158
Congressional District 2	7,500	828	8,419	436	7,198	404	5,065	347	100,800
Congressional District 3	10,124	384	10,467	486	8,687	279	5,749	298	108,826
Congressional District 4	8,131	351	9,081	662	7,042	348	5,544	370	107,441
Missouri									
Congressional District 1	10,051	1,152	10,121	942	7,850	722	5,124	546	94,420
Congressional District 2	12,270	688	14,955	1,134	11,357	423	8,008	438	116,276
Congressional District 3	10,596	587	11,416	717	8,815	540	5,509	444	104,569
Congressional District 4	9,366	755	9,869	408	9,096	381	6,668	460	112,597
Congressional District 5	10,331	606	11,893	776	9,114	658	6,505	400	102,490
Congressional District 6	10,429	646	12,364	393	9,467	667	7,124	325	108,286
Congressional District 7	9,825	937	11,748	856	9,500	629	6,856	550	119,173
Congressional District 8	9,635	519	10,050	542	8,641	611	6,336	264	130,930
Montana									
Congressional District (at Large)	17,085	1,143	18,231	807	15,753	583	10,980	536	153,503
Nebraska									
Congressional District 1	10,487	399	11,063	258	9,332	294	7,417	250	74,952
Congressional District 2	9,690	599	9,805	345	7,479	399	5,092	190	61,483
Congressional District 3	11,730	314	12,987	374	12,298	416	10,472	229	95,243
Nevada									
Congressional District 1	8,434	1,640	8,732	1,417	7,385	1,209	6,053	960	80,117
Congressional District 2	11,256	1,121	11,939	1,421	8,905	1,229	5,507	810	96,523
Congressional District 3	10,073	621	10,490	1,045	8,492	1,467	4,777	1,194	90,712
Congressional District 4	8,304	1,021	8,756	1,135	7,535	860	4,827	609	83,682
New Hampshire									
Congressional District 1	11,087	640	14,039	843	9,958	722	6,553	385	89,805
Congressional District 2	12,829	705	14,326	739	10,540	694	7,048	249	90,285
New Jersey									
Congressional District 1	9,772	887	12,426	1,335	9,637	1,123	6,594	870	95,888
Congressional District 2	12,249	1,183	12,505	1,246	10,367	1,438	8,413	976	112,905
Congressional District 3	11,954	1,111	13,526	1,480	10,264	1,443	8,522	703	124,179
Congressional District 4	10,405	1,069	13,383	1,313	10,698	1,777	8,035	721	118,755
Congressional District 5	12,910	1,401	14,932	1,149	13,615	1,254	9,685	929	97,382
Congressional District 6	10,546	1,470	11,865	1,272	9,668	782	5,995	694	84,697
Congressional District 7	12,603	1,025	13,410	1,437	11,898	954	8,175	645	90,430
Congressional District 8	7,235	816	8,653	595	6,214	757	3,771	498	72,660
Congressional District 9	10,354	1,402	10,322	1,321	10,029	1,028	6,974	698	92,191
Congressional District 10	8,952	1,350	9,603	1,161	8,508	789	5,066	520	83,687
Congressional District 11	13,954	1,194	15,336	1,532	14,283	1,395	9,974	824	103,848
Congressional District 12	10,939	866	12,198	976	10,324	1,596	7,214	645	91,215
New Mexico									
Congressional District 1	10,316	820	10,485	797	8,537	725	5,608	379	94,079
Congressional District 2	8,146	882	9,487	588	8,401	625	5,841	352	107,899
Congressional District 3	10,219	727	10,468	599	9,172	625	5,857	505	97,948

Table F-5: Congressional Districts—Employment and Labor Force Status, Civilian Labor Force—*Continued*

	60 and 61 Years		62 to 64 Years		65 to 69 Years		70 Years And Over		60 Years and Over Not In the Labor Force
	Employed	Unemployed	Employed	Unemployed	Employed	Unemployed	Employed	Unemployed	
New York									
Congressional District 1	10,453	419	12,654	888	10,426	996	7,606	651	103,803
Congressional District 2	9,835	841	10,445	898	8,606	727	6,834	557	93,570
Congressional District 3	12,855	870	15,745	1,016	14,478	911	11,815	859	115,064
Congressional District 4	12,900	890	13,075	1,016	11,259	578	7,953	753	100,430
Congressional District 5	9,620	1,029	11,684	1,048	7,280	1,190	5,195	236	93,172
Congressional District 6	10,212	1,134	12,341	1,180	8,526	951	6,357	451	111,064
Congressional District 7	7,189	524	6,716	723	4,182	567	2,197	73	76,613
Congressional District 8	9,399	975	9,262	878	6,956	562	3,195	355	96,935
Congressional District 9	10,832	1,159	11,995	969	8,703	691	4,126	322	88,141
Congressional District 10	11,188	729	14,344	1,089	11,229	1,262	8,402	715	89,199
Congressional District 11	10,247	1,015	10,144	950	7,680	500	4,270	398	112,295
Congressional District 12	8,732	820	11,456	1,087	14,069	1,222	11,586	702	84,188
Congressional District 13	8,003	1,054	7,236	575	5,633	559	2,935	175	89,880
Congressional District 14	7,424	714	9,360	1,017	6,656	601	4,183	305	88,278
Congressional District 15	5,207	629	5,020	492	4,564	274	1,567	182	71,543
Congressional District 16	10,886	816	12,959	1,100	11,056	1,152	8,127	605	103,292
Congressional District 17	12,067	961	12,398	1,050	12,647	863	9,221	664	94,268
Congressional District 18	10,321	898	11,192	914	9,335	980	6,749	571	90,696
Congressional District 19	12,746	831	12,875	1,451	11,346	1,042	8,430	551	116,588
Congressional District 20	10,442	724	12,011	718	8,610	825	5,800	518	107,110
Congressional District 21	10,178	596	9,723	932	8,105	758	5,109	331	113,332
Congressional District 22	10,410	529	11,421	1,074	8,377	653	6,807	465	120,081
Congressional District 23	11,336	782	12,182	753	8,762	424	6,752	272	115,993
Congressional District 24	10,268	711	10,681	829	8,989	439	5,978	209	107,197
Congressional District 25	10,029	529	10,009	778	9,723	621	5,555	373	105,733
Congressional District 26	8,551	608	10,208	674	7,928	953	7,370	628	115,094
Congressional District 27	12,288	670	11,153	675	9,654	581	7,714	472	117,846
North Carolina									
Congressional District 1	8,192	1,130	8,942	812	7,172	518	5,722	422	112,250
Congressional District 2	9,066	825	10,621	708	7,964	565	4,884	353	95,568
Congressional District 3	9,485	996	9,924	1,080	8,592	617	6,631	472	104,475
Congressional District 4	8,869	890	8,952	562	7,398	698	5,536	314	71,540
Congressional District 5	10,948	666	10,765	1,396	9,459	680	6,118	392	117,821
Congressional District 6	11,381	1,332	12,023	1,032	11,145	808	6,781	512	116,476
Congressional District 7	10,920	579	10,702	1,371	9,635	845	5,944	458	120,714
Congressional District 8	8,559	1,041	10,220	833	7,417	727	5,370	455	106,295
Congressional District 9	10,489	968	11,710	1,368	9,778	867	5,925	503	79,256
Congressional District 10	10,143	1,184	11,547	1,004	8,907	650	6,032	405	120,006
Congressional District 11	10,562	1,036	11,731	1,202	10,100	801	7,345	742	153,598
Congressional District 12	6,465	1,129	7,099	1,121	5,210	628	3,709	441	70,166
Congressional District 13	10,682	705	11,360	878	8,821	682	5,489	223	89,233
North Dakota									
Congressional District (at Large)	12,527	261	12,740	279	10,756	318	8,989	238	92,142
Ohio									
Congressional District 1	9,485	897	10,721	771	8,404	615	6,141	353	90,634
Congressional District 2	10,194	980	11,084	761	8,312	641	6,763	205	107,481
Congressional District 3	6,851	592	8,866	759	5,854	366	4,285	141	70,607
Congressional District 4	10,396	751	10,105	1,101	8,170	467	5,926	199	113,226
Congressional District 5	11,500	873	11,150	871	9,222	729	7,029	322	110,882
Congressional District 6	10,867	716	10,002	803	8,395	556	5,894	464	135,483
Congressional District 7	11,056	828	12,324	1,026	8,711	535	6,901	276	115,419
Congressional District 8	11,207	931	11,015	784	8,086	563	6,131	242	106,273
Congressional District 9	9,458	1,152	10,127	967	6,803	640	4,979	259	104,499
Congressional District 10	10,264	806	12,293	741	9,209	527	6,193	315	115,410
Congressional District 11	9,719	1,026	10,494	1,052	7,949	609	6,461	362	109,418
Congressional District 12	11,067	779	13,811	661	9,107	467	5,710	191	94,640
Congressional District 13	10,012	922	11,547	871	7,517	730	5,686	390	124,863
Congressional District 14	12,730	1,006	13,998	991	11,601	519	6,959	461	116,578
Congressional District 15	8,989	354	10,063	695	8,530	546	5,042	206	97,530
Congressional District 16	13,041	664	13,904	1,045	11,747	810	7,785	494	120,205
Oklahoma									
Congressional District 1	11,174	532	11,248	437	10,116	565	7,229	327	96,498
Congressional District 2	8,243	378	9,810	491	8,698	503	6,878	218	134,105
Congressional District 3	10,560	386	11,663	492	10,495	290	8,610	244	109,121
Congressional District 4	9,163	539	10,982	369	8,865	339	6,741	238	99,961
Congressional District 5	9,130	329	11,087	354	8,704	441	7,385	323	95,891
Oregon									
Congressional District 1	11,330	990	11,979	1,060	9,253	849	5,573	399	92,670
Congressional District 2	11,885	1,640	13,448	1,398	10,300	1,107	6,594	673	141,021
Congressional District 3	10,767	1,263	11,269	1,410	8,312	600	4,159	537	92,952
Congressional District 4	12,409	1,314	13,518	872	8,740	768	6,213	463	146,922
Congressional District 5	12,100	1,484	13,330	1,149	10,232	1,024	5,910	434	118,201

Table F-5: Congressional Districts—Employment and Labor Force Status, Civilian Labor Force—*Continued*

	60 and 61 Years		62 to 64 Years		65 to 69 Years		70 Years And Over		60 Years and Over Not In the Labor Force
	Employed	Unemployed	Employed	Unemployed	Employed	Unemployed	Employed	Unemployed	
Pennsylvania									
Congressional District 1	7,552	769	8,272	747	6,409	697	4,185	297	82,150
Congressional District 2	7,925	708	8,590	818	7,875	520	5,631	416	97,804
Congressional District 3	11,322	594	10,659	514	8,588	498	7,176	493	121,464
Congressional District 4	11,716	745	11,923	838	9,961	836	7,604	532	105,739
Congressional District 5	9,931	645	10,842	761	7,955	390	5,574	368	121,195
Congressional District 6	10,759	927	14,168	1,356	10,562	880	7,794	687	96,278
Congressional District 7	13,098	726	13,534	1,001	11,531	765	9,402	630	103,249
Congressional District 8	12,036	1,031	15,330	1,034	12,421	1,147	8,359	581	99,904
Congressional District 9	10,167	589	10,769	665	8,076	338	5,690	276	133,736
Congressional District 10	10,742	686	12,339	871	9,220	642	6,272	327	127,227
Congressional District 11	11,043	747	12,453	804	9,176	679	7,327	311	119,905
Congressional District 12	13,037	518	11,938	861	10,737	608	7,834	472	131,952
Congressional District 13	10,619	737	11,737	1,247	9,633	746	6,974	686	102,558
Congressional District 14	10,775	828	11,798	1,048	9,016	671	7,450	437	117,806
Congressional District 15	10,514	655	11,112	978	9,192	1,127	6,195	388	110,563
Congressional District 16	10,047	702	11,118	735	10,302	554	8,286	437	96,030
Congressional District 17	9,890	1,102	11,343	557	8,461	825	6,582	478	124,601
Congressional District 18	13,125	984	13,902	786	10,435	882	8,181	456	126,469
Rhode Island									
Congressional District 1	8,681	728	7,222	768	6,955	551	5,472	394	76,677
Congressional District 2	8,248	914	10,621	871	7,368	681	4,850	397	75,302
South Carolina									
Congressional District 1	9,637	643	11,446	425	8,843	845	5,880	574	102,906
Congressional District 2	9,001	632	10,760	546	7,833	390	5,265	413	90,637
Congressional District 3	8,061	944	8,514	819	6,717	870	5,221	611	113,659
Congressional District 4	9,271	985	9,481	751	8,231	743	5,140	295	93,288
Congressional District 5	9,093	1,029	9,173	835	6,320	734	4,948	363	100,521
Congressional District 6	7,128	668	8,390	835	6,849	476	4,298	401	93,965
Congressional District 7	8,946	1,136	10,496	910	9,143	726	5,758	698	117,847
South Dakota									
Congressional District (at Large)	13,973	414	15,424	353	12,971	295	10,921	163	111,955
Tennessee									
Congressional District 1	9,705	932	11,103	725	8,428	453	6,488	495	133,702
Congressional District 2	10,320	711	11,642	726	8,302	544	5,372	389	114,555
Congressional District 3	10,512	645	10,822	912	8,635	810	5,908	313	123,327
Congressional District 4	8,841	874	9,534	832	7,404	606	4,770	136	101,135
Congressional District 5	8,929	843	10,428	677	7,769	463	5,631	397	78,483
Congressional District 6	9,925	888	9,913	649	8,966	754	6,047	411	117,493
Congressional District 7	9,900	636	9,258	869	7,086	629	5,186	285	99,199
Congressional District 8	9,913	663	12,572	932	9,186	820	6,387	644	104,608
Congressional District 9	8,720	780	8,296	840	6,327	502	4,504	456	74,363
Texas									
Congressional District 1	10,239	637	10,485	592	8,333	445	7,118	257	105,112
Congressional District 2	10,869	506	12,272	525	9,467	539	5,760	279	60,237
Congressional District 3	8,825	355	11,170	652	9,314	696	4,724	199	56,261
Congressional District 4	8,753	655	10,839	695	9,697	457	7,029	434	111,146
Congressional District 5	9,365	531	9,031	456	7,706	542	5,652	217	91,535
Congressional District 6	9,304	770	10,794	713	8,087	737	4,667	202	68,316
Congressional District 7	9,399	565	11,940	791	9,850	679	6,078	460	58,509
Congressional District 8	8,968	420	9,784	1,278	8,287	539	5,777	472	86,772
Congressional District 9	8,682	740	8,658	452	6,713	786	3,581	380	58,382
Congressional District 10	8,604	687	9,698	649	8,125	328	5,878	328	75,424
Congressional District 11	10,354	202	10,160	391	10,076	313	8,191	475	104,575
Congressional District 12	10,495	719	10,865	730	8,242	655	5,301	220	78,185
Congressional District 13	9,382	462	11,007	457	8,669	411	7,705	406	96,972
Congressional District 14	9,411	660	10,455	542	7,964	578	5,079	436	88,331
Congressional District 15	6,040	509	6,651	396	5,558	243	2,643	248	76,971
Congressional District 16	6,869	420	6,981	505	6,127	302	3,804	172	83,251
Congressional District 17	8,546	348	9,801	383	7,599	490	5,299	328	76,199
Congressional District 18	7,282	644	8,428	754	5,805	547	3,463	217	63,419
Congressional District 19	8,253	394	10,067	347	8,683	316	8,148	187	87,229
Congressional District 20	7,870	216	7,307	396	6,165	271	4,317	102	77,165
Congressional District 21	10,279	417	12,931	713	10,679	379	6,411	343	98,654
Congressional District 22	7,691	624	9,980	433	8,000	392	4,440	118	62,004
Congressional District 23	8,169	456	8,122	565	7,273	481	5,016	254	82,471
Congressional District 24	9,232	690	11,135	672	9,407	640	5,702	267	60,057
Congressional District 25	9,204	737	9,466	580	8,789	411	5,009	316	87,261
Congressional District 26	8,033	766	9,769	318	7,311	591	3,438	243	53,787
Congressional District 27	9,102	544	12,053	574	8,611	359	7,018	277	98,671
Congressional District 28	6,896	550	6,745	272	5,223	271	3,402	187	78,753
Congressional District 29	6,220	742	5,576	550	4,280	441	2,052	268	55,242
Congressional District 30	7,917	803	8,039	703	5,900	445	3,068	277	68,229
Congressional District 31	7,798	564	8,101	851	6,142	605	4,275	303	72,832
Congressional District 32	9,634	896	11,370	862	9,653	686	6,634	580	69,020
Congressional District 33	5,873	317	6,825	580	4,796	563	2,919	295	57,037
Congressional District 34	6,721	726	7,109	503	5,987	346	3,962	228	92,672
Congressional District 35	6,912	439	7,480	382	5,276	304	3,591	350	65,990
Congressional District 36	8,459	508	9,911	714	7,186	521	4,616	513	94,112

Table F-5: Congressional Districts—Employment and Labor Force Status, Civilian Labor Force—*Continued*

	60 and 61 Years		62 to 64 Years		65 to 69 Years		70 Years And Over		60 Years and Over Not In the Labor Force
	Employed	Unemployed	Employed	Unemployed	Employed	Unemployed	Employed	Unemployed	
Utah									
Congressional District 1............	7,481	490	8,006	398	5,951	111	3,545	133	64,778
Congressional District 2............	7,661	529	8,632	496	7,595	459	4,968	193	79,613
Congressional District 3............	7,612	384	8,612	550	6,866	368	4,124	262	60,847
Congressional District 4............	7,198	501	8,130	418	6,288	305	4,016	160	56,748
Vermont									
Congressional District (at Large)	12,164	638	14,751	903	11,425	331	7,314	293	89,472
Virginia									
Congressional District 1............	10,410	504	10,936	640	10,512	407	5,959	254	94,771
Congressional District 2............	10,007	810	11,102	491	9,245	326	5,832	192	85,283
Congressional District 3............	8,422	648	8,787	673	6,528	477	4,932	248	87,930
Congressional District 4............	10,431	805	11,071	725	8,915	278	4,967	114	93,451
Congressional District 5............	11,173	1,024	13,503	645	10,851	394	8,417	291	127,294
Congressional District 6............	11,430	426	12,678	587	10,116	378	7,772	382	117,986
Congressional District 7............	12,121	445	14,020	522	11,478	360	6,852	251	95,650
Congressional District 8............	11,207	611	13,937	406	10,499	331	7,028	374	64,084
Congressional District 9............	10,566	619	10,707	698	9,090	374	6,547	184	134,111
Congressional District 10............	12,075	522	12,035	469	10,895	257	5,766	239	64,982
Congressional District 11............	12,423	674	15,217	580	10,959	494	6,134	292	66,586
Washington									
Congressional District 1............	10,568	788	11,511	915	7,889	676	3,789	412	78,122
Congressional District 2............	11,025	926	12,332	981	9,645	552	4,256	214	92,639
Congressional District 3............	9,710	950	10,000	943	7,346	863	3,594	452	106,710
Congressional District 4............	8,900	445	9,564	585	7,012	586	4,781	294	84,037
Congressional District 5............	9,796	812	12,418	652	7,854	673	4,242	324	102,229
Congressional District 6............	10,776	1,182	12,068	830	8,438	791	4,296	601	120,614
Congressional District 7............	10,414	519	14,237	960	9,550	698	5,595	330	83,338
Congressional District 8............	10,574	737	9,871	614	6,547	420	4,087	396	75,548
Congressional District 9............	9,219	981	9,917	823	7,294	574	4,595	428	82,826
Congressional District 10............	9,738	823	11,307	358	7,218	693	4,124	151	87,650
West Virginia									
Congressional District 1............	9,297	441	8,129	315	6,986	253	4,604	206	112,159
Congressional District 2............	9,324	565	8,791	465	7,387	418	5,111	244	109,206
Congressional District 3............	7,702	360	7,560	329	5,722	131	4,606	153	123,080
Wisconsin									
Congressional District 1............	10,561	639	11,415	1,299	8,771	577	5,532	352	95,744
Congressional District 2............	11,125	440	12,799	760	9,270	486	6,562	226	85,007
Congressional District 3............	10,587	607	12,049	600	7,940	589	7,335	300	108,522
Congressional District 4............	7,716	1,148	7,094	592	6,144	492	4,239	272	76,840
Congressional District 5............	12,618	832	13,302	843	8,873	417	6,677	749	105,245
Congressional District 6............	11,689	690	12,732	761	9,123	687	6,356	289	111,233
Congressional District 7............	12,278	1,008	12,398	728	9,857	645	6,779	348	124,976
Congressional District 8............	11,329	819	10,472	834	7,297	551	5,219	199	105,875
Wyoming									
Congressional District (at Large)	9,694	182	10,107	471	7,800	362	5,820	154	71,064

PART G

INCOME AND POVERTY

INCOME AND POVERTY

The Census Bureau reports that real median household income (adjusted for inflation) for all households in 2012 was statistically unchanged from the 2011 median income.[1] At the same time, inflation pushes prices higher, which disproportionately affects persons on fixed incomes, a group which includes many seniors. The Census definition of income includes sources of cash income: wages and salary, social security, retirement, interest, dividends and rent, for example. It does not include measures of assets and may not be a good measure of overall wealth. However, it still illustrates the wide variation across states and sub-state areas in income distributions and poverty. Most importantly poverty, because that population likely has very little in assets to offset their limited money income.

This historical data indicates that the median household income of householders age 65 and over is considerably below that of all householders. However, it also shows that the gap has narrowed in the last 5 years. This may be a result of the recessionary impact on households overall while many seniors have income sources that are indexed thereby helping them to keep pace.

Median Household Income, Adjusted for Inflation

	Householder 65 Years and Over	All Households	Gap
2008	$33,787	$52,029	$18,242
2009	$33,712	$50,221	$16,509
2010	$34,381	$50,046	$15,665
2011	$35,107	$50,502	$15,395
2012	$36,743	$51,371	$14,628

U.S. Census Bureau, American Community Survey 1-year Estimates, Table B19049.

---

1. U.S. Census Bureau, Current Population Reports, P60-245, *Income, Poverty, and health Insurance Coverage in the United States: 2012*, U.S. Government Printing Office, Washington, DC, 2013.

MEDIAN INCOME

The income data from the American Community Survey for the 2010–2012 period varies slightly from the data reported above as single-year measures. For example, the 2010–2012 national ACS median income for householders over the age of 65 is $36,236. There are 22 states above the national median. Hawaii has the highest median income at $55,085 followed by Maryland with $47,687. Mississippi has the lowest at $28,387 followed by West Virginia ($28,867) and Kentucky ($29,737).

The county with the highest median income, with nearly $82,000, is Fairfax County, Virginia followed by Loudon County, Virginia at $74,486. Forty-five counties have a median income over $50,000 while the median in 88 counties is below $30,000. Each of the counties in the states of Alaska, Connecticut, Delaware, Hawaii, Nebraska, Nevada, New Hampshire and Utah have median incomes above the national median. Among householders 65 and over, Newport Beach, California is the city with the highest median income at $88,737 and at $16,226, Miami, Florida has the lowest median income, less than one half the national figure. In 241 cities the median income is less than the national median and in 28 cities it is below $25,000. Fifty-eight cities have median incomes above $50,000. New York City, the city with the largest number of householders 65 and over, had a median income of $29,216, seven thousand dollars below the national figure.

The Washington-Arlington-Alexandria metropolitan statistical area has the highest median income for householders age 65 and over at $63,241 followed by the Honolulu, Hawaii metro area with a median of $59,292. Only five other areas, Anchorage, Alaska, Bridgeport-Stamford-Norwalk, Connecticut, Naples-Marco Island, Florida, Oxnard-Thousand Oaks-Ventura, California and San Jose-Sunnyvale-Santa Clara, California, have medians above $50,000. The Laredo, Texas metro area has the lowest median at $22,523 and 33 metro areas have median incomes below $30,000. Congressional districts with median incomes above the national figure number 228. The highest median ($76,957) is in Virginia's 11th Congressional District while the lowest is New York's 15th Congressional

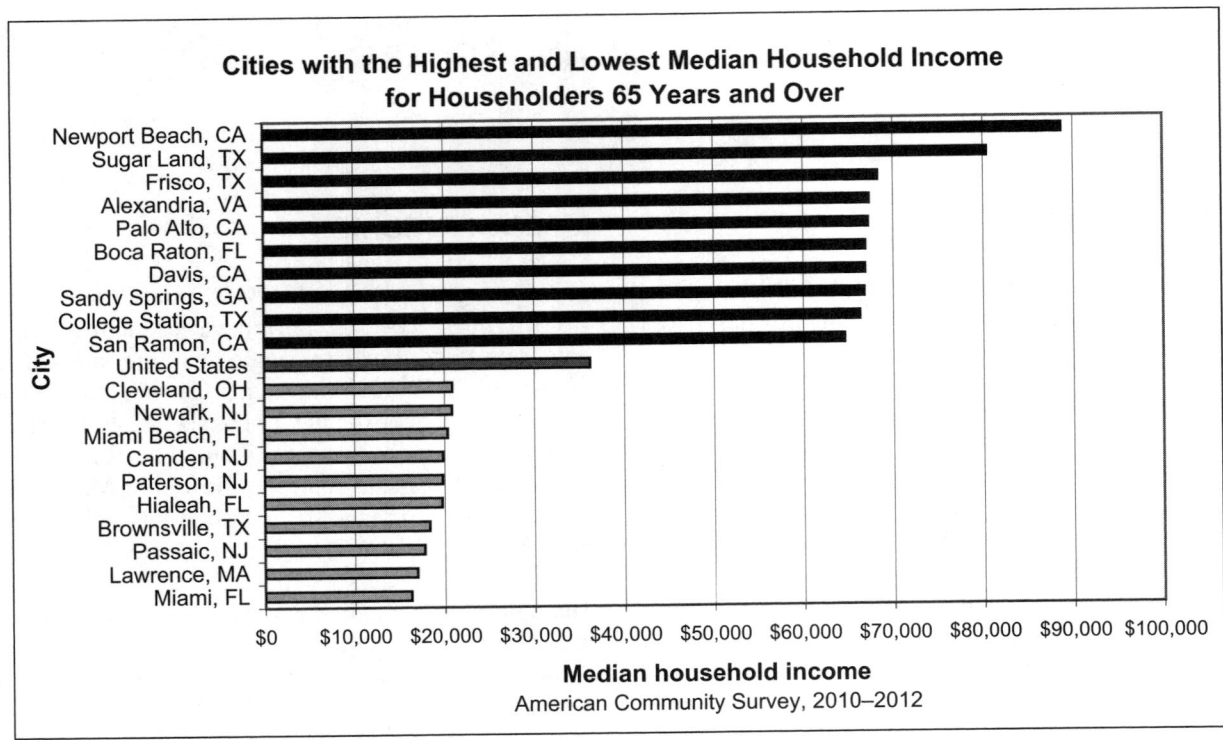

Cities with the Highest and Lowest Median Household Income for Householders 65 Years and Over

Median household income
American Community Survey, 2010–2012

District at only $15,813. Sixty-four congressional districts have median incomes that are less than $30,000 while 35 districts have medians above $50,000.

POVERTY STATUS AND RECEIPT OF FOOD STAMPS

Poverty status is determined by comparing total family or unrelated individual income to the established national poverty thresholds which vary by size and type of household and number of children. When a family or single person household is determined to be in poverty, every member of the family is so defined. The national poverty rate of persons age 55 to 64 years is 10.2 percent, for persons 65 to 74 years it declines to 8.4 percent then increases again to 10.5 percent for the 75 and over population. This pattern of decline to the 65 to 74 population followed by an increase in the 75 and over holds for every state except North Dakota where the poverty rate increases across each age. The pattern does not hold for other sub-state areas.

The poverty rate for the 55 to 64 population is higher than the national rate in 22 states and the highest rate (15.7 percent) is in the District of Columbia. New Hampshire has the lowest rate among this age category at 5.2 percent but Alaska has the lowest rate (6.5 percent) for the 75 and over population. Mississippi has the highest 75 and over rate at 14.7 percent followed by North and

South Dakota at 14.5 percent and 14.3 percent, respectively. Eighteen states are above the national rate for the 75 and over population. Food stamp recipient households are those containing one or more people age 60 and over. The District of Columbia (14.7 percent) and the State of New York (14.6 percent) have the highest percentages of food stamp recipient households. Wyoming has the lowest rate of food stamp recipients at 3.8 percent. Twenty-three states are above the national rate of 9.5 percent.

Apache County, Arizona has the highest rate of poverty among the 55 to 64 population at 27.4 percent and 24.5 percent of the 75 and over population is also in poverty. Both measures are more than two and a half times the national rates for their respective age groups. McKinley County, New Mexico has the highest rate among the 75 and over population. Hunterdon County, New Jersey has the lowest poverty rate for the 55 to 64 population at only 2.2 percent but Hamilton County, Indiana has the lowest rate (1.3 percent) for the 75 and over population. There are 308 counties with poverty rates above the national figure for the 55 to 64 population and 241 are above the nation for the 75 and over population. Bronx County, New York has the highest food stamp recipient rate at 34.5 percent while York County, Virginia is lowest at 1.1 percent. Ten percent or more households with a person 60 years or over receive food stamps in 251 counties and in 12 counties more than 20 percent are recipient households.

Median Household Income of Householders 65 Years and Over

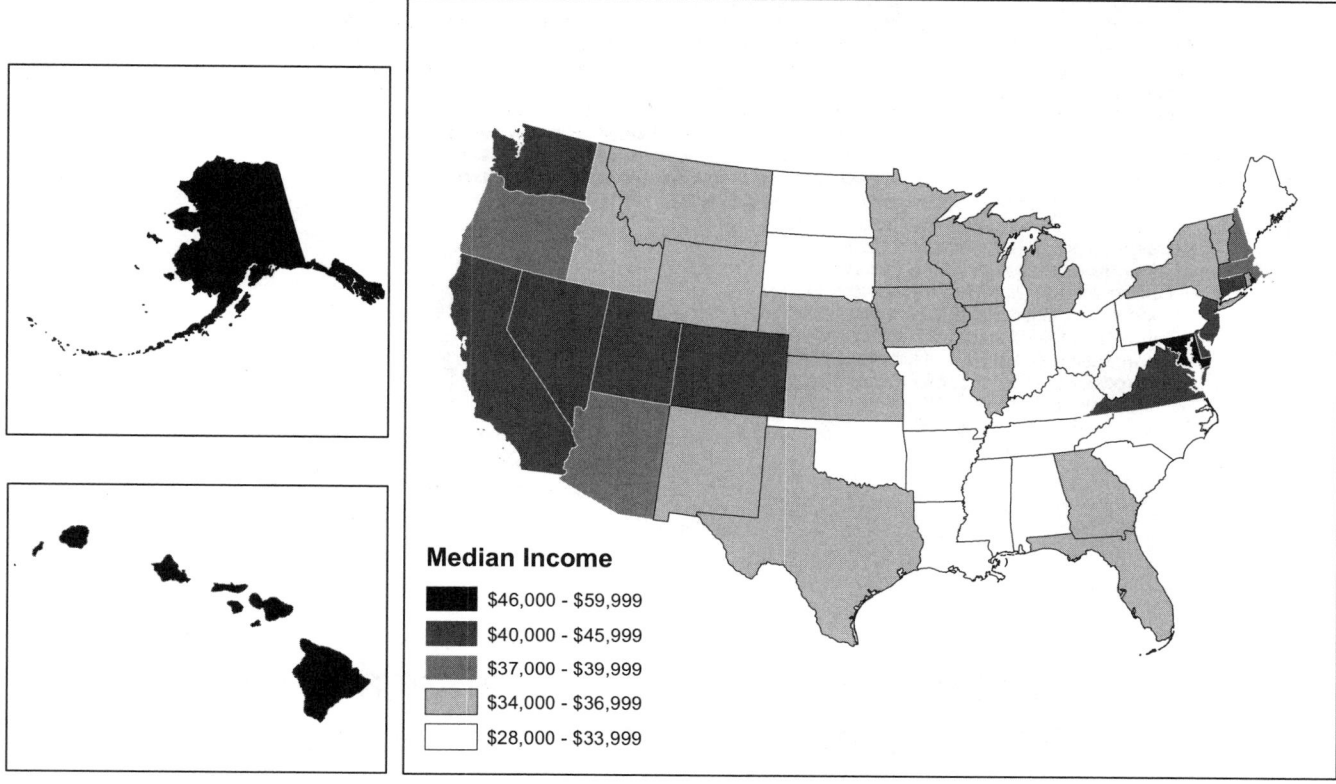

Median Income

- $46,000 - $59,999
- $40,000 - $45,999
- $37,000 - $39,999
- $34,000 - $36,999
- $28,000 - $33,999

In 11 cities, more than 25 percent of the 55 to 64 population is in poverty but the 75 and over poverty rate is over 25 percent in only 6 cities: Hialeah, Miami, and Miami Beach, Florida and Brownsville, Laredo, and Pharr Texas with Brownsville having the highest rate at 36.7 percent. Carmel, Indiana has the lowest percentage of 75 and over in poverty at 0.8 percent. Just over half (50.6 percent) of the households with a member 60 or over in Hialeah, Florida is receiving food stamps. In 22 cities, at least 25 percent of the households are receiving food stamps. San Ramon, California has the lowest rate at only 0.5 percent.

The McAllen-Edinburg-Mission, Texas metropolitan area has the highest rate of poverty (22.9 percent) among the 55 to 64 population while the Holland-Grand Haven, Michigan metro area is lowest at 3.9 percent. Among the 75 and over population, the Brownsville-Harlingen, Texas metropolitan area has the highest rate (27.2 percent) and the Iowa City, Iowa metro has the lowest rate at 3.0 percent. Only two metropolitan areas have more than 25 percent of households receiving food

stamps with both in Texas: the Laredo (33.5 percent) and McAllen-Edinburg-Mission (31.0 percent) metro areas. The San Luis Obispo, California metropolitan area has the lowest percent receiving food stamps at 3.1 percent and in 33 metros, less than 5 percent of the households receive food stamps.

New York's 15th Congressional District has the highest poverty rate (31.3 percent) among the 55 to 64 population and the next highest is also in New York at 25.1 percent in the 13th district. New Jersey's 12th district is the lowest at 3.1 percent but 25 districts have a poverty rate under 5 percent. Among the 75 and over population, seven congressional districts have poverty rates over 25 percent, led again by New York's 15th district. New York's 7th district is next highest at 32.0 percent. Virginia's 10th congressional district is the lowest at 5.0 percent. New York's 15th district also has the highest percent (50.2 percent) of households with members over 60 receiving food stamps. Three additional districts have more than a third of the households receiving food stamps: Florida's 27th district and New York's 7th and 13th districts.

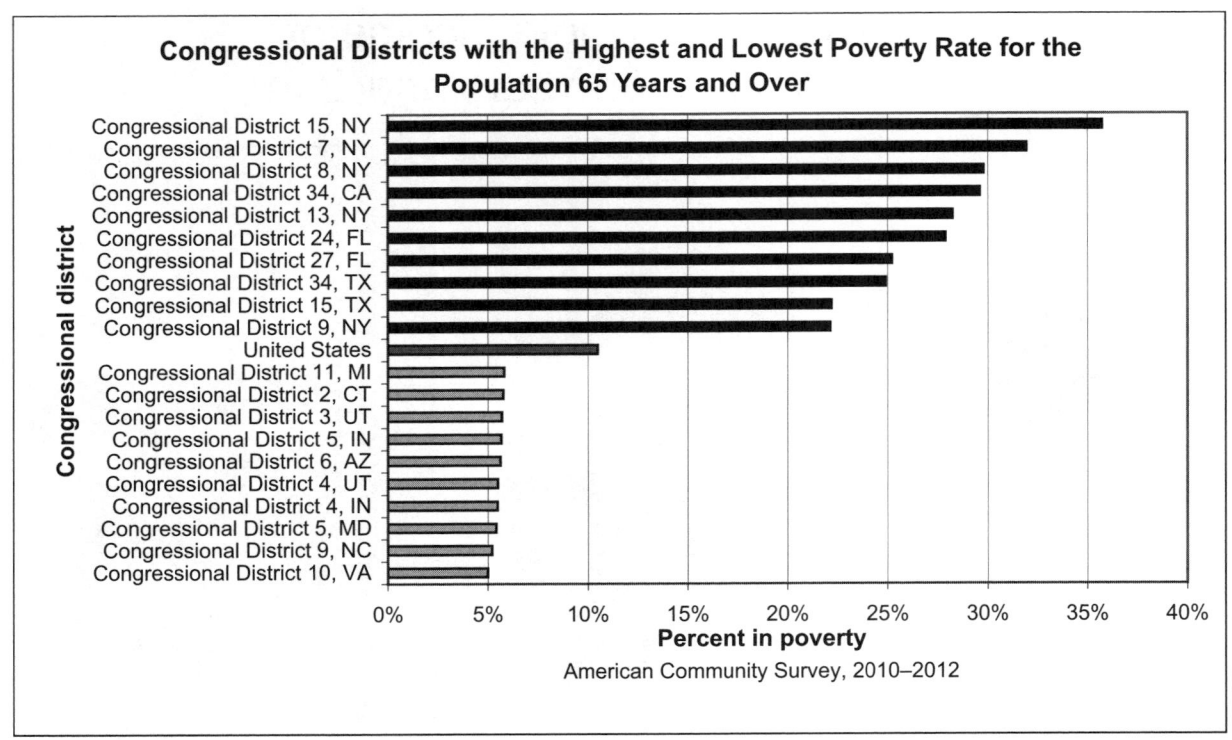

Congressional Districts with the Highest and Lowest Poverty Rate for the Population 65 Years and Over

American Community Survey, 2010–2012

Percent of the Population 75 Years and Over With Income Below the Poverty Level

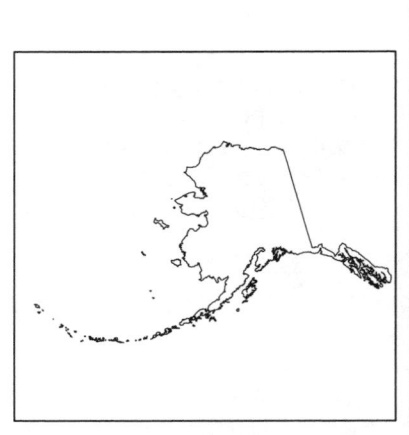

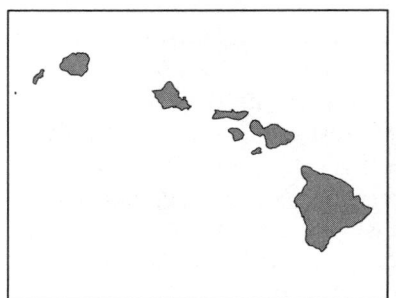

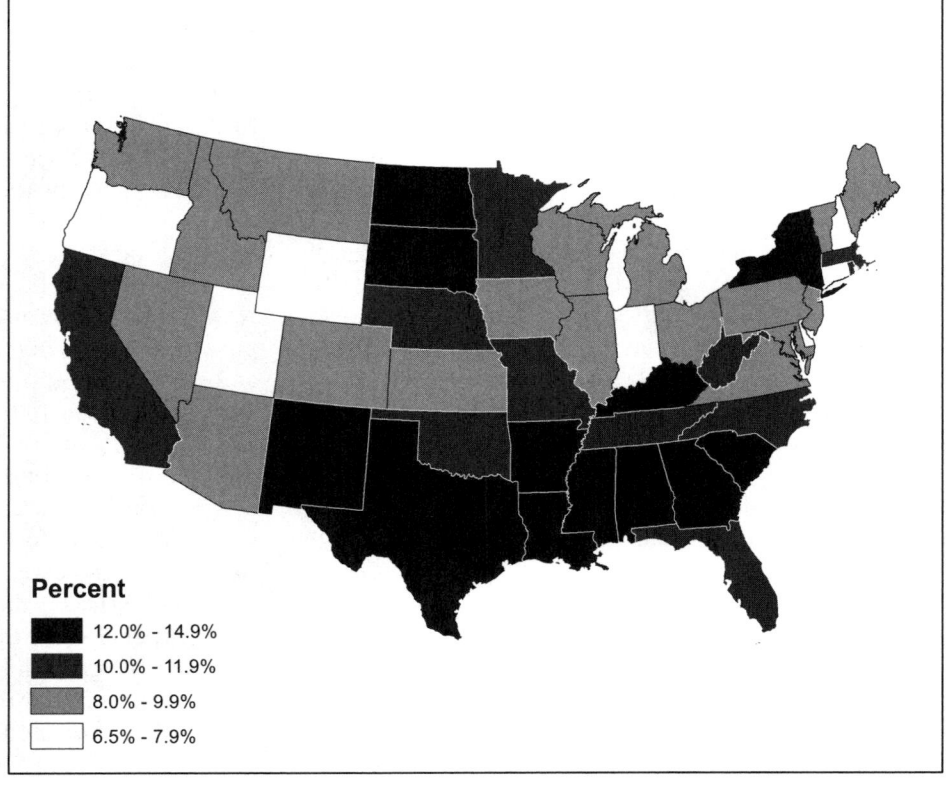

Percent

- 12.0% - 14.9%
- 10.0% - 11.9%
- 8.0% - 9.9%
- 6.5% - 7.9%

Table G-1: States—Income, Poverty Status and Receipt of Food Stamps (SNAP)

	Income of Households with Householder 65 and Over						Poverty Rate of Persons			Households with 1 or More Persons 60 Years and Over	
	Total Households	Less Than $25,000	$25,000-$49,999	$50,000-$99,999	$100,000 or More	Median Household Income	55 to 64 Years	65 to 74 Years	75 Years and Over	Receiving SNAP	Not Receiving SNAP
United States.............	25,624,042	8,841,048	7,545,800	6,157,671	3,079,523	$36,236	10.2%	8.4%	10.5%	3,798,624	36,361,376
Alabama...............	431,900	168,146	132,396	93,099	38,259	$32,180	12.0%	9.6%	12.3%	68,552	593,097
Alaska................	35,129	9,176	9,239	10,185	6,529	$47,441	6.4%	4.8%	6.5%	6,457	61,040
Arizona................	564,283	173,422	177,118	148,477	65,266	$38,790	11.9%	8.0%	8.5%	77,824	783,255
Arkansas..............	270,357	110,249	82,695	57,079	20,334	$30,824	11.7%	8.9%	13.0%	35,940	371,038
California..............	2,544,599	782,120	665,460	644,011	453,008	$42,116	10.9%	9.3%	11.1%	202,057	4,075,992
Colorado..............	364,159	111,784	104,394	98,435	49,546	$40,279	8.5%	7.1%	9.1%	35,864	559,730
Connecticut...........	315,972	94,428	85,686	80,542	55,316	$41,995	7.2%	6.1%	7.4%	45,355	448,741
Delaware.............	81,975	23,870	23,011	23,710	11,384	$42,892	8.1%	6.7%	7.1%	10,775	115,051
District of Columbia...........	49,026	16,300	10,109	10,567	12,050	$44,472	15.7%	12.0%	13.3%	11,191	64,715
Florida................	2,006,651	681,881	607,752	487,870	229,148	$36,344	12.6%	9.5%	10.6%	325,992	2,642,444
Georgia...............	659,443	244,031	189,782	153,979	71,651	$34,613	12.7%	9.8%	12.8%	128,682	963,582
Hawaii................	110,898	26,014	25,161	32,099	27,624	$55,085	9.3%	6.3%	8.4%	18,523	168,187
Idaho.................	127,817	44,620	41,847	30,568	10,782	$34,554	9.7%	6.6%	9.6%	14,525	182,876
Illinois................	1,032,851	345,481	311,884	250,009	125,477	$36,625	9.2%	7.6%	9.5%	146,027	1,455,458
Indiana...............	543,017	189,904	186,625	126,057	40,431	$33,892	8.7%	6.6%	7.8%	62,654	767,822
Iowa..................	289,929	101,938	94,561	69,089	24,341	$34,283	7.0%	5.8%	8.7%	27,008	401,145
Kansas...............	241,937	81,351	76,869	58,956	24,761	$36,226	7.6%	6.2%	8.3%	20,896	343,941
Kentucky.............	379,625	160,074	118,396	74,415	26,740	$29,737	12.5%	10.4%	13.7%	70,806	516,196
Louisiana.............	365,758	150,874	105,427	75,338	34,119	$30,795	13.7%	11.2%	13.7%	72,351	501,023
Maine.................	136,326	52,254	42,130	31,143	10,799	$32,241	9.3%	8.2%	9.4%	24,350	188,445
Maryland.............	447,752	122,884	109,450	122,806	92,612	$47,687	7.0%	6.6%	8.9%	57,542	675,206
Massachusetts........	576,645	203,726	149,204	136,742	86,973	$37,277	8.2%	8.0%	10.4%	97,373	802,820
Michigan.............	898,838	304,291	304,442	213,947	76,158	$34,943	10.5%	7.6%	8.9%	157,636	1,209,960
Minnesota............	449,498	151,867	136,547	116,506	44,578	$36,666	6.8%	6.1%	10.4%	37,604	639,955
Mississippi...........	248,897	111,441	70,379	48,111	18,966	$28,387	15.2%	12.6%	14.7%	48,107	336,739
Missouri..............	544,100	200,801	174,415	123,437	45,447	$33,519	10.1%	7.4%	10.5%	73,808	745,137
Montana..............	97,403	34,471	31,495	22,942	8,495	$34,371	10.3%	6.6%	9.8%	8,903	140,384
Nebraska.............	159,628	56,255	48,651	39,797	14,925	$35,247	6.9%	5.0%	10.2%	12,522	225,455
Nevada...............	204,680	61,495	60,847	55,430	26,908	$40,185	10.5%	8.2%	8.9%	28,642	311,915
New Hampshire........	113,302	33,691	35,602	28,949	15,060	$39,906	5.2%	5.0%	7.9%	10,211	172,771
New Jersey...........	733,601	219,707	193,732	189,500	130,662	$42,590	7.0%	6.7%	8.9%	79,301	1,085,279
New Mexico..........	177,448	64,137	50,958	41,390	20,963	$35,238	13.7%	11.2%	13.3%	25,927	254,723
New York.............	1,639,609	590,336	426,442	379,097	243,734	$36,404	10.7%	10.3%	12.6%	379,931	2,227,379
North Carolina........	808,175	304,535	238,097	189,916	75,627	$33,596	11.0%	8.7%	11.7%	133,181	1,121,086
North Dakota.........	62,826	23,993	18,858	14,082	5,893	$33,281	6.2%	7.6%	14.5%	5,255	87,400
Ohio..................	1,060,964	381,850	353,139	241,587	84,388	$33,541	9.8%	7.3%	8.5%	161,708	1,452,553
Oklahoma.............	331,413	124,883	102,513	75,403	28,614	$32,718	10.6%	8.5%	10.9%	45,703	451,908
Oregon...............	351,883	113,740	111,724	90,754	35,665	$37,114	10.9%	7.5%	7.8%	69,020	483,480
Pennsylvania.........	1,248,228	461,559	394,361	277,603	114,705	$33,198	9.0%	7.1%	9.2%	167,477	1,710,799
Rhode Island.........	96,289	36,808	24,391	21,949	13,141	$34,898	10.1%	8.7%	10.1%	19,129	130,521
South Carolina........	416,443	155,236	124,005	95,894	41,308	$33,851	12.1%	8.7%	12.1%	69,497	577,922
South Dakota.........	74,354	28,663	21,794	17,335	6,562	$33,317	8.3%	8.0%	14.3%	7,026	102,258
Tennessee...........	555,184	216,740	169,365	122,114	46,965	$31,877	11.7%	9.2%	11.5%	111,887	756,627
Texas.................	1,628,989	573,880	459,942	391,651	203,516	$36,076	11.1%	10.1%	12.8%	295,491	2,380,441
Utah..................	160,392	44,325	49,284	46,129	20,654	$41,944	7.3%	5.6%	6.7%	16,535	231,992
Vermont..............	60,018	20,711	17,718	14,367	7,222	$36,411	7.1%	6.4%	8.0%	10,038	84,498
Virginia...............	631,149	189,790	171,514	162,796	107,049	$41,996	7.6%	6.5%	9.3%	79,188	934,931
Washington...........	541,768	158,759	163,486	151,335	68,188	$40,960	8.9%	7.1%	8.8%	94,528	774,628
West Virginia.........	196,951	84,950	62,888	38,094	11,019	$28,867	12.3%	8.9%	10.1%	29,997	270,643
Wisconsin............	510,565	182,364	165,529	121,168	41,504	$34,081	7.5%	5.8%	9.4%	56,892	709,037
Wyoming.............	45,398	15,243	14,486	11,212	4,457	$36,211	6.4%	4.7%	7.2%	2,736	69,151

Table G-2: Counties—Income, Poverty Status and Receipt of Food Stamps (SNAP)

	Income of Households with Householder 65 and Over					Poverty Rate of Persons			Households with 1 or More Persons 60 Years and Over	
	Total Households	Less Than $25,000	$25,000- $49,999	$50,000- $99,999	$100,000 or More	Median Household Income	55 to 64 Years	65 to 74 Years	75 Years and Over	Receiving SNAP	Not Receiving SNAP
Alabama											
Baldwin County	19,751	5,281	6,300	5,852	2,318	$41,904	8.3%	3.4%	7.8%	1,364	28,014
Calhoun County	11,127	4,133	3,540	2,497	957	$33,589	12.8%	11.5%	11.6%	1,990	15,052
Cullman County	8,672	3,883	2,850	1,495	444	$27,420	10.0%	13.3%	12.2%	1,036	11,687
DeKalb County	6,209	2,798	2,295	860	256	$26,630	12.0%	8.9%	18.4%	966	8,564
Elmore County	5,647	1,823	1,783	1,380	661	$39,281	7.0%	5.3%	10.9%	601	8,466
Etowah County	10,485	4,792	3,517	1,673	503	$27,591	13.6%	9.8%	12.9%	1,666	14,848
Houston County	9,594	3,846	2,896	2,131	721	$31,220	11.1%	8.3%	11.8%	1,242	12,968
Jefferson County	56,890	22,222	16,860	12,135	5,673	$32,150	11.9%	9.4%	12.2%	8,638	78,921
Lauderdale County	10,481	3,836	3,374	2,398	873	$33,961	8.4%	10.5%	11.5%	1,123	13,993
Lee County	8,548	2,842	2,234	2,170	1,302	$40,559	12.0%	6.2%	13.8%	1,399	12,701
Limestone County	7,086	2,656	1,963	1,758	709	$35,196	8.0%	7.7%	13.1%	1,288	9,714
Madison County	26,641	7,159	7,302	6,989	5,191	$45,638	7.5%	5.3%	8.6%	2,667	38,792
Marshall County	9,209	4,120	2,654	1,856	579	$28,602	11.3%	7.3%	12.5%	1,390	12,186
Mobile County	34,830	12,452	10,903	8,768	2,707	$34,535	12.1%	11.7%	11.6%	7,610	47,896
Montgomery County	18,557	5,595	5,684	4,562	2,716	$39,968	10.4%	7.4%	11.5%	3,248	25,731
Morgan County	10,798	3,726	3,356	2,701	1,015	$35,818	9.4%	5.8%	10.7%	1,349	15,084
St. Clair County	7,275	2,617	2,434	1,675	549	$30,631	12.3%	7.5%	8.8%	1,088	10,355
Shelby County	13,741	3,264	4,125	4,024	2,328	$47,007	6.1%	3.6%	3.1%	850	21,074
Talladega County	7,542	3,719	2,186	1,350	287	$25,596	12.1%	12.5%	15.2%	1,449	10,507
Tuscaloosa County	12,736	4,342	4,333	2,876	1,185	$36,075	11.9%	7.5%	9.1%	1,851	19,262
Walker County	7,241	2,689	2,659	1,405	488	$32,557	15.0%	11.1%	7.6%	1,104	9,870
Alaska											
Fairbanks North Star Borough	4,117	915	1,152	1,319	731	$49,583	4.7%	5.2%	8.0%	373	7,961
Matanuska-Susitna Borough	4,302	1,233	1,128	1,301	640	$44,690	7.2%	3.5%	5.8%	759	7,765
Arizona											
Apache County	5,401	2,325	1,701	1,093	282	$29,950	27.4%	22.0%	24.5%	1,622	6,741
Cochise County	15,260	5,265	4,908	3,583	1,504	$35,200	15.0%	10.4%	9.3%	2,726	19,777
Coconino County	7,670	2,325	1,940	2,131	1,274	$44,983	13.5%	11.0%	15.8%	1,515	11,558
Maricopa County	293,480	85,907	90,077	79,072	38,424	$40,580	10.0%	7.3%	8.1%	35,994	420,287
Mohave County	30,103	10,901	10,903	6,940	1,359	$33,522	12.7%	7.0%	8.4%	4,958	38,586
Navajo County	9,553	3,936	2,951	2,122	544	$29,391	21.3%	12.8%	17.8%	2,450	12,247
Pima County	97,843	29,976	29,760	25,738	12,369	$38,861	12.5%	8.5%	7.9%	14,713	133,804
Pinal County	33,042	9,213	11,724	8,893	3,212	$39,037	13.4%	7.8%	8.1%	3,055	46,958
Yavapai County	34,015	9,441	11,282	9,963	3,329	$40,435	14.6%	5.6%	4.8%	3,303	45,714
Yuma County	18,834	6,772	6,061	4,546	1,455	$34,434	17.0%	11.0%	10.7%	3,969	23,225
Arkansas											
Benton County	16,868	4,731	5,785	4,972	1,380	$40,133	7.9%	4.5%	5.1%	1,610	24,661
Craighead County	7,167	2,282	2,405	1,779	701	$35,802	11.4%	5.2%	12.6%	903	11,108
Faulkner County	7,091	2,444	1,924	2,144	579	$36,015	10.3%	6.5%	8.8%	705	10,348
Garland County	12,591	4,291	3,768	3,324	1,208	$36,346	16.4%	8.5%	10.7%	962	16,885
Jefferson County	6,807	2,714	2,047	1,650	396	$31,813	16.2%	11.3%	13.8%	1,480	8,962
Lonoke County	4,849	1,694	1,624	1,213	318	$35,019	10.0%	8.3%	13.4%	471	7,161
Pulaski County	29,549	9,621	7,923	7,676	4,329	$38,721	8.6%	7.9%	8.8%	3,713	43,439
Saline County	10,363	2,758	3,242	3,233	1,130	$42,640	5.3%	4.0%	7.0%	759	14,536
Sebastian County	10,599	4,010	3,724	1,798	1,067	$31,235	12.9%	6.5%	10.5%	1,376	14,689
Washington County	13,001	4,587	4,226	2,698	1,490	$34,135	8.8%	7.3%	11.9%	1,451	19,184
White County	7,476	2,814	2,473	1,618	571	$32,323	10.4%	6.8%	17.2%	844	9,597
California											
Alameda County	101,384	31,075	23,690	25,303	21,316	$45,124	9.9%	8.8%	10.9%	6,685	170,008
Butte County	22,252	7,249	6,605	5,734	2,664	$37,881	13.0%	8.5%	7.2%	1,877	32,176
Contra Costa County	81,300	18,429	21,069	23,796	18,006	$51,817	7.0%	5.3%	8.2%	5,075	130,883
El Dorado County	16,779	3,427	5,164	5,187	3,001	$48,646	5.7%	3.0%	6.7%	908	26,905
Fresno County	56,190	18,962	16,354	13,802	7,072	$36,808	15.3%	12.5%	11.7%	8,576	85,481
Humboldt County	11,281	3,829	3,398	2,888	1,166	$34,904	13.4%	7.2%	7.9%	631	17,936
Imperial County	10,086	4,881	2,605	1,674	926	$26,184	18.1%	16.2%	17.9%	1,774	14,873
Kern County	45,718	15,942	13,309	10,971	5,496	$36,152	13.3%	10.1%	10.5%	5,721	72,832
Kings County	6,842	2,449	2,037	1,639	717	$33,543	10.0%	10.9%	13.9%	794	10,635
Lake County	7,633	2,839	2,439	1,672	683	$32,088	19.3%	8.1%	14.6%	611	11,251
Los Angeles County	615,860	216,244	149,475	141,494	108,647	$38,728	12.7%	12.0%	14.3%	49,307	1,015,612
Madera County	9,464	2,801	3,039	2,676	948	$39,354	13.1%	8.5%	7.6%	1,207	14,851
Marin County	28,524	5,692	6,175	7,288	9,369	$61,684	6.5%	4.1%	7.3%	713	43,091
Mendocino County	8,852	3,020	2,447	2,239	1,146	$36,383	14.1%	9.3%	7.5%	639	13,853
Merced County	13,739	5,587	3,724	3,005	1,423	$31,367	12.2%	13.6%	14.1%	1,839	21,704
Monterey County	25,539	6,535	6,349	7,086	5,569	$49,392	9.0%	7.9%	7.0%	1,433	42,475
Napa County	12,918	3,249	3,515	3,177	2,977	$47,462	9.4%	6.4%	6.6%	855	19,680
Nevada County	12,646	2,874	4,277	3,391	2,104	$44,231	10.6%	7.6%	5.9%	461	19,189
Orange County	206,912	52,555	52,454	55,785	46,118	$49,106	8.0%	7.4%	9.9%	10,466	333,202
Placer County	34,439	8,864	9,641	10,498	5,436	$45,786	6.3%	5.8%	8.6%	1,531	50,729
Riverside County	155,054	48,931	46,170	38,158	21,795	$39,149	11.7%	8.9%	9.2%	12,494	237,310
Sacramento County	99,171	29,332	28,348	27,511	13,980	$40,806	11.4%	9.4%	8.5%	9,609	157,455
San Bernardino County	103,717	36,726	29,873	24,807	12,311	$35,579	12.9%	11.8%	11.3%	16,806	175,034
San Diego County	209,064	58,746	54,454	56,951	38,913	$45,183	10.8%	8.0%	10.2%	13,629	335,011
San Francisco County	68,503	27,464	14,412	13,936	12,691	$35,240	12.7%	12.7%	17.0%	4,984	107,704
San Joaquin County	41,585	13,518	11,985	10,644	5,438	$39,214	11.7%	8.9%	10.4%	4,393	67,594
San Luis Obispo County	25,629	7,004	6,264	7,615	4,746	$47,935	8.2%	6.1%	7.3%	1,241	38,962
San Mateo County	56,479	12,004	13,571	15,959	14,945	$55,595	5.9%	5.5%	7.2%	1,834	93,327
Santa Barbara County	33,861	8,746	8,724	8,999	7,392	$48,911	8.7%	6.0%	7.8%	1,742	49,489
Santa Clara County	112,271	28,724	26,457	28,968	28,122	$51,255	8.7%	6.9%	10.9%	7,454	187,164

Table G-2: Counties—Income, Poverty Status and Receipt of Food Stamps (SNAP)—*Continued*

		Income of Households with Householder 65 and Over					Poverty Rate of Persons			Households with 1 or More Persons 60 Years and Over	
	Total Households	Less Than $25,000	$25,000-$49,999	$50,000-$99,999	$100,000 or More	Median Household Income	55 to 64 Years	65 to 74 Years	75 Years and Over	Receiving SNAP	Not Receiving SNAP
California—Cont.											
Santa Cruz County	19,970	5,297	5,208	5,538	3,927	$46,069	9.8%	8.3%	7.9%	1,463	32,212
Shasta County	19,897	7,073	6,717	4,511	1,596	$34,821	11.7%	7.9%	9.3%	1,030	28,595
Solano County	28,831	7,479	7,036	8,892	5,424	$49,557	8.0%	7.9%	9.0%	2,701	47,466
Sonoma County	44,296	11,622	12,081	12,607	7,986	$45,911	8.8%	5.1%	8.8%	2,281	69,984
Stanislaus County	33,059	11,186	10,874	7,543	3,456	$35,270	12.5%	10.9%	12.0%	4,358	50,636
Sutter County	7,275	2,684	1,907	1,860	824	$37,314	10.1%	9.7%	14.3%	616	11,624
Tulare County	24,691	9,261	7,269	5,421	2,740	$34,054	16.3%	11.0%	13.5%	4,541	37,626
Ventura County	59,887	14,998	14,488	16,643	13,758	$50,807	6.3%	6.6%	8.3%	3,689	93,852
Yolo County	12,783	3,875	3,489	3,130	2,289	$41,494	8.8%	10.2%	11.3%	1,093	20,034
Yuba County	4,379	1,496	1,307	1,140	436	$36,911	16.4%	10.3%	10.7%	796	7,004
Colorado											
Adams County	23,266	7,194	7,237	6,556	2,279	$38,776	8.9%	7.1%	6.6%	3,267	36,644
Arapahoe County	38,061	10,370	10,254	10,899	6,538	$45,127	6.4%	7.1%	8.6%	3,955	60,273
Boulder County	19,981	4,451	5,622	5,496	4,412	$49,597	7.1%	3.9%	7.6%	1,195	31,434
Denver County	43,278	17,043	11,116	9,480	5,639	$33,508	13.3%	11.7%	14.1%	7,350	62,082
Douglas County	13,496	2,225	3,511	4,481	3,279	$57,711	3.6%	3.9%	5.6%	647	23,784
El Paso County	40,618	11,478	11,397	11,866	5,877	$43,369	8.1%	7.2%	7.2%	3,416	64,453
Jefferson County	44,554	11,027	13,366	13,402	6,759	$45,096	7.0%	5.5%	5.2%	2,326	70,639
Larimer County	23,052	6,321	6,742	6,888	3,101	$42,472	6.9%	4.2%	7.1%	1,429	35,934
Mesa County	14,901	5,599	4,527	3,503	1,272	$33,330	10.1%	7.7%	11.1%	1,354	20,435
Pueblo County	15,828	5,841	5,422	3,524	1,041	$32,464	13.7%	9.3%	11.6%	2,673	21,166
Weld County	15,559	5,171	4,651	4,204	1,533	$36,890	6.1%	7.0%	8.6%	1,613	24,308
Connecticut											
Fairfield County	76,458	19,105	18,250	19,770	19,333	$51,423	7.4%	6.3%	6.4%	8,889	110,020
Hartford County	81,908	26,817	22,236	20,692	12,163	$38,502	8.6%	7.5%	9.2%	14,811	111,095
Litchfield County	19,301	5,634	5,972	4,094	3,601	$39,662	6.9%	3.1%	7.4%	1,613	28,029
Middlesex County	15,872	4,222	4,504	4,583	2,563	$43,435	3.7%	2.6%	5.7%	1,058	24,413
New Haven County	77,105	26,073	21,359	18,480	11,193	$37,415	8.0%	7.1%	7.5%	12,448	108,213
New London County	24,579	6,775	7,266	7,089	3,449	$43,825	5.0%	5.0%	7.3%	3,528	36,034
Tolland County	11,494	2,649	3,247	3,621	1,977	$47,895	3.3%	3.1%	5.0%	872	17,714
Windham County	9,255	3,153	2,852	2,213	1,037	$36,331	7.2%	5.5%	5.3%	2,128	13,223
Delaware											
Kent County	13,607	4,001	4,186	4,214	1,206	$42,006	9.3%	6.3%	7.2%	2,330	18,892
New Castle County	42,316	12,736	11,348	11,186	7,046	$42,721	7.5%	7.0%	7.7%	5,749	60,806
Sussex County	26,052	7,133	7,477	8,310	3,132	$43,796	8.8%	6.3%	5.9%	2,696	35,353
Florida											
Alachua County	16,705	4,878	4,058	5,153	2,616	$44,867	14.2%	7.8%	8.4%	2,447	25,243
Bay County	16,502	5,632	5,126	3,957	1,787	$37,069	11.6%	6.3%	11.1%	1,503	22,967
Brevard County	70,245	21,098	23,548	18,462	7,137	$38,133	11.8%	6.4%	7.4%	7,415	92,264
Broward County	154,109	62,746	41,779	32,324	17,260	$31,312	12.7%	12.2%	12.5%	27,488	218,444
Charlotte County	34,637	9,572	11,959	10,091	3,015	$39,128	12.3%	5.1%	6.7%	2,618	41,939
Citrus County	27,506	9,511	9,614	6,486	1,895	$34,736	11.0%	7.8%	9.1%	2,324	34,722
Clay County	13,066	2,877	4,431	4,275	1,483	$43,381	8.8%	5.8%	5.4%	1,680	20,095
Collier County	52,578	11,049	13,809	14,271	13,449	$52,992	10.9%	7.5%	6.7%	3,059	66,306
Columbia County	6,336	2,606	2,053	1,289	388	$31,057	12.6%	8.2%	6.2%	1,460	8,369
Duval County	62,242	21,924	17,410	15,659	7,249	$36,523	12.8%	8.4%	10.2%	11,945	90,108
Escambia County	28,334	9,359	8,351	7,679	2,945	$37,984	13.7%	7.7%	9.6%	4,663	37,473
Flagler County	13,858	4,259	4,268	3,779	1,552	$41,035	10.8%	12.3%	7.9%	1,188	18,625
Hernando County	27,698	9,554	9,896	6,844	1,404	$34,514	10.1%	6.5%	8.0%	2,909	34,999
Highlands County	19,350	6,693	7,569	4,220	868	$33,403	14.4%	11.1%	13.3%	2,322	22,105
Hillsborough County	90,712	32,947	26,927	21,714	9,124	$34,785	13.6%	11.3%	12.4%	19,290	127,262
Indian River County	24,390	7,627	6,921	5,672	4,170	$38,843	11.9%	7.6%	6.7%	1,565	29,991
Lake County	44,524	13,365	16,049	11,769	3,341	$36,367	9.7%	6.0%	6.8%	3,973	55,564
Lee County	87,499	22,647	27,569	24,042	13,241	$43,159	11.4%	6.3%	7.5%	7,026	114,956
Leon County	17,555	4,834	4,560	5,100	3,061	$45,860	9.6%	6.6%	11.5%	2,627	26,524
Manatee County	48,208	15,395	14,598	12,905	5,310	$38,532	10.9%	6.2%	7.7%	3,856	61,587
Marion County	53,390	17,092	20,508	13,202	2,588	$34,521	13.6%	7.2%	7.3%	7,396	64,752
Martin County	24,833	6,863	7,456	6,362	4,152	$42,611	7.9%	6.8%	5.0%	1,624	30,830
Miami-Dade County	185,793	91,710	42,136	32,333	19,614	$25,494	17.3%	19.7%	23.4%	95,881	218,745
Monroe County	8,057	2,092	1,942	2,355	1,668	$49,865	11.3%	7.7%	9.4%	700	12,174
Nassau County	7,596	1,680	2,486	2,010	1,420	$44,882	10.2%	5.6%	10.8%	1,114	10,998
Okaloosa County	15,915	3,746	4,750	4,745	2,674	$47,343	7.3%	5.3%	5.8%	1,469	22,456
Orange County	65,171	22,887	19,357	16,194	6,733	$35,006	10.6%	10.7%	11.0%	14,293	98,901
Osceola County	17,294	6,102	5,872	4,207	1,113	$33,830	9.2%	10.4%	11.2%	4,843	26,148
Palm Beach County	177,102	52,873	48,110	44,037	32,082	$42,518	10.9%	8.5%	8.2%	15,737	227,992
Pasco County	60,399	21,420	22,442	13,015	3,522	$32,932	13.8%	8.6%	7.5%	7,011	79,035
Pinellas County	126,874	45,859	40,500	28,786	11,729	$33,862	12.3%	8.1%	8.9%	15,064	166,864
Polk County	67,040	23,216	22,144	17,460	4,220	$34,466	11.9%	9.0%	8.6%	9,908	87,505
Putnam County	8,909	3,638	2,872	2,007	392	$30,074	17.9%	12.5%	11.8%	1,973	11,587
St. Johns County	19,214	4,860	5,436	5,425	3,493	$45,478	10.3%	6.1%	11.4%	1,949	27,191
St. Lucie County	34,902	10,709	12,296	8,299	3,598	$36,523	14.8%	7.1%	8.9%	4,068	45,016
Santa Rosa County	12,360	3,256	3,492	4,339	1,273	$43,509	8.0%	6.7%	5.4%	1,275	18,177
Sarasota County	75,984	19,839	23,938	20,689	11,518	$42,373	11.3%	5.8%	6.7%	4,169	93,805
Seminole County	29,449	8,752	9,015	7,877	3,805	$41,575	7.8%	7.7%	8.1%	3,665	46,231
Sumter County	27,991	6,343	9,806	8,835	3,007	$43,701	12.6%	3.0%	7.2%	1,147	33,955
Volusia County	65,197	21,979	22,162	15,846	5,210	$36,117	13.6%	7.3%	9.5%	8,078	84,036

Table G-2: Counties—Income, Poverty Status and Receipt of Food Stamps (SNAP)—*Continued*

	Income of Households with Householder 65 and Over						Poverty Rate of Persons			Households with 1 or More Persons 60 Years and Over	
	Total Households	Less Than $25,000	$25,000-$49,999	$50,000-$99,999	$100,000 or More	Median Household Income	55 to 64 Years	65 to 74 Years	75 Years and Over	Receiving SNAP	Not Receiving SNAP
Georgia											
Barrow County	3,742	1,241	1,501	818	182	$33,239	8.4%	6.7%	12.8%	895	5,821
Bartow County	6,660	2,633	1,741	1,634	652	$32,576	11.3%	11.1%	17.0%	1,365	9,603
Bibb County	12,547	5,031	3,319	3,099	1,098	$33,179	20.8%	11.5%	12.9%	2,778	17,139
Bulloch County	4,231	1,555	1,260	1,059	357	$33,983	16.8%	9.7%	18.5%	781	5,898
Carroll County	7,632	3,233	2,101	1,555	743	$32,320	12.4%	11.4%	12.5%	1,792	10,978
Catoosa County	5,795	1,992	2,027	1,464	312	$35,400	9.8%	7.0%	7.0%	625	8,336
Chatham County	21,924	6,949	6,412	5,561	3,002	$38,295	12.0%	7.6%	10.5%	2,550	31,006
Cherokee County	12,997	3,861	3,992	3,385	1,759	$39,482	6.6%	5.2%	7.5%	1,501	20,446
Clarke County	6,367	2,024	1,490	1,633	1,220	$43,302	15.3%	10.8%	11.6%	1,366	8,694
Clayton County	9,931	3,406	3,030	2,707	788	$33,551	14.5%	12.7%	18.4%	3,780	16,906
Cobb County	39,393	10,132	11,870	10,831	6,560	$44,247	7.9%	6.5%	9.6%	4,321	64,441
Columbia County	7,634	1,729	2,208	2,573	1,124	$47,917	5.8%	7.8%	4.1%	843	13,078
Coweta County	8,188	2,303	2,360	2,489	1,036	$43,035	11.0%	5.4%	8.3%	920	13,918
DeKalb County	40,015	14,224	10,470	9,846	5,475	$36,770	12.8%	14.1%	12.2%	9,775	59,230
Dougherty County	7,852	3,221	2,414	1,585	632	$29,158	21.7%	15.5%	15.0%	2,192	10,177
Douglas County	6,597	2,170	1,964	1,852	611	$39,849	10.0%	8.5%	15.2%	1,568	11,680
Fayette County	8,868	1,859	2,734	2,889	1,386	$48,522	5.8%	6.1%	3.6%	633	13,674
Floyd County	9,051	3,752	3,172	1,549	578	$28,144	13.9%	13.2%	13.2%	1,522	12,225
Forsyth County	8,366	2,676	2,221	2,151	1,318	$40,720	6.6%	3.3%	9.3%	758	14,556
Fulton County	56,248	20,475	12,998	12,264	10,511	$38,655	15.0%	11.8%	13.5%	12,736	82,905
Glynn County	8,374	2,536	2,409	2,006	1,423	$40,144	8.9%	6.6%	15.1%	1,303	11,470
Gwinnett County	30,096	7,400	9,245	8,810	4,641	$45,354	7.1%	7.4%	8.7%	5,131	57,560
Hall County	12,796	3,882	3,740	3,598	1,576	$40,159	10.4%	7.1%	10.6%	1,957	18,750
Henry County	9,972	3,055	2,925	3,026	966	$42,567	9.0%	6.0%	4.8%	1,465	16,391
Houston County	8,976	2,447	2,531	2,993	1,005	$44,748	8.2%	7.7%	8.4%	1,446	13,488
Liberty County	2,671	870	734	736	331	$39,458	11.7%	9.5%	20.0%	416	4,054
Lowndes County	6,975	2,733	1,960	1,571	711	$33,079	13.3%	7.6%	11.0%	1,534	9,652
Muscogee County	15,015	6,044	4,222	3,298	1,451	$31,268	13.1%	13.2%	14.3%	3,605	19,551
Newton County	5,917	1,971	2,035	1,493	418	$37,859	14.0%	6.9%	6.7%	1,338	8,721
Paulding County	6,247	2,164	2,019	1,712	352	$36,282	8.9%	9.1%	11.6%	1,470	10,420
Richmond County	14,145	5,834	3,925	3,003	1,383	$33,480	16.8%	9.9%	15.5%	2,565	19,899
Rockdale County	5,647	1,802	1,921	1,357	567	$36,191	10.4%	9.2%	8.4%	1,266	8,470
Troup County	5,337	2,252	1,477	1,226	382	$30,908	12.7%	10.3%	14.6%	1,203	7,438
Walker County	6,583	2,825	2,110	955	693	$29,048	16.2%	5.7%	7.9%	1,030	8,823
Walton County	5,978	1,962	2,190	1,371	455	$35,973	11.5%	5.1%	12.0%	857	8,969
Whitfield County	6,887	2,999	1,577	1,625	686	$29,738	15.5%	9.7%	12.0%	1,425	9,438
Hawaii											
Hawaii County	16,222	5,451	4,417	3,971	2,383	$38,999	16.6%	9.5%	11.5%	3,304	25,173
Honolulu County	77,959	16,667	17,007	22,684	21,601	$59,292	7.5%	5.8%	8.2%	12,382	115,391
Kauai County	5,565	1,396	1,506	1,687	976	$48,666	9.8%	8.4%	8.0%	927	8,920
Maui County	11,138	2,489	2,231	3,754	2,664	$57,509	8.6%	4.1%	6.0%	1,910	18,685
Idaho											
Ada County	27,658	8,346	8,904	7,213	3,195	$38,979	7.4%	6.4%	7.2%	3,328	41,866
Bannock County	5,794	1,874	1,712	1,602	606	$39,647	9.0%	2.6%	8.2%	580	8,303
Bonneville County	7,600	2,452	2,508	1,980	660	$37,875	8.0%	5.7%	5.5%	938	10,725
Canyon County	13,265	4,764	4,566	3,389	546	$34,528	12.6%	7.1%	9.4%	2,049	18,039
Kootenai County	13,114	3,964	4,681	3,327	1,142	$35,463	9.0%	6.5%	12.3%	1,785	19,088
Twin Falls County	6,465	2,244	2,391	1,143	687	$31,282	10.8%	3.8%	11.9%	663	9,357
Illinois											
Adams County	7,170	2,541	2,493	1,624	512	$33,025	12.0%	4.9%	7.1%	844	9,389
Champaign County	13,396	3,456	3,928	3,667	2,345	$44,214	7.6%	5.3%	8.1%	1,384	19,434
Cook County	399,022	144,848	112,020	91,503	50,651	$34,700	12.2%	10.9%	12.2%	85,214	543,624
DeKalb County	6,674	2,480	1,666	1,611	917	$35,945	9.2%	4.0%	4.7%	453	10,033
DuPage County	66,279	15,642	18,590	18,472	13,575	$48,145	4.5%	3.7%	6.8%	4,938	104,711
Kane County	31,517	8,279	9,302	8,595	5,341	$44,740	6.2%	4.8%	7.2%	3,284	49,616
Kankakee County	9,408	3,198	3,222	2,404	584	$33,980	11.4%	6.6%	9.6%	1,377	13,255
Kendall County	5,443	1,317	1,614	1,521	991	$43,590	2.5%	4.6%	6.6%	557	8,679
Lake County	45,604	11,237	12,432	12,291	9,644	$47,930	6.0%	5.2%	6.7%	4,306	72,533
LaSalle County	11,928	4,158	3,844	3,097	829	$35,667	8.7%	4.8%	7.8%	833	16,053
McHenry County	19,867	5,203	5,505	6,027	3,132	$45,482	5.5%	4.0%	6.8%	1,247	32,024
McLean County	11,076	3,033	3,262	3,067	1,714	$42,799	6.6%	4.8%	4.8%	1,154	16,338
Macon County	11,817	3,784	4,598	2,498	937	$34,506	10.1%	5.0%	5.7%	1,342	16,138
Madison County	25,080	8,242	8,397	6,102	2,339	$36,181	7.9%	5.1%	6.2%	2,523	34,664
Peoria County	17,184	5,069	5,679	4,887	1,549	$39,895	10.3%	7.7%	6.2%	1,484	24,226
Rock Island County	16,222	5,448	5,801	3,823	1,150	$34,778	7.8%	5.1%	7.1%	1,624	22,415
St. Clair County	22,614	7,903	6,692	5,848	2,171	$35,370	10.9%	8.2%	10.5%	2,975	30,872
Sangamon County	18,562	5,107	5,841	5,039	2,575	$41,572	6.6%	5.7%	7.2%	1,810	26,878
Tazewell County	13,854	4,110	4,991	3,565	1,188	$36,977	5.5%	4.8%	7.9%	829	19,032
Vermilion County	8,899	3,416	2,999	1,988	496	$32,331	8.0%	7.0%	9.0%	978	11,785
Will County	39,421	10,997	11,510	11,524	5,390	$42,902	4.8%	4.9%	6.8%	4,537	61,488
Williamson County	6,960	2,659	2,479	1,410	412	$30,858	9.9%	7.6%	11.0%	788	9,570
Winnebago County	25,799	9,209	8,559	6,011	2,020	$33,699	12.7%	7.4%	7.2%	3,709	36,282

Table G-2: Counties—Income, Poverty Status and Receipt of Food Stamps (SNAP)—*Continued*

	Income of Households with Householder 65 and Over					Poverty Rate of Persons			Households with 1 or More Persons 60 Years and Over	
	Total Households	Less Than $25,000	$25,000-$49,999	$50,000-$99,999	$100,000 or More	Median Household Income	55 to 64 Years	65 to 74 Years	75 Years and Over	Receiving SNAP	Not Receiving SNAP
Indiana										
Allen County	27,935	8,422	10,233	6,840	2,440	$36,020	8.6%	6.8%	7.2%	2,817	40,319
Bartholomew County	6,948	2,634	2,272	1,379	663	$33,309	6.7%	4.4%	6.1%	676	9,934
Clark County	9,165	3,391	3,069	1,985	720	$33,373	7.2%	6.6%	6.6%	857	13,455
Delaware County	11,532	4,178	4,515	2,006	833	$30,676	9.9%	6.3%	7.3%	1,302	15,026
Elkhart County	15,273	5,119	5,774	3,650	730	$34,766	7.9%	5.9%	8.5%	1,557	21,676
Floyd County	6,332	2,234	2,013	1,636	449	$36,147	7.3%	10.3%	8.6%	712	8,920
Grant County	7,615	3,112	2,630	1,484	389	$29,400	16.9%	7.1%	9.7%	943	9,795
Hamilton County	14,779	3,306	4,677	4,353	2,443	$46,560	2.7%	3.2%	1.3%	1,036	24,783
Hancock County	5,619	1,647	2,103	1,376	493	$37,982	6.3%	4.2%	4.7%	447	8,442
Hendricks County	10,047	3,024	3,707	2,468	848	$36,475	2.8%	10.5%	4.9%	760	15,415
Howard County	9,030	2,904	3,583	2,063	480	$33,324	9.9%	5.1%	4.1%	630	12,458
Johnson County	11,086	3,235	3,820	3,009	1,022	$37,736	4.1%	5.8%	5.4%	1,079	16,064
Kosciusko County	6,939	2,190	2,426	1,692	631	$36,356	9.1%	4.9%	6.4%	497	9,786
Lake County	41,018	14,448	12,808	10,403	3,359	$33,725	11.7%	7.5%	9.2%	7,433	58,389
LaPorte County	10,456	4,007	3,373	2,287	789	$32,642	9.5%	8.1%	8.7%	1,495	14,517
Madison County	13,929	4,803	4,895	3,554	677	$35,470	11.4%	8.6%	7.6%	1,396	18,253
Marion County	63,430	22,749	21,248	14,261	5,172	$33,564	11.2%	8.6%	10.1%	11,696	88,231
Monroe County	9,410	3,065	2,592	2,495	1,258	$40,764	7.7%	4.2%	9.5%	830	13,646
Morgan County	5,550	1,964	1,729	1,503	354	$33,010	4.0%	3.3%	5.0%	572	8,913
Porter County	12,514	3,984	3,830	3,253	1,447	$36,802	7.7%	6.9%	4.6%	1,221	19,494
St. Joseph County	22,588	7,687	8,309	4,772	1,820	$33,465	8.9%	4.8%	8.0%	2,507	31,941
Tippecanoe County	10,609	2,992	3,458	2,913	1,246	$39,755	5.7%	3.9%	4.3%	1,150	15,526
Vanderburgh County	16,819	6,000	5,805	3,765	1,249	$33,157	7.6%	6.0%	6.9%	1,542	23,197
Vigo County	8,907	3,237	3,094	1,828	748	$31,738	10.2%	4.4%	7.2%	1,098	12,321
Wayne County	7,535	3,180	2,716	1,331	308	$28,226	14.4%	7.4%	9.4%	864	9,847
Iowa										
Black Hawk County	11,863	3,768	4,485	2,675	935	$34,630	6.7%	3.3%	6.7%	1,297	16,259
Dallas County	4,323	1,330	1,753	779	461	$34,903	4.7%	4.4%	6.1%	342	6,743
Dubuque County	8,939	3,013	3,442	2,150	334	$32,122	5.3%	4.1%	15.3%	669	12,312
Johnson County	7,794	2,049	2,004	2,495	1,246	$46,648	4.8%	3.6%	2.3%	467	12,291
Linn County	18,216	5,282	6,177	4,969	1,788	$38,821	7.0%	5.3%	5.4%	1,658	25,522
Polk County	30,000	9,129	9,653	8,088	3,130	$37,550	8.2%	4.7%	5.1%	4,691	44,866
Pottawattamie County	8,432	2,951	2,727	1,940	814	$35,072	5.4%	7.0%	11.8%	1,022	12,161
Scott County	14,428	4,737	4,928	3,464	1,299	$36,918	9.0%	6.1%	6.6%	1,436	21,064
Story County	5,780	1,305	1,747	1,673	1,055	$47,975	5.8%	2.4%	4.1%	367	8,311
Woodbury County	8,837	3,606	2,893	1,852	486	$30,663	11.1%	6.7%	10.1%	1,141	11,787
Kansas										
Butler County	5,372	1,772	2,085	1,005	510	$33,289	5.7%	2.4%	7.3%	265	7,585
Douglas County	6,461	1,765	1,951	1,823	922	$40,815	5.8%	5.4%	4.0%	581	9,872
Johnson County	39,101	9,165	10,962	11,659	7,315	$48,587	3.8%	3.6%	5.8%	1,559	60,932
Leavenworth County	5,331	1,759	1,506	1,258	808	$38,695	8.0%	6.4%	13.6%	482	8,008
Riley County	3,449	883	914	1,001	651	$45,981	7.0%	4.0%	4.5%	166	4,953
Sedgwick County	37,312	12,184	12,438	9,271	3,419	$36,749	8.4%	8.7%	8.0%	4,742	53,552
Shawnee County	16,495	4,722	5,232	4,655	1,886	$42,444	8.6%	5.5%	5.0%	1,454	24,057
Wyandotte County	10,853	4,214	3,492	2,506	641	$31,705	15.8%	10.3%	11.4%	2,067	15,465
Kentucky										
Boone County	7,509	2,363	2,449	2,104	593	$40,252	5.8%	9.9%	9.8%	723	12,024
Bullitt County	5,983	2,248	2,017	1,413	305	$34,533	7.6%	5.2%	10.3%	770	8,278
Campbell County	7,577	2,661	2,632	1,867	417	$34,696	8.2%	3.7%	8.7%	775	10,820
Christian County	4,833	1,845	1,319	1,203	466	$32,344	11.8%	4.0%	16.0%	804	6,393
Daviess County	9,372	3,702	3,038	2,105	527	$32,350	9.1%	8.1%	11.9%	1,248	12,350
Fayette County	20,954	6,666	6,044	5,543	2,701	$38,105	10.0%	7.8%	8.0%	3,147	30,699
Hardin County	7,210	2,693	2,190	1,702	625	$33,568	8.8%	5.9%	9.5%	1,050	10,728
Jefferson County	65,238	23,548	20,861	14,245	6,584	$34,066	10.7%	9.6%	10.1%	9,845	91,628
Kenton County	11,711	4,016	3,775	2,833	1,087	$35,169	8.8%	7.4%	8.7%	1,800	16,898
McCracken County	6,928	2,470	2,449	1,465	544	$34,479	10.2%	8.8%	8.7%	907	9,312
Madison County	6,097	2,325	1,884	1,501	387	$32,366	16.3%	11.8%	7.7%	1,080	8,245
Pike County	6,227	3,036	2,124	673	394	$25,501	16.3%	14.4%	12.9%	1,945	8,065
Warren County	8,312	3,071	2,751	1,865	625	$32,883	12.0%	6.2%	7.0%	1,206	11,138
Louisiana										
Ascension Parish	6,304	2,148	2,183	1,486	487	$35,271	7.0%	12.3%	7.3%	935	9,530
Bossier Parish	9,301	3,036	2,510	2,438	1,317	$38,110	9.8%	5.8%	6.1%	1,129	12,618
Caddo Parish	22,588	8,174	6,353	5,493	2,568	$34,346	15.7%	9.5%	11.7%	3,872	30,391
Calcasieu Parish	15,754	6,776	4,868	2,764	1,346	$28,791	9.2%	10.3%	9.7%	2,276	22,745
East Baton Rouge Parish	30,978	9,743	9,081	7,668	4,486	$39,683	11.5%	7.9%	10.9%	5,398	45,085
Iberia Parish	6,097	2,394	1,863	1,296	544	$32,059	16.5%	11.8%	17.0%	1,291	7,591
Jefferson Parish	38,072	14,836	10,609	8,870	3,757	$32,565	11.0%	9.9%	11.7%	6,369	54,321
Lafayette Parish	14,646	5,773	4,056	2,824	1,993	$32,861	12.1%	9.8%	11.7%	1,793	21,385
Lafourche Parish	7,842	3,750	2,367	1,199	526	$25,796	10.7%	9.3%	13.3%	1,349	10,521
Livingston Parish	8,216	3,303	2,678	1,706	529	$30,240	12.4%	7.3%	15.2%	1,618	12,482

Table G-2: Counties—Income, Poverty Status and Receipt of Food Stamps (SNAP)—*Continued*

	Income of Households with Householder 65 and Over						Poverty Rate of Persons			Households with 1 or More Persons 60 Years and Over	
	Total Households	Less Than $25,000	$25,000-$49,999	$50,000-$99,999	$100,000 or More	Median Household Income	55 to 64 Years	65 to 74 Years	75 Years and Over	Receiving SNAP	Not Receiving SNAP
Louisiana—Cont.											
Orleans Parish	26,272	11,327	6,789	5,167	2,989	$29,206	20.0%	15.9%	17.5%	7,908	36,959
Ouachita Parish	12,544	5,116	3,931	2,245	1,252	$30,994	17.8%	13.5%	19.4%	2,141	16,437
Rapides Parish	11,646	4,609	3,652	2,493	892	$32,282	14.7%	12.2%	13.2%	2,055	15,231
St. Landry Parish	7,576	4,068	2,045	1,175	288	$22,289	16.0%	20.9%	19.4%	1,670	10,008
St. Tammany Parish	18,763	6,156	5,111	5,049	2,447	$38,570	9.6%	6.8%	9.1%	2,483	29,021
Tangipahoa Parish	9,082	3,701	2,862	1,720	799	$31,460	13.6%	12.6%	16.9%	2,509	12,349
Terrebonne Parish	8,315	3,163	2,418	1,919	815	$31,467	14.3%	10.2%	6.7%	1,355	11,172
Maine											
Androscoggin County	9,997	4,396	2,962	2,191	448	$28,182	8.1%	10.2%	10.3%	2,184	13,283
Aroostook County	8,899	4,603	2,763	1,354	179	$24,162	10.3%	11.5%	14.7%	2,184	10,725
Cumberland County	25,922	8,624	7,389	6,987	2,922	$38,269	8.3%	6.6%	8.0%	3,931	37,329
Kennebec County	12,060	4,317	4,108	2,729	906	$31,977	9.0%	8.1%	7.8%	2,222	16,845
Penobscot County	14,088	6,103	4,374	2,900	711	$28,555	9.0%	7.5%	10.7%	2,824	19,549
York County	20,159	7,139	6,130	5,025	1,865	$34,788	7.0%	7.6%	9.1%	3,154	27,970
Maryland											
Allegany County	8,459	3,434	3,014	1,599	412	$29,568	10.0%	8.1%	9.8%	1,191	11,065
Anne Arundel County	40,034	8,827	9,615	11,696	9,896	$56,784	5.4%	5.3%	6.1%	3,391	63,322
Baltimore County	74,636	22,272	20,546	20,554	11,264	$42,059	6.4%	5.5%	8.1%	7,594	108,801
Calvert County	5,903	1,121	1,213	2,068	1,501	$58,558	2.5%	6.0%	3.1%	527	9,918
Carroll County	13,690	3,532	3,883	4,021	2,254	$44,505	4.0%	4.7%	6.5%	1,020	21,315
Cecil County	7,182	2,080	2,334	1,639	1,129	$40,154	7.0%	4.2%	9.6%	949	11,649
Charles County	7,861	1,699	1,818	2,677	1,667	$58,431	5.8%	7.4%	6.6%	1,007	13,818
Frederick County	16,698	3,927	4,185	5,195	3,391	$51,875	4.0%	4.2%	7.1%	1,408	26,150
Harford County	19,247	4,871	5,419	5,461	3,496	$47,564	4.1%	4.5%	7.0%	1,685	29,598
Howard County	17,728	2,916	3,932	5,731	5,149	$68,030	3.2%	3.6%	8.4%	1,674	29,628
Montgomery County	73,571	13,628	13,955	19,635	26,353	$70,018	4.8%	4.8%	8.8%	5,993	117,861
Prince George's County	50,886	10,739	10,834	16,511	12,802	$58,683	5.8%	6.1%	8.0%	7,413	85,364
St. Mary's County	6,787	1,474	1,501	2,409	1,403	$58,544	7.1%	4.3%	3.7%	827	10,030
Washington County	13,680	5,156	4,119	3,032	1,373	$33,186	8.2%	6.9%	8.7%	1,510	18,898
Wicomico County	8,249	2,441	2,626	2,233	949	$39,206	9.6%	6.4%	11.0%	973	11,428
Massachusetts											
Barnstable County	34,374	10,092	8,998	9,712	5,572	$43,073	7.1%	5.4%	8.6%	2,702	45,811
Berkshire County	16,435	6,174	4,851	3,819	1,591	$34,356	9.4%	5.2%	8.5%	2,320	22,036
Bristol County	48,386	21,006	12,677	10,136	4,567	$30,199	9.7%	8.1%	14.0%	9,472	65,988
Essex County	66,454	22,947	17,418	15,959	10,130	$37,115	8.4%	9.4%	9.6%	12,447	94,108
Franklin County	6,942	2,354	2,163	1,737	688	$36,097	8.6%	8.5%	7.1%	1,122	10,509
Hampden County	41,761	17,246	11,651	9,187	3,677	$30,223	11.7%	9.4%	11.2%	10,446	54,040
Hampshire County	13,699	3,953	4,032	3,495	2,219	$41,093	6.7%	4.7%	7.1%	1,412	20,308
Middlesex County	125,401	39,229	30,502	30,785	24,885	$42,562	6.6%	6.4%	9.1%	15,142	182,208
Norfolk County	62,632	18,361	15,962	16,283	12,026	$44,670	4.6%	4.9%	9.5%	6,454	88,739
Plymouth County	43,633	12,580	12,163	12,004	6,886	$42,330	5.5%	5.7%	7.3%	5,876	63,927
Suffolk County	51,273	25,224	10,667	8,675	6,707	$25,754	16.5%	19.1%	19.7%	18,955	61,474
Worcester County	63,136	23,718	17,546	14,458	7,414	$34,307	7.8%	7.5%	9.4%	10,960	90,054
Michigan											
Allegan County	9,407	3,328	3,151	2,160	768	$35,035	10.9%	6.7%	11.9%	1,518	12,851
Bay County	11,597	3,886	4,284	2,762	665	$33,943	9.7%	6.0%	9.7%	1,825	15,230
Berrien County	16,237	6,135	5,253	3,620	1,229	$32,112	11.7%	9.3%	9.9%	2,632	21,039
Calhoun County	13,077	4,954	4,293	2,905	925	$31,735	12.2%	8.7%	8.3%	2,857	16,996
Clinton County	6,360	1,906	2,193	1,684	577	$38,671	7.3%	2.5%	7.1%	639	9,062
Eaton County	9,751	2,766	3,662	2,637	686	$39,071	5.4%	6.2%	6.6%	1,181	13,799
Genesee County	39,113	11,785	15,296	9,390	2,642	$35,461	12.6%	7.8%	5.9%	8,556	50,996
Grand Traverse County	8,457	2,762	2,181	2,311	1,203	$39,578	9.3%	4.8%	9.3%	907	11,969
Ingham County	19,912	5,688	6,447	5,294	2,483	$39,964	8.8%	6.2%	7.0%	3,245	28,831
Isabella County	4,332	1,557	1,334	1,002	439	$35,239	9.6%	7.6%	8.3%	725	5,823
Jackson County	14,626	5,142	5,535	3,057	892	$34,138	11.6%	5.0%	6.2%	2,363	20,113
Kalamazoo County	20,203	6,626	6,720	5,196	1,661	$35,562	9.6%	6.9%	8.7%	3,149	28,001
Kent County	43,911	14,076	15,145	10,697	3,993	$35,615	7.8%	5.5%	7.3%	7,186	61,245
Lapeer County	7,587	2,273	2,722	2,077	515	$37,012	6.5%	4.9%	7.5%	930	10,906
Lenawee County	9,461	3,431	3,261	2,184	585	$32,110	9.6%	6.1%	11.6%	1,164	13,280
Livingston County	14,436	3,065	4,498	5,118	1,755	$47,985	4.6%	3.3%	6.0%	1,270	21,132
Macomb County	79,675	26,162	27,836	19,531	6,146	$35,300	8.8%	6.6%	9.1%	12,596	108,863
Marquette County	6,460	2,426	2,107	1,492	435	$32,556	9.7%	4.9%	9.4%	755	8,908
Midland County	8,123	2,566	2,843	1,852	862	$35,412	9.4%	4.1%	5.7%	1,181	10,558
Monroe County	13,592	4,574	4,899	3,212	907	$34,487	9.3%	6.4%	8.1%	1,656	19,643
Muskegon County	15,242	5,798	5,262	3,184	998	$31,705	11.6%	6.6%	10.5%	3,149	19,930
Oakland County	106,767	29,612	31,731	29,246	16,178	$42,040	7.2%	6.0%	7.5%	13,898	153,126
Ottawa County	19,807	5,624	7,448	5,209	1,526	$36,404	3.9%	4.6%	5.6%	1,961	27,662
Saginaw County	20,511	7,329	7,659	4,652	871	$33,312	13.4%	8.5%	8.7%	3,555	25,814
St. Clair County	15,532	4,957	5,853	3,862	860	$34,320	8.9%	6.8%	7.7%	2,703	21,519
Shiawassee County	6,427	2,331	2,071	1,600	425	$35,679	7.3%	4.7%	7.7%	754	9,015
Van Buren County	6,789	2,707	2,334	1,265	483	$31,125	13.3%	8.6%	12.9%	1,231	9,489
Washtenaw County	24,398	6,046	7,173	6,225	4,954	$45,625	6.9%	5.0%	6.8%	3,253	35,346
Wayne County	154,962	60,558	48,586	34,159	11,659	$31,747	16.8%	13.2%	12.1%	44,410	194,977

Table G-2: Counties—Income, Poverty Status and Receipt of Food Stamps (SNAP)—*Continued*

	Income of Households with Householder 65 and Over						Poverty Rate of Persons			Households with 1 or More Persons 60 Years and Over	
	Total Households	Less Than $25,000	$25,000-$49,999	$50,000-$99,999	$100,000 or More	Median Household Income	55 to 64 Years	65 to 74 Years	75 Years and Over	Receiving SNAP	Not Receiving SNAP
Minnesota											
Anoka County	21,874	6,066	7,234	6,573	2,001	$41,186	5.2%	4.8%	7.1%	1,856	33,946
Blue Earth County	4,944	1,754	1,510	1,200	480	$35,068	4.8%	6.6%	8.8%	430	6,846
Carver County	5,237	1,511	1,708	1,306	712	$39,083	2.9%	3.8%	10.6%	197	8,143
Dakota County	26,628	6,981	7,869	8,038	3,740	$44,154	4.1%	3.4%	5.8%	1,486	42,044
Hennepin County	87,965	27,060	25,250	22,820	12,835	$40,351	8.0%	7.9%	9.0%	10,550	127,591
Olmsted County	11,322	3,302	3,409	3,408	1,203	$41,158	4.5%	5.3%	9.9%	770	16,269
Ramsey County	40,715	12,843	11,653	11,327	4,892	$40,250	10.0%	6.8%	11.3%	5,293	58,532
St. Louis County	20,875	8,093	6,588	4,974	1,220	$32,522	9.7%	8.1%	9.6%	1,771	29,364
Scott County	6,480	2,043	1,605	2,005	827	$42,145	5.2%	5.1%	9.5%	422	10,728
Sherburne County	4,524	1,042	1,631	1,416	435	$38,605	3.7%	3.0%	14.5%	177	7,210
Stearns County	11,817	4,407	3,895	2,663	852	$33,514	6.8%	7.4%	11.1%	801	16,643
Washington County	16,953	4,340	4,344	5,743	2,526	$48,332	4.3%	3.8%	8.2%	790	26,562
Wright County	7,685	2,311	2,725	2,045	604	$35,908	5.2%	4.3%	9.2%	616	11,186
Mississippi											
DeSoto County	10,554	3,222	3,208	3,030	1,094	$39,989	7.1%	5.5%	7.1%	1,070	15,872
Forrest County	5,577	2,268	1,920	1,024	365	$31,023	20.5%	19.5%	13.8%	1,144	7,504
Harrison County	14,816	5,021	4,503	3,871	1,421	$36,754	13.6%	8.6%	11.6%	2,501	21,044
Hinds County	17,118	6,237	4,957	3,965	1,959	$35,016	18.2%	11.3%	10.7%	3,498	23,944
Jackson County	11,224	3,640	3,760	2,593	1,231	$35,442	11.7%	7.9%	8.2%	1,249	15,987
Jones County	6,240	2,600	2,040	1,238	362	$28,145	14.2%	12.4%	12.8%	1,043	8,337
Lauderdale County	7,316	3,130	1,840	1,503	843	$29,379	12.6%	11.8%	15.6%	1,320	9,246
Lee County	7,122	2,883	1,734	2,142	363	$32,852	11.0%	7.9%	12.5%	922	10,047
Madison County	6,612	2,329	1,657	1,350	1,276	$36,824	11.5%	6.6%	13.1%	1,120	9,569
Rankin County	10,708	3,795	2,870	2,688	1,355	$36,177	7.5%	8.0%	6.9%	1,176	15,693
Missouri											
Boone County	9,695	2,710	2,901	2,623	1,461	$43,039	5.7%	4.6%	9.1%	1,221	14,454
Buchanan County	7,777	3,019	2,573	1,794	391	$31,685	13.2%	9.6%	8.3%	1,242	10,590
Cape Girardeau County	6,487	2,272	2,386	1,367	462	$32,652	8.0%	5.8%	13.2%	675	8,904
Cass County	8,700	2,595	2,698	2,529	878	$41,526	5.8%	2.1%	7.1%	812	11,610
Christian County	6,348	2,353	2,189	1,368	438	$31,792	6.4%	4.7%	15.6%	471	9,159
Clay County	16,195	4,457	6,122	3,858	1,758	$38,802	4.5%	4.0%	4.5%	1,178	24,551
Cole County	6,589	1,990	1,937	1,852	810	$38,916	6.9%	5.2%	7.7%	625	9,255
Franklin County	8,825	3,014	3,585	1,715	511	$32,881	9.9%	6.9%	8.5%	986	12,414
Greene County	25,202	8,791	8,644	5,754	2,013	$34,137	10.5%	6.6%	8.8%	2,577	35,168
Jackson County	56,156	20,211	17,636	13,165	5,144	$34,724	12.3%	7.8%	8.1%	8,232	77,739
Jasper County	9,733	4,179	3,348	1,596	610	$28,706	9.7%	7.6%	13.5%	1,726	13,132
Jefferson County	15,780	4,836	5,697	4,354	893	$37,721	6.8%	6.3%	6.3%	1,903	23,589
Platte County	6,619	1,719	2,309	1,688	903	$38,423	3.8%	3.1%	5.6%	449	10,279
St. Charles County	27,199	6,720	9,496	8,414	2,569	$42,300	5.1%	3.3%	6.5%	1,589	40,493
St. Francois County	6,033	2,675	1,956	1,023	379	$27,628	12.4%	11.3%	13.5%	1,186	7,484
St. Louis County	96,508	28,226	28,826	25,090	14,366	$40,963	6.6%	5.5%	7.9%	9,870	135,386
Montana											
Cascade County	8,117	2,610	2,945	2,062	500	$37,048	7.5%	5.9%	7.6%	772	11,433
Flathead County	8,779	2,785	2,927	2,068	999	$40,607	10.4%	5.9%	7.2%	942	12,701
Gallatin County	5,808	1,385	2,124	1,565	734	$42,899	8.1%	4.1%	5.8%	351	8,861
Missoula County	8,036	2,691	2,437	1,897	1,011	$37,381	8.4%	6.1%	10.3%	774	12,369
Yellowstone County	14,161	4,669	4,531	3,724	1,237	$35,717	7.1%	7.8%	8.9%	1,192	19,766
Nebraska											
Douglas County	37,242	12,034	10,974	9,722	4,512	$37,929	8.2%	4.9%	11.8%	4,244	54,426
Lancaster County	20,392	5,708	6,450	5,741	2,493	$42,166	7.0%	4.3%	6.6%	1,846	30,271
Sarpy County	8,953	2,114	3,001	2,949	889	$44,222	2.6%	2.7%	4.5%	432	14,389
Nevada											
Clark County	137,213	40,849	40,789	37,894	17,681	$40,374	10.6%	8.4%	9.3%	21,265	209,749
Washoe County	32,880	10,570	9,049	7,895	5,366	$39,267	10.7%	7.8%	9.0%	3,878	51,673
New Hampshire											
Cheshire County	7,472	2,318	2,548	1,913	693	$36,928	4.6%	6.7%	9.8%	838	11,139
Grafton County	8,927	2,709	2,949	1,892	1,377	$37,943	4.4%	5.2%	7.9%	671	12,662
Hillsborough County	29,700	8,994	9,361	7,380	3,965	$38,620	4.6%	5.1%	7.1%	2,843	46,134
Merrimack County	12,436	3,517	3,989	3,146	1,784	$39,462	6.5%	4.6%	6.8%	1,153	19,366
Rockingham County	24,103	6,556	6,324	7,374	3,849	$46,519	3.1%	4.4%	8.0%	1,628	38,120
Strafford County	9,381	2,817	3,227	2,290	1,047	$40,064	7.3%	5.0%	6.0%	1,340	13,414
New Jersey											
Atlantic County	24,270	7,853	7,096	5,904	3,417	$38,552	10.3%	10.7%	8.8%	3,345	35,621
Bergen County	83,020	22,794	19,514	20,468	20,244	$48,446	5.8%	5.8%	9.7%	6,509	123,404
Burlington County	39,411	9,137	11,412	12,255	6,607	$48,110	3.9%	3.7%	5.6%	2,792	58,977
Camden County	41,664	14,392	11,802	9,726	5,744	$36,004	7.5%	9.7%	9.0%	5,931	60,129
Cape May County	13,676	3,715	4,629	3,461	1,871	$40,135	5.9%	3.9%	9.5%	858	19,195
Cumberland County	12,301	4,940	3,449	2,885	1,027	$31,140	14.4%	12.2%	12.0%	2,061	17,321
Essex County	55,719	21,416	12,612	11,792	9,899	$35,698	11.9%	11.7%	12.0%	11,124	78,410
Gloucester County	22,640	6,162	7,289	6,537	2,652	$42,135	4.4%	4.7%	7.2%	1,825	35,493
Hudson County	40,421	17,688	9,997	8,303	4,433	$29,577	12.8%	12.8%	16.6%	9,946	59,719
Hunterdon County	10,475	2,021	2,231	3,262	2,961	$61,428	2.2%	2.4%	6.0%	516	16,334

Table G-2: Counties—Income, Poverty Status and Receipt of Food Stamps (SNAP)—*Continued*

	Income of Households with Householder 65 and Over					Poverty Rate of Persons			Households with 1 or More Persons 60 Years and Over	
Total Households	Less Than $25,000	$25,000-$49,999	$50,000-$99,999	$100,000 or More	Median Household Income	55 to 64 Years	65 to 74 Years	75 Years and Over	Receiving SNAP	Not Receiving SNAP
New Jersey—Cont.										
Mercer County	29,042	8,185	7,169	7,456	6,232	$46,458	7.4%	5.8%	8.3%	3,224	43,665
Middlesex County	58,029	16,014	15,233	16,163	10,619	$45,105	5.9%	4.8%	7.0%	5,341	91,876
Monmouth County	56,213	14,779	14,439	14,684	12,311	$47,966	4.7%	4.1%	7.2%	3,566	85,169
Morris County	41,827	8,836	9,673	12,511	10,807	$57,253	3.7%	3.2%	6.0%	2,427	64,089
Ocean County	79,232	24,279	25,975	19,923	9,055	$37,763	6.2%	5.1%	7.0%	4,616	104,311
Passaic County	34,527	12,563	8,415	8,251	5,298	$38,050	9.6%	11.6%	13.1%	6,921	51,232
Salem County	6,556	2,020	1,955	1,843	738	$39,630	9.0%	5.4%	7.4%	537	9,269
Somerset County	24,470	5,415	5,588	7,302	6,165	$56,680	3.7%	4.6%	8.3%	1,498	38,451
Sussex County	11,022	2,459	2,751	3,377	2,435	$52,590	3.5%	2.0%	5.8%	648	17,883
Union County	40,075	12,152	9,937	11,071	6,915	$43,832	7.6%	6.2%	10.2%	4,817	60,368
Warren County	9,011	2,887	2,566	2,326	1,232	$40,200	5.3%	5.1%	6.4%	799	14,363
New Mexico										
Bernalillo County	53,537	16,685	15,377	13,637	7,838	$39,839	12.3%	8.6%	10.2%	7,415	79,956
Chaves County	5,676	2,194	1,577	1,213	692	$35,080	15.4%	13.0%	15.9%	1,180	7,618
Doña Ana County	16,964	6,492	3,982	4,558	1,932	$35,520	14.0%	12.6%	17.9%	2,850	22,580
Lea County	4,453	1,884	1,257	879	433	$30,701	7.6%	11.0%	16.0%	805	5,937
McKinley County	4,378	2,542	891	723	222	$21,132	23.0%	27.3%	36.4%	974	6,065
Otero County	6,175	2,293	2,082	1,493	307	$33,873	16.7%	14.9%	6.5%	884	8,873
Sandoval County	10,240	2,738	2,962	2,999	1,541	$43,411	15.1%	7.0%	8.1%	1,266	15,888
San Juan County	8,792	3,183	2,644	1,900	1,065	$33,571	13.0%	15.0%	16.5%	815	13,226
Santa Fe County	15,667	4,477	4,055	4,176	2,959	$45,101	11.4%	7.9%	11.2%	1,549	23,986
Valencia County	6,177	2,351	2,031	1,326	469	$31,473	13.0%	19.5%	19.0%	1,322	8,883
New York										
Albany County	26,694	8,277	7,242	7,505	3,670	$41,516	6.8%	7.2%	8.6%	3,177	38,688
Bronx County	89,776	48,710	20,100	13,882	7,084	$22,147	22.6%	23.2%	24.8%	52,145	98,819
Broome County	20,716	7,460	7,036	4,303	1,917	$34,035	10.3%	7.0%	7.9%	3,106	27,716
Cattaraugus County	7,955	3,434	2,374	1,647	500	$28,674	7.8%	7.1%	11.2%	1,335	10,840
Cayuga County	8,022	2,824	2,652	1,880	666	$34,003	8.8%	4.9%	10.1%	1,182	11,349
Chautauqua County	14,404	5,811	4,994	2,786	813	$30,569	10.9%	6.5%	9.3%	2,411	19,415
Chemung County	8,794	3,438	2,591	1,998	767	$31,581	9.4%	6.2%	9.3%	1,254	12,166
Clinton County	7,230	2,746	1,968	1,844	672	$34,253	9.5%	7.6%	14.4%	1,211	9,539
Dutchess County	25,133	6,362	7,284	7,131	4,356	$45,404	6.8%	4.8%	6.3%	2,674	36,980
Erie County	94,461	34,532	28,699	22,775	8,455	$33,941	9.2%	6.6%	9.5%	15,517	123,171
Jefferson County	8,655	3,283	2,837	1,954	581	$32,900	10.9%	6.6%	7.9%	2,051	11,562
Kings County	180,377	93,658	40,017	29,431	17,271	$23,672	17.4%	20.0%	25.8%	87,215	218,741
Livingston County	5,743	2,119	1,837	1,354	433	$34,094	5.6%	7.0%	6.4%	602	8,185
Madison County	6,509	2,200	1,912	1,875	522	$37,038	8.1%	5.5%	9.3%	953	9,092
Monroe County	68,181	22,189	21,193	17,772	7,027	$36,817	8.3%	7.7%	8.1%	10,188	91,655
Nassau County	118,422	26,016	27,346	32,805	32,255	$56,527	4.4%	4.2%	6.0%	10,083	181,444
New York County	153,315	62,133	30,148	26,572	34,462	$34,727	17.6%	16.0%	20.2%	48,195	179,725
Niagara County	22,254	8,528	7,258	4,936	1,532	$33,186	9.8%	7.8%	10.7%	3,720	29,829
Oneida County	23,948	8,791	7,582	5,636	1,939	$34,977	9.8%	8.8%	10.6%	4,616	32,091
Onondaga County	42,609	15,456	12,177	10,323	4,653	$34,581	8.9%	7.8%	7.4%	7,164	56,650
Ontario County	10,730	3,551	3,124	2,820	1,235	$36,984	4.3%	5.4%	8.6%	1,329	15,895
Orange County	25,451	7,416	7,211	6,562	4,262	$42,222	7.7%	7.1%	6.8%	3,965	37,874
Oswego County	9,931	3,339	3,371	2,516	705	$32,833	11.5%	4.8%	11.1%	1,679	13,762
Putnam County	7,531	1,477	2,183	1,962	1,909	$51,628	3.3%	3.8%	6.0%	346	12,070
Queens County	164,595	63,328	40,354	37,774	23,139	$34,298	11.7%	13.0%	14.3%	52,039	232,879
Rensselaer County	13,772	4,265	4,312	3,901	1,294	$38,175	5.7%	6.9%	5.7%	1,721	20,706
Richmond County	35,919	11,321	8,634	9,542	6,422	$42,366	8.3%	9.1%	13.4%	6,845	55,067
Rockland County	24,214	5,508	5,429	7,017	6,260	$58,347	5.5%	5.1%	8.6%	2,719	35,822
St. Lawrence County	10,195	3,779	3,400	2,346	670	$31,900	11.5%	9.9%	7.0%	1,830	13,490
Saratoga County	19,879	5,390	5,900	6,011	2,578	$42,749	4.3%	4.7%	6.7%	2,297	28,384
Schenectady County	14,296	4,438	4,405	4,035	1,418	$37,583	6.7%	7.9%	5.7%	1,558	19,432
Steuben County	10,147	3,607	3,553	2,184	803	$33,147	9.7%	5.8%	10.7%	1,440	14,379
Suffolk County	120,129	27,547	30,068	35,144	27,370	$52,942	5.4%	4.7%	7.0%	12,022	182,072
Sullivan County	7,407	2,186	2,509	1,957	755	$38,841	12.0%	7.3%	9.4%	1,118	10,364
Tompkins County	7,172	2,168	1,659	1,984	1,361	$47,901	6.8%	5.0%	7.5%	916	10,961
Ulster County	17,228	5,513	4,917	4,589	2,209	$39,812	10.7%	5.6%	9.4%	2,678	25,706
Warren County	7,525	2,316	2,358	1,983	868	$37,445	8.6%	5.5%	10.4%	1,008	10,443
Wayne County	8,545	2,694	3,115	2,182	554	$35,752	8.2%	4.5%	8.9%	1,313	12,168
Westchester County	85,012	22,708	18,132	21,624	22,548	$52,858	6.2%	5.7%	8.5%	8,283	123,129
North Carolina										
Alamance County	15,143	6,411	4,552	3,070	1,110	$31,508	9.4%	8.7%	9.5%	1,865	19,944
Brunswick County	15,532	4,403	4,291	4,848	1,990	$45,008	13.2%	4.9%	6.1%	1,470	21,980
Buncombe County	24,525	8,252	7,485	6,015	2,773	$38,385	12.0%	6.7%	10.0%	3,424	34,610
Burke County	9,550	4,410	2,828	1,814	498	$26,294	15.0%	8.0%	9.6%	1,411	12,806
Cabarrus County	12,266	4,344	4,100	3,089	733	$35,139	7.9%	5.6%	9.4%	1,724	18,050
Caldwell County	8,715	4,762	2,174	1,530	249	$22,753	14.1%	12.5%	10.7%	1,497	11,995
Carteret County	8,027	2,387	2,218	2,510	912	$42,951	9.3%	6.8%	6.6%	978	11,342
Catawba County	13,927	5,130	4,955	2,754	1,088	$30,921	9.6%	6.1%	10.7%	1,978	19,805
Chatham County	7,609	1,934	2,369	2,036	1,270	$45,616	9.6%	3.0%	8.3%	625	11,232
Cleveland County	10,113	4,851	2,880	1,834	548	$26,186	14.1%	8.5%	15.1%	1,590	12,958

Table G-2: Counties—Income, Poverty Status and Receipt of Food Stamps (SNAP)—*Continued*

	Total Households	Income of Households with Householder 65 and Over					Poverty Rate of Persons			Households with 1 or More Persons 60 Years and Over	
		Less Than $25,000	$25,000-$49,999	$50,000-$99,999	$100,000 or More	Median Household Income	55 to 64 Years	65 to 74 Years	75 Years and Over	Receiving SNAP	Not Receiving SNAP
North Carolina—Cont.											
Craven County	10,411	3,234	2,847	3,139	1,191	$41,868	9.6%	5.4%	13.3%	1,801	13,773
Cumberland County	20,132	7,125	5,755	5,351	1,901	$36,058	10.6%	10.0%	12.8%	4,611	28,478
Davidson County	15,360	6,583	4,688	3,499	590	$28,904	12.2%	10.5%	11.8%	2,243	21,439
Durham County	17,478	5,437	4,924	4,268	2,849	$40,959	8.1%	8.4%	9.4%	3,190	25,593
Forsyth County	29,928	9,666	9,884	7,168	3,210	$36,023	9.6%	6.0%	7.6%	2,708	43,404
Gaston County	17,191	7,376	5,156	3,621	1,038	$29,063	13.6%	8.9%	13.1%	3,755	23,868
Guilford County	40,114	13,173	12,252	9,808	4,881	$36,849	10.0%	7.5%	9.7%	6,205	55,664
Harnett County	7,745	3,466	2,043	1,707	529	$27,200	13.5%	10.2%	12.4%	1,355	10,730
Henderson County	15,045	4,277	4,721	4,476	1,571	$40,789	9.3%	6.4%	5.9%	915	20,258
Iredell County	12,673	4,915	3,992	2,902	864	$31,571	10.3%	7.3%	10.4%	1,081	19,388
Johnston County	11,292	4,359	3,717	2,689	527	$33,115	8.9%	8.4%	11.8%	2,023	16,374
Lincoln County	6,568	2,516	2,010	1,411	631	$30,882	10.5%	10.2%	13.5%	847	9,560
Mecklenburg County	52,955	15,842	14,642	14,715	7,756	$41,517	10.3%	7.0%	8.0%	9,218	80,185
Moore County	12,681	4,137	3,257	3,273	2,014	$39,888	9.2%	8.0%	7.8%	1,111	16,236
Nash County	9,311	3,951	2,694	2,002	664	$30,176	10.6%	8.9%	19.1%	2,076	12,302
New Hanover County	18,801	5,469	5,126	5,459	2,747	$44,506	10.4%	6.7%	7.8%	2,365	26,010
Onslow County	8,668	2,851	2,722	2,657	438	$35,776	9.2%	8.1%	9.4%	1,334	12,535
Orange County	8,516	2,113	2,239	2,098	2,066	$47,500	9.9%	7.6%	4.7%	856	12,842
Pitt County	11,087	4,699	3,121	2,272	995	$32,019	10.7%	11.5%	17.6%	2,722	14,928
Randolph County	12,944	5,556	3,767	3,062	559	$28,327	12.0%	6.7%	16.4%	1,827	18,565
Robeson County	9,833	5,140	2,449	1,749	495	$23,898	18.2%	19.5%	21.7%	3,554	12,463
Rockingham County	9,877	4,390	3,171	1,758	558	$28,458	12.5%	12.5%	13.8%	1,876	13,033
Rowan County	13,295	5,379	4,489	2,769	658	$30,244	11.7%	9.5%	11.0%	1,681	17,979
Rutherford County	7,588	3,785	2,481	980	342	$25,075	13.9%	11.2%	13.2%	1,398	10,309
Surry County	8,442	4,176	2,275	1,433	558	$25,489	12.9%	15.0%	15.0%	1,671	10,705
Union County	11,867	3,724	3,643	3,300	1,200	$37,496	7.7%	5.3%	9.1%	1,765	18,079
Wake County	50,571	12,565	14,207	15,172	8,627	$46,529	6.0%	5.0%	7.9%	6,159	79,237
Wayne County	10,404	4,390	2,842	2,473	699	$31,184	12.8%	12.5%	12.9%	2,400	14,006
Wilkes County	7,838	3,850	2,434	1,155	399	$25,481	15.8%	10.6%	17.4%	1,347	10,207
Wilson County	7,792	3,506	2,500	1,495	291	$29,179	16.4%	7.1%	17.0%	1,437	10,202
North Dakota											
Burleigh County	7,417	2,301	2,295	2,071	750	$40,946	5.9%	5.0%	11.6%	564	10,467
Cass County	9,923	3,027	3,027	2,527	1,342	$38,866	4.7%	6.8%	8.3%	765	14,964
Grand Forks County	4,748	1,597	1,598	1,005	548	$35,974	3.8%	6.4%	14.5%	386	6,680
Ohio											
Allen County	9,963	3,606	3,647	2,313	397	$32,746	12.0%	7.8%	7.1%	1,392	13,291
Ashtabula County	10,295	4,888	3,174	1,738	495	$26,349	11.1%	12.0%	11.4%	1,885	13,505
Belmont County	7,881	3,218	3,245	1,180	238	$29,708	11.5%	5.9%	6.9%	1,009	11,004
Butler County	27,637	8,835	8,851	7,602	2,349	$37,351	8.2%	5.2%	6.4%	3,484	40,333
Clark County	14,890	5,098	5,159	3,430	1,203	$34,847	11.1%	6.9%	7.3%	3,285	18,662
Clermont County	15,326	4,698	5,175	4,194	1,259	$36,750	7.9%	5.0%	6.3%	1,720	22,714
Columbiana County	11,225	4,191	4,093	2,422	519	$30,591	12.3%	6.7%	6.4%	2,085	14,943
Cuyahoga County	131,447	54,019	39,298	26,981	11,149	$30,519	12.8%	10.3%	10.7%	25,045	171,902
Delaware County	10,771	2,670	2,942	3,210	1,949	$47,063	3.9%	2.9%	6.1%	1,215	17,216
Erie County	8,524	2,960	3,070	1,878	616	$35,517	6.8%	3.8%	8.4%	1,112	11,771
Fairfield County	11,630	3,400	3,909	3,447	874	$40,590	8.6%	3.9%	6.6%	2,018	16,157
Franklin County	76,037	25,779	22,078	18,881	9,299	$36,166	10.4%	8.6%	7.6%	14,856	109,754
Geauga County	8,947	2,289	2,682	2,677	1,299	$43,557	5.3%	4.9%	6.8%	548	13,721
Greene County	14,111	3,525	4,470	3,955	2,161	$43,349	6.6%	5.6%	5.4%	1,520	20,345
Hamilton County	70,311	24,922	20,146	16,222	9,021	$35,640	11.5%	7.2%	9.4%	9,629	96,500
Hancock County	6,948	2,365	2,218	1,823	542	$37,602	6.0%	4.6%	5.2%	530	9,655
Jefferson County	8,400	3,151	3,204	1,595	450	$32,103	9.7%	7.3%	7.0%	999	11,043
Lake County	24,006	7,964	8,369	5,701	1,972	$34,990	6.7%	5.5%	6.1%	2,431	33,451
Licking County	14,450	4,687	4,677	4,036	1,050	$35,778	7.3%	4.6%	6.7%	1,644	20,752
Lorain County	27,906	8,418	10,118	6,993	2,377	$36,675	7.5%	6.8%	6.5%	3,635	39,483
Lucas County	38,251	14,164	12,914	8,315	2,858	$32,353	12.2%	7.9%	9.8%	7,309	50,547
Mahoning County	28,479	11,600	10,146	5,391	1,342	$29,763	9.2%	8.2%	9.4%	5,218	36,542
Marion County	6,414	2,640	2,189	1,251	334	$29,359	12.1%	10.6%	5.1%	1,079	8,337
Medina County	14,720	4,003	5,163	4,176	1,378	$39,308	6.3%	4.2%	5.8%	1,626	21,288
Miami County	10,437	3,150	3,533	2,966	788	$36,586	7.5%	4.3%	7.8%	693	14,658
Montgomery County	55,283	19,933	18,621	12,411	4,318	$33,408	10.7%	9.0%	8.8%	8,142	74,458
Muskingum County	8,262	3,776	2,870	1,253	363	$27,556	10.9%	6.1%	10.6%	1,829	11,182
Portage County	13,015	3,667	4,469	3,905	974	$39,217	7.9%	4.1%	6.7%	1,516	18,979
Richland County	13,532	5,004	4,909	2,897	722	$32,471	11.9%	7.7%	6.5%	1,904	18,001
Ross County	6,824	2,670	2,495	1,290	369	$32,749	11.4%	7.9%	7.9%	1,193	8,601
Scioto County	8,017	3,953	2,472	1,398	194	$25,571	17.1%	14.4%	10.8%	2,797	9,185
Stark County	38,956	13,531	14,150	9,039	2,236	$33,976	9.3%	4.9%	8.0%	4,818	52,622
Summit County	51,983	17,687	17,656	11,857	4,783	$35,175	9.8%	7.4%	8.3%	7,758	71,593
Trumbull County	23,974	8,695	8,938	4,991	1,350	$32,801	9.5%	7.5%	7.7%	3,229	33,492
Tuscarawas County	9,621	3,782	3,769	1,741	329	$29,750	9.4%	7.1%	8.3%	1,240	12,886
Warren County	14,338	3,898	4,813	4,226	1,401	$40,313	3.8%	5.0%	5.4%	984	22,824
Wayne County	10,462	3,632	3,284	2,687	859	$35,737	8.7%	5.9%	7.7%	1,407	14,782
Wood County	10,464	3,245	3,699	2,485	1,035	$37,117	6.1%	3.8%	5.7%	785	14,988

Table G-2: Counties—Income, Poverty Status and Receipt of Food Stamps (SNAP)—*Continued*

	Income of Households with Householder 65 and Over						Poverty Rate of Persons			Households with 1 or More Persons 60 Years and Over	
	Total Households	Less Than $25,000	$25,000-$49,999	$50,000-$99,999	$100,000 or More	Median Household Income	55 to 64 Years	65 to 74 Years	75 Years and Over	Receiving SNAP	Not Receiving SNAP
Oklahoma											
Canadian County	8,051	2,317	2,417	2,240	1,077	$40,691	4.8%	2.8%	6.6%	859	11,980
Cleveland County	16,651	4,471	4,973	4,815	2,392	$43,839	7.3%	7.5%	7.4%	2,014	25,305
Comanche County	8,725	2,794	2,757	2,246	928	$37,332	10.5%	7.0%	14.0%	1,254	11,405
Creek County	6,708	2,763	2,027	1,421	497	$28,651	11.4%	9.7%	9.9%	988	9,280
Muskogee County	6,568	2,734	2,127	1,419	288	$30,706	16.4%	11.2%	5.8%	1,127	8,773
Oklahoma County	57,340	19,078	17,067	14,751	6,444	$37,140	11.3%	8.2%	8.6%	8,700	79,945
Payne County	5,209	1,690	1,555	1,521	443	$36,802	8.7%	4.4%	12.9%	639	7,108
Pottawatomie County	6,421	2,834	1,960	1,184	443	$28,697	14.0%	11.6%	10.5%	1,012	8,400
Rogers County	7,325	2,223	2,369	2,175	558	$38,649	7.1%	3.0%	10.2%	864	10,507
Tulsa County	48,412	16,539	14,804	11,175	5,894	$35,741	8.6%	6.7%	9.6%	5,406	69,085
Wagoner County	6,146	1,975	2,244	1,526	401	$35,125	7.8%	3.5%	10.7%	775	9,073
Oregon											
Benton County	6,771	1,527	1,924	2,025	1,295	$48,711	10.8%	2.6%	6.5%	571	9,985
Clackamas County	33,314	8,902	10,224	9,398	4,790	$42,735	7.4%	4.7%	6.4%	5,401	49,696
Deschutes County	15,950	5,112	5,070	3,764	2,004	$39,555	9.2%	6.6%	7.0%	1,774	22,771
Douglas County	14,506	5,268	5,225	3,255	758	$32,544	13.3%	10.8%	8.9%	2,938	18,544
Jackson County	23,740	8,208	7,682	5,307	2,543	$35,727	10.1%	9.1%	4.6%	3,741	31,346
Josephine County	11,849	4,661	3,799	2,600	789	$31,146	18.4%	8.9%	6.9%	2,348	15,216
Klamath County	7,609	2,810	2,424	1,991	384	$32,587	12.6%	10.1%	9.3%	1,953	9,684
Lane County	34,894	11,786	11,034	8,759	3,315	$36,205	13.3%	7.6%	8.3%	8,116	46,934
Linn County	12,108	4,509	4,201	2,788	610	$33,491	9.5%	8.7%	7.8%	2,456	15,743
Marion County	26,123	7,631	8,840	6,924	2,728	$39,005	12.7%	7.4%	5.0%	5,937	33,909
Multnomah County	52,357	17,555	14,758	13,516	6,528	$37,057	12.0%	10.1%	9.7%	14,116	74,027
Polk County	7,109	2,217	2,124	2,253	515	$38,035	8.8%	8.7%	7.9%	1,323	9,713
Umatilla County	6,242	2,153	1,884	1,791	414	$34,754	9.5%	5.9%	7.3%	1,456	8,538
Washington County	35,955	9,589	11,036	10,864	4,466	$41,937	7.3%	6.1%	9.4%	4,712	54,244
Yamhill County	8,356	2,437	2,931	2,152	836	$38,310	10.8%	5.0%	7.3%	1,730	10,661
Pennsylvania											
Adams County	9,970	3,423	2,759	2,819	969	$38,201	4.8%	4.8%	7.4%	745	14,376
Allegheny County	135,087	51,348	41,418	29,758	12,563	$32,415	8.6%	7.5%	9.3%	17,094	180,302
Armstrong County	8,268	3,652	2,961	1,331	324	$27,515	10.7%	6.2%	9.4%	1,017	11,135
Beaver County	20,859	8,199	6,998	4,508	1,154	$29,707	8.2%	7.0%	9.5%	2,896	27,019
Berks County	37,479	13,095	12,549	9,137	2,698	$33,621	9.5%	6.2%	7.5%	4,536	51,369
Blair County	14,484	6,077	5,056	2,610	741	$29,187	8.3%	6.8%	9.9%	2,352	18,734
Bucks County	56,346	15,096	16,785	15,229	9,236	$43,410	5.0%	4.2%	7.5%	4,942	83,756
Butler County	17,817	5,970	6,211	4,029	1,607	$34,865	6.8%	4.9%	6.9%	1,821	24,556
Cambria County	17,817	8,173	6,077	2,831	736	$27,373	9.0%	7.8%	8.8%	2,511	22,841
Carbon County	7,076	2,529	2,633	1,542	372	$33,918	6.6%	2.7%	10.0%	667	9,901
Centre County	11,231	3,172	3,610	2,994	1,455	$40,216	6.6%	2.7%	6.6%	980	15,895
Chester County	39,824	9,816	10,628	11,301	8,079	$48,521	4.6%	4.5%	6.2%	2,121	61,001
Clearfield County	9,071	4,171	3,061	1,462	377	$26,902	8.5%	6.9%	8.4%	1,330	11,860
Columbia County	7,062	3,360	2,194	1,096	412	$26,221	8.0%	6.4%	15.0%	866	9,432
Crawford County	9,560	3,766	3,416	1,981	397	$31,325	10.8%	7.6%	9.0%	1,629	12,593
Cumberland County	23,269	6,233	7,677	6,732	2,627	$41,181	4.4%	3.4%	7.4%	1,087	34,051
Dauphin County	24,168	7,697	8,143	5,778	2,550	$36,631	9.8%	4.8%	8.2%	2,740	35,186
Delaware County	50,131	14,631	15,539	12,423	7,538	$40,846	7.3%	6.1%	6.4%	5,666	70,406
Erie County	25,679	10,109	7,983	5,759	1,828	$31,693	9.4%	8.2%	10.1%	4,491	35,098
Fayette County	15,556	7,173	5,342	2,569	472	$26,739	16.2%	7.3%	11.7%	3,026	20,433
Franklin County	15,592	5,158	5,213	4,058	1,163	$36,160	7.9%	6.1%	6.3%	1,119	21,231
Indiana County	8,758	3,503	3,051	1,689	515	$29,588	8.4%	7.4%	10.2%	1,248	11,429
Lackawanna County	23,796	10,258	7,720	4,495	1,323	$28,761	9.0%	8.0%	9.2%	2,783	32,007
Lancaster County	47,590	15,142	16,079	11,994	4,375	$36,494	6.7%	5.7%	8.0%	4,336	67,203
Lawrence County	10,927	4,527	3,914	1,990	496	$28,984	8.9%	8.7%	8.4%	1,550	14,307
Lebanon County	14,277	4,582	4,630	3,715	1,350	$36,764	6.6%	4.6%	6.6%	1,062	19,449
Lehigh County	31,004	11,369	9,670	7,314	2,651	$34,052	9.0%	6.3%	7.6%	4,277	43,773
Luzerne County	36,834	16,636	11,420	6,679	2,099	$27,259	9.0%	7.6%	10.1%	5,451	48,464
Lycoming County	11,867	4,875	3,858	2,568	566	$30,382	9.1%	6.1%	8.8%	1,219	16,573
Mercer County	14,049	5,380	5,008	2,694	967	$30,991	10.6%	5.8%	9.7%	1,846	18,010
Monroe County	11,953	3,758	3,708	3,116	1,371	$37,659	10.2%	5.8%	8.4%	1,733	19,750
Montgomery County	74,581	19,369	20,326	20,081	14,805	$46,018	5.2%	4.3%	7.1%	4,789	109,038
Northampton County	29,061	9,364	9,572	6,822	3,303	$36,195	6.4%	5.9%	5.9%	2,523	41,140
Northumberland County	11,300	4,837	4,043	2,064	356	$27,715	8.6%	9.4%	9.2%	1,318	15,413
Philadelphia County	122,082	60,383	31,998	21,247	8,454	$25,335	20.9%	16.5%	17.9%	42,428	149,606
Schuylkill County	17,174	7,579	5,384	3,305	906	$28,738	7.6%	6.0%	8.8%	2,231	22,876
Somerset County	9,121	4,177	3,108	1,366	470	$26,961	8.2%	8.5%	13.0%	1,174	11,764
Washington County	23,892	8,655	7,686	5,855	1,696	$35,351	6.4%	7.1%	5.8%	2,752	32,778
Westmoreland County	45,195	17,694	15,311	9,196	2,994	$31,428	7.3%	4.9%	8.5%	4,874	60,364
York County	39,794	13,164	13,687	9,804	3,139	$35,473	7.1%	4.9%	6.1%	3,655	57,835
Rhode Island											
Kent County	17,045	6,043	4,746	4,094	2,162	$36,274	8.3%	6.6%	8.2%	2,539	23,338
Newport County	9,167	2,419	2,469	2,568	1,711	$46,508	8.9%	6.1%	4.9%	1,055	12,657
Providence County	52,402	23,573	12,666	10,451	5,712	$28,122	13.0%	11.6%	12.1%	13,416	69,057
Washington County	12,599	3,147	3,092	3,765	2,595	$50,655	4.2%	3.8%	6.0%	1,466	18,603

Table G-2: Counties—Income, Poverty Status and Receipt of Food Stamps (SNAP)—*Continued*

		Income of Households with Householder 65 and Over					Poverty Rate of Persons			Households with 1 or More Persons 60 Years and Over	
	Total Households	Less Than $25,000	$25,000-$49,999	$50,000-$99,999	$100,000 or More	Median Household Income	55 to 64 Years	65 to 74 Years	75 Years and Over	Receiving SNAP	Not Receiving SNAP
South Carolina											
Aiken County	16,110	6,014	4,912	3,639	1,545	$33,734	12.0%	9.9%	10.3%	2,262	21,869
Anderson County	18,798	7,683	5,900	3,869	1,346	$29,963	12.4%	8.2%	11.7%	2,935	25,403
Beaufort County	22,118	4,173	5,508	6,941	5,496	$59,472	6.4%	4.8%	7.2%	1,968	29,024
Berkeley County	11,717	3,832	3,769	3,080	1,036	$37,701	10.2%	6.2%	10.5%	2,165	17,545
Charleston County	30,038	9,516	7,885	7,697	4,940	$42,525	11.4%	8.7%	11.9%	4,331	43,546
Darlington County	6,784	2,939	2,217	1,151	477	$27,055	13.4%	11.9%	18.9%	1,760	8,730
Dorchester County	8,916	2,985	2,621	2,645	665	$37,403	8.2%	8.0%	8.7%	1,424	13,523
Florence County	11,261	4,270	3,541	2,207	1,243	$31,442	17.2%	8.7%	15.0%	2,378	15,557
Greenville County	37,562	13,790	11,523	8,282	3,967	$34,469	9.5%	8.1%	10.4%	4,770	53,001
Greenwood County	7,065	3,309	1,912	1,491	353	$27,398	13.9%	9.4%	11.2%	1,315	9,303
Horry County	31,520	9,498	10,878	8,223	2,921	$37,452	12.3%	6.5%	7.3%	3,537	45,184
Lancaster County	7,703	2,949	2,321	2,015	418	$34,491	10.9%	8.5%	12.9%	1,297	10,247
Laurens County	6,158	2,489	1,792	1,531	346	$32,382	9.1%	7.8%	5.6%	851	8,780
Lexington County	20,450	6,405	6,004	5,645	2,396	$39,845	10.3%	4.9%	7.8%	2,782	30,706
Oconee County	9,024	3,389	2,472	2,279	884	$33,170	9.1%	6.3%	11.5%	1,131	12,251
Orangeburg County	8,962	4,080	2,758	1,758	366	$28,278	14.6%	16.1%	21.7%	2,593	11,298
Pickens County	10,102	3,913	3,362	1,920	907	$31,080	12.7%	8.5%	9.3%	1,471	13,656
Richland County	24,800	8,548	6,602	5,940	3,710	$37,455	9.7%	8.8%	10.5%	3,867	36,862
Spartanburg County	24,662	9,956	7,791	4,928	1,987	$30,967	13.4%	10.7%	13.5%	4,029	35,227
Sumter County	9,106	3,717	2,932	1,785	672	$30,535	11.6%	9.1%	10.5%	2,360	11,988
York County	17,045	5,733	5,642	4,162	1,508	$37,257	9.0%	7.3%	10.1%	2,897	23,868
South Dakota											
Minnehaha County	12,106	4,336	3,737	2,896	1,137	$36,036	7.0%	6.6%	11.7%	1,113	17,502
Pennington County	8,758	2,746	2,351	2,729	932	$39,065	8.8%	6.9%	11.7%	1,045	12,465
Tennessee											
Anderson County	8,590	3,158	2,429	1,806	1,197	$32,744	13.0%	4.7%	8.2%	1,527	11,145
Blount County	12,826	4,218	4,332	3,381	895	$35,651	11.6%	4.8%	14.0%	1,990	17,440
Bradley County	9,145	3,852	3,123	1,778	392	$29,701	12.6%	11.4%	10.5%	1,839	12,440
Davidson County	42,599	14,524	12,489	10,335	5,251	$36,627	11.5%	9.4%	9.1%	8,240	61,446
Greene County	7,888	3,748	2,536	1,288	316	$26,384	13.1%	11.9%	22.4%	1,656	10,465
Hamilton County	32,214	11,459	10,010	7,622	3,123	$33,740	9.7%	7.8%	7.6%	5,338	44,427
Knox County	37,182	14,774	10,885	8,247	3,276	$31,331	9.0%	7.7%	6.4%	5,217	53,369
Madison County	8,034	2,749	2,587	1,915	783	$34,224	11.0%	8.6%	10.5%	1,752	10,536
Maury County	6,547	2,717	1,950	1,474	406	$29,954	10.1%	7.5%	15.8%	1,716	9,439
Montgomery County	8,609	2,441	2,732	2,564	872	$40,989	9.6%	9.9%	9.1%	1,302	12,922
Putnam County	6,939	2,756	2,057	1,627	499	$31,512	14.6%	7.4%	10.2%	856	9,520
Robertson County	5,220	1,612	1,682	1,687	239	$37,620	9.8%	5.5%	10.6%	684	7,261
Rutherford County	14,063	4,264	4,859	3,632	1,308	$39,987	7.3%	7.4%	4.6%	2,399	21,504
Sevier County	8,874	3,465	2,819	1,896	694	$30,325	8.6%	6.6%	12.3%	1,488	12,596
Shelby County	61,462	22,761	16,360	14,771	7,570	$35,522	13.5%	11.6%	12.0%	18,881	85,823
Sullivan County	20,031	7,753	6,740	4,119	1,419	$31,266	10.6%	7.2%	11.0%	3,115	25,483
Sumner County	12,748	3,882	4,156	3,427	1,283	$39,104	6.9%	5.5%	8.7%	1,934	18,515
Washington County	12,311	4,539	3,926	2,487	1,359	$32,888	10.2%	5.3%	9.4%	1,841	16,849
Williamson County	11,552	2,758	2,808	3,428	2,558	$53,074	3.4%	5.6%	7.8%	991	19,240
Wilson County	9,111	2,563	3,087	2,490	971	$41,888	6.2%	5.6%	7.7%	1,572	13,330
Texas											
Angelina County	7,547	2,760	2,296	1,893	598	$33,299	10.8%	8.8%	9.4%	1,494	9,991
Bastrop County	4,902	1,499	1,159	1,611	633	$45,367	5.5%	2.9%	9.5%	538	8,096
Bell County	16,529	5,151	4,838	4,718	1,822	$39,655	10.4%	7.3%	9.8%	2,460	23,879
Bexar County	110,503	37,758	30,112	28,683	13,950	$37,757	11.6%	11.0%	13.2%	23,275	158,329
Bowie County	8,732	3,396	2,906	1,948	482	$31,839	14.3%	13.5%	7.8%	1,420	11,657
Brazoria County	18,734	5,581	5,174	5,631	2,348	$41,343	8.8%	8.0%	9.2%	2,531	28,251
Brazos County	9,419	2,784	2,447	2,514	1,674	$42,304	9.8%	13.4%	9.8%	1,469	13,877
Cameron County	25,830	13,583	6,300	4,207	1,740	$23,237	22.0%	25.9%	27.2%	10,091	31,842
Collin County	36,949	8,476	9,452	10,374	8,647	$51,447	5.9%	5.9%	7.6%	2,862	65,016
Comal County	10,803	2,537	3,255	2,958	2,053	$45,543	7.9%	3.1%	8.6%	681	16,204
Coryell County	3,511	1,035	1,211	922	343	$36,956	9.9%	4.9%	9.3%	375	4,908
Dallas County	131,881	45,953	35,717	30,920	19,291	$37,121	11.6%	11.2%	11.6%	25,415	200,077
Denton County	28,022	6,080	8,072	9,017	4,853	$49,616	4.6%	4.6%	6.1%	2,374	50,035
Ector County	9,061	3,911	2,546	1,634	970	$28,502	11.5%	10.6%	15.0%	1,661	12,578
Ellis County	9,565	3,124	2,653	2,625	1,163	$39,144	6.8%	7.6%	9.4%	1,813	14,043
El Paso County	49,572	22,593	13,612	9,356	4,011	$28,213	18.4%	16.4%	22.6%	18,363	63,569
Fort Bend County	24,655	6,589	5,663	6,847	5,556	$50,208	5.8%	6.1%	9.1%	3,999	46,950
Galveston County	20,486	5,954	5,888	5,496	3,148	$40,679	9.6%	6.3%	9.8%	2,668	32,997
Grayson County	11,431	3,799	3,886	2,820	926	$35,299	9.9%	5.0%	12.3%	1,671	16,223
Gregg County	10,619	4,265	3,230	2,498	626	$30,537	12.0%	10.7%	12.7%	1,281	14,578
Guadalupe County	10,201	3,156	3,082	2,901	1,062	$39,570	7.0%	9.5%	9.8%	1,266	14,936
Harris County	205,093	69,103	52,680	49,114	34,196	$38,818	10.7%	11.3%	13.0%	39,805	329,895
Harrison County	5,890	2,367	1,750	1,315	458	$30,506	12.5%	8.6%	13.5%	1,018	8,414
Hays County	8,277	2,186	1,973	2,538	1,580	$49,834	7.4%	3.5%	9.2%	1,132	13,905
Henderson County	9,403	3,229	3,690	1,787	697	$34,080	15.0%	5.5%	9.1%	1,211	12,571
Hidalgo County	41,006	20,626	11,803	6,429	2,148	$24,814	22.9%	23.9%	25.9%	21,334	47,489
Hunt County	7,492	2,697	2,286	1,738	771	$35,992	11.4%	7.6%	11.5%	1,386	10,425
Jefferson County	21,674	8,704	6,637	4,435	1,898	$30,047	10.9%	9.3%	12.4%	3,495	28,936
Johnson County	10,832	2,948	3,354	3,118	1,412	$41,355	5.8%	6.0%	8.1%	1,146	15,926
Kaufman County	6,669	2,185	2,030	1,778	676	$35,854	8.5%	9.9%	11.9%	991	10,505

Table G-2: Counties—Income, Poverty Status and Receipt of Food Stamps (SNAP)—*Continued*

	Income of Households with Householder 65 and Over						Poverty Rate of Persons			Households with 1 or More Persons 60 Years and Over	
	Total Households	Less Than $25,000	$25,000-$49,999	$50,000-$99,999	$100,000 or More	Median Household Income	55 to 64 Years	65 to 74 Years	75 Years and Over	Receiving SNAP	Not Receiving SNAP
Texas—Cont.											
Liberty County	5,552	2,065	1,722	1,246	519	$31,305	15.8%	9.9%	6.1%	1,143	7,788
Lubbock County	20,165	6,387	6,166	5,270	2,342	$37,754	11.0%	6.3%	8.5%	3,332	27,391
McLennan County	18,149	6,494	6,283	4,032	1,340	$32,707	12.3%	8.4%	12.6%	2,594	24,927
Midland County	9,229	3,255	2,560	1,848	1,566	$35,681	8.2%	8.2%	8.8%	853	14,184
Montgomery County	30,909	8,509	9,528	8,043	4,829	$41,015	8.6%	6.7%	8.8%	3,354	47,727
Nacogdoches County	4,957	2,193	1,316	1,052	396	$28,501	13.1%	11.8%	13.7%	646	6,779
Nueces County	25,772	9,351	7,347	6,089	2,985	$35,157	12.5%	8.9%	13.5%	5,881	36,080
Orange County	7,230	2,645	2,419	1,714	452	$33,455	14.1%	9.1%	8.5%	1,040	10,036
Parker County	9,609	2,862	2,750	2,415	1,582	$43,197	7.5%	5.5%	10.2%	1,095	14,124
Potter County	8,181	3,433	2,315	1,600	833	$30,393	17.0%	14.6%	11.5%	1,931	11,266
Randall County	10,099	2,981	3,020	3,002	1,096	$40,195	5.4%	7.3%	5.0%	755	14,455
Rockwall County	4,518	1,090	1,087	1,365	976	$51,971	3.5%	1.4%	2.2%	456	7,656
San Patricio County	5,198	2,235	1,396	1,138	429	$30,321	10.0%	13.0%	18.2%	1,143	6,945
Smith County	19,347	7,008	6,021	4,314	2,004	$33,905	9.3%	12.9%	9.7%	1,999	26,707
Tarrant County	103,760	31,847	28,744	28,029	15,140	$41,212	8.9%	7.9%	10.2%	14,599	164,241
Taylor County	11,015	3,567	3,503	2,836	1,109	$36,966	9.7%	7.6%	14.9%	1,284	14,774
Tom Green County	10,089	3,696	2,761	2,568	1,064	$34,121	14.1%	8.5%	10.3%	1,393	13,109
Travis County	49,015	11,337	13,074	14,631	9,973	$50,257	9.8%	6.6%	9.7%	6,839	80,907
Victoria County	7,265	2,643	2,118	1,961	543	$35,091	8.4%	12.9%	10.5%	1,250	10,076
Walker County	4,461	1,337	1,303	1,250	571	$38,430	7.0%	4.6%	12.6%	415	5,927
Webb County	10,908	5,877	2,403	1,854	774	$22,523	18.5%	22.1%	26.0%	6,695	13,280
Wichita County	11,069	3,519	3,811	2,687	1,052	$35,844	10.3%	6.6%	9.4%	1,345	14,722
Williamson County	23,368	4,966	6,545	7,912	3,945	$51,032	6.1%	4.8%	5.0%	2,075	37,758
Utah											
Cache County	5,564	1,358	1,783	1,685	738	$43,482	6.8%	3.4%	5.3%	388	7,994
Davis County	15,780	3,135	4,795	5,425	2,425	$49,731	5.2%	2.8%	8.8%	1,278	23,326
Salt Lake County	57,796	16,634	16,732	16,025	8,405	$41,318	7.5%	6.4%	6.5%	7,434	86,198
Utah County	20,809	5,112	6,128	6,478	3,091	$46,522	6.2%	3.6%	5.9%	2,057	30,257
Washington County	15,283	4,168	5,170	4,368	1,577	$41,414	8.6%	4.8%	4.6%	765	19,499
Weber County	15,399	4,031	5,093	4,714	1,561	$42,281	6.8%	7.6%	6.1%	1,687	21,769
Vermont											
Chittenden County	11,803	3,432	3,321	3,154	1,896	$42,053	5.3%	3.5%	7.4%	1,507	17,488
Virginia											
Albemarle County	9,195	2,100	2,560	2,008	2,527	$49,352	8.1%	3.1%	4.4%	701	13,234
Arlington County	12,176	2,402	2,061	3,575	4,138	$69,497	4.8%	5.5%	7.9%	1,325	19,057
Augusta County	7,768	2,340	2,882	2,076	470	$37,007	9.1%	4.8%	8.0%	609	11,242
Bedford County	7,426	2,163	2,510	1,958	795	$37,410	4.3%	5.5%	6.7%	635	10,605
Chesterfield County	21,476	4,574	6,391	6,778	3,733	$49,162	5.6%	2.8%	5.7%	1,891	34,233
Fairfax County	64,675	9,270	10,528	18,542	26,335	$81,814	3.8%	3.9%	5.5%	6,004	114,360
Fauquier County	5,124	887	1,335	1,499	1,403	$58,838	5.3%	5.6%	6.4%	425	8,060
Frederick County	6,175	1,534	2,008	1,842	791	$42,982	5.3%	4.9%	5.5%	723	9,789
Hanover County	8,435	1,979	2,537	2,689	1,230	$46,757	4.7%	5.0%	5.1%	486	12,418
Henrico County	25,135	7,374	7,093	7,296	3,372	$41,743	6.0%	6.3%	6.2%	2,343	37,853
James City County	8,682	1,169	2,016	2,958	2,539	$66,696	5.5%	0.7%	6.3%	263	12,412
Loudoun County	11,937	1,446	2,550	3,464	4,477	$74,486	2.7%	3.6%	5.6%	784	22,743
Montgomery County	5,998	1,675	1,722	1,690	911	$44,186	6.1%	3.7%	4.4%	316	9,040
Prince William County	15,513	2,320	2,909	4,835	5,449	$72,093	3.8%	2.8%	2.9%	1,754	30,900
Roanoke County	10,426	3,194	3,071	3,078	1,083	$40,533	5.3%	5.5%	10.0%	424	14,991
Rockingham County	7,980	2,992	2,338	1,769	881	$33,286	6.6%	8.8%	11.0%	390	11,260
Spotsylvania County	7,813	1,855	1,967	2,315	1,676	$51,180	5.4%	2.7%	8.0%	1,043	12,406
Stafford County	5,781	1,270	1,319	1,602	1,590	$58,353	4.3%	4.5%	11.8%	392	9,888
York County	4,985	944	1,328	1,445	1,268	$56,998	2.9%	3.8%	7.5%	88	7,889
Washington											
Benton County	13,851	3,992	4,318	3,545	1,996	$43,110	5.5%	5.1%	7.7%	1,689	19,987
Chelan County	7,294	2,441	2,104	1,892	857	$39,381	12.7%	8.7%	10.6%	739	10,151
Clallam County	10,954	3,026	3,593	3,251	1,084	$41,074	11.2%	6.4%	6.7%	1,130	14,102
Clark County	32,636	9,111	10,268	9,585	3,672	$41,275	8.8%	7.9%	8.9%	6,326	46,911
Cowlitz County	10,586	3,648	3,540	2,773	625	$36,049	13.4%	7.9%	7.9%	2,098	13,846
Franklin County	3,448	1,147	945	1,112	244	$39,124	9.0%	9.9%	17.4%	833	5,552
Grant County	7,157	2,656	2,431	1,690	380	$33,129	10.9%	9.4%	7.7%	1,163	9,049
Grays Harbor County	7,566	2,343	3,023	1,653	547	$33,106	9.8%	9.5%	7.3%	1,436	10,591
Island County	9,195	1,753	2,640	3,329	1,473	$52,709	7.9%	4.3%	2.2%	833	13,183
King County	139,478	38,987	36,167	38,912	25,412	$45,624	8.6%	7.8%	11.3%	26,702	202,797
Kitsap County	21,257	5,246	6,386	7,146	2,479	$45,384	6.6%	5.6%	6.9%	3,414	32,297
Lewis County	8,882	3,074	3,040	2,281	487	$34,939	9.6%	7.4%	8.4%	1,448	11,338
Pierce County	56,645	16,264	16,803	16,484	7,094	$42,230	8.8%	7.7%	6.6%	10,270	82,718
Skagit County	12,155	3,180	4,138	3,319	1,518	$40,893	8.3%	6.8%	5.4%	1,781	16,834
Snohomish County	47,824	13,056	14,975	13,188	6,605	$42,182	7.4%	5.2%	7.7%	9,100	71,923
Spokane County	40,702	13,977	12,871	10,449	3,405	$36,159	8.7%	6.9%	10.6%	6,820	56,930
Thurston County	21,508	5,282	6,676	7,051	2,499	$44,225	6.6%	5.0%	6.7%	2,602	32,594
Whatcom County	17,606	5,084	5,646	5,331	1,545	$38,183	9.0%	5.3%	5.4%	3,009	24,737
Yakima County	16,886	6,075	5,220	4,117	1,474	$33,855	11.4%	11.1%	11.5%	4,353	22,586

Table G-2: Counties—Income, Poverty Status and Receipt of Food Stamps (SNAP)—*Continued*

	Income of Households with Householder 65 and Over						Poverty Rate of Persons			Households with 1 or More Persons 60 Years and Over	
	Total Households	Less Than $25,000	$25,000-$49,999	$50,000-$99,999	$100,000 or More	Median Household Income	55 to 64 Years	65 to 74 Years	75 Years and Over	Receiving SNAP	Not Receiving SNAP
West Virginia											
Berkeley County	7,552	2,367	2,209	2,238	738	$40,036	5.7%	4.0%	7.7%	943	12,533
Cabell County	10,095	4,228	3,039	2,301	527	$29,424	12.7%	8.8%	8.1%	1,428	13,409
Harrison County	7,720	3,421	2,551	1,313	435	$27,186	10.9%	9.1%	12.2%	1,010	10,196
Kanawha County	22,134	8,031	7,086	4,953	2,064	$32,952	9.9%	5.3%	7.3%	3,149	29,764
Monongalia County	5,975	2,121	1,514	1,426	914	$35,527	9.4%	8.3%	4.9%	596	8,967
Raleigh County	8,358	3,641	2,984	1,283	450	$28,485	11.2%	4.4%	8.6%	974	12,144
Wood County	9,880	4,080	3,168	2,011	621	$30,376	10.8%	8.0%	6.8%	1,077	13,210
Wisconsin											
Brown County	18,977	6,866	6,224	4,563	1,324	$34,453	5.9%	6.2%	11.0%	1,720	27,086
Dane County	34,303	7,976	9,179	11,113	6,035	$49,989	6.1%	3.5%	5.0%	2,954	52,029
Dodge County	8,083	3,075	2,890	1,638	480	$30,971	6.3%	5.8%	8.2%	497	11,411
Eau Claire County	8,546	3,343	2,491	1,910	802	$30,851	8.4%	8.4%	6.5%	1,041	11,802
Fond du Lac County	9,918	3,595	3,229	2,435	659	$34,195	5.2%	3.6%	11.3%	822	14,057
Jefferson County	7,181	2,324	2,527	1,735	595	$36,801	7.1%	4.6%	8.8%	668	10,150
Kenosha County	12,001	4,436	3,653	2,986	926	$32,831	7.4%	5.4%	7.5%	1,896	16,985
La Crosse County	10,188	3,929	3,417	1,991	851	$31,447	5.2%	8.8%	8.9%	718	14,051
Manitowoc County	8,800	3,362	3,440	1,638	360	$30,259	6.0%	3.7%	9.5%	512	12,276
Marathon County	11,818	4,514	3,849	2,773	682	$32,635	6.0%	6.1%	9.9%	1,375	17,011
Milwaukee County	73,522	29,915	22,056	15,332	6,219	$30,916	14.1%	9.8%	10.8%	15,406	96,460
Outagamie County	13,975	5,155	4,763	3,046	1,011	$32,393	4.9%	3.1%	10.9%	657	20,248
Ozaukee County	8,761	2,109	2,833	2,325	1,494	$43,017	3.8%	2.6%	5.7%	393	12,462
Portage County	6,118	2,154	2,148	1,404	412	$33,470	5.2%	2.9%	11.7%	595	9,017
Racine County	17,221	5,674	5,489	4,527	1,531	$36,396	6.6%	6.7%	9.3%	2,005	24,193
Rock County	14,192	4,918	4,959	3,569	746	$34,280	8.4%	6.3%	9.2%	2,344	18,666
St. Croix County	5,266	1,523	1,591	1,436	716	$40,355	5.9%	3.9%	7.4%	395	8,306
Sheboygan County	10,784	4,071	3,677	2,462	574	$31,884	7.0%	5.2%	9.6%	838	14,846
Walworth County	8,640	2,560	2,690	2,253	1,137	$38,912	5.6%	4.6%	3.9%	811	12,757
Washington County	11,986	3,669	4,577	2,742	998	$35,352	2.5%	3.8%	4.5%	602	16,943
Waukesha County	36,335	10,066	11,222	10,418	4,629	$41,056	3.4%	3.1%	6.3%	1,687	53,611
Winnebago County	14,435	5,113	4,708	3,557	1,057	$34,487	5.9%	5.8%	7.0%	1,148	20,560
Wood County	8,541	3,163	3,277	1,624	477	$31,450	6.4%	4.7%	8.0%	895	10,836
Wyoming											
Laramie County	7,710	2,713	2,149	2,033	815	$36,740	5.5%	6.5%	3.4%	585	10,980
Natrona County	6,257	2,062	2,207	1,280	708	$35,440	6.7%	3.2%	11.0%	388	9,486

Table G-3: Places—Income, Poverty Status and Receipt of Food Stamps (SNAP)

	Income of Households with Householder 65 and Over						Poverty Rate of Persons			Households with 1 or More Persons 60 Years and Over	
	Total Households	Less Than $25,000	$25,000-$49,999	$50,000-$99,999	$100,000 or More	Median Household Income	55 to 64 Years	65 to 74 Years	75 Years and Over	Receiving SNAP	Not Receiving SNAP
Alabama											
Birmingham city	18,290	9,435	4,745	3,113	997	$24,001	19.7%	17.4%	16.8%	5,120	22,667
Dothan city	6,154	2,293	1,843	1,417	601	$33,595	11.5%	7.7%	11.4%	848	8,250
Hoover city	6,100	1,107	1,655	1,788	1,550	$57,218	3.4%	2.3%	2.6%	218	9,614
Huntsville city	16,524	4,540	4,301	4,250	3,433	$46,279	8.5%	6.0%	9.0%	1,718	22,601
Mobile city	17,863	6,474	5,269	4,494	1,626	$35,352	12.4%	12.7%	11.5%	3,941	23,140
Montgomery city	16,232	4,818	5,081	3,823	2,510	$39,844	10.5%	7.5%	10.2%	2,846	22,292
Tuscaloosa city	5,512	1,925	1,719	1,194	674	$36,209	14.3%	9.9%	8.9%	986	7,956
Alaska											
Anchorage Municipality	13,374	3,146	3,252	3,804	3,172	$53,118	4.3%	3.6%	7.1%	2,333	23,752
Arizona											
Avondale city	2,137	545	746	748	98	$40,059	9.6%	2.1%	17.8%	866	4,024
Chandler city	12,219	2,980	3,577	3,849	1,813	$45,020	5.7%	4.7%	6.4%	1,220	20,280
Flagstaff city	2,804	638	605	943	618	$56,850	7.0%	9.3%	4.4%	357	4,388
Glendale city	12,528	4,652	3,349	3,068	1,459	$35,631	10.5%	8.9%	10.5%	2,789	18,759
Goodyear city	3,868	707	1,164	1,375	622	$51,445	5.4%	5.9%	4.9%	295	5,950
Mesa city	41,346	12,640	13,905	10,850	3,951	$38,153	9.5%	6.4%	8.2%	4,139	57,098
Peoria city	13,410	4,073	4,375	3,388	1,574	$37,757	5.2%	5.1%	6.0%	1,365	18,689
Phoenix city	77,061	26,643	22,206	19,208	9,004	$37,112	13.6%	11.1%	11.9%	16,725	118,993
Scottsdale city	28,373	6,845	7,037	7,777	6,714	$51,182	8.6%	6.3%	6.2%	1,181	38,988
Surprise city	13,145	2,867	4,404	4,495	1,379	$46,064	7.6%	5.7%	6.8%	943	16,831
Tempe city	8,421	1,926	2,301	2,685	1,509	$49,832	4.9%	2.4%	6.5%	1,085	13,499
Tucson city	41,664	16,360	12,865	9,048	3,391	$31,956	16.4%	13.5%	11.9%	9,021	55,371
Yuma city	7,471	2,750	2,338	1,782	601	$34,419	13.0%	8.7%	9.6%	1,461	9,246
Arkansas											
Fayetteville city	4,228	1,225	1,224	1,009	770	$40,551	11.0%	5.5%	7.5%	413	6,258
Fort Smith city	7,098	2,675	2,332	1,397	694	$31,461	14.0%	6.3%	11.0%	1,059	9,617
Jonesboro city	4,751	1,400	1,685	1,053	613	$36,499	12.0%	4.1%	12.7%	452	7,397
Little Rock city	14,384	4,292	3,656	3,830	2,606	$43,023	9.9%	7.8%	9.2%	2,012	20,817
Springdale city	3,706	1,280	1,336	752	338	$33,132	7.6%	5.7%	8.6%	498	5,078
California											
Alameda city	5,614	1,247	1,159	1,953	1,255	$54,954	10.4%	5.4%	5.7%	283	9,397
Alhambra city	6,093	2,388	1,410	1,511	784	$32,764	15.2%	11.8%	10.2%	517	10,375
Anaheim city	17,509	5,696	4,876	4,079	2,858	$39,512	8.9%	10.3%	12.0%	1,431	29,950
Antioch city	5,280	1,251	1,660	1,693	676	$45,671	8.5%	7.4%	12.6%	718	9,747
Bakersfield city	17,566	5,570	4,566	4,846	2,584	$40,963	11.8%	9.9%	7.6%	1,691	28,902
Baldwin Park city	2,679	883	791	777	228	$37,470	9.4%	7.0%	9.6%	567	5,831
Bellflower city	3,456	1,379	1,055	676	346	$32,315	11.0%	10.7%	10.7%	417	6,414
Berkeley city	9,832	2,744	1,515	2,421	3,152	$61,478	15.5%	10.5%	10.8%	237	14,685
Buena Park city	4,317	923	1,430	1,303	661	$42,993	9.1%	9.0%	5.6%	323	7,704
Burbank city	9,097	3,898	2,110	2,000	1,089	$31,519	8.7%	7.3%	14.3%	484	13,589
Camarillo city	7,463	1,801	1,938	2,176	1,548	$49,923	3.3%	2.9%	8.9%	430	10,098
Carlsbad city	9,689	1,982	2,282	3,019	2,406	$57,040	10.4%	5.1%	5.7%	266	14,641
Carson city	6,307	1,887	1,428	1,939	1,053	$46,147	7.8%	9.2%	9.7%	568	11,207
Chico city	5,979	2,082	1,749	1,296	852	$37,396	8.7%	9.2%	9.8%	408	9,244
Chino city	3,383	1,532	691	717	443	$30,326	8.8%	16.2%	20.5%	326	6,504
Chino Hills city	2,412	300	600	1,245	267	$56,661	3.6%	3.5%	2.9%	182	6,457
Chula Vista city	13,541	4,792	3,715	3,172	1,862	$38,159	6.7%	10.5%	9.7%	1,089	23,355
Citrus Heights city	7,453	2,005	2,367	2,402	679	$40,041	10.2%	5.7%	8.5%	621	10,892
Clovis city	6,390	1,888	1,717	1,905	880	$41,301	6.8%	8.7%	9.4%	731	9,903
Compton city	4,257	1,490	1,309	996	462	$35,063	20.8%	13.3%	13.1%	832	6,683
Concord city	9,029	2,296	2,453	2,848	1,432	$46,923	8.0%	4.1%	10.8%	530	13,754
Corona city	5,416	1,757	1,393	1,312	954	$39,311	7.1%	7.5%	7.2%	451	11,442
Costa Mesa city	6,028	1,626	1,454	1,565	1,383	$48,750	8.9%	7.3%	8.8%	284	10,112
Daly City city	6,493	1,842	1,257	1,843	1,551	$53,232	6.4%	6.6%	7.4%	302	12,475
Davis city	3,625	867	562	984	1,212	$66,905	6.5%	11.0%	6.4%	35	5,623
Downey city	6,050	1,933	1,479	1,678	960	$41,775	9.0%	13.5%	8.4%	404	10,584
El Cajon city	5,866	2,550	1,369	1,121	826	$30,401	19.3%	14.2%	16.3%	949	8,789
Elk Grove city	6,438	1,363	1,706	2,080	1,289	$52,799	3.9%	5.1%	7.6%	485	13,286
El Monte city	4,959	2,266	1,191	1,028	474	$30,292	14.9%	16.4%	19.3%	733	10,037
Escondido city	7,965	3,027	2,274	1,773	891	$32,761	19.8%	10.3%	9.6%	334	13,426
Fairfield city	6,404	1,848	1,533	1,951	1,072	$45,791	7.3%	11.7%	8.9%	585	10,077
Folsom city	4,582	1,386	977	1,190	1,029	$47,262	4.7%	10.0%	9.3%	103	6,942
Fontana city	4,711	1,709	1,336	1,365	301	$34,739	9.9%	9.6%	14.8%	1,199	11,029
Fremont city	11,261	3,156	2,715	2,935	2,455	$45,945	5.7%	6.1%	6.7%	526	21,051
Fresno city	28,015	10,464	8,180	6,189	3,182	$34,308	17.2%	13.3%	12.9%	4,995	42,077
Fullerton city	8,634	1,933	1,956	2,635	2,110	$55,830	7.2%	7.8%	9.2%	349	14,085
Garden Grove city	9,097	2,910	2,595	2,383	1,209	$36,998	13.6%	12.0%	15.2%	1,158	16,064
Glendale city	16,471	7,544	3,091	3,448	2,388	$30,343	9.4%	13.3%	17.9%	1,330	26,345
Hawthorne city	3,391	1,214	978	858	341	$36,415	10.8%	14.7%	11.6%	373	6,329
Hayward city	7,670	2,190	2,128	2,165	1,187	$42,112	9.8%	9.1%	7.8%	773	13,560
Hemet city	12,189	6,092	3,962	1,756	379	$25,009	20.2%	16.1%	9.7%	782	15,471
Hesperia city	5,067	1,982	1,840	825	420	$30,143	20.8%	20.5%	14.3%	1,413	7,564
Huntington Beach city	17,239	3,637	4,411	4,836	4,355	$53,221	6.6%	4.6%	8.8%	649	26,344
Indio city	5,756	2,072	1,286	1,464	934	$38,481	16.5%	10.2%	17.6%	466	9,237
Inglewood city	6,548	2,394	1,837	1,402	915	$34,245	15.9%	12.9%	12.7%	606	10,536
Irvine city	10,385	2,263	2,146	2,940	3,036	$62,196	4.4%	5.4%	11.4%	329	18,833
Jurupa Valley city[1]	3,998	1,620	1,174	912	292	$33,200	12.7%	15.3%	11.3%	536	7,025

[1] Jurupa Valley city was incorporated in 2011. The 2010 population is the U.S. Census Bureau's estimates base figure.

Table G-3: Places—Income, Poverty Status and Receipt of Food Stamps (SNAP)—*Continued*

	Income of Households with Householder 65 and Over					Poverty Rate of Persons			Households with 1 or More Persons 60 Years and Over	
	Total Households	Less Than $25,000	$25,000-$49,999	$50,000-$99,999	$100,000 or More	Median Household Income	55 to 64 Years	65 to 74 Years	75 Years and Over	Receiving SNAP	Not Receiving SNAP
California—Cont.											
Lake Forest city	4,442	943	1,206	1,405	888	$51,748	6.7%	4.6%	9.2%	207	7,680
Lakewood city	5,434	1,713	1,685	1,387	649	$39,331	5.4%	7.7%	11.4%	198	9,541
Lancaster city	7,390	2,915	2,122	1,585	768	$35,993	17.4%	11.4%	14.2%	768	13,444
Livermore city	5,198	1,386	955	1,570	1,287	$58,036	6.3%	5.4%	2.5%	286	8,633
Long Beach city	25,039	8,069	6,446	5,971	4,553	$40,771	15.1%	13.0%	13.6%	3,067	43,021
Los Angeles city	237,046	92,682	55,190	49,743	39,431	$35,019	16.3%	14.7%	17.8%	18,668	382,498
Lynwood city	1,648	581	603	304	160	$35,310	10.9%	14.5%	9.3%	461	3,535
Manteca city	4,198	1,318	1,067	1,230	583	$44,167	11.3%	6.3%	5.0%	348	6,851
Menifee city	8,860	2,470	3,936	1,894	560	$35,660	10.8%	4.6%	6.8%	699	11,527
Merced city	4,060	1,825	1,068	826	341	$27,551	13.3%	14.3%	14.9%	789	6,589
Milpitas city	2,848	725	741	689	693	$48,779	6.6%	5.7%	6.7%	333	6,182
Mission Viejo city	8,517	1,881	1,953	2,424	2,259	$54,814	3.7%	4.4%	7.5%	121	13,861
Modesto city	14,085	4,953	4,643	3,198	1,291	$34,022	11.9%	10.7%	11.9%	1,852	21,353
Moreno Valley city	6,104	1,687	1,778	1,712	927	$43,779	11.5%	11.9%	10.5%	1,639	11,819
Mountain View city	5,174	1,504	1,274	1,275	1,121	$43,553	7.9%	9.1%	14.5%	134	8,128
Murrieta city	6,159	1,840	1,989	1,640	690	$42,032	6.3%	5.9%	6.7%	354	10,158
Napa city	6,718	1,962	2,099	1,647	1,010	$42,987	10.0%	7.7%	6.6%	580	10,378
Newport Beach city	10,180	1,478	1,638	2,360	4,704	$88,737	7.8%	2.8%	5.9%	107	14,900
Norwalk city	5,292	1,812	1,331	1,600	549	$39,786	11.8%	9.6%	13.5%	641	8,855
Oakland city	29,723	11,925	6,716	5,804	5,278	$34,442	15.7%	12.3%	19.0%	2,724	46,618
Oceanside city	12,772	3,567	3,342	3,974	1,839	$42,789	10.2%	6.0%	13.0%	676	19,422
Ontario city	6,048	2,052	1,839	1,479	678	$37,214	13.2%	16.9%	10.7%	1,340	11,478
Orange city	8,077	1,774	1,962	2,249	2,092	$54,616	8.4%	5.5%	6.5%	523	13,690
Oxnard city	8,338	2,273	2,079	2,184	1,802	$46,378	9.7%	9.4%	9.5%	1,237	14,560
Palmdale city	5,191	1,796	1,626	1,329	440	$36,160	11.2%	10.4%	12.9%	842	9,957
Palo Alto city	7,239	1,377	1,423	1,659	2,780	$67,285	3.7%	3.6%	9.8%	121	9,839
Pasadena city	11,195	3,733	2,271	2,296	2,895	$45,898	9.5%	9.4%	14.7%	471	17,068
Perris city	1,558	528	624	240	166	$33,407	20.2%	10.3%	7.6%	252	2,737
Pleasanton city	4,777	1,399	1,013	1,145	1,220	$49,136	3.0%	3.8%	7.8%	120	7,872
Pomona city	6,121	1,893	1,927	1,559	742	$35,365	13.3%	17.5%	13.8%	858	10,905
Rancho Cordova city	4,373	1,228	1,502	1,210	433	$38,215	15.1%	8.5%	11.1%	493	6,886
Rancho Cucamonga city	7,504	2,077	2,440	1,928	1,059	$43,054	4.8%	3.7%	9.1%	526	14,539
Redding city	9,678	3,361	3,631	1,889	797	$34,628	12.4%	8.6%	7.7%	475	13,425
Redlands city	5,345	1,605	1,303	1,157	1,280	$45,677	9.2%	7.1%	13.5%	225	8,153
Redondo Beach city	4,936	1,491	1,034	1,171	1,240	$46,743	5.0%	4.0%	7.2%	232	7,517
Redwood City city	5,268	1,108	1,592	1,471	1,097	$48,636	6.9%	7.1%	6.4%	179	8,280
Rialto city	3,995	1,314	1,141	1,056	484	$37,456	15.0%	8.9%	7.6%	1,090	6,344
Richmond city	6,393	1,671	1,539	2,072	1,111	$49,810	10.0%	7.5%	8.1%	717	11,136
Riverside city	15,759	5,352	4,258	4,094	2,055	$38,611	12.6%	11.1%	11.6%	1,651	25,606
Roseville city	10,180	2,704	3,134	2,862	1,480	$43,101	5.3%	6.9%	8.5%	524	14,757
Sacramento city	32,016	11,608	8,099	8,168	4,141	$36,811	15.1%	12.3%	9.5%	3,800	50,529
Salinas city	5,951	2,328	1,553	1,421	649	$33,006	10.6%	13.2%	12.7%	582	10,570
San Bernardino city	9,607	3,930	2,800	2,087	790	$30,267	26.5%	20.2%	17.7%	2,156	15,056
San Buenaventura (Ventura) city	10,104	2,959	2,467	2,805	1,873	$46,915	10.4%	8.4%	6.7%	478	14,796
San Diego city	84,219	24,179	20,206	22,851	16,983	$46,629	10.6%	8.4%	11.1%	6,055	135,008
San Francisco city	68,503	27,464	14,412	13,936	12,691	$35,240	12.7%	12.7%	17.0%	4,984	107,704
San Jose city	52,773	15,117	13,344	13,651	10,661	$45,452	10.3%	8.0%	13.5%	5,196	92,684
San Leandro city	6,252	2,087	1,895	1,300	970	$39,156	6.5%	11.1%	11.8%	312	11,296
San Marcos city	5,474	1,914	1,978	1,183	399	$32,314	18.6%	10.2%	10.7%	168	8,321
San Mateo city	8,714	1,897	2,186	2,696	1,935	$52,095	8.0%	5.8%	8.8%	106	13,338
San Ramon city	2,920	455	815	684	966	$64,583	3.1%	2.6%	4.9%	27	5,539
Santa Ana city	9,878	3,433	2,397	2,835	1,213	$37,500	13.2%	13.4%	18.1%	1,558	18,662
Santa Barbara city	7,921	2,195	1,730	2,010	1,986	$50,439	8.4%	9.9%	6.3%	276	11,448
Santa Clara city	6,487	1,741	1,649	1,772	1,325	$45,650	6.8%	5.6%	8.3%	382	10,132
Santa Clarita city	10,565	2,862	3,013	2,907	1,783	$44,152	6.7%	6.4%	11.2%	464	17,838
Santa Maria city	5,330	1,809	1,336	1,556	629	$40,799	13.2%	5.6%	15.8%	641	7,906
Santa Monica city	9,500	3,855	1,741	1,702	2,202	$34,953	11.2%	9.5%	15.3%	328	13,690
Santa Rosa city	14,615	3,977	3,888	4,368	2,382	$45,061	11.4%	6.2%	8.3%	979	21,672
Simi Valley city	8,012	1,756	2,095	2,076	2,085	$51,296	4.1%	6.3%	4.1%	424	13,306
South Gate city	3,404	1,556	887	764	197	$29,110	16.7%	17.8%	18.2%	546	6,667
Stockton city	16,456	5,545	5,042	4,202	1,667	$36,166	16.1%	11.6%	13.5%	2,021	27,227
Sunnyvale city	9,181	2,089	2,397	2,625	2,070	$51,347	8.5%	3.2%	7.3%	327	14,212
Temecula city	4,246	1,057	1,363	1,076	750	$43,852	6.9%	3.9%	11.7%	192	7,928
Thousand Oaks city	11,638	2,352	2,832	3,220	3,234	$56,975	4.5%	2.7%	5.7%	388	17,944
Torrance city	14,053	3,817	3,436	4,184	2,616	$48,769	7.4%	9.5%	5.3%	203	20,516
Tracy city	2,799	895	581	627	696	$44,299	6.0%	4.9%	9.5%	429	6,248
Turlock city	4,676	2,020	1,516	688	452	$29,522	7.6%	9.4%	12.5%	378	6,891
Tustin city	3,721	1,188	834	982	717	$43,925	11.6%	7.8%	5.5%	258	6,235
Union City city	3,817	1,133	1,224	943	517	$41,412	4.3%	7.0%	14.5%	305	7,373
Upland city	5,168	1,052	1,381	1,667	1,068	$52,753	8.4%	5.4%	11.9%	403	8,682
Vacaville city	6,089	1,603	1,530	1,954	1,002	$48,817	6.3%	5.8%	7.8%	391	9,351
Vallejo city	7,994	2,471	1,974	2,334	1,215	$41,335	11.5%	11.9%	11.6%	1,134	14,336
Victorville city	5,023	2,208	1,512	961	342	$28,250	12.3%	17.5%	16.3%	1,326	7,643
Visalia city	8,055	2,556	2,514	1,943	1,042	$39,113	10.4%	9.0%	12.1%	1,066	12,654
Vista city	4,814	1,200	1,587	1,444	583	$41,594	13.0%	8.6%	6.9%	326	7,937
West Covina city	6,441	1,806	2,071	1,667	897	$39,883	6.1%	8.4%	5.5%	542	11,440
Westminster city	6,777	2,272	2,244	1,550	711	$35,371	15.9%	10.5%	9.1%	755	11,275
Whittier city	5,730	1,753	1,483	1,345	1,149	$42,380	8.5%	5.2%	12.9%	258	8,845
Yorba Linda city	4,885	963	1,000	1,440	1,482	$64,583	2.1%	2.5%	6.5%	98	7,927
Yuba City city	4,648	1,841	1,174	1,145	488	$34,947	10.7%	9.1%	19.3%	445	7,864

Table G-3: Places—Income, Poverty Status and Receipt of Food Stamps (SNAP)—*Continued*

	Income of Households with Householder 65 and Over						Poverty Rate of Persons			Households with 1 or More Persons 60 Years and Over	
	Total Households	Less Than $25,000	$25,000-$49,999	$50,000-$99,999	$100,000 or More	Median Household Income	55 to 64 Years	65 to 74 Years	75 Years and Over	Receiving SNAP	Not Receiving SNAP
Colorado											
Arvada city	10,077	2,680	3,375	2,817	1,205	$41,403	7.8%	4.3%	7.8%	465	15,222
Aurora city	19,195	5,480	5,298	5,864	2,553	$43,729	7.8%	9.4%	8.9%	2,847	30,355
Boulder city	5,772	1,029	1,525	1,763	1,455	$56,404	10.2%	4.0%	8.7%	322	8,701
Centennial city	7,538	1,370	2,000	2,631	1,537	$57,074	4.6%	3.2%	7.4%	390	12,648
Colorado Springs city	29,663	8,474	8,512	8,395	4,282	$42,487	8.3%	7.9%	7.2%	2,463	45,517
Denver city	43,278	17,043	11,116	9,480	5,639	$33,508	13.3%	11.7%	14.1%	7,350	62,082
Fort Collins city	7,907	2,307	2,142	2,407	1,051	$41,356	8.6%	6.1%	4.8%	626	12,731
Greeley city	6,143	2,205	1,505	1,791	642	$38,317	7.1%	8.3%	7.6%	729	9,063
Lakewood city	13,204	3,428	3,891	4,052	1,833	$43,884	8.6%	6.8%	4.4%	920	19,498
Longmont city	6,145	1,817	1,925	1,592	811	$39,984	8.8%	6.3%	8.5%	552	9,052
Loveland city	6,163	2,090	1,982	1,548	543	$36,772	5.8%	4.0%	9.6%	380	8,845
Pueblo city	10,932	4,351	3,903	2,095	583	$30,474	18.0%	11.0%	13.0%	2,309	13,750
Thornton city	4,526	1,221	1,811	1,239	255	$40,111	4.0%	4.1%	1.7%	670	8,058
Westminster city	6,626	1,856	1,673	1,900	1,197	$45,605	6.6%	4.8%	4.2%	530	10,659
Connecticut											
Bridgeport city	8,915	3,947	2,436	1,604	928	$27,888	15.8%	20.5%	11.7%	3,531	11,638
Danbury city	5,770	2,099	1,255	1,514	902	$38,007	12.0%	8.1%	11.0%	1,079	8,184
Hartford city	8,305	4,860	1,965	917	563	$22,134	24.8%	24.0%	24.9%	5,548	7,469
New Britain city	5,395	2,493	1,527	1,008	367	$27,282	18.9%	14.1%	10.6%	1,801	6,643
New Haven city	8,430	4,409	1,613	1,338	1,070	$22,825	15.9%	17.9%	11.5%	3,152	9,986
Norwalk city	8,293	2,059	2,326	2,144	1,764	$46,741	11.7%	4.8%	5.9%	1,043	12,528
Stamford city	9,437	2,502	2,048	2,531	2,356	$51,824	7.0%	9.2%	9.2%	1,050	13,101
Waterbury city	8,254	3,733	2,741	1,318	462	$27,312	15.9%	16.6%	14.4%	2,882	10,722
Delaware											
Wilmington city	6,344	3,521	1,298	934	591	$22,098	23.9%	17.4%	20.2%	1,756	7,553
District of Columbia											
Washington city	49,026	16,300	10,109	10,567	12,050	$44,472	15.7%	12.0%	13.3%	11,191	64,715
Florida											
Boca Raton city	10,681	1,821	2,121	3,152	3,587	$66,955	6.8%	2.6%	6.8%	526	15,469
Boynton Beach city	9,779	3,878	3,193	1,693	1,015	$30,359	16.4%	12.1%	9.9%	582	11,674
Cape Coral city	14,963	4,061	5,361	3,881	1,660	$39,876	13.0%	8.3%	9.4%	1,636	21,959
Clearwater city	14,824	5,967	4,168	3,024	1,665	$31,274	15.5%	10.0%	8.6%	2,023	19,296
Coral Springs city	6,257	1,692	1,609	1,914	1,042	$46,300	7.8%	7.4%	8.9%	1,204	10,616
Deerfield Beach city	10,330	4,957	2,933	1,672	768	$25,804	20.4%	12.5%	14.2%	1,500	12,631
Deltona city	6,715	2,404	2,552	1,509	250	$32,462	9.0%	7.1%	11.8%	1,697	9,053
Fort Lauderdale city	17,008	5,933	4,118	3,458	3,499	$39,239	18.7%	9.7%	12.6%	3,330	23,575
Gainesville city	6,416	1,815	1,377	2,190	1,034	$50,244	20.9%	8.0%	9.7%	1,093	9,728
Hialeah city	20,913	12,815	4,748	2,574	776	$19,731	22.9%	27.6%	27.7%	16,720	16,301
Hollywood city	12,296	4,711	3,328	2,842	1,415	$32,924	13.5%	14.9%	11.9%	2,504	18,001
Jacksonville city	57,872	20,883	16,267	14,396	6,326	$35,732	13.0%	8.7%	10.7%	11,438	84,055
Lakeland city	12,731	4,607	4,327	2,966	831	$31,902	12.9%	11.1%	8.6%	1,718	15,990
Largo city	12,557	5,016	4,305	2,462	774	$29,960	12.7%	9.5%	9.6%	900	15,674
Lauderhill city	5,317	2,439	1,341	1,222	315	$26,437	15.7%	18.3%	15.4%	1,508	7,273
Melbourne city	10,003	3,633	3,616	2,004	750	$31,755	15.4%	7.4%	5.8%	1,634	11,930
Miami city	35,694	23,272	6,509	3,905	2,008	$16,226	28.1%	32.9%	34.5%	24,376	31,494
Miami Beach city	9,362	5,425	1,593	1,091	1,253	$20,366	14.6%	14.3%	25.1%	3,160	10,188
Miami Gardens city	6,720	3,099	1,698	1,535	388	$28,041	17.6%	17.5%	20.7%	3,320	8,801
Miramar city	3,210	1,240	819	794	357	$38,631	8.4%	10.7%	12.8%	1,612	7,410
Orlando city	13,677	6,149	3,238	2,944	1,346	$29,069	15.5%	14.6%	13.5%	3,715	19,261
Palm Bay city	9,483	3,262	3,723	2,153	345	$31,437	14.3%	6.8%	7.3%	1,622	13,546
Palm Coast city	10,098	3,301	2,847	3,069	881	$39,343	10.7%	15.8%	9.0%	883	13,726
Pembroke Pines city	13,710	6,257	4,109	2,059	1,285	$26,947	8.0%	12.9%	12.9%	2,410	18,954
Plantation city	6,926	2,005	1,801	1,846	1,274	$45,622	6.8%	9.0%	11.3%	1,041	10,510
Pompano Beach city	12,414	5,140	3,188	2,932	1,154	$30,880	22.5%	11.3%	15.2%	1,973	15,371
Port St. Lucie city	15,429	4,433	5,543	4,170	1,283	$38,007	10.3%	6.7%	11.3%	2,107	21,173
St. Petersburg city	24,354	8,812	7,441	5,589	2,512	$33,431	13.7%	11.0%	11.9%	5,170	32,996
Sunrise city	8,033	3,970	2,265	1,432	366	$25,301	14.5%	19.0%	13.0%	1,469	10,579
Tallahassee city	9,945	3,029	2,513	2,612	1,791	$43,251	10.7%	7.5%	12.2%	1,455	14,291
Tampa city	24,456	11,866	5,467	4,676	2,447	$25,907	18.9%	16.2%	21.4%	7,717	31,099
Weston city	2,607	769	555	736	547	$47,950	5.1%	10.3%	10.5%	260	5,202
West Palm Beach city	10,164	3,571	2,457	2,806	1,330	$39,002	16.8%	11.8%	8.6%	1,702	14,271
Georgia											
Albany city	6,083	2,569	1,963	1,089	462	$28,434	26.1%	16.9%	15.7%	1,900	7,633
Athens-Clarke County unified govt (bal)	6,218	1,985	1,434	1,586	1,213	$43,621	15.4%	11.0%	11.5%	1,341	8,497
Atlanta city	28,912	13,952	5,749	4,798	4,413	$26,724	23.9%	18.6%	22.0%	9,072	37,031
Augusta-Richmond County consolidated govt (bal)	13,732	5,590	3,835	2,924	1,383	$33,900	17.2%	9.9%	15.0%	2,423	19,484
Columbus city	15,015	6,044	4,222	3,298	1,451	$31,268	13.1%	13.2%	14.3%	3,605	19,551
Johns Creek city	3,200	568	933	950	749	$52,802	3.7%	9.4%	9.6%	296	6,459
Macon city	6,957	3,644	1,707	1,107	499	$23,634	29.0%	19.0%	14.3%	2,215	9,000
Roswell city	6,430	993	1,924	1,913	1,600	$55,223	6.7%	2.5%	3.9%	355	10,100
Sandy Springs city	6,708	1,340	1,355	1,612	2,401	$66,815	9.9%	6.3%	5.4%	504	10,149
Savannah city	10,862	4,224	3,252	2,450	936	$30,858	16.2%	11.0%	11.8%	1,919	14,582
Warner Robins city	4,253	1,480	975	1,352	446	$41,028	12.1%	14.1%	9.5%	724	6,341

Table G-3: Places—Income, Poverty Status and Receipt of Food Stamps (SNAP)—*Continued*

	Income of Households with Householder 65 and Over					Poverty Rate of Persons			Households with 1 or More Persons 60 Years and Over	
	Total Households	Less Than $25,000	$25,000-$49,999	$50,000-$99,999	$100,000 or More	Median Household Income	55 to 64 Years	65 to 74 Years	75 Years and Over	Receiving SNAP	Not Receiving SNAP
Hawaii											
Urban Honolulu CDP	35,645	9,520	8,962	9,185	7,978	$47,488	8.6%	7.3%	9.7%	5,709	49,538
Idaho											
Boise City city	16,553	5,123	5,282	4,292	1,856	$38,370	9.9%	6.6%	7.8%	2,220	24,233
Meridian city	4,565	1,311	1,420	1,294	540	$43,225	1.6%	4.0%	6.8%	454	6,810
Nampa city	5,623	1,954	2,104	1,309	256	$34,188	13.6%	6.1%	6.4%	849	7,429
Illinois											
Aurora city	7,685	2,272	2,415	1,845	1,153	$41,036	8.2%	7.7%	8.7%	1,455	12,133
Bloomington city	5,079	1,612	1,371	1,392	704	$40,969	9.7%	4.8%	6.4%	868	7,302
Champaign city	4,507	1,270	1,352	1,058	827	$42,096	8.8%	6.2%	6.1%	583	6,798
Chicago city	182,180	81,269	47,178	34,781	18,952	$28,698	17.9%	16.3%	18.3%	58,980	234,406
Decatur city	8,228	2,737	3,354	1,574	563	$32,697	12.5%	7.0%	5.4%	1,088	11,060
Elgin city	5,952	1,617	1,732	1,956	647	$41,722	9.7%	4.6%	11.2%	943	9,257
Evanston city	5,710	1,208	1,336	1,626	1,540	$60,511	5.6%	8.0%	6.5%	460	8,462
Joliet city	7,585	2,784	2,225	1,663	913	$34,263	8.2%	6.9%	11.7%	1,311	11,067
Naperville city	7,421	1,372	1,985	1,698	2,366	$55,615	3.9%	3.6%	5.1%	292	13,208
Peoria city	10,009	3,044	3,078	2,795	1,092	$38,910	14.7%	10.2%	7.5%	1,201	13,701
Rockford city	13,412	5,516	4,219	2,723	954	$30,097	19.4%	9.5%	7.9%	2,805	17,196
Springfield city	11,949	3,620	3,563	3,265	1,501	$39,469	8.2%	7.2%	7.9%	1,403	16,466
Waukegan city	3,931	1,458	1,203	986	284	$30,457	11.6%	13.9%	11.9%	1,019	6,518
Indiana											
Bloomington city	4,483	1,425	1,063	1,223	772	$42,756	15.8%	6.2%	7.4%	614	5,879
Carmel city	4,936	798	1,753	1,077	1,308	$48,779	2.4%	3.5%	0.8%	98	8,422
Evansville city	11,492	4,622	3,939	2,202	729	$30,446	10.7%	8.1%	7.8%	1,379	15,077
Fort Wayne city	20,604	6,764	7,306	4,726	1,808	$34,162	11.0%	9.0%	7.8%	2,371	29,227
Gary city	7,903	3,360	2,417	1,554	572	$29,005	26.2%	14.6%	13.6%	2,653	9,842
Hammond city	5,621	2,302	1,828	1,277	214	$29,462	14.7%	8.7%	7.4%	1,453	7,413
Indianapolis city (bal)	56,836	20,927	18,639	12,712	4,558	$32,983	11.7%	8.8%	10.3%	10,795	79,119
Lafayette city	5,001	1,719	1,691	1,261	330	$34,308	9.3%	6.0%	2.6%	817	6,781
Muncie city	6,280	2,559	2,440	926	355	$28,599	16.8%	10.3%	8.6%	987	7,962
South Bend city	8,609	3,312	3,233	1,597	467	$29,937	15.5%	8.6%	11.4%	1,408	11,610
Iowa											
Cedar Rapids city	10,513	3,219	3,812	2,511	971	$36,482	7.7%	5.7%	5.1%	1,244	14,808
Davenport city	8,009	2,722	3,047	1,737	503	$34,639	12.8%	5.6%	7.5%	1,118	11,444
Des Moines city	14,491	5,329	4,601	3,491	1,070	$33,427	13.3%	6.9%	6.3%	3,515	20,102
Iowa City city	3,932	1,115	1,032	1,112	673	$43,065	8.5%	4.9%	2.6%	163	5,982
Sioux City city	7,036	2,756	2,440	1,518	322	$31,476	12.0%	7.4%	9.7%	984	9,213
Waterloo city	6,487	2,439	2,382	1,342	324	$30,732	9.8%	6.4%	9.0%	899	8,857
Kansas											
Kansas City city	10,001	3,944	3,187	2,303	567	$30,982	16.6%	10.7%	11.8%	2,022	14,048
Lawrence city	4,360	1,289	1,015	1,319	737	$43,012	5.5%	5.3%	3.5%	359	6,758
Olathe city	5,755	1,434	1,746	1,833	742	$45,813	3.5%	4.6%	4.6%	268	9,880
Overland Park city	14,305	3,187	4,231	4,319	2,568	$48,662	3.1%	3.2%	4.7%	535	21,908
Topeka city	11,733	4,166	3,631	2,791	1,145	$36,306	12.4%	7.6%	5.4%	1,328	16,650
Wichita city	28,688	9,672	9,543	7,047	2,426	$35,815	9.7%	10.6%	8.2%	4,193	40,999
Kentucky											
Lexington-Fayette urban county	20,954	6,666	6,044	5,543	2,701	$38,105	10.0%	7.8%	8.0%	3,147	30,699
Louisville/Jefferson County metro govt (bal)	49,976	19,244	16,049	10,665	4,018	$32,197	11.9%	10.9%	11.3%	9,043	70,357
Louisiana											
Baton Rouge city	16,907	6,131	4,431	3,873	2,472	$35,831	16.5%	10.6%	15.0%	3,733	22,157
Kenner city	5,491	2,160	1,705	1,199	427	$31,563	7.8%	12.5%	12.7%	1,321	7,669
Lafayette city	9,626	3,645	2,598	1,990	1,393	$34,288	11.9%	9.3%	9.7%	1,086	13,298
Lake Charles city	6,613	3,091	1,855	943	724	$27,113	13.0%	12.5%	12.9%	1,080	9,236
New Orleans city	26,272	11,327	6,789	5,167	2,989	$29,206	20.0%	15.9%	17.5%	7,908	36,959
Shreveport city	16,617	6,009	4,684	4,062	1,862	$34,271	17.4%	11.3%	11.0%	3,097	22,185
Maine											
Portland city	5,304	2,258	1,366	1,270	410	$31,591	15.9%	12.4%	7.1%	1,520	7,057
Maryland											
Baltimore city	50,955	24,907	12,179	9,293	4,576	$25,843	19.4%	18.3%	17.7%	16,489	63,366
Frederick city	4,734	1,238	1,068	1,583	845	$51,837	5.7%	7.3%	6.8%	774	6,991
Massachusetts											
Boston city	42,931	21,392	8,406	7,237	5,896	$25,171	17.0%	19.7%	21.2%	16,407	51,079
Brockton city	7,041	2,811	2,185	1,467	578	$30,736	11.6%	15.4%	14.4%	2,302	9,032
Cambridge city	7,952	2,641	1,507	1,903	1,901	$47,749	12.8%	9.0%	15.7%	1,312	10,779
Fall River city	8,833	5,049	2,184	1,219	381	$21,192	16.9%	12.4%	16.6%	2,591	10,064
Lawrence city	3,597	2,261	566	516	254	$16,908	28.1%	33.5%	22.0%	2,838	4,420
Lowell city	6,538	2,984	1,748	1,320	486	$26,759	15.3%	12.1%	10.7%	2,092	9,391
Lynn city	6,702	3,393	1,690	1,064	555	$24,746	18.8%	22.5%	18.9%	2,943	7,371
New Bedford city	9,128	4,839	2,336	1,488	465	$23,636	15.6%	14.1%	16.7%	2,794	10,735
Newton city	8,380	2,330	1,525	1,641	2,884	$56,662	2.7%	5.4%	11.2%	541	11,722
Quincy city	8,459	3,238	2,203	1,983	1,035	$33,803	8.8%	9.9%	13.6%	1,727	11,580

Table G-3: Places—Income, Poverty Status and Receipt of Food Stamps (SNAP)—*Continued*

	Income of Households with Householder 65 and Over					Poverty Rate of Persons			Households with 1 or More Persons 60 Years and Over	
	Total Households	Less Than $25,000	$25,000-$49,999	$50,000-$99,999	$100,000 or More	Median Household Income	55 to 64 Years	65 to 74 Years	75 Years and Over	Receiving SNAP	Not Receiving SNAP
Massachusetts—Cont.											
Somerville city	4,585	2,123	1,009	869	584	$27,702	16.7%	17.1%	9.4%	813	6,128
Springfield city	11,110	5,399	3,075	1,967	669	$25,863	21.0%	16.9%	14.7%	5,172	12,295
Worcester city	13,292	6,738	2,965	2,364	1,225	$24,643	13.9%	15.2%	15.0%	4,608	16,975
Michigan											
Ann Arbor city	8,021	2,043	1,914	2,149	1,915	$51,324	8.7%	6.8%	4.9%	960	11,069
Dearborn city	7,528	2,985	2,220	1,786	537	$32,656	20.5%	15.7%	12.1%	1,840	9,626
Detroit city	57,719	27,711	17,183	9,722	3,103	$26,074	27.6%	20.9%	19.8%	28,300	63,490
Farmington Hills city	8,126	2,578	1,875	2,361	1,312	$42,740	6.0%	5.4%	7.9%	708	12,148
Flint city	8,223	3,293	3,155	1,338	437	$29,494	22.9%	14.2%	11.4%	3,445	10,051
Grand Rapids city	13,491	5,006	4,762	2,613	1,110	$33,532	14.5%	8.3%	11.7%	3,590	16,397
Kalamazoo city	4,671	2,022	1,271	899	479	$30,082	17.5%	13.8%	16.2%	1,240	5,927
Lansing city	7,855	2,891	2,598	1,936	430	$32,504	12.5%	9.7%	9.4%	2,285	10,900
Livonia city	11,070	2,772	3,957	3,158	1,183	$41,607	5.9%	4.4%	6.1%	858	14,873
Rochester Hills city	6,177	1,627	1,862	1,818	870	$43,639	5.0%	4.1%	7.0%	446	9,085
Southfield city	8,403	2,775	2,363	2,358	907	$37,322	9.9%	7.6%	12.6%	1,936	11,364
Sterling Heights city	12,444	3,804	4,608	2,916	1,116	$35,175	6.7%	8.3%	8.2%	2,300	16,985
Troy city	7,155	1,856	1,910	2,241	1,148	$47,533	4.9%	6.0%	9.9%	1,120	10,486
Warren city	13,385	4,937	4,737	3,059	652	$33,436	13.1%	7.4%	6.9%	2,773	17,024
Westland city	7,783	3,197	2,397	1,805	384	$31,823	10.1%	8.9%	5.1%	1,332	10,547
Wyoming city	4,208	1,568	1,548	881	211	$32,318	9.3%	8.9%	11.2%	1,303	6,189
Minnesota											
Bloomington city	10,075	2,567	3,016	3,011	1,481	$46,194	7.6%	5.4%	6.6%	592	14,061
Brooklyn Park city	3,527	713	1,336	983	495	$43,871	6.6%	3.6%	9.1%	774	5,769
Duluth city	7,817	3,167	2,188	1,822	640	$32,163	11.2%	11.5%	9.9%	938	10,650
Minneapolis city	22,268	9,316	5,621	4,656	2,675	$31,653	16.4%	16.8%	14.7%	5,767	31,327
Plymouth city	5,630	1,253	1,609	1,806	962	$49,013	3.1%	4.5%	6.7%	251	8,312
Rochester city	8,501	2,550	2,429	2,684	838	$41,359	5.1%	5.6%	9.9%	597	11,927
St. Cloud city	4,355	1,549	1,256	1,045	505	$35,878	11.9%	8.9%	8.8%	414	6,085
St. Paul city	16,768	6,534	4,359	4,221	1,654	$33,798	14.4%	11.5%	17.8%	4,228	24,231
Mississippi											
Gulfport city	5,444	1,917	1,647	1,416	464	$34,691	15.1%	9.8%	11.5%	1,128	7,370
Jackson city	11,246	4,526	2,934	2,469	1,317	$32,332	20.6%	14.8%	10.8%	2,917	15,413
Missouri											
Columbia city	5,933	1,418	1,826	1,704	985	$44,785	6.7%	5.5%	8.9%	852	8,170
Independence city	12,340	4,783	3,850	2,823	884	$33,828	9.1%	7.1%	7.6%	1,407	16,050
Kansas City city	34,840	13,015	10,783	7,487	3,555	$34,328	13.2%	9.5%	9.7%	5,835	48,783
Lee's Summit city	6,916	1,651	2,343	2,197	725	$42,888	6.1%	4.0%	3.6%	355	10,258
O'Fallon city	4,802	1,313	1,584	1,489	416	$39,313	5.1%	1.7%	10.0%	330	7,152
St. Charles city	5,909	1,598	2,347	1,374	590	$38,869	7.0%	5.4%	8.1%	430	7,815
St. Joseph city	6,601	2,680	2,104	1,560	257	$30,291	14.9%	10.4%	8.1%	1,076	8,985
St. Louis city	25,167	12,815	6,486	4,331	1,535	$24,485	20.7%	16.6%	18.0%	9,138	30,836
Springfield city	15,397	6,048	5,198	3,137	1,014	$31,421	15.0%	9.3%	9.8%	1,913	20,152
Montana											
Billings city	10,499	3,657	3,336	2,554	952	$34,277	7.6%	8.5%	8.6%	775	14,545
Missoula city	4,841	1,685	1,345	1,157	654	$36,449	10.6%	7.0%	8.1%	392	6,813
Nebraska											
Lincoln city	18,487	5,416	5,879	5,098	2,094	$40,936	7.2%	4.5%	6.7%	1,774	26,916
Omaha city	31,656	10,772	9,546	7,952	3,386	$36,014	9.8%	5.5%	12.2%	4,006	44,935
Nevada											
Henderson city	23,115	5,698	6,022	7,249	4,146	$49,292	7.7%	5.2%	7.9%	1,586	36,184
Las Vegas city	45,369	14,556	13,215	12,508	5,090	$38,882	10.7%	10.2%	9.8%	7,641	65,424
North Las Vegas city	8,880	2,612	2,734	2,815	719	$40,605	8.9%	11.9%	10.0%	1,827	15,072
Reno city	17,420	6,483	4,591	3,650	2,696	$35,383	14.5%	10.3%	11.1%	2,567	25,783
Sparks city	6,451	1,945	2,101	1,769	636	$37,393	7.7%	5.3%	10.6%	645	10,536
New Hampshire											
Manchester city	8,305	2,915	2,821	1,898	671	$32,540	8.1%	6.0%	9.9%	1,285	12,181
Nashua city	6,921	2,302	2,044	1,577	998	$37,524	5.1%	7.2%	7.3%	736	9,819
New Jersey											
Camden city	4,296	2,350	997	723	226	$19,832	27.5%	29.5%	18.4%	1,948	5,005
Clifton city	6,499	2,153	1,844	1,520	982	$37,671	6.6%	5.3%	10.2%	628	9,850
Elizabeth city	6,269	3,033	1,500	1,312	424	$25,913	17.2%	11.8%	22.2%	1,778	9,362
Jersey City city	13,793	6,219	3,301	2,641	1,632	$27,636	12.9%	13.3%	13.9%	3,760	21,329
Newark city	14,658	8,303	3,205	2,207	943	$20,844	22.1%	23.0%	21.5%	5,802	18,887
Passaic city	3,248	2,009	525	480	234	$17,748	24.6%	24.6%	22.1%	1,547	3,941
Paterson city	7,259	4,259	1,348	1,246	406	$19,801	19.2%	24.0%	24.6%	3,843	9,549
Trenton city	4,865	2,083	1,278	1,164	340	$31,167	21.7%	19.5%	17.2%	1,826	6,361
Union City city	3,789	1,886	946	700	257	$25,217	20.7%	20.8%	24.7%	1,427	5,660
New Mexico											
Albuquerque city	44,318	13,968	13,047	11,135	6,168	$38,933	12.7%	8.7%	9.4%	6,081	64,615
Las Cruces city	8,434	3,014	2,147	2,321	952	$37,068	8.5%	8.3%	8.5%	1,267	11,264
Rio Rancho city	6,090	1,802	1,753	1,696	839	$41,213	13.3%	6.1%	4.3%	639	9,375
Santa Fe city	9,110	2,764	2,202	2,502	1,642	$44,935	12.4%	8.0%	9.9%	988	12,759

Table G-3: Places—Income, Poverty Status and Receipt of Food Stamps (SNAP)—*Continued*

		Income of Households with Householder 65 and Over					Poverty Rate of Persons			Households with 1 or More Persons 60 Years and Over	
	Total Households	Less Than $25,000	$25,000-$49,999	$50,000-$99,999	$100,000 or More	Median Household Income	55 to 64 Years	65 to 74 Years	75 Years and Over	Receiving SNAP	Not Receiving SNAP
New York											
Albany city	7,417	2,902	2,089	1,613	813	$34,469	14.1%	12.0%	13.2%	1,464	10,049
Buffalo city	20,530	9,953	5,774	3,516	1,287	$26,108	21.1%	14.4%	16.3%	8,006	24,232
Mount Vernon city	5,674	2,381	1,314	1,228	751	$31,687	9.1%	12.1%	11.1%	1,653	7,322
New Rochelle city	6,474	2,167	1,385	1,428	1,494	$43,079	6.6%	7.7%	9.6%	642	9,196
New York city	623,982	279,150	139,253	117,201	88,378	$29,216	16.0%	16.9%	20.4%	246,439	785,231
Rochester city	12,766	6,424	3,509	2,128	705	$24,856	18.7%	19.3%	16.9%	6,408	15,012
Schenectady city	4,988	1,994	1,439	1,238	317	$31,872	12.5%	11.2%	4.9%	1,009	6,236
Syracuse city	9,764	4,813	2,421	1,716	814	$25,483	19.8%	20.1%	14.5%	3,720	11,462
Yonkers city	17,880	6,546	4,111	4,321	2,902	$37,091	11.9%	8.1%	10.6%	3,504	25,036
North Carolina											
Asheville city	8,896	3,096	2,464	2,267	1,069	$38,190	17.9%	8.2%	8.7%	1,435	11,622
Charlotte city	41,262	12,673	11,615	10,743	6,231	$39,885	11.5%	7.9%	8.6%	8,072	61,790
Concord city	5,328	1,786	1,765	1,418	359	$37,756	4.7%	4.4%	7.8%	826	7,349
Durham city	13,814	4,497	3,970	3,291	2,056	$39,314	8.9%	9.0%	11.5%	2,874	20,389
Fayetteville city	13,108	4,173	3,781	3,849	1,305	$40,055	10.6%	9.0%	11.3%	2,714	17,706
Gastonia city	4,942	1,890	1,316	1,273	463	$33,176	16.1%	6.7%	11.2%	1,145	7,092
Greensboro city	20,939	7,261	6,086	4,833	2,759	$36,927	11.6%	9.0%	9.9%	3,616	28,955
Greenville city	4,084	1,426	1,118	977	563	$38,250	10.4%	9.8%	12.7%	989	5,671
High Point city	8,258	2,927	2,831	1,866	634	$32,950	12.9%	7.5%	10.0%	1,384	10,653
Jacksonville city	2,617	799	878	834	106	$35,030	12.6%	9.1%	13.8%	493	3,482
Raleigh city	22,166	6,030	6,050	6,429	3,657	$45,191	8.2%	7.3%	7.5%	3,432	32,981
Wilmington city	9,696	3,421	2,428	2,183	1,664	$39,429	13.4%	7.1%	8.5%	1,740	12,555
Winston-Salem city	19,117	6,360	6,404	4,253	2,100	$35,302	11.4%	8.0%	8.2%	2,140	26,839
North Dakota											
Fargo city	7,064	2,239	2,157	1,593	1,075	$37,706	5.9%	5.8%	7.8%	527	10,654
Ohio											
Akron city	17,030	7,331	5,247	3,338	1,114	$29,018	18.0%	13.0%	10.3%	4,526	22,105
Canton city	6,425	2,694	2,360	1,175	196	$29,274	19.6%	9.7%	11.2%	1,554	8,128
Cincinnati city	22,599	10,298	5,713	4,448	2,140	$28,072	21.0%	13.6%	13.1%	6,319	28,767
Cleveland city	33,934	19,674	8,437	4,795	1,028	$20,903	25.8%	22.5%	17.1%	13,815	39,135
Columbus city	46,612	17,886	14,063	10,368	4,295	$31,739	12.5%	11.2%	9.2%	11,774	65,419
Dayton city	11,844	6,240	3,430	1,940	234	$24,001	22.4%	15.7%	17.6%	3,730	14,726
Parma city	9,135	3,388	3,224	2,164	359	$32,717	6.6%	8.7%	5.8%	950	12,296
Toledo city	23,528	10,231	8,059	4,300	938	$28,217	16.6%	11.3%	11.9%	6,188	29,003
Youngstown city	7,091	3,664	2,152	1,119	156	$24,240	23.0%	11.5%	12.4%	2,666	7,884
Oklahoma											
Broken Arrow city	6,693	1,746	1,986	2,140	821	$45,066	4.3%	2.0%	7.1%	521	10,369
Edmond city	5,833	1,413	1,686	1,769	965	$47,878	3.0%	6.2%	7.3%	327	9,072
Lawton city	6,506	1,889	2,250	1,672	695	$39,050	11.8%	6.4%	14.1%	971	8,343
Norman city	7,900	2,045	2,038	2,242	1,575	$48,329	8.7%	8.2%	8.4%	1,121	11,035
Oklahoma City city	42,365	13,918	13,034	10,742	4,671	$36,951	10.7%	7.5%	8.7%	6,868	60,825
Tulsa city	33,014	11,888	9,632	7,138	4,356	$34,401	11.2%	8.5%	10.9%	4,202	46,151
Oregon											
Beaverton city	6,308	2,092	1,742	1,946	528	$36,860	10.3%	10.4%	12.5%	870	9,240
Bend city	7,490	2,630	2,194	1,683	983	$34,865	10.8%	6.9%	7.5%	809	10,413
Eugene city	13,664	4,482	4,127	3,280	1,775	$36,080	13.0%	9.2%	11.1%	2,696	18,631
Gresham city	7,368	2,825	2,022	1,936	585	$33,348	10.9%	9.6%	5.4%	1,944	9,987
Hillsboro city	4,410	1,116	1,423	1,426	445	$40,682	8.9%	8.8%	8.5%	1,072	6,845
Medford city	8,144	2,740	2,341	2,190	873	$38,615	13.0%	10.7%	5.5%	1,397	9,786
Portland city	41,715	14,144	11,896	10,335	5,340	$36,465	12.9%	11.0%	10.9%	11,610	58,345
Salem city	12,607	3,976	3,817	3,375	1,439	$38,968	15.6%	10.5%	7.3%	3,384	16,009
Pennsylvania											
Allentown city	8,216	3,944	2,144	1,748	380	$26,376	19.0%	12.8%	8.4%	2,399	11,198
Bethlehem city	7,150	2,846	2,126	1,638	540	$32,261	11.9%	7.1%	8.3%	1,020	9,461
Erie city	8,364	4,209	2,498	1,314	343	$24,880	19.7%	14.8%	13.2%	2,781	9,980
Philadelphia city	122,082	60,383	31,998	21,247	8,454	$25,335	20.9%	16.5%	17.9%	42,428	149,606
Pittsburgh city	29,182	13,844	7,646	4,882	2,810	$26,352	16.0%	12.7%	13.6%	6,507	36,505
Reading city	5,553	2,871	1,622	933	127	$23,650	34.3%	19.9%	16.8%	2,734	6,198
Scranton city	7,982	4,238	2,273	1,201	270	$23,184	14.1%	13.4%	11.3%	1,392	10,204
Rhode Island											
Cranston city	7,475	3,141	1,774	1,725	835	$32,151	7.9%	9.9%	8.5%	1,537	10,252
Pawtucket city	6,078	3,030	1,505	1,049	494	$25,085	18.6%	14.8%	14.7%	1,988	7,371
Providence city	9,006	4,371	1,847	1,616	1,172	$25,705	20.8%	20.5%	15.7%	4,721	11,403
Warwick city	9,705	3,678	2,452	2,405	1,170	$33,634	7.2%	5.7%	9.8%	1,364	12,877
South Carolina											
Charleston city	9,715	3,270	2,493	2,036	1,916	$40,267	12.0%	9.5%	10.7%	1,369	14,513
Columbia city	7,637	2,975	1,976	1,581	1,105	$34,276	13.3%	10.4%	12.1%	1,154	10,363
North Charleston city	5,604	2,295	1,621	1,479	209	$31,882	16.7%	12.3%	22.3%	1,664	7,697
Rock Hill city	4,457	1,800	1,271	1,104	282	$32,400	10.7%	10.6%	13.4%	983	6,065
South Dakota											
Rapid City city	6,316	2,178	1,779	1,821	538	$36,530	10.4%	8.9%	12.8%	833	8,790
Sioux Falls city	11,068	3,814	3,313	2,565	1,376	$37,652	7.8%	6.1%	9.0%	994	16,126

Table G-3: Places—Income, Poverty Status and Receipt of Food Stamps (SNAP)—*Continued*

	Income of Households with Householder 65 and Over					Poverty Rate of Persons			Households with 1 or More Persons 60 Years and Over	
	Total Households	Less Than $25,000	$25,000-$49,999	$50,000-$99,999	$100,000 or More	Median Household Income	55 to 64 Years	65 to 74 Years	75 Years and Over	Receiving SNAP	Not Receiving SNAP
Tennessee											
Chattanooga city	16,679	6,701	5,034	3,550	1,394	$30,669	13.7%	13.3%	9.7%	3,392	21,840
Clarksville city	6,113	1,762	2,052	1,703	596	$38,159	9.6%	10.8%	9.4%	961	9,105
Jackson city	5,420	1,923	1,726	1,282	489	$33,047	11.4%	10.6%	10.7%	1,368	6,557
Knoxville city	17,327	8,447	4,905	2,899	1,076	$25,920	15.5%	8.5%	6.3%	3,291	22,723
Memphis city	44,272	19,241	11,408	9,532	4,091	$29,670	17.9%	15.2%	14.3%	16,722	57,216
Murfreesboro city	5,957	1,802	1,922	1,623	610	$42,589	9.7%	6.0%	3.9%	902	9,031
Nashville-Davidson metropolitan government (bal)	40,491	14,196	12,091	9,769	4,435	$35,351	11.9%	9.8%	9.4%	8,090	58,245
Texas											
Abilene city	9,307	3,045	3,006	2,279	977	$36,479	10.1%	7.4%	15.4%	1,221	12,416
Allen city	2,485	604	563	802	516	$54,261	4.2%	2.8%	4.5%	308	5,093
Amarillo city	15,039	5,510	4,248	3,846	1,435	$33,947	11.2%	11.2%	7.9%	2,269	20,297
Arlington city	18,636	4,391	5,396	5,777	3,072	$47,105	7.4%	5.6%	9.9%	3,119	29,467
Austin city	36,373	9,147	10,429	10,099	6,698	$45,371	10.5%	8.6%	10.2%	5,804	59,476
Baytown city	4,056	1,253	1,417	1,064	322	$35,743	15.4%	11.8%	5.6%	1,086	6,298
Beaumont city	10,218	4,148	3,264	1,866	940	$29,210	14.1%	10.3%	15.6%	2,120	13,822
Brownsville city	9,563	5,683	2,087	1,335	458	$18,289	23.9%	33.0%	36.7%	4,705	11,566
Bryan city	4,904	1,847	1,204	1,389	464	$34,232	13.8%	19.4%	5.4%	1,154	6,450
Carrollton city	5,410	883	1,821	1,773	933	$50,036	2.7%	4.1%	3.7%	659	9,648
College Station city	2,918	553	709	781	875	$66,300	7.6%	4.9%	18.0%	208	4,635
Corpus Christi city	22,401	8,027	6,507	5,288	2,579	$35,435	12.3%	8.6%	12.8%	5,024	31,595
Dallas city	69,999	27,562	17,596	14,373	10,468	$33,578	15.3%	15.8%	14.9%	16,079	100,811
Denton city	6,081	1,289	1,784	1,849	1,159	$49,667	7.5%	5.9%	7.8%	690	8,970
Edinburg city	3,062	1,520	791	491	260	$25,491	19.1%	15.0%	18.9%	1,739	3,877
El Paso city	44,679	20,325	12,024	8,479	3,851	$28,370	16.7%	15.6%	21.7%	15,630	55,892
Fort Worth city	38,727	14,473	10,074	9,322	4,858	$35,414	12.8%	11.5%	13.2%	8,466	58,535
Frisco city	4,119	823	900	1,120	1,276	$68,350	1.9%	1.3%	2.6%	266	7,502
Garland city	12,289	3,500	3,896	3,313	1,580	$40,542	8.6%	8.2%	8.0%	1,984	19,241
Grand Prairie city	7,005	2,395	1,935	1,852	823	$39,316	11.3%	9.0%	8.9%	1,601	12,070
Harlingen city	5,079	2,351	1,424	1,005	299	$26,566	22.5%	25.7%	18.5%	1,512	6,191
Houston city	122,402	45,720	30,934	26,931	18,817	$35,617	14.4%	13.5%	15.6%	26,184	177,479
Irving city	8,690	2,621	2,563	2,101	1,405	$41,941	8.9%	7.3%	11.5%	1,603	14,049
Killeen city	4,053	1,253	1,258	1,121	421	$39,483	9.5%	8.7%	10.2%	932	6,252
Laredo city	10,430	5,630	2,302	1,761	737	$22,365	17.8%	21.8%	25.9%	6,319	12,848
League City city	3,994	707	945	1,336	1,006	$60,822	6.7%	1.0%	2.6%	189	7,418
Lewisville city	4,234	1,471	1,213	1,294	256	$33,271	6.7%	4.0%	2.5%	482	6,806
Longview city	7,090	2,786	2,136	1,694	474	$30,910	11.5%	7.8%	10.2%	869	9,521
Lubbock city	16,713	5,228	5,154	4,392	1,939	$38,225	11.4%	6.1%	8.3%	2,778	22,619
McAllen city	7,802	3,819	2,166	1,261	556	$25,629	18.8%	23.1%	20.7%	3,428	10,239
McKinney city	5,682	1,536	1,566	1,501	1,079	$46,094	8.6%	8.2%	5.0%	331	9,433
Mesquite city	7,112	2,469	2,055	2,101	487	$35,011	8.4%	6.2%	5.8%	987	11,130
Midland city	7,578	2,684	1,837	1,637	1,420	$36,977	8.3%	9.9%	9.9%	734	11,656
Mission city	4,644	2,197	1,379	829	239	$27,639	12.3%	10.2%	23.2%	1,462	6,078
Missouri City city	3,585	844	943	1,085	713	$50,382	5.2%	1.2%	13.6%	492	7,171
Odessa city	6,972	3,044	1,877	1,296	755	$28,364	10.2%	9.4%	14.8%	1,264	9,531
Pasadena city	7,980	3,188	2,169	1,954	669	$33,303	9.2%	12.9%	6.9%	1,712	12,412
Pearland city	4,038	784	850	1,514	890	$61,458	5.1%	2.5%	4.4%	270	7,163
Pharr city	4,435	2,324	1,140	725	246	$22,166	31.3%	26.6%	30.8%	2,605	4,360
Plano city	14,766	3,135	3,954	4,374	3,303	$52,019	4.7%	5.8%	9.5%	1,034	25,940
Richardson city	7,359	1,538	2,110	2,233	1,478	$50,529	3.6%	1.7%	4.5%	355	11,319
Round Rock city	3,438	797	835	1,146	660	$52,112	4.1%	5.8%	6.8%	392	6,399
San Angelo city	8,590	3,242	2,316	2,051	981	$33,547	15.4%	9.3%	9.5%	1,292	10,740
San Antonio city	89,493	32,839	25,346	21,801	9,507	$34,311	13.0%	12.5%	14.4%	20,684	123,346
Sugar Land city	4,077	526	860	1,048	1,643	$80,413	3.7%	2.9%	3.7%	427	9,056
Temple city	6,009	2,073	1,842	1,535	559	$36,925	11.1%	10.3%	10.5%	814	7,840
Tyler city	9,052	3,356	2,818	1,780	1,098	$35,280	9.6%	12.3%	10.2%	933	12,410
Waco city	8,666	3,627	2,718	1,735	586	$29,899	16.6%	13.5%	16.0%	1,815	11,181
Wichita Falls city	8,174	2,648	2,824	1,943	759	$37,605	11.5%	7.5%	9.4%	1,023	11,057
Utah											
Layton city	3,023	477	965	1,206	375	$52,849	7.6%	4.1%	3.3%	359	5,005
Ogden city	4,975	1,373	1,974	1,267	361	$37,511	13.2%	14.7%	7.2%	843	6,851
Orem city	4,539	1,253	1,146	1,431	709	$44,949	7.1%	5.8%	6.0%	520	6,675
Provo city	4,068	1,067	1,107	1,183	711	$45,672	10.4%	3.3%	5.0%	493	5,677
St. George city	8,087	2,169	2,975	2,114	829	$41,128	10.4%	6.0%	5.2%	451	10,246
Salt Lake City city	12,225	4,703	3,572	2,410	1,540	$31,993	12.2%	14.3%	12.3%	2,274	16,711
Sandy city	5,012	1,146	1,429	1,538	899	$48,948	5.1%	4.2%	5.8%	423	8,264
West Jordan city	3,049	705	933	1,033	378	$45,451	8.0%	4.4%	6.0%	467	6,031
West Valley City city	5,708	1,614	1,755	1,931	408	$42,182	9.4%	7.4%	7.4%	1,287	8,426
Virginia											
Alexandria city	8,939	1,820	1,587	2,381	3,151	$67,388	8.0%	8.3%	6.4%	1,191	13,685
Chesapeake city	14,794	3,896	4,436	4,216	2,246	$44,684	6.9%	5.1%	7.0%	1,574	23,090
Hampton city	11,080	3,446	3,355	2,992	1,287	$39,427	8.8%	7.3%	8.0%	1,097	15,625
Lynchburg city	6,872	2,498	2,230	1,472	672	$36,176	14.3%	10.1%	12.1%	945	9,097
Newport News city	12,796	3,353	4,238	3,915	1,290	$41,427	11.2%	4.5%	8.1%	2,216	17,916
Norfolk city	15,010	5,131	4,537	3,409	1,933	$36,629	12.4%	10.2%	10.2%	3,448	20,474
Portsmouth city	8,147	3,197	2,091	2,360	499	$34,562	11.8%	9.6%	11.9%	1,924	11,006
Richmond city	15,786	6,656	3,848	3,557	1,725	$32,102	16.6%	15.7%	14.1%	3,306	21,368
Roanoke city	9,667	4,096	3,038	1,909	624	$28,892	13.9%	11.3%	11.0%	2,118	12,710
Suffolk city	6,001	1,660	1,755	1,754	832	$42,781	6.2%	7.0%	10.5%	1,033	9,327
Virginia Beach city	30,003	6,866	8,131	9,141	5,865	$50,014	4.8%	4.2%	6.1%	2,639	46,107

Table G-3: Places—Income, Poverty Status and Receipt of Food Stamps (SNAP)—*Continued*

	Income of Households with Householder 65 and Over					Poverty Rate of Persons			Households with 1 or More Persons 60 Years and Over	
	Total Households	Less Than $25,000	$25,000-$49,999	$50,000-$99,999	$100,000 or More	Median Household Income	55 to 64 Years	65 to 74 Years	75 Years and Over	Receiving SNAP	Not Receiving SNAP
Washington											
Auburn city	4,927	1,524	1,710	1,225	468	$36,566	10.2%	7.5%	9.3%	1,380	6,910
Bellevue city	10,203	1,975	2,347	3,008	2,873	$60,735	8.3%	3.8%	7.4%	1,187	14,430
Bellingham city	7,002	2,192	2,067	2,043	700	$36,455	14.3%	7.5%	7.0%	1,215	9,305
Everett city	7,347	3,010	2,164	1,514	659	$31,852	11.3%	9.4%	10.4%	2,457	9,698
Federal Way city	6,032	1,868	1,786	1,627	751	$41,091	13.2%	7.4%	10.9%	2,101	7,984
Kennewick city	5,717	1,969	1,997	1,060	691	$33,602	7.3%	4.6%	9.6%	592	7,982
Kent city	6,667	2,393	1,511	1,967	796	$40,582	8.0%	8.7%	13.3%	2,185	9,772
Renton city	5,793	2,277	1,663	1,382	471	$32,381	11.4%	11.6%	12.5%	1,459	8,367
Seattle city	46,319	15,481	10,801	11,726	8,311	$41,193	11.0%	11.9%	16.7%	10,172	65,204
Spokane city	19,055	7,330	6,395	4,105	1,225	$32,467	11.3%	8.6%	12.2%	4,148	24,465
Spokane Valley city	8,182	2,714	2,826	2,124	518	$36,607	11.5%	7.3%	11.3%	1,262	11,763
Tacoma city	14,668	5,141	4,268	3,984	1,275	$36,207	10.5%	11.7%	7.4%	3,641	20,333
Vancouver city	14,025	4,820	4,478	3,366	1,361	$36,825	11.6%	13.5%	11.5%	3,558	18,229
Yakima city	7,758	2,899	2,418	1,818	623	$34,766	12.1%	13.2%	10.5%	1,813	9,654
Wisconsin											
Appleton city	5,622	1,934	2,126	1,202	360	$32,032	6.6%	4.0%	7.2%	338	8,562
Eau Claire city	5,188	2,109	1,442	1,174	463	$30,158	8.1%	8.5%	7.3%	604	7,039
Green Bay city	8,094	3,044	2,923	1,676	451	$32,163	8.7%	8.1%	13.6%	1,075	11,025
Kenosha city	6,898	2,849	2,064	1,657	328	$30,060	10.1%	6.6%	10.5%	1,432	9,275
Madison city	14,802	3,083	3,892	4,687	3,140	$53,329	8.1%	3.4%	4.1%	1,539	22,311
Milwaukee city	35,948	16,215	10,705	6,689	2,339	$27,780	18.9%	13.2%	13.3%	11,180	47,276
Oshkosh city	5,265	2,268	1,647	1,089	261	$28,091	4.7%	6.6%	9.8%	461	7,164
Racine city	5,985	2,573	1,731	1,388	293	$29,497	13.1%	12.5%	8.8%	1,371	7,701
Waukesha city	5,269	1,761	1,766	1,279	463	$35,748	4.5%	4.8%	6.8%	460	7,922

Table G-4: Metropolitan Statistical Areas—Income, Poverty Status and Receipt of Food Stamps (SNAP)

	Income of Households with Householder 65 and Over						Poverty Rate of Persons			Households with 1 or More Persons 60 Years and Over	
	Total Households	Less Than $25,000	$25,000-$49,999	$50,000-$99,999	$100,000 or More	Median Household Income	55 to 64 Years	65 to 74 Years	75 Years and Over	Receiving SNAP	Not Receiving SNAP
Abilene, TX	14,532	4,987	4,849	3,448	1,248	$34,856	9.3%	8.3%	14.7%	1,723	19,669
Akron, OH	64,998	21,354	22,125	15,762	5,757	$36,186	9.3%	6.6%	8.0%	9,274	90,572
Albany, GA	12,989	5,351	4,166	2,559	913	$29,189	18.5%	14.5%	15.2%	3,601	17,059
Albany-Schenectady-Troy, NY	78,336	23,683	23,055	22,238	9,360	$39,966	6.0%	6.7%	7.0%	9,324	112,331
Albuquerque, NM	71,559	22,482	20,932	18,197	9,948	$39,135	12.9%	9.4%	10.8%	10,202	107,173
Alexandria, LA	13,393	5,494	4,218	2,732	949	$31,132	14.5%	11.5%	13.7%	2,458	17,409
Allentown-Bethlehem-Easton, PA-NJ	76,152	26,149	24,441	18,004	7,558	$35,393	7.3%	5.6%	7.0%	8,266	109,177
Altoona, PA	14,484	6,077	5,056	2,610	741	$29,187	8.3%	6.8%	9.9%	2,352	18,734
Amarillo, TX	19,059	6,711	5,559	4,761	2,028	$34,473	10.5%	10.1%	8.2%	2,733	26,948
Ames, IA	5,780	1,305	1,747	1,673	1,055	$47,975	5.8%	2.4%	4.1%	367	8,311
Anchorage, AK	17,676	4,379	4,380	5,105	3,812	$50,591	5.0%	3.6%	6.8%	3,092	31,517
Anderson, IN	13,929	4,803	4,895	3,554	677	$35,470	11.4%	8.6%	7.6%	1,396	18,253
Anderson, SC	18,798	7,683	5,900	3,869	1,346	$29,963	12.4%	8.2%	11.7%	2,935	25,403
Ann Arbor, MI	24,398	6,046	7,173	6,225	4,954	$45,625	6.9%	5.0%	6.8%	3,253	35,346
Anniston-Oxford, AL	11,127	4,133	3,540	2,497	957	$33,589	12.8%	11.5%	11.6%	1,990	15,052
Appleton, WI	17,635	6,254	6,175	4,018	1,188	$33,016	4.4%	3.1%	9.9%	862	25,512
Asheville, NC	50,318	16,900	15,288	13,053	5,077	$37,639	10.6%	7.1%	8.5%	5,646	68,740
Athens-Clarke County, GA	12,485	4,120	3,531	2,952	1,882	$38,560	12.5%	8.6%	10.4%	2,095	17,749
Atlanta-Sandy Springs-Marietta, GA	295,043	95,319	84,293	75,366	40,065	$39,334	10.7%	9.0%	11.1%	56,570	466,145
Atlantic City-Hammonton, NJ	24,270	7,853	7,096	5,904	3,417	$38,552	10.3%	10.7%	8.8%	3,345	35,621
Auburn-Opelika, AL	8,548	2,842	2,234	2,170	1,302	$40,559	12.0%	6.2%	13.8%	1,399	12,701
Augusta-Richmond County, GA-SC	43,944	16,146	12,770	10,479	4,549	$35,363	12.8%	10.0%	11.5%	7,207	62,977
Austin-Round Rock-San Marcos, TX	88,351	20,989	23,590	27,343	16,429	$49,478	8.7%	5.6%	8.7%	11,283	144,322
Bakersfield-Delano, CA	45,718	15,942	13,309	10,971	5,496	$36,152	13.3%	10.1%	10.5%	5,721	72,832
Baltimore-Towson, MD	220,901	68,465	56,731	58,018	37,687	$41,991	8.1%	7.7%	9.6%	32,288	322,390
Bangor, ME	14,088	6,103	4,374	2,900	711	$28,555	9.0%	7.5%	10.7%	2,824	19,549
Barnstable Town, MA	34,374	10,092	8,998	9,712	5,572	$43,073	7.1%	5.4%	8.6%	2,702	45,811
Baton Rouge, LA	56,292	19,622	17,053	13,243	6,374	$35,643	11.2%	8.8%	11.6%	10,584	80,785
Battle Creek, MI	13,077	4,954	4,293	2,905	925	$31,735	12.2%	8.7%	8.3%	2,857	16,996
Bay City, MI	11,597	3,886	4,284	2,762	665	$33,943	9.7%	6.0%	9.7%	1,825	15,230
Beaumont-Port Arthur, TX	33,882	13,331	10,662	7,394	2,495	$31,191	11.8%	8.6%	11.0%	5,277	46,027
Bellingham, WA	17,606	5,084	5,646	5,331	1,545	$38,183	9.0%	5.3%	5.4%	3,009	24,737
Bend, OR	15,950	5,112	5,070	3,764	2,004	$39,555	9.2%	6.6%	7.0%	1,774	22,771
Billings, MT	15,467	5,181	4,901	4,054	1,331	$35,489	7.1%	7.3%	9.2%	1,249	21,670
Binghamton, NY	25,993	9,384	8,402	5,780	2,369	$34,240	9.6%	6.4%	7.5%	3,925	35,037
Birmingham-Hoover, AL	96,165	35,782	29,534	21,246	9,603	$32,907	11.0%	8.6%	10.4%	13,714	135,644
Bismarck, ND	9,938	3,318	3,178	2,499	943	$37,208	5.8%	4.6%	12.8%	631	14,334
Blacksburg-Christiansburg-Radford, VA	13,742	4,726	4,201	3,322	1,493	$36,605	8.2%	6.8%	6.9%	1,629	18,868
Bloomington, IN	15,036	5,435	4,511	3,568	1,522	$34,484	9.8%	5.8%	10.0%	1,628	21,569
Bloomington-Normal, IL	11,076	3,033	3,262	3,067	1,714	$42,799	6.6%	4.8%	4.8%	1,154	16,338
Boise City-Nampa, ID	44,817	14,679	14,695	11,484	3,959	$36,474	9.9%	7.0%	8.2%	5,906	65,113
Boston-Cambridge-Quincy, MA-NH	382,877	127,714	96,263	93,370	65,530	$40,089	7.5%	8.0%	10.2%	61,842	541,990
Boulder, CO	19,981	4,451	5,622	5,496	4,412	$49,597	7.1%	3.9%	7.6%	1,195	31,434
Bowling Green, KY	9,560	3,658	3,044	2,217	641	$32,477	13.0%	6.7%	8.2%	1,500	12,792
Bremerton-Silverdale, WA	21,257	5,246	6,386	7,146	2,479	$45,384	6.6%	5.6%	6.9%	3,414	32,297
Bridgeport-Stamford-Norwalk, CT	76,458	19,105	18,250	19,770	19,333	$51,423	7.4%	6.3%	6.4%	8,889	110,020
Brownsville-Harlingen, TX	25,830	13,583	6,300	4,207	1,740	$23,237	22.0%	25.9%	27.2%	10,091	31,842
Brunswick, GA	11,839	3,710	3,648	2,816	1,665	$38,920	11.2%	7.2%	15.5%	2,101	16,079
Buffalo-Niagara Falls, NY	116,715	43,060	35,957	27,711	9,987	$33,781	9.3%	6.8%	9.7%	19,237	153,000
Burlington, NC	15,143	6,411	4,552	3,070	1,110	$31,508	9.4%	8.7%	9.5%	1,865	19,944
Burlington-South Burlington, VT	16,287	5,194	4,588	4,146	2,359	$39,590	6.0%	3.9%	7.2%	2,610	23,660
Canton-Massillon, OH	41,933	14,607	15,345	9,632	2,349	$33,827	9.4%	5.1%	8.0%	5,122	56,730
Cape Coral-Fort Myers, FL	87,499	22,647	27,569	24,042	13,241	$43,159	11.4%	6.3%	7.5%	7,026	114,956
Cape Girardeau-Jackson, MO-IL	8,706	3,413	3,086	1,664	543	$30,605	9.6%	7.6%	15.4%	1,262	11,705
Casper, WY	6,257	2,062	2,207	1,280	708	$35,440	6.7%	3.2%	11.0%	388	9,486
Cedar Rapids, IA	23,070	6,873	7,844	6,304	2,049	$38,087	6.6%	5.6%	5.9%	2,030	32,277
Champaign-Urbana, IL	16,746	4,688	5,063	4,316	2,679	$41,943	7.1%	5.6%	7.6%	1,626	24,020
Charleston, WV	32,508	12,244	10,433	7,404	2,427	$31,927	11.0%	7.2%	8.4%	4,998	44,469
Charleston-North Charleston-Summerville, SC	50,671	16,333	14,275	13,422	6,641	$40,453	10.5%	7.9%	11.1%	7,920	74,614
Charlotte-Gastonia-Rock Hill, NC-SC	113,854	38,232	33,886	29,418	12,318	$36,876	10.1%	7.0%	9.4%	19,892	167,353
Charlottesville, VA	17,931	4,486	5,215	4,694	3,536	$45,325	8.8%	4.5%	5.7%	1,860	26,156
Chattanooga, TN-GA	50,496	18,613	16,121	11,141	4,621	$32,436	11.1%	7.8%	7.6%	8,282	69,596
Cheyenne, WY	7,710	2,713	2,149	2,033	815	$36,740	5.5%	6.5%	3.4%	585	10,980
Chicago-Joliet-Naperville, IL-IN-WI	687,259	225,416	195,432	170,441	95,965	$37,864	9.5%	8.3%	10.1%	115,775	988,847
Chico, CA	22,252	7,249	6,605	5,734	2,664	$37,881	13.0%	8.5%	7.2%	1,877	32,176
Cincinnati-Middletown, OH-KY-IN	169,699	57,442	52,855	42,617	16,785	$36,167	9.1%	6.5%	8.5%	21,258	243,430
Clarksville, TN-KY	16,678	5,525	5,196	4,412	1,545	$36,306	11.1%	7.6%	11.3%	2,551	23,186
Cleveland, TN	11,151	4,880	3,460	2,205	606	$29,078	12.3%	11.6%	12.0%	2,309	14,895
Cleveland-Elyria-Mentor, OH	207,026	76,693	65,630	46,528	18,175	$33,115	10.4%	8.4%	9.1%	33,285	279,845
Coeur d'Alene, ID	13,114	3,964	4,681	3,327	1,142	$35,463	9.0%	6.5%	12.3%	1,785	19,088
College Station-Bryan, TX	12,943	4,402	3,319	3,268	1,954	$38,507	10.5%	13.8%	11.8%	1,994	18,516
Colorado Springs, CO	42,773	12,035	11,938	12,494	6,306	$43,677	7.9%	6.8%	7.3%	3,698	68,060
Columbia, MO	10,703	3,107	3,251	2,818	1,527	$41,910	6.0%	4.9%	10.6%	1,357	15,804
Columbia, SC	57,244	19,769	16,393	14,113	6,969	$36,586	11.2%	7.4%	11.0%	9,341	83,733
Columbus, GA-AL	23,214	9,514	6,638	4,824	2,238	$30,501	13.2%	13.0%	14.2%	5,468	30,519
Columbus, IN	6,948	2,634	2,272	1,379	663	$33,309	6.7%	4.4%	6.1%	676	9,934
Columbus, OH	127,255	40,970	38,624	33,570	14,091	$36,913	9.0%	6.8%	7.3%	22,132	183,906
Corpus Christi, TX	34,267	12,760	9,718	7,992	3,797	$33,558	11.8%	9.1%	13.7%	7,487	47,343
Corvallis, OR	6,771	1,527	1,924	2,025	1,295	$48,711	10.8%	2.6%	6.5%	571	9,985
Crestview-Fort Walton Beach-Destin, FL	15,915	3,746	4,750	4,745	2,674	$47,343	7.3%	5.3%	5.8%	1,469	22,456

Table G-4: Metropolitan Statistical Areas—Income, Poverty Status and Receipt of Food Stamps (SNAP)—*Continued*

		Income of Households with Householder 65 and Over					Poverty Rate of Persons			Households with 1 or More Persons 60 Years and Over	
	Total Households	Less Than $25,000	$25,000-$49,999	$50,000-$99,999	$100,000 or More	Median Household Income	55 to 64 Years	65 to 74 Years	75 Years and Over	Receiving SNAP	Not Receiving SNAP
Cumberland, MD-WV	11,888	5,404	3,926	2,016	542	$27,364	11.1%	10.0%	12.0%	1,539	16,096
Dallas-Fort Worth-Arlington, TX	354,325	108,867	97,669	92,697	55,092	$41,135	8.8%	8.3%	10.0%	52,928	559,466
Dalton, GA	9,721	4,446	2,269	2,136	870	$28,045	17.5%	10.6%	13.1%	2,109	13,416
Danville, IL	8,899	3,416	2,999	1,988	496	$32,331	8.0%	7.0%	9.0%	978	11,785
Danville, VA	13,120	5,420	4,637	2,370	693	$29,362	10.1%	7.5%	14.1%	2,657	16,340
Davenport-Moline-Rock Island, IA-IL	38,299	12,748	13,418	9,077	3,056	$35,389	7.9%	5.2%	7.6%	3,536	53,655
Dayton, OH	84,112	28,012	28,287	20,350	7,463	$35,209	9.3%	7.6%	8.0%	10,916	115,610
Decatur, AL	14,058	5,201	4,568	3,188	1,101	$33,195	10.0%	6.8%	10.7%	2,030	19,232
Decatur, IL	11,817	3,784	4,598	2,498	937	$34,506	10.1%	5.0%	5.7%	1,342	16,138
Deltona-Daytona Beach-Ormond Beach, FL	65,197	21,979	22,162	15,846	5,210	$36,117	13.6%	7.3%	9.5%	8,078	84,036
Denver-Aurora-Broomfield, CO	170,199	49,798	47,547	47,284	25,570	$42,293	8.1%	7.2%	8.6%	18,045	266,018
Des Moines-West Des Moines, IA	41,036	12,450	13,847	10,568	4,171	$37,261	7.2%	4.7%	5.3%	5,490	61,051
Detroit-Warren-Livonia, MI	378,959	126,627	121,226	93,993	37,113	$36,032	11.3%	8.8%	9.7%	75,807	510,523
Dothan, AL	14,793	6,105	4,684	3,002	1,002	$29,554	12.4%	9.6%	12.8%	2,059	19,721
Dover, DE	13,607	4,001	4,186	4,214	1,206	$42,006	9.3%	6.3%	7.2%	2,330	18,892
Dubuque, IA	8,939	3,013	3,442	2,150	334	$32,122	5.3%	4.1%	15.3%	669	12,312
Duluth, MN-WI	28,720	10,927	9,293	6,915	1,585	$32,878	9.7%	7.6%	9.8%	2,547	40,465
Durham-Chapel Hill, NC	37,470	11,039	10,705	9,328	6,398	$41,858	9.0%	7.2%	8.7%	5,364	54,845
Eau Claire, WI	14,520	5,668	4,605	3,257	990	$31,257	8.5%	7.3%	8.8%	1,638	19,826
El Centro, CA	10,086	4,881	2,605	1,674	926	$26,184	18.1%	16.2%	17.9%	1,774	14,873
Elizabethtown, KY	8,592	3,213	2,720	1,984	675	$33,508	8.6%	6.1%	9.0%	1,192	12,635
Elkhart-Goshen, IN	15,273	5,119	5,774	3,650	730	$34,766	7.9%	5.9%	8.5%	1,557	21,676
Elmira, NY	8,794	3,438	2,591	1,998	767	$31,581	9.4%	6.2%	9.3%	1,254	12,166
El Paso, TX	49,572	22,593	13,612	9,356	4,011	$28,213	18.4%	16.4%	22.6%	18,363	63,569
Erie, PA	25,679	10,109	7,983	5,759	1,828	$31,693	9.4%	8.2%	10.1%	4,491	35,098
Eugene-Springfield, OR	34,894	11,786	11,034	8,759	3,315	$36,205	13.3%	7.6%	8.3%	8,116	46,934
Evansville, IN-KY	32,970	11,399	11,757	7,306	2,508	$34,259	7.4%	5.4%	6.6%	2,990	46,810
Fairbanks, AK	4,117	915	1,152	1,319	731	$49,583	4.7%	5.2%	8.0%	373	7,961
Fargo, ND-MN	14,513	4,724	4,561	3,468	1,760	$36,286	5.0%	6.2%	8.2%	1,223	21,343
Farmington, NM	8,792	3,183	2,644	1,900	1,065	$33,571	13.0%	15.0%	16.5%	815	13,226
Fayetteville, NC	22,266	7,932	6,314	5,899	2,121	$35,878	11.3%	10.1%	12.6%	5,135	31,698
Fayetteville-Springdale-Rogers, AR-MO	33,426	11,514	10,925	8,080	2,907	$35,534	8.9%	6.8%	8.9%	3,506	48,789
Flagstaff, AZ	7,670	2,325	1,940	2,131	1,274	$44,983	13.5%	11.0%	15.8%	1,515	11,558
Flint, MI	39,113	11,785	15,296	9,390	2,642	$35,461	12.6%	7.8%	5.9%	8,556	50,996
Florence, SC	18,045	7,209	5,758	3,358	1,720	$29,931	15.9%	9.8%	16.4%	4,138	24,287
Florence-Muscle Shoals, AL	16,800	6,454	5,283	3,915	1,148	$31,933	9.8%	10.7%	10.2%	2,083	22,005
Fond du Lac, WI	9,918	3,595	3,229	2,435	659	$34,195	5.2%	3.6%	11.3%	822	14,057
Fort Collins-Loveland, CO	23,052	6,321	6,742	6,888	3,101	$42,472	6.9%	4.2%	7.1%	1,429	35,934
Fort Smith, AR-OK	26,464	11,469	8,746	4,464	1,785	$28,032	13.5%	9.1%	12.2%	3,893	36,373
Fort Wayne, IN	33,792	10,408	12,158	8,491	2,735	$36,404	7.9%	6.3%	7.1%	3,196	48,696
Fresno, CA	56,190	18,962	16,354	13,802	7,072	$36,808	15.3%	12.5%	11.7%	8,576	85,481
Gadsden, AL	10,485	4,792	3,517	1,673	503	$27,591	13.6%	9.8%	12.9%	1,666	14,848
Gainesville, FL	18,310	5,399	4,671	5,478	2,762	$43,335	14.9%	7.6%	10.3%	2,739	27,456
Gainesville, GA	12,796	3,882	3,740	3,598	1,576	$40,159	10.4%	7.1%	10.6%	1,957	18,750
Glens Falls, NY	13,773	4,658	4,283	3,580	1,252	$34,454	8.6%	4.9%	9.9%	1,790	19,420
Goldsboro, NC	10,404	4,390	2,842	2,473	699	$31,184	12.8%	12.5%	12.9%	2,400	14,006
Grand Forks, ND-MN	8,067	2,939	2,425	1,904	799	$34,089	5.0%	6.4%	15.8%	641	11,147
Grand Junction, CO	14,901	5,599	4,527	3,503	1,272	$33,330	10.1%	7.7%	11.1%	1,354	20,435
Grand Rapids-Wyoming, MI	58,937	19,507	20,793	13,869	4,768	$34,906	7.9%	5.8%	7.3%	9,854	81,789
Great Falls, MT	8,117	2,610	2,945	2,062	500	$37,048	7.5%	5.9%	7.6%	772	11,433
Greeley, CO	15,559	5,171	4,651	4,204	1,533	$36,890	6.1%	7.0%	8.6%	1,613	24,308
Green Bay, WI	25,021	9,464	8,280	5,720	1,557	$32,220	6.0%	6.3%	10.9%	2,303	35,525
Greensboro-High Point, NC	62,935	23,119	19,190	14,628	5,998	$33,108	10.8%	8.1%	11.6%	9,908	87,262
Greenville, NC	12,947	5,500	3,738	2,642	1,067	$31,802	11.3%	11.0%	18.5%	3,300	17,030
Greenville-Mauldin-Easley, SC	53,822	20,192	16,677	11,733	5,220	$33,521	10.0%	8.1%	9.7%	7,092	75,437
Gulfport-Biloxi, MS	20,264	6,952	6,021	5,514	1,777	$37,086	14.0%	8.7%	12.4%	3,438	29,286
Hagerstown-Martinsburg, MD-WV	23,320	8,739	6,740	5,579	2,262	$33,973	7.9%	6.2%	8.8%	2,653	34,732
Hanford-Corcoran, CA	6,842	2,449	2,037	1,639	717	$33,543	10.0%	10.9%	13.9%	794	10,635
Harrisburg-Carlisle, PA	51,597	15,346	17,291	13,621	5,339	$38,161	7.1%	4.3%	7.8%	4,169	75,397
Harrisonburg, VA	10,301	3,686	3,328	2,227	1,060	$34,137	6.7%	9.6%	9.9%	638	14,309
Hartford-West Hartford-East Hartford, CT	109,274	33,688	29,987	28,896	16,703	$40,353	7.2%	6.2%	8.3%	16,749	153,222
Hattiesburg, MS	10,789	4,579	3,377	2,032	801	$29,442	16.6%	14.4%	12.9%	1,762	14,692
Hickory-Lenoir-Morganton, NC	35,767	15,870	11,348	6,567	1,982	$27,608	12.5%	8.3%	11.3%	5,440	49,627
Hinesville-Fort Stewart, GA	3,535	1,192	1,032	917	394	$36,915	14.7%	9.1%	14.5%	675	5,190
Holland-Grand Haven, MI	19,807	5,624	7,448	5,209	1,526	$36,404	3.9%	4.6%	5.6%	1,961	27,662
Honolulu, HI	77,959	16,667	17,007	22,684	21,601	$59,292	7.5%	5.8%	8.2%	12,382	115,391
Hot Springs, AR	12,591	4,291	3,768	3,324	1,208	$36,346	16.4%	8.5%	10.7%	962	16,885
Houma-Bayou Cane-Thibodaux, LA	16,157	6,913	4,785	3,118	1,341	$28,580	12.6%	9.7%	10.1%	2,704	21,693
Houston-Sugar Land-Baytown, TX	315,707	101,481	83,664	78,757	51,805	$39,914	10.0%	9.7%	11.7%	54,761	509,097
Huntington-Ashland, WV-KY-OH	30,945	13,373	9,921	6,201	1,450	$28,341	14.6%	10.2%	12.5%	5,240	40,992
Huntsville, AL	33,727	9,815	9,265	8,747	5,900	$43,324	7.6%	5.9%	9.4%	3,955	48,506
Idaho Falls, ID	9,202	2,939	3,207	2,291	765	$37,491	7.4%	4.9%	5.8%	1,112	12,998
Indianapolis-Carmel, IN	123,762	40,214	42,110	30,035	11,403	$35,984	7.8%	6.9%	7.3%	16,637	180,290
Iowa City, IA	10,229	2,807	2,767	3,163	1,492	$43,855	5.4%	3.6%	3.0%	658	15,553
Ithaca, NY	7,172	2,168	1,659	1,984	1,361	$47,901	6.8%	5.0%	7.5%	916	10,961
Jackson, MI	14,626	5,142	5,535	3,057	892	$34,138	11.6%	5.0%	6.2%	2,363	20,113
Jackson, MS	39,518	14,753	11,095	8,831	4,839	$34,028	13.9%	10.7%	10.8%	6,726	56,082
Jackson, TN	9,460	3,532	2,801	2,252	875	$32,981	11.4%	9.7%	15.6%	2,094	12,461
Jacksonville, FL	103,893	31,998	30,317	27,728	13,850	$39,923	11.6%	7.3%	9.9%	17,074	150,943
Jacksonville, NC	8,668	2,851	2,722	2,657	438	$35,776	9.2%	8.1%	9.4%	1,334	12,535

Table G-4: Metropolitan Statistical Areas—Income, Poverty Status and Receipt of Food Stamps (SNAP)—*Continued*

	Income of Households with Householder 65 and Over					Poverty Rate of Persons			Households with 1 or More Persons 60 Years and Over	
	Total Households	Less Than $25,000	$25,000-$49,999	$50,000-$99,999	$100,000 or More	Median Household Income	55 to 64 Years	65 to 74 Years	75 Years and Over	Receiving SNAP	Not Receiving SNAP
Janesville, WI	14,192	4,918	4,959	3,569	746	$34,280	8.4%	6.3%	9.2%	2,344	18,666
Jefferson City, MO	12,941	4,483	4,195	3,099	1,164	$34,796	7.7%	8.6%	11.2%	1,091	18,443
Johnson City, TN	21,283	8,916	6,599	4,024	1,744	$29,019	12.0%	7.4%	11.0%	3,770	28,352
Johnstown, PA	17,817	8,173	6,077	2,831	736	$27,373	9.0%	7.8%	8.8%	2,511	22,841
Jonesboro, AR	9,827	3,740	3,113	2,205	769	$32,798	11.7%	9.6%	15.7%	1,510	14,172
Joplin, MO	15,510	6,503	5,349	2,706	952	$29,233	9.0%	8.0%	13.1%	2,380	21,038
Kalamazoo-Portage, MI	26,992	9,333	9,054	6,461	2,144	$34,234	10.6%	7.4%	9.7%	4,380	37,490
Kankakee-Bradley, IL	9,408	3,198	3,222	2,404	584	$33,980	11.4%	6.6%	9.6%	1,377	13,255
Kansas City, MO-KS	160,004	50,296	50,606	40,391	18,711	$38,190	8.1%	5.7%	7.5%	16,112	232,435
Kennewick-Pasco-Richland, WA	17,299	5,139	5,263	4,657	2,240	$41,992	6.3%	6.1%	9.8%	2,522	25,539
Killeen-Temple-Fort Hood, TX	22,199	6,849	6,802	6,196	2,352	$38,892	10.1%	6.7%	10.4%	2,957	31,712
Kingsport-Bristol-Bristol, TN-VA	37,875	15,950	12,701	6,901	2,323	$28,767	11.5%	9.2%	12.5%	6,090	49,304
Kingston, NY	17,228	5,513	4,917	4,589	2,209	$39,812	10.7%	5.6%	9.4%	2,678	25,706
Knoxville, TN	67,028	24,694	20,210	15,759	6,365	$32,997	10.1%	6.5%	8.3%	9,778	93,325
Kokomo, IN	10,870	3,489	4,080	2,562	739	$34,190	9.8%	5.2%	4.1%	780	14,865
La Crosse, WI-MN	12,377	4,941	3,982	2,493	961	$30,915	5.3%	8.3%	10.3%	823	17,118
Lafayette, IN	13,741	4,245	4,395	3,637	1,464	$37,915	6.2%	4.1%	5.1%	1,357	19,776
Lafayette, LA	18,765	8,116	5,006	3,402	2,241	$30,388	11.7%	11.0%	12.5%	2,394	27,266
Lake Charles, LA	16,269	6,953	4,962	2,926	1,428	$29,004	9.0%	10.5%	9.5%	2,337	23,479
Lake Havasu City-Kingman, AZ	30,103	10,901	10,903	6,940	1,359	$33,522	12.7%	7.0%	8.4%	4,958	38,586
Lakeland-Winter Haven, FL	67,040	23,216	22,144	17,460	4,220	$34,466	11.9%	9.0%	8.6%	9,908	87,505
Lancaster, PA	47,590	15,142	16,079	11,994	4,375	$36,494	6.7%	5.7%	8.0%	4,336	67,203
Lansing-East Lansing, MI	36,023	10,360	12,302	9,615	3,746	$39,425	7.6%	5.5%	6.9%	5,065	51,692
Laredo, TX	10,908	5,877	2,403	1,854	774	$22,523	18.5%	22.1%	26.0%	6,695	13,280
Las Cruces, NM	16,964	6,492	3,982	4,558	1,932	$35,520	14.0%	12.6%	17.9%	2,850	22,580
Las Vegas-Paradise, NV	137,213	40,849	40,789	37,894	17,681	$40,374	10.6%	8.4%	9.3%	21,265	209,749
Lawrence, KS	6,461	1,765	1,951	1,823	922	$40,815	5.8%	5.4%	4.0%	581	9,872
Lawton, OK	8,725	2,794	2,757	2,246	928	$37,332	10.5%	7.0%	14.0%	1,254	11,405
Lebanon, PA	14,277	4,582	4,630	3,715	1,350	$36,764	6.6%	4.6%	6.6%	1,062	19,449
Lewiston-Auburn, ME	9,997	4,396	2,962	2,191	448	$28,182	8.1%	10.2%	10.3%	2,184	13,283
Lexington-Fayette, KY	34,928	11,313	10,653	8,756	4,206	$36,952	10.1%	7.4%	9.8%	5,706	50,491
Lima, OH	9,963	3,606	3,647	2,313	397	$32,746	12.0%	7.8%	7.1%	1,392	13,291
Lincoln, NE	21,994	6,212	7,002	6,127	2,653	$41,702	6.8%	4.0%	6.8%	1,892	32,516
Little Rock-North Little Rock-Conway, AR	54,676	17,622	15,627	14,937	6,490	$38,351	8.4%	6.9%	9.0%	5,910	79,384
Logan, UT-ID	6,708	1,783	2,117	2,014	794	$42,188	6.9%	3.7%	6.4%	432	9,423
Longview, TX	18,937	7,632	6,095	4,041	1,169	$31,185	11.1%	10.2%	11.6%	2,297	26,471
Longview, WA	10,586	3,648	3,540	2,773	625	$36,049	13.4%	7.9%	7.9%	2,098	13,846
Los Angeles-Long Beach-Santa Ana, CA	822,772	268,799	201,929	197,279	154,765	$41,207	11.6%	10.8%	13.2%	59,773	1,348,814
Louisville/Jefferson County, KY-IN	108,380	38,820	35,080	24,339	10,141	$34,455	9.4%	8.6%	10.0%	15,245	154,180
Lubbock, TX	20,867	6,642	6,424	5,409	2,392	$37,450	11.3%	6.3%	8.7%	3,502	28,270
Lynchburg, VA	25,581	8,743	8,586	5,965	2,287	$34,916	9.0%	7.4%	9.9%	3,058	35,281
Macon, GA	19,230	7,743	5,412	4,483	1,592	$32,141	17.8%	11.7%	13.2%	3,865	26,835
Madera-Chowchilla, CA	9,464	2,801	3,039	2,676	948	$39,354	13.1%	8.5%	7.6%	1,207	14,851
Madison, WI	41,825	10,615	11,724	12,944	6,542	$46,306	6.1%	3.6%	6.4%	3,815	62,609
Manchester-Nashua, NH	29,700	8,994	9,361	7,380	3,965	$38,620	4.6%	5.1%	7.1%	2,843	46,134
Manhattan, KS	6,642	1,875	2,058	1,838	871	$41,098	6.4%	4.2%	6.5%	465	10,032
Mankato-North Mankato, MN	7,670	2,665	2,320	1,934	751	$34,906	4.7%	6.1%	8.2%	610	10,519
Mansfield, OH	13,532	5,004	4,909	2,897	722	$32,471	11.9%	7.7%	6.5%	1,904	18,001
McAllen-Edinburg-Mission, TX	41,006	20,626	11,803	6,429	2,148	$24,814	22.9%	23.9%	25.9%	21,334	47,489
Medford, OR	23,740	8,208	7,682	5,307	2,543	$35,727	10.1%	9.1%	4.6%	3,741	31,346
Memphis, TN-MS-AR	89,448	32,836	24,704	21,830	10,078	$35,281	12.2%	10.3%	11.8%	23,936	126,725
Merced, CA	13,739	5,587	3,724	3,005	1,423	$31,367	12.2%	13.6%	14.1%	1,839	21,704
Miami-Fort Lauderdale-Pompano Beach, FL	517,004	207,329	132,025	108,694	68,956	$32,697	14.2%	14.3%	15.2%	139,106	665,181
Michigan City-La Porte, IN	10,456	4,007	3,373	2,287	789	$32,642	9.5%	8.1%	8.7%	1,495	14,517
Midland, TX	9,229	3,255	2,560	1,848	1,566	$35,681	8.2%	8.2%	8.8%	853	14,184
Milwaukee-Waukesha-West Allis, WI	130,604	45,759	40,688	30,817	13,340	$35,013	9.2%	6.7%	8.7%	18,088	179,476
Minneapolis-St. Paul-Bloomington, MN-WI	233,272	69,056	68,771	65,402	30,043	$40,900	6.7%	5.8%	9.0%	22,533	348,300
Missoula, MT	8,036	2,691	2,437	1,897	1,011	$37,381	8.4%	6.1%	10.3%	774	12,369
Mobile, AL	34,830	12,452	10,903	8,768	2,707	$34,535	12.1%	11.7%	11.6%	7,610	47,896
Modesto, CA	33,059	11,186	10,874	7,543	3,456	$35,270	12.5%	10.9%	12.0%	4,358	50,636
Monroe, LA	14,969	6,313	4,502	2,765	1,389	$30,581	17.5%	13.8%	18.6%	2,532	19,584
Monroe, MI	13,592	4,574	4,899	3,212	907	$34,487	9.3%	6.4%	8.1%	1,656	19,643
Montgomery, AL	29,334	9,344	9,086	7,058	3,846	$38,480	9.8%	7.6%	11.2%	4,610	41,407
Morgantown, WV	9,332	3,486	2,679	2,142	1,025	$33,531	9.9%	7.1%	7.3%	1,062	13,800
Morristown, TN	14,596	6,716	4,237	2,901	742	$27,544	13.7%	8.5%	14.2%	2,523	19,148
Mount Vernon-Anacortes, WA	12,155	3,180	4,138	3,319	1,518	$40,893	8.3%	6.8%	5.4%	1,781	16,834
Muncie, IN	11,532	4,178	4,515	2,006	833	$30,676	9.9%	6.3%	7.3%	1,302	15,026
Muskegon-Norton Shores, MI	15,242	5,798	5,262	3,184	998	$31,705	11.6%	6.6%	10.5%	3,149	19,930
Myrtle Beach-North Myrtle Beach-Conway, SC	31,520	9,498	10,878	8,223	2,921	$37,452	12.3%	6.5%	7.3%	3,537	45,184
Napa, CA	12,918	3,249	3,515	3,177	2,977	$47,462	9.4%	6.4%	6.6%	855	19,680
Naples-Marco Island, FL	52,578	11,049	13,809	14,271	13,449	$52,992	10.9%	7.5%	6.7%	3,059	66,306
Nashville-Davidson--Murfreesboro--Franklin, TN	110,342	35,799	34,104	28,033	12,406	$38,248	9.0%	8.1%	8.8%	19,555	161,475
New Haven-Milford, CT	77,105	26,073	21,359	18,480	11,193	$37,415	8.0%	7.1%	7.5%	12,448	108,213
New Orleans-Metairie-Kenner, LA	93,431	36,195	26,000	21,093	10,143	$32,639	13.3%	10.8%	12.3%	18,790	135,380
New York-Northern New Jersey-Long Island, NY-NJ-PA	1,520,309	524,210	360,693	354,877	280,529	$39,450	10.2%	10.4%	13.0%	338,357	2,119,773
Niles-Benton Harbor, MI	16,237	6,135	5,253	3,620	1,229	$32,112	11.7%	9.3%	9.9%	2,632	21,039
North Port-Bradenton-Sarasota, FL	124,192	35,234	38,536	33,594	16,828	$40,840	11.1%	6.0%	7.1%	8,025	155,392
Norwich-New London, CT	24,579	6,775	7,266	7,089	3,449	$43,825	5.0%	5.0%	7.3%	3,528	36,034
Ocala, FL	53,390	17,092	20,508	13,202	2,588	$34,521	13.6%	7.2%	7.3%	7,396	64,752
Ocean City, NJ	13,676	3,715	4,629	3,461	1,871	$40,135	5.9%	3.9%	9.5%	858	19,195

Table G-4: Metropolitan Statistical Areas—Income, Poverty Status and Receipt of Food Stamps (SNAP)—*Continued*

| | Income of Households with Householder 65 and Over | | | | | Poverty Rate of Persons | | | Households with 1 or More Persons 60 Years and Over | |
	Total Households	Less Than $25,000	$25,000-$49,999	$50,000-$99,999	$100,000 or More	Median Household Income	55 to 64 Years	65 to 74 Years	75 Years and Over	Receiving SNAP	Not Receiving SNAP
Odessa, TX	9,061	3,911	2,546	1,634	970	$28,502	11.5%	10.6%	15.0%	1,661	12,578
Ogden-Clearfield, UT	31,825	7,230	10,070	10,390	4,135	$45,972	6.1%	5.1%	7.4%	2,979	46,050
Oklahoma City, OK	97,069	31,320	29,196	25,482	11,071	$38,150	9.6%	7.4%	8.6%	13,632	137,558
Olympia, WA	21,508	5,282	6,676	7,051	2,499	$44,225	6.6%	5.0%	6.7%	2,602	32,594
Omaha-Council Bluffs, NE-IA	63,409	20,079	19,272	17,019	7,039	$38,175	6.3%	4.8%	10.3%	6,244	94,562
Orlando-Kissimmee-Sanford, FL	156,438	51,106	50,293	40,047	14,992	$36,246	9.7%	8.9%	9.3%	26,774	226,844
Oshkosh-Neenah, WI	14,435	5,113	4,708	3,557	1,057	$34,487	5.9%	5.8%	7.0%	1,148	20,560
Owensboro, KY	11,161	4,354	3,720	2,443	644	$32,044	8.8%	8.1%	11.9%	1,414	14,900
Oxnard-Thousand Oaks-Ventura, CA	59,887	14,998	14,488	16,643	13,758	$50,807	6.3%	6.6%	8.3%	3,689	93,852
Palm Bay-Melbourne-Titusville, FL	70,245	21,098	23,548	18,462	7,137	$38,133	11.8%	6.4%	7.4%	7,415	92,264
Palm Coast, FL	13,858	4,259	4,268	3,779	1,552	$41,035	10.8%	12.3%	7.9%	1,188	18,625
Panama City-Lynn Haven-Panama City Beach, FL	16,502	5,632	5,126	3,957	1,787	$37,069	11.6%	6.3%	11.1%	1,503	22,967
Parkersburg-Marietta-Vienna, WV-OH	18,054	7,274	6,062	3,709	1,009	$31,057	12.2%	9.7%	8.1%	2,440	23,478
Pascagoula, MS	13,309	4,587	4,445	2,990	1,287	$34,167	11.4%	8.0%	7.9%	1,588	18,474
Pensacola-Ferry Pass-Brent, FL	40,694	12,615	11,843	12,018	4,218	$39,523	11.8%	7.4%	8.4%	5,938	55,650
Peoria, IL	36,912	10,940	12,472	10,089	3,411	$38,678	7.8%	6.1%	7.1%	2,636	51,214
Philadelphia-Camden-Wilmington, PA-NJ-DE-MD	502,733	165,822	141,416	123,467	72,028	$38,131	9.2%	8.0%	9.6%	77,729	710,130
Phoenix-Mesa-Glendale, AZ	326,522	95,120	101,801	87,965	41,636	$40,428	10.4%	7.3%	8.1%	39,049	467,245
Pine Bluff, AR	8,567	3,450	2,708	1,948	461	$30,989	16.1%	11.2%	15.5%	1,787	11,437
Pittsburgh, PA	266,674	102,691	85,927	57,246	20,810	$31,814	8.6%	6.7%	8.9%	33,480	356,587
Pittsfield, MA	16,435	6,174	4,851	3,819	1,591	$34,356	9.4%	5.2%	8.5%	2,320	22,036
Pocatello, ID	6,496	2,048	1,938	1,869	641	$40,427	9.1%	3.0%	7.8%	632	9,261
Portland-South Portland-Biddeford, ME	49,863	16,780	14,718	13,128	5,237	$37,580	7.7%	6.9%	8.3%	7,494	70,700
Portland-Vancouver-Hillsboro, OR-WA	168,214	49,419	51,087	47,157	20,551	$40,190	9.3%	7.4%	8.7%	33,231	243,634
Port St. Lucie, FL	59,735	17,572	19,752	14,661	7,750	$38,570	12.2%	7.0%	7.2%	5,692	75,846
Poughkeepsie-Newburgh-Middletown, NY	50,584	13,778	14,495	13,693	8,618	$43,793	7.3%	5.9%	6.6%	6,639	74,854
Prescott, AZ	34,015	9,441	11,282	9,963	3,329	$40,435	14.6%	5.6%	4.8%	3,303	45,714
Providence-New Bedford-Fall River, RI-MA	144,675	57,814	37,068	32,085	17,708	$32,872	10.0%	8.5%	11.4%	28,601	196,509
Provo-Orem, UT	21,416	5,308	6,343	6,615	3,150	$46,104	6.3%	3.6%	6.0%	2,104	31,152
Pueblo, CO	15,828	5,841	5,422	3,524	1,041	$32,464	13.7%	9.3%	11.6%	2,673	21,166
Punta Gorda, FL	34,637	9,572	11,959	10,091	3,015	$39,128	12.3%	5.1%	6.7%	2,618	41,939
Racine, WI	17,221	5,674	5,489	4,527	1,531	$36,396	6.6%	6.7%	9.3%	2,005	24,193
Raleigh-Cary, NC	67,021	19,267	19,341	18,979	9,434	$41,993	6.9%	6.1%	9.5%	9,129	102,542
Rapid City, SD	10,675	3,337	3,101	3,262	975	$38,366	8.1%	7.4%	10.9%	1,148	15,482
Reading, PA	37,479	13,095	12,549	9,137	2,698	$33,621	9.5%	6.2%	7.5%	4,536	51,369
Redding, CA	19,897	7,073	6,717	4,511	1,596	$34,821	11.7%	7.9%	9.3%	1,030	28,595
Reno-Sparks, NV	33,271	10,634	9,225	7,992	5,420	$39,440	10.6%	7.7%	8.9%	3,920	52,471
Richmond, VA	100,701	30,253	29,051	27,340	14,057	$40,525	8.0%	6.6%	8.6%	13,183	148,243
Riverside-San Bernardino-Ontario, CA	258,771	85,657	76,043	62,965	34,106	$37,710	12.3%	10.1%	10.0%	29,300	412,344
Roanoke, VA	33,552	12,160	9,944	8,241	3,207	$35,099	8.3%	7.2%	9.9%	3,896	46,271
Rochester, MN	15,468	4,903	4,680	4,374	1,511	$38,887	4.5%	4.8%	10.3%	930	21,730
Rochester, NY	97,083	31,889	30,648	25,090	9,456	$36,452	7.7%	7.0%	8.1%	14,159	133,201
Rockford, IL	29,690	10,362	9,976	6,946	2,406	$34,444	12.0%	7.5%	7.8%	4,189	41,701
Rocky Mount, NC	14,820	6,494	4,546	2,957	823	$29,000	12.1%	11.3%	19.6%	3,895	18,737
Rome, GA	9,051	3,752	3,172	1,549	578	$28,144	13.9%	13.2%	13.2%	1,522	12,225
Sacramento--Arden-Arcade--Roseville, CA	163,172	45,498	46,642	46,326	24,706	$42,800	9.7%	8.0%	8.6%	13,141	255,123
Saginaw-Saginaw Township North, MI	20,511	7,329	7,659	4,652	871	$33,312	13.4%	8.5%	8.7%	3,555	25,814
St. Cloud, MN	14,791	5,871	4,519	3,380	1,021	$32,349	6.4%	8.3%	12.1%	1,094	20,649
St. George, UT	15,283	4,168	5,170	4,368	1,577	$41,414	8.6%	4.8%	4.6%	765	19,499
St. Joseph, MO-KS	11,423	4,495	3,731	2,641	556	$31,351	11.9%	7.6%	9.0%	1,584	15,442
St. Louis, MO-IL	246,259	80,534	77,368	61,836	26,521	$36,973	8.6%	6.6%	8.6%	31,481	342,605
Salem, OR	33,232	9,848	10,964	9,177	3,243	$38,666	11.9%	7.7%	5.6%	7,260	43,622
Salinas, CA	25,539	6,535	6,349	7,086	5,569	$49,392	9.0%	7.9%	7.0%	1,433	42,475
Salisbury, MD	10,516	3,392	3,183	2,876	1,065	$37,258	11.1%	5.9%	11.9%	1,419	14,446
Salt Lake City, UT	62,577	17,811	18,122	17,294	9,350	$41,650	7.3%	6.3%	6.5%	8,049	94,215
San Angelo, TX	10,206	3,731	2,792	2,612	1,071	$34,163	13.9%	8.4%	10.3%	1,402	13,279
San Antonio-New Braunfels, TX	148,360	49,078	40,873	39,051	19,358	$38,637	10.8%	10.0%	12.4%	27,669	214,223
San Diego-Carlsbad-San Marcos, CA	209,064	58,746	54,454	56,951	38,913	$45,183	10.8%	8.0%	10.2%	13,629	335,011
Sandusky, OH	8,524	2,960	3,070	1,878	616	$35,517	6.8%	3.8%	8.4%	1,112	11,771
San Francisco-Oakland-Fremont, CA	336,190	94,664	78,917	86,282	76,327	$48,167	8.8%	7.7%	10.7%	19,291	545,013
San Jose-Sunnyvale-Santa Clara, CA	115,635	29,982	27,261	29,884	28,508	$50,707	8.8%	7.0%	11.0%	7,770	192,537
San Luis Obispo-Paso Robles, CA	25,629	7,004	6,264	7,615	4,746	$47,935	8.2%	6.1%	7.3%	1,241	38,962
Santa Barbara-Santa Maria-Goleta, CA	33,861	8,746	8,724	8,999	7,392	$48,911	8.7%	6.0%	7.8%	1,742	49,489
Santa Cruz-Watsonville, CA	19,970	5,297	5,208	5,538	3,927	$46,069	9.8%	8.3%	7.9%	1,463	32,212
Santa Fe, NM	15,667	4,477	4,055	4,176	2,959	$45,101	11.4%	7.9%	11.2%	1,549	23,986
Santa Rosa-Petaluma, CA	44,296	11,622	12,081	12,607	7,986	$45,911	8.8%	5.1%	8.8%	2,281	69,984
Savannah, GA	26,733	8,890	7,434	7,019	3,390	$38,294	10.9%	7.8%	10.6%	3,550	38,798
Scranton--Wilkes-Barre, PA	63,550	27,934	19,962	11,927	3,727	$28,176	9.0%	7.6%	9.9%	8,494	84,716
Seattle-Tacoma-Bellevue, WA	243,947	68,307	67,945	68,584	39,111	$43,973	8.4%	7.2%	9.5%	46,072	357,438
Sebastian-Vero Beach, FL	24,390	7,627	6,921	5,672	4,170	$38,843	11.9%	7.6%	6.7%	1,565	29,991
Sheboygan, WI	10,784	4,071	3,677	2,462	574	$31,884	7.0%	5.2%	9.6%	838	14,846
Sherman-Denison, TX	11,431	3,799	3,886	2,820	926	$35,299	9.9%	5.0%	12.3%	1,671	16,223
Shreveport-Bossier City, LA	34,799	12,437	9,513	8,845	4,004	$35,252	14.0%	9.3%	11.3%	5,800	46,504
Sioux City, IA-NE-SD	12,252	4,892	3,809	2,670	881	$31,499	8.7%	6.7%	10.0%	1,309	16,773
Sioux Falls, SD	16,138	5,551	4,979	3,882	1,726	$37,251	6.4%	5.7%	11.4%	1,271	23,570
South Bend-Mishawaka, IN-MI	28,220	9,648	10,291	6,185	2,096	$33,329	9.4%	4.9%	8.3%	3,262	39,336
Spartanburg, SC	24,662	9,956	7,791	4,928	1,987	$30,967	13.4%	10.7%	13.5%	4,029	35,227
Spokane, WA	40,702	13,977	12,871	10,449	3,405	$36,159	8.7%	6.9%	10.6%	6,820	56,930
Springfield, IL	19,890	5,485	6,274	5,431	2,700	$41,491	6.6%	5.8%	7.7%	1,859	28,869
Springfield, MA	62,402	23,553	17,846	14,419	6,584	$33,256	10.1%	8.3%	9.9%	12,980	84,857

Table G-4: Metropolitan Statistical Areas—Income, Poverty Status and Receipt of Food Stamps (SNAP)—*Continued*

	Income of Households with Householder 65 and Over					Poverty Rate of Persons			Households with 1 or More Persons 60 Years and Over	
	Total Households	Less Than $25,000	$25,000-$49,999	$50,000-$99,999	$100,000 or More	Median Household Income	55 to 64 Years	65 to 74 Years	75 Years and Over	Receiving SNAP	Not Receiving SNAP
Springfield, MO	39,922	14,561	13,505	8,948	2,908	$32,860	10.5%	6.3%	11.2%	4,675	54,799
Springfield, OH	14,890	5,098	5,159	3,430	1,203	$34,847	11.1%	6.9%	7.3%	3,285	18,662
State College, PA	11,231	3,172	3,610	2,994	1,455	$40,216	6.6%	2.7%	6.6%	980	15,895
Steubenville-Weirton, OH-WV	15,188	5,794	5,656	3,071	667	$31,416	10.5%	6.3%	6.8%	1,698	20,520
Stockton, CA	41,585	13,518	11,985	10,644	5,438	$39,214	11.7%	8.9%	10.4%	4,393	67,594
Sumter, SC	9,106	3,717	2,932	1,785	672	$30,535	11.6%	9.1%	10.5%	2,360	11,988
Syracuse, NY	59,049	20,995	17,460	14,714	5,880	$34,601	9.3%	7.0%	8.1%	9,796	79,504
Tallahassee, FL	25,354	7,868	6,647	7,295	3,544	$41,753	10.6%	7.5%	12.5%	4,374	37,556
Tampa-St. Petersburg-Clearwater, FL	305,683	109,780	99,765	70,359	25,779	$33,938	12.9%	9.1%	9.5%	44,274	408,160
Terre Haute, IN	15,187	5,533	5,386	3,200	1,068	$31,686	10.5%	5.4%	7.2%	1,824	20,947
Texarkana, TX-Texarkana, AR	12,536	5,115	3,887	2,680	854	$31,348	13.0%	12.3%	11.4%	1,826	16,629
Toledo, OH	57,899	20,380	19,908	13,027	4,584	$33,754	10.3%	6.9%	8.7%	8,891	78,296
Topeka, KS	22,190	6,717	7,105	6,133	2,235	$40,119	8.3%	4.7%	5.5%	1,768	32,311
Trenton-Ewing, NJ	29,042	8,185	7,169	7,456	6,232	$46,458	7.4%	5.8%	8.3%	3,224	43,665
Tucson, AZ	97,843	29,976	29,760	25,738	12,369	$38,861	12.5%	8.5%	7.9%	14,713	133,804
Tulsa, OK	79,539	28,555	24,619	18,449	7,916	$34,007	9.1%	6.8%	10.3%	9,714	112,501
Tuscaloosa, AL	15,326	5,648	5,185	3,257	1,236	$33,765	14.0%	8.9%	10.3%	2,808	22,212
Tyler, TX	19,347	7,008	6,021	4,314	2,004	$33,905	9.3%	12.9%	9.7%	1,999	26,707
Utica-Rome, NY	31,249	12,009	9,909	6,915	2,416	$33,015	9.5%	8.7%	10.8%	6,279	41,263
Valdosta, GA	9,597	3,892	2,697	2,168	840	$31,134	15.1%	10.0%	13.6%	2,182	13,105
Vallejo-Fairfield, CA	28,831	7,479	7,036	8,892	5,424	$49,557	8.0%	7.9%	9.0%	2,701	47,466
Victoria, TX	10,442	3,905	3,243	2,505	789	$34,165	11.1%	12.1%	10.9%	1,557	14,384
Vineland-Millville-Bridgeton, NJ	12,301	4,940	3,449	2,885	1,027	$31,140	14.4%	12.2%	12.0%	2,061	17,321
Virginia Beach-Norfolk-Newport News, VA-NC	125,196	33,308	35,914	36,179	19,795	$44,897	7.7%	5.4%	8.1%	15,596	183,979
Visalia-Porterville, CA	24,691	9,261	7,269	5,421	2,740	$34,054	16.3%	11.0%	13.5%	4,541	37,626
Waco, TX	18,149	6,494	6,283	4,032	1,340	$32,707	12.3%	8.4%	12.6%	2,594	24,927
Warner Robins, GA	8,976	2,447	2,531	2,993	1,005	$44,748	8.2%	7.7%	8.4%	1,446	13,488
Washington-Arlington-Alexandria, DC-VA-MD-WV	350,684	72,789	69,822	99,339	108,734	$63,241	5.8%	5.7%	7.9%	42,580	571,494
Waterloo-Cedar Falls, IA	16,019	5,005	5,903	3,741	1,370	$35,195	5.9%	3.7%	7.2%	1,541	21,827
Wausau, WI	11,818	4,514	3,849	2,773	682	$32,635	6.0%	6.1%	9.9%	1,375	17,011
Wenatchee-East Wenatchee, WA	10,713	3,194	3,341	3,026	1,152	$40,293	10.7%	6.8%	8.4%	1,166	14,867
Wheeling, WV-OH	17,078	7,008	6,487	2,839	744	$29,755	11.5%	7.2%	7.1%	1,975	23,822
Wichita, KS	48,651	16,071	16,428	11,861	4,291	$35,868	8.3%	7.6%	8.1%	5,552	68,982
Wichita Falls, TX	13,139	4,211	4,446	3,313	1,169	$35,968	10.0%	6.3%	10.1%	1,611	17,445
Williamsport, PA	11,867	4,875	3,858	2,568	566	$30,382	9.1%	6.1%	8.8%	1,219	16,573
Wilmington, NC	39,482	11,683	10,962	11,538	5,299	$43,701	11.2%	6.7%	7.6%	4,667	55,128
Winchester, VA-WV	11,457	4,099	3,557	2,749	1,052	$33,573	9.7%	10.8%	9.7%	1,416	17,005
Winston-Salem, NC	43,386	15,894	13,888	9,579	4,025	$32,969	9.3%	7.9%	9.6%	4,849	61,372
Worcester, MA	63,136	23,718	17,546	14,458	7,414	$34,307	7.8%	7.5%	9.4%	10,960	90,054
Yakima, WA	16,886	6,075	5,220	4,117	1,474	$33,855	11.4%	11.1%	11.5%	4,353	22,586
York-Hanover, PA	39,794	13,164	13,687	9,804	3,139	$35,473	7.1%	4.9%	6.1%	3,655	57,835
Youngstown-Warren-Boardman, OH-PA	66,502	25,675	24,092	13,076	3,659	$31,190	9.6%	7.4%	8.9%	10,293	88,044
Yuba City, CA	11,654	4,180	3,214	3,000	1,260	$37,129	12.9%	9.9%	13.0%	1,412	18,628
Yuma, AZ	18,834	6,772	6,061	4,546	1,455	$34,434	17.0%	11.0%	10.7%	3,969	23,225

Table G-5: 113th Congressional Districts—Income, Poverty Status and Receipt of Food Stamps (SNAP)

		Income of Households with Householder 65 and Over					Poverty Rate of Persons			Households with 1 or More Persons 60 Years and Over	
	Total Households	Less Than $25,000	$25,000-$49,999	$50,000-$99,999	$100,000 or More	Median Household Income	55 to 64 Years	65 to 74 Years	75 Years and Over	Receiving SNAP	Not Receiving SNAP
Alabama											
Congressional District 1	63,296	21,942	19,982	15,870	5,502	$35,329	12.1%	9.3%	11.1%	10,496	87,207
Congressional District 2	62,194	24,200	18,752	13,823	5,419	$32,704	11.9%	9.6%	13.3%	9,253	84,128
Congressional District 3	60,439	24,701	17,974	12,603	5,161	$30,755	13.3%	9.9%	13.9%	10,707	83,648
Congressional District 4	70,393	31,082	23,254	12,271	3,786	$28,131	12.4%	10.5%	12.3%	10,186	95,008
Congressional District 5	61,062	20,355	17,861	14,756	8,090	$37,927	8.5%	7.1%	10.6%	7,277	85,391
Congressional District 6	57,022	18,296	17,145	14,075	7,506	$37,831	7.4%	6.1%	8.1%	4,858	83,008
Congressional District 7	57,494	27,570	17,428	9,701	2,795	$26,077	18.2%	14.9%	17.1%	15,775	74,707
Alaska											
Congressional District (at Large)	35,129	9,176	9,239	10,185	6,529	$47,441	6.4%	4.8%	6.5%	6,457	61,040
Arizona											
Congressional District 1	61,895	19,988	18,572	16,093	7,242	$38,246	15.7%	10.6%	10.4%	10,658	84,930
Congressional District 2	82,408	24,885	25,506	21,642	10,375	$39,038	11.9%	7.7%	7.3%	9,958	110,803
Congressional District 3	38,254	15,802	11,128	8,509	2,815	$30,805	16.2%	13.9%	16.1%	12,631	54,656
Congressional District 4	98,872	30,320	34,848	26,144	7,560	$36,981	13.1%	6.0%	7.1%	10,698	131,253
Congressional District 5	65,598	17,931	22,097	17,591	7,979	$40,530	6.9%	5.6%	7.3%	5,609	90,171
Congressional District 6	64,829	16,377	17,406	18,215	12,831	$47,456	7.5%	5.9%	5.6%	5,607	96,076
Congressional District 7	27,728	13,464	7,448	4,957	1,859	$25,974	21.2%	20.9%	21.4%	11,260	39,863
Congressional District 8	80,030	21,032	27,453	23,092	8,453	$41,194	6.9%	5.0%	6.1%	5,511	106,917
Congressional District 9	44,669	13,623	12,660	12,234	6,152	$40,946	11.5%	5.7%	8.1%	5,892	68,586
Arkansas											
Congressional District 1	74,629	34,680	22,473	13,348	4,128	$27,260	13.7%	11.7%	16.6%	11,985	99,056
Congressional District 2	60,603	20,421	17,428	15,713	7,041	$36,561	8.7%	7.2%	10.3%	6,531	86,022
Congressional District 3	58,181	20,837	19,332	13,415	4,597	$33,618	10.2%	7.1%	9.7%	6,796	83,459
Congressional District 4	76,944	34,311	23,462	14,603	4,568	$27,949	14.1%	8.9%	14.5%	10,628	102,501
California											
Congressional District 1	78,841	26,300	24,697	19,195	8,649	$36,785	12.3%	8.4%	8.5%	4,904	114,375
Congressional District 2	71,143	19,097	18,080	18,262	15,704	$47,132	9.5%	5.7%	7.9%	3,109	110,433
Congressional District 3	50,081	15,804	13,076	13,216	7,985	$40,831	9.8%	8.4%	10.6%	4,340	78,405
Congressional District 4	73,173	18,219	22,361	21,889	10,704	$44,865	7.6%	5.2%	7.4%	3,933	109,142
Congressional District 5	59,631	15,519	16,566	17,022	10,524	$46,010	9.7%	6.5%	8.8%	4,777	96,306
Congressional District 6	46,049	16,360	12,604	11,549	5,536	$36,767	15.6%	12.4%	9.7%	5,683	72,369
Congressional District 7	52,070	12,586	15,701	15,562	8,221	$44,895	8.5%	6.7%	7.6%	4,093	82,950
Congressional District 8	49,070	18,342	15,114	10,593	5,021	$32,655	14.1%	12.0%	9.4%	7,691	74,185
Congressional District 9	44,298	14,243	13,085	10,938	6,032	$38,731	10.7%	9.8%	11.1%	4,414	71,731
Congressional District 10	42,739	14,051	13,409	10,177	5,102	$36,871	11.5%	9.6%	10.6%	5,265	68,081
Congressional District 11	60,723	13,403	15,056	18,450	13,814	$53,753	7.4%	5.2%	8.2%	3,492	93,781
Congressional District 12	60,556	25,558	12,514	11,704	10,780	$33,142	13.6%	13.9%	18.3%	4,541	93,393
Congressional District 13	54,816	18,355	12,173	12,319	11,969	$43,502	13.3%	10.4%	14.4%	3,609	87,257
Congressional District 14	54,105	12,595	13,069	15,366	13,075	$52,736	6.4%	5.6%	8.1%	2,016	92,137
Congressional District 15	40,607	10,386	10,333	11,333	8,555	$48,851	6.3%	6.7%	7.8%	2,515	72,086
Congressional District 16	35,459	14,647	10,229	7,798	2,785	$29,988	17.2%	16.0%	14.1%	6,992	54,251
Congressional District 17	38,926	10,475	9,376	10,391	8,684	$48,594	8.1%	6.0%	9.1%	2,399	68,403
Congressional District 18	57,686	11,269	13,210	15,081	18,126	$61,287	6.4%	5.4%	7.6%	1,693	90,205
Congressional District 19	38,425	11,852	8,997	9,676	7,900	$44,404	10.7%	8.9%	14.3%	4,172	66,828
Congressional District 20	45,790	12,346	11,779	12,673	8,992	$46,324	9.8%	8.7%	8.1%	3,251	74,248
Congressional District 21	28,615	11,555	8,388	6,116	2,556	$30,996	18.3%	15.5%	15.5%	5,652	46,075
Congressional District 22	45,926	14,214	13,051	11,781	6,880	$40,445	11.9%	8.0%	10.2%	6,121	69,949
Congressional District 23	46,736	15,630	13,430	11,513	6,163	$37,730	11.0%	8.6%	9.1%	3,974	73,123
Congressional District 24	60,205	15,935	15,137	16,799	12,334	$48,669	8.6%	5.9%	7.6%	3,024	89,596
Congressional District 25	35,311	9,433	10,213	9,278	6,387	$44,628	8.3%	7.5%	9.7%	2,693	63,849
Congressional District 26	52,466	13,224	12,570	14,837	11,835	$50,925	6.5%	6.6%	8.7%	3,272	81,022
Congressional District 27	55,033	17,270	12,469	14,258	11,036	$44,314	10.2%	9.5%	11.9%	3,074	91,415
Congressional District 28	58,144	25,951	11,840	10,749	9,604	$30,416	14.4%	13.5%	18.7%	3,594	90,909
Congressional District 29	30,344	12,468	8,412	6,866	2,598	$32,002	16.1%	16.5%	18.5%	3,501	55,473
Congressional District 30	54,729	15,345	13,178	13,593	12,613	$47,651	10.0%	9.3%	10.6%	2,340	89,672
Congressional District 31	33,895	11,452	9,567	8,107	4,769	$37,332	13.7%	11.2%	12.9%	5,059	57,632
Congressional District 32	39,516	12,995	10,454	10,339	5,728	$38,876	8.9%	9.5%	11.6%	4,397	69,968
Congressional District 33	67,969	15,433	12,545	15,602	24,389	$65,169	6.5%	6.0%	7.8%	1,300	100,211
Congressional District 34	38,587	21,648	8,227	5,896	2,816	$21,079	23.2%	22.2%	29.6%	4,168	64,620
Congressional District 35	24,732	9,118	6,993	6,181	2,440	$34,361	12.1%	14.9%	13.4%	4,813	47,520
Congressional District 36	84,960	28,202	24,740	20,148	11,870	$38,124	14.4%	8.9%	9.1%	4,563	115,597
Congressional District 37	52,754	20,251	12,431	11,877	8,195	$35,794	16.4%	13.3%	16.7%	3,846	78,353
Congressional District 38	46,143	14,829	12,415	11,595	7,304	$40,120	9.7%	8.7%	12.0%	3,706	74,599
Congressional District 39	44,798	9,647	11,023	13,933	10,195	$53,995	6.1%	6.9%	9.0%	1,720	79,895
Congressional District 40	24,055	10,426	6,473	5,134	2,022	$29,486	18.2%	18.9%	17.6%	4,454	45,436
Congressional District 41	29,365	9,757	8,340	7,431	3,837	$38,192	13.3%	11.5%	11.4%	4,547	50,767
Congressional District 42	37,443	10,346	12,060	9,636	5,401	$41,009	7.7%	7.0%	7.5%	3,234	64,616
Congressional District 43	43,125	15,579	12,206	9,613	5,727	$35,643	13.3%	13.3%	14.1%	3,534	69,420
Congressional District 44	31,432	12,245	8,188	7,611	3,388	$33,772	15.0%	14.6%	14.3%	5,279	54,102
Congressional District 45	52,624	12,487	12,692	14,457	12,988	$52,893	5.9%	5.0%	8.5%	1,454	85,151
Congressional District 46	27,832	9,712	7,509	6,970	3,641	$36,944	11.0%	12.3%	13.8%	3,314	49,144
Congressional District 47	45,252	13,796	12,308	11,419	7,729	$40,887	12.9%	11.1%	11.8%	4,346	74,027
Congressional District 48	62,120	14,284	15,682	15,672	16,482	$52,401	8.2%	6.4%	9.7%	2,190	96,037
Congressional District 49	51,672	11,793	12,680	15,594	11,605	$52,381	9.0%	6.6%	9.4%	1,998	80,496
Congressional District 50	49,651	13,895	15,052	13,047	7,657	$41,951	13.2%	6.9%	9.4%	2,835	80,477

Table G-5: 113th Congressional Districts—Income, Poverty Status and Receipt of Food Stamps (SNAP)—Continued

	Income of Households with Householder 65 and Over						Poverty Rate of Persons			Households with 1 or More Persons 60 Years and Over	
	Total Households	Less Than $25,000	$25,000-$49,999	$50,000-$99,999	$100,000 or More	Median Household Income	55 to 64 Years	65 to 74 Years	75 Years and Over	Receiving SNAP	Not Receiving SNAP
California—Cont.											
Congressional District 51	37,498	16,670	9,577	7,684	3,567	$29,660	16.3%	15.2%	18.8%	6,181	59,381
Congressional District 52	51,293	12,255	11,432	14,579	13,027	$54,832	6.2%	5.8%	7.8%	1,699	81,352
Congressional District 53	46,186	12,868	12,749	12,502	8,067	$44,469	10.4%	8.2%	9.5%	3,286	75,542
Colorado											
Congressional District 1	52,387	19,776	13,813	11,727	7,071	$34,369	11.7%	10.8%	13.1%	7,962	76,437
Congressional District 2	50,240	11,917	13,662	15,000	9,661	$49,031	6.9%	3.6%	6.7%	2,750	82,532
Congressional District 3	66,323	23,770	20,095	16,124	6,334	$34,513	10.8%	9.1%	11.8%	7,491	96,490
Congressional District 4	48,484	15,899	13,766	13,015	5,804	$38,545	7.3%	6.7%	9.9%	4,577	74,141
Congressional District 5	51,265	15,024	15,142	14,202	6,897	$41,126	8.0%	6.6%	7.5%	4,381	80,299
Congressional District 6	42,773	10,695	11,716	12,888	7,474	$47,535	6.1%	6.2%	7.4%	4,281	69,529
Congressional District 7	52,687	14,703	16,200	15,479	6,305	$41,499	8.4%	6.4%	5.9%	4,422	80,302
Connecticut											
Congressional District 1	66,372	22,373	17,745	16,197	10,057	$38,024	8.1%	7.6%	9.8%	12,596	90,550
Congressional District 2	62,012	16,381	18,070	18,135	9,426	$44,258	4.7%	3.7%	5.8%	7,261	92,246
Congressional District 3	64,640	21,500	17,497	16,236	9,407	$38,160	7.1%	6.5%	6.8%	8,998	91,333
Congressional District 4	59,564	14,186	13,818	15,125	16,435	$54,159	7.4%	6.4%	6.6%	6,955	86,266
Congressional District 5	63,384	19,988	18,556	14,849	9,991	$38,571	8.8%	6.5%	7.8%	9,545	88,346
Delaware											
Congressional District (at Large)	81,975	23,870	23,011	23,710	11,384	$42,892	8.1%	6.7%	7.1%	10,775	115,051
District of Columbia											
Delegate District (at Large)	49,026	16,300	10,109	10,567	12,050	$44,472	15.7%	12.0%	13.3%	11,191	64,715
Florida											
Congressional District 1	63,862	18,997	18,473	18,763	7,629	$40,775	11.0%	6.9%	8.0%	8,356	87,817
Congressional District 2	57,302	20,210	16,316	14,591	6,185	$35,970	12.4%	8.3%	12.1%	8,781	80,022
Congressional District 3	62,566	20,982	19,787	16,241	5,556	$36,537	12.8%	7.6%	9.9%	9,679	87,663
Congressional District 4	53,158	15,280	15,560	14,455	7,863	$41,742	8.9%	6.2%	8.2%	7,199	80,208
Congressional District 5	45,734	21,302	12,850	9,059	2,523	$27,169	19.5%	15.5%	16.0%	15,639	59,694
Congressional District 6	91,244	28,458	29,422	23,449	9,915	$38,746	13.0%	8.3%	9.5%	10,076	121,056
Congressional District 7	52,401	16,192	16,327	13,590	6,292	$39,343	8.5%	7.4%	8.4%	6,698	78,071
Congressional District 8	95,706	29,027	30,881	24,423	11,375	$38,339	11.7%	6.7%	7.3%	9,251	123,793
Congressional District 9	42,093	14,515	13,835	11,017	2,726	$34,586	9.7%	9.5%	10.0%	9,774	64,435
Congressional District 10	72,215	22,786	23,452	19,217	6,760	$36,897	9.1%	7.0%	8.1%	8,345	97,511
Congressional District 11	130,399	40,264	47,988	33,531	8,616	$36,350	12.0%	6.5%	7.3%	12,592	159,373
Congressional District 12	86,993	29,059	31,071	20,153	6,710	$34,941	11.5%	7.8%	7.5%	8,971	116,633
Congressional District 13	99,789	36,574	31,390	22,396	9,429	$33,438	12.0%	7.9%	8.1%	10,619	131,192
Congressional District 14	50,835	21,952	14,704	10,205	3,974	$28,995	18.7%	15.7%	19.1%	16,688	66,610
Congressional District 15	56,084	18,987	17,560	14,644	4,893	$35,830	10.7%	8.5%	8.5%	8,908	80,354
Congressional District 16	123,819	35,026	38,500	33,501	16,792	$40,868	10.9%	5.8%	7.1%	7,890	154,769
Congressional District 17	107,005	34,177	37,404	27,584	7,840	$35,792	14.3%	8.7%	9.2%	11,246	130,677
Congressional District 18	96,368	27,117	29,342	23,519	16,330	$41,479	10.0%	6.4%	7.4%	7,624	124,932
Congressional District 19	109,884	25,407	32,437	29,876	22,164	$47,166	10.6%	6.0%	6.8%	6,960	141,869
Congressional District 20	57,393	26,690	16,907	10,293	3,503	$26,804	18.2%	17.3%	16.7%	14,640	75,266
Congressional District 21	96,018	30,445	26,922	25,040	13,611	$39,431	8.5%	7.7%	8.0%	7,182	122,112
Congressional District 22	90,806	28,098	22,623	21,988	18,097	$42,900	12.9%	8.6%	8.4%	8,873	122,511
Congressional District 23	66,819	29,579	16,295	11,967	8,978	$29,268	11.6%	13.4%	15.0%	12,459	90,579
Congressional District 24	41,211	21,572	9,505	7,318	2,816	$23,439	20.8%	24.5%	27.9%	21,729	51,553
Congressional District 25	49,231	19,380	13,383	10,919	5,549	$33,499	14.8%	14.8%	16.5%	22,741	61,625
Congressional District 26	47,260	18,539	12,155	10,439	6,127	$33,741	12.0%	13.0%	18.1%	20,492	66,266
Congressional District 27	60,456	31,206	12,663	9,692	6,895	$24,143	19.1%	22.4%	25.2%	32,580	65,853
Georgia											
Congressional District 1	54,470	19,503	16,091	12,736	6,140	$35,583	12.3%	9.3%	12.7%	8,662	76,704
Congressional District 2	57,264	26,729	15,810	11,365	3,360	$27,020	19.8%	14.3%	16.5%	16,261	72,899
Congressional District 3	52,125	18,241	15,498	12,819	5,567	$36,314	11.1%	8.5%	10.1%	9,414	76,267
Congressional District 4	35,772	11,539	10,388	9,757	4,088	$39,339	11.5%	11.6%	9.6%	9,139	57,917
Congressional District 5	42,195	20,085	9,565	7,929	4,616	$26,846	20.9%	18.4%	22.0%	14,176	56,741
Congressional District 6	42,234	8,998	11,495	12,055	9,686	$51,610	6.6%	5.9%	6.2%	3,060	68,795
Congressional District 7	27,528	7,339	7,992	7,703	4,494	$44,912	6.6%	6.0%	9.2%	3,774	50,395
Congressional District 8	55,875	22,549	15,882	12,768	4,676	$30,754	14.9%	9.9%	15.4%	11,623	75,641
Congressional District 9	63,534	23,869	19,598	14,636	5,431	$32,831	12.5%	8.4%	11.6%	9,947	88,979
Congressional District 10	48,726	17,614	14,509	11,262	5,341	$34,575	11.3%	8.3%	13.2%	8,745	71,722
Congressional District 11	41,487	12,270	11,686	10,401	7,130	$40,983	7.9%	6.7%	10.9%	4,649	64,347
Congressional District 12	51,734	22,331	14,380	10,920	4,103	$30,169	15.3%	12.4%	16.6%	10,684	72,494
Congressional District 13	34,488	11,141	10,509	9,472	3,366	$38,480	12.4%	8.9%	9.9%	8,835	56,924
Congressional District 14	52,011	21,823	16,379	10,156	3,653	$30,078	14.0%	9.8%	12.7%	9,713	73,757
Hawaii											
Congressional District 1	60,659	13,426	13,772	16,956	16,505	$57,217	7.0%	6.0%	8.2%	9,010	88,845
Congressional District 2	50,239	12,588	11,389	15,143	11,119	$52,729	11.4%	6.7%	8.8%	9,513	79,342
Idaho											
Congressional District 1	66,692	23,060	22,136	16,394	5,102	$34,582	10.0%	6.8%	9.9%	8,092	95,329
Congressional District 2	61,125	21,560	19,711	14,174	5,680	$34,517	9.5%	6.5%	9.3%	6,433	87,547

Table G-5: 113th Congressional Districts—Income, Poverty Status and Receipt of Food Stamps (SNAP)—*Continued*

		Income of Households with Householder 65 and Over					Poverty Rate of Persons			Households with 1 or More Persons 60 Years and Over	
	Total Households	Less Than $25,000	$25,000-$49,999	$50,000-$99,999	$100,000 or More	Median Household Income	55 to 64 Years	65 to 74 Years	75 Years and Over	Receiving SNAP	Not Receiving SNAP
Illinois											
Congressional District 1	63,639	24,206	18,352	14,625	6,456	$33,337	13.9%	11.1%	11.7%	15,599	81,177
Congressional District 2	60,904	22,175	18,746	14,610	5,373	$34,213	13.8%	10.3%	10.9%	13,364	80,383
Congressional District 3	53,766	17,573	16,918	13,622	5,653	$36,007	8.4%	7.2%	7.8%	6,615	78,923
Congressional District 4	32,366	13,718	9,972	6,089	2,587	$29,041	16.2%	16.4%	15.4%	11,135	47,688
Congressional District 5	52,736	20,038	14,053	11,166	7,479	$33,781	9.5%	8.0%	12.0%	6,898	75,779
Congressional District 6	53,412	12,491	14,167	14,472	12,282	$50,092	3.3%	3.4%	5.9%	2,989	84,142
Congressional District 7	49,877	22,649	11,377	9,453	6,398	$28,288	19.3%	19.0%	20.2%	19,395	60,449
Congressional District 8	44,160	12,072	13,823	13,035	5,230	$41,237	5.8%	3.9%	8.1%	5,625	70,086
Congressional District 9	69,300	20,658	18,129	17,571	12,942	$42,339	9.2%	8.7%	11.3%	10,386	93,893
Congressional District 10	51,370	13,229	14,209	13,726	10,206	$45,241	6.5%	6.3%	7.8%	5,670	77,864
Congressional District 11	42,364	11,774	12,319	11,781	6,490	$42,901	6.1%	5.3%	8.9%	5,063	65,968
Congressional District 12	67,007	25,226	21,791	14,672	5,318	$32,357	10.5%	7.9%	10.0%	8,893	89,150
Congressional District 13	62,715	20,557	20,347	15,231	6,580	$36,702	8.6%	5.9%	6.9%	6,405	87,746
Congressional District 14	43,461	10,510	12,257	12,424	8,270	$47,871	5.3%	4.2%	6.4%	2,738	70,566
Congressional District 15	75,149	28,924	24,786	16,055	5,384	$31,792	8.5%	6.9%	8.2%	7,390	100,019
Congressional District 16	65,819	21,969	21,769	16,262	5,819	$36,026	7.1%	5.1%	7.5%	4,885	93,131
Congressional District 17	74,168	26,907	26,164	16,164	4,933	$33,068	11.6%	6.6%	8.4%	8,493	99,492
Congressional District 18	70,638	20,805	22,705	19,051	8,077	$39,586	6.2%	5.1%	7.4%	4,484	99,002
Indiana											
Congressional District 1	59,248	20,456	18,490	15,061	5,241	$34,609	10.7%	7.3%	8.5%	9,476	85,614
Congressional District 2	62,647	22,175	22,433	13,841	4,198	$33,502	8.1%	6.0%	8.2%	6,463	88,191
Congressional District 3	60,316	20,274	21,357	14,233	4,452	$34,362	7.8%	6.2%	7.1%	5,229	86,216
Congressional District 4	59,975	19,361	21,858	14,512	4,244	$35,087	6.8%	5.8%	5.5%	5,413	84,741
Congressional District 5	56,560	16,722	18,316	14,788	6,734	$38,835	6.9%	5.4%	5.7%	5,057	81,865
Congressional District 6	68,201	26,122	24,096	13,913	4,070	$31,200	8.5%	6.9%	7.7%	7,016	94,221
Congressional District 7	48,994	18,893	17,071	10,417	2,613	$31,760	13.0%	9.4%	11.5%	10,477	67,009
Congressional District 8	66,676	24,490	23,253	14,625	4,308	$32,446	9.0%	6.0%	7.9%	6,832	93,636
Congressional District 9	60,400	21,411	19,751	14,667	4,571	$34,448	8.1%	6.6%	8.7%	6,691	86,329
Iowa											
Congressional District 1	74,800	24,485	26,026	18,322	5,967	$35,051	6.0%	5.1%	9.1%	5,958	102,856
Congressional District 2	71,833	26,102	22,776	17,267	5,688	$33,695	8.2%	7.2%	8.8%	7,686	100,206
Congressional District 3	61,362	20,378	20,088	14,941	5,955	$35,643	6.7%	5.6%	7.9%	7,458	88,877
Congressional District 4	81,934	30,973	25,671	18,559	6,731	$32,962	7.2%	5.4%	8.9%	5,906	109,206
Kansas											
Congressional District 1	66,555	24,588	21,408	14,858	5,701	$33,312	6.4%	5.9%	9.1%	4,919	91,587
Congressional District 2	65,186	22,962	20,813	15,470	5,941	$35,155	8.7%	6.4%	8.4%	5,852	91,346
Congressional District 3	50,782	13,658	14,701	14,309	8,114	$44,731	6.3%	5.0%	7.1%	3,655	77,738
Congressional District 4	59,414	20,143	19,947	14,319	5,005	$34,968	8.7%	7.3%	8.5%	6,470	83,270
Kentucky											
Congressional District 1	73,165	33,114	23,508	12,258	4,285	$27,477	12.3%	10.2%	15.2%	12,492	95,949
Congressional District 2	62,186	25,707	19,419	13,243	3,817	$30,540	10.2%	8.0%	13.9%	10,251	83,439
Congressional District 3	63,933	23,358	20,650	13,661	6,264	$33,690	11.0%	9.7%	10.3%	9,845	89,336
Congressional District 4	56,281	20,512	18,022	13,142	4,605	$34,078	9.1%	8.0%	11.6%	7,630	83,464
Congressional District 5	67,095	37,139	18,955	8,690	2,311	$22,388	20.1%	16.4%	19.2%	20,464	84,643
Congressional District 6	56,965	20,244	17,842	13,421	5,458	$34,111	12.2%	9.0%	12.0%	10,124	79,365
Louisiana											
Congressional District 1	64,336	22,690	18,441	15,240	7,965	$34,992	9.9%	7.6%	10.3%	8,529	92,993
Congressional District 2	55,094	25,258	15,308	10,422	4,106	$27,596	18.5%	15.2%	16.9%	17,306	75,359
Congressional District 3	58,991	27,147	16,460	10,196	5,188	$27,395	12.5%	12.1%	13.6%	10,692	80,296
Congressional District 4	67,450	27,900	18,790	14,914	5,846	$30,947	14.3%	10.8%	13.6%	13,180	87,859
Congressional District 5	66,226	30,114	20,132	11,461	4,519	$27,759	17.4%	13.8%	18.1%	14,830	85,757
Congressional District 6	53,661	17,765	16,296	13,105	6,495	$37,130	9.5%	7.5%	9.7%	7,814	78,759
Maine											
Congressional District 1	67,165	22,481	20,229	17,370	7,085	$37,135	8.5%	7.0%	8.0%	10,058	95,065
Congressional District 2	69,161	29,773	21,901	13,773	3,714	$28,834	10.2%	9.5%	10.8%	14,292	93,380
Maryland											
Congressional District 1	67,990	18,315	18,591	19,882	11,202	$44,779	6.1%	4.3%	7.7%	6,832	98,366
Congressional District 2	52,049	16,644	15,300	13,789	6,316	$38,687	8.8%	7.1%	8.5%	8,496	78,379
Congressional District 3	60,493	18,486	13,934	15,132	12,941	$44,327	7.0%	7.2%	10.0%	6,833	89,932
Congressional District 4	45,816	9,880	10,122	14,656	11,158	$57,977	6.1%	5.8%	7.4%	5,835	74,632
Congressional District 5	44,843	8,271	9,732	14,799	12,041	$62,767	4.6%	5.4%	5.4%	4,825	75,429
Congressional District 6	53,783	15,651	13,876	13,213	11,043	$43,920	6.1%	5.8%	9.3%	6,266	82,291
Congressional District 7	61,093	23,144	14,643	14,770	8,536	$36,370	12.5%	12.2%	13.5%	14,335	80,717
Congressional District 8	61,685	12,493	13,252	16,565	19,375	$62,030	4.6%	5.4%	8.0%	4,120	95,460
Massachusetts											
Congressional District 1	70,654	27,460	20,692	15,901	6,601	$32,257	10.2%	7.4%	10.0%	14,363	94,707
Congressional District 2	58,359	21,051	15,750	14,091	7,467	$35,889	7.8%	8.2%	8.6%	9,915	83,403
Congressional District 3	54,213	19,211	14,907	13,017	7,078	$36,248	9.5%	8.1%	9.7%	10,201	80,834
Congressional District 4	59,690	19,302	14,284	14,442	11,662	$42,788	5.3%	5.1%	10.3%	6,614	87,668
Congressional District 5	65,582	20,309	15,639	15,295	14,339	$43,289	6.3%	6.1%	10.1%	8,029	93,772
Congressional District 6	68,756	21,418	18,077	17,926	11,335	$40,578	6.2%	7.6%	7.6%	9,196	98,131
Congressional District 7	48,752	25,905	9,328	8,261	5,258	$22,893	16.5%	20.4%	20.4%	18,900	58,032
Congressional District 8	66,721	20,438	18,775	16,474	11,034	$40,942	7.0%	6.8%	9.5%	9,379	92,979
Congressional District 9	83,918	28,632	21,752	21,335	12,199	$38,986	7.9%	6.5%	10.7%	10,776	113,294

Table G-5: 113th Congressional Districts—Income, Poverty Status and Receipt of Food Stamps (SNAP)—*Continued*

	Income of Households with Householder 65 and Over						Poverty Rate of Persons			Households with 1 or More Persons 60 Years and Over	
	Total Households	Less Than $25,000	$25,000-$49,999	$50,000-$99,999	$100,000 or More	Median Household Income	55 to 64 Years	65 to 74 Years	75 Years and Over	Receiving SNAP	Not Receiving SNAP
Michigan											
Congressional District 1	86,476	31,519	29,416	19,676	5,865	$33,050	10.1%	6.4%	9.2%	11,570	114,115
Congressional District 2	58,368	20,381	20,716	13,661	3,610	$33,228	8.3%	5.8%	8.2%	10,015	78,521
Congressional District 3	56,348	18,533	19,708	13,203	4,904	$35,140	8.6%	6.1%	7.0%	9,156	77,604
Congressional District 4	70,829	25,249	26,210	15,173	4,197	$33,240	10.5%	6.5%	8.5%	10,389	93,261
Congressional District 5	70,085	22,699	26,648	16,566	4,172	$34,339	12.9%	7.9%	7.3%	14,478	89,798
Congressional District 6	63,960	22,980	21,452	14,786	4,742	$33,267	10.9%	7.9%	10.0%	9,988	86,299
Congressional District 7	63,933	21,164	23,250	14,685	4,834	$35,089	8.8%	5.6%	8.4%	8,279	90,688
Congressional District 8	52,661	12,918	16,566	16,168	7,009	$44,565	6.3%	4.4%	6.5%	6,046	78,472
Congressional District 9	72,707	25,663	24,166	15,990	6,888	$33,937	10.5%	8.0%	8.7%	12,549	95,609
Congressional District 10	63,850	19,445	22,876	16,435	5,094	$36,695	7.7%	6.4%	9.1%	8,440	90,564
Congressional District 11	60,804	15,018	19,334	18,317	8,135	$43,830	5.5%	4.2%	5.8%	5,228	88,228
Congressional District 12	55,781	17,938	17,719	13,857	6,267	$37,653	10.1%	8.4%	7.2%	9,264	76,649
Congressional District 13	59,820	27,500	18,840	10,928	2,552	$27,343	22.0%	17.5%	14.8%	23,923	69,093
Congressional District 14	63,216	23,284	17,541	14,502	7,889	$34,176	16.1%	12.7%	13.2%	18,311	81,059
Minnesota											
Congressional District 1	64,269	23,640	19,497	16,068	5,064	$34,099	5.4%	6.2%	11.5%	4,414	86,608
Congressional District 2	44,625	12,853	13,070	13,304	5,398	$41,571	4.4%	4.0%	8.3%	2,343	68,963
Congressional District 3	52,318	12,828	15,703	15,199	8,588	$45,635	4.3%	4.4%	6.6%	3,605	79,149
Congressional District 4	52,030	15,672	14,386	15,141	6,831	$41,850	8.5%	6.0%	10.7%	5,781	76,054
Congressional District 5	49,190	18,080	14,179	11,379	5,552	$35,223	12.0%	11.6%	10.5%	8,040	68,014
Congressional District 6	40,864	12,483	13,286	11,344	3,751	$38,206	4.7%	4.7%	10.5%	2,838	62,935
Congressional District 7	73,648	28,934	22,725	17,012	4,977	$32,318	6.4%	5.7%	12.8%	4,918	98,260
Congressional District 8	72,554	27,377	23,701	17,059	4,417	$32,818	8.8%	6.6%	10.4%	5,665	99,972
Mississippi											
Congressional District 1	63,562	28,385	18,500	12,281	4,396	$28,448	12.5%	10.2%	13.4%	10,535	87,571
Congressional District 2	58,279	28,735	15,382	10,425	3,737	$25,476	21.0%	17.0%	19.5%	16,174	75,078
Congressional District 3	65,405	29,371	17,691	12,199	6,144	$28,521	12.6%	13.2%	13.7%	10,790	89,223
Congressional District 4	61,651	24,950	18,806	13,206	4,689	$30,990	14.8%	10.6%	12.4%	10,608	84,867
Missouri											
Congressional District 1	61,438	26,209	17,610	12,922	4,697	$29,727	14.5%	12.0%	13.6%	15,990	80,456
Congressional District 2	73,521	18,329	22,854	20,116	12,222	$44,116	4.4%	3.7%	6.6%	4,105	105,086
Congressional District 3	62,537	19,394	21,317	16,700	5,126	$37,425	7.9%	5.5%	8.7%	5,780	90,139
Congressional District 4	67,398	25,032	21,507	15,770	5,089	$33,526	10.3%	6.8%	11.1%	8,613	91,250
Congressional District 5	66,508	24,487	22,068	14,963	4,990	$33,320	12.2%	7.7%	8.3%	9,245	90,894
Congressional District 6	65,556	24,451	21,089	14,872	5,144	$33,565	7.6%	6.0%	10.5%	6,322	92,181
Congressional District 7	71,462	27,504	24,234	15,200	4,524	$31,703	10.9%	7.2%	11.3%	9,425	97,224
Congressional District 8	75,680	35,395	23,736	12,894	3,655	$27,066	13.4%	11.2%	14.1%	14,328	97,907
Montana											
Congressional District (at Large)	97,403	34,471	31,495	22,942	8,495	$34,371	10.3%	6.6%	9.8%	8,903	140,384
Nebraska											
Congressional District 1	50,998	16,297	16,149	13,509	5,043	$38,005	5.8%	4.5%	8.0%	3,495	73,199
Congressional District 2	41,658	13,117	12,423	11,118	5,000	$38,525	7.3%	4.8%	11.0%	4,475	61,966
Congressional District 3	66,972	26,841	20,079	15,170	4,882	$31,409	7.4%	5.6%	11.4%	4,552	90,290
Nevada											
Congressional District 1	49,790	19,976	15,131	10,604	4,079	$30,669	15.8%	10.9%	11.6%	12,062	69,619
Congressional District 2	57,060	16,918	16,609	14,919	8,614	$41,519	10.4%	7.5%	7.8%	6,154	88,393
Congressional District 3	49,698	11,406	13,765	15,354	9,173	$49,311	7.9%	6.1%	8.3%	4,087	81,021
Congressional District 4	48,132	13,195	15,342	14,553	5,042	$41,165	8.5%	8.6%	7.9%	6,339	72,882
New Hampshire											
Congressional District 1	55,685	15,987	17,300	14,946	7,452	$41,541	5.5%	4.4%	8.0%	5,204	84,917
Congressional District 2	57,617	17,704	18,302	14,003	7,608	$38,296	4.9%	5.6%	7.7%	5,007	87,854
New Jersey											
Congressional District 1	60,165	19,584	18,068	14,655	7,858	$37,256	6.6%	8.2%	8.3%	7,334	88,411
Congressional District 2	70,540	22,090	21,132	18,172	9,146	$38,864	9.3%	8.2%	9.1%	7,734	101,970
Congressional District 3	78,363	21,268	24,144	21,920	11,031	$42,197	4.4%	4.5%	6.3%	5,022	112,079
Congressional District 4	78,391	21,438	22,995	20,752	13,206	$42,916	4.9%	3.5%	7.0%	4,291	110,046
Congressional District 5	62,712	15,117	14,796	16,949	15,850	$53,436	4.5%	3.9%	8.5%	3,877	96,651
Congressional District 6	49,969	15,150	12,511	13,297	9,011	$43,282	6.6%	6.0%	7.6%	5,281	80,395
Congressional District 7	58,088	13,326	13,252	17,083	14,427	$55,026	3.6%	3.4%	6.7%	3,493	89,974
Congressional District 8	41,136	19,589	9,544	8,032	3,971	$26,614	14.9%	14.2%	18.5%	11,527	60,071
Congressional District 9	58,242	21,280	14,038	13,055	9,869	$36,744	10.1%	11.4%	12.3%	9,811	83,524
Congressional District 10	51,555	22,067	12,662	10,453	6,373	$30,439	13.3%	12.6%	14.8%	12,171	73,012
Congressional District 11	66,166	14,049	15,989	19,169	16,959	$56,339	3.1%	3.2%	6.1%	3,169	101,753
Congressional District 12	58,274	14,749	14,601	15,963	12,961	$49,485	6.3%	5.3%	8.1%	5,591	87,393
New Mexico											
Congressional District 1	56,382	17,820	16,381	14,159	8,022	$38,994	12.7%	8.9%	10.3%	7,932	84,548
Congressional District 2	63,242	25,546	18,635	13,613	5,448	$31,997	14.4%	12.3%	15.1%	10,381	84,774
Congressional District 3	57,824	20,771	15,942	13,618	7,493	$35,994	14.0%	12.1%	14.3%	7,614	85,401

Table G-5: 113th Congressional Districts—Income, Poverty Status and Receipt of Food Stamps (SNAP)—*Continued*

	Income of Households with Householder 65 and Over						Poverty Rate of Persons			Households with 1 or More Persons 60 Years and Over	
	Total Households	Less Than $25,000	$25,000-$49,999	$50,000-$99,999	$100,000 or More	Median Household Income	55 to 64 Years	65 to 74 Years	75 Years and Over	Receiving SNAP	Not Receiving SNAP
New York											
Congressional District 1	61,352	13,902	15,507	17,768	14,175	$53,161	5.8%	5.3%	6.2%	4,943	92,727
Congressional District 2	53,807	12,685	13,696	16,614	10,812	$51,412	4.2%	3.9%	7.2%	6,970	82,760
Congressional District 3	72,842	15,891	15,559	20,333	21,059	$58,983	4.7%	3.9%	6.2%	4,839	107,318
Congressional District 4	60,479	14,116	14,705	16,078	15,580	$53,113	5.2%	4.5%	6.4%	5,913	92,210
Congressional District 5	46,869	15,935	11,162	12,031	7,741	$40,907	9.4%	12.2%	12.7%	18,882	69,373
Congressional District 6	61,218	24,362	15,193	13,298	8,365	$32,749	11.4%	13.0%	13.9%	15,986	87,950
Congressional District 7	40,174	24,241	7,471	4,984	3,478	$19,588	23.5%	27.8%	32.0%	25,112	45,924
Congressional District 8	57,410	30,246	12,607	9,606	4,951	$22,739	17.9%	22.6%	29.8%	29,373	65,298
Congressional District 9	52,588	24,697	11,729	10,086	6,076	$27,132	16.0%	18.1%	22.1%	23,985	68,116
Congressional District 10	63,915	23,867	13,920	12,250	13,878	$37,008	12.3%	11.3%	17.5%	15,264	84,401
Congressional District 11	61,466	24,092	15,306	13,274	8,794	$33,209	9.9%	11.0%	16.2%	15,566	85,901
Congressional District 12	69,281	22,668	12,820	13,618	20,175	$47,576	13.4%	11.0%	14.2%	11,579	88,369
Congressional District 13	51,805	30,409	11,898	6,186	3,312	$20,118	25.1%	25.3%	28.2%	34,720	50,133
Congressional District 14	47,181	19,805	12,522	10,071	4,783	$30,565	14.2%	14.0%	18.9%	16,312	64,226
Congressional District 15	39,856	27,142	7,300	3,870	1,544	$15,813	31.3%	32.8%	35.7%	34,177	33,906
Congressional District 16	65,395	22,030	14,468	15,623	13,274	$41,706	9.3%	8.7%	10.9%	11,170	90,558
Congressional District 17	59,751	13,888	13,219	16,515	16,129	$57,358	4.8%	4.9%	8.3%	4,636	88,980
Congressional District 18	54,771	14,189	15,338	13,799	11,445	$45,410	6.3%	5.8%	6.9%	6,375	80,880
Congressional District 19	71,306	22,063	22,125	18,909	8,209	$38,888	8.9%	5.9%	8.0%	8,878	103,314
Congressional District 20	64,691	19,890	18,797	18,320	7,684	$39,651	6.6%	7.1%	7.1%	8,013	91,370
Congressional District 21	66,841	24,270	20,938	16,098	5,535	$33,597	9.7%	7.3%	9.4%	11,025	90,580
Congressional District 22	71,222	26,299	23,450	16,048	5,425	$33,515	9.9%	7.6%	9.6%	12,646	95,661
Congressional District 23	69,521	26,448	21,423	15,544	6,106	$32,651	8.7%	6.3%	9.1%	10,320	97,371
Congressional District 24	65,266	22,925	20,071	16,037	6,233	$34,708	9.0%	6.6%	8.2%	10,694	88,755
Congressional District 25	65,975	21,616	20,650	17,038	6,671	$36,482	8.4%	8.0%	8.1%	10,093	88,104
Congressional District 26	74,605	30,386	22,408	15,961	5,850	$31,453	12.3%	8.5%	10.6%	14,912	94,006
Congressional District 27	70,022	22,274	22,160	19,138	6,450	$37,230	5.4%	4.8%	7.8%	7,548	99,188
North Carolina											
Congressional District 1	66,554	32,151	18,583	12,434	3,386	$26,256	17.4%	14.7%	20.0%	21,811	79,110
Congressional District 2	55,632	20,438	15,740	13,925	5,529	$33,960	9.7%	8.1%	11.1%	7,531	80,590
Congressional District 3	62,436	21,299	18,467	16,466	6,204	$37,229	9.5%	8.0%	10.6%	10,406	86,266
Congressional District 4	45,224	14,428	11,772	11,904	7,120	$41,183	10.4%	7.5%	10.5%	8,198	65,201
Congressional District 5	70,921	26,649	22,645	16,003	5,624	$32,488	10.1%	7.3%	11.1%	7,791	98,998
Congressional District 6	72,716	26,173	22,338	16,595	7,610	$34,719	8.2%	8.2%	9.8%	9,236	100,135
Congressional District 7	71,476	26,285	20,195	17,913	7,083	$35,480	11.6%	8.7%	11.6%	11,072	97,630
Congressional District 8	62,266	27,322	18,587	13,006	3,351	$28,539	13.5%	10.3%	14.8%	12,459	84,074
Congressional District 9	48,157	13,110	12,850	14,367	7,830	$45,632	6.4%	4.5%	5.2%	4,185	76,266
Congressional District 10	69,278	27,868	21,646	14,419	5,345	$30,626	12.2%	7.8%	11.9%	11,404	96,292
Congressional District 11	89,001	35,269	26,586	20,357	6,789	$32,528	11.9%	8.7%	10.1%	10,517	120,147
Congressional District 12	41,118	18,104	12,983	7,886	2,145	$28,185	17.1%	13.5%	15.1%	12,523	56,310
Congressional District 13	53,396	15,439	15,705	14,641	7,611	$41,591	6.3%	6.1%	9.6%	6,048	80,067
North Dakota											
Congressional District (at Large)	62,826	23,993	18,858	14,082	5,893	$33,281	6.2%	7.6%	14.5%	5,255	87,400
Ohio											
Congressional District 1	56,278	19,189	17,164	13,461	6,464	$36,136	10.0%	7.6%	8.1%	7,990	78,730
Congressional District 2	65,963	23,989	20,724	15,083	6,167	$33,674	11.4%	6.9%	10.0%	9,881	90,917
Congressional District 3	43,825	17,339	13,898	9,310	3,278	$30,542	14.1%	12.5%	9.4%	12,362	59,185
Congressional District 4	67,395	24,264	24,558	15,234	3,339	$32,603	8.8%	6.4%	7.1%	8,514	92,574
Congressional District 5	69,228	23,259	23,929	16,563	5,477	$35,197	7.1%	5.0%	7.3%	5,889	96,080
Congressional District 6	77,660	31,282	28,825	14,357	3,196	$30,150	11.6%	8.8%	9.3%	13,966	102,452
Congressional District 7	68,916	23,579	25,459	15,627	4,251	$34,061	8.4%	5.6%	8.3%	7,962	96,138
Congressional District 8	64,548	21,332	21,742	16,594	4,880	$35,663	8.4%	5.3%	7.5%	8,617	89,254
Congressional District 9	64,955	26,729	21,638	12,850	3,738	$30,074	12.7%	9.6%	10.0%	13,654	85,160
Congressional District 10	71,934	24,754	23,832	16,763	6,585	$34,537	9.9%	8.5%	8.1%	10,288	97,807
Congressional District 11	69,855	32,974	18,913	12,378	5,590	$26,628	19.2%	15.5%	14.7%	20,242	86,819
Congressional District 12	57,210	18,091	16,943	15,179	6,997	$37,375	6.8%	4.6%	7.7%	7,733	84,976
Congressional District 13	75,629	29,028	26,697	15,704	4,200	$31,535	10.7%	7.1%	8.9%	12,943	101,341
Congressional District 14	73,757	23,619	24,152	18,367	7,619	$37,095	5.8%	5.8%	7.0%	6,652	104,187
Congressional District 15	57,635	19,167	18,278	14,719	5,471	$36,302	8.4%	6.3%	7.0%	8,915	80,104
Congressional District 16	76,176	23,255	26,387	19,398	7,136	$37,297	5.7%	4.3%	5.9%	6,100	106,829
Oklahoma											
Congressional District 1	62,489	21,056	19,335	15,039	7,059	$35,871	8.4%	6.1%	9.4%	6,896	88,733
Congressional District 2	77,562	34,624	24,613	14,471	3,854	$27,885	14.5%	11.0%	14.4%	12,645	101,437
Congressional District 3	68,953	26,010	21,625	15,712	5,606	$32,219	9.4%	8.1%	10.6%	8,493	93,014
Congressional District 4	61,389	21,575	18,947	15,392	5,475	$35,471	8.5%	7.7%	10.2%	8,081	84,785
Congressional District 5	61,020	21,618	17,993	14,789	6,620	$35,212	11.9%	9.0%	9.2%	9,588	83,939
Oregon											
Congressional District 1	57,497	16,015	17,720	16,730	7,032	$40,879	7.9%	6.3%	8.6%	8,623	84,166
Congressional District 2	84,449	30,036	27,218	19,573	7,622	$34,202	11.1%	7.6%	7.2%	14,843	112,373
Congressional District 3	54,792	17,955	16,000	14,552	6,285	$37,434	12.0%	9.5%	9.6%	14,694	77,709
Congressional District 4	84,442	29,266	27,633	20,702	6,841	$35,206	13.2%	8.0%	7.9%	17,569	111,859
Congressional District 5	70,703	20,468	23,153	19,197	7,885	$40,208	10.0%	6.5%	6.3%	13,291	97,373

Table G-5: 113th Congressional Districts—Income, Poverty Status and Receipt of Food Stamps (SNAP)—*Continued*

	Total Households	Income of Households with Householder 65 and Over				Median Household Income	Poverty Rate of Persons			Households with 1 or More Persons 60 Years and Over	
		Less Than $25,000	$25,000-$49,999	$50,000-$99,999	$100,000 or More		55 to 64 Years	65 to 74 Years	75 Years and Over	Receiving SNAP	Not Receiving SNAP
Pennsylvania											
Congressional District 1	49,999	23,906	13,601	8,161	4,331	$26,251	19.3%	12.8%	14.5%	16,774	64,188
Congressional District 2	63,296	29,354	15,277	11,874	6,791	$27,429	22.7%	17.7%	18.8%	21,070	74,555
Congressional District 3	73,915	28,757	25,589	14,930	4,639	$31,043	10.0%	7.1%	8.9%	10,851	97,975
Congressional District 4	66,376	21,475	21,866	17,259	5,776	$36,422	7.2%	5.4%	7.3%	6,369	95,477
Congressional District 5	72,084	28,494	25,052	14,218	4,320	$30,679	7.5%	6.4%	8.5%	8,571	97,887
Congressional District 6	62,853	17,973	18,636	17,412	8,832	$41,146	5.0%	4.0%	6.2%	3,815	91,359
Congressional District 7	66,840	16,766	19,906	18,181	11,987	$44,830	4.6%	4.2%	6.0%	3,813	97,198
Congressional District 8	63,106	16,680	19,183	17,218	10,025	$43,438	4.9%	4.1%	7.1%	5,258	94,474
Congressional District 9	78,422	33,124	26,427	15,020	3,851	$29,191	10.6%	7.4%	9.3%	11,350	103,132
Congressional District 10	72,892	27,074	25,136	15,949	4,733	$32,577	8.5%	6.7%	8.6%	7,581	103,087
Congressional District 11	72,457	27,633	23,661	15,914	5,249	$32,133	7.2%	5.7%	9.7%	7,448	101,897
Congressional District 12	83,948	31,919	27,755	17,499	6,775	$31,838	6.3%	6.2%	8.9%	8,531	112,000
Congressional District 13	62,168	22,928	17,126	14,401	7,713	$34,923	9.5%	9.6%	12.2%	10,674	87,387
Congressional District 14	78,595	35,123	23,710	14,367	5,395	$27,806	12.3%	9.7%	11.3%	14,454	100,705
Congressional District 15	65,964	22,338	21,219	15,992	6,415	$35,554	7.8%	5.8%	6.6%	6,628	93,323
Congressional District 16	61,178	20,365	20,521	14,577	5,715	$35,190	9.3%	7.0%	8.1%	7,699	84,466
Congressional District 17	73,422	30,710	23,297	14,434	4,981	$29,729	9.0%	6.1%	9.3%	9,589	100,593
Congressional District 18	80,713	26,940	26,399	20,197	7,177	$35,646	5.8%	5.4%	7.0%	7,002	111,096
Rhode Island											
Congressional District 1	48,757	19,431	12,504	10,420	6,402	$32,424	12.2%	9.5%	10.6%	10,339	63,658
Congressional District 2	47,532	17,377	11,887	11,529	6,739	$36,642	8.2%	7.8%	9.5%	8,790	66,863
South Carolina											
Congressional District 1	60,335	14,806	16,129	17,950	11,450	$48,455	7.7%	5.2%	7.1%	6,004	87,974
Congressional District 2	53,496	17,603	15,455	13,437	7,001	$38,423	9.6%	7.4%	9.2%	7,207	77,413
Congressional District 3	64,787	26,938	19,310	13,908	4,631	$29,997	12.0%	8.5%	10.7%	10,369	87,783
Congressional District 4	56,127	20,923	17,528	12,108	5,568	$33,596	11.1%	8.9%	11.5%	7,512	79,830
Congressional District 5	58,130	23,124	18,338	12,644	4,024	$31,783	12.1%	8.3%	13.3%	11,863	78,775
Congressional District 6	54,028	25,442	15,490	10,139	2,957	$26,733	17.5%	14.8%	20.6%	14,865	71,099
Congressional District 7	69,540	26,400	21,755	15,708	5,677	$32,114	14.8%	8.7%	13.5%	11,677	95,048
South Dakota											
Congressional District (at Large)	74,354	28,663	21,794	17,335	6,562	$33,317	8.3%	8.0%	14.3%	7,026	102,258
Tennessee											
Congressional District 1	78,559	33,537	25,094	14,722	5,206	$28,921	11.9%	8.8%	13.8%	14,249	103,593
Congressional District 2	67,244	25,722	20,239	15,713	5,570	$32,174	10.9%	7.4%	8.9%	10,388	93,544
Congressional District 3	71,872	28,601	21,687	15,473	6,111	$31,124	11.5%	9.4%	9.9%	13,781	96,012
Congressional District 4	57,673	22,531	18,410	12,413	4,319	$31,545	11.8%	8.8%	10.7%	11,751	79,211
Congressional District 5	48,840	16,844	14,484	11,808	5,704	$36,302	11.5%	9.5%	9.1%	9,531	70,371
Congressional District 6	67,865	25,715	22,048	15,666	4,436	$33,073	11.4%	8.5%	12.0%	11,980	91,572
Congressional District 7	56,764	22,849	16,514	12,414	4,987	$31,805	11.3%	10.5%	13.6%	10,961	78,436
Congressional District 8	61,894	21,034	19,259	14,396	7,205	$35,897	8.8%	7.3%	11.3%	11,556	85,167
Congressional District 9	44,473	19,907	11,630	9,509	3,427	$28,746	17.2%	15.4%	14.9%	17,690	58,721
Texas											
Congressional District 1	63,924	24,827	19,478	14,513	5,106	$31,846	11.7%	10.7%	11.8%	8,246	88,129
Congressional District 2	35,897	8,055	9,227	9,765	8,850	$52,648	5.6%	6.0%	9.3%	3,620	62,892
Congressional District 3	33,448	7,609	8,457	9,339	8,043	$51,968	5.6%	5.7%	7.1%	2,554	58,791
Congressional District 4	64,787	24,228	20,216	14,989	5,354	$33,082	11.4%	9.0%	10.7%	9,948	88,934
Congressional District 5	53,103	19,877	16,145	12,558	4,523	$33,691	12.7%	9.2%	11.9%	7,429	75,631
Congressional District 6	40,426	11,018	11,574	11,507	6,327	$43,942	7.5%	6.5%	8.9%	6,275	63,847
Congressional District 7	40,123	9,375	8,863	10,247	11,638	$56,533	6.2%	7.3%	8.0%	3,208	65,820
Congressional District 8	49,965	15,144	15,625	12,181	7,015	$38,005	9.5%	6.7%	9.9%	5,790	74,112
Congressional District 9	31,161	12,210	8,213	7,559	3,179	$34,538	13.3%	14.8%	19.2%	9,612	52,073
Congressional District 10	43,255	13,518	11,471	11,405	6,861	$41,041	8.2%	7.5%	9.4%	4,132	68,613
Congressional District 11	65,403	25,329	19,809	13,574	6,691	$31,893	11.5%	8.8%	11.8%	7,900	89,229
Congressional District 12	48,788	14,717	13,292	13,257	7,522	$42,220	8.6%	5.9%	9.0%	5,162	73,935
Congressional District 13	60,794	22,463	18,144	14,330	5,857	$33,953	10.6%	8.6%	10.7%	7,433	83,061
Congressional District 14	52,832	18,006	15,851	12,947	6,028	$35,600	10.0%	7.9%	11.2%	7,766	77,070
Congressional District 15	40,468	19,527	11,205	6,863	2,873	$26,154	19.6%	20.7%	22.2%	17,311	49,075
Congressional District 16	45,848	20,695	12,430	8,826	3,897	$28,742	16.7%	15.4%	21.3%	15,742	58,068
Congressional District 17	46,729	16,431	14,514	11,079	4,705	$33,855	10.7%	9.6%	12.4%	6,863	66,136
Congressional District 18	36,168	16,903	9,535	6,722	3,008	$27,171	18.2%	16.8%	21.0%	10,845	53,012
Congressional District 19	56,285	20,620	17,050	12,987	5,628	$33,183	11.1%	9.0%	12.5%	8,490	74,802
Congressional District 20	43,172	16,057	12,337	11,073	3,705	$33,741	12.4%	13.4%	14.2%	9,889	60,819
Congressional District 21	60,200	13,913	16,012	18,588	11,687	$50,282	7.5%	5.1%	6.8%	3,364	90,586
Congressional District 22	32,218	8,280	7,386	9,253	7,299	$50,979	5.8%	5.7%	6.4%	4,198	56,843
Congressional District 23	45,265	19,101	11,506	9,293	5,365	$30,472	14.1%	12.6%	19.5%	13,754	61,693
Congressional District 24	38,054	8,945	11,207	10,757	7,145	$46,297	4.8%	6.1%	6.7%	3,188	63,972
Congressional District 25	50,768	13,733	14,305	14,255	8,475	$44,309	8.1%	6.2%	8.7%	5,352	74,176
Congressional District 26	30,049	7,096	8,466	9,197	5,290	$48,587	4.8%	4.0%	7.0%	2,327	53,113
Congressional District 27	58,692	22,629	17,062	13,473	5,528	$32,237	11.5%	9.2%	13.5%	10,842	80,788
Congressional District 28	38,665	17,176	9,719	8,572	3,198	$30,028	16.0%	16.0%	21.9%	15,059	52,051
Congressional District 29	28,978	13,850	8,069	5,468	1,591	$26,299	16.3%	17.5%	17.4%	9,159	43,130
Congressional District 30	38,028	17,130	10,112	7,700	3,086	$28,074	16.3%	16.7%	18.0%	11,463	56,273
Congressional District 31	39,647	10,117	11,254	12,630	5,646	$46,040	7.7%	5.8%	7.1%	4,301	61,005
Congressional District 32	44,912	10,953	12,021	11,632	10,306	$48,770	6.1%	5.9%	6.8%	4,645	69,081
Congressional District 33	32,269	15,656	8,859	6,122	1,632	$26,109	18.3%	19.6%	19.1%	10,671	45,645
Congressional District 34	48,254	23,700	13,185	8,182	3,187	$25,657	20.5%	22.1%	24.9%	17,814	59,145
Congressional District 35	37,093	16,221	10,943	7,519	2,410	$28,865	17.5%	14.3%	20.1%	12,815	50,913
Congressional District 36	53,321	18,771	16,400	13,289	4,861	$34,621	11.2%	8.4%	8.4%	8,324	77,978

Table G-5: 113th Congressional Districts—Income, Poverty Status and Receipt of Food Stamps (SNAP)—*Continued*

	Income of Households with Householder 65 and Over						Poverty Rate of Persons			Households with 1 or More Persons 60 Years and Over	
	Total Households	Less Than $25,000	$25,000-$49,999	$50,000-$99,999	$100,000 or More	Median Household Income	55 to 64 Years	65 to 74 Years	75 Years and Over	Receiving SNAP	Not Receiving SNAP
Utah											
Congressional District 1	39,016	9,889	12,594	11,871	4,662	$43,113	6.1%	5.7%	6.0%	3,613	57,438
Congressional District 2	49,485	15,019	15,734	13,094	5,638	$38,688	9.1%	6.9%	8.8%	5,001	67,733
Congressional District 3	36,967	8,903	10,393	11,496	6,175	$48,082	6.2%	4.2%	5.7%	3,339	54,736
Congressional District 4	34,924	10,514	10,563	9,668	4,179	$39,257	7.6%	5.0%	5.5%	4,582	52,085
Vermont											
Congressional District (at Large)	60,018	20,711	17,718	14,367	7,222	$36,411	7.1%	6.4%	8.0%	10,038	84,498
Virginia											
Congressional District 1	56,291	13,308	14,022	16,315	12,646	$51,696	4.8%	5.4%	9.1%	5,089	84,651
Congressional District 2	54,078	14,273	14,906	16,053	8,846	$45,788	6.6%	5.0%	8.2%	5,585	79,686
Congressional District 3	53,307	21,353	15,445	12,366	4,143	$32,868	13.8%	11.7%	12.7%	12,407	72,976
Congressional District 4	53,177	15,852	16,103	14,428	6,794	$40,021	8.7%	5.8%	9.7%	8,153	80,279
Congressional District 5	77,295	27,730	23,580	17,210	8,775	$34,012	9.9%	7.5%	11.0%	11,267	105,393
Congressional District 6	74,617	26,822	23,482	17,897	6,416	$34,960	8.8%	8.0%	10.2%	7,952	102,316
Congressional District 7	59,890	14,146	16,512	18,159	11,073	$48,801	5.5%	3.6%	5.8%	4,258	90,591
Congressional District 8	44,714	7,864	7,844	13,337	15,669	$70,981	5.8%	5.4%	6.0%	4,511	72,484
Congressional District 9	80,517	36,167	24,801	15,063	4,486	$27,371	11.6%	9.3%	14.0%	12,435	106,744
Congressional District 10	38,090	6,162	7,831	10,745	13,352	$69,788	3.5%	4.2%	5.0%	2,763	68,426
Congressional District 11	39,173	6,113	6,988	11,223	14,849	$76,957	3.4%	3.4%	5.9%	4,768	71,385
Washington											
Congressional District 1	45,144	10,569	13,613	13,705	7,257	$46,273	6.5%	4.2%	6.9%	6,163	70,916
Congressional District 2	56,310	15,690	17,339	16,130	7,151	$41,614	8.3%	5.8%	6.2%	10,096	79,919
Congressional District 3	60,556	19,076	19,791	16,485	5,204	$38,120	10.2%	7.5%	8.6%	11,329	83,504
Congressional District 4	49,062	16,466	15,682	12,277	4,637	$36,518	9.3%	9.2%	9.5%	9,395	67,773
Congressional District 5	61,573	21,188	19,864	15,491	5,030	$35,675	10.4%	7.1%	9.9%	10,379	84,994
Congressional District 6	68,148	18,900	22,028	19,780	7,440	$41,296	9.0%	6.7%	7.1%	10,424	97,368
Congressional District 7	56,152	15,286	14,184	15,608	11,074	$47,154	9.6%	7.9%	10.9%	8,486	80,833
Congressional District 8	43,636	11,608	12,923	12,752	6,353	$44,580	8.1%	6.4%	8.3%	7,247	66,707
Congressional District 9	49,636	15,731	12,783	13,249	7,873	$41,760	10.4%	9.8%	13.4%	12,790	67,808
Congressional District 10	51,551	14,245	15,279	15,858	6,169	$42,960	7.3%	6.8%	7.1%	8,219	74,806
West Virginia											
Congressional District 1	66,039	28,457	21,331	12,611	3,640	$28,917	11.1%	8.7%	9.5%	8,054	90,057
Congressional District 2	63,481	25,911	19,148	13,930	4,492	$30,709	11.3%	8.2%	9.5%	9,242	89,152
Congressional District 3	67,431	30,582	22,409	11,553	2,887	$27,293	14.3%	9.9%	11.3%	12,701	91,434
Wisconsin											
Congressional District 1	59,452	18,692	18,574	16,506	5,680	$37,441	6.7%	5.4%	6.7%	7,045	84,936
Congressional District 2	55,307	15,984	15,882	15,958	7,483	$41,548	6.4%	4.2%	7.3%	5,890	80,764
Congressional District 3	67,859	26,312	22,533	14,850	4,164	$31,320	7.3%	6.6%	10.5%	7,107	92,605
Congressional District 4	48,766	20,714	14,404	9,581	4,067	$29,735	16.9%	11.5%	12.4%	12,849	63,694
Congressional District 5	68,769	22,583	22,803	16,643	6,740	$35,976	4.7%	4.1%	7.6%	4,491	96,306
Congressional District 6	69,461	24,539	23,788	15,964	5,170	$33,902	6.0%	4.7%	8.8%	5,395	96,749
Congressional District 7	76,850	29,600	25,789	17,234	4,227	$31,935	8.5%	5.8%	11.3%	8,989	104,380
Congressional District 8	64,101	23,940	21,756	14,432	3,973	$32,374	5.6%	5.3%	10.4%	5,126	89,603
Wyoming											
Congressional District (at Large)	45,398	15,243	14,486	11,212	4,457	$36,211	6.4%	4.7%	7.2%	2,736	69,151

PART H

DISABILITY STATUS AND TYPE

DISABILITY STATUS AND TYPE

Life expectancy at birth in the United States has steadily increased and the latest data from the National Center for Health Statistics says women's life expectancy has increased from 77.4 years in 1980 to 81.3 years in 2010. Male life expectancy has also increased from 70.0 years in 1980 to 76.2 years in 2010.[1] It is unclear whether the increasing life span will bring increased incidence of disability or if medical advances will ease the process of aging. Part of the uncertainty lies in the data. While life expectancy can be calculated based on detailed mortality data, measuring basic functions of activity that are defined as disabilities is much more difficult.

The Census Bureau's American Community Survey asks a series of questions about activities of daily living to measure the extent of identified disabilities. These are not clinical measures but the respondent's identification of difficulties they experience. These include difficulties

1. U.S. Department of Health and Human Services, Centers for Disease Control and Prevention, National Center for Health Statistics, National Vital Statistics Reports, Vol. 61, No. 4, *Deaths: Final Data for 2010.*

in: vision, hearing, cognitive ability, ambulatory ability, and self-care ability.

States

In the United States, just over 25 percent of the population age 65 to 74 indicated that they experience some disability but that percentage doubles for those age 75 and over where 50.3 percent have a disability. Ambulatory difficulty is most prevalent at 33.1 percent followed by hearing difficulty (22.5 percent), cognitive difficulty (14.4 percent), self-care difficulty (14.0 percent) and vision difficulty at 10.1 percent. Among the states, Mississippi has the highest percent of 75 and over population (58.7 percent) indicating that they have a disability. Mississippi is also highest for those with cognitive or self-care difficulties. Alaskans 75 and over have the highest percentage for hearing difficulties (29.9 percent), vision difficulties (29.5 percent) and ambulatory difficulties (15.6 percent). Iowa has the lowest percent for disabilities overall at 44.2 percent and for ambulatory difficulty (7.5 percent). The states with the lowest percent of persons 75 and over experiencing difficulties are New Jersey for hearing difficulty at 7.1 percent; the District of Columbia for vision difficulty at 14.6 percent and North Dakota for cognitive difficulty (2.8 percent) and self-care difficulty at 3.7 percent.

Metro Areas with the Highest and Lowest Percentage by Disability Type

Vision Difficulty	Hearing Difficulty	Cognitive Difficulty	Ambulatory Difficulty
Highest Percentage			
Hattiesburg, MS - 21.9%	Fairbanks, AK - 36.5%	Laredo, TX - 31.2%	Laredo, TX - 53.5%
Merced, CA - 21.5%	Laredo, TX - 35.3%	Gadsden, AL - 27.3%	Hattiesburg, MS - 51%
Laredo, TX - 21.2%	Madera-Chowcilla, CA - 34.6%	El Centro, CA - 27.1%	El Centro, CA - 48.5%
Fairbanks, AK - 20.9%	McAllen-Edinburg-Mission, TX - 32.6%	Hattiesburg, MS - 26.1%	Pine Bluff, AR - 44.7%
McAllen-Edinburg-Mission, TX - 19.0%	Gadsden, AL - 32.4%	Merced, CA - 24.9%	Valdosta, GA - 44.4%
Lowest Percentage			
Cedar Rapids, IA - 6.2%	New York-Northern New Jersey-Long Island, NY-NJ-PA - 17.5%	Danville, IL - 7.9%	Punta Gorda, FL - 23.8%
Appleton, WI - 6.2%	Grand Forks, ND-MN - 17.5%	Grand Forks, ND-MN - 7.5%	Logan, UT-ID - 23.2%
Holland-Grand Haven, MI - 5.0%	Palm Coast, FL - 17.5%	St. Cloud, MN - 7.5%	Palm Coast, FL - 23.0%
St. Cloud, MN - 4.9%	Winston-Salem, NC - 17.1%	Lebanon, PA - 7.5%	Naples-Marco Island, FL - 22.4%
Sheboygan, WI - 4.8%	Lebanon, PA - 16.1%	Barnstable Town, MA - 7.0%	Barnstable Town, MA - 21.7%

Counties and Cities

There is wide variation across the nation's counties in the percentage of 75 and over population with a disability or experiencing difficulty. Riley County, Kansas has the lowest experience of any county with only 0.2 percent of the population experiencing cognitive difficulties while Apache County, Arizona has the highest percentage of persons experiencing vision difficulties at 44.1 percent. Overall, Webb County, Texas has the highest percent reporting any disability at 73.0 percent. In 415 counties, greater than 50 percent of the population 75 and over report some disability and no county has less than one-third of the population reporting any disability.

In Laredo, Texas, 71.9 percent of the 75 and over population (the highest of all cities) reports some disability while Layton, Utah is the lowest at 35.7 percent. Like counties, at least one-third of the population in each city reports some disability. Among all cities, ambulatory difficulty is most common and reported by 35.6 percent of the 75 and over population. Vision difficulty is the least often reported at 10.8 percent. Avondale, Arizona has the highest percent reporting a hearing difficulty at 30.9 percent while Pharr, Texas reports the highest percentage with a vision difficulty. Merced, California (41.0 percent) has the highest rate of cognitive difficulty while 277 counties report a rate of less than 5 percent. Cognitive difficulty and self-care difficulty are reported by about 16 percent of the population of all cities for each disability.

Metropolitan Areas and Congressional Districts

Across all metropolitan areas, nearly half (49.7 percent) of the 75 and over population report some form of disability. The Laredo, Texas metro area is highest where nearly three of every four people 75 and over (73.0 percent) report a disability. The Laredo area also has the highest rate for cognitive difficulty (31.2 percent), ambulatory difficulty (53.5 percent) and self-care difficulty (29.9 percent). The Barnstable Town metro area in Massachusetts is lowest at 36.9 percent, indicating that at least one-third of all 75 and over residents of metropolitan areas have reported some disability. The Barnstable Town metro area also has the lowest percentage for cognitive difficulty (7.0 percent) and ambulatory difficulty at 21.7 percent. The percent with hearing difficulty is highest in the Fairbanks, Alaska metropolitan area at 36.5 percent and lowest in the Lebanon, Pennsylvania metro area at 16.1 percent. In nearly 200 metropolitan areas, more than 50 percent of the 75 and over population report some type of disability.

Two-thirds of the 75 and over population report some type of disability in Kentucky's 5th Congressional District, the highest of all districts. In more than half of all districts (226) over 50 percent of the population reports a disability. Even in Florida's 16th district, the lowest, 41.3 percent have some type of disability. Kentucky's 5th district also has the highest percent of persons with a hearing difficulty (26.8 percent), cognitive difficulty at 17.2 percent, as well as self-care difficulty at 20.8 percent. Texas' 15th Congressional District has the highest percent of persons with a vision difficulty at 33.2 percent.

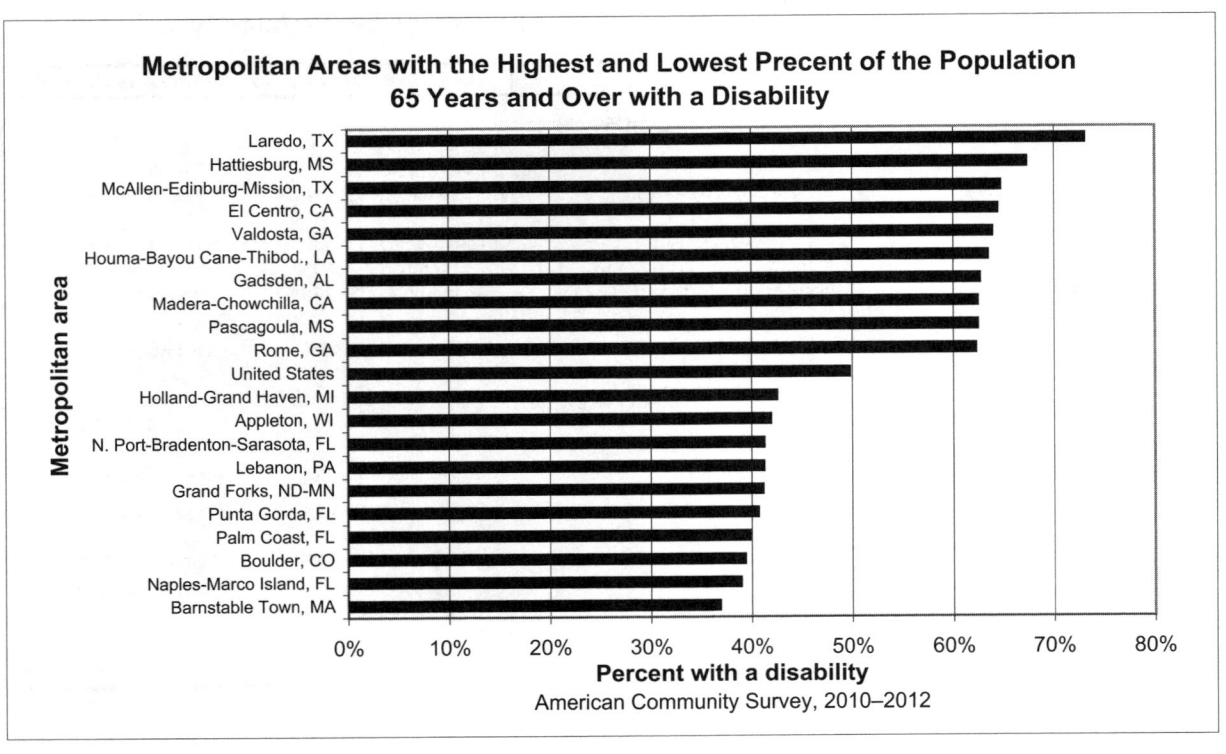

Metropolitan Areas with the Highest and Lowest Precent of the Population 65 Years and Over with a Disability

American Community Survey, 2010–2012

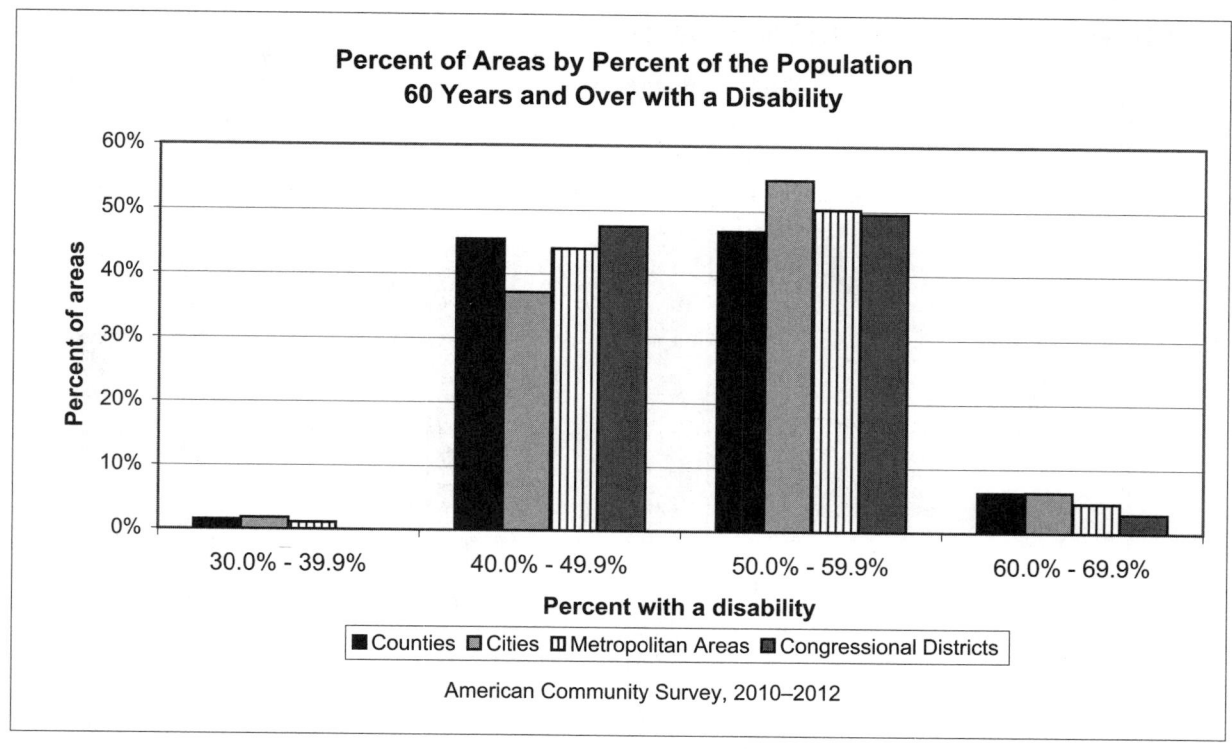

Percent of the Population 75 Years and Over With a Disability

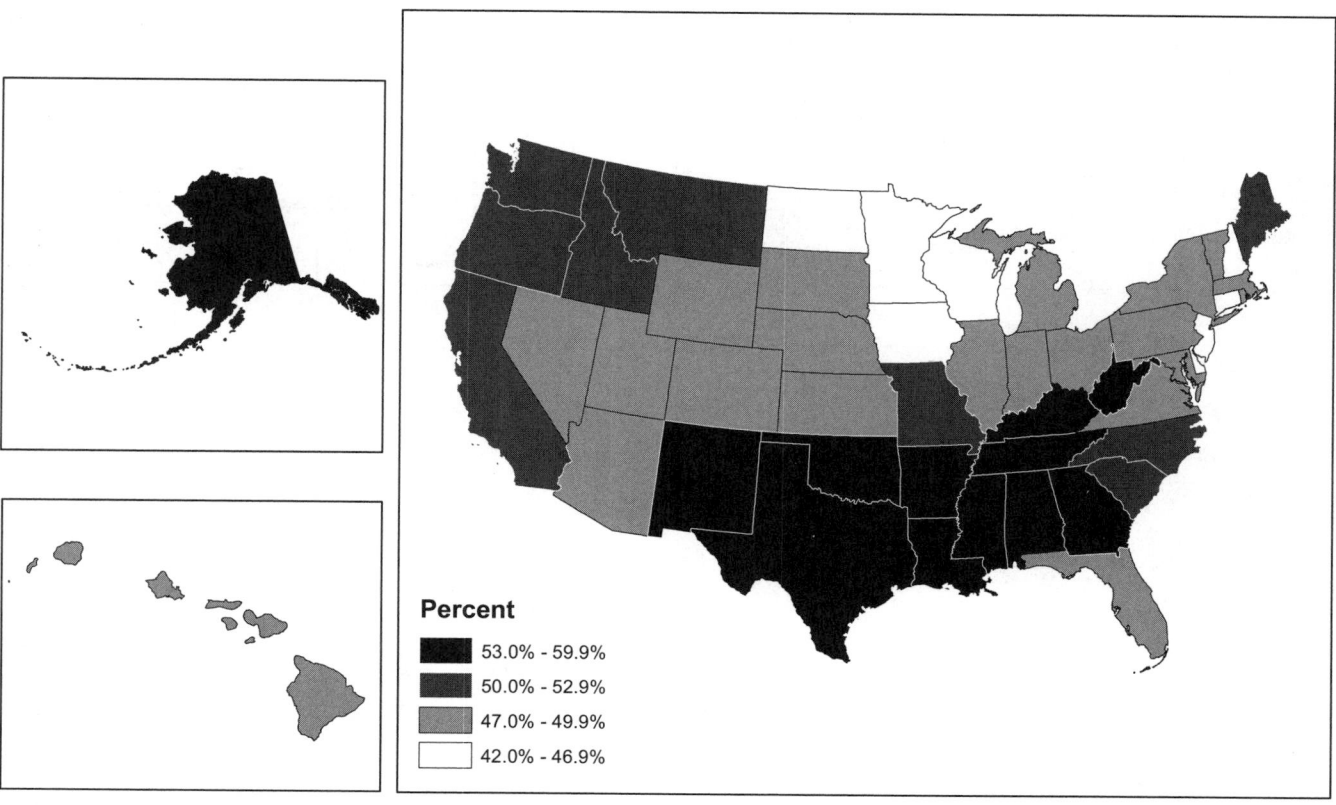

Table H-1: States—Disability Status and Type of Disability

	Total Population		With a Disability		With a Hearing Difficulty		With a Vision Difficulty		With a Cognitive Difficulty		With an Ambulatory Difficulty	
	65 to 74 Years	75 Years and Over	65 to 74 Years	75 Years and Over	65 to 74 Years	75 Years and Over	65 to 74 Years	75 Years and Over	65 to 74 Years	75 Years and Over	65 to 74 Years	75 Years and Over
United States	22,520,076	17,829,686	5,707,638	8,963,150	2,021,265	4,004,862	922,593	1,797,446	1,223,688	2,568,838	3,577,015	5,906,776
Alabama	380,585	276,738	123,590	159,734	42,665	69,516	22,957	34,319	29,555	52,019	82,464	111,776
Alaska	37,249	19,970	11,945	11,247	5,972	5,895	1,987	3,109	2,367	3,415	6,536	7,336
Arizona	525,277	390,174	120,129	184,342	45,415	91,623	18,834	38,099	24,261	48,959	72,279	118,972
Arkansas	238,513	175,549	78,568	97,810	30,829	45,341	14,262	22,024	17,486	29,239	50,734	65,212
California	2,381,539	1,948,100	579,053	1,010,072	187,356	443,833	93,946	203,353	136,645	324,462	362,153	674,266
Colorado	329,835	235,638	73,202	116,600	31,624	60,498	10,884	25,238	13,108	30,556	40,381	71,648
Connecticut	264,243	231,834	54,773	106,973	17,456	48,092	7,316	18,793	11,186	27,543	32,648	66,291
Delaware	75,755	54,968	16,756	25,274	5,102	10,734	2,500	5,169	3,217	6,490	10,442	16,594
District of Columbia	37,724	30,328	9,429	14,182	2,225	4,435	1,866	2,976	2,020	4,175	6,857	9,962
Florida	1,790,731	1,525,939	405,719	719,136	137,388	325,905	63,394	142,784	88,352	211,152	251,308	472,681
Georgia	636,945	416,810	182,238	225,511	59,699	94,656	33,809	50,242	41,776	75,999	120,216	154,718
Hawaii	105,304	93,168	21,826	45,436	8,429	21,712	3,849	7,028	5,237	14,982	13,095	28,160
Idaho	114,982	84,024	30,598	43,974	13,737	23,379	4,508	9,731	6,500	10,813	17,379	26,781
Illinois	873,132	713,727	206,298	349,670	62,812	145,819	31,708	66,992	39,854	91,752	134,531	234,832
Indiana	462,909	364,224	124,033	181,457	46,447	83,683	19,258	33,967	23,046	47,551	77,198	119,168
Iowa	228,673	207,163	49,946	91,523	19,830	43,658	6,036	15,466	8,874	20,403	29,006	55,654
Kansas	195,564	170,210	48,928	84,734	19,641	39,904	6,679	15,737	9,682	21,166	30,064	55,298
Kentucky	333,504	237,693	108,558	133,679	39,077	60,980	18,745	28,316	26,067	38,916	71,711	90,696
Louisiana	320,370	234,250	104,665	132,735	36,117	56,518	21,676	28,442	23,549	43,750	68,428	91,644
Maine	117,471	93,858	30,500	47,603	13,159	24,691	3,840	8,823	6,843	12,687	16,959	28,208
Maryland	402,351	309,266	89,636	146,612	27,037	60,506	13,692	27,417	17,552	42,483	57,570	95,754
Massachusetts	475,435	415,005	102,950	196,388	35,438	87,899	15,203	37,976	22,887	51,023	61,415	122,446
Michigan	748,277	611,339	193,890	304,604	71,364	138,337	27,690	56,520	39,997	87,228	119,077	196,216
Minnesota	367,334	308,189	75,583	139,171	33,214	66,529	9,143	23,487	14,201	30,391	40,524	83,156
Mississippi	219,355	158,052	78,035	92,724	25,143	37,365	15,807	22,102	19,517	31,415	54,626	68,022
Missouri	460,677	361,187	127,454	185,266	46,030	86,521	19,037	36,761	25,836	48,606	80,738	119,670
Montana	83,660	63,461	21,862	32,238	10,559	18,066	3,202	7,129	3,527	7,200	11,594	18,925
Nebraska	124,955	113,183	28,151	54,119	12,884	27,222	3,547	10,439	4,474	11,854	15,244	32,427
Nevada	208,628	129,993	54,197	63,875	19,679	28,554	8,591	12,630	9,752	17,087	33,780	42,425
New Hampshire	101,592	76,422	22,332	35,077	8,934	18,099	2,879	6,722	4,182	8,525	12,758	20,849
New Jersey	632,400	545,149	132,963	253,883	38,786	103,144	22,068	50,658	27,221	71,102	85,478	169,969
New Mexico	161,209	117,273	47,534	66,370	19,785	34,544	8,982	16,779	10,478	21,388	28,850	42,798
New York	1,398,272	1,185,838	307,288	568,940	86,712	220,435	50,172	112,226	67,997	159,384	204,083	392,801
North Carolina	728,109	519,005	196,379	274,190	66,887	121,890	35,152	58,114	44,526	79,575	125,026	184,392
North Dakota	47,935	45,172	11,298	20,987	5,011	10,206	1,251	4,476	1,669	4,554	6,047	11,933
Ohio	868,878	720,322	219,724	352,678	78,558	153,458	32,675	65,892	44,391	91,273	138,908	227,625
Oklahoma	287,232	214,207	92,296	118,203	37,111	56,377	15,508	25,279	17,851	32,108	59,468	79,350
Oregon	307,433	240,264	80,487	125,340	35,546	61,449	11,490	23,586	18,287	37,884	45,730	80,015
Pennsylvania	1,001,061	912,591	237,724	437,232	86,783	192,983	35,459	80,737	46,636	114,737	143,545	278,896
Rhode Island	76,205	70,815	16,553	34,901	5,412	15,360	2,251	5,602	3,351	8,556	10,008	21,695
South Carolina	388,767	256,118	108,722	134,823	36,279	56,863	19,938	29,196	25,870	42,746	69,795	91,796
South Dakota	58,820	53,733	13,669	26,564	6,237	14,042	1,699	5,367	2,489	5,980	7,706	15,959
Tennessee	504,327	354,342	154,868	194,638	55,334	87,512	26,799	42,171	36,615	63,444	102,894	132,864
Texas	1,537,461	1,102,511	453,252	604,660	165,418	271,966	86,733	132,856	100,685	186,810	294,445	417,648
Utah	145,056	111,331	33,667	54,301	14,962	28,056	4,199	11,153	6,142	14,430	18,657	31,962
Vermont	51,972	39,268	11,218	19,480	5,079	9,972	1,305	4,038	2,317	5,216	6,113	11,581
Virginia	576,564	415,872	136,839	205,741	47,263	87,354	21,356	41,369	28,881	60,664	86,053	135,721
Washington	484,988	362,744	123,395	189,392	51,004	93,035	16,604	36,468	26,244	54,331	69,310	120,238
West Virginia	166,968	127,695	56,976	71,614	23,387	34,971	10,248	16,679	13,217	21,805	37,214	48,827
Wisconsin	412,917	355,839	87,248	163,022	35,126	73,393	10,797	29,471	15,611	37,569	50,594	102,227
Wyoming	40,933	29,135	10,694	14,425	5,323	7,882	1,062	3,538	1,660	3,441	5,376	8,692

Table H-2: Counties—Disability Status and Type of Disability

	Total Population		With a Disability		With a Hearing Difficulty		With a Vision Difficulty		With a Cognitive Difficulty		With an Ambulatory Difficulty	
	65 to 74 Years	75 Years and Over	65 to 74 Years	75 Years and Over	65 to 74 Years	75 Years and Over	65 to 74 Years	75 Years and Over	65 to 74 Years	75 Years and Over	65 to 74 Years	75 Years and Over
Alabama												
Baldwin County	18,895	12,708	5,029	6,593	2,006	2,918	968	1,147	1,215	1,885	3,052	4,651
Calhoun County	9,623	7,405	4,131	4,093	1,213	1,629	690	718	937	1,364	2,993	3,031
Cullman County	7,682	5,270	2,496	3,155	932	1,590	319	844	578	877	1,710	2,220
DeKalb County	5,787	3,874	1,733	2,122	844	1,242	308	447	485	533	1,065	1,374
Elmore County	5,816	3,570	1,823	2,031	634	1,103	445	444	642	748	1,156	1,611
Etowah County	9,299	6,886	3,165	4,313	1,082	2,234	450	1,047	853	1,882	2,352	2,865
Houston County	8,555	6,331	3,178	3,672	1,037	1,681	677	595	943	1,303	2,086	2,573
Jefferson County	45,142	39,601	12,784	21,117	3,192	8,150	1,974	3,983	3,022	6,331	9,367	14,785
Lauderdale County	8,602	6,719	2,501	3,767	843	1,712	252	648	571	1,183	1,644	2,704
Lee County	8,128	5,062	2,602	2,795	788	905	248	409	767	853	1,630	1,779
Limestone County	6,472	3,971	2,243	2,333	1,052	1,368	400	559	315	808	1,220	1,190
Madison County	23,766	17,595	6,222	9,576	2,423	4,559	1,259	2,004	1,439	3,179	3,690	6,324
Marshall County	8,097	5,672	2,751	3,700	936	1,723	393	929	533	1,345	1,878	2,688
Mobile County	31,054	22,627	10,010	13,353	3,637	5,587	1,989	3,027	2,447	4,368	6,778	9,283
Montgomery County	14,906	12,311	4,829	6,538	1,562	2,580	1,335	1,359	1,101	2,418	3,423	4,585
Morgan County	9,889	6,882	2,710	3,823	1,228	1,524	479	714	690	1,279	1,576	2,588
St. Clair County	6,941	4,113	2,225	2,450	787	1,142	203	457	689	777	1,475	1,433
Shelby County	13,279	8,661	3,462	4,849	1,290	2,371	481	1,164	561	1,545	2,207	3,530
Talladega County	6,929	4,686	2,236	2,939	563	1,263	353	845	411	775	1,360	1,981
Tuscaloosa County	11,750	9,222	3,335	5,166	1,142	2,007	546	914	760	1,386	2,556	3,649
Walker County	6,499	4,287	2,372	2,751	866	1,211	488	803	541	911	1,669	1,705
Alaska												
Fairbanks North Star Borough	4,329	2,253	1,451	1,254	632	823	194	471	280	439	842	904
Matanuska-Susitna Borough	5,048	2,537	1,744	1,310	819	591	352	404	505	320	976	879
Arizona												
Apache County	5,525	3,267	2,253	2,366	1,282	1,441	716	1,001	709	1,042	1,101	1,485
Cochise County	13,850	9,273	3,917	5,191	1,325	2,642	207	916	612	1,601	2,562	3,550
Coconino County	7,965	4,599	2,076	2,571	803	1,422	395	696	392	810	1,168	1,648
Maricopa County	271,038	210,354	58,688	95,954	21,873	46,212	9,121	18,195	12,459	25,602	35,710	62,738
Mohave County	29,079	19,004	7,496	9,226	2,281	4,725	910	1,862	1,351	2,237	4,841	5,811
Navajo County	9,365	5,574	3,270	3,386	1,542	1,873	794	1,124	937	1,095	1,866	2,107
Pima County	85,619	69,752	19,433	33,444	7,294	17,335	3,261	7,739	3,932	8,424	11,642	21,480
Pinal County	35,794	20,171	7,177	9,526	2,944	4,189	929	1,667	1,136	2,510	4,298	6,190
Yavapai County	30,610	21,868	6,577	10,157	2,496	5,229	953	1,922	1,209	2,475	3,634	6,136
Yuma County	17,674	13,693	4,755	6,450	1,994	3,305	812	1,679	779	1,471	2,719	4,187
Arkansas												
Benton County	15,051	11,776	3,026	6,301	1,039	2,922	285	1,517	494	1,522	2,026	3,886
Craighead County	6,580	4,659	2,258	2,608	1,070	1,145	480	623	581	750	1,361	1,854
Faulkner County	6,732	4,810	2,004	2,711	808	1,383	297	534	359	652	1,242	1,596
Garland County	10,750	8,753	3,572	4,730	1,169	2,441	328	841	891	986	2,094	2,923
Jefferson County	5,750	4,173	2,086	2,561	757	1,024	395	787	408	771	1,350	1,877
Lonoke County	4,651	2,838	1,532	1,633	738	587	333	478	337	392	1,029	1,171
Pulaski County	25,513	20,197	7,415	10,826	2,217	4,919	1,656	2,482	1,673	3,565	5,206	7,602
Saline County	10,321	6,483	2,944	3,268	1,164	1,817	528	613	636	1,125	1,845	1,892
Sebastian County	9,107	6,842	2,894	3,503	1,071	1,651	571	589	710	724	1,983	2,489
Washington County	11,388	8,477	3,355	4,493	1,272	2,137	474	791	649	1,365	1,840	2,864
White County	6,347	4,487	2,110	2,788	1,119	1,370	530	760	538	701	1,376	1,778
California												
Alameda County	95,406	76,047	21,399	38,607	6,287	14,148	3,065	7,548	4,660	12,236	12,879	26,310
Butte County	17,642	15,960	4,940	8,529	1,637	4,220	660	1,366	1,224	2,491	2,928	5,184
Contra Costa County	75,536	59,044	16,160	29,950	4,625	12,226	1,918	5,122	2,896	8,289	9,995	18,931
El Dorado County	16,347	11,267	3,270	5,287	1,393	2,661	315	815	682	1,356	1,780	3,213
Fresno County	51,649	42,785	15,241	23,017	6,298	10,956	3,045	4,644	3,826	7,234	9,339	15,824
Humboldt County	10,120	7,909	3,100	4,592	1,277	2,106	748	639	587	1,354	1,895	2,990
Imperial County	9,931	8,619	3,925	5,551	975	2,662	952	1,405	946	2,335	2,560	4,179
Kern County	44,840	31,840	12,690	18,220	4,643	8,169	2,274	3,937	2,632	5,619	8,657	12,419
Kings County	6,375	5,062	1,838	2,883	648	1,202	202	503	304	812	1,204	2,028
Lake County	6,665	4,752	2,151	2,705	917	1,187	236	571	431	879	1,460	1,770
Los Angeles County	589,987	488,344	148,839	260,699	39,236	104,855	26,582	53,849	39,375	89,479	97,623	180,857
Madera County	10,117	7,193	3,485	4,490	1,710	2,487	648	1,209	685	1,151	2,195	2,625
Marin County	24,610	18,999	3,098	7,740	1,101	3,410	190	1,146	556	2,391	1,850	4,470
Mendocino County	8,151	5,868	2,186	3,436	927	1,939	323	841	489	933	1,344	2,018
Merced County	14,083	10,543	4,926	6,536	1,812	3,214	2,129	2,269	1,504	2,630	2,876	4,350
Monterey County	23,863	20,789	4,741	10,186	1,578	4,887	601	2,031	1,258	3,539	2,924	6,760
Napa County	11,013	9,556	2,226	5,147	754	2,331	250	898	558	1,281	1,402	3,247
Nevada County	11,352	8,326	2,795	3,657	1,414	2,314	159	777	333	1,087	1,492	1,776
Orange County	197,432	162,730	36,413	76,354	12,022	33,979	5,427	15,267	8,798	26,571	20,882	50,372
Placer County	30,833	25,193	6,744	11,602	2,361	5,382	665	2,290	1,098	3,261	4,269	7,778
Riverside County	147,467	119,671	37,811	59,234	13,779	28,420	5,452	12,280	7,470	16,178	23,727	38,589
Sacramento County	87,688	74,240	25,803	40,104	8,559	17,787	4,227	7,157	6,393	12,639	16,760	26,178
San Bernardino County	108,636	77,657	33,121	44,651	10,808	19,850	5,883	11,133	7,996	14,470	21,855	31,547
San Diego County	190,140	168,134	42,676	85,810	12,757	40,168	6,360	16,350	11,085	28,414	25,670	55,902
San Francisco County	55,902	54,835	13,582	28,929	4,078	10,708	2,848	6,567	3,967	10,396	8,711	20,040
San Joaquin County	40,377	32,065	11,612	17,446	3,541	8,116	1,713	3,806	2,944	5,675	7,482	11,987
San Luis Obispo County	22,118	19,530	4,596	9,972	2,504	4,787	826	1,952	690	2,755	2,106	6,321
San Mateo County	52,441	45,171	8,608	20,464	2,836	8,727	1,151	3,373	1,637	6,395	4,995	14,053
Santa Barbara County	27,894	26,956	5,986	13,209	2,550	6,038	1,242	2,679	1,525	3,750	3,466	8,402
Santa Clara County	111,034	90,420	22,103	45,463	7,360	19,719	3,142	8,736	4,764	14,327	12,123	29,995

Table H-2: Counties—Disability Status and Type of Disability—*Continued*

	Total Population		With a Disability		With a Hearing Difficulty		With a Vision Difficulty		With a Cognitive Difficulty		With an Ambulatory Difficulty	
	65 to 74 Years	75 Years and Over	65 to 74 Years	75 Years and Over	65 to 74 Years	75 Years and Over	65 to 74 Years	75 Years and Over	65 to 74 Years	75 Years and Over	65 to 74 Years	75 Years and Over
California—Cont.												
Santa Cruz County	17,254	12,856	3,325	6,303	1,072	3,202	562	1,268	851	1,684	1,974	3,780
Shasta County	17,372	13,216	5,422	7,354	2,134	3,950	780	1,411	1,035	2,187	3,305	4,551
Solano County	26,958	20,639	6,818	11,207	2,245	5,010	1,091	2,128	1,009	2,835	4,199	6,959
Sonoma County	38,370	31,185	7,695	15,732	3,029	7,611	963	2,998	1,846	4,994	4,657	9,888
Stanislaus County	30,896	24,430	10,090	15,084	3,699	6,689	1,425	3,090	2,512	5,062	6,279	10,161
Sutter County	6,900	5,185	2,005	2,400	665	1,126	104	438	404	573	1,327	1,453
Tulare County	23,646	18,020	7,560	10,035	2,313	4,339	1,076	1,566	1,692	3,067	5,357	6,737
Ventura County	54,312	44,744	11,884	22,343	4,052	10,115	2,028	4,583	2,187	6,894	7,487	15,158
Yolo County	11,192	8,956	3,214	4,979	1,292	2,222	539	666	858	1,484	2,041	3,138
Yuba County	4,162	3,149	1,167	1,757	634	902	139	310	208	537	527	1,298
Colorado												
Adams County	22,716	15,663	6,142	8,866	2,429	4,795	1,010	1,987	1,033	2,308	4,024	6,123
Arapahoe County	35,036	24,976	6,919	11,820	2,652	6,064	1,241	2,524	1,222	3,651	3,651	7,285
Boulder County	18,134	12,381	2,981	4,872	1,335	2,401	266	1,129	565	1,483	1,486	3,117
Denver County	33,764	28,860	8,410	14,971	2,655	6,736	1,381	3,704	1,709	4,157	5,378	9,249
Douglas County	14,853	7,899	2,589	3,333	1,290	1,886	219	487	322	897	1,195	1,784
El Paso County	37,423	26,564	8,551	12,897	3,930	6,467	1,320	2,567	1,598	3,010	4,633	7,801
Jefferson County	39,710	28,897	8,304	13,325	3,985	6,310	1,256	2,944	1,269	3,326	4,051	8,250
Larimer County	21,065	15,665	4,272	7,664	1,991	4,426	442	1,321	1,038	1,763	1,925	4,371
Mesa County	12,109	10,012	2,871	5,107	1,385	2,910	338	917	391	1,361	1,641	2,966
Pueblo County	12,889	11,168	3,533	5,768	1,253	2,955	668	1,361	660	1,394	2,156	3,781
Weld County	15,216	10,112	3,599	5,589	1,783	2,821	578	932	832	1,783	1,975	3,594
Connecticut												
Fairfield County	64,611	57,679	11,421	25,878	3,252	11,925	1,955	4,714	2,150	7,134	6,589	16,376
Hartford County	65,330	60,800	14,906	29,163	4,894	12,767	2,305	5,473	3,517	7,560	8,834	17,870
Litchfield County	16,660	13,287	2,961	5,695	1,074	2,577	321	871	597	1,362	1,534	3,547
Middlesex County	14,129	11,301	2,536	5,090	883	2,305	160	679	299	1,085	1,520	2,984
New Haven County	62,741	57,717	14,442	27,057	3,931	11,922	1,882	5,007	2,869	7,264	9,031	16,644
New London County	21,609	16,975	4,714	7,657	2,007	3,496	380	1,187	1,023	1,695	2,681	5,024
Tolland County	10,688	7,706	1,793	3,622	573	1,711	142	482	348	731	1,170	2,084
Windham County	8,475	6,369	2,000	2,811	842	1,389	171	380	383	712	1,289	1,762
Delaware												
Kent County	13,232	9,226	3,081	4,156	828	1,715	403	952	617	1,196	1,991	2,822
New Castle County	36,821	29,158	8,255	13,165	2,086	5,776	1,364	2,597	1,567	3,449	5,425	8,508
Sussex County	25,702	16,584	5,420	7,953	2,188	3,243	733	1,620	1,033	1,845	3,026	5,264
Florida												
Alachua County	15,017	11,869	3,687	5,925	1,457	2,807	827	1,260	868	1,678	2,302	3,843
Bay County	14,272	10,418	3,984	4,805	1,940	2,378	838	937	608	1,798	2,488	3,204
Brevard County	59,271	52,589	13,152	25,608	4,717	11,344	2,170	4,985	2,732	7,151	7,913	16,666
Broward County	131,307	122,798	29,595	63,037	7,923	24,873	5,639	13,336	6,948	19,561	19,137	44,250
Charlotte County	30,062	25,700	6,646	10,449	2,969	5,248	929	1,942	1,503	2,703	3,652	6,122
Citrus County	24,651	20,209	5,443	8,874	2,028	4,935	745	2,237	815	2,080	3,555	5,146
Clay County	14,403	8,810	4,247	4,510	1,144	1,719	525	701	691	1,762	3,043	2,884
Collier County	48,188	40,624	5,934	15,821	2,507	8,200	872	3,270	1,065	4,138	3,201	9,101
Columbia County	6,158	4,079	1,893	2,496	476	1,344	499	628	386	907	1,496	1,723
Duval County	55,652	41,859	15,126	21,114	4,319	8,861	2,599	4,944	3,210	6,184	10,014	14,779
Escambia County	24,371	18,618	7,242	10,321	2,867	4,982	925	2,354	1,112	3,200	5,034	7,326
Flagler County	14,682	10,123	3,088	4,033	1,155	1,768	602	819	338	1,338	1,576	2,327
Hernando County	23,671	21,222	6,648	9,922	2,827	4,439	1,198	2,035	1,281	3,278	3,740	6,147
Highlands County	16,305	15,058	3,918	6,274	1,865	2,988	402	1,052	467	1,389	2,125	3,507
Hillsborough County	82,679	66,512	21,998	34,022	6,482	15,092	3,244	8,087	4,898	10,616	14,844	23,437
Indian River County	19,063	19,668	3,041	8,922	1,084	5,031	260	1,728	826	2,090	1,732	5,393
Lake County	40,353	32,613	9,279	13,634	3,720	7,565	1,220	2,692	1,716	3,465	5,677	7,926
Lee County	85,960	65,873	16,660	28,205	7,002	13,709	1,696	4,989	3,251	8,647	9,926	17,784
Leon County	15,624	11,096	3,398	5,519	1,346	2,417	658	1,014	774	1,790	1,848	3,518
Manatee County	40,947	36,293	7,295	15,110	3,254	8,074	1,190	3,216	1,580	3,981	3,847	9,452
Marion County	48,244	38,269	11,263	17,778	4,685	9,150	1,722	3,674	2,173	5,241	6,307	10,417
Martin County	20,093	20,312	3,870	8,694	1,382	4,775	437	944	651	1,670	2,272	5,383
Miami-Dade County	191,681	166,984	45,664	83,395	8,124	29,489	7,697	19,585	15,812	34,125	29,520	60,347
Monroe County	8,143	4,970	1,768	2,165	728	829	268	434	419	585	1,042	1,345
Nassau County	7,908	4,617	2,086	2,336	729	969	261	325	283	499	1,476	1,602
Okaloosa County	14,425	11,022	3,706	5,462	1,286	2,831	532	1,137	836	1,579	2,433	4,119
Orange County	64,611	48,437	16,198	24,322	4,068	9,389	2,837	5,302	3,527	6,628	10,790	17,055
Osceola County	18,885	12,465	5,194	6,899	1,814	3,126	1,201	1,293	1,608	2,225	3,527	4,987
Palm Beach County	134,453	152,492	22,904	66,393	7,697	30,243	3,657	11,183	4,366	14,918	13,472	42,074
Pasco County	52,319	44,618	12,489	21,195	4,464	10,664	1,911	3,875	2,245	6,172	7,706	13,593
Pinellas County	97,366	95,107	21,802	44,864	7,749	20,934	2,906	8,708	4,212	12,336	13,547	29,870
Polk County	62,370	47,437	14,912	23,338	5,076	10,614	2,719	4,324	3,563	6,172	9,275	15,591
Putnam County	8,102	6,041	1,832	3,102	717	1,359	378	475	366	1,123	984	1,865
St. Johns County	18,242	13,186	3,806	5,962	1,469	2,400	368	791	622	1,567	2,072	3,653
St. Lucie County	30,929	26,556	6,919	11,601	2,369	5,979	962	1,988	915	3,230	4,558	7,137
Santa Rosa County	12,570	7,409	3,290	3,936	1,284	1,860	410	591	690	1,049	2,336	2,647
Sarasota County	60,342	58,707	10,993	24,088	5,141	11,897	1,302	3,533	1,584	5,752	5,729	14,726
Seminole County	29,696	23,203	6,759	11,305	1,996	4,955	703	1,969	1,561	3,284	4,304	7,676
Sumter County	29,314	15,681	4,961	5,824	2,567	2,768	306	816	698	1,371	2,667	3,232
Volusia County	55,341	49,069	11,711	22,739	4,749	11,162	1,881	4,083	2,230	5,950	6,809	14,557

Table H-2: Counties—Disability Status and Type of Disability—*Continued*

	Total Population		With a Disability		With a Hearing Difficulty		With a Vision Difficulty		With a Cognitive Difficulty		With an Ambulatory Difficulty	
	65 to 74 Years	75 Years and Over	65 to 74 Years	75 Years and Over	65 to 74 Years	75 Years and Over	65 to 74 Years	75 Years and Over	65 to 74 Years	75 Years and Over	65 to 74 Years	75 Years and Over
Georgia												
Barrow County	4,022	2,560	1,224	1,490	563	965	220	299	344	676	714	1,012
Bartow County	6,825	4,052	2,290	2,111	1,014	851	451	583	699	703	1,579	1,329
Bibb County	10,637	8,727	2,919	4,395	505	1,927	531	1,001	632	1,452	2,051	3,059
Bulloch County	3,802	2,530	908	1,463	241	686	132	341	204	315	522	909
Carroll County	7,630	4,586	2,561	2,668	1,027	1,222	270	679	586	972	1,640	1,745
Catoosa County	5,479	3,605	1,541	2,124	455	1,011	280	436	322	598	963	1,254
Chatham County	18,524	14,645	4,522	7,556	1,275	2,965	782	1,299	998	2,360	3,040	5,099
Cherokee County	13,766	7,276	3,074	3,896	1,153	2,165	471	940	829	1,322	2,074	2,525
Clarke County	5,799	4,336	1,803	2,364	304	956	203	418	414	741	1,297	1,382
Clayton County	11,690	6,537	3,864	4,117	1,037	1,809	624	986	975	1,440	2,121	2,976
Cobb County	38,804	24,154	7,669	11,137	2,757	4,701	815	2,234	1,500	3,509	4,604	7,271
Columbia County	8,228	5,014	2,281	2,558	778	1,045	294	607	757	997	1,510	1,715
Coweta County	8,670	5,043	2,489	2,433	904	1,008	287	576	506	861	1,673	1,851
DeKalb County	37,235	25,602	8,853	12,859	1,901	4,752	1,493	2,391	1,918	4,236	6,020	8,503
Dougherty County	6,358	5,158	2,007	2,832	639	1,308	379	768	464	1,048	1,509	2,058
Douglas County	7,803	4,084	2,190	2,268	567	1,042	318	517	490	708	1,373	1,348
Fayette County	8,813	5,506	1,759	2,812	716	1,192	321	557	515	764	882	1,693
Floyd County	7,497	5,966	2,321	3,713	860	1,447	390	1,039	521	1,274	1,421	2,390
Forsyth County	11,184	6,521	2,396	3,014	1,110	1,141	518	658	502	604	1,349	2,024
Fulton County	50,738	36,152	12,338	18,792	3,258	6,497	2,472	3,505	2,601	7,085	8,555	13,653
Glynn County	7,260	5,035	1,912	2,345	592	1,092	363	350	520	663	1,258	1,585
Gwinnett County	37,352	21,990	8,301	11,571	2,319	4,984	1,488	2,655	1,613	4,273	5,613	7,903
Hall County	12,670	8,552	3,127	4,342	1,023	1,785	381	620	884	1,400	2,173	3,074
Henry County	11,523	6,469	2,742	3,307	717	1,446	420	889	399	711	2,099	2,341
Houston County	8,692	5,958	3,172	3,072	1,181	1,267	366	656	795	996	2,107	2,182
Liberty County	2,708	1,264	926	806	364	359	316	190	299	177	688	558
Lowndes County	6,403	4,299	1,920	2,694	696	1,117	462	641	269	899	1,289	1,930
Muscogee County	11,408	10,100	4,510	5,747	1,502	2,309	1,243	1,479	1,340	1,770	3,170	4,270
Newton County	6,403	3,805	1,930	1,849	643	787	369	607	627	803	969	1,291
Paulding County	7,291	3,738	2,261	2,205	1,014	859	131	382	455	610	1,542	1,500
Richmond County	13,053	9,491	4,548	5,554	1,654	2,368	833	1,497	1,307	2,167	3,131	4,014
Rockdale County	5,836	3,499	1,381	2,009	377	741	241	423	255	481	963	1,496
Troup County	4,773	3,504	1,319	2,037	399	955	437	261	461	729	792	1,305
Walker County	5,954	4,208	2,219	2,434	749	864	464	392	481	847	1,553	1,668
Walton County	6,296	3,957	1,797	2,332	748	969	253	331	294	557	833	1,594
Whitfield County	6,548	4,853	2,066	2,771	737	1,437	496	730	474	1,073	1,196	2,031
Hawaii												
Hawaii County	16,205	11,872	4,479	6,624	2,004	3,842	1,257	1,452	1,004	1,999	2,650	3,916
Honolulu County	71,444	68,200	13,982	31,612	5,131	14,713	2,115	4,420	3,272	10,511	8,601	19,843
Kauai County	5,696	4,480	1,453	2,465	631	1,248	183	393	442	776	810	1,390
Maui County	11,945	8,611	1,912	4,733	663	1,907	294	763	519	1,696	1,034	3,011
Idaho												
Ada County	24,533	18,405	5,529	8,869	2,361	4,479	810	2,435	1,337	2,098	3,129	5,341
Bannock County	5,141	4,127	1,610	2,326	711	1,339	195	337	361	452	1,019	1,320
Bonneville County	6,282	5,227	1,650	3,146	674	1,642	220	541	202	813	906	1,867
Canyon County	12,462	8,721	3,961	4,898	1,721	2,872	407	1,024	770	1,025	2,315	3,153
Kootenai County	12,144	8,561	2,811	4,016	1,483	1,892	354	631	591	1,056	1,260	2,442
Twin Falls County	5,810	4,954	1,318	2,268	609	1,136	259	697	295	459	864	1,519
Illinois												
Adams County	5,676	5,293	1,312	2,457	414	1,120	167	402	155	354	973	1,609
Champaign County	10,918	9,090	2,623	4,174	740	1,897	293	790	422	1,007	1,985	2,563
Cook County	331,877	282,215	82,763	143,403	19,505	52,954	15,019	28,504	18,254	41,177	56,958	101,084
DeKalb County	5,569	4,366	1,075	2,032	383	1,036	111	349	149	521	781	1,145
DuPage County	60,786	46,076	11,166	21,731	3,544	9,768	1,340	3,777	2,148	5,757	6,644	13,860
Kane County	30,129	21,282	6,287	9,503	1,970	4,006	631	2,008	1,125	2,509	3,796	6,212
Kankakee County	7,882	6,589	2,314	3,412	600	1,315	390	694	653	910	1,455	2,331
Kendall County	5,251	3,292	1,104	1,521	435	704	44	210	188	302	683	1,169
Lake County	42,238	31,107	7,904	14,489	2,552	5,346	939	2,500	1,175	3,769	5,026	9,506
LaSalle County	9,078	8,676	2,127	3,884	932	1,715	270	650	331	662	1,172	2,320
McHenry County	19,697	12,160	3,873	5,470	1,449	2,576	358	957	660	1,578	2,227	3,717
McLean County	9,492	7,621	2,046	3,667	871	1,683	200	540	332	776	1,317	2,378
Macon County	9,261	8,022	2,323	3,706	861	1,987	286	855	475	672	1,543	2,439
Madison County	20,502	17,141	4,530	8,666	1,600	3,948	666	1,472	795	2,338	3,021	5,784
Peoria County	13,704	11,584	2,860	5,288	1,001	2,272	387	740	561	1,202	1,900	3,314
Rock Island County	12,512	10,971	2,927	5,653	1,126	2,858	592	1,328	450	1,549	1,846	3,522
St. Clair County	17,486	15,352	5,012	7,551	1,324	3,478	1,178	1,988	1,130	2,313	3,238	4,961
Sangamon County	14,647	12,313	3,468	6,205	1,204	2,782	488	1,175	634	1,768	2,085	3,965
Tazewell County	10,871	9,594	2,145	4,664	677	1,944	239	859	433	1,285	1,460	3,142
Vermilion County	6,938	5,820	2,287	2,657	689	1,305	265	479	656	457	1,550	1,665
Will County	38,672	25,992	7,549	12,193	2,412	4,925	1,254	2,445	1,197	3,202	4,517	7,967
Williamson County	6,127	4,508	1,880	2,185	546	775	283	464	225	506	1,360	1,469
Winnebago County	22,260	17,891	5,527	8,620	1,833	4,069	971	1,454	770	1,866	3,499	5,411

Table H-2: Counties—Disability Status and Type of Disability—*Continued*

	Total Population		With a Disability		With a Hearing Difficulty		With a Vision Difficulty		With a Cognitive Difficulty		With an Ambulatory Difficulty	
	65 to 74 Years	75 Years and Over	65 to 74 Years	75 Years and Over	65 to 74 Years	75 Years and Over	65 to 74 Years	75 Years and Over	65 to 74 Years	75 Years and Over	65 to 74 Years	75 Years and Over
Indiana												
Allen County	22,663	19,008	5,407	8,834	1,925	3,794	780	1,589	1,036	2,560	3,312	5,939
Bartholomew County	6,199	4,446	1,493	2,071	612	984	203	571	293	570	810	1,356
Clark County	8,245	5,869	2,509	3,093	773	1,429	311	668	264	1,394	1,582	2,360
Delaware County	9,156	7,667	2,814	3,784	1,257	1,902	440	743	751	841	1,713	2,556
Elkhart County	12,769	10,586	3,366	5,187	1,361	2,625	805	1,244	597	1,082	1,766	3,102
Floyd County	5,412	3,925	1,593	1,644	699	815	479	282	414	363	903	1,126
Grant County	6,106	4,887	2,006	2,538	732	1,564	223	652	518	586	1,415	1,470
Hamilton County	14,640	9,941	2,673	4,380	1,463	1,964	310	398	432	1,195	1,457	2,991
Hancock County	5,430	3,583	1,293	1,919	480	947	105	138	186	469	854	1,309
Hendricks County	9,266	6,568	2,106	2,911	818	1,232	196	466	235	1,002	1,501	2,065
Howard County	7,547	5,945	2,337	3,051	939	1,100	440	458	300	829	1,444	2,164
Johnson County	9,963	7,173	2,022	3,782	588	1,708	199	758	319	761	1,464	2,505
Kosciusko County	6,020	4,241	1,288	2,039	630	1,108	183	384	162	367	664	1,330
Lake County	35,151	29,601	10,210	15,393	3,126	6,367	1,821	3,019	2,047	4,617	6,862	10,351
LaPorte County	8,578	7,006	2,218	3,313	771	1,698	304	470	344	858	1,576	2,083
Madison County	10,937	8,953	3,483	4,834	1,404	2,490	631	903	693	1,461	2,252	3,144
Marion County	51,396	42,242	14,614	20,925	4,675	8,354	2,384	3,608	2,971	5,929	9,576	14,441
Monroe County	7,689	6,422	1,446	3,289	502	1,616	359	873	333	750	901	1,966
Morgan County	5,674	3,595	1,476	1,855	624	771	248	420	224	456	836	1,330
Porter County	11,919	8,507	2,895	3,791	1,011	1,570	347	663	544	993	1,725	2,353
St. Joseph County	17,666	17,184	4,920	8,900	1,712	4,360	743	1,529	894	2,498	2,832	5,676
Tippecanoe County	8,852	7,141	2,163	3,340	833	1,321	227	535	330	723	1,415	2,126
Vanderburgh County	12,742	11,926	3,206	5,765	1,038	2,610	323	1,073	420	1,226	2,231	4,047
Vigo County	7,495	6,337	2,337	3,243	749	1,566	196	541	596	959	1,494	1,963
Wayne County	6,010	4,979	2,175	2,363	912	1,379	509	546	428	511	1,180	1,480
Iowa												
Black Hawk County	9,064	8,562	2,275	3,857	881	1,610	132	737	336	954	1,270	2,292
Dallas County	3,807	2,807	980	1,286	417	788	82	147	114	166	588	655
Dubuque County	7,108	6,661	1,195	3,335	473	1,461	189	556	167	911	617	2,070
Johnson County	6,413	4,857	1,341	2,271	311	1,231	202	376	232	414	884	1,480
Linn County	14,762	12,536	2,778	5,536	1,279	2,363	289	846	531	1,513	1,420	3,470
Polk County	25,769	20,229	5,569	9,165	2,025	4,352	663	1,676	1,099	2,446	3,684	5,904
Pottawattamie County	7,064	6,002	1,663	2,707	730	1,164	295	567	370	573	1,002	1,861
Scott County	12,036	9,519	2,684	3,879	1,163	1,761	361	721	428	1,020	1,465	2,594
Story County	4,562	4,223	973	1,857	330	911	123	282	233	364	673	1,028
Woodbury County	6,841	6,000	1,534	2,696	535	1,207	159	676	159	758	1,049	1,689
Kansas												
Butler County	4,225	3,801	1,205	2,118	595	1,146	244	440	228	491	657	1,284
Douglas County	5,590	4,462	1,015	2,226	458	1,185	186	632	192	668	607	1,551
Johnson County	33,293	27,107	5,656	12,403	2,314	5,580	730	1,767	958	3,316	3,079	8,277
Leavenworth County	4,958	3,447	1,413	1,826	612	973	186	358	409	401	867	1,207
Riley County	2,653	2,352	310	991	136	406	4	225	28	264	194	622
Sedgwick County	30,819	26,264	8,571	13,199	2,900	6,176	1,145	2,366	1,765	3,639	5,650	8,659
Shawnee County	13,559	11,445	3,163	5,447	1,289	2,081	366	942	646	1,415	2,097	3,611
Wyandotte County	9,211	7,372	2,976	4,404	842	2,191	445	662	624	1,146	2,044	2,951
Kentucky												
Boone County	7,294	4,426	1,977	2,728	720	1,147	252	496	193	723	1,225	1,844
Bullitt County	5,774	3,195	1,817	1,760	733	718	293	343	650	456	1,007	1,120
Campbell County	6,289	4,985	1,532	2,490	719	1,220	137	562	299	839	874	1,402
Christian County	4,120	3,292	1,276	1,663	396	805	134	246	206	353	836	1,043
Daviess County	7,488	6,397	1,783	3,727	597	1,779	228	727	377	1,023	1,141	2,341
Fayette County	17,511	13,304	4,734	7,091	1,769	3,154	511	1,385	1,086	2,061	2,786	4,924
Hardin County	6,621	4,732	1,857	2,924	507	1,361	296	647	480	867	1,349	2,052
Jefferson County	52,403	45,050	14,246	23,535	3,827	9,693	2,362	4,665	3,850	7,096	9,189	15,449
Kenton County	9,998	7,491	2,772	3,832	733	1,919	346	671	833	996	1,728	2,375
McCracken County	5,899	4,723	1,751	2,496	612	1,112	218	481	432	731	1,109	1,539
Madison County	5,508	3,798	1,578	1,774	651	934	256	369	350	405	1,127	1,252
Pike County	5,442	3,448	2,662	2,407	970	1,245	417	554	827	988	2,040	1,813
Warren County	7,162	5,284	2,135	2,838	675	1,285	309	496	480	710	1,523	2,080
Louisiana												
Ascension Parish	6,381	3,500	2,077	1,818	794	865	687	368	393	444	995	1,243
Bossier Parish	8,138	5,535	2,186	3,056	724	1,096	299	559	388	1,167	1,488	2,041
Caddo Parish	18,276	15,407	5,730	8,355	1,951	3,455	1,364	1,726	1,420	2,724	3,750	5,433
Calcasieu Parish	13,935	10,348	5,381	5,642	2,280	2,582	1,241	1,168	1,370	2,057	3,269	3,464
East Baton Rouge Parish	27,394	20,766	8,174	11,019	2,723	4,432	1,327	2,163	1,538	3,386	5,655	7,662
Iberia Parish	5,148	3,755	1,284	2,177	426	1,102	265	420	344	555	932	1,376
Jefferson Parish	32,926	26,428	9,797	14,063	3,064	6,092	1,589	2,439	2,109	4,005	6,077	9,803
Lafayette Parish	12,736	9,697	3,162	5,222	971	1,722	452	801	671	1,865	2,199	3,597
Lafourche Parish	7,068	4,994	2,514	3,158	890	1,310	517	553	704	958	1,519	2,143
Livingston Parish	8,397	4,967	2,952	3,032	839	1,236	496	565	393	916	2,246	2,143
Orleans Parish	22,397	16,609	6,689	9,584	1,695	3,206	1,883	2,729	1,741	3,743	4,671	6,817
Ouachita Parish	10,285	8,171	3,067	4,069	1,054	1,707	583	597	610	1,419	2,075	3,057
Rapides Parish	10,027	7,553	3,856	4,500	1,229	2,381	1,047	1,357	1,080	1,631	2,602	3,320
St. Landry Parish	6,342	4,707	2,097	2,748	756	943	445	518	384	875	1,301	1,970
St. Tammany Parish	18,351	12,380	5,184	6,572	2,268	2,759	927	1,185	865	2,197	3,291	4,615
Tangipahoa Parish	8,376	5,561	3,402	3,349	917	1,264	711	782	770	947	2,324	2,425
Terrebonne Parish	7,532	4,858	2,021	3,092	793	1,200	283	755	308	1,024	1,262	2,002

Table H-2: Counties—Disability Status and Type of Disability—*Continued*

	Total Population		With a Disability		With a Hearing Difficulty		With a Vision Difficulty		With a Cognitive Difficulty		With an Ambulatory Difficulty	
	65 to 74 Years	75 Years and Over	65 to 74 Years	75 Years and Over	65 to 74 Years	75 Years and Over	65 to 74 Years	75 Years and Over	65 to 74 Years	75 Years and Over	65 to 74 Years	75 Years and Over
Maine												
Androscoggin County	8,148	6,865	2,296	3,835	876	1,694	287	762	629	994	1,379	2,402
Aroostook County	7,417	5,878	2,682	3,064	1,136	1,659	275	524	614	817	1,617	1,902
Cumberland County	21,658	18,611	4,455	9,031	1,855	4,823	667	1,803	914	2,344	2,386	5,661
Kennebec County	10,240	8,588	2,838	4,259	1,175	2,398	288	733	662	1,142	1,511	2,302
Penobscot County	12,011	9,992	3,880	5,076	1,616	2,459	522	883	1,108	1,408	2,319	3,294
York County	17,326	13,548	3,998	6,405	1,744	3,260	474	885	887	1,942	2,030	3,633
Maryland												
Allegany County	6,926	5,853	2,242	3,186	779	1,578	456	874	334	695	1,540	1,913
Anne Arundel County	38,808	26,461	8,002	11,242	2,934	4,894	1,055	2,214	1,759	3,243	4,892	7,499
Baltimore County	58,529	57,305	12,956	26,855	4,788	11,276	1,682	4,611	2,445	7,448	7,721	17,328
Calvert County	5,931	3,931	1,121	2,155	356	906	153	328	305	993	729	1,699
Carroll County	12,702	9,305	2,286	4,366	737	1,849	255	743	366	1,088	1,213	2,544
Cecil County	7,269	4,776	2,055	2,250	848	1,229	342	419	501	767	1,187	1,544
Charles County	8,955	5,426	2,571	2,858	802	1,406	288	776	745	1,131	1,975	1,912
Frederick County	15,162	11,238	3,291	5,388	1,037	2,660	394	974	619	1,176	1,841	3,363
Harford County	18,222	13,014	3,560	6,134	1,337	2,795	473	883	529	1,782	2,221	3,839
Howard County	19,017	11,985	2,874	5,605	731	2,446	430	1,054	550	1,627	1,696	3,284
Montgomery County	65,639	55,393	11,108	25,107	3,039	10,532	2,089	4,530	2,236	6,547	6,809	16,454
Prince George's County	52,568	31,398	11,829	14,350	2,450	4,850	1,718	2,169	2,457	4,723	8,329	10,039
St. Mary's County	6,642	4,215	1,416	2,011	394	866	205	394	113	579	1,046	1,280
Washington County	10,991	9,540	2,390	5,033	972	2,475	377	794	367	1,231	1,566	3,324
Wicomico County	7,048	5,679	2,134	2,545	759	981	230	619	364	629	1,318	1,715
Massachusetts												
Barnstable County	28,143	25,869	3,850	9,536	1,237	4,708	358	1,638	887	1,804	2,285	5,608
Berkshire County	12,201	11,673	2,552	5,922	861	2,726	290	911	419	1,328	1,581	3,629
Bristol County	40,845	34,937	10,076	17,439	3,557	8,199	1,401	2,814	2,060	4,524	6,304	11,418
Essex County	55,047	49,087	11,762	23,372	4,396	10,726	1,893	4,832	2,492	6,676	6,874	14,125
Franklin County	6,016	4,796	1,405	2,203	552	934	88	405	308	538	853	1,423
Hampden County	33,174	30,638	8,444	15,541	3,026	7,111	1,503	2,913	1,758	3,897	5,566	10,058
Hampshire County	10,854	9,268	1,916	4,355	534	2,011	211	868	411	1,174	1,417	2,474
Middlesex County	103,233	91,714	19,823	40,761	6,663	17,356	2,581	7,336	4,090	10,414	11,556	25,327
Norfolk County	49,658	46,576	9,735	21,705	3,604	9,238	1,386	4,000	2,366	5,569	5,112	13,321
Plymouth County	39,961	28,824	8,299	13,719	3,230	6,739	1,118	3,107	1,610	3,520	4,792	8,029
Suffolk County	40,522	33,775	12,336	18,758	3,310	7,303	2,719	4,195	3,752	5,889	7,649	12,484
Worcester County	53,395	46,024	12,459	22,540	4,428	10,463	1,586	4,860	2,608	5,575	7,216	14,284
Michigan												
Allegan County	8,589	6,110	1,684	3,015	608	1,398	204	467	332	754	901	1,819
Bay County	9,508	7,849	2,784	3,829	1,280	2,050	417	677	742	1,183	1,608	2,298
Berrien County	13,546	11,534	3,439	5,818	1,192	2,761	386	784	577	1,713	2,310	3,920
Calhoun County	10,534	9,152	3,159	4,579	1,028	2,164	518	1,025	702	1,406	2,129	2,979
Clinton County	5,904	4,104	1,271	1,863	441	741	241	218	216	475	819	1,026
Eaton County	8,837	6,481	2,242	3,236	880	1,687	153	464	651	789	1,087	1,941
Genesee County	31,967	26,344	9,485	13,372	2,876	5,879	1,525	2,152	2,106	4,364	5,863	8,923
Grand Traverse County	7,011	5,916	1,242	2,880	602	1,221	267	305	213	754	626	1,906
Ingham County	16,443	13,316	4,287	6,892	1,508	2,722	813	1,316	1,015	2,288	2,555	4,607
Isabella County	3,716	3,027	1,052	1,461	420	768	84	283	127	343	607	776
Jackson County	11,876	10,386	3,200	5,488	1,228	2,739	387	992	685	1,870	2,090	3,805
Kalamazoo County	16,512	14,021	3,699	6,523	1,403	3,479	583	1,208	833	1,783	2,305	4,021
Kent County	35,243	31,482	7,962	15,092	3,139	6,977	885	2,731	1,534	4,130	4,737	9,210
Lapeer County	7,438	4,640	1,846	2,265	776	1,030	218	250	446	586	978	1,346
Lenawee County	8,248	6,421	2,166	3,484	780	1,631	148	548	375	914	1,320	2,155
Livingston County	14,026	8,753	2,451	4,277	961	1,948	289	854	440	1,168	1,325	2,728
Macomb County	63,125	56,806	15,765	29,135	5,594	12,823	2,185	5,467	3,267	8,594	9,609	19,292
Marquette County	5,288	4,362	1,123	2,081	428	987	170	429	255	600	616	1,278
Midland County	6,564	5,655	1,673	2,645	704	1,175	252	305	233	798	923	1,595
Monroe County	11,639	8,921	3,144	4,707	1,282	2,310	514	758	547	1,117	1,793	2,770
Muskegon County	12,427	10,597	3,037	5,342	1,142	2,563	440	1,072	744	1,292	1,826	3,413
Oakland County	89,150	73,439	19,437	34,201	6,856	15,122	2,705	6,631	3,410	10,166	11,864	22,134
Ottawa County	17,100	14,035	3,530	5,968	1,547	2,969	346	701	529	1,637	1,792	3,564
Saginaw County	16,387	13,681	4,747	6,414	1,601	3,211	649	1,094	828	1,865	3,077	4,287
St. Clair County	13,369	10,228	3,702	5,190	1,506	2,638	205	1,006	537	1,199	2,238	3,385
Shiawassee County	5,798	4,394	1,446	2,284	589	997	207	381	250	538	897	1,423
Van Buren County	6,097	4,463	1,579	2,451	609	1,096	151	534	293	565	952	1,420
Washtenaw County	21,020	15,257	4,726	6,569	1,432	2,921	520	1,486	775	2,124	3,241	4,071
Wayne County	119,568	106,813	36,225	57,120	9,601	22,047	6,634	11,874	9,367	17,379	25,355	39,306
Minnesota												
Anoka County	20,589	13,066	4,342	5,665	2,198	2,609	439	1,044	787	1,365	2,033	3,343
Blue Earth County	3,618	3,683	756	1,694	329	739	101	331	191	426	362	1,093
Carver County	4,553	3,497	637	1,666	409	628	31	245	127	254	238	1,144
Dakota County	23,974	17,194	4,216	7,382	2,024	3,244	312	1,246	868	2,105	2,196	4,441
Hennepin County	69,308	60,466	13,645	26,471	4,357	12,058	1,779	4,477	3,089	5,862	8,147	16,000
Olmsted County	9,686	8,212	1,603	3,589	829	1,734	130	822	140	899	771	2,082
Ramsey County	31,667	28,480	6,537	13,304	2,635	5,870	1,094	2,357	1,491	3,098	3,799	7,975
St. Louis County	16,252	14,443	4,201	6,788	1,937	3,344	451	1,167	895	1,406	2,417	3,879
Scott County	6,584	4,050	1,380	1,776	731	777	29	286	232	484	697	970
Sherburne County	4,449	2,800	1,096	1,376	396	704	74	283	185	197	706	708
Stearns County	9,422	8,573	1,951	3,635	1,048	2,078	371	405	199	599	806	1,888
Washington County	15,427	10,650	2,720	4,683	1,163	1,860	260	671	515	726	1,467	3,242
Wright County	7,232	4,833	1,433	2,313	739	1,103	234	382	247	535	701	1,489

Table H-2: Counties—Disability Status and Type of Disability—*Continued*

	Total Population		With a Disability		With a Hearing Difficulty		With a Vision Difficulty		With a Cognitive Difficulty		With an Ambulatory Difficulty	
	65 to 74 Years	75 Years and Over	65 to 74 Years	75 Years and Over	65 to 74 Years	75 Years and Over	65 to 74 Years	75 Years and Over	65 to 74 Years	75 Years and Over	65 to 74 Years	75 Years and Over
Mississippi												
DeSoto County	10,470	6,556	2,730	3,453	931	1,821	262	796	468	961	2,018	2,097
Forrest County	4,869	3,710	1,921	2,444	659	950	527	653	733	1,019	1,214	1,862
Harrison County	12,921	9,540	4,233	5,246	1,385	2,036	630	890	920	1,710	3,289	3,635
Hinds County	14,670	11,466	4,710	6,614	1,006	2,092	1,017	1,475	1,011	2,328	3,440	5,046
Jackson County	10,678	6,960	4,113	4,329	1,528	1,808	892	887	690	1,091	2,727	3,118
Jones County	5,302	4,177	2,112	2,373	659	1,079	524	650	527	900	1,642	1,672
Lauderdale County	5,865	5,017	2,298	2,604	907	1,130	281	482	468	974	1,463	2,071
Lee County	6,236	4,439	2,581	2,580	887	947	498	681	670	1,035	1,649	1,950
Madison County	5,899	4,352	1,445	2,232	679	874	36	552	195	800	851	1,750
Rankin County	10,152	6,349	3,358	3,780	1,207	1,578	748	1,051	1,035	1,453	2,157	2,592
Missouri												
Boone County	8,492	6,677	2,110	3,340	799	1,775	393	605	396	894	1,320	2,026
Buchanan County	6,278	5,415	2,140	2,913	504	1,547	315	655	479	752	1,382	1,845
Cape Girardeau County	5,504	4,592	1,384	2,658	627	1,057	175	350	356	801	755	1,717
Cass County	7,835	5,645	1,890	2,629	737	1,334	182	447	308	766	1,195	1,543
Christian County	6,003	3,799	1,611	1,564	590	919	75	204	403	130	1,216	930
Clay County	14,505	10,874	3,853	5,154	1,787	2,497	472	1,034	739	1,329	2,261	3,015
Cole County	5,312	4,105	1,554	1,998	651	1,137	503	601	250	507	801	1,351
Franklin County	7,837	5,960	1,847	2,903	803	1,310	154	395	371	629	991	1,687
Greene County	20,503	17,535	5,321	8,817	1,705	3,938	836	1,793	1,158	2,466	3,463	5,798
Jackson County	44,625	37,779	11,990	18,994	3,574	8,082	1,899	3,590	2,719	5,072	8,053	12,487
Jasper County	8,400	6,667	2,688	3,557	910	1,835	337	833	319	1,037	1,886	2,364
Jefferson County	15,687	8,996	4,404	5,038	1,809	2,336	611	1,139	740	1,537	2,652	3,264
Platte County	6,267	4,082	1,259	2,217	579	946	86	458	221	643	597	1,516
St. Charles County	24,339	17,471	5,682	8,615	2,048	4,055	643	1,751	1,158	2,493	3,396	5,550
St. Francois County	4,929	3,760	1,524	1,919	607	987	269	368	344	585	1,007	1,266
St. Louis County	76,104	68,852	15,964	32,567	4,804	13,668	1,877	5,867	3,447	8,149	10,281	21,124
Montana												
Cascade County	6,795	5,758	1,957	3,137	759	1,652	198	815	214	743	1,269	1,879
Flathead County	7,748	5,543	1,701	2,532	783	1,538	195	432	306	531	903	1,441
Gallatin County	5,090	3,731	1,009	1,907	528	926	215	252	199	403	429	1,227
Missoula County	7,304	5,326	1,573	2,616	850	1,514	191	632	189	612	827	1,664
Yellowstone County	11,092	9,600	2,914	4,296	1,433	2,241	441	1,086	562	825	1,353	2,602
Nebraska												
Douglas County	29,502	24,716	6,070	12,213	2,616	5,508	909	2,770	1,180	3,432	3,210	7,932
Lancaster County	16,567	14,537	3,267	7,192	1,386	3,501	260	1,361	701	1,367	1,847	4,296
Sarpy County	8,530	5,414	1,698	2,562	773	1,087	228	381	161	762	897	1,663
Nevada												
Clark County	142,736	88,295	36,311	43,337	11,995	19,183	6,206	8,727	6,430	11,340	23,145	28,731
Washoe County	32,552	20,675	7,701	9,727	2,853	4,193	879	1,781	1,384	2,838	4,896	6,550
New Hampshire												
Cheshire County	6,278	4,939	1,666	2,088	631	972	186	509	184	536	1,027	1,172
Grafton County	7,727	6,200	1,841	2,785	728	1,442	113	588	477	565	1,190	1,539
Hillsborough County	26,880	20,190	5,636	9,372	2,300	4,801	626	1,768	1,080	2,063	3,075	5,338
Merrimack County	10,956	8,612	2,275	4,203	849	2,140	378	581	333	1,048	1,378	2,653
Rockingham County	22,510	15,933	4,101	6,871	1,685	3,762	689	1,342	646	1,696	2,205	4,057
Strafford County	8,125	6,495	2,512	3,307	923	1,471	337	601	579	683	1,367	2,301
New Jersey												
Atlantic County	21,807	16,910	5,296	7,567	1,585	3,139	675	1,254	1,016	1,863	3,470	4,999
Bergen County	69,891	66,308	11,482	28,467	3,648	11,629	1,813	5,389	2,021	8,504	6,656	18,859
Burlington County	33,506	28,470	7,920	13,371	2,567	5,463	1,205	2,062	1,519	3,266	4,891	8,639
Camden County	35,168	29,986	9,470	14,325	2,605	5,952	1,753	3,010	2,264	3,690	6,323	9,833
Cape May County	11,311	9,668	1,962	4,330	843	1,759	210	640	439	1,245	1,202	2,996
Cumberland County	10,874	8,427	3,543	4,582	1,239	1,930	815	1,029	897	1,671	2,317	3,135
Essex County	48,629	40,169	12,590	20,238	2,868	7,048	3,125	5,284	2,470	6,015	8,542	14,005
Gloucester County	20,180	15,668	5,388	8,020	1,916	3,436	355	1,526	1,188	2,306	3,524	5,442
Hudson County	36,739	28,684	9,798	13,945	1,993	4,580	1,912	3,342	2,605	3,790	7,036	9,739
Hunterdon County	9,776	6,912	1,488	3,238	684	1,610	147	610	247	926	744	1,900
Mercer County	24,275	21,414	4,491	10,178	1,057	4,128	772	1,997	847	2,958	3,041	6,644
Middlesex County	52,992	46,232	10,705	21,505	2,759	9,196	1,566	4,054	1,997	5,978	7,292	14,521
Monmouth County	46,853	40,298	8,181	18,566	2,817	7,576	1,118	3,626	1,947	4,858	5,047	12,198
Morris County	36,949	31,813	6,096	13,889	1,951	6,027	611	2,699	1,232	3,491	3,417	8,721
Ocean County	59,866	59,312	12,095	26,104	3,539	11,332	1,436	4,930	1,943	6,783	7,726	16,755
Passaic County	32,824	27,051	8,069	13,620	2,380	5,471	2,170	3,446	1,906	4,748	5,367	9,536
Salem County	5,225	4,495	1,393	2,053	467	892	346	386	278	685	951	1,537
Somerset County	22,186	18,110	3,301	8,485	879	3,582	136	1,283	527	2,070	2,170	5,537
Sussex County	10,707	7,004	1,943	3,165	750	1,405	113	409	364	887	1,201	2,023
Union County	34,543	31,617	6,178	15,081	1,703	5,853	1,448	3,147	1,047	4,402	3,741	10,789
Warren County	8,099	6,601	1,574	3,154	536	1,136	342	535	467	966	820	2,161
New Mexico												
Bernalillo County	46,237	36,946	11,837	19,199	4,304	8,917	2,141	3,999	2,018	5,907	7,611	12,659
Chaves County	4,762	4,251	1,512	2,293	615	1,213	198	434	545	562	715	1,251
Doña Ana County	15,091	11,534	3,922	6,413	1,615	2,874	786	1,520	977	1,709	2,420	4,326
Lea County	3,934	3,058	982	1,662	341	776	215	316	208	315	605	1,087
McKinley County	4,186	2,729	2,030	1,755	925	993	393	620	396	697	1,319	1,075
Otero County	5,491	3,932	2,264	2,556	1,013	1,283	481	749	456	808	1,364	1,462
Sandoval County	10,371	6,495	2,670	3,524	983	2,218	349	1,176	737	969	1,574	2,283
San Juan County	8,080	6,065	2,255	3,225	1,070	1,832	330	751	523	1,258	1,427	1,897
Santa Fe County	14,637	8,709	2,951	4,651	1,523	2,518	357	1,115	832	1,279	1,503	2,753
Valencia County	6,153	4,068	2,235	2,583	1,115	1,563	506	649	465	964	1,249	1,772

Table H-2: Counties—Disability Status and Type of Disability—*Continued*

	Total Population		With a Disability		With a Hearing Difficulty		With a Vision Difficulty		With a Cognitive Difficulty		With an Ambulatory Difficulty	
	65 to 74 Years	75 Years and Over	65 to 74 Years	75 Years and Over	65 to 74 Years	75 Years and Over	65 to 74 Years	75 Years and Over	65 to 74 Years	75 Years and Over	65 to 74 Years	75 Years and Over
New York												
Albany County	21,318	19,683	4,530	9,453	1,607	4,293	715	1,751	815	2,555	2,882	6,089
Bronx County	80,661	60,016	26,543	32,729	5,200	10,123	5,690	8,354	7,340	10,272	19,818	25,617
Broome County	15,980	15,268	3,548	7,142	1,106	3,136	345	1,412	523	1,429	2,284	4,273
Cattaraugus County	6,498	5,598	1,655	2,642	770	1,111	162	427	304	636	1,028	1,692
Cayuga County	6,323	5,674	1,313	2,757	475	1,289	55	444	162	664	833	1,595
Chautauqua County	11,247	10,115	2,495	4,571	935	2,162	282	708	345	904	1,515	2,731
Chemung County	6,752	6,096	1,501	3,078	499	1,418	192	552	230	781	960	1,951
Clinton County	6,005	4,666	1,606	2,159	532	1,055	315	434	404	400	1,181	1,286
Dutchess County	22,035	17,643	5,156	8,515	1,834	3,747	612	980	1,129	2,122	3,169	5,389
Erie County	71,201	68,769	15,648	31,269	5,368	13,525	2,014	5,447	2,632	7,210	10,155	20,150
Jefferson County	7,192	5,576	1,966	2,822	957	1,399	289	503	226	557	1,098	1,630
Kings County	156,416	132,306	41,626	74,331	9,306	24,283	8,724	18,689	11,879	27,204	30,298	58,921
Livingston County	4,934	4,064	1,068	1,883	524	972	108	386	312	513	534	1,101
Madison County	5,814	4,366	996	1,939	334	848	166	244	290	572	725	1,157
Monroe County	54,000	47,976	9,650	22,086	2,699	9,003	1,450	3,524	1,905	5,781	6,394	14,160
Nassau County	101,100	101,000	15,947	42,247	4,235	16,270	1,953	7,340	2,864	11,129	10,614	28,314
New York County	118,191	96,021	24,789	45,278	4,224	13,550	4,759	8,988	6,111	13,741	18,482	34,780
Niagara County	17,732	15,758	4,011	7,118	1,598	3,102	507	1,097	636	1,791	2,507	4,437
Oneida County	18,733	17,413	4,548	8,685	1,826	3,835	585	1,986	896	2,348	2,755	5,566
Onondaga County	32,782	30,812	6,717	13,246	2,269	6,013	1,174	2,803	1,477	3,339	4,201	8,599
Ontario County	9,344	7,303	2,179	3,356	910	1,402	372	314	372	731	1,238	2,267
Orange County	23,472	17,413	5,683	9,427	2,172	4,130	941	2,384	1,244	3,065	2,981	6,253
Oswego County	8,775	6,339	2,151	3,133	939	1,744	249	600	347	891	1,203	1,927
Putnam County	7,704	5,087	1,483	2,459	309	1,014	175	442	126	616	1,036	1,592
Queens County	153,834	129,632	34,895	64,486	8,622	21,795	6,564	12,790	8,719	18,709	23,081	47,598
Rensselaer County	11,412	9,521	2,227	4,496	717	1,809	218	715	475	1,271	1,441	2,915
Richmond County	34,150	25,433	6,827	12,091	1,358	4,505	945	1,791	1,149	3,428	4,504	8,780
Rockland County	23,065	19,282	4,054	8,542	1,175	3,340	682	1,538	810	2,201	2,265	5,303
St. Lawrence County	8,545	6,561	2,751	3,493	1,137	1,602	544	686	659	921	1,629	2,488
Saratoga County	17,732	12,653	3,707	5,912	1,322	2,853	679	992	818	1,379	2,022	3,212
Schenectady County	11,086	11,052	2,392	5,608	938	2,374	435	986	553	1,627	1,432	3,492
Steuben County	8,493	6,913	1,934	3,415	916	1,414	228	864	238	861	951	2,376
Suffolk County	112,607	88,694	19,917	38,780	5,392	15,669	2,495	6,916	3,758	10,352	13,648	24,560
Sullivan County	7,073	4,410	1,667	2,071	477	992	221	507	141	619	1,257	1,270
Tompkins County	5,969	5,067	1,243	2,399	432	1,362	259	520	331	661	844	1,467
Ulster County	14,964	11,992	3,547	6,050	1,250	2,614	616	1,086	600	1,525	2,096	3,875
Warren County	6,264	5,106	1,228	2,465	469	1,042	122	433	389	578	721	1,578
Wayne County	7,722	5,556	1,786	2,682	609	1,230	233	566	440	558	984	1,850
Westchester County	70,326	66,114	11,502	29,053	2,978	11,551	1,494	5,118	2,167	7,502	7,461	18,631
North Carolina												
Alamance County	11,825	10,242	3,030	5,544	1,110	2,363	554	1,315	917	1,617	1,813	3,451
Brunswick County	16,723	7,941	2,963	3,813	993	1,705	530	732	654	1,125	1,761	2,817
Buncombe County	20,695	16,946	4,930	9,522	1,767	4,392	804	1,976	1,117	2,484	2,602	6,436
Burke County	8,490	5,979	3,228	3,263	1,656	1,497	446	706	764	997	2,041	2,496
Cabarrus County	11,616	8,597	2,576	4,377	917	2,036	252	744	380	1,307	1,755	2,977
Caldwell County	7,853	5,117	2,674	2,815	1,074	1,398	671	526	407	786	1,920	1,941
Carteret County	7,593	5,167	1,866	2,686	875	1,284	276	489	408	595	1,119	1,676
Catawba County	12,936	9,345	3,101	4,933	1,112	2,526	531	740	857	1,055	1,792	3,055
Chatham County	7,052	5,363	1,544	2,584	473	1,172	211	490	252	797	938	1,545
Cleveland County	8,825	6,103	2,893	3,390	1,077	1,675	558	764	708	925	1,989	2,363
Craven County	9,124	7,048	2,796	3,594	1,192	1,489	464	990	574	1,003	1,582	2,260
Cumberland County	18,284	12,199	5,879	6,705	1,696	2,410	908	1,286	1,257	1,996	4,020	4,842
Davidson County	14,470	9,488	3,865	5,074	1,413	2,507	617	1,017	758	1,580	2,323	3,068
Durham County	14,937	11,223	3,019	6,046	924	2,849	725	1,439	696	1,770	1,790	4,074
Forsyth County	25,056	20,240	4,938	9,076	1,409	3,120	960	1,769	1,085	2,537	2,840	6,195
Gaston County	15,743	11,291	5,036	6,133	2,008	3,050	700	1,536	1,499	1,894	3,091	4,453
Guilford County	33,540	27,226	6,967	13,220	2,512	5,749	894	3,046	1,569	3,543	4,433	8,487
Harnett County	7,107	4,954	2,200	3,045	852	1,302	456	627	405	937	1,290	1,988
Henderson County	12,888	11,043	2,768	5,213	1,186	2,325	618	967	497	1,299	1,540	3,125
Iredell County	12,432	8,338	2,918	4,668	1,164	2,131	458	977	459	1,208	1,704	3,166
Johnston County	11,345	6,707	3,839	3,544	931	1,227	457	546	1,259	1,078	2,165	2,638
Lincoln County	6,722	3,898	2,015	1,999	531	1,062	230	492	463	582	1,350	1,374
Mecklenburg County	48,681	34,994	10,293	17,642	2,950	7,181	1,383	3,435	2,147	5,239	6,678	11,914
Moore County	10,318	9,522	2,328	3,767	920	2,014	475	817	656	956	1,430	2,243
Nash County	7,884	5,524	2,558	2,950	823	1,266	486	478	622	1,045	1,680	1,959
New Hanover County	16,583	12,107	4,492	5,937	1,228	2,616	443	1,065	794	1,704	2,824	3,773
Onslow County	8,216	5,265	2,885	2,695	1,164	1,471	422	602	605	838	1,921	1,784
Orange County	8,154	5,203	1,501	2,571	471	1,094	174	544	372	841	916	1,635
Pitt County	9,748	7,123	2,701	4,051	905	1,560	509	596	636	1,329	2,096	2,690
Randolph County	11,773	8,344	2,991	4,446	917	1,703	521	1,005	687	1,306	2,109	3,008
Robeson County	9,390	5,785	3,854	3,588	1,303	1,589	850	787	1,189	1,203	2,743	2,666
Rockingham County	8,648	6,464	2,319	3,501	594	1,512	467	778	632	1,182	1,698	2,204
Rowan County	11,231	8,372	3,263	4,716	1,141	2,006	718	1,026	681	1,263	2,302	3,353
Rutherford County	6,726	4,785	2,354	2,813	1,064	1,591	486	739	659	895	1,460	1,931
Surry County	6,857	5,165	2,034	2,433	686	1,085	255	572	414	778	1,422	1,725
Union County	12,845	7,216	2,847	3,837	927	1,846	451	593	627	1,239	1,744	2,738
Wake County	48,001	32,113	9,707	15,067	2,623	6,413	1,465	3,020	2,088	4,458	5,932	10,511
Wayne County	9,301	6,536	3,193	3,637	1,059	1,467	693	843	720	955	2,366	2,414
Wilkes County	6,861	5,011	1,997	2,736	794	1,089	389	513	350	994	1,289	2,268
Wilson County	6,624	4,707	2,155	2,637	549	1,186	296	446	294	645	1,397	1,854

Table H-2: Counties—Disability Status and Type of Disability—*Continued*

	Total Population		With a Disability		With a Hearing Difficulty		With a Vision Difficulty		With a Cognitive Difficulty		With an Ambulatory Difficulty	
	65 to 74 Years	75 Years and Over	65 to 74 Years	75 Years and Over	65 to 74 Years	75 Years and Over	65 to 74 Years	75 Years and Over	65 to 74 Years	75 Years and Over	65 to 74 Years	75 Years and Over
North Dakota												
Burleigh County	5,745	5,241	1,211	2,514	498	1,147	119	469	186	755	625	1,574
Cass County	7,642	7,056	1,754	2,990	749	1,183	147	809	236	643	941	1,623
Grand Forks County	3,802	3,018	821	1,259	282	428	114	194	149	219	545	817
Ohio												
Allen County	7,944	7,015	1,887	3,306	672	1,752	271	678	498	937	1,186	2,173
Ashtabula County	8,513	6,776	2,351	3,444	1,090	1,717	463	618	416	792	1,388	2,026
Belmont County	6,191	5,535	1,639	2,867	594	1,446	244	569	260	780	1,065	1,736
Butler County	23,781	18,457	5,521	9,655	2,420	3,977	754	1,710	934	2,351	3,373	6,748
Clark County	12,037	9,452	3,424	4,823	1,338	2,396	503	819	496	1,451	2,074	3,096
Clermont County	14,276	9,494	3,999	4,859	1,495	2,308	763	1,120	1,027	1,277	2,320	3,206
Columbiana County	9,424	7,879	2,819	3,943	1,050	1,595	480	632	668	937	1,571	2,519
Cuyahoga County	96,170	94,622	23,708	46,475	7,127	17,356	3,854	9,778	4,845	12,023	16,230	30,216
Delaware County	10,830	6,678	2,135	2,681	934	1,280	293	400	381	872	1,140	1,765
Erie County	7,243	5,626	1,962	2,554	819	1,170	384	464	218	617	1,264	1,741
Fairfield County	10,625	7,460	2,645	3,738	980	1,754	272	670	797	1,078	1,678	2,517
Franklin County	65,095	50,545	17,357	26,025	5,618	10,840	2,791	5,079	4,364	7,486	11,480	17,518
Geauga County	8,439	6,100	1,433	2,660	665	944	57	407	270	584	591	1,697
Greene County	12,299	9,811	2,764	4,549	976	2,067	377	820	495	1,240	1,702	2,736
Hamilton County	53,574	48,834	12,289	24,294	3,635	9,220	1,978	4,195	2,198	6,044	8,111	16,342
Hancock County	5,894	4,727	1,165	2,267	399	877	93	375	274	441	742	1,617
Jefferson County	6,619	5,806	1,765	2,742	557	1,120	166	354	257	576	1,193	1,807
Lake County	20,051	16,721	3,956	7,472	1,610	3,060	538	1,196	620	1,726	2,154	4,428
Licking County	13,203	9,116	3,153	4,739	1,258	1,981	363	1,072	477	1,168	1,853	3,362
Lorain County	23,801	18,849	5,963	9,028	2,071	4,069	735	1,795	1,216	2,153	3,560	5,778
Lucas County	30,247	26,365	8,004	13,119	2,629	6,132	1,124	2,427	1,724	3,637	5,656	8,161
Mahoning County	20,157	20,384	5,130	9,238	1,742	4,220	935	1,535	900	2,273	3,157	6,043
Marion County	5,004	4,232	1,602	2,227	556	1,203	376	426	278	835	951	1,306
Medina County	13,369	9,409	2,573	4,416	947	2,078	359	734	368	1,542	1,350	2,462
Miami County	9,033	6,683	1,954	2,910	757	1,414	337	554	273	764	963	1,855
Montgomery County	42,109	37,459	11,617	18,689	4,042	8,408	1,714	3,762	2,717	4,391	7,940	11,394
Muskingum County	6,949	5,736	1,851	2,846	719	1,377	398	454	302	661	1,187	1,939
Portage County	12,150	8,685	2,976	3,657	1,390	1,682	482	570	797	1,219	1,726	2,059
Richland County	10,708	9,247	2,743	4,046	1,225	1,706	323	660	529	1,129	1,524	2,739
Ross County	6,054	4,121	2,003	2,500	715	1,278	315	578	480	765	1,361	1,805
Scioto County	6,458	5,176	2,518	2,859	824	1,184	405	611	697	913	1,904	1,928
Stark County	31,526	27,128	7,133	13,095	2,551	5,436	971	2,199	1,564	3,527	4,539	8,589
Summit County	40,572	37,430	9,981	17,744	3,036	7,637	1,379	3,112	1,793	4,220	6,517	11,615
Trumbull County	18,917	16,881	4,337	8,081	1,755	3,590	526	1,657	756	2,275	2,308	5,233
Tuscarawas County	7,655	6,824	1,736	3,092	658	1,372	181	436	320	713	990	1,989
Warren County	13,778	9,592	3,453	4,148	1,262	1,796	684	785	738	711	2,170	2,366
Wayne County	9,332	7,138	2,365	3,917	985	2,036	288	629	318	862	1,376	2,117
Wood County	8,325	7,035	1,468	2,904	673	1,441	267	625	314	629	775	1,889
Oklahoma												
Canadian County	7,942	5,098	2,327	2,732	944	1,286	216	494	480	836	1,362	1,807
Cleveland County	16,031	10,596	5,011	5,919	2,318	2,898	667	1,015	998	1,892	3,041	3,900
Comanche County	6,981	5,453	2,677	3,336	1,239	1,734	515	673	464	917	1,724	2,297
Creek County	6,313	4,167	2,382	2,290	1,134	1,198	354	432	565	624	1,524	1,522
Muskogee County	5,611	4,409	1,822	2,481	768	952	390	804	382	747	1,165	1,683
Oklahoma County	46,439	38,736	13,370	20,837	4,832	9,293	2,369	3,831	2,277	5,255	8,578	13,900
Payne County	4,354	3,540	1,244	1,848	443	1,059	123	230	211	398	793	1,202
Pottawatomie County	5,971	3,775	2,383	2,290	863	1,000	522	705	611	686	1,594	1,465
Rogers County	7,247	4,414	1,916	2,236	897	1,161	255	325	267	555	1,295	1,696
Tulsa County	39,678	32,541	10,930	16,240	4,261	7,902	1,907	3,415	1,769	3,960	6,817	10,630
Wagoner County	6,427	3,364	2,034	1,784	1,082	1,022	428	438	205	598	1,228	1,315
Oregon												
Benton County	5,720	4,971	1,209	2,391	508	1,332	34	504	143	586	675	1,426
Clackamas County	30,863	22,709	7,272	11,733	3,190	5,524	891	1,912	1,929	3,507	3,995	7,706
Deschutes County	15,013	10,034	2,805	4,825	1,149	2,649	326	1,013	636	1,189	1,385	3,003
Douglas County	12,687	10,208	4,300	5,671	2,319	2,954	745	746	739	1,663	2,327	3,770
Jackson County	19,772	17,091	5,237	8,753	2,517	4,599	931	1,602	1,271	2,475	2,735	5,377
Josephine County	10,267	8,332	2,544	4,393	1,015	2,416	173	577	654	1,355	1,306	3,002
Klamath County	6,741	5,003	2,222	2,617	931	1,249	295	462	650	688	1,497	1,398
Lane County	29,921	24,328	7,610	13,048	3,676	5,746	837	2,425	1,544	3,904	4,171	8,670
Linn County	10,455	8,099	3,493	4,298	1,623	2,194	392	682	732	1,349	2,231	2,631
Marion County	22,309	18,569	5,862	8,510	2,252	4,268	1,081	1,520	1,337	2,441	3,709	5,358
Multnomah County	43,804	34,809	11,021	18,903	3,790	7,859	1,593	4,220	2,568	5,787	6,356	12,320
Polk County	6,310	5,357	1,809	2,597	729	1,205	413	381	353	819	1,232	1,537
Umatilla County	5,433	4,057	1,458	2,123	469	1,199	307	468	191	871	795	1,306
Washington County	31,252	24,500	7,012	11,996	2,872	5,310	1,011	2,363	1,883	4,275	3,756	7,887
Yamhill County	7,279	6,379	1,791	3,565	681	1,949	220	631	370	1,312	1,089	2,416
Pennsylvania												
Adams County	8,900	6,931	2,131	3,424	863	1,398	208	680	255	725	1,250	2,233
Allegheny County	96,735	101,329	21,620	47,499	6,622	20,772	3,489	8,195	4,420	11,865	13,767	30,927
Armstrong County	6,471	6,129	2,040	3,023	820	1,473	165	701	401	720	1,219	1,658
Beaver County	15,401	15,828	3,782	7,565	1,572	3,913	456	1,215	642	1,919	2,267	4,502
Berks County	30,487	27,721	6,979	13,676	2,339	6,305	1,036	2,020	1,406	3,737	4,100	8,371
Blair County	11,182	10,085	2,814	4,708	1,185	2,245	453	1,060	718	1,278	1,761	3,350
Bucks County	49,376	42,261	9,103	19,817	2,894	8,421	1,199	3,541	1,588	5,224	5,551	12,506
Butler County	14,676	13,019	3,429	6,545	1,570	3,269	624	1,071	688	1,906	1,744	3,902
Cambria County	12,871	13,381	3,576	6,994	1,492	3,244	305	1,450	637	1,912	2,162	4,479
Carbon County	6,173	5,267	1,651	2,595	454	1,111	260	429	312	642	1,184	1,798

Table H-2: Counties—Disability Status and Type of Disability—*Continued*

	Total Population		With a Disability		With a Hearing Difficulty		With a Vision Difficulty		With a Cognitive Difficulty		With an Ambulatory Difficulty	
	65 to 74 Years	75 Years and Over	65 to 74 Years	75 Years and Over	65 to 74 Years	75 Years and Over	65 to 74 Years	75 Years and Over	65 to 74 Years	75 Years and Over	65 to 74 Years	75 Years and Over
Pennsylvania—Cont.												
Centre County	9,231	7,824	2,038	3,503	838	1,752	192	668	325	830	1,099	2,407
Chester County	35,833	28,240	5,530	10,967	2,171	4,719	956	1,545	1,049	2,804	2,625	7,123
Clearfield County	7,386	6,321	1,839	3,325	784	1,604	169	800	377	671	1,007	2,067
Columbia County	5,564	4,843	1,035	2,182	411	883	177	394	162	518	586	1,391
Crawford County	8,024	6,428	2,006	3,217	863	1,653	279	590	390	665	1,104	2,042
Cumberland County	18,843	17,124	3,883	7,960	1,491	3,145	356	1,319	596	2,339	2,203	4,836
Dauphin County	19,234	16,968	4,261	8,571	1,701	3,593	789	1,673	734	1,937	2,556	5,344
Delaware County	38,024	39,173	7,577	18,535	2,299	7,338	1,060	3,491	1,547	5,136	4,781	12,072
Erie County	20,763	18,573	5,198	9,495	2,059	4,614	608	1,677	969	2,425	3,309	5,521
Fayette County	12,410	11,402	3,912	5,753	1,760	2,772	568	1,511	968	1,754	2,459	3,865
Franklin County	13,390	11,392	2,769	4,597	1,134	2,092	341	714	420	1,187	1,746	2,695
Indiana County	7,172	6,400	1,945	3,315	788	1,407	277	514	416	850	1,245	2,098
Lackawanna County	18,499	17,657	4,879	8,739	1,868	3,656	513	1,668	852	1,572	3,092	5,804
Lancaster County	39,833	35,948	8,066	15,896	3,290	7,280	863	2,545	1,890	3,755	4,464	9,833
Lawrence County	8,108	8,420	1,835	3,591	730	1,719	139	450	308	1,008	1,025	2,226
Lebanon County	11,496	10,248	2,344	4,225	1,231	1,652	197	642	469	768	912	2,613
Lehigh County	25,585	24,223	5,746	11,485	1,844	4,473	1,230	2,200	1,387	2,960	3,574	7,794
Luzerne County	27,980	27,433	7,396	13,438	2,809	5,864	1,148	2,599	1,185	3,112	4,613	8,960
Lycoming County	9,575	8,796	2,576	4,237	1,293	2,514	392	864	384	1,252	1,338	2,337
Mercer County	10,413	10,226	2,752	4,940	1,277	2,321	308	873	618	1,316	1,544	3,166
Monroe County	12,988	8,912	3,430	4,543	1,046	2,204	961	1,100	490	1,444	2,095	2,914
Montgomery County	59,968	57,711	9,997	24,307	3,653	10,300	1,347	4,448	1,590	6,982	5,568	15,407
Northampton County	23,416	22,389	5,445	10,820	1,904	5,061	751	2,171	793	3,284	3,626	6,992
Northumberland County	8,685	7,936	2,518	3,877	1,051	1,963	277	725	392	773	1,588	2,341
Philadelphia County	95,260	84,603	30,288	45,955	6,780	16,040	5,971	9,580	7,630	14,369	21,689	32,016
Schuylkill County	13,016	12,572	3,866	6,283	1,512	3,132	518	1,146	650	1,687	2,259	3,993
Somerset County	7,297	6,699	2,148	3,812	1,000	1,758	376	848	424	968	1,104	2,307
Washington County	18,586	17,265	4,728	8,534	1,721	4,059	527	1,564	1,066	1,880	2,873	4,844
Westmoreland County	34,331	33,325	7,496	16,288	3,228	7,176	1,061	3,181	1,244	4,274	4,073	10,336
York County	33,981	27,296	7,583	12,606	3,564	5,940	1,232	2,330	1,525	3,374	3,988	7,627
Rhode Island												
Kent County	13,142	12,420	2,509	6,332	772	2,565	339	957	767	1,733	1,508	3,889
Newport County	7,728	6,306	1,127	2,956	446	1,417	130	707	239	745	630	1,683
Providence County	40,471	39,875	10,592	20,120	3,302	8,909	1,461	3,218	1,768	4,663	6,588	12,847
Washington County	10,862	8,245	1,624	3,340	636	1,402	161	343	453	923	770	1,984
South Carolina												
Aiken County	14,778	10,358	3,897	5,286	1,487	2,067	596	928	1,160	1,487	2,296	3,743
Anderson County	16,614	11,862	5,464	6,326	1,398	3,194	1,200	1,588	1,315	1,731	3,713	3,873
Beaufort County	21,610	13,565	3,464	5,329	1,446	2,784	435	920	527	1,328	1,986	3,206
Berkeley County	12,648	6,631	3,918	4,092	1,671	1,625	697	772	978	1,313	2,661	3,052
Charleston County	26,831	19,268	6,180	9,890	1,859	3,563	923	2,144	1,402	2,555	3,823	6,761
Darlington County	5,965	3,851	1,435	1,977	316	681	337	346	427	562	1,153	1,334
Dorchester County	9,203	5,215	2,269	2,660	807	1,056	455	483	536	921	1,306	1,821
Florence County	10,851	7,020	3,519	4,003	951	1,471	765	940	857	1,305	2,274	2,730
Greenville County	34,550	24,415	7,967	12,277	3,119	5,102	1,447	2,506	1,975	4,076	5,121	8,203
Greenwood County	5,828	4,543	1,931	2,718	683	1,089	174	612	601	835	1,180	2,140
Horry County	30,310	18,029	7,925	8,355	2,905	3,945	1,180	1,966	1,445	2,609	5,118	5,401
Lancaster County	7,755	4,675	1,997	2,535	1,032	1,231	234	482	244	850	1,056	1,373
Laurens County	5,736	3,836	1,955	2,351	794	1,079	438	541	562	903	1,141	1,698
Lexington County	20,058	12,702	5,066	6,245	1,542	2,669	690	1,202	924	1,915	3,319	4,374
Oconee County	8,849	5,588	2,364	2,793	999	1,415	225	603	572	782	1,479	1,852
Orangeburg County	8,159	5,697	2,710	3,644	829	1,506	751	796	912	1,603	1,654	2,561
Pickens County	9,377	6,792	2,717	3,889	928	1,730	263	913	654	1,137	1,642	2,762
Richland County	22,284	15,666	6,032	8,203	1,483	3,484	995	1,758	1,669	2,587	3,914	5,796
Spartanburg County	22,761	15,492	6,997	8,970	1,841	3,579	1,193	1,587	1,519	2,819	4,804	5,791
Sumter County	8,005	5,675	2,816	3,021	887	1,016	539	726	680	1,055	1,897	2,244
York County	16,283	10,022	4,749	4,992	1,497	1,732	816	861	1,135	1,591	2,957	3,278
South Dakota												
Minnehaha County	9,788	8,702	2,063	4,126	777	1,999	257	858	301	1,207	1,213	2,502
Pennington County	7,411	6,180	1,496	3,029	676	1,706	128	509	346	674	843	1,995
Tennessee												
Anderson County	6,826	5,977	2,016	3,413	832	1,620	451	813	436	906	1,206	2,390
Blount County	11,902	8,118	2,929	4,154	1,005	2,000	292	922	598	1,322	1,815	2,632
Bradley County	8,604	5,658	3,413	3,316	1,556	1,540	828	843	756	1,211	2,310	2,259
Davidson County	36,153	29,277	9,149	15,237	3,122	6,548	1,381	2,658	2,387	4,377	6,332	9,821
Greene County	7,316	4,736	2,649	3,018	1,307	1,534	419	784	707	1,200	1,712	2,047
Hamilton County	27,458	22,267	7,600	11,989	2,479	5,042	1,031	2,806	1,941	4,198	5,067	8,161
Knox County	31,957	24,944	7,761	12,435	2,661	5,280	1,388	2,459	2,027	3,931	5,561	8,861
Madison County	7,192	5,533	2,064	3,207	870	1,580	222	803	304	1,138	1,286	2,120
Maury County	6,094	4,452	1,625	2,749	690	1,173	304	803	355	801	853	1,883
Montgomery County	8,364	5,593	2,714	2,824	752	1,015	280	648	707	1,059	1,929	2,038
Putnam County	6,044	4,440	1,687	2,362	584	856	190	352	421	734	1,063	1,793
Robertson County	4,778	3,097	1,548	1,647	603	983	166	380	417	404	1,088	1,139
Rutherford County	13,845	8,603	3,659	4,255	1,137	1,957	481	940	714	1,559	2,620	2,987
Sevier County	8,867	5,406	2,578	2,906	1,215	1,377	521	614	568	1,342	1,648	1,724
Shelby County	54,314	41,160	15,646	22,744	4,210	9,005	2,798	5,032	4,034	7,448	10,655	15,864
Sullivan County	16,493	12,555	5,278	6,666	1,935	3,128	865	1,118	1,165	1,779	3,675	4,630
Sumner County	13,170	7,927	3,593	4,189	1,054	1,826	479	571	687	1,430	2,337	2,732
Washington County	10,777	7,747	3,238	4,393	1,317	2,349	718	857	693	1,618	2,116	2,743
Williamson County	11,237	7,418	2,224	3,453	654	1,351	457	617	478	860	1,023	2,259
Wilson County	9,363	5,297	2,650	2,745	998	1,380	414	350	396	672	1,712	1,757

Table H-2: Counties—Disability Status and Type of Disability—*Continued*

	Total Population		With a Disability		With a Hearing Difficulty		With a Vision Difficulty		With a Cognitive Difficulty		With an Ambulatory Difficulty	
	65 to 74 Years	75 Years and Over	65 to 74 Years	75 Years and Over	65 to 74 Years	75 Years and Over	65 to 74 Years	75 Years and Over	65 to 74 Years	75 Years and Over	65 to 74 Years	75 Years and Over
Texas												
Angelina County	6,483	5,164	2,331	3,196	798	1,428	524	944	594	1,061	1,594	2,251
Bastrop County	4,826	3,678	1,471	1,971	673	841	106	424	378	428	892	1,351
Bell County	15,704	11,642	4,974	6,364	2,035	2,700	944	970	1,188	1,951	3,119	4,291
Bexar County	100,803	78,218	32,086	44,779	11,670	19,627	6,272	10,572	7,480	14,243	21,098	32,047
Bowie County	7,298	5,516	1,866	2,981	733	1,359	386	571	435	786	1,242	2,179
Brazoria County	18,604	11,787	5,815	6,262	2,257	2,823	839	1,478	1,412	2,041	3,889	4,244
Brazos County	8,261	6,089	2,216	2,856	798	1,280	315	493	276	956	1,530	2,001
Cameron County	25,305	20,226	8,828	11,835	3,060	5,157	2,015	2,536	2,484	4,098	6,080	8,186
Collin County	42,617	22,912	7,511	11,045	2,784	5,647	826	1,658	1,079	3,303	4,936	7,314
Comal County	10,570	6,981	2,603	3,570	769	1,490	577	509	176	1,292	1,650	2,303
Coryell County	3,588	2,354	1,228	1,466	510	680	34	353	294	419	801	1,169
Dallas County	121,415	88,783	32,643	45,918	10,133	18,278	5,714	10,164	7,709	15,536	21,662	32,626
Denton County	32,161	17,317	6,712	8,552	2,589	3,361	916	1,710	1,155	3,546	4,339	5,660
Ector County	7,713	5,996	2,650	3,621	966	1,770	490	678	620	702	1,671	2,129
Ellis County	9,858	5,588	3,171	3,075	1,139	1,380	718	477	778	980	2,217	2,057
El Paso County	45,342	38,152	15,410	22,016	4,520	9,576	3,083	5,202	3,645	7,006	10,577	15,878
Fort Bend County	30,232	16,952	6,454	8,756	2,053	3,444	1,105	1,397	1,258	2,589	4,187	5,563
Galveston County	19,713	13,819	5,960	7,519	2,624	3,500	1,363	1,808	1,268	2,473	4,140	5,619
Grayson County	10,501	7,910	3,650	4,314	1,497	2,161	644	762	768	1,121	2,389	2,897
Gregg County	8,240	7,498	2,574	3,845	871	1,766	349	789	523	1,122	1,712	2,581
Guadalupe County	9,346	6,446	2,759	3,519	1,153	1,791	311	693	375	1,031	1,502	2,555
Harris County	207,466	138,019	55,758	72,980	18,902	30,551	10,512	15,581	13,936	22,473	36,646	50,731
Harrison County	5,202	3,693	1,831	2,021	814	679	252	446	209	500	1,230	1,533
Hays County	8,819	5,250	1,598	2,874	792	1,519	120	426	296	682	857	1,691
Henderson County	8,837	5,960	2,315	3,570	862	1,543	298	640	469	951	1,587	2,513
Hidalgo County	41,760	32,392	17,308	20,952	5,766	10,565	4,892	6,166	4,452	7,043	11,456	14,118
Hunt County	7,051	4,622	2,870	2,660	1,148	1,139	818	342	617	681	1,666	1,779
Jefferson County	15,917	15,174	5,565	8,976	2,042	3,860	1,340	2,399	1,246	3,106	3,872	6,117
Johnson County	11,106	6,526	3,162	3,200	1,364	1,231	474	396	419	945	1,953	2,292
Kaufman County	6,850	3,961	2,288	2,076	694	916	597	281	466	373	1,371	1,294
Liberty County	5,204	3,223	2,192	2,022	979	960	669	692	531	614	1,439	1,349
Lubbock County	16,676	13,648	5,238	7,626	2,036	3,829	732	1,725	1,073	2,173	3,445	5,362
McLennan County	15,416	12,914	5,128	6,674	1,806	2,704	1,082	1,474	1,039	1,824	3,820	4,626
Midland County	7,730	7,148	2,899	4,094	1,071	1,651	568	1,164	512	1,179	1,865	3,041
Montgomery County	31,573	18,676	8,420	9,511	2,651	4,477	1,265	1,524	1,901	2,637	4,956	6,220
Nacogdoches County	4,102	3,272	1,538	1,893	564	982	209	300	261	469	1,060	1,292
Nueces County	22,773	18,302	7,932	10,571	3,064	5,139	1,708	2,605	2,000	3,626	5,361	7,861
Orange County	6,323	4,972	2,257	3,149	947	1,678	385	854	585	981	1,376	2,067
Parker County	9,291	5,643	2,309	3,125	1,082	1,391	421	617	514	849	1,488	1,931
Potter County	6,886	5,549	2,142	3,038	830	1,291	455	684	437	952	1,417	2,146
Randall County	8,657	6,634	2,180	3,377	924	1,700	256	615	252	722	1,264	2,419
Rockwall County	4,928	2,857	639	1,041	229	434	48	185	69	328	493	688
San Patricio County	4,818	3,418	1,781	2,135	716	1,053	466	735	494	871	1,180	1,417
Smith County	16,519	13,524	4,762	7,076	1,955	3,585	858	1,817	900	2,393	2,960	4,722
Tarrant County	96,928	68,155	24,631	35,238	9,175	14,939	3,935	7,091	4,741	10,601	15,609	24,051
Taylor County	9,049	7,825	2,979	4,503	1,400	2,457	671	1,282	573	1,586	1,965	3,010
Tom Green County	8,065	7,126	2,154	3,290	759	1,548	419	694	296	803	1,271	2,176
Travis County	46,138	31,985	9,879	16,233	3,727	7,141	1,562	3,318	2,029	5,105	6,136	11,136
Victoria County	6,301	5,168	2,152	2,916	599	1,293	334	772	623	808	1,584	1,999
Walker County	4,024	2,595	864	1,158	300	403	67	165	148	255	620	815
Webb County	11,393	8,474	5,193	6,189	1,252	2,994	1,635	1,794	1,691	2,647	3,370	4,536
Wichita County	8,563	7,812	2,636	4,205	881	1,930	420	1,141	374	1,273	1,820	2,926
Williamson County	25,231	15,166	5,887	7,083	1,719	3,336	1,222	1,249	1,325	2,303	3,670	4,458
Utah												
Cache County	4,942	3,981	1,293	1,865	509	864	134	470	207	557	615	928
Davis County	14,539	11,352	3,616	5,508	1,674	2,562	281	1,011	648	1,069	1,986	3,573
Salt Lake County	51,910	39,269	11,443	19,642	4,713	10,784	1,776	4,006	2,308	5,323	6,697	11,126
Utah County	19,615	15,232	4,268	7,742	2,080	3,774	578	1,534	657	2,140	2,248	4,573
Washington County	13,576	11,557	2,757	5,034	1,425	2,243	233	1,037	338	1,347	1,382	2,869
Weber County	12,807	11,029	3,262	5,069	1,091	2,779	330	910	625	1,342	1,803	3,207
Vermont												
Chittenden County	10,040	7,817	1,779	4,034	687	1,983	264	642	332	1,062	974	2,445
Virginia												
Albemarle County	7,808	6,678	1,616	3,067	632	1,672	236	821	440	1,038	946	1,761
Arlington County	10,837	7,610	1,619	3,349	511	1,169	341	905	245	924	719	2,442
Augusta County	7,207	4,992	1,709	2,271	770	1,070	241	368	453	484	887	1,650
Bedford County	7,376	4,433	1,269	2,085	467	1,283	200	283	200	382	695	1,176
Chesterfield County	21,257	13,605	4,351	6,894	1,569	2,746	444	1,555	1,257	2,395	2,748	4,987
Fairfax County	67,715	43,949	10,202	19,800	3,387	8,506	1,191	4,235	1,952	5,469	6,016	11,874
Fauquier County	5,482	3,344	1,225	1,857	397	398	152	306	206	425	730	1,210
Frederick County	6,099	4,136	1,543	1,670	580	780	161	355	255	545	817	972
Hanover County	7,795	5,657	1,846	2,586	701	1,063	237	473	510	928	1,050	1,529
Henrico County	20,021	17,893	3,281	8,575	1,188	3,436	449	1,623	532	2,389	1,810	5,613

Table H-2: Counties—Disability Status and Type of Disability—*Continued*

	Total Population		With a Disability		With a Hearing Difficulty		With a Vision Difficulty		With a Cognitive Difficulty		With an Ambulatory Difficulty	
	65 to 74 Years	75 Years and Over	65 to 74 Years	75 Years and Over	65 to 74 Years	75 Years and Over	65 to 74 Years	75 Years and Over	65 to 74 Years	75 Years and Over	65 to 74 Years	75 Years and Over
Virginia—Cont.												
James City County	7,864	6,341	1,075	2,138	382	920	123	205	115	513	607	1,327
Loudoun County	13,614	8,784	2,152	4,099	845	1,708	296	584	479	1,171	1,292	2,433
Montgomery County	5,260	3,976	1,097	2,121	411	1,127	263	425	143	353	743	1,314
Prince William County	19,659	9,735	4,254	4,523	1,090	1,816	642	696	508	1,796	2,970	3,115
Roanoke County	8,584	7,024	1,572	2,943	511	1,431	166	711	231	813	996	2,100
Rockingham County	6,667	5,642	1,574	2,794	621	1,097	185	526	274	714	881	2,047
Spotsylvania County	7,652	4,942	2,005	2,651	768	1,032	201	593	363	846	1,206	1,710
Stafford County	6,598	3,450	1,417	1,783	459	720	199	305	357	554	875	1,067
York County	4,878	3,274	901	1,369	287	638	92	384	117	367	571	899
Washington												
Benton County	12,534	8,883	2,783	4,305	1,252	2,226	495	622	660	1,190	1,404	2,707
Chelan County	5,913	5,155	1,124	2,333	579	1,282	168	688	251	580	584	1,354
Clallam County	9,429	7,847	2,314	3,846	1,327	1,892	234	581	500	865	1,052	2,406
Clark County	30,473	21,134	7,882	11,427	3,129	5,451	1,004	2,361	1,659	3,610	4,626	7,480
Cowlitz County	9,346	6,738	3,474	3,855	1,739	1,996	287	845	524	1,050	1,915	2,376
Franklin County	3,327	2,513	982	1,385	414	756	189	339	195	432	496	835
Grant County	6,287	4,476	1,895	2,842	756	1,699	187	504	390	528	1,244	1,526
Grays Harbor County	7,049	4,819	2,388	2,497	1,054	1,375	360	335	639	608	1,445	1,538
Island County	9,023	5,865	1,561	2,791	734	1,524	110	470	216	840	731	1,576
King County	120,656	95,944	26,497	48,765	9,177	21,488	3,702	9,255	6,299	14,560	14,917	31,127
Kitsap County	20,772	13,194	6,052	6,916	2,559	4,028	810	1,591	1,243	2,085	3,373	3,949
Lewis County	7,467	5,626	2,236	3,076	1,029	1,608	169	720	562	920	1,239	1,767
Pierce County	51,564	38,109	14,506	19,901	6,189	9,362	1,960	4,107	2,852	6,354	8,325	13,056
Skagit County	10,957	8,371	2,800	4,292	1,550	2,202	343	803	496	824	1,483	2,770
Snohomish County	44,153	32,251	10,231	17,068	3,532	7,858	1,297	2,888	2,340	5,307	6,436	11,521
Spokane County	34,004	27,429	9,217	14,684	4,123	7,142	1,244	2,997	1,749	3,836	5,574	9,354
Thurston County	19,460	14,307	4,512	7,180	1,766	3,453	704	1,137	948	1,656	2,314	4,945
Whatcom County	15,585	11,768	3,949	5,777	1,974	2,955	709	1,301	1,068	1,666	1,869	3,073
Yakima County	15,610	12,403	5,020	7,339	1,889	3,902	874	1,418	1,374	2,059	2,781	4,895
West Virginia												
Berkeley County	7,681	4,617	1,907	2,296	801	959	289	571	289	715	1,140	1,515
Cabell County	7,972	7,040	2,553	4,286	949	2,194	368	1,113	632	1,581	1,795	2,933
Harrison County	6,156	5,045	2,320	2,969	825	1,557	709	514	525	804	1,470	1,953
Kanawha County	17,301	14,681	5,415	7,877	1,962	3,281	975	1,678	1,246	2,348	3,795	5,632
Monongalia County	5,334	4,325	1,377	2,154	505	929	191	402	384	585	819	1,261
Raleigh County	6,772	5,753	3,313	3,247	1,380	1,529	442	907	620	969	2,212	1,905
Wood County	8,382	6,106	2,098	3,074	914	1,650	363	397	496	790	1,271	1,843
Wisconsin												
Brown County	15,435	13,159	3,218	6,503	1,168	2,477	506	1,037	496	1,933	1,963	4,368
Dane County	28,443	22,685	4,913	10,292	2,308	4,659	505	1,976	779	2,669	2,660	6,333
Dodge County	6,604	5,875	1,343	2,585	574	948	142	468	197	481	790	1,655
Eau Claire County	6,440	5,904	1,547	2,675	434	1,226	88	359	439	662	911	1,657
Fond du Lac County	7,729	7,276	1,479	3,379	654	1,623	126	693	385	831	824	2,266
Jefferson County	6,299	4,730	1,226	1,854	440	780	83	233	162	472	748	1,202
Kenosha County	9,851	8,597	2,544	4,210	899	2,009	238	915	429	889	1,720	2,672
La Crosse County	7,733	7,267	1,549	3,076	588	1,619	212	732	290	589	1,009	1,869
Manitowoc County	7,084	6,383	1,177	2,901	435	1,264	169	302	163	561	786	1,670
Marathon County	10,171	8,761	1,844	3,998	765	1,848	199	642	221	787	1,114	2,727
Milwaukee County	52,750	53,604	13,907	26,270	3,803	10,325	2,263	4,644	3,335	6,966	9,206	17,830
Outagamie County	11,140	9,528	2,112	4,012	1,035	1,734	169	623	324	969	1,063	2,512
Ozaukee County	7,234	6,153	1,164	2,371	399	1,146	134	295	198	448	511	1,481
Portage County	4,888	4,159	847	2,048	379	932	86	276	111	370	419	1,408
Racine County	13,894	11,987	3,210	5,398	1,216	2,418	515	995	595	1,213	1,945	3,578
Rock County	11,659	9,782	2,845	4,577	1,165	2,350	622	1,003	655	1,192	1,482	2,592
St. Croix County	4,994	3,458	1,082	1,462	576	652	69	349	123	355	537	944
Sheboygan County	8,559	7,889	1,934	3,403	805	1,552	175	377	255	828	997	2,094
Walworth County	7,648	5,930	1,423	2,688	437	1,072	166	553	268	581	765	1,603
Washington County	9,791	7,978	1,500	3,309	682	1,273	203	473	187	775	769	2,176
Waukesha County	29,868	26,321	5,238	12,209	2,299	5,364	469	2,056	771	2,997	3,026	7,143
Winnebago County	11,304	10,448	2,273	4,562	1,218	2,177	463	823	691	987	1,423	2,757
Wood County	6,426	5,995	1,425	2,713	528	1,438	145	633	269	507	623	1,580
Wyoming												
Laramie County	6,812	4,942	2,030	2,363	802	1,100	193	588	420	518	1,087	1,567
Natrona County	4,976	4,232	1,406	1,900	585	923	222	516	270	573	848	1,035

Table H-3: Places—Disability Status and Type of Disability

	Total Population		With a Disability		With a Hearing Difficulty		With a Vision Difficulty		With a Cognitive Difficulty		With an Ambulatory Difficulty	
	65 to 74 Years	75 Years and Over	65 to 74 Years	75 Years and Over	65 to 74 Years	75 Years and Over	65 to 74 Years	75 Years and Over	65 to 74 Years	75 Years and Over	65 to 74 Years	75 Years and Over
Alabama												
Birmingham city	13,442	12,426	4,281	6,818	696	1,855	744	1,437	1,083	2,344	3,346	4,994
Dothan city	5,268	4,216	1,855	2,426	549	1,022	365	389	482	826	1,232	1,732
Hoover city	5,463	4,173	915	2,182	254	851	47	423	267	502	679	1,540
Huntsville city	13,605	11,122	3,338	5,742	1,245	2,795	900	1,189	605	1,862	1,973	3,511
Mobile city	14,136	11,857	4,314	6,666	1,335	2,532	1,013	1,751	1,081	2,348	2,894	4,552
Montgomery city	13,172	10,513	4,172	5,497	1,194	2,272	1,189	1,137	1,003	1,836	3,086	3,699
Tuscaloosa city	4,482	4,778	1,459	2,422	459	871	241	362	371	603	1,044	1,691
Alaska												
Anchorage Municipality	14,045	7,941	3,740	4,384	1,858	2,047	385	1,142	709	1,582	2,026	3,059
Arizona												
Avondale city	3,264	1,135	819	722	351	256	53	82	111	233	515	634
Chandler city	12,205	8,028	2,704	4,337	909	2,078	261	531	495	968	1,660	2,981
Flagstaff city	2,617	1,756	465	734	137	473	44	122	45	114	277	412
Glendale city	12,219	8,113	3,756	4,412	1,193	2,184	943	872	860	1,175	2,483	3,076
Goodyear city	5,234	2,287	579	909	244	488	18	215	188	280	380	685
Mesa city	35,483	31,817	7,566	13,486	2,760	6,222	1,169	3,456	1,614	3,616	4,528	8,533
Peoria city	11,110	10,518	2,317	4,992	853	2,395	344	1,186	473	1,139	1,292	3,022
Phoenix city	74,389	52,756	18,857	26,888	6,633	12,169	3,401	5,356	4,307	8,015	11,884	17,815
Scottsdale city	25,502	19,443	3,712	7,203	1,772	3,603	433	1,163	734	1,928	2,049	4,849
Surprise city	14,861	8,501	2,854	3,329	1,146	1,336	210	530	685	821	1,908	2,217
Tempe city	8,124	5,395	1,560	2,725	591	1,284	335	455	218	725	847	1,985
Tucson city	33,875	29,329	9,578	15,026	3,285	7,409	1,793	3,607	2,612	3,851	6,169	10,451
Yuma city	6,580	5,333	1,830	2,732	711	1,460	340	610	264	693	1,068	1,613
Arkansas												
Fayetteville city	3,026	2,989	866	1,554	263	776	85	191	188	347	691	1,028
Fort Smith city	5,445	4,823	1,810	2,382	756	1,138	382	501	359	561	1,124	1,773
Jonesboro city	3,690	3,426	1,312	2,005	633	843	230	521	344	683	823	1,481
Little Rock city	11,946	9,878	3,486	5,249	944	2,250	656	1,039	812	1,508	2,336	3,735
Springdale city	3,083	2,695	893	1,374	450	562	172	317	279	513	448	852
California												
Alameda city	5,082	3,895	1,027	1,722	281	617	188	226	228	489	492	1,009
Alhambra city	6,219	5,803	1,311	2,976	353	1,406	85	695	404	937	795	1,906
Anaheim city	17,550	14,589	3,993	7,535	1,285	2,945	668	1,280	684	2,838	2,635	5,084
Antioch city	6,255	3,187	1,844	1,799	400	916	271	237	150	476	1,158	1,007
Bakersfield city	17,455	13,183	5,314	7,484	2,175	3,199	997	1,781	1,097	2,421	3,584	4,934
Baldwin Park city	4,005	2,685	1,118	1,588	202	606	148	263	265	628	776	1,077
Bellflower city	3,504	2,917	1,156	1,776	467	846	212	376	198	689	649	1,255
Berkeley city	8,563	5,515	1,389	2,895	403	947	272	545	307	1,025	811	2,011
Buena Park city	5,033	4,016	1,059	2,129	446	771	160	505	323	896	511	1,468
Burbank city	7,065	7,402	1,806	4,014	406	1,253	220	631	634	1,322	1,183	2,741
Camarillo city	5,270	6,112	1,036	3,209	392	1,479	126	474	71	992	555	2,263
Carlsbad city	7,810	8,026	881	3,602	464	1,643	135	508	40	1,028	355	2,085
Carson city	7,590	5,041	1,888	2,777	489	1,115	328	617	381	1,026	1,238	2,014
Chico city	4,158	4,787	1,116	2,372	233	953	114	320	453	762	728	1,590
Chino city	4,416	2,383	1,344	1,585	411	607	89	327	205	529	960	1,202
Chino Hills city	3,646	1,903	842	1,235	339	426	131	314	252	356	566	908
Chula Vista city	13,920	11,205	3,104	6,029	650	2,886	542	1,319	576	2,217	2,016	4,396
Citrus Heights city	6,217	5,271	1,702	2,790	640	1,319	172	359	226	923	1,037	2,037
Clovis city	6,062	4,532	1,554	2,223	865	1,349	200	555	381	639	647	1,456
Compton city	4,405	2,880	1,786	1,718	388	632	619	517	669	428	1,309	1,204
Concord city	7,695	6,663	1,605	3,470	406	1,586	232	669	259	800	1,169	2,390
Corona city	7,085	4,618	1,970	2,264	632	1,044	239	856	437	965	1,330	1,595
Costa Mesa city	5,373	4,376	1,056	2,202	411	921	145	479	462	843	621	1,715
Daly City city	7,809	5,636	1,378	3,062	194	1,114	240	419	197	1,182	990	2,210
Davis city	2,967	2,261	385	1,112	156	530	53	117	15	205	296	573
Downey city	6,177	5,148	1,695	2,572	456	1,210	506	836	421	696	1,110	1,750
El Cajon city	5,433	4,514	1,602	2,755	291	901	128	709	465	796	1,057	1,798
Elk Grove city	8,160	6,151	2,580	3,567	1,108	1,661	323	823	605	1,175	1,901	2,209
El Monte city	6,439	4,854	1,437	2,523	344	1,239	201	553	288	1,006	1,125	1,695
Escondido city	6,780	7,529	2,175	4,179	492	1,657	316	1,085	916	1,815	1,001	2,599
Fairfield city	5,945	5,063	1,812	2,766	453	1,419	402	561	308	814	1,288	1,809
Folsom city	3,649	2,981	952	1,470	399	573	82	153	247	567	466	955
Fontana city	7,262	4,674	2,742	3,071	673	1,086	355	501	905	1,400	1,949	2,168
Fremont city	12,587	10,902	2,516	5,325	752	2,457	158	1,359	496	1,456	1,596	3,426
Fresno city	24,866	20,473	8,014	11,492	3,241	5,274	1,865	2,539	2,362	3,820	5,182	8,227
Fullerton city	8,092	7,985	1,394	3,826	518	1,775	133	888	193	1,219	763	2,523
Garden Grove city	10,222	8,749	2,279	4,592	628	1,834	244	688	680	2,075	1,319	3,173
Glendale city	14,761	14,793	4,910	9,505	904	2,863	741	1,396	1,985	4,888	2,600	6,136
Hawthorne city	3,842	2,162	1,099	932	209	381	250	395	196	520	803	707
Hayward city	7,790	6,823	2,320	3,610	568	1,460	282	642	502	1,193	1,271	2,435
Hemet city	8,239	9,501	2,570	5,336	1,096	2,388	549	891	401	1,450	1,476	3,307
Hesperia city	5,104	3,936	1,571	2,382	501	1,144	251	626	412	1,057	1,233	1,392
Huntington Beach city	15,636	12,072	2,360	5,480	918	2,758	355	949	507	1,675	1,383	3,181
Indio city	6,528	3,939	1,729	2,106	870	968	154	530	320	592	979	1,523
Inglewood city	6,271	3,785	1,730	1,942	341	507	357	366	346	831	1,182	1,358
Irvine city	11,634	7,408	2,116	3,795	572	1,639	258	698	400	1,272	1,110	2,665
Jurupa Valley city[1]	4,440	2,642	1,252	1,428	411	635	151	368	217	315	799	1,043

[1] Jurupa Valley city was incorporated in 2011. The 2010 population is the U.S. Census Bureau's estimates base figure.

Table H-3: Places—Disability Status and Type of Disability—*Continued*

	Total Population		With a Disability		With a Hearing Difficulty		With a Vision Difficulty		With a Cognitive Difficulty		With an Ambulatory Difficulty	
	65 to 74 Years	75 Years and Over	65 to 74 Years	75 Years and Over	65 to 74 Years	75 Years and Over	65 to 74 Years	75 Years and Over	65 to 74 Years	75 Years and Over	65 to 74 Years	75 Years and Over
California—Cont.												
Lake Forest city	4,717	3,099	810	1,332	332	627	19	198	257	399	537	746
Lakewood city	4,782	4,907	1,195	2,486	442	1,050	228	620	235	787	833	1,648
Lancaster city	7,426	5,658	2,387	3,063	623	1,464	585	588	806	1,305	1,697	2,164
Livermore city	4,889	3,630	1,264	1,658	511	536	176	232	197	387	717	1,107
Long Beach city	23,896	18,255	6,821	9,704	1,804	4,098	1,414	1,852	2,046	2,981	4,499	6,474
Los Angeles city	217,388	181,171	59,113	99,001	14,592	38,440	10,787	22,001	15,996	34,216	39,568	70,803
Lynwood city	2,290	1,911	550	1,157	161	421	225	358	164	449	466	767
Manteca city	3,984	2,813	1,014	1,572	260	759	95	263	270	444	690	1,117
Menifee city	7,532	6,830	1,927	3,338	560	1,556	168	844	247	820	1,248	2,164
Merced city	4,260	2,663	2,016	1,748	699	901	1,091	615	544	737	1,216	1,281
Milpitas city	3,827	2,851	748	1,406	134	491	140	286	189	409	434	1,077
Mission Viejo city	7,528	6,575	1,309	3,120	456	1,474	148	626	296	1,317	805	2,354
Modesto city	11,626	10,761	4,229	6,415	1,582	2,908	523	1,129	793	2,260	2,644	4,444
Moreno Valley city	7,481	5,617	2,655	3,303	703	1,729	347	734	583	1,471	1,892	2,407
Mountain View city	4,471	3,540	683	1,902	187	745	31	207	163	563	453	1,275
Murrieta city	5,386	5,058	1,316	2,096	502	819	0	412	291	544	865	1,150
Napa city	5,115	5,143	1,179	2,678	407	1,119	110	444	246	645	831	1,549
Newport Beach city	8,674	7,173	724	2,716	303	1,193	76	398	161	642	447	1,806
Norwalk city	5,759	4,473	1,765	2,350	439	783	147	651	446	798	1,156	1,549
Oakland city	25,055	19,807	6,029	10,646	1,570	3,606	928	2,118	1,475	3,633	4,147	7,644
Oceanside city	10,319	10,549	2,211	5,567	723	2,713	253	1,096	723	1,945	1,141	3,408
Ontario city	6,481	5,549	1,738	2,911	557	992	402	524	171	992	960	2,243
Orange city	8,632	6,264	1,491	2,898	440	1,266	203	705	276	969	744	1,708
Oxnard city	9,173	7,042	2,823	3,553	785	1,448	707	823	584	1,226	1,977	2,426
Palmdale city	6,019	4,714	1,817	2,721	383	1,052	177	446	425	995	1,258	1,741
Palo Alto city	5,569	5,389	802	2,057	264	756	167	385	135	926	412	1,361
Pasadena city	8,845	9,661	2,081	5,514	448	2,363	508	807	581	1,955	1,302	3,793
Perris city	2,072	973	633	633	261	264	180	173	215	359	379	482
Pleasanton city	4,526	3,373	856	1,589	403	581	37	244	123	415	363	984
Pomona city	6,643	4,600	1,860	2,426	275	1,018	383	751	483	772	1,348	1,658
Rancho Cordova city	3,818	3,170	1,386	1,503	481	702	129	355	304	471	885	961
Rancho Cucamonga city	7,527	6,345	1,739	3,817	555	1,575	189	1,191	240	1,558	992	2,678
Redding city	7,492	6,970	2,353	3,852	751	1,967	278	845	464	1,239	1,591	2,307
Redlands city	4,586	4,019	1,241	1,852	596	805	46	482	251	615	558	1,100
Redondo Beach city	4,264	3,311	716	1,585	312	634	115	471	201	464	444	986
Redwood City city	4,721	3,870	897	1,949	277	752	185	385	246	642	394	1,315
Rialto city	4,477	2,837	1,510	1,864	342	996	268	392	189	829	1,279	1,412
Richmond city	6,064	4,045	1,351	2,268	171	969	181	210	301	668	1,003	1,533
Riverside city	15,674	12,139	4,260	6,523	1,432	2,820	566	1,101	1,015	1,600	2,740	4,597
Roseville city	8,010	8,024	1,882	3,458	577	1,178	237	454	371	989	1,256	2,396
Sacramento city	27,061	24,136	8,219	13,480	2,485	5,907	1,638	2,371	1,995	3,940	5,618	9,015
Salinas city	6,445	4,619	1,751	2,389	421	1,189	336	523	660	832	1,227	1,627
San Bernardino city	9,685	6,797	3,692	3,885	977	1,677	620	768	1,234	1,195	2,474	2,866
San Buenaventura (Ventura) city	7,776	7,292	1,202	3,555	372	1,932	227	666	315	1,166	835	2,399
San Diego city	76,194	66,762	16,708	33,092	5,131	13,933	2,562	6,033	3,870	10,424	10,552	22,189
San Francisco city	55,902	54,835	13,582	28,929	4,078	10,708	2,848	6,567	3,967	10,396	8,711	20,040
San Jose city	56,434	43,568	12,841	23,381	4,040	9,935	2,078	4,713	3,004	7,826	6,922	15,626
San Leandro city	5,867	5,396	1,439	2,839	194	876	351	367	298	960	749	2,103
San Marcos city	4,477	4,976	1,333	2,902	286	1,541	97	339	635	1,596	620	1,979
San Mateo city	6,728	7,251	1,061	3,404	396	1,557	174	516	178	998	692	2,281
San Ramon city	3,350	2,062	502	1,159	170	465	85	239	18	318	288	842
Santa Ana city	12,194	8,857	3,355	4,769	816	2,073	1,044	1,370	871	1,664	1,705	3,092
Santa Barbara city	5,978	6,130	856	2,921	274	1,374	155	661	331	664	527	1,790
Santa Clara city	5,214	5,431	1,069	2,649	243	1,166	75	510	212	652	606	1,765
Santa Clarita city	10,461	7,097	2,872	4,261	962	1,640	315	569	733	975	1,469	3,124
Santa Maria city	4,900	4,445	1,548	2,363	681	1,041	324	540	379	795	774	1,693
Santa Monica city	6,981	6,031	1,664	3,275	303	1,025	228	563	588	918	1,149	2,168
Santa Rosa city	10,826	10,860	2,490	5,384	976	2,530	258	1,099	710	1,497	1,648	3,211
Simi Valley city	8,052	5,380	1,760	2,892	672	1,273	245	569	215	617	1,162	2,025
South Gate city	4,535	2,809	1,529	1,794	368	633	196	427	409	599	942	1,169
Stockton city	16,083	12,308	5,136	6,643	1,428	2,882	785	1,265	1,455	2,634	3,235	4,825
Sunnyvale city	8,017	7,438	1,454	3,767	419	1,764	173	844	199	1,222	893	2,494
Temecula city	4,394	3,353	1,124	1,608	455	947	86	284	171	532	542	1,065
Thousand Oaks city	10,212	8,508	1,788	4,030	775	1,702	198	900	440	1,469	950	2,552
Torrance city	11,705	10,960	1,890	5,422	538	2,445	287	1,029	258	1,625	1,175	3,536
Tracy city	4,110	2,231	712	1,279	210	481	52	158	176	377	448	878
Turlock city	4,141	3,662	1,409	2,362	455	908	225	342	639	1,041	798	1,606
Tustin city	3,842	2,463	753	1,152	249	486	148	210	144	429	461	787
Union City city	4,705	3,352	1,194	1,430	486	450	291	167	197	433	766	1,051
Upland city	5,469	4,014	1,382	1,943	647	928	235	496	239	409	722	1,341
Vacaville city	5,473	3,582	1,352	2,026	686	973	235	334	106	528	634	1,113
Vallejo city	7,522	6,292	1,907	3,616	371	1,301	201	581	381	851	1,224	2,436
Victorville city	4,989	3,440	1,229	2,252	478	866	434	608	330	646	600	1,665
Visalia city	7,194	5,995	2,041	3,183	596	1,239	309	338	477	1,176	1,365	2,163
Vista city	4,377	4,366	1,159	2,568	243	1,352	76	531	412	890	695	1,760
West Covina city	6,408	6,370	1,543	3,739	383	1,757	122	751	230	1,356	974	2,571
Westminster city	7,357	6,232	1,575	2,906	422	1,228	142	548	383	1,208	1,042	1,898
Whittier city	4,350	5,401	936	2,964	180	1,328	198	582	159	1,017	706	2,003
Yorba Linda city	4,949	3,267	927	1,567	313	632	69	338	123	466	576	1,012
Yuba City city	4,501	3,473	1,172	1,719	309	796	57	353	341	426	775	1,129

Table H-3: Places—Disability Status and Type of Disability—*Continued*

	Total Population		With a Disability		With a Hearing Difficulty		With a Vision Difficulty		With a Cognitive Difficulty		With an Ambulatory Difficulty	
	65 to 74 Years	75 Years and Over	65 to 74 Years	75 Years and Over	65 to 74 Years	75 Years and Over	65 to 74 Years	75 Years and Over	65 to 74 Years	75 Years and Over	65 to 74 Years	75 Years and Over
Colorado												
Arvada city	8,703	6,869	1,908	3,037	879	1,329	388	624	279	671	995	1,984
Aurora city	18,021	11,997	4,380	5,952	1,595	3,039	970	1,106	1,027	2,128	2,516	3,834
Boulder city	4,835	3,822	759	1,594	322	717	54	166	91	547	461	1,002
Centennial city	7,132	5,335	1,136	2,273	509	1,215	294	427	59	545	612	1,383
Colorado Springs city	25,845	19,727	6,406	9,673	2,938	4,928	975	2,080	1,225	2,307	3,540	5,957
Denver city	33,764	28,860	8,410	14,971	2,655	6,736	1,381	3,704	1,709	4,157	5,378	9,249
Fort Collins city	6,836	5,305	1,290	2,821	438	1,497	210	553	448	676	643	1,591
Greeley city	5,345	4,498	1,153	2,465	463	1,179	127	202	270	739	688	1,543
Lakewood city	10,674	9,112	2,487	4,491	1,128	2,005	421	1,126	394	1,131	1,332	2,896
Longmont city	5,266	4,160	1,023	1,756	452	990	128	481	162	473	507	1,140
Loveland city	4,717	4,753	992	2,312	405	1,343	117	402	275	441	537	1,451
Pueblo city	7,868	7,927	2,538	4,209	827	2,122	460	1,078	558	1,027	1,630	2,959
Thornton city	5,119	3,286	1,321	1,919	457	1,025	135	456	253	555	862	1,371
Westminster city	5,867	4,541	1,261	2,536	555	1,207	291	410	185	696	849	1,759
Connecticut												
Bridgeport city	7,428	6,299	2,164	3,295	331	1,475	491	705	532	883	1,465	2,379
Danbury city	5,118	4,091	605	2,019	108	955	60	472	138	586	393	1,440
Hartford city	6,509	4,714	2,654	2,733	643	766	699	595	785	771	1,786	1,817
New Britain city	4,137	4,295	1,114	2,291	347	832	126	400	262	719	711	1,525
New Haven city	6,236	5,952	1,921	2,877	470	994	339	646	566	810	1,375	1,878
Norwalk city	6,872	5,974	1,621	2,574	499	1,154	501	491	142	613	919	1,546
Stamford city	7,575	7,585	1,094	3,426	276	1,472	227	552	251	880	673	2,209
Waterbury city	6,541	5,758	2,321	2,902	472	1,025	394	604	372	853	1,474	1,878
Delaware												
Wilmington city	4,659	3,503	1,478	1,869	227	660	247	385	410	536	1,068	1,362
District of Columbia												
Washington city	37,724	30,328	9,429	14,182	2,225	4,435	1,866	2,976	2,020	4,175	6,857	9,962
Florida												
Boca Raton city	9,068	8,622	852	3,516	360	1,729	212	603	191	698	587	1,904
Boynton Beach city	5,856	8,636	1,316	3,965	265	1,696	424	1,000	245	909	692	2,613
Cape Coral city	16,447	11,640	3,314	5,263	1,411	2,832	217	845	809	1,634	2,299	3,318
Clearwater city	10,700	11,350	2,177	5,170	632	1,977	220	1,138	494	1,565	1,501	4,001
Coral Springs city	7,048	4,048	1,681	2,452	560	1,247	205	536	205	747	1,155	1,723
Deerfield Beach city	6,928	9,066	1,991	4,618	514	2,066	240	873	431	1,356	1,344	2,947
Deltona city	6,273	5,480	1,561	2,694	446	1,290	240	526	353	808	1,124	1,519
Fort Lauderdale city	14,799	11,783	3,621	5,685	1,235	2,258	840	1,085	756	1,860	2,207	4,296
Gainesville city	4,879	5,138	1,414	2,549	646	1,084	254	421	353	847	897	1,553
Hialeah city	21,980	21,525	5,947	11,198	1,283	4,255	1,677	3,572	3,054	6,202	3,662	7,943
Hollywood city	10,706	10,412	2,570	5,318	608	2,037	631	914	837	1,972	1,662	3,570
Jacksonville city	52,512	38,575	14,463	19,731	4,089	8,195	2,492	4,489	2,946	5,920	9,495	14,017
Lakeland city	9,973	9,412	2,435	4,150	677	1,930	353	744	448	969	1,698	2,784
Largo city	9,170	9,522	1,910	4,378	1,014	2,189	206	1,070	433	1,072	846	2,969
Lauderhill city	4,661	3,510	1,951	1,762	341	694	517	233	662	534	1,277	1,223
Melbourne city	7,331	8,016	1,682	3,775	631	1,363	118	745	383	1,186	1,251	2,951
Miami city	30,572	31,586	8,876	17,020	1,187	5,736	1,512	4,130	3,256	7,136	6,031	12,388
Miami Beach city	6,485	6,759	1,505	3,819	303	1,393	139	1,296	447	1,502	940	3,039
Miami Gardens city	7,355	4,892	1,990	2,318	538	527	316	473	640	864	1,304	1,810
Miramar city	4,900	4,401	864	2,189	370	439	119	589	211	735	579	1,579
Orlando city	12,319	9,918	3,265	4,720	897	1,683	751	939	650	1,059	2,029	3,147
Palm Bay city	8,873	7,839	2,239	3,978	820	1,503	534	964	319	1,189	1,211	2,529
Palm Coast city	10,823	7,572	2,532	3,219	840	1,474	552	726	238	989	1,272	1,758
Pembroke Pines city	11,473	12,118	2,251	6,195	390	2,273	594	908	574	2,208	1,590	4,662
Plantation city	6,641	5,597	1,322	2,721	278	1,172	235	709	254	764	915	1,871
Pompano Beach city	8,062	10,420	1,471	5,405	431	1,943	293	1,039	320	1,617	903	3,786
Port St. Lucie city	14,883	11,931	3,541	5,204	1,357	2,407	382	1,017	255	1,425	2,103	3,412
St. Petersburg city	20,655	16,931	5,090	8,701	1,530	3,539	665	1,471	983	2,727	3,263	6,068
Sunrise city	6,161	6,546	1,713	3,673	378	1,361	270	968	491	1,342	1,077	2,656
Tallahassee city	7,746	6,688	1,970	3,304	759	1,548	396	643	396	970	967	2,206
Tampa city	19,663	17,056	5,566	9,265	1,663	3,622	921	2,344	1,367	3,051	3,903	6,509
Weston city	3,198	1,909	126	764	26	174	42	131	25	385	58	596
West Palm Beach city	8,661	7,846	1,333	3,948	275	1,647	339	764	239	1,109	872	2,886
Georgia												
Albany city	4,655	4,198	1,562	2,390	454	1,172	273	674	362	844	1,175	1,744
Athens-Clarke County unified govt (bal)	5,684	4,196	1,769	2,270	298	912	203	367	397	711	1,263	1,324
Atlanta city	23,399	17,575	6,796	9,487	1,382	2,880	1,553	1,958	1,641	3,526	5,160	7,122
Augusta-Richmond County consolidated govt (bal)	12,657	9,292	4,370	5,409	1,539	2,253	803	1,453	1,247	2,127	3,003	3,913
Columbus city	11,408	10,100	4,510	5,747	1,502	2,309	1,243	1,479	1,340	1,770	3,170	4,270
Johns Creek city	3,728	2,336	396	997	213	280	0	158	0	318	223	623
Macon city	5,387	5,028	1,540	2,636	278	1,126	271	445	414	895	1,066	1,931
Roswell city	6,792	3,815	1,124	1,863	524	755	94	320	201	609	398	1,455
Sandy Springs city	5,965	4,562	803	2,027	166	935	174	405	197	770	368	1,175
Savannah city	8,278	7,723	2,494	4,553	568	1,737	375	844	649	1,653	1,910	3,093
Warner Robins city	3,634	2,938	1,348	1,361	390	363	131	272	160	401	950	902
Hawaii												
Urban Honolulu CDP	27,731	31,831	4,794	14,293	1,808	6,753	700	1,845	1,139	4,902	3,048	9,229

Table H-3: Places—Disability Status and Type of Disability—*Continued*

	Total Population		With a Disability		With a Hearing Difficulty		With a Vision Difficulty		With a Cognitive Difficulty		With an Ambulatory Difficulty	
	65 to 74 Years	75 Years and Over	65 to 74 Years	75 Years and Over	65 to 74 Years	75 Years and Over	65 to 74 Years	75 Years and Over	65 to 74 Years	75 Years and Over	65 to 74 Years	75 Years and Over
Idaho												
Boise City city	13,874	10,759	3,322	5,229	1,325	2,769	604	1,584	914	1,144	2,004	2,869
Meridian city	3,824	3,233	564	1,624	353	793	0	533	2	389	232	1,104
Nampa city	5,094	3,693	1,722	2,170	750	1,060	259	258	274	481	1,060	1,581
Illinois												
Aurora city	8,098	4,642	1,442	2,230	414	1,138	277	562	305	606	654	1,444
Bloomington city	3,710	3,881	858	2,119	342	996	71	349	169	495	542	1,404
Champaign city	3,667	2,957	804	1,248	223	484	73	282	37	207	632	792
Chicago city	152,494	122,834	44,016	66,898	9,224	22,860	8,908	14,750	10,035	20,819	31,772	48,476
Decatur city	5,845	5,925	1,322	2,809	602	1,465	197	717	183	506	835	1,914
Elgin city	5,339	3,946	1,457	1,915	274	877	80	579	212	796	1,135	1,449
Evanston city	4,443	3,670	748	1,896	270	720	306	445	249	578	390	1,214
Joliet city	6,347	5,553	1,441	2,948	576	1,102	378	558	387	1,059	920	1,991
Naperville city	7,625	5,308	1,104	2,452	375	1,238	135	539	90	620	795	1,651
Peoria city	7,433	7,021	1,561	3,115	478	1,174	232	491	345	785	1,058	2,033
Rockford city	10,382	9,443	2,920	4,538	968	1,931	646	796	542	1,172	1,929	2,980
Springfield city	8,333	8,247	2,255	4,255	770	1,838	234	848	397	1,148	1,311	2,826
Waukegan city	3,443	2,862	950	1,395	341	488	115	451	309	271	687	906
Indiana												
Bloomington city	3,113	3,267	618	1,491	204	795	97	412	141	379	419	851
Carmel city	5,394	3,032	828	1,452	503	571	94	186	145	447	443	1,136
Evansville city	8,080	8,157	2,378	4,102	722	1,833	254	694	289	777	1,669	2,919
Fort Wayne city	15,458	14,487	3,860	6,622	1,029	2,858	630	1,210	877	2,020	2,619	4,577
Gary city	6,390	5,245	2,371	2,951	408	1,142	429	633	394	1,033	1,738	1,936
Hammond city	4,232	4,146	1,564	2,045	575	1,047	258	280	383	654	1,073	1,306
Indianapolis city (bal)	46,003	37,440	13,220	18,394	4,273	7,442	2,260	3,188	2,692	5,208	8,643	12,840
Lafayette city	3,844	3,490	1,123	1,698	456	731	81	313	209	455	828	1,246
Muncie city	4,540	4,114	1,472	2,111	696	977	226	435	404	492	887	1,439
South Bend city	6,134	6,459	1,790	3,459	551	1,602	336	496	394	1,107	1,071	2,393
Iowa												
Cedar Rapids city	7,732	8,110	1,844	3,986	877	1,652	192	667	264	1,282	1,011	2,394
Davenport city	6,432	5,503	1,703	2,391	612	1,144	258	467	343	728	952	1,608
Des Moines city	11,574	9,649	2,796	4,668	928	2,140	403	890	671	1,342	1,968	3,284
Iowa City city	2,902	2,683	602	1,396	170	627	26	180	135	328	388	1,018
Sioux City city	5,490	4,699	1,264	2,185	406	970	123	587	116	659	888	1,423
Waterloo city	4,542	4,647	1,330	2,244	423	945	57	354	256	571	834	1,402
Kansas												
Kansas City city	8,593	6,675	2,800	4,001	832	1,998	445	540	598	1,007	1,878	2,676
Lawrence city	3,422	3,290	787	1,641	316	870	96	517	163	488	520	1,175
Olathe city	5,312	3,615	855	2,101	254	749	128	221	182	367	579	1,551
Overland Park city	11,677	10,231	2,123	4,411	898	2,092	124	885	444	1,344	1,165	2,863
Topeka city	8,590	8,417	2,127	4,287	852	1,634	292	674	481	998	1,376	2,882
Wichita city	23,537	19,988	6,782	10,382	2,310	4,897	950	1,946	1,596	2,951	4,467	6,896
Kentucky												
Lexington-Fayette urban county	17,511	13,304	4,734	7,091	1,769	3,154	511	1,385	1,086	2,061	2,786	4,924
Louisville/Jefferson County metro govt (bal)	39,979	34,195	11,669	18,437	2,966	7,650	1,815	3,892	3,175	5,737	7,733	12,190
Louisiana												
Baton Rouge city	13,824	11,344	4,698	5,849	1,423	2,308	752	1,170	1,006	1,960	3,365	4,093
Kenner city	5,405	3,311	1,759	1,720	303	740	399	395	376	553	1,110	1,204
Lafayette city	8,230	6,316	1,967	3,134	597	887	229	531	509	1,048	1,396	2,095
Lake Charles city	5,175	4,477	1,730	2,344	782	819	312	353	422	847	921	1,511
New Orleans city	22,397	16,609	6,689	9,584	1,695	3,206	1,883	2,729	1,741	3,743	4,671	6,817
Shreveport city	13,034	11,486	4,320	6,342	1,251	2,559	1,103	1,438	1,068	2,149	2,804	4,199
Maine												
Portland city	3,415	4,044	802	2,074	272	895	175	446	310	582	504	1,457
Maryland												
Baltimore city	38,649	31,835	13,247	16,840	2,652	5,137	2,548	3,905	2,806	5,445	9,786	11,613
Frederick city	3,832	2,859	938	1,403	243	895	155	282	282	330	354	834
Massachusetts												
Boston city	33,411	28,515	10,214	16,013	2,713	5,933	2,184	3,622	3,048	5,033	6,328	10,498
Brockton city	6,159	5,101	2,022	2,883	444	1,345	424	805	329	1,188	1,400	1,879
Cambridge city	6,370	4,911	1,436	1,970	270	653	180	387	445	438	978	1,401
Fall River city	6,629	5,963	2,223	3,034	574	1,186	503	389	567	612	1,484	2,171
Lawrence city	3,341	2,657	1,117	1,607	284	715	329	464	417	527	869	1,059
Lowell city	5,782	4,863	1,822	2,398	485	1,140	222	492	458	811	1,146	1,689
Lynn city	5,438	4,676	1,751	2,547	485	1,082	479	627	476	725	1,231	1,464
New Bedford city	6,592	6,710	1,899	3,521	513	1,397	305	548	465	1,019	1,372	2,381
Newton city	6,527	6,502	1,124	2,834	375	1,172	181	364	274	657	705	1,613
Quincy city	6,959	6,161	1,603	2,866	561	1,349	278	559	372	955	912	1,739
Somerville city	3,165	3,193	836	1,545	331	776	82	268	273	354	584	934
Springfield city	9,243	7,272	3,171	4,102	833	1,424	772	723	942	1,240	2,387	3,001
Worcester city	10,939	10,008	3,237	5,082	974	1,965	525	1,193	848	1,347	1,921	3,542

Table H-3: Places—Disability Status and Type of Disability—*Continued*

	Total Population		With a Disability		With a Hearing Difficulty		With a Vision Difficulty		With a Cognitive Difficulty		With an Ambulatory Difficulty	
	65 to 74 Years	75 Years and Over	65 to 74 Years	75 Years and Over	65 to 74 Years	75 Years and Over	65 to 74 Years	75 Years and Over	65 to 74 Years	75 Years and Over	65 to 74 Years	75 Years and Over
Michigan												
Ann Arbor city	6,112	5,295	1,233	2,074	297	808	263	439	181	762	950	1,201
Dearborn city	5,217	5,595	1,352	2,695	399	1,118	382	525	472	733	823	1,788
Detroit city	43,903	37,551	16,935	21,948	3,152	6,871	3,969	5,566	4,763	7,520	12,781	16,047
Farmington Hills city	6,302	6,512	1,328	2,651	400	1,082	152	374	349	663	831	1,765
Flint city	6,301	5,233	2,255	2,750	355	1,125	376	436	465	1,030	1,606	2,151
Grand Rapids city	8,704	10,558	2,495	5,048	715	2,329	374	889	693	1,353	1,550	3,130
Kalamazoo city	3,135	3,475	737	1,713	192	856	264	290	209	491	575	1,211
Lansing city	6,471	4,950	2,247	2,735	641	943	546	720	519	985	1,379	1,732
Livonia city	7,822	8,724	1,616	3,801	593	1,876	154	503	268	875	1,035	2,686
Rochester Hills city	4,949	4,459	845	2,257	378	861	141	268	130	700	502	1,584
Southfield city	6,340	5,950	1,456	3,414	383	1,173	349	561	458	1,153	899	2,269
Sterling Heights city	10,905	8,993	2,707	4,731	948	2,198	410	1,009	460	1,817	1,660	3,149
Troy city	6,591	4,959	1,358	2,075	453	981	266	476	184	672	767	1,226
Warren city	9,286	10,742	2,411	5,473	778	2,351	415	879	507	1,577	1,570	3,840
Westland city	6,217	5,509	1,777	2,964	510	1,271	253	540	302	790	1,256	2,059
Wyoming city	3,312	2,978	712	1,564	301	583	134	274	181	508	444	1,166
Minnesota												
Bloomington city	8,290	7,033	1,596	2,793	651	1,295	118	385	256	495	804	1,614
Brooklyn Park city	3,916	2,273	860	1,296	310	622	133	172	213	426	527	925
Duluth city	5,507	5,774	1,597	2,654	707	1,264	173	405	416	549	886	1,567
Minneapolis city	17,299	13,366	4,579	5,998	1,206	2,307	743	1,001	1,197	1,346	2,957	3,772
Plymouth city	5,133	3,756	631	1,690	215	951	122	342	129	410	315	953
Rochester city	6,827	6,378	1,086	2,854	587	1,325	84	604	100	672	500	1,628
St. Cloud city	3,246	3,322	555	1,370	271	647	152	158	110	228	338	853
St. Paul city	13,376	11,067	3,739	5,875	1,432	2,607	809	913	1,124	1,551	2,256	3,585
Mississippi												
Gulfport city	4,382	3,705	1,425	2,129	316	688	113	336	169	754	1,132	1,577
Jackson city	9,505	7,578	3,142	4,408	476	1,407	749	910	743	1,501	2,313	3,269
Missouri												
Columbia city	4,952	4,295	1,234	2,321	506	1,158	184	453	223	765	757	1,515
Independence city	9,658	8,645	2,782	4,628	937	1,963	232	875	770	1,155	2,256	3,274
Kansas City city	27,221	22,896	7,055	11,343	2,395	4,721	1,237	2,214	1,506	3,320	4,131	7,417
Lee's Summit city	5,509	5,103	1,065	2,723	241	1,085	185	570	263	782	626	1,780
O'Fallon city	4,095	3,248	1,040	1,757	317	731	102	474	233	568	658	1,143
St. Charles city	4,311	4,085	829	2,007	265	857	136	280	205	612	652	1,418
St. Joseph city	5,013	4,838	1,823	2,643	429	1,422	311	635	335	694	1,229	1,670
St. Louis city	17,855	16,347	6,225	8,155	1,376	3,008	1,618	1,605	1,441	2,266	4,303	5,546
Springfield city	10,818	11,203	3,365	5,780	950	2,536	649	1,175	796	1,643	2,123	3,758
Montana												
Billings city	7,714	7,302	1,881	3,139	837	1,628	340	859	430	592	938	1,970
Missoula city	3,726	3,536	656	1,772	383	964	119	429	21	397	438	1,224
Nebraska												
Lincoln city	14,499	13,326	2,843	6,701	1,072	3,167	247	1,316	695	1,309	1,740	4,082
Omaha city	23,845	21,778	4,772	10,712	1,938	4,729	692	2,503	908	3,048	2,781	7,135
Nevada												
Henderson city	24,778	14,607	5,577	6,704	2,339	3,020	777	1,027	876	1,459	2,978	4,689
Las Vegas city	43,906	31,065	11,634	15,827	3,339	7,077	1,963	3,081	1,841	4,044	7,741	10,545
North Las Vegas city	10,469	5,324	2,484	2,990	962	1,136	359	550	439	1,040	1,594	1,682
Reno city	15,369	11,553	3,784	5,305	1,406	2,189	506	948	630	1,543	2,318	3,514
Sparks city	6,940	3,890	1,995	1,980	672	934	113	360	413	552	1,424	1,335
New Hampshire												
Manchester city	7,278	5,347	1,777	2,761	564	1,428	256	617	361	660	995	1,542
Nashua city	5,720	4,864	1,451	1,991	654	998	100	368	227	464	663	1,296
New Jersey												
Camden city	3,871	2,040	1,387	1,028	314	283	540	345	490	423	1,042	745
Clifton city	5,582	5,091	1,606	2,641	510	1,024	432	642	417	838	1,190	1,930
Elizabeth city	6,500	4,586	1,406	2,428	488	842	391	531	266	627	870	1,859
Jersey City city	13,754	8,649	4,265	4,221	676	1,332	823	1,069	1,029	1,117	3,254	3,048
Newark city	13,069	9,406	4,782	5,916	796	1,270	1,503	1,793	905	1,663	3,219	4,327
Passaic city	3,131	2,190	1,062	1,327	451	639	655	542	428	445	642	1,016
Paterson city	8,362	5,069	2,527	2,614	507	984	454	845	554	1,126	1,942	1,930
Trenton city	3,865	3,095	1,270	1,535	222	515	327	360	283	419	890	1,179
Union City city	3,421	2,871	1,154	1,751	318	583	293	450	294	444	785	1,185
New Mexico												
Albuquerque city	36,803	30,370	9,715	15,950	3,470	7,416	1,675	3,346	1,607	4,819	6,163	10,412
Las Cruces city	6,890	5,800	1,791	3,012	739	1,285	355	649	468	715	966	2,080
Rio Rancho city	6,149	3,881	1,748	2,161	624	1,312	180	666	569	570	1,057	1,409
Santa Fe city	7,538	5,365	1,813	2,826	876	1,545	234	624	426	790	896	1,616

Table H-3: Places—Disability Status and Type of Disability—*Continued*

	Total Population		With a Disability		With a Hearing Difficulty		With a Vision Difficulty		With a Cognitive Difficulty		With an Ambulatory Difficulty	
	65 to 74 Years	75 Years and Over	65 to 74 Years	75 Years and Over	65 to 74 Years	75 Years and Over	65 to 74 Years	75 Years and Over	65 to 74 Years	75 Years and Over	65 to 74 Years	75 Years and Over
New York												
Albany city	5,781	5,058	1,420	2,580	324	1,031	220	540	267	679	992	1,656
Buffalo city	14,994	13,847	4,724	7,535	1,299	2,995	776	1,293	1,004	2,081	3,592	5,455
Mount Vernon city	4,855	3,836	1,267	1,959	217	567	221	433	181	602	985	1,452
New Rochelle city	5,071	5,034	1,052	2,232	282	898	131	443	235	602	732	1,504
New York city	543,252	443,408	134,680	228,915	28,710	74,256	26,682	50,612	35,198	73,354	96,183	175,696
Rochester city	10,168	7,440	3,098	4,131	663	1,334	536	864	670	1,266	2,210	2,935
Schenectady city	3,771	3,660	873	1,976	228	595	201	391	221	540	563	1,297
Syracuse city	6,907	6,544	1,702	3,128	424	1,474	449	960	514	663	1,150	2,011
Yonkers city	14,662	13,648	2,811	6,567	835	2,692	474	1,324	651	1,416	1,881	4,542
North Carolina												
Asheville city	6,267	6,015	1,618	3,577	443	1,425	230	742	400	926	903	2,526
Charlotte city	36,818	27,965	8,059	14,442	2,161	5,786	1,161	2,810	1,714	4,162	5,322	9,557
Concord city	5,259	3,394	1,055	1,742	393	804	125	382	193	472	812	1,123
Durham city	11,596	8,897	2,388	5,021	756	2,370	601	1,179	583	1,529	1,499	3,542
Fayetteville city	11,181	8,323	3,515	4,313	935	1,690	545	694	818	1,250	2,496	2,992
Gastonia city	4,437	3,448	1,339	1,917	455	866	169	415	341	595	893	1,233
Greensboro city	16,077	15,188	3,206	7,095	1,078	3,162	307	1,629	718	1,985	1,942	4,655
Greenville city	3,410	2,699	700	1,610	243	890	166	181	155	444	575	959
High Point city	6,669	5,368	1,387	2,985	280	1,267	249	625	281	627	1,051	1,756
Jacksonville city	2,339	1,745	957	781	288	387	223	241	135	322	696	588
Raleigh city	18,976	14,968	4,355	6,862	1,295	2,844	640	1,300	884	2,024	2,763	4,612
Wilmington city	7,913	6,487	2,170	3,517	567	1,584	386	641	523	998	1,398	2,256
Winston-Salem city	15,033	13,056	3,081	5,872	704	1,804	675	1,091	743	1,577	1,700	4,026
North Dakota												
Fargo city	5,019	5,384	946	2,125	354	856	94	673	152	435	534	1,172
Ohio												
Akron city	12,964	11,681	3,991	5,662	924	2,223	510	1,062	707	1,360	2,998	3,713
Canton city	4,513	4,652	1,251	2,370	417	706	237	438	283	837	830	1,602
Cincinnati city	16,466	14,343	4,714	7,952	1,164	2,580	884	1,526	891	1,983	3,341	5,517
Cleveland city	24,587	22,152	8,620	12,466	2,118	3,968	1,570	3,162	2,138	3,891	6,405	9,131
Columbus city	38,888	29,451	11,394	15,080	3,360	6,345	2,057	3,241	3,106	4,636	7,763	10,125
Dayton city	8,752	7,406	3,507	4,247	1,169	1,402	607	974	1,098	1,094	2,710	2,899
Parma city	6,805	7,176	1,330	3,392	294	1,390	207	457	143	973	861	2,154
Toledo city	17,194	16,222	5,532	8,403	1,558	3,910	915	1,679	1,213	2,393	4,128	5,148
Youngstown city	4,371	5,417	1,224	2,631	359	928	221	541	286	703	841	1,734
Oklahoma												
Broken Arrow city	6,301	4,102	1,468	1,866	568	956	201	321	167	496	761	1,304
Edmond city	5,405	3,873	1,159	1,985	532	793	96	322	238	544	599	1,376
Lawton city	5,036	4,046	1,935	2,486	788	1,242	350	444	395	706	1,309	1,798
Norman city	6,925	5,025	2,058	2,681	976	1,422	245	413	418	1,026	1,187	1,702
Oklahoma City city	35,599	28,700	10,887	15,760	3,890	6,728	2,099	3,129	1,827	3,953	6,746	10,728
Tulsa city	25,402	22,643	6,777	11,074	2,470	5,124	1,318	2,409	1,198	2,578	4,396	7,242
Oregon												
Beaverton city	5,435	4,260	1,198	2,342	293	868	206	595	394	1,071	679	1,676
Bend city	6,120	5,065	1,041	2,550	362	1,378	117	426	223	648	545	1,684
Eugene city	10,730	9,784	2,717	5,359	1,407	2,205	339	1,029	553	1,740	1,347	3,400
Gresham city	6,500	5,048	1,832	2,721	689	1,426	330	539	347	924	1,031	1,949
Hillsboro city	4,617	2,543	1,269	1,494	480	574	198	345	331	489	868	1,085
Medford city	5,720	6,335	1,647	2,888	705	1,260	342	381	434	690	913	1,837
Portland city	33,837	27,707	8,373	15,360	2,782	6,021	1,209	3,526	2,147	4,659	4,831	9,736
Salem city	10,789	8,581	2,851	3,909	922	2,278	827	748	787	1,028	2,028	2,631
Pennsylvania												
Allentown city	6,131	7,019	2,081	3,483	659	1,215	732	766	732	926	1,277	2,574
Bethlehem city	4,740	5,560	1,331	2,485	436	925	275	493	284	561	962	1,447
Erie city	6,209	6,280	1,840	3,269	421	1,471	150	652	324	886	1,275	2,088
Philadelphia city	95,260	84,603	30,288	45,955	6,780	16,040	5,971	9,580	7,630	14,369	21,689	32,016
Pittsburgh city	20,411	20,469	4,969	10,173	1,300	4,170	847	1,889	1,068	2,552	3,394	6,952
Reading city	4,321	3,807	1,393	2,211	328	765	172	213	360	814	1,013	1,615
Scranton city	5,141	6,423	1,367	3,404	523	1,310	189	715	232	570	925	2,361
Rhode Island												
Cranston city	5,625	6,320	1,138	2,894	384	1,306	174	467	159	513	667	1,593
Pawtucket city	4,579	4,228	1,528	2,085	524	799	175	568	239	571	940	1,475
Providence city	7,470	6,664	2,302	3,924	427	1,672	436	686	629	873	1,409	2,415
Warwick city	7,006	7,071	1,559	3,478	425	1,394	236	548	454	880	828	1,906
South Carolina												
Charleston city	8,361	6,432	2,027	3,184	488	1,138	428	659	600	941	1,450	2,256
Columbia city	5,541	5,360	1,446	3,181	519	1,067	264	517	308	928	816	2,266
North Charleston city	5,117	3,096	1,553	1,597	553	619	233	383	352	447	888	1,096
Rock Hill city	3,305	2,982	1,122	1,477	219	505	220	344	201	560	744	1,075
South Dakota												
Rapid City city	4,933	4,608	1,113	2,337	502	1,344	100	399	267	563	608	1,499
Sioux Falls city	8,832	8,123	1,854	3,938	628	1,951	258	804	264	1,034	1,196	2,373

Table H-3: Places—Disability Status and Type of Disability—*Continued*

	Total Population		With a Disability		With a Hearing Difficulty		With a Vision Difficulty		With a Cognitive Difficulty		With an Ambulatory Difficulty	
	65 to 74 Years	75 Years and Over	65 to 74 Years	75 Years and Over	65 to 74 Years	75 Years and Over	65 to 74 Years	75 Years and Over	65 to 74 Years	75 Years and Over	65 to 74 Years	75 Years and Over
Tennessee												
Chattanooga city	13,049	11,287	3,903	6,107	1,194	2,253	552	1,532	1,095	2,105	2,873	4,356
Clarksville city	5,832	3,872	1,781	2,048	492	736	206	515	466	716	1,291	1,386
Jackson city	4,605	3,811	1,482	2,230	595	1,000	120	501	157	687	941	1,382
Knoxville city	13,528	11,332	3,317	5,910	897	2,357	515	1,209	798	1,954	2,439	4,235
Memphis city	36,400	29,840	12,076	16,558	3,003	6,339	2,511	3,681	2,863	5,516	8,374	11,690
Murfreesboro city	5,583	3,804	1,295	1,755	299	755	68	386	158	688	961	1,150
Nashville-Davidson metropolitan government (bal)	34,356	27,512	8,941	14,466	3,043	6,230	1,343	2,577	2,371	4,128	6,250	9,286
Texas												
Abilene city	7,480	6,735	2,489	4,068	1,207	2,176	547	1,194	476	1,417	1,624	2,710
Allen city	3,410	1,867	721	1,073	121	651	87	175	22	214	523	604
Amarillo city	11,937	10,248	3,370	5,575	1,185	2,542	596	1,158	583	1,509	2,262	3,996
Arlington city	17,967	11,634	4,711	5,665	2,030	2,530	613	1,098	813	1,899	2,753	4,015
Austin city	32,164	24,327	7,251	12,666	2,456	5,282	1,067	2,844	1,637	3,993	4,657	8,714
Baytown city	3,024	3,352	1,076	2,326	315	998	101	391	163	788	800	1,574
Beaumont city	7,649	6,768	2,915	4,128	1,082	1,686	832	1,051	696	1,497	2,080	2,810
Brownsville city	9,758	7,128	3,709	4,763	1,240	2,027	959	1,047	1,050	1,915	2,698	3,400
Bryan city	4,039	3,128	1,264	1,511	478	679	182	224	151	512	878	1,072
Carrollton city	6,614	3,415	1,383	1,596	569	676	242	326	139	533	877	1,159
College Station city	2,855	1,742	570	709	234	337	105	148	60	248	407	465
Corpus Christi city	19,469	16,021	6,457	9,055	2,368	4,451	1,200	2,280	1,665	3,056	4,357	6,812
Dallas city	61,010	47,708	16,860	24,972	4,506	9,431	3,294	5,679	4,340	8,212	11,765	18,018
Denton city	6,296	3,431	1,527	1,469	768	478	256	301	429	435	904	991
Edinburg city	3,244	2,289	1,317	1,377	484	512	384	307	398	402	907	981
El Paso city	39,880	34,033	13,173	19,333	3,983	8,314	2,653	4,305	2,883	6,167	8,908	13,844
Fort Worth city	34,496	26,491	9,853	14,090	3,499	5,844	1,986	2,673	2,218	4,326	6,634	9,739
Frisco city	5,225	2,328	904	1,077	396	350	26	111	37	309	616	853
Garland city	12,277	8,322	3,406	4,550	1,183	1,971	709	938	825	1,663	2,317	3,407
Grand Prairie city	7,953	4,333	2,098	1,925	740	880	141	586	433	640	1,334	1,458
Harlingen city	4,537	3,820	1,270	2,056	479	808	280	365	501	718	978	1,540
Houston city	110,662	82,278	30,753	43,845	9,571	17,465	6,145	9,771	8,043	13,282	20,544	31,226
Irving city	8,178	6,144	1,687	3,225	610	1,527	243	743	460	872	1,009	2,147
Killeen city	4,129	2,491	1,524	1,407	533	495	433	281	456	360	830	1,092
Laredo city	10,958	8,011	4,923	5,761	1,213	2,758	1,570	1,634	1,597	2,348	3,136	4,249
League City city	4,430	2,539	1,307	1,358	706	745	361	250	146	544	874	865
Lewisville city	4,332	2,573	1,048	1,476	215	603	274	255	155	666	815	1,035
Longview city	4,770	5,712	1,434	2,823	402	1,244	203	588	366	968	944	1,997
Lubbock city	13,557	11,384	4,303	6,254	1,612	3,108	471	1,445	908	1,689	2,904	4,375
McAllen city	8,079	5,411	3,060	3,402	973	1,443	632	843	1,027	965	2,058	2,349
McKinney city	5,835	3,886	834	1,880	424	815	87	182	117	560	368	1,599
Mesquite city	6,610	5,176	1,971	2,647	516	1,168	244	683	340	1,057	1,317	1,814
Midland city	6,170	6,357	2,216	3,648	812	1,335	360	1,075	414	1,162	1,497	2,694
Mission city	4,481	3,694	1,681	2,166	499	867	505	589	291	375	1,050	1,234
Missouri City city	4,532	2,449	946	1,021	245	361	167	219	262	303	565	638
Odessa city	5,340	4,815	1,766	2,827	747	1,258	343	574	431	519	1,066	1,723
Pasadena city	7,014	5,776	2,213	3,096	1,182	1,283	427	724	450	1,007	1,367	1,947
Pearland city	4,037	3,027	581	1,399	190	371	85	326	115	441	341	867
Pharr city	3,481	4,448	1,096	2,844	363	1,739	423	801	400	923	701	1,877
Plano city	15,976	9,333	2,379	4,697	892	2,243	279	842	533	1,737	1,700	2,936
Richardson city	6,906	5,265	1,360	2,547	612	1,104	175	498	175	813	783	1,511
Round Rock city	4,515	1,924	1,285	870	388	474	303	151	371	319	737	560
San Angelo city	6,610	6,023	1,738	2,794	646	1,286	325	655	235	724	1,078	1,935
San Antonio city	79,545	62,731	26,579	36,318	9,247	15,404	5,250	8,942	6,275	11,653	17,822	26,126
Sugar Land city	5,313	3,316	675	1,454	226	559	20	268	130	423	475	952
Temple city	4,925	4,527	1,522	2,544	765	1,139	162	275	368	806	782	1,672
Tyler city	6,729	7,098	1,569	3,862	525	1,713	370	1,072	347	1,359	1,187	2,627
Waco city	6,317	6,679	2,199	3,572	758	1,394	403	868	383	1,019	1,620	2,474
Wichita Falls city	6,086	5,709	1,661	3,078	594	1,471	326	997	271	885	1,052	2,243
Utah												
Layton city	3,046	2,163	682	772	282	353	28	185	128	93	394	475
Ogden city	3,820	3,724	992	1,736	308	832	142	322	222	438	578	1,109
Orem city	4,251	3,117	939	1,434	472	667	123	295	93	353	504	946
Provo city	3,255	3,347	715	1,806	399	863	41	380	101	590	308	1,215
St. George city	6,227	6,658	1,307	2,864	687	1,293	151	514	182	635	654	1,646
Salt Lake City city	9,319	8,130	2,182	4,441	918	2,349	369	1,308	499	1,402	1,335	2,780
Sandy city	5,673	2,873	1,096	1,303	361	876	101	384	170	418	637	841
West Jordan city	3,031	2,083	792	1,128	373	512	95	313	187	233	426	744
West Valley City city	5,939	3,515	1,666	1,544	776	762	178	166	328	509	958	801
Virginia												
Alexandria city	7,710	5,295	1,261	2,227	238	719	154	426	132	528	832	1,671
Chesapeake city	14,178	9,624	3,487	4,703	1,200	1,889	332	733	794	1,111	2,348	3,311
Hampton city	9,710	7,316	2,441	3,661	650	1,244	284	738	462	888	1,556	2,535
Lynchburg city	4,790	4,982	1,284	2,493	255	838	122	354	251	724	785	1,569
Newport News city	10,582	8,287	2,830	4,534	859	1,767	517	772	553	1,282	1,908	3,206
Norfolk city	11,755	10,598	3,579	5,771	994	2,352	877	1,006	893	1,654	2,246	3,929
Portsmouth city	6,511	5,981	2,471	2,905	683	967	627	548	547	968	1,644	2,133
Richmond city	11,868	10,587	3,887	5,117	865	1,390	908	1,001	1,021	1,644	2,771	3,345
Roanoke city	6,725	6,392	2,122	3,098	690	1,199	329	667	564	874	1,283	2,033
Suffolk city	5,762	3,966	1,551	1,957	525	822	213	560	253	509	1,033	1,203
Virginia Beach city	26,995	20,359	5,706	10,033	1,759	3,904	652	1,523	1,292	3,046	3,921	6,688

Table H-3: Places—Disability Status and Type of Disability—*Continued*

	Total Population		With a Disability		With a Hearing Difficulty		With a Vision Difficulty		With a Cognitive Difficulty		With an Ambulatory Difficulty	
	65 to 74 Years	75 Years and Over	65 to 74 Years	75 Years and Over	65 to 74 Years	75 Years and Over	65 to 74 Years	75 Years and Over	65 to 74 Years	75 Years and Over	65 to 74 Years	75 Years and Over
Washington												
Auburn city	4,173	3,680	1,304	2,122	392	874	174	315	124	458	886	1,373
Bellevue city	8,102	8,903	1,256	3,941	288	1,850	148	678	324	695	699	2,363
Bellingham city	5,513	4,562	1,145	2,219	582	844	190	525	185	529	476	1,290
Everett city	5,623	4,831	1,428	2,825	338	1,182	187	614	381	919	988	2,040
Federal Way city	5,410	4,070	1,396	2,416	559	928	280	781	366	740	707	1,517
Kennewick city	4,396	3,821	1,054	1,734	337	896	164	249	185	387	636	1,273
Kent city	6,631	4,783	2,111	2,569	752	1,004	234	587	636	797	1,111	1,544
Renton city	5,076	4,139	1,240	2,424	518	631	89	393	203	956	596	1,884
Seattle city	36,996	29,542	8,106	15,043	2,606	6,088	1,256	2,766	1,997	4,915	4,687	9,751
Spokane city	13,935	13,696	4,052	7,001	1,571	3,400	675	1,507	889	2,100	2,766	4,466
Spokane Valley city	7,242	5,371	2,217	3,022	1,111	1,285	206	678	423	702	1,235	2,106
Tacoma city	11,626	10,383	3,893	5,584	1,406	2,605	718	1,335	796	1,662	2,494	3,611
Vancouver city	11,682	9,602	3,630	5,032	1,371	2,287	634	1,024	764	1,635	2,311	3,407
Yakima city	6,294	5,838	2,024	3,415	736	1,723	404	862	492	1,025	1,189	2,362
Wisconsin												
Appleton city	4,027	3,734	673	1,715	282	715	81	303	129	493	333	1,161
Eau Claire city	3,572	3,566	807	1,492	257	771	8	179	254	358	448	1,014
Green Bay city	5,686	6,018	1,418	3,143	426	1,062	174	408	205	995	983	2,259
Kenosha city	5,418	4,998	1,479	2,478	425	1,297	178	466	313	498	1,036	1,550
Madison city	11,423	10,323	1,812	4,693	686	2,138	188	820	303	1,200	1,049	2,911
Milwaukee city	26,801	25,598	8,300	12,851	2,076	4,578	1,178	2,364	2,081	3,873	5,669	8,832
Oshkosh city	3,881	3,751	1,062	1,636	526	793	329	328	412	309	829	976
Racine city	4,676	3,904	1,326	1,693	353	773	233	295	341	363	877	1,099
Waukesha city	3,933	3,451	875	1,972	342	949	50	292	54	415	528	1,231

Table H-4: Metropolitan Statistical Areas—Disability Status and Type of Disability

	Total Population		With a Disability		With a Hearing Difficulty		With a Vision Difficulty		With a Cognitive Difficulty		With an Ambulatory Difficulty	
	65 to 74 Years	75 Years and Over	65 to 74 Years	75 Years and Over	65 to 74 Years	75 Years and Over	65 to 74 Years	75 Years and Over	65 to 74 Years	75 Years and Over	65 to 74 Years	75 Years and Over
Abilene, TX	11,979	10,122	3,785	5,856	1,802	3,149	957	1,554	751	1,961	2,409	3,909
Akron, OH	52,722	46,115	12,957	21,401	4,426	9,319	1,861	3,682	2,590	5,439	8,243	13,674
Albany, GA	11,192	8,211	3,498	4,374	1,096	2,033	714	1,246	935	1,581	2,577	3,028
Albany-Schenectady-Troy, NY	64,576	55,204	13,814	26,691	4,997	12,008	2,102	4,824	2,884	7,038	8,335	16,391
Albuquerque, NM	64,645	48,250	17,615	25,579	6,664	12,890	3,049	5,884	3,432	7,890	11,074	16,838
Alexandria, LA	11,641	8,578	4,610	5,100	1,476	2,669	1,205	1,529	1,352	1,782	3,184	3,761
Allentown-Bethlehem-Easton, PA-NJ	63,273	58,480	14,416	28,054	4,738	11,781	2,583	5,335	2,959	7,852	9,204	18,745
Altoona, PA	11,182	10,085	2,814	4,708	1,185	2,245	453	1,060	718	1,278	1,761	3,350
Amarillo, TX	16,266	12,784	4,577	6,743	1,843	3,139	769	1,349	742	1,760	2,808	4,762
Ames, IA	4,562	4,223	973	1,857	330	911	123	282	233	364	673	1,028
Anchorage, AK	19,093	10,478	5,484	5,694	2,677	2,638	737	1,546	1,214	1,902	3,002	3,938
Anderson, IN	10,937	8,953	3,483	4,834	1,404	2,490	631	903	693	1,461	2,252	3,144
Anderson, SC	16,614	11,862	5,464	6,326	1,398	3,194	1,200	1,588	1,315	1,731	3,713	3,873
Ann Arbor, MI	21,020	15,257	4,726	6,569	1,432	2,921	520	1,486	775	2,124	3,241	4,071
Anniston-Oxford, AL	9,623	7,405	4,131	4,093	1,213	1,629	690	718	937	1,364	2,993	3,031
Appleton, WI	14,218	12,165	2,649	5,100	1,225	2,174	205	749	395	1,188	1,391	3,189
Asheville, NC	42,949	34,653	9,615	17,687	3,745	8,345	1,868	3,579	1,903	4,434	5,260	11,443
Athens-Clarke County, GA	12,009	7,845	3,840	4,367	891	1,990	378	1,114	723	1,561	2,760	2,876
Atlanta-Sandy Springs-Marietta, GA	304,411	188,640	76,533	98,010	24,380	40,296	12,593	20,757	16,493	32,467	49,769	66,717
Atlantic City-Hammonton, NJ	21,807	16,910	5,296	7,567	1,585	3,139	675	1,254	1,016	1,863	3,470	4,999
Auburn-Opelika, AL	8,128	5,062	2,602	2,795	788	905	248	409	767	853	1,630	1,779
Augusta-Richmond County, GA-SC	41,905	28,238	12,389	15,247	4,321	6,261	2,096	3,547	3,577	5,050	8,196	10,826
Austin-Round Rock-San Marcos, TX	87,567	57,967	19,670	29,272	7,190	13,514	3,154	5,661	4,208	8,763	12,207	19,237
Bakersfield-Delano, CA	44,840	31,840	12,690	18,220	4,643	8,169	2,274	3,937	2,632	5,619	8,657	12,419
Baltimore-Towson, MD	190,416	152,846	43,782	72,434	13,548	28,965	6,505	13,635	8,564	21,018	28,011	46,896
Bangor, ME	12,011	9,992	3,880	5,076	1,616	2,459	522	883	1,108	1,408	2,319	3,294
Barnstable Town, MA	28,143	25,869	3,850	9,536	1,237	4,708	358	1,638	887	1,804	2,285	5,608
Baton Rouge, LA	51,505	35,575	16,330	19,795	5,519	8,565	3,075	4,078	2,940	6,232	10,755	13,460
Battle Creek, MI	10,534	9,152	3,159	4,579	1,028	2,164	518	1,025	702	1,406	2,129	2,979
Bay City, MI	9,508	7,849	2,784	3,829	1,280	2,050	417	677	742	1,183	1,608	2,298
Beaumont-Port Arthur, TX	26,490	23,230	9,268	13,845	3,852	6,325	2,125	3,752	2,322	4,779	6,224	9,513
Bellingham, WA	15,585	11,768	3,949	5,777	1,974	2,955	709	1,301	1,068	1,666	1,869	3,073
Bend, OR	15,013	10,034	2,805	4,825	1,149	2,649	326	1,013	636	1,189	1,385	3,003
Billings, MT	12,291	10,320	3,242	4,676	1,525	2,468	502	1,167	591	912	1,549	2,767
Binghamton, NY	20,518	18,897	4,615	8,904	1,619	4,030	573	1,703	751	1,947	2,974	5,448
Birmingham-Hoover, AL	82,553	63,565	24,557	35,193	7,277	14,877	3,799	7,374	5,630	11,220	17,305	24,426
Bismarck, ND	7,771	7,012	1,828	3,544	803	1,856	254	758	256	988	929	2,148
Blacksburg-Christiansburg-Radford, VA	11,825	8,293	3,271	4,430	1,530	2,320	886	869	566	973	2,229	2,888
Bloomington, IN	12,686	9,988	2,794	5,200	1,010	2,504	563	1,262	793	1,124	1,694	3,401
Bloomington-Normal, IL	9,492	7,621	2,046	3,667	871	1,683	200	540	332	776	1,317	2,378
Boise City-Nampa, ID	40,591	29,507	10,600	15,148	4,599	7,963	1,365	3,623	2,309	3,419	5,971	9,479
Boston-Cambridge-Quincy, MA-NH	319,056	272,404	68,568	128,493	23,811	56,595	10,723	25,413	15,535	34,447	39,555	79,644
Boulder, CO	18,134	12,381	2,981	4,872	1,335	2,401	266	1,129	565	1,483	1,486	3,117
Bowling Green, KY	8,421	6,047	2,548	3,273	811	1,585	338	619	571	836	1,773	2,302
Bremerton-Silverdale, WA	20,772	13,194	6,052	6,916	2,559	4,028	810	1,591	1,243	2,085	3,373	3,949
Bridgeport-Stamford-Norwalk, CT	64,611	57,679	11,421	25,878	3,252	11,925	1,955	4,714	2,150	7,134	6,589	16,376
Brownsville-Harlingen, TX	25,305	20,226	8,828	11,835	3,060	5,157	2,015	2,536	2,484	4,098	6,080	8,186
Brunswick, GA	10,727	6,623	3,495	3,386	1,318	1,570	693	703	910	991	2,299	2,452
Buffalo-Niagara Falls, NY	88,933	84,527	19,659	38,387	6,966	16,627	2,521	6,544	3,268	9,001	12,662	24,587
Burlington, NC	11,825	10,242	3,030	5,544	1,110	2,363	554	1,315	917	1,617	1,813	3,451
Burlington-South Burlington, VT	14,035	10,717	2,850	5,499	1,138	2,783	394	1,071	531	1,432	1,496	3,340
Canton-Massillon, OH	34,415	29,011	7,762	13,993	2,901	5,804	1,123	2,345	1,688	3,771	4,943	9,064
Cape Coral-Fort Myers, FL	85,960	65,873	16,660	28,205	7,002	13,709	1,696	4,989	3,251	8,647	9,926	17,784
Cape Girardeau-Jackson, MO-IL	7,596	6,042	2,222	3,641	902	1,541	304	652	533	1,138	1,306	2,504
Casper, WY	4,976	4,232	1,406	1,900	585	923	222	516	270	573	848	1,035
Cedar Rapids, IA	18,524	16,056	3,478	6,959	1,544	2,993	375	1,002	655	1,806	1,861	4,319
Champaign-Urbana, IL	13,643	11,490	3,286	5,354	985	2,422	419	1,010	512	1,369	2,349	3,353
Charleston, WV	27,103	21,186	9,199	11,677	3,566	5,129	1,639	2,584	2,199	3,631	6,366	8,641
Charleston-North Charleston-Summerville, SC	48,682	31,114	12,367	16,642	4,337	6,244	2,075	3,399	2,916	4,789	7,790	11,634
Charlotte-Gastonia-Rock Hill, NC-SC	107,360	73,656	26,178	37,833	8,482	16,145	3,719	7,307	6,082	11,598	16,665	25,963
Charlottesville, VA	15,807	12,092	3,324	5,644	1,138	2,933	543	1,158	801	1,774	1,995	3,424
Chattanooga, TN-GA	44,611	33,508	13,433	18,995	4,414	7,996	2,301	4,132	3,275	6,458	9,026	12,922
Cheyenne, WY	6,812	4,942	2,030	2,363	802	1,100	193	588	420	518	1,087	1,567
Chicago-Joliet-Naperville, IL-IN-WI	598,536	478,240	139,319	236,288	38,124	92,515	22,483	45,924	28,160	65,802	92,030	161,750
Chico, CA	17,642	15,960	4,940	8,529	1,637	4,220	660	1,366	1,224	2,491	2,928	5,184
Cincinnati-Middletown, OH-KY-IN	143,403	112,558	36,072	56,640	12,969	23,902	5,612	10,379	7,161	14,196	22,678	37,271
Clarksville, TN-KY	15,349	10,643	5,068	5,373	1,528	2,166	478	1,248	1,030	1,573	3,531	3,707
Cleveland, TN	10,500	6,708	4,145	3,824	1,918	1,699	877	947	972	1,314	2,839	2,576
Cleveland-Elyria-Mentor, OH	161,830	145,701	37,633	70,051	12,420	27,507	5,543	13,910	7,319	18,028	23,885	44,581
Coeur d'Alene, ID	12,144	8,561	2,811	4,016	1,483	1,892	354	631	591	1,056	1,260	2,442

Table H-4: Metropolitan Statistical Areas—Disability Status and Type of Disability—*Continued*

	Total Population		With a Disability		With a Hearing Difficulty		With a Vision Difficulty		With a Cognitive Difficulty		With an Ambulatory Difficulty	
	65 to 74 Years	75 Years and Over	65 to 74 Years	75 Years and Over	65 to 74 Years	75 Years and Over	65 to 74 Years	75 Years and Over	65 to 74 Years	75 Years and Over	65 to 74 Years	75 Years and Over
College Station-Bryan, TX	11,556	8,752	3,135	4,483	1,120	2,077	497	860	486	1,503	2,186	3,114
Colorado Springs, CO	39,814	27,484	8,899	13,211	4,029	6,682	1,343	2,673	1,618	3,108	4,874	8,009
Columbia, MO	9,364	7,340	2,290	3,711	861	1,923	409	658	415	971	1,441	2,344
Columbia, SC	53,264	35,682	14,738	18,607	4,111	7,850	2,579	3,763	3,330	5,702	9,568	13,161
Columbus, GA-AL	18,858	15,043	7,292	8,763	2,592	3,635	1,744	2,253	2,135	2,880	4,700	6,431
Columbus, IN	6,199	4,446	1,493	2,071	612	984	203	571	293	570	810	1,356
Columbus, OH	112,743	82,873	28,836	41,887	9,768	18,036	4,365	7,992	6,863	11,661	18,580	28,310
Corpus Christi, TX	31,102	23,978	11,161	13,840	4,457	6,765	2,330	3,731	2,916	4,932	7,580	9,964
Corvallis, OR	5,720	4,971	1,209	2,391	508	1,332	34	504	143	586	675	1,426
Crestview-Fort Walton Beach-Destin, FL	14,425	11,022	3,706	5,462	1,286	2,831	532	1,137	836	1,579	2,433	4,119
Cumberland, MD-WV	9,843	7,776	3,235	4,101	1,172	2,103	662	1,025	625	1,172	2,381	2,644
Dallas-Fort Worth-Arlington, TX	347,642	229,507	87,999	117,604	31,051	49,516	14,859	23,259	18,049	37,647	57,067	80,752
Dalton, GA	9,353	6,429	2,911	3,716	1,038	1,703	723	898	639	1,338	1,696	2,699
Danville, IL	6,938	5,820	2,287	2,657	689	1,305	265	479	656	457	1,550	1,665
Danville, VA	10,492	8,253	2,993	4,372	930	1,725	334	780	515	1,052	1,899	2,698
Davenport-Moline-Rock Island, IA-IL	30,862	25,713	7,104	11,753	2,883	5,924	1,115	2,471	1,098	3,065	4,281	7,427
Dayton, OH	67,159	56,588	17,343	27,465	6,144	12,474	2,646	5,380	3,723	6,792	11,272	16,965
Decatur, AL	13,036	8,678	4,154	5,037	1,687	2,074	646	962	1,039	1,605	2,526	3,499
Decatur, IL	9,261	8,022	2,323	3,706	861	1,987	286	855	475	672	1,543	2,439
Deltona-Daytona Beach-Ormond Beach, FL	55,341	49,069	11,711	22,739	4,749	11,162	1,881	4,083	2,230	5,950	6,809	14,557
Denver-Aurora-Broomfield, CO	154,014	110,506	33,778	54,899	13,840	27,272	5,153	12,162	5,726	14,930	18,945	34,096
Des Moines-West Des Moines, IA	35,360	27,607	7,633	12,584	2,836	6,111	848	2,121	1,480	3,118	4,828	7,831
Detroit-Warren-Livonia, MI	306,676	260,679	79,426	132,188	25,294	55,608	12,236	26,082	17,467	39,092	51,369	88,191
Dothan, AL	13,065	9,613	4,776	5,567	1,710	2,635	837	1,137	1,393	1,999	3,129	3,918
Dover, DE	13,232	9,226	3,081	4,156	828	1,715	403	952	617	1,196	1,991	2,822
Dubuque, IA	7,108	6,661	1,195	3,335	473	1,461	189	556	167	911	617	2,070
Duluth, MN-WI	22,460	19,513	5,505	9,078	2,570	4,564	611	1,648	1,059	1,853	3,123	5,172
Durham-Chapel Hill, NC	33,635	24,224	7,287	12,611	2,270	5,741	1,323	2,939	1,659	3,712	4,560	7,915
Eau Claire, WI	11,260	10,056	2,666	4,628	891	2,167	231	756	584	1,074	1,624	2,966
El Centro, CA	9,931	8,619	3,925	5,551	975	2,662	952	1,405	946	2,335	2,560	4,179
Elizabethtown, KY	7,777	5,650	2,305	3,430	748	1,597	351	782	607	1,044	1,591	2,385
Elkhart-Goshen, IN	12,769	10,586	3,366	5,187	1,361	2,625	805	1,244	597	1,082	1,766	3,102
Elmira, NY	6,752	6,096	1,501	3,078	499	1,418	192	552	230	781	960	1,951
El Paso, TX	45,342	38,152	15,410	22,016	4,520	9,576	3,083	5,202	3,645	7,006	10,577	15,878
Erie, PA	20,763	18,573	5,198	9,495	2,059	4,614	608	1,677	969	2,425	3,309	5,521
Eugene-Springfield, OR	29,921	24,328	7,610	13,048	3,676	5,746	837	2,425	1,544	3,904	4,171	8,670
Evansville, IN-KY	27,243	22,267	6,756	10,814	2,305	5,049	793	2,087	1,047	2,599	4,597	7,492
Fairbanks, AK	4,329	2,253	1,451	1,254	632	823	194	471	280	439	842	904
Fargo, ND-MN	11,110	10,374	2,372	4,555	1,056	1,876	172	991	347	1,141	1,288	2,609
Farmington, NM	8,080	6,065	2,255	3,225	1,070	1,832	330	751	523	1,258	1,427	1,897
Fayetteville, NC	20,298	13,470	6,854	7,624	2,049	2,783	1,055	1,411	1,442	2,336	4,763	5,605
Fayetteville-Springdale-Rogers, AR-MO	29,768	22,254	7,782	12,137	2,924	5,807	1,178	2,699	1,590	3,299	4,858	7,517
Flagstaff, AZ	7,965	4,599	2,076	2,571	803	1,422	395	696	392	810	1,168	1,648
Flint, MI	31,967	26,344	9,485	13,372	2,876	5,879	1,525	2,152	2,106	4,364	5,863	8,923
Florence, SC	16,816	10,871	4,954	5,980	1,267	2,152	1,102	1,286	1,284	1,867	3,427	4,064
Florence-Muscle Shoals, AL	13,847	10,747	4,198	6,166	1,546	2,710	559	1,390	893	1,974	2,714	4,130
Fond du Lac, WI	7,729	7,276	1,479	3,379	654	1,623	126	693	385	831	824	2,266
Fort Collins-Loveland, CO	21,065	15,665	4,272	7,664	1,991	4,426	442	1,321	1,038	1,763	1,925	4,371
Fort Smith, AR-OK	24,313	16,672	8,628	9,321	3,166	4,164	1,407	1,843	2,162	2,523	5,848	6,500
Fort Wayne, IN	27,455	22,996	6,532	10,621	2,510	4,518	992	1,991	1,196	3,006	3,914	7,132
Fresno, CA	51,649	42,785	15,241	23,017	6,298	10,956	3,045	4,644	3,826	7,234	9,339	15,824
Gadsden, AL	9,299	6,886	3,165	4,313	1,082	2,234	450	1,047	853	1,882	2,352	2,865
Gainesville, FL	16,711	13,061	4,271	6,655	1,568	3,181	894	1,460	995	1,868	2,650	4,357
Gainesville, GA	12,670	8,552	3,127	4,342	1,023	1,785	381	620	884	1,400	2,173	3,074
Glens Falls, NY	11,639	9,255	2,579	4,764	1,002	2,046	191	695	647	1,013	1,560	2,963
Goldsboro, NC	9,301	6,536	3,193	3,637	1,059	1,467	693	843	720	955	2,366	2,414
Grand Forks, ND-MN	6,340	5,326	1,406	2,190	501	932	217	397	229	401	885	1,331
Grand Junction, CO	12,109	10,012	2,871	5,107	1,385	2,910	338	917	391	1,361	1,641	2,966
Grand Rapids-Wyoming, MI	49,127	41,342	11,772	20,261	4,901	9,603	1,335	3,561	2,302	5,666	6,837	12,648
Great Falls, MT	6,795	5,758	1,957	3,137	759	1,652	198	815	214	743	1,269	1,879
Greeley, CO	15,216	10,112	3,599	5,589	1,783	2,821	578	932	832	1,783	1,975	3,594
Green Bay, WI	20,822	17,297	4,362	8,419	1,722	3,456	611	1,364	639	2,255	2,440	5,529
Greensboro-High Point, NC	53,961	42,034	12,277	21,167	4,023	8,964	1,882	4,829	2,888	6,031	8,240	13,699
Greenville, NC	11,127	8,376	3,174	4,754	1,023	1,918	568	814	691	1,548	2,471	3,167
Greenville-Mauldin-Easley, SC	49,663	35,043	12,639	18,517	4,841	7,911	2,148	3,960	3,191	6,116	7,904	12,663
Gulfport-Biloxi, MS	18,584	13,028	5,890	7,087	1,848	3,105	991	1,360	1,252	2,304	4,519	4,784
Hagerstown-Martinsburg, MD-WV	20,591	15,422	4,980	8,144	2,152	3,897	767	1,587	793	2,210	3,175	5,495
Hanford-Corcoran, CA	6,375	5,062	1,838	2,883	648	1,202	202	503	304	812	1,204	2,028
Harrisburg-Carlisle, PA	41,833	36,566	8,997	17,766	3,446	7,299	1,304	3,147	1,439	4,652	5,284	10,937
Harrisonburg, VA	8,331	7,490	2,048	3,633	768	1,532	274	681	352	1,003	1,178	2,545
Hartford-West Hartford-East Hartford, CT	90,147	79,807	19,235	37,875	6,350	16,783	2,607	6,634	4,164	9,376	11,524	22,938
Hattiesburg, MS	9,638	6,852	3,626	4,612	1,343	1,884	906	1,503	1,179	1,790	2,503	3,494
Hickory-Lenoir-Morganton, NC	32,898	22,625	10,221	12,120	4,260	5,772	1,740	2,252	2,254	3,179	6,510	8,304
Hinesville-Fort Stewart, GA	3,562	1,741	1,246	1,035	527	439	418	247	308	223	884	741
Holland-Grand Haven, MI	17,100	14,035	3,530	5,968	1,547	2,969	346	701	529	1,637	1,792	3,564
Honolulu, HI	71,444	68,200	13,982	31,612	5,131	14,713	2,115	4,420	3,272	10,511	8,601	19,843
Hot Springs, AR	10,750	8,753	3,572	4,730	1,169	2,441	328	841	891	986	2,094	2,923
Houma-Bayou Cane-Thibodaux, LA	14,600	9,852	4,535	6,250	1,683	2,510	800	1,308	1,012	1,982	2,781	4,145
Houston-Sugar Land-Baytown, TX	323,061	209,354	87,548	110,860	30,470	47,541	16,230	23,421	20,949	34,182	57,188	76,216
Huntington-Ashland, WV-KY-OH	25,728	20,094	8,733	11,769	2,947	5,442	1,324	2,846	1,761	3,592	6,057	8,181

Table H-4: Metropolitan Statistical Areas—Disability Status and Type of Disability—*Continued*

	Total Population		With a Disability		With a Hearing Difficulty		With a Vision Difficulty		With a Cognitive Difficulty		With an Ambulatory Difficulty	
	65 to 74 Years	75 Years and Over	65 to 74 Years	75 Years and Over	65 to 74 Years	75 Years and Over	65 to 74 Years	75 Years and Over	65 to 74 Years	75 Years and Over	65 to 74 Years	75 Years and Over
Huntsville, AL	30,238	21,566	8,465	11,909	3,475	5,927	1,659	2,563	1,754	3,987	4,910	7,514
Idaho Falls, ID	7,913	6,254	2,208	3,501	839	1,870	228	641	353	922	1,216	2,049
Indianapolis-Carmel, IN	108,438	81,491	26,671	39,315	9,702	16,428	3,854	6,442	4,762	10,696	17,200	26,905
Iowa City, IA	8,231	6,605	1,810	2,997	584	1,629	266	450	259	593	1,081	1,915
Ithaca, NY	5,969	5,067	1,243	2,399	432	1,362	259	520	331	661	844	1,467
Jackson, MI	11,876	10,386	3,200	5,488	1,228	2,739	387	992	685	1,870	2,090	3,805
Jackson, MS	35,212	25,401	10,911	14,239	3,288	5,245	2,001	3,437	2,434	5,090	7,369	10,505
Jackson, TN	8,527	6,640	2,483	3,972	906	1,842	304	967	389	1,353	1,650	2,761
Jacksonville, FL	98,037	69,401	26,185	34,414	7,986	14,201	3,905	6,948	4,966	10,177	17,203	23,247
Jacksonville, NC	8,216	5,265	2,885	2,695	1,164	1,471	422	602	605	838	1,921	1,784
Janesville, WI	11,659	9,782	2,845	4,577	1,165	2,350	622	1,003	655	1,192	1,482	2,592
Jefferson City, MO	10,827	8,114	3,228	4,175	1,292	2,266	838	940	443	1,006	1,769	2,728
Johnson City, TN	18,805	13,119	6,355	7,441	2,400	4,030	1,424	1,744	1,455	2,660	4,362	4,745
Johnstown, PA	12,871	13,381	3,576	6,994	1,492	3,244	305	1,450	637	1,912	2,162	4,479
Jonesboro, AR	8,928	6,176	2,950	3,569	1,360	1,563	554	819	754	1,013	1,847	2,529
Joplin, MO	13,758	10,324	4,147	5,633	1,616	3,057	501	1,316	564	1,580	2,804	3,776
Kalamazoo-Portage, MI	22,609	18,484	5,278	8,974	2,012	4,575	734	1,742	1,126	2,348	3,257	5,441
Kankakee-Bradley, IL	7,882	6,589	2,314	3,412	600	1,315	390	694	653	910	1,455	2,331
Kansas City, MO-KS	135,496	107,150	33,195	53,114	12,018	24,037	4,489	9,442	6,807	14,097	20,552	34,401
Kennewick-Pasco-Richland, WA	15,861	11,396	3,765	5,690	1,666	2,982	684	961	855	1,622	1,900	3,542
Killeen-Temple-Fort Hood, TX	21,266	15,198	6,718	8,437	2,780	3,720	1,040	1,469	1,588	2,665	4,259	5,950
Kingsport-Bristol-Bristol, TN-VA	32,640	23,674	10,993	13,044	4,229	5,995	2,191	2,791	2,535	4,010	7,038	9,061
Kingston, NY	14,964	11,992	3,547	6,050	1,250	2,614	616	1,086	600	1,525	2,096	3,875
Knoxville, TN	59,277	43,987	14,937	22,547	5,423	10,236	2,374	4,832	3,549	6,979	9,776	15,166
Kokomo, IN	9,124	7,086	2,780	3,741	1,112	1,459	526	582	360	988	1,756	2,620
La Crosse, WI-MN	9,331	8,889	1,891	3,854	713	2,069	228	886	359	734	1,234	2,354
Lafayette, IN	11,456	9,021	2,991	4,314	1,168	1,720	386	732	477	961	1,963	2,760
Lafayette, LA	16,530	12,078	4,375	6,710	1,280	2,423	632	1,187	1,086	2,323	3,132	4,549
Lake Charles, LA	14,426	10,559	5,498	5,738	2,293	2,616	1,241	1,176	1,383	2,083	3,386	3,500
Lake Havasu City-Kingman, AZ	29,079	19,004	7,496	9,226	2,281	4,725	910	1,862	1,351	2,237	4,841	5,811
Lakeland-Winter Haven, FL	62,370	47,437	14,912	23,338	5,076	10,614	2,719	4,324	3,563	6,172	9,275	15,591
Lancaster, PA	39,833	35,948	8,066	15,896	3,290	7,280	863	2,545	1,890	3,755	4,464	9,833
Lansing-East Lansing, MI	31,184	23,901	7,800	11,991	2,829	5,150	1,207	1,998	1,882	3,552	4,461	7,574
Laredo, TX	11,393	8,474	5,193	6,189	1,252	2,994	1,635	1,794	1,691	2,647	3,370	4,536
Las Cruces, NM	15,091	11,534	3,922	6,413	1,615	2,874	786	1,520	977	1,709	2,420	4,326
Las Vegas-Paradise, NV	142,736	88,295	36,311	43,337	11,995	19,183	6,206	8,727	6,430	11,340	23,145	28,731
Lawrence, KS	5,590	4,462	1,015	2,226	458	1,185	186	632	192	668	607	1,551
Lawton, OK	6,981	5,453	2,677	3,336	1,239	1,734	515	673	464	917	1,724	2,297
Lebanon, PA	11,496	10,248	2,344	4,225	1,231	1,652	197	642	469	768	912	2,613
Lewiston-Auburn, ME	8,148	6,865	2,296	3,835	876	1,694	287	762	629	994	1,379	2,402
Lexington-Fayette, KY	30,289	22,255	8,438	11,799	2,926	5,310	1,062	2,274	1,870	3,216	5,476	8,321
Lima, OH	7,944	7,015	1,887	3,306	672	1,752	271	678	498	937	1,186	2,173
Lincoln, NE	17,872	15,671	3,456	7,747	1,474	3,818	290	1,513	719	1,395	1,915	4,599
Little Rock-North Little Rock-Conway, AR	49,826	36,039	14,864	19,213	5,399	9,132	2,888	4,351	3,192	6,032	9,788	12,802
Logan, UT-ID	5,952	4,671	1,433	2,190	560	1,083	160	566	223	671	715	1,084
Longview, TX	16,011	13,039	4,922	7,428	1,681	3,375	716	1,576	886	2,248	3,379	5,192
Longview, WA	9,346	6,738	3,474	3,855	1,739	1,996	287	845	524	1,050	1,915	2,376
Los Angeles-Long Beach-Santa Ana, CA	787,419	651,074	185,252	337,053	51,258	138,834	32,009	69,116	48,173	116,050	118,505	231,229
Louisville/Jefferson County, KY-IN	92,674	70,909	25,740	37,057	8,463	15,557	4,197	7,191	6,280	11,601	15,930	25,071
Lubbock, TX	17,349	14,124	5,541	7,933	2,217	3,966	768	1,791	1,165	2,274	3,618	5,577
Lynchburg, VA	22,763	17,212	5,350	8,538	1,537	3,727	586	1,701	984	2,491	3,331	5,718
Macon, GA	17,028	13,080	5,053	6,756	1,342	2,892	834	1,388	968	2,243	3,505	4,353
Madera-Chowchilla, CA	10,117	7,193	3,485	4,490	1,710	2,487	648	1,209	685	1,151	2,195	2,625
Madison, WI	34,809	27,807	6,165	12,584	2,855	5,680	598	2,451	924	3,317	3,429	7,755
Manchester-Nashua, NH	26,880	20,190	5,636	9,372	2,300	4,801	626	1,768	1,080	2,063	3,075	5,338
Manhattan, KS	5,407	4,551	861	2,088	373	956	49	453	112	611	589	1,370
Mankato-North Mankato, MN	5,786	5,552	1,183	2,559	636	1,115	121	424	271	659	466	1,647
Mansfield, OH	10,708	9,247	2,743	4,046	1,225	1,706	323	660	529	1,129	1,524	2,739
McAllen-Edinburg-Mission, TX	41,760	32,392	17,308	20,952	5,766	10,565	4,892	6,166	4,452	7,043	11,456	14,118
Medford, OR	19,772	17,091	5,237	8,753	2,517	4,599	931	1,602	1,271	2,475	2,735	5,377
Memphis, TN-MS-AR	81,656	58,269	24,202	32,236	7,097	13,123	4,114	7,118	5,804	10,401	16,528	22,260
Merced, CA	14,083	10,543	4,926	6,536	1,812	3,214	2,129	2,269	1,504	2,630	2,876	4,350
Miami-Fort Lauderdale-Pompano Beach, FL	457,441	442,274	98,163	212,825	23,744	84,605	16,993	44,104	27,126	68,604	62,129	146,671
Michigan City-La Porte, IN	8,578	7,006	2,218	3,313	771	1,698	304	470	344	858	1,576	2,083
Midland, TX	7,730	7,148	2,899	4,094	1,071	1,651	568	1,164	512	1,179	1,865	3,041
Milwaukee-Waukesha-West Allis, WI	99,643	94,056	21,809	44,159	7,183	18,108	3,069	7,468	4,491	11,186	13,512	28,630
Minneapolis-St. Paul-Bloomington, MN-WI	197,864	154,790	39,157	68,729	16,078	30,792	4,732	11,863	8,037	15,575	21,607	41,650
Missoula, MT	7,304	5,326	1,573	2,616	850	1,514	191	632	189	612	827	1,664
Mobile, AL	31,054	22,627	10,010	13,353	3,637	5,587	1,989	3,027	2,447	4,368	6,778	9,283
Modesto, CA	30,896	24,430	10,090	15,084	3,699	6,689	1,425	3,090	2,512	5,062	6,279	10,161
Monroe, LA	12,509	9,746	3,739	4,910	1,324	2,048	689	777	723	1,720	2,548	3,592
Monroe, MI	11,639	8,921	3,144	4,707	1,282	2,310	514	758	547	1,117	1,793	2,770
Montgomery, AL	25,959	18,881	8,124	10,245	2,727	4,509	2,115	2,244	2,115	3,679	5,562	7,354
Morgantown, WV	8,405	6,381	2,491	3,341	1,144	1,577	451	648	727	851	1,459	2,024
Morristown, TN	13,668	8,404	4,373	4,926	1,941	2,384	764	1,143	884	1,805	2,544	3,385
Mount Vernon-Anacortes, WA	10,957	8,371	2,800	4,292	1,550	2,202	343	803	496	824	1,483	2,770
Muncie, IN	9,156	7,667	2,814	3,784	1,257	1,902	440	743	751	841	1,713	2,556
Muskegon-Norton Shores, MI	12,427	10,597	3,037	5,342	1,142	2,563	440	1,072	744	1,292	1,826	3,413
Myrtle Beach-North Myrtle Beach-Conway, SC	30,310	18,029	7,925	8,355	2,905	3,945	1,180	1,966	1,445	2,609	5,118	5,401
Napa, CA	11,013	9,556	2,226	5,147	754	2,331	250	898	558	1,281	1,402	3,247

Table H-4: Metropolitan Statistical Areas—Disability Status and Type of Disability—*Continued*

	Total Population		With a Disability		With a Hearing Difficulty		With a Vision Difficulty		With a Cognitive Difficulty		With an Ambulatory Difficulty	
	65 to 74 Years	75 Years and Over	65 to 74 Years	75 Years and Over	65 to 74 Years	75 Years and Over	65 to 74 Years	75 Years and Over	65 to 74 Years	75 Years and Over	65 to 74 Years	75 Years and Over
Naples-Marco Island, FL	48,188	40,624	5,934	15,821	2,507	8,200	872	3,270	1,065	4,138	3,201	9,101
Nashville-Davidson--Murfreesboro--Franklin, TN....	102,819	70,860	28,210	36,650	9,543	16,365	4,330	6,553	6,100	10,683	18,807	24,128
New Haven-Milford, CT	62,741	57,717	14,442	27,057	3,931	11,922	1,882	5,007	2,869	7,264	9,031	16,644
New Orleans-Metairie-Kenner, LA	83,141	62,066	24,669	33,936	8,036	13,785	4,977	7,071	5,600	11,176	15,939	23,848
New York-Northern New Jersey-Long Island, NY-NJ-PA	1,326,363	1,130,841	281,166	537,904	69,392	198,163	49,441	110,607	63,435	157,913	191,272	379,655
Niles-Benton Harbor, MI	13,546	11,534	3,439	5,818	1,192	2,761	386	784	577	1,713	2,310	3,920
North Port-Bradenton-Sarasota, FL	101,289	95,000	18,288	39,198	8,395	19,971	2,492	6,749	3,164	9,733	9,576	24,178
Norwich-New London, CT	21,609	16,975	4,714	7,657	2,007	3,496	380	1,187	1,023	1,695	2,681	5,024
Ocala, FL	48,244	38,269	11,263	17,778	4,685	9,150	1,722	3,674	2,173	5,241	6,307	10,417
Ocean City, NJ	11,311	9,668	1,962	4,330	843	1,759	210	640	439	1,245	1,202	2,996
Odessa, TX	7,713	5,996	2,650	3,621	966	1,770	490	678	620	702	1,671	2,129
Ogden-Clearfield, UT	28,132	22,613	6,950	10,643	2,811	5,370	611	1,949	1,273	2,411	3,815	6,811
Oklahoma City, OK	84,415	63,186	25,242	34,730	9,993	16,122	3,723	6,353	4,586	9,343	15,862	23,223
Olympia, WA	19,460	14,307	4,512	7,180	1,766	3,453	704	1,137	948	1,656	2,314	4,945
Omaha-Council Bluffs, NE-IA	52,739	42,222	11,212	20,508	4,936	9,418	1,716	4,231	2,140	5,265	6,108	13,191
Orlando-Kissimmee-Sanford, FL	153,545	116,718	37,430	56,160	11,598	25,035	5,961	11,256	8,412	15,602	24,298	37,644
Oshkosh-Neenah, WI	11,304	10,448	2,273	4,562	1,218	2,177	463	823	691	987	1,423	2,757
Owensboro, KY	9,168	7,511	2,461	4,352	860	2,101	309	872	525	1,160	1,524	2,748
Oxnard-Thousand Oaks-Ventura, CA	54,312	44,744	11,884	22,343	4,052	10,115	2,028	4,583	2,187	6,894	7,487	15,158
Palm Bay-Melbourne-Titusville, FL	59,271	52,589	13,152	25,608	4,717	11,344	2,170	4,985	2,732	7,151	7,913	16,666
Palm Coast, FL	14,682	10,123	3,088	4,033	1,155	1,768	602	819	338	1,338	1,576	2,327
Panama City-Lynn Haven-Panama City Beach, FL...	14,272	10,418	3,984	4,805	1,940	2,378	838	937	608	1,798	2,488	3,204
Parkersburg-Marietta-Vienna, WV-OH	15,453	11,367	4,090	6,092	1,666	3,189	758	967	892	1,377	2,480	3,647
Pascagoula, MS	12,630	7,972	4,750	4,976	1,756	2,234	1,012	1,036	915	1,226	3,227	3,512
Pensacola-Ferry Pass-Brent, FL	36,941	26,027	10,532	14,257	4,151	6,842	1,335	2,945	1,802	4,249	7,370	9,973
Peoria, IL	29,526	25,165	6,015	11,528	2,153	4,926	717	1,791	1,078	2,850	3,959	7,396
Philadelphia-Camden-Wilmington, PA-NJ-DE-MD ..	416,630	364,541	96,976	172,765	28,286	69,566	15,898	32,605	20,721	48,678	62,515	114,627
Phoenix-Mesa-Glendale, AZ	306,832	230,525	65,865	105,480	24,817	50,401	10,050	19,862	13,595	28,112	40,008	68,928
Pine Bluff, AR	7,424	5,475	2,597	3,362	975	1,490	487	1,003	526	1,137	1,643	2,449
Pittsburgh, PA	198,610	198,297	47,007	95,207	17,293	43,434	6,890	17,438	9,429	24,318	28,402	60,034
Pittsfield, MA	12,201	11,673	2,552	5,922	861	2,726	290	911	419	1,328	1,581	3,629
Pocatello, ID	5,727	4,576	1,777	2,563	810	1,405	246	430	372	542	1,150	1,496
Portland-South Portland-Biddeford, ME	42,449	34,562	9,274	16,664	4,033	8,738	1,141	3,024	1,950	4,718	4,842	10,037
Portland-Vancouver-Hillsboro, OR-WA	149,082	112,896	36,466	59,389	14,421	26,900	4,821	11,838	8,866	18,997	20,737	38,969
Port St. Lucie, FL	51,022	46,868	10,789	20,295	3,751	10,754	1,399	2,932	1,566	4,900	6,830	12,520
Poughkeepsie-Newburgh-Middletown, NY	45,507	35,056	10,839	17,942	4,006	7,877	1,553	3,364	2,373	5,187	6,150	11,642
Prescott, AZ	30,610	21,868	6,577	10,157	2,496	5,229	953	1,922	1,209	2,475	3,634	6,136
Providence-New Bedford-Fall River, RI-MA	117,050	105,752	26,629	52,340	8,969	23,559	3,652	8,416	5,411	13,080	16,312	33,113
Provo-Orem, UT	20,211	15,667	4,400	8,069	2,160	4,031	587	1,622	661	2,298	2,297	4,779
Pueblo, CO	12,889	11,168	3,533	5,768	1,253	2,955	668	1,361	660	1,394	2,156	3,781
Punta Gorda, FL	30,062	25,700	6,646	10,449	2,969	5,248	929	1,942	1,503	2,703	3,652	6,122
Racine, WI	13,894	11,987	3,210	5,398	1,216	2,418	515	995	595	1,213	1,945	3,578
Raleigh-Cary, NC	64,145	41,775	14,871	20,142	4,198	8,168	2,254	3,947	3,606	5,872	8,655	14,161
Rapid City, SD	9,151	7,541	2,230	3,810	1,072	2,144	203	683	578	869	1,171	2,508
Reading, PA	30,487	27,721	6,979	13,676	2,339	6,305	1,036	2,020	1,406	3,737	4,100	8,371
Redding, CA	17,372	13,216	5,422	7,354	2,134	3,950	780	1,411	1,035	2,187	3,305	4,551
Reno-Sparks, NV	32,981	20,901	7,765	9,773	2,887	4,204	909	1,781	1,384	2,853	4,932	6,570
Richmond, VA	89,755	66,152	21,277	32,801	6,727	13,139	3,038	6,587	5,207	11,015	14,007	22,023
Riverside-San Bernardino-Ontario, CA	256,103	197,328	70,932	103,885	24,587	48,270	11,335	23,413	15,466	30,648	45,582	70,136
Roanoke, VA	27,489	21,909	6,545	10,360	2,574	4,767	1,086	2,110	1,199	2,662	3,857	6,907
Rochester, MN	13,115	10,920	2,160	4,893	1,111	2,535	205	1,154	236	1,138	1,067	2,905
Rochester, NY	79,453	67,500	15,458	31,201	5,059	13,213	2,234	4,987	3,177	7,878	9,663	20,072
Rockford, IL	26,197	20,368	6,204	9,664	1,995	4,589	1,086	1,644	872	2,092	3,935	5,965
Rocky Mount, NC	12,655	8,874	4,089	4,913	1,113	2,014	820	1,009	1,036	1,661	2,926	3,128
Rome, GA	7,497	5,966	2,321	3,713	860	1,447	390	1,039	521	1,274	1,421	2,390
Sacramento--Arden-Arcade--Roseville, CA	146,060	119,656	39,031	61,972	13,605	28,052	5,746	10,928	9,031	18,740	24,850	40,307
Saginaw-Saginaw Township North, MI	16,387	13,681	4,747	6,414	1,601	3,211	649	1,094	828	1,865	3,077	4,287
St. Cloud, MN	11,734	10,671	2,456	4,888	1,276	2,708	411	527	298	800	1,130	2,656
St. George, UT	13,576	11,557	2,757	5,034	1,425	2,243	233	1,037	338	1,347	1,382	2,869
St. Joseph, MO-KS	9,363	7,786	2,834	4,136	789	2,064	440	892	574	990	1,764	2,651
St. Louis, MO-IL	201,749	166,804	49,537	81,859	16,125	36,198	7,562	15,609	10,232	21,711	31,727	53,190
Salem, OR	28,619	23,926	7,671	11,107	2,981	5,473	1,494	1,901	1,690	3,260	4,941	6,895
Salinas, CA	23,863	20,789	4,741	10,186	1,578	4,887	601	2,031	1,258	3,539	2,924	6,760
Salisbury, MD	8,996	7,141	2,748	3,407	900	1,336	304	841	364	808	1,760	2,339
Salt Lake City, UT	56,766	41,791	12,528	20,874	5,231	11,469	1,936	4,320	2,519	5,651	7,240	11,800
San Angelo, TX	8,155	7,205	2,198	3,328	784	1,568	426	701	303	815	1,286	2,202
San Antonio-New Braunfels, TX	137,304	102,639	42,342	58,129	15,963	26,097	8,053	13,156	8,809	18,169	26,926	41,547
San Diego-Carlsbad-San Marcos, CA	190,140	168,134	42,676	85,810	12,757	40,168	6,360	16,350	11,085	28,414	25,670	55,902
Sandusky, OH	7,243	5,626	1,962	2,554	819	1,170	384	464	218	617	1,264	1,741
San Francisco-Oakland-Fremont, CA	303,895	254,096	62,847	125,690	18,927	49,219	9,172	23,756	13,716	39,707	38,430	83,804

Table H-4: Metropolitan Statistical Areas—Disability Status and Type of Disability—*Continued*

	Total Population		With a Disability		With a Hearing Difficulty		With a Vision Difficulty		With a Cognitive Difficulty		With an Ambulatory Difficulty	
	65 to 74 Years	75 Years and Over	65 to 74 Years	75 Years and Over	65 to 74 Years	75 Years and Over	65 to 74 Years	75 Years and Over	65 to 74 Years	75 Years and Over	65 to 74 Years	75 Years and Over
San Jose-Sunnyvale-Santa Clara, CA	114,295	92,866	23,096	46,506	7,753	20,290	3,266	8,871	5,049	14,604	12,706	30,613
San Luis Obispo-Paso Robles, CA	22,118	19,530	4,596	9,972	2,504	4,787	826	1,952	690	2,755	2,106	6,321
Santa Barbara-Santa Maria-Goleta, CA	27,894	26,956	5,986	13,209	2,550	6,038	1,242	2,679	1,525	3,750	3,466	8,402
Santa Cruz-Watsonville, CA	17,254	12,856	3,325	6,303	1,072	3,202	562	1,268	851	1,684	1,974	3,780
Santa Fe, NM	14,637	8,709	2,951	4,651	1,523	2,518	357	1,115	832	1,279	1,503	2,753
Santa Rosa-Petaluma, CA	38,370	31,185	7,695	15,732	3,029	7,611	963	2,998	1,846	4,994	4,657	9,888
Savannah, GA	23,623	17,392	5,944	9,177	1,859	3,782	938	1,706	1,175	3,053	3,913	6,395
Scranton--Wilkes-Barre, PA	49,206	46,886	12,866	23,170	4,984	9,987	1,788	4,462	2,077	4,946	7,978	15,352
Seattle-Tacoma-Bellevue, WA	216,373	166,304	51,234	85,734	18,898	38,708	6,959	16,250	11,491	26,221	29,678	55,704
Sebastian-Vero Beach, FL	19,063	19,668	3,041	8,922	1,084	5,031	260	1,728	826	2,090	1,732	5,393
Sheboygan, WI	8,559	7,889	1,934	3,403	805	1,552	175	377	255	828	997	2,094
Sherman-Denison, TX	10,501	7,910	3,650	4,314	1,497	2,161	644	762	768	1,121	2,389	2,897
Shreveport-Bossier City, LA	28,725	22,527	8,757	12,251	2,817	4,946	1,789	2,540	2,009	4,143	5,832	8,031
Sioux City, IA-NE-SD	9,792	8,366	2,118	3,641	855	1,752	264	843	227	944	1,271	2,212
Sioux Falls, SD	13,345	11,591	2,663	5,485	975	2,733	311	1,062	384	1,432	1,653	3,301
South Bend-Mishawaka, IN-MI	22,891	20,747	6,291	10,619	2,243	5,136	1,048	1,891	1,187	2,872	3,577	6,698
Spartanburg, SC	22,761	15,492	6,997	8,970	1,841	3,579	1,193	1,587	1,519	2,819	4,804	5,791
Spokane, WA	34,004	27,429	9,217	14,684	4,123	7,142	1,244	2,997	1,749	3,836	5,574	9,354
Springfield, IL	15,806	13,130	3,712	6,513	1,265	2,909	544	1,223	662	1,858	2,236	4,132
Springfield, MA	50,044	44,702	11,765	22,099	4,112	10,056	1,802	4,186	2,477	5,609	7,836	13,955
Springfield, MO	33,764	26,749	8,626	13,389	2,992	6,061	1,221	2,637	1,715	3,511	5,689	8,964
Springfield, OH	12,037	9,452	3,424	4,823	1,338	2,396	503	819	496	1,451	2,074	3,096
State College, PA	9,231	7,824	2,038	3,503	838	1,752	192	668	325	830	1,099	2,407
Steubenville-Weirton, OH-WV	11,703	10,703	2,758	5,209	925	2,398	350	937	409	1,140	1,719	3,437
Stockton, CA	40,377	32,065	11,612	17,446	3,541	8,116	1,713	3,806	2,944	5,675	7,482	11,987
Sumter, SC	8,005	5,675	2,816	3,021	887	1,016	539	726	680	1,055	1,897	2,244
Syracuse, NY	47,371	41,517	9,864	18,318	3,542	8,605	1,589	3,647	2,114	4,802	6,129	11,683
Tallahassee, FL	22,931	15,822	5,711	8,285	2,142	3,783	1,042	1,582	1,263	2,333	3,248	5,319
Tampa-St. Petersburg-Clearwater, FL	256,035	227,459	62,937	110,003	21,522	51,129	9,259	22,705	12,636	32,402	39,837	73,047
Terre Haute, IN	13,032	10,525	4,202	5,602	1,384	2,736	526	963	1,029	1,487	2,713	3,459
Texarkana, TX-Texarkana, AR	10,834	7,990	2,804	4,253	1,004	1,972	498	943	606	1,216	1,721	2,936
Toledo, OH	46,452	39,342	11,198	19,170	4,017	9,005	1,589	3,432	2,272	4,963	7,367	12,123
Topeka, KS	18,601	15,005	4,497	7,356	1,886	3,059	549	1,229	840	1,776	2,785	4,771
Trenton-Ewing, NJ	24,275	21,414	4,491	10,178	1,057	4,128	772	1,997	847	2,958	3,041	6,644
Tucson, AZ	85,619	69,752	19,433	33,444	7,294	17,335	3,261	7,739	3,932	8,424	11,642	21,480
Tulsa, OK	69,566	51,250	20,889	26,436	8,633	12,904	3,487	5,368	3,529	6,841	13,397	18,008
Tuscaloosa, AL	13,874	10,865	4,388	6,209	1,517	2,398	777	1,047	1,063	1,856	3,235	4,454
Tyler, TX	16,519	13,524	4,762	7,076	1,955	3,585	858	1,817	900	2,393	2,960	4,722
Utica-Rome, NY	24,332	22,441	5,659	11,043	2,232	5,121	720	2,596	1,106	2,889	3,410	6,934
Valdosta, GA	8,680	5,928	3,145	3,789	1,039	1,637	879	952	435	1,156	2,246	2,631
Vallejo-Fairfield, CA	26,958	20,639	6,818	11,207	2,245	5,010	1,091	2,128	1,009	2,835	4,199	6,959
Victoria, TX	9,075	7,284	3,081	4,273	1,117	2,143	502	1,227	770	1,435	1,989	2,751
Vineland-Millville-Bridgeton, NJ	10,874	8,427	3,543	4,582	1,239	1,930	815	1,029	897	1,671	2,317	3,135
Virginia Beach-Norfolk-Newport News, VA-NC	111,334	83,965	26,823	40,847	8,539	16,247	4,122	7,062	5,444	11,427	17,414	27,814
Visalia-Porterville, CA	23,646	18,020	7,560	10,035	2,313	4,339	1,076	1,566	1,692	3,067	5,357	6,737
Waco, TX	15,416	12,914	5,128	6,674	1,806	2,704	1,082	1,474	1,039	1,824	3,820	4,626
Warner Robins, GA	8,692	5,958	3,172	3,072	1,181	1,267	366	656	795	996	2,107	2,182
Washington-Arlington-Alexandria, DC-VA-MD-WV	339,497	234,789	66,331	108,884	18,542	42,907	10,051	20,561	13,177	31,602	42,957	71,882
Waterloo-Cedar Falls, IA	12,408	11,463	2,968	5,086	1,267	2,120	172	821	407	1,116	1,559	3,040
Wausau, WI	10,171	8,761	1,844	3,998	765	1,848	199	642	221	787	1,114	2,727
Wenatchee-East Wenatchee, WA	8,932	7,537	1,781	3,743	958	1,947	329	936	338	999	870	2,273
Wheeling, WV-OH	13,187	11,967	3,497	5,771	1,373	2,603	522	1,214	746	1,467	2,286	3,600
Wichita, KS	39,389	34,570	10,753	17,278	3,913	8,182	1,469	3,154	2,182	4,574	6,964	11,203
Wichita Falls, TX	10,553	9,184	3,336	4,837	1,192	2,269	554	1,270	541	1,378	2,236	3,354
Williamsport, PA	9,575	8,796	2,576	4,237	1,293	2,514	392	864	384	1,252	1,338	2,337
Wilmington, NC	38,228	23,271	8,871	11,482	2,703	5,262	1,230	2,062	1,736	3,204	5,464	7,786
Winchester, VA-WV	10,171	7,495	3,401	3,306	1,319	1,777	344	627	818	1,008	2,174	2,142
Winston-Salem, NC	37,285	28,618	8,112	13,111	2,415	4,881	1,474	2,658	1,693	3,873	4,775	8,995
Worcester, MA	53,395	46,024	12,459	22,540	4,428	10,463	1,586	4,860	2,608	5,575	7,216	14,284
Yakima, WA	15,610	12,403	5,020	7,339	1,889	3,902	874	1,418	1,374	2,059	2,781	4,895
York-Hanover, PA	33,981	27,296	7,583	12,606	3,564	5,940	1,232	2,330	1,525	3,374	3,988	7,627
Youngstown-Warren-Boardman, OH-PA	49,487	47,491	12,219	22,259	4,774	10,131	1,769	4,065	2,274	5,864	7,009	14,442
Yuba City, CA	11,062	8,334	3,172	4,157	1,299	2,028	243	748	612	1,110	1,854	2,751
Yuma, AZ	17,674	13,693	4,755	6,450	1,994	3,305	812	1,679	779	1,471	2,719	4,187

Table H-5: 113th Congressional Districts—Disability Status and Type of Disability

	Total Population		With a Disability		With a Hearing Difficulty		With a Vision Difficulty		With a Cognitive Difficulty		With an Ambulatory Difficulty	
	65 to 74 Years	75 Years and Over	65 to 74 Years	75 Years and Over	65 to 74 Years	75 Years and Over	65 to 74 Years	75 Years and Over	65 to 74 Years	75 Years and Over	65 to 74 Years	75 Years and Over
Alabama												
Congressional District 1	57,579	40,778	17,989	23,160	6,666	9,951	3,597	4,913	4,300	7,181	11,814	16,436
Congressional District 2	54,625	40,336	18,803	23,111	6,289	10,248	3,923	4,952	4,985	7,652	12,618	16,627
Congressional District 3	54,233	37,186	19,217	22,107	6,433	9,006	3,128	4,536	4,441	7,074	12,261	15,395
Congressional District 4	62,513	43,370	21,695	27,035	7,996	12,805	3,633	6,927	5,022	8,977	14,811	18,504
Congressional District 5	54,098	38,561	15,546	21,496	6,228	10,091	2,976	4,432	3,421	7,026	9,368	14,223
Congressional District 6	50,420	38,497	13,882	20,483	4,334	9,678	2,228	4,323	3,016	6,400	9,569	14,384
Congressional District 7	47,117	38,010	16,458	22,342	4,719	7,737	3,472	4,236	4,370	7,709	12,023	16,207
Alaska												
Congressional District (at Large)	37,249	19,970	11,945	11,247	5,972	5,895	1,987	3,109	2,367	3,415	6,536	7,336
Arizona												
Congressional District 1	61,757	39,525	15,590	21,190	6,847	11,364	3,452	5,107	3,448	5,627	9,025	12,692
Congressional District 2	69,250	57,579	15,394	28,541	5,654	14,728	2,027	6,198	2,795	7,357	9,309	18,739
Congressional District 3	39,940	25,808	12,390	13,187	4,456	6,601	2,321	3,328	2,795	3,848	7,608	9,240
Congressional District 4	95,886	63,867	21,377	29,003	8,024	14,518	2,233	5,746	3,464	7,485	12,410	18,198
Congressional District 5	59,812	48,594	12,500	21,143	4,646	10,542	1,810	4,449	2,612	5,328	7,381	13,692
Congressional District 6	62,182	42,933	11,167	18,406	4,671	8,318	1,854	2,634	2,281	5,103	6,320	12,266
Congressional District 7	27,628	18,542	9,162	10,343	2,693	4,732	2,393	2,716	2,431	2,954	6,418	7,098
Congressional District 8	69,810	62,986	13,671	27,745	4,957	14,066	1,481	5,079	2,871	7,106	8,656	17,319
Congressional District 9	39,012	30,340	8,878	14,784	3,467	6,754	1,263	2,842	1,564	4,151	5,152	9,728
Arkansas												
Congressional District 1	65,059	47,353	22,869	27,088	9,379	11,874	4,314	6,112	5,040	8,279	14,825	18,131
Congressional District 2	54,108	39,888	16,060	21,494	6,107	10,389	3,248	4,765	3,482	6,573	10,647	14,147
Congressional District 3	51,850	38,755	14,699	21,241	5,620	10,074	2,215	4,605	3,130	5,900	9,158	14,006
Congressional District 4	67,496	49,553	24,940	27,987	9,723	13,004	4,485	6,542	5,834	8,487	16,104	18,928
California												
Congressional District 1	68,358	53,340	19,168	27,848	7,740	14,973	2,490	5,149	3,934	8,144	11,417	16,691
Congressional District 2	64,048	46,995	12,978	23,501	5,175	11,265	1,997	4,133	2,543	7,105	7,765	14,438
Congressional District 3	45,308	34,945	12,603	18,731	4,786	9,049	1,800	3,470	2,217	5,046	7,779	11,772
Congressional District 4	67,534	50,445	15,202	24,047	5,987	12,125	1,646	4,687	2,767	6,452	9,514	14,726
Congressional District 5	52,930	43,949	11,551	22,664	3,974	9,831	1,283	4,119	2,721	6,605	7,331	14,600
Congressional District 6	39,635	34,360	13,033	19,488	4,214	8,282	2,543	3,272	3,449	6,490	8,689	13,048
Congressional District 7	46,738	39,087	12,810	20,196	4,574	9,359	1,653	3,694	3,019	6,174	7,974	12,701
Congressional District 8	46,459	33,359	14,123	18,568	5,111	9,310	2,890	4,940	3,462	5,347	9,099	12,431
Congressional District 9	43,662	33,586	13,510	18,487	4,143	8,551	1,964	4,025	2,935	5,865	8,540	12,370
Congressional District 10	41,532	31,674	12,421	19,134	4,286	8,545	1,757	3,752	3,117	6,218	7,845	12,846
Congressional District 11	52,548	44,375	10,357	21,868	2,930	8,860	1,273	3,745	2,011	5,986	6,426	13,822
Congressional District 12	47,454	46,725	11,809	24,986	3,627	9,353	2,580	5,779	3,489	8,984	7,533	17,369
Congressional District 13	47,779	36,476	10,401	19,149	2,644	6,386	1,820	3,429	2,387	6,390	6,499	13,524
Congressional District 14	51,706	45,839	9,218	21,321	2,692	8,685	1,306	3,564	1,870	6,958	5,641	14,823
Congressional District 15	41,187	32,537	9,462	16,260	3,119	6,333	1,199	3,500	1,789	4,996	5,292	10,899
Congressional District 16	34,802	26,455	13,101	16,513	5,297	7,640	4,003	4,676	3,648	5,877	8,216	11,474
Congressional District 17	40,249	34,835	7,665	17,128	2,310	7,637	870	3,360	1,613	4,891	4,444	11,398
Congressional District 18	50,409	43,836	7,479	20,118	2,814	9,129	708	3,564	1,230	5,889	4,016	12,305
Congressional District 19	42,481	30,118	10,362	16,214	3,627	6,655	1,719	3,380	2,597	5,623	5,614	11,027
Congressional District 20	41,617	34,594	8,913	17,110	2,997	8,300	1,376	3,321	2,465	5,441	5,438	11,134
Congressional District 21	29,511	21,959	9,458	12,676	3,317	5,582	1,751	2,715	1,728	3,934	6,515	9,079
Congressional District 22	41,393	34,942	10,550	18,112	4,013	8,540	1,642	3,120	2,642	5,510	6,225	11,890
Congressional District 23	44,686	31,794	12,435	17,816	4,450	8,382	2,041	3,538	2,727	5,522	8,624	11,893
Congressional District 24	50,770	46,822	10,706	23,302	5,068	10,931	2,068	4,690	2,221	6,520	5,602	14,751
Congressional District 25	38,346	26,237	10,136	14,397	3,174	6,079	1,602	2,607	2,367	4,273	6,155	9,622
Congressional District 26	46,626	39,946	10,091	19,602	3,456	8,895	1,783	3,965	1,978	6,324	6,296	13,220
Congressional District 27	52,513	49,522	11,011	24,241	3,574	10,563	1,843	4,405	2,492	8,179	6,689	16,542
Congressional District 28	50,604	45,603	14,222	26,459	3,013	8,947	2,251	5,163	4,785	11,341	8,905	18,339
Congressional District 29	34,084	25,484	11,653	14,962	3,142	5,740	2,752	4,095	3,512	5,604	7,601	10,105
Congressional District 30	50,067	44,160	12,047	23,616	3,436	9,799	1,863	4,465	3,220	8,225	7,637	16,463
Congressional District 31	33,516	26,397	10,200	15,127	3,066	6,722	1,685	3,846	2,408	5,326	6,760	10,618
Congressional District 32	43,102	33,668	10,128	18,012	2,853	7,746	1,289	3,479	2,141	6,463	6,897	12,280
Congressional District 33	56,162	50,344	8,759	22,551	2,372	9,530	1,186	3,820	2,384	6,287	5,336	14,884
Congressional District 34	36,945	30,686	10,046	17,444	2,415	6,675	1,950	3,972	2,745	5,634	6,922	13,155
Congressional District 35	30,810	20,562	9,723	12,219	2,461	4,630	1,500	2,932	2,330	4,312	6,886	9,205
Congressional District 36	70,737	63,985	16,719	30,435	6,913	15,102	2,731	5,599	2,929	7,275	10,032	19,212
Congressional District 37	41,897	36,888	10,831	19,832	2,270	7,353	1,703	4,097	2,712	6,129	7,567	14,312
Congressional District 38	44,594	39,147	11,010	21,223	3,508	8,710	1,661	4,136	2,618	7,173	7,060	14,862
Congressional District 39	48,739	37,037	8,685	18,545	3,023	7,577	1,157	3,578	1,681	5,938	4,799	12,679
Congressional District 40	27,719	21,459	8,449	12,212	2,108	4,893	2,148	2,955	2,484	4,136	5,909	8,999
Congressional District 41	31,907	23,049	9,294	12,847	2,904	5,968	1,360	2,759	2,129	4,029	6,182	9,092
Congressional District 42	41,394	29,937	10,888	14,667	3,605	6,597	1,275	3,733	2,288	4,495	7,090	9,438
Congressional District 43	39,791	31,039	9,777	15,878	2,358	6,364	1,684	3,804	1,892	5,738	6,714	11,013
Congressional District 44	34,995	23,396	11,527	13,556	3,008	5,483	2,723	3,593	3,278	4,720	8,188	9,279
Congressional District 45	48,770	40,956	8,148	18,246	2,837	8,400	1,090	3,315	1,798	6,349	4,705	12,086
Congressional District 46	29,415	24,124	7,460	12,737	2,061	5,242	1,625	2,878	1,571	4,694	4,386	8,231
Congressional District 47	42,515	36,615	10,244	18,765	2,842	8,312	1,736	3,670	2,990	6,597	6,488	12,282
Congressional District 48	58,291	45,048	9,346	20,332	3,119	9,253	1,275	3,919	2,728	6,722	5,304	13,679
Congressional District 49	45,377	41,175	7,878	19,130	2,803	9,446	922	3,693	2,105	6,438	4,177	11,976
Congressional District 50	45,487	40,193	11,572	21,028	3,389	10,601	1,534	4,188	3,649	7,428	6,469	12,920
Congressional District 51	36,779	32,331	11,989	19,042	3,260	8,383	2,791	4,399	3,049	7,160	7,956	13,797
Congressional District 52	45,494	39,372	7,880	18,065	2,999	8,323	1,356	2,695	1,600	4,867	4,698	11,864
Congressional District 53	42,067	36,693	10,025	19,655	2,492	8,797	1,092	3,971	2,201	6,639	6,307	13,101

Table H-5: 113th Congressional Districts—Disability Status and Type of Disability—*Continued*

	Total Population		With a Disability		With a Hearing Difficulty		With a Vision Difficulty		With a Cognitive Difficulty		With an Ambulatory Difficulty	
	65 to 74 Years	75 Years and Over	65 to 74 Years	75 Years and Over	65 to 74 Years	75 Years and Over	65 to 74 Years	75 Years and Over	65 to 74 Years	75 Years and Over	65 to 74 Years	75 Years and Over
Colorado												
Congressional District 1....................	41,878	34,413	9,809	17,549	3,342	8,157	1,489	4,363	1,914	4,958	6,019	10,952
Congressional District 2....................	48,806	31,095	8,316	14,257	4,121	7,788	710	2,736	1,632	3,482	3,793	8,098
Congressional District 3....................	58,893	41,858	14,422	21,229	6,522	11,643	2,234	5,035	2,403	5,279	8,020	12,908
Congressional District 4....................	45,614	31,830	10,462	16,485	4,796	8,881	1,482	3,171	2,017	4,539	5,803	10,230
Congressional District 5....................	47,324	32,724	10,717	15,906	4,813	8,424	1,583	3,263	1,870	3,686	5,920	9,533
Congressional District 6....................	41,142	27,687	8,256	12,929	3,375	6,732	1,546	2,739	1,500	4,131	4,267	8,101
Congressional District 7....................	46,178	36,031	11,220	18,245	4,655	8,873	1,840	3,931	1,772	4,481	6,559	11,826
Connecticut												
Congressional District 1....................	52,572	49,701	12,557	24,233	3,912	10,336	1,906	4,517	3,064	6,194	7,826	15,096
Congressional District 2....................	56,064	43,004	11,030	19,400	4,459	9,247	949	2,892	2,088	4,259	6,419	11,982
Congressional District 3....................	52,273	47,867	11,288	22,399	3,096	10,094	1,397	4,075	2,168	5,653	7,211	13,858
Congressional District 4....................	50,270	45,069	9,099	19,845	2,600	9,248	1,751	3,592	1,609	5,324	5,206	12,425
Congressional District 5....................	53,064	46,193	10,799	21,096	3,389	9,167	1,313	3,717	2,257	6,113	5,986	12,930
Delaware												
Congressional District (at Large)	75,755	54,968	16,756	25,274	5,102	10,734	2,500	5,169	3,217	6,490	10,442	16,594
District of Columbia												
Delegate District (at Large)	37,724	30,328	9,429	14,182	2,225	4,435	1,866	2,976	2,020	4,175	6,857	9,962
Florida												
Congressional District 1....................	58,401	41,313	16,212	21,729	6,091	10,845	2,135	4,570	3,062	6,339	11,094	15,404
Congressional District 2....................	51,451	36,321	14,817	19,746	6,214	9,246	3,095	4,031	2,945	6,420	9,070	13,039
Congressional District 3....................	59,763	43,331	17,189	22,972	6,255	11,053	2,755	4,949	3,435	7,677	10,980	14,852
Congressional District 4....................	49,785	35,148	12,779	17,179	4,418	7,651	1,729	4,004	2,387	5,073	8,505	11,876
Congressional District 5....................	41,859	31,240	13,337	16,552	3,144	6,120	2,717	3,583	2,897	4,678	9,171	11,558
Congressional District 6....................	83,443	65,303	17,235	29,194	6,903	13,376	2,817	4,803	2,925	7,830	9,399	18,334
Congressional District 7....................	49,124	41,181	10,933	20,678	3,418	9,108	1,253	3,749	2,226	5,873	7,301	13,878
Congressional District 8....................	79,511	72,744	16,646	34,713	5,993	16,451	2,454	6,713	3,802	9,241	9,886	22,217
Congressional District 9....................	46,172	29,551	12,028	15,396	3,431	6,428	2,994	3,105	3,583	4,925	7,605	10,995
Congressional District 10..................	67,365	53,591	15,168	23,941	5,488	11,817	2,124	4,680	2,961	6,132	9,350	14,833
Congressional District 11..................	118,340	91,932	26,462	40,383	11,240	20,509	3,633	8,390	4,733	10,937	15,397	23,616
Congressional District 12..................	74,728	64,672	17,073	30,553	6,107	15,659	2,691	5,546	2,970	8,746	10,504	19,674
Congressional District 13..................	76,075	74,677	16,506	34,979	6,181	16,129	2,096	6,956	3,375	9,136	10,129	23,223
Congressional District 14..................	45,213	35,554	13,786	18,962	3,610	8,015	2,126	4,922	3,256	6,626	9,501	13,519
Congressional District 15..................	52,777	40,564	12,972	20,667	4,097	9,231	2,042	4,055	2,645	6,362	8,559	14,118
Congressional District 16..................	100,714	94,861	18,081	39,198	8,228	19,971	2,475	6,749	3,164	9,733	9,536	24,178
Congressional District 17..................	94,951	80,729	22,990	36,156	9,588	17,762	3,155	6,682	4,866	9,466	13,178	22,129
Congressional District 18..................	81,279	76,962	15,122	33,826	5,437	16,695	2,020	5,171	2,086	9,114	9,323	20,857
Congressional District 19..................	103,653	83,049	17,231	34,324	7,309	16,675	1,731	5,951	3,162	10,065	9,956	21,130
Congressional District 20..................	48,065	43,370	13,626	23,667	3,148	8,413	3,068	5,375	3,563	7,027	8,786	17,196
Congressional District 21..................	70,073	85,334	13,267	39,623	4,693	19,098	1,473	6,767	1,852	7,877	8,339	25,649
Congressional District 22..................	68,703	73,720	11,967	31,177	3,772	14,165	2,185	5,991	3,101	8,102	6,864	20,034
Congressional District 23..................	55,547	53,391	10,787	26,140	2,579	9,940	1,937	5,677	2,729	8,700	7,017	18,834
Congressional District 24..................	42,475	30,702	11,002	15,398	1,876	3,794	1,766	3,253	3,582	5,614	7,393	11,738
Congressional District 25..................	56,200	46,424	11,728	21,058	3,001	8,977	2,686	5,555	4,183	8,676	7,529	13,860
Congressional District 26..................	56,548	45,073	12,933	21,291	2,774	6,933	1,669	3,604	3,618	8,246	7,850	14,278
Congressional District 27..................	58,516	55,202	13,842	29,634	2,393	11,844	2,568	7,953	5,244	12,537	9,086	21,662
Georgia												
Congressional District 1....................	48,316	33,859	14,156	17,874	4,800	7,338	2,913	3,559	3,448	5,663	9,447	12,435
Congressional District 2....................	49,163	35,392	17,050	19,614	5,148	8,249	4,002	5,069	4,663	6,870	11,648	13,964
Congressional District 3....................	50,467	32,645	15,263	17,746	5,022	7,380	2,711	3,787	3,720	5,694	10,230	11,883
Congressional District 4....................	37,160	23,649	9,747	12,007	2,356	4,282	1,988	2,945	2,072	4,199	6,096	8,457
Congressional District 5....................	36,279	25,379	11,295	14,464	2,559	4,932	2,303	3,134	2,535	5,416	7,952	10,569
Congressional District 6....................	42,071	27,665	7,240	12,434	2,250	5,212	674	1,782	1,310	4,077	4,398	7,880
Congressional District 7....................	33,938	19,534	6,538	9,990	2,026	4,396	1,126	2,012	1,410	2,907	4,335	6,735
Congressional District 8....................	50,588	36,052	17,034	20,164	6,045	8,540	3,739	5,026	3,806	6,728	11,663	13,675
Congressional District 9....................	63,710	40,449	18,441	21,926	6,697	10,050	3,242	4,904	4,151	7,669	11,575	14,194
Congressional District 10..................	49,611	30,486	14,153	17,526	5,271	7,577	2,453	3,826	2,910	5,622	8,907	12,186
Congressional District 11..................	40,815	24,513	8,679	11,752	3,636	5,406	1,293	2,696	2,215	3,865	5,437	7,961
Congressional District 12..................	48,468	31,497	16,017	17,963	5,019	7,472	2,841	4,227	3,798	6,356	11,096	12,957
Congressional District 13..................	36,899	22,806	10,300	12,540	2,692	5,398	1,750	2,767	2,358	4,019	6,799	8,390
Congressional District 14..................	49,460	32,884	16,325	19,511	6,178	8,424	2,774	4,508	3,380	6,914	10,633	13,432
Hawaii												
Congressional District 1....................	54,095	53,672	9,776	24,502	3,769	11,356	1,411	3,358	2,425	8,299	5,822	15,548
Congressional District 2....................	51,209	39,496	12,050	20,934	4,660	10,356	2,438	3,670	2,812	6,683	7,273	12,612
Idaho												
Congressional District 1....................	62,082	42,822	16,379	22,316	7,668	11,692	2,215	4,356	3,401	5,854	8,829	14,055
Congressional District 2....................	52,900	41,202	14,219	21,658	6,069	11,687	2,293	5,375	3,099	4,959	8,550	12,726

Table H-5: 113th Congressional Districts—Disability Status and Type of Disability—*Continued*

	Total Population		With a Disability		With a Hearing Difficulty		With a Vision Difficulty		With a Cognitive Difficulty		With an Ambulatory Difficulty	
	65 to 74 Years	75 Years and Over	65 to 74 Years	75 Years and Over	65 to 74 Years	75 Years and Over	65 to 74 Years	75 Years and Over	65 to 74 Years	75 Years and Over	65 to 74 Years	75 Years and Over
Illinois												
Congressional District 1..................	50,215	44,135	13,732	22,270	2,886	7,173	2,506	4,709	3,319	7,358	9,751	15,803
Congressional District 2..................	50,963	40,200	14,460	21,073	3,023	7,501	2,663	4,688	3,176	5,946	10,217	14,743
Congressional District 3..................	45,402	41,633	10,004	20,629	3,054	8,116	1,334	3,370	1,654	4,672	6,468	13,684
Congressional District 4..................	31,377	22,500	9,222	12,292	2,284	5,071	2,197	2,370	1,881	3,637	6,336	8,618
Congressional District 5..................	42,849	38,988	9,676	18,979	2,801	7,326	1,508	4,204	1,890	4,860	6,081	12,884
Congressional District 6..................	49,335	37,015	8,666	16,067	2,479	6,721	911	2,653	1,787	4,645	5,491	10,614
Congressional District 7..................	42,336	30,478	13,300	17,127	2,353	4,847	2,829	3,370	3,314	5,561	9,949	12,943
Congressional District 8..................	39,384	30,828	8,877	15,308	2,553	6,828	1,220	2,974	1,946	4,249	5,616	10,573
Congressional District 9..................	55,064	51,994	10,547	25,335	2,880	10,623	2,074	4,866	2,455	7,041	6,607	17,358
Congressional District 10..................	45,799	36,580	8,178	16,947	2,474	6,358	965	2,892	1,419	4,366	5,172	11,608
Congressional District 11..................	40,113	28,059	8,088	13,622	2,684	5,915	1,072	2,728	1,482	3,776	4,837	9,378
Congressional District 12..................	53,430	45,700	15,368	23,753	4,725	11,000	2,390	5,256	3,001	6,803	9,948	15,987
Congressional District 13..................	50,376	42,027	12,480	20,154	4,324	9,332	1,463	3,914	2,048	4,449	8,205	13,205
Congressional District 14..................	43,902	27,080	8,153	12,398	2,970	5,356	720	2,171	1,052	3,049	4,747	7,816
Congressional District 15..................	60,160	51,505	16,508	25,981	6,222	12,179	2,328	4,747	3,210	5,980	11,041	16,647
Congressional District 16..................	55,750	45,160	12,097	20,544	4,907	9,653	1,725	3,644	1,574	4,347	7,219	12,775
Congressional District 17..................	58,991	50,817	14,651	24,277	5,275	11,330	2,399	4,401	2,696	5,796	9,360	15,741
Congressional District 18..................	57,686	49,028	12,291	22,914	4,918	10,490	1,404	4,035	1,950	5,217	7,486	14,455
Indiana												
Congressional District 1..................	51,906	41,699	14,461	20,784	4,679	8,747	2,442	3,893	2,881	6,051	9,518	13,758
Congressional District 2..................	51,393	44,485	13,944	22,643	5,037	11,404	2,374	4,345	2,261	5,523	8,152	14,209
Congressional District 3..................	50,362	40,273	12,379	19,424	4,994	8,918	1,719	3,795	1,907	5,170	7,318	12,126
Congressional District 4..................	51,872	39,439	13,793	19,115	5,708	8,509	2,066	3,652	2,159	4,731	8,683	12,869
Congressional District 5..................	47,303	38,495	11,142	18,909	4,747	8,852	1,431	3,266	2,107	4,899	6,754	12,448
Congressional District 6..................	58,548	44,550	17,141	22,285	7,128	11,108	2,642	4,343	3,488	5,624	10,246	14,312
Congressional District 7..................	40,956	31,278	12,720	15,785	3,922	6,452	2,337	2,713	2,684	4,770	8,603	10,878
Congressional District 8..................	56,740	45,381	14,775	22,596	5,216	10,420	1,907	3,956	2,951	5,408	9,349	14,906
Congressional District 9..................	53,829	38,624	13,678	19,916	5,016	9,273	2,340	4,004	2,608	5,375	8,575	13,662
Iowa												
Congressional District 1..................	58,935	53,736	11,758	23,709	5,062	10,532	1,257	3,614	1,942	5,391	6,268	14,441
Congressional District 2..................	57,848	49,850	13,641	22,686	5,034	11,007	1,667	3,857	2,276	5,216	8,154	14,314
Congressional District 3..................	51,367	42,358	11,569	19,149	4,523	9,175	1,597	3,299	2,288	4,649	7,155	12,067
Congressional District 4..................	60,523	61,219	12,978	25,979	5,211	12,944	1,515	4,696	2,368	5,147	7,429	14,832
Kansas												
Congressional District 1..................	50,287	48,947	12,355	23,807	5,079	11,456	1,434	4,640	2,340	5,311	7,478	15,098
Congressional District 2..................	53,938	44,075	14,326	22,948	6,159	10,731	2,116	4,759	2,905	5,731	8,792	15,288
Congressional District 3..................	43,320	35,043	8,803	17,065	3,227	7,876	1,191	2,478	1,601	4,516	5,244	11,375
Congressional District 4..................	48,019	42,145	13,444	20,914	5,176	9,841	1,938	3,860	2,836	5,608	8,550	13,537
Kentucky												
Congressional District 1..................	63,745	45,477	20,403	23,882	7,439	10,851	3,187	5,075	4,201	6,370	13,027	15,855
Congressional District 2..................	55,182	39,348	16,894	23,152	6,292	10,914	2,362	4,769	3,756	6,676	10,957	15,692
Congressional District 3..................	50,891	44,380	13,857	23,286	3,792	9,607	2,311	4,665	3,814	6,975	8,878	15,271
Congressional District 4..................	51,458	34,536	15,059	18,232	5,454	8,251	1,903	3,489	2,874	5,138	9,657	11,921
Congressional District 5..................	62,147	38,761	27,438	25,699	10,400	12,660	6,674	6,425	8,054	8,181	19,346	18,182
Congressional District 6..................	50,081	35,191	14,907	19,428	5,700	8,697	2,308	3,893	3,368	5,576	9,846	13,775
Louisiana												
Congressional District 1..................	55,501	44,580	15,883	24,492	5,893	10,254	3,029	4,604	2,700	7,580	10,137	16,591
Congressional District 2..................	49,563	33,794	17,137	19,650	4,728	7,272	3,556	4,817	4,569	6,979	11,544	13,974
Congressional District 3..................	51,560	37,420	17,474	20,867	6,041	8,993	3,874	4,075	4,076	6,948	11,537	13,666
Congressional District 4..................	56,975	42,734	18,785	24,337	6,524	10,398	3,989	5,020	4,269	8,055	12,308	16,552
Congressional District 5..................	56,507	42,151	20,649	24,977	7,350	11,337	4,326	6,231	5,124	8,568	13,854	18,194
Congressional District 6..................	50,264	33,571	14,737	18,412	5,581	8,264	2,902	3,695	2,811	5,620	9,048	12,667
Maine												
Congressional District 1..................	57,026	47,078	12,544	22,494	5,231	11,911	1,460	4,144	2,881	6,235	6,626	13,068
Congressional District 2..................	60,445	46,780	17,956	25,109	7,928	12,780	2,380	4,679	3,962	6,452	10,333	15,140
Maryland												
Congressional District 1..................	64,081	46,250	14,234	21,772	5,406	9,891	1,830	3,870	2,318	6,616	8,192	13,677
Congressional District 2..................	43,806	38,139	11,160	18,557	3,704	7,332	1,936	3,444	2,313	5,370	7,228	12,222
Congressional District 3..................	47,437	45,213	10,881	20,566	3,613	8,632	1,934	4,395	2,327	6,078	7,031	13,827
Congressional District 4..................	46,277	27,906	10,027	12,166	2,287	4,504	1,437	2,102	2,112	3,903	6,952	8,697
Congressional District 5..................	47,107	29,351	10,345	14,192	3,040	5,978	1,174	2,343	2,109	4,860	7,019	9,552
Congressional District 6..................	50,903	36,001	10,581	17,999	3,454	8,598	1,600	3,743	1,945	4,493	6,546	11,345
Congressional District 7..................	51,133	39,884	13,233	20,377	2,947	6,671	2,216	3,953	2,702	6,016	8,989	13,080
Congressional District 8..................	51,607	46,522	9,175	20,983	2,586	8,900	1,565	3,567	1,726	5,147	5,613	13,354
Massachusetts												
Congressional District 1..................	55,547	51,440	13,211	25,911	4,503	11,982	2,091	4,665	2,611	6,204	8,560	16,251
Congressional District 2..................	49,184	41,701	10,973	20,457	3,893	9,242	1,285	4,389	2,294	5,014	6,546	13,117
Congressional District 3..................	47,732	38,832	10,889	18,198	4,140	8,231	1,614	3,659	2,123	4,993	6,447	11,493
Congressional District 4..................	51,054	43,731	10,166	19,813	3,881	9,288	1,351	3,482	2,085	4,820	5,877	11,986
Congressional District 5..................	51,595	49,244	9,018	21,112	2,666	9,156	1,375	4,145	2,152	5,240	5,298	13,418
Congressional District 6..................	58,002	49,372	11,444	23,292	4,346	10,822	1,462	4,370	2,172	6,828	6,324	13,889
Congressional District 7..................	38,195	32,498	12,721	18,270	3,146	6,727	2,672	4,034	3,754	5,565	8,256	12,197
Congressional District 8..................	52,580	49,568	11,361	23,967	4,035	10,845	1,750	4,726	2,808	6,903	6,164	14,675
Congressional District 9..................	71,546	58,619	13,167	25,368	4,828	11,606	1,603	4,506	2,888	5,456	7,943	15,420

Table H-5: 113th Congressional Districts—Disability Status and Type of Disability—*Continued*

	Total Population		With a Disability		With a Hearing Difficulty		With a Vision Difficulty		With a Cognitive Difficulty		With an Ambulatory Difficulty	
	65 to 74 Years	75 Years and Over	65 to 74 Years	75 Years and Over	65 to 74 Years	75 Years and Over	65 to 74 Years	75 Years and Over	65 to 74 Years	75 Years and Over	65 to 74 Years	75 Years and Over
Michigan												
Congressional District 1....................	73,419	57,805	18,434	27,943	8,831	13,937	2,750	5,197	3,509	7,217	9,964	16,830
Congressional District 2....................	49,372	40,763	11,663	19,635	4,870	9,480	1,508	3,361	2,139	5,303	6,709	12,312
Congressional District 3....................	46,776	39,506	11,733	18,958	4,609	9,009	1,396	3,471	2,445	5,448	7,002	11,724
Congressional District 4....................	62,192	46,521	17,466	22,585	7,886	10,935	2,263	3,955	3,109	6,051	10,035	13,908
Congressional District 5....................	57,676	46,872	17,165	23,578	5,791	11,134	2,644	3,796	3,787	7,213	10,565	15,567
Congressional District 6....................	54,755	43,393	12,885	21,475	4,819	10,544	1,758	3,741	2,433	5,714	7,946	13,406
Congressional District 7....................	55,808	42,854	14,294	21,988	5,727	10,698	1,485	3,715	2,892	5,910	8,517	13,611
Congressional District 8....................	48,491	33,093	10,240	16,422	4,235	7,087	1,457	3,141	2,122	5,083	5,879	10,542
Congressional District 9....................	53,680	52,908	13,536	26,852	4,644	11,828	2,036	5,100	2,518	7,495	8,686	17,765
Congressional District 10..................	57,214	42,584	14,476	21,122	5,677	10,041	1,378	3,774	2,868	6,110	8,638	13,747
Congressional District 11..................	51,078	42,358	9,921	19,230	3,466	8,910	1,416	3,331	1,529	5,249	5,771	12,602
Congressional District 12..................	44,271	37,330	12,060	18,549	3,939	7,978	1,665	3,599	2,727	5,541	7,982	11,878
Congressional District 13..................	44,500	40,692	15,976	22,423	3,449	7,708	3,160	4,799	4,258	6,987	11,770	15,396
Congressional District 14..................	49,045	44,660	14,041	23,844	3,421	9,048	2,774	5,540	3,661	7,907	9,613	16,928
Minnesota												
Congressional District 1....................	48,930	47,222	9,224	21,097	4,124	10,386	847	3,758	1,677	4,693	4,901	12,581
Congressional District 2....................	39,808	29,338	7,269	12,767	3,686	5,762	576	2,170	1,434	3,482	3,795	7,838
Congressional District 3....................	44,793	35,438	7,461	15,084	2,901	7,028	645	2,354	1,377	3,564	3,990	8,989
Congressional District 4....................	42,011	35,300	8,106	16,382	3,270	7,078	1,256	2,793	1,813	3,514	4,604	10,132
Congressional District 5....................	35,606	33,910	8,556	15,175	2,593	6,550	1,299	2,779	2,077	3,201	5,302	9,285
Congressional District 6....................	38,355	25,760	7,921	12,108	3,937	6,079	1,047	1,791	1,335	2,250	3,984	7,199
Congressional District 7....................	56,723	53,320	12,177	23,917	5,757	11,930	1,400	4,063	2,026	4,824	6,111	13,931
Congressional District 8....................	61,108	47,901	14,869	22,641	6,946	11,716	2,073	3,779	2,462	4,863	7,837	13,201
Mississippi												
Congressional District 1....................	56,643	40,592	19,387	24,062	6,349	9,506	3,458	5,158	4,890	8,373	13,524	17,647
Congressional District 2....................	50,067	37,478	16,767	21,697	4,494	7,554	3,649	5,390	4,220	7,843	11,768	16,609
Congressional District 3....................	55,966	41,652	21,121	24,067	7,139	10,293	4,356	5,729	5,576	7,874	14,004	17,509
Congressional District 4....................	56,679	38,330	20,760	22,898	7,161	10,012	4,344	5,825	4,831	7,325	15,330	16,257
Missouri												
Congressional District 1....................	45,614	40,705	13,999	20,824	3,440	8,017	2,708	4,098	3,016	5,728	9,604	14,047
Congressional District 2....................	60,042	52,694	10,982	24,046	3,703	10,517	1,293	4,247	2,331	6,097	6,554	15,314
Congressional District 3....................	57,353	38,734	15,601	19,460	6,220	9,885	2,148	3,796	2,876	4,836	9,436	12,357
Congressional District 4....................	59,271	44,911	16,687	23,966	6,551	11,901	2,326	4,851	2,722	5,812	10,525	14,710
Congressional District 5....................	51,943	44,640	14,444	22,590	4,465	9,735	2,375	4,338	3,382	5,876	9,608	14,837
Congressional District 6....................	56,998	43,709	15,247	22,171	5,955	10,710	1,816	4,154	2,779	5,618	9,226	13,884
Congressional District 7....................	63,704	46,783	17,618	23,998	6,416	11,643	2,467	4,812	3,404	6,332	11,461	15,640
Congressional District 8....................	65,752	49,011	22,876	28,211	9,280	14,113	3,904	6,465	5,326	8,307	14,324	18,881
Montana												
Congressional District (at Large)	83,660	63,461	21,862	32,238	10,559	18,066	3,202	7,129	3,527	7,200	11,594	18,925
Nebraska												
Congressional District 1....................	40,828	36,387	8,345	17,430	3,498	8,967	914	3,125	1,412	3,343	4,679	10,227
Congressional District 2....................	33,734	27,423	6,849	13,555	3,089	6,045	1,034	2,971	1,269	3,831	3,474	8,838
Congressional District 3....................	50,393	49,373	12,957	23,134	6,297	12,210	1,599	4,343	1,793	4,680	7,091	13,362
Nevada												
Congressional District 1....................	48,696	31,911	14,826	16,140	4,404	7,127	2,868	3,748	2,658	4,263	10,149	11,303
Congressional District 2....................	55,779	35,407	14,603	17,259	6,369	8,087	1,828	3,208	2,640	4,590	8,795	11,393
Congressional District 3....................	55,123	31,630	12,245	14,595	4,524	6,399	2,125	2,667	2,231	3,798	7,074	9,656
Congressional District 4....................	49,030	31,045	12,523	15,881	4,382	6,941	1,770	3,007	2,223	4,436	7,762	10,073
New Hampshire												
Congressional District 1....................	50,654	37,486	10,486	17,341	4,106	9,053	1,588	3,533	2,079	4,281	5,618	10,198
Congressional District 2....................	50,938	38,936	11,846	17,736	4,828	9,046	1,291	3,189	2,103	4,244	7,140	10,651
New Jersey												
Congressional District 1....................	51,042	42,750	13,851	20,812	4,203	8,751	2,089	4,179	3,241	5,458	9,091	14,405
Congressional District 2....................	61,750	48,756	14,647	22,782	4,997	9,549	2,302	4,136	3,085	6,589	9,446	15,402
Congressional District 3....................	63,094	59,056	14,225	27,286	4,464	11,334	1,924	4,611	2,578	6,760	8,766	17,633
Congressional District 4....................	60,930	58,362	11,163	26,775	3,355	11,236	1,184	5,326	2,321	7,497	7,495	17,188
Congressional District 5....................	56,372	47,794	9,130	20,815	3,088	8,622	1,178	3,816	1,900	5,897	5,346	13,491
Congressional District 6....................	46,527	37,771	9,533	17,369	2,788	7,512	1,753	3,234	1,815	4,968	6,012	11,972
Congressional District 7....................	51,169	43,483	7,600	19,854	2,585	8,726	847	3,489	1,207	5,424	4,189	13,034
Congressional District 8....................	37,511	30,797	10,458	15,624	2,777	4,907	3,072	3,959	2,607	4,243	6,415	10,884
Congressional District 9....................	50,287	45,610	10,906	21,437	3,156	8,535	2,547	5,038	2,283	7,230	7,157	15,051
Congressional District 10..................	46,754	33,180	12,494	17,459	2,336	5,896	2,593	4,339	2,737	5,538	9,463	12,572
Congressional District 11..................	57,240	53,686	9,689	23,714	3,023	10,210	1,216	4,775	1,829	6,296	5,627	15,154
Congressional District 12..................	49,724	43,904	9,267	19,956	2,014	7,866	1,363	3,756	1,618	5,202	6,471	13,183
New Mexico												
Congressional District 1....................	49,728	38,535	13,062	20,053	4,688	9,546	2,312	4,367	2,359	6,168	8,407	13,044
Congressional District 2....................	56,559	43,169	17,877	25,905	7,708	13,480	3,801	6,781	4,165	8,056	10,644	16,577
Congressional District 3....................	54,922	35,569	16,595	20,412	7,389	11,518	2,869	5,631	3,954	7,164	9,799	13,177

Table H-5: 113th Congressional Districts—Disability Status and Type of Disability—*Continued*

	Total Population		With a Disability		With a Hearing Difficulty		With a Vision Difficulty		With a Cognitive Difficulty		With an Ambulatory Difficulty	
	65 to 74 Years	75 Years and Over	65 to 74 Years	75 Years and Over	65 to 74 Years	75 Years and Over	65 to 74 Years	75 Years and Over	65 to 74 Years	75 Years and Over	65 to 74 Years	75 Years and Over
New York												
Congressional District 1	57,838	43,413	9,824	18,999	3,001	8,050	1,160	3,372	2,188	4,894	6,644	11,989
Congressional District 2	48,305	44,302	9,701	20,125	2,417	7,584	1,177	3,512	1,438	5,132	6,759	13,450
Congressional District 3	60,993	60,898	8,738	25,745	2,503	10,549	1,011	4,300	1,509	7,235	5,817	16,512
Congressional District 4	51,844	49,870	8,889	20,855	2,268	8,106	1,180	3,853	1,704	5,317	5,877	13,993
Congressional District 5	49,039	36,567	13,037	18,816	2,470	5,378	2,798	4,331	3,328	6,218	9,088	14,034
Congressional District 6	56,632	48,838	11,091	23,545	3,194	8,257	2,185	4,514	2,784	6,277	6,960	17,329
Congressional District 7	34,988	30,977	9,676	16,465	1,737	5,416	1,955	4,175	2,917	6,348	7,524	12,806
Congressional District 8	49,151	39,415	15,465	23,700	3,564	8,095	3,809	7,076	4,836	8,740	11,148	18,788
Congressional District 9	47,433	36,788	11,546	19,375	2,529	6,008	2,345	4,243	2,738	7,062	8,362	15,457
Congressional District 10	50,069	43,980	9,731	22,044	2,133	7,113	1,536	4,224	2,196	7,036	6,331	16,565
Congressional District 11	55,642	45,769	11,138	23,395	2,452	8,511	1,548	4,425	2,336	7,412	7,515	17,714
Congressional District 12	52,994	42,701	8,194	17,654	2,088	5,935	1,362	3,383	2,048	4,327	5,570	13,061
Congressional District 13	44,075	33,837	14,219	19,345	1,874	4,694	2,849	4,453	3,532	6,417	11,578	15,930
Congressional District 14	42,963	36,729	10,591	18,757	2,594	6,380	1,795	3,753	2,802	5,756	7,154	14,390
Congressional District 15	36,287	23,395	14,126	13,908	2,790	3,713	3,396	3,605	4,287	4,560	10,961	11,289
Congressional District 16	54,081	48,072	11,203	22,214	2,411	8,262	2,055	4,812	2,487	5,749	7,710	15,473
Congressional District 17	52,322	47,953	8,367	20,739	2,255	8,272	1,095	3,348	1,549	5,622	4,922	12,643
Congressional District 18	49,553	38,466	10,621	19,003	3,591	8,144	1,419	3,626	2,125	5,439	6,125	12,292
Congressional District 19	63,466	47,285	14,288	22,517	5,342	10,634	2,177	4,200	2,469	5,426	8,155	14,209
Congressional District 20	51,459	47,255	10,989	23,297	3,777	10,199	1,817	4,262	2,408	6,201	6,602	14,582
Congressional District 21	57,111	44,027	14,292	21,557	5,887	10,189	1,968	3,874	2,948	4,667	8,626	13,040
Congressional District 22	57,984	50,582	13,112	24,257	4,575	11,151	1,521	5,070	2,455	6,084	8,280	15,206
Congressional District 23	57,057	48,137	13,139	23,092	5,382	10,610	1,733	4,169	2,352	5,544	7,900	14,776
Congressional District 24	51,783	46,210	11,127	20,700	3,979	9,639	1,661	4,150	2,344	5,084	6,677	13,315
Congressional District 25	51,888	46,718	9,339	21,523	2,616	8,730	1,319	3,387	1,871	5,571	6,284	13,737
Congressional District 26	53,246	55,054	12,854	25,513	4,162	10,652	1,653	4,310	2,279	6,252	8,685	16,979
Congressional District 27	60,069	48,600	11,991	21,800	5,121	10,164	1,648	3,799	2,067	5,014	6,829	13,242
North Carolina												
Congressional District 1	55,009	42,844	19,288	26,056	4,858	10,226	4,831	6,663	4,099	8,789	12,904	18,860
Congressional District 2	51,185	37,065	13,693	19,006	4,731	8,264	2,256	4,116	2,907	5,128	8,817	12,705
Congressional District 3	57,221	39,385	16,923	21,296	6,812	10,096	2,790	4,263	3,525	5,598	10,772	13,671
Congressional District 4	39,903	28,904	10,670	14,350	2,651	5,844	1,605	2,836	2,280	4,001	7,199	9,555
Congressional District 5	62,057	46,665	14,988	22,939	5,107	9,309	2,384	4,275	2,981	6,695	8,769	15,806
Congressional District 6	62,461	48,530	13,729	23,837	5,107	11,130	2,092	5,538	3,426	7,055	8,891	15,086
Congressional District 7	68,214	41,709	20,101	22,445	6,155	9,941	3,059	4,452	5,440	6,670	13,100	15,504
Congressional District 8	56,757	38,208	17,242	21,552	5,948	10,216	3,139	4,217	4,103	6,719	11,957	14,814
Congressional District 9	46,918	31,916	8,909	15,817	3,228	7,084	995	3,185	1,642	4,432	5,390	10,671
Congressional District 10	62,449	45,017	17,981	24,385	6,582	11,981	2,944	5,368	4,907	6,607	10,885	16,184
Congressional District 11	79,715	59,399	20,887	31,832	9,070	15,795	4,462	7,030	4,178	8,725	12,579	20,704
Congressional District 12	35,718	26,099	10,157	14,534	2,601	5,181	1,952	3,091	2,198	4,352	6,724	9,792
Congressional District 13	50,502	33,264	11,811	16,141	4,037	6,823	2,643	3,080	2,840	4,804	7,039	11,040
North Dakota												
Congressional District (at Large)	47,935	45,172	11,298	20,987	5,011	10,206	1,251	4,476	1,669	4,554	6,047	11,933
Ohio												
Congressional District 1	47,312	37,832	11,715	18,377	3,570	7,287	2,078	3,370	2,165	4,311	7,605	11,751
Congressional District 2	53,144	44,381	14,483	23,128	5,376	9,998	2,492	4,393	3,716	6,404	9,444	15,491
Congressional District 3	36,374	28,149	11,272	15,187	3,164	6,149	2,207	2,991	3,013	4,544	7,821	10,289
Congressional District 4	55,567	45,854	14,666	21,800	5,204	10,981	1,959	3,585	2,546	5,336	9,146	13,599
Congressional District 5	56,539	47,416	11,794	22,694	4,778	10,777	1,300	3,912	2,205	5,343	7,102	14,391
Congressional District 6	66,202	51,471	19,285	25,615	7,051	11,445	3,076	4,954	3,886	6,457	11,993	16,759
Congressional District 7	58,970	46,415	14,065	22,316	5,377	9,918	1,660	3,927	3,008	5,786	8,395	14,328
Congressional District 8	54,278	42,347	13,252	20,904	5,387	9,396	1,956	3,889	2,138	5,617	7,886	13,978
Congressional District 9	49,275	44,454	14,291	22,189	4,762	9,318	2,509	4,660	2,558	5,802	9,581	14,284
Congressional District 10	56,455	48,872	15,031	24,149	5,272	10,842	2,221	4,825	3,357	5,827	10,048	14,801
Congressional District 11	50,398	48,628	14,356	24,764	3,730	8,621	2,646	5,226	3,151	7,172	10,213	16,673
Congressional District 12	51,169	37,479	11,770	17,395	4,750	7,880	1,604	3,219	2,132	4,474	6,854	11,710
Congressional District 13	57,174	53,863	14,836	26,133	5,098	11,799	2,147	4,938	2,700	6,693	9,315	16,667
Congressional District 14	61,369	52,092	11,980	23,345	5,168	9,868	1,535	4,006	2,093	5,627	6,615	14,609
Congressional District 15	51,354	37,557	13,611	19,815	4,952	8,531	1,666	3,870	3,328	5,568	8,870	13,204
Congressional District 16	63,298	53,512	13,317	24,867	4,919	10,648	1,619	4,127	2,395	6,312	8,020	15,091
Oklahoma												
Congressional District 1	52,639	41,222	14,923	20,760	6,185	10,228	2,621	4,474	2,336	5,252	9,273	13,768
Congressional District 2	70,444	48,214	25,708	27,975	10,367	13,017	4,731	7,039	5,662	8,353	17,328	19,168
Congressional District 3	59,577	45,407	18,327	25,203	7,484	12,291	2,509	4,848	3,638	6,557	11,410	16,564
Congressional District 4	54,336	38,920	18,273	22,158	7,565	11,135	2,658	4,383	3,526	6,179	11,789	15,034
Congressional District 5	50,236	40,444	15,065	22,107	5,510	9,706	2,989	4,535	2,689	5,767	9,668	14,816
Oregon												
Congressional District 1	51,090	38,683	11,521	19,673	4,638	9,128	1,482	3,518	3,066	6,853	6,719	13,042
Congressional District 2	73,724	57,433	19,684	30,112	9,229	16,313	2,877	5,864	4,538	8,740	10,621	18,407
Congressional District 3	47,230	36,678	12,663	19,712	4,783	8,394	1,862	4,352	3,257	6,017	7,133	12,476
Congressional District 4	73,584	58,232	21,330	31,727	10,706	15,906	2,933	5,543	4,144	9,303	12,021	20,301
Congressional District 5	61,805	49,238	15,289	24,116	6,190	11,708	2,336	4,309	3,282	6,971	9,236	15,789

Table H-5: 113th Congressional Districts—Disability Status and Type of Disability—*Continued*

	Total Population		With a Disability		With a Hearing Difficulty		With a Vision Difficulty		With a Cognitive Difficulty		With an Ambulatory Difficulty	
	65 to 74 Years	75 Years and Over	65 to 74 Years	75 Years and Over	65 to 74 Years	75 Years and Over	65 to 74 Years	75 Years and Over	65 to 74 Years	75 Years and Over	65 to 74 Years	75 Years and Over
Pennsylvania												
Congressional District 1	41,033	34,241	11,987	18,855	3,177	6,877	1,991	4,156	2,721	5,562	8,269	12,651
Congressional District 2	47,903	40,579	14,048	19,689	2,701	5,909	3,213	3,622	3,663	6,362	10,193	14,008
Congressional District 3	58,550	53,533	15,005	26,222	6,210	12,752	1,803	4,663	2,955	6,922	8,697	15,813
Congressional District 4	55,086	46,693	12,315	21,874	5,336	9,351	1,679	4,028	2,332	6,034	6,839	13,427
Congressional District 5	58,712	50,612	15,373	24,760	6,801	12,393	1,717	4,684	3,089	5,648	8,702	14,728
Congressional District 6	52,763	45,190	9,249	19,549	4,046	8,363	1,340	2,803	1,738	4,742	4,281	12,451
Congressional District 7	52,537	54,092	9,035	23,955	3,170	10,229	1,019	4,117	1,366	6,607	5,280	15,221
Congressional District 8	55,700	47,733	10,047	21,727	3,199	9,208	1,301	3,832	1,744	5,637	6,020	13,610
Congressional District 9	63,083	56,498	16,485	27,431	6,975	12,803	2,545	5,663	3,668	7,611	10,247	17,589
Congressional District 10	65,062	51,047	17,373	24,424	7,371	12,656	2,966	4,581	2,690	5,861	9,633	15,320
Congressional District 11	59,276	50,636	13,839	24,807	5,411	10,799	2,220	4,443	2,102	5,657	8,232	15,835
Congressional District 12	62,455	64,655	14,599	30,959	5,929	14,924	1,876	5,646	2,554	8,220	8,262	18,943
Congressional District 13	48,592	49,477	12,197	24,909	3,329	10,610	2,148	5,215	2,897	7,827	8,076	16,483
Congressional District 14	54,388	57,231	13,779	28,439	3,840	11,859	2,340	5,358	2,853	7,450	9,037	19,232
Congressional District 15	55,224	49,082	12,285	23,511	4,428	9,719	2,127	4,604	2,480	5,868	7,373	15,438
Congressional District 16	50,175	45,916	10,570	20,696	3,913	9,191	1,304	3,254	2,519	5,182	6,187	13,009
Congressional District 17	58,429	56,349	16,454	27,942	5,854	12,862	2,242	5,645	2,793	7,320	10,578	18,265
Congressional District 18	62,093	59,027	13,084	27,483	5,093	12,478	1,628	4,423	2,472	6,227	7,639	16,873
Rhode Island												
Congressional District 1	37,992	36,011	8,541	18,587	2,853	8,429	1,203	3,260	1,294	4,562	5,313	11,988
Congressional District 2	38,213	34,804	8,012	16,314	2,559	6,931	1,048	2,342	2,057	3,994	4,695	9,707
South Carolina												
Congressional District 1	58,942	37,783	12,223	17,926	4,263	7,742	1,818	3,392	2,510	4,906	7,632	12,026
Congressional District 2	50,539	33,424	13,191	17,502	4,233	7,716	2,027	3,747	3,464	5,496	8,163	12,393
Congressional District 3	59,508	40,655	17,962	22,724	6,146	10,468	2,905	5,312	4,565	6,817	11,480	15,568
Congressional District 4	51,588	36,274	13,066	19,033	4,086	7,605	2,342	3,731	2,857	6,295	8,620	12,538
Congressional District 5	53,814	35,255	16,976	18,994	5,819	7,967	3,087	3,415	3,517	5,926	10,687	12,852
Congressional District 6	49,235	32,825	16,571	18,957	5,292	6,826	4,211	4,897	4,812	6,761	10,955	13,240
Congressional District 7	65,141	39,902	18,733	19,687	6,440	8,539	3,548	4,702	4,145	6,545	12,258	13,179
South Dakota												
Congressional District (at Large)	58,820	53,733	13,669	26,564	6,237	14,042	1,699	5,367	2,489	5,980	7,706	15,959
Tennessee												
Congressional District 1	70,495	48,159	23,664	27,765	9,575	13,769	4,677	6,169	5,298	9,742	15,435	18,424
Congressional District 2	61,209	43,071	16,077	22,159	6,000	10,200	2,505	4,818	3,818	6,992	10,639	15,083
Congressional District 3	64,234	46,952	20,830	25,610	7,853	11,295	3,436	5,633	5,334	8,817	13,472	17,706
Congressional District 4	54,201	35,423	17,972	20,034	6,654	9,764	3,845	4,650	4,491	6,669	12,472	13,896
Congressional District 5	42,324	33,162	11,363	17,240	3,882	7,574	1,683	3,023	2,746	4,835	7,834	11,217
Congressional District 6	64,749	41,764	19,242	22,521	6,787	10,146	2,851	4,250	4,274	6,864	12,676	14,995
Congressional District 7	52,390	35,832	16,776	19,771	5,652	8,584	2,884	4,380	3,876	6,809	10,895	14,044
Congressional District 8	57,455	40,552	16,618	22,790	5,790	9,662	2,365	5,342	3,829	7,097	10,820	15,495
Congressional District 9	37,270	29,427	12,326	16,748	3,141	6,518	2,553	3,906	2,949	5,619	8,651	12,004
Texas												
Congressional District 1	54,731	43,373	17,429	24,191	6,780	11,341	3,030	5,729	3,423	7,020	11,305	16,392
Congressional District 2	38,598	23,452	7,463	10,927	3,093	4,593	998	2,121	1,460	3,169	4,321	7,205
Congressional District 3	38,318	20,815	6,590	10,076	2,475	5,014	713	1,524	923	3,067	4,260	6,749
Congressional District 4	60,321	40,911	19,006	22,325	7,385	10,016	4,060	4,354	4,119	6,103	12,465	15,666
Congressional District 5	48,353	34,727	14,431	19,172	4,964	8,333	2,579	3,430	2,893	5,185	9,194	13,158
Congressional District 6	39,631	25,592	10,713	13,212	4,038	5,949	1,760	2,514	2,216	4,240	6,845	9,188
Congressional District 7	37,622	27,135	7,425	12,295	2,536	5,329	1,507	2,190	1,948	3,618	4,381	8,323
Congressional District 8	49,799	31,336	13,002	16,096	4,010	7,415	1,760	2,710	2,804	4,286	7,930	10,901
Congressional District 9	33,684	21,257	9,702	11,311	2,974	4,298	1,895	2,503	2,600	3,771	6,214	8,290
Congressional District 10	41,994	29,594	9,609	14,763	3,622	6,374	1,270	2,898	2,117	4,251	5,874	10,161
Congressional District 11	57,095	44,659	17,106	24,927	6,871	11,631	3,250	5,671	3,122	6,068	10,544	16,813
Congressional District 12	42,574	32,540	11,320	16,898	4,145	7,691	1,885	3,404	2,574	4,773	7,170	11,041
Congressional District 13	50,808	41,492	15,782	21,683	6,118	10,555	2,546	4,244	2,815	5,724	10,048	14,477
Congressional District 14	46,264	34,858	15,205	19,679	6,061	8,923	3,358	4,942	3,504	6,464	10,617	13,961
Congressional District 15	39,345	29,651	15,814	19,484	5,088	9,837	4,212	5,482	4,022	6,837	10,862	13,654
Congressional District 16	41,505	35,016	13,979	19,851	4,103	8,321	2,768	4,560	3,275	6,215	9,516	14,215
Congressional District 17	42,206	31,228	13,052	17,002	4,481	7,346	2,296	3,296	2,492	4,989	9,134	12,039
Congressional District 18	34,966	23,809	12,111	14,297	3,446	6,021	2,907	3,590	3,394	4,737	9,154	10,285
Congressional District 19	47,036	39,179	15,659	21,748	6,382	11,017	2,758	5,068	3,092	6,592	10,227	15,087
Congressional District 20	39,085	30,582	13,684	18,137	4,531	7,486	2,851	4,256	3,538	5,771	8,962	13,161
Congressional District 21	54,102	40,928	11,685	21,253	4,710	10,488	1,780	4,063	1,882	6,510	7,166	14,436
Congressional District 22	36,641	22,806	8,053	11,853	2,645	4,661	1,125	2,119	1,563	3,714	5,138	7,468
Congressional District 23	44,586	31,201	14,895	19,243	6,090	9,253	3,782	4,781	3,905	6,194	8,973	13,139
Congressional District 24	37,406	24,812	7,383	11,914	2,913	4,971	1,022	2,350	1,309	3,608	4,304	8,471
Congressional District 25	49,288	32,519	12,828	17,189	5,029	7,682	1,829	3,112	2,378	5,338	7,933	11,648
Congressional District 26	34,670	18,209	7,671	9,048	3,153	3,577	1,024	1,788	1,281	3,538	4,919	5,505
Congressional District 27	51,735	40,984	18,210	23,459	7,185	11,365	3,469	5,823	4,216	7,345	11,715	16,644
Congressional District 28	39,900	29,409	16,413	18,977	6,155	9,183	4,368	5,477	4,389	6,860	10,395	13,560
Congressional District 29	29,132	20,162	10,750	12,124	3,561	4,962	2,111	3,151	2,792	3,400	7,247	8,544
Congressional District 30	35,886	23,931	12,160	13,391	2,975	4,442	1,961	3,400	3,262	5,125	8,712	9,869

Table H-5: 113th Congressional Districts—Disability Status and Type of Disability—*Continued*

	Total Population		With a Disability		With a Hearing Difficulty		With a Vision Difficulty		With a Cognitive Difficulty		With an Ambulatory Difficulty	
	65 to 74 Years	75 Years and Over	65 to 74 Years	75 Years and Over	65 to 74 Years	75 Years and Over	65 to 74 Years	75 Years and Over	65 to 74 Years	75 Years and Over	65 to 74 Years	75 Years and Over
Texas—Cont.												
Congressional District 31	40,521	26,576	10,665	13,353	3,754	6,016	2,121	2,199	2,419	4,219	6,642	8,690
Congressional District 32	41,455	31,408	9,133	15,022	3,459	6,844	1,585	3,021	1,982	5,093	5,846	10,241
Congressional District 33	30,671	21,144	9,442	12,289	3,009	4,619	2,323	2,933	2,338	3,889	6,411	9,082
Congressional District 34	45,659	36,864	16,607	22,071	6,288	9,953	3,731	5,188	4,208	7,758	10,826	15,260
Congressional District 35	33,028	25,555	11,424	14,852	3,858	6,516	2,353	3,791	2,358	4,541	8,085	10,552
Congressional District 36	48,846	34,797	16,851	20,548	7,531	9,944	3,746	5,174	4,072	6,798	11,110	13,773
Utah												
Congressional District 1	34,965	26,641	8,766	12,083	3,551	6,216	957	2,563	1,786	3,013	4,778	7,255
Congressional District 2	43,276	35,074	10,211	17,294	4,825	8,456	923	3,776	1,739	4,853	5,786	10,480
Congressional District 3	35,435	25,158	7,470	12,603	3,428	6,820	1,200	2,492	1,417	3,121	4,038	7,199
Congressional District 4	31,380	24,458	7,220	12,321	3,158	6,564	1,119	2,322	1,200	3,443	4,055	7,028
Vermont												
Congressional District (at Large)	51,972	39,268	11,218	19,480	5,079	9,972	1,305	4,038	2,317	5,216	6,113	11,581
Virginia												
Congressional District 1	55,389	35,982	12,303	16,148	4,422	6,888	1,392	2,774	1,979	4,749	7,692	10,262
Congressional District 2	47,139	36,433	10,421	17,627	3,193	7,367	1,332	2,996	2,348	4,850	6,756	11,844
Congressional District 3	43,677	35,069	13,772	19,110	3,427	6,383	2,926	3,757	3,408	6,042	9,540	13,210
Congressional District 4	51,299	34,232	13,728	17,353	4,359	6,971	1,652	3,190	3,416	5,275	9,473	12,274
Congressional District 5	69,349	49,631	16,765	25,527	5,604	10,937	2,344	4,826	3,279	7,442	10,335	16,596
Congressional District 6	61,461	50,392	15,185	24,323	5,663	10,871	2,010	5,005	3,426	6,733	8,976	15,917
Congressional District 7	53,447	40,930	10,325	19,605	3,992	8,287	1,464	3,826	1,965	6,299	5,744	12,822
Congressional District 8	40,268	29,425	6,831	12,720	1,922	5,385	992	3,147	995	3,436	4,116	8,416
Congressional District 9	68,973	50,961	23,364	29,537	9,979	14,396	5,367	7,602	5,191	8,939	15,057	19,852
Congressional District 10	41,721	25,795	7,731	11,302	2,951	4,939	944	1,912	1,513	2,957	4,424	6,662
Congressional District 11	43,841	27,022	6,414	12,489	1,751	4,930	933	2,334	1,361	3,942	3,940	7,866
Washington												
Congressional District 1	44,258	29,331	10,275	15,405	4,432	7,926	1,508	2,776	2,270	4,205	5,357	9,507
Congressional District 2	49,404	38,380	10,976	19,962	4,429	9,372	1,338	3,806	2,283	5,935	6,440	12,667
Congressional District 3	55,597	38,466	16,271	21,368	7,130	10,908	1,724	4,673	3,262	6,390	9,341	13,635
Congressional District 4	44,987	33,664	12,775	19,043	5,157	10,428	2,124	3,697	2,849	5,391	7,066	12,046
Congressional District 5	52,132	41,099	14,327	21,769	6,394	10,972	1,902	3,939	2,635	5,787	8,425	13,674
Congressional District 6	63,100	44,177	17,728	22,470	7,961	11,949	2,385	4,527	3,517	5,997	9,666	13,642
Congressional District 7	46,643	35,941	9,429	17,502	3,013	7,653	1,316	3,005	2,416	5,223	5,281	11,418
Congressional District 8	41,567	28,690	10,181	14,633	4,283	7,778	1,304	2,820	2,080	4,347	5,687	9,072
Congressional District 9	41,932	37,267	10,115	18,739	3,823	7,655	1,394	3,949	2,491	5,704	5,677	12,158
Congressional District 10	45,368	35,729	11,318	18,501	4,382	8,394	1,609	3,276	2,441	5,352	6,370	12,419
West Virginia												
Congressional District 1	54,342	43,175	15,120	22,266	6,377	10,754	2,720	4,277	3,610	5,877	9,529	14,381
Congressional District 2	56,137	40,421	17,720	21,925	6,698	9,954	2,644	4,654	3,883	6,440	11,878	15,774
Congressional District 3	56,489	44,099	24,136	27,423	10,312	14,263	4,884	7,748	5,724	9,488	15,807	18,672
Wisconsin												
Congressional District 1	50,901	40,854	11,197	19,002	4,141	8,677	1,488	3,756	2,008	4,495	6,707	11,963
Congressional District 2	45,518	37,605	9,063	17,306	3,964	7,916	1,193	3,397	1,655	4,153	5,178	10,271
Congressional District 3	54,693	46,998	11,412	21,454	4,638	10,250	1,292	4,104	2,183	4,226	6,550	13,444
Congressional District 4	35,960	34,754	10,436	17,056	2,773	6,559	1,770	3,101	2,540	4,731	6,871	11,493
Congressional District 5	51,752	50,332	9,159	22,945	3,640	9,629	907	3,710	1,494	5,388	5,425	14,572
Congressional District 6	55,976	49,949	10,993	22,079	4,856	10,094	1,466	3,575	2,099	5,008	6,241	13,742
Congressional District 7	64,818	51,499	14,203	23,273	6,391	11,641	1,512	4,435	2,104	4,793	7,865	14,320
Congressional District 8	53,299	43,848	10,785	19,907	4,723	8,627	1,169	3,393	1,528	4,775	5,757	12,422
Wyoming												
Congressional District (at Large)	40,933	29,135	10,694	14,425	5,323	7,882	1,062	3,538	1,660	3,441	5,376	8,692

PART I

HEALTH INSURANCE

HEALTH INSURANCE COVERAGE AND TYPE OF INSURANCE

At age 65, most Americans become eligible and obtain health insurance coverage through the national Medicare program. Of the 40.3 million civilian non-institutional population, 96.5 percent are insured by Medicare. Some have earlier eligibility and 9 percent of the population age 55 to 64 have coverage through Medicare. The District of Columbia has the lowest Medicare coverage at 91.4 percent while Iowa, South Dakota, and West Virginia have the highest coverage level at 98.4 percent. Among the 55 to 64 population, Medicare coverage is highest in West Virginia at 16.4 percent and lowest in Hawaii at 6.2 percent.

However, the categories reported in the ACS are not mutually exclusive. People can obtain coverage through multiple plans depending on their individual and family situations and the benefits offered by different plans. This is seen in the ACS data on insurance coverage where the percentage by coverage type far exceeds 100 percent. For example, while 96.5 percent of the 65 and

over population is covered by Medicare, 37.3 percent hold employer based coverage, 34.5 percent are in direct pay plans, and 14.6 percent obtain Medicaid.

Coverage through TRICARE/Military and the VA account for relatively small percentages for the 65 and over population. TRICARE/Military is highest in Virginia at 13.6 percent and only 4 states are above 10 percent. South Dakota has the highest VA coverage at 14.8 percent but in 16 states more than 10 percent of the 65 and over population has VA coverage. Nationally, the percentage of VA coverage for the 55 to 64 population is 4.1 percent, about half the level for the 65 and over population (8.0 percent). Similarly, the coverage of TRICARE/ Military for the 55 to 64 population (3.0 percent) is half of the 65 and over at 6.1 percent.

Private employer based coverage is most important for the 55 to 64 population as 63.6 percent are covered by such plans. Coverage is highest in New Hampshire at 73.3 percent but even the lowest level of coverage (Mississippi) is over 50 percent. Employer based plans cover only 36.9 percent of the 65 and over population where

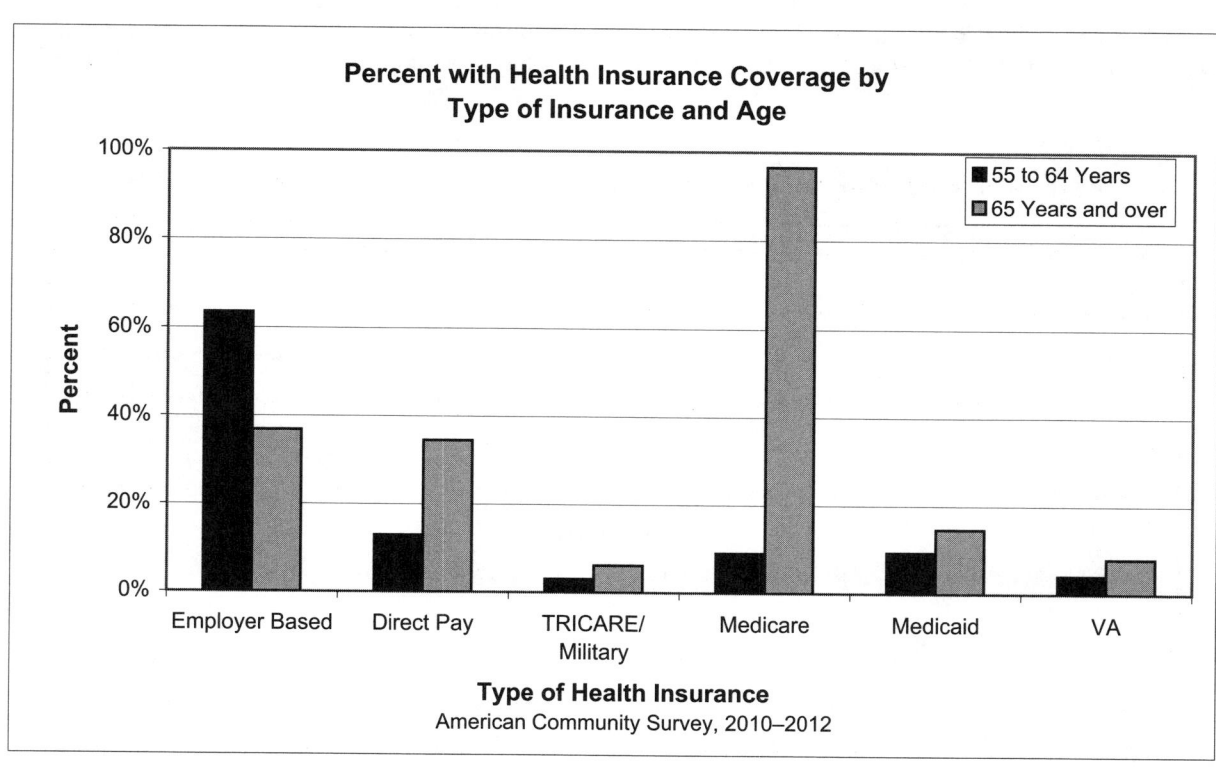

American Community Survey, 2010–2012

the District of Columbia is highest at 57.3 percent and South Dakota is lowest at 23.0 percent.

South Dakota has the highest percentage of the 55 to 64 population covered by direct purchase plans with 20.8 percent. Among the 65 and over group, 57.7 percent of North Dakota's population has direct purchase plans. Alaska is lowest at 18.0 percent. Forty-three states have at least 30 percent of the 65 and over population covered by direct purchase plans. For the 55 to 64 population, in all but four states, direct purchase covers between 10 and 20 percent of the population.

The national Medicare program covers only 9 percent of the 55 to 64 population and this is mainly for persons with eligible disabilities. By contrast, 96.5 percent of the 65 and over population has Medicare coverage and even in the District of Columbia (the lowest), 91.4 percent are have Medicare. Medicaid coverage is more evenly distributed between the 55 to 64 and 65 and over populations. Nationwide, 9.3 percent of the 55 to 64 population has Medicaid compared to 14.6 percent of the 65 and over. The District of Columbia has the highest Medicaid coverage rate for both age categories at 24.9 percent (55 to 64) and 23.1 percent for the 65 and over. North Dakota has the lowest Medicaid coverage among the 55 to 64 group at 3.6 percent while New Hampshire has the lowest (9.5 percent) for the 65 and over population.

Counties and Cities

County coverage of the 55 to 64 population through employer based plans varied from a low of 31.8 percent in McKinley County, New Mexico to a high of 85.2 percent in Putnam County, New York. There is a wider range among the 65 and over population from the low of 12.1 percent in Miami-Dade County, Florida to the highest coverage of 70.0 percent in Midland County, Michigan. Direct purchase plans are more prevalent among the 65 and over than then the 55 to 64 population. The county with the highest percent of direct purchase for the 55 to 64 is Marin County, California at 27.6 percent while Burleigh County, North Dakota is highest among the 65 and over population at 58.6 percent.

Coverage through Medicare shows a narrow range for the 65 and over population where 99.7 percent of the population in Wilkes County, North Carolina is the highest, while the lowest coverage is 88.1 percent in Fort Bend County, Texas. Among the 55 to 64 population only a little more than one-third of the population (34.9 percent) is covered in Pike County, Kentucky, the highest coverage level. Medicaid covers more than half of the 65 and over population (51.6 percent) in Imperial County, California.

Employer based plans cover 62.9 percent of the 65 and over population in Ann Arbor, Michigan but only 4.2 percent in Hialeah, Florida. Among the 55 to 64 population, 83.3 percent coverage is the highest in Newton, Massachusetts and lowest (26.2 percent) again in Hialeah, Florida where 93.3 percent are covered by Medicare. Jackson, Tennessee has the highest rate of coverage among the 65 and over population at 99.8 percent but it still has a moderate rate of direct purchase coverage at 39.5 percent. The Medicaid program covers 48 percent of the 55 to 64 population in Lawrence, Massachusetts, the highest of all cities but less than 1 percent in Roswell, Georgia.

Highest and Lowest Metropolitan Area Percent of Coverage for the Population 65 Years and Over by Health Insurance Type

Employer Based	Direct Pay	Medicare	Medicaid
Highest Percentage			
Congressional District 5, MI - 60.8%	Congressional District 7, MN - 59.4%	Congressional District 1, MI - 99.1%	Congressional District 15, NY - 53.4%
Congressional District 4, MD - 59.9%	Congressional District 4, IA - 58.9%	Congressional District 4, MI - 99.0%	Congressional District 13, NY - 46.6%
Congressional District 5, MD - 58.8%	Congressional District (at Large), ND - 57.7%	Congressional District 1, TN - 98.8%	Congressional District 7, NY - 43.2%
Congressional District 12, MI - 58.0%	Congressional District 3, NE - 56.3%	Congressional District 3, SC - 98.8%	Congressional District 34, CA - 42.2%
Congressional District 20, NY - 57.3%	Congressional District 1, MN - 54.3%	Congressional District 11, NC - 98.8%	Congressional District 40, CA - 40.8%
Lowest Percentage			
Congressional District 25, FL - 17.4%	Congressional District 29, CA - 11.0%	Congressional District 35, CA - 90.8%	Congressional District 4, VA 7.8%
Congressional District 34, CA - 17.0%	Congressional District 7, NY - 10.6%	Congressional District 22, TX - 90.6%	Congressional District 1, VA - 7.7%
Congressional District 26, F:L - 15.6%	Congressional District 13, NY - 9.5%	Congressional District 11, VA - 90.6%	Congressional District 6, IL - 7.7%
Congressional District 24, FL - 14.1%	Congressional District 40, CA - 9.2%	Congressional District 8, NJ - 90.5%	Congressional District 14, IL - 7.7%
Congressional District 27, FL - 11.5%	Congressional District 34, CA - 8.2%	Congressional District 9, TX - 89.9%	Congressional District 2, MO - 6.0%

Metropolitan Areas and Congressional Districts

Employer based plans for the 55 to 64 population cover at least 50 percent in 349 metropolitan areas. In comparison to the 65 and over population, only 28 metro areas have coverage rates over 50 percent. The Ames, Iowa metropolitan area has the highest coverage for the 55 to 64 population (79.6 percent) while the Flint, Michigan metro is highest among the 65 and over population at 63.2 percent. Direct purchase plans are more prevalent among the 65 and over than the 55 to 64 population. The coverage range for the 65 and over population is from a low of 12.9 percent in the Fairbanks, Alaska metro area to a high of 58.9 percent in the Bismarck, North Dakota metro area. For the 55 to 64 population, the Santa Fe, New Mexico metro is the highest at 22.8 percent and the lowest is 6.8 percent in the Laredo, Texas metropolitan area. The Crestview-Fort Walton Beach-Destin, Florida metropolitan area has the highest percent of TRICARE/Military coverage for both the 55 to 64 (31.6 percent) and the 65 and over (45.1 percent) populations – a likely indicator of an area with a high proportion of military, or former military, personnel.

Nearly 100 percent (99.2 percent) of the 65 and over population in the Bay City, Michigan and Owensboro, Kentucky metropolitan areas are covered by Medicare. The Laredo, Texas metro area has the lowest percent of Medicare coverage at 91.0 percent. VA coverage is held by more than 10 percent of the 65 and over population in 123 metropolitan areas with the highest (21.4 percent) being Rapid City, South Dakota.

Among congressional districts, every district but one (Texas' 9th) has a Medicare coverage rate over 90 percent for the 65 and over population and two districts, both in Michigan, have coverage rates over 99 percent – district 1 and 4. Medicaid coverage for the 65 and over population is highest in New York's 15th Congressional District. In 250 congressional districts more than one-third of the 65 and over population carries direct pay coverage as do 301 districts for employer based coverage. Michigan's 5th Congressional District has the highest coverage rate for employer based plans at 60.8 percent. Minnesota's 7th district is highest at 59.4 percent for direct pay coverage.

COVERAGE OPTIONS DEFINED

Health insurance coverage in the ACS defines coverage to include plans and programs that provide comprehensive health coverage. Plans that provide insurance for specific conditions or situations such as cancer and long-term care policies are not considered comprehensive coverage. The types of coverage are derived from a series of questions asked of all respondents by their "yes" or "no" response for each type. The types of coverage are further identified as either private or public insurance coverage. While the question is asked of all respondents, the data is reported for only the civilian non-institutional population.

Private Insurance Coverage

Employer Based – Insurance through a current or former employer or union (of this person or another family member)

Direct Purchase – Insurance purchased directly from an insurance company (by this person or another family member)

TRICARE/Military – Insurance coverage through TRICARE or other military health care; TRICARE services uniformed service members, retirees and their families

Public Insurance Coverage

Medicare – Insurance coverage by Medicare for people 65 and over, or people with certain disabilities

Medicaid – Insurance coverage by Medicaid, Medical Assistance, or any kind of government-assistance plan for those with low incomes or a disability

VA – Insurance coverage for veterans through the Veterans Administration (including those who have ever used or enrolled for VA health care)

Percent of the Population 65 Years and Over With Direct Pay Health Insurance Coverage

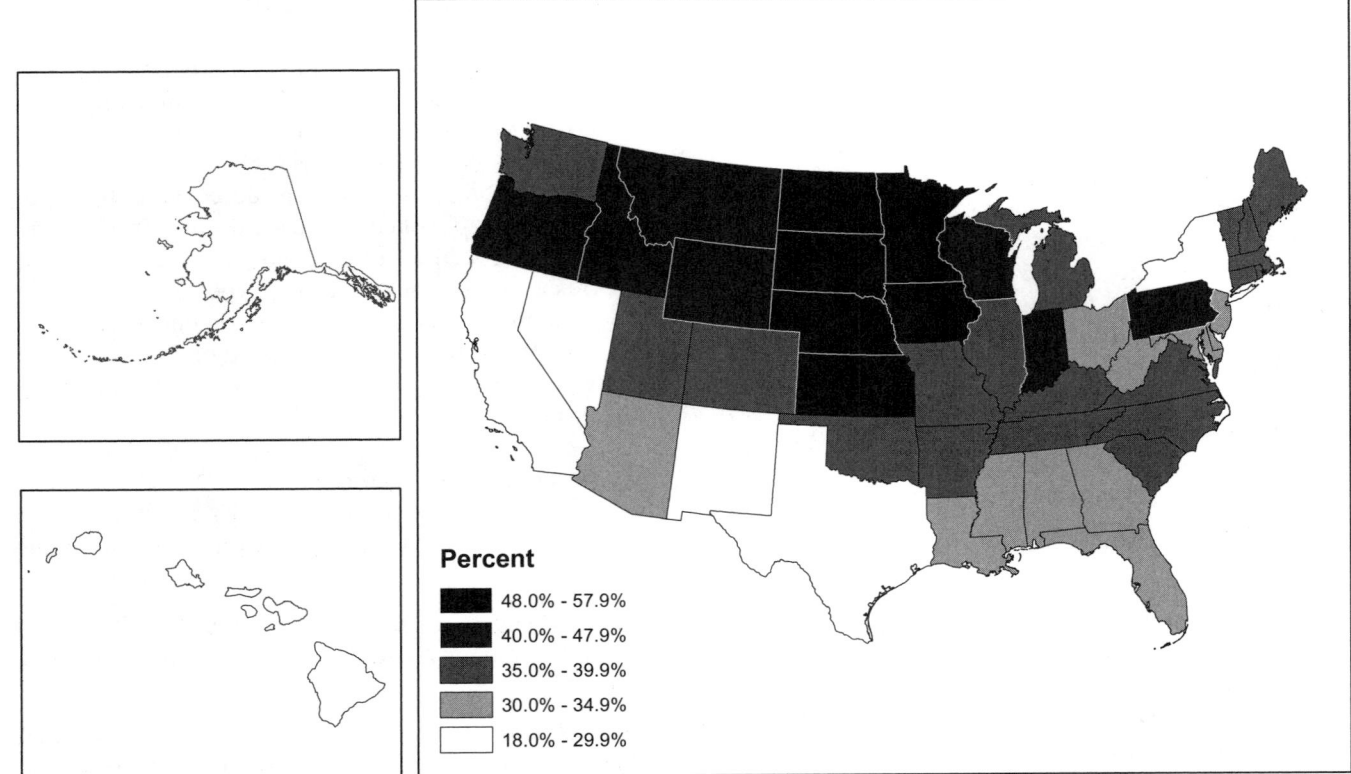

Percent

- 48.0% - 57.9%
- 40.0% - 47.9%
- 35.0% - 39.9%
- 30.0% - 34.9%
- 18.0% - 29.9%

Table I-1: States—Persons With Health Insurance by Source of Insurance

| | Private Health Insurance Coverage | | | | | | Public Health Insurance Coverage | | | | | |
| | Employer Based | | | Direct Purchase | | | Medicare | | | Medicaid/CHIP | | |
	55 to 64 Years	65 to 74 Years	75 Years and Over	55 to 64 Years	65 to 74 Years	75 Years and Over	55 to 64 Years	65 to 74 Years	75 Years and Over	55 to 64 Years	65 to 74 Years	75 Years and Over
United States........	23,857,968	8,786,754	6,087,763	4,846,840	6,958,501	6,979,921	3,391,160	21,400,015	17,547,313	3,506,781	2,937,673	2,949,259
Alabama..............	375,809	151,541	93,681	81,976	118,667	105,944	89,463	369,894	274,052	65,893	55,492	51,865
Alaska................	57,780	18,725	8,425	8,054	5,812	4,466	5,559	34,508	19,632	6,739	5,596	4,720
Arizona...............	429,867	174,092	124,116	109,131	160,289	140,838	62,122	501,332	382,287	80,654	58,600	53,529
Arkansas.............	199,748	72,604	44,786	48,847	83,730	72,597	54,716	232,488	174,474	36,766	32,598	32,244
California............	2,414,025	862,978	595,045	564,563	541,575	570,794	299,322	2,201,940	1,897,531	469,669	420,027	448,754
Colorado.............	383,945	124,330	79,383	102,494	106,871	93,511	39,232	312,382	231,440	45,275	35,195	34,929
Connecticut..........	332,098	123,584	90,344	55,897	78,890	96,290	32,404	246,551	228,314	33,294	29,793	34,826
Delaware.............	82,003	40,295	28,065	12,902	21,792	18,856	10,883	72,990	54,435	11,703	7,773	7,191
District of Columbia......	40,810	22,291	16,711	9,436	8,845	9,221	5,322	33,397	28,770	16,208	8,349	7,394
Florida...............	1,303,851	567,197	440,053	328,761	497,393	546,022	226,372	1,696,719	1,496,049	210,859	227,243	242,384
Georgia..............	670,891	244,421	134,568	130,454	173,427	146,588	115,212	608,641	409,950	94,570	89,291	77,830
Hawaii...............	127,636	59,686	46,243	30,434	25,544	29,237	11,032	96,767	90,720	15,442	12,631	14,190
Idaho................	108,743	34,418	23,699	33,677	47,968	41,568	17,309	111,673	83,521	12,083	10,474	11,065
Illinois..............	1,025,686	355,590	249,897	177,536	289,606	312,904	112,347	821,099	701,186	104,616	97,654	96,084
Indiana..............	538,269	178,156	131,825	90,649	174,707	170,949	74,766	447,716	361,213	58,195	45,354	40,196
Iowa.................	266,490	74,364	56,606	66,386	112,050	124,137	28,198	222,519	206,268	31,657	26,113	29,628
Kansas..............	234,428	63,490	44,216	49,704	85,562	94,285	26,758	188,112	168,832	20,674	19,321	21,992
Kentucky............	337,382	130,514	85,726	68,612	109,959	97,845	82,710	324,631	235,752	63,449	50,410	38,681
Louisiana...........	316,311	116,754	74,749	73,187	89,944	84,284	67,382	304,630	230,538	61,807	51,002	46,106
Maine...............	122,835	41,844	30,536	25,649	40,570	41,428	20,536	112,878	93,171	22,947	21,452	20,163
Maryland............	522,247	222,570	144,737	85,550	110,071	113,294	47,659	370,643	302,110	50,664	43,172	45,430
Massachusetts......	600,997	225,187	161,462	95,676	148,106	163,295	60,314	442,632	408,045	131,819	76,297	82,565
Michigan............	888,802	386,694	304,642	155,966	260,464	256,411	133,660	729,362	606,382	132,312	90,696	83,967
Minnesota..........	456,875	122,757	89,788	102,260	180,556	178,507	43,776	354,960	305,568	51,216	33,820	40,082
Mississippi.........	189,243	61,327	37,697	47,147	71,651	59,970	58,215	213,705	156,764	48,491	41,620	38,020
Missouri............	476,443	165,175	114,101	96,333	164,269	159,739	82,623	446,647	357,446	57,661	47,852	44,579
Montana.............	80,988	25,949	18,022	25,687	33,482	32,837	12,466	81,439	62,831	9,968	7,503	7,022
Nebraska............	148,381	39,416	27,353	38,868	55,563	63,032	16,220	120,103	112,203	13,025	11,524	14,325
Nevada..............	196,925	76,831	40,612	38,301	48,669	37,087	24,617	193,713	126,440	19,009	21,422	17,311
New Hampshire......	135,139	44,395	28,804	19,449	33,629	33,658	13,296	97,000	75,444	8,563	8,013	8,926
New Jersey.........	769,634	301,303	201,845	118,032	171,009	205,564	74,949	585,643	535,391	75,503	71,159	83,230
New Mexico.........	142,594	59,130	39,297	37,085	39,418	34,067	25,792	152,973	114,722	30,432	20,548	20,113
New York............	1,586,824	645,271	447,151	261,076	324,661	373,168	199,365	1,307,219	1,165,820	343,842	236,167	247,882
North Carolina......	702,854	269,061	170,009	168,103	249,835	217,709	140,402	707,915	513,935	100,613	87,373	83,790
North Dakota........	57,111	15,367	9,955	17,520	24,229	29,510	5,798	46,265	44,786	3,054	4,861	5,459
Ohio.................	1,033,883	393,582	308,379	160,235	264,724	279,739	130,074	836,068	711,666	103,608	86,536	84,044
Oklahoma...........	267,831	103,690	69,554	56,230	96,198	89,388	51,250	277,941	211,367	31,588	32,288	29,638
Oregon..............	318,532	103,995	77,718	79,601	121,471	115,943	45,620	297,084	237,525	42,402	34,212	35,458
Pennsylvania........	1,155,802	392,752	310,401	228,196	395,854	451,785	144,143	959,067	902,451	157,965	118,826	129,715
Rhode Island........	91,169	30,284	20,678	15,863	24,486	31,375	13,607	72,499	69,972	14,744	11,530	11,308
South Carolina......	354,388	141,315	83,816	73,655	125,921	99,305	75,606	378,043	253,959	55,147	48,678	41,732
South Dakota.......	64,498	15,107	10,833	21,231	26,322	30,297	7,921	57,473	53,257	5,405	6,625	6,959
Tennessee..........	494,590	171,594	110,572	102,562	173,487	145,629	97,642	489,494	350,884	78,912	69,819	57,861
Texas...............	1,575,861	558,453	338,686	302,201	401,565	358,797	227,484	1,441,885	1,076,048	229,604	218,921	209,701
Utah................	175,005	60,249	44,607	32,064	47,148	45,624	16,564	138,145	109,735	16,319	14,013	13,314
Vermont.............	61,739	20,527	13,281	12,440	17,364	16,427	7,727	50,430	38,872	13,148	6,649	7,484
Virginia.............	653,850	253,940	161,093	130,030	182,462	167,420	84,949	546,452	408,506	48,737	56,676	50,927
Washington.........	554,159	185,971	121,259	130,681	165,604	155,985	67,317	461,382	358,426	70,441	57,233	59,215
West Virginia........	167,708	76,578	58,057	25,271	45,164	43,708	43,899	163,024	126,900	31,894	19,801	17,930
Wisconsin..........	515,191	146,854	116,180	89,481	166,740	174,872	51,506	400,678	352,739	63,997	45,406	53,484
Wyoming............	50,098	14,556	8,500	11,697	15,178	14,015	5,054	39,264	28,984	4,198	4,065	4,017

Table I-2: Counties—Persons With Health Insurance by Source of Insurance

| | Private Health Insurance Coverage | | | | | | Public Health Insurance Coverage | | | | | |
| | Employer Based | | | Direct Purchase | | | Medicare | | | Medicaid/CHIP | | |
	55 to 64 Years	65 to 74 Years	75 Years and Over	55 to 64 Years	65 to 74 Years	75 Years and Over	55 to 64 Years	65 to 74 Years	75 Years and Over	55 to 64 Years	65 to 74 Years	75 Years and Over
Alabama												
Baldwin County	16,646	7,063	4,905	3,898	5,141	4,705	2,857	18,424	12,478	1,907	1,424	1,570
Calhoun County	9,558	4,154	2,744	2,606	2,973	2,787	2,686	9,366	7,345	1,778	1,461	1,172
Cullman County	6,338	2,804	1,229	1,313	2,522	2,199	1,790	7,543	5,270	1,057	1,145	967
DeKalb County	4,752	1,574	1,209	1,136	1,557	1,546	1,695	5,670	3,853	1,278	1,023	959
Elmore County	6,658	2,603	1,515	1,317	1,610	1,436	870	5,594	3,515	615	391	662
Etowah County	8,388	3,761	2,260	2,184	3,064	2,814	2,802	9,211	6,786	2,044	1,336	1,626
Houston County	7,814	3,065	1,851	1,720	3,107	2,679	1,928	8,365	6,313	1,253	1,117	1,092
Jefferson County	54,590	17,780	13,882	10,287	14,295	15,426	11,043	43,420	39,315	9,359	6,849	6,814
Lauderdale County	8,298	4,435	3,044	1,769	3,054	2,921	1,235	8,330	6,571	915	1,244	1,086
Lee County	8,889	3,665	1,663	1,737	3,035	2,411	2,084	7,822	5,007	972	1,059	709
Limestone County	6,699	2,929	1,570	1,461	1,999	1,569	1,372	6,276	3,940	743	902	807
Madison County	26,842	13,025	8,236	5,335	6,892	6,657	3,844	22,634	17,286	2,500	2,342	2,088
Marshall County	6,908	3,594	2,136	1,561	2,534	2,003	1,558	7,803	5,581	1,141	890	1,191
Mobile County	31,727	10,717	7,203	5,855	8,482	8,541	7,447	30,249	22,403	5,362	5,243	3,547
Montgomery County	16,607	7,023	5,370	3,316	3,827	3,933	3,575	14,646	12,255	3,231	2,505	2,329
Morgan County	9,824	4,752	2,930	2,147	3,378	2,615	2,022	9,420	6,882	1,470	901	1,011
St. Clair County	6,999	2,835	1,289	1,296	2,314	1,713	1,450	6,828	4,084	881	830	634
Shelby County	17,460	6,761	3,602	3,412	4,168	3,343	1,823	12,768	8,380	1,507	865	1,145
Talladega County	6,603	2,570	1,141	1,491	2,441	1,986	1,792	6,784	4,686	1,268	974	1,018
Tuscaloosa County	15,421	5,706	3,721	2,394	3,515	3,236	3,325	11,425	9,127	2,074	1,840	1,787
Walker County	5,364	2,964	1,943	918	1,989	1,372	2,312	6,456	4,270	1,096	1,174	757
Alaska												
Fairbanks North Star Borough	7,309	2,496	1,174	1,014	496	354	703	4,017	2,218	967	382	422
Matanuska-Susitna Borough	6,942	2,224	1,167	1,049	975	801	1,092	4,893	2,468	882	778	428
Arizona												
Apache County	2,999	1,034	331	610	959	486	939	5,010	3,077	2,207	1,617	1,473
Cochise County	8,531	4,563	2,703	2,294	3,308	3,047	1,667	13,559	9,172	2,269	1,676	1,222
Coconino County	8,530	2,729	1,744	2,613	2,440	1,521	1,202	7,642	4,443	1,771	1,211	959
Maricopa County	254,817	90,898	66,124	60,000	80,012	74,286	31,933	256,402	205,917	37,973	29,291	28,452
Mohave County	16,098	8,497	6,034	4,969	11,652	8,289	3,623	28,675	18,830	4,022	3,369	2,266
Navajo County	6,376	2,583	1,302	1,635	3,109	1,677	1,350	8,917	5,554	2,701	1,302	1,395
Pima County	71,359	29,198	24,074	16,009	23,407	23,835	10,057	82,234	68,403	15,962	9,826	8,857
Pinal County	23,215	12,287	7,050	7,277	12,513	8,415	4,509	34,276	19,720	4,971	3,504	2,651
Yavapai County	18,623	11,542	7,192	7,580	10,613	9,152	3,075	29,982	21,661	3,122	1,785	1,830
Yuma County	7,993	4,972	3,807	2,923	6,754	5,746	1,823	16,571	13,141	2,928	2,408	2,298
Arkansas												
Benton County	14,558	5,493	2,978	3,342	5,173	5,386	2,626	14,462	11,636	1,402	1,513	1,574
Craighead County	6,178	1,805	1,061	1,618	2,807	2,396	1,569	6,460	4,654	1,253	813	691
Faulkner County	7,804	2,309	1,436	1,367	2,391	1,912	1,698	6,512	4,774	962	1,235	645
Garland County	7,225	3,779	3,232	2,336	4,734	4,411	1,761	10,541	8,740	1,372	954	1,210
Jefferson County	5,136	1,651	804	1,402	2,182	1,838	1,685	5,628	4,157	1,554	957	1,034
Lonoke County	4,320	1,285	789	1,215	1,703	929	956	4,597	2,838	646	494	539
Pulaski County	30,702	11,126	6,121	5,356	7,702	7,315	5,392	24,520	20,039	4,692	3,314	3,629
Saline County	8,739	4,338	2,831	1,886	4,115	2,565	1,524	10,160	6,483	604	1,323	895
Sebastian County	9,379	2,564	1,692	1,494	3,036	2,838	2,167	9,011	6,829	1,451	1,307	978
Washington County	12,403	3,775	2,358	2,869	3,749	2,836	2,037	11,027	8,419	1,277	1,325	1,347
White County	4,753	2,219	1,488	647	2,064	1,905	1,193	6,163	4,432	815	661	836
California												
Alameda County	114,496	40,796	26,843	23,998	22,875	23,429	11,921	86,880	73,694	19,945	15,966	17,590
Butte County	15,522	6,962	6,489	3,908	5,735	7,293	3,746	17,177	15,709	5,336	2,783	2,763
Contra Costa County	90,980	37,063	25,378	20,520	21,582	22,084	8,876	69,163	57,515	11,533	8,746	10,392
El Dorado County	19,870	7,847	4,411	4,633	4,869	4,451	1,594	15,622	11,047	2,272	992	1,017
Fresno County	48,682	18,436	12,640	9,454	12,573	14,185	7,924	48,159	41,763	13,663	11,095	11,576
Humboldt County	10,648	3,642	2,643	2,691	3,069	3,465	2,005	9,906	7,860	3,082	1,028	745
Imperial County	6,676	1,848	1,118	1,232	1,566	1,551	1,831	9,447	8,494	4,598	4,518	5,063
Kern County	42,985	15,716	9,460	7,507	10,934	9,923	8,756	42,357	30,968	11,674	8,913	6,897
Kings County	6,949	2,249	1,259	960	1,532	1,552	1,484	5,881	4,908	1,915	1,109	1,214
Lake County	5,181	1,923	1,163	1,224	2,074	1,537	1,405	6,427	4,654	2,206	929	792
Los Angeles County	541,118	190,257	126,285	132,809	93,468	101,937	69,060	535,177	473,006	133,708	139,540	153,217
Madera County	9,355	3,554	2,187	1,246	2,871	2,251	1,468	9,746	7,109	2,003	1,830	1,439
Marin County	25,303	11,001	7,916	11,058	8,822	8,369	1,625	22,951	18,731	1,810	1,776	1,906
Mendocino County	6,700	2,253	1,503	2,702	2,488	2,261	1,382	7,819	5,800	1,985	1,191	1,009
Merced County	11,364	3,929	2,316	2,749	3,461	3,144	2,652	13,216	10,358	3,979	3,899	3,626
Monterey County	24,515	8,947	6,999	7,195	6,918	7,306	3,619	22,480	20,523	3,606	3,157	4,216
Napa County	12,164	5,365	4,156	2,802	3,051	3,795	1,039	10,345	9,245	1,692	1,206	1,382
Nevada County	9,946	5,037	3,249	3,685	4,118	3,486	1,905	10,955	8,326	1,409	1,057	572
Orange County	206,981	66,430	45,859	50,444	41,116	41,109	16,107	181,032	159,404	26,509	26,829	31,197
Placer County	30,433	15,412	11,720	7,945	10,022	9,614	3,710	29,471	24,624	2,848	2,193	2,505
Riverside County	122,649	46,019	32,816	28,135	33,457	36,099	18,085	138,227	116,497	23,663	22,433	22,842
Sacramento County	101,389	40,985	31,127	16,851	20,276	21,546	14,681	82,491	71,429	23,109	15,515	16,313
San Bernardino County	112,718	32,731	18,511	20,842	17,364	16,599	17,444	99,273	74,594	25,113	20,053	18,511
San Diego County	203,369	63,516	46,729	48,459	42,089	49,619	21,104	174,934	163,334	28,573	27,479	32,981
San Francisco County	56,712	17,667	16,319	15,905	11,439	15,001	7,459	51,820	53,690	17,785	14,872	17,206
San Joaquin County	41,609	14,370	10,411	7,583	10,688	12,254	6,954	37,830	30,899	11,032	7,860	6,525
San Luis Obispo County	23,472	9,592	6,811	6,705	7,457	8,489	3,263	21,193	19,229	2,675	1,862	2,152
San Mateo County	63,489	24,465	16,596	15,506	14,085	17,150	4,761	47,854	44,269	6,630	6,604	7,716
Santa Barbara County	27,165	10,269	9,246	7,560	9,522	10,121	2,926	26,383	26,293	3,676	3,061	3,764
Santa Clara County	123,347	45,244	29,332	28,974	28,375	28,169	9,693	102,167	88,793	19,154	20,733	23,520

Table I-2: Counties—Persons With Health Insurance by Source of Insurance—Continued

| | Private Health Insurance Coverage | | | | | | Public Health Insurance Coverage | | | | | |
| | Employer Based | | | Direct Purchase | | | Medicare | | | Medicaid/CHIP | | |
	55 to 64 Years	65 to 74 Years	75 Years and Over	55 to 64 Years	65 to 74 Years	75 Years and Over	55 to 64 Years	65 to 74 Years	75 Years and Over	55 to 64 Years	65 to 74 Years	75 Years and Over
California—Cont.												
Santa Cruz County	23,279	6,130	4,088	6,065	5,032	5,571	2,147	16,188	12,620	2,640	2,404	1,655
Shasta County	14,621	5,651	4,069	2,808	6,016	5,872	3,813	17,053	13,057	3,794	2,189	1,878
Solano County	35,747	14,329	8,852	5,995	6,111	5,646	3,886	24,896	19,841	4,526	3,331	4,298
Sonoma County	44,515	15,441	11,144	13,058	13,978	13,910	4,544	36,006	30,657	6,047	4,140	4,043
Stanislaus County	29,792	9,489	5,929	7,303	9,597	9,054	5,597	28,838	24,172	7,319	6,073	5,638
Sutter County	5,527	2,131	1,656	1,268	2,118	1,794	725	6,506	5,009	1,434	1,561	943
Tulare County	21,053	6,228	4,495	4,210	5,707	6,251	3,375	22,372	17,703	6,604	5,438	4,810
Ventura County	63,865	22,953	14,994	14,559	14,753	15,880	5,918	49,777	44,056	7,312	6,723	7,869
Yolo County	13,884	5,353	3,596	2,113	2,615	3,001	1,501	10,558	8,788	1,755	2,324	1,632
Yuba County	3,873	1,592	977	754	888	806	1,041	4,002	3,034	1,645	608	920
Colorado												
Adams County	27,822	9,112	5,583	4,732	6,246	5,497	3,024	20,902	15,131	3,598	3,708	2,772
Arapahoe County	45,812	13,977	8,971	10,826	10,428	9,153	3,901	32,680	24,427	4,614	3,460	3,737
Boulder County	24,499	8,482	4,872	7,432	6,059	5,226	1,517	16,911	12,247	1,926	1,421	1,278
Denver County	35,614	11,853	9,314	9,596	8,719	10,453	5,186	31,383	28,263	8,805	6,194	6,247
Douglas County	23,989	6,201	2,543	6,212	5,372	3,494	886	14,235	7,753	476	1,081	697
El Paso County	40,625	11,608	8,124	9,470	11,290	9,703	5,179	36,071	26,236	4,711	3,830	2,901
Jefferson County	54,902	18,286	11,183	11,918	13,334	12,541	3,392	37,260	28,392	3,543	2,788	3,424
Larimer County	25,432	8,615	5,543	6,685	7,093	7,139	2,122	20,055	15,500	2,388	1,326	2,069
Mesa County	11,341	4,529	3,376	2,366	4,808	4,406	1,323	11,584	9,910	1,235	1,516	1,466
Pueblo County	11,656	4,942	5,274	2,992	4,402	3,849	3,160	12,448	10,977	3,469	1,657	1,574
Weld County	17,861	5,602	2,830	4,324	4,477	3,966	1,810	14,442	9,912	2,055	1,679	2,009
Connecticut												
Fairfield County	77,495	28,624	22,412	17,438	19,784	23,702	6,169	59,577	56,385	7,621	6,552	7,812
Hartford County	83,068	31,186	24,364	11,462	18,467	24,566	9,574	60,940	59,962	9,059	8,391	9,769
Litchfield County	20,984	7,354	5,190	4,578	5,678	5,889	1,355	15,952	13,196	1,613	1,070	2,099
Middlesex County	18,763	7,780	4,682	2,647	4,299	4,933	1,264	13,395	11,205	913	1,211	1,344
New Haven County	77,882	28,456	21,370	12,316	17,671	24,540	8,878	58,040	56,832	9,758	7,114	8,715
New London County	26,944	11,294	7,129	4,162	6,165	6,534	2,727	20,401	16,872	2,115	2,780	2,814
Tolland County	15,671	4,990	3,031	1,635	4,021	3,437	921	10,192	7,677	1,003	1,225	992
Windham County	11,291	3,900	2,166	1,659	2,805	2,689	1,516	8,054	6,185	1,212	1,450	1,281
Delaware												
Kent County	12,304	6,810	4,323	2,087	3,961	3,079	2,384	12,830	9,171	2,727	1,504	1,615
New Castle County	48,577	20,505	15,205	6,504	9,469	9,559	5,187	35,165	28,762	6,314	4,039	3,614
Sussex County	21,122	12,980	8,537	4,311	8,362	6,218	3,312	24,995	16,502	2,662	2,230	1,962
Florida												
Alachua County	16,219	6,584	4,559	4,335	4,574	4,697	2,725	14,339	11,550	3,224	1,752	1,770
Bay County	11,217	4,609	3,242	3,168	4,188	3,878	2,434	13,762	10,390	1,540	1,370	1,078
Brevard County	42,907	21,924	17,468	8,962	16,491	18,962	9,835	56,864	52,092	6,440	4,637	6,621
Broward County	118,562	33,396	24,675	29,909	28,882	41,376	15,488	120,125	118,369	17,287	19,083	20,438
Charlotte County	15,222	11,671	11,432	4,873	10,236	10,604	3,247	29,082	25,186	1,532	2,413	2,690
Citrus County	12,178	9,279	7,211	3,641	9,519	7,906	3,097	24,386	19,986	1,945	2,678	2,383
Clay County	13,713	4,333	2,600	1,955	3,720	3,576	2,656	13,977	8,763	1,759	1,289	942
Collier County	23,201	17,254	14,636	8,133	19,630	18,756	2,327	46,325	39,612	2,286	2,865	3,357
Columbia County	4,616	1,704	1,050	804	1,713	1,541	848	5,934	4,039	1,558	955	649
Duval County	60,885	19,420	11,247	11,377	14,904	14,621	10,477	52,220	41,550	11,126	7,421	6,254
Escambia County	19,462	8,128	5,658	4,879	7,734	6,766	4,922	23,899	18,423	3,101	2,909	2,620
Flagler County	9,193	6,816	3,992	1,967	4,102	3,855	1,375	13,660	9,890	1,211	1,895	1,635
Hernando County	12,624	8,175	6,900	4,083	7,486	8,285	3,521	23,021	20,918	2,570	1,785	2,311
Highlands County	6,565	6,206	5,998	1,411	6,278	6,092	2,021	15,821	14,821	1,759	2,107	2,190
Hillsborough County	80,131	26,037	17,072	16,359	18,397	21,218	15,181	77,790	65,795	17,559	11,123	12,383
Indian River County	11,684	7,204	8,021	4,251	6,712	9,245	1,745	18,730	19,507	1,510	1,724	1,745
Lake County	23,828	15,014	12,126	5,198	12,768	13,453	4,590	39,547	32,307	2,425	2,623	3,050
Lee County	50,127	32,034	22,013	14,927	30,195	27,676	7,784	81,885	65,035	5,761	7,816	8,578
Leon County	22,059	8,140	5,327	3,531	4,872	3,229	1,859	15,084	10,917	2,074	1,690	1,815
Manatee County	27,450	14,769	13,723	6,345	14,727	15,344	4,303	39,232	35,105	3,115	3,731	3,386
Marion County	22,188	15,006	13,637	6,517	15,567	14,111	5,699	47,134	37,922	4,368	4,645	4,661
Martin County	12,245	7,617	7,689	4,348	6,738	8,898	1,902	19,728	20,188	1,546	1,037	1,463
Miami-Dade County	117,506	29,739	13,643	30,337	21,461	23,646	21,297	172,310	160,362	31,469	59,688	68,932
Monroe County	6,270	2,763	1,508	2,849	2,321	1,560	572	7,735	4,936	849	852	815
Nassau County	6,877	2,864	1,326	1,709	2,938	1,782	991	7,672	4,609	893	726	708
Okaloosa County	10,875	4,558	3,211	3,496	4,364	3,966	1,749	14,029	10,819	813	1,470	1,092
Orange County	70,826	19,755	13,294	13,071	13,935	15,502	9,057	58,815	47,353	8,285	9,681	8,431
Osceola County	16,559	4,955	3,204	3,647	3,673	2,988	2,550	17,790	12,031	2,494	2,712	2,328
Palm Beach County	91,436	43,149	43,190	30,402	41,400	65,923	11,413	126,327	149,907	10,717	12,341	15,597
Pasco County	32,392	16,392	13,943	8,679	15,840	16,645	8,379	49,987	44,096	7,052	5,340	5,111
Pinellas County	78,585	29,636	28,378	18,417	27,191	34,941	12,456	92,375	93,023	11,527	10,304	12,224
Polk County	42,129	20,571	14,817	10,205	15,986	17,800	9,055	59,819	46,573	8,339	6,880	6,105
Putnam County	5,324	2,202	1,193	1,161	2,171	1,970	1,533	7,924	5,995	1,247	1,200	1,172
St. Johns County	17,179	7,108	4,950	5,019	6,019	5,918	2,057	17,902	12,985	1,616	1,183	1,016
St. Lucie County	18,738	10,798	8,547	4,925	10,378	10,581	4,655	30,173	26,276	3,562	3,158	3,137
Santa Rosa County	11,779	4,078	2,787	2,368	4,546	2,712	1,788	12,229	7,282	1,128	991	992
Sarasota County	31,765	23,292	23,300	12,614	20,905	26,758	4,498	58,175	57,958	3,393	3,960	5,070
Seminole County	34,603	9,439	6,790	6,455	7,524	7,770	3,450	27,602	22,549	2,888	2,615	2,838
Sumter County	11,893	12,370	5,918	2,759	11,196	7,740	1,457	28,787	15,608	943	1,453	848
Volusia County	40,266	20,002	18,616	8,882	16,833	18,928	8,611	53,443	48,511	7,690	5,972	6,605

Table I-2: Counties—Persons With Health Insurance by Source of Insurance—*Continued*

| | Private Health Insurance Coverage | | | | | | Public Health Insurance Coverage | | | | | |
| | Employer Based | | | Direct Purchase | | | Medicare | | | Medicaid/CHIP | | |
	55 to 64 Years	65 to 74 Years	75 Years and Over	55 to 64 Years	65 to 74 Years	75 Years and Over	55 to 64 Years	65 to 74 Years	75 Years and Over	55 to 64 Years	65 to 74 Years	75 Years and Over
Georgia												
Barrow County	4,124	1,794	1,063	609	697	1,016	910	3,656	2,549	641	535	398
Bartow County	6,726	2,597	1,321	1,486	2,152	1,290	1,959	6,734	4,052	1,582	860	518
Bibb County	10,600	3,997	3,395	2,280	2,826	3,021	2,572	10,171	8,494	2,501	1,623	1,402
Bulloch County	3,408	1,467	685	708	995	614	574	3,730	2,525	666	591	249
Carroll County	7,047	3,368	1,559	1,127	1,742	1,962	1,360	7,497	4,534	1,356	1,127	815
Catoosa County	5,090	1,878	1,058	855	2,148	1,852	830	5,378	3,605	453	596	665
Chatham County	18,425	6,884	4,707	3,717	4,443	4,385	2,602	18,065	14,513	2,595	1,880	2,327
Cherokee County	17,161	5,514	2,559	3,209	4,683	2,897	1,639	13,278	7,203	925	720	951
Clarke County	5,977	2,860	2,029	1,389	1,572	1,390	1,195	5,607	4,306	1,216	862	719
Clayton County	15,152	4,131	1,831	2,539	2,734	1,742	2,364	10,543	6,298	2,535	2,008	1,677
Cobb County	52,503	16,386	8,697	11,234	11,283	9,675	4,094	36,103	23,687	2,925	3,010	2,465
Columbia County	11,205	3,508	1,707	1,521	2,063	1,446	1,263	7,991	4,969	887	1,375	836
Coweta County	10,556	3,533	1,605	1,344	2,782	1,769	1,045	8,526	5,002	684	807	717
DeKalb County	45,838	14,477	8,529	9,257	8,354	7,851	6,340	34,362	25,235	4,732	5,964	4,728
Dougherty County	5,682	2,518	2,017	1,042	1,921	1,679	1,563	6,239	5,058	1,791	1,277	1,093
Douglas County	8,806	3,076	1,269	1,026	2,552	1,400	1,502	7,394	3,978	1,080	1,097	499
Fayette County	12,197	4,245	2,523	2,090	2,778	1,924	699	8,385	5,403	346	625	334
Floyd County	7,213	2,424	2,118	1,206	2,425	2,557	1,492	7,434	5,888	1,186	1,085	1,120
Forsyth County	12,849	4,474	1,605	2,489	3,638	2,806	892	10,378	6,251	639	703	1,135
Fulton County	60,172	20,885	12,312	14,351	12,710	12,423	8,133	46,824	35,052	9,653	8,868	7,088
Glynn County	5,726	3,145	1,867	1,925	2,749	2,611	1,279	6,912	4,947	1,224	1,081	1,023
Gwinnett County	56,452	17,030	7,160	9,216	8,486	7,865	4,042	33,189	20,871	2,616	4,386	4,359
Hall County	12,400	4,921	2,858	2,342	4,100	3,663	1,503	12,258	8,487	1,178	1,480	1,203
Henry County	14,628	4,789	2,768	1,765	3,412	2,196	1,685	11,012	6,244	884	1,000	925
Houston County	10,129	4,085	3,040	1,508	2,200	2,042	1,590	8,506	5,865	1,112	1,285	687
Liberty County	2,313	1,062	388	564	638	334	530	2,654	1,256	321	503	188
Lowndes County	5,823	2,217	1,446	1,086	1,877	1,531	1,493	6,296	4,299	1,205	861	765
Muscogee County	11,148	3,696	2,918	2,228	3,023	3,812	2,751	11,097	9,985	2,758	2,414	1,989
Newton County	7,061	2,290	1,698	1,250	2,396	1,427	1,372	6,129	3,782	990	1,037	893
Paulding County	8,967	2,756	1,495	1,402	2,447	1,488	1,435	7,059	3,715	679	816	698
Richmond County	11,567	4,666	2,640	2,663	3,041	2,433	3,406	12,731	9,402	3,382	2,155	1,594
Rockdale County	7,095	2,585	1,212	1,472	1,517	1,494	939	5,598	3,466	873	751	688
Troup County	4,565	1,739	888	1,211	1,405	1,278	1,215	4,637	3,488	959	1,038	578
Walker County	4,673	1,716	1,166	1,126	2,170	2,018	1,258	5,830	4,202	855	874	801
Walton County	6,969	2,824	1,605	1,404	1,959	1,877	1,232	6,182	3,957	948	1,000	683
Whitfield County	6,972	2,149	1,036	893	1,481	1,703	1,163	6,305	4,670	928	1,109	1,012
Hawaii												
Hawaii County	17,915	7,230	3,668	4,663	4,046	3,580	2,266	15,112	11,565	3,197	2,107	1,848
Honolulu County	86,913	43,051	36,369	20,251	17,254	22,042	7,011	65,409	66,301	9,808	8,950	10,709
Kauai County	7,400	2,969	2,081	1,517	1,396	1,065	552	5,217	4,352	594	411	516
Maui County	15,398	6,429	4,123	4,003	2,845	2,548	1,203	11,015	8,497	1,843	1,160	1,115
Idaho												
Ada County	30,243	7,920	5,654	6,989	8,923	8,025	3,294	23,810	18,269	2,281	2,228	2,248
Bannock County	5,903	1,574	1,545	1,490	2,243	1,907	927	4,907	4,103	611	422	560
Bonneville County	7,837	1,809	1,483	1,587	2,940	2,962	1,020	6,143	5,166	538	487	747
Canyon County	9,862	3,201	1,694	3,139	5,104	4,106	2,161	12,080	8,619	1,998	1,399	1,437
Kootenai County	10,322	3,976	2,174	3,750	5,404	5,105	2,011	11,936	8,500	1,202	905	1,000
Twin Falls County	4,173	1,722	1,299	1,661	2,942	2,756	860	5,560	4,940	538	745	764
Illinois												
Adams County	5,550	2,026	2,007	1,342	2,608	2,670	811	5,344	5,279	1,084	562	575
Champaign County	14,690	5,748	4,698	2,248	3,635	3,807	1,210	10,073	8,691	827	1,159	973
Cook County	361,369	122,321	84,759	61,085	89,239	107,040	46,050	304,963	275,886	55,231	47,422	47,399
DeKalb County	7,242	2,556	1,895	1,539	1,941	2,048	542	5,385	4,354	309	694	465
DuPage County	89,264	26,918	16,465	15,072	20,798	23,350	4,374	55,777	45,151	3,779	4,277	4,581
Kane County	42,124	12,863	7,425	5,786	10,378	9,591	2,707	28,152	20,739	2,004	3,249	2,398
Kankakee County	9,129	2,700	2,442	1,333	2,869	3,226	1,605	7,623	6,503	1,145	836	806
Kendall County	8,530	2,347	1,134	806	1,745	1,700	500	5,198	3,269	458	379	293
Lake County	59,723	18,293	10,218	12,200	14,321	14,262	3,976	39,114	30,245	3,109	3,355	3,239
LaSalle County	10,400	4,111	2,992	2,304	3,890	4,888	1,205	8,881	8,636	775	813	1,080
McHenry County	27,825	7,462	4,424	4,244	8,621	5,979	1,944	18,712	12,061	1,078	1,215	1,059
McLean County	13,625	5,120	3,748	2,956	3,163	3,834	960	9,165	7,589	850	762	689
Macon County	10,308	4,135	3,690	1,641	3,460	3,447	1,441	8,956	7,963	1,028	790	964
Madison County	24,224	8,803	6,890	3,520	7,393	8,270	3,518	19,787	16,987	2,424	1,343	1,447
Peoria County	17,494	6,335	5,398	2,112	5,483	5,514	1,679	13,257	11,537	1,582	1,185	1,076
Rock Island County	14,307	6,872	6,054	2,305	3,955	4,584	1,715	12,007	10,923	1,184	1,043	1,476
St. Clair County	19,930	6,869	5,684	3,575	5,475	6,009	3,795	17,151	15,094	2,928	2,116	2,137
Sangamon County	20,833	8,347	6,770	3,261	4,718	4,856	2,185	13,944	12,071	1,643	1,725	1,111
Tazewell County	13,711	5,500	4,600	2,222	4,360	3,935	1,009	10,704	9,554	811	854	1,082
Vermilion County	7,255	2,826	2,359	1,713	2,939	3,137	1,058	6,674	5,746	819	870	646
Will County	55,819	18,807	10,154	7,094	12,722	10,742	4,016	35,977	25,542	2,486	3,012	3,039
Williamson County	5,230	2,929	1,984	1,065	1,869	1,775	1,143	5,987	4,451	583	660	544
Winnebago County	24,925	7,743	6,194	4,293	9,106	9,007	3,222	21,421	17,736	2,919	2,760	2,184

Table I-2: Counties—Persons With Health Insurance by Source of Insurance—*Continued*

	Private Health Insurance Coverage						Public Health Insurance Coverage					
	Employer Based			Direct Purchase			Medicare			Medicaid/CHIP		
	55 to 64 Years	65 to 74 Years	75 Years and Over	55 to 64 Years	65 to 74 Years	75 Years and Over	55 to 64 Years	65 to 74 Years	75 Years and Over	55 to 64 Years	65 to 74 Years	75 Years and Over
Indiana												
Allen County	29,532	7,411	6,530	5,124	7,100	8,464	3,125	22,238	18,801	3,096	1,758	1,866
Bartholomew County	6,500	2,335	1,636	1,174	2,275	2,078	944	6,090	4,425	664	433	602
Clark County	10,332	3,195	1,765	1,761	2,901	2,950	1,715	8,092	5,780	810	970	753
Delaware County	8,691	4,311	3,552	1,343	3,483	3,550	1,847	9,000	7,617	1,233	1,110	885
Elkhart County	14,182	3,592	2,919	3,112	4,958	5,513	1,967	12,158	10,420	1,464	1,243	881
Floyd County	7,137	2,458	1,661	1,200	2,197	2,138	899	5,317	3,865	677	535	525
Grant County	5,217	2,923	2,515	996	2,038	2,039	1,333	5,930	4,867	943	970	643
Hamilton County	23,448	6,006	4,575	3,377	6,383	4,295	952	13,743	9,561	709	920	396
Hancock County	6,290	3,248	2,029	1,037	2,173	1,517	606	5,334	3,583	525	247	291
Hendricks County	13,348	3,920	2,776	1,800	3,628	3,254	909	8,758	6,537	764	1,090	420
Howard County	7,789	3,784	2,988	1,403	2,718	2,618	1,432	7,442	5,933	838	631	355
Johnson County	11,675	3,806	2,954	1,927	4,207	3,459	1,025	9,716	7,169	639	817	800
Kosciusko County	6,755	1,728	918	1,361	2,215	2,236	831	5,923	4,241	509	422	398
Lake County	43,185	14,767	11,765	6,769	11,650	10,970	6,398	33,613	29,397	5,703	4,044	4,224
LaPorte County	9,994	2,960	2,076	1,565	3,357	2,781	1,118	8,331	6,965	999	751	893
Madison County	11,330	6,128	4,655	1,810	3,645	3,889	1,929	10,653	8,926	1,323	1,175	1,091
Marion County	62,956	20,161	15,835	10,303	17,508	18,666	10,482	49,001	41,712	11,275	7,167	6,212
Monroe County	9,827	2,933	2,103	1,540	3,473	3,329	1,226	7,307	6,359	594	363	677
Morgan County	6,420	2,618	1,410	930	2,097	1,861	887	5,535	3,595	532	516	387
Porter County	16,603	4,670	3,127	2,681	4,627	4,073	1,441	11,410	8,330	1,023	1,212	762
St. Joseph County	22,980	6,984	5,543	3,452	6,365	7,639	2,956	17,020	17,135	1,966	1,405	2,076
Tippecanoe County	12,267	3,677	3,054	1,599	3,537	4,157	1,091	8,614	7,111	804	621	551
Vanderburgh County	15,924	4,940	3,687	2,600	5,071	6,213	2,316	12,209	11,891	1,559	1,296	1,243
Vigo County	8,114	2,491	2,396	1,287	2,811	3,204	1,705	7,326	6,259	1,287	1,040	818
Wayne County	5,100	1,715	1,618	970	2,618	2,639	1,074	5,878	4,942	903	536	494
Iowa												
Black Hawk County	12,292	4,801	3,877	1,753	3,736	4,451	1,175	8,852	8,562	1,527	1,129	1,362
Dallas County	5,172	1,180	892	1,135	1,665	1,501	440	3,714	2,807	402	394	165
Dubuque County	9,105	2,838	2,276	2,366	3,820	3,608	770	7,002	6,635	741	622	1,166
Johnson County	11,024	2,899	1,815	1,629	2,986	2,690	866	6,101	4,857	963	715	467
Linn County	18,946	5,093	3,885	3,344	6,134	7,243	1,633	14,397	12,481	1,858	1,517	1,379
Polk County	34,740	9,675	7,804	6,005	10,683	10,276	3,834	24,951	20,114	5,729	3,051	3,051
Pottawattamie County	8,451	2,302	1,585	1,819	3,026	3,074	955	6,812	5,946	735	739	707
Scott County	15,628	5,049	4,056	2,392	5,428	4,782	1,902	11,607	9,462	2,017	1,159	1,363
Story County	6,696	2,129	1,903	1,205	1,701	2,526	218	4,463	4,208	435	315	414
Woodbury County	7,650	1,928	1,278	1,618	3,207	3,358	1,113	6,604	5,929	1,545	899	1,207
Kansas												
Butler County	5,879	1,190	981	1,068	1,997	2,004	772	4,126	3,801	376	233	386
Douglas County	7,581	2,898	1,966	1,619	2,337	2,287	694	5,287	4,392	563	590	492
Johnson County	50,508	12,995	9,790	9,595	13,630	13,563	2,651	31,841	26,758	1,661	1,908	3,058
Leavenworth County	5,816	2,398	1,082	1,450	1,847	2,026	606	4,812	3,447	536	303	321
Riley County	3,436	1,247	591	806	1,040	1,473	173	2,463	2,339	143	80	377
Sedgwick County	40,127	8,318	5,659	6,203	12,281	14,308	4,869	29,297	26,061	4,345	3,914	3,581
Shawnee County	16,794	6,117	4,778	2,552	6,051	5,807	2,321	13,175	11,291	1,922	1,269	1,386
Wyandotte County	10,389	2,873	2,143	1,919	3,304	3,488	2,037	8,825	7,187	1,546	1,350	1,262
Kentucky												
Boone County	10,651	3,405	1,966	1,424	2,274	1,898	1,175	6,926	4,382	736	866	767
Bullitt County	7,007	2,666	1,321	900	2,138	1,462	1,052	5,647	3,133	692	806	429
Campbell County	7,898	2,328	1,643	2,120	2,315	2,169	1,111	6,217	4,918	643	788	526
Christian County	3,420	1,565	1,005	921	1,410	1,109	938	3,890	3,275	742	473	541
Daviess County	8,588	3,241	2,786	1,374	2,539	2,681	1,768	7,409	6,369	1,115	727	1,121
Fayette County	22,252	8,156	5,214	4,824	5,404	5,490	2,745	16,699	13,205	2,433	2,006	1,597
Hardin County	7,410	2,540	1,548	1,287	2,076	1,956	1,219	6,451	4,628	1,090	731	735
Jefferson County	64,314	22,979	17,931	12,310	19,474	21,046	10,656	50,153	44,620	8,192	6,875	6,390
Kenton County	13,309	4,492	2,745	2,646	2,849	3,522	1,796	9,805	7,444	1,533	1,094	867
McCracken County	5,900	2,531	1,734	1,132	2,056	2,051	1,024	5,815	4,573	768	518	481
Madison County	5,751	1,838	1,478	982	1,994	1,514	1,443	5,357	3,779	1,526	910	493
Pike County	3,975	2,054	1,575	885	1,192	776	3,230	5,325	3,406	1,796	1,212	528
Warren County	7,665	2,758	1,909	2,016	2,969	2,420	1,315	6,846	5,284	1,078	766	625
Louisiana												
Ascension Parish	8,407	2,361	1,547	1,231	1,664	995	1,149	6,063	3,444	675	748	623
Bossier Parish	7,475	3,140	2,027	1,211	2,454	2,104	1,489	7,832	5,375	998	1,008	633
Caddo Parish	18,583	6,699	5,844	3,560	5,772	5,679	3,965	17,537	15,266	3,591	2,967	2,678
Calcasieu Parish	14,664	4,668	4,603	3,186	4,985	4,636	2,953	13,650	10,141	1,959	1,958	1,501
East Baton Rouge Parish	33,524	11,961	8,683	6,783	6,735	6,706	5,025	25,483	19,962	5,583	3,644	3,399
Iberia Parish	4,941	2,430	1,137	1,001	1,943	1,473	1,173	4,659	3,752	1,159	565	878
Jefferson Parish	35,677	10,242	6,637	7,305	8,155	8,731	5,172	31,179	26,070	5,210	4,361	4,290
Lafayette Parish	15,441	5,212	3,523	3,959	5,096	4,254	1,948	11,884	9,561	1,961	1,352	1,403
Lafourche Parish	6,042	2,144	1,346	1,590	2,589	2,357	1,375	6,815	4,986	1,134	895	709
Livingston Parish	7,946	2,863	1,568	1,874	2,001	1,437	1,595	8,093	4,847	1,420	868	627
Orleans Parish	22,065	6,862	3,801	6,899	4,676	4,758	6,034	21,215	16,264	7,626	5,715	4,432
Ouachita Parish	8,848	3,579	2,394	1,949	3,275	2,943	1,895	9,562	8,085	2,136	1,407	1,538
Rapides Parish	8,099	3,844	2,230	2,032	2,726	2,208	2,574	9,511	7,482	2,653	2,403	2,400
St. Landry Parish	5,879	2,114	1,457	1,069	1,667	1,493	1,673	6,044	4,671	978	1,029	1,157
St. Tammany Parish	21,222	7,319	3,964	3,836	4,015	4,471	2,840	17,285	12,303	2,184	1,580	1,590
Tangipahoa Parish	8,011	3,215	1,944	2,550	3,008	2,167	2,224	8,099	5,449	1,658	1,595	1,072
Terrebonne Parish	6,824	2,943	1,243	1,849	2,459	2,087	2,129	7,013	4,842	1,947	1,080	867

Table I-2: Counties—Persons With Health Insurance by Source of Insurance—*Continued*

	Private Health Insurance Coverage						Public Health Insurance Coverage					
	Employer Based			Direct Purchase			Medicare			Medicaid/CHIP		
	55 to 64 Years	65 to 74 Years	75 Years and Over	55 to 64 Years	65 to 74 Years	75 Years and Over	55 to 64 Years	65 to 74 Years	75 Years and Over	55 to 64 Years	65 to 74 Years	75 Years and Over
Maine												
Androscoggin County	9,163	2,563	1,808	1,354	2,928	3,249	1,763	7,754	6,809	1,854	1,985	2,156
Aroostook County	6,312	1,787	1,526	1,613	2,337	2,259	1,672	7,291	5,767	1,957	2,275	1,879
Cumberland County	27,749	9,028	7,306	4,604	7,055	8,578	2,843	20,664	18,486	3,323	2,978	3,339
Kennebec County	11,476	4,202	3,036	2,280	3,353	3,398	1,988	9,891	8,512	2,352	1,790	1,815
Penobscot County	12,848	3,859	3,189	2,124	4,571	4,065	2,566	11,590	9,972	2,640	3,049	2,312
York County	19,977	6,790	4,840	3,957	5,760	6,031	2,629	16,526	13,515	2,758	2,358	2,700
Maryland												
Allegany County	6,056	3,138	2,342	1,249	2,560	2,501	1,378	6,756	5,853	946	969	1,032
Anne Arundel County	53,042	23,557	14,035	9,057	9,867	9,083	3,814	36,432	26,041	3,295	3,547	3,132
Baltimore County	77,319	30,166	25,775	12,946	19,292	25,367	7,863	54,719	56,649	6,754	5,778	6,818
Calvert County	9,226	3,746	2,048	1,148	1,606	1,143	463	5,341	3,812	499	392	444
Carroll County	16,811	7,196	4,154	2,700	4,191	3,874	911	11,974	9,236	794	1,021	1,155
Cecil County	9,911	3,634	2,602	1,328	1,845	1,518	1,179	7,161	4,550	1,481	751	724
Charles County	12,466	5,315	2,638	1,564	1,800	1,357	1,446	8,643	5,298	1,153	954	715
Frederick County	22,276	8,072	4,974	2,797	4,522	4,420	1,622	14,613	11,026	1,369	1,259	1,002
Harford County	24,974	9,978	6,516	3,852	5,838	5,170	1,851	17,596	12,739	1,157	1,793	1,651
Howard County	29,271	11,880	6,167	4,480	5,436	4,683	1,048	16,975	11,596	1,527	1,317	1,800
Montgomery County	92,988	39,323	28,621	15,953	15,891	18,966	3,598	56,928	53,263	3,529	5,628	7,860
Prince George's County	74,984	33,863	16,269	9,914	11,509	8,545	5,345	46,137	29,950	5,963	6,096	4,916
St. Mary's County	7,959	3,489	2,027	1,156	1,570	1,228	905	6,239	4,126	822	669	373
Washington County	12,811	5,491	4,071	1,712	3,428	3,670	1,663	10,408	9,421	1,609	1,079	1,380
Wicomico County	7,666	3,316	2,029	1,552	2,057	2,715	1,366	6,614	5,585	1,385	806	725
Massachusetts												
Barnstable County	24,961	14,547	11,616	6,105	10,530	11,439	2,610	26,865	25,557	5,205	2,344	3,121
Berkshire County	13,921	5,733	5,045	2,247	3,885	5,552	2,002	11,666	11,624	3,401	1,550	1,852
Bristol County	47,564	17,165	11,220	7,315	13,176	13,421	7,382	38,731	34,434	12,927	6,844	7,854
Essex County	71,727	27,089	20,291	11,753	17,406	19,016	7,106	51,452	48,411	15,967	9,243	10,573
Franklin County	9,062	2,903	2,282	1,552	1,890	2,035	1,179	5,586	4,700	2,220	837	508
Hampden County	39,331	14,379	11,226	5,631	10,375	11,977	5,736	31,470	30,260	12,761	6,608	6,593
Hampshire County	16,297	5,278	4,363	2,687	3,405	4,037	1,158	10,057	9,044	2,468	1,399	1,333
Middlesex County	138,857	52,054	36,523	23,118	32,167	37,155	10,590	95,115	90,255	22,494	14,398	16,155
Norfolk County	69,115	25,584	19,874	10,163	15,706	18,466	4,625	45,662	45,769	9,544	6,169	8,304
Plymouth County	52,324	19,728	10,900	7,125	12,917	11,249	4,559	37,529	28,220	8,903	5,841	5,522
Suffolk County	40,779	15,036	10,069	7,880	8,170	8,829	6,309	36,788	32,740	20,284	12,311	11,471
Worcester County	74,312	24,757	17,362	9,186	17,796	19,209	6,996	49,478	45,331	15,180	8,521	9,080
Michigan												
Allegan County	9,676	3,728	2,381	3,040	3,409	2,831	1,498	8,375	6,110	1,184	793	932
Bay County	10,646	5,872	4,736	1,758	3,350	2,791	2,002	9,441	7,777	1,573	1,307	1,025
Berrien County	13,551	5,517	4,107	2,824	4,472	5,215	2,635	13,236	11,406	2,341	1,699	1,776
Calhoun County	11,027	5,667	5,474	2,060	3,209	3,061	2,337	10,327	9,109	2,648	1,744	1,335
Clinton County	7,789	3,712	2,143	1,584	1,991	1,682	759	5,800	4,093	590	390	446
Eaton County	12,606	5,600	4,023	1,504	2,765	2,463	1,175	8,752	6,406	937	908	707
Genesee County	38,378	20,233	16,644	5,720	9,679	8,907	7,160	31,395	26,229	8,052	4,720	3,637
Grand Traverse County	8,909	3,427	3,217	1,761	2,610	2,268	839	6,938	5,896	842	477	626
Ingham County	24,678	10,380	7,930	3,072	4,085	5,112	2,885	16,117	13,279	3,598	1,993	1,858
Isabella County	4,432	1,968	1,906	757	1,262	1,231	919	3,694	3,018	765	506	531
Jackson County	14,364	6,066	5,374	2,247	4,070	3,820	2,273	11,613	10,344	2,127	1,233	1,088
Kalamazoo County	20,909	8,584	7,140	4,126	5,866	5,927	2,971	16,265	13,856	3,263	1,425	1,569
Kent County	48,631	15,566	11,470	8,637	13,097	14,970	5,375	34,444	31,364	5,129	3,542	4,667
Lapeer County	9,212	4,195	2,813	1,376	2,535	1,857	1,064	7,361	4,627	842	633	430
Lenawee County	9,505	4,342	2,933	1,829	3,058	2,731	1,249	8,143	6,363	1,005	835	659
Livingston County	19,496	7,410	3,774	3,045	4,972	4,735	1,596	13,750	8,738	1,079	884	768
Macomb County	76,489	32,606	29,578	12,837	23,556	24,406	9,860	61,444	56,408	9,643	6,866	6,710
Marquette County	6,715	3,031	2,324	1,114	1,702	1,476	864	5,157	4,362	777	726	793
Midland County	7,997	4,368	4,183	1,288	1,961	1,872	907	6,439	5,646	905	443	488
Monroe County	16,478	6,679	4,932	2,489	3,893	3,560	2,057	11,214	8,900	1,514	1,152	1,443
Muskegon County	14,065	6,053	4,667	2,430	4,450	4,449	2,988	12,209	10,575	2,447	1,622	1,720
Oakland County	121,694	44,132	34,784	23,171	35,320	33,065	11,578	85,787	72,405	10,978	9,036	9,315
Ottawa County	22,521	7,263	5,371	4,559	6,582	6,747	2,069	16,700	13,952	1,307	1,404	1,461
Saginaw County	18,542	9,892	7,738	2,943	5,651	5,809	3,572	16,047	13,549	3,397	2,281	1,977
St. Clair County	15,547	7,321	5,458	2,803	5,205	4,635	2,596	13,120	10,228	2,203	1,308	1,170
Shiawassee County	7,073	3,569	2,220	848	1,862	2,118	904	5,773	4,353	786	457	445
Van Buren County	6,994	2,790	1,647	1,071	2,401	2,135	923	6,022	4,435	996	711	623
Washtenaw County	31,596	13,317	9,269	4,367	6,421	5,613	2,877	19,907	15,129	2,808	2,199	2,153
Wayne County	141,210	62,220	54,915	20,630	33,156	38,852	29,233	114,832	105,357	35,894	22,539	18,262
Minnesota												
Anoka County	30,232	7,571	3,990	4,815	9,958	7,824	2,552	20,017	12,870	2,258	1,678	1,709
Blue Earth County	4,937	1,088	758	1,098	1,812	2,060	414	3,512	3,650	473	228	493
Carver County	7,187	1,383	850	1,807	2,474	2,131	368	4,382	3,481	309	219	229
Dakota County	37,404	9,957	6,119	5,170	11,426	10,060	2,841	22,834	17,097	2,303	1,497	1,785
Hennepin County	97,724	24,599	18,967	19,285	31,394	33,938	8,138	65,593	59,811	12,487	7,853	8,288
Olmsted County	13,163	5,169	3,659	1,972	3,606	3,885	813	9,304	8,161	1,005	573	1,018
Ramsey County	43,661	12,856	10,683	6,835	13,559	14,296	4,857	30,184	28,252	6,712	3,030	3,709
St. Louis County	19,451	6,630	5,839	4,660	7,515	8,197	3,113	15,682	14,326	3,240	1,763	1,921
Scott County	8,948	1,895	1,031	2,051	2,761	2,290	814	6,183	3,955	684	491	570
Sherburne County	6,627	1,552	1,003	1,033	2,289	1,647	442	4,381	2,791	554	232	336
Stearns County	11,473	2,619	2,220	3,165	4,935	4,813	1,311	9,070	8,468	1,116	766	1,105
Washington County	23,888	7,123	4,533	4,256	7,461	5,612	1,344	14,959	10,573	1,327	1,387	1,156
Wright County	8,883	2,278	977	1,943	3,806	3,129	346	7,037	4,806	798	843	444

Table I-2: Counties—Persons With Health Insurance by Source of Insurance—*Continued*

| | Private Health Insurance Coverage | | | | | | Public Health Insurance Coverage | | | | | |
| | Employer Based | | | Direct Purchase | | | Medicare | | | Medicaid/CHIP | | |
	55 to 64 Years	65 to 74 Years	75 Years and Over	55 to 64 Years	65 to 74 Years	75 Years and Over	55 to 64 Years	65 to 74 Years	75 Years and Over	55 to 64 Years	65 to 74 Years	75 Years and Over
Mississippi												
DeSoto County	12,025	4,608	2,572	2,153	3,401	2,682	1,852	10,092	6,466	1,151	743	806
Forrest County	3,321	1,447	1,026	1,230	1,647	1,509	1,311	4,827	3,608	1,198	1,008	857
Harrison County	12,319	3,987	2,854	2,822	4,236	3,036	2,838	12,525	9,449	2,623	1,792	1,455
Hinds County	15,330	4,913	2,785	3,511	4,714	4,204	3,842	14,058	11,356	4,193	3,218	2,718
Jackson County	10,199	3,343	1,986	1,668	2,856	2,370	2,628	10,308	6,925	1,537	920	869
Jones County	4,147	1,424	1,061	850	1,716	1,467	1,609	5,145	4,177	1,099	1,175	885
Lauderdale County	5,609	1,948	1,399	1,449	1,310	1,954	1,276	5,683	4,997	1,218	957	1,661
Lee County	5,375	1,384	1,249	1,568	2,122	1,308	1,580	5,931	4,439	1,315	869	942
Madison County	7,308	2,181	1,224	2,109	1,770	1,838	1,400	5,597	4,314	1,116	786	981
Rankin County	10,982	3,548	1,511	2,058	3,802	2,989	1,629	9,985	6,252	1,251	1,192	742
Missouri												
Boone County	12,370	4,894	3,079	2,179	2,438	2,680	1,217	8,033	6,604	928	600	622
Buchanan County	6,829	2,124	1,613	1,340	2,594	2,666	1,364	6,121	5,415	1,136	820	452
Cape Girardeau County	6,282	1,816	1,575	1,098	1,891	1,984	1,330	5,246	4,555	622	510	616
Cass County	7,965	3,171	1,967	1,674	2,989	2,552	734	7,725	5,627	644	451	692
Christian County	5,471	1,673	1,033	1,540	2,157	1,902	876	5,872	3,781	413	381	452
Clay County	19,609	5,942	3,841	3,302	6,229	5,916	1,620	14,084	10,705	898	964	667
Cole County	7,404	2,987	1,740	805	1,619	1,935	792	4,996	4,105	576	275	374
Franklin County	8,660	2,974	2,119	1,734	2,018	2,222	1,162	7,565	5,875	698	533	700
Greene County	20,438	5,360	4,471	3,921	8,095	8,247	4,198	20,147	17,402	2,840	2,431	2,158
Jackson County	49,525	17,566	13,304	9,400	15,572	16,954	8,001	42,657	37,256	6,534	4,929	4,278
	8,100	2,344	1,538	986	3,358	2,983	1,628	8,225	6,642	1,603	1,125	1,008
Jasper County	20,467	6,279	4,002	3,111	4,079	3,031	2,835	15,317	8,924	1,669	1,248	1,056
Jefferson County												
Platte County	9,170	2,732	1,279	1,446	2,563	2,070	486	5,834	3,986	201	259	307
St. Charles County	33,954	10,778	7,120	5,162	7,988	7,128	2,369	23,737	17,364	983	1,197	1,123
St. Francois County	4,383	2,059	1,627	805	1,936	1,979	1,311	4,833	3,760	1,009	772	594
St. Louis County	97,840	33,753	25,687	16,835	25,043	28,129	9,510	72,983	67,985	5,948	5,844	6,537
Montana												
Cascade County	5,770	1,980	1,534	1,605	2,777	2,532	874	6,614	5,707	949	979	724
Flathead County	7,402	2,812	2,106	3,103	3,075	3,178	826	7,521	5,440	782	602	554
Gallatin County	6,285	1,651	1,109	2,290	1,643	1,573	430	4,924	3,693	363	345	205
Missoula County	8,698	2,310	1,401	2,232	2,640	2,972	1,365	7,024	5,285	948	530	597
Yellowstone County	12,854	3,860	2,926	2,714	4,967	5,568	1,610	10,753	9,503	1,413	802	1,340
Nebraska												
Douglas County	41,216	10,928	7,780	8,043	11,071	10,724	4,467	28,268	24,409	4,055	2,770	3,390
Lancaster County	24,075	6,532	4,455	4,134	6,934	7,621	2,203	15,567	14,264	1,986	1,380	1,765
Sarpy County	11,699	3,092	2,033	2,274	2,684	2,131	669	8,269	5,346	289	515	400
Nevada												
Clark County	135,338	52,556	27,519	24,632	29,365	22,904	16,916	130,635	85,252	13,316	15,578	12,310
Washoe County	33,609	12,036	6,655	7,854	8,964	6,769	3,703	30,634	20,337	3,082	3,132	3,068
New Hampshire												
Cheshire County	7,405	2,678	1,527	1,389	2,093	2,517	1,058	6,041	4,935	531	480	704
Grafton County	9,301	2,900	2,370	1,406	2,543	2,640	796	7,289	6,112	483	639	701
Hillsborough County	40,218	12,330	7,552	4,495	8,112	8,828	3,141	25,292	19,900	2,404	1,995	2,642
Merrimack County	15,807	4,807	3,545	2,009	3,769	3,877	1,516	10,683	8,578	1,152	1,176	575
Rockingham County	33,038	10,139	6,378	4,443	7,321	6,320	2,550	21,303	15,573	1,428	1,394	1,529
Strafford County	10,284	3,506	2,682	1,563	2,721	2,394	1,432	7,805	6,434	791	875	828
New Jersey												
Atlantic County	24,384	10,839	5,994	5,683	6,762	7,002	3,257	20,202	16,703	3,320	2,963	2,963
Bergen County	84,370	31,438	21,736	14,223	17,138	24,004	5,348	63,468	65,109	4,752	5,897	8,686
Burlington County	43,815	17,919	11,695	6,123	10,516	11,870	3,898	32,059	28,184	2,512	3,241	3,726
Camden County	44,422	15,447	11,043	6,301	9,825	12,423	4,965	33,230	29,540	6,132	5,000	4,742
Cape May County	10,944	5,515	3,846	2,370	4,221	4,201	958	11,002	9,570	1,079	851	1,037
Cumberland County	10,644	4,143	2,391	1,701	3,330	3,846	2,659	10,503	8,300	2,696	1,508	1,828
Essex County	54,279	20,343	12,876	10,362	9,277	11,779	7,217	44,243	39,548	9,663	8,311	8,194
Gloucester County	27,918	9,820	7,304	3,640	6,978	6,286	2,992	19,426	15,501	2,096	1,723	1,995
Hudson County	34,808	11,879	6,828	6,458	6,400	7,796	5,840	31,646	27,390	8,964	7,142	8,311
Hunterdon County	15,917	5,658	3,206	2,038	3,311	2,824	582	9,254	6,806	447	598	936
Mercer County	33,291	14,770	10,342	3,853	6,000	7,258	3,177	22,605	20,820	3,509	2,886	2,969
Middlesex County	69,662	26,108	18,096	8,131	12,398	16,362	5,286	47,468	44,666	5,122	5,748	7,649
Monmouth County	66,434	23,923	15,905	10,761	14,831	17,907	4,264	44,365	39,796	3,434	4,006	4,897
Morris County	52,235	21,283	13,898	7,120	10,748	12,857	2,332	34,119	31,681	2,183	3,057	3,383
Ocean County	51,519	30,068	24,746	9,532	21,225	27,107	7,592	58,390	58,896	4,268	4,451	5,794
Passaic County	35,773	12,795	7,124	4,862	6,027	7,875	4,710	29,570	26,483	5,965	5,954	6,460
Salem County	6,689	2,685	2,153	857	1,435	1,402	835	5,174	4,430	896	523	500
Somerset County	31,666	11,728	7,069	4,403	6,089	6,920	1,993	19,907	17,770	1,632	1,792	2,108
Sussex County	16,903	5,953	2,773	2,216	3,235	3,140	1,798	10,143	6,894	906	585	686
Union County	43,124	14,948	10,532	5,906	8,507	10,042	4,002	31,199	30,733	4,861	4,074	5,418
Warren County	10,837	4,041	2,288	1,492	2,756	2,663	1,244	7,670	6,571	1,066	849	948

Table I-2: Counties—Persons With Health Insurance by Source of Insurance—*Continued*

| | Private Health Insurance Coverage | | | | | | Public Health Insurance Coverage | | | | | |
| | Employer Based | | | Direct Purchase | | | Medicare | | | Medicaid/CHIP | | |
	55 to 64 Years	65 to 74 Years	75 Years and Over	55 to 64 Years	65 to 74 Years	75 Years and Over	55 to 64 Years	65 to 74 Years	75 Years and Over	55 to 64 Years	65 to 74 Years	75 Years and Over
New Mexico												
Bernalillo County	49,322	19,533	13,780	10,609	8,772	9,807	7,487	43,974	36,136	9,606	6,221	5,908
Chaves County	3,802	1,597	1,479	1,358	1,025	1,069	698	4,606	4,096	1,190	832	773
Doña Ana County	12,160	5,154	3,858	2,552	3,892	3,041	1,506	14,278	11,144	3,203	2,000	2,400
Lea County	3,808	1,212	1,038	865	1,341	1,067	742	3,756	3,002	1,032	713	697
McKinley County	2,366	681	260	681	420	283	510	3,759	2,666	1,402	1,270	1,151
Otero County	2,782	1,544	1,973	1,407	1,935	998	1,265	5,371	3,919	1,027	1,023	565
Sandoval County	10,529	3,859	2,004	2,685	2,334	1,877	1,511	9,883	6,263	1,231	883	732
San Juan County	8,359	2,762	1,778	1,396	1,546	1,722	1,482	7,358	6,049	969	865	1,356
Santa Fe County	12,997	6,067	3,370	5,601	4,577	3,252	1,802	13,492	8,530	1,602	1,190	763
Valencia County	5,882	2,224	1,447	1,133	1,441	1,285	1,130	6,007	3,978	805	817	763
New York												
Albany County	31,727	14,021	11,259	4,039	5,531	6,637	3,279	20,470	19,501	3,405	2,420	2,880
Bronx County	66,128	26,059	14,861	12,826	10,781	10,610	14,316	72,661	58,699	44,279	30,430	24,633
Broome County	18,075	8,036	8,587	2,904	4,804	6,028	2,624	15,665	15,165	2,813	1,563	1,934
Cattaraugus County	7,440	2,593	1,769	1,668	2,676	2,498	1,201	6,350	5,576	1,562	873	886
Cayuga County	7,457	3,195	2,657	1,029	1,893	1,850	1,507	6,186	5,661	1,268	650	691
Chautauqua County	12,781	4,238	3,405	2,320	4,558	5,264	2,314	10,922	10,021	2,398	1,406	1,440
Chemung County	8,440	3,494	2,953	1,028	2,068	2,364	1,577	6,646	6,089	1,645	763	925
Clinton County	7,539	3,470	2,361	994	1,687	1,737	1,041	5,900	4,662	1,104	660	560
Dutchess County	29,448	13,843	8,954	3,788	6,159	6,133	3,172	21,132	17,498	2,756	2,020	2,338
Erie County	88,105	36,227	28,088	12,742	24,704	30,100	12,373	68,975	68,100	15,142	7,754	10,506
Jefferson County	7,687	3,228	1,935	1,039	2,560	2,451	1,322	6,999	5,576	1,552	776	949
Kings County	148,748	50,606	27,808	23,384	17,521	21,033	21,236	141,914	129,195	69,220	49,839	55,572
Livingston County	7,016	2,436	1,869	919	1,529	1,946	563	4,645	4,057	513	409	521
Madison County	6,974	2,924	1,758	1,315	1,845	1,785	734	5,664	4,366	1,025	543	746
Monroe County	71,015	29,699	26,875	10,779	17,673	17,521	7,697	52,058	47,546	9,288	6,276	5,864
Nassau County	137,170	52,975	42,260	23,375	25,383	38,021	10,982	93,949	99,111	10,311	9,105	11,505
New York County	97,999	45,763	27,366	25,369	24,320	22,908	15,100	106,652	93,049	41,333	28,590	29,160
Niagara County	22,267	9,409	6,950	4,499	5,620	6,570	4,013	17,309	15,669	3,799	2,470	2,669
Oneida County	21,152	9,127	7,582	3,185	5,159	6,617	3,382	18,085	17,158	3,814	2,648	2,850
Onondaga County	44,286	17,925	14,230	6,007	8,840	12,081	5,213	31,336	30,498	6,007	3,577	4,308
Ontario County	11,874	4,871	2,997	1,733	3,807	3,549	1,210	9,015	7,283	1,149	1,018	1,110
Orange County	32,047	12,154	8,086	4,106	5,734	5,845	3,854	22,693	17,315	3,906	2,610	2,969
Oswego County	10,684	4,111	2,430	1,657	2,357	2,550	2,063	8,641	6,263	2,176	851	1,097
Putnam County	11,634	4,550	2,571	1,261	2,597	1,811	902	7,460	5,017	592	587	595
Queens County	148,663	53,067	35,223	26,251	21,980	28,475	19,150	138,029	126,065	50,276	35,553	33,843
Rensselaer County	16,917	6,479	5,191	1,484	3,109	3,449	1,502	11,066	9,449	1,790	1,107	1,228
Richmond County	43,899	15,988	8,607	6,376	4,943	5,220	5,494	32,094	24,910	7,469	4,476	4,801
Rockland County	28,623	14,203	9,032	3,739	5,121	5,393	2,253	21,291	18,873	2,985	2,185	3,139
St. Lawrence County	9,617	4,565	3,403	1,567	2,530	2,256	1,993	8,167	6,478	1,773	1,127	1,132
Saratoga County	24,615	9,572	6,380	3,191	6,404	5,782	2,134	17,320	12,612	1,923	1,543	1,588
Schenectady County	14,762	5,955	6,016	2,025	2,706	4,307	1,933	10,586	10,952	2,396	1,256	1,320
Steuben County	9,750	4,838	3,481	1,458	2,472	2,694	1,637	8,216	6,863	1,502	840	973
Suffolk County	142,135	64,409	38,353	24,441	28,318	32,063	13,492	105,754	87,780	11,729	9,312	10,091
Sullivan County	6,834	3,379	1,498	1,090	2,109	1,899	1,144	6,679	4,376	1,387	647	565
Tompkins County	9,015	3,626	3,201	1,302	1,277	1,378	1,008	5,632	4,948	1,021	636	690
Ulster County	17,693	7,833	5,116	3,171	3,340	4,171	2,453	14,382	11,907	2,920	1,236	1,688
Warren County	7,352	3,496	2,368	906	2,278	2,263	870	6,088	5,033	867	499	839
Wayne County	9,337	3,612	2,454	1,755	2,717	2,434	1,452	7,597	5,531	1,364	771	750
Westchester County	88,026	35,412	26,168	14,934	16,652	23,186	6,511	64,643	64,778	8,581	7,162	8,698
North Carolina												
Alamance County	11,781	3,863	3,279	1,901	3,400	4,587	2,267	11,544	10,242	1,344	1,198	1,256
Brunswick County	12,253	8,111	3,661	2,836	6,089	3,502	2,226	16,317	7,918	1,363	880	689
Buncombe County	18,470	7,316	5,910	5,749	7,467	7,125	3,828	20,388	16,772	2,662	2,023	2,743
Burke County	6,498	2,601	1,459	1,751	2,930	2,430	1,991	8,441	5,945	1,227	1,172	868
Cabarrus County	13,837	4,436	2,303	2,300	4,066	4,341	1,821	11,066	8,521	1,158	899	1,172
Caldwell County	5,924	1,289	719	1,625	2,835	2,318	2,219	7,632	5,117	1,088	881	743
Carteret County	6,834	3,817	1,887	1,682	2,536	2,297	1,212	7,368	5,162	615	544	576
Catawba County	12,075	3,759	2,352	2,803	5,163	4,204	2,447	12,598	9,255	1,110	1,162	1,540
Chatham County	6,059	3,247	2,183	1,642	2,225	1,804	444	6,836	5,337	594	513	595
Cleveland County	7,505	2,584	1,473	1,782	2,957	2,794	2,049	8,554	6,091	1,570	1,288	1,215
Craven County	7,077	3,946	2,807	1,906	3,574	3,058	1,694	8,877	6,982	1,093	855	952
Cumberland County	15,850	6,545	2,853	3,941	4,696	3,828	4,071	17,566	12,132	3,739	2,885	2,359
Davidson County	12,853	4,646	2,684	2,888	4,361	3,888	2,450	14,151	9,452	1,833	1,595	1,275
Durham County	19,863	7,683	5,389	4,188	4,035	4,708	2,421	14,329	11,155	2,110	2,027	2,046
Forsyth County	28,659	10,828	8,195	6,219	8,054	8,461	4,198	23,880	20,098	2,997	2,816	2,980
Gaston County	15,510	5,219	2,847	2,979	6,054	4,751	4,073	15,372	11,034	3,330	2,234	2,107
Guilford County	37,224	11,462	9,028	7,721	10,018	11,341	5,467	32,256	26,880	3,898	3,366	3,356
Harnett County	6,331	2,259	1,206	1,462	2,417	1,920	1,937	6,944	4,887	1,467	911	687
Henderson County	8,989	4,669	4,595	3,298	5,610	5,206	1,802	12,784	10,953	651	747	1,127
Iredell County	12,860	3,626	1,997	2,655	4,898	3,965	1,939	12,093	8,294	1,543	867	850
Johnston County	12,154	3,935	2,241	2,832	3,555	3,252	2,783	11,051	6,608	1,462	1,727	962
Lincoln County	7,072	2,055	1,036	1,473	2,799	1,758	1,210	6,677	3,898	831	900	612
Mecklenburg County	58,310	18,757	13,243	13,443	16,084	15,092	7,528	46,274	34,193	6,348	5,460	4,982
Moore County	7,443	3,494	3,498	2,151	3,871	3,635	1,488	10,180	9,503	823	1,004	1,232
Nash County	7,890	2,889	1,598	1,548	2,732	2,770	2,157	7,749	5,454	1,282	1,320	1,426
New Hanover County	15,983	7,010	5,377	4,302	6,653	5,679	2,513	16,130	12,088	2,130	1,140	1,599
Onslow County	6,665	3,567	1,582	2,160	2,080	2,026	1,310	8,068	5,232	975	1,250	748
Orange County	10,687	4,451	2,346	2,580	2,312	1,877	1,414	7,788	5,109	717	827	414
Pitt County	10,386	4,322	2,851	2,243	2,914	2,799	2,048	9,236	6,984	1,814	1,541	1,408
Randolph County	11,028	3,245	1,700	2,663	3,617	3,448	2,179	11,563	8,344	1,339	1,353	761

Table I-2: Counties—Persons With Health Insurance by Source of Insurance—*Continued*

| | Private Health Insurance Coverage | | | | | | Public Health Insurance Coverage | | | | | |
| | Employer Based | | | Direct Purchase | | | Medicare | | | Medicaid/CHIP | | |
	55 to 64 Years	65 to 74 Years	75 Years and Over	55 to 64 Years	65 to 74 Years	75 Years and Over	55 to 64 Years	65 to 74 Years	75 Years and Over	55 to 64 Years	65 to 74 Years	75 Years and Over
North Carolina—Cont.												
Robeson County	7,037	2,248	1,462	2,081	2,091	1,906	3,325	8,943	5,691	2,903	2,044	1,447
Rockingham County	7,344	2,411	2,011	1,526	3,249	2,647	2,190	8,510	6,382	1,785	1,478	1,026
Rowan County	9,963	3,619	2,357	2,151	4,326	3,857	2,887	10,956	8,361	1,555	1,123	1,069
Rutherford County	4,950	1,690	1,035	1,500	2,173	2,191	1,370	6,669	4,735	1,052	1,188	738
Surry County	5,567	1,793	1,203	1,636	3,173	2,470	2,145	6,761	5,141	1,288	1,014	1,087
Union County	13,557	4,907	1,959	3,259	4,937	3,526	2,025	12,553	7,174	988	1,007	1,091
Wake County	67,634	24,557	14,321	11,880	16,138	12,564	6,470	45,987	31,537	4,811	4,212	3,968
Wayne County	8,069	3,473	1,845	1,851	2,648	2,324	2,396	9,078	6,495	1,659	1,555	1,632
Wilkes County	5,262	1,953	1,003	1,908	2,674	2,472	1,553	6,824	5,011	1,018	1,101	920
Wilson County	6,230	2,459	1,367	1,501	2,306	1,983	1,593	6,302	4,707	1,257	996	1,050
North Dakota												
Burleigh County	8,167	2,356	1,470	1,591	3,137	3,302	681	5,577	5,221	250	490	549
Cass County	11,721	2,773	1,968	2,618	3,386	4,712	988	7,201	6,851	501	648	795
Grand Forks County	5,368	1,358	859	822	1,595	1,589	468	3,597	3,018	223	368	226
Ohio												
Allen County	9,232	3,985	3,165	1,488	2,353	2,868	1,700	7,750	6,922	1,404	882	834
Ashtabula County	9,143	3,355	2,622	1,220	2,834	2,504	1,564	8,174	6,762	1,258	917	616
Belmont County	7,241	3,382	2,633	1,214	1,782	2,230	995	6,009	5,491	859	497	700
Butler County	31,992	11,232	8,921	4,715	6,711	6,739	3,751	22,901	18,309	2,428	1,613	1,940
Clark County	12,315	5,984	4,973	2,107	3,212	3,390	1,962	11,724	9,291	1,727	1,334	1,120
Clermont County	18,603	5,731	3,699	2,625	4,653	3,747	1,960	13,675	9,473	1,355	1,301	927
Columbiana County	9,910	3,084	2,392	1,612	3,363	3,258	1,500	9,160	7,835	1,166	1,069	825
Cuyahoga County	112,949	44,135	38,642	16,340	25,312	33,034	14,107	91,497	92,940	16,284	12,518	14,078
Delaware County	16,798	5,682	3,510	2,556	3,736	2,567	912	10,527	6,602	555	851	584
Erie County	8,466	3,881	3,000	1,573	2,228	2,351	1,151	7,075	5,538	728	622	586
Fairfield County	13,025	4,935	3,133	2,214	3,378	3,016	1,454	10,234	7,383	999	905	845
Franklin County	88,127	31,575	20,962	12,230	17,055	18,441	10,843	60,814	49,723	9,400	7,648	5,797
Geauga County	10,140	3,965	2,375	2,044	2,869	2,908	840	7,807	5,958	380	645	692
Greene County	15,034	5,952	4,530	2,198	3,040	3,012	1,055	11,796	9,743	772	745	661
Hamilton County	68,509	23,783	19,936	10,652	15,447	18,734	8,478	51,155	48,418	6,784	4,473	5,627
Hancock County	7,001	2,757	2,652	1,259	2,817	2,131	485	5,687	4,720	339	358	372
Jefferson County	6,815	3,120	2,666	1,192	2,283	2,515	954	6,471	5,703	779	639	753
Lake County	24,763	9,234	7,085	3,417	7,259	7,265	1,724	19,003	16,618	999	1,021	1,219
Licking County	14,968	5,876	4,021	2,376	4,498	3,639	1,523	12,893	9,041	966	1,026	1,030
Lorain County	30,533	13,274	9,846	3,945	6,894	6,856	3,246	22,916	18,660	2,058	1,936	1,719
Lucas County	37,631	15,124	12,157	5,628	9,832	10,963	5,898	29,081	26,162	4,849	3,626	3,593
Mahoning County	22,986	8,187	7,214	3,977	5,183	7,121	3,328	19,597	20,175	2,742	1,998	2,046
Marion County	5,632	2,222	1,717	885	1,568	2,163	828	4,863	4,180	635	590	483
Medina County	18,224	6,602	4,498	3,306	4,218	3,943	1,554	13,075	9,303	731	719	785
Miami County	9,993	3,628	2,499	1,422	3,214	2,725	1,283	8,816	6,596	903	675	751
Montgomery County	46,612	17,325	15,543	7,397	11,955	13,010	6,671	40,683	37,018	5,208	4,475	4,419
Muskingum County	7,427	2,720	2,362	865	2,130	2,295	1,521	6,811	5,722	805	871	599
Portage County	14,993	6,397	3,475	1,938	3,286	3,303	1,411	11,747	8,566	1,128	976	903
Richland County	10,627	4,671	3,427	1,781	4,142	4,353	1,676	10,413	9,234	1,129	1,020	998
Ross County	6,135	2,645	1,852	769	1,749	1,543	852	5,661	4,040	769	739	441
Scioto County	5,822	2,559	1,747	819	1,934	1,864	1,361	6,333	5,176	1,656	1,332	885
Stark County	37,100	14,739	12,217	6,048	9,812	12,021	3,621	30,414	26,975	2,995	2,740	3,353
Summit County	52,194	17,984	18,794	7,876	10,416	13,061	5,909	38,856	37,171	4,875	4,290	4,888
Trumbull County	20,909	7,663	6,438	3,491	6,424	7,057	2,869	18,392	16,760	2,043	1,560	1,840
Tuscarawas County	8,761	2,845	2,078	1,712	2,765	3,160	1,215	7,519	6,678	839	809	878
Warren County	18,957	6,371	3,829	2,907	4,547	4,130	1,753	13,354	9,280	725	1,024	509
Wayne County	9,846	4,411	2,798	1,765	2,897	3,348	954	8,972	6,916	1,129	1,304	826
Wood County	11,994	4,213	3,667	1,869	2,693	2,755	1,004	7,955	6,937	846	447	602
Oklahoma												
Canadian County	9,981	3,683	2,180	1,507	2,656	2,170	635	7,569	4,902	452	528	640
Cleveland County	19,711	7,891	4,998	3,630	4,746	4,057	2,426	15,483	10,410	1,253	1,148	944
Comanche County	5,632	2,623	1,580	1,489	1,914	1,647	1,492	6,777	5,370	763	915	803
Creek County	4,885	1,484	827	1,259	2,397	2,322	1,111	6,158	4,150	782	790	360
Muskogee County	4,254	1,872	1,224	1,014	1,601	1,641	1,391	5,366	4,384	901	776	562
Oklahoma County	51,887	18,172	14,236	8,607	14,316	16,199	9,268	44,569	37,991	5,748	5,331	5,033
Payne County	4,300	2,000	1,705	996	1,483	1,784	749	4,149	3,497	649	427	506
Pottawatomie County	4,965	2,077	1,408	839	1,916	1,245	994	5,789	3,745	770	651	427
Rogers County	7,325	2,818	1,368	1,182	2,899	2,031	1,102	6,954	4,388	602	640	454
Tulsa County	46,306	15,269	10,809	8,865	14,299	15,092	5,948	37,704	32,090	4,035	3,832	3,637
Wagoner County	5,778	2,046	888	1,135	2,294	1,319	1,116	6,278	3,301	460	528	550
Oregon												
Benton County	7,437	2,483	2,160	1,380	2,305	1,988	590	5,486	4,887	741	361	550
Clackamas County	38,379	11,525	7,959	10,011	12,231	11,299	3,599	29,246	22,494	2,984	3,044	2,865
Deschutes County	13,400	5,097	2,944	4,805	6,298	5,266	1,355	14,673	9,951	1,024	847	1,028
Douglas County	10,214	3,668	3,127	2,626	5,351	4,013	1,786	12,293	10,129	1,558	1,350	1,273
Jackson County	17,263	5,364	5,996	5,120	7,521	7,808	3,198	19,366	16,926	2,280	2,244	2,223
Josephine County	6,353	2,926	2,192	2,204	4,704	4,459	1,738	10,102	8,276	2,051	1,555	949
Klamath County	4,607	1,411	1,264	1,978	2,034	2,059	1,253	6,532	4,974	1,072	905	861
Lane County	29,971	9,329	7,276	6,985	13,234	13,524	4,722	29,277	24,105	5,002	3,494	3,607
Linn County	10,040	3,292	2,521	2,102	4,459	3,940	1,579	10,255	7,944	1,269	1,230	1,268
Marion County	23,632	8,675	6,582	4,665	9,726	9,267	3,137	21,451	18,284	3,293	2,748	2,389

Table I-2: Counties—Persons With Health Insurance by Source of Insurance—*Continued*

| | Private Health Insurance Coverage | | | | | | Public Health Insurance Coverage | | | | | |
| | Employer Based | | | Direct Purchase | | | Medicare | | | Medicaid/CHIP | | |
	55 to 64 Years	65 to 74 Years	75 Years and Over	55 to 64 Years	65 to 74 Years	75 Years and Over	55 to 64 Years	65 to 74 Years	75 Years and Over	55 to 64 Years	65 to 74 Years	75 Years and Over
Oregon—Cont.												
Multnomah County	56,296	17,031	11,126	11,804	14,897	15,928	8,080	42,135	34,413	8,942	5,751	6,595
Polk County	6,356	1,889	2,119	1,124	2,375	2,861	1,158	6,090	5,293	890	648	981
Umatilla County	5,727	1,526	1,050	1,534	2,079	1,836	989	5,043	3,977	528	693	567
Washington County	41,717	11,258	8,556	8,648	11,477	11,215	3,384	29,605	23,950	2,752	2,998	3,711
Yamhill County	7,776	2,447	1,688	2,077	2,985	3,217	930	7,000	6,366	796	859	1,080
Pennsylvania												
Adams County	10,486	3,583	2,420	1,730	3,829	3,728	1,151	8,568	6,908	870	845	773
Allegheny County	120,845	38,242	37,285	22,958	40,039	53,197	12,704	92,036	100,499	14,707	12,821	16,115
Armstrong County	6,892	2,551	2,445	1,338	2,798	3,177	1,042	6,363	6,012	1,179	689	890
Beaver County	17,793	5,779	5,263	3,645	7,370	8,842	2,576	15,116	15,686	2,222	2,222	2,496
Berks County	35,105	11,920	9,996	6,923	13,219	13,829	4,671	29,056	27,495	4,895	2,637	3,592
Blair County	11,759	4,316	3,466	2,613	4,923	5,779	2,318	11,057	9,977	1,991	1,242	1,552
Bucks County	66,533	22,008	15,143	12,757	18,740	21,759	4,995	46,538	41,799	4,207	3,711	4,750
Butler County	18,044	5,999	5,406	3,960	6,390	6,259	1,704	14,263	12,872	1,743	1,428	1,362
Cambria County	14,561	5,147	4,671	2,527	6,016	7,315	2,254	12,669	13,344	2,166	1,704	2,316
Carbon County	6,370	2,216	1,967	1,552	3,048	2,866	1,102	6,022	5,210	473	455	557
Centre County	11,918	4,655	3,736	1,293	3,290	3,160	1,244	8,761	7,685	1,245	856	1,036
Chester County	48,721	15,885	10,062	8,851	14,245	14,202	2,638	33,651	27,962	2,670	2,623	2,524
Clearfield County	6,781	2,123	1,531	1,915	2,998	3,010	1,130	7,228	6,299	1,290	818	936
Columbia County	6,487	2,046	1,184	1,224	2,749	2,893	735	5,441	4,823	545	459	771
Crawford County	7,468	2,663	1,870	1,705	3,200	3,584	1,549	7,718	6,331	1,885	1,075	791
Cumberland County	24,522	8,343	7,244	4,124	7,696	7,594	1,374	18,188	16,835	1,280	1,691	1,718
Dauphin County	26,819	9,302	7,827	3,820	6,586	6,933	3,370	18,279	16,772	3,499	1,963	2,172
Delaware County	50,871	18,593	14,782	9,445	13,184	18,823	4,917	35,629	38,681	5,496	3,649	4,207
Erie County	26,262	7,473	5,871	4,159	8,947	10,027	3,450	20,289	18,429	3,104	2,648	3,165
Fayette County	12,154	3,763	3,434	2,220	5,231	5,182	2,309	12,190	11,279	3,104	1,962	1,716
Franklin County	13,199	6,434	4,935	2,633	4,447	4,546	1,655	12,845	11,327	1,211	1,381	1,382
Indiana County	8,443	3,394	2,634	1,446	2,870	2,664	1,043	7,092	6,336	1,202	992	668
Lackawanna County	19,806	7,092	5,347	4,423	7,931	9,470	2,764	17,896	17,384	2,963	1,990	2,786
Lancaster County	46,757	14,831	12,585	8,539	14,991	16,968	3,976	37,648	34,927	4,512	2,899	3,610
Lawrence County	8,249	2,346	2,267	2,081	3,664	4,637	1,659	7,765	8,387	1,492	1,028	853
Lebanon County	13,303	5,075	4,264	2,209	4,807	4,722	1,174	11,201	10,132	1,083	852	1,276
Lehigh County	30,025	9,365	8,446	6,102	9,435	12,531	4,165	24,909	23,929	3,447	3,443	3,127
Luzerne County	29,188	9,493	7,702	6,320	12,778	14,345	4,919	27,081	27,231	3,947	3,804	4,267
Lycoming County	10,939	2,981	3,034	2,014	3,961	4,300	999	9,244	8,780	1,553	987	1,045
Mercer County	10,438	2,958	2,670	2,025	4,411	5,715	1,933	10,135	10,077	2,212	1,082	1,297
Monroe County	15,683	5,803	2,841	3,415	4,556	4,230	1,944	12,521	8,866	1,644	1,919	1,424
Montgomery County	77,321	28,306	20,470	15,567	21,942	29,072	5,749	56,670	56,940	4,848	4,744	5,451
Northampton County	29,637	8,456	6,698	5,068	10,018	13,380	3,142	22,451	22,227	2,504	2,362	2,640
Northumberland County	8,738	2,654	2,054	2,265	4,333	4,426	1,537	8,351	7,912	1,256	1,299	1,197
Philadelphia County	87,988	31,730	21,374	20,065	27,072	30,870	20,521	88,874	82,924	38,395	22,210	21,380
Schuylkill County	13,296	4,469	3,771	3,134	5,546	6,982	2,236	12,702	12,502	1,754	1,355	1,690
Somerset County	7,527	2,155	2,179	1,770	3,661	3,422	1,187	7,085	6,660	1,007	1,011	1,016
Washington County	21,978	7,508	6,608	3,973	7,935	8,880	2,878	17,950	17,064	2,610	2,294	2,262
Westmoreland County	39,932	14,132	12,590	8,576	14,070	17,420	4,603	33,240	33,097	4,247	3,986	4,793
York County	42,277	12,965	8,273	6,677	13,734	14,174	4,159	32,998	27,088	4,115	3,142	3,066
Rhode Island												
Kent County	17,046	6,155	3,673	2,786	4,127	5,434	2,582	12,481	12,386	2,297	1,773	2,250
Newport County	8,305	3,554	2,477	1,966	2,714	3,364	629	7,331	6,254	705	885	985
Providence County	46,535	13,861	10,434	7,522	11,962	16,434	8,151	38,590	39,266	10,341	8,013	6,779
Washington County	14,337	5,003	2,905	2,484	4,060	4,315	1,634	10,299	8,159	1,030	647	642
South Carolina												
Aiken County	14,502	6,648	4,365	2,258	4,348	3,889	1,954	14,243	10,320	1,922	1,374	1,384
Anderson County	14,399	5,100	3,752	2,522	5,674	5,535	4,399	16,340	11,805	2,189	1,914	1,721
Beaufort County	13,689	10,224	6,075	4,801	7,777	5,782	1,442	20,858	13,372	1,348	1,571	999
Berkeley County	12,727	4,670	1,896	2,141	2,800	1,786	2,275	12,233	6,584	1,483	1,259	1,009
Charleston County	24,807	11,744	7,004	6,999	8,658	7,477	3,952	25,582	18,893	3,656	3,611	3,541
Darlington County	4,976	1,752	948	1,019	2,135	1,641	1,781	5,823	3,800	1,295	891	877
Dorchester County	9,397	3,038	2,055	1,379	3,352	1,853	2,196	8,967	5,104	1,033	1,124	571
Florence County	9,373	3,747	2,135	2,308	3,182	2,626	2,676	10,625	6,977	2,420	1,533	1,884
Greenville County	36,133	10,934	7,027	6,757	12,622	10,086	5,142	33,549	24,244	3,994	3,554	2,988
Greenwood County	4,926	2,050	1,252	1,166	2,076	1,955	1,662	5,674	4,542	1,016	909	528
Horry County	23,196	11,418	7,489	5,951	11,119	7,597	4,021	29,342	17,805	2,961	2,758	2,083
Lancaster County	5,841	2,664	1,250	1,435	3,332	1,996	1,281	7,630	4,648	926	1,032	681
Laurens County	5,056	2,026	912	1,701	1,975	1,442	1,846	5,724	3,784	1,146	616	355
Lexington County	23,265	9,395	5,162	2,796	5,671	4,826	2,701	19,734	12,611	1,798	1,537	1,360
Oconee County	6,608	3,594	2,029	1,502	2,767	2,126	1,274	8,692	5,558	800	1,039	884
Orangeburg County	6,492	2,246	1,544	1,586	2,651	1,616	1,771	7,815	5,643	1,608	1,644	1,905
Pickens County	8,504	2,984	2,288	1,410	3,365	2,870	2,065	9,275	6,746	1,191	1,116	1,081
Richland County	27,712	9,897	6,196	4,824	5,753	5,164	4,692	21,175	15,446	3,442	3,307	3,012
Spartanburg County	20,461	6,892	4,070	4,159	7,172	6,833	5,813	22,065	15,456	4,137	2,922	2,146
Sumter County	6,563	2,613	1,572	1,218	2,030	1,890	1,791	7,784	5,615	1,679	1,538	1,386
York County	19,031	5,838	3,166	3,091	5,423	4,699	2,482	15,909	10,001	1,710	1,975	1,317

Table I-2: Counties—Persons With Health Insurance by Source of Insurance—*Continued*

| | Private Health Insurance Coverage | | | | | | Public Health Insurance Coverage | | | | | |
| | Employer Based | | | Direct Purchase | | | Medicare | | | Medicaid/CHIP | | |
	55 to 64 Years	65 to 74 Years	75 Years and Over	55 to 64 Years	65 to 74 Years	75 Years and Over	55 to 64 Years	65 to 74 Years	75 Years and Over	55 to 64 Years	65 to 74 Years	75 Years and Over
South Dakota												
Minnehaha County	14,303	2,952	2,050	3,306	4,173	5,165	1,439	9,514	8,664	949	1,052	1,452
Pennington County	7,694	2,326	2,020	2,362	2,981	3,171	1,216	7,300	6,125	699	725	524
Tennessee												
Anderson County	7,198	2,824	2,508	1,046	2,256	2,664	1,591	6,658	5,926	1,323	866	590
Blount County	11,289	4,079	2,828	2,274	5,134	3,893	1,693	11,663	8,086	1,298	1,046	1,070
Bradley County	7,429	2,367	1,320	1,682	3,463	2,530	1,701	8,530	5,643	1,022	1,455	1,166
Davidson County	45,707	14,216	10,778	9,127	9,978	10,394	5,740	33,762	28,711	6,580	4,359	4,685
Greene County	5,694	2,251	1,252	1,401	2,790	2,059	1,507	7,160	4,705	1,039	1,087	1,191
Hamilton County	29,906	10,446	7,764	5,893	9,559	10,026	4,465	26,547	22,068	4,687	3,361	3,043
Knox County	36,650	13,848	9,398	6,354	10,414	10,200	5,511	30,986	24,804	4,449	3,462	2,849
Madison County	7,445	2,374	1,794	1,529	2,607	2,436	1,539	7,143	5,519	1,510	856	935
Maury County	7,194	2,688	1,279	1,260	2,503	1,484	1,319	5,861	4,452	1,207	749	747
Montgomery County	7,794	2,274	1,642	1,704	2,190	2,114	1,388	8,112	5,507	1,085	884	655
Putnam County	4,800	1,935	1,226	1,329	2,525	2,343	1,201	5,898	4,393	593	697	776
Robertson County	5,284	1,585	877	1,450	1,435	1,134	671	4,674	3,053	663	611	531
Rutherford County	18,113	4,480	3,009	3,366	3,500	2,935	2,033	13,524	8,509	1,823	1,806	1,281
Sevier County	7,450	2,584	1,189	2,125	3,670	2,612	1,202	8,857	5,374	665	1,141	848
Shelby County	69,237	21,257	14,865	12,210	14,868	13,866	11,343	51,460	40,393	11,349	9,857	7,566
Sullivan County	13,216	5,549	4,744	2,762	6,690	5,436	3,629	16,236	12,456	2,707	2,066	1,734
Sumner County	14,218	3,944	2,495	2,170	3,613	2,977	2,085	12,633	7,845	1,012	1,955	1,286
Washington County	10,429	3,598	2,782	1,431	4,444	3,262	2,443	10,614	7,686	1,355	1,232	910
Williamson County	17,278	5,420	3,219	4,780	3,997	2,954	745	10,703	7,303	659	755	550
Wilson County	10,296	3,311	2,026	1,961	2,633	2,183	1,140	9,094	5,297	1,022	952	610
Texas												
Angelina County	5,317	2,266	1,922	1,133	2,124	1,535	1,440	6,323	5,164	1,268	953	955
Bastrop County	6,810	2,141	1,531	843	1,286	883	567	4,797	3,620	318	330	546
Bell County	15,190	6,890	4,660	2,275	4,624	4,269	2,711	15,210	11,519	2,804	2,540	2,560
Bexar County	98,762	36,446	24,447	19,179	22,389	19,753	17,868	95,286	75,318	20,310	17,280	17,088
Bowie County	7,031	2,763	2,326	1,223	1,888	2,019	1,266	6,879	5,449	1,092	1,007	906
Brazoria County	22,756	7,719	4,343	3,026	5,040	3,981	2,198	17,433	11,539	1,714	2,367	1,546
Brazos County	9,496	4,384	2,978	1,524	2,095	2,244	682	7,765	6,031	985	733	852
Cameron County	13,900	4,525	2,853	3,544	4,617	3,619	3,628	23,109	19,235	5,019	7,464	7,588
Collin County	57,319	17,934	7,493	10,401	12,588	7,394	3,581	38,866	22,201	2,591	2,916	3,547
Comal County	10,565	3,907	2,610	2,776	3,133	2,387	876	10,313	6,928	666	658	1,036
Coryell County	2,824	1,428	906	652	1,054	1,042	465	3,280	2,325	433	527	654
Dallas County	134,381	40,856	25,539	27,916	28,863	30,184	17,511	111,304	85,979	21,126	18,534	16,317
Denton County	46,540	14,387	6,622	8,320	8,481	6,273	3,415	29,578	17,180	2,355	2,410	1,899
Ector County	7,229	2,347	1,366	1,888	2,236	2,347	1,792	7,415	5,804	1,460	1,438	1,220
Ellis County	11,410	3,579	1,724	1,877	2,866	1,977	1,461	9,378	5,571	1,219	1,154	667
El Paso County	30,950	10,589	7,676	6,281	7,584	6,788	9,291	42,453	36,443	10,134	10,935	13,930
Fort Bend County	47,596	12,972	4,692	5,661	6,632	4,489	3,288	25,933	15,652	3,162	3,577	2,862
Galveston County	23,543	8,535	5,381	4,605	5,523	4,629	2,951	19,168	13,785	2,216	2,193	2,187
Grayson County	9,593	4,164	2,934	2,163	3,864	2,993	1,697	10,237	7,796	1,586	833	1,297
Gregg County	7,443	2,488	2,143	1,479	2,937	2,931	1,237	7,740	7,342	1,582	728	1,210
Guadalupe County	9,371	2,926	1,840	1,589	3,359	1,819	1,150	9,147	6,353	749	942	1,066
Harris County	248,916	72,919	41,320	40,315	43,009	40,728	29,275	186,909	133,080	40,786	31,915	27,541
Harrison County	5,212	1,783	1,173	912	1,686	915	729	5,037	3,603	549	370	751
Hays County	11,883	4,582	2,007	2,494	2,303	1,743	782	8,471	5,139	679	777	723
Henderson County	5,062	2,848	2,043	1,434	3,080	2,446	1,410	8,551	5,956	951	842	692
Hidalgo County	22,896	7,994	6,447	4,755	7,553	7,662	7,436	37,792	30,929	9,334	14,454	13,428
Hunt County	6,289	2,356	1,592	1,271	2,358	1,766	1,282	6,905	4,602	858	654	635
Jefferson County	17,039	6,867	5,844	3,191	4,538	5,157	3,586	15,231	14,958	3,011	2,719	2,300
Johnson County	11,469	3,645	1,598	1,609	2,718	2,017	1,320	10,495	6,450	624	1,088	803
Kaufman County	7,696	2,785	1,358	867	2,286	1,294	1,176	6,669	3,956	835	569	579
Liberty County	5,005	1,611	561	1,126	1,430	1,414	877	5,022	3,193	747	671	338
Lubbock County	16,827	7,153	4,808	3,908	5,447	5,212	2,711	16,169	13,333	2,284	2,780	2,314
McLennan County	15,414	5,941	4,933	2,795	5,519	6,182	2,274	14,723	12,858	2,443	2,321	2,082
Midland County	9,754	2,960	2,215	2,068	2,341	2,808	1,095	7,181	7,099	1,199	808	1,078
Montgomery County	36,666	12,501	6,221	7,229	8,501	6,187	3,912	29,979	18,179	2,643	3,140	1,871
Nacogdoches County	4,049	1,618	986	718	1,122	1,299	858	3,937	3,272	802	640	482
Nueces County	22,723	7,207	4,793	3,923	5,285	6,440	3,926	21,712	18,016	5,205	3,836	3,676
Orange County	6,230	2,691	2,018	1,848	1,664	1,986	1,336	6,129	4,915	1,058	701	867
Parker County	10,013	3,841	2,346	1,599	2,991	2,207	1,212	9,082	5,495	740	801	451
Potter County	6,306	2,043	1,673	1,299	1,953	2,095	1,311	6,630	5,529	1,467	1,418	898
Randall County	10,212	3,946	2,475	2,051	2,709	2,716	1,183	8,363	6,585	559	530	623
Rockwall County	6,332	1,866	1,004	1,043	1,765	1,129	475	4,776	2,857	391	392	339
San Patricio County	4,247	1,618	789	752	1,173	883	605	4,671	3,418	868	726	859
Smith County	15,335	6,015	4,592	2,724	5,643	5,860	2,479	15,728	13,208	1,529	1,807	2,353
Tarrant County	122,407	36,207	20,822	20,213	22,996	20,127	13,132	90,143	66,719	12,897	10,269	9,090
Taylor County	7,788	3,262	2,621	2,086	2,634	2,806	1,277	8,748	7,697	1,027	1,319	1,214
Tom Green County	7,832	3,648	2,896	1,536	2,825	3,054	1,425	7,821	7,060	991	676	964
Travis County	65,128	22,856	14,222	13,780	11,999	10,310	6,783	42,675	31,316	7,740	4,963	5,308
Victoria County	7,213	2,826	1,703	1,635	2,014	2,245	710	6,185	5,127	708	868	865
Walker County	3,567	2,145	1,236	727	1,080	640	407	3,771	2,563	364	378	314

Table I-2: Counties—Persons With Health Insurance by Source of Insurance—*Continued*

| | Private Health Insurance Coverage | | | | | | Public Health Insurance Coverage | | | | | |
| | Employer Based | | | Direct Purchase | | | Medicare | | | Medicaid/CHIP | | |
	55 to 64 Years	65 to 74 Years	75 Years and Over	55 to 64 Years	65 to 74 Years	75 Years and Over	55 to 64 Years	65 to 74 Years	75 Years and Over	55 to 64 Years	65 to 74 Years	75 Years and Over
Texas—Cont.												
Webb County	7,420	2,156	1,075	1,335	1,622	1,068	1,794	10,126	7,948	2,462	3,367	4,048
Wichita County	8,187	3,819	2,589	1,857	2,801	3,236	1,782	8,291	7,812	1,307	1,012	1,014
Williamson County	30,585	12,225	5,949	5,311	8,891	6,012	2,743	23,971	14,771	1,851	1,880	2,040
Utah												
Cache County	6,281	2,014	1,305	1,314	1,636	1,935	504	4,798	3,955	352	345	421
Davis County	21,159	7,499	5,533	3,399	4,187	4,255	1,474	13,986	11,102	1,269	1,400	1,040
Salt Lake County	68,863	21,906	14,468	11,595	15,449	15,889	6,158	48,974	38,745	7,064	5,664	5,279
Utah County	23,605	8,559	6,789	4,085	6,893	6,088	1,603	18,360	14,952	1,869	1,832	1,941
Washington County	9,312	4,621	4,616	2,503	5,236	4,900	1,538	13,314	11,444	920	714	1,063
Weber County	15,757	5,421	5,312	2,849	3,882	4,428	1,725	12,093	10,853	1,458	1,202	1,403
Vermont												
Chittenden County	13,850	5,203	3,623	2,658	2,963	2,755	1,194	9,861	7,700	2,127	1,157	1,368
Virginia												
Albemarle County	8,788	3,607	3,010	2,904	2,796	3,145	943	7,420	6,597	334	550	831
Arlington County	16,248	7,145	3,836	2,624	2,844	2,272	761	9,482	7,310	595	860	1,063
Augusta County	6,661	2,931	1,915	2,008	3,147	2,332	1,217	7,060	4,918	376	460	599
Bedford County	7,442	2,522	1,425	1,605	3,300	2,241	1,099	7,182	4,401	338	255	368
Chesterfield County	31,756	10,971	6,199	5,153	6,949	5,132	2,667	20,357	13,490	1,548	1,322	966
Fairfax County	101,196	39,784	21,547	16,370	15,249	12,800	4,059	60,005	42,122	2,928	4,805	5,896
Fauquier County	6,691	2,533	1,325	1,384	1,697	1,308	484	5,102	3,298	284	461	208
Frederick County	6,730	2,555	1,649	1,636	1,878	1,882	746	5,783	4,112	287	673	496
Hanover County	10,606	3,545	2,578	2,131	3,100	2,619	812	7,517	5,647	425	714	683
Henrico County	27,030	9,372	7,941	4,660	6,226	8,292	2,381	19,139	17,776	1,230	1,442	1,617
James City County	7,656	4,210	3,352	1,446	2,667	2,609	523	7,705	6,341	59	228	377
Loudoun County	21,457	7,482	3,879	3,087	3,192	2,834	1,139	12,123	8,340	495	858	1,229
Montgomery County	6,711	2,340	1,758	1,008	2,077	1,851	743	5,041	3,946	249	294	353
Prince William County	28,709	9,931	4,720	4,395	4,052	3,021	1,511	17,254	9,261	902	1,471	861
Roanoke County	10,113	3,615	2,509	2,229	3,411	3,362	1,038	8,107	6,949	451	678	564
Rockingham County	6,807	2,577	1,641	1,700	2,883	2,221	763	6,382	5,490	392	707	537
Spotsylvania County	10,330	3,881	2,129	1,690	2,002	1,704	925	7,377	4,879	448	668	693
Stafford County	9,847	3,823	1,601	1,676	2,040	1,116	709	6,182	3,268	294	537	452
York County	5,763	2,566	1,356	841	1,436	1,359	339	4,767	3,233	121	181	49
Washington												
Benton County	16,772	5,747	4,417	2,704	4,206	3,248	1,857	12,036	8,837	1,454	1,155	1,095
Chelan County	6,333	2,681	2,152	2,118	2,549	2,386	932	5,635	5,045	967	433	1,003
Clallam County	6,599	3,389	2,683	2,434	3,310	3,158	1,587	9,194	7,809	1,163	662	714
Clark County	36,391	11,363	6,874	7,303	11,031	9,504	3,818	29,008	20,633	3,901	3,165	3,129
Cowlitz County	8,694	3,188	2,927	2,015	4,158	3,169	1,580	9,083	6,710	1,672	1,345	1,203
Franklin County	4,262	1,255	565	1,074	1,070	899	507	3,166	2,435	706	588	497
Grant County	5,680	1,938	1,145	1,495	2,124	1,918	780	6,123	4,326	939	1,025	694
Grays Harbor County	6,431	2,579	1,523	1,624	2,799	2,195	1,396	6,988	4,792	1,138	901	553
Island County	7,101	3,164	2,068	2,870	3,212	2,311	716	8,706	5,738	552	462	571
King County	163,993	49,677	32,684	35,223	39,206	38,656	13,056	111,114	94,382	17,282	15,789	17,845
Kitsap County	22,929	9,914	5,480	5,483	6,362	5,431	2,784	19,955	13,038	2,961	2,442	1,991
Lewis County	5,737	2,128	1,491	1,759	3,084	3,055	1,572	7,273	5,547	1,201	873	678
Pierce County	57,799	18,771	12,434	11,256	17,050	14,753	8,675	49,138	37,816	7,969	5,815	6,055
Skagit County	10,079	3,794	3,197	3,135	4,114	3,889	1,174	10,657	8,228	1,204	1,256	1,046
Snohomish County	60,767	17,272	10,097	12,588	13,580	13,717	5,608	41,341	31,814	6,565	4,902	6,291
Spokane County	38,185	12,362	8,024	9,435	11,300	12,849	6,070	33,249	27,373	5,920	4,129	4,335
Thurston County	23,668	9,739	6,247	4,829	5,821	6,012	3,016	18,672	14,307	2,283	1,865	1,726
Whatcom County	16,212	5,585	3,838	5,400	5,789	5,675	2,019	15,091	11,722	2,402	2,217	1,502
Yakima County	14,264	4,165	3,163	3,909	5,122	5,210	2,748	14,821	12,261	2,610	2,489	2,677
West Virginia												
Berkeley County	9,290	4,375	2,104	956	2,297	1,913	1,432	7,344	4,584	1,135	856	732
Cabell County	7,467	3,768	3,081	1,026	2,264	2,193	1,776	7,715	6,942	1,918	1,068	945
Harrison County	6,594	2,328	2,184	772	1,994	2,290	1,429	6,102	5,028	1,363	713	506
Kanawha County	20,113	8,651	8,013	2,227	4,351	5,369	4,118	16,785	14,582	3,035	1,772	1,987
Monongalia County	7,288	2,815	2,455	925	1,345	1,058	1,384	5,133	4,298	944	477	351
Raleigh County	8,092	3,738	3,308	3,140	2,824	2,125	2,468	6,741	5,725	1,373	521	628
Wood County	8,141	3,801	2,793	1,199	2,676	2,622	1,886	8,178	6,048	1,320	816	665

Table I-2: Counties—Persons With Health Insurance by Source of Insurance—Continued

| | Private Health Insurance Coverage | | | | | | Public Health Insurance Coverage | | | | | |
| | Employer Based | | | Direct Purchase | | | Medicare | | | Medicaid/CHIP | | |
	55 to 64 Years	65 to 74 Years	75 Years and Over	55 to 64 Years	65 to 74 Years	75 Years and Over	55 to 64 Years	65 to 74 Years	75 Years and Over	55 to 64 Years	65 to 74 Years	75 Years and Over
Wisconsin												
Brown County	21,129	4,365	3,708	3,777	5,816	5,454	1,813	15,039	12,983	1,988	1,262	1,490
Dane County	46,528	15,819	10,834	7,195	10,764	11,468	3,239	26,792	22,322	4,077	2,072	2,605
Dodge County	8,193	2,340	1,768	1,791	2,907	3,079	624	6,450	5,856	665	768	775
Eau Claire County	8,496	2,514	2,289	1,373	2,868	3,455	856	6,307	5,864	1,079	877	729
Fond du Lac County	9,876	1,950	1,561	1,501	3,872	3,807	1,064	7,608	7,246	961	887	1,373
Jefferson County	8,264	2,202	1,501	1,158	3,120	2,664	632	6,148	4,700	715	635	736
Kenosha County	13,351	4,516	3,572	1,989	3,194	3,385	1,432	9,464	8,539	1,601	1,199	1,364
La Crosse County	10,495	2,144	1,646	1,234	3,256	3,714	1,046	7,487	7,206	1,189	1,028	893
Manitowoc County	8,383	2,191	1,725	1,339	2,772	3,374	1,021	6,980	6,333	927	883	1,176
Marathon County	12,558	2,938	2,123	2,331	4,829	5,348	974	9,707	8,731	1,045	1,280	1,217
Milwaukee County	67,260	19,941	21,679	8,915	15,785	19,272	10,179	50,299	52,919	16,334	9,083	10,736
Outagamie County	16,327	3,083	2,960	2,453	4,398	4,409	1,147	10,959	9,470	1,184	1,370	1,287
Ozaukee County	9,775	2,891	2,211	2,065	2,699	3,262	546	7,008	6,135	516	591	659
Portage County	5,997	1,802	1,324	1,160	2,199	2,247	652	4,839	4,144	836	342	735
Racine County	18,355	5,891	4,499	2,649	4,682	4,641	1,568	13,646	11,900	1,858	1,358	1,593
Rock County	13,898	5,305	3,332	2,179	5,018	5,348	1,921	11,442	9,761	2,343	1,140	1,573
St. Croix County	7,392	1,916	1,149	1,511	2,262	2,024	579	4,935	3,403	655	298	599
Sheboygan County	11,435	2,552	2,063	1,821	3,801	4,258	913	8,368	7,836	1,377	898	1,136
Walworth County	9,436	2,697	1,873	1,823	2,986	3,220	929	7,515	5,865	849	809	726
Washington County	14,120	3,493	2,956	2,100	3,952	3,598	871	9,560	7,887	980	872	885
Waukesha County	44,079	12,437	9,323	6,546	10,653	13,241	2,014	28,895	26,033	2,345	1,913	3,431
Winnebago County	15,487	3,621	3,123	2,120	4,866	5,368	1,239	10,949	10,285	1,394	918	1,116
Wood County	7,269	2,040	1,767	1,569	3,064	3,516	493	6,266	5,947	992	613	982
Wyoming												
Laramie County	8,270	3,019	1,937	1,050	2,326	1,706	993	6,519	4,900	846	638	524
Natrona County	7,069	1,436	1,096	1,320	2,101	2,151	629	4,805	4,216	561	442	436

Table I-3: Places—Persons With Health Insurance by Source of Insurance

| | Private Health Insurance Coverage | | | | | | Public Health Insurance Coverage | | | | | |
| | Employer Based | | | Direct Purchase | | | Medicare | | | Medicaid/CHIP | | |
	55 to 64 Years	65 to 74 Years	75 Years and Over	55 to 64 Years	65 to 74 Years	75 Years and Over	55 to 64 Years	65 to 74 Years	75 Years and Over	55 to 64 Years	65 to 74 Years	75 Years and Over
Alabama												
Birmingham city	13,758	4,402	3,687	3,050	3,716	3,775	4,523	13,000	12,388	5,071	3,696	3,549
Dothan city	5,030	1,887	1,322	1,066	1,941	1,847	1,273	5,124	4,198	795	676	721
Hoover city	8,156	2,596	1,932	1,635	1,703	1,771	322	5,386	4,148	200	246	397
Huntsville city	13,096	8,020	5,509	2,467	3,543	4,116	1,951	13,071	10,871	1,403	1,141	1,196
Mobile city	14,233	4,880	4,184	2,969	4,110	4,656	3,270	13,611	11,707	2,191	2,482	1,786
Montgomery city	14,178	6,303	4,891	2,773	3,325	3,457	3,179	12,919	10,457	2,983	2,267	1,838
Tuscaloosa city	6,020	1,892	1,808	1,113	1,375	1,514	1,304	4,361	4,709	844	657	938
Alaska												
Anchorage Municipality	23573	7624	3306	3,401	2,404	1,766	2,085	12,651	7,787	2,432	1,781	2,035
Arizona												
Avondale city	3,786	477	255	246	521	134	446	2,940	1,124	407	634	391
Chandler city	16,414	4,625	3,140	3,454	3,577	2,716	1,142	11,544	7,722	1,540	1,059	1,028
Flagstaff city	3,685	1,123	838	825	793	619	459	2,605	1,756	338	210	221
Glendale city	15,428	4,170	2,380	2,295	3,046	2,192	1,917	11,555	7,920	2,820	1,954	1,426
Goodyear city	4,415	1,859	835	2,008	1,587	887	678	5,105	2,060	370	505	179
Mesa city	30,610	11,626	10,661	7,544	13,093	13,553	4,022	33,539	31,177	4,914	3,692	4,020
Peoria city	12,133	4,036	3,024	2,054	2,884	3,055	1,294	10,667	10,318	1,283	1,102	1,030
Phoenix city	82,650	24,046	14,038	16,336	17,115	15,603	13,232	69,019	51,268	18,316	10,875	9,447
Scottsdale city	20,846	9,089	6,783	7,453	10,267	8,797	1,117	23,837	19,085	1,596	1,911	2,431
Surprise city	6,861	5,690	2,508	1,921	4,572	3,445	997	14,366	8,444	780	1,376	721
Tempe city	11,270	3,339	1,914	2,922	2,383	1,488	927	7,549	5,337	661	590	1,255
Tucson city	28,427	9,387	8,573	5,655	8,612	9,287	5,326	32,436	28,548	9,773	5,562	5,087
Yuma city	3,960	1,856	1,762	1,148	2,381	2,119	742	5,995	4,949	1,222	1,019	858
Arkansas												
Fayetteville city	4,075	1,215	1,192	896	927	834	567	2,930	2,962	464	319	153
Fort Smith city	6,379	1,642	1,226	1,164	1,643	1,977	1,363	5,391	4,810	1,103	760	642
Jonesboro city	3,997	949	621	1,248	1,514	1,888	1,004	3,645	3,426	721	421	537
Little Rock city	16,242	5,761	3,357	2,632	3,586	3,616	2,376	11,319	9,811	2,609	1,295	1,841
Springdale city	3,466	893	610	777	1,077	1,082	714	2,986	2,664	339	223	436
California												
Alameda city	6,312	2,176	1,467	1,590	1,499	1,506	367	4,812	3,846	964	513	823
Alhambra city	4,936	1,905	1,119	1,809	616	920	573	5,769	5,766	1,236	1,622	2,302
Anaheim city	19,172	5,376	3,313	2,953	2,174	3,035	2,259	16,004	14,227	3,395	3,745	4,263
Antioch city	9,145	3,042	1,127	1,874	1,712	1,119	1,023	5,737	3,094	1,562	755	660
Bakersfield city	19,578	6,418	3,763	2,899	4,842	4,294	3,002	16,245	12,708	4,132	3,326	2,752
Baldwin Park city	2,948	715	301	385	260	257	444	3,705	2,584	1,295	1,339	1,194
Bellflower city	3,828	1,205	506	1,064	435	382	564	3,224	2,810	1,178	869	964
Berkeley city	7,774	4,200	2,383	2,540	2,332	1,956	959	7,724	5,308	1,312	1,043	938
Buena Park city	4,652	1,082	1,113	1,063	928	795	414	4,402	3,770	841	773	845
Burbank city	6,964	2,303	1,779	1,343	1,487	1,895	411	6,464	7,201	1,083	1,631	2,618
Camarillo city	5,247	2,529	2,167	1,308	1,262	1,972	426	4,719	6,051	524	419	728
Carlsbad city	10,351	2,875	2,730	2,160	2,587	2,732	318	7,635	7,894	367	759	1,326
Carson city	6,492	3,276	1,646	758	932	857	718	6,977	4,865	1,504	1,532	1,757
Chico city	5,273	1,728	2,041	1,133	1,674	1,775	698	3,955	4,623	1,143	754	1,130
Chino city	4,785	1,301	349	762	606	414	319	4,097	2,317	464	933	835
Chino Hills city	6,485	1,030	620	1,203	817	244	407	3,112	1,753	226	569	551
Chula Vista city	13,072	4,297	2,732	2,333	2,092	2,324	1,508	12,228	10,752	2,075	3,358	4,368
Citrus Heights city	6,476	3,059	2,072	1,286	1,982	1,672	1,237	5,840	5,078	1,279	645	948
Clovis city	6,850	2,653	1,878	1,223	1,748	1,725	696	5,758	4,272	894	822	714
Compton city	3,249	1,231	871	417	346	344	647	4,089	2,694	1,769	1,605	1,063
Concord city	9,613	4,050	3,067	1,773	2,309	2,262	835	6,679	6,527	1,231	928	1,097
Corona city	9,708	2,041	1,200	1,626	1,222	823	817	6,442	4,618	1,060	1,528	1,486
Costa Mesa city	6,696	1,941	978	1,555	1,255	1,218	719	4,831	4,307	831	697	684
Daly City city	10,334	3,403	1,864	1,673	1,561	1,551	943	7,074	5,509	917	1,524	2,100
Davis city	5,135	1,806	1,400	633	609	588	180	2,820	2,141	278	307	155
Downey city	6,124	1,693	1,322	1,871	666	826	780	5,684	5,081	1,012	1,528	1,479
El Cajon city	4,376	1,950	1,191	890	1,142	1,353	1,084	5,006	4,357	2,150	1,257	947
Elk Grove city	11,117	4,145	2,477	2,236	1,420	1,538	1,112	7,917	5,758	1,529	1,396	1,486
El Monte city	4,243	986	459	878	345	253	672	5,787	4,687	1,911	2,688	2,386
Escondido city	7,768	1,601	1,805	2,040	1,211	2,257	768	6,269	7,406	917	1,014	1,451
Fairfield city	6,961	3,171	1,637	1,411	1,292	1,066	819	5,423	4,944	914	765	1,089
Folsom city	5,304	1,692	1,236	898	1,223	998	262	3,280	2,910	396	166	462
Fontana city	8,841	1,800	1,294	1,311	563	514	1,369	6,477	4,493	1,498	1,930	1,536
Fremont city	16,435	4,427	3,034	3,172	2,769	2,768	978	11,152	10,431	1,843	2,357	2,632
Fresno city	23,659	8,860	5,592	4,885	5,283	6,569	4,573	23,260	20,175	8,887	6,393	6,304
Fullerton city	8,332	2,924	2,352	1,901	1,224	1,783	889	7,389	7,812	1,150	808	1,384
Garden Grove city	9,492	2,629	2,337	1,485	1,103	1,358	1,424	9,431	8,630	3,320	2,827	2,523
Glendale city	10,781	3,462	2,764	2,886	2,115	2,159	1,579	13,709	14,494	6,039	6,048	8,126
Hawthorne city	4,330	1,203	238	570	529	487	429	3,253	2,091	973	1,261	779
Hayward city	9,407	3,239	2,565	1,693	1,386	2,076	1,524	7,300	6,564	1,974	1,638	1,710
Hemet city	3,337	1,804	3,003	650	1,673	2,656	1,496	7,939	9,336	1,942	1,457	1,448
Hesperia city	4,328	1,218	682	986	930	821	1,027	4,629	3,856	1,607	648	892
Huntington Beach city	17,701	6,502	3,814	3,755	3,664	3,328	972	14,340	11,993	1,197	888	2,366
Indio city	3,901	1,907	1,105	1,014	2,180	1,398	677	6,372	3,874	784	1,182	1,199
Inglewood city	6,199	2,443	1,394	1,008	951	742	790	5,458	3,619	1,449	1,615	1,297
Irvine city	14,178	4,329	2,129	4,273	2,231	1,344	588	10,181	7,244	1,350	1,544	2,150
Jurupa Valley city[1]	4,877	1,535	447	757	558	324	721	4,129	2,517	1,031	793	813

[1] Jurupa Valley city was incorporated in 2011. The 2010 population is the U.S. Census Bureau's estimates base figure.

Table I-3: Places—Persons With Health Insurance by Source of Insurance—*Continued*

	Private Health Insurance Coverage						Public Health Insurance Coverage					
	Employer Based			Direct Purchase			Medicare			Medicaid/CHIP		
	55 to 64 Years	65 to 74 Years	75 Years and Over	55 to 64 Years	65 to 74 Years	75 Years and Over	55 to 64 Years	65 to 74 Years	75 Years and Over	55 to 64 Years	65 to 74 Years	75 Years and Over
California—Cont.												
Lake Forest city	6,305	1,654	911	1,321	894	620	373	4,256	3,013	377	590	496
Lakewood city	8,303	1,680	1,586	1,352	755	1,308	486	4,256	4,798	588	818	903
Lancaster city	9,451	3,220	1,919	1,044	1,055	1,039	1,184	6,932	5,462	2,492	1,543	1,661
Livermore city	7,741	2,829	1,953	996	1,021	1,246	731	4,428	3,463	616	436	533
Long Beach city	26,567	9,519	6,460	5,066	3,820	4,436	3,809	21,943	17,632	6,869	5,529	4,536
Los Angeles city	174,842	67,602	46,364	50,622	33,531	37,198	27,886	195,298	175,082	59,958	57,077	61,408
Lynwood city	1,882	545	351	203	164	263	318	2,014	1,815	680	746	811
Manteca city	4,943	1,827	1,188	667	1,321	1,334	687	3,914	2,769	1,003	533	439
Menifee city	4,712	2,434	2,069	798	1,528	2,039	885	7,358	6,592	1,205	692	1,035
Merced city	3,629	1,398	646	1,041	890	887	1,058	3,937	2,598	1,870	1,499	873
Milpitas city	4,538	1,414	503	935	356	322	374	3,471	2,834	1,100	907	1,126
Mission Viejo city	9,269	2,697	2,134	2,362	2,118	2,287	562	7,217	6,486	543	547	695
Modesto city	12,461	4,002	2,956	2,886	3,955	3,989	2,446	11,026	10,736	3,108	2,174	2,287
Moreno Valley city	9,445	2,212	1,047	1,126	758	645	1,236	6,840	5,311	2,355	1,906	2,321
Mountain View city	5,168	1,661	982	1,275	1,490	1,414	290	3,732	3,410	541	577	1,036
Murrieta city	6,485	1,689	1,546	1,004	1,423	1,288	410	5,075	5,035	325	324	739
Napa city	6,458	2,505	2,181	1,272	1,292	2,030	664	4,811	4,884	1,017	638	960
Newport Beach city	7,665	3,116	2,325	3,471	3,055	2,961	385	8,099	7,166	354	393	537
Norwalk city	5,445	1,178	993	820	649	538	711	5,145	4,367	1,133	1,560	1,337
Oakland city	24,732	9,674	6,032	5,760	5,343	5,352	4,452	23,126	19,253	8,375	4,868	6,151
Oceanside city	10,438	3,075	3,255	2,308	2,385	3,700	1,239	9,424	10,444	1,103	1,320	1,518
Ontario city	8,556	1,809	901	923	1,088	986	1,190	5,737	5,189	1,696	1,202	1,817
Orange city	9,464	3,157	1,876	1,545	1,828	1,337	636	7,951	6,151	841	1,207	913
Oxnard city	9,174	2,926	1,777	1,568	1,717	1,592	1,775	8,351	6,827	3,035	2,145	2,602
Palmdale city	7,065	2,252	1,419	827	836	848	1,274	5,540	4,584	1,800	1,135	1,476
Palo Alto city	5,665	2,750	2,102	1,661	1,699	2,466	239	5,243	5,210	282	521	809
Pasadena city	8,361	3,447	2,166	2,036	2,043	2,606	966	7,812	9,501	1,547	1,812	2,692
Perris city	1,867	368	280	232	130	160	512	1,952	973	1,042	644	323
Pleasanton city	6,700	2,518	1,523	1,491	1,626	1,172	235	4,124	3,234	146	421	467
Pomona city	6,101	1,946	759	1,190	691	707	1,178	5,828	4,415	2,036	1,726	1,587
Rancho Cordova city	4,330	1,470	1,194	596	862	678	686	3,595	2,997	1,059	622	834
Rancho Cucamonga city	12,662	2,475	1,531	2,211	1,347	1,292	708	7,027	5,718	1,113	998	888
Redding city	6,568	2,648	2,247	1,259	2,850	3,319	1,406	7,431	6,927	1,769	965	873
Redlands city	5,665	1,825	1,065	1,141	725	1,225	518	4,326	3,967	539	339	535
Redondo Beach city	5,233	1,635	1,025	872	1,066	1,144	376	3,798	3,281	260	436	522
Redwood City city	5,180	1,984	1,180	964	1,504	1,771	293	4,236	3,855	724	712	364
Rialto city	3,775	1,206	524	291	427	301	723	3,752	2,681	1,300	1,215	857
Richmond city	7,396	3,363	1,668	1,214	1,217	1,371	1,409	5,240	3,942	1,890	856	873
Riverside city	16,123	4,943	2,935	2,252	2,684	2,866	1,806	14,452	11,822	3,261	2,966	3,263
Roseville city	8,370	3,620	3,940	2,403	1,853	2,619	868	7,792	7,875	711	527	705
Sacramento city	30,736	12,388	9,605	4,347	5,320	6,796	4,822	25,320	23,192	9,097	5,914	6,176
Salinas city	6,587	1,788	1,369	1,014	1,432	1,402	1,089	6,015	4,432	1,380	1,472	1,508
San Bernardino city	7,737	2,559	1,729	1,059	1,391	1,365	2,274	8,718	6,620	4,262	2,782	2,155
San Buenaventura (Ventura) city	9,334	3,382	2,973	1,986	2,350	3,348	901	7,299	7,166	1,073	702	653
San Diego city	78,693	26,758	18,488	19,589	15,307	17,497	8,272	69,181	64,583	12,428	12,534	14,669
San Francisco city	56,712	17,667	16,319	15,905	11,439	15,001	7,459	51,820	53,690	17,785	14,872	17,206
San Jose city	61,277	21,507	12,319	12,501	12,565	11,121	5,561	52,183	42,728	12,935	13,128	14,616
San Leandro city	8,029	2,119	1,814	1,337	1,408	1,511	523	5,367	5,344	933	1,296	1,113
San Marcos city	4,291	1,132	1,032	1,262	891	1,419	586	4,083	4,894	683	359	572
San Mateo city	7,110	3,103	2,953	2,026	2,063	2,828	914	6,162	7,100	1,001	635	1,068
San Ramon city	5,090	1,787	853	979	912	951	88	2,976	2,008	185	319	389
Santa Ana city	11,510	2,106	1,370	1,441	1,463	1,352	1,640	10,750	8,415	3,416	3,079	2,828
Santa Barbara city	6,095	1,907	1,966	2,205	2,312	2,738	615	5,700	6,038	609	753	1,103
Santa Clara city	6,456	2,041	2,167	1,185	1,259	1,831	950	4,953	5,367	804	802	1,043
Santa Clarita city	15,214	4,569	2,496	2,877	1,922	2,288	1,212	9,599	6,955	790	1,425	1,258
Santa Maria city	3,288	1,483	1,411	707	1,137	1,097	624	4,573	4,231	1,170	794	1,011
Santa Monica city	6,796	2,440	1,642	2,729	1,643	1,415	573	6,448	5,872	947	1,174	1,629
Santa Rosa city	13,776	4,083	3,914	2,803	3,958	4,670	1,742	10,391	10,589	2,220	1,323	1,299
Simi Valley city	11,331	3,697	2,067	2,323	2,025	1,782	792	7,439	5,380	733	817	1,078
South Gate city	2,972	582	427	532	325	251	799	4,231	2,720	1,583	1,910	1,423
Stockton city	16,012	5,506	3,881	2,601	3,318	4,013	3,441	14,975	11,718	5,982	4,064	2,991
Sunnyvale city	9,618	3,728	2,756	1,954	2,627	2,982	648	7,258	7,293	1,170	851	1,072
Temecula city	6,006	1,544	849	1,578	959	1,172	669	3,891	3,243	602	471	665
Thousand Oaks city	12,388	4,667	3,040	2,873	3,160	3,559	607	9,506	8,386	444	908	984
Torrance city	10,937	4,608	4,022	2,574	2,403	2,686	849	10,936	10,800	1,234	1,512	1,620
Tracy city	5,067	1,136	667	571	946	614	388	3,559	2,067	751	896	604
Turlock city	4,159	907	533	934	1,182	1,568	619	3,942	3,615	879	1,192	1,075
Tustin city	3,981	1,163	503	923	630	694	192	3,496	2,417	699	530	589
Union City city	5,804	1,870	944	678	814	1,031	381	4,163	3,173	853	1,171	1,080
Upland city	5,693	2,010	1,075	1,372	1,212	1,107	377	5,057	3,885	607	567	658
Vacaville city	6,896	2,583	1,689	913	1,307	1,422	628	5,232	3,510	600	663	586
Vallejo city	10,679	4,212	2,802	1,631	1,323	1,359	1,464	6,726	5,970	2,079	1,327	2,050
Victorville city	4,190	1,351	894	447	662	524	1,160	4,294	3,380	1,422	988	1,133
Visalia city	7,649	2,498	1,807	1,058	1,684	2,206	779	6,759	5,964	1,260	1,274	1,288
Vista city	4,434	1,276	1,038	975	685	1,580	562	3,814	4,294	780	333	528
West Covina city	7,042	1,862	1,552	1,227	722	1,190	669	6,055	6,270	802	1,124	2,084
Westminster city	4,816	1,627	1,509	1,164	915	1,332	783	6,810	6,109	2,403	2,281	2,204
Whittier city	5,266	1,644	1,477	762	1,016	1,130	782	4,046	5,244	652	502	1,083
Yorba Linda city	6,844	1,935	1,015	1,932	1,037	941	296	4,779	3,187	175	269	482
Yuba City city	3,549	1,248	955	712	1,314	1,133	512	4,204	3,301	1,136	988	680

Table I-3: Places—Persons With Health Insurance by Source of Insurance—*Continued*

	Private Health Insurance Coverage						Public Health Insurance Coverage					
	Employer Based			Direct Purchase			Medicare			Medicaid/CHIP		
	55 to 64 Years	65 to 74 Years	75 Years and Over	55 to 64 Years	65 to 74 Years	75 Years and Over	55 to 64 Years	65 to 74 Years	75 Years and Over	55 to 64 Years	65 to 74 Years	75 Years and Over
Colorado												
Arvada city	10,659	3,806	2,738	2,163	3,060	2,769	554	8,224	6,698	720	726	958
Aurora city	21,897	7,314	3,750	4,386	5,021	4,215	2,666	16,661	11,807	3,182	2,391	2,291
Boulder city	5,897	2,519	1,772	2,303	1,312	1,588	369	4,476	3,775	539	365	406
Centennial city	11,335	3,270	2,286	2,291	2,086	2,001	433	6,607	5,226	446	566	478
Colorado Springs city	27,824	8,120	6,477	6,710	7,986	7,560	3,595	24,890	19,412	3,416	2,927	2,241
Denver city	35,614	11,853	9,314	9,596	8,719	10,453	5,186	31,383	28,263	8,805	6,194	6,247
Fort Collins city	10,059	2,661	2,175	2,208	2,617	2,350	879	6,504	5,258	895	602	600
Greeley city	6,100	2,238	1,344	1,463	1,353	1,712	725	5,063	4,412	888	927	755
Lakewood city	12,061	5,124	3,275	2,807	3,895	3,917	1,073	10,152	8,972	1,430	834	1,054
Longmont city	5,756	2,067	1,494	1,570	2,028	1,616	535	4,996	4,099	943	519	429
Loveland city	4,844	1,673	1,632	1,275	1,502	2,548	467	4,627	4,707	439	351	684
Pueblo city	6,911	2,872	3,922	1,927	2,487	2,770	2,559	7,637	7,802	2,779	1,260	1,252
Thornton city	7,269	1,963	1,217	1,028	1,386	718	400	4,722	3,175	683	458	427
Westminster city	9,103	2,424	1,547	1,694	1,855	2,012	925	5,516	4,510	588	503	662
Connecticut												
Bridgeport city	6,794	2,403	1,756	1,541	1,898	2,368	1,694	6,889	6,116	2,924	1,638	1,421
Danbury city	6,094	2,049	1,582	988	1,124	1,466	555	4,639	3,985	552	1,102	762
Hartford city	5,340	2,129	1,265	861	1,029	849	2,055	6,041	4,603	2,936	2,575	1,637
New Britain city	4,386	1,656	1,523	361	958	1,372	986	3,582	4,208	1,466	927	1,069
New Haven city	6,393	2,131	1,570	874	1,087	1,894	1,603	5,844	5,746	2,359	1,430	1,567
Norwalk city	7,530	2,922	2,211	2,101	1,918	2,250	1,054	6,343	5,733	1,134	822	801
Stamford city	7,886	3,153	3,386	1,466	1,927	2,795	779	6,491	7,313	938	718	883
Waterbury city	6,812	1,911	1,876	944	1,437	2,212	1,679	6,037	5,676	1,964	1,334	1,729
Delaware												
Wilmington city	3,846	1,796	1,160	982	810	799	1,400	4,374	3,472	1,982	1,104	812
District of Columbia												
Washington city	40,810	22,291	16,711	9,436	8,845	9,221	5,322	33,397	28,770	16,208	8,349	7,394
Florida												
Boca Raton city	6,967	3,037	2,781	3,718	2,800	3,774	530	8,585	8,314	294	419	522
Boynton Beach city	4,160	1,827	2,329	1,227	1,856	3,751	627	5,408	8,381	793	552	961
Cape Coral city	11,901	6,335	3,186	3,156	5,051	4,246	2,439	15,571	11,430	1,617	1,786	2,023
Clearwater city	8,489	3,272	3,372	1,699	3,013	3,831	1,154	9,860	11,185	1,110	1,030	1,493
Coral Springs city	9,111	1,553	594	2,074	1,571	758	557	6,688	3,916	765	827	752
Deerfield Beach city	4,278	1,960	2,441	1,243	1,980	3,942	1,086	6,460	8,459	969	1,137	1,292
Deltona city	6,187	2,313	1,993	534	1,227	1,666	1,477	5,982	5,370	1,221	963	982
Fort Lauderdale city	10,494	3,998	2,449	4,008	4,036	4,660	2,278	13,749	11,376	2,874	1,714	2,073
Gainesville city	5,681	2,344	2,032	1,552	1,347	1,982	1,261	4,695	4,902	1,917	582	805
Hialeah city	6,396	1,227	583	1,058	924	1,185	2,203	20,081	20,504	4,008	11,119	12,335
Hollywood city	9,089	2,109	1,883	2,529	2,460	3,162	1,229	9,940	10,265	1,442	1,918	1,979
Jacksonville city	56,684	18,109	10,133	10,509	13,863	13,273	10,087	49,205	38,266	10,675	7,160	5,916
Lakeland city	5,570	3,295	3,271	1,305	2,883	4,061	1,378	9,566	9,096	1,385	1,509	1,148
Largo city	4,824	3,190	2,802	1,277	2,735	3,706	1,172	8,416	9,324	1,114	884	994
Lauderhill city	4,545	865	523	789	601	951	628	4,163	3,300	908	1,188	396
Melbourne city	5,022	2,766	2,207	912	1,621	2,811	1,147	7,051	7,958	1,445	754	1,068
Miami city	12,438	3,042	1,845	3,973	2,849	3,177	4,584	28,596	30,554	7,956	13,683	15,795
Miami Beach city	4,204	1,531	661	1,867	1,243	1,764	882	5,817	6,579	1,354	1,547	2,119
Miami Gardens city	6,335	1,050	608	941	707	700	1,521	6,961	4,749	1,575	1,812	2,123
Miramar city	6,367	1,115	720	1,188	383	494	618	4,156	3,959	844	797	1,537
Orlando city	10,901	3,394	2,342	2,225	2,474	2,856	1,768	10,799	9,601	2,392	2,816	1,559
Palm Bay city	7,299	2,871	1,851	1,239	2,232	2,130	2,295	8,151	7,836	1,320	523	1,299
Palm Coast city	6,967	5,019	3,019	1,385	2,728	2,656	921	10,070	7,372	1,028	1,774	1,184
Pembroke Pines city	10,386	2,942	2,431	1,802	1,925	3,869	1,485	10,527	11,766	1,185	2,707	2,374
Plantation city	7,698	1,778	1,262	1,840	1,524	1,755	506	6,285	5,497	648	640	860
Pompano Beach city	5,122	2,039	2,347	2,236	2,116	4,188	1,160	7,595	10,200	1,321	873	1,456
Port St. Lucie city	10,713	5,454	3,398	2,635	4,611	4,623	2,217	14,345	11,833	1,345	1,500	1,326
St. Petersburg city	18,641	5,753	4,303	4,402	5,499	6,150	3,593	19,946	16,625	3,990	3,297	2,801
Sunrise city	5,010	1,598	1,126	974	1,084	2,393	648	5,640	6,232	710	1,253	1,160
Tallahassee city	10,606	3,758	3,278	1,705	2,397	1,927	954	7,455	6,633	1,030	1,124	1,002
Tampa city	18,373	5,157	3,739	4,006	3,970	5,660	4,232	18,533	16,637	5,437	3,562	4,069
Weston city	4,266	947	408	839	699	624	45	2,715	1,909	174	385	478
West Palm Beach city	6,713	2,714	1,574	1,731	2,708	3,097	1,191	7,962	7,504	1,317	882	1,339
Georgia												
Albany city	3,828	1,883	1,714	767	1,355	1,510	1,289	4,536	4,098	1,550	977	840
Athens-Clarke County unified govt (bal)	5,871	2,784	1,967	1,378	1,513	1,330	1,189	5,497	4,166	1,187	856	694
Atlanta city	20,794	9,262	5,367	6,406	5,387	5,480	5,405	21,888	17,168	6,810	5,874	4,935
Augusta-Richmond County consolidated govt (bal)	11,306	4,609	2,595	2,556	2,972	2,387	3,274	12,335	9,203	3,382	2,111	1,591
Columbus city	11,148	3,696	2,918	2,228	3,023	3,812	2,751	11,097	9,985	2,758	2,414	1,989
Johns Creek city	6,517	1,339	857	1,277	1,323	935	120	3,003	2,058	86	250	393
Macon city	4,295	1,918	1,658	1,201	1,441	1,671	1,838	5,156	4,889	2,149	1,122	1,055
Roswell city	8,339	3,537	1,089	1,921	1,638	1,510	245	6,484	3,788	105	404	465
Sandy Springs city	6,341	2,493	1,726	1,890	1,762	2,061	408	5,535	4,547	401	639	272
Savannah city	7,952	2,944	1,985	1,417	1,642	2,353	1,792	8,074	7,611	1,907	1,297	1,594
Warner Robins city	3,977	1,457	1,403	746	730	844	845	3,490	2,938	556	537	287
Hawaii												
Urban Honolulu CDP	31,785	14,980	15,682	8,273	6,652	10,452	2,403	25,031	31,038	4,388	4,000	5,652

Table I-3: Places—Persons With Health Insurance by Source of Insurance—*Continued*

	Private Health Insurance Coverage						Public Health Insurance Coverage					
	Employer Based			Direct Purchase			Medicare			Medicaid/CHIP		
	55 to 64 Years	65 to 74 Years	75 Years and Over	55 to 64 Years	65 to 74 Years	75 Years and Over	55 to 64 Years	65 to 74 Years	75 Years and Over	55 to 64 Years	65 to 74 Years	75 Years and Over
Idaho												
Boise City city	15,820	4,428	3,458	3,886	5,369	4,671	2,292	13,305	10,759	1,658	1,546	1,341
Meridian city	5,230	1,501	1,121	952	1,224	1,272	391	3,744	3,179	132	172	606
Nampa city	2,889	1,040	778	874	2,153	1,788	804	4,983	3,666	765	514	636
Illinois												
Aurora city	10,893	3,273	1,760	1,104	2,302	2,016	1,026	7,082	4,549	933	1,265	884
Bloomington city	5,984	2,063	1,858	1,068	1,154	1,981	506	3,466	3,881	436	339	480
Champaign city	5,211	2,153	1,779	825	1,095	1,249	304	3,345	2,640	321	449	224
Chicago city	144,006	49,916	31,520	21,673	30,646	36,387	25,528	139,098	119,281	36,424	28,572	26,814
Decatur city	6,416	2,408	2,784	1,232	2,161	2,423	1,188	5,716	5,870	871	634	792
Elgin city	7,697	2,261	1,243	837	1,984	1,890	608	4,828	3,701	550	540	422
Evanston city	5,838	1,958	1,271	1,605	1,380	1,531	311	4,173	3,647	476	414	303
Joliet city	8,295	3,241	1,903	660	1,811	2,216	826	5,784	5,388	863	669	1,091
Naperville city	13,973	3,683	2,219	2,509	2,361	2,429	405	6,514	5,028	328	330	639
Peoria city	8,621	3,316	3,208	1,085	2,804	3,199	1,025	7,161	7,002	1,214	720	578
Rockford city	10,295	3,303	3,082	1,773	4,251	4,739	1,831	9,969	9,380	1,924	1,943	1,274
Springfield city	12,163	4,654	4,448	1,808	2,453	3,053	1,608	7,963	8,066	1,277	1,226	806
Waukegan city	5,420	975	1,072	737	914	1,038	795	3,150	2,716	684	642	478
Indiana												
Bloomington city	3,226	1,191	1,128	519	1,264	1,739	652	2,915	3,267	474	240	305
Carmel city	7,879	1,755	1,421	1,441	2,752	1,376	206	5,015	3,016	117	186	67
Evansville city	8,583	2,613	2,237	1,463	3,034	4,110	1,828	7,700	8,122	1,330	989	923
Fort Wayne city	19,457	4,786	4,956	3,104	4,748	6,361	2,719	15,066	14,309	2,792	1,514	1,531
Gary city	5,860	2,525	2,072	945	1,474	1,422	1,698	6,088	5,193	2,126	1,121	1,347
Hammond city	5,134	1,873	1,787	699	1,460	1,213	1,209	4,154	4,114	1,225	488	625
Indianapolis city (bal)	57,039	17,818	14,356	9,234	16,087	16,454	9,788	44,059	36,991	10,779	6,756	5,616
Lafayette city	4,646	1,612	1,426	526	1,603	2,112	547	3,751	3,490	512	393	211
Muncie city	3,939	2,152	1,912	563	1,578	1,841	1,269	4,419	4,098	952	833	658
South Bend city	7,042	2,290	2,256	1,005	2,312	2,696	1,253	5,853	6,433	1,162	697	936
Iowa												
Cedar Rapids city	11,046	2,717	2,560	2,036	3,165	4,569	954	7,497	8,059	1,343	912	1,050
Davenport city	8,352	2,626	2,159	1,340	2,764	2,772	1,431	6,109	5,469	1,607	850	988
Des Moines city	13,446	4,484	3,505	2,359	4,367	4,997	2,288	11,162	9,579	4,014	1,955	1,794
Iowa City city	4,576	1,629	1,087	796	990	1,230	424	2,788	2,683	455	277	251
Sioux City city	5,752	1,659	994	1,235	2,459	2,573	899	5,314	4,628	1,344	735	956
Waterloo city	5,989	2,277	2,213	922	1,797	2,158	708	4,462	4,647	1,121	751	741
Kansas												
Kansas City city	9,358	2,660	2,016	1,710	2,974	3,116	1,877	8,207	6,490	1,424	1,342	1,163
Lawrence city	5,135	1,901	1,611	1,098	1,386	1,645	305	3,144	3,251	297	371	302
Olathe city	10,200	2,146	1,075	1,493	2,177	1,778	700	5,078	3,556	270	512	413
Overland Park city	17,143	4,831	4,167	3,371	4,564	4,889	532	11,021	10,154	567	446	1,309
Topeka city	10,055	3,696	3,238	1,247	3,913	4,446	1,760	8,365	8,318	1,734	998	1,103
Wichita city	29,401	6,377	4,563	4,614	9,033	10,699	4,144	22,305	19,861	3,792	3,221	2,760
Kentucky												
Lexington-Fayette urban county	22,252	8,156	5,214	4,824	5,404	5,490	2,745	16,699	13,205	2,433	2,006	1,597
Louisville/Jefferson County metro govt (bal)	50,045	16,969	13,565	9,199	14,736	15,686	9,151	38,317	33,961	7,382	5,859	5,506
Louisiana												
Baton Rouge city	12,877	5,604	4,570	3,232	2,955	3,336	2,785	12,985	10,923	3,829	2,405	2,266
Kenner city	5,890	1,542	835	970	1,128	1,059	737	5,075	3,311	591	985	606
Lafayette city	8,025	3,310	2,452	2,046	3,397	3,071	1,040	7,585	6,301	1,024	974	822
Lake Charles city	5,264	1,790	2,187	1,324	1,703	2,082	1,346	5,036	4,341	1,038	1,034	814
New Orleans city	22,065	6,862	3,801	6,899	4,676	4,758	6,034	21,215	16,264	7,626	5,715	4,432
Shreveport city	13,501	4,638	4,495	2,299	3,735	4,131	2,835	12,370	11,352	2,917	2,312	2,218
Maine												
Portland city	4,925	1,270	1,815	956	905	1,599	894	3,215	4,032	1,691	645	1,036
Maryland												
Baltimore city	38,637	15,155	11,108	7,693	9,722	10,227	9,698	36,146	31,438	15,089	8,262	8,702
Frederick city	5,170	1,997	1,516	923	1,269	913	648	3,711	2,821	704	578	305
Massachusetts												
Boston city	33,693	12,362	8,369	6,883	6,515	7,309	5,019	30,329	27,520	17,054	10,990	10,463
Brockton city	6,788	2,002	1,261	517	1,598	1,499	1,106	5,769	4,833	2,552	1,904	1,884
Cambridge city	6,658	2,667	2,015	1,759	2,088	1,900	765	5,708	4,786	1,483	1,180	991
Fall River city	5,746	2,060	1,353	886	1,707	1,841	1,740	6,441	5,911	3,130	1,789	1,994
Lawrence city	2,918	947	829	375	530	554	1,207	3,099	2,502	3,601	1,571	1,091
Lowell city	6,714	2,149	1,443	1,003	1,349	1,920	1,523	5,230	4,760	3,427	1,538	1,423
Lynn city	4,645	1,979	1,577	644	1,231	1,497	939	5,380	4,648	2,909	2,051	1,882
New Bedford city	5,940	2,607	2,103	1,140	1,804	2,641	1,462	6,122	6,510	3,257	1,683	1,687
Newton city	9,317	3,654	2,593	1,623	1,935	2,997	173	5,980	6,429	573	927	957
Quincy city	7,349	2,713	2,729	1,238	2,187	2,099	974	6,378	6,122	2,498	1,401	1,322
Somerville city	3,250	1,619	1,090	629	674	1,076	504	2,861	3,155	1,402	839	816
Springfield city	8,663	3,208	2,566	1,100	2,564	2,722	2,300	8,755	7,151	6,104	3,368	2,077
Worcester city	11,713	3,948	3,557	1,649	2,402	3,927	1,867	10,134	9,866	5,092	2,936	2,769

Table I-3: Places—Persons With Health Insurance by Source of Insurance—*Continued*

| | Private Health Insurance Coverage | | | | | | Public Health Insurance Coverage | | | | | |
| | Employer Based | | | Direct Purchase | | | Medicare | | | Medicaid/CHIP | | |
	55 to 64 Years	65 to 74 Years	75 Years and Over	55 to 64 Years	65 to 74 Years	75 Years and Over	55 to 64 Years	65 to 74 Years	75 Years and Over	55 to 64 Years	65 to 74 Years	75 Years and Over
Michigan												
Ann Arbor city	8,981	3,830	3,346	1,236	1,725	1,798	684	5,591	5,253	743	677	839
Dearborn city	7,333	2,394	3,197	905	1,558	2,114	1,042	4,942	5,478	1,806	946	815
Detroit city	41,135	21,185	17,942	5,625	7,541	8,032	14,907	41,814	36,967	21,606	12,480	10,173
Farmington Hills city	9,200	2,983	2,888	1,484	2,879	2,988	570	6,153	6,399	562	601	634
Flint city	6,372	3,693	3,397	930	1,248	1,390	2,528	6,184	5,219	3,351	1,570	923
Grand Rapids city	10,536	3,840	4,189	2,006	2,722	4,926	2,426	8,454	10,521	2,743	1,249	2,055
Kalamazoo city	3,799	1,395	1,844	853	992	1,275	1,002	3,118	3,459	1,558	435	692
Lansing city	8,779	3,720	2,902	1,259	1,417	1,662	1,604	6,320	4,950	2,254	1,121	982
Livonia city	10,934	4,563	4,612	1,647	2,856	4,255	685	7,516	8,606	874	813	806
Rochester Hills city	8,316	2,387	1,499	1,324	1,935	2,104	605	4,792	4,459	446	454	458
Southfield city	8,015	4,005	3,217	1,432	1,805	2,278	1,398	5,844	5,910	1,170	888	1,255
Sterling Heights city	12,211	5,626	4,504	1,550	3,879	3,183	1,425	10,364	8,943	1,788	1,331	1,579
Troy city	8,647	3,196	2,175	1,802	2,639	2,262	608	6,274	4,796	483	623	683
Warren city	9,813	4,634	5,398	1,966	3,161	4,691	1,800	9,140	10,676	2,076	1,072	969
Westland city	7,007	3,091	3,270	1,256	2,401	2,515	1,694	6,116	5,486	1,054	1,053	651
Wyoming city	5,051	1,205	874	819	1,239	1,087	696	3,252	2,953	555	330	531
Minnesota												
Bloomington city	8,651	3,209	2,335	1,519	3,962	4,452	756	7,988	6,973	749	646	795
Brooklyn Park city	5,867	1,374	637	676	1,427	1,156	572	3,639	2,243	967	598	366
Duluth city	6,731	2,386	2,237	1,157	2,099	3,132	885	5,305	5,720	1,117	724	673
Minneapolis city	23,493	5,618	4,205	3,997	6,649	6,245	3,463	16,181	13,094	6,876	3,284	2,584
Plymouth city	7,411	1,772	1,296	1,665	2,443	2,169	256	4,904	3,721	216	419	594
Rochester city	9,030	3,904	3,067	1,206	2,331	2,915	626	6,539	6,338	741	368	847
St. Cloud city	4,115	931	1,000	855	1,577	1,945	695	3,136	3,251	761	325	592
St. Paul city	18,636	5,048	4,326	2,997	4,999	4,547	2,977	12,671	10,940	4,926	2,126	2,001
Mississippi												
Gulfport city	3,944	1,449	1,020	1,163	1,300	1,143	888	4,184	3,639	962	659	652
Jackson city	9,251	2,975	1,691	2,292	2,583	2,781	2,552	8,990	7,488	3,229	2,403	2,110
Missouri												
Columbia city	6,616	3,044	2,076	1,007	1,271	1,741	708	4,591	4,248	557	379	414
Independence city	9,358	3,687	2,848	1,484	3,719	3,948	1,762	9,445	8,577	1,156	1,285	1,038
Kansas City city	32,890	10,283	7,956	5,784	10,040	10,221	4,895	25,661	22,431	4,520	2,955	3,098
Lee's Summit city	7,531	2,752	1,836	1,533	2,046	2,561	370	5,306	5,042	267	342	396
O'Fallon city	5,415	2,110	1,287	933	1,220	1,392	478	3,954	3,248	296	325	231
St. Charles city	5,715	1,579	1,614	780	1,416	1,958	415	4,154	4,077	145	271	274
St. Joseph city	5,460	1,680	1,455	966	2,108	2,331	1,192	4,898	4,838	1,066	691	403
St. Louis city	18,148	6,923	4,708	3,540	3,856	5,080	5,186	16,801	16,074	5,702	3,811	3,411
Springfield city	9,483	2,523	2,980	1,480	3,906	5,470	2,700	10,607	11,121	1,913	1,639	1,464
Montana												
Billings city	8,816	2,866	2,305	1,777	3,271	4,090	1,267	7,427	7,231	1,160	487	977
Missoula city	4,233	1,227	914	1,018	1,375	2,158	672	3,560	3,495	567	335	429
Nebraska												
Lincoln city	20,621	5,794	4,129	3,588	6,057	6,946	2,036	13,671	13,100	1,909	1,280	1,580
Omaha city	31,927	8,799	6,752	6,451	8,981	9,509	3,971	22,883	21,485	3,741	2,492	3,076
Nevada												
Henderson city	23,182	9,935	4,570	5,565	5,984	4,102	1,988	23,631	14,269	993	1,397	2,150
Las Vegas city	39,506	15,481	9,844	7,082	8,766	8,412	5,180	40,031	30,262	4,606	4,745	3,928
North Las Vegas city	12,239	3,692	1,728	1,602	1,186	1,111	1,297	9,206	5,116	1,276	934	612
Reno city	14,163	6,114	3,498	3,480	3,783	3,922	2,198	14,191	11,404	2,092	2,247	2,160
Sparks city	7,673	2,489	1,607	1,110	1,773	1,078	695	6,633	3,796	492	322	562
New Hampshire												
Manchester city	9,397	2,863	1,697	971	2,122	2,542	1,148	6,785	5,298	1,093	748	878
Nashua city	7,810	2,658	1,923	842	1,860	1,934	857	5,532	4,751	567	606	580
New Jersey												
Camden city	2,785	898	484	607	641	508	1,019	3,712	1,963	2,248	1,573	605
Clifton city	6,615	2,379	1,407	643	907	1,675	540	4,666	4,955	686	757	1,326
Elizabeth city	5,400	1,541	718	594	1,060	763	705	5,768	4,350	2,021	1,470	1,673
Jersey City city	12,489	3,971	1,806	2,511	1,805	1,655	2,251	11,934	8,190	3,463	2,955	2,586
Newark city	10,247	3,382	1,956	1,906	1,975	1,693	3,175	11,747	9,228	5,067	4,156	3,200
Passaic city	2,052	599	386	346	330	385	715	2,716	2,189	1,205	1,173	1,005
Paterson city	5,599	1,718	497	313	880	743	1,815	7,403	4,885	2,507	2,432	1,963
Trenton city	4,099	1,520	932	480	541	758	1,426	3,643	3,095	2,004	1,038	812
Union City city	2,829	822	576	701	657	604	715	2,771	2,773	1,137	806	1,212
New Mexico												
Albuquerque city	38,301	15,414	11,681	8,342	7,189	8,120	5,891	35,252	29,750	8,057	4,847	4,616
Las Cruces city	6,361	2,592	2,390	1,463	2,126	2,283	667	6,646	5,630	1,328	725	761
Rio Rancho city	6,177	2,245	1,136	1,321	1,424	1,139	698	5,904	3,750	475	463	246
Santa Fe city	5,816	2,920	2,099	2,738	2,492	2,038	1,029	7,068	5,290	781	784	430

Table I-3: Places—Persons With Health Insurance by Source of Insurance—*Continued*

| | Private Health Insurance Coverage | | | | | | Public Health Insurance Coverage | | | | | |
| | Employer Based | | | Direct Purchase | | | Medicare | | | Medicaid/CHIP | | |
	55 to 64 Years	65 to 74 Years	75 Years and Over	55 to 64 Years	65 to 74 Years	75 Years and Over	55 to 64 Years	65 to 74 Years	75 Years and Over	55 to 64 Years	65 to 74 Years	75 Years and Over
New York												
Albany city	7,799	3,401	2,417	799	1,169	1,765	961	5,639	5,029	1,558	925	826
Buffalo city	16,015	6,307	4,833	2,920	4,018	4,458	4,985	14,590	13,682	8,657	3,357	3,183
Mount Vernon city	5,143	2,043	1,276	685	1,003	981	790	4,343	3,697	977	924	603
New Rochelle city	6,841	1,974	1,697	1,248	958	1,780	605	4,466	4,978	916	761	897
New York city	505,437	191,483	113,865	94,206	79,545	88,246	75,296	491,350	431,918	212,577	148,888	148,009
Rochester city	11,738	3,959	3,170	2,199	2,890	2,308	3,128	9,813	7,389	5,489	2,902	1,954
Schenectady city	4,030	1,849	1,791	713	739	1,455	1,091	3,698	3,590	1,243	739	578
Syracuse city	8,284	2,850	2,637	1,215	1,545	2,294	2,338	6,531	6,400	3,600	1,367	1,464
Yonkers city	16,380	6,908	4,916	1,913	2,801	4,179	2,125	13,594	13,361	3,711	2,313	2,934
North Carolina												
Asheville city	5,074	2,121	1,981	2,043	2,615	2,451	1,215	6,208	5,967	1,335	733	1,161
Charlotte city	43,803	13,527	10,529	10,748	11,825	11,554	6,203	34,862	27,180	5,589	4,700	4,220
Concord city	5,388	2,048	1,073	1,029	1,845	1,764	700	4,975	3,394	488	294	590
Durham city	15,488	5,928	4,231	3,134	2,868	3,567	2,130	11,044	8,845	1,862	1,651	1,843
Fayetteville city	9,235	4,335	2,081	2,414	2,736	2,534	2,220	10,669	8,256	2,105	1,927	1,578
Gastonia city	4,784	1,624	1,090	1,069	1,637	1,506	1,276	4,221	3,404	1,195	537	682
Greensboro city	18,969	5,364	5,081	3,800	4,292	6,038	3,100	15,433	14,873	2,047	1,846	2,005
Greenville city	4,271	1,635	1,628	990	901	1,022	596	3,196	2,699	735	358	404
High Point city	6,426	1,969	1,659	1,264	2,228	2,534	997	6,361	5,354	1,179	767	772
Jacksonville city	1,582	902	422	540	502	651	196	2,317	1,712	286	448	308
Raleigh city	24,888	9,445	7,281	4,741	6,026	6,240	2,938	18,243	14,599	2,574	2,078	1,884
Wilmington city	6,980	3,441	2,515	2,218	2,728	3,191	1,712	7,691	6,468	1,590	883	1,029
Winston-Salem city	15,069	6,454	5,595	3,488	4,759	5,315	2,854	14,127	12,991	2,217	2,055	2,163
North Dakota												
Fargo city	8,075	1,933	1,533	1,473	2,002	3,542	630	4,787	5,201	436	369	555
Ohio												
Akron city	14,513	5,184	6,225	2,534	2,508	3,439	3,233	12,362	11,586	3,113	2,189	1,832
Canton city	5,567	2,097	1,793	670	1,096	2,143	989	4,304	4,589	986	809	759
Cincinnati city	18,186	6,831	5,152	2,657	4,247	5,246	4,263	15,435	14,074	4,238	2,045	2,289
Cleveland city	23,573	8,627	7,846	3,121	4,657	6,077	6,502	23,469	21,671	9,491	6,026	5,647
Columbus city	49,738	17,773	12,320	7,491	9,189	10,732	7,938	35,909	28,812	7,249	5,862	4,001
Dayton city	8,943	3,405	2,998	1,419	2,029	2,068	1,988	8,398	7,281	2,665	1,498	1,406
Parma city	7,263	2,884	3,240	1,077	2,119	2,427	668	6,477	7,059	502	684	456
Toledo city	19,491	8,152	7,263	3,146	4,975	5,860	4,403	16,520	16,127	3,885	3,036	2,734
Youngstown city	4,225	1,526	1,630	780	1,070	1,821	1,365	4,295	5,341	1,656	733	881
Oklahoma												
Broken Arrow city	9,123	2,563	1,123	1,521	2,424	1,940	827	6,003	4,091	503	516	507
Edmond city	7,965	2,493	1,232	958	2,106	1,826	704	5,125	3,811	272	315	349
Lawton city	3,914	1,921	1,207	991	1,267	1,211	1,147	4,859	4,033	607	629	537
Norman city	8,740	3,842	2,691	1,505	2,048	1,751	969	6,681	4,900	408	517	374
Oklahoma City city	42,315	13,693	10,453	7,471	10,442	11,664	6,796	34,163	28,138	4,744	4,373	4,257
Tulsa city	28,117	9,850	7,472	5,650	8,748	10,616	4,037	24,139	22,239	3,032	2,826	2,574
Oregon												
Beaverton city	7,023	1,397	1,494	1,337	1,759	1,833	464	5,266	4,192	573	774	664
Bend city	5,677	2,650	1,601	2,050	2,355	2,477	402	5,993	5,022	344	417	619
Eugene city	11,984	3,908	2,911	2,842	4,473	5,491	1,575	10,469	9,644	1,366	1,186	1,457
Gresham city	7,976	2,562	1,501	1,328	2,197	2,521	1,009	6,333	5,008	1,324	1,016	1,073
Hillsboro city	5,835	1,412	1,153	650	1,700	1,079	501	4,256	2,543	586	425	493
Medford city	4,761	1,522	2,659	777	1,978	2,933	1,020	5,609	6,226	970	599	808
Portland city	43,374	12,955	8,797	9,501	11,171	12,453	6,512	32,482	27,374	7,309	4,528	5,222
Salem city	11,102	4,218	3,154	2,360	4,005	4,240	1,813	10,460	8,425	1,987	1,473	1,235
Pennsylvania												
Allentown city	6,656	1,829	2,051	1,301	1,893	3,434	1,491	5,876	6,938	2,095	1,374	1,315
Bethlehem city	5,595	1,612	1,855	857	1,692	3,510	1,010	4,391	5,509	1,070	705	666
Erie city	6,738	1,980	1,919	1,134	2,483	3,362	1,540	6,021	6,266	2,379	1,204	1,521
Philadelphia city	87,988	31,730	21,374	20,065	27,072	30,870	20,521	88,874	82,924	38,395	22,210	21,380
Pittsburgh city	21,957	8,509	6,868	4,556	7,275	10,721	3,500	18,996	20,254	5,171	3,998	4,507
Reading city	3,012	1,102	948	529	1,285	1,722	1,529	3,973	3,807	2,697	845	784
Scranton city	5,369	1,584	1,713	1,356	2,019	3,366	971	4,942	6,316	1,260	751	1,056
Rhode Island												
Cranston city	7,340	2,255	1,603	872	1,496	2,478	659	5,435	6,253	921	865	1,103
Pawtucket city	4,892	1,467	758	767	1,174	1,641	1,674	4,294	4,132	1,845	1,277	728
Providence city	7,967	2,466	1,505	1,693	1,168	2,145	1,832	7,015	6,471	2,934	2,564	1,833
Warwick city	8,713	3,347	1,939	1,500	2,195	3,145	1,349	6,611	7,055	1,296	892	1,431
South Carolina												
Charleston city	8,196	3,971	2,667	2,367	2,224	2,772	1,332	7,936	6,284	1,123	1,267	847
Columbia city	6,752	2,574	2,106	1,260	1,461	1,577	1,358	5,228	5,313	1,216	907	1,017
North Charleston city	5,004	1,628	831	565	1,425	768	1,109	4,864	3,047	1,482	834	767
Rock Hill city	4,752	1,027	888	499	1,124	1,463	794	3,224	2,982	721	666	515
South Dakota												
Rapid City city	5,278	1,591	1,542	1,699	2,027	2,418	965	4,844	4,588	598	555	445
Sioux Falls city	13,264	2,927	2,047	3,092	3,762	4,822	1,288	8,572	8,085	907	886	1,294

Table I-3: Places—Persons With Health Insurance by Source of Insurance—*Continued*

| | Private Health Insurance Coverage | | | | | | Public Health Insurance Coverage | | | | | |
| | Employer Based | | | Direct Purchase | | | Medicare | | | Medicaid/CHIP | | |
	55 to 64 Years	65 to 74 Years	75 Years and Over	55 to 64 Years	65 to 74 Years	75 Years and Over	55 to 64 Years	65 to 74 Years	75 Years and Over	55 to 64 Years	65 to 74 Years	75 Years and Over
Tennessee												
Chattanooga city	12,968	4,597	3,539	2,619	4,678	4,812	2,593	12,638	11,227	3,152	1,992	1,752
Clarksville city	5,091	1,477	1,100	1,067	1,365	1,305	965	5,658	3,786	814	675	457
Jackson city	4,321	1,403	1,346	836	1,542	1,784	827	4,605	3,797	1,069	579	590
Knoxville city	11,986	6,160	4,134	2,221	3,506	4,309	2,530	13,159	11,254	3,045	1,637	1,598
Memphis city	42,092	12,711	10,017	8,020	9,012	9,231	9,239	34,487	29,319	10,277	8,560	6,600
Murfreesboro city	6,365	1,658	1,539	1,519	1,690	1,441	863	5,511	3,714	806	727	492
Nashville-Davidson metropolitan government (bal)....	43,240	13,329	10,098	8,451	9,366	9,721	5,535	32,126	26,971	6,444	4,202	4,526
Texas												
Abilene city	6,711	2,687	2,141	1,544	2,059	2,343	1,124	7,208	6,607	981	1,121	1,007
Allen city	5,923	1,352	407	736	1,019	830	388	3,204	1,867	306	198	671
Amarillo city	12,717	4,544	3,493	2,518	3,666	4,130	2,080	11,483	10,184	1,778	1,607	1,414
Arlington city	24,185	8,055	4,362	3,638	4,357	2,976	1,982	16,670	11,384	2,243	2,160	1,498
Austin city	46,058	15,420	10,846	8,796	8,720	7,843	5,174	29,834	23,930	5,999	3,927	4,193
Baytown city	4,478	842	1,259	611	615	1,198	629	2,706	3,211	797	358	507
Beaumont city	7,419	2,988	2,618	1,817	2,432	2,176	2,080	7,326	6,638	1,516	1,490	1,124
Brownsville city	5,052	1,538	723	1,054	1,251	1,197	1,526	8,573	6,631	2,121	3,415	3,256
Bryan city	3,734	1,918	1,469	661	1,172	1,046	422	3,864	3,100	666	504	583
Carrollton city	9,518	2,467	994	2,110	1,480	1,212	387	6,061	3,405	297	396	511
College Station city	3,637	1,827	871	550	568	664	185	2,604	1,712	211	151	183
Corpus Christi city	20,824	6,551	4,356	3,373	4,489	5,774	3,305	18,474	15,868	4,452	3,263	3,038
Dallas city	56,446	18,581	12,269	14,121	14,139	16,335	10,091	55,310	45,991	12,673	11,100	9,799
Denton city	6,719	3,014	1,548	756	1,478	1,244	727	5,743	3,367	601	482	299
Edinburg city	2,538	826	490	522	665	590	865	3,212	2,255	969	1,036	928
El Paso city	27,799	9,787	7,137	5,722	6,920	6,476	7,295	37,380	32,896	7,914	9,444	12,130
Fort Worth city	39,123	11,244	7,576	7,292	7,746	7,481	6,177	31,839	25,715	6,712	4,325	4,232
Frisco city	6,032	2,582	620	1,689	1,993	893	525	4,470	2,195	156	422	261
Garland city	13,920	5,045	2,392	2,222	2,475	2,694	1,550	11,411	8,155	2,031	1,584	1,313
Grand Prairie city	9,583	2,753	1,494	1,270	1,700	1,525	902	7,319	4,252	984	967	803
Harlingen city	3,048	991	712	737	995	993	751	4,274	3,665	868	1,127	971
Houston city	112,348	37,385	23,735	20,639	23,107	24,416	16,052	100,355	79,248	24,804	19,644	17,515
Irving city	10,923	2,381	1,515	2,119	2,234	1,802	1,000	7,361	5,746	1,357	1,100	853
Killeen city	3,657	1,706	818	540	754	761	927	3,919	2,468	1,005	882	741
Laredo city	7,185	2,106	1,011	1,324	1,567	1,056	1,687	9,713	7,485	2,353	3,205	3,739
League City city	6,898	2,220	1,315	972	929	842	312	4,242	2,539	78	376	330
Lewisville city	5,449	1,801	1,012	759	842	1,092	724	3,892	2,573	409	571	279
Longview city	4,538	1,378	1,614	897	1,791	2,239	707	4,495	5,596	1,012	455	914
Lubbock city	13,272	5,710	4,136	3,175	4,563	4,555	2,243	13,070	11,100	1,910	2,421	1,695
McAllen city	5,019	1,258	865	1,173	1,391	1,244	1,273	7,159	5,184	1,326	2,528	2,316
McKinney city	7,328	3,039	1,564	1,135	2,038	1,506	548	5,082	3,886	545	366	624
Mesquite city	8,407	2,338	2,068	1,399	2,112	2,043	861	6,221	5,111	874	841	790
Midland city	7,783	2,404	2,023	1,733	1,892	2,593	961	5,699	6,308	1,127	651	1,025
Mission city	2,895	1,429	1,207	390	1,140	935	487	4,038	3,570	1,255	1,100	941
Missouri City city	6,975	1,972	654	922	1,078	434	469	3,887	2,294	267	609	303
Odessa city	6,105	1,709	1,206	1,421	1,749	2,055	1,116	5,125	4,802	936	918	882
Pasadena city	8,572	2,228	1,813	1,346	1,222	1,884	1,167	6,516	5,620	2,068	894	1,014
Pearland city	6,179	2,096	975	735	844	822	512	3,564	2,838	369	352	269
Pharr city	1,881	560	836	308	369	1,120	628	3,004	4,367	817	1,321	2,135
Plano city	23,088	6,126	3,138	4,315	4,045	2,523	885	14,595	8,899	467	1,407	1,292
Richardson city	8,204	3,293	2,056	1,978	1,837	2,138	599	6,431	5,222	378	460	544
Round Rock city	6,063	1,977	667	753	1,414	693	543	4,239	1,777	322	488	257
San Angelo city	6,387	3,024	2,349	1,118	2,284	2,511	1,104	6,373	5,957	801	614	792
San Antonio city	74,858	27,770	19,236	14,536	17,441	15,687	14,834	75,310	60,333	17,693	15,059	14,659
Sugar Land city	9,208	2,395	1,164	1,357	1,198	823	259	4,384	2,772	179	417	553
Temple city	4,821	2,405	1,814	716	1,570	1,704	906	4,693	4,461	951	778	1,099
Tyler city	6,379	2,633	2,243	1,088	2,278	3,307	980	6,319	6,962	648	848	1,257
Waco city	6,155	2,446	2,242	1,120	2,106	3,018	1,058	5,960	6,629	1,500	1,353	1,407
Wichita Falls city	5,946	2,766	2,108	1,581	1,804	2,388	1,269	5,889	5,709	975	761	808
Utah												
Layton city	4,699	1,590	1,112	835	853	379	337	2,893	2,087	345	326	247
Ogden city	4,179	1,510	1,515	640	1,022	1,447	1,023	3,443	3,692	872	463	734
Orem city	5,598	2,075	1,370	763	1,311	1,215	396	3,968	3,016	397	388	401
Provo city	3,710	1,339	1,407	761	962	1,417	319	2,830	3,347	425	432	476
St. George city	4,545	2,009	2,307	1,474	2,478	3,152	944	6,164	6,608	469	208	607
Salt Lake City city	10,897	3,771	2,788	2,133	2,374	3,245	1,333	8,815	7,930	2,153	1,432	1,152
Sandy city	7,806	2,402	1,058	1,423	1,573	1,074	360	5,351	2,832	386	687	328
West Jordan city	6,897	1,327	671	645	908	750	638	2,808	2,017	603	327	352
West Valley City city	7,479	2,710	1,490	713	1,544	1,220	985	5,491	3,455	969	860	638
Virginia												
Alexandria city	11,576	4,789	2,730	1,390	1,507	1,803	371	6,856	5,050	558	948	433
Chesapeake city	18,629	6,840	4,339	2,672	4,216	3,794	2,173	13,507	9,477	1,072	1,529	1,053
Hampton city	10,248	3,360	3,106	1,566	2,512	2,589	1,516	9,207	7,124	965	1,129	647
Lynchburg city	4,444	1,908	2,072	1,258	1,770	2,496	881	4,625	4,974	506	646	570
Newport News city	10,909	5,339	3,235	2,074	3,601	3,392	1,450	10,003	8,149	1,253	1,214	966
Norfolk city	13,376	4,240	3,114	2,342	2,827	4,294	2,171	11,118	10,491	2,049	1,870	1,597
Portsmouth city	6,670	3,006	2,303	1,047	1,643	2,275	1,609	6,275	5,841	795	950	984
Richmond city	12,451	4,190	3,743	3,338	3,322	4,217	3,675	11,047	10,302	3,732	2,482	1,844
Roanoke city	6,447	2,066	1,655	1,825	2,550	2,922	2,030	6,433	6,276	1,191	857	645
Suffolk city	6,716	2,865	1,469	1,417	1,442	1,502	883	5,461	3,941	706	503	726
Virginia Beach city	30,973	10,418	7,014	7,124	8,029	8,001	2,805	25,760	19,867	1,523	2,182	1,917

Table I-3: Places—Persons With Health Insurance by Source of Insurance—*Continued*

| | Private Health Insurance Coverage | | | | | | Public Health Insurance Coverage | | | | | |
| | Employer Based | | | Direct Purchase | | | Medicare | | | Medicaid/CHIP | | |
	55 to 64 Years	65 to 74 Years	75 Years and Over	55 to 64 Years	65 to 74 Years	75 Years and Over	55 to 64 Years	65 to 74 Years	75 Years and Over	55 to 64 Years	65 to 74 Years	75 Years and Over
Washington												
Auburn city	5,915	1,231	984	937	1,469	1,380	698	3,840	3,592	741	810	592
Bellevue city	10,540	3,914	3,376	2,778	2,645	3,798	618	7,406	8,649	765	741	1,020
Bellingham city	5,443	2,325	1,637	1,329	1,831	2,202	848	5,449	4,545	1,316	965	952
Everett city	7,731	2,003	1,148	1,124	1,528	1,815	1,208	5,295	4,831	1,754	1,217	1,405
Federal Way city	6,179	1,854	1,361	1,060	1,172	1,158	469	5,127	3,954	907	1,097	999
Kennewick city	5,907	1,962	1,727	1,002	1,557	1,505	893	4,309	3,821	665	415	411
Kent city	7,977	2,385	1,197	1,175	2,248	2,189	743	6,197	4,733	1,402	1,195	1,159
Renton city	5,629	2,137	1,268	1,134	1,443	1,657	516	4,721	4,113	1,008	806	906
Seattle city	47,480	14,916	9,301	12,109	11,511	11,860	5,405	34,126	29,045	6,749	5,762	6,510
Spokane city	14,314	4,830	3,709	2,973	4,230	6,858	2,756	13,455	13,696	3,333	2,152	2,147
Spokane Valley city	6,951	2,413	1,678	1,524	2,752	2,480	1,238	7,141	5,371	1,190	1,020	945
Tacoma city	12,965	3,876	2,840	2,427	3,771	3,940	2,129	10,955	10,322	2,583	2,016	1,916
Vancouver city	12,388	3,913	2,928	2,251	3,778	4,529	1,604	11,227	9,226	1,835	1,734	1,459
Yakima city	5,279	1,837	1,983	1,106	2,093	2,646	1,193	5,923	5,825	1,262	1,132	1,148
Wisconsin												
Appleton city	6,636	1,509	1,408	936	1,368	1,567	647	3,889	3,676	630	429	393
Eau Claire city	5,007	1,430	1,559	686	1,557	2,001	466	3,498	3,566	606	441	504
Green Bay city	7,310	1,398	1,504	1,325	2,120	2,707	994	5,543	5,965	1,211	684	795
Kenosha city	6,600	2,283	2,414	693	1,698	1,766	975	5,268	4,940	1,132	832	1,040
Madison city	18,767	6,840	5,769	2,594	3,848	4,762	1,429	10,700	10,205	1,988	886	1,091
Milwaukee city	31,967	9,552	9,230	3,935	6,721	8,012	7,315	25,362	25,142	12,294	5,884	6,099
Oshkosh city	4,367	1,033	946	311	2,018	2,075	323	3,792	3,716	434	384	441
Racine city	5,195	1,798	1,400	599	1,314	1,473	712	4,577	3,861	1,232	672	718
Waukesha city	6,405	1,444	1,082	985	1,291	1,747	566	3,820	3,421	691	194	580

Table I-4: Metropolitan Statistical Areas—Persons With Health Insurance by Source of Insurance

| | Private Health Insurance Coverage | | | | | | Public Health Insurance Coverage | | | | | |
| | Employer Based | | | Direct Purchase | | | Medicare | | | Medicaid/CHIP | | |
	55 to 64 Years	65 to 74 Years	75 Years and Over	55 to 64 Years	65 to 74 Years	75 Years and Over	55 to 64 Years	65 to 74 Years	75 Years and Over	55 to 64 Years	65 to 74 Years	75 Years and Over
Abilene, TX	10,080	4,423	3,337	2,778	3,731	3,788	1,721	11,495	9,994	1,254	1,693	1,797
Akron, OH	67,187	24,381	22,269	9,814	13,702	16,364	7,320	50,603	45,737	6,003	5,266	5,791
Albany, GA	9,966	4,302	2,658	2,024	3,066	2,719	2,441	11,036	8,050	2,594	2,234	1,907
Albany-Schenectady-Troy, NY	91,750	37,641	29,972	11,264	18,477	20,945	9,345	62,414	54,786	9,894	6,706	7,355
Albuquerque, NM	66,988	26,136	17,346	14,830	12,830	13,242	10,366	61,579	47,118	11,890	8,064	7,453
Alexandria, LA	9,291	4,165	2,652	2,444	3,056	2,470	3,006	11,055	8,477	3,041	2,777	2,608
Allentown-Bethlehem-Easton, PA-NJ	76,869	24,078	19,399	14,214	25,257	31,440	9,653	61,052	57,937	7,490	7,109	7,272
Altoona, PA	11,759	4,316	3,466	2,613	4,923	5,779	2,318	11,057	9,977	1,991	1,242	1,552
Amarillo, TX	17,123	6,282	4,301	3,466	4,853	5,028	2,631	15,668	12,715	2,056	2,012	1,572
Ames, IA	6,696	2,129	1,903	1,205	1,701	2,526	218	4,463	4,208	435	315	414
Anchorage, AK	30,515	9,848	4,473	4,450	3,379	2,567	3,177	17,544	10,255	3,314	2,559	2,463
Anderson, IN	11,330	6,128	4,655	1,810	3,645	3,889	1,929	10,653	8,926	1,323	1,175	1,091
Anderson, SC	14,399	5,100	3,752	2,522	5,674	5,535	4,399	16,340	11,805	2,189	1,914	1,721
Ann Arbor, MI	31,596	13,317	9,269	4,367	6,421	5,613	2,877	19,907	15,129	2,808	2,199	2,153
Anniston-Oxford, AL	9,558	4,154	2,744	2,606	2,973	2,787	2,686	9,366	7,345	1,778	1,461	1,172
Appleton, WI	20,826	3,848	3,653	3,300	5,694	5,878	1,580	13,957	12,087	1,518	1,533	1,605
Asheville, NC	34,824	15,387	12,887	10,784	16,700	15,053	7,380	42,349	34,315	4,224	3,758	4,687
Athens-Clarke County, GA	13,118	5,524	3,148	2,495	3,438	2,494	2,173	11,683	7,812	1,968	1,466	1,147
Atlanta-Sandy Springs-Marietta, GA	372,603	124,537	64,916	70,962	82,456	68,036	45,653	284,917	184,218	37,431	38,484	32,373
Atlantic City-Hammonton, NJ	24,384	10,839	5,994	5,683	6,762	7,002	3,257	20,202	16,703	3,320	2,963	2,963
Auburn-Opelika, AL	8,889	3,665	1,663	1,737	3,035	2,411	2,084	7,822	5,007	972	1,059	709
Augusta-Richmond County, GA-SC	42,759	16,891	9,850	7,853	11,442	9,105	7,805	40,609	28,055	7,406	6,207	4,538
Austin-Round Rock-San Marcos, TX	116,249	42,773	24,073	22,918	25,057	19,715	11,459	82,328	56,734	11,051	8,242	8,872
Bakersfield-Delano, CA	42,985	15,716	9,460	7,507	10,934	9,923	8,756	42,357	30,968	11,674	8,913	6,897
Baltimore-Towson, MD	245,321	100,636	69,061	41,791	55,734	59,601	25,580	178,116	150,579	28,824	21,933	23,709
Bangor, ME	12,848	3,859	3,189	2,124	4,571	4,065	2,566	11,590	9,972	2,640	3,049	2,312
Barnstable Town, MA	24,961	14,547	11,616	6,105	10,530	11,439	2,610	26,865	25,557	5,205	2,344	3,121
Baton Rouge, LA	59,131	21,480	14,007	11,975	13,173	11,716	9,305	48,543	34,438	8,936	6,607	6,029
Battle Creek, MI	11,027	5,667	5,474	2,060	3,209	3,061	2,337	10,327	9,109	2,648	1,744	1,335
Bay City, MI	10,646	5,872	4,736	1,758	3,350	2,791	2,002	9,441	7,777	1,573	1,307	1,025
Beaumont-Port Arthur, TX	27,496	11,315	9,044	5,613	7,460	8,164	5,873	25,558	22,935	4,634	3,670	3,593
Bellingham, WA	16,212	5,585	3,838	5,400	5,789	5,675	2,019	15,091	11,722	2,402	2,217	1,502
Bend, OR	13,400	5,097	2,944	4,805	6,298	5,266	1,355	14,673	9,951	1,024	847	1,028
Billings, MT	13,805	4,043	2,989	3,220	5,521	6,003	1,833	11,942	10,220	1,551	857	1,430
Binghamton, NY	23,921	10,574	10,527	3,460	6,202	7,257	3,081	20,115	18,701	3,401	1,868	2,356
Birmingham-Hoover, AL	94,514	33,422	22,268	18,132	25,701	24,641	19,144	79,800	62,952	14,573	11,575	10,983
Bismarck, ND	10,703	2,952	1,812	2,436	4,275	4,435	1,087	7,603	6,975	353	656	882
Blacksburg-Christiansburg-Radford, VA	12,661	4,787	3,504	2,255	4,638	3,909	1,856	11,591	8,216	829	1,008	876
Bloomington, IN	14,559	4,874	3,463	2,472	5,317	5,155	2,103	12,180	9,886	1,020	937	1,006
Bloomington-Normal, IL	13,625	5,120	3,748	2,956	3,163	3,834	960	9,165	7,589	850	762	689
Boise City-Nampa, ID	42,958	11,903	7,996	11,119	15,465	13,147	6,070	39,305	29,249	4,557	3,971	3,953
Boston-Cambridge-Quincy, MA-NH	416,124	153,136	106,717	66,045	96,408	103,429	37,171	295,654	267,402	79,411	50,231	54,422
Boulder, CO	24,499	8,482	4,872	7,432	6,059	5,226	1,517	16,911	12,247	1,926	1,421	1,278
Bowling Green, KY	8,423	3,157	1,979	2,071	3,373	2,643	1,646	8,092	6,047	1,464	999	829
Bremerton-Silverdale, WA	22,929	9,914	5,480	5,483	6,362	5,431	2,784	19,955	13,038	2,961	2,442	1,991
Bridgeport-Stamford-Norwalk, CT	77,495	28,624	22,412	17,438	19,784	23,702	6,169	59,577	56,385	7,621	6,552	7,812
Brownsville-Harlingen, TX	13,900	4,525	2,853	3,544	4,617	3,619	3,628	23,109	19,235	5,019	7,464	7,588
Brunswick, GA	7,797	4,335	2,242	2,435	3,411	3,025	2,005	10,280	6,535	1,646	1,488	1,383
Buffalo-Niagara Falls, NY	110,372	45,636	35,038	17,241	30,324	36,670	16,386	86,284	83,769	18,941	10,224	13,175
Burlington, NC	11,781	3,863	3,279	1,901	3,400	4,587	2,267	11,544	10,242	1,344	1,198	1,256
Burlington-South Burlington, VT	19,152	6,688	4,586	3,398	4,246	4,050	1,968	13,712	10,593	3,301	1,846	2,107
Canton-Massillon, OH	40,020	15,711	12,833	6,641	10,929	12,970	4,050	33,171	28,858	3,309	3,228	3,558
Cape Coral-Fort Myers, FL	50,127	32,034	22,013	14,927	30,195	27,676	7,784	81,885	65,035	5,761	7,816	8,578
Cape Girardeau-Jackson, MO-IL	7,738	2,236	1,971	1,365	2,465	2,403	1,879	7,311	6,001	1,191	811	909
Casper, WY	7,069	1,436	1,096	1,320	2,101	2,151	629	4,805	4,216	561	442	436
Cedar Rapids, IA	22,943	6,237	4,824	4,688	8,277	9,653	2,294	18,117	15,964	2,387	1,974	1,788
Champaign-Urbana, IL	17,368	6,845	5,589	3,044	4,826	5,155	1,651	12,750	11,031	1,006	1,359	1,180
Charleston, WV	30,949	13,614	11,436	3,743	6,407	7,407	6,838	26,255	21,031	4,905	2,935	2,987
Charleston-North Charleston-Summerville, SC	46,931	19,452	10,955	10,519	14,810	11,116	8,423	46,782	30,581	6,172	5,994	5,121
Charlotte-Gastonia-Rock Hill, NC-SC	122,167	39,885	23,967	25,419	37,291	32,985	18,442	103,363	72,459	13,901	11,860	11,038
Charlottesville, VA	16,684	7,286	5,065	4,589	5,364	5,798	2,148	15,007	11,992	923	1,453	1,524
Chattanooga, TN-GA	44,736	15,689	10,996	8,975	16,075	15,280	7,693	43,469	33,303	6,944	5,701	5,088
Cheyenne, WY	8,270	3,019	1,937	1,050	2,326	1,706	993	6,519	4,900	846	638	524
Chicago-Joliet-Naperville, IL-IN-WI	733,253	238,713	157,091	120,582	182,006	195,470	74,423	554,902	468,532	77,265	70,491	69,274
Chico, CA	15,522	6,962	6,489	3,908	5,735	7,293	3,746	17,177	15,709	5,336	2,783	2,763
Cincinnati-Middletown, OH-KY-IN	185,612	62,567	45,683	29,735	43,289	45,321	23,006	137,952	111,440	16,277	12,652	12,446
Clarksville, TN-KY	13,237	4,683	3,181	3,369	4,663	3,916	3,119	14,850	10,477	2,281	1,785	1,534
Cleveland, TN	8,798	2,732	1,511	1,995	4,097	3,072	2,046	10,393	6,658	1,251	1,726	1,345
Cleveland-Elyria-Mentor, OH	196,609	77,210	62,446	29,052	46,552	54,006	21,471	154,298	143,479	20,452	16,839	18,493
Coeur d'Alene, ID	10,322	3,976	2,174	3,750	5,404	5,105	2,011	11,936	8,500	1,202	905	1,000
College Station-Bryan, TX	12,108	5,828	3,955	2,207	3,224	3,318	1,124	10,842	8,616	1,398	1,098	1,182
Colorado Springs, CO	43,617	12,590	8,524	10,309	12,134	9,867	5,651	38,364	27,156	5,063	3,860	3,029
Columbia, MO	13,138	5,232	3,279	2,418	2,773	2,078	1,414	8,883	7,267	1,103	699	701
Columbia, SC	61,009	23,463	13,854	9,543	15,442	12,332	9,692	51,638	35,304	7,303	6,615	6,104
Columbus, GA-AL	18,780	6,287	4,357	3,716	4,934	5,488	4,438	18,398	14,916	4,052	3,682	3,366
Columbus, IN	6,500	2,335	1,636	1,174	2,275	2,078	944	6,090	4,425	664	433	602
Columbus, OH	148,496	53,355	36,371	22,001	33,237	30,657	16,824	107,139	81,622	13,275	11,584	9,249
Corpus Christi, TX	29,082	9,761	6,282	5,054	7,370	7,936	4,874	29,722	23,684	6,381	4,917	4,946
Corvallis, OR	7,437	2,483	2,160	1,380	2,305	1,988	590	5,486	4,887	741	361	550
Crestview-Fort Walton Beach-Destin, FL	10,875	4,558	3,211	3,496	4,364	3,966	1,749	14,029	10,819	813	1,470	1,092

Table I-4: Metropolitan Statistical Areas—Persons With Health Insurance by Source of Insurance—*Continued*

| | Private Health Insurance Coverage | | | | | | Public Health Insurance Coverage | | | | | |
| | Employer Based | | | Direct Purchase | | | Medicare | | | Medicaid/CHIP | | |
	55 to 64 Years	65 to 74 Years	75 Years and Over	55 to 64 Years	65 to 74 Years	75 Years and Over	55 to 64 Years	65 to 74 Years	75 Years and Over	55 to 64 Years	65 to 74 Years	75 Years and Over
Cumberland, MD-WV	7,943	4,360	2,894	1,575	3,256	2,899	2,010	9,554	7,748	1,390	1,356	1,380
Dallas-Fort Worth-Arlington, TX	418,416	129,498	71,326	76,140	89,421	75,486	45,453	322,440	224,153	44,173	39,532	34,840
Dalton, GA	9,357	2,582	1,339	1,243	2,189	2,070	2,023	9,110	6,246	1,659	1,520	1,560
Danville, IL	7,255	2,826	2,359	1,713	2,939	3,137	1,058	6,674	5,746	819	870	646
Danville, VA	9,193	3,561	2,079	2,448	3,661	4,050	2,031	10,255	8,205	1,339	1,351	1,209
Davenport-Moline-Rock Island, IA-IL	36,556	14,571	12,003	5,813	11,866	12,156	4,240	29,680	25,590	3,572	2,731	3,394
Dayton, OH	75,371	28,619	23,539	11,754	19,260	19,856	9,614	64,947	55,992	7,243	6,108	6,161
Decatur, AL	12,536	5,870	3,362	2,749	4,469	3,252	2,815	12,541	8,584	1,967	1,578	1,411
Decatur, IL	10,308	4,135	3,690	1,641	3,460	3,447	1,441	8,956	7,963	1,028	790	964
Deltona-Daytona Beach-Ormond Beach, FL	40,266	20,002	18,616	8,882	16,833	18,928	8,611	53,443	48,511	7,690	5,972	6,605
Denver-Aurora-Broomfield, CO	198,843	62,271	39,012	46,076	46,517	42,811	17,266	143,977	108,103	22,051	17,777	17,584
Des Moines-West Des Moines, IA	46,832	12,808	9,921	8,912	15,124	14,657	4,628	34,322	27,492	6,573	3,971	3,747
Detroit-Warren-Livonia, MI	383,648	157,884	131,322	63,862	104,744	107,550	55,927	296,294	257,763	60,639	41,266	36,655
Dothan, AL	11,390	4,478	2,631	2,742	4,396	3,845	2,863	12,805	9,567	2,140	1,871	1,773
Dover, DE	12,304	6,810	4,323	2,087	3,961	3,079	2,384	12,830	9,171	2,727	1,504	1,615
Dubuque, IA	9,105	2,838	2,276	2,366	3,820	3,608	770	7,002	6,635	741	622	1,166
Duluth, MN-WI	26,550	8,856	7,485	5,924	10,254	11,010	4,165	21,788	19,334	4,460	2,436	2,605
Durham-Chapel Hill, NC	39,935	16,652	10,646	9,190	9,848	9,284	4,885	32,413	24,034	4,053	3,889	3,532
Eau Claire, WI	14,293	4,048	3,527	2,378	5,440	5,455	1,531	11,035	10,010	1,917	1,502	1,447
El Centro, CA	6,676	1,848	1,118	1,232	1,566	1,551	1,831	9,447	8,494	4,598	4,518	5,063
Elizabethtown, KY	8,635	2,889	1,743	1,577	2,434	2,411	1,416	7,607	5,546	1,291	966	857
Elkhart-Goshen, IN	14,182	3,592	2,919	3,112	4,958	5,513	1,967	12,158	10,420	1,464	1,243	881
Elmira, NY	8,440	3,494	2,953	1,028	2,068	2,364	1,577	6,646	6,089	1,645	763	925
El Paso, TX	30,950	10,589	7,676	6,281	7,584	6,788	9,291	42,453	36,443	10,134	10,935	13,930
Erie, PA	26,262	7,473	5,871	4,159	8,947	10,027	3,450	20,289	18,429	4,145	2,648	3,165
Eugene-Springfield, OR	29,971	9,329	7,276	6,985	13,234	13,524	4,722	29,277	24,105	5,002	3,494	3,607
Evansville, IN-KY	32,830	10,289	7,248	5,797	11,534	12,193	4,703	26,454	22,196	3,165	2,597	2,442
Fairbanks, AK	7,309	2,496	1,174	1,014	496	354	703	4,017	2,218	967	382	422
Fargo, ND-MN	16,213	3,771	2,643	3,377	5,152	6,994	1,372	10,553	10,164	1,035	1,069	1,075
Farmington, NM	8,359	2,762	1,778	1,396	1,546	1,722	1,482	7,358	6,049	969	865	1,356
Fayetteville, NC	18,325	6,955	3,018	4,261	5,301	4,096	4,704	19,474	13,388	4,304	3,246	2,781
Fayetteville-Springdale-Rogers, AR-MO	29,446	9,764	5,605	6,874	10,376	8,980	5,540	28,732	21,992	3,093	3,435	3,247
Flagstaff, AZ	8,530	2,729	1,744	2,613	2,440	1,521	1,202	7,642	4,443	1,771	1,211	959
Flint, MI	38,378	20,233	16,644	5,720	9,679	8,907	7,160	31,395	26,229	8,052	4,720	3,637
Florence, SC	14,349	5,499	3,083	3,327	5,317	4,267	4,457	16,448	10,777	3,715	2,424	2,761
Florence-Muscle Shoals, AL	12,870	6,894	4,809	3,024	4,794	4,724	2,598	13,444	10,592	1,690	2,094	1,654
Fond du Lac, WI	9,876	1,950	1,561	1,501	3,872	3,807	1,064	7,608	7,246	961	887	1,373
Fort Collins-Loveland, CO	25,432	8,615	5,543	6,685	7,093	7,139	2,122	20,055	15,500	2,388	1,326	2,069
Fort Smith, AR-OK	20,078	5,974	3,582	3,781	7,178	6,159	5,655	23,824	16,616	3,777	3,527	2,733
Fort Wayne, IN	35,183	8,920	7,940	6,581	9,013	10,427	3,710	26,995	22,764	3,617	2,112	2,056
Fresno, CA	48,682	18,436	12,640	9,454	12,573	14,185	7,924	48,159	41,763	13,663	11,095	11,576
Gadsden, AL	8,388	3,761	2,260	2,184	3,064	2,814	2,802	9,211	6,786	2,044	1,336	1,626
Gainesville, FL	17,199	7,142	4,839	4,401	5,033	4,917	3,103	15,929	12,742	3,568	1,930	1,942
Gainesville, GA	12,400	4,921	2,858	2,342	4,100	3,663	1,503	12,258	8,487	1,178	1,480	1,203
Glens Falls, NY	13,515	6,318	4,063	1,910	4,094	4,032	1,855	11,305	9,161	1,473	881	1,391
Goldsboro, NC	8,069	3,473	1,845	1,851	2,648	2,324	2,396	9,078	6,495	1,659	1,555	1,632
Grand Forks, ND-MN	7,971	1,836	1,277	1,620	2,986	3,028	746	6,085	5,315	627	776	462
Grand Junction, CO	11,341	4,529	3,376	2,366	4,808	4,406	1,323	11,584	9,910	1,235	1,516	1,466
Grand Rapids-Wyoming, MI	63,958	21,734	15,924	11,394	18,511	19,456	7,966	48,000	41,180	7,416	5,019	5,928
Great Falls, MT	5,770	1,980	1,534	1,605	2,777	2,532	874	6,614	5,707	949	979	724
Greeley, CO	17,861	5,602	2,830	4,324	4,477	3,966	1,810	14,442	9,912	2,055	1,679	2,009
Green Bay, WI	26,730	5,573	4,570	5,032	7,623	7,455	2,553	20,325	17,117	2,708	1,801	2,169
Greensboro-High Point, NC	55,596	17,118	12,739	11,910	16,884	17,436	9,836	52,329	41,606	7,022	6,197	5,143
Greenville, NC	11,559	4,737	3,233	2,632	3,439	3,211	2,520	10,583	8,152	2,264	1,730	1,854
Greenville-Mauldin-Easley, SC	49,693	15,944	10,227	9,868	17,962	14,398	9,053	48,548	34,774	6,331	5,286	4,424
Gulfport-Biloxi, MS	17,130	5,407	3,641	3,629	6,272	4,365	3,646	17,939	12,937	3,720	2,507	2,103
Hagerstown-Martinsburg, MD-WV	23,592	10,766	6,507	2,860	6,000	5,852	3,351	19,608	15,270	3,135	2,097	2,265
Hanford-Corcoran, CA	6,949	2,249	1,259	960	1,532	1,552	1,484	5,881	4,908	1,915	1,109	1,214
Harrisburg-Carlisle, PA	56,435	19,378	15,882	8,776	15,888	15,773	5,297	40,124	36,029	5,120	4,014	4,180
Harrisonburg, VA	8,972	3,087	2,424	2,139	3,488	3,295	966	7,946	7,310	555	809	597
Hartford-West Hartford-East Hartford, CT	117,502	43,956	32,077	15,744	26,787	32,936	11,759	84,527	78,844	10,975	10,827	12,105
Hattiesburg, MS	7,381	2,636	1,836	2,667	3,442	2,768	2,528	9,476	6,677	2,162	1,747	1,589
Hickory-Lenoir-Morganton, NC	27,423	8,648	4,867	7,088	12,242	10,059	7,204	32,236	22,355	3,703	3,776	3,513
Hinesville-Fort Stewart, GA	2,934	1,397	479	575	793	447	626	3,508	1,733	506	662	225
Holland-Grand Haven, MI	22,521	7,263	5,371	4,559	6,582	6,747	2,069	16,707	13,952	1,307	1,404	1,461
Honolulu, HI	86,913	43,051	36,369	20,251	17,254	22,042	7,011	65,409	66,301	9,808	8,950	10,709
Hot Springs, AR	7,225	3,779	3,232	2,336	4,734	4,411	1,761	10,541	8,740	1,372	954	1,210
Houma-Bayou Cane-Thibodaux, LA	12,866	5,087	2,589	3,439	5,048	4,444	3,504	13,828	9,828	3,081	1,975	1,576
Houston-Sugar Land-Baytown, TX	394,998	119,937	64,555	64,344	72,983	64,013	43,560	294,197	202,004	52,408	44,849	36,975
Huntington-Ashland, WV-KY-OH	22,079	12,273	8,669	3,598	6,542	6,066	7,325	25,133	19,902	5,664	3,314	3,085
Huntsville, AL	33,541	15,954	9,806	6,796	8,891	8,226	5,216	28,910	21,226	3,243	3,244	2,895
Idaho Falls, ID	9,602	2,356	1,821	1,846	3,535	3,475	1,164	7,743	6,193	640	668	925
Indianapolis-Carmel, IN	137,659	44,738	32,496	21,642	40,761	36,992	16,509	103,716	80,526	15,673	11,697	9,278
Iowa City, IA	12,966	3,271	2,139	2,251	3,969	3,827	1,039	7,829	6,598	1,189	910	675
Ithaca, NY	9,015	3,626	3,201	1,302	1,277	1,378	1,008	5,632	4,948	1,021	636	690
Jackson, MI	14,364	6,066	5,374	2,247	4,070	3,820	2,273	11,613	10,344	2,127	1,233	1,088
Jackson, MS	37,053	11,564	6,213	8,561	11,570	10,217	7,963	33,991	25,137	7,221	6,345	5,185
Jackson, TN	8,528	2,834	2,096	1,914	3,011	2,712	1,768	8,478	6,546	1,582	1,234	1,295
Jacksonville, FL	100,293	34,305	20,349	20,363	28,053	26,208	16,641	93,548	68,822	15,633	10,984	9,050
Jacksonville, NC	6,665	3,567	1,582	2,160	2,080	2,026	1,310	8,068	5,232	975	1,250	748

Table I-4: Metropolitan Statistical Areas—Persons With Health Insurance by Source of Insurance—*Continued*

	Private Health Insurance Coverage						Public Health Insurance Coverage					
	Employer Based			Direct Purchase			Medicare			Medicaid/CHIP		
	55 to 64 Years	65 to 74 Years	75 Years and Over	55 to 64 Years	65 to 74 Years	75 Years and Over	55 to 64 Years	65 to 74 Years	75 Years and Over	55 to 64 Years	65 to 74 Years	75 Years and Over
Janesville, WI	13,898	5,305	3,332	2,179	5,018	5,348	1,921	11,442	9,761	2,343	1,140	1,573
Jefferson City, MO	13,713	5,433	3,206	1,831	4,148	4,121	1,898	10,351	8,044	1,070	677	829
Johnson City, TN	16,467	5,742	4,219	2,674	7,270	5,695	4,541	18,413	13,037	2,686	2,667	2,086
Johnstown, PA	14,561	5,147	4,671	2,527	6,016	7,315	2,254	12,669	13,344	2,166	1,704	2,316
Jonesboro, AR	7,313	2,126	1,257	2,061	3,437	2,952	2,431	8,800	6,171	1,597	1,259	1,092
Joplin, MO	11,820	3,497	2,379	2,179	5,590	4,861	2,642	13,503	10,299	2,112	1,801	1,393
Kalamazoo-Portage, MI	27,903	11,374	8,787	5,197	8,267	8,062	3,894	22,287	18,291	4,259	2,136	2,192
Kankakee-Bradley, IL	9,129	2,700	2,442	1,333	2,869	3,226	1,605	7,623	6,503	1,145	836	806
Kansas City, MO-KS	167,940	53,123	36,921	32,487	52,418	51,845	18,460	130,244	105,728	13,298	11,173	11,824
Kennewick-Pasco-Richland, WA	21,034	7,002	4,982	3,778	5,276	4,147	2,364	15,202	11,272	2,160	1,743	1,592
Killeen-Temple-Fort Hood, TX	19,153	9,160	5,890	3,257	6,177	5,867	3,279	20,428	14,988	3,313	3,188	3,331
Kingsport-Bristol-Bristol, TN-VA	25,630	10,394	7,598	5,982	12,912	10,928	7,872	32,128	23,515	5,398	4,782	3,635
Kingston, NY	17,693	7,833	5,116	3,171	3,340	4,171	2,453	14,382	11,907	2,920	1,236	1,688
Knoxville, TN	61,753	24,131	16,820	11,361	20,644	18,878	9,928	57,632	43,738	8,008	6,067	4,935
Kokomo, IN	9,272	4,645	3,591	1,701	3,322	3,070	1,590	8,996	7,074	940	731	486
La Crosse, WI-MN	12,215	2,562	1,990	1,931	4,121	4,584	1,322	9,070	8,828	1,358	1,194	1,155
Lafayette, IN	14,929	4,490	3,616	2,030	4,840	5,041	1,436	11,153	8,970	1,041	854	612
Lafayette, LA	19,204	6,343	4,145	4,637	6,042	5,266	2,911	15,537	11,922	2,603	1,781	1,840
Lake Charles, LA	15,193	4,937	4,737	3,275	5,084	4,713	2,999	14,125	10,352	1,959	2,055	1,566
Lake Havasu City-Kingman, AZ	16,098	8,497	6,034	4,969	11,652	8,289	3,623	28,675	18,830	4,022	3,369	2,266
Lakeland-Winter Haven, FL	42,129	20,571	14,817	10,205	15,986	17,800	9,055	59,819	46,573	8,339	6,880	6,105
Lancaster, PA	46,757	14,831	12,585	8,539	14,991	16,968	3,976	37,648	34,927	4,512	2,899	3,610
Lansing-East Lansing, MI	45,073	19,692	14,096	6,160	8,841	9,257	4,819	30,669	23,778	5,125	3,291	3,011
Laredo, TX	7,420	2,156	1,075	1,335	1,622	1,068	1,794	10,126	7,948	2,462	3,367	4,048
Las Cruces, NM	12,160	5,154	3,858	2,552	3,892	3,041	1,506	14,278	11,144	3,203	2,000	2,400
Las Vegas-Paradise, NV	135,338	52,556	27,519	24,632	29,365	22,904	16,916	130,635	85,252	13,316	15,578	12,310
Lawrence, KS	7,581	2,898	1,966	1,619	2,337	2,287	694	5,287	4,392	563	590	492
Lawton, OK	5,632	2,623	1,580	1,489	1,914	1,647	1,492	6,777	5,370	763	915	803
Lebanon, PA	13,303	5,075	4,264	2,209	4,807	4,722	1,174	11,201	10,132	1,083	852	1,276
Lewiston-Auburn, ME	9,163	2,563	1,808	1,354	2,928	3,249	1,763	7,754	6,809	1,854	1,985	2,156
Lexington-Fayette, KY	36,690	13,860	8,458	7,358	9,879	9,595	5,672	29,034	22,064	4,506	3,662	3,377
Lima, OH	9,232	3,985	3,165	1,488	2,353	2,868	1,700	7,750	6,922	1,404	882	834
Lincoln, NE	25,522	6,920	4,644	4,681	7,475	8,413	2,333	16,788	15,398	2,083	1,513	1,858
Little Rock-North Little Rock-Conway, AR	53,581	19,978	11,476	10,211	16,777	13,342	10,309	48,371	35,842	7,365	6,801	6,064
Logan, UT-ID	7,042	2,335	1,531	1,459	1,940	2,307	546	5,800	4,645	399	486	559
Longview, TX	14,362	4,913	3,865	2,794	5,480	4,754	2,425	15,141	12,864	2,695	1,709	1,917
Longview, WA	8,694	3,188	2,927	2,015	4,158	3,169	1,580	9,083	6,710	1,672	1,345	1,203
Los Angeles-Long Beach-Santa Ana, CA	748,099	256,687	172,144	183,253	134,584	143,046	85,167	716,209	632,410	160,217	166,369	184,414
Louisville/Jefferson County, KY-IN	113,265	39,618	26,974	21,373	35,355	33,670	17,850	89,244	70,218	12,913	11,305	9,795
Lubbock, TX	17,269	7,291	4,944	4,029	5,626	5,428	2,782	16,829	13,809	2,340	2,873	2,354
Lynchburg, VA	21,094	8,052	5,666	5,286	9,328	7,887	3,547	22,227	17,150	1,986	2,003	2,221
Macon, GA	17,260	6,245	4,764	3,337	4,408	4,349	4,256	16,474	12,845	3,218	2,737	2,390
Madera-Chowchilla, CA	9,355	3,554	2,187	1,246	2,871	2,251	1,468	9,746	7,109	2,003	1,830	1,439
Madison, WI	54,549	18,229	12,222	8,661	13,978	14,156	3,852	33,033	27,418	4,881	2,767	3,425
Manchester-Nashua, NH	40,218	12,330	7,552	4,495	8,112	8,828	3,141	25,292	19,900	2,404	1,995	2,642
Manhattan, KS	6,442	2,486	1,217	1,733	1,992	2,512	835	5,058	4,538	568	255	707
Mankato-North Mankato, MN	8,098	1,673	1,498	1,744	3,173	3,251	629	5,648	5,499	734	318	653
Mansfield, OH	10,627	4,671	3,427	1,781	4,142	4,353	1,676	10,413	9,234	1,129	1,020	998
McAllen-Edinburg-Mission, TX	22,896	7,994	6,447	4,755	7,553	7,662	7,436	37,792	30,929	9,334	14,454	13,428
Medford, OR	17,263	5,364	5,996	5,120	7,521	7,808	3,198	19,366	16,926	2,280	2,244	2,223
Memphis, TN-MS-AR	98,557	31,415	19,790	17,894	23,522	20,305	16,816	77,727	57,266	14,967	13,636	10,837
Merced, CA	11,364	3,929	2,316	2,749	3,461	3,144	2,652	13,216	10,358	3,979	3,899	3,626
Miami-Fort Lauderdale-Pompano Beach, FL	327,504	106,284	81,508	90,648	91,743	130,945	48,198	418,762	428,638	59,473	91,112	104,967
Michigan City-La Porte, IN	9,994	2,960	2,076	1,565	3,357	2,781	1,118	8,331	6,965	999	751	893
Midland, TX	9,754	2,960	2,215	2,068	2,341	2,808	1,095	7,181	7,099	1,199	808	1,078
Milwaukee-Waukesha-West Allis, WI	135,234	38,762	36,169	19,626	33,089	39,373	13,610	95,762	92,974	20,175	12,459	15,711
Minneapolis-St. Paul-Bloomington, MN-WI	283,044	74,043	51,008	50,621	92,016	86,397	23,381	189,444	153,310	29,442	18,066	19,635
Missoula, MT	8,698	2,310	1,401	2,232	2,640	2,972	1,365	7,024	5,285	948	530	597
Mobile, AL	31,727	10,717	7,203	5,855	8,482	8,541	7,447	30,249	22,403	5,362	5,243	3,547
Modesto, CA	29,792	9,489	5,929	7,303	9,597	9,054	5,597	28,838	24,172	7,319	6,073	5,638
Monroe, LA	10,489	4,335	2,852	2,311	4,010	3,629	2,438	11,668	9,660	2,586	1,757	1,908
Monroe, MI	16,478	6,679	4,932	2,489	3,893	3,560	2,057	11,214	8,900	1,514	1,152	1,443
Montgomery, AL	27,785	11,459	8,068	5,805	6,721	6,506	5,466	25,351	18,770	4,846	3,748	3,457
Morgantown, WV	10,428	4,113	3,415	1,357	2,017	1,696	2,121	8,170	6,338	1,604	695	723
Morristown, TN	10,025	3,630	2,281	2,753	5,845	4,370	2,878	13,489	8,327	2,329	1,945	1,031
Mount Vernon-Anacortes, WA	10,079	3,794	3,197	3,135	4,114	3,889	1,174	10,657	8,228	1,204	1,256	1,046
Muncie, IN	8,691	4,311	3,552	1,343	3,483	3,550	1,847	9,000	7,617	1,233	1,110	885
Muskegon-Norton Shores, MI	14,065	6,053	4,667	2,430	4,450	4,449	2,988	12,209	10,575	2,447	1,622	1,720
Myrtle Beach-North Myrtle Beach-Conway, SC	23,196	11,418	7,489	5,951	11,119	7,597	4,021	29,342	17,805	2,961	2,758	2,083
Napa, CA	12,164	5,365	4,156	2,802	3,051	3,795	1,039	10,345	9,245	1,692	1,206	1,382
Naples-Marco Island, FL	23,201	17,254	14,636	8,133	19,630	18,756	2,327	46,325	39,612	2,286	2,865	3,357
Nashville-Davidson--Murfreesboro--Franklin, TN	124,143	37,043	24,920	25,866	29,445	26,110	15,341	98,145	69,887	14,283	12,584	10,571
New Haven-Milford, CT	77,882	28,456	21,370	12,316	17,671	24,540	8,878	58,040	56,832	9,758	7,114	8,715
New Orleans-Metairie-Kenner, LA	90,840	27,912	16,426	20,681	18,999	20,039	16,625	78,719	61,168	17,270	13,047	11,829
New York-Northern New Jersey-Long Island, NY-NJ-PA.	1,474,834	582,183	378,728	249,196	279,244	338,682	161,409	1,214,373	1,106,964	299,424	229,535	244,938
Niles-Benton Harbor, MI	13,551	5,517	4,107	2,824	4,472	5,215	2,635	13,236	11,406	2,341	1,699	1,776
North Port-Bradenton-Sarasota, FL	59,215	38,061	37,023	18,959	35,632	42,102	8,801	97,407	93,063	6,508	7,691	8,456
Norwich-New London, CT	26,944	11,294	7,129	4,162	6,165	6,534	2,727	20,401	16,872	2,115	2,780	2,814
Ocala, FL	22,188	15,006	13,637	6,517	15,567	14,111	5,699	47,134	37,922	4,368	4,645	4,661
Ocean City, NJ	10,944	5,515	3,846	2,370	4,221	4,201	958	11,002	9,570	1,079	851	1,037

Table I-4: Metropolitan Statistical Areas—Persons With Health Insurance by Source of Insurance—*Continued*

| | Private Health Insurance Coverage | | | | | | Public Health Insurance Coverage | | | | | |
| | Employer Based | | | Direct Purchase | | | Medicare | | | Medicaid/CHIP | | |
	55 to 64 Years	65 to 74 Years	75 Years and Over	55 to 64 Years	65 to 74 Years	75 Years and Over	55 to 64 Years	65 to 74 Years	75 Years and Over	55 to 64 Years	65 to 74 Years	75 Years and Over
Odessa, TX	7,229	2,347	1,366	1,888	2,236	2,347	1,792	7,415	5,804	1,460	1,438	1,220
Ogden-Clearfield, UT	37,676	13,107	10,952	6,522	8,464	8,741	3,261	26,849	22,187	2,812	2,638	2,452
Oklahoma City, OK	94,142	35,517	24,217	16,646	26,517	26,060	15,009	81,326	61,888	8,878	8,437	7,972
Olympia, WA	23,668	9,739	6,247	4,829	5,821	6,012	3,016	18,672	14,307	2,283	1,865	1,726
Omaha-Council Bluffs, NE-IA	71,060	18,976	13,002	14,406	20,299	19,757	7,207	50,827	41,791	5,888	4,819	5,291
Orlando-Kissimmee-Sanford, FL	145,816	49,163	35,414	28,371	37,900	39,713	19,647	143,754	114,240	16,092	17,631	16,647
Oshkosh-Neenah, WI	15,487	3,621	3,123	2,120	4,866	5,368	1,239	10,949	10,285	1,394	918	1,116
Owensboro, KY	10,135	4,008	3,113	1,672	3,140	3,146	2,158	9,058	7,483	1,333	899	1,273
Oxnard-Thousand Oaks-Ventura, CA	63,865	22,953	14,994	14,559	14,753	15,880	5,918	49,777	44,056	7,312	6,723	7,869
Palm Bay-Melbourne-Titusville, FL	42,907	21,924	17,468	8,962	16,491	18,962	9,835	56,864	52,092	6,440	4,637	6,621
Palm Coast, FL	9,193	6,816	3,992	1,967	4,102	3,855	1,375	13,660	9,890	1,211	1,895	1,635
Panama City-Lynn Haven-Panama City Beach, FL	11,217	4,609	3,242	3,168	4,188	3,878	2,434	13,762	10,390	1,540	1,370	1,078
Parkersburg-Marietta-Vienna, WV-OH	15,469	6,919	5,245	2,137	5,193	4,808	3,275	15,103	11,244	2,245	1,596	1,149
Pascagoula, MS	11,284	3,803	2,241	2,093	3,530	2,841	3,036	12,237	7,902	1,808	1,156	1,018
Pensacola-Ferry Pass-Brent, FL	31,241	12,206	8,445	7,247	12,280	9,478	6,710	36,128	25,705	4,229	3,900	3,612
Peoria, IL	37,031	13,839	11,427	5,511	12,147	11,667	3,250	28,748	25,028	2,675	2,324	2,497
Philadelphia-Camden-Wilmington, PA-NJ-DE-MD	512,766	186,532	131,833	91,438	135,251	157,784	57,876	393,577	359,273	75,047	52,214	53,613
Phoenix-Mesa-Glendale, AZ	278,032	103,185	73,174	67,277	92,525	82,701	36,442	290,678	225,637	42,944	32,795	31,103
Pine Bluff, AR	6,474	1,975	1,035	1,653	2,725	2,379	2,068	7,266	5,447	1,755	1,227	1,518
Pittsburgh, PA	237,638	77,974	73,031	46,670	83,833	102,957	27,816	191,158	196,509	29,812	25,402	29,634
Pittsfield, MA	13,921	5,733	5,045	2,247	3,885	5,552	2,002	11,666	11,624	3,401	1,550	1,852
Pocatello, ID	6,434	1,758	1,807	1,663	2,559	2,074	1,024	5,493	4,552	644	466	592
Portland-South Portland-Biddeford, ME	50,891	17,203	12,872	9,205	14,122	15,600	6,015	40,516	34,385	6,692	5,745	6,467
Portland-Vancouver-Hillsboro, OR-WA	186,729	55,461	37,428	41,052	54,750	52,674	20,807	142,238	111,159	20,119	16,562	17,990
Port St. Lucie, FL	30,983	18,415	16,236	9,273	17,116	19,479	6,557	49,901	46,464	5,108	4,195	4,600
Poughkeepsie-Newburgh-Middletown, NY	61,495	25,997	17,040	7,894	11,893	11,978	7,026	43,825	34,813	6,662	4,630	5,307
Prescott, AZ	18,623	11,542	7,192	7,580	10,613	9,152	3,075	29,982	21,661	3,122	1,785	1,830
Providence-New Bedford-Fall River, RI-MA	138,733	47,449	31,898	23,178	37,662	44,796	20,989	111,230	104,406	27,671	18,374	19,162
Provo-Orem, UT	24,191	8,777	6,842	4,242	7,141	6,365	1,684	18,922	15,387	1,938	1,952	1,979
Pueblo, CO	11,656	4,942	5,274	2,992	4,402	3,849	3,160	12,448	10,977	3,469	1,657	1,574
Punta Gorda, FL	15,222	11,671	11,432	4,873	10,236	10,604	3,247	29,082	25,186	1,532	2,413	2,690
Racine, WI	18,355	5,891	4,499	2,649	4,682	4,641	1,568	13,646	11,900	1,858	1,358	1,593
Raleigh-Cary, NC	84,258	30,234	17,696	16,306	21,185	16,591	10,353	61,677	41,081	7,111	6,595	5,619
Rapid City, SD	9,821	2,651	2,367	2,986	3,742	3,786	1,438	9,033	7,486	945	1,052	841
Reading, PA	35,105	11,920	9,996	6,923	13,219	13,829	4,671	29,056	27,495	4,895	2,637	3,592
Redding, CA	14,621	5,651	4,069	2,808	6,016	5,872	3,813	17,053	13,057	3,794	2,189	1,878
Reno-Sparks, NV	34,223	12,231	6,696	8,134	9,225	6,873	3,721	31,009	20,563	3,122	3,144	3,099
Richmond, VA	110,693	39,096	27,784	21,130	29,494	28,104	14,381	85,903	65,453	9,558	8,843	7,516
Riverside-San Bernardino-Ontario, CA	235,367	78,750	51,627	48,977	50,821	52,698	35,529	237,500	191,091	48,776	42,486	41,353
Roanoke, VA	28,543	10,268	7,066	7,284	11,359	10,318	4,921	26,516	21,603	2,498	2,479	1,826
Rochester, MN	16,908	6,484	4,678	3,266	5,415	5,299	1,064	12,638	10,865	1,351	850	1,596
Rochester, NY	103,134	42,584	35,391	15,978	26,918	26,682	11,481	76,739	67,005	12,984	8,846	8,453
Rockford, IL	29,202	9,272	7,126	4,880	10,698	10,164	3,675	25,284	20,193	3,250	3,084	2,406
Rocky Mount, NC	12,087	4,221	2,277	2,443	4,517	4,386	3,451	12,463	8,758	2,665	2,335	2,223
Rome, GA	7,213	2,424	2,118	1,206	2,425	2,557	1,492	7,434	5,888	1,186	1,085	1,120
Sacramento--Arden-Arcade--Roseville, CA	165,576	69,597	50,854	31,542	37,782	38,612	21,486	138,142	115,888	29,984	21,024	21,467
Saginaw-Saginaw Township North, MI	18,542	9,892	7,738	2,943	5,651	5,809	3,572	16,047	13,549	3,397	2,281	1,977
St. Cloud, MN	14,301	3,184	2,635	3,852	6,062	6,125	1,624	11,363	10,543	1,318	1,099	1,647
St. George, UT	9,312	4,621	4,616	2,503	5,236	4,900	1,538	13,314	11,444	920	714	1,063
St. Joseph, MO-KS	9,448	3,073	2,277	2,265	3,948	3,872	1,909	9,160	7,753	1,479	1,057	771
St. Louis, MO-IL	247,388	85,391	61,859	42,121	64,013	67,992	31,775	194,627	164,822	22,659	18,334	18,470
Salem, OR	29,988	10,564	8,701	5,789	12,101	12,128	4,295	27,541	23,577	4,183	3,396	3,370
Salinas, CA	24,515	8,947	6,999	7,195	6,918	7,306	3,619	22,480	20,523	3,606	3,157	4,216
Salisbury, MD	9,094	4,163	2,609	2,049	2,636	3,341	1,852	8,500	7,036	1,751	1,064	914
Salt Lake City, UT	76,480	24,422	15,735	12,938	17,225	16,899	6,500	53,593	41,203	7,729	6,044	5,669
San Angelo, TX	7,962	3,682	2,928	1,553	2,859	3,101	1,459	7,904	7,139	991	678	973
San Antonio-New Braunfels, TX	133,755	49,436	32,176	27,058	33,741	27,558	21,756	130,840	99,484	23,228	20,592	20,808
San Diego-Carlsbad-San Marcos, CA	203,369	63,516	46,729	48,459	42,089	49,619	21,104	174,934	163,334	28,573	27,479	32,981
Sandusky, OH	8,466	3,881	3,000	1,573	2,228	2,351	1,151	7,075	5,538	728	622	586
San Francisco-Oakland-Fremont, CA	350,980	130,992	93,052	86,987	78,803	86,033	34,642	278,668	247,899	57,703	47,964	54,810
San Jose-Sunnyvale-Santa Clara, CA	127,187	46,323	29,918	29,655	29,449	29,112	10,073	105,235	91,227	19,875	21,132	23,806
San Luis Obispo-Paso Robles, CA	23,472	9,592	6,811	6,705	7,457	8,489	3,263	21,193	19,229	2,675	1,862	2,152
Santa Barbara-Santa Maria-Goleta, CA	27,165	10,269	9,246	7,560	9,522	10,121	2,926	26,383	26,293	3,676	3,061	3,764
Santa Cruz-Watsonville, CA	23,279	6,130	4,088	6,065	5,032	5,571	2,147	16,188	12,620	2,640	2,404	1,655
Santa Fe, NM	12,997	6,067	3,370	5,601	4,577	3,252	1,802	13,492	8,530	1,602	1,190	763
Santa Rosa-Petaluma, CA	44,515	15,441	11,144	13,058	13,978	13,910	4,544	36,006	30,657	6,047	4,140	4,043
Savannah, GA	24,449	9,222	5,625	4,705	5,557	5,202	3,648	22,828	17,260	3,389	2,091	2,804
Scranton--Wilkes-Barre, PA	51,446	17,740	13,677	11,525	22,012	24,825	8,134	47,626	46,392	7,249	5,958	7,358
Seattle-Tacoma-Bellevue, WA	282,559	85,720	55,215	59,067	69,836	67,126	27,339	201,593	164,012	31,816	26,506	30,191
Sebastian-Vero Beach, FL	11,684	7,204	8,021	4,251	6,712	9,245	1,745	18,730	19,507	1,510	1,724	1,745
Sheboygan, WI	11,435	2,552	2,063	1,821	3,801	4,258	913	8,368	7,836	1,377	898	1,136
Sherman-Denison, TX	9,593	4,164	2,934	2,163	3,864	2,993	1,697	10,237	7,796	1,586	833	1,297
Shreveport-Bossier City, LA	28,338	10,881	8,425	5,104	8,815	8,326	5,963	27,641	22,201	5,045	4,586	3,710
Sioux City, IA-NE-SD	11,489	2,737	1,640	2,687	4,653	4,822	1,512	9,485	8,293	1,661	1,336	1,487
Sioux Falls, SD	19,515	4,062	2,556	5,030	5,906	6,990	1,681	12,995	11,550	1,114	1,361	1,738
South Bend-Mishawaka, IN-MI	27,944	8,785	6,713	4,251	8,413	9,264	3,591	22,038	20,689	2,592	2,154	2,624
Spartanburg, SC	20,461	6,892	4,070	4,159	7,172	6,833	5,813	22,065	15,456	4,137	2,922	2,146
Spokane, WA	38,185	12,362	8,024	9,435	11,300	12,849	6,070	33,249	27,373	5,920	4,129	4,335
Springfield, IL	22,204	8,926	7,131	3,585	4,999	5,180	2,259	15,030	12,888	1,677	1,773	1,159
Springfield, MA	64,690	22,560	17,871	9,870	15,670	18,049	8,073	47,113	44,004	17,449	8,844	8,434

Table I-4: Metropolitan Statistical Areas—Persons With Health Insurance by Source of Insurance—*Continued*

	Private Health Insurance Coverage						Public Health Insurance Coverage					
	Employer Based			Direct Purchase			Medicare			Medicaid/CHIP		
	55 to 64 Years	65 to 74 Years	75 Years and Over	55 to 64 Years	65 to 74 Years	75 Years and Over	55 to 64 Years	65 to 74 Years	75 Years and Over	55 to 64 Years	65 to 74 Years	75 Years and Over
Springfield, MO	31,443	9,075	6,724	7,095	12,708	12,544	6,553	33,107	26,509	4,077	3,570	3,661
Springfield, OH	12,315	5,984	4,973	2,107	3,212	3,390	1,962	11,724	9,291	1,727	1,334	1,120
State College, PA	11,918	4,655	3,736	1,293	3,290	3,160	1,244	8,761	7,685	1,245	856	1,036
Steubenville-Weirton, OH-WV	12,691	5,156	4,229	2,270	4,301	5,054	1,887	11,376	10,559	1,843	1,095	1,311
Stockton, CA	41,609	14,370	10,411	7,583	10,688	12,254	6,954	37,830	30,899	11,032	7,860	6,525
Sumter, SC	6,563	2,613	1,572	1,218	2,030	1,890	1,791	7,784	5,615	1,679	1,538	1,386
Syracuse, NY	61,944	24,960	18,418	8,979	13,042	16,416	8,010	45,641	41,127	9,208	4,971	6,151
Tallahassee, FL	29,680	10,696	6,692	5,171	7,177	4,627	2,998	22,093	15,593	3,333	2,820	2,788
Tampa-St. Petersburg-Clearwater, FL	203,732	80,240	66,293	47,538	68,914	81,089	39,537	243,173	223,832	38,708	28,552	32,029
Terre Haute, IN	13,338	4,465	3,768	2,347	5,064	5,197	2,593	12,789	10,438	2,146	1,756	1,542
Texarkana, TX-Texarkana, AR	10,134	3,816	3,124	1,985	3,181	2,949	2,086	10,336	7,844	1,819	1,527	1,577
Toledo, OH	58,892	22,835	18,640	9,045	15,823	16,275	7,805	44,687	39,002	6,049	4,513	4,665
Topeka, KS	21,940	8,275	6,154	3,873	8,371	7,709	3,063	18,103	14,845	2,398	1,750	1,765
Trenton-Ewing, NJ	33,291	14,770	10,342	3,853	6,000	7,258	3,177	22,605	20,820	3,509	2,886	2,969
Tucson, AZ	71,359	29,198	24,074	16,009	23,407	23,835	10,057	82,234	68,403	15,962	9,826	8,857
Tulsa, OK	72,253	24,783	15,935	14,116	25,330	23,405	10,949	66,844	50,617	6,790	7,209	6,277
Tuscaloosa, AL	17,274	6,390	4,265	2,844	4,090	3,743	4,207	13,466	10,732	2,932	2,452	2,259
Tyler, TX	15,335	6,015	4,592	2,724	5,643	5,860	2,479	15,728	13,208	1,529	1,807	2,353
Utica-Rome, NY	27,353	11,670	9,550	4,128	6,914	8,802	4,447	23,552	22,142	4,894	3,475	3,825
Valdosta, GA	7,369	2,966	1,982	1,721	2,335	2,128	2,025	8,524	5,928	1,690	1,250	1,344
Vallejo-Fairfield, CA	35,747	14,329	8,852	5,995	6,111	5,646	3,886	24,896	19,841	4,526	3,331	4,298
Victoria, TX	9,535	3,784	2,355	2,201	2,797	2,997	1,159	8,893	7,225	1,069	1,135	1,312
Vineland-Millville-Bridgeton, NJ	10,644	4,143	2,391	1,701	3,330	3,846	2,659	10,503	8,300	2,696	1,508	1,828
Virginia Beach-Norfolk-Newport News, VA-NC	124,166	48,558	33,042	22,826	32,754	32,798	15,227	106,506	82,558	9,540	10,771	9,070
Visalia-Porterville, CA	21,053	6,228	4,495	4,210	5,707	6,251	3,375	22,372	17,703	6,604	5,438	4,810
Waco, TX	15,414	5,941	4,933	2,795	5,519	6,182	2,274	14,723	12,858	2,443	2,321	2,082
Warner Robins, GA	10,129	4,085	3,040	1,508	2,200	2,042	1,590	8,506	5,865	1,112	1,285	687
Washington-Arlington-Alexandria, DC-VA-MD-WV	477,220	198,930	116,887	76,883	81,352	74,313	29,464	303,140	225,444	36,334	34,813	34,136
Waterloo-Cedar Falls, IA	15,843	5,967	4,418	2,698	5,447	6,210	1,360	12,083	11,456	1,724	1,403	1,692
Wausau, WI	12,558	2,938	2,123	2,331	4,829	5,348	974	9,707	8,731	1,045	1,280	1,217
Wenatchee-East Wenatchee, WA	9,659	3,522	2,733	2,793	3,750	3,687	1,344	8,593	7,399	1,328	616	1,542
Wheeling, WV-OH	15,653	6,591	5,594	2,437	4,096	5,039	2,366	12,865	11,898	1,986	1,427	1,523
Wichita, KS	51,497	10,514	7,566	8,486	16,377	18,823	6,481	37,686	34,330	5,405	4,452	4,604
Wichita Falls, TX	9,839	4,658	2,872	2,280	3,508	3,843	2,084	10,218	9,184	1,532	1,131	1,110
Williamsport, PA	10,939	2,981	3,034	2,014	3,961	4,300	999	9,244	8,780	1,553	987	1,045
Wilmington, NC	32,585	17,703	9,990	8,805	14,237	10,571	5,572	37,233	23,169	3,938	2,359	2,770
Winchester, VA-WV	10,245	3,820	2,802	2,406	2,850	3,174	1,348	9,697	7,419	994	996	847
Winston-Salem, NC	40,000	15,253	10,756	9,596	12,936	12,255	6,286	35,712	28,437	4,343	3,988	3,954
Worcester, MA	74,312	24,757	17,362	9,186	17,796	19,209	6,996	49,478	45,331	15,180	8,521	9,080
Yakima, WA	14,264	4,165	3,163	3,909	5,122	5,210	2,748	14,821	12,261	2,610	2,489	2,677
York-Hanover, PA	42,277	12,965	8,273	6,677	13,734	14,174	4,159	32,998	27,088	4,115	3,142	3,066
Youngstown-Warren-Boardman, OH-PA	54,333	18,808	16,322	9,493	16,018	19,893	8,130	48,124	47,012	6,997	4,640	5,183
Yuba City, CA	9,400	3,723	2,633	2,022	3,006	2,600	1,766	10,508	8,043	3,079	2,169	1,863
Yuma, AZ	7,993	4,972	3,807	2,923	6,754	5,746	1,823	16,571	13,141	2,928	2,408	2,298

Table I-5: 113th Congressional Districts—Persons With Health Insurance by Source of Insurance

	Private Health Insurance Coverage						Public Health Insurance Coverage					
	Employer Based			Direct Purchase			Medicare			Medicaid/CHIP		
	55 to 64 Years	65 to 74 Years	75 Years and Over	55 to 64 Years	65 to 74 Years	75 Years and Over	55 to 64 Years	65 to 74 Years	75 Years and Over	55 to 64 Years	65 to 74 Years	75 Years and Over
Alabama												
Congressional District 1	53,778	20,337	13,524	11,381	16,368	15,351	12,821	56,097	40,268	9,213	8,014	6,315
Congressional District 2	51,213	20,444	12,775	11,885	16,455	14,534	11,893	53,471	40,064	9,283	7,790	7,883
Congressional District 3	51,481	21,837	11,353	12,821	17,819	14,701	14,581	52,970	36,958	10,306	7,997	7,859
Congressional District 4	54,533	24,102	14,043	12,537	20,731	17,598	16,131	61,299	42,965	10,271	9,715	8,632
Congressional District 5	56,251	26,941	16,544	11,644	17,681	15,233	9,662	51,898	38,055	6,431	6,060	5,855
Congressional District 6	61,524	21,120	13,661	11,415	16,314	16,559	8,377	48,380	38,018	5,635	4,813	5,352
Congressional District 7	47,029	16,760	11,781	10,293	13,299	11,968	15,998	45,779	37,724	14,754	11,103	9,969
Alaska												
Congressional District (at Large)	57,780	18,725	8,425	8,054	5,812	4,466	5,559	34,508	19,632	6,739	5,596	4,720
Arizona												
Congressional District 1	47,574	20,094	13,745	13,085	19,217	13,028	8,560	59,043	38,956	12,929	8,151	7,196
Congressional District 2	54,745	24,353	19,880	13,747	19,304	20,679	7,561	66,825	56,523	11,611	7,246	6,579
Congressional District 3	33,168	10,016	5,817	6,901	8,613	6,044	6,055	37,888	24,965	10,095	7,977	5,903
Congressional District 4	53,484	32,381	20,336	19,096	35,902	28,431	10,292	92,876	62,562	10,654	7,830	6,904
Congressional District 5	51,394	19,666	16,499	12,326	21,472	20,477	4,881	57,108	47,503	5,226	5,701	5,535
Congressional District 6	61,673	21,890	13,172	17,359	21,478	16,932	5,569	58,593	42,209	5,817	5,454	5,465
Congressional District 7	25,257	6,402	3,799	3,592	4,081	3,620	6,511	24,972	17,662	10,684	6,239	5,030
Congressional District 8	54,287	24,435	21,190	11,736	19,934	21,742	7,038	67,659	62,018	5,657	5,862	6,224
Congressional District 9	48,285	14,855	9,678	11,289	10,288	9,885	5,655	36,368	29,889	7,981	4,140	4,693
Arkansas												
Congressional District 1	47,569	16,077	10,252	12,900	23,865	20,180	16,350	63,821	47,093	11,220	9,727	9,795
Congressional District 2	55,140	21,461	12,815	10,109	17,555	15,150	11,200	52,407	39,614	7,761	7,378	6,708
Congressional District 3	48,409	16,317	9,781	11,572	17,966	15,760	10,284	50,331	38,452	6,389	6,172	5,737
Congressional District 4	48,630	18,749	11,938	14,266	24,344	21,507	16,882	65,929	49,315	11,396	9,321	10,004
California												
Congressional District 1	57,407	26,741	19,544	15,412	23,173	22,713	13,087	66,693	52,474	14,203	8,668	7,648
Congressional District 2	64,492	25,309	16,497	23,632	21,942	20,648	7,757	60,578	46,449	9,929	6,207	5,801
Congressional District 3	49,966	19,774	12,984	9,221	12,048	11,413	6,821	42,895	33,927	9,274	6,750	6,196
Congressional District 4	67,822	31,745	22,163	16,741	21,972	20,079	7,811	65,046	49,820	8,454	4,968	4,328
Congressional District 5	64,986	24,410	17,764	13,483	15,042	16,422	7,195	48,911	42,509	10,318	6,615	7,187
Congressional District 6	43,027	17,613	13,244	5,985	8,040	9,366	7,037	37,327	33,242	13,876	9,265	8,842
Congressional District 7	56,076	22,651	17,139	10,397	11,492	11,926	7,334	43,929	37,518	9,018	6,596	7,499
Congressional District 8	40,367	14,152	8,832	9,746	9,231	8,699	9,074	43,556	32,789	11,373	7,424	6,600
Congressional District 9	44,524	16,375	10,956	9,037	12,165	12,501	7,904	41,191	32,449	10,759	8,073	6,716
Congressional District 10	42,833	13,511	8,386	9,222	12,507	11,926	6,858	38,700	31,181	9,312	7,688	6,986
Congressional District 11	61,264	25,996	19,929	15,174	15,311	16,730	5,904	47,993	43,329	8,130	5,891	7,754
Congressional District 12	47,857	14,586	13,259	13,249	10,048	12,813	6,513	43,916	45,889	15,404	12,668	15,483
Congressional District 13	50,536	19,885	12,436	12,279	11,465	11,147	6,389	43,808	35,575	11,783	7,901	9,174
Congressional District 14	61,570	23,164	16,843	15,445	12,389	16,059	5,226	47,495	44,782	8,451	8,219	8,959
Congressional District 15	56,493	19,274	12,858	10,494	9,905	11,090	4,701	37,303	31,468	6,973	6,487	6,507
Congressional District 16	28,422	9,859	5,833	5,342	7,711	7,982	7,072	32,613	26,003	12,512	10,610	9,301
Congressional District 17	47,280	15,268	10,742	10,125	9,296	10,106	3,648	36,675	33,982	6,922	7,872	8,660
Congressional District 18	62,007	23,500	16,476	15,526	15,947	17,427	3,283	46,270	42,946	4,687	5,396	6,795
Congressional District 19	43,945	15,710	8,334	9,714	9,609	7,062	4,359	39,169	29,585	9,589	10,005	10,832
Congressional District 20	45,566	14,929	10,898	12,564	12,156	12,999	5,949	39,147	34,138	6,857	5,906	6,168
Congressional District 21	24,716	8,308	4,269	3,876	5,632	5,849	6,736	27,303	21,157	9,942	8,156	7,852
Congressional District 22	42,782	14,682	11,311	8,849	11,000	12,529	5,409	39,178	34,368	8,315	6,862	7,958
Congressional District 23	44,909	17,265	10,826	7,824	11,548	10,358	6,710	41,915	30,922	9,676	7,116	5,206
Congressional District 24	51,446	20,073	16,165	14,407	17,161	18,710	6,326	48,300	45,840	6,526	4,940	5,982
Congressional District 25	50,521	15,856	8,572	8,778	7,281	6,686	4,726	35,444	25,647	6,016	5,675	5,955
Congressional District 26	52,588	19,610	13,126	12,211	12,893	14,454	5,063	42,614	39,276	6,368	6,026	6,814
Congressional District 27	51,918	17,388	11,408	15,269	9,360	10,920	4,630	48,433	48,576	8,036	11,295	14,967
Congressional District 28	40,117	14,253	9,645	11,591	8,334	9,083	5,222	46,146	44,430	14,947	16,712	19,936
Congressional District 29	28,372	9,946	5,696	4,960	3,198	3,352	4,586	30,274	24,510	12,204	10,692	10,639
Congressional District 30	47,062	18,087	13,704	17,153	10,559	12,639	4,679	45,990	42,848	8,415	8,972	10,321
Congressional District 31	39,334	10,506	6,592	6,140	5,088	5,583	4,919	30,577	25,029	8,927	6,535	6,026
Congressional District 32	39,764	11,109	6,394	6,885	4,879	5,701	4,744	39,532	32,590	9,081	10,187	10,902
Congressional District 33	55,439	24,012	17,539	22,470	16,844	17,669	3,489	51,231	49,367	3,849	5,531	6,643
Congressional District 34	22,105	7,146	4,326	4,346	2,779	2,775	5,401	32,700	29,646	13,022	13,491	15,017
Congressional District 35	31,633	8,451	3,744	4,743	3,237	3,119	4,668	27,179	19,454	7,125	7,411	6,980
Congressional District 36	39,443	22,167	18,648	13,306	19,846	23,591	8,391	67,048	62,540	9,567	9,405	9,369
Congressional District 37	35,146	15,474	11,537	9,497	6,997	8,336	6,353	37,518	35,371	10,638	8,947	10,735
Congressional District 38	45,106	13,592	9,998	7,779	6,438	7,115	5,200	40,740	38,233	7,757	8,496	10,419
Congressional District 39	54,908	16,432	9,971	13,560	8,593	7,443	3,769	43,913	35,716	4,947	6,026	8,702
Congressional District 40	19,814	5,169	3,473	4,801	2,292	2,245	4,808	24,522	20,337	10,240	10,208	9,842
Congressional District 41	34,459	9,596	5,043	4,821	4,492	4,512	4,645	29,455	22,231	8,253	6,772	7,221
Congressional District 42	43,864	13,099	8,277	8,752	8,349	7,018	4,646	38,587	29,122	5,443	5,841	5,727
Congressional District 43	37,506	14,093	9,218	6,710	5,654	5,934	5,463	35,619	29,726	9,753	10,010	9,469
Congressional District 44	28,752	10,463	6,050	4,535	3,544	3,472	4,688	32,014	22,308	11,193	10,374	8,560
Congressional District 45	57,281	17,799	11,745	14,993	11,538	11,377	2,849	44,816	40,181	4,271	4,638	6,857
Congressional District 46	30,246	7,173	5,378	3,773	3,513	4,177	4,044	26,595	23,415	7,107	7,402	6,803
Congressional District 47	43,817	15,464	12,050	7,954	6,586	8,878	5,573	38,884	35,661	10,461	8,987	8,593
Congressional District 48	56,458	20,330	12,857	15,979	14,466	12,676	3,693	53,671	44,370	5,778	6,914	8,301
Congressional District 49	50,226	15,810	13,296	14,326	12,959	14,617	3,239	42,375	40,528	3,091	3,937	5,268
Congressional District 50	52,309	14,434	10,945	13,000	11,145	13,376	5,271	42,369	39,359	6,556	4,945	6,030

Table I-5: 113th Congressional Districts—Persons With Health Insurance by Source of Insurance—*Continued*

| | Private Health Insurance Coverage | | | | | | Public Health Insurance Coverage | | | | | |
| | Employer Based | | | Direct Purchase | | | Medicare | | | Medicaid/CHIP | | |
	55 to 64 Years	65 to 74 Years	75 Years and Over	55 to 64 Years	65 to 74 Years	75 Years and Over	55 to 64 Years	65 to 74 Years	75 Years and Over	55 to 64 Years	65 to 74 Years	75 Years and Over
California—Cont.												
Congressional District 51	27,792	8,105	5,151	4,596	4,834	5,490	6,624	33,390	31,012	13,038	12,256	14,037
Congressional District 52	53,542	17,970	12,128	13,480	10,538	12,014	3,376	41,905	38,244	3,766	5,415	6,776
Congressional District 53	44,210	14,664	10,846	10,411	8,549	9,988	5,460	38,488	35,462	7,537	6,644	7,411
Colorado												
Congressional District 1	47,785	15,211	11,667	12,408	11,147	12,642	5,818	39,017	33,697	9,563	6,848	6,782
Congressional District 2	66,307	21,062	11,692	20,008	15,483	13,411	4,366	45,905	30,749	4,677	3,108	3,942
Congressional District 3	54,845	20,210	14,565	19,537	21,895	17,061	8,224	56,619	41,031	8,930	6,637	6,202
Congressional District 4	53,373	16,200	8,357	15,010	16,154	12,859	5,075	43,650	31,403	5,728	4,765	5,077
Congressional District 5	49,774	14,847	9,947	12,172	14,971	12,119	6,521	45,705	32,381	5,742	4,592	3,630
Congressional District 6	54,552	16,973	9,833	12,430	12,332	10,771	4,185	38,223	26,976	5,178	4,247	4,227
Congressional District 7	57,309	19,827	13,322	10,929	14,889	14,648	5,043	43,263	35,203	5,457	4,998	5,069
Connecticut												
Congressional District 1	68,578	24,806	19,620	9,436	14,830	19,850	8,120	49,096	49,019	7,236	6,749	7,887
Congressional District 2	72,174	28,459	17,567	10,545	17,854	18,341	6,452	53,344	42,608	5,293	6,474	6,415
Congressional District 3	65,757	24,411	18,325	10,194	14,542	19,965	6,176	48,534	47,195	6,920	5,576	6,902
Congressional District 4	59,265	22,119	17,524	14,564	15,796	18,816	5,030	46,331	44,093	6,308	4,768	6,016
Congressional District 5	66,324	23,789	17,308	11,158	15,868	19,318	6,626	49,246	45,399	7,537	6,226	7,606
Delaware												
Congressional District (at Large)	82,003	40,295	28,065	12,902	21,792	18,856	10,883	72,990	54,435	11,703	7,773	7,191
District of Columbia												
Delegate District (at Large)	40,810	22,291	16,711	9,436	8,845	9,221	5,322	33,397	28,770	16,208	8,349	7,394
Florida												
Congressional District 1	46,783	19,043	12,565	12,553	18,825	15,183	9,861	57,024	40,572	5,695	6,215	5,212
Congressional District 2	50,262	19,329	12,774	10,796	16,122	11,539	8,854	49,790	36,022	7,346	6,410	5,674
Congressional District 3	47,090	19,150	13,858	10,392	17,776	16,867	9,953	57,902	42,945	9,266	6,469	5,771
Congressional District 4	55,067	18,732	10,454	10,591	14,739	13,273	7,304	46,807	34,921	6,033	4,928	4,273
Congressional District 5	37,479	11,261	6,321	6,806	9,134	9,719	10,089	38,953	30,759	12,471	8,564	7,040
Congressional District 6	60,385	31,480	24,087	15,643	25,729	26,176	10,730	80,572	64,417	8,965	8,488	8,373
Congressional District 7	54,157	16,723	13,758	9,730	12,779	14,376	6,530	46,066	40,221	5,861	4,340	5,143
Congressional District 8	55,652	29,450	25,659	13,389	23,500	28,413	11,725	76,744	72,086	8,041	6,696	8,366
Congressional District 9	42,275	14,407	7,171	7,879	8,848	7,981	6,542	43,379	28,604	5,481	6,729	5,145
Congressional District 10	53,153	23,872	18,622	12,681	18,868	19,869	8,067	63,868	52,856	5,435	5,410	7,231
Congressional District 11	55,281	42,576	32,362	15,693	41,255	36,866	13,225	116,052	91,078	9,305	10,101	9,699
Congressional District 12	55,528	24,059	20,621	13,722	22,524	23,996	10,654	71,447	63,744	8,755	7,181	7,819
Congressional District 13	59,059	23,383	22,048	13,932	21,016	27,686	9,178	71,622	73,031	8,194	7,763	8,837
Congressional District 14	39,606	12,219	7,406	8,613	9,467	10,733	9,533	42,249	35,018	13,144	7,912	9,278
Congressional District 15	49,587	16,502	11,952	10,189	12,834	14,291	9,086	50,715	39,963	9,139	6,498	4,933
Congressional District 16	58,735	37,917	37,023	18,924	35,432	42,045	8,616	96,884	92,924	6,392	7,691	8,456
Congressional District 17	49,599	34,179	30,212	13,154	31,010	32,102	11,751	91,093	79,570	8,228	9,659	10,318
Congressional District 18	55,304	29,119	25,053	17,006	27,186	32,070	8,789	78,438	76,114	6,595	6,546	7,407
Congressional District 19	57,340	38,878	28,501	18,692	38,759	36,885	7,696	99,146	81,733	6,022	7,915	8,931
Congressional District 20	35,370	11,301	7,885	7,722	8,907	13,522	7,256	43,753	41,473	9,048	8,840	8,080
Congressional District 21	49,516	22,142	23,032	13,798	21,294	37,363	6,001	66,438	83,509	4,864	5,767	8,369
Congressional District 22	52,329	20,801	20,333	20,206	20,045	31,370	5,513	64,032	72,232	6,231	6,406	7,814
Congressional District 23	48,002	12,874	9,093	13,794	12,906	17,423	6,405	50,248	51,819	6,557	8,977	10,575
Congressional District 24	31,695	7,349	2,987	8,103	4,766	4,773	6,878	37,853	29,143	10,487	12,807	12,874
Congressional District 25	31,950	10,785	7,055	6,766	9,756	8,201	5,104	51,556	44,212	7,134	15,845	16,211
Congressional District 26	39,803	11,063	4,790	9,999	7,119	5,893	5,293	51,023	43,183	6,459	13,542	16,694
Congressional District 27	32,844	8,603	4,431	7,988	6,797	7,407	5,739	53,065	53,900	9,711	19,544	23,861
Georgia												
Congressional District 1	43,591	18,203	10,452	9,274	12,876	11,555	9,219	46,935	33,576	7,547	5,820	6,149
Congressional District 2	42,216	16,723	10,518	8,666	12,801	11,508	12,291	47,830	34,856	12,425	10,080	8,466
Congressional District 3	53,984	19,417	10,642	8,682	14,500	12,856	8,612	49,291	32,229	6,614	6,626	5,369
Congressional District 4	50,878	15,659	8,645	8,177	8,876	8,228	7,278	34,309	23,150	4,918	6,097	4,748
Congressional District 5	36,174	14,256	7,711	9,021	7,592	6,963	8,177	33,178	24,841	10,054	8,241	6,923
Congressional District 6	58,710	17,849	9,926	13,824	11,955	10,670	2,844	38,862	26,982	1,665	3,437	2,705
Congressional District 7	47,073	14,861	6,085	8,377	8,454	7,744	3,497	30,350	18,722	2,338	3,223	3,518
Congressional District 8	44,954	18,670	11,551	8,737	13,073	12,367	11,341	49,223	35,620	8,737	8,115	7,504
Congressional District 9	52,604	23,665	12,342	11,529	19,425	14,986	9,365	62,211	40,216	6,599	6,928	6,499
Congressional District 10	51,981	21,820	11,668	10,015	13,467	10,728	9,382	47,589	29,998	7,184	7,344	5,859
Congressional District 11	49,015	16,360	8,659	10,265	13,273	9,612	5,505	39,141	24,245	3,856	3,024	2,885
Congressional District 12	45,294	16,952	8,500	8,693	11,158	8,801	10,995	46,912	31,149	9,675	8,481	6,609
Congressional District 13	46,588	14,365	7,739	7,510	10,129	7,160	6,427	34,254	21,911	5,717	4,958	3,848
Congressional District 14	47,829	15,621	10,130	7,684	15,848	13,410	10,279	48,556	32,455	7,241	6,917	6,748
Hawaii												
Congressional District 1	63,643	32,185	28,249	14,630	13,193	17,338	4,966	49,311	52,303	6,961	6,907	8,655
Congressional District 2	63,993	27,501	17,994	15,804	12,351	11,899	6,066	47,456	38,417	8,481	5,724	5,535
Idaho												
Congressional District 1	55,146	19,309	11,425	17,869	25,217	21,476	9,447	60,179	42,542	6,837	5,318	5,591
Congressional District 2	53,597	15,109	12,274	15,808	22,751	20,092	7,862	51,494	40,979	5,246	5,156	5,474

Table I-5: 113th Congressional Districts—Persons With Health Insurance by Source of Insurance—Continued

| | Private Health Insurance Coverage | | | | | | Public Health Insurance Coverage | | | | | |
| | Employer Based | | | Direct Purchase | | | Medicare | | | Medicaid/CHIP | | |
	55 to 64 Years	65 to 74 Years	75 Years and Over	55 to 64 Years	65 to 74 Years	75 Years and Over	55 to 64 Years	65 to 74 Years	75 Years and Over	55 to 64 Years	65 to 74 Years	75 Years and Over
Illinois												
Congressional District 1	54,388	21,318	16,419	7,750	13,408	14,724	7,731	46,910	43,171	10,134	7,910	7,578
Congressional District 2	55,039	22,351	15,171	8,948	14,598	15,105	8,354	47,668	39,530	9,034	7,651	6,560
Congressional District 3	56,559	17,528	14,364	7,338	13,622	18,196	5,532	42,459	40,863	5,105	4,555	5,396
Congressional District 4	28,886	7,898	4,406	4,097	5,247	7,134	5,587	27,723	21,623	6,832	5,099	4,416
Congressional District 5	49,771	15,920	10,428	8,645	11,770	15,748	5,357	38,900	38,151	4,689	5,064	6,063
Congressional District 6	73,358	21,725	14,500	13,015	17,511	18,383	3,255	46,023	36,212	2,449	3,481	3,184
Congressional District 7	39,251	14,305	7,073	6,912	8,627	7,808	7,604	39,136	29,618	11,341	8,703	7,323
Congressional District 8	59,969	14,793	8,762	8,666	13,690	13,414	3,933	36,127	30,221	3,327	3,336	4,039
Congressional District 9	60,307	19,941	15,698	12,407	17,517	23,445	5,376	50,675	50,942	7,301	6,980	7,508
Congressional District 10	58,155	18,020	10,937	11,997	15,324	17,074	4,408	42,098	35,972	3,310	4,540	4,329
Congressional District 11	54,715	18,622	10,456	7,297	13,148	12,048	4,251	36,825	27,296	3,229	3,722	3,746
Congressional District 12	56,443	22,360	18,269	9,611	17,886	19,231	10,432	51,814	44,979	7,746	6,147	6,033
Congressional District 13	60,254	24,247	18,859	10,228	17,400	18,975	7,233	48,445	41,339	5,487	4,841	4,774
Congressional District 14	62,784	19,180	9,048	10,608	16,515	13,259	3,662	41,274	26,562	2,480	2,744	2,707
Congressional District 15	59,310	23,172	18,294	13,361	23,830	26,040	8,476	58,251	50,862	5,959	6,642	6,373
Congressional District 16	64,703	22,311	15,439	12,533	23,437	24,358	6,565	54,048	44,810	4,253	4,728	5,074
Congressional District 17	61,937	24,018	20,348	10,467	23,662	24,453	8,440	57,307	50,434	7,457	6,559	6,208
Congressional District 18	69,857	27,881	21,426	13,656	22,414	23,509	6,151	55,436	48,601	4,483	4,952	4,773
Indiana												
Congressional District 1	64,648	20,973	15,963	10,320	18,137	16,509	8,440	49,684	41,304	7,313	5,646	5,474
Congressional District 2	59,443	17,336	12,867	10,567	19,189	21,307	8,217	49,638	44,220	5,798	4,557	4,877
Congressional District 3	59,805	16,082	12,737	11,635	18,249	19,016	7,177	49,281	39,940	5,665	3,970	3,546
Congressional District 4	60,614	20,713	15,252	9,642	20,888	20,354	6,647	50,291	39,277	5,034	4,563	3,037
Congressional District 5	63,314	21,777	16,827	10,567	17,900	17,173	6,110	45,169	38,038	4,257	4,126	3,857
Congressional District 6	60,978	24,137	16,672	10,070	21,716	20,838	10,200	57,247	44,308	7,125	5,561	4,877
Congressional District 7	45,435	16,069	12,345	6,956	13,626	13,320	9,131	39,144	30,771	10,380	6,410	4,886
Congressional District 8	62,400	20,106	15,122	11,003	23,384	23,339	9,918	55,202	45,052	6,754	5,631	5,066
Congressional District 9	61,632	20,963	14,040	9,889	21,609	19,093	8,926	52,060	38,303	5,869	4,890	4,576
Iowa												
Congressional District 1	69,886	21,272	15,795	16,506	28,728	32,111	6,571	57,646	53,575	6,758	6,182	7,341
Congressional District 2	68,776	19,658	15,443	15,062	28,561	28,906	8,165	55,949	49,657	8,925	7,158	7,948
Congressional District 3	64,080	17,345	13,512	13,685	22,794	23,334	6,786	49,926	42,158	8,523	5,965	5,663
Congressional District 4	63,748	16,089	11,856	21,133	31,967	39,786	6,676	58,998	60,878	7,451	6,808	8,676
Kansas												
Congressional District 1	54,724	13,909	9,061	14,767	23,874	29,363	6,308	48,043	48,717	4,504	4,951	6,470
Congressional District 2	58,988	20,575	14,038	12,471	23,637	24,018	7,823	52,403	43,712	6,507	5,769	5,691
Congressional District 3	61,981	16,231	12,149	11,808	17,257	17,283	4,850	41,482	34,509	3,273	3,324	4,424
Congressional District 4	58,735	12,775	8,968	10,658	20,794	23,621	7,777	46,184	41,894	6,390	5,277	5,407
Kentucky												
Congressional District 1	55,857	24,090	15,337	13,052	21,051	19,436	14,879	62,469	45,020	10,952	8,830	7,329
Congressional District 2	57,365	22,026	13,749	11,315	19,927	17,070	11,497	53,963	39,085	9,210	7,462	6,345
Congressional District 3	61,930	22,017	17,574	11,683	18,924	20,743	10,557	48,806	43,950	8,156	6,712	6,233
Congressional District 4	62,632	21,552	12,889	11,889	16,909	15,017	10,101	50,086	34,216	7,408	6,581	4,726
Congressional District 5	44,407	18,977	12,658	10,105	16,603	11,362	24,751	60,997	38,597	17,908	13,961	8,418
Congressional District 6	55,191	21,852	13,519	10,568	16,545	14,217	10,925	48,310	34,884	9,815	6,864	5,630
Louisiana												
Congressional District 1	61,796	21,264	12,786	14,326	15,209	16,469	9,459	52,740	44,062	7,820	5,448	6,852
Congressional District 2	47,888	14,496	8,373	12,069	10,132	9,316	12,611	46,932	33,151	15,154	11,900	8,812
Congressional District 3	52,087	18,722	12,978	12,771	18,104	16,729	10,789	49,366	36,995	8,411	7,244	6,271
Congressional District 4	50,254	21,274	14,488	10,466	16,756	15,369	12,327	55,025	42,188	10,415	9,602	8,330
Congressional District 5	45,716	20,206	13,037	11,618	15,439	13,962	13,416	52,993	41,576	12,676	11,646	11,310
Congressional District 6	58,570	20,792	13,087	11,937	14,304	12,439	8,780	47,574	32,566	7,331	5,162	4,531
Maine												
Congressional District 1	64,987	22,886	16,792	12,928	19,491	20,884	8,294	54,587	46,771	9,590	7,740	8,918
Congressional District 2	57,848	18,958	13,744	12,721	21,079	20,544	12,242	58,291	46,400	13,357	13,712	11,245
Maryland												
Congressional District 1	72,562	34,704	21,813	13,270	19,502	18,752	7,285	61,351	45,361	6,693	5,896	5,925
Congressional District 2	60,457	21,668	16,467	9,406	13,917	15,807	7,758	40,887	37,725	8,123	5,179	5,330
Congressional District 3	66,378	25,405	20,554	11,958	13,392	17,105	5,228	44,036	44,313	5,861	4,776	6,617
Congressional District 4	63,375	30,041	14,397	10,042	10,140	8,360	4,895	40,463	26,883	5,035	4,943	4,277
Congressional District 5	68,165	29,270	15,650	8,362	10,696	8,327	4,679	43,694	28,426	4,651	4,632	3,518
Congressional District 6	63,999	26,736	16,273	10,495	14,651	13,114	5,572	46,244	34,924	5,014	5,249	5,251
Congressional District 7	56,117	24,403	16,837	10,369	14,209	14,432	8,957	47,621	39,262	12,205	8,654	8,547
Congressional District 8	71,194	30,343	22,746	11,648	13,564	17,397	3,285	46,347	45,216	3,082	3,843	5,965
Massachusetts												
Congressional District 1	69,001	24,390	19,538	10,578	17,820	21,389	9,180	52,554	50,898	18,838	9,268	9,855
Congressional District 2	67,907	23,371	17,005	8,438	15,460	17,411	6,389	45,524	41,008	13,982	7,550	7,630
Congressional District 3	65,686	21,672	15,011	10,143	14,653	15,135	7,087	44,730	38,096	15,748	8,676	8,378
Congressional District 4	73,707	25,321	16,710	10,445	17,005	18,359	6,193	47,135	42,887	9,335	6,643	8,153
Congressional District 5	68,064	27,220	20,323	11,734	16,283	18,862	5,279	47,293	48,504	11,205	6,398	8,291
Congressional District 6	76,750	29,042	20,740	12,350	19,447	20,790	5,985	54,088	48,739	12,487	7,981	9,177
Congressional District 7	38,054	13,598	8,472	7,745	7,486	8,555	5,675	34,826	31,775	19,430	12,667	12,041
Congressional District 8	67,841	25,760	20,814	9,301	15,367	18,483	6,144	48,679	48,371	14,316	8,466	9,557
Congressional District 9	73,987	34,813	22,779	14,942	24,585	24,311	8,382	67,803	57,767	16,478	8,648	9,483

Table I-5: 113th Congressional Districts—Persons With Health Insurance by Source of Insurance—*Continued*

	Private Health Insurance Coverage						Public Health Insurance Coverage					
	Employer Based			Direct Purchase			Medicare			Medicaid/CHIP		
	55 to 64 Years	65 to 74 Years	75 Years and Over	55 to 64 Years	65 to 74 Years	75 Years and Over	55 to 64 Years	65 to 74 Years	75 Years and Over	55 to 64 Years	65 to 74 Years	75 Years and Over
Michigan												
Congressional District 1	69,669	35,102	26,879	16,035	28,279	25,670	12,272	72,523	57,493	10,048	7,624	8,124
Congressional District 2	58,709	21,520	15,822	11,091	18,432	18,212	8,557	48,345	40,572	6,865	5,365	5,817
Congressional District 3	58,555	22,276	17,727	10,587	17,086	17,955	8,181	45,799	39,355	8,275	5,118	5,342
Congressional District 4	64,872	35,189	25,962	10,894	21,346	19,935	10,507	61,435	46,216	9,201	6,486	5,494
Congressional District 5	64,780	35,542	28,057	10,498	18,528	17,171	12,748	56,679	46,586	13,312	8,383	6,480
Congressional District 6	61,242	24,241	18,207	12,701	20,166	19,331	9,544	53,513	43,063	9,152	5,941	6,010
Congressional District 7	71,586	30,488	22,082	11,353	19,377	17,618	8,927	54,663	42,553	7,046	5,424	4,923
Congressional District 8	71,108	26,774	16,771	10,967	17,081	14,894	6,180	47,331	32,928	6,184	4,434	3,865
Congressional District 9	60,529	25,914	25,837	11,911	20,404	24,113	8,694	51,911	52,510	9,558	6,367	6,592
Congressional District 10	69,767	30,826	22,376	12,451	21,711	18,653	9,001	56,122	42,385	7,469	5,665	5,078
Congressional District 11	71,916	25,745	21,634	12,056	19,767	19,073	5,618	49,132	41,780	4,563	4,314	4,026
Congressional District 12	62,494	25,834	21,460	8,567	13,887	15,161	8,308	42,458	36,823	8,913	5,450	5,077
Congressional District 13	45,733	21,517	19,922	6,696	10,268	13,021	13,103	42,573	40,067	17,591	11,380	8,180
Congressional District 14	57,842	25,726	21,906	10,159	14,132	15,604	12,020	46,878	44,051	14,135	8,745	8,959
Minnesota												
Congressional District 1	57,092	15,511	13,108	14,835	25,064	27,125	4,875	47,535	46,940	5,593	4,217	6,088
Congressional District 2	58,385	15,262	9,983	10,132	19,121	17,037	4,354	38,077	29,103	3,858	2,711	3,414
Congressional District 3	66,242	16,018	10,725	13,508	21,269	20,965	3,804	42,710	35,254	4,052	3,658	4,492
Congressional District 4	59,726	17,667	13,649	9,446	18,711	17,789	5,773	40,341	35,034	7,491	4,201	4,493
Congressional District 5	46,405	12,244	10,976	8,107	15,623	18,317	5,807	33,604	33,390	9,893	5,159	4,774
Congressional District 6	54,321	13,237	7,156	11,251	19,340	15,342	3,899	37,222	25,399	3,944	3,037	3,311
Congressional District 7	54,699	12,951	9,284	19,111	30,987	34,372	6,139	55,575	52,924	6,843	5,176	6,722
Congressional District 8	60,005	19,867	14,907	15,870	30,441	27,560	9,125	59,896	47,524	9,542	5,661	6,788
Mississippi												
Congressional District 1	49,801	16,171	10,053	11,461	20,072	16,533	14,933	55,380	40,287	11,258	9,116	9,533
Congressional District 2	41,612	12,631	7,221	11,232	14,762	12,224	16,501	48,569	37,219	15,655	13,147	12,267
Congressional District 3	51,090	16,799	10,064	13,232	18,713	17,316	13,228	54,618	41,287	10,521	10,425	9,373
Congressional District 4	46,740	15,726	10,359	11,222	18,104	13,897	13,553	55,138	37,971	11,057	8,932	6,847
Missouri												
Congressional District 1	52,219	19,054	14,019	8,806	11,376	13,563	11,442	43,345	40,202	9,656	7,278	6,895
Congressional District 2	80,282	26,737	20,006	13,533	21,010	22,677	4,512	57,762	51,966	2,810	3,137	3,635
Congressional District 3	67,307	24,220	14,308	11,976	18,847	16,129	8,756	55,857	38,442	4,874	3,937	3,876
Congressional District 4	53,550	21,011	14,407	13,058	21,993	20,200	9,970	57,707	44,551	6,815	5,893	5,854
Congressional District 5	55,199	19,687	15,130	10,665	19,272	20,910	9,404	50,031	44,077	7,373	5,463	5,161
Congressional District 6	61,664	20,185	11,485	13,626	24,132	23,042	8,585	55,097	43,213	5,748	5,058	4,446
Congressional District 7	52,716	16,195	11,073	12,046	24,756	22,330	12,424	62,464	46,389	8,527	7,350	5,715
Congressional District 8	53,506	18,086	13,673	12,623	22,883	20,888	17,530	64,384	48,606	11,858	9,736	8,997
Montana												
Congressional District (at Large)	80,988	25,949	18,022	25,687	33,482	32,837	12,466	81,439	62,831	9,968	7,503	7,022
Nebraska												
Congressional District 1	51,056	14,039	9,428	10,781	17,242	20,768	4,662	39,000	36,002	3,754	3,425	4,375
Congressional District 2	48,299	12,504	8,844	9,635	12,606	11,809	4,810	32,360	27,086	4,164	2,972	3,629
Congressional District 3	49,026	12,873	9,081	18,452	25,715	30,455	6,748	48,743	49,115	5,107	5,127	6,321
Nevada												
Congressional District 1	39,682	15,371	8,187	5,610	8,803	7,891	6,744	43,238	30,364	6,721	8,123	5,409
Congressional District 2	56,024	20,806	11,877	12,471	16,419	12,458	5,796	53,148	34,954	4,698	5,047	4,426
Congressional District 3	55,063	22,620	10,666	12,039	12,396	8,427	5,550	51,326	30,769	2,909	4,568	4,597
Congressional District 4	46,156	18,034	9,882	8,181	11,051	8,311	6,527	46,001	30,353	4,681	3,684	2,879
New Hampshire												
Congressional District 1	65,536	22,802	14,077	9,956	16,625	16,765	6,745	48,164	36,958	4,265	3,687	4,302
Congressional District 2	69,603	21,593	14,727	9,493	17,004	16,893	6,551	48,836	38,486	4,298	4,326	4,624
New Jersey												
Congressional District 1	65,341	22,996	16,743	9,192	15,309	17,811	7,497	48,526	42,171	7,842	6,577	6,322
Congressional District 2	67,475	29,642	18,621	12,837	20,379	20,333	9,061	59,081	48,182	9,231	6,490	7,284
Congressional District 3	72,687	33,445	24,959	11,295	20,704	25,259	7,489	60,762	58,511	3,988	5,372	6,802
Congressional District 4	68,367	32,075	24,525	10,502	20,092	26,432	6,323	58,919	57,761	4,558	4,951	6,099
Congressional District 5	77,269	28,353	17,056	12,170	15,389	19,029	4,532	51,997	47,084	3,881	3,937	5,508
Congressional District 6	64,925	22,179	14,116	8,808	11,180	13,111	5,343	41,449	36,497	5,072	5,368	6,611
Congressional District 7	78,038	28,229	17,602	10,680	14,514	16,829	4,326	46,516	42,826	3,444	3,741	4,995
Congressional District 8	33,896	10,356	6,534	5,980	6,456	7,487	6,335	32,431	29,386	10,405	8,034	9,523
Congressional District 9	50,297	18,265	12,428	7,150	9,732	13,972	6,586	44,675	44,657	7,097	7,800	9,255
Congressional District 10	47,133	18,179	9,603	7,985	7,984	8,583	7,782	41,770	32,402	10,732	9,078	8,501
Congressional District 11	79,197	31,288	21,556	13,170	16,117	20,729	4,309	53,796	53,076	3,563	4,631	6,190
Congressional District 12	65,009	26,296	18,102	8,263	13,153	15,989	5,366	45,721	42,838	5,690	5,180	6,140
New Mexico												
Congressional District 1	52,797	20,514	14,195	11,604	9,256	10,552	7,889	47,169	37,673	10,168	6,590	5,946
Congressional District 2	42,396	18,784	14,255	11,699	16,048	13,157	9,166	54,299	42,239	11,582	7,760	8,240
Congressional District 3	47,401	19,832	10,847	13,782	14,114	10,358	8,737	51,505	34,810	8,682	6,198	5,927

Table I-5: 113th Congressional Districts—Persons With Health Insurance by Source of Insurance—*Continued*

| | Private Health Insurance Coverage | | | | | | Public Health Insurance Coverage | | | | | |
| | Employer Based | | | Direct Purchase | | | Medicare | | | Medicaid/CHIP | | |
	55 to 64 Years	65 to 74 Years	75 Years and Over	55 to 64 Years	65 to 74 Years	75 Years and Over	55 to 64 Years	65 to 74 Years	75 Years and Over	55 to 64 Years	65 to 74 Years	75 Years and Over
New York												
Congressional District 1	70,031	34,595	20,300	14,208	14,337	16,438	6,398	54,963	43,106	5,108	4,177	4,142
Congressional District 2	67,759	26,457	17,813	8,863	11,596	15,483	7,232	44,844	43,619	6,246	5,096	5,778
Congressional District 3	75,714	32,660	24,744	17,811	17,356	23,701	5,250	56,862	59,717	5,337	4,483	7,175
Congressional District 4	70,870	26,884	20,772	10,414	12,818	18,713	5,831	48,132	49,205	5,952	4,985	6,029
Congressional District 5	54,966	19,279	11,230	6,989	6,259	6,449	6,017	43,875	35,271	15,936	12,333	9,899
Congressional District 6	52,156	17,682	12,912	9,690	7,841	11,186	6,901	50,603	47,541	16,131	12,174	12,265
Congressional District 7	26,291	7,704	5,043	5,724	3,324	3,695	6,266	31,905	30,228	24,368	14,488	14,040
Congressional District 8	48,311	16,445	8,347	6,633	6,040	6,118	7,019	44,808	38,427	17,904	16,206	17,118
Congressional District 9	49,894	17,900	8,359	6,514	5,392	6,037	6,112	41,981	35,592	18,557	13,740	14,486
Congressional District 10	51,262	20,255	12,883	12,611	10,402	10,556	4,965	44,952	42,574	15,003	9,218	12,352
Congressional District 11	60,441	23,278	13,765	9,523	7,662	8,657	7,783	52,025	44,983	14,220	9,701	12,737
Congressional District 12	45,414	22,620	13,412	12,278	12,974	13,755	5,710	47,528	41,607	9,396	8,353	8,101
Congressional District 13	30,882	11,767	6,513	5,351	3,817	3,586	7,727	40,422	33,107	30,510	19,356	16,926
Congressional District 14	38,738	13,468	9,259	6,522	6,114	7,528	5,851	38,698	35,752	16,574	10,650	11,291
Congressional District 15	22,210	8,711	3,214	6,267	4,634	2,845	7,928	32,996	22,846	28,941	18,497	13,357
Congressional District 16	60,690	25,832	17,683	9,261	9,972	14,506	6,869	48,679	47,115	10,510	8,535	9,088
Congressional District 17	68,042	29,791	21,047	10,452	12,908	16,019	4,308	48,487	46,880	5,336	4,414	6,357
Congressional District 18	67,283	27,768	18,497	9,011	13,136	13,206	7,131	47,555	38,087	6,449	4,798	5,369
Congressional District 19	75,712	33,330	20,685	11,092	17,985	18,030	9,318	61,065	46,943	9,728	5,527	6,180
Congressional District 20	73,219	30,617	25,972	8,843	14,111	17,789	7,560	49,714	46,758	8,796	5,722	6,030
Congressional District 21	65,705	29,233	19,568	9,607	18,544	17,952	9,902	55,448	43,775	9,926	6,297	6,885
Congressional District 22	65,102	27,781	23,854	10,342	17,533	20,023	10,060	56,527	50,094	11,212	6,840	7,576
Congressional District 23	68,595	27,558	21,235	10,803	18,803	19,488	10,696	55,421	47,672	10,905	6,238	6,904
Congressional District 24	67,978	27,272	21,004	9,704	14,669	18,094	9,509	49,971	45,793	9,940	5,399	6,502
Congressional District 25	67,264	28,366	26,097	9,994	17,020	17,078	7,587	50,061	46,294	9,005	6,142	5,735
Congressional District 26	61,850	26,334	22,096	10,083	17,648	23,262	11,044	51,642	54,518	14,774	7,432	8,914
Congressional District 27	80,445	31,684	20,847	12,486	21,766	22,974	8,391	58,055	48,316	7,078	5,366	6,646
North Carolina												
Congressional District 1	47,315	19,052	12,835	13,472	15,608	15,972	14,050	53,751	42,567	13,978	11,934	12,869
Congressional District 2	48,249	17,523	10,059	11,187	16,587	13,938	9,254	49,919	36,718	6,843	5,620	4,636
Congressional District 3	51,147	25,084	14,169	13,717	19,588	16,722	10,732	55,721	39,034	7,490	6,409	6,265
Congressional District 4	44,438	18,724	12,246	9,349	10,714	10,205	7,073	38,091	28,441	6,209	5,975	4,551
Congressional District 5	60,592	23,487	16,008	15,437	22,373	20,324	10,089	60,045	46,305	6,474	6,634	6,123
Congressional District 6	65,477	21,570	15,959	14,580	22,630	21,701	11,149	60,742	48,199	6,966	6,227	6,306
Congressional District 7	60,037	27,310	15,288	13,849	23,826	18,281	13,052	66,721	41,296	8,515	7,774	6,710
Congressional District 8	52,116	17,720	10,093	11,413	18,969	16,672	13,618	55,342	37,990	9,997	6,935	6,543
Congressional District 9	57,094	18,562	11,364	13,425	16,961	14,929	5,140	44,946	31,609	3,170	3,418	3,548
Congressional District 10	58,065	19,197	11,693	14,663	23,504	19,733	13,338	61,269	44,488	9,410	7,808	7,811
Congressional District 11	57,774	26,124	19,970	17,020	30,413	25,654	14,807	78,333	59,083	8,206	7,850	8,764
Congressional District 12	36,122	11,339	7,278	7,145	10,012	10,073	9,712	34,142	25,307	8,479	6,328	5,327
Congressional District 13	64,428	23,369	13,047	12,846	18,650	13,505	8,388	48,893	32,898	4,876	4,461	4,337
North Dakota												
Congressional District (at Large)	57,111	15,367	9,955	17,520	24,229	29,510	5,798	46,265	44,786	3,054	4,861	5,459
Ohio												
Congressional District 1	59,420	20,959	15,089	8,463	14,542	14,836	7,644	45,576	37,268	5,533	4,155	4,098
Congressional District 2	63,519	21,856	17,708	10,502	15,630	17,476	8,613	50,912	44,134	7,364	5,631	5,249
Congressional District 3	44,929	15,958	11,275	6,117	8,779	9,835	8,004	33,690	27,540	8,059	5,951	3,843
Congressional District 4	66,029	25,657	20,740	10,491	19,487	19,585	8,533	54,188	45,396	6,029	4,894	4,894
Congressional District 5	72,905	27,173	21,728	11,400	21,230	21,295	6,657	54,612	46,974	4,588	3,823	4,380
Congressional District 6	66,268	27,944	21,154	10,688	20,763	20,413	11,916	64,536	51,105	9,117	7,385	6,751
Congressional District 7	69,043	28,001	19,717	11,237	18,918	20,333	8,094	56,886	45,412	4,784	5,367	5,415
Congressional District 8	64,746	24,521	19,026	10,260	16,648	16,225	8,244	52,732	41,897	5,803	4,409	4,749
Congressional District 9	58,377	22,705	19,674	8,446	14,787	16,500	9,750	47,394	43,898	8,587	6,074	5,987
Congressional District 10	63,609	24,074	20,626	9,718	15,790	16,590	8,148	54,489	48,349	6,365	5,553	5,391
Congressional District 11	54,906	22,523	19,528	8,601	11,635	15,294	10,286	48,071	47,703	13,212	9,315	9,816
Congressional District 12	68,202	24,989	17,192	10,252	16,371	15,093	6,472	49,677	37,102	3,927	4,411	3,594
Congressional District 13	66,301	23,965	22,039	10,396	15,707	19,562	9,144	55,584	53,316	7,689	6,070	6,164
Congressional District 14	77,246	27,978	21,649	11,735	21,152	22,125	6,111	58,136	51,680	3,606	4,369	4,763
Congressional District 15	62,220	24,274	16,200	9,647	15,200	13,748	7,205	49,101	37,256	4,625	4,766	4,095
Congressional District 16	76,163	31,005	25,034	12,282	18,085	20,829	5,253	60,484	52,636	4,320	4,363	4,855
Oklahoma												
Congressional District 1	58,764	19,738	13,327	11,443	19,460	19,259	7,879	50,325	40,680	4,950	4,896	4,559
Congressional District 2	47,711	21,739	13,334	12,155	22,567	17,882	14,909	68,920	47,883	9,110	9,848	9,026
Congressional District 3	54,288	21,171	14,127	12,103	21,159	20,399	9,467	57,595	44,797	6,046	5,795	5,925
Congressional District 4	53,977	21,921	13,975	11,307	17,397	15,450	9,107	52,821	38,187	5,052	5,758	4,631
Congressional District 5	53,091	19,121	14,791	9,222	15,615	16,398	9,888	48,280	39,820	6,430	5,991	5,497
Oregon												
Congressional District 1	63,751	18,096	12,823	13,761	19,781	18,179	6,231	48,724	38,046	5,042	5,339	5,863
Congressional District 2	61,236	21,106	17,078	20,326	29,439	28,034	10,726	71,695	57,027	9,271	7,789	7,780
Congressional District 3	59,543	18,038	12,052	13,578	16,186	16,552	8,831	45,488	36,281	9,128	6,191	6,834
Congressional District 4	66,249	24,025	18,496	16,217	31,257	28,271	11,575	71,914	57,510	11,298	8,214	8,192
Congressional District 5	67,753	22,730	17,269	15,719	24,808	24,907	8,257	59,263	48,661	7,663	6,679	6,789

Table I-5: 113th Congressional Districts—Persons With Health Insurance by Source of Insurance—*Continued*

	Private Health Insurance Coverage						Public Health Insurance Coverage					
	Employer Based			Direct Purchase			Medicare			Medicaid/CHIP		
	55 to 64 Years	65 to 74 Years	75 Years and Over	55 to 64 Years	65 to 74 Years	75 Years and Over	55 to 64 Years	65 to 74 Years	75 Years and Over	55 to 64 Years	65 to 74 Years	75 Years and Over
Pennsylvania												
Congressional District 1	40,350	13,790	8,698	8,688	12,427	13,552	8,839	38,238	33,524	15,623	8,556	7,261
Congressional District 2	42,782	17,072	10,703	10,542	13,730	14,577	9,057	45,080	39,849	18,609	10,753	10,105
Congressional District 3	64,171	20,224	17,415	13,067	24,875	28,074	10,002	56,853	52,925	11,278	6,900	6,958
Congressional District 4	69,334	22,381	16,153	10,710	21,657	23,094	6,941	53,093	46,271	6,873	5,370	5,290
Congressional District 5	64,145	20,721	16,668	12,569	24,239	25,536	9,478	57,204	50,252	8,814	6,601	7,422
Congressional District 6	67,113	22,802	16,347	13,024	22,407	23,172	4,893	50,114	44,737	3,900	3,946	4,573
Congressional District 7	72,102	26,033	20,681	14,156	19,604	26,629	4,656	49,411	53,177	4,534	3,765	5,146
Congressional District 8	74,961	24,696	16,808	14,241	21,132	24,205	5,611	52,559	47,236	4,638	4,110	5,185
Congressional District 9	64,070	25,325	21,189	13,006	24,787	25,674	10,549	61,577	55,992	10,701	8,398	8,413
Congressional District 10	67,171	23,957	17,047	14,966	27,523	25,321	8,960	62,841	50,644	8,006	7,058	6,891
Congressional District 11	68,798	22,912	16,391	13,822	26,603	25,350	8,368	57,263	50,174	6,721	6,197	7,111
Congressional District 12	76,213	23,818	23,196	15,210	28,451	34,743	8,234	60,567	64,330	7,204	7,415	8,892
Congressional District 13	58,106	20,550	16,020	10,594	15,094	21,971	8,022	45,221	48,602	9,874	7,137	8,164
Congressional District 14	62,618	21,375	20,423	12,267	21,320	29,859	9,153	51,752	56,705	12,076	9,281	11,320
Congressional District 15	66,591	21,484	17,714	12,197	21,247	25,598	8,301	53,243	48,610	6,552	5,943	5,996
Congressional District 16	57,549	18,514	15,980	10,698	19,295	22,060	6,292	47,353	45,145	8,122	4,327	5,287
Congressional District 17	62,933	21,852	17,252	13,519	24,441	30,737	9,363	56,993	55,794	8,066	6,857	8,225
Congressional District 18	76,795	25,246	21,716	14,920	27,022	31,633	7,424	59,705	58,484	6,374	6,212	7,476
Rhode Island												
Congressional District 1	41,502	13,907	10,476	7,907	12,227	15,827	7,085	36,261	35,481	8,015	6,394	5,885
Congressional District 2	49,667	16,377	10,202	7,956	12,259	15,548	6,522	36,238	34,491	6,729	5,136	5,423
South Carolina												
Congressional District 1	51,367	26,009	15,114	13,759	19,423	15,548	7,195	56,647	37,146	4,447	5,713	4,283
Congressional District 2	57,937	23,284	13,974	8,544	13,917	12,542	7,286	48,813	33,098	5,158	5,010	4,374
Congressional District 3	52,259	19,303	12,281	10,373	20,416	17,228	13,757	58,513	40,453	7,995	7,531	6,066
Congressional District 4	50,131	16,194	10,107	9,793	17,151	15,417	9,390	49,983	36,067	7,352	5,564	4,586
Congressional District 5	51,074	19,202	10,035	9,748	19,080	14,212	11,759	52,771	35,129	8,305	7,902	6,115
Congressional District 6	40,175	15,058	8,812	7,781	14,049	8,657	12,606	47,735	32,554	12,250	9,248	9,029
Congressional District 7	51,445	22,265	13,493	13,657	21,885	15,701	13,613	63,581	39,512	9,640	7,710	7,279
South Dakota												
Congressional District (at Large)	64,498	15,107	10,833	21,231	26,322	30,297	7,921	57,473	53,257	5,405	6,625	6,959
Tennessee												
Congressional District 1	57,744	21,587	13,957	11,941	28,088	21,640	15,360	69,394	47,867	10,880	9,861	8,171
Congressional District 2	60,414	23,402	15,886	11,693	22,147	18,620	10,437	59,795	42,795	8,333	6,724	5,080
Congressional District 3	60,523	22,392	14,916	12,360	22,392	21,177	13,384	62,468	46,575	10,798	8,227	6,763
Congressional District 4	53,240	17,151	9,775	10,783	18,883	14,792	10,472	53,163	35,109	8,118	7,677	6,218
Congressional District 5	51,570	16,131	12,206	10,678	11,669	11,794	6,876	39,706	32,542	7,721	5,269	5,148
Congressional District 6	55,807	19,779	11,358	12,461	21,540	17,048	11,207	63,179	41,479	8,251	9,098	7,214
Congressional District 7	50,270	16,932	9,894	12,700	18,048	14,442	9,405	50,823	35,491	6,986	6,963	6,188
Congressional District 8	60,011	20,906	12,911	11,603	22,005	17,518	10,562	55,639	40,120	7,091	7,271	6,345
Congressional District 9	45,011	13,314	9,669	8,343	8,715	8,598	9,939	35,327	28,906	10,734	8,729	6,734
Texas												
Congressional District 1	48,950	18,921	13,945	9,504	18,318	16,339	9,129	52,305	42,786	7,502	5,969	7,208
Congressional District 2	54,300	15,790	8,062	9,331	8,653	8,020	3,862	34,899	22,563	3,618	3,369	3,012
Congressional District 3	51,272	16,218	6,799	9,298	11,384	7,034	3,025	34,832	20,168	1,909	2,680	3,246
Congressional District 4	51,716	22,071	13,429	11,344	19,558	15,817	10,629	58,466	40,418	8,219	6,909	6,262
Congressional District 5	42,791	16,654	11,120	8,929	16,015	13,380	8,596	46,429	34,440	7,344	5,861	5,241
Congressional District 6	51,605	15,835	8,728	8,045	9,951	7,832	5,501	37,531	25,182	4,384	4,452	3,552
Congressional District 7	53,915	15,549	10,137	9,749	9,542	10,113	2,897	32,963	26,655	3,290	3,734	3,563
Congressional District 8	52,347	20,638	10,522	10,627	13,224	10,023	5,738	46,964	30,529	4,576	5,133	3,490
Congressional District 9	37,207	11,273	5,446	5,345	6,474	5,129	5,505	29,779	19,632	7,811	7,229	5,972
Congressional District 10	52,133	17,822	11,714	9,828	12,018	10,981	4,845	39,225	28,773	4,555	4,434	3,624
Congressional District 11	49,062	21,233	14,144	11,712	18,887	17,999	8,582	54,809	44,132	6,997	6,758	7,038
Congressional District 12	51,613	16,158	11,181	9,285	11,094	10,681	5,438	40,571	31,930	4,996	3,827	3,208
Congressional District 13	47,892	19,813	12,935	10,179	16,642	17,922	8,221	49,019	41,275	6,083	6,288	5,346
Congressional District 14	52,280	19,668	13,594	9,619	13,026	11,667	7,909	44,569	34,582	6,219	6,518	5,352
Congressional District 15	26,430	7,742	5,930	5,279	8,414	7,281	6,616	36,764	28,606	7,636	11,913	11,519
Congressional District 16	28,367	10,233	7,610	5,929	7,219	6,470	7,360	38,860	33,559	8,046	9,582	12,365
Congressional District 17	43,560	18,248	12,563	8,192	13,245	13,044	5,862	40,103	30,982	6,056	5,272	5,147
Congressional District 18	33,260	9,262	4,678	5,939	6,574	5,711	7,798	32,078	22,978	12,074	7,890	6,469
Congressional District 19	40,966	17,889	11,646	10,221	14,602	15,560	7,261	45,476	38,679	6,099	7,242	6,490
Congressional District 20	37,420	14,543	10,143	8,207	8,703	7,754	7,180	36,740	29,182	8,642	7,160	7,382
Congressional District 21	55,293	23,346	15,783	13,797	15,177	13,680	4,932	51,689	40,422	3,826	4,203	4,493
Congressional District 22	53,363	16,184	7,381	6,313	8,071	6,928	3,880	32,320	21,556	3,566	3,988	3,260
Congressional District 23	35,512	13,698	7,389	7,484	9,685	7,235	8,406	42,498	29,990	8,752	8,853	9,353
Congressional District 24	51,443	13,980	8,152	10,195	10,048	8,918	3,044	33,669	24,402	3,051	3,068	2,719
Congressional District 25	50,626	20,784	11,397	11,353	14,170	12,110	5,415	46,773	32,040	4,379	4,071	4,429
Congressional District 26	50,004	15,433	6,557	7,159	9,374	6,984	4,018	32,219	17,970	2,416	2,686	2,031
Congressional District 27	49,597	17,957	11,475	9,669	13,793	14,496	7,535	49,904	40,575	7,832	7,301	7,604
Congressional District 28	28,361	10,563	6,471	4,360	7,131	5,648	6,101	36,915	28,212	6,990	9,386	9,863
Congressional District 29	26,062	6,540	3,806	3,842	4,014	4,282	5,395	26,263	19,372	9,548	6,786	5,662
Congressional District 30	37,280	10,898	6,080	7,253	7,029	5,874	7,145	33,077	22,979	9,367	7,436	6,622
Congressional District 31	45,227	18,968	10,570	7,586	13,515	10,241	5,341	38,914	26,058	4,555	4,244	4,463
Congressional District 32	48,491	16,786	9,585	11,328	10,754	12,161	3,981	38,273	30,712	4,150	4,006	3,711
Congressional District 33	24,562	7,542	4,387	4,197	5,702	4,843	6,430	27,420	20,084	7,972	6,216	5,124
Congressional District 34	28,093	10,083	6,316	6,458	10,057	8,502	7,999	42,223	35,597	9,473	11,600	12,717
Congressional District 35	31,791	10,425	6,341	5,142	6,512	5,400	7,777	30,797	24,824	10,087	7,950	7,561
Congressional District 36	53,070	19,706	12,670	9,503	12,990	12,738	8,131	46,549	34,204	7,584	4,907	4,603

Table I-5: 113th Congressional Districts—Persons With Health Insurance by Source of Insurance—*Continued*

| | Private Health Insurance Coverage | | | | | | Public Health Insurance Coverage | | | | | |
| | Employer Based | | | Direct Purchase | | | Medicare | | | Medicaid/CHIP | | |
	55 to 64 Years	65 to 74 Years	75 Years and Over	55 to 64 Years	65 to 74 Years	75 Years and Over	55 to 64 Years	65 to 74 Years	75 Years and Over	55 to 64 Years	65 to 74 Years	75 Years and Over
Utah												
Congressional District 1	45,918	15,503	11,858	8,548	11,100	10,558	4,273	33,313	26,184	3,589	3,282	3,122
Congressional District 2	44,587	17,075	13,312	8,736	14,232	14,936	4,789	41,775	34,561	5,511	3,986	3,892
Congressional District 3	42,792	14,813	10,326	8,832	11,854	10,551	3,049	33,263	24,770	3,017	3,414	2,986
Congressional District 4	41,708	12,858	9,111	5,948	9,962	9,579	4,453	29,794	24,220	4,202	3,331	3,314
Vermont												
Congressional District (at Large)	61,739	20,527	13,281	12,440	17,364	16,427	7,727	50,430	38,872	13,148	6,649	7,484
Virginia												
Congressional District 1	60,631	27,920	17,158	10,501	16,829	13,756	5,099	52,939	35,471	2,572	3,844	3,227
Congressional District 2	51,475	18,994	13,000	10,602	13,769	14,939	5,212	45,038	35,674	3,184	4,233	4,093
Congressional District 3	47,650	16,634	12,088	9,623	11,976	13,130	11,125	41,511	34,480	8,725	7,268	5,880
Congressional District 4	61,304	22,609	13,912	10,955	16,317	13,906	8,374	49,272	33,879	5,406	5,580	4,497
Congressional District 5	60,607	25,242	14,670	16,872	26,253	22,370	11,639	67,153	49,234	6,829	7,241	7,404
Congressional District 6	60,395	22,746	16,933	15,206	24,318	23,001	9,837	59,579	49,777	4,702	5,666	4,839
Congressional District 7	68,395	25,613	18,569	13,072	17,989	17,917	6,019	51,074	40,496	2,722	3,949	3,379
Congressional District 8	58,514	24,577	15,204	10,035	9,358	9,195	3,139	35,666	28,343	2,603	3,880	3,453
Congressional District 9	57,877	22,872	15,446	13,542	25,118	22,800	18,844	67,676	50,651	8,753	9,162	7,270
Congressional District 10	63,750	23,185	11,342	10,770	10,927	9,027	3,258	37,926	24,950	1,520	2,683	3,068
Congressional District 11	63,252	23,548	12,771	8,852	9,608	7,379	2,403	38,618	25,551	1,721	3,170	3,817
Washington												
Congressional District 1	59,852	16,692	9,340	15,550	14,847	13,097	4,088	41,229	28,856	4,499	4,288	4,452
Congressional District 2	56,512	18,689	12,498	14,313	16,996	16,575	6,322	47,008	38,003	7,322	5,508	6,467
Congressional District 3	56,900	19,292	12,712	13,071	21,428	18,593	8,351	53,582	37,818	8,024	6,216	5,726
Congressional District 4	47,599	14,954	10,513	11,325	15,039	13,608	6,993	43,137	33,171	6,965	6,399	6,095
Congressional District 5	53,932	18,574	12,147	14,490	18,439	19,747	8,791	50,972	40,974	9,100	6,229	6,378
Congressional District 6	60,094	25,694	15,789	15,370	21,092	18,652	9,250	60,885	43,788	8,598	6,785	6,055
Congressional District 7	58,779	20,116	13,165	14,917	15,427	15,301	5,252	43,290	35,506	6,755	5,585	5,564
Congressional District 8	59,225	16,573	10,260	11,301	15,510	11,868	5,572	39,087	28,243	5,562	4,147	4,374
Congressional District 9	50,382	16,339	11,903	10,223	12,762	14,393	5,063	38,893	36,499	7,274	7,040	8,824
Congressional District 10	50,884	19,048	12,932	10,121	14,064	14,151	7,635	43,299	35,568	6,342	5,036	5,280
West Virginia												
Congressional District 1	56,792	23,654	18,876	7,851	16,846	16,826	12,031	53,070	42,943	9,243	6,058	5,603
Congressional District 2	57,923	26,434	18,788	7,622	14,670	14,142	11,715	54,598	40,105	9,795	6,326	5,673
Congressional District 3	52,993	26,490	20,393	9,798	13,648	12,740	20,153	55,356	43,852	12,856	7,417	6,654
Wisconsin												
Congressional District 1	67,765	21,898	15,845	10,131	17,923	17,511	5,853	49,369	40,600	6,842	4,856	5,527
Congressional District 2	67,331	22,269	14,812	10,802	18,244	20,102	5,351	43,349	37,155	6,802	3,915	4,678
Congressional District 3	63,521	17,922	13,618	11,704	24,668	24,987	7,014	53,396	46,701	8,356	6,359	7,039
Congressional District 4	43,114	13,149	12,796	5,944	9,817	11,472	8,184	34,200	34,286	13,556	7,353	8,128
Congressional District 5	74,216	20,012	19,212	10,978	20,453	24,807	4,862	50,248	49,739	5,720	4,496	6,865
Congressional District 6	69,773	18,048	14,159	12,214	24,426	26,171	6,248	54,594	49,585	7,019	5,616	7,339
Congressional District 7	64,944	19,392	13,827	15,338	29,861	28,793	7,320	63,259	51,117	9,457	7,775	8,039
Congressional District 8	64,527	14,164	11,911	12,370	21,348	21,029	6,674	52,263	43,556	6,245	5,036	5,869
Wyoming												
Congressional District (at Large)	50,098	14,556	8,500	11,697	15,178	14,015	5,054	39,264	28,984	4,198	4,065	4,017

PART J
HOUSING SUMMARY

HOUSING SUMMARY

As the Baby Boom entered its household formation years in the late 1960's and 1970's, housing development grew to accommodate the growing adult population and their children. The Baby Boomers are now between the ages of 50 and 68 and their housing needs are changing. Senior residences take a number of forms from independent living apartments to full nursing care, often right within the same residential complex. Virtually every community has seen the development of some type of senior living arrangement. This generation grew up in an era of homeownership and many have the resources for seasonal and second homes. As they age, there will be changes in the market forces affecting housing markets both for primary residences and second homes. A challenge in the market will be location. Will the growing inventory of homes for sale be in the same locations as the demand from younger generations?

Nationwide, 78.6 percent of householders 65 and over are home owners while 21.4 percent are renters. Of the home owners, 34.4 percent are still paying on a mortgage. Home ownership is highest in South Carolina where 85.3 percent are owners but, like the nation, the same percentage has a mortgage to pay. The District of Columbia has the lowest ownership rate at 60.4 percent and therefore the highest rental rate at 39.6 percent. They also have the highest percent of owners with a mortgage (49.4 percent). In 44 states the percentage of home owners among householders 65 and over is greater than 75 percent. South Carolina has the lowest percentage of householders 65 and over who are renters at 14.7 percent. North Dakota has the lowest percentage of mortgage holders at 17.5 percent.

The Census obtains data on meals included in rent for rental occupied units. This is often used as a measurement of congregate housing within the housing inventory. Renters in continuing care or life facilities are included here if their contracts cover meal services. Nationwide, 11.7 percent of renter households have meals included in their rent. This varies from a low of 3.4 percent in West Virginia to a high of 26.0 percent in Oregon.

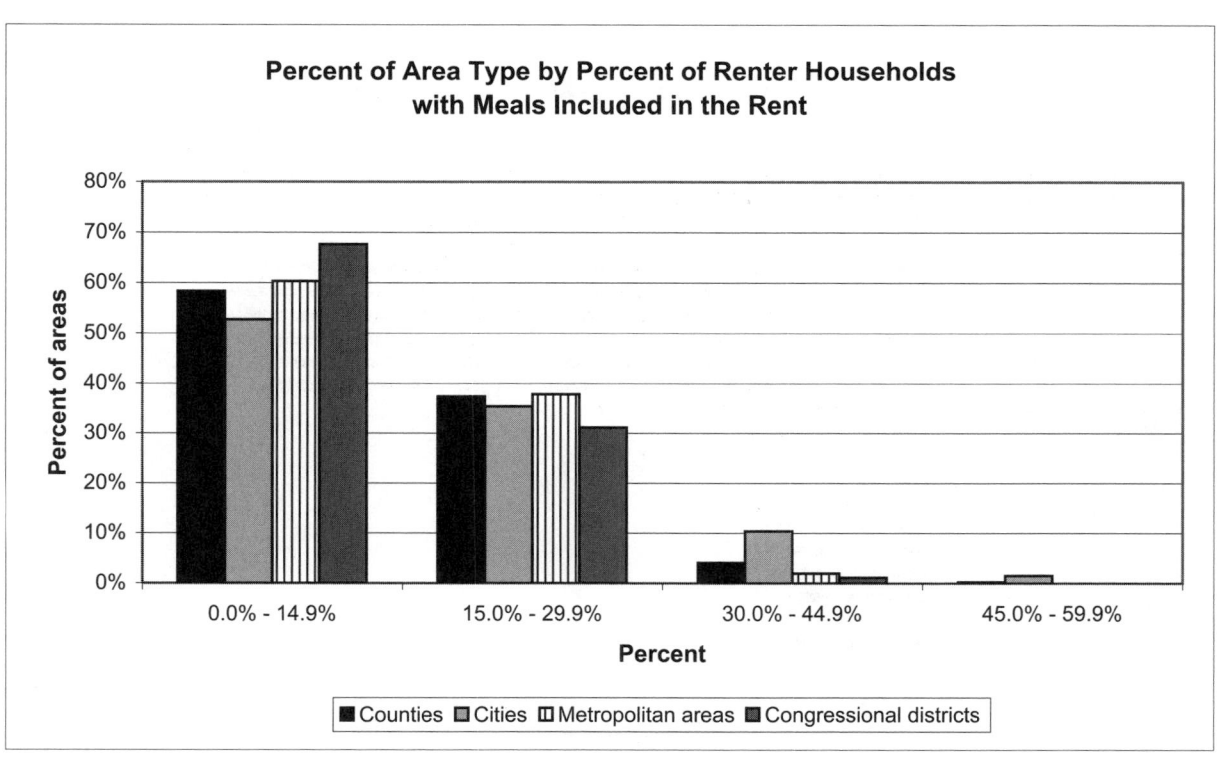

The nation's Consumer Expenditure Survey shows that housing accounts for about 33 percent of consumer units (roughly households) total expenditures.[1] The Census obtains data on owner and renter affordability of housing based on a measure of owner or renter costs as a percentage of income. When a household spends more than 35 percent of its income on housing costs it is considered a housing cost burden. Using this basis, 22.6 percent of owner householders 65 and over pay more than 35 percent on housing costs and would be considered to have a cost burden. For renters, 45.3 percent pay more than 35 percent of their income for rental costs nationwide. New Jersey has the highest owner cost burden at 36.4 percent while California has the highest percentage of householders with renter cost burden at 53.0 percent. West Virginia ranks lowest on both owner and renter costs at 11.5 percent and 27.2 percent, respectively.

Sumter County, Florida has the highest percentage of owner occupied units at 96.0 percent. At 27.7 percent, New York County, New York (Manhattan) has the lowest percent of home owners among the 65 and over population. Almost 90 percent of the counties (88.9 percent) have home ownership rates over 75 percent. Prince George's County, Maryland has the highest percentage of home owners who still have a mortgage at 58.2 percent.

1. U.S. Bureau of Labor Statistics, Consumer Expenditures, 2012, www.bls.gov/news.release/cesan.nr0.htm.

McKinley County, New Mexico is lowest at 12.4 percent. James City County, Virginia, home of Colonial Williamsburg, has the highest percentage of householders 65 and over with meals included in their rent at 58.8 percent. Hawaii County, Hawaii is lowest with only less than one-half percent. Nearly half (46.2 percent) of owners in Hunterdon County, New Jersey pay 35 percent or more of income on housing costs while Walker County, Georgia is lowest at 7.2 percent. For renters, Forsyth County, Georgia has the highest percentage of cost burden households at 69.8 percent while Cochise County, Arizona is lowest at 10.1 percent.

Missouri, Texas is the city with the highest percentage (93.2 percent) of householders 65 and over who are home owners. At 76.0 percent, Union City, New Jersey has the highest percentage of renter householders. New York City by far has the largest absolute number of renter householders with 362,000 and more than three times the next largest (Los Angeles) at 99,000. Only 15 cities have fewer than 50 percent owner occupied householders over 65. In Temecula, Texas 68.2 percent of owner occupied households have a mortgage and in 62 cities, more than 50 percent of homeowners still pay on a mortgage. Peoria, Arizona is the city with the highest percentage (54.9 percent) of rental households with meals included in the rent. Union City, New Jersey and Mount Vernon, New York are the only cities where more than 50 percent of homeowners pay more than 35 percent of their incomes

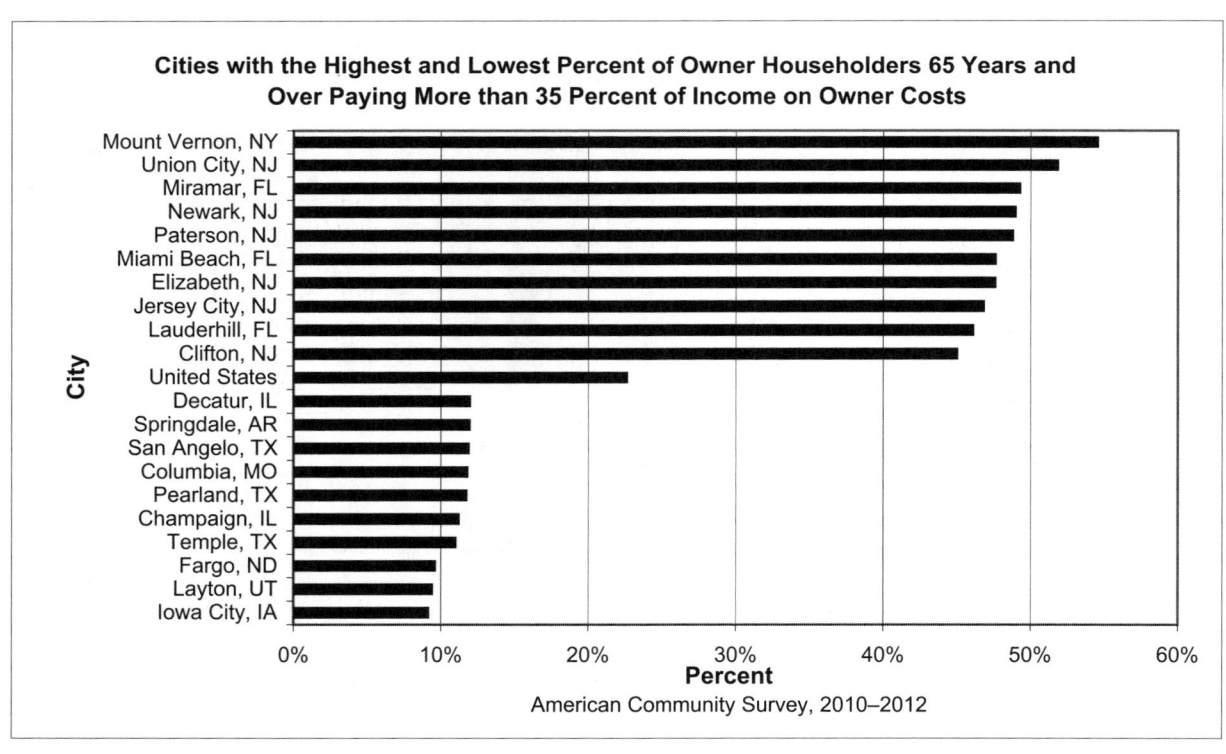

Cities with the Highest and Lowest Percent of Owner Householders 65 Years and Over Paying More than 35 Percent of Income on Owner Costs

American Community Survey, 2010–2012

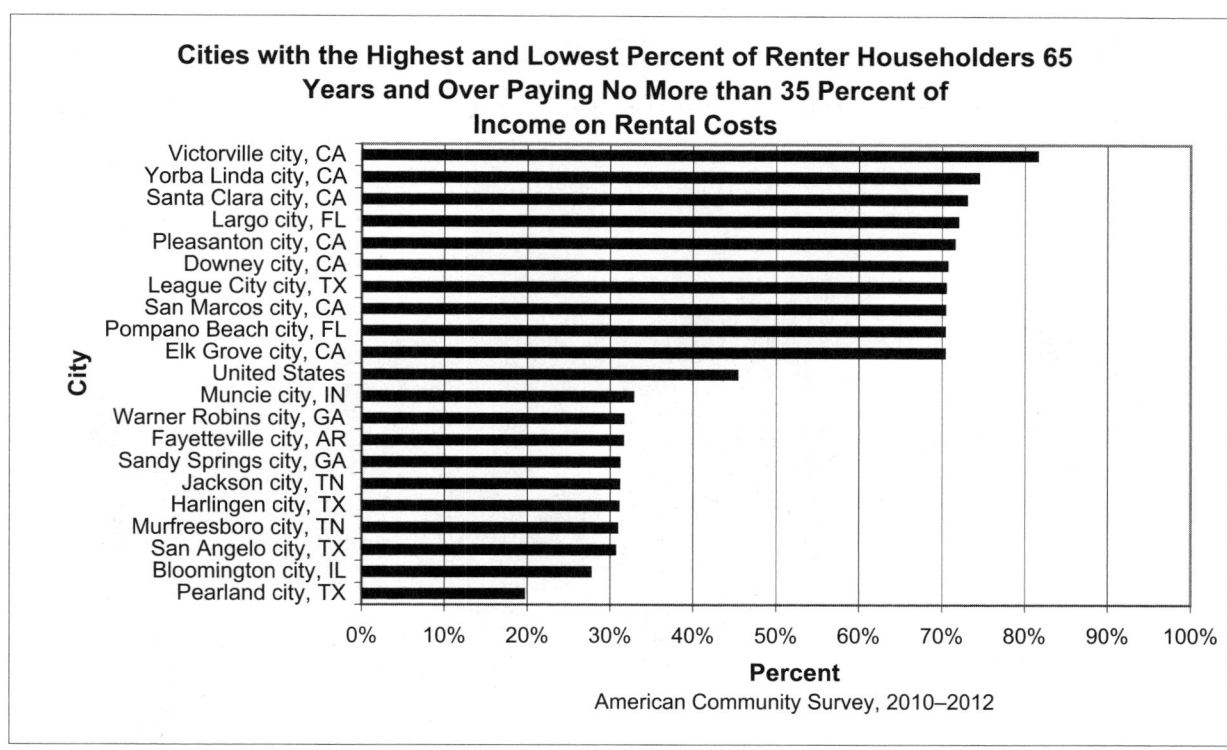

Cities with the Highest and Lowest Percent of Renter Householders 65 Years and Over Paying No More than 35 Percent of Income on Rental Costs

American Community Survey, 2010–2012

for housing costs. In Victorville, California more than 80 percent (81.5 percent) of rental householders pay more than 35 percent of their income on rental costs.

The range between the highest and lowest homeownership rate at the metropolitan level is less than that for counties and cities. The lowest rate is 63 percent found in the New York-Northern New Jersey-Long Island metropolitan area while the highest, at 91.0 percent, is in the Palm Coast, Florida metro area. Forty-two metropolitan areas have ownership rates over 85 percent. In the Las Vegas-Paradise, Nevada metropolitan area, 52.6 percent of owner householders still pay on their mortgage while only 14.6 percent still hold mortgages in the Odessa, Texas metro area. In the Atlantic City-Hammonton, New Jersey metropolitan area, 37.6 percent of owner householders pay more than 35 percent of their incomes on housing costs. In the Ames, Iowa metro area only 8.6 percent have that cost burden. For renters, the Medford, Oregon metro is highest at 57.0 percent and in 240 metro areas, more than 40 percent of renters are burdened by rental costs.

Florida's 11th Congressional District has the highest home ownership rate at 91.8 percent among householders 65 and over though more than one-third (35.3 percent) are currently paying on a mortgage. In New York's 13th Congressional District renters dominate with only 10.5 percent of older householders owning their home. Of those that do own, 35.0 percent still hold a mortgage. The homeownership rate for householders over 65 exceeds 75 percent in 332 congressional districts. In Maryland's 4th and 5th Congressional Districts more than 50 percent of the owner householders have a mortgage to pay. In 19 congressional districts, more than 25 percent of all renter householders have meals included in their rent payment. Over one-third of all congressional districts have more than 25 percent of older householders experiencing an owner cost burden in relation to their income. It's highest in New Jersey's 10th Congressional District at 49.1 percent and lowest in West Virginia's 1st district at 10.2 percent. The rental cost burden is highest in the 49th Congressional District of California where nearly two-thirds (61.3 percent) of rental householders pay more than 35 percent of their income in rental costs.

Percent of Renter Householders 65 Years and Over Paying 35 Percent or More of Income on Rental Costs

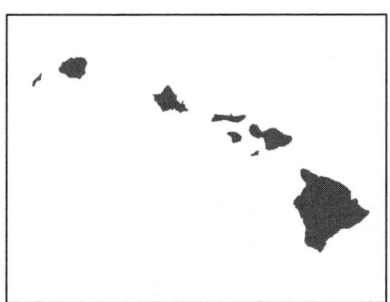

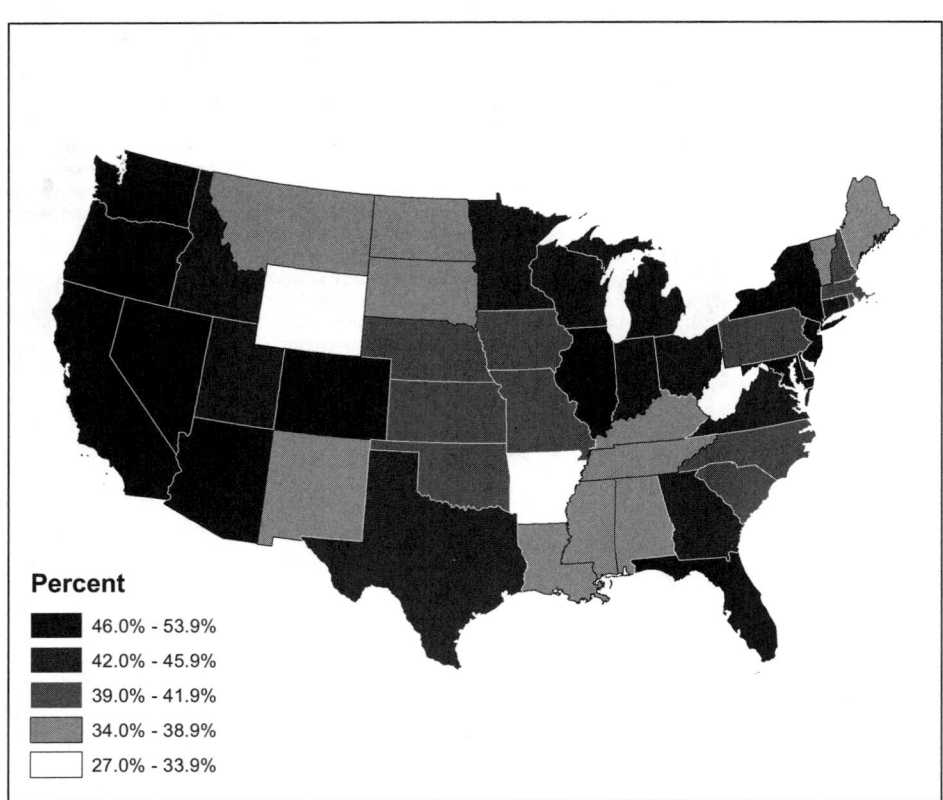

Percent

- 46.0% - 53.9%
- 42.0% - 45.9%
- 39.0% - 41.9%
- 34.0% - 38.9%
- 27.0% - 33.9%

Table J-1: States—Summary of Housing and Householder Characteristics

| | | | | Householders 65 Years and Over | | | | | |
| | | | | | Owner Householders | | | | |
	Total Housing Units	Total Households	Owner Occupied	Renter Occupied	With a Mortgage	Without a Mortgage	Renter Households With Meals Included in Rent	Percent of Owner Householders Who Pay 35% or More of Income for Housing Costs	Percent of Renter Householders Who Pay 35% or More of Income for Rental Costs
United States	132,114,283	25,624,042	20,141,371	5,482,671	6,918,707	13,222,664	644,013	22.6%	45.3%
Alabama	2,181,814	431,900	361,626	70,274	112,789	248,837	5,579	18.4%	35.0%
Alaska	307,367	35,129	28,658	6,471	10,114	18,544	430	20.1%	42.4%
Arizona	2,858,823	564,283	467,386	96,897	192,421	274,965	15,629	21.3%	48.0%
Arkansas	1,322,947	270,357	222,407	47,950	61,929	160,478	4,624	14.8%	33.3%
California	13,695,007	2,544,599	1,870,845	673,754	844,915	1,025,930	69,563	27.5%	53.0%
Colorado	2,222,093	364,159	290,101	74,058	121,758	168,343	12,659	21.9%	48.2%
Connecticut	1,488,177	315,972	241,133	74,839	84,497	156,636	8,055	32.5%	43.1%
Delaware	408,428	81,975	68,524	13,451	26,280	42,244	1,562	21.2%	42.9%
District of Columbia	297,918	49,026	29,590	19,436	14,625	14,965	1,434	25.9%	44.6%
Florida	9,011,721	2,006,651	1,676,679	329,972	598,345	1,078,334	47,919	26.1%	50.9%
Georgia	4,099,090	659,443	536,090	123,353	203,760	332,330	12,541	22.6%	43.2%
Hawaii	522,197	110,898	84,335	26,563	36,103	48,232	1,101	22.9%	39.9%
Idaho	670,858	127,817	106,326	21,491	38,801	67,525	4,159	18.2%	42.8%
Illinois	5,294,412	1,032,851	821,378	211,473	270,543	550,835	30,217	24.1%	47.4%
Indiana	2,802,784	543,017	445,121	97,896	161,200	283,921	11,757	16.6%	42.2%
Iowa	1,341,551	289,929	236,208	53,721	56,340	179,868	9,824	14.6%	39.2%
Kansas	1,236,407	241,937	192,770	49,167	53,210	139,560	8,917	16.1%	40.4%
Kentucky	1,932,905	379,625	311,926	67,699	91,571	220,355	5,326	16.5%	34.7%
Louisiana	1,977,240	365,758	304,230	61,528	74,892	229,338	4,243	15.5%	38.0%
Maine	723,305	136,326	107,056	29,270	33,852	73,204	3,303	22.6%	37.2%
Maryland	2,387,867	447,752	351,896	95,856	151,245	200,651	13,814	25.0%	48.5%
Massachusetts	2,809,746	576,645	408,982	167,663	148,874	260,108	15,726	29.7%	40.1%
Michigan	4,528,042	898,838	743,131	155,707	249,604	493,527	21,165	22.0%	43.5%
Minnesota	2,354,562	449,498	351,112	98,386	112,735	238,377	18,759	20.5%	45.9%
Mississippi	1,280,057	248,897	210,290	38,607	54,532	155,758	2,973	17.9%	37.2%
Missouri	2,717,060	544,100	439,796	104,304	138,918	300,878	12,856	18.2%	40.1%
Montana	484,745	97,403	77,984	19,419	21,812	56,172	3,699	16.6%	37.9%
Nebraska	800,926	159,628	125,346	34,282	31,307	94,039	7,575	16.7%	40.0%
Nevada	1,179,007	204,680	153,590	51,090	75,635	77,955	3,297	26.2%	52.1%
New Hampshire	616,027	113,302	88,478	24,824	29,540	58,938	2,740	29.8%	40.3%
New Jersey	3,565,222	733,601	558,001	175,600	194,563	363,438	13,761	36.4%	49.9%
New Mexico	904,519	177,448	148,323	29,125	48,070	100,253	2,399	17.1%	36.4%
New York	8,116,133	1,639,609	1,063,283	576,326	334,267	729,016	24,210	29.3%	47.8%
North Carolina	4,354,216	808,175	662,447	145,728	240,123	422,324	17,587	21.5%	41.3%
North Dakota	323,146	62,826	46,176	16,650	8,061	38,115	2,798	13.2%	37.1%
Ohio	5,128,144	1,060,964	844,720	216,244	292,495	552,225	27,311	19.6%	42.3%
Oklahoma	1,671,230	331,413	273,404	58,009	75,126	198,278	7,647	15.7%	40.3%
Oregon	1,679,365	351,883	271,277	80,606	105,532	165,745	20,958	23.0%	50.6%
Pennsylvania	5,571,122	1,248,228	961,319	286,909	266,438	694,881	38,272	21.7%	41.8%
Rhode Island	462,981	96,289	66,435	29,854	24,945	41,490	2,833	31.3%	39.4%
South Carolina	2,148,151	416,443	355,230	61,213	122,139	233,091	6,742	20.1%	41.4%
South Dakota	366,175	74,354	55,371	18,983	11,707	43,664	2,939	15.9%	36.7%
Tennessee	2,825,006	555,184	458,523	96,661	137,749	320,774	10,158	18.1%	37.5%
Texas	10,073,268	1,628,989	1,313,122	315,867	368,675	944,447	36,995	18.3%	44.9%
Utah	989,091	160,392	136,010	24,382	49,517	86,493	4,284	16.9%	45.6%
Vermont	323,419	60,018	47,944	12,074	16,344	31,600	1,471	29.5%	36.3%
Virginia	3,383,270	631,149	514,471	116,678	198,767	315,704	16,421	20.3%	43.7%
Washington	2,901,351	541,768	415,302	126,466	160,137	255,165	27,007	22.9%	48.9%
West Virginia	882,461	196,951	167,779	29,172	38,911	128,868	989	11.5%	27.2%
Wisconsin	2,629,234	510,565	391,280	119,285	113,617	277,663	17,135	22.4%	45.6%
Wyoming	263,696	45,398	37,960	7,438	9,377	28,583	650	14.7%	32.4%

Table J-2: Counties—Summary of Housing and Householder Characteristics

| | | Householders 65 Years and Over | | | | | | | |
| | | | | | Owner Householders | | | Percent of Owner Householders Who Pay 35% or More of Income for Housing Costs | Percent of Renter Householders Who Pay 35% or More of Income for Rental Costs |
	Total Housing Units	Total Households	Owner Occupied	Renter Occupied	With a Mortgage	Without a Mortgage	Renter Households With Meals Included in Rent		
Alabama									
Baldwin County	104,757	19,751	17,075	2,676	6,279	10,796	369	17.7%	48.0%
Calhoun County	53,317	11,127	9,287	1,840	2,876	6,411	133	19.6%	29.0%
Cullman County	37,062	8,672	7,075	1,597	1,978	5,097	133	20.3%	25.4%
DeKalb County	31,090	6,209	5,193	1,016	1,232	3,961	62	15.9%	28.5%
Elmore County	32,785	5,647	5,059	588	2,052	3,007	17	19.6%	36.6%
Etowah County	47,467	10,485	8,700	1,785	1,808	6,892	201	15.6%	39.1%
Houston County	45,556	9,594	8,034	1,560	2,536	5,498	68	15.1%	37.9%
Jefferson County	301,257	56,890	46,283	10,607	16,092	30,191	1,606	21.7%	48.8%
Lauderdale County	43,879	10,481	8,599	1,882	2,135	6,464	71	12.9%	29.7%
Lee County	63,521	8,548	7,259	1,289	2,849	4,410	214	21.1%	41.8%
Limestone County	35,132	7,086	6,099	987	1,812	4,287	na	13.8%	29.3%
Madison County	148,812	26,641	22,948	3,693	8,903	14,045	529	16.0%	37.7%
Marshall County	40,342	9,209	7,721	1,488	1,985	5,736	104	16.4%	25.6%
Mobile County	179,528	34,830	28,782	6,048	10,123	18,659	522	19.6%	41.1%
Montgomery County	102,132	18,557	15,230	3,327	6,490	8,740	231	18.7%	37.2%
Morgan County	51,273	10,798	9,002	1,796	2,892	6,110	136	15.2%	25.1%
St. Clair County	35,637	7,275	6,251	1,024	2,046	4,205	na	16.2%	41.3%
Shelby County	81,540	13,741	12,535	1,206	5,015	7,520	237	17.5%	31.2%
Talladega County	37,135	7,542	6,153	1,389	1,582	4,571	na	18.5%	22.2%
Tuscaloosa County	85,540	12,736	10,563	2,173	3,940	6,623	335	17.9%	36.7%
Walker County	30,789	7,241	6,331	910	1,334	4,997	na	11.3%	20.5%
Alaska									
Fairbanks North Star Borough	41,743	4,117	3,507	610	1,261	2,246	77	24.7%	27.4%
Matanuska-Susitna Borough	41,326	4,302	3,616	686	1,272	2,344	26	17.0%	55.0%
Arizona									
Apache County	32,571	5,401	4,652	749	873	3,779	na	13.4%	10.1%
Cochise County	59,496	15,260	13,050	2,210	5,029	8,021	143	17.0%	56.5%
Coconino County	63,653	7,670	6,723	947	2,535	4,188	109	14.8%	33.1%
Maricopa County	1,647,256	293,480	239,344	54,136	106,872	132,472	10,618	23.4%	52.9%
Mohave County	111,162	30,103	25,779	4,324	10,752	15,027	115	19.1%	38.1%
Navajo County	57,091	9,553	8,426	1,127	2,440	5,986	52	19.2%	43.4%
Pima County	442,702	97,843	78,794	19,049	32,081	46,713	3,819	20.7%	47.5%
Pinal County	161,115	33,042	29,257	3,785	11,064	18,193	142	23.7%	36.0%
Yavapai County	110,858	34,015	29,023	4,992	11,664	17,359	438	19.5%	43.1%
Yuma County	88,460	18,834	16,486	2,348	4,169	12,317	193	13.4%	29.8%
Arkansas									
Benton County	93,980	16,868	13,849	3,019	5,059	8,790	638	14.4%	45.4%
Craighead County	41,183	7,167	5,741	1,426	1,858	3,883	356	13.8%	48.0%
Faulkner County	47,634	7,091	5,442	1,649	2,174	3,268	194	12.5%	39.5%
Garland County	50,521	12,591	10,552	2,039	3,891	6,661	369	16.4%	38.9%
Jefferson County	33,069	6,807	5,822	985	1,817	4,005	74	19.5%	35.8%
Lonoke County	27,575	4,849	4,031	818	1,290	2,741	94	14.1%	36.7%
Pulaski County	177,041	29,549	23,928	5,621	8,313	15,615	716	16.0%	37.7%
Saline County	45,520	10,363	9,157	1,206	3,057	6,100	248	10.6%	40.5%
Sebastian County	55,112	10,599	8,129	2,470	2,180	5,949	315	15.9%	35.7%
Washington County	88,272	13,001	10,278	2,723	3,034	7,244	453	14.8%	37.1%
White County	32,655	7,476	5,909	1,567	1,448	4,461	110	13.7%	28.2%
California									
Alameda County	583,058	101,384	70,753	30,631	31,746	39,007	3,249	25.1%	48.3%
Butte County	96,025	22,252	17,431	4,821	6,958	10,473	776	20.5%	45.6%
Contra Costa County	401,058	81,300	65,294	16,006	30,289	35,005	3,166	28.4%	54.8%
El Dorado County	88,155	16,779	14,276	2,503	6,612	7,664	310	27.8%	40.0%
Fresno County	317,269	56,190	40,601	15,589	16,902	23,699	1,651	20.8%	49.0%
Humboldt County	61,603	11,281	9,039	2,242	3,673	5,366	231	21.1%	49.3%
Imperial County	56,077	10,086	6,395	3,691	2,070	4,325	121	22.4%	47.1%
Kern County	285,366	45,718	36,044	9,674	14,470	21,574	793	21.1%	46.6%
Kings County	44,040	6,842	4,810	2,032	1,649	3,161	140	19.9%	40.4%
Lake County	35,388	7,633	6,183	1,450	2,539	3,644	na	30.8%	58.1%
Los Angeles County	3,444,189	615,860	404,026	211,834	193,153	210,873	12,069	30.3%	55.2%
Madera County	49,274	9,464	7,750	1,714	3,567	4,183	187	28.6%	46.1%
Marin County	111,137	28,524	21,808	6,716	10,327	11,481	817	30.4%	52.2%
Mendocino County	40,311	8,852	6,794	2,058	2,131	4,663	159	23.7%	38.2%
Merced County	83,622	13,739	9,933	3,806	4,007	5,926	128	26.4%	46.8%
Monterey County	138,964	25,539	18,478	7,061	7,702	10,776	755	24.2%	50.5%
Napa County	54,745	12,918	9,915	3,003	4,346	5,569	605	27.2%	55.2%
Nevada County	52,615	12,646	10,889	1,757	4,800	6,089	375	29.2%	57.0%
Orange County	1,050,598	206,912	160,709	46,203	74,884	85,825	6,103	28.8%	55.9%
Placer County	153,681	34,439	28,239	6,200	12,627	15,612	1,069	28.6%	58.6%
Riverside County	803,396	155,054	124,000	31,054	56,578	67,422	3,571	29.8%	56.2%
Sacramento County	556,091	99,171	73,597	25,574	33,803	39,794	3,612	23.2%	53.2%
San Bernardino County	700,153	103,717	80,393	23,324	37,288	43,105	2,384	27.3%	56.7%
San Diego County	1,166,740	209,064	157,744	51,320	73,992	83,752	6,463	28.4%	55.2%
San Francisco County	376,653	68,503	35,712	32,791	14,863	20,849	1,528	29.1%	46.3%
San Joaquin County	234,161	41,585	30,901	10,684	13,112	17,789	1,432	24.9%	54.4%
San Luis Obispo County	117,476	25,629	20,851	4,778	8,814	12,037	752	25.4%	48.1%
San Mateo County	270,776	56,479	44,731	11,748	19,938	24,793	2,424	27.0%	54.3%
Santa Barbara County	152,750	33,861	25,861	8,000	11,123	14,738	1,831	25.9%	50.5%
Santa Clara County	634,321	112,271	84,098	28,173	35,612	48,486	4,412	24.5%	53.6%

Table J-2: Counties—Summary of Housing and Householder Characteristics—*Continued*

| | | | | Householders 65 Years and Over | | | | | |
| | | | | | Owner Householders | | | Percent of Owner Householders Who Pay 35% or More of Income for Housing Costs | Percent of Renter Householders Who Pay 35% or More of Income for Rental Costs |
	Total Housing Units	Total Households	Owner Occupied	Renter Occupied	With a Mortgage	Without a Mortgage	Renter Households With Meals Included in Rent		
California—Cont.									
Santa Cruz County	104,376	19,970	15,351	4,619	6,585	8,766	462	27.7%	44.5%
Shasta County	77,370	19,897	16,022	3,875	6,051	9,971	550	24.2%	52.7%
Solano County	152,947	28,831	22,320	6,511	10,918	11,402	773	25.4%	51.1%
Sonoma County	204,652	44,296	34,235	10,061	15,414	18,821	1,620	28.6%	56.0%
Stanislaus County	179,394	33,059	24,223	8,836	10,301	13,922	1,247	28.5%	52.9%
Sutter County	33,886	7,275	5,575	1,700	2,184	3,391	171	25.0%	33.6%
Tulare County	142,747	24,691	18,702	5,989	7,554	11,148	406	23.2%	44.9%
Ventura County	281,723	59,887	47,070	12,817	23,284	23,786	2,037	28.4%	50.9%
Yolo County	75,176	12,783	8,940	3,843	3,542	5,398	635	19.1%	47.9%
Yuba County	27,612	4,379	3,363	1,016	1,561	1,802	72	20.8%	42.9%
Colorado									
Adams County	163,598	23,266	18,272	4,994	8,072	10,200	795	23.2%	51.2%
Arapahoe County	239,284	38,061	29,645	8,416	13,957	15,688	1,656	23.4%	56.6%
Boulder County	127,595	19,981	15,710	4,271	6,053	9,657	1,251	18.4%	50.2%
Denver County	286,732	43,278	28,888	14,390	12,361	16,527	2,051	25.5%	42.7%
Douglas County	108,022	13,496	11,271	2,225	6,425	4,846	514	27.1%	44.1%
El Paso County	254,496	40,618	33,136	7,482	14,805	18,331	1,373	20.0%	51.6%
Jefferson County	230,350	44,554	36,335	8,219	16,046	20,289	1,874	21.0%	54.1%
Larimer County	133,763	23,052	19,089	3,963	7,717	11,372	920	21.4%	51.9%
Mesa County	62,945	14,901	12,318	2,583	4,618	7,700	719	22.4%	54.1%
Pueblo County	69,588	15,828	13,268	2,560	4,647	8,621	135	19.5%	44.9%
Weld County	96,948	15,559	12,488	3,071	5,466	7,022	471	23.0%	51.3%
Connecticut									
Fairfield County	361,355	76,458	60,781	15,677	23,808	36,973	1,753	37.6%	42.4%
Hartford County	374,118	81,908	60,297	21,611	19,664	40,633	2,600	29.5%	46.4%
Litchfield County	87,506	19,301	15,150	4,151	4,975	10,175	264	30.7%	31.2%
Middlesex County	74,979	15,872	12,676	3,196	4,343	8,333	623	30.0%	46.3%
New Haven County	361,932	77,105	56,065	21,040	19,374	36,691	2,011	35.6%	45.8%
New London County	121,056	24,579	18,983	5,596	6,459	12,524	565	26.7%	34.5%
Tolland County	58,110	11,494	9,650	1,844	3,200	6,450	132	22.6%	32.8%
Windham County	49,121	9,255	7,531	1,724	2,674	4,857	107	27.4%	35.7%
Delaware									
Kent County	66,050	13,607	11,532	2,075	4,051	7,481	209	18.0%	39.0%
New Castle County	217,823	42,316	33,652	8,664	13,375	20,277	1,033	21.8%	46.4%
Sussex County	124,555	26,052	23,340	2,712	8,854	14,486	320	21.7%	34.9%
Florida									
Alachua County	113,011	16,705	13,516	3,189	4,469	9,047	855	19.9%	51.1%
Bay County	99,738	16,502	13,830	2,672	4,490	9,340	211	22.0%	48.5%
Brevard County	270,428	70,245	60,941	9,304	24,092	36,849	852	23.2%	43.7%
Broward County	810,642	154,109	126,575	27,534	49,396	77,179	4,448	36.5%	57.1%
Charlotte County	100,804	34,637	30,969	3,668	10,682	20,287	1,143	24.1%	39.4%
Citrus County	78,006	27,506	25,222	2,284	8,434	16,788	346	18.5%	51.8%
Clay County	75,879	13,066	11,372	1,694	5,154	6,218	277	21.8%	51.9%
Collier County	198,373	52,578	45,813	6,765	15,750	30,063	1,960	27.3%	45.0%
Columbia County	28,566	6,336	5,590	746	1,628	3,962	na	14.2%	42.6%
Duval County	389,605	62,242	49,126	13,116	20,292	28,834	1,661	25.2%	42.9%
Escambia County	137,306	28,334	23,275	5,059	8,251	15,024	590	18.6%	46.3%
Flagler County	48,782	13,858	12,608	1,250	5,885	6,723	256	29.2%	48.6%
Hernando County	84,596	27,698	25,315	2,383	9,259	16,056	414	19.5%	47.3%
Highlands County	55,283	19,350	17,014	2,336	4,554	12,460	369	16.3%	40.8%
Hillsborough County	539,508	90,712	71,431	19,281	28,032	43,399	3,196	25.7%	52.1%
Indian River County	76,535	24,390	20,709	3,681	6,075	14,634	813	19.7%	53.4%
Lake County	145,131	44,524	38,590	5,934	11,970	26,620	1,110	19.8%	52.8%
Lee County	371,630	87,499	75,469	12,030	27,018	48,451	1,761	24.5%	48.8%
Leon County	124,560	17,555	14,324	3,231	5,759	8,565	679	20.0%	53.8%
Manatee County	173,715	48,208	40,915	7,293	13,325	27,590	1,262	23.9%	50.1%
Marion County	163,884	53,390	48,080	5,310	16,899	31,181	801	21.4%	46.1%
Martin County	78,143	24,833	22,172	2,661	6,873	15,299	363	24.8%	56.0%
Miami-Dade County	990,428	185,793	128,817	56,976	49,975	78,842	1,465	38.1%	54.0%
Monroe County	52,824	8,057	6,607	1,450	2,369	4,238	10	31.6%	56.8%
Nassau County	35,212	7,596	6,709	887	2,480	4,229	53	20.7%	25.4%
Okaloosa County	92,905	15,915	13,675	2,240	4,850	8,825	399	19.8%	46.9%
Orange County	490,427	65,171	52,399	12,772	24,482	27,917	1,078	32.2%	54.2%
Osceola County	128,892	17,294	13,294	4,000	6,497	6,797	49	31.3%	47.5%
Palm Beach County	665,541	177,102	153,801	23,301	51,097	102,704	5,655	29.3%	54.6%
Pasco County	229,979	60,399	52,830	7,569	16,366	36,464	910	20.4%	52.3%
Pinellas County	502,937	126,874	101,715	25,159	32,597	69,118	5,884	27.2%	55.6%
Polk County	281,291	67,040	58,097	8,943	17,872	40,225	1,256	22.3%	44.7%
Putnam County	37,141	8,909	8,246	663	2,523	5,723	na	20.9%	24.1%
St. Johns County	91,167	19,214	15,841	3,373	6,661	9,180	787	26.1%	49.2%
St. Lucie County	137,077	34,902	31,513	3,389	10,658	20,855	384	25.2%	49.0%
Santa Rosa County	65,368	12,360	10,933	1,427	4,368	6,565	277	23.1%	30.8%
Sarasota County	228,664	75,984	64,523	11,461	20,994	43,529	2,802	23.9%	44.4%
Seminole County	182,133	29,449	24,189	5,260	11,650	12,539	1,036	28.5%	61.9%
Sumter County	55,740	27,991	26,868	1,123	10,022	16,846	82	16.3%	34.3%
Volusia County	254,452	65,197	54,674	10,523	18,690	35,984	2,041	23.0%	51.3%

Table J-2: Counties—Summary of Housing and Householder Characteristics—*Continued*

| | | | | | Householders 65 Years and Over | | | | |
| | | | | | Owner Householders | | | Percent of Owner Householders Who Pay 35% or More of Income for Housing Costs | Percent of Renter Householders Who Pay 35% or More of Income for Rental Costs |
	Total Housing Units	Total Households	Owner Occupied	Renter Occupied	With a Mortgage	Without a Mortgage	Renter Households With Meals Included in Rent		
Georgia								18.9%	35.9%
Barrow County	26,407	3,742	3,366	376	1,397	1,969	na	22.9%	46.0%
Bartow County	39,827	6,660	5,739	921	2,301	3,438	na	23.7%	49.9%
Bibb County	69,751	12,547	9,272	3,275	3,527	5,745	487	19.8%	34.5%
Bulloch County	29,054	4,231	3,337	894	1,102	2,235	60	20.1%	55.9%
Carroll County	44,609	7,632	5,996	1,636	2,292	3,704	156	15.9%	40.5%
Catoosa County	26,643	5,795	4,938	857	1,446	3,492	na	22.8%	53.3%
Chatham County	120,222	21,924	18,044	3,880	6,341	11,703	685	24.0%	49.8%
Cherokee County	82,824	12,997	11,161	1,836	4,798	6,363	138	15.5%	48.7%
Clarke County	51,096	6,367	4,910	1,457	1,869	3,041	348	24.6%	54.2%
Clayton County	104,625	9,931	7,880	2,051	4,121	3,759	300		
								21.9%	44.0%
Cobb County	287,404	39,393	33,166	6,227	16,298	16,868	1,222	16.7%	57.7%
Columbia County	50,019	7,634	6,792	842	2,775	4,017	273	24.1%	42.2%
Coweta County	50,515	8,188	6,886	1,302	3,118	3,768	140	29.1%	52.0%
DeKalb County	304,974	40,015	30,516	9,499	14,144	16,372	1,059	25.9%	50.8%
Dougherty County	40,752	7,852	5,824	2,028	2,341	3,483	209	21.3%	39.3%
Douglas County	51,656	6,597	5,578	1,019	2,329	3,249	na	20.5%	47.8%
Fayette County	40,826	8,868	7,975	893	3,719	4,256	255	12.5%	42.1%
Floyd County	40,512	9,051	6,545	2,506	1,928	4,617	366	26.1%	69.8%
Forsyth County	65,237	8,366	7,217	1,149	3,535	3,682	312	27.8%	46.9%
Fulton County	437,864	56,248	37,950	18,298	17,644	20,306	2,582		
								25.4%	44.8%
Glynn County	40,948	8,374	6,754	1,620	3,136	3,618	177	23.6%	48.2%
Gwinnett County	292,451	30,096	25,411	4,685	12,677	12,734	677	18.2%	46.0%
Hall County	68,868	12,796	10,511	2,285	4,000	6,511	508	29.5%	54.5%
Henry County	76,700	9,972	8,957	1,015	4,847	4,110	na	16.5%	26.7%
Houston County	58,953	8,976	7,671	1,305	2,588	5,083	66	25.3%	36.8%
Liberty County	26,865	2,671	2,405	266	964	1,441	na	16.0%	31.9%
Lowndes County	44,660	6,975	5,239	1,736	1,840	3,399	108	21.6%	49.7%
Muscogee County	82,895	15,015	11,500	3,515	4,389	7,111	395	32.5%	52.1%
Newton County	38,317	5,917	5,132	785	2,589	2,543	na	28.2%	29.3%
Paulding County	52,343	6,247	5,504	743	2,822	2,682	na		
								20.0%	44.9%
Richmond County	86,535	14,145	11,387	2,758	4,238	7,149	69	25.3%	67.3%
Rockdale County	33,269	5,647	4,772	875	2,099	2,673	104	25.9%	45.1%
Troup County	28,157	5,337	4,321	1,016	1,581	2,740	89	7.9%	28.6%
Walker County	30,082	6,583	5,712	871	1,273	4,439	na	19.4%	49.6%
Walton County	32,434	5,978	5,056	922	1,943	3,113	100	20.7%	32.5%
Whitfield County	39,851	6,887	5,772	1,115	1,894	3,878	92		
Hawaii								23.0%	36.1%
Hawaii County	83,301	16,222	12,670	3,552	5,057	7,613	19	22.0%	40.6%
Honolulu County	338,168	77,959	58,744	19,215	25,024	33,720	954	23.4%	47.3%
Kauai County	30,026	5,565	4,401	1,164	1,775	2,626	42	29.1%	36.1%
Maui County	70,618	11,138	8,520	2,618	4,247	4,273	86		
Idaho								20.2%	52.1%
Ada County	160,782	27,658	22,000	5,658	10,103	11,897	1,811	16.3%	48.8%
Bannock County	33,235	5,794	5,069	725	1,959	3,110	145	11.7%	45.9%
Bonneville County	39,946	7,600	6,414	1,186	1,917	4,497	315	21.6%	35.2%
Canyon County	69,636	13,265	11,089	2,176	4,891	6,198	267	20.4%	48.0%
Kootenai County	63,800	13,114	10,532	2,582	4,443	6,089	450	17.7%	27.0%
Twin Falls County	31,200	6,465	5,703	762	1,780	3,923	58		
Illinois								14.9%	33.5%
Adams County	29,891	7,170	5,599	1,571	1,421	4,178	200	12.6%	47.2%
Champaign County	87,921	13,396	10,834	2,562	3,680	7,154	803	31.0%	52.2%
Cook County	2,176,932	399,022	294,236	104,786	107,268	186,968	10,586	20.6%	46.3%
DeKalb County	41,045	6,674	5,187	1,487	1,439	3,748	275	27.5%	50.3%
DuPage County	356,252	66,279	55,291	10,988	20,402	34,889	3,317	29.2%	62.9%
Kane County	182,241	31,517	26,935	4,582	12,119	14,816	847	19.1%	55.9%
Kankakee County	45,201	9,408	7,608	1,800	2,024	5,584	313	24.2%	32.1%
Kendall County	40,524	5,443	4,766	677	2,193	2,573	57	32.2%	47.0%
Lake County	260,519	45,604	37,553	8,051	15,739	21,814	1,971	19.6%	37.4%
LaSalle County	49,947	11,928	9,939	1,989	2,446	7,493	231		
								31.1%	55.3%
McHenry County	116,270	19,867	17,548	2,319	7,819	9,729	491	17.0%	30.3%
McLean County	70,054	11,076	9,294	1,782	3,099	6,195	408	12.5%	41.0%
Macon County	50,453	11,817	9,814	2,003	2,372	7,442	401	15.5%	49.4%
Madison County	117,385	25,080	20,979	4,101	6,259	14,720	569	14.6%	40.2%
Peoria County	83,217	17,184	13,775	3,409	3,931	9,844	513	16.2%	44.8%
Rock Island County	65,766	16,222	12,706	3,516	3,414	9,292	927	18.6%	47.3%
St. Clair County	117,011	22,614	18,373	4,241	5,471	12,902	649	14.1%	41.3%
Sangamon County	90,133	18,562	15,036	3,526	4,928	10,108	610	13.6%	33.0%
Tazewell County	57,608	13,854	11,448	2,406	3,236	8,212	531	15.2%	37.2%
Vermilion County	36,221	8,899	7,221	1,678	1,992	5,229	171		
								29.1%	51.4%
Will County	237,819	39,421	33,940	5,481	13,697	20,243	1,120	15.3%	35.1%
Williamson County	30,465	6,960	5,579	1,381	1,453	4,126	103	20.8%	41.8%
Winnebago County	125,894	25,799	20,195	5,604	7,006	13,189	815		

Table J-2: Counties—Summary of Housing and Householder Characteristics—*Continued*

| | | | | | Householders 65 Years and Over | | | | |
| | | | | | Owner Householders | | | Percent of Owner Householders Who Pay 35% or More of Income for Housing Costs | Percent of Renter Householders Who Pay 35% or More of Income for Rental Costs |
	Total Housing Units	Total Households	Owner Occupied	Renter Occupied	With a Mortgage	Without a Mortgage	Renter Households With Meals Included in Rent		
Indiana									
Allen County	152,621	27,935	22,304	5,631	8,123	14,181	602	11.5%	46.8%
Bartholomew County	33,179	6,948	5,943	1,005	2,008	3,935	290	13.9%	47.9%
Clark County	47,985	9,165	7,334	1,831	2,797	4,537	335	18.6%	39.1%
Delaware County	52,239	11,532	9,741	1,791	3,569	6,172	121	13.2%	40.9%
Elkhart County	77,764	15,273	12,697	2,576	4,595	8,102	386	18.9%	37.0%
Floyd County	32,037	6,332	5,167	1,165	1,555	3,612	28	18.7%	36.0%
Grant County	30,392	7,615	6,387	1,228	2,200	4,187	115	14.0%	22.1%
Hamilton County	109,061	14,779	12,291	2,488	5,979	6,312	492	18.2%	35.2%
Hancock County	28,314	5,619	4,971	648	2,328	2,643	56	21.6%	29.0%
Hendricks County	56,196	10,047	8,536	1,511	3,397	5,139	275	20.8%	47.4%
Howard County	38,588	9,030	7,424	1,606	3,003	4,421	239	13.4%	55.3%
Johnson County	57,251	11,086	8,785	2,301	3,598	5,187	269	14.6%	48.2%
Kosciusko County	37,164	6,939	6,083	856	2,099	3,984	45	14.6%	39.1%
Lake County	209,083	41,018	34,052	6,966	12,739	21,313	441	19.5%	44.3%
LaPorte County	48,508	10,456	8,780	1,676	3,028	5,752	218	18.0%	53.2%
Madison County	58,958	13,929	11,755	2,174	4,087	7,668	321	16.4%	46.9%
Marion County	418,276	63,430	46,731	16,699	21,743	24,988	2,291	21.2%	51.9%
Monroe County	59,263	9,410	7,678	1,732	2,891	4,787	517	16.7%	42.7%
Morgan County	27,776	5,550	4,821	729	1,654	3,167	45	18.4%	43.3%
Porter County	66,321	12,514	10,912	1,602	4,230	6,682	306	19.5%	61.3%
St. Joseph County	114,883	22,588	18,208	4,380	6,715	11,493	454	14.6%	40.1%
Tippecanoe County	71,722	10,609	8,386	2,223	3,277	5,109	628	14.5%	43.5%
Vanderburgh County	83,049	16,819	13,334	3,485	4,037	9,297	500	15.5%	49.6%
Vigo County	46,099	8,907	7,325	1,582	2,492	4,833	164	14.5%	43.8%
Wayne County	31,241	7,535	5,944	1,591	2,051	3,893	89	18.5%	28.2%
Iowa									
Black Hawk County	56,104	11,863	9,569	2,294	2,829	6,740	601	13.3%	44.9%
Dallas County	27,801	4,323	3,594	729	1,034	2,560	94	16.9%	44.4%
Dubuque County	39,425	8,939	7,259	1,680	1,392	5,867	439	13.5%	50.0%
Johnson County	56,576	7,794	6,288	1,506	2,073	4,215	455	8.0%	41.7%
Linn County	92,964	18,216	15,456	2,760	4,649	10,807	699	16.6%	41.2%
Polk County	184,241	30,000	24,126	5,874	8,535	15,591	1,097	19.0%	46.4%
Pottawattamie County	39,387	8,432	6,627	1,805	1,965	4,662	235	18.0%	42.2%
Scott County	72,177	14,428	11,128	3,300	3,483	7,645	813	16.2%	43.2%
Story County	36,965	5,780	4,588	1,192	1,239	3,349	135	8.6%	37.7%
Woodbury County	41,429	8,837	6,518	2,319	1,575	4,943	546	14.0%	52.2%
Kansas									
Butler County	26,154	5,372	4,239	1,133	1,291	2,948	352	17.5%	27.2%
Douglas County	47,048	6,461	4,810	1,651	1,977	2,833	283	19.2%	49.5%
Johnson County	227,652	39,101	30,339	8,762	12,641	17,698	2,943	20.0%	53.0%
Leavenworth County	28,777	5,331	4,485	846	1,593	2,892	44	22.2%	37.0%
Riley County	28,734	3,449	2,686	763	775	1,911	222	14.4%	47.6%
Sedgwick County	212,320	37,312	29,328	7,984	8,958	20,370	1,598	15.8%	49.6%
Shawnee County	79,260	16,495	12,590	3,905	3,915	8,675	522	12.2%	39.0%
Wyandotte County	66,727	10,853	8,558	2,295	2,636	5,922	237	22.0%	48.6%
Kentucky									
Boone County	46,630	7,509	5,931	1,578	2,461	3,470	322	23.6%	33.5%
Bullitt County	29,662	5,983	5,241	742	1,918	3,323	123	17.7%	31.0%
Campbell County	39,597	7,577	6,380	1,197	2,397	3,983	43	20.1%	31.2%
Christian County	29,522	4,833	3,994	839	953	3,041	na	13.3%	31.0%
Daviess County	41,710	9,372	7,446	1,926	1,980	5,466	178	11.7%	36.0%
Fayette County	135,963	20,954	15,570	5,384	6,151	9,419	712	16.6%	40.9%
Hardin County	44,276	7,210	6,050	1,160	1,929	4,121	121	13.4%	27.9%
Jefferson County	337,934	65,238	51,429	13,809	18,417	33,012	1,769	19.0%	38.7%
Kenton County	69,122	11,711	9,322	2,389	3,645	5,677	385	21.4%	48.7%
McCracken County	31,150	6,928	5,498	1,430	1,605	3,893	92	9.4%	27.8%
Madison County	35,245	6,097	5,104	993	1,438	3,666	89	16.1%	35.6%
Pike County	30,312	6,227	5,362	865	830	4,532	na	9.7%	22.1%
Warren County	47,856	8,312	6,756	1,556	2,245	4,511	310	16.3%	56.0%
Louisiana									
Ascension Parish	41,675	6,304	5,633	671	1,716	3,917	na	17.5%	31.4%
Bossier Parish	50,547	9,301	7,834	1,467	2,820	5,014	307	12.1%	42.4%
Caddo Parish	112,205	22,588	18,566	4,022	5,431	13,135	478	12.9%	39.1%
Calcasieu Parish	83,192	15,754	13,263	2,491	2,832	10,431	298	12.9%	32.9%
East Baton Rouge Parish	188,362	30,978	25,576	5,402	8,899	16,677	856	15.6%	47.5%
Iberia Parish	29,817	6,097	5,225	872	655	4,570	139	9.6%	45.6%
Jefferson Parish	189,079	38,072	30,664	7,408	7,753	22,911	435	17.5%	42.3%
Lafayette Parish	94,439	14,646	12,460	2,186	3,309	9,151	230	15.7%	41.7%
Lafourche Parish	38,907	7,842	6,662	1,180	1,048	5,614	57	12.8%	25.2%
Livingston Parish	51,265	8,216	7,218	998	1,959	5,259	78	11.2%	43.3%
Orleans Parish	190,707	26,272	18,292	7,980	5,607	12,685	324	27.1%	50.4%
Ouachita Parish	64,882	12,544	9,935	2,609	2,966	6,969	140	17.4%	47.3%
Rapides Parish	56,053	11,646	9,349	2,297	2,209	7,140	214	14.2%	39.5%
St. Landry Parish	35,812	7,576	6,460	1,116	1,115	5,345	0	16.6%	43.2%
St. Tammany Parish	96,141	18,763	16,147	2,616	5,509	10,638	365	18.9%	45.8%
Tangipahoa Parish	50,799	9,082	7,855	1,227	2,319	5,536	na	17.1%	17.9%
Terrebonne Parish	43,974	8,315	7,222	1,093	1,538	5,684	na	11.9%	25.0%

Table J-2: Counties—Summary of Housing and Householder Characteristics—*Continued*

| | | | | Householders 65 Years and Over | | | | | |
| | | | | Owner Householders | | | | Percent of Owner Householders Who Pay 35% or More of Income for Housing Costs | Percent of Renter Householders Who Pay 35% or More of Income for Rental Costs |
	Total Housing Units	Total Households	Owner Occupied	Renter Occupied	With a Mortgage	Without a Mortgage	Renter Households With Meals Included in Rent		
Maine									
Androscoggin County	49,137	9,997	7,315	2,682	2,256	5,059	364	22.4%	31.7%
Aroostook County	39,501	8,899	6,633	2,266	1,478	5,155	61	19.5%	30.4%
Cumberland County	138,966	25,922	19,365	6,557	7,118	12,247	1,208	25.6%	41.8%
Kennebec County	61,133	12,060	9,699	2,361	3,347	6,352	28	20.4%	36.3%
Penobscot County	73,971	14,088	10,251	3,837	3,016	7,235	581	18.2%	37.7%
York County	106,116	20,159	15,788	4,371	5,939	9,849	564	28.3%	45.4%
Maryland									
Allegany County	33,328	8,459	6,630	1,829	1,724	4,906	38	17.9%	27.5%
Anne Arundel County	214,291	40,034	34,928	5,106	16,250	18,678	691	24.2%	48.9%
Baltimore County	336,021	74,636	56,186	18,450	20,064	36,122	4,422	23.2%	54.7%
Calvert County	33,998	5,903	4,965	938	2,609	2,356	298	23.0%	60.1%
Carroll County	62,504	13,690	11,237	2,453	4,512	6,725	813	21.0%	49.0%
Cecil County	41,385	7,182	5,956	1,226	2,057	3,899	0	24.5%	41.6%
Charles County	55,637	7,861	6,768	1,093	3,444	3,324	27	22.1%	66.7%
Frederick County	90,980	16,698	13,650	3,048	6,047	7,603	650	21.6%	47.9%
Harford County	96,303	19,247	16,046	3,201	5,433	10,613	290	22.5%	36.1%
Howard County	110,627	17,728	14,698	3,030	7,889	6,809	688	24.5%	51.9%
Montgomery County	377,361	73,571	57,310	16,261	26,275	31,035	4,114	24.0%	53.2%
Prince George's County	328,653	50,886	40,650	10,236	23,650	17,000	394	30.0%	47.1%
St. Mary's County	41,817	6,787	5,820	967	2,512	3,308	72	24.3%	37.2%
Washington County	60,899	13,680	10,733	2,947	3,439	7,294	337	26.2%	38.7%
Wicomico County	41,257	8,249	6,474	1,775	2,110	4,364	99	18.7%	50.5%
Massachusetts									
Barnstable County	160,420	34,374	29,333	5,041	11,513	17,820	524	31.3%	39.6%
Berkshire County	68,450	16,435	12,336	4,099	4,196	8,140	384	26.2%	29.1%
Bristol County	230,424	48,386	33,592	14,794	11,330	22,262	755	29.9%	41.7%
Essex County	306,706	66,454	45,646	20,808	17,322	28,324	1,933	29.7%	40.0%
Franklin County	33,691	6,942	5,566	1,376	1,781	3,785	45	23.5%	46.4%
Hampden County	191,935	41,761	29,960	11,801	9,817	20,143	1,092	26.9%	43.9%
Hampshire County	62,674	13,699	10,657	3,042	3,299	7,358	314	21.8%	37.7%
Middlesex County	612,448	125,401	91,915	33,486	33,894	58,021	3,826	31.1%	41.4%
Norfolk County	271,056	62,632	44,592	18,040	15,484	29,108	2,582	28.5%	43.2%
Plymouth County	200,634	43,633	35,171	8,462	13,369	21,802	948	31.1%	38.8%
Suffolk County	315,048	51,273	24,182	27,091	10,664	13,518	1,356	34.9%	36.5%
Worcester County	327,329	63,136	43,876	19,260	15,426	28,450	1,967	27.8%	40.1%
Michigan									
Allegan County	49,457	9,407	8,398	1,009	2,810	5,588	122	21.6%	45.5%
Bay County	48,157	11,597	9,898	1,699	2,183	7,715	188	18.9%	36.7%
Berrien County	76,797	16,237	13,715	2,522	4,767	8,948	293	21.8%	34.6%
Calhoun County	60,871	13,077	10,478	2,599	3,395	7,083	193	19.7%	35.2%
Clinton County	30,711	6,360	5,941	419	1,629	4,312	na	20.5%	35.1%
Eaton County	47,031	9,751	8,014	1,737	3,254	4,760	295	20.0%	42.7%
Genesee County	191,631	39,113	32,420	6,693	11,072	21,348	556	22.1%	48.9%
Grand Traverse County	41,720	8,457	6,973	1,484	2,794	4,179	334	22.5%	48.5%
Ingham County	121,293	19,912	15,022	4,890	6,321	8,701	539	17.9%	42.9%
Isabella County	28,342	4,332	3,676	656	1,102	2,574	58	19.9%	27.1%
Jackson County	69,289	14,626	11,788	2,838	3,768	8,020	768	19.9%	51.4%
Kalamazoo County	110,006	20,203	16,427	3,776	6,003	10,424	520	20.9%	47.4%
Kent County	247,032	43,911	35,577	8,334	10,665	24,912	1,832	18.7%	40.7%
Lapeer County	36,247	7,587	6,832	755	2,614	4,218	45	18.5%	49.8%
Lenawee County	43,443	9,461	7,877	1,584	2,644	5,233	150	22.3%	46.7%
Livingston County	72,866	14,436	13,066	1,370	5,804	7,262	272	23.4%	46.5%
Macomb County	356,864	79,675	65,839	13,836	22,727	43,112	2,540	23.0%	46.5%
Marquette County	34,354	6,460	5,048	1,412	1,126	3,922	59	12.9%	25.8%
Midland County	36,016	8,123	6,868	1,255	1,821	5,047	418	18.4%	39.2%
Monroe County	62,876	13,592	11,361	2,231	3,788	7,573	148	21.8%	34.5%
Muskegon County	73,420	15,242	13,130	2,112	3,855	9,275	248	18.1%	41.7%
Oakland County	527,173	106,767	84,609	22,158	35,583	49,026	4,515	25.8%	49.9%
Ottawa County	102,778	19,807	16,830	2,977	5,326	11,504	895	17.9%	47.2%
Saginaw County	86,739	20,511	17,038	3,473	4,771	12,267	498	19.7%	44.2%
St. Clair County	71,662	15,532	13,066	2,466	4,156	8,910	295	20.6%	38.3%
Shiawassee County	30,245	6,427	5,525	902	1,653	3,872	84	19.2%	35.4%
Van Buren County	36,738	6,789	5,806	983	1,886	3,920	74	28.3%	44.3%
Washtenaw County	147,636	24,398	19,093	5,305	7,737	11,356	1,445	24.3%	46.4%
Wayne County	819,572	154,962	120,059	34,903	41,258	78,801	2,565	26.0%	44.6%
Minnesota									
Anoka County	127,382	21,874	18,249	3,625	7,423	10,826	575	22.0%	57.6%
Blue Earth County	26,345	4,944	3,714	1,230	857	2,857	350	14.4%	39.5%
Carver County	34,917	5,237	3,700	1,537	1,564	2,136	249	23.5%	50.5%
Dakota County	160,374	26,628	20,923	5,705	8,987	11,936	1,337	22.0%	53.5%
Hennepin County	511,343	87,965	65,993	21,972	25,464	40,529	4,052	23.9%	50.7%
Olmsted County	60,816	11,322	9,034	2,288	2,606	6,428	604	16.2%	47.0%
Ramsey County	217,333	40,715	29,617	11,098	10,570	19,047	1,974	18.6%	47.1%
St. Louis County	103,039	20,875	15,896	4,979	4,070	11,826	786	17.5%	41.5%
Scott County	47,719	6,480	5,107	1,373	2,034	3,073	251	25.5%	37.6%
Sherburne County	32,468	4,524	3,693	831	1,730	1,963	90	23.9%	36.8%
Stearns County	62,182	11,817	9,436	2,381	2,335	7,101	344	18.2%	36.7%
Washington County	93,458	16,953	13,632	3,321	5,860	7,772	943	23.7%	53.4%
Wright County	49,114	7,685	6,201	1,484	2,209	3,992	315	22.3%	43.6%

Table J-2: Counties—Summary of Housing and Householder Characteristics—*Continued*

| | | | | | Householders 65 Years and Over | | | | |
| | | | | | Owner Householders | | | Percent of Owner Householders Who Pay 35% or More of Income for Housing Costs | Percent of Renter Householders Who Pay 35% or More of Income for Rental Costs |
	Total Housing Units	Total Households	Owner Occupied	Renter Occupied	With a Mortgage	Without a Mortgage	Renter Households With Meals Included in Rent		
Mississippi									
DeSoto County	62,125	10,554	9,223	1,331	3,885	5,338	200	15.3%	56.6%
Forrest County	32,313	5,577	4,566	1,011	1,306	3,260	na	18.9%	43.0%
Harrison County	86,792	14,816	12,313	2,503	4,128	8,185	119	18.2%	39.3%
Hinds County	103,626	17,118	13,992	3,126	4,968	9,024	242	16.5%	35.4%
Jackson County	60,454	11,224	10,006	1,218	2,779	7,227	na	18.3%	46.3%
Jones County	28,482	6,240	5,502	738	1,113	4,389	na	16.7%	21.4%
Lauderdale County	34,766	7,316	6,018	1,298	1,375	4,643	187	16.7%	48.7%
Lee County	35,996	7,122	5,770	1,352	1,564	4,206	294	12.1%	46.2%
Madison County	39,156	6,612	5,296	1,316	2,012	3,284	525	18.0%	60.5%
Rankin County	56,932	10,708	9,422	1,286	2,742	6,680	217	11.5%	45.6%
Missouri									
Boone County	70,281	9,695	7,906	1,789	2,660	5,246	347	13.9%	45.9%
Buchanan County	38,426	7,777	6,033	1,744	1,497	4,536	216	15.3%	45.1%
Cape Girardeau County	32,675	6,487	5,209	1,278	1,432	3,777	242	13.9%	44.8%
Cass County	40,157	8,700	6,987	1,713	2,448	4,539	310	16.9%	53.7%
Christian County	31,847	6,348	5,070	1,278	1,840	3,230	105	20.4%	41.9%
Clay County	93,975	16,195	13,458	2,737	4,955	8,503	97	17.4%	42.2%
Cole County	32,410	6,589	4,951	1,638	1,083	3,868	291	10.3%	36.1%
Franklin County	43,534	8,825	7,646	1,179	1,669	5,977	150	14.7%	41.7%
Greene County	126,254	25,202	19,977	5,225	6,618	13,359	848	14.0%	49.4%
Jackson County	312,172	56,156	42,760	13,396	15,672	27,088	1,619	23.0%	46.5%
Jasper County	50,728	9,733	7,579	2,154	2,047	5,532	295	17.1%	42.6%
Jefferson County	88,063	15,780	13,926	1,854	5,010	8,916	166	15.3%	37.2%
Platte County	39,357	6,619	5,184	1,435	1,899	3,285	700	21.7%	49.5%
St. Charles County	142,639	27,199	23,029	4,170	9,870	13,159	1,237	20.1%	50.4%
St. Francois County	28,770	6,033	4,792	1,241	1,353	3,439	92	11.6%	48.0%
St. Louis County	437,773	96,508	78,850	17,658	29,208	49,642	4,246	21.6%	47.4%
Montana									
Cascade County	37,378	8,117	6,515	1,602	1,717	4,798	378	12.6%	47.8%
Flathead County	47,103	8,779	7,031	1,748	2,129	4,902	356	22.7%	31.2%
Gallatin County	42,680	5,808	4,677	1,131	1,315	3,362	264	18.0%	50.9%
Missoula County	50,385	8,036	6,356	1,680	2,048	4,308	578	15.8%	53.8%
Yellowstone County	64,397	14,161	11,196	2,965	3,582	7,614	678	15.4%	43.4%
Nebraska									
Douglas County	221,426	37,242	28,570	8,672	9,915	18,655	2,210	19.2%	48.2%
Lancaster County	121,725	20,392	14,797	5,595	4,620	10,177	1,695	14.6%	45.1%
Sarpy County	62,939	8,953	6,989	1,964	2,781	4,208	567	19.5%	43.7%
Nevada									
Clark County	845,485	137,213	99,687	37,526	52,462	47,225	2,263	27.0%	53.7%
Washoe County	185,112	32,880	24,661	8,219	11,368	13,293	652	27.8%	55.4%
New Hampshire									
Cheshire County	34,766	7,472	5,730	1,742	1,780	3,950	200	35.4%	55.9%
Grafton County	51,337	8,927	7,261	1,666	2,005	5,256	291	24.7%	23.6%
Hillsborough County	166,446	29,700	21,718	7,982	8,122	13,596	871	32.0%	48.2%
Merrimack County	63,547	12,436	9,550	2,886	2,974	6,576	312	29.4%	42.7%
Rockingham County	127,017	24,103	19,426	4,677	7,126	12,300	688	31.7%	35.0%
Strafford County	51,885	9,381	7,258	2,123	2,294	4,964	162	29.0%	43.2%
New Jersey									
Atlantic County	127,046	24,270	19,217	5,053	7,288	11,929	244	37.8%	39.4%
Bergen County	353,499	83,020	61,742	21,278	20,205	41,537	1,463	40.1%	49.0%
Burlington County	176,315	39,411	33,496	5,915	13,025	20,471	765	30.9%	58.1%
Camden County	205,363	41,664	30,159	11,505	10,592	19,567	1,521	36.5%	56.0%
Cape May County	98,503	13,676	11,304	2,372	3,729	7,575	446	32.7%	44.4%
Cumberland County	56,073	12,301	9,387	2,914	2,548	6,839	17	32.1%	51.1%
Essex County	313,130	55,719	32,793	22,926	13,147	19,646	1,056	44.7%	48.9%
Gloucester County	110,569	22,640	19,098	3,542	6,904	12,194	536	33.6%	46.4%
Hudson County	271,671	40,421	19,170	21,251	6,605	12,565	272	46.2%	44.4%
Hunterdon County	49,797	10,475	9,399	1,076	3,677	5,722	38	33.9%	48.3%
Mercer County	143,667	29,042	22,036	7,006	7,906	14,130	515	31.0%	46.7%
Middlesex County	296,423	58,029	46,106	11,923	15,056	31,050	609	35.9%	49.1%
Monmouth County	259,141	56,213	43,631	12,582	15,612	28,019	2,013	36.0%	51.8%
Morris County	190,382	41,827	34,024	7,803	12,188	21,836	1,110	32.5%	51.5%
Ocean County	278,935	79,232	71,988	7,244	23,643	48,345	1,203	32.1%	51.0%
Passaic County	175,988	34,527	23,201	11,326	7,658	15,543	304	44.3%	51.4%
Salem County	27,496	6,556	5,092	1,464	1,507	3,585	199	29.7%	54.2%
Somerset County	123,771	24,470	20,542	3,928	7,536	13,006	965	37.0%	57.7%
Sussex County	62,249	11,022	9,619	1,403	3,832	5,787	214	31.7%	57.7%
Union County	200,104	40,075	28,932	11,143	9,695	19,237	206	41.3%	52.9%
Warren County	45,100	9,011	7,065	1,946	2,210	4,855	65	33.8%	49.6%

Table J-2: Counties—Summary of Housing and Householder Characteristics—*Continued*

| | | | | Householders 65 Years and Over | | | | | |
| | | | | | Owner Householders | | | Percent of Owner Householders Who Pay 35% or More of Income for Housing Costs | Percent of Renter Householders Who Pay 35% or More of Income for Rental Costs |
	Total Housing Units	Total Households	Owner Occupied	Renter Occupied	With a Mortgage	Without a Mortgage	Renter Households With Meals Included in Rent		
New Mexico									
Bernalillo County	285,288	53,537	42,527	11,010	16,295	26,232	1,315	19.5%	41.6%
Chaves County	26,691	5,676	4,541	1,135	1,121	3,420	141	12.2%	28.2%
Doña Ana County	82,346	16,964	14,185	2,779	4,854	9,331	150	14.4%	40.1%
Lea County	24,936	4,453	3,613	840	743	2,870	na	13.0%	34.0%
McKinley County	25,812	4,378	3,722	656	461	3,261	0	12.0%	32.8%
Otero County	30,989	6,175	5,498	677	1,491	4,007	86	15.3%	25.8%
Sandoval County	52,807	10,240	9,023	1,217	3,793	5,230	129	15.7%	49.0%
San Juan County	49,481	8,792	7,803	989	2,107	5,696	35	13.4%	35.8%
Santa Fe County	71,444	15,667	12,521	3,146	5,215	7,306	418	24.7%	37.7%
Valencia County	30,152	6,177	5,564	613	1,944	3,620	na	22.9%	31.5%
New York									
Albany County	137,714	26,694	19,634	7,060	6,319	13,315	579	23.2%	44.5%
Bronx County	513,229	89,776	26,833	62,943	9,887	16,946	913	38.5%	49.7%
Broome County	90,309	20,716	16,101	4,615	4,049	12,052	582	17.6%	43.2%
Cattaraugus County	41,075	7,955	6,582	1,373	1,522	5,060	14	17.2%	35.6%
Cayuga County	36,438	8,022	5,944	2,078	1,660	4,284	374	17.6%	25.4%
Chautauqua County	66,820	14,404	11,382	3,022	2,810	8,572	102	18.5%	37.7%
Chemung County	38,342	8,794	6,934	1,860	1,785	5,149	149	14.4%	36.1%
Clinton County	35,904	7,230	5,430	1,800	1,266	4,164	196	17.9%	42.0%
Dutchess County	118,678	25,133	19,026	6,107	6,624	12,402	418	30.3%	51.4%
Erie County	420,008	94,461	72,621	21,840	21,528	51,093	2,200	18.3%	45.2%
Jefferson County	58,072	8,655	6,545	2,110	1,575	4,970	45	23.1%	20.7%
Kings County	1,001,986	180,377	70,894	109,483	24,927	45,967	1,108	41.6%	51.2%
Livingston County	27,131	5,743	4,621	1,122	1,473	3,148	85	20.9%	42.0%
Madison County	31,765	6,509	5,447	1,062	1,709	3,738	0	23.4%	31.7%
Monroe County	320,821	68,181	50,776	17,405	19,024	31,752	3,042	22.6%	53.1%
Nassau County	467,357	118,422	100,212	18,210	31,033	69,179	1,712	38.3%	50.0%
New York County	848,768	153,315	42,526	110,789	13,024	29,502	1,871	27.2%	44.1%
Niagara County	99,132	22,254	17,136	5,118	4,350	12,786	148	18.4%	46.2%
Oneida County	104,094	23,948	18,105	5,843	4,610	13,495	556	17.7%	39.2%
Onondaga County	202,793	42,609	32,711	9,898	10,624	22,087	1,091	20.5%	47.8%
Ontario County	48,382	10,730	8,303	2,427	3,051	5,252	496	20.4%	48.9%
Orange County	137,750	25,451	19,457	5,994	7,075	12,382	391	33.0%	53.8%
Oswego County	53,628	9,931	8,070	1,861	1,940	6,130	79	18.1%	21.5%
Putnam County	38,225	7,531	6,363	1,168	2,333	4,030	62	36.6%	54.6%
Queens County	837,509	164,595	94,477	70,118	28,940	65,537	1,067	35.5%	53.1%
Rensselaer County	71,553	13,772	10,576	3,196	3,119	7,457	239	20.9%	41.7%
Richmond County	177,124	35,919	27,063	8,856	9,879	17,184	81	34.3%	43.6%
Rockland County	104,118	24,214	19,178	5,036	6,782	12,396	634	33.6%	52.8%
St. Lawrence County	52,154	10,195	8,019	2,176	1,848	6,171	47	16.9%	29.7%
Saratoga County	99,333	19,879	15,175	4,704	5,031	10,144	507	20.0%	48.2%
Schenectady County	68,127	14,296	10,757	3,539	3,151	7,606	441	23.1%	50.8%
Steuben County	48,871	10,147	8,344	1,803	1,841	6,503	0	13.5%	29.6%
Suffolk County	569,677	120,129	101,280	18,849	34,703	66,577	1,728	37.3%	55.8%
Sullivan County	49,329	7,407	5,979	1,428	1,431	4,548	0	25.3%	28.5%
Tompkins County	41,710	7,172	5,385	1,787	1,600	3,785	351	17.7%	36.2%
Ulster County	83,696	17,228	13,419	3,809	4,565	8,854	336	33.6%	43.9%
Warren County	38,822	7,525	5,650	1,875	1,615	4,035	130	19.6%	49.1%
Wayne County	41,060	8,545	7,076	1,469	2,485	4,591	0	19.2%	34.9%
Westchester County	370,235	85,012	62,013	22,999	21,441	40,572	1,838	39.2%	47.9%
North Carolina									
Alamance County	67,098	15,143	11,998	3,145	4,164	7,834	522	20.1%	53.5%
Brunswick County	78,425	15,532	13,633	1,899	6,545	7,088	na	23.5%	51.3%
Buncombe County	114,340	24,525	19,240	5,285	6,472	12,768	1,229	19.1%	42.3%
Burke County	40,846	9,550	7,540	2,010	2,112	5,428	150	15.5%	26.6%
Cabarrus County	72,665	12,266	10,042	2,224	4,095	5,947	268	21.9%	32.8%
Caldwell County	37,656	8,715	7,179	1,536	1,879	5,300	10	15.8%	49.6%
Carteret County	48,360	8,027	6,869	1,158	2,515	4,354	134	21.9%	28.4%
Catawba County	67,834	13,927	12,170	1,757	3,971	8,199	153	16.0%	30.7%
Chatham County	29,006	7,609	6,554	1,055	2,165	4,389	340	18.4%	32.3%
Cleveland County	43,360	10,113	8,219	1,894	2,415	5,804	21	18.5%	45.9%
Craven County	45,334	10,411	8,806	1,605	3,547	5,259	159	22.3%	38.9%
Cumberland County	138,423	20,132	16,183	3,949	6,361	9,822	259	22.3%	39.6%
Davidson County	72,746	15,360	13,003	2,357	4,132	8,871	223	19.8%	40.4%
Durham County	121,602	17,478	12,935	4,543	5,928	7,007	938	21.0%	49.6%
Forsyth County	157,794	29,928	24,458	5,470	9,991	14,467	976	18.9%	43.1%
Gaston County	89,057	17,191	14,303	2,888	4,970	9,333	384	20.0%	45.8%
Guilford County	219,391	40,114	31,795	8,319	13,067	18,728	1,746	21.5%	41.6%
Harnett County	47,509	7,745	6,442	1,303	2,262	4,180	50	25.7%	32.6%
Henderson County	54,815	15,045	12,964	2,081	4,230	8,734	541	15.6%	45.9%
Iredell County	69,267	12,673	10,975	1,698	4,054	6,921	31	20.4%	35.2%
Johnston County	68,200	11,292	9,035	2,257	3,486	5,549	135	22.1%	36.9%
Lincoln County	33,677	6,568	5,667	901	2,159	3,508	na	16.9%	29.2%
Mecklenburg County	401,260	52,955	41,156	11,799	20,152	21,004	2,340	25.4%	51.2%
Moore County	44,228	12,681	10,755	1,926	4,055	6,700	492	18.4%	31.0%
Nash County	42,340	9,311	7,092	2,219	2,568	4,524	134	23.4%	37.4%
New Hanover County	101,921	18,801	14,517	4,284	6,795	7,722	861	25.1%	51.2%
Onslow County	70,717	8,668	7,051	1,617	2,612	4,439	na	19.5%	46.6%
Orange County	55,990	8,516	6,674	1,842	2,700	3,974	241	20.3%	45.7%
Pitt County	75,439	11,087	8,690	2,397	2,951	5,739	330	28.2%	37.0%
Randolph County	61,168	12,944	11,121	1,823	3,098	8,023	45	19.4%	30.6%

Table J-2: Counties—Summary of Housing and Householder Characteristics—*Continued*

| | | | | Householders 65 Years and Over | | | | | |
| | | | | | Owner Householders | | | Percent of Owner Householders | Percent of Renter Householders Who |
	Total Housing Units	Total Households	Owner Occupied	Renter Occupied	With a Mortgage	Without a Mortgage	Renter Households With Meals Included in Rent	Who Pay 35% or More of Income for Housing Costs	Pay 35% or More of Income for Rental Costs
North Carolina—Cont.									
Robeson County	52,661	9,833	8,072	1,761	1,773	6,299	na	21.4%	35.9%
Rockingham County	43,638	9,877	8,230	1,647	2,349	5,881	96	19.7%	34.7%
Rowan County	60,184	13,295	11,292	2,003	3,658	7,634	115	22.2%	34.8%
Rutherford County	33,853	7,588	6,357	1,231	1,772	4,585	0	16.3%	21.5%
Surry County	33,631	8,442	6,961	1,481	1,987	4,974	97	22.9%	35.2%
Union County	73,397	11,867	10,473	1,394	4,592	5,881	162	24.5%	57.9%
Wake County	376,811	50,571	39,338	11,233	18,957	20,381	2,238	21.4%	53.1%
Wayne County	53,027	10,404	8,077	2,327	2,719	5,358	180	21.5%	44.2%
Wilkes County	33,043	7,838	6,864	974	1,787	5,077	31	20.9%	44.9%
Wilson County	35,607	7,792	5,657	2,135	1,790	3,867	140	27.2%	47.0%
North Dakota									
Burleigh County	36,486	7,417	5,629	1,788	1,517	4,112	348	11.8%	48.7%
Cass County	69,412	9,923	6,282	3,641	1,758	4,524	601	10.5%	43.4%
Grand Forks County	29,611	4,748	3,445	1,303	784	2,661	181	16.0%	19.6%
Ohio									
Allen County	44,935	9,963	8,244	1,719	2,428	5,816	327	16.2%	46.2%
Ashtabula County	46,022	10,295	8,343	1,952	2,463	5,880	132	21.9%	36.0%
Belmont County	32,346	7,881	6,474	1,407	1,419	5,055	54	9.0%	23.7%
Butler County	148,492	27,637	23,021	4,616	9,902	13,119	614	24.4%	44.7%
Clark County	61,319	14,890	11,976	2,914	4,053	7,923	574	13.7%	31.4%
Clermont County	81,021	15,326	12,636	2,690	5,026	7,610	315	19.0%	45.9%
Columbiana County	46,951	11,225	9,265	1,960	2,748	6,517	117	16.5%	25.2%
Cuyahoga County	620,220	131,447	97,680	33,767	34,910	62,770	4,253	25.6%	49.5%
Delaware County	67,066	10,771	9,372	1,399	4,585	4,787	118	24.5%	52.7%
Erie County	37,797	8,524	7,007	1,517	2,389	4,618	81	21.2%	29.9%
Fairfield County	58,805	11,630	9,768	1,862	3,781	5,987	473	16.2%	39.9%
Franklin County	529,610	76,037	56,099	19,938	24,935	31,164	2,571	23.2%	45.4%
Geauga County	36,585	8,947	7,982	965	2,946	5,036	289	21.8%	34.3%
Greene County	68,514	14,111	12,416	1,695	4,453	7,963	205	16.7%	32.6%
Hamilton County	376,835	70,311	51,452	18,859	20,711	30,741	3,006	24.4%	47.7%
Hancock County	33,184	6,948	5,865	1,083	1,673	4,192	325	14.9%	47.4%
Jefferson County	32,725	8,400	7,007	1,393	1,635	5,372	13	11.5%	39.1%
Lake County	101,268	24,006	19,401	4,605	6,674	12,727	697	19.2%	46.1%
Licking County	69,440	14,450	11,924	2,526	4,530	7,394	630	18.0%	47.8%
Lorain County	127,393	27,906	23,107	4,799	8,292	14,815	855	20.2%	41.5%
Lucas County	202,323	38,251	30,007	8,244	10,920	19,087	915	19.7%	43.6%
Mahoning County	111,588	28,479	22,454	6,025	7,199	15,255	732	18.5%	37.5%
Marion County	27,803	6,414	4,894	1,520	1,575	3,319	316	15.2%	40.3%
Medina County	69,590	14,720	12,141	2,579	4,462	7,679	552	18.5%	43.9%
Miami County	44,246	10,437	8,705	1,732	3,174	5,531	153	16.1%	46.3%
Montgomery County	254,379	55,283	42,378	12,905	16,064	26,314	1,510	20.9%	47.3%
Muskingum County	37,983	8,262	6,583	1,679	1,578	5,005	193	17.8%	41.4%
Portage County	67,629	13,015	11,197	1,818	4,618	6,579	189	21.4%	35.6%
Richland County	54,463	13,532	10,923	2,609	3,510	7,413	295	14.9%	38.3%
Ross County	32,048	6,824	5,449	1,375	1,673	3,776	219	16.9%	34.8%
Scioto County	34,096	8,017	6,229	1,788	1,545	4,684	132	16.7%	33.8%
Stark County	165,178	38,956	31,473	7,483	10,193	21,280	1,119	15.5%	41.2%
Summit County	245,046	51,983	41,299	10,684	16,060	25,239	1,856	19.6%	44.2%
Trumbull County	95,913	23,974	19,662	4,312	5,819	13,843	241	14.8%	36.4%
Tuscarawas County	40,117	9,621	7,816	1,805	1,896	5,920	161	14.6%	31.7%
Warren County	81,432	14,338	11,717	2,621	4,390	7,327	172	20.0%	49.2%
Wayne County	45,873	10,462	8,589	1,873	2,610	5,979	160	14.8%	32.6%
Wood County	53,499	10,464	8,590	1,874	3,031	5,559	186	16.8%	37.4%
Oklahoma									
Canadian County	46,041	8,051	6,512	1,539	2,237	4,275	395	17.4%	55.1%
Cleveland County	105,977	16,651	14,182	2,469	5,283	8,899	470	18.0%	50.9%
Comanche County	51,094	8,725	7,413	1,312	2,484	4,929	195	16.5%	36.9%
Creek County	29,853	6,708	5,498	1,210	1,289	4,209	87	13.6%	33.7%
Muskogee County	30,912	6,568	5,398	1,170	1,254	4,144	118	17.2%	34.3%
Oklahoma County	321,306	57,340	44,626	12,714	14,492	30,134	2,588	17.1%	47.6%
Payne County	34,123	5,209	4,233	976	1,073	3,160	213	13.2%	44.8%
Pottawatomie County	29,276	6,421	5,462	959	1,406	4,056	68	13.6%	37.1%
Rogers County	35,477	7,325	6,407	918	1,847	4,560	74	15.3%	35.4%
Tulsa County	270,462	48,412	38,007	10,405	12,743	25,264	2,000	17.2%	49.4%
Wagoner County	29,979	6,146	5,562	584	1,613	3,949	na	15.2%	32.2%
Oregon									
Benton County	36,429	6,771	5,547	1,224	1,607	3,940	382	15.2%	34.3%
Clackamas County	157,602	33,314	25,559	7,755	10,660	14,899	2,814	24.6%	56.5%
Deschutes County	80,406	15,950	12,856	3,094	5,766	7,090	892	30.4%	53.1%
Douglas County	48,942	14,506	12,096	2,410	4,111	7,985	355	20.0%	40.5%
Jackson County	91,090	23,740	18,849	4,891	7,650	11,199	1,546	26.6%	57.0%
Josephine County	38,027	11,849	8,878	2,971	3,333	5,545	930	20.3%	51.5%
Klamath County	32,811	7,609	6,250	1,359	2,477	3,773	180	20.9%	51.4%
Lane County	156,327	34,894	27,607	7,287	10,468	17,139	1,571	21.1%	47.8%
Linn County	48,884	12,108	9,671	2,437	3,335	6,336	519	18.2%	43.0%
Marion County	121,388	26,123	19,949	6,174	7,455	12,494	1,756	21.9%	53.6%

Table J-2: Counties—Summary of Housing and Householder Characteristics—*Continued*

| | | | | Householders 65 Years and Over | | | | | |
| | | | | | Owner Householders | | | Percent of Owner Householders Who Pay 35% or More of Income for Housing Costs | Percent of Renter Householders Who Pay 35% or More of Income for Rental Costs |
	Total Housing Units	Total Households	Owner Occupied	Renter Occupied	With a Mortgage	Without a Mortgage	Renter Households With Meals Included in Rent		
Oregon—Cont.									
Multnomah County	325,301	52,357	35,614	16,743	14,498	21,116	3,696	26.1%	52.9%
Polk County	30,376	7,109	5,638	1,471	2,425	3,213	534	21.8%	43.8%
Umatilla County	29,703	6,242	4,848	1,394	1,556	3,292	493	17.9%	35.9%
Washington County	213,514	35,955	26,062	9,893	11,669	14,393	2,739	26.4%	52.8%
Yamhill County	37,196	8,356	6,247	2,109	2,490	3,757	774	22.2%	52.7%
Pennsylvania									
Adams County	40,984	9,970	8,081	1,889	2,522	5,559	169	23.8%	37.3%
Allegheny County	588,854	135,087	101,041	34,046	28,640	72,401	4,983	19.4%	42.4%
Armstrong County	32,483	8,268	6,511	1,757	1,211	5,300	359	14.9%	38.1%
Beaver County	78,251	20,859	16,283	4,576	4,486	11,797	511	18.9%	29.4%
Berks County	164,760	37,479	28,552	8,927	7,857	20,695	1,493	24.5%	46.7%
Blair County	56,205	14,484	10,994	3,490	2,486	8,508	389	16.1%	38.3%
Bucks County	245,877	56,346	44,880	11,466	14,643	30,237	3,208	28.4%	59.7%
Butler County	78,551	17,817	13,813	4,004	3,937	9,876	1,013	16.3%	44.3%
Cambria County	65,538	17,817	14,256	3,561	2,835	11,421	124	15.9%	27.9%
Carbon County	34,352	7,076	5,895	1,181	1,670	4,225	228	24.2%	35.6%
Centre County	63,554	11,231	8,755	2,476	2,267	6,488	573	15.7%	42.9%
Chester County	193,257	39,824	32,283	7,541	12,222	20,061	2,086	29.6%	51.3%
Clearfield County	38,647	9,071	7,809	1,262	1,397	6,412	87	19.6%	43.8%
Columbia County	29,521	7,062	5,713	1,349	1,236	4,477	125	21.0%	33.7%
Crawford County	44,624	9,560	7,598	1,962	2,124	5,474	71	18.5%	37.8%
Cumberland County	100,657	23,269	17,783	5,486	5,114	12,669	1,113	16.4%	47.5%
Dauphin County	120,779	24,168	18,195	5,973	5,683	12,512	675	19.1%	39.0%
Delaware County	222,501	50,131	37,562	12,569	11,662	25,900	3,365	27.6%	58.7%
Erie County	119,356	25,679	18,846	6,833	5,461	13,385	860	16.6%	37.9%
Fayette County	62,782	15,556	12,482	3,074	2,823	9,659	79	16.2%	27.5%
Franklin County	63,582	15,592	12,807	2,785	3,393	9,414	188	18.3%	34.9%
Indiana County	38,259	8,758	7,203	1,555	1,235	5,968	224	15.7%	25.0%
Lackawanna County	96,776	23,796	17,480	6,316	4,533	12,947	191	26.5%	32.8%
Lancaster County	203,966	47,590	34,836	12,754	9,257	25,579	2,941	19.8%	47.7%
Lawrence County	40,943	10,927	8,515	2,412	2,094	6,421	118	17.9%	26.2%
Lebanon County	55,692	14,277	10,997	3,280	3,057	7,940	382	16.6%	44.5%
Lehigh County	142,939	31,004	23,225	7,779	7,038	16,187	592	23.6%	45.2%
Luzerne County	148,587	36,834	27,374	9,460	6,870	20,504	527	23.8%	32.3%
Lycoming County	52,505	11,867	9,372	2,495	2,446	6,926	288	18.8%	40.4%
Mercer County	51,705	14,049	11,286	2,763	2,868	8,418	222	16.2%	28.8%
Monroe County	80,523	11,953	9,990	1,963	4,054	5,936	332	30.2%	48.1%
Montgomery County	326,041	74,581	56,543	18,038	18,393	38,150	4,040	26.0%	53.5%
Northampton County	120,519	29,061	22,626	6,435	7,188	15,438	1,260	25.2%	44.1%
Northumberland County	45,063	11,300	8,394	2,906	1,655	6,739	268	17.2%	17.1%
Philadelphia County	668,947	122,082	85,262	36,820	23,336	61,926	1,605	25.4%	45.6%
Schuylkill County	69,248	17,174	13,745	3,429	2,430	11,315	135	19.8%	26.0%
Somerset County	38,092	9,121	7,310	1,811	1,355	5,955	114	18.7%	30.0%
Washington County	93,215	23,892	19,179	4,713	5,521	13,658	441	15.9%	31.9%
Westmoreland County	168,230	45,195	36,632	8,563	9,119	27,513	965	18.9%	28.5%
York County	179,327	39,794	32,197	7,597	9,810	22,387	925	25.2%	41.3%
Rhode Island									
Kent County	73,653	17,045	12,426	4,619	4,714	7,712	718	30.4%	34.3%
Newport County	41,796	9,167	6,928	2,239	2,664	4,264	304	29.9%	36.7%
Providence County	264,330	52,402	33,018	19,384	11,924	21,094	1,358	32.2%	39.8%
Washington County	62,386	12,599	10,222	2,377	4,205	6,017	282	28.0%	41.2%
South Carolina									
Aiken County	72,820	16,110	13,985	2,125	4,727	9,258	250	16.7%	44.6%
Anderson County	84,848	18,798	15,616	3,182	4,629	10,987	410	13.4%	51.6%
Beaufort County	93,178	22,118	19,964	2,154	8,888	11,076	310	26.6%	46.9%
Berkeley County	74,552	11,717	10,507	1,210	3,753	6,754	109	19.4%	49.5%
Charleston County	171,341	30,038	25,095	4,943	10,506	14,589	573	28.6%	57.1%
Darlington County	30,299	6,784	5,638	1,146	1,676	3,962	0	20.2%	33.6%
Dorchester County	55,727	8,916	7,463	1,453	3,078	4,385	260	23.7%	32.1%
Florence County	58,825	11,261	9,108	2,153	2,998	6,110	93	17.4%	33.6%
Greenville County	196,435	37,562	31,723	5,839	10,948	20,775	806	17.2%	45.3%
Greenwood County	31,002	7,065	5,724	1,341	2,106	3,618	365	21.6%	29.8%
Horry County	187,398	31,520	27,403	4,117	10,554	16,849	411	20.7%	39.0%
Lancaster County	32,704	7,703	6,948	755	2,321	4,627	na	15.3%	46.2%
Laurens County	30,637	6,158	5,266	892	1,282	3,984	91	18.6%	32.8%
Lexington County	115,256	20,450	17,668	2,782	6,608	11,060	727	16.4%	52.8%
Oconee County	38,854	9,024	8,178	846	2,391	5,787	122	13.3%	33.7%
Orangeburg County	42,420	8,962	7,336	1,626	2,007	5,329	53	25.7%	36.9%
Pickens County	51,325	10,102	8,440	1,662	2,159	6,281	276	13.5%	38.0%
Richland County	162,945	24,800	21,311	3,489	8,057	13,254	305	22.3%	49.6%
Spartanburg County	122,932	24,662	20,575	4,087	6,786	13,789	622	16.3%	41.4%
Sumter County	46,278	9,106	7,357	1,749	2,343	5,014	279	17.2%	43.1%
York County	95,335	17,045	14,466	2,579	6,261	8,205	395	20.9%	48.6%

Table J-2: Counties—Summary of Housing and Householder Characteristics—*Continued*

| | | | | Householders 65 Years and Over | | | | | |
| | | | | Owner Householders | | | | | |
	Total Housing Units	Total Households	Owner Occupied	Renter Occupied	With a Mortgage	Without a Mortgage	Renter Households With Meals Included in Rent	Percent of Owner Householders Who Pay 35% or More of Income for Housing Costs	Percent of Renter Householders Who Pay 35% or More of Income for Rental Costs
South Dakota									
Minnehaha County	72,441	12,106	8,785	3,321	2,733	6,052	543	16.1%	52.8%
Pennington County	45,339	8,758	6,328	2,430	2,097	4,231	568	15.2%	45.4%
Tennessee									
Anderson County	34,751	8,590	7,022	1,568	1,722	5,300	185	12.1%	40.6%
Blount County	55,347	12,826	11,122	1,704	3,292	7,830	139	16.9%	27.7%
Bradley County	41,729	9,145	7,239	1,906	2,138	5,101	303	21.5%	48.1%
Davidson County	285,430	42,599	32,575	10,024	11,548	21,027	1,533	19.6%	44.0%
Greene County	32,053	7,888	6,528	1,360	1,642	4,886	na	16.4%	22.1%
Hamilton County	151,795	32,214	25,924	6,290	8,912	17,012	1,394	21.6%	45.4%
Knox County	196,083	37,182	29,415	7,767	7,833	21,582	1,050	16.8%	44.5%
Madison County	42,015	8,034	6,459	1,575	1,880	4,579	79	15.5%	26.3%
Maury County	35,409	6,547	5,432	1,115	1,688	3,744	na	22.5%	46.8%
Montgomery County	72,079	8,609	7,440	1,169	2,556	4,884	159	16.1%	33.7%
Putnam County	32,165	6,939	5,770	1,169	1,795	3,975	67	16.4%	41.2%
Robertson County	26,182	5,220	4,458	762	1,483	2,975	na	17.6%	19.6%
Rutherford County	104,054	14,063	11,317	2,746	4,168	7,149	188	18.9%	31.5%
Sevier County	56,062	8,874	7,521	1,353	2,075	5,446	na	15.0%	31.2%
Shelby County	399,094	61,462	47,075	14,387	19,383	27,692	2,131	25.0%	48.7%
Sullivan County	73,872	20,031	17,402	2,629	4,499	12,903	287	14.7%	25.5%
Sumner County	66,426	12,748	10,506	2,242	4,412	6,094	400	19.8%	48.7%
Washington County	57,644	12,311	10,373	1,938	3,357	7,016	199	15.2%	24.0%
Williamson County	69,434	11,552	9,694	1,858	3,886	5,808	398	16.6%	45.3%
Wilson County	46,438	9,111	8,108	1,003	3,098	5,010	160	19.5%	38.9%
Texas									
Angelina County	35,791	7,547	6,010	1,537	1,285	4,725	140	10.7%	35.5%
Bastrop County	29,375	4,902	4,246	656	1,367	2,879	na	21.1%	31.9%
Bell County	127,742	16,529	13,318	3,211	3,441	9,877	384	13.1%	41.5%
Bexar County	667,117	110,503	86,699	23,804	27,903	58,796	3,170	16.2%	45.8%
Bowie County	38,722	8,732	7,202	1,530	1,415	5,787	192	13.3%	48.4%
Brazoria County	120,529	18,734	15,972	2,762	4,667	11,305	276	17.4%	38.8%
Brazos County	78,892	9,419	7,581	1,838	2,321	5,260	284	17.3%	37.8%
Cameron County	143,106	25,830	20,174	5,656	3,792	16,382	45	20.1%	38.4%
Collin County	306,324	36,949	27,893	9,056	12,926	14,967	1,403	22.2%	55.0%
Comal County	48,044	10,803	9,237	1,566	2,992	6,245	226	14.9%	49.7%
Coryell County	25,459	3,511	3,057	454	730	2,327	na	11.9%	24.7%
Dallas County	947,776	131,881	99,994	31,887	32,291	67,703	4,020	23.5%	52.5%
Denton County	261,401	28,022	21,660	6,362	10,263	11,397	1,349	20.1%	50.5%
Ector County	53,662	9,061	7,392	1,669	1,077	6,315	193	15.4%	35.2%
Ellis County	54,953	9,565	7,884	1,681	2,682	5,202	120	18.8%	50.3%
El Paso County	274,924	49,572	38,395	11,177	9,942	28,453	628	16.4%	38.8%
Fort Bend County	203,252	24,655	20,942	3,713	9,272	11,670	862	27.8%	54.2%
Galveston County	134,389	20,486	16,336	4,150	4,936	11,400	197	16.7%	60.8%
Grayson County	53,920	11,431	9,748	1,683	2,120	7,628	276	15.5%	33.5%
Gregg County	49,905	10,619	8,313	2,306	2,156	6,157	573	19.0%	53.1%
Guadalupe County	51,263	10,201	8,884	1,317	3,072	5,812	84	18.7%	27.3%
Harris County	1,614,656	205,093	158,283	46,810	48,961	109,322	5,995	20.7%	52.2%
Harrison County	27,792	5,890	5,148	742	993	4,155	60	11.3%	36.8%
Hays County	62,009	8,277	6,863	1,414	3,066	3,797	138	19.5%	55.5%
Henderson County	39,662	9,403	8,541	862	2,072	6,469	0	17.1%	27.4%
Hidalgo County	251,951	41,006	32,581	8,425	5,929	26,652	251	17.5%	35.8%
Hunt County	36,780	7,492	5,912	1,580	1,498	4,414	185	13.7%	46.8%
Jefferson County	105,513	21,674	17,623	4,051	3,255	14,368	474	16.8%	45.3%
Johnson County	57,332	10,832	9,559	1,273	2,672	6,887	21	15.9%	30.1%
Kaufman County	38,529	6,669	5,659	1,010	1,384	4,275	46	14.6%	44.1%
Liberty County	29,004	5,552	4,808	744	1,366	3,442	na	14.4%	29.0%
Lubbock County	116,519	20,165	16,167	3,998	4,590	11,577	747	16.3%	46.2%
McLennan County	95,677	18,149	14,727	3,422	3,713	11,014	379	15.3%	41.8%
Midland County	54,792	9,229	7,702	1,527	1,677	6,025	361	18.4%	53.4%
Montgomery County	181,429	30,909	25,371	5,538	10,344	15,027	902	21.9%	45.8%
Nacogdoches County	27,575	4,957	3,970	987	593	3,377	na	15.3%	31.7%
Nueces County	141,893	25,772	20,499	5,273	5,511	14,988	616	19.1%	45.8%
Orange County	35,583	7,230	6,573	657	1,155	5,418	0	13.4%	36.7%
Parker County	46,911	9,609	8,364	1,245	2,686	5,678	238	19.5%	36.9%
Potter County	47,633	8,181	6,167	2,014	1,357	4,810	416	16.1%	44.7%
Randall County	52,001	10,099	8,335	1,764	2,448	5,887	161	17.5%	37.0%
Rockwall County	28,703	4,518	3,979	539	1,459	2,520	na	21.0%	#N/A
San Patricio County	26,637	5,198	4,287	911	1,021	3,266	38	21.3%	39.7%
Smith County	87,578	19,347	16,163	3,184	4,152	12,011	829	18.8%	48.3%
Tarrant County	720,214	103,760	81,910	21,850	28,630	53,280	3,495	20.6%	53.0%
Taylor County	55,980	11,015	8,857	2,158	2,003	6,854	453	12.9%	42.1%
Tom Green County	46,773	10,089	8,127	1,962	1,958	6,169	213	12.8%	29.6%
Travis County	446,383	49,015	37,180	11,835	13,838	23,342	1,933	21.6%	46.9%
Victoria County	35,430	7,265	6,152	1,113	1,132	5,020	225	15.1%	54.1%
Walker County	24,442	4,461	3,982	479	927	3,055	na	18.9%	27.8%
Webb County	74,316	10,908	7,980	2,928	1,699	6,281	0	24.6%	42.0%
Wichita County	55,603	11,069	9,017	2,052	2,072	6,945	482	15.2%	52.3%
Williamson County	165,230	23,368	18,762	4,606	8,380	10,382	651	19.2%	45.8%

Table J-2: Counties—Summary of Housing and Householder Characteristics—*Continued*

| | | | | | Householders 65 Years and Over | | | | |
| | | | | | Owner Householders | | | Percent of Owner Householders | Percent of Renter Householders Who |
	Total Housing Units	Total Households	Owner Occupied	Renter Occupied	With a Mortgage	Without a Mortgage	Renter Households With Meals Included in Rent	Who Pay 35% or More of Income for Housing Costs	Pay 35% or More of Income for Rental Costs
Utah									
Cache County	37,623	5,564	4,872	692	1,371	3,501	119	14.3%	38.6%
Davis County	98,688	15,780	13,873	1,907	5,579	8,294	530	14.6%	51.0%
Salt Lake County	366,833	57,796	46,932	10,864	17,853	29,079	1,647	17.8%	50.2%
Utah County	150,353	20,809	17,603	3,206	6,826	10,777	954	16.9%	45.0%
Washington County	58,643	15,283	13,033	2,250	4,743	8,290	344	16.8%	41.9%
Weber County	86,606	15,399	13,293	2,106	4,865	8,428	377	18.3%	40.8%
Vermont									
Chittenden County	66,111	11,803	8,853	2,950	3,651	5,202	901	28.1%	50.6%
Virginia									
Albemarle County	42,751	9,195	7,283	1,912	2,963	4,320	577	20.7%	49.1%
Arlington County	106,444	12,176	8,133	4,043	3,911	4,222	495	21.9%	48.4%
Augusta County	31,413	7,768	7,066	702	2,116	4,950	na	14.1%	42.9%
Bedford County	32,197	7,426	6,936	490	2,209	4,727	na	19.9%	15.7%
Chesterfield County	123,353	21,476	18,305	3,171	8,332	9,973	1,038	19.9%	57.3%
Fairfax County	408,321	64,675	53,859	10,816	26,962	26,897	2,736	19.5%	48.7%
Fauquier County	25,723	5,124	4,289	835	1,914	2,375	99	25.7%	26.6%
Frederick County	31,626	6,175	5,519	656	2,042	3,477	169	18.1%	53.7%
Hanover County	38,642	8,435	7,646	789	2,860	4,786	136	19.3%	38.3%
Henrico County	133,250	25,135	19,244	5,891	8,013	11,231	1,713	20.4%	48.1%
James City County	30,288	8,682	6,635	2,047	3,065	3,570	1,204	22.2%	49.6%
Loudoun County	112,205	11,937	9,225	2,712	5,256	3,969	936	24.0%	53.7%
Montgomery County	38,722	5,998	5,132	866	1,327	3,805	131	12.1%	41.6%
Prince William County	139,317	15,513	13,067	2,446	7,448	5,619	388	19.6%	49.1%
Roanoke County	40,204	10,426	8,745	1,681	3,046	5,699	177	19.8%	39.0%
Rockingham County	33,871	7,980	6,832	1,148	1,756	5,076	127	19.0%	40.2%
Spotsylvania County	45,406	7,813	6,520	1,293	3,345	3,175	282	21.5%	48.0%
Stafford County	44,537	5,781	5,066	715	2,644	2,422	36	22.6%	56.9%
York County	26,829	4,985	4,609	376	2,036	2,573	90	18.3%	46.3%
Washington									
Benton County	69,703	13,851	11,042	2,809	3,428	7,614	718	13.9%	44.4%
Chelan County	35,571	7,294	5,690	1,604	2,008	3,682	439	22.1%	35.3%
Clallam County	35,652	10,954	9,188	1,766	3,103	6,085	367	16.9%	49.5%
Clark County	168,223	32,636	24,993	7,643	10,944	14,049	1,671	21.2%	52.3%
Cowlitz County	43,440	10,586	8,436	2,150	2,848	5,588	355	19.7%	54.0%
Franklin County	25,133	3,448	2,526	922	942	1,584	166	14.1%	22.1%
Grant County	35,151	7,157	5,623	1,534	1,839	3,784	194	15.0%	38.3%
Grays Harbor County	35,215	7,566	6,444	1,122	2,370	4,074	136	21.6%	25.5%
Island County	40,366	9,195	7,906	1,289	3,132	4,774	208	20.1%	38.5%
King County	855,599	139,478	97,726	41,752	39,422	58,304	9,964	27.1%	52.9%
Kitsap County	107,781	21,257	16,940	4,317	7,300	9,640	627	24.9%	38.9%
Lewis County	34,122	8,882	7,346	1,536	2,339	5,007	306	21.1%	43.8%
Pierce County	326,979	56,645	43,047	13,598	18,681	24,366	2,574	25.3%	53.0%
Skagit County	51,581	12,155	10,057	2,098	3,562	6,495	375	19.4%	41.9%
Snohomish County	288,774	47,824	36,613	11,211	15,560	21,053	2,538	26.8%	48.6%
Spokane County	202,856	40,702	31,261	9,441	11,779	19,482	2,229	21.3%	51.7%
Thurston County	109,278	21,508	17,317	4,191	6,481	10,836	759	20.7%	47.1%
Whatcom County	90,980	17,606	13,487	4,119	4,695	8,792	925	22.0%	45.9%
Yakima County	85,783	16,886	12,944	3,942	4,319	8,625	865	18.3%	52.6%
West Virginia									
Berkeley County	45,150	7,552	6,349	1,203	2,374	3,975	90	14.4%	38.0%
Cabell County	46,183	10,095	8,412	1,683	2,109	6,303	134	11.7%	28.6%
Harrison County	31,431	7,720	6,486	1,234	1,223	5,263	75	10.3%	34.5%
Kanawha County	92,475	22,134	18,488	3,646	4,325	14,163	291	11.7%	30.4%
Monongalia County	43,523	5,975	4,978	997	1,080	3,898	112	8.7%	40.1%
Raleigh County	35,976	8,358	7,303	1,055	1,790	5,513	na	10.8%	18.2%
Wood County	40,229	9,880	8,539	1,341	2,597	5,942	0	14.0%	37.8%
Wisconsin									
Brown County	105,161	18,977	14,020	4,957	4,345	9,675	892	20.0%	48.0%
Dane County	216,919	34,303	26,522	7,781	9,841	16,681	1,148	20.7%	50.2%
Dodge County	37,034	8,083	6,152	1,931	1,518	4,634	168	24.3%	37.6%
Eau Claire County	42,318	8,546	6,287	2,259	1,606	4,681	357	18.3%	45.2%
Fond du Lac County	44,035	9,918	7,567	2,351	2,056	5,511	426	21.6%	37.2%
Jefferson County	35,222	7,181	5,535	1,646	1,632	3,903	167	22.6%	41.4%
Kenosha County	69,366	12,001	9,119	2,882	2,994	6,125	133	25.7%	45.1%
La Crosse County	48,615	10,188	7,495	2,693	2,359	5,136	719	22.5%	50.4%
Manitowoc County	37,168	8,800	7,000	1,800	1,517	5,483	289	16.7%	47.3%
Marathon County	57,895	11,818	9,286	2,532	2,118	7,168	399	19.3%	48.1%

Table J-2: Counties—Summary of Housing and Householder Characteristics—*Continued*

| | | | | Householders 65 Years and Over | | | | | |
| | | | | Owner Householders | | | Percent of Owner Householders Who Pay 35% or More of Income for Housing Costs | Percent of Renter Householders Who Pay 35% or More of Income for Rental Costs |
	Total Housing Units	Total Households	Owner Occupied	Renter Occupied	With a Mortgage	Without a Mortgage	Renter Households With Meals Included in Rent		
Wisconsin—Cont.									
Milwaukee County	417,772	73,522	48,382	25,140	15,679	32,703	3,482	28.2%	50.4%
Outagamie County	73,586	13,975	10,928	3,047	2,800	8,128	369	21.9%	50.3%
Ozaukee County	36,338	8,761	7,193	1,568	2,137	5,056	304	21.5%	43.7%
Portage County	30,145	6,118	4,810	1,308	1,165	3,645	401	15.7%	50.2%
Racine County	82,197	17,221	13,739	3,482	4,198	9,541	324	21.8%	47.4%
Rock County	68,355	14,192	10,983	3,209	3,609	7,374	289	18.0%	48.5%
St. Croix County	34,119	5,266	3,977	1,289	1,285	2,692	240	16.9%	38.8%
Sheboygan County	50,707	10,784	8,323	2,461	2,036	6,287	550	21.3%	38.8%
Walworth County	51,550	8,640	7,103	1,537	2,258	4,845	260	24.9%	41.6%
Washington County	54,925	11,986	9,538	2,448	2,556	6,982	264	23.5%	51.0%
Waukesha County	161,130	36,335	27,853	8,482	8,964	18,889	1,470	22.9%	63.4%
Winnebago County	73,588	14,435	11,024	3,411	2,989	8,035	795	19.2%	49.8%
Wood County	34,133	8,541	6,485	2,056	1,532	4,953	258	13.9%	40.7%
Wyoming									
Laramie County	40,667	7,710	6,303	1,407	2,085	4,218	205	17.9%	32.1%
Natrona County	34,454	6,257	5,126	1,131	1,324	3,802	124	10.9%	38.9%

Table J-3: Places—Summary of Housing and Householder Characteristics

		Householders 65 Years and Over							
			Owner Households					Percent of Owner Householders Who Pay 35% or More of Income for Housing Costs	Percent of Renter Householders Who Pay 35% or More of Income for Rental Costs
	Total Housing Units	Total Households	Owner Occupied	Renter Occupied	With a Mortgage	Without a Mortgage	Renter Households With Meals Included in Rent		
Alabama									
Birmingham city	110,511	18,290	13,660	4,630	4,901	8,759	65	26.2%	47.1%
Dothan city	29,562	6,154	5,016	1,138	1,813	3,203	64	15.5%	42.1%
Hoover city	34,408	6,100	5,084	1,016	2,382	2,702	469	15.1%	43.2%
Huntsville city	85,840	16,524	13,804	2,720	5,287	8,517	506	16.5%	39.7%
Mobile city	90,256	17,863	13,871	3,992	5,105	8,766	522	21.2%	44.9%
Montgomery city	92,345	16,232	13,214	3,018	5,805	7,409	231	18.1%	37.0%
Tuscaloosa city	43,421	5,512	4,143	1,369	1,363	2,780	213	19.9%	38.2%
Alaska									
Anchorage Municipality	113,370	13,374	10,736	2,638	4,664	6,072	168	23.5%	46.0%
Arizona									
Avondale city	26,021	2,137	1,709	428	736	973	0	20.2%	32.7%
Chandler city	95,522	12,219	9,680	2,539	5,764	3,916	531	23.4%	51.7%
Flagstaff city	26,247	2,804	2,434	370	1,224	1,210	109	14.2%	36.5%
Glendale city	89,934	12,528	9,160	3,368	4,702	4,458	499	23.5%	50.9%
Goodyear city	26,104	3,868	3,393	475	1,691	1,702	na	23.3%	na
Mesa city	198,721	41,346	33,818	7,528	11,594	22,224	2,156	19.7%	53.1%
Peoria city	64,276	13,410	10,473	2,937	5,149	5,324	1,612	23.9%	60.8%
Phoenix city	599,724	77,061	58,938	18,123	28,974	29,964	1,882	28.5%	48.9%
Scottsdale city	124,501	28,373	23,590	4,783	10,964	12,626	1,139	26.7%	60.5%
Surprise city	51,830	13,145	12,160	985	5,530	6,630	240	20.6%	57.8%
Tempe city	71,515	8,421	6,661	1,760	3,190	3,471	399	19.6%	49.7%
Tucson city	229,779	41,664	30,397	11,267	12,359	18,038	1,616	23.2%	50.1%
Yuma city	40,066	7,471	6,198	1,273	1,693	4,505	193	17.4%	36.6%
Arkansas									
Fayetteville city	36,211	4,228	2,940	1,288	857	2,083	210	12.6%	31.5%
Fort Smith city	38,429	7,098	5,049	2,049	1,352	3,697	257	16.7%	36.0%
Jonesboro city	28,756	4,751	3,825	926	1,328	2,497	356	14.4%	59.9%
Little Rock city	91,853	14,384	11,480	2,904	4,080	7,400	500	16.9%	38.4%
Springdale city	26,713	3,706	2,842	864	984	1,858	188	11.9%	44.4%
California									
Alameda city	31,758	5,614	3,923	1,691	1,665	2,258	80	26.2%	48.1%
Alhambra city	31,113	6,093	3,458	2,635	1,473	1,985	47	25.2%	47.3%
Anaheim city	104,443	17,509	11,593	5,916	5,315	6,278	726	26.9%	59.1%
Antioch city	35,348	5,280	4,144	1,136	2,255	1,889	283	28.4%	46.7%
Bakersfield city	119,106	17,566	13,465	4,101	6,070	7,395	681	20.9%	49.0%
Baldwin Park city	17,389	2,679	1,971	708	1,100	871	0	28.5%	39.0%
Bellflower city	24,467	3,456	1,987	1,469	683	1,304	70	21.3%	61.5%
Berkeley city	48,525	9,832	6,888	2,944	3,179	3,709	58	20.0%	42.1%
Buena Park city	23,819	4,317	3,607	710	1,740	1,867	0	25.9%	53.8%
Burbank city	43,275	9,097	5,031	4,066	2,632	2,399	310	35.0%	69.8%
Camarillo city	24,968	7,463	5,873	1,590	2,695	3,178	380	26.4%	56.0%
Carlsbad city	45,968	9,689	7,386	2,303	3,811	3,575	955	31.9%	58.3%
Carson city	25,855	6,307	5,479	828	2,844	2,635	0	28.0%	48.4%
Chico city	37,972	5,979	4,034	1,945	1,481	2,553	323	19.1%	51.8%
Chino city	23,342	3,383	2,427	956	1,364	1,063	113	38.8%	58.9%
Chino Hills city	24,409	2,412	1,979	433	1,246	733	214	33.4%	53.1%
Chula Vista city	84,752	13,541	9,807	3,734	4,269	5,538	64	22.7%	64.6%
Citrus Heights city	34,491	7,453	5,467	1,986	2,247	3,220	190	23.7%	59.6%
Clovis city	35,689	6,390	4,427	1,963	2,139	2,288	206	19.4%	56.9%
Compton city	25,380	4,257	3,376	881	2,019	1,357	0	37.6%	36.8%
Concord city	48,025	9,029	7,004	2,025	3,006	3,998	351	25.5%	64.7%
Corona city	47,096	5,416	3,894	1,522	2,188	1,706	289	30.4%	54.7%
Costa Mesa city	43,272	6,028	4,533	1,495	1,949	2,584	164	25.7%	53.4%
Daly City city	32,460	6,493	4,861	1,632	2,249	2,612	137	26.0%	52.0%
Davis city	25,045	3,625	2,570	1,055	1,108	1,462	391	17.2%	50.0%
Downey city	34,146	6,050	4,517	1,533	2,077	2,440	27	26.9%	70.6%
El Cajon city	34,351	5,866	3,677	2,189	1,591	2,086	87	27.2%	65.5%
Elk Grove city	49,869	6,438	5,224	1,214	3,334	1,890	279	30.1%	70.3%
El Monte city	30,961	4,959	2,752	2,207	1,076	1,676	8	26.6%	54.1%
Escondido city	47,089	7,965	5,333	2,632	2,233	3,100	597	28.1%	61.2%
Fairfield city	36,197	6,404	4,990	1,414	2,141	2,849	365	25.6%	54.5%
Folsom city	26,229	4,582	3,528	1,054	2,063	1,465	318	31.9%	60.5%
Fontana city	51,154	4,711	3,468	1,243	1,903	1,565	61	35.6%	51.5%
Fremont city	74,048	11,261	8,875	2,386	3,507	5,368	491	22.1%	61.0%
Fresno city	171,673	28,015	18,461	9,554	8,058	10,403	1,228	20.5%	51.7%
Fullerton city	46,391	8,634	6,830	1,804	2,697	4,133	310	25.2%	45.1%
Garden Grove city	48,329	9,097	6,646	2,451	3,021	3,625	102	22.8%	45.2%
Glendale city	73,853	16,471	7,608	8,863	3,580	4,028	378	33.5%	69.0%
Hawthorne city	29,926	3,391	1,762	1,629	950	812	0	35.1%	45.9%
Hayward city	47,743	7,670	5,918	1,752	2,517	3,401	243	26.8%	52.2%
Hemet city	34,746	12,189	8,748	3,441	2,530	6,218	603	23.8%	68.2%
Hesperia city	29,210	5,067	4,015	1,052	1,919	2,096	0	29.0%	67.5%
Huntington Beach city	77,370	17,239	14,083	3,156	6,571	7,512	309	27.7%	63.4%
Indio city	28,974	5,756	4,668	1,088	2,106	2,562	0	36.0%	43.1%
Inglewood city	39,141	6,548	3,649	2,899	2,292	1,357	46	34.7%	58.2%
Irvine city	84,167	10,385	7,238	3,147	4,313	2,925	484	28.6%	35.0%
Jurupa Valley city[1]	25,669	3,998	2,743	1,255	1,406	1,337	117	31.7%	62.2%

[1] Jurupa Valley city was incorporated in 2011. The 2010 population is the U.S. Census Bureau's estimates base figure.

Table J-3: Places—Summary of Housing and Householder Characteristics—*Continued*

		Householders 65 Years and Over							
					Owner Householders			Percent of Owner Householders Who Pay 35% or More of Income for Housing Costs	Percent of Renter Householders Who Pay 35% or More of Income for Rental Costs
	Total Housing Units	Total Households	Owner Occupied	Renter Occupied	With a Mortgage	Without a Mortgage	Renter Households With Meals Included in Rent		
California—Cont.									
Lake Forest city	28,626	4,442	3,668	774	1,780	1,888	153	34.2%	48.7%
Lakewood city	27,796	5,434	4,437	997	1,851	2,586	na	24.0%	45.3%
Lancaster city	51,990	7,390	5,333	2,057	2,543	2,790	50	27.3%	61.7%
Livermore city	30,590	5,198	3,949	1,249	1,814	2,135	161	18.3%	59.6%
Long Beach city	172,803	25,039	16,272	8,767	7,308	8,964	575	25.3%	51.9%
Los Angeles city	1,424,961	237,046	138,027	99,019	68,507	69,520	4,952	34.9%	55.5%
Lynwood city	15,850	1,648	1,056	592	598	458	0	35.2%	45.9%
Manteca city	23,592	4,198	3,123	1,075	1,486	1,637	136	23.1%	67.0%
Menifee city	29,291	8,860	7,421	1,439	3,674	3,747	88	23.6%	64.2%
Merced city	27,210	4,060	2,583	1,477	1,189	1,394	104	24.7%	50.2%
Milpitas city	20,109	2,848	2,091	757	924	1,167	99	25.8%	64.2%
Mission Viejo city	34,042	8,517	7,146	1,371	3,417	3,729	481	23.3%	65.4%
Modesto city	74,145	14,085	9,621	4,464	4,069	5,552	762	28.0%	57.5%
Moreno Valley city	53,467	6,104	4,780	1,324	3,108	1,672	167	33.5%	67.0%
Mountain View city	33,484	5,174	3,210	1,964	1,111	2,099	72	24.8%	53.7%
Murrieta city	35,283	6,159	4,768	1,391	2,380	2,388	50	32.9%	61.2%
Napa city	29,890	6,718	4,713	2,005	1,995	2,718	406	27.9%	52.8%
Newport Beach city	43,153	10,180	8,511	1,669	4,219	4,292	156	31.0%	64.0%
Norwalk city	27,770	5,292	3,893	1,399	1,860	2,033	8	26.3%	40.2%
Oakland city	172,519	29,723	17,065	12,658	8,545	8,520	972	31.1%	41.5%
Oceanside city	63,385	12,722	10,063	2,659	4,658	5,405	321	28.4%	48.4%
Ontario city	47,040	6,048	4,192	1,856	2,258	1,934	67	31.9%	59.6%
Orange city	45,316	8,077	6,253	1,824	3,042	3,211	60	22.5%	54.5%
Oxnard city	53,741	8,338	6,524	1,814	3,318	3,206	76	24.7%	37.7%
Palmdale city	44,330	5,191	3,961	1,230	2,137	1,824	85	33.7%	64.8%
Palo Alto city	28,134	7,239	5,006	2,233	1,813	3,193	627	15.6%	39.4%
Pasadena city	58,098	11,195	7,187	4,008	3,358	3,829	888	25.9%	41.4%
Perris city	17,020	1,558	1,131	427	760	371	na	33.9%	45.7%
Pleasanton city	25,403	4,777	3,380	1,397	1,700	1,680	242	36.5%	71.4%
Pomona city	40,841	6,121	4,502	1,619	2,208	2,294	301	34.9%	65.5%
Rancho Cordova city	25,776	4,373	3,240	1,133	1,453	1,787	0	24.3%	41.9%
Rancho Cucamonga city	57,104	7,504	5,416	2,088	3,010	2,406	301	34.3%	68.3%
Redding city	38,251	9,678	6,899	2,779	2,557	4,342	493	24.9%	54.8%
Redlands city	26,407	5,345	3,945	1,400	1,567	2,378	499	18.7%	55.2%
Redondo Beach city	31,069	4,936	3,344	1,592	1,816	1,528	24	26.4%	61.5%
Redwood City city	29,253	5,268	4,072	1,196	1,841	2,231	478	31.3%	65.5%
Rialto city	26,346	3,995	3,135	860	1,655	1,480	77	23.0%	55.1%
Richmond city	40,071	6,393	5,199	1,194	2,597	2,602	na	29.2%	46.0%
Riverside city	98,065	15,759	11,017	4,742	5,058	5,959	605	24.7%	50.7%
Roseville city	48,560	10,180	7,885	2,295	3,439	4,446	433	25.3%	68.9%
Sacramento city	192,314	32,016	21,986	10,030	9,747	12,239	1,107	23.6%	53.2%
Salinas city	43,047	5,951	3,774	2,177	1,653	2,121	197	29.9%	53.7%
San Bernardino city	64,175	9,607	6,766	2,841	2,788	3,978	206	25.8%	44.7%
San Buenaventura (Ventura) city	43,232	10,104	7,386	2,718	3,123	4,263	481	28.2%	46.8%
San Diego city	512,184	84,219	61,453	22,766	28,621	32,832	1,806	27.9%	50.4%
San Francisco city	376,653	68,503	35,712	32,791	14,863	20,849	1,528	29.1%	46.3%
San Jose city	318,644	52,773	38,300	14,473	17,014	21,286	1,087	26.6%	50.2%
San Leandro city	31,753	6,252	4,415	1,837	1,461	2,954	327	15.4%	52.7%
San Marcos city	29,105	5,474	4,079	1,395	1,419	2,660	379	30.3%	70.3%
San Mateo city	39,265	8,714	6,154	2,560	2,548	3,606	514	22.9%	63.4%
San Ramon city	25,811	2,920	2,161	759	1,238	923	333	23.0%	61.0%
Santa Ana city	74,993	9,878	6,736	3,142	3,249	3,487	188	25.2%	46.4%
Santa Barbara city	36,993	7,921	5,011	2,910	2,402	2,609	709	30.6%	44.4%
Santa Clara city	44,368	6,487	4,508	1,979	1,661	2,847	625	22.8%	73.0%
Santa Clarita city	61,132	10,565	8,083	2,482	4,602	3,481	103	34.1%	62.7%
Santa Maria city	29,105	5,330	4,029	1,301	1,612	2,417	140	24.5%	51.0%
Santa Monica city	49,723	9,500	3,664	5,836	1,919	1,745	530	32.9%	53.8%
Santa Rosa city	66,962	14,615	10,581	4,034	4,428	6,153	942	27.4%	52.9%
Simi Valley city	42,447	8,012	6,512	1,500	3,438	3,074	124	25.0%	57.5%
South Gate city	24,271	3,404	2,237	1,167	1,085	1,152	na	30.4%	55.9%
Stockton city	99,962	16,456	11,139	5,317	5,502	5,637	840	28.5%	54.0%
Sunnyvale city	56,329	9,181	7,027	2,154	2,475	4,552	567	19.1%	57.1%
Temecula city	33,597	4,246	3,246	1,000	2,214	1,032	197	37.9%	69.2%
Thousand Oaks city	46,942	11,638	9,516	2,122	5,448	4,068	844	33.9%	59.4%
Torrance city	58,913	14,053	10,787	3,266	3,906	6,881	292	20.6%	52.8%
Tracy city	25,387	2,799	2,084	715	1,152	932	136	26.6%	49.7%
Turlock city	24,756	4,676	3,048	1,628	1,356	1,692	237	36.2%	55.2%
Tustin city	26,299	3,721	2,843	878	1,606	1,237	88	34.8%	68.9%
Union City city	21,567	3,817	2,839	978	1,161	1,678	126	25.5%	48.6%
Upland city	27,866	5,168	4,374	794	2,021	2,353	119	25.9%	41.7%
Vacaville city	32,813	6,089	4,404	1,685	2,156	2,248	69	28.3%	51.2%
Vallejo city	45,252	7,994	5,868	2,126	3,212	2,656	339	24.7%	51.7%
Victorville city	34,796	5,023	4,019	1,004	2,096	1,923	45	28.9%	81.5%
Visalia city	44,391	8,055	6,058	1,997	2,640	3,418	278	22.9%	56.6%
Vista city	31,651	4,814	4,184	630	1,840	2,344	81	28.2%	49.2%
West Covina city	32,086	6,441	4,733	1,708	1,959	2,774	143	22.0%	52.3%
Westminster city	28,405	6,777	4,333	2,444	1,450	2,883	13	27.3%	54.1%
Whittier city	28,433	5,730	4,505	1,225	2,012	2,493	227	27.8%	60.7%
Yorba Linda city	22,350	4,885	3,916	969	2,431	1,485	388	32.8%	74.4%
Yuba City city	23,228	4,648	3,418	1,230	1,397	2,021	166	26.9%	34.5%

Table J-3: Places—Summary of Housing and Householder Characteristics—*Continued*

| | | Householders 65 Years and Over | | | | | | | |
| | | | | | Owner Householders | | | | |
	Total Housing Units	Total Households	Owner Occupied	Renter Occupied	With a Mortgage	Without a Mortgage	Renter Households With Meals Included in Rent	Percent of Owner Householders Who Pay 35% or More of Income for Housing Costs	Percent of Renter Householders Who Pay 35% or More of Income for Rental Costs
Colorado									
Arvada city	45,260	10,077	8,313	1,764	3,341	4,972	412	20.2%	41.7%
Aurora city	130,639	19,195	14,678	4,517	7,823	6,855	651	25.6%	58.0%
Boulder city	43,327	5,772	4,198	1,574	1,483	2,715	595	18.4%	48.0%
Centennial city	39,301	7,538	6,599	939	3,134	3,465	350	19.8%	63.6%
Colorado Springs city	179,660	29,663	23,004	6,659	9,950	13,054	1,373	18.9%	52.1%
Denver city	286,732	43,278	28,888	14,390	12,361	16,527	2,051	25.5%	42.7%
Fort Collins city	58,782	7,907	6,141	1,766	2,488	3,653	491	19.2%	50.4%
Greeley city	36,326	6,143	4,557	1,586	1,955	2,602	362	18.1%	51.4%
Lakewood city	63,639	13,204	10,315	2,889	4,097	6,218	967	17.6%	59.2%
Longmont city	35,069	6,145	4,667	1,478	1,758	2,909	363	16.3%	40.9%
Loveland city	29,995	6,163	4,658	1,505	1,784	2,874	349	18.2%	53.1%
Pueblo city	47,958	10,932	8,772	2,160	2,898	5,874	39	18.0%	40.9%
Thornton city	43,466	4,526	3,659	867	1,780	1,879	68	24.4%	59.6%
Westminster city	44,362	6,626	4,928	1,698	2,198	2,730	544	21.5%	50.9%
Connecticut									
Bridgeport city	57,834	8,915	4,909	4,006	1,872	3,037	127	42.8%	43.6%
Danbury city	32,223	5,770	4,231	1,539	1,805	2,426	215	39.9%	33.4%
Hartford city	53,848	8,305	3,048	5,257	1,455	1,593	143	40.0%	43.9%
New Britain city	30,654	5,395	3,141	2,254	918	2,223	92	36.1%	46.4%
New Haven city	57,648	8,430	3,654	4,776	1,631	2,023	170	41.2%	42.8%
Norwalk city	39,550	8,293	6,722	1,571	2,450	4,272	98	38.2%	58.6%
Stamford city	48,627	9,437	6,816	2,621	2,784	4,032	376	40.6%	45.4%
Waterbury city	48,423	8,254	5,264	2,990	1,712	3,552	113	44.9%	46.0%
Delaware									
Wilmington city	34,500	6,344	3,348	2,996	1,447	1,901	263	31.5%	45.7%
District of Columbia									
Washington city	297,918	49,026	29,590	19,436	14,625	14,965	1,434	25.9%	44.6%
Florida									
Boca Raton city	44,667	10,681	9,067	1,614	3,032	6,035	470	25.6%	59.2%
Boynton Beach city	35,807	9,779	8,372	1,407	2,382	5,990	581	28.6%	60.3%
Cape Coral city	75,630	14,963	12,718	2,245	5,832	6,886	244	30.6%	59.3%
Clearwater city	61,044	14,824	10,698	4,126	3,696	7,002	1,116	30.2%	54.8%
Coral Springs city	44,647	6,257	4,651	1,606	2,607	2,044	176	40.7%	42.2%
Deerfield Beach city	41,489	10,330	8,549	1,781	2,929	5,620	505	34.7%	60.4%
Deltona city	32,877	6,715	5,913	802	3,054	2,859	160	29.3%	52.7%
Fort Lauderdale city	93,376	17,008	13,332	3,676	4,996	8,336	93	39.1%	58.4%
Gainesville city	56,633	6,416	4,750	1,666	1,702	3,048	331	22.1%	43.9%
Hialeah city	72,244	20,913	12,719	8,194	4,688	8,031	289	38.7%	51.6%
Hollywood city	70,443	12,296	9,574	2,722	3,531	6,043	323	29.6%	54.5%
Jacksonville city	367,903	57,872	46,042	11,830	19,148	26,894	1,437	25.3%	42.2%
Lakeland city	48,929	12,731	10,035	2,696	2,676	7,359	742	22.1%	46.6%
Largo city	46,066	12,557	9,412	3,145	2,400	7,012	1,208	24.9%	71.9%
Lauderhill city	29,783	5,317	3,954	1,363	1,885	2,069	550	46.1%	60.3%
Melbourne city	39,775	10,003	7,497	2,506	2,738	4,759	260	22.6%	35.1%
Miami city	189,380	35,694	16,500	19,194	5,366	11,134	326	38.6%	54.9%
Miami Beach city	67,601	9,362	4,993	4,369	1,338	3,655	21	47.6%	47.4%
Miami Gardens city	34,700	6,720	5,412	1,308	2,684	2,728	0	39.8%	50.5%
Miramar city	41,816	3,210	2,897	313	1,628	1,269	na	49.3%	60.4%
Orlando city	119,182	13,677	8,838	4,839	3,701	5,137	303	31.3%	59.3%
Palm Bay city	44,506	9,483	8,357	1,126	4,099	4,258	146	31.0%	48.4%
Palm Coast city	34,287	10,098	9,271	827	4,489	4,782	256	28.6%	na
Pembroke Pines city	62,933	13,710	11,336	2,374	3,866	7,470	0	36.1%	60.5%
Plantation city	37,333	6,926	5,995	931	2,915	3,080	384	33.2%	62.5%
Pompano Beach city	56,272	12,414	9,376	3,038	3,388	5,988	1,368	33.5%	70.3%
Port St. Lucie city	68,249	15,429	14,277	1,152	6,237	8,040	307	28.4%	49.4%
St. Petersburg city	127,722	24,354	19,078	5,276	6,807	12,271	693	28.3%	45.9%
Sunrise city	36,684	8,033	6,822	1,211	2,743	4,079	241	43.5%	48.6%
Tallahassee city	84,120	9,945	7,625	2,320	3,030	4,595	494	22.7%	55.6%
Tampa city	158,719	24,456	16,472	7,984	6,401	10,071	401	28.7%	44.6%
Weston city	24,664	2,607	2,373	234	1,157	1,216	na	39.0%	na
West Palm Beach city	54,749	10,164	7,440	2,724	2,870	4,570	537	27.2%	58.3%
Georgia									
Albany city	33,562	6,083	4,311	1,772	1,639	2,672	134	25.6%	52.1%
Athens-Clarke County unified govt (bal)	50,565	6,218	4,775	1,443	1,816	2,959	334	15.2%	48.2%
Atlanta city	224,143	28,912	17,453	11,459	7,575	9,878	1,038	32.8%	47.1%
Augusta-Richmond County consolidated govt (bal)	84,484	13,732	10,974	2,758	4,115	6,859	69	20.1%	44.9%
Columbus city	82,895	15,015	11,500	3,515	4,389	7,111	395	21.6%	49.7%
Johns Creek city	27,205	3,200	2,755	445	1,349	1,406	na	23.1%	na
Macon city	42,677	6,957	4,730	2,227	1,861	2,869	277	27.3%	47.1%
Roswell city	37,351	6,430	4,942	1,488	2,494	2,448	456	20.7%	54.3%
Sandy Springs city	46,247	6,708	5,026	1,682	2,162	2,864	553	22.1%	31.1%
Savannah city	61,358	10,862	8,089	2,773	2,941	5,148	655	25.1%	57.0%
Warner Robins city	30,219	4,253	3,306	947	1,147	2,159	46	16.7%	31.6%
Hawaii									
Urban Honolulu CDP	142,334	35,645	22,562	13,083	7,921	14,641	556	22.0%	41.0%

Table J-3: Places—Summary of Housing and Householder Characteristics—*Continued*

| | | Householders 65 Years and Over | | | | | | |
| | Total Housing Units | Total Households | Owner Occupied | Renter Occupied | Owner Householders | | Renter Households With Meals Included in Rent | Percent of Owner Householders Who Pay 35% or More of Income for Housing Costs | Percent of Renter Householders Who Pay 35% or More of Income for Rental Costs |
					With a Mortgage	Without a Mortgage			
Idaho									
Boise City city	92,163	16,553	12,474	4,079	5,449	7,025	1,296	17.9%	50.4%
Meridian city	28,431	4,565	3,775	790	2,108	1,667	359	23.7%	63.9%
Nampa city	29,832	5,623	4,394	1,229	1,935	2,459	184	20.6%	36.0%
Illinois									
Aurora city	66,094	7,685	5,917	1,768	2,963	2,954	197	29.6%	52.1%
Bloomington city	33,797	5,079	3,914	1,165	1,219	2,695	243	19.1%	27.6%
Champaign city	35,877	4,507	3,747	760	1,246	2,501	na	11.2%	38.7%
Chicago city	1,192,775	182,180	114,481	67,699	45,144	69,337	3,728	33.5%	50.9%
Decatur city	36,115	8,228	6,597	1,631	1,618	4,979	328	11.9%	39.4%
Elgin city	37,276	5,952	5,094	858	2,260	2,834	na	29.2%	62.6%
Evanston city	31,709	5,710	3,975	1,735	1,647	2,328	365	23.9%	47.6%
Joliet city	50,420	7,585	5,695	1,890	2,196	3,499	235	26.3%	49.7%
Naperville city	52,243	7,421	6,062	1,359	2,385	3,677	494	23.5%	47.6%
Peoria city	52,340	10,009	7,301	2,708	2,264	5,037	513	16.5%	43.0%
Rockford city	66,975	13,412	9,369	4,043	3,382	5,987	707	22.0%	47.7%
Springfield city	56,723	11,949	9,126	2,823	3,028	6,098	594	13.9%	42.8%
Waukegan city	32,665	3,931	2,893	1,038	1,084	1,809	na	29.5%	47.2%
Indiana									
Bloomington city	32,601	4,483	3,265	1,218	1,179	2,086	505	18.3%	46.5%
Carmel city	31,134	4,936	4,024	912	2,035	1,989	373	13.8%	41.9%
Evansville city	58,928	11,492	8,419	3,073	2,416	6,003	387	18.7%	46.5%
Fort Wayne city	113,469	20,604	15,809	4,795	5,873	9,936	486	12.0%	47.7%
Gary city	41,428	7,903	6,208	1,695	2,622	3,586	20	24.2%	46.5%
Hammond city	33,250	5,621	4,586	1,035	1,404	3,182	0	18.6%	38.9%
Indianapolis city (bal)	381,117	56,836	41,994	14,842	19,612	22,382	2,024	22.0%	52.8%
Lafayette city	31,177	5,001	3,883	1,118	1,579	2,304	144	13.0%	45.6%
Muncie city	31,874	6,280	4,999	1,281	1,784	3,215	17	14.6%	32.7%
South Bend city	46,708	8,609	6,597	2,012	2,530	4,067	292	17.8%	37.4%
Iowa									
Cedar Rapids city	57,379	10,513	8,876	1,637	2,385	6,491	459	14.1%	39.8%
Davenport city	44,559	8,009	5,880	2,129	1,763	4,117	529	17.2%	39.5%
Des Moines city	88,824	14,491	10,988	3,503	3,716	7,272	513	21.8%	41.6%
Iowa City city	29,426	3,932	2,993	939	738	2,255	359	9.1%	39.0%
Sioux City city	33,412	7,036	4,980	2,056	1,302	3,678	494	13.4%	56.2%
Waterloo city	31,024	6,487	4,895	1,592	1,618	3,277	413	17.5%	46.9%
Kansas									
Kansas City city	61,847	10,001	8,027	1,974	2,457	5,570	237	22.6%	48.3%
Lawrence city	37,261	4,360	2,988	1,372	1,346	1,642	262	19.4%	50.0%
Olathe city	47,521	5,755	4,124	1,631	1,909	2,215	465	21.5%	43.1%
Overland Park city	76,497	14,305	10,538	3,767	4,274	6,264	1,371	15.7%	54.6%
Topeka city	59,255	11,733	8,380	3,353	2,572	5,808	451	12.5%	36.7%
Wichita city	167,914	28,688	22,056	6,632	6,971	15,085	1,308	16.2%	50.6%
Kentucky									
Lexington-Fayette urban county	135,963	20,954	15,570	5,384	6,151	9,419	712	16.6%	40.9%
Louisville/Jefferson County metro govt (bal)	272,300	49,976	38,911	11,065	14,106	24,805	1,209	19.5%	37.2%
Louisiana									
Baton Rouge city	100,524	16,907	13,374	3,533	4,526	8,848	590	16.6%	51.1%
Kenner city	28,584	5,491	4,007	1,484	1,282	2,725	115	21.6%	53.6%
Lafayette city	54,185	9,626	8,106	1,520	2,448	5,658	196	17.3%	43.9%
Lake Charles city	34,239	6,613	5,127	1,486	1,301	3,826	269	16.2%	42.4%
New Orleans city	190,707	26,272	18,292	7,980	5,607	12,685	324	27.1%	50.4%
Shreveport city	88,423	16,617	13,215	3,402	4,155	9,060	471	12.7%	42.6%
Maine									
Portland city	34,098	5,304	3,150	2,154	1,165	1,985	568	27.6%	40.2%
Maryland									
Baltimore city	296,227	50,955	32,436	18,519	12,949	19,487	559	32.3%	44.8%
Frederick city	27,651	4,734	3,319	1,415	1,737	1,582	185	17.1%	42.7%
Massachusetts									
Boston city	272,568	42,931	19,368	23,563	8,744	10,624	1,102	33.9%	35.6%
Brockton city	36,289	7,041	4,290	2,751	1,762	2,528	264	34.0%	39.7%
Cambridge city	48,050	7,952	4,893	3,059	1,934	2,959	423	24.9%	37.6%
Fall River city	43,683	8,833	4,118	4,715	1,197	2,921	167	27.6%	49.9%
Lawrence city	28,238	3,597	1,269	2,328	607	662	101	40.6%	35.8%
Lowell city	42,840	6,538	4,116	2,422	1,515	2,601	0	33.6%	35.3%
Lynn city	35,289	6,702	3,562	3,140	1,363	2,199	0	34.1%	36.2%
New Bedford city	43,769	9,128	5,241	3,887	1,505	3,736	66	35.5%	42.7%
Newton city	32,060	8,380	6,325	2,055	1,993	4,332	507	28.7%	40.9%
Quincy city	41,596	8,459	4,678	3,781	1,380	3,298	530	34.7%	36.0%
Somerville city	32,730	4,585	2,814	1,771	846	1,968	70	41.6%	35.1%
Springfield city	61,499	11,110	6,989	4,121	2,684	4,305	299	31.2%	43.8%
Worcester city	76,526	13,292	7,034	6,258	2,608	4,426	635	32.7%	44.0%

Table J-3: Places—Summary of Housing and Householder Characteristics—*Continued*

		Householders 65 Years and Over						
		Total Households	Owner Occupied	Renter Occupied	Owner Householders		Renter Households With Meals Included in Rent	Percent of Owner Householders Who Pay 35% or More of Income for Housing Costs	Percent of Renter Householders Who Pay 35% or More of Income for Rental Costs
	Total Housing Units				With a Mortgage	Without a Mortgage			
Michigan									
Ann Arbor city	49,539	8,021	5,680	2,341	2,145	3,535	604	22.5%	45.1%
Dearborn city	35,594	7,528	5,801	1,727	1,553	4,248	210	26.5%	46.3%
Detroit city	363,099	57,719	40,432	17,287	15,066	25,366	157	32.1%	43.3%
Farmington Hills city	36,562	8,126	5,752	2,374	2,440	3,312	328	28.1%	54.9%
Flint city	53,505	8,223	6,670	1,553	2,217	4,453	12	22.2%	48.1%
Grand Rapids city	80,995	13,491	9,829	3,662	2,864	6,965	785	16.5%	40.2%
Kalamazoo city	32,213	4,671	3,110	1,561	1,108	2,002	264	18.4%	42.9%
Lansing city	55,077	7,855	5,725	2,130	2,556	3,169	43	22.6%	35.1%
Livonia city	39,349	11,070	9,602	1,468	3,153	6,449	365	20.1%	43.0%
Rochester Hills city	29,056	6,177	4,824	1,353	2,079	2,745	490	25.8%	51.5%
Southfield city	35,718	8,403	4,677	3,726	2,527	2,150	784	32.9%	53.1%
Sterling Heights city	52,056	12,444	9,649	2,795	3,241	6,408	919	23.2%	55.0%
Troy city	32,306	7,155	5,541	1,614	2,232	3,309	170	19.5%	40.5%
Warren city	58,224	13,385	11,569	1,816	3,227	8,342	233	19.7%	51.7%
Westland city	37,540	7,783	5,700	2,083	1,911	3,789	448	18.1%	52.1%
Wyoming city	28,935	4,208	3,103	1,105	852	2,251	206	17.6%	39.1%
Minnesota									
Bloomington city	38,108	10,075	8,077	1,998	3,004	5,073	253	18.9%	45.5%
Brooklyn Park city	27,230	3,527	2,914	613	1,299	1,615	217	17.3%	61.0%
Duluth city	38,112	7,817	5,170	2,647	1,603	3,567	416	18.7%	43.0%
Minneapolis city	180,974	22,268	14,803	7,465	5,697	9,106	350	30.1%	36.9%
Plymouth city	30,511	5,630	4,786	844	1,878	2,908	141	19.7%	56.3%
Rochester city	45,995	8,501	6,593	1,908	1,992	4,601	583	15.3%	42.0%
St. Cloud city	27,701	4,355	3,365	990	965	2,400	14	16.0%	33.5%
St. Paul city	120,237	16,768	10,707	6,061	4,244	6,463	617	22.4%	40.9%
Mississippi									
Gulfport city	31,950	5,444	4,498	946	1,808	2,690	52	23.9%	41.4%
Jackson city	74,460	11,246	8,717	2,529	3,226	5,491	77	17.8%	37.0%
Missouri									
Columbia city	47,362	5,933	4,582	1,351	1,627	2,955	347	11.8%	54.5%
Independence city	53,689	12,340	9,790	2,550	3,017	6,773	401	20.5%	48.2%
Kansas City city	224,119	34,840	26,314	8,526	9,868	16,446	1,270	23.8%	46.0%
Lee's Summit city	35,851	6,916	4,610	2,306	1,865	2,745	556	22.8%	59.8%
O'Fallon city	30,163	4,802	3,783	1,019	1,792	1,991	538	20.8%	58.2%
St. Charles city	27,561	5,909	4,612	1,297	1,690	2,922	397	16.0%	46.2%
St. Joseph city	33,149	6,601	4,945	1,656	1,259	3,686	216	15.0%	45.2%
St. Louis city	175,577	25,167	15,776	9,391	5,382	10,394	148	24.9%	40.1%
Springfield city	77,840	15,397	11,068	4,329	3,573	7,495	822	14.6%	49.9%
Montana									
Billings city	46,542	10,499	7,971	2,528	2,645	5,326	602	16.0%	44.0%
Missoula city	31,025	4,841	3,436	1,405	985	2,451	578	12.9%	57.4%
Nebraska									
Lincoln city	111,150	18,487	13,084	5,403	4,166	8,918	1,684	14.9%	46.0%
Omaha city	180,105	31,656	24,176	7,480	7,977	16,199	1,601	18.6%	49.8%
Nevada									
Henderson city	112,669	23,115	18,265	4,850	9,963	8,302	101	25.2%	57.5%
Las Vegas city	249,165	45,369	32,102	13,267	16,453	15,649	1,037	27.5%	51.5%
North Las Vegas city	77,590	8,880	6,653	2,227	4,404	2,249	13	31.1%	48.3%
Reno city	101,442	17,420	11,548	5,872	4,984	6,564	372	25.5%	54.9%
Sparks city	37,523	6,451	4,823	1,628	2,252	2,571	150	29.0%	56.1%
New Hampshire									
Manchester city	49,174	8,305	4,936	3,369	1,897	3,039	294	35.3%	45.3%
Nashua city	36,922	6,921	4,950	1,971	1,667	3,283	291	28.9%	47.9%
New Jersey									
Camden city	30,181	4,296	2,856	1,440	931	1,925	30	39.0%	63.2%
Clifton city	30,560	6,499	4,608	1,891	1,252	3,356	39	45.0%	53.8%
Elizabeth city	44,402	6,269	2,826	3,443	986	1,840	30	47.6%	53.1%
Jersey City city	110,015	13,793	6,050	7,743	2,388	3,662	175	46.8%	45.4%
Newark city	109,187	14,658	5,746	8,912	2,748	2,998	22	49.0%	46.9%
Passaic city	22,148	3,248	1,277	1,971	326	951	0	na	45.8%
Paterson city	48,826	7,259	2,736	4,523	1,139	1,597	0	48.8%	56.0%
Trenton city	34,432	4,865	2,783	2,082	1,171	1,612	0	30.8%	42.9%
Union City city	25,216	3,789	909	2,880	239	670	0	51.8%	52.0%
New Mexico									
Albuquerque city	241,565	44,318	33,901	10,417	13,299	20,602	1,315	19.9%	42.0%
Las Cruces city	41,976	8,434	6,624	1,810	2,724	3,900	150	15.4%	47.1%
Rio Rancho city	34,608	6,090	5,069	1,021	2,371	2,698	129	18.8%	50.9%
Santa Fe city	37,134	9,110	6,594	2,516	2,534	4,060	418	23.2%	39.0%

Table J-3: Places—Summary of Housing and Householder Characteristics—*Continued*

	Total Housing Units	Householders 65 Years and Over						
		Total Households	Owner Occupied	Renter Occupied	Owner Householders		Renter Households With Meals Included in Rent	Percent of Owner Householders Who Pay 35% or More of Income for Housing Costs	Percent of Renter Householders Who Pay 35% or More of Income for Rental Costs
					With a Mortgage	Without a Mortgage			
New York									
Albany city	46,956	7,417	4,583	2,834	1,567	3,016	310	23.4%	43.7%
Buffalo city	134,513	20,530	13,180	7,350	4,797	8,383	195	20.1%	44.2%
Mount Vernon city	29,850	5,674	2,876	2,798	1,353	1,523	53	54.6%	55.9%
New Rochelle city	29,713	6,474	4,054	2,420	1,342	2,712	51	39.0%	49.8%
New York city	3,378,616	623,982	261,793	362,189	86,657	175,136	5,040	36.0%	48.9%
Rochester city	99,469	12,766	7,366	5,400	3,265	4,101	217	25.5%	49.1%
Schenectady city	31,073	4,988	3,263	1,725	1,091	2,172	132	25.7%	53.0%
Syracuse city	64,375	9,764	6,119	3,645	1,931	4,188	157	22.1%	48.0%
Yonkers city	80,513	17,880	11,070	6,810	3,617	7,453	273	42.2%	44.0%
North Carolina									
Asheville city	41,661	8,896	5,823	3,073	2,204	3,619	662	20.1%	39.4%
Charlotte city	325,545	41,262	31,431	9,831	15,376	16,055	1,810	25.8%	48.5%
Concord city	33,641	5,328	4,091	1,237	1,836	2,255	96	22.3%	37.1%
Durham city	105,518	13,814	9,452	4,362	4,551	4,901	882	20.7%	49.4%
Fayetteville city	88,988	13,108	10,473	2,635	4,393	6,080	198	23.5%	35.1%
Gastonia city	29,902	4,942	3,682	1,260	1,621	2,061	305	24.6%	43.5%
Greensboro city	125,661	20,939	15,608	5,331	6,469	9,139	1,166	22.0%	38.9%
Greenville city	40,026	4,084	3,027	1,057	1,193	1,834	303	19.4%	49.3%
High Point city	46,135	8,258	6,107	2,151	2,517	3,590	565	26.3%	50.6%
Jacksonville city	22,445	2,617	1,910	707	628	1,282	na	14.8%	64.6%
Raleigh city	177,988	22,166	15,929	6,237	7,545	8,384	1,193	22.6%	60.3%
Wilmington city	53,653	9,696	6,686	3,010	3,151	3,535	590	25.7%	49.3%
Winston-Salem city	104,615	19,117	15,109	4,008	6,509	8,600	627	20.7%	39.9%
North Dakota									
Fargo city	50,832	7,064	4,284	2,780	1,179	3,105	501	9.6%	41.0%
Ohio									
Akron city	97,050	17,030	12,499	4,531	4,972	7,527	226	18.2%	40.2%
Canton city	35,696	6,425	4,635	1,790	1,609	3,026	276	15.3%	37.9%
Cincinnati city	163,115	22,599	12,973	9,626	5,633	7,340	1,029	29.7%	45.8%
Cleveland city	214,218	33,934	22,396	11,538	8,950	13,446	412	30.6%	43.5%
Columbus city	375,672	46,612	31,779	14,833	15,037	16,742	1,714	25.2%	46.1%
Dayton city	73,409	11,844	8,344	3,500	3,314	5,030	138	22.9%	45.7%
Parma city	35,870	9,135	7,770	1,365	1,887	5,883	58	17.7%	49.5%
Toledo city	138,430	23,528	17,893	5,635	6,450	11,443	372	19.7%	43.5%
Youngstown city	33,347	7,091	5,496	1,595	1,462	4,034	88	15.1%	36.9%
Oklahoma									
Broken Arrow city	38,419	6,693	5,641	1,052	2,600	3,041	212	18.2%	52.1%
Edmond city	32,662	5,833	4,644	1,189	1,811	2,833	255	15.1%	45.7%
Lawton city	40,340	6,506	5,461	1,045	2,106	3,355	195	17.6%	34.6%
Norman city	50,503	7,900	6,576	1,324	2,707	3,869	176	17.0%	48.6%
Oklahoma City city	257,325	42,365	32,354	10,011	11,199	21,155	2,396	19.4%	49.5%
Tulsa city	186,676	33,014	24,888	8,126	7,748	17,140	1,553	17.3%	50.1%
Oregon									
Beaverton city	38,350	6,308	3,691	2,617	1,892	1,799	882	29.3%	53.6%
Bend city	36,594	7,490	5,507	1,983	2,426	3,081	790	30.0%	56.1%
Eugene city	69,871	13,664	9,724	3,940	3,608	6,116	1,185	20.4%	52.8%
Gresham city	41,028	7,368	5,147	2,221	2,015	3,132	646	23.4%	57.0%
Hillsboro city	34,653	4,410	3,231	1,179	1,668	1,563	469	31.7%	58.2%
Medford city	32,681	8,144	5,630	2,514	2,129	3,501	1,150	21.5%	65.7%
Portland city	265,710	41,715	27,733	13,982	11,317	16,416	3,025	26.6%	53.1%
Salem city	61,316	12,607	8,844	3,763	3,349	5,495	807	21.0%	52.5%
Pennsylvania									
Allentown city	47,474	8,216	4,954	3,262	1,614	3,340	176	23.0%	46.4%
Bethlehem city	31,806	7,150	4,569	2,581	1,233	3,336	219	17.8%	42.9%
Erie city	45,918	8,364	5,116	3,248	1,459	3,657	331	19.7%	39.8%
Philadelphia city	668,947	122,082	85,262	36,820	23,336	61,926	1,605	25.4%	45.6%
Pittsburgh city	155,635	29,182	19,301	9,881	5,678	13,623	1,000	20.1%	39.3%
Reading city	35,345	5,553	2,906	2,647	943	1,963	225	24.4%	40.2%
Scranton city	34,168	7,982	4,797	3,185	1,067	3,730	30	30.7%	34.1%
Rhode Island									
Cranston city	32,543	7,475	5,425	2,050	1,747	3,678	41	34.3%	43.1%
Pawtucket city	33,137	6,078	3,666	2,412	1,130	2,536	0	31.0%	37.3%
Providence city	71,137	9,006	4,722	4,284	1,875	2,847	277	37.3%	37.7%
Warwick city	37,629	9,705	6,963	2,742	3,074	3,889	497	32.4%	42.5%
South Carolina									
Charleston city	59,904	9,715	7,286	2,429	3,210	4,076	256	31.4%	56.6%
Columbia city	52,560	7,637	5,798	1,839	1,887	3,911	149	19.1%	43.9%
North Charleston city	42,449	5,604	4,476	1,128	1,846	2,630	0	22.5%	55.7%
Rock Hill city	29,731	4,457	3,150	1,307	1,311	1,839	395	22.7%	56.9%

Table J-3: Places—Summary of Housing and Householder Characteristics—*Continued*

		Householders 65 Years and Over							
					Owner Householders			Percent of Owner Householders Who Pay 35% or More of Income for Housing Costs	Percent of Renter Householders Who Pay 35% or More of Income for Rental Costs
	Total Housing Units	Total Households	Owner Occupied	Renter Occupied	With a Mortgage	Without a Mortgage	Renter Households With Meals Included in Rent		
South Dakota									
Rapid City city	30,241	6,316	4,091	2,225	1,433	2,658	568	16.0%	45.7%
Sioux Falls city	67,363	11,068	7,799	3,269	2,449	5,350	678	12.4%	55.2%
Tennessee									
Chattanooga city	80,435	16,679	12,524	4,155	4,570	7,954	972	23.9%	49.2%
Clarksville city	56,532	6,113	5,115	998	1,937	3,178	159	17.3%	37.3%
Jackson city	29,496	5,420	4,187	1,233	1,244	2,943	79	17.8%	31.1%
Knoxville city	91,928	17,327	12,025	5,302	3,126	8,899	725	18.5%	52.2%
Memphis city	294,881	44,272	32,145	12,127	12,723	19,422	1,572	26.6%	47.6%
Murfreesboro city	45,457	5,957	4,283	1,674	1,428	2,855	173	19.9%	30.8%
Nashville-Davidson metropolitan government (bal)	275,676	40,491	30,704	9,787	11,044	19,660	1,533	20.0%	44.5%
Texas									
Abilene city	48,006	9,307	7,215	2,092	1,729	5,486	453	13.1%	42.4%
Allen city	29,670	2,485	1,975	510	1,150	825	0	33.4%	41.8%
Amarillo city	81,029	15,039	11,682	3,357	3,158	8,524	549	17.0%	40.5%
Arlington city	146,134	18,636	15,005	3,631	5,621	9,384	627	17.3%	52.6%
Austin city	357,710	36,373	26,817	9,556	9,649	17,168	1,575	21.1%	46.0%
Baytown city	28,167	4,056	3,104	952	720	2,384	149	15.0%	59.0%
Beaumont city	51,338	10,218	7,794	2,424	1,713	6,081	408	19.4%	47.2%
Brownsville city	55,852	9,563	6,704	2,859	1,665	5,039	0	24.5%	42.9%
Bryan city	31,490	4,904	3,642	1,262	1,070	2,572	260	21.6%	42.5%
Carrollton city	45,655	5,410	4,098	1,312	1,947	2,151	290	21.4%	41.3%
College Station city	37,767	2,918	2,443	475	767	1,676	24	15.0%	33.3%
Corpus Christi city	125,596	22,401	17,466	4,935	4,902	12,564	616	19.5%	45.6%
Dallas city	519,305	69,999	49,674	20,325	15,508	34,166	2,417	27.1%	49.8%
Denton city	45,059	6,081	4,692	1,389	1,985	2,707	175	15.3%	45.5%
Edinburg city	25,975	3,062	2,358	704	547	1,811	na	21.6%	37.4%
El Paso city	232,625	44,679	34,006	10,673	8,950	25,056	628	15.5%	39.1%
Fort Worth city	295,419	38,727	29,128	9,599	10,298	18,830	1,292	22.5%	49.9%
Frisco city	42,941	4,119	3,255	864	1,855	1,400	153	25.0%	49.0%
Garland city	78,502	12,289	10,153	2,136	3,531	6,622	504	19.8%	49.7%
Grand Prairie city	62,117	7,005	5,576	1,429	1,957	3,619	140	21.8%	54.0%
Harlingen city	25,071	5,079	3,732	1,347	724	3,008	45	19.8%	31.0%
Houston city	904,039	122,402	89,061	33,341	23,834	65,227	4,676	21.3%	51.8%
Irving city	91,621	8,690	6,733	1,957	2,057	4,676	296	19.9%	56.9%
Killeen city	54,605	4,053	3,232	821	960	2,272	0	12.6%	49.5%
Laredo city	69,259	10,430	7,595	2,835	1,685	5,910	0	25.6%	42.4%
League City city	32,705	3,994	3,315	679	1,319	1,996	na	13.3%	70.4%
Lewisville city	41,573	4,234	2,287	1,947	1,072	1,215	515	22.9%	66.4%
Longview city	32,903	7,090	5,237	1,853	1,370	3,867	537	18.9%	54.8%
Lubbock city	97,832	16,713	13,139	3,574	3,738	9,401	671	15.8%	46.5%
McAllen city	48,471	7,802	5,664	2,138	1,417	4,247	54	19.1%	37.3%
McKinney city	48,083	5,682	3,980	1,702	1,753	2,227	217	18.5%	61.2%
Mesquite city	52,499	7,112	5,804	1,308	1,642	4,162	176	16.7%	61.5%
Midland city	44,567	7,578	6,270	1,308	1,411	4,859	293	20.0%	57.2%
Mission city	27,554	4,644	3,880	764	728	3,152	na	19.2%	33.2%
Missouri City city	23,456	3,585	3,341	244	1,743	1,598	na	24.4%	na
Odessa city	40,371	6,972	5,492	1,480	868	4,624	261	16.5%	44.3%
Pasadena city	54,500	7,980	5,955	2,025	1,665	4,290	145	15.3%	49.4%
Pearland city	34,241	4,038	3,491	547	1,298	2,193	117	11.7%	19.6%
Pharr city	23,001	4,435	3,037	1,398	784	2,253	103	22.7%	38.3%
Plano city	105,780	14,766	10,495	4,271	4,634	5,861	903	21.9%	53.8%
Richardson city	41,067	7,359	6,160	1,199	1,886	4,274	238	16.7%	50.5%
Round Rock city	36,857	3,438	2,528	910	1,527	1,001	73	22.0%	42.6%
San Angelo city	39,456	8,590	6,690	1,900	1,626	5,064	213	11.9%	30.6%
San Antonio city	529,614	89,493	68,374	21,119	21,361	47,013	2,747	16.7%	46.0%
Sugar Land city	28,350	4,077	3,469	608	1,677	1,792	na	18.4%	na
Temple city	30,732	6,009	4,419	1,590	997	3,422	353	11.0%	43.6%
Tyler city	42,700	9,052	6,883	2,169	1,570	5,313	806	20.0%	53.9%
Waco city	52,128	8,666	6,274	2,392	1,754	4,520	379	18.6%	41.2%
Wichita Falls city	42,996	8,174	6,420	1,754	1,600	4,820	482	16.2%	56.8%
Utah									
Layton city	22,361	3,023	2,726	297	1,196	1,530	na	9.4%	55.9%
Ogden city	31,457	4,975	3,877	1,098	1,455	2,422	131	16.1%	39.3%
Orem city	27,321	4,539	3,926	613	1,433	2,493	119	13.8%	50.4%
Provo city	33,780	4,068	3,340	728	1,006	2,334	259	12.9%	39.4%
St. George city	32,123	8,087	6,844	1,243	2,207	4,637	261	16.4%	53.2%
Salt Lake City city	80,199	12,225	8,419	3,806	2,867	5,552	102	21.1%	41.9%
Sandy city	29,243	5,012	4,137	875	1,697	2,440	302	16.4%	61.0%
West Jordan city	32,342	3,049	2,559	490	1,428	1,131	159	24.9%	36.3%
West Valley City city	39,689	5,708	4,637	1,071	1,988	2,649	na	13.6%	48.6%

Table J-3: Places—Summary of Housing and Householder Characteristics—*Continued*

	Total Housing Units	Householders 65 Years and Over						
		Total Households	Owner Occupied	Renter Occupied	Owner Householders		Renter Households With Meals Included in Rent	Percent of Owner Householders Who Pay 35% or More of Income for Housing Costs	Percent of Renter Householders Who Pay 35% or More of Income for Rental Costs
					With a Mortgage	Without a Mortgage			
Virginia									
Alexandria city	72,809	8,939	5,941	2,998	3,014	2,927	477	21.6%	46.9%
Chesapeake city	84,278	14,794	12,551	2,243	6,218	6,333	308	26.6%	50.1%
Hampton city	59,877	11,080	8,905	2,175	3,643	5,262	185	23.4%	50.3%
Lynchburg city	32,050	6,872	4,693	2,179	1,433	3,260	566	19.8%	37.7%
Newport News city	76,616	12,796	9,152	3,644	3,903	5,249	380	21.5%	39.9%
Norfolk city	95,238	15,010	10,703	4,307	4,178	6,525	279	24.7%	47.5%
Portsmouth city	40,781	8,147	6,450	1,697	2,782	3,668	48	28.4%	41.1%
Richmond city	98,613	15,786	10,202	5,584	4,491	5,711	343	32.0%	50.7%
Roanoke city	47,321	9,667	6,971	2,696	2,550	4,421	398	24.0%	41.4%
Suffolk city	33,346	6,001	4,887	1,114	1,887	3,000	69	20.6%	40.7%
Virginia Beach city	178,796	30,003	24,167	5,836	11,541	12,626	668	25.9%	58.7%
Washington									
Auburn city	29,012	4,927	3,434	1,493	1,091	2,343	331	27.3%	67.1%
Bellevue city	55,348	10,203	7,940	2,263	2,836	5,104	569	26.3%	45.7%
Bellingham city	36,185	7,002	4,727	2,275	1,519	3,208	636	17.3%	53.8%
Everett city	43,935	7,347	4,651	2,696	1,881	2,770	502	27.9%	49.4%
Federal Way city	36,441	6,032	4,085	1,947	1,684	2,401	763	29.0%	53.5%
Kennewick city	28,947	5,717	4,263	1,454	1,350	2,913	407	16.8%	42.5%
Kent city	44,932	6,667	4,352	2,315	1,871	2,481	490	21.6%	62.6%
Renton city	38,528	5,793	3,711	2,082	1,496	2,215	638	35.1%	46.5%
Seattle city	307,084	46,319	28,480	17,839	11,159	17,321	3,700	26.1%	51.3%
Spokane city	95,609	19,055	13,533	5,522	4,886	8,647	1,061	21.6%	49.6%
Spokane Valley city	38,724	8,182	5,788	2,394	2,222	3,566	872	19.0%	60.5%
Tacoma city	85,273	14,668	9,405	5,263	4,069	5,336	1,212	23.7%	50.4%
Vancouver city	69,959	14,025	8,934	5,091	3,819	5,115	995	19.4%	52.5%
Yakima city	35,543	7,758	5,400	2,358	1,729	3,671	758	17.3%	56.3%
Wisconsin									
Appleton city	30,706	5,622	4,406	1,216	1,164	3,242	264	24.3%	54.7%
Eau Claire city	28,240	5,188	3,605	1,583	963	2,642	227	18.5%	50.7%
Green Bay city	46,263	8,094	5,633	2,461	1,866	3,767	319	17.2%	41.2%
Kenosha city	41,030	6,898	4,770	2,128	1,520	3,250	113	25.7%	39.9%
Madison city	106,814	14,802	10,972	3,830	3,949	7,023	407	19.7%	50.2%
Milwaukee city	258,068	35,948	23,822	12,126	8,466	15,356	1,104	30.6%	48.2%
Oshkosh city	27,572	5,265	3,812	1,453	1,018	2,794	313	20.2%	46.2%
Racine city	33,965	5,985	4,430	1,555	1,435	2,995	55	24.2%	43.4%
Waukesha city	29,844	5,269	3,463	1,806	1,103	2,360	254	23.3%	50.3%

Table J-4: Metropolitan Statistical Areas—Summary of Housing and Householder Characteristics

| | | Households 65 Years and Over | | | | | | | |
| | | | | | Owner Householders | | Renter Households With Meals Included in Rent | Percent of Owner Householders Who Pay 35% or More of Income for Housing Costs | Percent of Renter Householders Who Pay 35% or More of Income for Rental Costs |
	Total Housing Units	Total Households	Owner Occupied	Renter Occupied	With a Mortgage	Without a Mortgage			
Abilene, TX	70,104	14,532	11,855	2,677	2,596	9,259	462	13.6%	38.0%
Akron, OH	312,675	64,998	52,496	12,502	20,678	31,818	2,045	20.0%	42.9%
Albany, GA	65,920	12,989	10,346	2,643	3,556	6,790	209	23.7%	47.4%
Albany-Schenectady-Troy, NY	393,957	78,336	59,130	19,206	18,393	40,737	1,771	21.9%	46.3%
Albuquerque, NM	376,038	71,559	58,646	12,913	22,476	36,170	1,462	19.2%	41.8%
Alexandria, LA	64,981	13,393	10,923	2,470	2,444	8,479	214	13.9%	38.0%
Allentown-Bethlehem-Easton, PA-NJ	342,910	76,152	58,811	17,341	18,106	40,705	2,145	25.5%	44.6%
Altoona, PA	56,205	14,484	10,994	3,490	2,486	8,508	389	16.1%	38.3%
Amarillo, TX	103,275	19,059	15,213	3,846	3,869	11,344	580	16.4%	40.8%
Ames, IA	36,965	5,780	4,588	1,192	1,239	3,349	135	8.6%	37.7%
Anchorage, AK	154,696	17,676	14,352	3,324	5,936	8,416	194	21.8%	47.8%
Anderson, IN	58,958	13,929	11,755	2,174	4,087	7,668	321	16.4%	46.9%
Anderson, SC	84,848	18,798	15,616	3,182	4,629	10,987	410	13.4%	51.6%
Ann Arbor, MI	147,636	24,398	19,093	5,305	7,737	11,356	1,445	24.3%	46.4%
Anniston-Oxford, AL	53,317	11,127	9,287	1,840	2,876	6,411	133	19.6%	29.0%
Appleton, WI	93,351	17,635	13,933	3,702	3,366	10,567	543	20.3%	50.6%
Asheville, NC	214,799	50,318	41,581	8,737	13,781	27,800	1,832	18.4%	41.2%
Athens-Clarke County, GA	81,797	12,485	9,798	2,687	3,443	6,355	459	16.7%	44.8%
Atlanta-Sandy Springs-Marietta, GA	2,170,360	295,043	237,158	57,885	108,952	128,206	7,199	25.0%	48.0%
Atlantic City-Hammonton, NJ	127,046	24,270	19,217	5,053	7,288	11,929	244	37.8%	39.4%
Auburn-Opelika, AL	63,521	8,548	7,259	1,289	2,849	4,410	214	21.1%	41.8%
Augusta-Richmond County, GA-SC	239,117	43,944	37,196	6,748	13,173	24,023	616	18.3%	46.2%
Austin-Round Rock-San Marcos, TX	716,795	88,351	69,235	19,116	27,205	42,030	2,736	20.7%	47.1%
Bakersfield-Delano, CA	285,366	45,718	36,044	9,674	14,470	21,574	793	21.1%	46.6%
Baltimore-Towson, MD	1,136,255	220,901	169,580	51,321	69,098	100,482	7,463	25.2%	48.9%
Bangor, ME	73,971	14,088	10,251	3,837	3,016	7,235	581	18.2%	37.7%
Barnstable Town, MA	160,420	34,374	29,333	5,041	11,513	17,820	524	31.3%	39.6%
Baton Rouge, LA	332,754	56,292	47,782	8,510	14,464	33,318	1,027	14.8%	40.3%
Battle Creek, MI	60,871	13,077	10,478	2,599	3,395	7,083	193	19.7%	35.2%
Bay City, MI	48,157	11,597	9,898	1,699	2,183	7,715	188	18.9%	36.7%
Beaumont-Port Arthur, TX	163,918	33,882	28,631	5,251	5,140	23,491	474	15.5%	42.8%
Bellingham, WA	90,980	17,606	13,487	4,119	4,695	8,792	925	22.0%	45.9%
Bend, OR	80,406	15,950	12,856	3,094	5,766	7,090	892	30.4%	53.1%
Billings, MT	71,125	15,467	12,301	3,166	3,938	8,363	708	16.3%	41.8%
Binghamton, NY	112,510	25,935	20,676	5,259	5,176	15,500	615	17.7%	41.1%
Birmingham-Hoover, AL	501,350	96,165	80,576	15,589	26,900	53,676	1,927	19.6%	42.7%
Bismarck, ND	48,787	9,938	7,603	2,335	1,875	5,728	355	13.4%	45.8%
Blacksburg-Christiansburg-Radford, VA	71,285	13,742	11,501	2,241	3,041	8,460	131	15.2%	40.5%
Bloomington, IN	84,484	15,036	12,679	2,357	4,318	8,361	532	16.3%	40.3%
Bloomington-Normal, IL	70,054	11,076	9,294	1,782	3,099	6,195	408	17.0%	30.3%
Boise City-Nampa, ID	247,372	44,817	36,163	8,654	15,967	20,196	2,111	19.9%	45.7%
Boston-Cambridge-Quincy, MA-NH	1,884,794	382,877	268,190	114,687	100,153	168,037	11,495	30.8%	39.8%
Boulder, CO	127,595	19,981	15,710	4,271	6,053	9,657	1,251	18.4%	50.2%
Bowling Green, KY	54,321	9,560	7,846	1,714	2,548	5,298	310	16.1%	51.3%
Bremerton-Silverdale, WA	107,781	21,257	16,940	4,317	7,300	9,640	627	24.9%	38.9%
Bridgeport-Stamford-Norwalk, CT	361,355	76,458	60,781	15,677	23,808	36,973	1,753	37.6%	42.4%
Brownsville-Harlingen, TX	143,106	25,830	20,174	5,656	3,792	16,382	45	20.1%	38.4%
Brunswick, GA	59,004	11,839	9,674	2,165	4,362	5,312	177	27.0%	35.6%
Buffalo-Niagara Falls, NY	519,140	116,715	89,757	26,958	25,878	63,879	2,348	18.4%	45.4%
Burlington, NC	67,098	15,143	11,998	3,145	4,164	7,834	522	20.1%	53.5%
Burlington-South Burlington, VT	92,875	16,287	12,466	3,821	4,831	7,635	921	28.2%	50.2%
Canton-Massillon, OH	178,844	41,933	33,899	8,034	10,990	22,909	1,119	15.2%	40.0%
Cape Coral-Fort Myers, FL	371,630	87,499	75,469	12,030	27,018	48,451	1,761	24.5%	48.8%
Cape Girardeau-Jackson, MO-IL	42,539	8,706	7,116	1,590	1,762	5,354	242	15.5%	38.7%
Casper, WY	34,454	6,257	5,126	1,131	1,324	3,802	124	10.9%	38.9%
Cedar Rapids, IA	112,957	23,070	19,465	3,605	5,462	14,003	814	16.0%	40.9%
Champaign-Urbana, IL	101,484	16,746	13,733	3,013	4,267	9,466	883	12.9%	45.5%
Charleston, WV	141,438	32,508	27,885	4,623	6,583	21,302	297	11.4%	35.6%
Charleston-North Charleston-Summerville, SC	301,620	50,671	43,065	7,606	17,337	25,728	942	25.5%	51.1%
Charlotte-Gastonia-Rock Hill, NC-SC	743,273	113,854	92,643	21,211	40,720	51,923	3,571	23.4%	48.3%
Charlottesville, VA	90,147	17,931	14,693	3,238	5,286	9,407	599	20.0%	43.1%
Chattanooga, TN-GA	235,325	50,496	41,639	8,857	13,198	28,441	1,500	18.4%	41.5%
Cheyenne, WY	40,667	7,710	6,303	1,407	2,085	4,218	205	17.9%	32.1%
Chicago-Joliet-Naperville, IL-IN-WI	3,795,676	687,259	536,258	151,001	202,687	333,571	19,613	29.1%	51.5%
Chico, CA	96,025	22,252	17,431	4,821	6,958	10,473	776	20.5%	45.6%
Cincinnati-Middletown, OH-KY-IN	919,244	169,699	133,185	36,514	52,856	80,329	4,964	22.4%	45.7%
Clarksville, TN-KY	116,238	16,678	14,203	2,475	4,257	9,946	197	15.1%	31.6%
Cleveland, TN	49,815	11,151	8,949	2,202	2,497	6,452	303	20.1%	44.4%
Cleveland-Elyria-Mentor, OH	955,056	207,026	160,311	46,715	57,284	103,027	6,646	23.3%	47.7%
Coeur d'Alene, ID	63,800	13,114	10,532	2,582	4,443	6,089	450	20.4%	48.0%
College Station-Bryan, TX	96,221	12,943	10,663	2,280	2,891	7,772	302	17.7%	39.6%
Colorado Springs, CO	267,164	42,773	34,965	7,808	15,984	18,981	1,373	20.4%	52.9%
Columbia, MO	74,856	10,703	8,794	1,909	2,802	5,992	353	14.2%	44.3%
Columbia, SC	334,145	57,244	49,566	7,678	17,887	31,679	1,050	19.9%	45.6%
Columbus, GA-AL	129,134	23,214	18,436	4,778	7,080	11,356	409	23.8%	43.4%
Columbus, IN	33,179	6,948	5,943	1,005	2,008	3,935	290	13.9%	47.9%
Columbus, OH	795,713	127,255	98,825	28,430	42,128	56,697	4,065	21.7%	44.6%
Corpus Christi, TX	183,971	34,267	27,864	6,403	7,357	20,507	654	19.2%	44.9%
Corvallis, OR	36,429	6,771	5,547	1,224	1,607	3,940	382	15.2%	34.3%
Crestview-Fort Walton Beach-Destin, FL	92,905	15,915	13,675	2,240	4,850	8,825	399	19.8%	46.9%

Table J-4: Metropolitan Statistical Areas—Summary of Housing and Householder Characteristics—*Continued*

| | | | | Householders 65 Years and Over | | | | |
| | | | | Owner Householders | | Renter Households With Meals Included in Rent | Percent of Owner Householders Who Pay 35% or More of Income for Housing Costs | Percent of Renter Householders Who Pay 35% or More of Income for Rental Costs |
	Total Housing Units	Total Households	Owner Occupied	Renter Occupied	With a Mortgage	Without a Mortgage			
Cumberland, MD-WV	46,380	11,888	8,857	3,031	2,207	6,650	55	15.5%	21.8%
Dallas-Fort Worth-Arlington, TX	2,525,359	354,325	277,283	77,042	97,571	179,712	10,899	21.2%	51.9%
Dalton, GA	55,780	9,721	8,287	1,434	2,592	5,695	92	20.0%	34.4%
Danville, IL	36,221	8,899	7,221	1,678	1,992	5,229	171	15.2%	37.2%
Danville, VA	53,728	13,120	10,709	2,411	2,859	7,850	101	15.4%	31.7%
Davenport-Moline-Rock Island, IA-IL	167,449	38,299	30,278	8,021	8,289	21,989	2,008	15.5%	42.4%
Dayton, OH	385,015	84,112	67,329	16,783	24,993	42,336	1,868	19.6%	44.9%
Decatur, AL	66,487	14,058	11,675	2,383	3,444	8,231	136	14.9%	22.6%
Decatur, IL	50,453	11,817	9,814	2,003	2,372	7,442	401	12.5%	41.0%
Deltona-Daytona Beach-Ormond Beach, FL	254,452	65,197	54,674	10,523	18,690	35,984	2,041	23.0%	51.3%
Denver-Aurora-Broomfield, CO	1,083,106	170,199	130,780	39,419	60,279	70,501	7,132	23.6%	49.4%
Des Moines-West Des Moines, IA	242,970	41,036	33,475	7,561	11,063	22,412	1,305	18.6%	44.5%
Detroit-Warren-Livonia, MI	1,884,384	378,959	303,471	75,488	112,142	191,329	10,232	24.8%	46.4%
Dothan, AL	67,162	14,793	12,528	2,265	3,581	8,947	203	15.6%	38.6%
Dover, DE	66,050	13,607	11,532	2,075	4,051	7,481	209	18.0%	39.0%
Dubuque, IA	39,425	8,939	7,259	1,680	1,392	5,867	439	13.5%	50.0%
Duluth, MN-WI	141,567	28,720	21,768	6,952	5,721	16,047	981	17.8%	41.2%
Durham-Chapel Hill, NC	224,804	37,470	29,520	7,950	11,965	17,555	1,557	19.4%	46.4%
Eau Claire, WI	69,566	14,520	10,746	3,774	2,832	7,914	771	19.8%	41.8%
El Centro, CA	56,077	10,086	6,395	3,691	2,070	4,325	121	22.4%	47.1%
Elizabethtown, KY	50,472	8,592	7,241	1,351	2,288	4,953	121	12.5%	31.1%
Elkhart-Goshen, IN	77,764	15,273	12,697	2,576	4,595	8,102	386	18.9%	37.0%
Elmira, NY	38,342	8,794	6,934	1,860	1,785	5,149	149	14.4%	36.1%
El Paso, TX	274,924	49,572	38,395	11,177	9,942	28,453	628	16.4%	38.8%
Erie, PA	119,356	25,679	18,846	6,833	5,461	13,385	860	16.6%	37.9%
Eugene-Springfield, OR	156,327	34,894	27,607	7,287	10,468	17,139	1,571	21.1%	47.8%
Evansville, IN-KY	159,602	32,970	27,161	5,809	8,352	18,809	726	14.5%	43.8%
Fairbanks, AK	41,743	4,117	3,507	610	1,261	2,246	77	24.7%	27.4%
Fargo, ND-MN	93,581	14,513	9,604	4,909	2,706	6,898	995	13.2%	42.8%
Farmington, NM	49,481	8,792	7,803	989	2,107	5,696	35	13.4%	35.8%
Fayetteville, NC	157,156	22,266	18,065	4,201	7,191	10,874	259	22.9%	38.5%
Fayetteville-Springdale-Rogers, AR-MO	199,438	33,426	27,035	6,391	8,529	18,506	1,091	15.3%	39.2%
Flagstaff, AZ	63,653	7,670	6,723	947	2,535	4,188	109	14.8%	33.1%
Flint, MI	191,631	39,113	32,420	6,693	11,072	21,348	556	20.0%	48.9%
Florence, SC	89,124	18,045	14,746	3,299	4,674	10,072	93	18.5%	33.6%
Florence-Muscle Shoals, AL	69,721	16,800	14,049	2,751	3,525	10,524	172	14.7%	28.3%
Fond du Lac, WI	44,035	9,918	7,567	2,351	2,056	5,511	426	21.6%	37.2%
Fort Collins-Loveland, CO	133,763	23,052	19,089	3,963	7,717	11,372	920	21.4%	51.9%
Fort Smith, AR-OK	129,571	26,464	21,712	4,752	5,271	16,441	335	14.5%	28.4%
Fort Wayne, IN	178,654	33,792	27,043	6,749	9,757	17,286	728	11.7%	47.6%
Fresno, CA	317,269	56,190	40,601	15,589	16,902	23,699	1,651	20.8%	49.0%
Gadsden, AL	47,467	10,485	8,700	1,785	1,808	6,892	201	15.6%	39.1%
Gainesville, FL	120,293	18,310	15,045	3,265	4,897	10,148	855	19.6%	49.9%
Gainesville, GA	68,868	12,796	10,511	2,285	4,000	6,511	508	18.2%	46.0%
Glens Falls, NY	67,703	13,773	10,769	3,004	3,121	7,648	180	23.4%	41.4%
Goldsboro, NC	53,027	10,404	8,077	2,327	2,719	5,358	180	21.5%	44.2%
Grand Forks, ND-MN	44,242	8,067	6,087	1,980	1,300	4,787	342	16.3%	29.2%
Grand Junction, CO	62,945	14,901	12,318	2,583	4,618	7,700	719	22.4%	54.1%
Grand Rapids-Wyoming, MI	323,714	58,937	48,801	10,136	14,216	34,585	1,898	18.7%	39.5%
Great Falls, MT	37,378	8,117	6,515	1,602	1,717	4,798	378	12.6%	47.8%
Greeley, CO	96,948	15,559	12,488	3,071	5,466	7,022	471	23.0%	51.3%
Green Bay, WI	138,047	25,021	19,082	5,939	5,758	13,324	963	21.4%	44.7%
Greensboro-High Point, NC	324,197	62,935	51,146	11,789	18,514	32,632	1,887	20.8%	39.0%
Greenville, NC	83,623	12,947	10,221	2,726	3,561	6,660	330	27.9%	36.9%
Greenville-Mauldin-Easley, SC	278,397	53,822	45,429	8,393	14,389	31,040	1,173	16.7%	42.5%
Gulfport-Biloxi, MS	116,302	20,264	17,161	3,103	5,383	11,778	119	19.1%	38.9%
Hagerstown-Martinsburg, MD-WV	115,829	23,320	18,406	4,914	6,164	12,242	439	21.7%	36.5%
Hanford-Corcoran, CA	44,040	6,842	4,810	2,032	1,649	3,161	140	19.9%	40.4%
Harrisburg-Carlisle, PA	241,888	51,597	39,491	12,106	11,693	27,798	1,788	17.9%	42.9%
Harrisonburg, VA	51,499	10,301	8,268	2,033	2,242	6,026	356	18.0%	39.0%
Hartford-West Hartford-East Hartford, CT	507,207	109,274	82,623	26,651	27,207	55,416	3,355	28.8%	45.4%
Hattiesburg, MS	61,941	10,789	9,052	1,737	2,487	6,565	385	16.4%	43.5%
Hickory-Lenoir-Morganton, NC	162,519	35,767	30,029	5,738	8,688	21,341	313	15.8%	34.2%
Hinesville-Fort Stewart, GA	33,205	3,535	3,133	402	1,309	1,824	na	27.5%	43.5%
Holland-Grand Haven, MI	102,778	19,807	16,830	2,977	5,326	11,504	895	17.9%	47.2%
Honolulu, HI	338,168	77,959	58,744	19,215	25,024	33,720	954	22.0%	40.6%
Hot Springs, AR	50,521	12,591	10,552	2,039	3,891	6,661	369	16.4%	38.9%
Houma-Bayou Cane-Thibodaux, LA	82,881	16,157	13,884	2,273	2,586	11,298	99	12.3%	25.1%
Houston-Sugar Land-Baytown, TX	2,338,856	315,707	250,852	64,855	81,612	169,240	8,232	20.7%	51.1%
Huntington-Ashland, WV-KY-OH	130,974	30,945	25,996	4,949	6,408	19,588	240	13.1%	29.4%
Huntsville, AL	183,944	33,727	29,047	4,680	10,715	18,332	529	15.6%	36.0%
Idaho Falls, ID	48,716	9,202	7,939	1,263	2,362	5,577	315	13.1%	44.8%
Indianapolis-Carmel, IN	762,522	123,762	96,826	26,936	42,720	54,106	3,741	19.8%	47.7%
Iowa City, IA	66,102	10,229	8,072	2,157	2,701	5,371	514	9.3%	42.9%
Ithaca, NY	41,710	7,172	5,385	1,787	1,600	3,785	351	17.7%	36.2%
Jackson, MI	69,289	14,626	11,788	2,838	3,768	8,020	768	19.9%	51.4%
Jackson, MS	223,804	39,518	33,134	6,384	10,395	22,739	984	15.8%	40.7%
Jackson, TN	49,017	9,460	7,684	1,776	2,091	5,593	79	16.9%	27.6%
Jacksonville, FL	601,534	103,893	84,641	19,252	34,998	49,643	2,778	24.5%	44.0%
Jacksonville, NC	70,717	8,668	7,051	1,617	2,612	4,439	na	19.5%	46.6%

Table J-4: Metropolitan Statistical Areas—Summary of Housing and Householder Characteristics—*Continued*

				Householders 65 Years and Over					
				Owner Householders		Renter Households With Meals Included in Rent	Percent of Owner Householders Who Pay 35% or More of Income for Housing Costs	Percent of Renter Householders Who Pay 35% or More of Income for Rental Costs
	Total Housing Units	Total Households	Owner Occupied	Renter Occupied	With a Mortgage	Without a Mortgage			
Janesville, WI	68,355	14,192	10,983	3,209	3,609	7,374	289	18.0%	48.5%
Jefferson City, MO	63,684	12,941	10,319	2,622	2,486	7,833	459	12.9%	31.1%
Johnson City, TN	94,264	21,283	17,960	3,323	4,543	13,417	199	13.4%	25.3%
Johnstown, PA	65,538	17,817	14,256	3,561	2,835	11,421	124	15.9%	27.9%
Jonesboro, AR	52,100	9,827	7,644	2,183	2,209	5,435	356	14.7%	43.7%
Joplin, MO	75,052	15,510	12,225	3,285	3,448	8,777	332	17.0%	44.0%
Kalamazoo-Portage, MI	146,744	26,992	22,233	4,759	7,889	14,344	594	22.8%	46.8%
Kankakee-Bradley, IL	45,201	9,408	7,608	1,800	2,024	5,584	313	19.1%	55.9%
Kansas City, MO-KS	884,650	160,004	125,842	34,162	45,395	80,447	6,207	20.5%	46.9%
Kennewick-Pasco-Richland, WA	94,836	17,299	13,568	3,731	4,370	9,198	884	14.0%	38.9%
Killeen-Temple-Fort Hood, TX	162,184	22,199	18,294	3,905	4,815	13,479	457	13.8%	39.3%
Kingsport-Bristol-Bristol, TN-VA	147,164	37,875	32,211	5,664	7,831	24,380	500	15.4%	29.0%
Kingston, NY	83,696	17,228	13,419	3,809	4,565	8,854	336	33.6%	43.9%
Knoxville, TN	317,175	67,028	55,202	11,826	15,277	39,925	1,462	16.0%	40.3%
Kokomo, IN	45,570	10,870	8,995	1,875	3,357	5,638	263	12.5%	52.0%
La Crosse, WI-MN	57,234	12,377	9,288	3,089	2,617	6,671	763	22.1%	47.5%
Lafayette, IN	85,208	13,741	11,122	2,619	4,107	7,015	647	15.1%	41.2%
Lafayette, LA	116,575	18,765	16,083	2,682	3,897	12,186	230	15.2%	38.9%
Lake Charles, LA	86,698	16,269	13,755	2,514	2,919	10,836	298	12.7%	33.2%
Lake Havasu City-Kingman, AZ	111,162	30,103	25,779	4,324	10,752	15,027	115	19.1%	38.1%
Lakeland-Winter Haven, FL	281,291	67,040	58,097	8,943	17,872	40,225	1,256	22.3%	44.7%
Lancaster, PA	203,966	47,590	34,836	12,754	9,257	25,579	2,941	19.8%	47.7%
Lansing-East Lansing, MI	199,035	36,023	28,977	7,046	11,204	17,773	834	21.0%	42.4%
Laredo, TX	74,316	10,908	7,980	2,928	1,699	6,281	0	24.6%	42.0%
Las Cruces, NM	82,346	16,964	14,185	2,779	4,854	9,331	150	14.4%	40.1%
Las Vegas-Paradise, NV	845,485	137,213	99,687	37,526	52,462	47,225	2,263	27.0%	53.7%
Lawrence, KS	47,048	6,461	4,810	1,651	1,977	2,833	283	19.2%	49.5%
Lawton, OK	51,094	8,725	7,413	1,312	2,484	4,929	195	16.5%	36.9%
Lebanon, PA	55,692	14,277	10,997	3,280	3,057	7,940	382	16.6%	44.5%
Lewiston-Auburn, ME	49,137	9,997	7,315	2,682	2,256	5,059	364	22.4%	31.7%
Lexington-Fayette, KY	210,510	34,928	26,960	7,968	10,877	16,083	814	17.0%	36.9%
Lima, OH	44,935	9,963	8,244	1,719	2,428	5,816	327	16.2%	46.2%
Lincoln, NE	128,644	21,994	16,133	5,861	4,881	11,252	1,752	14.9%	44.4%
Little Rock-North Little Rock-Conway, AR	310,478	54,676	45,033	9,643	15,458	29,575	1,306	14.0%	37.6%
Logan, UT-ID	42,173	6,708	5,884	824	1,563	4,321	119	13.8%	33.9%
Longview, TX	87,739	18,937	15,822	3,115	3,418	12,404	620	16.6%	48.5%
Longview, WA	43,440	10,586	8,436	2,150	2,848	5,588	355	19.7%	54.0%
Los Angeles-Long Beach-Santa Ana, CA	4,494,787	822,772	564,735	258,037	268,037	296,698	18,172	29.9%	55.3%
Louisville/Jefferson County, KY-IN	561,138	108,380	88,131	20,249	30,996	57,135	2,617	18.9%	38.4%
Lubbock, TX	119,509	20,867	16,726	4,141	4,671	12,055	766	16.1%	45.3%
Lynchburg, VA	112,812	25,581	21,559	4,022	6,902	14,657	583	19.1%	33.0%
Macon, GA	101,883	19,230	15,114	4,116	5,233	9,881	528	22.0%	48.3%
Madera-Chowchilla, CA	49,274	9,464	7,750	1,714	3,567	4,183	187	28.6%	46.1%
Madison, WI	253,826	41,825	32,470	9,355	11,579	20,891	1,253	21.4%	47.3%
Manchester-Nashua, NH	166,446	29,700	21,718	7,982	8,122	13,596	871	32.0%	48.2%
Manhattan, KS	52,237	6,642	5,385	1,257	1,446	3,939	278	18.6%	43.7%
Mankato-North Mankato, MN	39,321	7,670	5,835	1,835	1,418	4,417	579	14.9%	45.1%
Mansfield, OH	54,463	13,532	10,923	2,609	3,510	7,413	295	14.9%	38.3%
McAllen-Edinburg-Mission, TX	251,951	41,006	32,581	8,425	5,929	26,652	251	17.5%	35.8%
Medford, OR	91,090	23,740	18,849	4,891	7,650	11,199	1,546	26.6%	57.0%
Memphis, TN-MS-AR	552,538	89,448	71,025	18,423	28,264	42,761	2,438	23.1%	47.3%
Merced, CA	83,622	13,739	9,933	3,806	4,007	5,926	128	26.4%	46.8%
Miami-Fort Lauderdale-Pompano Beach, FL	2,466,611	517,004	409,193	107,811	150,468	258,725	11,568	34.3%	54.9%
Michigan City-La Porte, IN	48,508	10,456	8,780	1,676	3,028	5,752	218	18.0%	53.2%
Midland, TX	54,792	9,229	7,702	1,527	1,677	6,025	361	18.4%	53.4%
Milwaukee-Waukesha-West Allis, WI	670,165	130,604	92,966	37,638	29,336	63,630	5,520	25.6%	53.1%
Minneapolis-St. Paul-Bloomington, MN-WI	1,360,961	233,272	179,310	53,962	70,278	109,032	10,297	22.5%	49.7%
Missoula, MT	50,385	8,036	6,356	1,680	2,048	4,308	578	15.8%	53.8%
Mobile, AL	179,528	34,830	28,782	6,048	10,123	18,659	522	19.6%	41.1%
Modesto, CA	179,394	33,059	24,223	8,836	10,301	13,922	1,247	28.5%	52.9%
Monroe, LA	76,250	14,969	12,219	2,750	3,391	8,828	146	17.0%	46.4%
Monroe, MI	62,876	13,592	11,361	2,231	3,788	7,573	148	21.8%	34.5%
Montgomery, AL	162,252	29,334	24,865	4,469	10,144	14,721	284	20.0%	38.4%
Morgantown, WV	58,611	9,332	8,007	1,325	1,854	6,153	112	9.5%	39.1%
Morristown, TN	61,417	14,596	12,802	1,794	3,239	9,563	124	15.5%	45.5%
Mount Vernon-Anacortes, WA	51,581	12,155	10,057	2,098	3,562	6,495	375	19.4%	41.9%
Muncie, IN	52,239	11,532	9,741	1,791	3,569	6,172	121	13.2%	40.9%
Muskegon-Norton Shores, MI	73,420	15,242	13,130	2,112	3,855	9,275	248	18.1%	41.7%
Myrtle Beach-North Myrtle Beach-Conway, SC	187,398	31,520	27,403	4,117	10,554	16,849	411	20.7%	39.0%
Napa, CA	54,745	12,918	9,915	3,003	4,346	5,569	605	27.2%	55.2%
Naples-Marco Island, FL	198,373	52,578	45,813	6,765	15,750	30,063	1,960	27.3%	45.0%
Nashville-Davidson--Murfreesboro--Franklin, TN	672,778	110,342	89,322	21,020	32,024	57,298	2,737	18.6%	40.6%
New Haven-Milford, CT	361,932	77,105	56,065	21,040	19,374	36,691	2,011	35.6%	45.8%
New Orleans-Metairie-Kenner, LA	539,970	93,431	74,368	19,063	20,566	53,802	1,124	19.7%	46.0%
New York-Northern New Jersey-Long Island, NY-NJ-PA	7,541,788	1,520,309	957,308	563,001	324,346	632,962	20,567	37.2%	49.4%
Niles-Benton Harbor, MI	76,797	16,237	13,715	2,522	4,767	8,948	293	21.8%	34.6%
North Port-Bradenton-Sarasota, FL	402,379	124,192	105,438	18,754	34,319	71,119	4,064	23.9%	46.6%
Norwich-New London, CT	121,056	24,579	18,983	5,596	6,459	12,524	565	26.7%	34.5%
Ocala, FL	163,884	53,390	48,080	5,310	16,899	31,181	801	21.4%	46.1%
Ocean City, NJ	98,503	13,676	11,304	2,372	3,729	7,575	446	32.7%	44.4%

Table J-4: Metropolitan Statistical Areas—Summary of Housing and Householder Characteristics—*Continued*

				Householders 65 Years and Over				
				Owner Householders		Renter Households With Meals Included in Rent	Percent of Owner Householders Who Pay 35% or More of Income for Housing Costs	Percent of Renter Householders Who Pay 35% or More of Income for Rental Costs
	Total Housing Units	Total Households	Owner Occupied	Renter Occupied	With a Mortgage	Without a Mortgage			
Odessa, TX	53,662	9,061	7,392	1,669	1,077	6,315	193	15.4%	35.2%
Ogden-Clearfield, UT	188,656	31,825	27,779	4,046	10,628	17,151	907	16.3%	45.3%
Oklahoma City, OK	542,161	97,069	78,300	18,769	25,853	52,447	3,533	17.1%	47.0%
Olympia, WA	109,278	21,508	17,317	4,191	6,481	10,836	759	20.7%	47.1%
Omaha-Council Bluffs, NE-IA	365,305	63,409	49,351	14,058	16,624	32,727	3,199	18.8%	44.5%
Orlando-Kissimmee-Sanford, FL	946,583	156,438	128,472	27,966	54,599	73,873	3,273	27.7%	54.4%
Oshkosh-Neenah, WI	73,588	14,435	11,024	3,411	2,989	8,035	795	19.2%	49.8%
Owensboro, KY	49,700	11,161	9,084	2,077	2,396	6,688	178	11.1%	33.9%
Oxnard-Thousand Oaks-Ventura, CA	281,723	59,887	47,070	12,817	23,284	23,786	2,037	28.4%	50.9%
Palm Bay-Melbourne-Titusville, FL	270,428	70,245	60,941	9,304	24,092	36,849	852	23.2%	43.7%
Palm Coast, FL	48,782	13,858	12,608	1,250	5,885	6,723	256	29.2%	48.6%
Panama City-Lynn Haven-Panama City Beach, FL	99,738	16,502	13,830	2,672	4,490	9,340	211	22.0%	48.5%
Parkersburg-Marietta-Vienna, WV-OH	75,089	18,054	15,436	2,618	4,047	11,389	128	14.4%	36.9%
Pascagoula, MS	69,791	13,309	11,949	1,360	3,111	8,838	na	16.8%	43.8%
Pensacola-Ferry Pass-Brent, FL	202,674	40,694	34,208	6,486	12,619	21,589	867	20.1%	42.8%
Peoria, IL	164,703	36,912	30,242	6,670	8,453	21,789	1,044	14.6%	35.8%
Philadelphia-Camden-Wilmington, PA-NJ-DE-MD	2,435,574	502,733	383,983	118,750	127,716	256,267	18,358	27.9%	51.7%
Phoenix-Mesa-Glendale, AZ	1,808,371	326,522	268,601	57,921	117,936	150,665	10,760	23.4%	51.8%
Pine Bluff, AR	42,040	8,567	7,328	1,239	2,092	5,236	74	18.7%	32.4%
Pittsburgh, PA	1,102,366	266,674	205,941	60,733	55,737	150,204	8,351	18.4%	37.9%
Pittsfield, MA	68,450	16,435	12,336	4,099	4,196	8,140	384	26.2%	29.1%
Pocatello, ID	36,165	6,496	5,735	761	2,111	3,624	145	15.0%	46.5%
Portland-South Portland-Biddeford, ME	263,419	49,863	38,224	11,639	14,049	24,175	1,859	26.2%	43.5%
Portland-Vancouver-Hillsboro, OR-WA	928,150	168,214	123,336	44,878	52,027	71,309	11,764	24.4%	53.2%
Port St. Lucie, FL	215,220	59,735	53,685	6,050	17,531	36,154	747	25.0%	52.1%
Poughkeepsie-Newburgh-Middletown, NY	256,428	50,584	38,483	12,101	13,699	24,784	809	31.6%	52.6%
Prescott, AZ	110,858	34,015	29,023	4,992	11,664	17,359	438	19.5%	43.1%
Providence-New Bedford-Fall River, RI-MA	693,405	144,675	100,027	44,648	36,275	63,752	3,588	30.8%	40.1%
Provo-Orem, UT	153,874	21,416	18,101	3,315	6,994	11,107	970	17.0%	44.6%
Pueblo, CO	69,588	15,828	13,268	2,560	4,647	8,621	135	19.5%	44.9%
Punta Gorda, FL	100,804	34,637	30,969	3,668	10,682	20,287	1,143	24.1%	39.4%
Racine, WI	82,197	17,221	13,739	3,482	4,198	9,541	324	21.8%	47.4%
Raleigh-Cary, NC	471,662	67,021	52,608	14,413	23,975	28,633	2,399	22.3%	50.0%
Rapid City, SD	56,492	10,675	7,834	2,841	2,482	5,352	568	15.8%	40.8%
Reading, PA	164,760	37,479	28,552	8,927	7,857	20,695	1,493	24.5%	46.7%
Redding, CA	77,370	19,897	16,022	3,875	6,051	9,971	550	24.2%	52.7%
Reno-Sparks, NV	187,136	33,271	25,052	8,219	11,527	13,525	652	27.6%	55.4%
Richmond, VA	534,162	100,701	80,844	19,857	32,627	48,217	3,366	21.8%	48.6%
Riverside-San Bernardino-Ontario, CA	1,503,549	258,771	204,393	54,378	93,866	110,527	5,955	28.8%	56.4%
Roanoke, VA	145,157	33,552	27,594	5,958	8,925	18,669	661	19.0%	37.9%
Rochester, MN	78,772	15,468	12,461	3,007	3,420	9,041	672	16.2%	47.4%
Rochester, NY	455,782	97,083	74,136	22,947	27,163	46,973	3,623	22.0%	50.4%
Rockford, IL	145,875	29,690	23,735	5,955	8,477	15,258	815	21.0%	42.1%
Rocky Mount, NC	67,134	14,820	11,143	3,677	3,921	7,222	201	24.9%	38.1%
Rome, GA	40,512	9,051	6,545	2,506	1,928	4,617	366	12.5%	42.1%
Sacramento--Arden-Arcade--Roseville, CA	873,103	163,172	125,052	38,120	56,584	68,468	5,626	24.7%	52.7%
Saginaw-Saginaw Township North, MI	86,739	20,511	17,038	3,473	4,771	12,267	498	19.7%	44.2%
St. Cloud, MN	78,354	14,791	11,482	3,309	2,963	8,519	467	19.1%	41.8%
St. George, UT	58,643	15,283	13,033	2,250	4,743	8,290	344	16.8%	41.9%
St. Joseph, MO-KS	53,336	11,423	8,707	2,716	2,284	6,423	323	15.6%	40.6%
St. Louis, MO-IL	1,238,949	246,259	200,203	46,056	68,829	131,374	7,535	19.4%	44.8%
Salem, OR	151,764	33,232	25,587	7,645	9,880	15,707	2,290	21.9%	51.7%
Salinas, CA	138,964	25,539	18,478	7,061	7,702	10,776	755	24.2%	50.5%
Salisbury, MD	52,427	10,516	8,486	2,030	2,686	5,800	99	21.1%	49.3%
Salt Lake City, UT	413,334	62,577	51,014	11,563	19,839	31,175	1,647	17.6%	50.1%
San Angelo, TX	47,595	10,206	8,244	1,962	1,972	6,272	213	12.8%	29.6%
San Antonio-New Braunfels, TX	844,767	148,360	119,438	28,922	38,277	81,161	3,650	16.6%	44.1%
San Diego-Carlsbad-San Marcos, CA	1,166,740	209,064	157,744	51,320	73,992	83,752	6,463	28.4%	55.2%
Sandusky, OH	37,797	8,524	7,007	1,517	2,389	4,618	81	21.2%	29.9%
San Francisco-Oakland-Fremont, CA	1,742,682	336,190	238,298	97,892	107,163	131,135	11,184	27.5%	49.7%
San Jose-Sunnyvale-Santa Clara, CA	652,202	115,635	86,963	28,672	36,848	50,115	4,412	24.9%	53.6%
San Luis Obispo-Paso Robles, CA	117,476	25,629	20,851	4,778	8,814	12,037	752	25.4%	48.1%
Santa Barbara-Santa Maria-Goleta, CA	152,750	33,861	25,861	8,000	11,123	14,738	1,831	25.9%	50.5%
Santa Cruz-Watsonville, CA	104,376	19,970	15,351	4,619	6,585	8,766	462	27.7%	44.5%
Santa Fe, NM	71,444	15,667	12,521	3,146	5,215	7,306	418	24.7%	37.7%
Santa Rosa-Petaluma, CA	204,652	44,296	34,235	10,061	15,414	18,821	1,620	28.6%	56.0%
Savannah, GA	152,337	26,733	22,019	4,714	7,888	14,131	725	23.5%	53.1%
Scranton--Wilkes-Barre, PA	258,653	63,550	47,317	16,233	12,065	35,252	735	24.4%	32.3%
Seattle-Tacoma-Bellevue, WA	1,471,352	243,947	177,386	66,561	73,663	103,723	15,076	26.6%	52.2%
Sebastian-Vero Beach, FL	76,535	24,390	20,709	3,681	6,075	14,634	813	19.7%	53.4%
Sheboygan, WI	50,707	10,784	8,323	2,461	2,036	6,287	550	21.3%	38.8%
Sherman-Denison, TX	53,920	11,431	9,748	1,683	2,120	7,628	276	15.5%	33.5%
Shreveport-Bossier City, LA	175,061	34,799	28,850	5,949	9,060	19,790	785	13.2%	39.7%
Sioux City, IA-NE-SD	58,223	12,252	9,225	3,027	2,199	7,026	623	14.8%	47.8%
Sioux Falls, SD	97,005	16,138	11,879	4,259	3,589	8,290	833	15.7%	50.7%
South Bend-Mishawaka, IN-MI	140,774	28,220	23,266	4,954	8,393	14,873	454	15.9%	38.5%
Spartanburg, SC	122,932	24,662	20,575	4,087	6,786	13,789	622	16.3%	41.4%
Spokane, WA	202,856	40,702	31,261	9,441	11,779	19,482	2,229	21.3%	51.7%
Springfield, IL	95,792	19,890	16,157	3,733	5,242	10,915	673	14.4%	40.6%
Springfield, MA	288,300	62,402	46,183	16,219	14,897	31,286	1,451	25.3%	43.0%

Table J-4: Metropolitan Statistical Areas—Summary of Housing and Householder Characteristics—*Continued*

| | | | | Householders 65 Years and Over | | | | |
| | | | | Owner Householders | | Renter Households With Meals Included in Rent | Percent of Owner Householders Who Pay 35% or More of Income for Housing Costs | Percent of Renter Householders Who Pay 35% or More of Income for Rental Costs |
	Total Housing Units	Total Households	Owner Occupied	Renter Occupied	With a Mortgage	Without a Mortgage			
Springfield, MO	193,469	39,922	32,069	7,853	10,387	21,682	1,005	15.7%	48.0%
Springfield, OH	61,319	14,890	11,976	2,914	4,053	7,923	574	13.7%	31.4%
State College, PA	63,554	11,231	8,755	2,476	2,267	6,488	573	15.7%	42.9%
Steubenville-Weirton, OH-WV	58,166	15,188	12,855	2,333	3,064	9,791	46	10.6%	29.1%
Stockton, CA	234,161	41,585	30,901	10,684	13,112	17,789	1,432	24.9%	54.4%
Sumter, SC	46,278	9,106	7,357	1,749	2,343	5,014	279	17.2%	43.1%
Syracuse, NY	288,186	59,049	46,228	12,821	14,273	31,955	1,170	20.4%	42.6%
Tallahassee, FL	163,514	25,354	21,292	4,062	7,814	13,478	691	21.1%	49.3%
Tampa-St. Petersburg-Clearwater, FL	1,357,020	305,683	251,291	54,392	86,254	165,037	10,404	24.5%	53.6%
Terre Haute, IN	74,192	15,187	12,671	2,516	4,239	8,432	238	14.6%	38.5%
Texarkana, TX-Texarkana, AR	58,035	12,536	10,381	2,155	1,803	8,578	282	12.3%	47.1%
Toledo, OH	301,155	57,899	46,391	11,508	16,265	30,126	1,428	18.9%	40.8%
Topeka, KS	103,944	22,190	17,463	4,727	5,050	12,413	582	13.0%	36.8%
Trenton-Ewing, NJ	143,667	29,042	22,036	7,006	7,906	14,130	515	31.0%	46.7%
Tucson, AZ	442,702	97,843	78,794	19,049	32,081	46,713	3,819	20.7%	47.5%
Tulsa, OK	412,623	79,539	64,836	14,703	19,686	45,150	2,187	16.4%	44.6%
Tuscaloosa, AL	98,287	15,326	12,574	2,752	4,425	8,149	335	18.0%	32.6%
Tyler, TX	87,578	19,347	16,163	3,184	4,152	12,011	829	18.8%	48.3%
Utica-Rome, NY	137,450	31,249	23,625	7,624	5,765	17,860	570	17.5%	38.5%
Valdosta, GA	58,013	9,597	7,575	2,022	2,538	5,037	134	16.9%	34.8%
Vallejo-Fairfield, CA	152,947	28,831	22,320	6,511	10,918	11,402	773	25.4%	51.1%
Victoria, TX	50,681	10,442	9,101	1,341	1,571	7,530	249	14.0%	45.9%
Vineland-Millville-Bridgeton, NJ	56,073	12,301	9,387	2,914	2,548	6,839	17	32.1%	51.1%
Virginia Beach-Norfolk-Newport News, VA-NC	690,440	125,196	100,162	25,034	44,356	55,806	3,378	24.1%	48.1%
Visalia-Porterville, CA	142,747	24,691	18,702	5,989	7,554	11,148	406	23.2%	44.9%
Waco, TX	95,677	18,149	14,727	3,422	3,713	11,014	379	15.3%	41.8%
Warner Robins, GA	58,953	8,976	7,671	1,305	2,588	5,083	66	16.5%	26.7%
Washington-Arlington-Alexandria, DC-VA-MD-WV	2,226,819	350,684	271,064	79,620	136,023	135,041	12,457	23.4%	48.7%
Waterloo-Cedar Falls, IA	71,584	16,019	13,142	2,877	3,573	9,569	663	13.0%	42.5%
Wausau, WI	57,895	11,818	9,286	2,532	2,118	7,168	399	19.3%	48.1%
Wenatchee-East Wenatchee, WA	51,643	10,713	8,697	2,016	3,025	5,672	583	19.6%	41.1%
Wheeling, WV-OH	69,387	17,078	13,957	3,121	3,107	10,850	99	9.5%	22.9%
Wichita, KS	263,865	48,651	38,419	10,232	11,610	26,809	1,991	16.4%	45.5%
Wichita Falls, TX	64,873	13,139	10,881	2,258	2,360	8,521	482	15.4%	49.3%
Williamsport, PA	52,505	11,867	9,372	2,495	2,446	6,926	288	18.8%	40.4%
Wilmington, NC	207,154	39,482	32,786	6,696	15,120	17,666	945	24.5%	51.0%
Winchester, VA-WV	57,212	11,457	9,290	2,167	2,937	6,353	243	16.1%	38.1%
Winston-Salem, NC	215,256	43,386	36,209	7,177	13,027	23,182	1,036	18.4%	41.9%
Worcester, MA	327,329	63,136	43,876	19,260	15,426	28,450	1,967	27.8%	40.1%
Yakima, WA	85,783	16,886	12,944	3,942	4,319	8,625	865	18.3%	52.6%
York-Hanover, PA	179,327	39,794	32,197	7,597	9,810	22,387	925	25.2%	41.3%
Youngstown-Warren-Boardman, OH-PA	259,206	66,502	53,402	13,100	15,886	37,516	1,195	16.7%	35.3%
Yuba City, CA	61,498	11,654	8,938	2,716	3,745	5,193	243	23.5%	37.1%
Yuma, AZ	88,460	18,834	16,486	2,348	4,169	12,317	193	13.4%	29.8%

Table J-5: 113th Congressional Districts—Summary of Housing and Householder Characteristics

					Householders 65 Years and Over				
					Owner Householders		Renter Households With Meals Included in Rent	Percent of Owner Householders Who Pay 35% or More of Income for Housing Costs	Percent of Renter Householders Who Pay 35% or More of Income for Rental Costs
	Total Housing Units	Total Households	Owner Occupied	Renter Occupied	With a Mortgage	Without a Mortgage			
Alabama									
Congressional District 1	324,503	63,296	53,401	9,895	17,780	35,621	922	18.3%	41.1%
Congressional District 2	307,405	62,194	52,399	9,795	16,602	35,797	519	17.7%	34.5%
Congressional District 3	318,198	60,439	50,431	10,008	16,594	33,837	496	20.2%	31.1%
Congressional District 4	310,797	70,393	58,720	11,673	13,594	45,126	810	15.4%	27.8%
Congressional District 5	303,835	61,062	51,769	9,293	16,793	34,976	736	15.1%	31.2%
Congressional District 6	291,733	57,022	49,283	7,739	16,683	32,600	1,610	18.8%	44.1%
Congressional District 7	325,343	57,494	45,623	11,871	14,743	30,880	486	24.4%	38.0%
Alaska									
Congressional District (at Large)	307,367	35,129	28,658	6,471	10,114	18,544	430	20.1%	42.4%
Arizona									
Congressional District 1	324,662	61,895	53,625	8,270	19,241	34,384	675	18.7%	33.8%
Congressional District 2	343,733	82,408	66,150	16,258	26,418	39,732	3,549	19.3%	51.8%
Congressional District 3	261,691	38,254	30,567	7,687	12,148	18,419	323	22.2%	37.3%
Congressional District 4	377,848	98,872	86,454	12,418	31,890	54,564	507	18.6%	37.0%
Congressional District 5	300,290	65,598	56,523	9,075	22,434	34,089	1,858	20.2%	51.8%
Congressional District 6	347,671	64,829	54,018	10,811	26,484	27,534	1,653	28.9%	54.3%
Congressional District 7	258,641	27,728	19,467	8,261	8,967	10,500	253	29.7%	45.6%
Congressional District 8	311,466	80,030	67,874	12,156	29,479	38,395	4,041	19.5%	58.2%
Congressional District 9	332,821	44,669	32,708	11,961	15,360	17,348	2,770	24.5%	53.3%
Arkansas									
Congressional District 1	334,629	74,629	60,820	13,809	15,201	45,619	751	15.3%	33.3%
Congressional District 2	327,511	60,603	49,802	10,801	16,222	33,580	1,309	14.2%	36.0%
Congressional District 3	318,543	58,181	47,332	10,849	15,033	32,299	1,535	15.1%	36.2%
Congressional District 4	342,264	76,944	64,453	12,491	15,473	48,980	1,029	14.7%	28.4%
California									
Congressional District 1	319,540	78,841	64,629	14,212	24,942	39,687	2,061	24.3%	48.4%
Congressional District 2	316,425	71,143	55,966	15,177	24,285	31,681	1,663	27.0%	49.9%
Congressional District 3	263,259	50,081	38,900	11,181	16,294	22,606	1,286	23.7%	45.1%
Congressional District 4	349,058	73,173	62,169	11,004	27,410	34,759	1,426	28.2%	48.9%
Congressional District 5	284,165	59,631	45,490	14,141	21,055	24,435	2,377	27.9%	56.2%
Congressional District 6	283,853	46,049	31,613	14,436	14,133	17,480	1,425	23.3%	51.3%
Congressional District 7	269,552	52,070	40,461	11,609	18,777	21,684	2,213	22.9%	55.1%
Congressional District 8	305,273	49,070	40,148	8,922	17,232	22,916	349	25.6%	57.5%
Congressional District 9	241,178	44,298	33,500	10,798	15,104	18,396	1,493	28.1%	52.5%
Congressional District 10	241,253	42,739	31,391	11,348	13,677	17,714	1,588	27.3%	54.6%
Congressional District 11	278,818	60,723	49,009	11,714	21,731	27,278	2,232	27.5%	54.0%
Congressional District 12	341,935	60,556	29,402	31,154	11,781	17,621	1,359	29.0%	46.0%
Congressional District 13	303,637	54,816	34,882	19,934	16,269	18,613	1,607	25.6%	43.2%
Congressional District 14	259,326	54,105	42,368	11,737	19,007	23,361	2,058	27.2%	53.9%
Congressional District 15	246,578	40,607	31,160	9,447	13,980	17,180	1,532	25.1%	58.9%
Congressional District 16	221,397	35,459	24,060	11,399	10,239	13,821	627	25.2%	49.9%
Congressional District 17	249,019	38,926	29,574	9,352	11,364	18,210	2,153	21.7%	59.7%
Congressional District 18	284,270	57,686	45,801	11,885	19,166	26,635	2,481	23.9%	50.8%
Congressional District 19	224,006	38,425	27,469	10,956	13,064	14,405	897	29.3%	51.5%
Congressional District 20	244,364	45,790	33,974	11,816	14,490	19,484	1,076	26.5%	48.2%
Congressional District 21	194,108	28,615	20,709	7,906	8,096	12,613	300	22.6%	44.1%
Congressional District 22	245,591	45,926	34,864	11,062	14,649	20,215	1,478	20.0%	49.8%
Congressional District 23	264,321	46,736	36,995	9,741	15,215	21,780	914	21.8%	48.4%
Congressional District 24	275,495	60,205	47,095	13,110	20,121	26,974	2,583	25.7%	49.0%
Congressional District 25	230,738	35,311	28,099	7,212	15,441	12,658	348	32.0%	59.4%
Congressional District 26	238,877	52,466	41,228	11,238	20,326	20,902	1,913	29.3%	51.1%
Congressional District 27	255,733	55,033	38,441	16,592	16,609	21,832	2,101	25.8%	50.2%
Congressional District 28	317,381	58,144	29,224	28,920	14,097	15,127	1,098	34.2%	59.7%
Congressional District 29	210,415	30,344	18,985	11,359	8,973	10,012	705	35.1%	54.7%
Congressional District 30	285,140	54,729	39,637	15,092	20,338	19,299	2,015	36.1%	58.1%
Congressional District 31	230,391	33,895	24,813	9,082	11,190	13,623	1,503	26.1%	56.5%
Congressional District 32	201,744	39,516	29,489	10,027	12,983	16,506	658	24.3%	49.6%
Congressional District 33	327,203	67,969	48,889	19,080	22,974	25,915	1,759	28.3%	55.9%
Congressional District 34	251,981	38,587	13,893	24,694	6,203	7,690	601	29.5%	51.3%
Congressional District 35	192,281	24,732	17,962	6,770	9,148	8,814	619	33.4%	58.1%
Congressional District 36	341,448	84,960	69,086	15,874	28,273	40,813	1,626	30.4%	56.1%
Congressional District 37	289,011	52,754	30,056	22,698	15,691	14,365	1,011	35.9%	60.1%
Congressional District 38	211,790	46,143	35,139	11,004	15,610	19,529	696	24.9%	50.3%
Congressional District 39	230,450	44,798	37,075	7,723	18,264	18,811	1,215	28.2%	55.6%
Congressional District 40	184,110	24,055	14,707	9,348	6,677	8,030	87	28.6%	58.7%
Congressional District 41	206,395	29,365	21,244	8,121	11,019	10,225	1,122	28.4%	55.1%
Congressional District 42	228,338	37,443	30,841	6,602	15,305	15,536	823	28.1%	57.8%
Congressional District 43	248,076	43,125	28,332	14,793	13,554	14,778	126	32.1%	53.4%
Congressional District 44	192,861	31,432	21,822	9,610	10,972	10,850	108	30.9%	49.9%
Congressional District 45	268,135	52,624	41,796	10,828	21,032	20,764	2,115	30.5%	52.9%
Congressional District 46	191,128	27,832	18,146	9,686	8,022	10,124	785	24.6%	54.6%
Congressional District 47	255,673	45,252	31,872	13,380	14,047	17,825	840	25.8%	49.4%
Congressional District 48	282,685	62,120	50,384	11,736	22,563	27,821	1,167	29.3%	58.9%
Congressional District 49	268,017	51,672	41,847	9,825	20,462	21,385	2,457	30.8%	61.3%
Congressional District 50	255,207	49,651	39,317	10,334	19,157	20,160	1,552	31.5%	60.6%

Table J-5: 113th Congressional Districts—Summary of Housing and Householder Characteristics—*Continued*

				Householders 65 Years and Over					
					Owner Householders				
	Total Housing Units	Total Households	Owner Occupied	Renter Occupied	With a Mortgage	Without a Mortgage	Renter Households With Meals Included in Rent	Percent of Owner Householders Who Pay 35% or More of Income for Housing Costs	Percent of Renter Householders Who Pay 35% or More of Income for Rental Costs
California—*Cont.*									
Congressional District 51..................	218,205	37,498	23,611	13,887	8,888	14,723	288	23.6%	50.6%
Congressional District 52..................	295,336	51,293	39,129	12,164	18,707	20,422	1,656	28.8%	51.7%
Congressional District 53..................	279,837	46,186	34,152	12,034	16,309	17,843	1,391	26.4%	56.4%
Colorado									
Congressional District 1....................	337,987	52,387	36,238	16,149	15,424	20,814	2,327	25.2%	43.9%
Congressional District 2....................	353,843	50,240	41,615	8,625	18,041	23,574	2,115	21.7%	51.1%
Congressional District 3....................	358,411	66,323	55,448	10,875	19,716	35,732	1,218	21.1%	43.4%
Congressional District 4....................	286,546	48,484	39,797	8,687	16,049	23,748	1,208	21.3%	43.3%
Congressional District 5....................	305,965	51,265	41,884	9,381	18,378	23,506	1,389	20.3%	50.8%
Congressional District 6....................	284,558	42,773	33,720	9,053	16,494	17,226	2,067	23.4%	55.3%
Congressional District 7....................	294,783	52,687	41,399	11,288	17,656	23,743	2,335	20.9%	52.8%
Connecticut									
Congressional District 1....................	304,455	66,372	48,258	18,114	16,075	32,183	2,232	30.5%	44.5%
Congressional District 2....................	300,648	62,012	50,735	11,277	17,199	33,536	1,082	25.7%	38.4%
Congressional District 3....................	301,251	64,640	46,856	17,784	15,912	30,944	1,771	34.7%	45.2%
Congressional District 4....................	279,982	59,564	47,179	12,385	18,517	28,662	1,456	38.1%	43.7%
Congressional District 5....................	301,841	63,384	48,105	15,279	16,794	31,311	1,514	34.1%	41.8%
Delaware									
Congressional District (at Large)	408,428	81,975	68,524	13,451	26,280	42,244	1,562	21.2%	42.9%
District of Columbia									
Delegate District (at Large)	297,918	49,026	29,590	19,436	14,625	14,965	1,434	25.9%	44.6%
Florida									
Congressional District 1....................	346,243	63,862	53,956	9,906	19,486	34,470	1,427	20.1%	46.6%
Congressional District 2....................	337,441	57,302	48,838	8,464	15,805	33,033	964	20.0%	47.3%
Congressional District 3....................	305,917	62,566	54,081	8,485	17,526	36,555	1,431	18.6%	41.5%
Congressional District 4....................	309,660	53,158	43,027	10,131	17,772	25,255	1,643	23.5%	41.1%
Congressional District 5....................	306,594	45,734	35,784	9,950	14,838	20,946	182	29.4%	48.9%
Congressional District 6....................	363,786	91,244	78,041	13,203	28,227	49,814	2,229	23.8%	46.9%
Congressional District 7....................	297,689	52,401	43,649	8,752	19,828	23,821	2,461	29.2%	61.2%
Congressional District 8....................	352,750	95,706	82,609	13,097	30,537	52,072	1,665	22.4%	46.4%
Congressional District 9....................	313,232	42,093	33,951	8,142	16,592	17,359	150	32.8%	52.2%
Congressional District 10..................	335,441	72,215	61,545	10,670	20,747	40,798	1,717	22.0%	51.4%
Congressional District 11..................	359,009	130,399	119,651	10,748	42,233	77,418	1,503	18.6%	47.6%
Congressional District 12..................	337,263	86,993	74,167	12,826	24,660	49,507	2,811	21.6%	55.5%
Congressional District 13..................	390,924	99,789	81,273	18,516	24,895	56,378	4,160	27.4%	56.2%
Congressional District 14..................	329,966	50,835	36,012	14,823	14,861	21,151	1,227	28.7%	49.1%
Congressional District 15..................	291,599	56,084	47,930	8,154	16,476	31,454	1,416	24.5%	45.1%
Congressional District 16..................	400,263	123,819	105,147	18,672	34,191	70,956	4,064	23.9%	46.8%
Congressional District 17..................	357,109	107,005	94,841	12,164	29,540	65,301	2,823	20.8%	45.8%
Congressional District 18..................	364,288	96,368	85,930	10,438	28,621	57,309	1,846	26.2%	54.4%
Congressional District 19..................	447,418	109,884	94,447	15,437	33,635	60,812	3,534	26.1%	46.2%
Congressional District 20..................	296,129	57,393	44,407	12,986	18,441	25,966	2,492	38.6%	55.2%
Congressional District 21..................	326,672	96,018	85,942	10,076	29,558	56,384	2,365	30.7%	51.3%
Congressional District 22..................	396,807	90,806	76,009	14,797	25,462	50,547	3,775	31.4%	58.5%
Congressional District 23..................	380,539	66,819	52,367	14,452	17,657	34,710	565	38.1%	53.8%
Congressional District 24..................	275,388	41,211	28,180	13,031	12,956	15,224	270	38.8%	49.1%
Congressional District 25..................	252,541	49,231	38,641	10,590	15,211	23,430	498	31.3%	51.2%
Congressional District 26..................	259,515	47,260	38,279	8,981	16,139	22,140	266	36.4%	58.8%
Congressional District 27..................	277,538	60,456	37,975	22,481	12,451	25,524	435	35.8%	57.7%
Georgia									
Congressional District 1....................	308,558	54,470	45,509	8,961	16,487	29,022	1,069	23.8%	45.2%
Congressional District 2....................	301,232	57,264	44,767	12,497	14,676	30,091	512	24.2%	37.2%
Congressional District 3....................	280,490	52,125	43,101	9,024	17,155	25,946	918	22.6%	49.6%
Congressional District 4....................	278,576	35,772	29,686	6,086	14,949	14,737	610	28.6%	56.6%
Congressional District 5....................	342,502	42,195	26,392	15,803	12,268	14,124	1,367	31.4%	50.9%
Congressional District 6....................	291,338	42,234	33,926	8,308	15,015	18,911	2,022	21.2%	43.6%
Congressional District 7....................	253,511	27,528	22,729	4,799	11,294	11,435	904	24.1%	53.6%
Congressional District 8....................	294,953	55,875	45,299	10,576	13,090	32,209	857	18.0%	35.0%
Congressional District 9....................	318,626	63,534	54,414	9,120	17,337	37,077	854	19.6%	38.9%
Congressional District 10..................	288,363	48,726	41,738	6,988	14,660	27,078	636	21.8%	38.8%
Congressional District 11..................	287,750	41,487	34,832	6,655	15,958	18,874	802	24.7%	42.3%
Congressional District 12..................	292,776	51,734	41,860	9,874	13,400	28,460	728	21.0%	40.0%
Congressional District 13..................	281,411	34,488	28,539	5,949	14,105	14,434	718	24.8%	47.2%
Congressional District 14..................	279,004	52,011	43,298	8,713	13,366	29,932	544	18.1%	33.4%
Hawaii									
Congressional District 1....................	252,140	60,659	44,426	16,233	18,616	25,810	762	22.0%	39.5%
Congressional District 2....................	270,057	50,239	39,909	10,330	17,487	22,422	339	23.9%	40.5%
Idaho									
Congressional District 1....................	338,836	66,692	55,317	11,375	21,965	33,352	1,920	19.6%	43.5%
Congressional District 2....................	332,022	61,125	51,009	10,116	16,836	34,173	2,239	16.7%	41.9%

Table J-5: 113th Congressional Districts—Summary of Housing and Householder Characteristics—*Continued*

| | | | | Householders 65 Years and Over | | | | |
| | | | | Owner Householders | | Renter Households With Meals Included in Rent | Percent of Owner Householders Who Pay 35% or More of Income for Housing Costs | Percent of Renter Householders Who Pay 35% or More of Income for Rental Costs |
	Total Housing Units	Total Households	Owner Occupied	Renter Occupied	With a Mortgage	Without a Mortgage			
Illinois									
Congressional District 1	302,024	63,639	46,940	16,699	19,549	27,391	930	30.1%	48.3%
Congressional District 2	298,413	60,904	46,799	14,105	19,249	27,550	1,521	28.7%	53.4%
Congressional District 3	260,153	53,766	45,787	7,979	13,668	32,119	1,255	27.4%	55.0%
Congressional District 4	247,503	32,366	22,505	9,861	8,131	14,374	392	34.9%	57.2%
Congressional District 5	326,990	52,736	39,016	13,720	11,458	27,558	1,430	30.3%	51.9%
Congressional District 6	274,485	53,412	45,003	8,409	17,437	27,566	2,939	29.5%	52.0%
Congressional District 7	339,837	49,877	28,164	21,713	12,736	15,428	699	39.3%	49.6%
Congressional District 8	268,510	44,160	36,730	7,430	15,086	21,644	1,603	27.6%	55.2%
Congressional District 9	314,261	69,300	52,314	16,986	15,808	36,506	3,141	29.0%	51.3%
Congressional District 10	266,434	51,370	41,827	9,543	16,602	25,225	2,690	33.1%	50.1%
Congressional District 11	259,096	42,364	35,299	7,065	14,953	20,346	1,310	28.5%	54.3%
Congressional District 12	317,330	67,007	55,261	11,746	14,000	41,261	1,675	16.0%	39.3%
Congressional District 13	316,822	62,715	51,599	11,116	14,338	37,261	2,122	13.3%	39.7%
Congressional District 14	261,667	43,461	38,042	5,419	16,422	21,620	890	28.6%	56.2%
Congressional District 15	313,688	75,149	63,177	11,972	13,998	49,179	1,944	14.8%	37.2%
Congressional District 16	296,835	65,819	54,423	11,396	15,724	38,699	1,633	19.6%	39.7%
Congressional District 17	323,530	74,168	59,457	14,711	15,583	43,874	2,452	15.4%	39.2%
Congressional District 18	306,834	70,638	59,035	11,603	15,801	43,234	1,591	14.5%	34.7%
Indiana									
Congressional District 1	301,427	59,248	49,784	9,464	18,665	31,119	850	19.5%	48.0%
Congressional District 2	306,275	62,647	52,132	10,515	18,032	34,100	1,453	15.9%	39.8%
Congressional District 3	311,479	60,316	49,520	10,796	16,732	32,788	1,014	13.1%	41.4%
Congressional District 4	303,731	59,975	49,626	10,349	18,136	31,490	1,381	15.6%	39.1%
Congressional District 5	307,769	56,560	45,191	11,369	18,324	26,867	2,251	16.5%	43.5%
Congressional District 6	310,553	68,201	56,626	11,575	20,051	36,575	1,085	17.1%	35.1%
Congressional District 7	334,572	48,994	36,758	12,236	17,055	19,703	1,195	21.9%	51.9%
Congressional District 8	316,742	66,676	55,669	11,007	16,545	39,124	991	14.0%	39.0%
Congressional District 9	310,236	60,400	49,815	10,585	17,660	32,155	1,537	17.2%	42.1%
Iowa									
Congressional District 1	333,351	74,800	62,358	12,442	14,411	47,947	2,466	14.0%	41.4%
Congressional District 2	335,619	71,833	57,661	14,172	14,338	43,323	2,369	15.2%	37.0%
Congressional District 3	328,189	61,362	49,851	11,511	14,920	34,931	1,873	17.8%	41.1%
Congressional District 4	344,392	81,934	66,338	15,596	12,671	53,667	3,116	12.4%	38.0%
Kansas									
Congressional District 1	315,424	66,555	53,721	12,834	11,227	42,494	1,989	14.8%	33.1%
Congressional District 2	314,017	65,186	52,213	12,973	13,470	38,743	1,486	14.9%	36.0%
Congressional District 3	298,966	50,782	39,550	11,232	15,467	24,083	3,217	20.5%	52.4%
Congressional District 4	308,000	59,414	47,286	12,128	13,046	34,240	2,225	15.3%	41.8%
Kentucky									
Congressional District 1	332,208	73,165	61,748	11,417	14,466	47,282	421	14.3%	29.5%
Congressional District 2	314,753	62,186	52,332	9,854	15,128	37,204	876	15.1%	37.3%
Congressional District 3	330,489	63,933	50,138	13,795	17,702	32,436	1,769	18.7%	38.6%
Congressional District 4	303,591	56,281	46,079	10,202	16,440	29,639	956	19.0%	36.2%
Congressional District 5	326,897	67,095	56,357	10,738	11,243	45,114	212	15.7%	28.8%
Congressional District 6	324,967	56,965	45,272	11,693	16,592	28,680	1,092	17.2%	37.0%
Louisiana									
Congressional District 1	326,461	64,336	54,106	10,230	14,350	39,756	850	17.3%	36.9%
Congressional District 2	350,449	55,094	42,262	12,832	11,846	30,416	352	21.0%	48.6%
Congressional District 3	321,612	58,991	49,786	9,205	9,438	40,348	693	13.2%	35.1%
Congressional District 4	337,050	67,450	57,083	10,367	14,077	43,006	809	13.4%	35.2%
Congressional District 5	324,236	66,226	54,689	11,537	11,927	42,762	491	15.2%	31.9%
Congressional District 6	317,432	53,661	46,304	7,357	13,254	33,050	1,048	14.0%	38.2%
Maine									
Congressional District 1	347,892	67,165	52,493	14,672	18,522	33,971	1,974	25.1%	41.7%
Congressional District 2	375,413	69,161	54,563	14,598	15,330	39,233	1,329	20.3%	32.7%
Maryland									
Congressional District 1	334,001	67,990	58,177	9,813	21,140	37,037	635	23.1%	41.7%
Congressional District 2	298,494	52,049	40,350	11,699	14,791	25,559	1,281	24.3%	52.4%
Congressional District 3	304,641	60,493	43,416	17,077	18,440	24,976	3,758	24.9%	52.2%
Congressional District 4	282,616	45,816	36,958	8,858	20,910	16,048	833	29.9%	50.5%
Congressional District 5	270,249	44,843	38,876	5,967	19,528	19,348	492	24.3%	48.4%
Congressional District 6	290,953	53,783	42,684	11,099	17,621	25,063	1,670	22.9%	44.6%
Congressional District 7	319,564	61,093	42,149	18,944	18,460	23,689	2,300	28.6%	47.2%
Congressional District 8	287,349	61,685	49,286	12,399	20,355	28,931	2,845	23.3%	49.3%
Massachusetts									
Congressional District 1	319,193	70,654	51,757	18,897	16,875	34,882	1,948	25.9%	40.1%
Congressional District 2	295,683	58,359	41,230	17,129	14,511	26,719	1,736	25.7%	42.3%
Congressional District 3	292,126	54,213	38,572	15,641	14,291	24,281	1,169	29.9%	37.6%
Congressional District 4	285,616	59,690	44,566	15,124	15,502	29,064	1,771	28.9%	40.2%
Congressional District 5	303,440	65,582	46,763	18,819	17,656	29,107	2,016	31.3%	42.8%
Congressional District 6	299,376	68,756	50,611	18,145	19,007	31,604	2,116	30.4%	40.1%
Congressional District 7	304,064	48,752	22,181	26,571	9,367	12,814	1,171	37.1%	36.6%
Congressional District 8	309,136	66,721	46,671	20,050	16,797	29,874	2,742	29.7%	41.3%
Congressional District 9	401,112	83,918	66,631	17,287	24,868	41,763	1,057	31.5%	41.6%

Table J-5: 113th Congressional Districts—Summary of Housing and Householder Characteristics—*Continued*

					Householders 65 Years and Over				
					Owner Householders		Renter Households With Meals Included in Rent	Percent of Owner Householders Who Pay 35% or More of Income for Housing Costs	Percent of Renter Householders Who Pay 35% or More of Income for Rental Costs
	Total Housing Units	Total Households	Owner Occupied	Renter Occupied	With a Mortgage	Without a Mortgage			
Michigan									
Congressional District 1	442,790	86,476	75,451	11,025	21,165	54,286	916	18.2%	35.0%
Congressional District 2	311,969	58,368	49,293	9,075	14,859	34,434	1,701	18.6%	41.6%
Congressional District 3	294,609	56,348	46,637	9,711	14,040	32,597	1,629	18.9%	39.2%
Congressional District 4	344,322	70,829	62,467	8,362	18,651	43,816	1,147	20.4%	35.8%
Congressional District 5	329,918	70,085	58,847	11,238	18,074	40,773	872	19.3%	44.5%
Congressional District 6	325,398	63,960	54,256	9,704	18,477	35,779	1,078	22.0%	41.8%
Congressional District 7	302,929	63,933	53,421	10,512	18,097	35,324	1,982	21.3%	44.6%
Congressional District 8	291,018	52,661	43,985	8,676	19,212	24,773	1,384	23.3%	44.9%
Congressional District 9	319,964	72,707	59,627	13,080	19,938	39,689	1,710	23.3%	44.9%
Congressional District 10	303,542	63,850	55,073	8,777	18,571	36,502	1,539	22.2%	43.6%
Congressional District 11	293,896	60,804	50,393	10,411	20,005	30,388	2,905	24.2%	49.2%
Congressional District 12	295,818	55,781	44,112	11,669	14,831	29,281	1,599	22.4%	41.1%
Congressional District 13	342,602	59,820	43,008	16,812	14,447	28,561	773	26.1%	46.8%
Congressional District 14	329,267	63,216	46,561	16,655	19,237	27,324	1,930	31.0%	48.8%
Minnesota									
Congressional District 1	282,828	64,269	51,514	12,755	12,761	38,753	3,093	17.5%	44.8%
Congressional District 2	262,672	44,625	35,224	9,401	14,094	21,130	2,069	22.7%	48.9%
Congressional District 3	275,025	52,318	41,709	10,609	17,359	24,350	2,402	21.8%	53.8%
Congressional District 4	278,134	52,030	38,523	13,507	14,481	24,042	2,698	19.6%	48.3%
Congressional District 5	307,305	49,190	34,816	14,374	12,341	22,475	2,083	25.8%	48.9%
Congressional District 6	255,897	40,864	33,064	7,800	12,488	20,576	1,232	21.9%	47.9%
Congressional District 7	325,274	73,648	57,546	16,102	12,212	45,334	3,076	17.6%	40.0%
Congressional District 8	367,427	72,554	58,716	13,838	16,999	41,717	2,106	20.2%	39.1%
Mississippi									
Congressional District 1	319,223	63,562	54,103	9,459	14,615	39,488	1,055	17.7%	43.2%
Congressional District 2	309,509	58,279	46,400	11,879	12,065	34,335	298	19.4%	31.5%
Congressional District 3	323,356	65,405	56,300	9,105	13,537	42,763	1,116	16.2%	38.4%
Congressional District 4	327,969	61,651	53,487	8,164	14,315	39,172	504	18.5%	37.3%
Missouri									
Congressional District 1	371,131	61,438	44,299	17,139	16,888	27,411	871	24.9%	42.8%
Congressional District 2	312,478	73,521	61,513	12,008	22,186	39,327	4,525	19.7%	50.3%
Congressional District 3	332,546	62,537	53,445	9,092	17,424	36,021	1,075	16.4%	35.4%
Congressional District 4	340,546	67,398	56,641	10,757	16,250	40,391	1,194	16.3%	36.4%
Congressional District 5	352,462	66,508	50,648	15,860	17,502	33,146	1,709	21.1%	45.2%
Congressional District 6	325,112	65,556	53,477	12,079	14,429	39,048	1,253	16.7%	32.9%
Congressional District 7	343,964	71,462	57,642	13,820	18,451	39,191	1,430	16.6%	43.0%
Congressional District 8	338,821	75,680	62,131	13,549	15,788	46,343	799	15.6%	31.5%
Montana									
Congressional District (at Large)	484,745	97,403	77,984	19,419	21,812	56,172	3,699	16.6%	37.9%
Nebraska									
Congressional District 1	260,898	50,998	39,561	11,437	10,428	29,133	2,730	16.1%	41.1%
Congressional District 2	256,809	41,658	31,820	9,838	11,327	20,493	2,447	19.3%	46.8%
Congressional District 3	283,219	66,972	53,965	13,007	9,552	44,413	2,398	15.6%	33.8%
Nevada									
Congressional District 1	297,862	49,790	30,998	18,792	14,455	16,543	945	27.5%	58.7%
Congressional District 2	295,676	57,060	45,025	12,035	19,585	25,440	1,032	24.5%	50.2%
Congressional District 3	308,590	49,698	38,531	11,167	21,012	17,519	816	25.6%	51.7%
Congressional District 4	276,879	48,132	39,036	9,096	20,583	18,453	504	27.8%	41.5%
New Hampshire									
Congressional District 1	311,986	55,685	43,319	12,366	14,839	28,480	1,272	29.1%	40.5%
Congressional District 2	304,041	57,617	45,159	12,458	14,701	30,458	1,468	30.4%	40.1%
New Jersey									
Congressional District 1	293,532	60,165	45,558	14,607	16,363	29,195	1,859	35.8%	54.3%
Congressional District 2	383,514	70,540	57,315	13,225	19,575	37,740	1,104	34.4%	45.7%
Congressional District 3	314,091	78,363	69,669	8,694	25,063	44,606	987	32.1%	54.8%
Congressional District 4	297,779	78,391	64,544	13,847	21,513	43,031	2,883	32.5%	53.6%
Congressional District 5	279,750	62,712	50,913	11,799	18,266	32,647	1,307	37.5%	54.2%
Congressional District 6	271,029	49,969	37,831	12,138	12,979	24,852	599	36.6%	49.2%
Congressional District 7	278,486	58,088	47,984	10,104	16,267	31,717	1,146	35.4%	56.2%
Congressional District 8	300,665	41,136	18,648	22,488	6,778	11,870	155	48.3%	46.6%
Congressional District 9	281,776	58,242	37,072	21,170	10,788	26,284	571	43.6%	49.0%
Congressional District 10	300,814	51,555	27,321	24,234	11,442	15,879	377	49.1%	45.5%
Congressional District 11	282,247	66,166	54,312	11,854	18,839	35,473	2,024	36.3%	51.3%
Congressional District 12	281,539	58,274	46,834	11,440	16,690	30,144	749	33.8%	46.9%
New Mexico									
Congressional District 1	296,732	56,382	45,256	11,126	17,329	27,927	1,315	19.4%	41.5%
Congressional District 2	301,183	63,242	54,013	9,229	14,929	39,084	490	14.5%	31.2%
Congressional District 3	306,604	57,824	49,054	8,770	15,812	33,242	594	17.9%	35.5%

Table J-5: 113th Congressional Districts—Summary of Housing and Householder Characteristics—*Continued*

| | | Householders 65 Years and Over | | | | | | | |
| | | | | | Owner Householders | | | | |
	Total Housing Units	Total Households	Owner Occupied	Renter Occupied	With a Mortgage	Without a Mortgage	Renter Households With Meals Included in Rent	Percent of Owner Householders Who Pay 35% or More of Income for Housing Costs	Percent of Renter Householders Who Pay 35% or More of Income for Rental Costs
New York									
Congressional District 1	304,609	61,352	52,377	8,975	17,637	34,740	608	34.9%	52.5%
Congressional District 2	243,313	53,807	44,830	8,977	15,019	29,811	725	40.2%	57.3%
Congressional District 3	264,284	72,842	62,196	10,646	19,117	43,079	1,078	36.5%	52.4%
Congressional District 4	249,273	60,479	50,463	10,016	15,842	34,621	1,035	38.4%	51.3%
Congressional District 5	240,865	46,869	30,116	16,753	13,125	16,991	168	37.7%	46.8%
Congressional District 6	286,673	61,218	33,849	27,369	8,059	25,790	706	34.1%	56.8%
Congressional District 7	270,158	40,174	10,863	29,311	3,611	7,252	174	37.5%	46.9%
Congressional District 8	298,314	57,410	23,572	33,838	9,502	14,070	418	42.3%	45.3%
Congressional District 9	294,612	52,588	21,627	30,961	8,822	12,805	403	41.4%	53.0%
Congressional District 10	349,382	63,915	23,042	40,873	6,291	16,751	1,224	35.1%	47.4%
Congressional District 11	279,716	61,466	38,482	22,984	12,647	25,835	154	35.9%	54.6%
Congressional District 12	424,432	69,281	27,803	41,478	7,994	19,809	433	28.4%	45.0%
Congressional District 13	292,780	51,805	5,449	46,356	1,906	3,543	582	27.7%	46.9%
Congressional District 14	263,884	47,181	21,965	25,216	6,268	15,697	306	39.4%	52.0%
Congressional District 15	255,302	39,856	5,814	34,042	2,799	3,015	179	43.8%	48.8%
Congressional District 16	290,165	65,395	39,620	25,775	13,540	26,080	1,266	38.8%	48.3%
Congressional District 17	256,006	59,751	46,636	13,115	16,292	30,344	1,493	37.2%	49.8%
Congressional District 18	272,586	54,771	42,767	12,004	15,333	27,434	644	32.1%	51.9%
Congressional District 19	359,082	71,306	58,137	13,169	17,193	40,944	757	26.8%	41.4%
Congressional District 20	322,972	64,691	47,444	17,247	14,772	32,672	1,518	21.5%	45.9%
Congressional District 21	367,458	66,841	52,717	14,124	13,202	39,515	777	20.9%	36.2%
Congressional District 22	321,890	71,222	55,741	15,481	14,105	41,636	1,225	18.9%	37.5%
Congressional District 23	338,215	69,521	56,082	13,439	13,883	42,199	800	16.5%	34.2%
Congressional District 24	311,552	65,266	50,552	14,714	15,713	34,839	1,544	19.4%	40.9%
Congressional District 25	309,825	65,975	48,920	17,055	18,331	30,589	2,996	22.3%	53.0%
Congressional District 26	343,479	74,605	55,351	19,254	16,203	39,148	1,640	19.0%	47.0%
Congressional District 27	305,306	70,022	56,868	13,154	17,061	39,807	1,357	19.0%	42.5%
North Carolina									
Congressional District 1	335,551	66,554	47,721	18,833	17,117	30,604	1,319	28.8%	42.3%
Congressional District 2	311,240	55,632	46,030	9,602	16,564	29,466	1,048	20.0%	37.6%
Congressional District 3	366,561	62,436	52,510	9,926	19,278	33,232	783	23.8%	35.2%
Congressional District 4	324,317	45,224	34,514	10,710	14,338	20,176	1,306	22.2%	48.2%
Congressional District 5	348,546	70,921	60,525	10,396	19,691	40,834	1,231	18.3%	40.0%
Congressional District 6	329,333	72,716	60,987	11,729	21,580	39,407	2,292	19.3%	43.3%
Congressional District 7	361,297	71,476	59,964	11,512	23,354	36,610	1,043	24.0%	38.9%
Congressional District 8	313,051	62,266	52,265	10,001	16,944	35,321	853	22.8%	36.6%
Congressional District 9	308,444	48,157	40,160	7,997	18,946	21,214	1,903	23.8%	50.8%
Congressional District 10	332,676	69,278	57,695	11,583	19,391	38,304	1,164	17.6%	37.6%
Congressional District 11	394,897	89,001	75,570	13,431	22,019	53,551	1,889	17.2%	35.8%
Congressional District 12	323,385	41,118	30,003	11,115	12,438	17,565	835	25.3%	43.6%
Congressional District 13	304,918	53,396	44,503	8,893	18,463	26,040	1,921	22.4%	50.6%
North Dakota									
Congressional District (at Large)	323,146	62,826	46,176	16,650	8,061	38,115	2,798	13.2%	37.1%
Ohio									
Congressional District 1	317,271	56,278	42,369	13,909	16,702	25,667	1,559	23.1%	47.1%
Congressional District 2	324,787	65,963	50,957	15,006	18,380	32,577	2,310	20.8%	44.7%
Congressional District 3	334,205	43,825	29,971	13,854	14,396	15,575	1,218	24.6%	43.5%
Congressional District 4	306,368	67,395	55,856	11,539	16,353	39,503	1,645	17.5%	39.1%
Congressional District 5	309,814	69,228	57,791	11,437	17,640	40,151	1,902	16.7%	38.0%
Congressional District 6	323,053	77,660	64,222	13,438	16,240	47,982	739	14.9%	31.6%
Congressional District 7	304,594	68,916	57,494	11,422	18,660	38,834	1,078	15.9%	34.4%
Congressional District 8	301,061	64,548	53,337	11,211	19,520	33,817	1,601	19.4%	38.8%
Congressional District 9	350,312	64,955	50,225	14,730	16,777	33,448	1,113	21.2%	39.5%
Congressional District 10	333,836	71,934	56,678	15,256	21,033	35,645	1,715	19.8%	46.4%
Congressional District 11	371,667	69,855	48,983	20,872	20,068	28,915	1,965	28.9%	48.8%
Congressional District 12	302,442	57,210	46,973	10,237	18,404	28,569	1,769	20.1%	44.7%
Congressional District 13	336,633	75,629	60,375	15,254	19,915	40,460	1,143	16.9%	34.6%
Congressional District 14	305,256	73,757	60,394	13,363	21,325	39,069	2,499	21.6%	47.7%
Congressional District 15	302,364	57,635	47,059	10,576	16,332	30,727	1,553	17.9%	41.2%
Congressional District 16	304,481	76,176	62,036	14,140	20,750	41,286	3,502	19.2%	49.7%
Oklahoma									
Congressional District 1	333,406	62,489	50,390	12,099	16,322	34,068	2,351	16.6%	47.2%
Congressional District 2	350,028	77,562	65,643	11,919	15,135	50,508	404	15.6%	28.9%
Congressional District 3	331,378	68,953	57,737	11,216	13,232	44,505	1,099	14.2%	36.9%
Congressional District 4	321,699	61,389	51,975	9,414	15,457	36,518	1,234	15.6%	40.9%
Congressional District 5	334,719	61,020	47,659	13,361	14,980	32,679	2,559	16.7%	46.6%
Oregon									
Congressional District 1	321,178	57,497	42,554	14,943	18,200	24,354	4,009	25.1%	51.6%
Congressional District 2	355,420	84,449	66,915	17,534	25,779	41,136	5,028	23.9%	50.1%
Congressional District 3	329,744	54,792	38,936	15,856	16,169	22,767	3,395	26.0%	51.7%
Congressional District 4	343,347	84,442	68,574	15,868	24,120	44,454	3,208	19.6%	44.9%
Congressional District 5	329,676	70,703	54,298	16,405	21,264	33,034	5,318	22.7%	54.7%

Table J-5: 113th Congressional Districts—Summary of Housing and Householder Characteristics—*Continued*

					Householders 65 Years and Over				
					Owner Householders		Renter Households With Meals Included in Rent	Percent of Owner Householders Who Pay 35% or More of Income for Housing Costs	Percent of Renter Householders Who Pay 35% or More of Income for Rental Costs
	Total Housing Units	Total Households	Owner Occupied	Renter Occupied	With a Mortgage	Without a Mortgage			
Pennsylvania									
Congressional District 1	297,887	49,999	36,581	13,418	9,804	26,777	185	26.0%	45.7%
Congressional District 2	330,588	63,296	43,857	19,439	13,120	30,737	996	26.9%	43.5%
Congressional District 3	316,361	73,915	57,396	16,519	15,054	42,342	2,230	16.7%	35.7%
Congressional District 4	298,611	66,376	51,754	14,622	16,126	35,628	2,106	23.5%	44.4%
Congressional District 5	340,192	72,084	57,316	14,768	12,792	44,524	1,327	16.1%	32.8%
Congressional District 6	284,835	62,853	50,434	12,419	16,162	34,272	2,762	26.3%	50.3%
Congressional District 7	271,492	66,840	52,055	14,785	16,615	35,440	5,144	25.6%	56.1%
Congressional District 8	277,460	63,106	49,900	13,206	16,148	33,752	3,533	27.9%	59.0%
Congressional District 9	318,222	78,422	63,275	15,147	13,955	49,320	1,070	17.0%	30.2%
Congressional District 10	344,008	72,892	59,466	13,426	15,983	43,483	1,357	20.7%	34.4%
Congressional District 11	318,345	72,457	57,173	15,284	15,005	42,168	1,239	20.3%	30.7%
Congressional District 12	317,395	83,948	67,684	16,264	17,395	50,289	2,711	18.4%	38.5%
Congressional District 13	287,408	62,168	44,590	17,578	13,714	30,876	2,317	25.8%	54.5%
Congressional District 14	366,038	78,595	55,247	23,348	15,635	39,612	2,090	20.0%	36.7%
Congressional District 15	288,388	65,964	50,924	15,040	14,854	36,070	1,698	22.7%	43.2%
Congressional District 16	278,206	61,178	43,312	17,866	12,216	31,096	3,887	21.5%	48.0%
Congressional District 17	321,992	73,422	55,604	17,818	14,331	41,273	1,400	24.5%	34.9%
Congressional District 18	313,694	80,713	64,751	15,962	17,529	47,222	2,220	18.0%	38.2%
Rhode Island									
Congressional District 1	233,045	48,757	31,959	16,798	11,777	20,182	1,514	32.6%	39.9%
Congressional District 2	229,936	47,532	34,476	13,056	13,168	21,308	1,319	30.2%	38.7%
South Carolina									
Congressional District 1	324,098	60,335	52,583	7,752	22,972	29,611	1,252	25.4%	50.6%
Congressional District 2	289,048	53,496	46,745	6,751	16,800	29,945	1,100	18.2%	47.4%
Congressional District 3	300,325	64,787	55,155	9,632	15,801	39,354	1,358	16.1%	40.8%
Congressional District 4	287,909	56,127	46,932	9,195	16,191	30,741	1,321	16.8%	43.3%
Congressional District 5	287,418	58,130	49,867	8,263	16,741	33,126	769	18.1%	37.1%
Congressional District 6	293,530	54,028	44,707	9,321	13,276	31,431	315	25.4%	39.6%
Congressional District 7	365,823	69,540	59,241	10,299	20,358	38,883	627	20.9%	34.6%
South Dakota									
Congressional District (at Large)	366,175	74,354	55,371	18,983	11,707	43,664	2,939	15.9%	36.7%
Tennessee									
Congressional District 1	344,700	78,559	66,785	11,774	16,688	50,097	753	14.4%	29.9%
Congressional District 2	320,523	67,244	56,029	11,215	15,563	40,466	1,277	16.4%	39.2%
Congressional District 3	321,129	71,872	59,709	12,163	17,135	42,574	1,734	18.7%	37.0%
Congressional District 4	300,031	57,673	47,566	10,107	13,666	33,900	730	16.8%	33.6%
Congressional District 5	317,781	48,840	37,811	11,029	12,968	24,843	1,533	18.9%	44.6%
Congressional District 6	309,111	67,865	58,373	9,492	18,668	39,705	886	18.3%	35.4%
Congressional District 7	303,564	56,764	47,618	9,146	13,729	33,889	772	17.9%	32.9%
Congressional District 8	291,416	61,894	52,442	9,452	15,975	36,467	1,048	18.5%	33.2%
Congressional District 9	316,751	44,473	32,190	12,283	13,357	18,833	1,425	27.2%	48.7%
Texas									
Congressional District 1	298,749	63,924	53,488	10,436	11,433	42,055	1,716	15.3%	42.8%
Congressional District 2	282,915	35,897	29,455	6,442	10,480	18,975	1,331	18.6%	51.7%
Congressional District 3	275,671	33,448	24,818	8,630	11,574	13,244	1,376	22.9%	55.1%
Congressional District 4	299,592	64,787	53,994	10,793	12,214	41,780	819	15.8%	40.1%
Congressional District 5	284,521	53,103	43,824	9,279	10,423	33,401	691	18.6%	42.4%
Congressional District 6	274,265	40,426	33,507	6,919	11,975	21,532	1,186	19.2%	51.5%
Congressional District 7	307,212	40,123	29,591	10,532	9,966	19,625	2,868	22.9%	58.7%
Congressional District 8	282,592	49,965	42,364	7,601	14,713	27,651	959	20.7%	42.5%
Congressional District 9	275,102	31,161	22,207	8,954	7,663	14,544	666	22.4%	47.4%
Congressional District 10	287,017	43,255	35,825	7,430	10,621	25,204	769	21.5%	44.6%
Congressional District 11	317,627	65,403	54,275	11,128	11,213	43,062	1,440	14.9%	36.4%
Congressional District 12	295,184	48,788	38,336	10,452	12,232	26,104	1,893	19.2%	51.3%
Congressional District 13	300,034	60,794	50,556	10,238	9,697	40,859	1,167	15.3%	37.2%
Congressional District 14	299,730	52,832	42,980	9,852	10,293	32,687	830	16.9%	52.6%
Congressional District 15	238,254	40,468	32,703	7,765	7,200	25,503	373	19.6%	32.6%
Congressional District 16	246,474	45,848	34,999	10,849	9,166	25,833	628	16.2%	39.1%
Congressional District 17	298,303	46,729	37,941	8,788	9,864	28,077	1,069	15.9%	42.1%
Congressional District 18	285,083	36,168	27,266	8,902	6,513	20,753	179	21.8%	53.1%
Congressional District 19	290,564	56,285	45,677	10,608	9,205	36,472	1,538	13.8%	37.6%
Congressional District 20	263,152	43,172	33,357	9,815	10,097	23,260	1,199	15.6%	47.3%
Congressional District 21	333,315	60,200	48,239	11,961	15,935	32,304	2,700	17.2%	46.1%
Congressional District 22	254,538	32,218	27,151	5,067	10,654	16,497	1,163	22.7%	47.6%
Congressional District 23	253,252	45,265	38,821	6,444	9,420	29,401	249	16.0%	28.5%
Congressional District 24	309,195	38,054	28,185	9,869	10,377	17,808	1,797	20.8%	51.8%
Congressional District 25	288,035	50,768	43,238	7,530	13,722	29,516	1,192	20.4%	38.0%
Congressional District 26	263,135	30,049	24,094	5,955	11,645	12,449	1,154	21.5%	56.1%
Congressional District 27	304,172	58,692	48,833	9,859	11,084	37,749	990	17.2%	44.5%
Congressional District 28	236,893	38,665	31,683	6,982	7,321	24,362	135	17.4%	39.0%
Congressional District 29	233,556	28,978	22,577	6,401	5,361	17,216	90	20.5%	46.7%
Congressional District 30	267,976	38,028	28,459	9,569	9,833	18,626	425	26.9%	54.4%

Table J-5: 113th Congressional Districts—Summary of Housing and Householder Characteristics—*Continued*

| | | | | | Householders 65 Years and Over | | | | |
| | | | | | Owner Householders | | | | |
	Total Housing Units	Total Households	Owner Occupied	Renter Occupied	With a Mortgage	Without a Mortgage	Renter Households With Meals Included in Rent	Percent of Owner Householders Who Pay 35% or More of Income for Housing Costs	Percent of Renter Householders Who Pay 35% or More of Income for Rental Costs
Texas—Cont.									
Congressional District 31	281,563	39,647	31,846	7,801	11,734	20,112	1,035	16.7%	44.1%
Congressional District 32	297,134	44,912	36,089	8,823	12,131	23,958	1,957	21.7%	48.2%
Congressional District 33	239,537	32,269	23,986	8,283	6,420	17,566	399	21.7%	51.5%
Congressional District 34	251,922	48,254	38,802	9,452	6,594	32,208	132	17.9%	34.8%
Congressional District 35	267,752	37,093	27,577	9,516	8,983	18,594	418	19.1%	42.7%
Congressional District 36	289,252	53,321	46,379	6,942	10,919	35,460	462	14.4%	38.5%
Utah									
Congressional District 1	259,069	39,016	34,157	4,859	12,158	21,999	841	15.5%	43.8%
Congressional District 2	268,785	49,485	41,190	8,295	14,747	26,443	804	17.9%	40.3%
Congressional District 3	226,803	36,967	31,845	5,122	11,428	20,417	1,162	16.2%	48.5%
Congressional District 4	234,434	34,924	28,818	6,106	11,184	17,634	1,477	18.0%	51.7%
Vermont									
Congressional District (at Large)	323,419	60,018	47,944	12,074	16,344	31,600	1,471	29.5%	36.3%
Virginia									
Congressional District 1	296,443	56,291	47,556	8,735	20,502	27,054	2,045	20.4%	42.5%
Congressional District 2	305,006	54,078	43,570	10,508	18,502	25,068	1,101	23.1%	50.3%
Congressional District 3	321,489	53,307	38,735	14,572	16,050	22,685	715	27.2%	47.4%
Congressional District 4	283,339	53,177	44,275	8,902	18,493	25,782	763	23.0%	47.5%
Congressional District 5	342,359	77,295	65,667	11,628	20,914	44,753	910	19.0%	30.0%
Congressional District 6	325,528	74,617	60,133	14,484	18,521	41,612	2,100	18.7%	41.5%
Congressional District 7	301,075	59,890	49,709	10,181	21,382	28,327	2,864	20.2%	47.9%
Congressional District 8	327,361	44,714	33,258	11,456	15,814	17,444	1,918	21.5%	47.1%
Congressional District 9	343,489	80,517	67,292	13,225	15,905	51,387	690	15.3%	32.0%
Congressional District 10	262,684	38,090	32,093	5,997	16,308	15,785	1,448	20.8%	54.5%
Congressional District 11	274,497	39,173	32,183	6,990	16,376	15,807	1,867	18.5%	50.6%
Washington									
Congressional District 1	280,206	45,144	35,758	9,386	15,302	20,456	2,597	26.4%	52.0%
Congressional District 2	299,043	56,310	42,880	13,430	16,539	26,341	2,845	23.6%	48.1%
Congressional District 3	284,444	60,556	47,911	12,645	18,304	29,607	2,404	20.6%	49.1%
Congressional District 4	255,736	49,062	38,323	10,739	12,466	25,857	2,221	16.4%	42.8%
Congressional District 5	296,604	61,573	48,271	13,302	16,826	31,445	3,000	19.6%	48.8%
Congressional District 6	313,981	68,148	54,531	13,617	22,283	32,248	2,529	22.8%	42.9%
Congressional District 7	335,252	56,152	38,575	17,577	15,114	23,461	3,884	25.0%	48.9%
Congressional District 8	273,624	43,636	35,089	8,547	14,528	20,561	2,351	26.5%	55.5%
Congressional District 9	283,223	49,636	34,058	15,578	13,334	20,724	3,281	28.5%	50.9%
Congressional District 10	279,238	51,551	39,906	11,645	15,441	24,465	1,895	21.9%	52.3%
West Virginia									
Congressional District 1	289,126	66,039	55,954	10,085	12,740	43,214	300	10.2%	26.1%
Congressional District 2	294,019	63,481	52,769	10,712	13,676	39,093	466	12.8%	30.7%
Congressional District 3	299,316	67,431	59,056	8,375	12,495	46,561	223	11.5%	24.0%
Wisconsin									
Congressional District 1	303,217	59,452	47,165	12,287	15,274	31,891	1,318	23.1%	49.3%
Congressional District 2	317,008	55,307	42,745	12,562	14,410	28,335	1,599	21.0%	46.9%
Congressional District 3	318,525	67,859	52,842	15,017	13,654	39,188	2,602	20.3%	42.1%
Congressional District 4	311,029	48,766	32,334	16,432	11,258	21,076	1,816	29.1%	48.2%
Congressional District 5	306,239	68,769	49,896	18,873	14,353	35,543	3,156	24.2%	55.9%
Congressional District 6	320,388	69,461	54,252	15,209	14,195	40,057	2,748	20.4%	41.4%
Congressional District 7	413,187	76,850	61,359	15,491	16,673	44,686	2,017	22.0%	35.8%
Congressional District 8	339,641	64,101	50,687	13,414	13,800	36,887	1,879	21.5%	43.3%
Wyoming									
Congressional District (at Large)	263,696	45,398	37,960	7,438	9,377	28,583	650	14.7%	32.4%

APPENDIXES

APPENDIX A. CORE BASED STATISTICAL AREAS AND COMPONENTS

Core Based Statistical Areas and Components (as defined February 2013)		
Core based statistical area	State/County FIPS code	Title and Geographic Components
10180		Abilene, TX Metro area
	48059	Callahan County, TX
	48253	Jones County, TX
	48441	Taylor County, TX
10420		Akron, OH Metro area
	39133	Portage County, OH
	39153	Summit County, OH
10500		Albany, GA Metro area
	13007	Baker County, GA
	13095	Dougherty County, GA
	13177	Lee County, GA
	13273	Terrell County, GA
	13321	Worth County, GA
10580		Albany-Schenectady-Troy, NY Metro area
	36001	Albany County, NY
	36083	Rensselaer County, NY
	36091	Saratoga County, NY
	36093	Schenectady County, NY
	36095	Schoharie County, NY
10740		Albuquerque, NM Metro area
	35001	Bernalillo County, NM
	35043	Sandoval County, NM
	35057	Torrance County, NM
	35061	Valencia County, NM
10780		Alexandria, LA Metro area
	22043	Grant Parish, LA
	22079	Rapides Parish, LA
10900		Allentown-Bethlehem-Easton, PA-NJ Metro area
	34041	Warren County, NJ
	42025	Carbon County, PA
	42077	Lehigh County, PA
	42095	Northampton County, PA
11020		Altoona, PA Metro area
	42013	Blair County, PA
11100		Amarillo, TX Metro area
	48011	Armstrong County, TX
	48065	Carson County, TX
	48359	Oldham County, TX
	48375	Potter County, TX
	48381	Randall County, TX
11180		Ames, IA Metro area
	19169	Story County, IA
11260		Anchorage, AK Metro area
	02020	Anchorage Municipality, AK
	02170	Matanuska-Susitna Borough, AK
11460		Ann Arbor, MI Metro area
	26161	Washtenaw County, MI
11500		Anniston-Oxford-Jacksonville, AL Metro area
	01015	Calhoun County, AL
11540		Appleton, WI Metro area
	55015	Calumet County, WI
	55087	Outagamie County, WI
11700		Asheville, NC Metro area
	37021	Buncombe County, NC
	37087	Haywood County, NC
	37089	Henderson County, NC
	37115	Madison County, NC
12020		Athens-Clarke County, GA Metro area
	13059	Clarke County, GA
	13195	Madison County, GA
	13219	Oconee County, GA
	13221	Oglethorpe County, GA
12060		Atlanta-Sandy Springs-Roswell, GA Metro area
	13013	Barrow County, GA
	13015	Bartow County, GA
	13035	Butts County, GA
	13045	Carroll County, GA
	13057	Cherokee County, GA
	13063	Clayton County, GA
	13067	Cobb County, GA
	13077	Coweta County, GA
	13085	Dawson County, GA
	13089	DeKalb County, GA
	13097	Douglas County, GA
	13113	Fayette County, GA
	13117	Forsyth County, GA
	13121	Fulton County, GA
	13135	Gwinnett County, GA
	13143	Haralson County, GA
	13149	Heard County, GA
	13151	Henry County, GA
	13159	Jasper County, GA
	13171	Lamar County, GA

Core Based Statistical Areas and Components (as defined February 2013)		
Core based statistical area	State/County FIPS code	Title and Geographic Components
	13199	Meriwether County, GA
	13211	Morgan County, GA
	13217	Newton County, GA
	13223	Paulding County, GA
	13227	Pickens County, GA
	13231	Pike County, GA
	13247	Rockdale County, GA
	13255	Spalding County, GA
	13297	Walton County, GA
12100		Atlantic City-Hammonton, NJ Metro area
	34001	Atlantic County, NJ
12220		Auburn-Opelika, AL Metro area
	01081	Lee County, AL
12260		Augusta-Richmond County, GA-SC Metro area
	13033	Burke County, GA
	13073	Columbia County, GA
	13181	Lincoln County, GA
	13189	McDuffie County, GA
	13245	Richmond County, GA
	45003	Aiken County, SC
	45037	Edgefield County, SC
12420		Austin-Round Rock, TX Metro area
	48021	Bastrop County, TX
	48055	Caldwell County, TX
	48209	Hays County, TX
	48453	Travis County, TX
	48491	Williamson County, TX
12540		Bakersfield, CA Metro area
	06029	Kern County, CA
12580		Baltimore-Columbia-Towson, MD Metro area
	24003	Anne Arundel County, MD
	24005	Baltimore County, MD
	24013	Carroll County, MD
	24025	Harford County, MD
	24027	Howard County, MD
	24035	Queen Anne's County, MD
	24510	Baltimore city, MD
12620		Bangor, ME Metro area
	23019	Penobscot County, ME
12700		Barnstable Town, MA Metro area
	25001	Barnstable County, MA
12940		Baton Rouge, LA Metro area
	22005	Ascension Parish, LA
	22033	East Baton Rouge Parish, LA
	22037	East Feliciana Parish, LA
	22047	Iberville Parish, LA
	22063	Livingston Parish, LA
	22077	Pointe Coupee Parish, LA
	22091	St. Helena Parish, LA
	22121	West Baton Rouge Parish, LA
	22125	West Feliciana Parish, LA
12980		Battle Creek, MI Metro area
	26025	Calhoun County, MI
13020		Bay City, MI Metro area
	26017	Bay County, MI
13140		Beaumont-Port Arthur, TX Metro area
	48199	Hardin County, TX
	48245	Jefferson County, TX
	48351	Newton County, TX
	48361	Orange County, TX
13380		Bellingham, WA Metro area
	53073	Whatcom County, WA
13460		Bend-Redmond, OR Metro area
	41017	Deschutes County, OR
13740		Billings, MT Metro area
	30009	Carbon County, MT
	30037	Golden Valley County, MT
	30111	Yellowstone County, MT
13780		Binghamton, NY Metro area
	36007	Broome County, NY
	36107	Tioga County, NY
13820		Birmingham-Hoover, AL Metro area
	01007	Bibb County, AL
	01009	Blount County, AL
	01021	Chilton County, AL
	01073	Jefferson County, AL
	01115	St. Clair County, AL
	01117	Shelby County, AL
	01127	Walker County, AL
13900		Bismarck, ND Metro area
	38015	Burleigh County, ND
	38059	Morton County, ND
	38065	Oliver County, ND
	38085	Sioux County, ND

Core based statistical area	State/County FIPS code	Title and Geographic Components
		Core Based Statistical Areas and Components (as defined February 2013)
13980		Blacksburg-Christiansburg-Radford, VA Metro area
	51063	Floyd County, VA
	51071	Giles County, VA
	51121	Montgomery County, VA
	51155	Pulaski County, VA
	51750	Radford city, VA
14010		Bloomington, IL Metro area
	17039	De Witt County, IL
	17113	McLean County, IL
14020		Bloomington, IN Metro area
	18105	Monroe County, IN
	18119	Owen County, IN
14260		Boise City, ID Metro area
	16001	Ada County, ID
	16015	Boise County, ID
	16027	Canyon County, ID
	16045	Gem County, ID
	16073	Owyhee County, ID
14460		Boston-Cambridge Newton, MA-NH Metro area
14460		Boston, MA Metro Div 14454
	25021	Norfolk County, MA
	25023	Plymouth County, MA
	25025	Suffolk County, MA
14460		Cambridge-Newton-Framingham, MA Metro Div 15764
	25009	Essex County, MA
	25017	Middlesex County, MA
14460		Rockingham County-Strafford County-NH Metro Div 40484
	33015	Rockingham County, NH
	33017	Strafford County, NH
14500		Boulder, CO Metro area
	08013	Boulder County, CO
14540		Bowling Green, KY Metro area
	21003	Allen County, KY
	21031	Butler County, KY
	21061	Edmonson County, KY
	21227	Warren County, KY
14740		Bremerton-Silverdale, WA Metro area
	53035	Kitsap County, WA
14860		Bridgeport-Stamford-Norwalk, CT Metro area
	09001	Fairfield County, CT
15180		Brownsville-Harlingen, TX Metro area
	48061	Cameron County, TX
15260		Brunswick, GA Metro area
	13025	Brantley County, GA
	13127	Glynn County, GA
	13191	McIntosh County, GA
15380		Buffalo-Cheektowaga-Niagara Falls, NY Metro area
	36029	Erie County, NY
	36063	Niagara County, NY
15500		Burlington, NC Metro area
	37001	Alamance County, NC
15540		Burlington-South Burlington, VT Metro area
	50007	Chittenden County, VT
	50011	Franklin County, VT
	50013	Grand Isle County, VT
15940		Canton-Massillon, OH Metro area
	39019	Carroll County, OH
	39151	Stark County, OH
15980		Cape Coral-Fort Myers, FL Metro area
	12071	Lee County, FL
16020		Cape Girardeau, MO-IL Metro area
	17003	Alexander County, IL
	29017	Bollinger County, MO
	29031	Cape Girardeau County, MO
16220		Casper, WY Metro area
	56025	Natrona County, WY
16300		Cedar Rapids, IA Metro area
	19011	Benton County, IA
	19105	Jones County, IA
	19113	Linn County, IA
16580		Champaign-Urbana, IL Metro area
	17019	Champaign County, IL
	17053	Ford County, IL
	17147	Piatt County, IL
16620		Charleston, WV Metro area
	54005	Boone County, WV
	54015	Clay County, WV
	54039	Kanawha County, WV
16700		Charleston-North Charleston, SC Metro area
	45015	Berkeley County, SC
	45019	Charleston County, SC
	45035	Dorchester County, SC
16740		Charlotte-Concord-Gastonia, NC-SC Metro area
	37025	Cabarrus County, NC
	37071	Gaston County, NC
	37097	Iredell County, NC
	37109	Lincoln County, NC
	37119	Mecklenburg County, NC
	37159	Rowan County, NC
	37179	Union County, NC
	45023	Chester County, SC
	45057	Lancaster County, SC
	45091	York County, SC
16820		Charlottesville, VA Metro area
	51003	Albemarle County, VA
	51029	Buckingham County, VA
	51065	Fluvanna County, VA
	51079	Greene County, VA
	51125	Nelson County, VA
	51540	Charlottesville city, VA
16860		Chattanooga, TN-GA Metro area
	13047	Catoosa County, GA
	13083	Dade County, GA
	13295	Walker County, GA
	47065	Hamilton County, TN
	47115	Marion County, TN
	47153	Sequatchie County, TN
16940		Cheyenne, WY Metro area
	56021	Laramie County, WY
16980		Chicago-Naperville-Elgin, IL-IN-WI Metro area
16980		Chicago-Naperville-Arlington Heights, IL Metro Div 16974
	17031	Cook County, IL
	17043	DuPage County, IL
	17063	Grundy County, IL
	17093	Kendall County, IL
	17111	McHenry County, IL
	17197	Will County, IL
16980		Gary, IN Metro Div 23844
	18073	Jasper County, IN
	18089	Lake County, IN
	18111	Newton County, IN
	18127	Porter County, IN
16980		Lake County-Kenosha County, IL-WI Metro Div 29404
	17097	Lake County, IL
	55059	Kenosha County, WI
17020		Chico, CA Metro area
	06007	Butte County, CA
17140		Cincinnati, OH-KY-IN Metro area
	18029	Dearborn County, IN
	18115	Ohio County, IN
	18161	Union County, IN
	21015	Boone County, KY
	21023	Bracken County, KY
	21037	Campbell County, KY
	21077	Gallatin County, KY
	21081	Grant County, KY
	21117	Kenton County, KY
	21191	Pendleton County, KY
	39015	Brown County, OH
	39017	Butler County, OH
	39025	Clermont County, OH
	39061	Hamilton County, OH
	39165	Warren County, OH
17300		Clarksville, TN-KY Metro area
	21047	Christian County, KY
	21221	Trigg County, KY
	47125	Montgomery County, TN
17420		Cleveland, TN Metro area
	47011	Bradley County, TN
	47139	Polk County, TN
17460		Cleveland-Elyria, OH Metro area
	39035	Cuyahoga County, OH
	39055	Geauga County, OH
	39085	Lake County, OH
	39093	Lorain County, OH
	39103	Medina County, OH
17660		Coeur d'Alene, ID Metro area
	16055	Kootenai County, ID
17780		College Station-Bryan, TX Metro area
	48041	Brazos County, TX
	48051	Burleson County, TX
	48395	Robertson County, TX
17820		Colorado Springs, CO Metro area
	08041	El Paso County, CO
	08119	Teller County, CO
17860		Columbia, MO Metro area
	29019	Boone County, MO
17900		Columbia, SC Metro area
	45017	Calhoun County, SC
	45039	Fairfield County, SC
	45055	Kershaw County, SC
	45063	Lexington County, SC
	45079	Richland County, SC
	45081	Saluda County, SC
17980		Columbus, GA-AL Metro area
	01113	Russell County, AL
	13053	Chattahoochee County, GA
	13145	Harris County, GA
	13197	Marion County, GA
	13215	Muscogee County, GA

Core Based Statistical Areas and Components (as defined February 2013)

Core based statistical area	State/County FIPS code	Title and Geographic Components
18020		Columbus, IN Metro area
	18005	Bartholomew County, IN
18140		Columbus, OH Metro area
	39041	Delaware County, OH
	39045	Fairfield County, OH
	39049	Franklin County, OH
	39073	Hocking County, OH
	39089	Licking County, OH
	39097	Madison County, OH
	39117	Morrow County, OH
	39127	Perry County, OH
	39129	Pickaway County, OH
	39159	Union County, OH
18580		Corpus Christi, TX Metro area
	48007	Aransas County, TX
	48355	Nueces County, TX
	48409	San Patricio County, TX
18700		Corvallis, OR Metro area
	41003	Benton County, OR
18880		Crestview-Fort Walton Beach-Destin, FL Metro area
	12091	Okaloosa County, FL
	12131	Walton County, FL
19060		Cumberland, MD-WV Metro area
	24001	Allegany County, MD
	54057	Mineral County, WV
19100		Dallas-Fort Worth-Arlington, TX Metro area
19100		Dallas-Plano-Irving, TX Metro Div 19124
	48085	Collin County, TX
	48113	Dallas County, TX
	48121	Denton County, TX
	48139	Ellis County, TX
	48231	Hunt County, TX
	48257	Kaufman County, TX
	48397	Rockwall County, TX
19100		Fort Worth-Arlington, TX Metro Div 23104
	48221	Hood County, TX
	48251	Johnson County, TX
	48367	Parker County, TX
	48425	Somervell County, TX
	48439	Tarrant County, TX
	48497	Wise County, TX
19140		Dalton, GA Metro area
	13213	Murray County, GA
	13313	Whitfield County, GA
19180		Danville, IL Metro area
	17183	Vermilion County, IL
19260		Danville, VA Micro area
	51143	Pittsylvania County, VA
	51590	Danville city, VA
19340		Davenport-Moline-Rock Island, IA-IL Metro area
	17073	Henry County, IL
	17131	Mercer County, IL
	17161	Rock Island County, IL
	19163	Scott County, IA
19380		Dayton, OH Metro area
	39057	Greene County, OH
	39109	Miami County, OH
	39113	Montgomery County, OH
19460		Decatur, AL Metro area
	01079	Lawrence County, AL
	01103	Morgan County, AL
19500		Decatur, IL Metro area
	17115	Macon County, IL
19660		Deltona-Daytona Beach-Ormond Beach, FL Metro area
	12035	Flagler County, FL
	12127	Volusia County, FL
19740		Denver-Aurora-Lakewood, CO Metro area
	08001	Adams County, CO
	08005	Arapahoe County, CO
	08014	Broomfield County, CO
	08019	Clear Creek County, CO
	08031	Denver County, CO
	08035	Douglas County, CO
	08039	Elbert County, CO
	08047	Gilpin County, CO
	08059	Jefferson County, CO
	08093	Park County, CO
19780		Des Moines-West Des Moines, IA Metro area
	19049	Dallas County, IA
	19077	Guthrie County, IA
	19121	Madison County, IA
	19153	Polk County, IA
	19181	Warren County, IA
19820		Detroit-Warren-Dearborn, MI Metro area
19820		Detroit-Dearborn-Livonia, MI Metro Div 19804
	26163	Wayne County, MI
19820		Warren-Troy-Farmington Hills, MI Metro Div 47664
	26087	Lapeer County, MI
	26093	Livingston County, MI
	26099	Macomb County, MI
	26125	Oakland County, MI
	26147	St. Clair County, MI

Core Based Statistical Areas and Components (as defined February 2013)

Core based statistical area	State/County FIPS code	Title and Geographic Components
20020		Dothan, AL Metro area
	01061	Geneva County, AL
	01067	Henry County, AL
	01069	Houston County, AL
20100		Dover, DE Metro area
	10001	Kent County, Delaware
20220		Dubuque, IA Metro area
	19061	Dubuque County, IA
20260		Duluth, MN-WI Metro area
	27017	Carlton County, MN
	27137	St. Louis County, MN
	55031	Douglas County, WI
20500		Durham-Chapel Hill, NC Metro area
	37037	Chatham County, NC
	37063	Durham County, NC
	37135	Orange County, NC
	37145	Person County, NC
20740		Eau Claire, WI Metro area
	55017	Chippewa County, WI
	55035	Eau Claire County, WI
20940		El Centro, CA Metro area
	06025	Imperial County, CA
21060		Elizabethtown-Fort Knox, KY Metro area
	21093	Hardin County, KY
	21123	Larue County, KY
	21163	Meade County, KY
21140		Elkhart-Goshen, IN Metro area
	18039	Elkhart County, IN
21300		Elmira, NY Metro area
	36015	Chemung County, NY
21340		El Paso, TX Metro area
	48141	El Paso County, TX
	48229	Hudspeth County, TX
21500		Erie, PA Metro area
	42049	Erie County, PA
21660		Eugene, OR Metro area
	41039	Lane County, OR
21780		Evansville, IN-KY Metro area
	18129	Posey County, IN
	18163	Vanderburgh County, IN
	18173	Warrick County, IN
	21101	Henderson County, KY
21820		Fairbanks, AK Metro area
	02090	Fairbanks North Star Borough, AK
22020		Fargo, ND-MN Metro area
	27027	Clay County, MN
	38017	Cass County, ND
22140		Farmington, NM Metro area
	35045	San Juan County, NM
22180		Fayetteville, NC Metro area
	37051	Cumberland County, NC
	37093	Hoke County, NC
22220		Fayetteville-Springdale-Rogers, AR-MO Metro area
	05007	Benton County, AR
	05087	Madison County, AR
	05143	Washington County, AR
	29119	McDonald County, MO
22380		Flagstaff, AZ Metro area
	04005	Coconino County, AZ
22420		Flint, MI Metro area
	26049	Genesee County, MI
22500		Florence, SC Metro area
	45031	Darlington County, SC
	45041	Florence County, SC
22520		Florence-Muscle Shoals, AL Metro area
	01033	Colbert County, AL
	01077	Lauderdale County, AL
22540		Fond du Lac, WI Metro area
	55039	Fond du Lac County, WI
22660		Fort Collins, CO Metro area
	08069	Larimer County, CO
22900		Fort Smith, AR-OK Metro area
	05033	Crawford County, AR
	05131	Sebastian County, AR
	40079	Le Flore County, OK
	40135	Sequoyah County, OK
23060		Fort Wayne, IN Metro area
	18003	Allen County, IN
	18179	Wells County, IN
	18183	Whitley County, IN
23420		Fresno, CA Metro area
	06019	Fresno County, CA
23460		Gadsden, AL Metro area
	01055	Etowah County, AL
23540		Gainesville, FL Metro area
	12001	Alachua County, FL
	12041	Gilchrist County, FL
23580		Gainesville, GA Metro area
	13139	Hall County, GA
24020		Glens Falls, NY Metro area
	36113	Warren County, NY
	36115	Washington County, NY

Core Based Statistical Areas and Components (as defined February 2013)

Core based statistical area	State/County FIPS code	Title and Geographic Components
24140		Goldsboro, NC Metro area
	37191	Wayne County, NC
24220		Grand Forks, ND-MN Metro area
	27119	Polk County, MN
	38035	Grand Forks County, ND
24300		Grand Junction, CO Metro area
	08077	Mesa County, CO
24340		Grand Rapids-Wyoming, MI Metro area
	26015	Barry County, MI
	26081	Kent County, MI
	26117	Montcalm County, MI
	26139	Ottawa County, MI
24500		Great Falls, MT Metro area
	30013	Cascade County, MT
24540		Greeley, CO Metro area
	08123	Weld County, CO
24580		Green Bay, WI Metro area
	55009	Brown County, WI
	55061	Kewaunee County, WI
	55083	Oconto County, WI
24660		Greensboro-High Point, NC Metro area
	37081	Guilford County, NC
	37151	Randolph County, NC
	37157	Rockingham County, NC
24780		Greenville, NC Metro area
	37147	Pitt County, NC
24860		Greenville-Anderson-Mauldin, SC Metro area
	45007	Anderson County, SC
	45045	Greenville County, SC
	45059	Laurens County, SC
	45077	Pickens County, SC
25060		Gulfport-Biloxi-Pascagoula, MS Metro area
	28045	Hancock County, MS
	28047	Harrison County, MS
	28059	Jackson County, MS
25180		Hagerstown-Martinsburg, MD-WV Metro area
	24043	Washington County, MD
	54003	Berkeley County, WV
25260		Hanford-Corcoran, CA Metro area
	06031	Kings County, CA
25420		Harrisburg-Carlisle, PA Metro area
	42041	Cumberland County, PA
	42043	Dauphin County, PA
	42099	Perry County, PA
25500		Harrisonburg, VA Metro area
	51165	Rockingham County, VA
	51660	Harrisonburg city, VA
25540		Hartford-West Hartford-East Hartford, CT Metro area
	09003	Hartford County, CT
	09007	Middlesex County, CT
	09013	Tolland County, CT
25620		Hattiesburg, MS Metro area
	28035	Forrest County, MS
	28073	Lamar County, MS
	28111	Perry County, MS
25860		Hickory-Lenoir-Morganton, NC Metro area
	37003	Alexander County, NC
	37023	Burke County, NC
	37027	Caldwell County, NC
	37035	Catawba County, NC
25980		Hinesville, GA Metro area
	13179	Liberty County, GA
	13183	Long County, GA
26090		Holland, MI Micro area
	26005	Allegan County, MI
26300		Hot Springs, AR Metro area
	05051	Garland County, AR
26380		Houma-Thibodaux, LA Metro area
	22057	Lafourche Parish, LA
	22109	Terrebonne Parish, LA
26420		Houston-The Woodlands-Sugar Land, TX Metro area
	48015	Austin County, TX
	48039	Brazoria County, TX
	48071	Chambers County, TX
	48157	Fort Bend County, TX
	48167	Galveston County, TX
	48201	Harris County, TX
	48291	Liberty County, TX
	48339	Montgomery County, TX
	48473	Waller County, TX
26580		Huntington-Ashland, WV-KY-OH Metro area
	21019	Boyd County, KY
	21089	Greenup County, KY
	39087	Lawrence County, OH
	54011	Cabell County, WV
	54043	Lincoln County, WV
	54079	Putnam County, WV
	54099	Wayne County, WV
26620		Huntsville, AL Metro area
	01083	Limestone County, AL
	01089	Madison County, AL

Core Based Statistical Areas and Components (as defined February 2013)

Core based statistical area	State/County FIPS code	Title and Geographic Components
26820		Idaho Falls, ID Metro area
	16019	Bonneville County, ID
	16023	Butte County, ID
	16051	Jefferson County, ID
26900		Indianapolis-Carmel-Anderson, IN Metro area
	18011	Boone County, IN
	18013	Brown County, IN
	18057	Hamilton County, IN
	18059	Hancock County, IN
	18063	Hendricks County, IN
	18081	Johnson County, IN
	18095	Madison County, IN
	18097	Marion County, IN
	18109	Morgan County, IN
	18133	Putnam County, IN
	18145	Shelby County, IN
26980		Iowa City, IA Metro area
	19103	Johnson County, IA
	19183	Washington County, IA
27060		Ithaca, NY Metro area
	36109	Tompkins County, NY
27100		Jackson, MI Metro area
	26075	Jackson County, MI
27140		Jackson, MS Metro area
	28029	Copiah County, MS
	28049	Hinds County, MS
	28089	Madison County, MS
	28121	Rankin County, MS
	28127	Simpson County, MS
	28163	Yazoo County, MS
27180		Jackson, TN Metro area
	47023	Chester County, TN
	47033	Crockett County, TN
	47113	Madison County, TN
27260		Jacksonville, FL Metro area
	12003	Baker County, FL
	12019	Clay County, FL
	12031	Duval County, FL
	12089	Nassau County, FL
	12109	St. Johns County, FL
27340		Jacksonville, NC Metro area
	37133	Onslow County, NC
27500		Janesville-Beloit, WI Metro area
	55105	Rock County, WI
27620		Jefferson City, MO Metro area
	29027	Callaway County, MO
	29051	Cole County, MO
	29135	Moniteau County, MO
	29151	Osage County, MO
27740		Johnson City, TN Metro area
	47019	Carter County, TN
	47171	Unicoi County, TN
	47179	Washington County, TN
27780		Johnstown, PA Metro area
	42021	Cambria County, PA
27860		Jonesboro, AR Metro area
	05031	Craighead County, AR
	05111	Poinsett County, AR
27900		Joplin, MO Metro area
	29097	Jasper County, MO
	29145	Newton County, MO
27920		Junction City, KS Micro area
	20061	Geary County, KS
27940		Juneau, AK Micro area
	02110	Juneau City and Borough, AK
27980		Kahului-Wailuku-Lahaina, HI Metro area
	15005	Kalawao County, HI
	15009	Maui County, HI
28020		Kalamazoo-Portage, MI Metro area
	26077	Kalamazoo County, MI
	26159	Van Buren County, MI
28100		Kankakee, IL Metro area
	17091	Kankakee County, IL
28140		Kansas City, MO-KS Metro area
	20091	Johnson County, KS
	20103	Leavenworth County, KS
	20107	Linn County, KS
	20121	Miami County, KS
	20209	Wyandotte County, KS
	29013	Bates County, MO
	29025	Caldwell County, MO
	29037	Cass County, MO
	29047	Clay County, MO
	29049	Clinton County, MO
	29095	Jackson County, MO
	29107	Lafayette County, MO
	29165	Platte County, MO
	29177	Ray County, MO
28420		Kennewick-Richland, WA Metro area
	53005	Benton County, WA
	53021	Franklin County, WA

Core based statistical area	State/County FIPS code	Title and Geographic Components
28660		Killeen-Temple, TX Metro area
	48027	Bell County, TX
	48099	Coryell County, TX
	48281	Lampasas County, TX
28700		Kingsport-Bristol-Bristol, TN-VA Metro area
	47073	Hawkins County, TN
	47163	Sullivan County, TN
	51169	Scott County, VA
	51191	Washington County, VA
	51520	Bristol city, VA
28740		Kingston, NY Metro area
	36111	Ulster County, NY
28940		Knoxville, TN Metro area
	47001	Anderson County, TN
	47009	Blount County, TN
	47013	Campbell County, TN
	47057	Grainger County, TN
	47093	Knox County, TN
	47105	Loudon County, TN
	47129	Morgan County, TN
	47145	Roane County, TN
	47173	Union County, TN
29020		Kokomo, IN Metro area
	18067	Howard County, IN
29100		La Crosse-Onalaska, WI-MN Metro area
	27055	Houston County, MN
	55063	La Crosse County, WI
29180		Lafayette, LA Metro area
	22001	Acadia Parish, LA
	22045	Iberia Parish, LA
	22055	Lafayette Parish, LA
	22099	St. Martin Parish, LA
	22113	Vermilion Parish, LA
29200		Lafayette-West Lafayette, IN Metro area
	18007	Benton County, IN
	18015	Carroll County, IN
	18157	Tippecanoe County, IN
29340		Lake Charles, LA Metro area
	22019	Calcasieu Parish, LA
	22023	Cameron Parish, LA
29420		Lake Havasu City-Kingman, AZ Metro area
	04015	Mohave County, AZ
29460		Lakeland-Winter Haven, FL Metro area
	12105	Polk County, FL
29540		Lancaster, PA Metro area
	42071	Lancaster County, PA
29620		Lansing-East Lansing, MI Metro area
	26037	Clinton County, MI
	26045	Eaton County, MI
	26065	Ingham County, MI
29700		Laredo, TX Metro area
	48479	Webb County, TX
29740		Las Cruces, NM Metro area
	35013	Doña Ana County, NM
29820		Las Vegas-Henderson-Paradise, NV Metro area
	32003	Clark County, NV
29940		Lawrence, KS Metro area
	20045	Douglas County, KS
30020		Lawton, OK Metro area
	40031	Comanche County, OK
	40033	Cotton County, OK
30060		Lebanon, MO Micro area
	29105	Laclede County, MO
30340		Lewiston-Auburn, ME Metro area
	23001	Androscoggin County, ME
30460		Lexington-Fayette, KY Metro area
	21017	Bourbon County, KY
	21049	Clark County, KY
	21067	Fayette County, KY
	21113	Jessamine County, KY
	21209	Scott County, KY
	21239	Woodford County, KY
30620		Lima, OH Metro area
	39003	Allen County, OH
30660		Lincoln, IL Micro area
	17107	Logan County, IL
30780		Little Rock-North Little Rock-Conway, AR Metro area
	05045	Faulkner County, AR
	05053	Grant County, AR
	05085	Lonoke County, AR
	05105	Perry County, AR
	05119	Pulaski County, AR
	05125	Saline County, AR
30860		Logan, UT-ID Metro area
30980		Longview, TX Metro area
	48183	Gregg County, TX
	48401	Rusk County, TX
	48459	Upshur County, TX
31020		Longview, WA Metro area
	53015	Cowlitz County, WA

Core based statistical area	State/County FIPS code	Title and Geographic Components
31080		Los Angeles-Long Beach-Anaheim, CA Metro area
31080		Anaheim-Santa Ana-Irvine, CA Metro Div 11244
	06059	Orange County, CA
31080		Los Angeles-Long Beach-Glendale, CA Metro Div 31084
	06037	Los Angeles County, CA
31140		Louisville/Jefferson County, KY-IN Metro area
	18019	Clark County, IN
	18043	Floyd County, IN
	18061	Harrison County, IN
	18143	Scott County, IN
	18175	Washington County, IN
	21029	Bullitt County, KY
	21103	Henry County, KY
	21111	Jefferson County, KY
	21185	Oldham County, KY
	21211	Shelby County, KY
	21215	Spencer County, KY
	21223	Trimble County, KY
31180		Lubbock, TX Metro area
	48107	Crosby County, TX
	48303	Lubbock County, TX
	48305	Lynn County, TX
31340		Lynchburg, VA Metro area
	51009	Amherst County, VA
	51011	Appomattox County, VA
	51019	Bedford County, VA
	51031	Campbell County, VA
	51515	Bedford city, VA
	51680	Lynchburg city, VA
31420		Macon, GA Metro area
	13021	Bibb County, GA
	13079	Crawford County, GA
	13169	Jones County, GA
	13207	Monroe County, GA
	13289	Twiggs County, GA
31460		Madera, CA Metro area
	06039	Madera County, CA
31540		Madison, WI Metro area
	55021	Columbia County, WI
	55025	Dane County, WI
	55045	Green County, WI
	55049	Iowa County, WI
31700		Manchester-Nashua, NH Metro area
	33011	Hillsborough County, NH
31740		Manhattan, KS Metro area
	20149	Pottawatomie County, KS
	20161	Riley County, KS
31860		Mankato-North Mankato, MN Metro area
	27013	Blue Earth County, MN
	27103	Nicollet County, MN
31900		Mansfield, OH Metro area
	39139	Richland County, OH
32580		McAllen-Edinburg-Mission, TX Metro area
	48215	Hidalgo County, TX
32780		Medford, OR Metro area
	41029	Jackson County, OR
32820		Memphis, TN-MS-AR Metro area
	05035	Crittenden County, AR
	28009	Benton County, MS
	28033	DeSoto County, MS
	28093	Marshall County, MS
	28137	Tate County, MS
	28143	Tunica County, MS
	47047	Fayette County, TN
	47157	Shelby County, TN
	47167	Tipton County, TN
32900		Merced, CA Metro area
	06047	Merced County, CA
33100		Miami-Fort Lauderdale-West Palm Beach, FL Metro area
33100		Fort Lauderdale-Pompano Beach-Deerfield Beach, FL Metro Div 22744
	12011	Broward County, FL
33100		Miami-Miami Beach-Kendall, FL Metro Div 33124
	12086	Miami-Dade County, FL
33100		West Palm Beach-Boca Raton-Delray Beach, FL Metro Div 48424
	12099	Palm Beach County, FL
33140		Michigan City-La Porte, IN Metro area
	18091	LaPorte County, IN
33260		Midland, TX Metro area
	48317	Martin County, TX
	48329	Midland County, TX
33340		Milwaukee-Waukesha-West Allis, WI Metro area
	55079	Milwaukee County, WI
	55089	Ozaukee County, WI
	55131	Washington County, WI
	55133	Waukesha County, WI
33460		Minneapolis-St. Paul-Bloomington, MN Metro area
	27003	Anoka County, MN
	27019	Carver County, MN

Core based statistical area	State/County FIPS code	Title and Geographic Components
	27025	Chisago County, MN
	27037	Dakota County, MN
	27053	Hennepin County, MN
	27059	Isanti County, MN
	27079	Le Sueur County, MN
	27095	Mille Lacs County, MN
	27123	Ramsey County, MN
	27139	Scott County, MN
	27141	Sherburne County, MN
	27143	Sibley County, MN
	27163	Washington County, MN
	27171	Wright County, MN
	55093	Pierce County, WI
	55109	St. Croix County, WI
33540		Missoula, MT Metro area
	30063	Missoula County, MT
33660		Mobile, AL Metro area
	01097	Mobile County, AL
33700		Modesto, CA Metro area
	06099	Stanislaus County, CA
33740		Monroe, LA Metro area
	22073	Ouachita Parish, LA
	22111	Union Parish, LA
33780		Monroe, MI Metro area
	26115	Monroe County, MI
33860		Montgomery, AL Metro area
	01001	Autauga County, AL
	01051	Elmore County, AL
	01085	Lowndes County, AL
	01101	Montgomery County, AL
34060		Morgantown, WV Metro area
	54061	Monongalia County, WV
	54077	Preston County, WV
34100		Morristown, TN Metro area
	47063	Hamblen County, TN
	47089	Jefferson County, TN
34540		Mount Vernon, OH Micro area
	39083	Knox County, OH
34620		Muncie, IN Metro area
	18035	Delaware County, IN
34740		Muskegon, MI Metro area
	26121	Muskegon County, MI
34820		Myrtle Beach-Conway-North Myrtle Beach, NC-SC Metro area
	37019	Brunswick County, NC
	45051	Horry County, SC
34900		Napa, CA Metro area
	06055	Napa County, CA
34940		Naples-Immokalee-Marco Island, FL Metro area
	12021	Collier County, FL
34980		Nashville-Davidson--Murfreesboro--Franklin, TN Metro area
	47015	Cannon County, TN
	47021	Cheatham County, TN
	47037	Davidson County, TN
	47043	Dickson County, TN
	47081	Hickman County, TN
	47111	Macon County, TN
	47119	Maury County, TN
	47147	Robertson County, TN
	47149	Rutherford County, TN
	47159	Smith County, TN
	47165	Sumner County, TN
	47169	Trousdale County, TN
	47187	Williamson County, TN
	47189	Wilson County, TN
35300		New Haven-Milford, CT Metro area
	09009	New Haven County, CT
35380		New Orleans-Metairie, LA Metro area
	22051	Jefferson Parish, LA
	22071	Orleans Parish, LA
	22075	Plaquemines Parish, LA
	22087	St. Bernard Parish, LA
	22089	St. Charles Parish, LA
	22093	St. James Parish, LA
	22095	St. John the Baptist Parish, LA
	22103	St. Tammany Parish, LA
35620		New York-Newark-Jersey City, NY-NJ-PA Metro area
35620		Dutchess County-Putnam County, NY Metro Div 20524
	36027	Dutchess County, NY
	36079	Putnam County, NY
35620		Nassau County-Suffolk County, NY Metro Div 35004
	36059	Nassau County, NY
	36103	Suffolk County, NY
35620		Newark, NJ-PA Metro Div 35084
	34013	Essex County, NJ
	34019	Hunterdon County, NJ
	34027	Morris County, NJ
	34035	Somerset County, NJ
	34037	Sussex County, NJ
	34039	Union County, NJ

Core based statistical area	State/County FIPS code	Title and Geographic Components
	42103	Pike County, PA
35620		New York-Jersey City-White Plains, NY-NJ Metro Div 35614
	34003	Bergen County, NJ
	34017	Hudson County, NJ
	34023	Middlesex County, NJ
	34025	Monmouth County, NJ
	34029	Ocean County, NJ
	34031	Passaic County, NJ
	36005	Bronx County, NY
	36047	Kings County, NY
	36061	New York County, NY
	36071	Orange County, NY
	36081	Queens County, NY
	36085	Richmond County, NY
	36087	Rockland County, NY
	36119	Westchester County, NY
35660		Niles-Benton Harbor, MI Metro area
	26021	Berrien County, MI
35840		North Port-Sarasota-Bradenton, FL Metro area
	12081	Manatee County, FL
	12115	Sarasota County, FL
35980		Norwich-New London, CT Metro area
	09011	New London County, CT
36100		Ocala, FL Metro area
	12083	Marion County, FL
36140		Ocean City, NJ Metro area
	34009	Cape May County, NJ
36220		Odessa, TX Metro area
	48135	Ector County, TX
36260		Ogden-Clearfield, UT Metro area
	49003	Box Elder County, UT
	49011	Davis County, UT
	49029	Morgan County, UT
	49057	Weber County, UT
36420		Oklahoma City, OK Metro area
	40017	Canadian County, OK
	40027	Cleveland County, OK
	40051	Grady County, OK
	40081	Lincoln County, OK
	40083	Logan County, OK
	40087	McClain County, OK
	40109	Oklahoma County, OK
36500		Olympia-Tumwater, WA Metro area
	53067	Thurston County, WA
36540		Omaha-Council Bluffs, NE-IA Metro area
	19085	Harrison County, IA
	19129	Mills County, IA
	19155	Pottawattamie County, IA
	31025	Cass County, NE
	31055	Douglas County, NE
	31153	Sarpy County, NE
	31155	Saunders County, NE
	31177	Washington County, NE
36740		Orlando-Kissimmee-Sanford, FL Metro
	12069	Lake County, FL
	12095	Orange County, FL
	12097	Osceola County, FL
	12117	Seminole County, FL
36780		Oshkosh-Neenah, WI Metro area
	55139	Winnebago County, WI
36980		Owensboro, KY Metro area
	21059	Daviess County, KY
	21091	Hancock County, KY
	21149	McLean County, KY
37100		Oxnard-Thousand Oaks-Ventura, CA Metro area
	06111	Ventura County, CA
37340		Palm Bay-Melbourne-Titusville, FL Metro area
	12009	Brevard County, FL
37460		Panama City, FL Metro area
37620		Parkersburg-Vienna, WV Metro area
37860		Pensacola-Ferry Pass-Brent, FL Metro area
	12033	Escambia County, FL
	12113	Santa Rosa County, FL
37900		Peoria, IL Metro area
	17123	Marshall County, IL
	17143	Peoria County, IL
	17175	Stark County, IL
	17179	Tazewell County, IL
	17203	Woodford County, IL
37980		Philadelphia-Camden-Wilmington, PA-NJ-DE-MD Metro area
37980		Camden, NJ Metro Div 15804
	34005	Burlington County, NJ
	34007	Camden County, NJ
	34015	Gloucester County, NJ
37980		Montgomery County-Bucks County-Chester County, PA Metro Div 33874
	42017	Bucks County, PA
	42029	Chester County, PA
	42091	Montgomery County, PA

Core Based Statistical Areas and Components (as defined February 2013)

Core based statistical area	State/County FIPS code	Title and Geographic Components
37980		Philadelphia, PA Metro Div 37964
	42045	Delaware County, PA
	42101	Philadelphia County, PA
37980		Wilmington, DE-MD-NJ Metro Div 48864
	10003	New Castle County, Delaware
	24015	Cecil County, MD
	34033	Salem County, NJ
38060		Phoenix-Mesa-Scottsdale, AZ Metro area
	04013	Maricopa County, AZ
	04021	Pinal County, AZ
38220		Pine Bluff, AR Metro area
	05025	Cleveland County, AR
	05069	Jefferson County, AR
	05079	Lincoln County, AR
38300		Pittsburgh, PA Metro area
	42003	Allegheny County, PA
	42005	Armstrong County, PA
	42007	Beaver County, PA
	42019	Butler County, PA
	42051	Fayette County, PA
	42125	Washington County, PA
	42129	Westmoreland County, PA
38340		Pittsfield, MA Metro area
	25003	Berkshire County, MA
38540		Pocatello, ID Metro area
	16005	Bannock County, ID
38860		Portland-South Portland, ME Metro area
	23005	Cumberland County, ME
	23023	Sagadahoc County, ME
	23031	York County, ME
38900		Portland-Vancouver-Hillsboro, OR-WA Metro area
	41005	Clackamas County, OR
	41009	Columbia County, OR
	41051	Multnomah County, OR
	41067	Washington County, OR
	41071	Yamhill County, OR
	53011	Clark County, WA
	53059	Skamania County, WA
38940		Port St. Lucie, FL Metro area
	12085	Martin County, FL
	12111	St. Lucie County, FL
39140		Prescott, AZ Metro area
	04025	Yavapai County, AZ
39300		Providence-Warwick, RI-MA Metro area
	25005	Bristol County, MA
	44001	Bristol County, RI
	44003	Kent County, RI
	44005	Newport County, RI
	44007	Providence County, RI
	44009	Washington County, RI
39340		Provo-Orem, UT Metro area
	49023	Juab County, UT
	49049	Utah County, UT
39380		Pueblo, CO Metro area
	08101	Pueblo County, CO
39460		Punta Gorda, FL Metro area
	12015	Charlotte County, FL
39540		Racine, WI Metro area
	55101	Racine County, WI
39580		Raleigh, NC Metro area
	37069	Franklin County, NC
	37101	Johnston County, NC
	37183	Wake County, NC
39660		Rapid City, SD Metro area
	46033	Custer County, SD
	46093	Meade County, SD
	46103	Pennington County, SD
39740		Reading, PA Metro area
	42011	Berks County, PA
39820		Redding, CA Metro area
	06089	Shasta County, CA
39900		Reno, NV Metro area
	32029	Storey County, NV
	32031	Washoe County, NV
40060		Richmond, VA Metro area
	51007	Amelia County, VA
	51033	Caroline County, VA
	51036	Charles City County, VA
	51041	Chesterfield County, VA
	51053	Dinwiddie County, VA
	51075	Goochland County, VA
	51085	Hanover County, VA
	51087	Henrico County, VA
	51101	King William County, VA
	51127	New Kent County, VA
	51145	Powhatan County, VA
	51149	Prince George County, VA
	51183	Sussex County, VA
	51570	Colonial Heights city, VA
	51670	Hopewell city, VA
	51730	Petersburg city, VA
	51760	Richmond city, VA

Core based statistical area	State/County FIPS code	Title and Geographic Components
40140		Riverside-San Bernardino-Ontario, CA
	06065	Riverside County, CA
	06071	San Bernardino County, CA
40220		Roanoke, VA Metro area
	51023	Botetourt County, VA
	51045	Craig County, VA
	51067	Franklin County, VA
	51161	Roanoke County, VA
	51770	Roanoke city, VA
	51775	Salem city, VA
40340		Rochester, MN Metro area
	27039	Dodge County, MN
	27045	Fillmore County, MN
	27109	Olmsted County, MN
	27157	Wabasha County, MN
40380		Rochester, NY Metro area
	36051	Livingston County, NY
	36055	Monroe County, NY
	36069	Ontario County, NY
	36073	Orleans County, NY
	36117	Wayne County, NY
	36123	Yates County, NY
40420		Rockford, IL Metro area
	17007	Boone County, IL
	17201	Winnebago County, IL
40580		Rocky Mount, NC Metro area
	37065	Edgecombe County, NC
	37127	Nash County, NC
40660		Rome, GA Metro area
	13115	Floyd County, GA
40900		Sacramento--Roseville--Arden-Arcade, CA Metro area
	06017	El Dorado County, CA
	06061	Placer County, CA
	06067	Sacramento County, CA
	06113	Yolo County, CA
40980		Saginaw, MI Metro area
	26145	Saginaw County, MI
41060		St. Cloud, MN Metro area
	27009	Benton County, MN
	27145	Stearns County, MN
41100		St. George, UT Metro area
	49053	Washington County, UT
41140		St. Joseph, MO-KS Metro area
	20043	Doniphan County, KS
	29003	Andrew County, MO
	29021	Buchanan County, MO
	29063	DeKalb County, MO
41180		St. Louis, MO-IL Metro area
	17005	Bond County, IL
	17013	Calhoun County, IL
	17027	Clinton County, IL
	17083	Jersey County, IL
	17117	Macoupin County, IL
	17119	Madison County, IL
	17133	Monroe County, IL
	17163	St. Clair County, IL
	29071	Franklin County, MO
	29099	Jefferson County, MO
	29113	Lincoln County, MO
	29183	St. Charles County, MO
	29189	St. Louis County, MO
	29219	Warren County, MO
	29510	St. Louis city, MO
41420		Salem, OR Metro area
	41047	Marion County, OR
	41053	Polk County, OR
41500		Salinas, CA Metro area
	06053	Monterey County, CA
41540		Salisbury, MD-DE Metro area
	10005	Sussex County, DE
	24039	Somerset County, MD
	24045	Wicomico County, MD
	24047	Worcester County, MD
41620		Salt Lake City, UT Metro area
	49035	Salt Lake County, UT
	49045	Tooele County, UT
41660		San Angelo, TX Metro area
	48235	Irion County, TX
	48451	Tom Green County, TX
41700		San Antonio-New Braunfels, TX Metro
	48013	Atascosa County, TX
	48019	Bandera County, TX
	48029	Bexar County, TX
	48091	Comal County, TX
	48187	Guadalupe County, TX
	48259	Kendall County, TX
	48325	Medina County, TX
	48493	Wilson County, TX
41740		San Diego-Carlsbad, CA Metro area
	06073	San Diego County, CA
41780		Sandusky, OH Micro area
	39043	Erie County, OH

Core based statistical area	State/County FIPS code	Title and Geographic Components
		Core Based Statistical Areas and Components (as defined February 2013)
41860		San Francisco-Oakland-Hayward, CA Metro area
41860		Oakland-Hayward-Berkeley, CA Metro Div 36084
	06001	Alameda County, CA
	06013	Contra Costa County, CA
41860		San Francisco-Redwood City-South San Francisco, CA Metro Div 41884
	06075	San Francisco County, CA
	06081	San Mateo County, CA
41860		San Rafael, CA Metropolitan Div 42034
	06041	Marin County, CA
41940		San Jose-Sunnyvale-Santa Clara, CA Metro area
	06069	San Benito County, CA
	06085	Santa Clara County, CA
42020		San Luis Obispo-Paso Robles-Arroyo Grande, CA Metro area
	06079	San Luis Obispo County, CA
42100		Santa Cruz-Watsonville, CA Metro area
	06087	Santa Cruz County, CA
42140		Santa Fe, NM Metro area
	35049	Santa Fe County, NM
42200		Santa Maria-Santa Barbara, CA Metro
	06083	Santa Barbara County, CA
42220		Santa Rosa, CA Metro area
	06097	Sonoma County, CA
42340		Savannah, GA Metro area
	13029	Bryan County, GA
	13051	Chatham County, GA
	13103	Effingham County, GA
42540		Scranton--Wilkes-Barre--Hazleton, PA Metro area
	42069	Lackawanna County, PA
	42079	Luzerne County, PA
	42131	Wyoming County, PA
42660		Seattle-Tacoma-Bellevue, WA Metro area
42660		Seattle-Bellevue-Everett, WA Metro Div 42644
	53033	King County, WA
	53061	Snohomish County, WA
42660		Tacoma-Lakewood, WA Metro Div 45104
	53053	Pierce County, WA
42680		Sebastian-Vero Beach, FL Metro area
	12061	Indian River County, FL
43100		Sheboygan, WI Metro area
	55117	Sheboygan County, WI
43300		Sherman-Denison, TX Metro area
	48181	Grayson County, TX
43340		Shreveport-Bossier City, LA Metro area
	22015	Bossier Parish, LA
	22017	Caddo Parish, LA
	22031	De Soto Parish, LA
	22119	Webster Parish, LA
43580		Sioux City, IA-NE-SD Metro area
	19149	Plymouth County, IA
	19193	Woodbury County, IA
	31043	Dakota County, NE
	31051	Dixon County, NE
	46127	Union County, SD
43620		Sioux Falls, SD Metro area
	46083	Lincoln County, SD
	46087	McCook County, SD
	46099	Minnehaha County, SD
	46125	Turner County, SD
43780		South Bend-Mishawaka, IN-MI Metro area
	18141	St. Joseph County, IN
	26027	Cass County, MI
43900		Spartanburg, SC Metro area
	45083	Spartanburg County, SC
	45087	Union County, SC
44060		Spokane-Spokane Valley, WA Metro area
	53051	Pend Oreille County, WA
	53063	Spokane County, WA
	53065	Stevens County, WA
44100		Springfield, IL Metro area
	17129	Menard County, IL
	17167	Sangamon County, IL
44140		Springfield, MA Metro area
	25013	Hampden County, MA
	25015	Hampshire County, MA
44180		Springfield, MO Metro area
	29043	Christian County, MO
	29059	Dallas County, MO
	29077	Greene County, MO
	29167	Polk County, MO
	29225	Webster County, MO
44220		Springfield, OH Metro area
	39023	Clark County, OH
44300		State College, PA Metro area
	42027	Centre County, PA
44700		Stockton-Lodi, CA Metro area
	06077	San Joaquin County, CA
44940		Sumter, SC Metro area
	45085	Sumter County, SC
45060		Syracuse, NY Metro area
	36053	Madison County, NY
	36067	Onondaga County, NY
	36075	Oswego County, NY

Core based statistical area	State/County FIPS code	Title and Geographic Components
		Core Based Statistical Areas and Components (as defined February 2013)
45220		Tallahassee, FL Metro area
	12039	Gadsden County, FL
	12065	Jefferson County, FL
	12073	Leon County, FL
	12129	Wakulla County, FL
45300		Tampa-St. Petersburg-Clearwater, FL Metro area
	12053	Hernando County, FL
	12057	Hillsborough County, FL
	12101	Pasco County, FL
	12103	Pinellas County, FL
45460		Terre Haute, IN Metro area
	18021	Clay County, IN
	18153	Sullivan County, IN
	18165	Vermillion County, IN
	18167	Vigo County, IN
45500		Texarkana, TX-AR Metro area
	05081	Little River County, AR
	05091	Miller County, AR
	48037	Bowie County, TX
45780		Toledo, OH Metro area
	39051	Fulton County, OH
	39095	Lucas County, OH
	39173	Wood County, OH
45820		Topeka, KS Metro area
	20085	Jackson County, KS
	20087	Jefferson County, KS
	20139	Osage County, KS
	20177	Shawnee County, KS
	20197	Wabaunsee County, KS
45940		Trenton, NJ Metro area
	34021	Mercer County, NJ
46060		Tucson, AZ Metro area
	04019	Pima County, AZ
46140		Tulsa, OK Metro area
	40037	Creek County, OK
	40111	Okmulgee County, OK
	40113	Osage County, OK
	40117	Pawnee County, OK
	40131	Rogers County, OK
	40143	Tulsa County, OK
	40145	Wagoner County, OK
46220		Tuscaloosa, AL Metro area
	01065	Hale County, AL
	01107	Pickens County, AL
	01125	Tuscaloosa County, AL
46340		Tyler, TX Metro area
	48423	Smith County, TX
46520		Urban Honolulu, HI Metro area
	15003	Honolulu County, HI
46540		Utica-Rome, NY Metro area
	36043	Herkimer County, NY
	36065	Oneida County, NY
46660		Valdosta, GA Metro area
	13027	Brooks County, GA
	13101	Echols County, GA
	13173	Lanier County, GA
	13185	Lowndes County, GA
46700		Vallejo-Fairfield, CA Metro area
	06095	Solano County, CA
47020		Victoria, TX Metro area
	48175	Goliad County, TX
	48469	Victoria County, TX
47220		Vineland-Bridgeton, NJ Metro area
	34011	Cumberland County, NJ
47260		Virginia Beach-Norfolk-Newport News, VA-NC Metro area
	37053	Currituck County, NC
	37073	Gates County, NC
	51073	Gloucester County, VA
	51093	Isle of Wight County, VA
	51095	James City County, VA
	51115	Mathews County, VA
	51199	York County, VA
	51550	Chesapeake city, VA
	51650	Hampton city, VA
	51700	Newport News city, VA
	51710	Norfolk city, VA
	51735	Poquoson city, VA
	51740	Portsmouth city, VA
	51800	Suffolk city, VA
	51810	Virginia Beach city, VA
	51830	Williamsburg city, VA
47300		Visalia-Porterville, CA Metro area
	06107	Tulare County, CA
47380		Waco, TX Metro area
	48145	Falls County, TX
	48309	McLennan County, TX
47580		Warner Robins, GA Metro area
	13153	Houston County, GA
	13225	Peach County, GA
	13235	Pulaski County, GA
47900		Washington-Arlington-Alexandria, DC-VA-MD-WV Metro area
47900		Silver Spring-Frederick-Rockville, MD Metro Div 43524
	24021	Frederick County, MD

Core based statistical area	State/County FIPS code	Title and Geographic Components
		Core Based Statistical Areas and Components (as defined February 2013)
	24031	Montgomery County, MD
47900		Washington-Arlington-Alexandria, DC-VA-MD-WV Metro Div 47894
	11001	District of Columbia, DC
	24009	Calvert County, MD
	24017	Charles County, MD
	24033	Prince George's County, MD
	51013	Arlington County, VA
	51043	Clarke County, VA
	51047	Culpeper County, VA
	51059	Fairfax County, VA
	51061	Fauquier County, VA
	51107	Loudoun County, VA
	51153	Prince William County, VA
	51157	Rappahannock County, VA
	51177	Spotsylvania County, VA
	51179	Stafford County, VA
	51187	Warren County, VA
	51510	Alexandria city, VA
	51600	Fairfax city, VA
	51610	Falls Church city, VA
	51630	Fredericksburg city, VA
	51683	Manassas city, VA
	51685	Manassas Park city, VA
	54037	Jefferson County, WV
47920		Washington Court House, OH Micro area
	39047	Fayette County, OH
47940		Waterloo-Cedar Falls, IA Metro area
	19013	Black Hawk County, IA
	19017	Bremer County, IA
	19075	Grundy County, IA
48140		Wausau, WI Metro area
	55073	Marathon County, WI
48300		Wenatchee, WA Metro area
	53007	Chelan County, WA
	53017	Douglas County, WA
48260		Weirton-Steubenville, WV-OH Metro area
	39081	Jefferson County, OH
	54009	Brooke County, WV
	54029	Hancock County, WV
48540		Wheeling, WV-OH Metro area
	39013	Belmont County, OH
	54051	Marshall County, WV
	54069	Ohio County, WV

Core based statistical area	State/County FIPS code	Title and Geographic Components
		Core Based Statistical Areas and Components (as defined February 2013)
48620		Wichita, KS Metro area
	20015	Butler County, KS
	20079	Harvey County, KS
	20095	Kingman County, KS
	20173	Sedgwick County, KS
	20191	Sumner County, KS
48660		Wichita Falls, TX Metro area
	48009	Archer County, TX
	48077	Clay County, TX
	48485	Wichita County, TX
48700		Williamsport, PA Metro area
	42081	Lycoming County, PA
48900		Wilmington, NC Metro area
	37129	New Hanover County, NC
	37141	Pender County, NC
49020		Winchester, VA-WV Metro area
	51069	Frederick County, VA
	51840	Winchester city, VA
	54027	Hampshire County, WV
49180		Winston-Salem, NC Metro area
	37057	Davidson County, NC
	37059	Davie County, NC
	37067	Forsyth County, NC
	37169	Stokes County, NC
	37197	Yadkin County, NC
49340		Worcester, MA-CT Metro area
	09015	Windham County, CT
	25027	Worcester County, MA
49420		Yakima, WA Metro area
	53077	Yakima County, WA
49460		Yankton, SD Micro area
	46135	Yankton County, SD
49620		York-Hanover, PA Metro area
	42133	York County, PA
49660		Youngstown-Warren-Boardman, OH-PA Metro area
	39099	Mahoning County, OH
	39155	Trumbull County, OH
	42085	Mercer County, PA
49700		Yuba City, CA Metro area
	06101	Sutter County, CA
	06115	Yuba County, CA
49740		Yuma, AZ Metro area
	04027	Yuma County, AZ

APPENDIX B. CITIES BY COUNTY

The following table is arranged alphabetically by state. Under each state heading are listed all cities with a 2010–2012 ACS population of 65,000 or more, along with their component counties. The population in each component reflects the 2010 Census population which in some cases is less than 65,000.

State code	Place code	County code	Geographic Area Name	2010 census population
01			**ALABAMA**	4,779,736
01		07000	Birmingham city	212,237
01	073	07000	Jefferson County	210,609
01	117	07000	Shelby County	1,628
01		21184	Dothan city	65,496
01	045	21184	Dale County	887
01	067	21184	Henry County	5
01	069	21184	Houston County	64,604
01		35896	Hoover city	81,619
01	073	35896	Jefferson County	58,582
01	117	35896	Shelby County	23,037
01		37000	Huntsville city	180,105
01	083	37000	Limestone County	1,521
01	089	37000	Madison County	178,584
01		50000	Mobile city	195,111
01	097	50000	Mobile County	195,111
01		51000	Montgomery city	205,764
01	101	51000	Montgomery County	205,764
01		77256	Tuscaloosa city	90,468
01	125	77256	Tuscaloosa County	90,468
02			**ALASKA**	710,231
02		03000	Anchorage municipality	291,826
02	020	03000	Anchorage Municipality	291,826
04			**ARIZONA**	6,392,017
04		04720	Avondale city	76,238
04	013	04720	Maricopa County	76,238
04		12000	Chandler city	236,123
04	013	12000	Maricopa County	236,123
04		23620	Flagstaff city	65,870
04	005	23620	Coconino County	65,870
04		27820	Glendale city	226,721
04	013	27820	Maricopa County	226,721
04		28380	Goodyear city	65,275
04	013	28380	Maricopa County	65,275
04		46000	Mesa city	439,041
04	013	46000	Maricopa County	439,041
04		54050	Peoria city	154,065
04	013	54050	Maricopa County	154,058
04	025	54050	Yavapai County	7
04		55000	Phoenix city	1,445,632
04	013	55000	Maricopa County	1,445,632
04		65000	Scottsdale city	217,385
04	013	65000	Maricopa County	217,385
04		71510	Surprise city	117,517
04	013	71510	Maricopa County	117,517
04		73000	Tempe city	161,719
04	013	73000	Maricopa County	161,719
04		77000	Tucson city	520,116
04	019	77000	Pima County	520,116
04		85540	Yuma city	93,064
04	027	85540	Yuma County	93,064
05			**ARKANSAS**	2,915,918
05		23290	Fayetteville city	73,580
05	143	23290	Washington County	73,580
05		24550	Fort Smith city	86,209
05	131	24550	Sebastian County	86,209
05		35710	Jonesboro city	67,263
05	031	35710	Craighead County	67,263
05		41000	Little Rock city	193,524
05	119	41000	Pulaski County	193,524
05		66080	Springdale city	69,797
05	007	66080	Benton County	6,054
05	143	66080	Washington County	63,743
06			**CALIFORNIA**	37,253,956
06		00562	Alameda city	73,812
06	001	00562	Alameda County	73,812
06		00884	Alhambra city	83,089
06	037	00884	Los Angeles County	83,089
06		02000	Anaheim city	336,265
06	059	02000	Orange County	336,265
06		02252	Antioch city	102,372
06	013	02252	Contra Costa County	102,372
06		03526	Bakersfield city	347,483
06	029	03526	Kern County	347,483
06		03666	Baldwin Park city	75,390
06	037	03666	Los Angeles County	75,390
06		04982	Bellflower city	76,616
06	037	04982	Los Angeles County	76,616
06		06000	Berkeley city	112,580
06	001	06000	Alameda County	112,580
06		08786	Buena Park city	80,530
06	059	08786	Orange County	80,530
06		08954	Burbank city	103,340
06	037	08954	Los Angeles County	103,340
06		10046	Camarillo city	65,201
06	111	10046	Ventura County	65,201
06		11194	Carlsbad city	105,328
06	073	11194	San Diego County	105,328
06		11530	Carson city	91,714
06	037	11530	Los Angeles County	91,714
06		13014	Chico city	86,187
06	007	13014	Butte County	86,187
06		13210	Chino city	77,983
06	071	13210	San Bernardino County	77,983
06		13214	Chino Hills city	74,799
06	071	13214	San Bernardino County	74,799
06		13392	Chula Vista city	243,916
06	073	13392	San Diego County	243,916
06		13588	Citrus Heights city	83,301
06	067	13588	Sacramento County	83,301
06		14218	Clovis city	95,631
06	019	14218	Fresno County	95,631
06		15044	Compton city	96,455
06	037	15044	Los Angeles County	96,455
06		16000	Concord city	122,067
06	013	16000	Contra Costa County	122,067
06		16350	Corona city	152,374
06	065	16350	Riverside County	152,374
06		16532	Costa Mesa city	109,960
06	059	16532	Orange County	109,960
06		17918	Daly City city	101,123
06	081	17918	San Mateo County	101,123

State code	Place code	County code	Geographic Area Name	2010 census population
06		18100	Davis city	65,622
06	113	18100	Yolo County	65,622
06		19766	Downey city	111,772
06	037	19766	Los Angeles County	111,772
06		21712	El Cajon city	99,478
06	073	21712	San Diego County	99,478
06		22020	Elk Grove city	153,015
06	067	22020	Sacramento County	153,015
06		22230	El Monte city	113,475
06	037	22230	Los Angeles County	113,475
06		22804	Escondido city	143,911
06	073	22804	San Diego County	143,911
06		23182	Fairfield city	105,321
06	095	23182	Solano County	105,321
06		24638	Folsom city	72,203
06	067	24638	Sacramento County	72,203
06		24680	Fontana city	196,069
06	071	24680	San Bernardino County	196,069
06		26000	Fremont city	214,089
06	001	26000	Alameda County	214,089
06		27000	Fresno city	494,665
06	019	27000	Fresno County	494,665
06		28000	Fullerton city	135,161
06	059	28000	Orange County	135,161
06		29000	Garden Grove city	170,883
06	059	29000	Orange County	170,883
06		30000	Glendale city	191,719
06	037	30000	Los Angeles County	191,719
06		32548	Hawthorne city	84,293
06	037	32548	Los Angeles County	84,293
06		33000	Hayward city	144,186
06	001	33000	Alameda County	144,186
06		33182	Hemet city	78,657
06	065	33182	Riverside County	78,657
06		33434	Hesperia city	90,173
06	071	33434	San Bernardino County	90,173
06		36000	Huntington Beach city	189,992
06	059	36000	Orange County	189,992
06		36448	Indio city	76,036
06	065	36448	Riverside County	76,036
06		36546	Inglewood city	109,673
06	037	36546	Los Angeles County	109,673
06		36770	Irvine city	212,375
06	059	36770	Orange County	212,375
06		37692	Jurupa Valley city	95,004
06	065	37692	Riverside County	95,004
06		39496	Lake Forest city	77,264
06	059	39496	Orange County	77,264
06		39892	Lakewood city	80,048
06	037	39892	Los Angeles County	80,048
06		40130	Lancaster city	156,633
06	037	40130	Los Angeles County	156,633
06		41992	Livermore city	80,968
06	001	41992	Alameda County	80,968
06		43000	Long Beach city	462,257
06	037	43000	Los Angeles County	462,257
06		44000	Los Angeles city	3,792,621
06	037	44000	Los Angeles County	3,792,621
06		44574	Lynwood city	69,772
06	037	44574	Los Angeles County	69,772
06		45484	Manteca city	67,096
06	077	45484	San Joaquin County	67,096

State code	Place code	County code	Geographic Area Name	2010 census population
06		46842	Menifee city	77,519
06	065	46842	Riverside County	77,519
06		46898	Merced city	78,958
06	047	46898	Merced County	78,958
06		47766	Milpitas city	66,790
06	085	47766	Santa Clara County	66,790
06		48256	Mission Viejo city	93,305
06	059	48256	Orange County	93,305
06		48354	Modesto city	201,165
06	099	48354	Stanislaus County	201,165
06		49270	Moreno Valley city	193,365
06	065	49270	Riverside County	193,365
06		49670	Mountain View city	74,066
06	085	49670	Santa Clara County	74,066
06		50076	Murrieta city	103,466
06	065	50076	Riverside County	103,466
06		50258	Napa city	76,915
06	055	50258	Napa County	76,915
06		51182	Newport Beach city	85,186
06	059	51182	Orange County	85,186
06		52526	Norwalk city	105,549
06	037	52526	Los Angeles County	105,549
06		53000	Oakland city	390,724
06	001	53000	Alameda County	390,724
06		53322	Oceanside city	167,086
06	073	53322	San Diego County	167,086
06		53896	Ontario city	163,924
06	071	53896	San Bernardino County	163,924
06		53980	Orange city	136,416
06	059	53980	Orange County	136,416
06		54652	Oxnard city	197,899
06	111	54652	Ventura County	197,899
06		55156	Palmdale city	152,750
06	037	55156	Los Angeles County	152,750
06		55282	Palo Alto city	64,403
06	085	55282	Santa Clara County	64,403
06		56000	Pasadena city	137,122
06	037	56000	Los Angeles County	137,122
06		56700	Perris city	68,386
06	065	56700	Riverside County	68,386
06		57792	Pleasanton city	70,285
06	001	57792	Alameda County	70,285
06		58072	Pomona city	149,058
06	037	58072	Los Angeles County	149,058
06		59444	Rancho Cordova city	64,776
06	067	59444	Sacramento County	64,776
06		59451	Rancho Cucamonga city	165,269
06	071	59451	San Bernardino County	165,269
06		59920	Redding city	89,861
06	089	59920	Shasta County	89,861
06		59962	Redlands city	68,747
06	071	59962	San Bernardino County	68,747
06		60018	Redondo Beach city	66,748
06	037	60018	Los Angeles County	66,748
06		60102	Redwood City city	76,815
06	081	60102	San Mateo County	76,815
06		60466	Rialto city	99,171
06	071	60466	San Bernardino County	99,171
06		60620	Richmond city	103,701
06	013	60620	Contra Costa County	103,701
06		62000	Riverside city	303,871
06	065	62000	Riverside County	303,871

State code	Place code	County code	Geographic Area Name	2010 census population
06		62938	Roseville city	118,788
06	061	62938	Placer County	118,788
06		64000	Sacramento city	466,488
06	067	64000	Sacramento County	466,488
06		64224	Salinas city	150,441
06	053	64224	Monterey County	150,441
06		65000	San Bernardino city	209,924
06	071	65000	San Bernardino County	209,924
06		65042	San Buenaventura (Ventura) city	106,433
06	111	65042	Ventura County	106,433
06		66000	San Diego city	1,307,402
06	073	66000	San Diego County	1,307,402
06		67000	San Francisco city	805,235
06	075	67000	San Francisco County	805,235
06		68000	San Jose city	945,942
06	085	68000	Santa Clara County	945,942
06		68084	San Leandro city	84,950
06	001	68084	Alameda County	84,950
06		68196	San Marcos city	83,781
06	073	68196	San Diego County	83,781
06		68252	San Mateo city	97,207
06	081	68252	San Mateo County	97,207
06		68378	San Ramon city	72,148
06	013	68378	Contra Costa County	72,148
06		69000	Santa Ana city	324,528
06	059	69000	Orange County	324,528
06		69070	Santa Barbara city	88,410
06	083	69070	Santa Barbara County	88,410
06		69084	Santa Clara city	116,468
06	085	69084	Santa Clara County	116,468
06		69088	Santa Clarita city	176,320
06	037	69088	Los Angeles County	176,320
06		69196	Santa Maria city	99,553
06	083	69196	Santa Barbara County	99,553
06		70000	Santa Monica city	89,736
06	037	70000	Los Angeles County	89,736
06		70098	Santa Rosa city	167,815
06	097	70098	Sonoma County	167,815
06		72016	Simi Valley city	124,237
06	111	72016	Ventura County	124,237
06		73080	South Gate city	94,396
06	037	73080	Los Angeles County	94,396
06		75000	Stockton city	291,707
06	077	75000	San Joaquin County	291,707
06		77000	Sunnyvale city	140,081
06	085	77000	Santa Clara County	140,081
06		78120	Temecula city	100,097
06	065	78120	Riverside County	100,097
06		78582	Thousand Oaks city	126,683
06	111	78582	Ventura County	126,683
06		80000	Torrance city	145,438
06	037	80000	Los Angeles County	145,438
06		80238	Tracy city	82,922
06	077	80238	San Joaquin County	82,922
06		80812	Turlock city	68,549
06	099	80812	Stanislaus County	68,549
06		80854	Tustin city	75,540
06	059	80854	Orange County	75,540
06		81204	Union City city	69,516
06	001	81204	Alameda County	69,516
06		81344	Upland city	73,732
06	071	81344	San Bernardino County	73,732
06		81554	Vacaville city	92,428
06	095	81554	Solano County	92,428
06		81666	Vallejo city	115,942
06	095	81666	Solano County	115,942
06		82590	Victorville city	115,903
06	071	82590	San Bernardino County	115,903
06		82954	Visalia city	124,442
06	107	82954	Tulare County	124,442
06		82996	Vista city	93,834
06	073	82996	San Diego County	93,834
06		84200	West Covina city	106,098
06	037	84200	Los Angeles County	106,098
06		84550	Westminster city	89,701
06	059	84550	Orange County	89,701
06		85292	Whittier city	85,331
06	037	85292	Los Angeles County	85,331
06		86832	Yorba Linda city	64,234
06	059	86832	Orange County	64,234
06		86972	Yuba City city	64,925
06	101	86972	Sutter County	64,925
08			**COLORADO**	5,029,196
08		03455	Arvada city	106,433
08	001	03455	Adams County	2,849
08	059	03455	Jefferson County	103,584
08		04000	Aurora city	325,078
08	001	04000	Adams County	39,871
08	005	04000	Arapahoe County	285,090
08	035	04000	Douglas County	117
08		07850	Boulder city	97,385
08	013	07850	Boulder County	97,385
08		12815	Centennial city	100,377
08	005	12815	Arapahoe County	100,377
08		16000	Colorado Springs city	416,427
08	041	16000	El Paso County	416,427
08		20000	Denver city	600,158
08	031	20000	Denver County	600,158
08		27425	Fort Collins city	143,986
08	069	27425	Larimer County	143,986
08		32155	Greeley city	92,889
08	123	32155	Weld County	92,889
08		43000	Lakewood city	142,980
08	059	43000	Jefferson County	142,980
08		45970	Longmont city	86,270
08	013	45970	Boulder County	86,240
08	123	45970	Weld County	30
08		46465	Loveland city	66,859
08	069	46465	Larimer County	66,859
08		62000	Pueblo city	106,595
08	101	62000	Pueblo County	106,595
08		77290	Thornton city	118,772
08	001	77290	Adams County	118,772
08	123	77290	Weld County	0
08		83835	Westminster city	106,114
08	001	83835	Adams County	63,696
08	059	83835	Jefferson County	42,418
09			**CONNECTICUT**	3,574,097
09		08000	Bridgeport city	144,229
09	001	08000	Fairfield County	144,229
09		18430	Danbury city	80,893
09	001	18430	Fairfield County	80,893
09		37000	Hartford city	124,775
09	003	37000	Hartford County	124,775
09		50370	New Britain city	73,206
09	003	50370	Hartford County	73,206
09		52000	New Haven city	129,779
09	009	52000	New Haven County	129,779
09		55990	Norwalk city	85,603
09	001	55990	Fairfield County	85,603

State code	Place code	County code	Geographic Area Name	2010 census population
09		73000	Stamford city	122,643
09	001	73000	Fairfield County	122,643
09		80000	Waterbury city	110,366
09	009	80000	New Haven County	110,366
10			**DELAWARE**	897,934
10		77580	Wilmington city	70,851
10	003	77580	New Castle County	70,851
11			**DISTRICT OF COLUMBIA**	601,723
11		50000	Washington city	601,723
11	001	50000	District of Columbia	601,723
12			**FLORIDA**	18,801,310
12		07300	Boca Raton city	84,392
12	099	07300	Palm Beach County	84,392
12		07875	Boynton Beach city	68,217
12	099	07875	Palm Beach County	68,217
12		10275	Cape Coral city	154,305
12	071	10275	Lee County	154,305
12		12875	Clearwater city	107,685
12	103	12875	Pinellas County	107,685
12		14400	Coral Springs city	121,096
12	011	14400	Broward County	121,096
12		16725	Deerfield Beach city	75,018
12	011	16725	Broward County	75,018
12		17200	Deltona city	85,182
12	127	17200	Volusia County	85,182
12		24000	Fort Lauderdale city	165,521
12	011	24000	Broward County	165,521
12		25175	Gainesville city	124,354
12	001	25175	Alachua County	124,354
12		30000	Hialeah city	224,669
12	086	30000	Miami-Dade County	224,669
12		32000	Hollywood city	140,768
12	011	32000	Broward County	140,768
12		35000	Jacksonville city	821,784
12	031	35000	Duval County	821,784
12		38250	Lakeland city	97,422
12	105	38250	Polk County	97,422
12		39425	Largo city	77,648
12	103	39425	Pinellas County	77,648
12		39550	Lauderhill city	66,887
12	011	39550	Broward County	66,887
12		43975	Melbourne city	76,068
12	009	43975	Brevard County	76,068
12		45000	Miami city	399,457
12	086	45000	Miami-Dade County	399,457
12		45025	Miami Beach city	87,779
12	086	45025	Miami-Dade County	87,779
12		45060	Miami Gardens city	107,167
12	086	45060	Miami-Dade County	107,167
12		45975	Miramar city	122,041
12	011	45975	Broward County	122,041
12		53000	Orlando city	238,300
12	095	53000	Orange County	238,300
12		54000	Palm Bay city	103,190
12	009	54000	Brevard County	103,190
12		54200	Palm Coast city	75,180
12	035	54200	Flagler County	75,180
12		55775	Pembroke Pines city	154,750
12	011	55775	Broward County	154,750
12		57425	Plantation city	84,955
12	011	57425	Broward County	84,955

State code	Place code	County code	Geographic Area Name	2010 census population
12		58050	Pompano Beach city	99,845
12	011	58050	Broward County	99,845
12		58715	Port St. Lucie city	164,603
12	111	58715	St. Lucie County	164,603
12		63000	St. Petersburg city	244,769
12	103	63000	Pinellas County	244,769
12		69700	Sunrise city	84,439
12	011	69700	Broward County	84,439
12		70600	Tallahassee city	181,376
12	073	70600	Leon County	181,376
12		71000	Tampa city	335,709
12	057	71000	Hillsborough County	335,709
12		76582	Weston city	65,333
12	011	76582	Broward County	65,333
12		76600	West Palm Beach city	99,919
12	099	76600	Palm Beach County	99,919
13			**GEORGIA**	9,687,653
13		01052	Albany city	77,434
13	095	01052	Dougherty County	77,434
13		04000	Atlanta city	420,003
13	089	04000	DeKalb County	28,292
13	121	04000	Fulton County	391,711
13		19000	Columbus city	189,885
13	215	19000	Muscogee County	189,885
13		42425	Johns Creek city	76,728
13	121	42425	Fulton County	76,728
13		49000	Macon city	91,351
13	021	49000	Bibb County	90,885
13	169	49000	Jones County	466
13		67284	Roswell city	88,346
13	121	67284	Fulton County	88,346
13		68516	Sandy Springs city	93,853
13	121	68516	Fulton County	93,853
13		69000	Savannah city	136,286
13	051	69000	Chatham County	136,286
13		80508	Warner Robins city	66,588
13	153	80508	Houston County	66,224
13	225	80508	Peach County	364
15			**HAWAII**	1,360,301
15		71550	Urban Honolulu CDP	337,256
15	003	71550	Honolulu County	337,256
16			**IDAHO**	1,567,582
16		08830	Boise City city	205,671
16	001	08830	Ada County	205,671
16		52120	Meridian city	75,092
16	001	52120	Ada County	75,092
16		56260	Nampa city	81,557
16	027	56260	Canyon County	81,557
17			**ILLINOIS**	12,830,632
17		03012	Aurora city	197,899
17	043	03012	DuPage County	49,433
17	089	03012	Kane County	130,976
17	093	03012	Kendall County	6,019
17	197	03012	Will County	11,471
17		06613	Bloomington city	76,610
17	113	06613	McLean County	76,610
17		12385	Champaign city	81,055
17	019	12385	Champaign County	81,055
17		14000	Chicago city	2,695,598
17	031	14000	Cook County	2,695,598
17	043	14000	DuPage County	0
17		18823	Decatur city	76,122
17	115	18823	Macon County	76,122

State code	Place code	County code	Geographic Area Name	2010 census population
17		23074	Elgin city	108,188
17	031	23074	Cook County	24,032
17	089	23074	Kane County	84,156
17		24582	Evanston city	74,486
17	031	24582	Cook County	74,486
17		38570	Joliet city	147,433
17	093	38570	Kendall County	9,749
17	197	38570	Will County	137,684
17		51622	Naperville city	141,853
17	043	51622	DuPage County	94,533
17	197	51622	Will County	47,320
17		59000	Peoria city	115,007
17	143	59000	Peoria County	115,007
17		65000	Rockford city	152,871
17	201	65000	Winnebago County	152,871
17		72000	Springfield city	116,250
17	167	72000	Sangamon County	116,250
17		79293	Waukegan city	89,078
17	097	79293	Lake County	89,078
18			**INDIANA**	6,483,802
18		05860	Bloomington city	80,405
18	105	05860	Monroe County	80,405
18		10342	Carmel city	79,191
18	057	10342	Hamilton County	79,191
18		22000	Evansville city	117,429
18	163	22000	Vanderburgh County	117,429
18		25000	Fort Wayne city	253,691
18	003	25000	Allen County	253,691
18		27000	Gary city	80,294
18	089	27000	Lake County	80,294
18		31000	Hammond city	80,830
18	089	31000	Lake County	80,830
18		40788	Lafayette city	67,140
18	157	40788	Tippecanoe County	67,140
18		51876	Muncie city	70,085
18	035	51876	Delaware County	70,085
18		71000	South Bend city	101,168
18	141	71000	St. Joseph County	101,168
19			**IOWA**	3,046,355
19		12000	Cedar Rapids city	126,326
19	113	12000	Linn County	126,326
19		19000	Davenport city	99,685
19	163	19000	Scott County	99,685
19		21000	Des Moines city	203,433
19	153	21000	Polk County	203,419
19	181	21000	Warren County	14
19		38595	Iowa City city	67,862
19	103	38595	Johnson County	67,862
19		73335	Sioux City city	82,684
19	149	73335	Plymouth County	6
19	193	73335	Woodbury County	82,678
19		82425	Waterloo city	68,406
19	013	82425	Black Hawk County	68,406
20			**KANSAS**	2,853,118
20		36000	Kansas City city	145,786
20	209	36000	Wyandotte County	145,786
20		38900	Lawrence city	87,643
20	045	38900	Douglas County	87,643
20		52575	Olathe city	125,872
20	091	52575	Johnson County	125,872
20		53775	Overland Park city	173,372
20	091	53775	Johnson County	173,372
20		71000	Topeka city	127,473
20	177	71000	Shawnee County	127,473

State code	Place code	County code	Geographic Area Name	2010 census population
20		79000	Wichita city	382,368
20	173	79000	Sedgwick County	382,368
21			**KENTUCKY**	4,339,367
21		46027	Lexington-Fayette urban county	295,803
21	067	46027	Fayette County	295,803
22			**LOUISIANA**	4,533,372
22		05000	Baton Rouge city	229,493
22	033	05000	East Baton Rouge Parish	229,493
22		39475	Kenner city	66,702
22	051	39475	Jefferson Parish	66,702
22		40735	Lafayette city	120,623
22	055	40735	Lafayette Parish	120,623
22		41155	Lake Charles city	71,993
22	019	41155	Calcasieu Parish	71,993
22		55000	New Orleans city	343,829
22	071	55000	Orleans Parish	343,829
22		70000	Shreveport city	199,311
22	015	70000	Bossier Parish	2,702
22	017	70000	Caddo Parish	196,609
23			**MAINE**	1,328,361
23		60545	Portland city	66,194
23	005	60545	Cumberland County	66,194
24			**MARYLAND**	5,773,552
24		04000	Baltimore city	620,961
24	510	04000	Baltimore city	620,961
24		30325	Frederick city	65,239
24	021	30325	Frederick County	65,239
25			**MASSACHUSETTS**	6,547,629
25		07000	Boston city	617,594
25	025	07000	Suffolk County	617,594
25		09000	Brockton city	93,810
25	023	09000	Plymouth County	93,810
25		11000	Cambridge city	105,162
25	017	11000	Middlesex County	105,162
25		23000	Fall River city	88,857
25	005	23000	Bristol County	88,857
25		34550	Lawrence city	76,377
25	009	34550	Essex County	76,377
25		37000	Lowell city	106,519
25	017	37000	Middlesex County	106,519
25		37490	Lynn city	90,329
25	009	37490	Essex County	90,329
25		45000	New Bedford city	95,072
25	005	45000	Bristol County	95,072
25		45560	Newton city	85,146
25	017	45560	Middlesex County	85,146
25		55745	Quincy city	92,271
25	021	55745	Norfolk County	92,271
25		62535	Somerville city	75,754
25	017	62535	Middlesex County	75,754
25		67000	Springfield city	153,060
25	013	67000	Hampden County	153,060
25		82000	Worcester city	181,045
25	027	82000	Worcester County	181,045
26			**MICHIGAN**	9,883,640
26		03000	Ann Arbor city	113,934
26	161	03000	Washtenaw County	113,934
26		21000	Dearborn city	98,153
26	163	21000	Wayne County	98,153
26		22000	Detroit city	713,777
26	163	22000	Wayne County	713,777

State code	Place code	County code	Geographic Area Name	2010 census population
26		27440	Farmington Hills city	79,740
26	125	27440	Oakland County	79,740
26		29000	Flint city	102,434
26	049	29000	Genesee County	102,434
26		34000	Grand Rapids city	188,040
26	081	34000	Kent County	188,040
26		42160	Kalamazoo city	74,262
26	077	42160	Kalamazoo County	74,262
26		46000	Lansing city	114,297
26	045	46000	Eaton County	4,734
26	065	46000	Ingham County	109,563
26		49000	Livonia city	96,942
26	163	49000	Wayne County	96,942
26		50560	Madison Heights city	29,694
26		69035	Rochester Hills city	70,995
26	125	69035	Oakland County	70,995
26		74900	Southfield city	71,739
26	125	74900	Oakland County	71,739
26		76460	Sterling Heights city	129,699
26	099	76460	Macomb County	129,699
26		80700	Troy city	80,980
26	125	80700	Oakland County	80,980
26		84000	Warren city	134,056
26	099	84000	Macomb County	134,056
26		86000	Westland city	84,094
26	163	86000	Wayne County	84,094
26		88940	Wyoming city	72,125
26	081	88940	Kent County	72,125
27			**MINNESOTA**	5,303,925
27		06616	Bloomington city	82,893
27	053	06616	Hennepin County	82,893
27		07966	Brooklyn Park city	75,781
27	053	07966	Hennepin County	75,781
27		17000	Duluth city	86,265
27	137	17000	St. Louis County	86,265
27		43000	Minneapolis city	382,578
27	053	43000	Hennepin County	382,578
27		51730	Plymouth city	70,576
27	053	51730	Hennepin County	70,576
27		54880	Rochester city	106,769
27	109	54880	Olmsted County	106,769
27		56896	St. Cloud city	65,842
27	009	56896	Benton County	6,396
27	141	56896	Sherburne County	6,785
27	145	56896	Stearns County	52,661
27		58000	St. Paul city	285,068
27	123	58000	Ramsey County	285,068
28			**MISSISSIPPI**	2,967,297
28		29700	Gulfport city	67,793
28	047	29700	Harrison County	67,793
28		36000	Jackson city	173,514
28	049	36000	Hinds County	172,891
28	089	36000	Madison County	622
28	121	36000	Rankin County	1
29			**MISSOURI**	5,988,927
29		15670	Columbia city	108,500
29	019	15670	Boone County	108,500
29		35000	Independence city	116,830
29	047	35000	Clay County	0
29	095	35000	Jackson County	116,830
29		38000	Kansas City city	459,787
29	037	38000	Cass County	197
29	047	38000	Clay County	113,415
29	095	38000	Jackson County	302,499
29	165	38000	Platte County	43,676

State code	Place code	County code	Geographic Area Name	2010 census population
29		41348	Lee's Summit city	91,364
29	037	41348	Cass County	1,917
29	095	41348	Jackson County	89,447
29		42032	Liberty city	29,149
29		54074	O'Fallon city	79,329
29	183	54074	St. Charles County	79,329
29		64082	St. Charles city	65,794
29	183	64082	St. Charles County	65,794
29		64550	St. Joseph city	76,780
29	021	64550	Buchanan County	76,780
29		65000	St. Louis city	319,294
29	510	65000	St. Louis city	319,294
29		70000	Springfield city	159,498
29	043	70000	Christian County	2
29	077	70000	Greene County	159,496
30			**MONTANA**	989,415
30		06550	Billings city	104,170
30	111	06550	Yellowstone County	104,170
30		50200	Missoula city	66,788
30	063	50200	Missoula County	66,788
31			**NEBRASKA**	1,826,341
31		28000	Lincoln city	258,379
31	109	28000	Lancaster County	258,379
31		37000	Omaha city	408,958
31	055	37000	Douglas County	408,958
32			**NEVADA**	2,700,551
32		31900	Henderson city	257,729
32	003	31900	Clark County	257,729
32		40000	Las Vegas city	583,756
32	003	40000	Clark County	583,756
32		51800	North Las Vegas city	216,961
32	003	51800	Clark County	216,961
32		60600	Reno city	225,221
32	031	60600	Washoe County	225,221
32		68400	Sparks city	90,264
32	031	68400	Washoe County	90,264
33			**NEW HAMPSHIRE**	1,316,470
33		45140	Manchester city	109,565
33	011	45140	Hillsborough County	109,565
33		50260	Nashua city	86,494
33	011	50260	Hillsborough County	86,494
34			**NEW JERSEY**	8,791,894
34		10000	Camden city	77,344
34	007	10000	Camden County	77,344
34		13690	Clifton city	84,136
34	031	13690	Passaic County	84,136
34		21000	Elizabeth city	124,969
34	039	21000	Union County	124,969
34		36000	Jersey City city	247,597
34	017	36000	Hudson County	247,597
34		51000	Newark city	277,140
34	013	51000	Essex County	277,140
34		56550	Passaic city	69,781
34	031	56550	Passaic County	69,781
34		57000	Paterson city	146,199
34	031	57000	Passaic County	146,199
34		74000	Trenton city	84,913
34	021	74000	Mercer County	84,913
34		74630	Union City city	66,455
34	017	74630	Hudson County	66,455
35			**NEW MEXICO**	2,059,179
35		02000	Albuquerque city	545,852
35	001	02000	Bernalillo County	545,852

State code	Place code	County code	Geographic Area Name	2010 census population
35		39380	Las Cruces city	97,618
35	013	39380	Doña Ana County	97,618
35		63460	Rio Rancho city	87,521
35	001	63460	Bernalillo County	130
35	043	63460	Sandoval County	87,391
35		70500	Santa Fe city	67,947
35	049	70500	Santa Fe County	67,947
36			**NEW YORK**	19,378,102
36		01000	Albany city	97,856
36	001	01000	Albany County	97,856
36		11000	Buffalo city	261,310
36	029	11000	Erie County	261,310
36		49121	Mount Vernon city	67,292
36	119	49121	Westchester County	67,292
36		50617	New Rochelle city	77,062
36	119	50617	Westchester County	77,062
36		51000	New York city	8,175,133
36	005	51000	Bronx County	1,385,108
36	047	51000	Kings County	2,504,700
36	061	51000	New York County	1,585,873
36	081	51000	Queens County	2,230,722
36	085	51000	Richmond County	468,730
36		63000	Rochester city	210,565
36	055	63000	Monroe County	210,565
36		65508	Schenectady city	66,135
36	093	65508	Schenectady County	66,135
36		73000	Syracuse city	145,170
36	067	73000	Onondaga County	145,170
36		84000	Yonkers	195,976
36	119	84000	Westchester County	195,976
37			**NORTH CAROLINA**	9,535,483
37		02140	Asheville city	83,393
37	021	02140	Buncombe County	83,393
37		12000	Charlotte city	731,424
37	119	12000	Mecklenburg County	731,424
37		14100	Concord city	79,066
37	025	14100	Cabarrus County	79,066
37		19000	Durham city	228,330
37	063	19000	Durham County	228,300
37	135	19000	Orange County	30
37	183	19000	Wake County	0
37		22920	Fayetteville city	200,564
37	051	22920	Cumberland County	200,564
37		25580	Gastonia city	71,741
37	071	25580	Gaston County	71,741
37		28000	Greensboro city	269,666
37	081	28000	Guilford County	269,666
37		28080	Greenville city	84,554
37	147	28080	Pitt County	84,554
37		31400	High Point city	104,371
37	057	31400	Davidson County	5,310
37	067	31400	Forsyth County	8
37	081	31400	Guilford County	99,042
37	151	31400	Randolph County	11
37		34200	Jacksonville city	70,145
37	133	34200	Onslow County	70,145
37		55000	Raleigh city	403,892
37	063	55000	Durham County	1,067
37	183	55000	Wake County	402,825
37		74440	Wilmington city	106,476
37	129	74440	New Hanover County	106,476
37		75000	Winston-Salem city	229,617
37	067	75000	Forsyth County	229,617
38			**NORTH DAKOTA**	672,591
38		25700	Fargo city	105,549
38	017	25700	Cass County	105,549

State code	Place code	County code	Geographic Area Name	2010 census population
39			**OHIO**	11,536,504
39		01000	Akron city	199,110
39	153	01000	Summit County	199,110
39		12000	Canton city	73,007
39	151	12000	Stark County	73,007
39		15000	Cincinnati city	296,943
39	061	15000	Hamilton County	296,943
39		16000	Cleveland city	396,815
39	035	16000	Cuyahoga County	396,815
39		16014	Cleveland Heights city	46,121
39	035	16014	Cuyahoga County	46,121
39		18000	Columbus city	787,033
39	041	18000	Delaware County	7,245
39	045	18000	Fairfield County	9,666
39	049	18000	Franklin County	770,122
39		21000	Dayton city	141,527
39	113	21000	Montgomery County	141,527
39		61000	Parma city	81,601
39	035	61000	Cuyahoga County	81,601
39		77000	Toledo city	287,208
39	095	77000	Lucas County	287,208
39		88000	Youngstown city	66,982
39	099	88000	Mahoning County	66,971
39	155	88000	Trumbull County	11
40			**OKLAHOMA**	3,751,351
40		09050	Broken Arrow city	98,850
40	143	09050	Tulsa County	80,634
40	145	09050	Wagoner County	18,216
40		23200	Edmond city	81,405
40	109	23200	Oklahoma County	81,405
40		41850	Lawton city	96,867
40	031	41850	Comanche County	96,867
40		52500	Norman city	110,925
40	027	52500	Cleveland County	110,925
40		55000	Oklahoma City city	579,999
40	017	55000	Canadian County	44,541
40	027	55000	Cleveland County	63,723
40	109	55000	Oklahoma County	471,671
40	125	55000	Pottawatomie County	64
40		75000	Tulsa city	391,906
40	113	75000	Osage County	6,136
40	131	75000	Rogers County	0
40	143	75000	Tulsa County	385,613
40	145	75000	Wagoner County	157
41			**OREGON**	3,831,074
41		05350	Beaverton city	89,803
41	067	05350	Washington County	89,803
41		05800	Bend city	76,639
41	017	05800	Deschutes County	76,639
41		23850	Eugene city	156,185
41	039	23850	Lane County	156,185
41		31250	Gresham city	105,594
41	051	31250	Multnomah County	105,594
41		34100	Hillsboro city	91,611
41	067	34100	Washington County	91,611
41		47000	Medford city	74,907
41	029	47000	Jackson County	74,907
41		59000	Portland city	583,776
41	005	59000	Clackamas County	744
41	051	59000	Multnomah County	581,485
41	067	59000	Washington County	1,547
41		64900	Salem city	154,637
41	047	64900	Marion County	130,398
41	053	64900	Polk County	24,239
42			**PENNSYLVANIA**	12,702,379
42		02000	Allentown city	118,032
42	077	02000	Lehigh County	118,032

State code	Place code	County code	Geographic Area Name	2010 census population
42		06088	Bethlehem city	74,982
42	077	06088	Lehigh County	19,343
42	095	06088	Northampton County	55,639
42		24000	Erie city	101,786
42	049	24000	Erie County	101,786
42		60000	Philadelphia city	1,526,006
42	101	60000	Philadelphia County	1,526,006
42		61000	Pittsburgh city	305,704
42	003	61000	Allegheny County	305,704
42		63624	Reading city	88,082
42	011	63624	Berks County	88,082
42		69000	Scranton city	76,089
42	069	69000	Lackawanna County	76,089
44			**RHODE ISLAND**	1,052,567
44		19180	Cranston city	80,387
44	007	19180	Providence County	80,387
44		54640	Pawtucket city	71,148
44	007	54640	Providence County	71,148
44		59000	Providence city	178,042
44	007	59000	Providence County	178,042
44		74300	Warwick city	82,672
44	003	74300	Kent County	82,672
45			**SOUTH CAROLINA**	4,625,364
45		13330	Charleston city	120,083
45	015	13330	Berkeley County	8,095
45	019	13330	Charleston County	111,988
45		16000	Columbia city	129,272
45	063	16000	Lexington County	559
45	079	16000	Richland County	128,713
45		50875	North Charleston city	97,471
45	015	50875	Berkeley County	0
45	019	50875	Charleston County	78,393
45	035	50875	Dorchester County	19,078
45		61405	Rock Hill city	66,154
45	091	61405	York County	66,154
46			**SOUTH DAKOTA**	814,180
46		52980	Rapid City city	67,956
46	103	52980	Pennington County	67,956
46		59020	Sioux Falls city	153,888
46	083	59020	Lincoln County	21,095
46	099	59020	Minnehaha County	132,793
47			**TENNESSEE**	6,346,105
47		14000	Chattanooga city	167,674
47	065	14000	Hamilton County	167,674
47		15160	Clarksville city	132,929
47	125	15160	Montgomery County	132,929
47		37640	Jackson city	65,211
47	113	37640	Madison County	65,211
47		40000	Knoxville city	178,874
47	093	40000	Knox County	178,874
47		48000	Memphis city	646,889
47	157	48000	Shelby County	646,889
47		51560	Murfreesboro city	108,755
47	149	51560	Rutherford County	108,755
48			**TEXAS**	25,145,561
48		01000	Abilene city	117,063
48	253	01000	Jones County	5,145
48	441	01000	Taylor County	111,918
48		01924	Allen city	84,246
48	085	01924	Collin County	84,246
48		03000	Amarillo city	190,695
48	375	03000	Potter County	105,486
48	381	03000	Randall County	85,209
48		04000	Arlington city	365,438
48	439	04000	Tarrant County	365,438
48		05000	Austin city	790,390
48	209	05000	Hays County	2
48	453	05000	Travis County	754,691
48	491	05000	Williamson County	35,697
48		06128	Baytown city	71,802
48	071	06128	Chambers County	4,116
48	201	06128	Harris County	67,686
48		07000	Beaumont city	118,296
48	245	07000	Jefferson County	118,296
48		10768	Brownsville city	175,023
48	061	10768	Cameron County	175,023
48		10912	Bryan city	76,201
48	041	10912	Brazos County	76,201
48		13024	Carrollton city	119,097
48	085	13024	Collin County	2
48	113	13024	Dallas County	49,352
48	121	13024	Denton County	69,743
48		15976	College Station city	93,857
48	041	15976	Brazos County	93,857
48		17000	Corpus Christi city	305,215
48	007	17000	Aransas County	0
48	273	17000	Kleberg County	0
48	355	17000	Nueces County	305,215
48	409	17000	San Patricio County	0
48		19000	Dallas city	1,197,816
48	085	19000	Collin County	46,885
48	113	19000	Dallas County	1,124,296
48	121	19000	Denton County	26,579
48	257	19000	Kaufman County	0
48	397	19000	Rockwall County	56
48		19972	Denton city	113,383
48	121	19972	Denton County	113,383
48		22660	Edinburg city	77,100
48	215	22660	Hidalgo County	77,100
48		24000	El Paso city	649,121
48	141	24000	El Paso County	649,121
48		27000	Fort Worth city	741,206
48	121	27000	Denton County	7,813
48	367	27000	Parker County	7
48	439	27000	Tarrant County	733,386
48	497	27000	Wise County	0
48		27684	Frisco city	116,989
48	085	27684	Collin County	72,489
48	121	27684	Denton County	44,500
48		29000	Garland city	226,876
48	085	29000	Collin County	266
48	113	29000	Dallas County	226,608
48	397	29000	Rockwall County	2
48		30464	Grand Prairie city	175,396
48	113	30464	Dallas County	123,487
48	139	30464	Ellis County	45
48	439	30464	Tarrant County	51,864
48		32372	Harlingen city	64,849
48	061	32372	Cameron County	64,849
48		35000	Houston city	2,099,451
48	157	35000	Fort Bend County	38,124
48	201	35000	Harris County	2,057,280
48	339	35000	Montgomery County	4,047
48		37000	Irving city	216,290
48	113	37000	Dallas County	216,290
48		39148	Killeen city	127,921
48	027	39148	Bell County	127,921
48		41464	Laredo city	236,091
48	479	41464	Webb County	236,091
48		41980	League City city	83,560
48	167	41980	Galveston County	81,998
48	201	41980	Harris County	1,562

State code	Place code	County code	Geographic Area Name	2010 census population
48		42508	Lewisville city	95,290
48	113	42508	Dallas County	841
48	121	42508	Denton County	94,449
48		43888	Longview city	80,455
48	183	43888	Gregg County	78,585
48	203	43888	Harrison County	1,870
48		45000	Lubbock city	229,573
48	303	45000	Lubbock County	229,573
48		45384	McAllen city	129,877
48	215	45384	Hidalgo County	129,877
48		45744	McKinney city	131,117
48	085	45744	Collin County	131,117
48		48072	Midland city	111,147
48	317	48072	Martin County	0
48	329	48072	Midland County	111,147
48		48768	Mission city	77,058
48	215	48768	Hidalgo County	77,058
48		48804	Missouri City city	67,358
48	157	48804	Fort Bend County	61,755
48	201	48804	Harris County	5,603
48		53388	Odessa city	99,940
48	135	53388	Ector County	98,270
48	329	53388	Midland County	1,670
48		56000	Pasadena city	149,043
48	201	56000	Harris County	149,043
48		56348	Pearland city	91,252
48	039	56348	Brazoria County	86,706
48	157	56348	Fort Bend County	721
48	201	56348	Harris County	3,825
48		57200	Pharr city	70,400
48	215	57200	Hidalgo County	70,400
48		58016	Plano city	259,841
48	085	58016	Collin County	254,525
48	121	58016	Denton County	5,316
48		61796	Richardson city	99,223
48	085	61796	Collin County	28,569
48	113	61796	Dallas County	70,654
48		63500	Round Rock city	99,887
48	453	63500	Travis County	1,362
48	491	63500	Williamson County	98,525
48		64472	San Angelo city	93,200
48	451	64472	Tom Green County	93,200
48		65000	San Antonio city	1,327,407
48	029	65000	Bexar County	1,327,381
48	091	65000	Comal County	0
48	325	65000	Medina County	26
48		70808	Sugar Land city	78,817
48	157	70808	Fort Bend County	78,817
48		72176	Temple city	66,102
48	027	72176	Bell County	66,102
48		74144	Tyler city	96,900
48	423	74144	Smith County	96,900
48		76000	Waco city	124,805
48	309	76000	McLennan County	124,805
48		79000	Wichita Falls city	104,553
48	485	79000	Wichita County	104,553
49			**UTAH**	2,763,885
49		43660	Layton city	67,311
49	011	43660	Davis County	67,311
49		55980	Ogden city	82,825
49	057	55980	Weber County	82,825
49		57300	Orem city	88,328
49	049	57300	Utah County	88,328
49		62470	Provo city	112,488
49	049	62470	Utah County	112,488
49		65330	St. George city	72,897
49	053	65330	Washington County	72,897

State code	Place code	County code	Geographic Area Name	2010 census population
49		67000	Salt Lake City city	186,440
49	035	67000	Salt Lake County	186,440
49		67440	Sandy city	87,461
49	035	67440	Salt Lake County	87,461
49		82950	West Jordan city	103,712
49	035	82950	Salt Lake County	103,712
49		83470	West Valley City city	129,480
49	035	83470	Salt Lake County	129,480
51			**VIRGINIA**	8,001,024
51		01000	Alexandria city	139,966
51	510	01000	Alexandria city	139,966
51		16000	Chesapeake city	222,209
51	550	16000	Chesapeake city	222,209
51		35000	Hampton city	137,436
51	650	35000	Hampton city	137,436
51		47672	Lynchburg city	75,568
51	680	47672	Lynchburg city	75,568
51		56000	Newport News city	180,719
51	700	56000	Newport News city	180,719
51		57000	Norfolk city	242,803
51	710	57000	Norfolk city	242,803
51		64000	Portsmouth city	95,535
51	740	64000	Portsmouth city	95,535
51		67000	Richmond city	204,214
51	760	67000	Richmond city	204,214
51		68000	Roanoke city	97,032
51	770	68000	Roanoke city	97,032
51		76432	Suffolk city	84,585
51	800	76432	Suffolk city	84,585
51		82000	Virginia Beach city	437,994
51	810	82000	Virginia Beach city	437,994
53			**WASHINGTON**	6,724,540
53		03180	Auburn city	70,180
53	033	03180	King County	62,761
53	053	03180	Pierce County	7,419
53		05210	Bellevue city	122,363
53	033	05210	King County	122,363
53		05280	Bellingham city	80,885
53	073	05280	Whatcom County	80,885
53		22640	Everett city	103,019
53	061	22640	Snohomish County	103,019
53		23515	Federal Way city	89,306
53	033	23515	King County	89,306
53		35275	Kennewick city	73,917
53	005	35275	Benton County	73,917
53		35415	Kent city	92,411
53	033	35415	King County	92,411
53		57745	Renton city	90,927
53	033	57745	King County	90,927
53		63000	Seattle city	608,660
53	033	63000	King County	608,660
53		67000	Spokane city	208,916
53	063	67000	Spokane County	208,916
53		67167	Spokane Valley city	89,755
53	063	67167	Spokane County	89,755
53		70000	Tacoma city	198,397
53	053	70000	Pierce County	198,397
53		74060	Vancouver city	161,791
53	011	74060	Clark County	161,791
53		80010	Yakima city	91,067
53	077	80010	Yakima County	91,067

State code	Place code	County code	Geographic Area Name	2010 census population
55			**WISCONSIN**	5,686,986
55		02375	Appleton city	72,623
55	015	02375	Calumet County	11,088
55	087	02375	Outagamie County	60,045
55	139	02375	Winnebago County	1,490
55		22300	Eau Claire city	65,883
55	017	22300	Chippewa County	1,981
55	035	22300	Eau Claire County	63,902
55		31000	Green Bay city	104,057
55	009	31000	Brown County	104,057
55		39225	Kenosha city	99,218
55	059	39225	Kenosha County	99,218
55		48000	Madison city	233,209
55	025	48000	Dane County	233,209
55		53000	Milwaukee city	594,833
55	079	53000	Milwaukee County	594,833
55	131	53000	Washington County	0
55	133	53000	Waukesha County	0
55		60500	Oshkosh city	66,083
55	139	60500	Winnebago County	66,083
55		66000	Racine city	78,860
55	101	66000	Racine County	78,860
55		84250	Waukesha city	70,718
55	133	84250	Waukesha County	70,718

The following consolidated cities are included here. They are listed here with their 2010 census populations followed by the separate entities that make up the consolidated city. Data from the American Community Survey include only the "balance," the major city of each consolidated city.

State code	Place code	County code	Geographic Area Name	2010 census population
13			**GEORGIA**	9,687,653
13		03436	Athens-Clark county	116,714
13		03440	Athens-Clark county (balance)	115,452
13		09068	Bogart town	140
13		83728	Winterville city	1,122
13		04200	Augusta-Richmond county	200,549
13		04204	Augusta-Richmond county (balance)	195,844
13		09040	Blythe city	694
13		38040	Hephzibah city	4,011
18			**INDIANA**	6,483,802
18		36000	Indianapolis city	829,718
18		04204	Beech Grove city	0
18		13492	Clermont town	1,356
18		16156	Crows Nest town	73
18		16336	Cumberland town	2,597
18		34420	Homecroft town	722
18		36003	Indianapolis city (balance)	820,445
18		42426	Lawrence city	42
18		48456	Meridian Hills town	1,616
18		54612	North Crows Nest town	45
18		65556	Rocky Ripple town	606
18		72232	Spring Hill town	98
18		80234	Warren Park town	1,480
18		84374	Williams Creek town	407
18		85742	Wynnedale town	231
21			**KENTUCKY**	4,339,367
21		46003	Louisville/Jefferson County	741,096
21		01504	Anchorage city	2,348
21		02656	Audubon Park city	1,473
21		03376	Bancroft city	494
21		03556	Barbourmeade city	1,218
21		05068	Beechwood Village city	1,324
21		05392	Bellemeade city	865
21		05464	Bellewood city	321
21		07858	Blue Ridge Manor city	767
21		09532	Briarwood city	435
21		09847	Broeck Pointe city	272
21		10162	Brownsboro Farm city	648
21		10198	Brownsboro Village city	319

State code	Place code	County code	Geographic Area Name	2010 census population
21		12066	Cambridge city	175
21		16395	Coldstream city	1,100
21		18270	Creekside city	305
21		18766	Crossgate city	225
21		22204	Douglass Hills city	5,484
21		22474	Druid Hills city	308
21		27262	Fincastle city	817
21		28342	Forest Hills city	444
21		31348	Glenview city	531
21		31402	Glenview Hills city	319
21		31420	Glenview Manor city	191
21		31870	Goose Creek city	294
21		32523	Graymoor-Devondale city	2,870
21		32986	Green Spring city	715
21		36102	Heritage Creek city	1,076
21		36374	Hickory Hill city	114
21		36865	Hills and Dales city	142
21		37576	Hollow Creek city	783
21		37630	Hollyvilla city	537
21		38170	Houston Acres city	507
21		38814	Hurstbourne city	4,216
21		38818	Hurstbourne Acres city	1,811
21		39304	Indian Hills city	2,868
21		40222	Jeffersontown city	26,595
21		42598	Kingsley city	381
21		43900	Langdon Place city	936
21		46540	Lincolnshire city	148
21		48006	Louisville/Jefferson County (balance)	597,337
21		48558	Lyndon city	11,002
21		48648	Lynnview city	914
21		49800	Manor Creek city	140
21		50412	Maryhill Estates city	179
21		51193	Meadowbrook Farm city	136
21		51258	Meadow Vale city	736
21		51294	Meadowview Estates city	363
21		51978	Middletown city	7,218
21		52842	Mockingbird Valley city	167
21		53328	Moorland city	431
21		54660	Murray Hill city	582
21		56550	Norbourne Estates city	441
21		56730	Northfield city	1,020
21		56928	Norwood city	370
21		57658	Old Brownsboro Place city	353
21		59322	Parkway Village city	650
21		61554	Plantation city	832
21		62370	Poplar Hills city	362
21		63264	Prospect city	4,636
21		65208	Richlawn city	405
21		65766	Riverwood city	446
21		66486	Rolling Fields city	646
21		66504	Rolling Hills city	959
21		67944	St. Matthews city	17,472
21		67998	St. Regis Park city	1,454
21		69384	Seneca Gardens city	696
21		70284	Shively city	15,264
21		72138	South Park View city	7
21		72770	Spring Mill city	287
21		72790	Spring Valley city	654
21		74064	Strathmoor Manor city	337
21		74082	Strathmoor Village city	648
21		75190	Sycamore city	160
21		75963	Ten Broeck city	103
21		76380	Thornhill city	178
21		80913	Watterson Park city	976
21		81372	Wellington city	565
21		81624	West Buechel city	1,230
21		82164	Westwood city	634
21		83208	Wildwood city	261
21		83784	Windy Hills city	2,385
21		84486	Woodland Hills city	696
21		84576	Woodlawn Park city	942
21		84891	Worthington Hills city	1,446
47			**TENNESSEE**	6,346,105
47		52004	Nashville-Davidson	626,681
47		04620	Belle Meade city	2,912
47		05140	Berry Hill city	537
47		27020	Forest Hills city	4,812
47		29920	Goodlettsville city	10,319
47		40720	Lakewood city	2,302
47		52006	Nashville-Davidson (balance)	601,222
47		54780	Oak Hill city	4,529
47		63140	Ridgetop city	48

INDEX

INDEX